Literature

X.J. Kennedy • Dana Gioia

For English 1020 at the Cuyahoga Community College

Taken from:

Literature: An Introduction to Fiction, Poetry, and Drama, Seventh
Edition
by X.J. Kennedy and Dana Gioia
Copyright © 1999 by X.J. Kennedy and Dana Gioia
Published by Longman, an imprint of Addison Wesley Longman,
Inc.
A Pearson Education Company
Boston, Massachusetts 02116

Printed in the United States of America

10 9 8 7 6 5 4 3 2 1

Please visit our web site at www.pearsoncustom.com

ISBN 0–536–63808–X

BA 993513

PEARSON CUSTOM PUBLISHING
75 Arlington Street, Suite 300, Boston, MA 02116
A Pearson Education Company

Contents

13 Listening to a Voice   667

19 Sound 807

20 *Rhythm* *831*

21 *Closed Form* *854*

23 Symbol 902

24 Myth and Narrative 919

28 What Is Poetry? 1009

29 Two Poets in Depth 1013

Geoffrey Hartman, On Wordsworth's "A Slumber Did My Spirit Seal" 1971

CULTURAL STUDIES 1972

Vincent B. Leitch, Poststructuralist Cultural Critique 1974

Mark Bauerlein, What Is Cultural Studies? 1975

Heather Glen, The Stance of Observation in William Blake's "London" 1976

Acknowledgments 1981

Index of Major Themes 1995

Index of First Lines of Poetry 2003

Index of Authors and Titles 2011

12 Reading a Poem

How do you read a poem? The literal-minded might say, "Just let your eye light on it"; but there is more to poetry than meets the eye. What Shakespeare called "the mind's eye" also plays a part. Many a reader who has no trouble understanding and enjoying prose finds poetry difficult. This is to be expected. At first glance, a poem usually will make some sense and give some pleasure, but it may not yield everything at once. Sometimes it only hints at meaning still to come if we will keep after it. Poetry is not to be galloped over like the daily news: a poem differs from most prose in that it is to be read slowly, carefully, and attentively. Not all poems are difficult, of course, and some can be understood and enjoyed on first seeing. But good poems yield more if read twice; and the best poems— after ten, twenty, or a hundred readings—still go on yielding.

Approaching a thing written in lines and surrounded with white space, we need not expect it to be a poem just because it is **verse.** (Any composition in lines of more or less regular rhythm, usually ending in rimes, is verse.) Here, for instance, is a specimen of verse that few will call poetry:

Thirty days hath September,
April, June, and November;
All the rest have thirty-one
Excepting February alone,
To which we twenty-eight assign
Till leap year makes it twenty-nine.

To a higher degree than that classic memory-tickler, poetry appeals to the mind and arouses feelings. Poetry may state facts, but, more important, it makes imaginative statements that we may value even if its facts are incorrect. Coleridge's error in placing a star within the horns of the crescent moon in "The Rime of the Ancient Mariner" does not stop the passage from being good poetry, though it is faulty astronomy. According to one poet, Gerard Manley Hopkins, poetry is "to be heard for its own sake and interest even over and above its interest of meaning." There are other elements in a poem besides plain prose sense: sounds, images, rhythms, figures of speech. These may strike us and please us even before we ask, "But what does it all mean?"

This is a truth not readily grasped by anyone who regards a poem as a kind of puzzle written in secret code with a message slyly concealed. The effect of a poem (one's whole mental and emotional response to it) consists in much more than simply a message. By its musical qualities, by its suggestions, it can work on the reader's unconscious. T. S. Eliot put it well when he said in *The Use of Poetry and the Use of Criticism* that the prose sense of a poem is chiefly useful in keeping the reader's mind "diverted and quiet, while the poem does its work upon him." Eliot went on to liken the meaning of a poem to the bit of meat a burglar brings along to throw to the family dog. What is the work of a poem? To touch us, to stir us, to make us glad, and possibly even to tell us something.

How to set about reading a poem? Here are a few suggestions.

To begin with, read the poem once straight through, with no particular expectations; read open-mindedly. Let yourself experience whatever you find, without worrying just yet about the large general and important ideas the poem contains (if indeed it contains any). Don't dwell on a troublesome word or difficult passage—just push on. Some of the difficulties may seem smaller when you read the poem for a second time; at least, they will have become parts of a whole for you.

On the second reading, read for the exact sense of all the words; if there are words you don't understand, look them up in a dictionary. Dwell on any difficult parts as long as you need to.

If you read the poem silently to yourself, sound its words in your mind. (This is a technique that will get you nowhere in a speed-reading course, but it may help the poem to do its work on you.) Better still, read the poem aloud, or hear someone else read it. You may discover meanings you didn't perceive in it before. Even if you are no actor, to decide how to speak a poem can be an excellent method of getting to understand it. Some poems, like bells, seem heavy till heard. Listen while reading the following lines from Alexander Pope's *Dunciad*. Attacking the minor poet James Ralph, who had sung the praises of a mistress named Cynthia, Pope makes the goddess of Dullness exclaim:

"Silence, ye wolves! while Ralph to Cynthia howls,
And makes night hideous—answer him, ye owls!"

When *ye owls* slide together and become *yowls*, poor Ralph's serenade is turned into the nightly outcry of a cat.

Try to **paraphrase** the poem as a whole, or perhaps just the more difficult lines. In paraphrasing, we put into our own words what we understand the poem to say, restating ideas that seem essential, coming out and stating what the poem may only suggest. This may sound like a heartless thing to do to a poem, but good poems can stand it. In fact, to compare a poem to its paraphrase is a good way to see the distance between poetry and prose. In making a paraphrase, we generally work through a poem or a passage line by line. The statement that results may take as many words as the original, if not more. A paraphrase, then, is ampler than a **summary,** a brief condensation of gist, main idea, or story. (Summary of a horror film in *TV Guide:* "Demented biologist, coveting power over New York, swells sewer rats to hippopotamus-size.") Here is a poem worth considering line by line. The poet writes of an island in a lake in the west of Ireland, in a region where he spent many summers as a boy.

William Butler Yeats   (1865–1939)*

THE LAKE ISLE OF INNISFREE   1892

I will arise and go now, and go to Innisfree,
And a small cabin build there, of clay and wattles made:
Nine bean-rows will I have there, a hive for the honey-bee,
And live alone in the bee-loud glade.

And I shall have some peace there, for peace comes dropping slow,   5
Dropping from the veils of the morning to where the cricket sings;
There midnight's all a glimmer, and noon a purple glow,
And evening full of the linnet's wings.

I will arise and go now, for always night and day
I hear lake water lapping with low sounds by the shore;   10
While I stand on the roadway, or on the pavements gray,
I hear it in the deep heart's core.

Though relatively simple, this poem is far from simple-minded. We need to absorb it slowly and thoughtfully. At the start, for most of us, it raises problems: what are *wattles,* from which the speaker's dream-cabin is to be made? We might guess, but in this case it will help to consult a dictionary: they are "poles interwoven with sticks or branches, formerly used in building as frameworks to support walls or roofs." Evidently, this getaway house will be built in an old-fashioned way: it won't be a prefabricated log cabin or A-frame house, nothing modern or citified. The phrase *bee-loud glade* certainly isn't commonplace language of the sort we find on a cornflakes package, but right away, we can understand it, at least partially: it's a place loud with bees. What is a *glade?* Experience might tell us that it is an open space in woods, but if that word stops us, we can look it up. Although the *linnet* doesn't live in North America, it is a creature with wings—a songbird of the finch family, adds the dictionary. But even if we don't make a special trip to the dictionary to find *linnet,* we probably recognize that the word means "bird," and the line makes sense to us.

A paraphrase of the whole poem might go something like this (in language easier to forget than that of the original): "I'm going to get up now, go to Innisfree,

*The asterisk indicates a poet who is described in Chapter Thirty-one, "Lives of the Poets."

build a cabin, plant beans, keep bees, and live peacefully by myself amid nature and beautiful light. I want to, because I can't forget the sound of that lake water. When I'm in the city, a gray and dingy place, I seem to hear it deep inside me."

These dull remarks, roughly faithful to what Yeats is saying, seem a long way from poetry. Nevertheless, they make certain things clear. For one, they spell out what the poet merely hints at in his choice of the word *gray:* that he finds the city dull and depressing. He stresses the word; instead of saying *gray pavements,* in the usual word order, he turns the phrase around and makes *gray* stand at the end of the line, where it rimes with *day* and so takes extra emphasis. The grayness of the city therefore seems important to the poem, and the paraphrase tries to make its meaning obvious.

Whenever you paraphrase, you stick your neck out. You affirm what the poem gives you to understand. And making a paraphrase can help you see the central thought of the poem, its **theme.** Theme isn't the same as **subject,** the main topic, whatever the poem is "about." In Yeats's poem, the subject is the lake isle of Innisfree, or a wish to retreat to it. But the theme is, "I yearn for an ideal place where I will find perfect peace and happiness." Themes can be stated variously, depending on what you believe most matters in the poem. Taking a different view of the poem, placing more weight on the speaker's wish to escape the city, you might instead state the theme: "This city is getting me down—I want to get back to nature." But after taking a second look at that statement, you might want to sharpen it. After all, this Innisfree seems a special, particular place, where the natural world means more to the poet than just any old trees and birds he might see in a park. Perhaps a stronger statement of theme, one closer to what matters most in the poem, might be: "I want to quit the city for my heaven on earth." That, of course, is saying in an obvious way what Yeats says more subtly, more memorably.

Not all poems clearly assert a proposition, but many do; some even declare their themes in their opening lines: "Gather ye rose-buds while ye may!"—that is, enjoy love before it's too late. This theme, stated in that famous first line of Robert Herrick's "To the Virgins, to Make Much of Time" (page 1081), is so familiar that we give it a name: **carpe diem,** Latin for "seize the day." (For the original *carpe diem* poem, see the Latin poet Horace's ode on page 969.) Seizing the joys of the present moment is a favorite argument of poets. You will meet it in more than these two poems in this book.

A paraphrase, of course, never tells *all* that a poem contains; nor will every reader agree that a particular paraphrase is accurate. We all make our own interpretations; and sometimes the total meaning of a poem evades even the poet who wrote it. Asked to explain his difficult *Sordello,* Robert Browning replied that when he had written the poem only God and he knew what it meant; but "Now, only God knows." Still, to analyze a poem *as if* we could be certain of its meaning is, in general, more fruitful than to proceed as if no certainty could ever be had. The latter approach is likely to end in complete subjectivity: the attitude of the reader who says, "Yeats's 'Lake Isle of Innisfree' is really about the lost island of Atlantis. It is, because I think it is. How can you prove me wrong?" Interpretations can't be proven "wrong." A more fruitful question might be, "What can we understand from the poem's very words?"

All of us bring personal associations to the poems we read. "The Lake Isle of Innisfree" might give you special pleasure if you have ever vacationed on a small island or on the shore of a lake. Such associations are inevitable, even to be welcomed, as long as they don't interfere with our reading the words on the page. We need to distinguish irrelevant responses from those the poem calls for. The reader who can't stand "The Lake Isle of Innisfree" because she is afraid of bees isn't reading a poem by Yeats, but one of her own invention.

Now and again we meet a poem—perhaps startling and memorable—into which the method of paraphrase won't take us far. Some portion of any deep poem resists explanation, but certain poems resist it almost entirely. Many poems of religious mystics seem closer to dream than waking. So do poems that purport to record drug experiences, such as Coleridge's "Kubla Khan" (page 1050), as well as poems that embody some private system of beliefs, such as Blake's "The Sick Rose" (page 1041), or the same poet's lines from *Jerusalem,*

> For a Tear is an Intellectual thing,
> And a Sigh is the Sword of an Angel King.

So do nonsense poems, translations of primitive folk songs, and surreal poems.[1] Such poetry may move us and give pleasure (although not, perhaps, the pleasure of mental understanding). We do it no harm by trying to paraphrase it, though we may fail. Whether logically clear or strangely opaque, good poems appeal to the intelligence and do not shrink from it.

So far, we have taken for granted that poetry differs from prose; yet all our strategies for reading poetry—plowing straight on through and then going back, isolating difficulties, trying to paraphrase, reading aloud, using a dictionary—are no different from those we might employ in unraveling a complicated piece of prose. Poetry, after all, is similar to prose in most respects. At the very least, it is written in the same language. Like prose, poetry shares knowledge with us. It tells us, for instance, of a beautiful island in Lake Gill, County Sligo, Ireland, of how one man feels toward it. Maybe the poet knows no more about Innisfree than a writer of a travel guidebook knows. And yet Yeats's poem indicates a kind of knowledge that tourist guidebooks do not ordinarily reveal: that the human heart can yearn for peace and happiness, that the lake isle of Innisfree with its "low sounds by the shore" can echo and reecho in memory forever.

---

[1]The French poet André Breton, founder of **surrealism,** a movement in art and writing, declared that a higher reality exists, which to mortal eyes looks absurd. To mirror that reality, surrealist poets are fond of bizarre and dreamlike objects such as soluble fish and white-haired revolvers.

LYRIC POETRY

Originally, as its Greek name suggests, a *lyric* was a poem sung to the music of a lyre. This earlier meaning—a poem made for singing—is still current today, when we use *lyrics* to mean the words of a popular song. But the kind of printed poem we now call a *lyric* is usually something else, for over the past five hundred years, the nature of lyric poetry has changed greatly. Ever since the rise of the printing press in the fifteenth century, poets have written less often for singers, more often for readers. In general, this tendency has made lyric poems contain less word-music and (since they can be pondered on a page) more thought—and perhaps more complicated feelings.

Here is a rough definition of a **lyric** as it is written today: a short poem expressing the thoughts and feelings of a single speaker. Often a poet will write a lyric in the first person ("I will arise and go now, and go to Innisfree"), but not always. Instead, a lyric might describe an object or recall an experience without the speaker's ever bringing himself or herself into it. (For an example of such a lyric, one in which the poet refrains from saying "I," see William Carlos Williams's "The Red Wheelbarrow" on page 680, Theodore Roethke's "Root Cellar" on page 743, or Gerard Manley Hopkins's "Pied Beauty" on page 748.)

Perhaps because, rightly or wrongly, some people still think of lyrics as lyre-strummings, they expect a lyric to be an outburst of feeling, somewhat resembling a song, at least containing musical elements such as rime, rhythm, or sound effects. Such expectations are fulfilled in "The Lake Isle of Innisfree," that impassioned lyric full of language rich in sound (as you will hear if you'll read it aloud). In practice, though, many contemporary poets write short poems in which they voice opinions or complicated feelings—poems that no reader would dream of trying to sing. Most people would call such poems lyrics, too; one recent commentator has argued that a lyric may contain an argument.[2]

But in the sense in which we use it, *lyric* will usually apply to a kind of poem you can easily recognize. Here, for instance, are two lyrics. They differ sharply in subject and theme, but they have traits in common: both are short, and (as you will find) both set forth one speaker's definite, unmistakable feelings.

D. H. Lawrence (1885–1930)*

PIANO   1918

Softly, in the dusk, a woman is singing to me;
Taking me back down the vista of years, till I see
A child sitting under the piano, in the boom of the tingling strings
And pressing the small, poised feet of a mother who smiles as she sings.

---

[2]Jeffrey Walker, "Aristotle's Lyric," *College English* 51 (January, 1989) 5–26.

In spite of myself, the insidious mastery of song   5
Betrays me back, till the heart of me weeps to belong
To the old Sunday evenings at home, with winter outside
And hymns in the cozy parlor, the tinkling piano our guide.

So now it is vain for the singer to burst into clamor
With the great black piano appassionato. The glamor   10
Of childish days is upon me, my manhood is cast
Down in the flood of remembrance, I weep like a child for the past.

QUESTIONS

1. Jot down a brief paraphrase of this poem. In your paraphrase, clearly show what the speaker says is happening at present and also what he finds himself remembering. Make clear which seems the more powerful in its effect on him.
2. What are the speaker's various feelings? What do you understand from the words *insidious* and *betrays*?
3. With what specific details does the poem make the past seem real?
4. What is the subject of Lawrence's poem? How would you state its theme?

Adrienne Rich   (b. 1929)*

AUNT JENNIFER'S TIGERS   1951

Aunt Jennifer's tigers prance across a screen,
Bright topaz denizens of a world of green.
They do not fear the men beneath the tree;
They pace in sleek chivalric certainty.

Aunt Jennifer's fingers fluttering through her wool   5
Find even the ivory needle hard to pull.
The massive weight of Uncle's wedding band
Sits heavily upon Aunt Jennifer's hand.

When Aunt is dead, her terrified hands will lie
Still ringed with ordeals she was mastered by.   10
The tigers in the panel that she made
Will go on prancing, proud and unafraid.

COMPARE

"Aunt Jennifer's Tigers" with Adrienne Rich's critical comments on the poem (page 664).

NARRATIVE POETRY

Although a lyric sometimes relates an incident, or like "Piano" draws a scene, it does not usually relate a series of events. That happens in a **narrative poem,** one whose main purpose is to tell a story.

In Western literature, narrative poetry dates back to the Babylonian epic of Gilgamesh (composed before 2000 B.C.) and Homer's epic Iliad and Odyssey (composed before 700 B.C.). It may well have originated much earlier. In England and Scotland, storytelling poems have long been popular; in the late Middle Ages, ballads—or storytelling songs—circulated widely. Some, like "Sir Patrick Spence" and "Bonny Barbara Allan," survive in our day, and folksingers sometimes perform them.

Evidently the art of narrative poetry invites the skills of a writer of fiction: the ability to draw characters and settings briefly, to engage attention, to shape a plot. Needless to say, it calls for all the skills of a poet besides. Here are two narrative poems: one medieval, one modern. How would you paraphrase the stories they tell? How do they hold your attention to their stories?

Anonymous   (traditional Scottish ballad)

Sir Patrick Spence

The king sits in Dumferling toune,
  Drinking the blude-reid wine:
"O whar will I get guid sailor
  To sail this schip of mine?"

Up and spak an eldern knicht°,   *knight*   5
  Sat at the kings richt kne:
"Sir Patrick Spence is the best sailor
  That sails upon the se."

The king has written a braid letter,
  And signed it wi' his hand,   10
And sent it to Sir Patrick Spence,
  Was walking on the sand.

The first line that Sir Patrick red,
  A loud lauch lauchèd he;
The next line that Sir Patrick red,   15
  The teir blinded his ee.

"O wha° is this has don this deid,   *who*
  This ill deid don to me,
To send me out this time o' the yeir,
  To sail upon the se!   20

"Mak haste, mak haste, my mirry men all,
  Our guid schip sails the morne."
"O say na sae°, my master deir,   *so*
  For I feir a deadlie storme.

"Late late yestreen I saw the new moone,   25
  Wi' the auld moone in hir arme,
And I feir, I feir, my deir master,
  That we will cum to harme."

O our Scots nobles wer richt laith°   *loath*
  To weet° their cork-heild schoone°,   *wet; shoes*   30
Bot lang owre° a' the play wer playd,   *before*
  Their hats they swam aboone°.   *above (their heads)*

O lang, lang may their ladies sit,
  Wi' their fans into their hand,
Or ere° they se Sir Patrick Spence   *long before*   35
  Cum sailing to the land.

O lang, lang may the ladies stand,
  Wi' their gold kems° in their hair,   *combs*
Waiting for their ain° deir lords,   *own*
  For they'll se thame na mair.   40

Haf owre°, haf owre to Aberdour,   *halfway over*
  It's fiftie fadom deip,
And thair lies guid Sir Patrick Spence,
  Wi' the Scots lords at his feit.

SIR PATRICK SPENCE. 9 *braid:* Broad, but broad in what sense? Among guesses are *plain-spoken, offi-cial,* and *on wide paper.*

QUESTIONS

1. That the king drinks "blood-red wine" (line 2)—what meaning do you find in that detail? What does it hint, or foreshadow?
2. What do you make of this king and his motives for sending Spence and the Scots lords into an impending storm? Is he a fool, is he cruel and inconsiderate, is he deliberately trying to drown Sir Patrick and his crew, or can't we possibly know? Let your answer depend on the poem alone, not on anything you read into it.
3. Comment on this ballad's methods of storytelling. Is the story told too briefly for us to care what happens to Spence and his men, or does the poet by any means make us feel compassion for them? Do you resent the lack of a detailed account of the shipwreck?
4. Lines 25–28—the new moon with the old moon in her arm—has been much admired as poetry. What does this stanza contribute to the story as well?

Robert Frost   (1874–1963)*

"OUT, OUT—"   1916

The buzz-saw snarled and rattled in the yard
And made dust and dropped stove-length sticks of wood,
Sweet-scented stuff when the breeze drew across it.
And from there those that lifted eyes could count
Five mountain ranges one behind the other   5
Under the sunset far into Vermont.
And the saw snarled and rattled, snarled and rattled,
As it ran light, or had to bear a load.
And nothing happened: day was all but done.
Call it a day, I wish they might have said   10
To please the boy by giving him the half hour
That a boy counts so much when saved from work.
His sister stood beside them in her apron
To tell them "Supper." At the word, the saw,
As if to prove saws knew what supper meant,   15
Leaped out at the boy's hand, or seemed to leap—
He must have given the hand. However it was,
Neither refused the meeting. But the hand!
The boy's first outcry was a rueful laugh,
As he swung toward them holding up the hand   20
Half in appeal, but half as if to keep
The life from spilling. Then the boy saw all—
Since he was old enough to know, big boy
Doing a man's work, though a child at heart—
He saw all spoiled. "Don't let him cut my hand off—   25
The doctor, when he comes. Don't let him, sister!"
So. But the hand was gone already.
The doctor put him in the dark of ether.
He lay and puffed his lips out with his breath.
And then—the watcher at his pulse took fright.   30
No one believed. They listened at his heart.
Little—less—nothing!—and that ended it.
No more to build on there. And they, since they
Were not the one dead, turned to their affairs.

"OUT, OUT—" The title of this poem echoes the words of Shakespeare's *Macbeth* on receiving news
that his queen is dead: "Out, out, brief candle! / Life's but a walking shadow, a poor player / That
struts and frets his hour upon the stage / And then is heard no more. It is a tale / Told by an idiot, full
of sound and fury, / Signifying nothing" (*Macbeth* V, v, 23–28).

QUESTIONS

1. How does Frost make the buzz-saw appear sinister? How does he make it seem, in another way, like a friend?

2. What do you make of the people who surround the boy—the "they" of the poem? Who might they be? Do they seem to you concerned and compassionate, cruel, indifferent, or what?
3. What does Frost's reference to *Macbeth* contribute to your understanding of "Out, Out—"? How would you state the theme of Frost's poem?
4. Set this poem side by side with "Sir Patrick Spence." How does "Out, Out—" resemble that medieval folk ballad in subject, or differ from it? How is Frost's poem similar or different in its way of telling a story?

DRAMATIC POETRY

A third kind of poetry is **dramatic poetry** that presents the voice of an imaginary character (or characters) speaking directly, without any additional narration by the author. A dramatic poem, according to T. S. Eliot, does not consist of "what the poet would say in his own person, but only what he can say within the limits of one imaginary character addressing another imaginary character." Strictly speaking, the term *dramatic poetry* describes any verse written for the stage (and until a few centuries ago most playwrights, like Shakespeare and Molière, wrote their plays mainly in verse). But the term most often refers to the **dramatic monologue,** a poem written as a speech made by a character (other than the author) at some decisive moment. A dramatic monologue is usually addressed by the speaker to some other character who remains silent. If the listener replies, the poem becomes a dialogue (like the traditional ballad "Edward" on page 1028) in which the story unfolds in the conversation between two speakers.

The Victorian poet Robert Browning, who developed the form of the dramatic monologue, liked to put words in the mouths of characters who were conspicuously nasty, weak, reckless, or crazy: see, for instance, Browning's "Soliloquy of the Spanish Cloister" (page 1047) in which the speaker is an obsessively proud and jealous monk. The dramatic monologue has been a popular form among American poets, including Edwin Arlington Robinson, Robert Frost, Ezra Pound, Randall Jarrell, and Sylvia Plath. The most famous dramatic monologue ever written is probably Browning's "My Last Duchess" in which the poet creates a Renaissance Italian Duke whose words reveal more about himself than the aristocratic speaker intends.

Robert Browning (1812–1889)*

MY LAST DUCHESS 1842

Ferrara

That's my last Duchess painted on the wall,
Looking as if she were alive. I call
That piece a wonder, now; Frà Pandolf's hands
Worked busily a day, and there she stands.

Will't please you sit and look at her? I said   5
"Frà Pandolf" by design, for never read
Strangers like you that pictured countenance,
The depth and passion of its earnest glance,
But to myself they turned (since none puts by
The curtain I have drawn for you, but I)   10
And seemed as they would ask me, if they durst,
How such a glance came there; so, not the first
Are you to turn and ask thus. Sir, 'twas not
Her husband's presence only, called that spot
Of joy into the Duchess' cheek; perhaps   15
Frà Pandolf chanced to say, "Her mantle laps
Over my lady's wrist too much," or "Paint
Must never hope to reproduce the faint
Half-flush that dies along her throat." Such stuff
Was courtesy, she thought, and cause enough   20
For calling up that spot of joy. She had
A heart—how shall I say?—too soon made glad,
Too easily impressed; she liked whate'er
She looked on, and her looks went everywhere.
Sir, 'twas all one! My favor at her breast,   25
The dropping of the daylight in the West,
The bough of cherries some officious fool
Broke in the orchard for her, the white mule
She rode with round the terrace—all and each
Would draw from her alike the approving speech,   30
Or blush, at least. She thanked men,—good! but thanked
Somehow—I know not how—as if she ranked
My gift of a nine-hundred-years-old name
With anybody's gift. Who'd stoop to blame
This sort of trifling? Even had you skill   35
In speech—which I have not—to make your will
Quite clear to such an one, and say "Just this
Or that in you disgusts me; here you miss,
Or there exceed the mark"—and if she let
Herself be lessoned so, nor plainly set   40
Her wits to yours, forsooth, and made excuse—
E'en then would be some stooping; and I choose
Never to stoop. Oh, sir, she smiled, no doubt,
Whene'er I passed her; but who passed without
Much the same smile? This grew; I gave commands;   45
Then all smiles stopped together. There she stands
As if alive. Will't please you rise? We'll meet
The company below, then. I repeat,
The Count your master's known munificence

Is ample warrant that no just pretense 50
Of mine for dowry will be disallowed;
Though his fair daughter's self, as I avowed
At starting, is my object. Nay, we'll go
Together down, sir. Notice Neptune, though,
Taming a sea-horse, thought a rarity, 55
Which Claus of Innsbruck cast in bronze for me!

MY LAST DUCHESS. Ferrara, a city in northern Italy, is the scene. Browning may have modeled his speaker after Alonzo, Duke of Ferrara (1533–1598). 3 *Frà Pandolf* and, 56 *Claus of Innsbruck*: fictitious names of artists.

QUESTIONS

1. Who is the Duke addressing? What is this person's business in Ferrara?
2. What is the Duke's opinion of his last Duchess's personality? Do we see her character differently?
3. If the Duke was unhappy with the Duchess's behavior, why didn't he make his displeasure known? Cite a specific passage to explain his reticence.
4. How much do we know about the fate of the last Duchess? Would it help our understanding of the poem to know more?
5. Does Browning imply any connection between the Duke's art collection and his attitude toward his wife?

Today, lyrics in the English language seem more plentiful than other kinds of poetry. Although there has recently been a revival of interest in writing narrative poems, they have a far smaller audience today than long verse narratives, like Henry Wadsworth Longfellow's *Evangeline* and Alfred, Lord Tennyson's *Idylls of the King*, enjoyed in the nineteenth century.

Also more fashionable in former times was a fourth variety of poetry, **didactic poetry:** that was apparently written to state a message or teach a body of knowledge. In a lyric, a speaker may express sadness; in a didactic poem, he or she may explain that sadness is inherent in life. Poems that impart a body of knowledge, like Ovid's *Art of Love* and Lucretius's *On the Nature of Things*, are didactic. Such instructive poetry was favored especially by classical Latin poets and by English poets of the eighteenth century. In *The Fleece* (1757), John Dyer celebrated the British woolen industry and included practical advice on raising sheep:

In cold stiff soils the bleaters oft complain
Of gouty ails, by shepherds termed the halt:
Those let the neighboring fold or ready crook
Detain, and pour into their cloven feet
Corrosive drugs, deep-searching arsenic,
Dry alum, verdegris, or vitriol keen.

One might agree with Dr. Johnson's comment on Dyer's effort: "The subject, Sir, cannot be made poetical." But it may be argued that the subject of didactic poetry does not make it any less poetical. Good poems, it seems, can be written about anything under the sun. Like Dyer, John Milton also described sick sheep in "Lycidas," a poem few readers have thought unpoetic:

The hungry sheep look up, and are not fed,
But, swoll'n with wind and the rank mist they draw,
Rot inwardly, and foul contagion spread . . .

What makes Milton's lines better poetry than Dyer's is, among other things, a difference in attitude. Sick sheep to Dyer mean the loss of a few shillings and pence; to Milton, whose sheep stand for English Christendom, they mean a moral catastrophe.

WRITER'S PERSPECTIVE

Adrienne Rich

Adrienne Rich on Writing
RECALLING "AUNT JENNIFER'S TIGERS"   1971

I know that my style was formed first by male poets: by the men I was reading as an undergraduate—Frost, Dylan Thomas, Donne, Auden, MacNeice, Stevens, Yeats. What I chiefly learned from them was craft. But poems are like dreams: in them you put what you don't know you know. Looking back at poems I wrote before I was 21, I'm startled because beneath the conscious craft are glimpses of the split I even then experienced between the girl who wrote poems, who defined herself in writing poems, and the girl who was to define herself by her relationships with men. "Aunt Jennifer's Tigers," written while I was a student, looks with deliberate detachment at this split. In writing this poem, composed and apparently cool as it is, I thought I was creating a portrait of an imaginary woman. But this woman suffers from the opposition of her imagination, worked out in tapestry, and her life-style, "ringed with ordeals she was mastered by." It was important to me that Aunt Jennifer was a person as distinct from myself as possible—distanced by the formalism of the poem, by its objective, observant tone—even by putting the woman in a different generation.

In those years formalism was part of the strategy—like asbestos gloves, it allowed me to handle materials I couldn't pick up bare-handed.

"When We Dead Awaken: Writing as Re-Vision"

Can a Poem Be Paraphrased?

Since the full meaning of a poem is so completely wedded to its exact wording, some people maintain that no poem can be truly paraphrased. As we have discussed earlier in the chapter, however, such an opinion misses the point of paraphrasing. A paraphrase doesn't attempt to re-create the full effect of a poem; it only tries to map out clearly the key images, actions, and ideas. A map is no substitute for a landscape, but a good map often helps us find our way through the landscape without getting lost.

Let's look at an example of a paraphrase written, not by a critic, but by an author about one of his own poems. When an editor asked William Stafford if one of his poems could be paraphrased, Stafford responded by providing his own paraphrase of a short poem. Here is the poem he chose, along with his own restatement in prose of what the poem says.

William Stafford   (1914–1993)*
ASK ME   1975

Some time when the river is ice ask me
mistakes I have made. Ask me whether
what I have done is my life. Others
have come in their slow way into
my thought, and some have tried to help   5
or to hurt—ask me what difference
their strongest love or hate has made.

I will listen to what you say.
You and I can turn and look
at the silent river and wait. We know   10
the current is there, hidden; and there
are comings and goings from miles away
that hold the stillness exactly before us.
What the river says, that is what I say.

William Stafford   (1914–1993)*
A PARAPHRASE OF "ASK ME"   1977

I think my poem can be paraphrased—and that any poem can be paraphrased. But every pass through the material, using other words, would have to be achieved at certain costs, either in momentum, or nuance, or dangerously explicit (and therefore misleading in tone) adjustments. I'll try one such pass through the poem:

When it's quiet and cold and we have some chance to interchange without hurry, confront me if you like with a challenge about whether I think I have made mistakes in my life—and ask me, if you want to, whether to me my life is actually the sequence of events or exploits others would see. Well, those others tag along in my living, and some of them in fact have played significant roles in the narrative run of my world; they have intended either helping or hurting (but by implication in the way I am saying this you will know that neither effort is conclusive). So—ask me how important their good or bad intentions have been (both intentions get a drastic *leveling* judgment from this cool stating of it all). You, too, will be entering that realm of maybe-help-maybe-hurt, by entering that far into my life by asking this serious question—so: I will stay still and consider. Out there will be the world confronting us both; we will both know we are surrounded by mystery, tremendous things that do not reveal themselves to us. That river, that world— and our lives—all share the depth and stillness of much more sig- nificance than our talk, or intentions. There is a steadiness and somehow a solace in knowing that what is around us so greatly sur- passes our human concerns.

"Ask Me"

Writing Assignment

Write a concise, accurate paraphrase of a short poem from "Poems for Further Reading" (pages 1027–1164). Your instructor may suggest a particular poem or poems. Although your paraphrase should cover the entire poem, it need not mention everything. Try to in- clude the most vital points and details and try to state the poem's main thought or theme. Be as specific as possible, but explain the poem in your own words without quoting any original passages.

Be prepared to share your paraphrase with the rest of the class and to compare it with other paraphrases of the same poem. You may then be able to test yourself as a reader of poetry. What in the poem whizzed by you that other students noticed? What did you catch that others ignored?

13 *Listening to a Voice*

TONE

In old Western movies, when one hombre taunts another, it is customary for the second to drawl, "Smile when you say that, pardner" or "Mister, I don't like your tone of voice." Sometimes in reading a poem, although we can neither see a face nor hear a voice, we can infer the poet's attitude from other evidence.

Like tone of voice, **tone** in literature often conveys an attitude toward the person addressed. Like the manner of a person, the manner of a poem may be friendly or belligerent toward its reader, condescending or respectful. Again like tone of voice, the tone of a poem may tell us how the speaker feels about himself or herself: cocksure or humble, sad or glad. But usually when we ask, "What is the tone of a poem?" we mean, "What attitude does the poet take toward a theme or a subject?" Is the poet being affectionate, hostile, earnest, playful, sarcastic, or what? We may never be able to know, of course, the poet's personal feelings. All we need know is how to feel when we read the poem.

Strictly speaking, tone isn't an attitude; it is whatever in the poem makes an attitude clear to us: the choice of certain words instead of others, the picking out of certain details. In A. E. Housman's "Loveliest of trees," for example, the poet communicates his admiration for a cherry tree's beauty by singling out for attention its white blossoms; had he wanted to show his dislike for the tree, he might have concentrated on its broken branches, birdlime, or snails. Rightly to perceive the tone of a poem, we need to read the poem carefully, paying attention to whatever suggestions we find in it.

Theodore Roethke   (1908–1963)*

MY PAPA'S WALTZ   1948

The whiskey on your breath
Could make a small boy dizzy;
But I hung on like death:
Such waltzing was not easy.

We romped until the pans   5
Slid from the kitchen shelf;
My mother's countenance
Could not unfrown itself.

The hand that held my wrist
Was battered on one knuckle;   10
At every step you missed
My right ear scraped a buckle.

You beat time on my head
With a palm caked hard by dirt,
Then waltzed me off to bed   15
Still clinging to your shirt.

What is the tone of this poem? Most readers find the speaker's attitude toward his father critical, but nonetheless affectionate. They take this recollection of childhood to be an odd but happy one. Other readers, however, concentrate on other details, such as the father's rough manners and drunkenness. One reader has written that "Roethke expresses his resentment for his father, a drunken brute with dirty hands and whiskey breath who carelessly hurt the child's ear and manhandled him." Although this reader accurately noticed some of the events in the poem and perceived that there was something desperate in the son's hanging onto the father "like death," he simplifies the tone of the poem and so misses its humorous side.

While "My Papa's Waltz" contains the dark elements of manhandling and drunkenness, the tone remains grotesquely comic. The rollicking rhythms of the poem underscore Roethke's complex humor—half loving and half censuring of the unwashed, intoxicated father. The humor is further reinforced by playful rimes like *dizzy* and *easy*, *knuckle* and *buckle*, as well as the joyful suggestions of the words *waltz, waltzing,* and *romped.* The scene itself is comic, with kitchen pans falling due to the father's roughhousing while the mother looks on unamused. However much the speaker satirizes the overly rambunctious father, he does not have the boy identify with the soberly disapproving mother. Not all comedy is comfortable and reassuring. Certainly, this small boy's family life has its frightening side, but the last line suggests the boy is *still clinging* to his father with persistent if also complicated love.

Such a poem, though it includes lifelike details that aren't pretty, has a tone relatively easy to recognize. So does **satiric poetry,** a kind of comic poetry that generally conveys a message. Usually its tone is one of detached amusement, withering contempt, and implied superiority. In a satiric poem, the poet ridicules some person or persons (or perhaps some kind of human behavior), examining the victim by the light of certain principles and implying that the reader, too, ought to feel contempt for the victim.

Countee Cullen (1903–1946)

FOR A LADY I KNOW
1925

She even thinks that up in heaven
  Her class lies late and snores,
While poor black cherubs rise at seven
  To do celestial chores.

QUESTIONS

1. What is Cullen's message?
2. How would you characterize the tone of this poem? Wrathful? Amused?

In some poems the poet's attitude may be plain enough; while in other poems attitudes may be so mingled that it is hard to describe them tersely without doing injustice to the poem. Does Andrew Marvell in "To His Coy Mistress" (page 1101) take a serious or playful attitude toward the fact that he and his lady are destined to be food for worms? No one-word answer will suffice. And what of T. S. Eliot's "The Love Song of J. Alfred Prufrock" (page 1059)? In his attitude toward his redemption-seeking hero who wades with trousers rolled, Eliot is seriously funny. Such a mingled tone may be seen in the following poem by the wife of a governor of the Massachusetts Bay Colony and the earliest American poet of note. Anne Bradstreet's first book, *The Tenth Muse Lately Sprung Up in America* (1650), had been published in England without her consent. She wrote these lines to preface a second edition:

Anne Bradstreet (1612?–1672)

THE AUTHOR TO HER BOOK
1678

Thou ill-formed offspring of my feeble brain,
Who after birth did'st by my side remain,
Till snatched from thence by friends, less wise than true,
Who thee abroad exposed to public view;
Made thee in rags, halting, to the press to trudge,   5
Where errors were not lessened, all may judge.
At thy return my blushing was not small,
My rambling brat (in print) should mother call;
I cast thee by as one unfit for light,

Thy visage was so irksome in my sight;   10
Yet being mine own, at length affection would
Thy blemishes amend, if so I could:
I washed thy face, but more defects I saw,
And rubbing off a spot, still made a flaw.
I stretched thy joints to make thee even feet,   15
Yet still thou run'st more hobbling than is meet;
In better dress to trim thee was my mind,
But nought save homespun cloth in the house I find.
In this array, 'mongst vulgars may'st thou roam;
In critics' hands beware thou dost not come;   20
And take thy way where yet thou are not known.
If for thy Father asked, say thou had'st none;
And for thy Mother, she alas is poor,
Which caused her thus to send thee out of door.

In the author's comparison of her book to an illegitimate ragamuffin, we may be
struck by the details of scrubbing and dressing a child: details that might well
occur to a mother who had scrubbed and dressed many. As she might feel toward
such a child, so she feels toward her book. She starts by deploring it but, as the
poem goes on, cannot deny it her affection. Humor enters (as in the pun in line
15). She must dress the creature in *homespun cloth,* something both crude and
serviceable. By the end of her poem, Bradstreet seems to regard her book-child
with tenderness, amusement, and a certain indulgent awareness of its faults. To
read this poem is to sense its mingling of several attitudes. Simultaneously, a
poet can be merry and in earnest.

Walt Whitman   (1819–1892)*

TO A LOCOMOTIVE IN WINTER   1881

Thee for my recitative,
Thee in the driving storm even as now, the snow, the winter-day
    declining,
Thee in thy panoply°, thy measur'd dual throbbing and thy beat
    convulsive,   *suit of armor*
Thy black cylindric body, golden brass and silvery steel,
Thy ponderous side-bars, parallel and connecting rods, gyrating,
    shuttling at thy sides,   5
Thy metrical, now swelling pant and roar, now tapering in the distance,
Thy great protruding head-light fix'd in front,
Thy long, pale, floating vapor-pennants, tinged with delicate purple,
The dense and murky clouds out-belching from thy smoke-stack,
Thy knitted frame, thy springs and valves, the tremulous twinkle of
    thy wheels,   10

Thy train of cars behind, obedient, merrily following,
Through gale or calm, now swift, now slack, yet steadily careering;
Type of the modern—emblem of motion and power—pulse of the
     continent,
For once come serve the Muse and merge in verse, even as here I see
     thee,
With storm and buffeting gusts of wind and falling snow,   15
By day thy warning ringing bell to sound its notes,
By night thy silent signal lamps to swing.
Fierce-throated beauty!
Roll through my chant with all thy lawless music, thy swinging lamps
     at night,
Thy madly-whistled laughter, echoing, rumbling like an earthquake,
     rousing all,   20
Law of thyself complete, thine own track firmly holding,
(No sweetness debonair of tearful harp or glib piano thine,)
Thy trills of shrieks by rocks and hills return'd,
Launch'd o'er the prairies wide, across the lakes,
To the free skies unpent and glad and strong.   25

Emily Dickinson   (1830–1886)*

I LIKE TO SEE IT LAP THE MILES   (ABOUT 1862)[1]

I like to see it lap the Miles –
And lick the Valleys up –
And stop to feed itself at Tanks –
And then – prodigious step

Around a Pile of Mountains –   5
And supercilious peer
In Shanties – by the sides of Roads –
And then a Quarry pare

To fit its Ribs
And crawl between   10
Complaining all the while
In horrid – hooting stanza –
Then chase itself down Hill –

And neigh like Boanerges –
Then – punctual as a Star   15
Stop – docile and omnipotent
At its own stable door –

---

[1] Parentheses around a date that follows a poem title indicate the poem's date of composition, when
it was composed much earlier than its first publication date.

1. What differences in tone do you find between Whitman's and Dickinson's poems? Point out in each poem whatever contributes to these differences.
2. *Boanerges* in Dickinson's last stanza means "sons of thunder," a name given by Jesus to the disciples John and James (see Mark 3:17). How far should the reader work out the particulars of this comparison? Does it make the tone of the poem serious?
3. In Whitman's opening line, what is a *recitative?* What other specialized terms from the vocabulary of music and poetry does each poem contain? How do they help underscore Whitman's theme?
4. Poets and songwriters probably have regarded the locomotive with more affection than they have shown most other machines. Why do you suppose this is so? Can you think of any other poems or songs for example?
5. What do these two poems tell you about locomotives that you would not be likely to find in a technical book on railroading?
6. Are the subjects of the two poems identical? Discuss.

Langston Hughes   (1902–1967)*

HOMECOMING   1959

I went back in the alley
And I opened up my door.
All her clothes was gone:
She wasn't home no more.

I pulled back the covers,   5
I made down the bed.
A *whole* lot of room
Was the only thing I had.

QUESTIONS

1. How does the speaker feel about this sudden disappearance? Exactly what in the poem makes his feelings clear?
2. Suppose the speaker had ranted, cried, felt sorry for himself, and discussed his anger, frustration, and grief at great length. Do you suppose a better poem might have resulted? What do you find to admire in the poem as it is?

Weldon Kees   (1914–1955)

FOR MY DAUGHTER   1940

Looking into my daughter's eyes I read
Beneath the innocence of morning flesh
Concealed, hintings of death she does not heed.
Coldest of winds have blown this hair, and mesh
Of seaweed snarled these miniatures of hands;   5
The night's slow poison, tolerant and bland,

Has moved her blood. Parched years that I have seen
That may be hers appear: foul, lingering
Death in certain war, the slim legs green.
Or, fed on hate, she relishes the sting   10
Of others' agony; perhaps the cruel
Bride of a syphilitic or a fool.
These speculations sour in the sun.
I have no daughter. I desire none.

QUESTIONS

1. How does the last line of this sonnet affect the meaning of the poem?
2. "For My Daughter" was first published in 1940. What considerations might a potential American parent have felt at that time? Are these historical concerns mirrored
   in the poem?
3. Donald Justice has said that "Kees is one of the bitterest poets in history." Is bitterness the only attitude the speaker reveals in this poem?

THE PERSON IN THE POEM

The tone of a poem, we said, is like tone of voice in that both communicate feelings. Still, this comparison raises a question: When we read a poem, whose
"voice" speaks to us?

"The poet's" is one possible answer; and in the case of many a poem, that
answer may be right. Reading Anne Bradstreet's "The Author to Her Book," we
can be reasonably sure that the poet speaks of her very own book, and of her own
experiences. In order to read a poem, we seldom need to read a poet's biography;
but in truth there are certain poems whose full effect depends upon our knowing
at least a fact or two of the poet's life. Here is one such poem.

Carter Revard (b. 1931)
BIRCH CANOE   1992

Red men embraced   my body's whiteness,
cutting into me   carved it free,
sewed it tight   with sinews taken
from lightfoot deer   who leaped this stream—
now in my ghost-skin   they glide over clouds   5
at home in the fish's   fallen heaven.

Although Revard's poem may initially seem dreamlike and mysterious, it depicts neither a nightmare nor a vision. The poem will mean more to you if you
know that Revard is part white, part Osage Indian. Raised in poverty on a reservation, he eventually became a Rhodes scholar and earned a Ph.D. from Yale.
The form of the poem may become clear when you learn that Revard teaches

Medieval English literature and patterned the poem after an Anglo-Saxon riddle. The title is the answer to the riddle posed by the six lines that follow. The poem is spoken by the canoe, but the reader who knows something of the author's life will also detect a subtle autobiographical element in the theme of a white birch tree shaped into a new entity by Native American custom. As Revard has remarked, "To become a good *human* poem this should be a good Indian poem." Surely "Birch Canoe" succeeds in both ways. A knowing celebration of tribal life and values, the poem's distinction comes from its ability to speak memorably about a significant aspect of human experience and the world.

Most of us can tell the difference between a person we meet in life and a person we meet in a work of art—unlike the moviegoer in the Philippines who, watching a villain in an exciting film, pulled out a revolver and peppered the screen. And yet, in reading poems, we are liable to temptation.

When the poet says "I," we may want to assume that he or she is making a personal statement. But reflect: do all poems have to be personal? Here is a brief poem inscribed on the tombstone of an infant in Burial Hill cemetery, Plymouth, Massachusetts:

> Since I have been so quickly done for,
> I wonder what I was begun for.

We do not know who wrote those lines, but it is clear that the poet was not a short-lived infant writing from personal experience. In other poems, the speaker is obviously a **persona** or fictitious character: not the poet, but the poet's creation. As a grown man, William Blake, a skilled professional engraver, wrote a poem in the voice of a boy, an illiterate chimney sweeper. (The poem appears on page 688.)

Let's consider a poem spoken not by a poet, but by a persona—in this case a mysterious one. Edwin Arlington Robinson's "Luke Havergal" is a dramatic monologue, but the identity of the speaker is never clearly stated. Upon first reading the poem in Robinson's *The Children of the Night* (1897), President Theodore Roosevelt was so moved that he wrote a review of the book that made the author famous. Roosevelt, however, admitted that he found the musically seductive poem difficult. "I am not sure I understand 'Luke Havergal,'" he wrote, "but I am entirely sure I like it." Possibly what most puzzled our twenty-sixth president was who was speaking in the poem. How much does Robinson let us know about the voice and the person it addresses?

Edwin Arlington Robinson   (1869–1935)*

LUKE HAVERGAL   1897

Go to the western gate, Luke Havergal,
There where the vines cling crimson on the wall,
And in the twilight wait for what will come.
The leaves will whisper there of her, and some,

Like flying words, will strike you as they fall; 5
But go, and if you listen she will call.
Go to the western gate, Luke Havergal—
Luke Havergal.

No, there is not a dawn in eastern skies
To rift the fiery night that's in your eyes; 10
But there, where western glooms are gathering,
The dark will end the dark, if anything:
God slays Himself with every leaf that flies,
And hell is more than half of paradise.
No, there is not a dawn in eastern skies— 15
In eastern skies.

Out of a grave I come to tell you this,
Out of a grave I come to quench the kiss
That flames upon your forehead with a glow
That blinds you to the way that you must go. 20
Yes, there is yet one way to where she is,
Bitter, but one that faith may never miss.
Out of a grave I come to tell you this—
To tell you this.

There is the western gate, Luke Havergal, 25
There are the crimson leaves upon the wall.
Go, for the winds are tearing them away,—
Nor think to riddle the dead words they say,
Nor any more to feel them as they fall;
But go, and if you trust her she will call. 30
There is the western gate, Luke Havergal—
Luke Havergal.

QUESTIONS

1. Who is the speaker of the poem? What specific details does the author reveal about the speaker?
2. What does the speaker ask Luke Havergal to do?
3. What do you understand "the western gate" to be?
4. Would you advise Luke Havergal to follow the speaker's advice? Why or why not?

No literary law decrees that the speaker in a poem even has to be human. Carter Revard's poem is spoken by a birch-bark canoe. Good poems have been uttered by clouds, pebbles, clocks, and cats. Here is a recent poem spoken by a flower, a dramatic monologue that expresses the thoughts and desires of a persona at a moment of particularly intense emotion—as the speaker faces death. The poem seems to be a sort of a prayer, but to whom is the prayer addressed?

Louise Glück (b. 1943)*

THE GOLD LILY   1992

As I perceive
I am dying now, and know
I will not speak again, will not
survive the earth, be summoned
out of it again, not   5
a flower yet, a spine only, raw dirt
catching my ribs, I call you
father and master: all around,
my companions are failing, thinking
you do not see. How   10
can they know you see
unless you save us?
In the summer twilight, are you
close enough to hear
your child's terror? Or   15
are you not my father,
you who raised me?

QUESTION

To what "father and master" does the flower speak? Support your answer with evidence
from the poem.

In a famous definition, William Wordsworth calls poetry "the spontaneous
overflow of powerful feelings . . . recollected in tranquillity." But in the case of
the following poem, Wordsworth's feelings weren't all his; they didn't just overflow spontaneously; and the process of tranquil recollection had to go on for
years.

William Wordsworth (1770–1850)*

I WANDERED LONELY AS A CLOUD   1807

I wandered lonely as a cloud
   That floats on high o'er vales and hills,
When all at once I saw a crowd,
   A host, of golden daffodils,
Beside the lake, beneath the trees,   5
Fluttering and dancing in the breeze.

Continuous as the stars that shine
  And twinkle on the milky way,
They stretched in never-ending line
  Along the margin of a bay: 10
Ten thousand saw I at a glance,
Tossing their heads in sprightly dance.

The waves beside them danced; but they
  Out-did the sparkling waves in glee;
A poet could not but be gay,   15
  In such a jocund company;
I gazed—and gazed—but little thought
What wealth the show to me had brought:

For oft, when on my couch I lie
  In vacant or in pensive mood,   20
They flash upon that inward eye
  Which is the bliss of solitude;
And then my heart with pleasure fills,
And dances with the daffodils.

Between the first printing of the poem in 1807 and the version of 1815 given here, Wordsworth made several deliberate improvements. He changed *dancing* to *golden* in line 4, *Along* to *Beside* in line 5, *Ten thousand* to *Fluttering and* in line 6, *laughing* to *jocund* in line 16, and he added a whole stanza (the second). In fact, the writing of the poem was unspontaneous enough for Wordsworth, at a loss for lines 21–22, to take them from his wife Mary. It is likely that the experience of daffodil-watching was not entirely his to begin with but was derived in part from the recollections his sister Dorothy Wordsworth had set down in her journal of April 15, 1802, two years before he first drafted his poem:

When we were in the woods beyond Gowbarrow Park we saw a few daffodils close to the water-side. We fancied that the lake had floated the seeds ashore, and that the little colony had so sprung up. But as we went along there were more and yet more; and at last, under the boughs of the trees, we saw that there was a long belt of them along the shore, about the breadth of a country turnpike road. I never saw daffodils so beautiful. They grew among the mossy stones about and about them; some rested their heads upon these stones as on a pillow for weariness; and the rest tossed and reeled and danced, and seemed as if they verily laughed with the wind, that flew upon them over the Lake; they looked so gay, ever glancing, ever changing. This wind blew directly over the Lake to them. There was here and there a little knot, and a few stragglers a few yards higher up; but they were so few as not to disturb the simplicity, unity, and life of that one busy highway.

Notice that Wordsworth's poem echoes a few of his sister's observations. Weaving poetry out of their mutual memories, Wordsworth has offered the experience as if altogether his own, made himself lonely, and left Dorothy out. The point is not that Wordsworth is a liar or a plagiarist but that, like any other good poet, he has transformed ordinary life into art. A process of interpreting, shaping, and ordering had to intervene between the experience of looking at daffodils and the finished poem.

We need not deny that a poet's experience can contribute to a poem nor that the emotion in the poem can indeed be the poet's. Still, to write a good poem one has to do more than live and feel. It seems a pity that, as Randall Jarrell has said, a cardinal may write verses worse than his youngest choirboy's. But writing poetry takes skill and imagination—qualities that extensive travel and wide experience do not necessarily give. For much of her life, Emily Dickinson seldom strayed from her family's house and grounds in Amherst, Massachusetts; yet her rimed lifestudies of a snake, a bee, and a hummingbird contain more poetry than we find in any firsthand description (so far) of the surface of the moon.

James Stephens   (1882–1950)*

A Glass of Beer   1918

The lanky hank of a she in the inn over there
Nearly killed me for asking the loan of a glass of beer;
May the devil grip the whey-faced slut by the hair,
And beat bad manners out of her skin for a year.

That parboiled ape, with the toughest jaw you will see   5
On virtue's path, and a voice that would rasp the dead,
Came roaring and raging the minute she looked at me,
And threw me out of the house on the back of my head!

If I asked her master he'd give me a cask a day;
But she, with the beer at hand, not a gill° would arrange!   *quarter-pint*   10
May she marry a ghost and bear him a kitten, and may
The High King of Glory permit her to get the mange.

QUESTIONS

1. Who do you take to be the speaker? Is it the poet? The speaker may be angry, but what is the tone of this poem?

2. Would you agree with a commentator who said, "To berate anyone in truly memorable language is practically a lost art in America"? How well does the speaker (an Irishman) succeed? Which of his epithets and curses strike you as particularly imaginative?

Anne Sexton   (1928–1974)*

HER KIND   1960

I have gone out, a possessed witch,
haunting the black air, braver at night;
dreaming evil, I have done my hitch
over the plain houses, light by light:
lonely thing, twelve-fingered, out of mind.   5
A woman like that is not a woman, quite.
I have been her kind.

I have found the warm caves in the woods,
filled them with skillets, carvings, shelves,
closets, silks, innumerable goods;   10
fixed the suppers for the worms and the elves:
whining, rearranging the disaligned.
A woman like that is misunderstood.
I have been her kind.

I have ridden in your cart, driver,   15
waved my nude arms at villages going by,
learning the last bright routes, survivor
where your flames still bite my thigh
and my ribs crack where your wheels wind.
A woman like that is not ashamed to die.   20
I have been her kind.

QUESTIONS

1. Who is the speaker of this poem? What do we know about her?
2. What does the speaker mean by ending each stanza with the statement, "I have been her kind?"
3. Who are the figures with whom the speaker identifies? What do these figures tell us about the speaker's state of mind?

EXPERIMENT: *Reading with and without Biography*

Read the following poem and state what you understand from it. Then consider the circumstances in which it probably came to be written. (Some information is offered in a note on page 697.) Does the meaning of the poem change? To what extent does an appreciation of the poem need the support of biography?

William Carlos Williams (1883–1963)*

THE RED WHEELBARROW   1923

so much depends
upon

a red wheel
barrow

glazed with rain   5
water

beside the white
chickens.

IRONY

To see a distinction between the poet and the words of a fictitious character—between Robert Browning and "My Last Duchess"—is to be aware of **irony:** a manner of speaking that implies a discrepancy. If the mask says one thing and we sense that the writer is in fact saying something else, the writer has adopted an **ironic point of view.** No finer illustration exists in English than Jonathan Swift's "A Modest Proposal," an essay in which Swift speaks as an earnest, humorless citizen who sets forth his reasonable plan to aid the Irish poor. The plan is so monstrous no sane reader can assent to it: the poor are to sell their children as meat for the tables of their landlords. From behind his falseface, Swift is actually recommending not cannibalism but love and Christian charity.

A poem is often made complicated and more interesting by another kind of irony. **Verbal irony** occurs whenever words say one thing but mean something else, usually the opposite. The word *love* means *hate* here: "I just *love* to stay home and do my hair on a Saturday night!" If the verbal irony is conspicuously bitter, heavy-handed, and mocking, it is **sarcasm:** "Oh, he's the biggest spender in the world, all right!" (The sarcasm, if that statement were spoken, would be underscored by the speaker's tone of voice.) A famous instance of sarcasm is Mark Antony's line in his oration over the body of slain Julius Caesar: "Brutus is an honorable man." Antony repeats this line until the enraged populace begins shouting exactly what he means to call Brutus and the other conspirators: traitors, villains, murderers. We had best be alert for irony on the printed page, for if we miss it, our interpretations of a poem may go wild.

Robert Creeley   (b. 1926)

Oh No   1959

If you wander far enough
you will come to it
and when you get there
they will give you a place to sit

for yourself only, in a nice chair,   5
and all your friends will be there
with smiles on their faces
and they will likewise all have places.

This poem is rich in verbal irony. The title helps point out that between the speaker's words and attitude lie deep differences. In line 2, what is *it?* Old age? The wandering suggests a conventional metaphor: the journey of life. Is *it* literally a rest home for "senior citizens," or perhaps some naïve popular concept of heaven (such as we meet in comic strips: harps, angels with hoops for halos) in which the saved all sit around in a ring, smugly congratulating one another? We can't be sure, but the speaker's attitude toward this final sitting-place is definite. It is a place for the selfish, as we infer from the phrase *for yourself only*. And *smiles on their faces* may hint that the smiles are unchanging and forced. There is a difference between saying "They had smiles on their faces" and "They smiled": the latter suggests that the smiles came from within. The word *nice* is to be regarded with distrust. If we see through this speaker, as Creeley implies we can do, we realize that, while pretending to be sweet-talking us into a seat, actually he is revealing the horror of a little hell. And the title is the poet's reaction to it (or the speaker's unironic, straightforward one): "Oh no! Not *that!*"

Dramatic irony, like verbal irony, contains an element of contrast, but it usually refers to a situation in a play wherein a character, whose knowledge is limited, says, does, or encounters something of greater significance than he or she knows. We, the spectators, realize the meaning of this speech or action, for the playwright has afforded us superior knowledge. In Sophocles' *King Oedipus*, when Oedipus vows to punish whoever has brought down a plague upon the city of Thebes, we know—as he does not—that the man he would punish is himself. (Referring to such a situation that precedes the downfall of a hero in a tragedy, some critics speak of **tragic irony** instead of dramatic irony.) Superior knowledge can be enjoyed not only by spectators in a theater but by readers of poetry as well. In *Paradise Lost*, we know in advance that Adam will fall into temptation, and we recognize his overconfidence when he neglects a warning. The situation of Oedipus contains also **cosmic irony,** or **irony of fate:** some Fate with a grim sense of humor seems cruelly to trick a human being. Cosmic irony clearly exists in poems in which fate or the Fates are personified and seen as hostile, as in Thomas Hardy's "The Convergence of the Twain" (page 1070); and it may be said to occur also in Robinson's "Richard Cory" (page 793). Evidently it is a twist of fate for the most envied man in town to kill himself.

To sum up: the effect of irony depends upon the reader's noticing some incongruity or discrepancy between two things. In *verbal irony*, there is a contrast between the speaker's words and meaning; in an *ironic point of view*, between the writer's attitude and what is spoken by a fictitious character; in *dramatic irony*, between the limited knowledge of a character and the fuller knowledge of the reader or spectator; in *cosmic irony*, between a character's aspiration and the treatment he or she receives at the hands of Fate. Although, in the work of an inept poet, irony can be crude and obvious sarcasm, it is invaluable to a poet of more complicated mind, who imagines more than one perspective.

W. H. Auden (1907–1973)*

THE UNKNOWN CITIZEN   1940

(To JS/07/M/378
This Marble Monument
Is Erected by the State)

He was found by the Bureau of Statistics to be
One against whom there was no official complaint,
And all the reports on his conduct agree
That, in the modern sense of an old-fashioned word, he was a saint,
For in everything he did he served the Greater Community.   5
Except for the War till the day he retired
He worked in a factory and never got fired,
But satisfied his employers, Fudge Motors Inc.
Yet he wasn't a scab or odd in his views,
For his Union reports that he paid his dues,   10
(Our report on his Union shows it was sound)
And our Social Psychology workers found
That he was popular with his mates and liked a drink.
The Press are convinced that he bought a paper every day
And that his reactions to advertisements were normal in every way. 15
Policies taken out in his name prove that he was fully insured,
And his Health-card shows he was once in hospital but left it cured.
Both Producers Research and High-Grade Living declare
He was fully sensible to the advantages of the Installment Plan
And had everything necessary to the Modern Man,   20
A phonograph, a radio, a car and a frigidaire.
Our researchers into Public Opinion are content
That he held the proper opinions for the time of year;
When there was peace, he was for peace; when there was war, he went.
He was married and added five children to the population,   25

Which our Eugenist says was the right number for a parent of his
    generation,
And our teachers report that he never interfered with their education.
Was he free? Was he happy? The question is absurd:
Had anything been wrong, we should certainly have heard.

QUESTIONS

1. Read the three-line epitaph at the beginning of the poem as carefully as you read
   what follows. How does the epitaph help establish the voice by which the rest of the
   poem is spoken?
2. Who is speaking?
3. What ironic discrepancies do you find between the speaker's attitude toward the subject and that of the poet himself? By what is the poet's attitude made clear?
4. In the phrase "The Unknown Soldier" (of which "The Unknown Citizen" reminds
   us), what does the word *unknown* mean? What does it mean in the title of Auden's
   poem?
5. What tendencies in our civilization does Auden satirize?
6. How would you expect the speaker to define a Modern Man, if a CD player, a radio,
   a car, and a refrigerator are "everything" a Modern Man needs?

Sharon Olds   (b. 1942)*

RITES OF PASSAGE   1983

As the guests arrive at my son's party
they gather in the living room—
short men, men in first grade
with smooth jaws and chins.
Hands in pockets, they stand around   5
jostling, jockeying for place, small fights
breaking out and calming. One says to another
How old are you? Six. I'm seven. So?
They eye each other, seeing themselves
tiny in the other's pupils. They clear their   10
throats a lot, a room of small bankers,
they fold their arms and frown. *I could beat you
up*, a seven says to a six,
the dark cake, round and heavy as a
turret, behind them on the table. My son,   15
freckles like specks of nutmeg on his cheeks,
chest narrow as the balsa keel of a
model boat, long hands
cool and thin as the day they guided him
out of me, speaks up as a host   20
for the sake of the group.
We could easily kill a two-year-old,

he says in his clear voice. The other
men agree, they clear their throats
like Generals, they relax and get down to   25
playing war, celebrating my son's life.

QUESTIONS

1. What is ironic about the way the speaker describes the first grade boys at her son's birthday party?
2. What other irony does the author underscore in the last two lines?
3. Does this mother sentimentalize her own son by seeing him as better than the other little boys?

John Betjeman   (1906–1984)

IN WESTMINSTER ABBEY   1940

Let me take this other glove off
    As the *vox humana* swells,
And the beauteous fields of Eden
    Bask beneath the Abbey bells.
Here, where England's statesmen lie,   5
Listen to a lady's cry.

Gracious Lord, oh bomb the Germans.
    Spare their women for Thy Sake,
And if that is not too easy
    We will pardon Thy Mistake.   10
But, gracious Lord, whate'er shall be,
Don't let anyone bomb me.

Keep our Empire undismembered,
    Guide our Forces by Thy Hand,
Gallant blacks from far Jamaica,   15
    Honduras and Togoland;
Protect them Lord in all their fights,
And, even more, protect the whites.

Think of what our Nation stands for:
    Books from Boots' and country lanes,   20
Free speech, free passes, class distinction,
    Democracy and proper drains.
Lord, put beneath Thy special care
One-eighty-nine Cadogan Square.

Although dear Lord I am a sinner,
  I have done no major crime;
Now I'll come to Evening Service
  Whensoever I have the time.
So, Lord, reserve for me a crown,
And do not let my shares° go down.   *stocks*   30

I will labor for Thy Kingdom,
  Help our lads to win the war,
Send white feathers to the cowards,
  Join the Women's Army Corps,
Then wash the Steps around Thy Throne   35
In the Eternal Safety Zone.

Now I feel a little better,
  What a treat to hear Thy Word,
Where the bones of leading statesmen
  Have so often been interred.   40
And now, dear Lord, I cannot wait
Because I have a luncheon date.

IN WESTMINSTER ABBEY. First printed during World War II. 2 *vox humana*: an organ stop that makes tones similar to those of the human voice. 20 *Boots'*: a chain of pharmacies whose branches had lending libraries.

QUESTIONS

1. Who is the speaker? What do we know about her life-style? About her prejudices?
2. Point out some of the places in which she contradicts herself.
3. How would you describe the speaker's attitude toward religion?
4. Through the medium of irony, what positive points do you believe Betjeman makes?

Sarah N. Cleghorn   (1876–1959)

THE GOLF LINKS   1917

The golf links lie so near the mill
  That almost every day
The laboring children can look out
  And see the men at play.

QUESTIONS

1. Is this brief poem satiric? Does it contain any verbal irony? Is the poet making a matter-of-fact statement in words that mean just what they say?

2. What other kind of irony is present in the poem?
3. Sarah N. Cleghorn's poem dates from before the enactment of legislation against child labor. Is it still a good poem, or is it hopelessly dated?
4. How would you state its theme?
5. Would you call this poem lyric, narrative, or didactic?

Tess Gallagher (b. 1943)

I Stop Writing the Poem   1992

to fold the clothes. No matter who lives
or who dies, I'm still a woman.
I'll always have plenty to do.
I bring the arms of his shirt
together. Nothing can stop   5
our tenderness. I'll get back
to the poem. I'll get back to being
a woman. But for now
there's a shirt, a giant shirt
in my hands, and somewhere a small girl   10
standing next to her mother
watching to see how it's done.

QUESTIONS

1. What is the speaker's attitude toward her situation? How do her real attitudes emerge in her words?
2. In what ways is the ending of the poem ironic?

Charles Causley (b. 1917)

I Saw a Jolly Hunter   1970

I saw a jolly hunter
  With a jolly gun
Walking in the country
  In the jolly sun.

In the jolly meadow   5
  Sat a jolly hare.
Saw the jolly hunter.
  Took jolly care.

Hunter jolly eager—
  Sight of jolly prey.   10
Forgot gun pointing
  Wrong jolly way.

Jolly hunter jolly head
  Over heels gone.
Jolly old safety catch   15
  Not jolly on.

Bang went the jolly gun.
  Hunter jolly dead.
Jolly hare got clean away.
  Jolly good, I said.   20

QUESTIONS

1. Is this poem written for adults or children—or both? Use reasoning to support your answer.
2. What features of the poem seem ironic?
3. What does the author gain by repeating *jolly* so many times?
4. In what way does the tone of the final line differ from earlier portions of the poem?

EXERCISE: *Detecting Irony*

Point out the kinds of irony that occur in the following poem.

Thomas Hardy (1840–1928)*

THE WORKBOX   1914

"See, here's the workbox, little wife,
  That I made of polished oak."
He was a joiner°, of village life;   *carpenter*
  She came of borough folk.

He holds the present up to her   5
  As with a smile she nears
And answers to the profferer,
  "'Twill last all my sewing years!"

"I warrant it will. And longer too.
  'Tis a scantling that I got   10
Off poor John Wayward's coffin, who
  Died of they knew not what.

"The shingled pattern that seems to cease
  Against your box's rim
Continues right on in the piece   15
  That's underground with him.

"And while I worked it made me think
  Of timber's varied doom:
One inch where people eat and drink,
  The next inch in a tomb.   20

"But why do you look so white, my dear,
    And turn aside your face?
You knew not that good lad, I fear,
    Though he came from your native place?"

"How could I know that good young man,   25
    Though he came from my native town,
When he must have left far earlier than
    I was a woman grown?"

"Ah, no. I should have understood!
    It shocked you that I gave   30
To you one end of a piece of wood
    Whose other is in a grave?"

"Don't, dear, despise my intellect,
    Mere accidental things
Of that sort never have effect   35
    On my imaginings."

Yet still her lips were limp and wan,
    Her face still held aside,
As if she had known not only John,
    But known of what he died.   40

FOR REVIEW AND FURTHER STUDY

William Blake   (1757–1827)*

THE CHIMNEY SWEEPER   1789

When my mother died I was very young,
And my father sold me while yet my tongue
Could scarcely cry "'weep! 'weep! 'weep! 'weep!"
So your chimneys I sweep, and in soot I sleep.

There's little Tom Dacre, who cried when his head,   5
That curled like a lamb's back, was shaved: so I said
"Hush, Tom! never mind it, for when your head's bare
You know that the soot cannot spoil your white hair."

And so he was quiet, and that very night,
As Tom was a-sleeping, he had such a sight!   10
That thousands of sweepers, Dick, Joe, Ned, and Jack,
Were all of them locked up in coffins of black.

And by came an Angel who had a bright key,
And he opened the coffins and set them all free;
Then down a green plain leaping, laughing, they run,   15
And wash in a river, and shine in the sun.

Then naked and white, all their bags left behind,
They rise upon clouds and sport in the wind;
And the Angel told Tom, if he'd be a good boy,
He'd have God for his father, and never want joy.   20

And so Tom awoke; and we rose in the dark,
And got with our bags and our brushes to work.
Though the morning was cold, Tom was happy and warm;
So if all do their duty they need not fear harm.

QUESTIONS

1. What does Blake's poem reveal about conditions of life in the London of his day?
2. What does this poem have in common with "The Golf Links" (page 685)?
3. Sum up your impressions of the speaker's character. What does he say and do that displays it to us?
4. What pun do you find in line 3? Is its effect comic or serious?
5. In Tom Dacre's dream (lines 11–20), what wishes come true? Do you understand them to be the wishes of the chimney sweepers, of the poet, or of both?
6. In the last line, what is ironic in the speaker's assurance that the dutiful *need not fear harm?* What irony is there in his urging all to *do their duty?* (Who have failed in their duty to *him?*)
7. What is the tone of Blake's poem? Angry? Hopeful? Sorrowful? Compassionate? (Don't feel obliged to sum it up in a single word.)

Bettie Sellers   (b. 1926)

IN THE COUNSELOR'S WAITING ROOM   1981

The terra cotta girl
with the big flat farm feet
traces furrows in the rug
with her toes,
reads an existentialist paperback   5
from psychology class,
finds no ease there
from the guilt of loving
the quiet girl down the hall.
Their home soil has seen to this visit,   10
their Baptist mothers,
who weep for the waste of sturdy hips
ripe for grandchildren.

IN THE COUNSELOR'S WAITING ROOM.   The poet is a teacher and administrator at a small college in Georgia. 1 *terra cotta:* fired clay, light brownish orange in hue. 5 *existentialist:* of the twentieth-century school of philosophy that holds (among other tenets) that an individual is alone and isolated, free and yet responsible, and ordinarily subject to guilt, anxiety, and dread.

1. For what sort of counseling is this girl waiting?
2. Point out all the words that refer to plowing, to clay and earth. Why are the mothers called "home soil"? How do these references to earth relate to the idea in the last line?
3. What irony inheres in this situation?
4. Does the poet appear to sympathize with the girls? With their weeping mothers? In what details does this poem hint at any of the poet's own attitude or attitudes?

José Emilio Pacheco (b. 1939)

HIGH TREASON   1969

I do not love my country. Its abstract lustre
is beyond my grasp.
But (although it sounds bad) I would give my life
for ten places in it, for certain people,
seaports, pinewoods, fortresses,   5
a run-down city, gray, grotesque,
various figures from its history,
mountains
(and three or four rivers).

> —*Translated from Spanish*
> *by Alastair Reid**

HIGH TREASON. José Emilio Pacheco, one of Mexico's leading poets, was born in Mexico City in 1939. He currently teaches at the University of Maryland.

QUESTION

Does this speaker truly not love his country? Explain what he means by his opening remark.

William Stafford (1914–1993)*

AT THE UN-NATIONAL MONUMENT   1977
ALONG THE CANADIAN BORDER

This is the field where the battle did not happen,
where the unknown soldier did not die.
This is the field where grass joined hands,
where no monument stands,
and the only heroic thing is the sky.   5

Birds fly here without any sound,
unfolding their wings across the open.
No people killed—or were killed—on this ground
hallowed by neglect and an air so tame
that people celebrate it by forgetting its name.   10

QUESTIONS

1. What nonevent does this poem celebrate? What is the speaker's attitude toward it?
2. The speaker describes an empty field. What is odd about the way in which he describes it?
3. What words does the speaker appear to use ironically?

EXERCISE: *Telling Tone*

Here are two radically different poems on a similar subject. Try stating the theme of each poem in your own words. How is tone (the speaker's attitude) different in the two poems?

Richard Lovelace (1618–1658)

TO LUCASTA
On Going to the Wars

1649

Tell me not, Sweet, I am unkind
　　That from the nunnery
Of thy chaste breast and quiet mind,
　　To war and arms I fly.

True, a new mistress now I chase,　　　　　　　　　　5
　　The first foe in the field;
And with a stronger faith embrace
　　A sword, a horse, a shield.

Yet this inconstancy is such
　　As you too shall adore;　　　　　　　　　　　　10
I could not love thee, Dear, so much,
　　Loved I not Honor more.

Wilfred Owen (1893–1918)*

DULCE ET DECORUM EST

1920

Bent double, like old beggars under sacks,
Knock-kneed, coughing like hags, we cursed through sludge,
Till on the haunting flares we turned our backs
And towards our distant rest began to trudge.
Men marched asleep. Many had lost their boots　　　　5
But limped on, blood-shod. All went lame; all blind;
Drunk with fatigue; deaf even to the hoots
Of tired, outstripped Five-Nines that dropped behind.

Gas! Gas! Quick, boys!—An ecstasy of fumbling,
Fitting the clumsy helmets just in time;   10
But someone still was yelling out and stumbling
And flound'ring like a man in fire or lime . . .
Dim, through the misty panes and thick green light,
As under a green sea, I saw him drowning.
In all my dreams, before my helpless sight,   15
He plunges at me, guttering, choking, drowning.

If in some smothering dreams you too could pace
Behind the wagon that we flung him in,
And watch the white eyes writhing in his face,
His hanging face, like a devil's sick of sin;   20
If you could hear, at every jolt, the blood
Come gargling from the froth-corrupted lungs,
Obscene as cancer, bitter as the cud
Of vile, incurable sores on innocent tongues,—
My friend, you would not tell with such high zest   25
To children ardent for some desperate glory,
The old Lie: Dulce et decorum est
Pro patria mori.

DULCE ET DECORUM EST.   8 *Five-Nines:* German howitzers often used to shoot poison gas shells
17 *you too:* Some manuscript versions of this poem carry the dedication "To Jessie Pope" (a writer of
patriotic verse) or "To a certain Poetess." 27–28 *Dulce et . . . mori:* a quotation from the Latin poet
Horace, "It is sweet and fitting to die for one's country."

WRITER'S PERSPECTIVE

Wilfred Owen

Wilfred Owen was only twenty years old when World War I broke out in 1914.
Twice wounded in battle, Owen was rapidly promoted and eventually became a
company commander. The shocking violence of modern war summoned Owen's

poetic genius, and in a two-year period he grew from a negligible minor poet into the most important English-language poet of World War I. Owen, however, did not live to see his talent recognized. He was killed one week before the end of the war; he was twenty-five years old. Owen published only four poems during his lifetime. Shortly before his death he drafted out a few lines of prose for the preface of a book of poems. (For a short biography of Owen, consult "Lives of the Poets," beginning on page 1165.)

Wilfred Owen on Writing   WAR POETRY   1917?

This book is not about heroes. English poetry is not yet fit to speak of them.
Nor is it about deeds, or lands, nor anything about glory, honour, might, majesty, dominion, or power, except War.
Above all I am not concerned with Poetry.
My subject is War, and the pity of War.
The Poetry is in the pity.
Yet these elegies are to this generation in no sense consolatory. They may be to the next. All a poet can do today is warn. That is why the true Poets must be truthful.

◁▬◌WRITING CRITICALLY▬▷

Paying Attention to the Obvious

If tone is a speaker's attitude toward his or her material, then to understand the tone of a poem, we need mostly just to listen—as we might listen to a real conversation. The key is to hear not only *what* is being said but *how* it is being said. Does the speaker sound noticeably surprised, angry, nostalgic, tender, or expectant? A common mistake in analyzing poetry is to discuss subtle points of interpretation before you fully understand the *obvious* features of a poem. In critical writing it almost never hurts to begin by asking obvious questions:

1. Does the speaker reveal any obvious emotion or attitude about the subject or the setting of the poem? (When D. H. Lawrence, for example, ends his poem "Piano" on page 656 by saying, "I weep like a child for the past," he makes his nostalgic and tender tone explicit.)
2. If there is an implied listener or listeners to the poem, how does the speaker address them? Is there anything obviously unusual about the tone? (In Betjeman's "In Westminster Abbey," for example, the speaker addresses God with astonishing egocentricity and snooty nonchalance.)
3. Is there any obvious difference between the reaction of the speaker to what is happening in the poem and your own honest reaction? If the gap between the two reactions is large (as it is in Robert Browning's "My Last Duchess," for instance), what does it suggest?

4. If the difference between your honest reaction and the speaker's is enormous, is the poem in some way ironic?

Writing Assignment

Using any poetry selection from this chapter, analyze the speaker's attitude toward the poem's main subject. Support your argument by examining the author's choice of specific words and images to create the particular tone used to convey the speaker's attitudes. (Possible subjects might include Wilfred Owen's attitude toward war in "Dulce et Decorum Est," the tone and imagery of Weldon Kees's "For My Daughter," Charles Causley's attitude toward sports hunting in "I Saw a Jolly Hunter," or Anne Bradstreet's attitude toward her own poetry in "The Author to Her Book.")

Here is an example of an essay written for this assignment by Kim Larsen, a student of Karen Locke at Lane Community College in Eugene, Oregon.

Word Choice, Tone, and Point of View in

Roethke's "My Papa's Waltz"

Some readers may find Theodore Roethke's "My Papa's Waltz" a reminiscence of a happy childhood scene. I believe, however, that the poem depicts a more painful and complicated series of emotions. By examining the choice of words that Roethke uses to convey the tone of his scene, I will demonstrate that beneath the seemingly comic situation of the poem is a darker story. The true point of view of "My Papa's Waltz" is that of a resentful adult reliving his fear of a domineering parent.

The first clue that the dance may not have been a mutually enjoyable experience is in the title itself. The author did not title the poem "Our Waltz" or "Waltzing with My Papa," either of which would set an initial tone for readers to expect a shared, loving sentiment. It does not even have a neutral title, such as "The Waltz." The title specifically implies that the waltz was exclusively the father's. Since a waltz normally involves two people, it can be reasoned that the father dances his waltz without regard for his young partner.

Examining each stanza of the poem offers numerous examples where the choice of words sustains the tone implied in the title. The first line, "The whiskey on your breath," conjures up an olfactory image that most would find unpleasant. The small boy finds it so overpowering he is made "dizzy." This stanza contains the only simile in the poem, "I hung on like death" (3), which creates a ghastly and stark visual image. There are innumerable choices of similes to portray hanging on: a vine, an infant, an animal cub, all of which would have illustrated a lighthearted romp. The choice of "death" was purposefully used to convey an intended image. The first stanza ends by stating the "waltzing was not easy." The definitions of easy, as found in Webster's New Collegiate Dictionary, include "free from pain, annoyance or anxiety," and "not difficult to endure or undergo" ("Easy"). Obviously the speaker did not find those qualities in the waltz.

Further evidence of this harsh and oppressive scene are brought to mind by reckless disregard for "the pans / Slid from the kitchen shelf" (5-6), which the reader can almost hear crashing on the floor in loud cacophony, and the "mother's countenance," which "[c]ould not unfrown itself" (8). If this was only a silly, playful romp between father and son, even a stern, fastidious mother might be expected to at least make an unsuccessful attempt to suppress a grin. Instead, the reader gets a visual image of a silent, unhappy woman, afraid, probably due to past experience, to interfere in the domestic destruction around her. Once more, this detail suggests a domineering father who controls the family.

The third stanza relates the father's "battered" hand holding the boy's wrist. The tactile image of holding a wrist suggests dragging or forcing an unwilling person, not holding hands as would be expected with a mutual dance partner. Further disregard for the son's feelings is displayed by the lines "At every step you missed / My right ear scraped a buckle" (11-12). In each missed step, probably due to his drunkenness, the father causes the boy physical pain.

The tone continues in the final stanza as the speaker recalls "You beat time on my head / With a palm caked hard by dirt" (13-14). The visual and tactile image of a dirt-hardened hand beating on a child's head as if it were a drum is distinctly unpleasant. The last lines "Then waltzed me off to bed / Still clinging to your shirt" (15-16) are the most ambiguous in the poem. It can be reasoned, as X.J. Kennedy and Dana Gioia do, that the lines suggest "the boy is still clinging to his father with persistent if also complicated love" (668). On the other hand, if one notices the earlier dark images, the conclusion could describe a boy clinging out of fear, the physical fear of being dropped by one who is drunk and the emotional fear of not being loved and nurtured as a child needs to be by his father.

It can also be argued that the poem's rollicking rhythm contributes to a sense of fun, and in truth, the poem can be read in that fashion. On the other hand, it can be read in such a way as to deemphasize the rhythm, as the author himself does in his recording of "My Papa's Waltz" (Roethke, Reads). The joyful, rollicking rhythm can be seen as ironic. By reminding readers of a waltzing tempo, it is highlighting the discrepancy of what a waltz should be and the bleak, frightening picture painted in the words.

While "My Papa's Waltz" can be read as a roughhouse comedy, by examining Roethke's title and choice of words closely to interpret the meaning of their images and sounds, it is also plausible to hear an entirely different tone. I believe "My Papa's Waltz" employs the voice of an embittered adult remembering a harsh scene in which both he and his mother were powerless in the presence of a drunk and domineering father.

Works Cited

"Easy." Merriam-Webster's New Collegiate Dictionary. 7th ed. 1971.

Kennedy, X.J., and Dana Gioia, eds. Literature: An Introduction to Fiction, Poetry, and Drama. 7th ed. New York: Longman, 1999. 668.

Roethke, Theodore. "My Papa's Waltz." Literature: An Introduction to Fiction, Poetry, and Drama. Ed. X.J. Kennedy and Dana Gioia. 7th ed. New York: Longman, 1999. 668.

---. Theodore Roethke Reads His Poetry. Audiocassette. Caedmon, 1972.

INFORMATION FOR EXPERIMENT: *Reading with and without Biography*

THE RED WHEELBARROW (page 680). Dr. Williams's poem reportedly contains a personal experience: he was gazing from the window of the house where one of his patients, a small girl, lay suspended between life and death. (This account, from the director of the public library in Williams's native Rutherford, N.J., is given by Geri M. Rhodes in "The Paterson Metaphor in William Carlos Williams's *Paterson*," master's essay, Tufts U, 1965.)

Further Suggestions for Writing

1. Do you think Wilfred Owen's "Dulce et Decorum Est" (page 691) fulfills his intentions as stated in "On War Poetry"? Write a brief essay comparing Owen's poem to his goals as a writer. Cite specific instances of where the poem meets or fails to meet his criteria.

2. In a paragraph, sum up your initial reactions to "The Red Wheelbarrow." Then, taking another look at the poem in light of information noted above, write a second paragraph summing up your further reactions.

3. Write a short essay titled "What Thomas Hardy Leaves Unsaid in 'The Workbox'."

4. Write a verbal profile or short character sketch of the speaker of John Betjeman's "In Westminster Abbey."

5. In a brief essay, consider the tone of two poems on a similar subject. Compare and contrast Walt Whitman and Emily Dickinson as locomotive-fanciers; or, in the poems by Richard Lovelace and Wilfred Owen, compare and contrast attitudes toward war. (For advice on writing about poetry by the method of comparison and contrast, see page 1902.)

14 *Words*

LITERAL MEANING: WHAT A POEM SAYS FIRST

Although successful as a painter, Edgar Degas struggled to produce sonnets, and found poetry discouragingly hard to write. To his friend, the poet Stéphane Mallarmé, he complained, "What a business! My whole day gone on a blasted sonnet, without getting an inch further . . . and it isn't ideas I'm short of . . . I'm full of them, I've got too many . . ."

"But Degas," said Mallarmé, "you can't make a poem with ideas—you make it with *words!*"[1]

Like the celebrated painter, some people assume that all it takes to make a poem is a bright idea. Poems state ideas, to be sure, and sometimes the ideas are invaluable; and yet the most impressive idea in the world will not make a poem, unless its words are selected and arranged with loving art. Some poets take great pains to find the right word. Unable to fill a two-syllable gap in an unfinished line that went, "The seal's wide—gaze toward Paradise," Hart Crane paged through an unabridged dictionary. When he reached S, he found the object of his quest in *spindrift:* "spray skimmed from the sea by a strong wind." The word is exact and memorable. Any word can be the right word, however, if artfully chosen and placed. It may be a word as ordinary as *from.* Consider the difference between "The sedge is withered *on* the lake" (a misquotation of a line by Keats) and "The sedge is withered *from* the lake" (what Keats in fact wrote). Keats's original line suggests, as the altered line doesn't, that because the sedge (a growth of grasslike plants) has withered *from* the lake, it has withdrawn mysteriously.

In reading a poem, some people assume that its words can be skipped over rapidly, and they try to leap at once to the poem's general theme. It is as if they

[1]Paul Valéry, *Degas . . . Manet . . . Morisot,* translated by David Paul (New York: Pantheon, 1960) 62.

fear being thought clods unless they can find huge ideas in the poem (whether or not there are any). Such readers often ignore the literal meanings of words: the ordinary, matter-of-fact sense to be found in a dictionary. (As you will see in Chapter Fifteen, "Saying and Suggesting," words possess not only dictionary meanings—**denotations**—but also many associations and suggestions—**connotations.**) Consider the following poem and see what you make of it.

William Carlos Williams (1883–1963)*
THIS IS JUST TO SAY 1934

I have eaten
the plums
that were in
the icebox
and which
you were probably   5
saving
for breakfast

Forgive me
they were delicious   10
so sweet
and so cold

Some readers distrust a poem so simple and candid. They think, "What's wrong with me? There has to be more to it than this!" But poems seldom are puzzles in need of solutions. We can begin by accepting the poet's statements, without suspecting the poet of trying to hoodwink us. On later reflection, of course, we might possibly decide that the poet is playfully teasing or being ironic; but Williams gives us no reason to think that. There seems no need to look beyond the literal sense of his words, no profit in speculating that the plums symbolize worldly joys and that the icebox stands for the universe. Clearly, a reader who held such a grand theory would have overlooked (in eagerness to find a significant idea) the plain truth that the poet makes clear to us: that ice-cold plums are a joy to taste.

To be sure, Williams's small poem is simpler than most poems are; and yet in reading any poem, no matter how complicated, you will do well to reach slowly and reluctantly for a theory to explain it by. To find the general theme of a poem, you first need to pay attention to its words. Recall Yeats's "The Lake Isle of Innisfree" (page 653), a poem that makes a statement—crudely summed up, "I yearn to leave the city and retreat to a place of ideal peace and happiness." And yet before we can realize this theme, we have to notice details: nine bean rows, a glade loud with bees, "lake water lapping with low sounds by the shore," the gray of a pavement. These details and not some abstract remark make clear what the poem is saying: that the city is drab, while the island hideaway is sublimely beautiful.

Poets often strive for words that point to physical details and solid objects. They may do so even when speaking of an abstract idea:

> Beauty is but a flower
> Which wrinkles will devour;
> Brightness falls from the air,
> Queens have died young and fair,
> Dust hath closed Helen's eye.
> I am sick, I must die:
> > Lord, have mercy on us!

In these lines by Thomas Nashe, the abstraction *beauty* has grown petals that shrivel. Brightness may be a general name for light, but Nashe succeeds in giving it the weight of a falling body.

If a poem reads *daffodils* instead of *plant life*, *diaper years* instead of *infancy*, we call its **diction,** or choice of words, **concrete** rather than **abstract.** Concrete words refer to what we can immediately perceive with our senses: *dog, actor, chemical,* or particular individuals who belong to those general classes: *Bonzo the fox terrier, Clint Eastwood, hydrogen sulfate.* Abstract words express ideas or concepts: *love, time, truth.* In abstracting, we leave out some characteristics found in each individual, and instead observe a quality common to many. The word *beauty,* for instance, denotes what may be observed in numerous persons, places, and things.

Ezra Pound gave a famous piece of advice to his fellow poets: "Go in fear of abstractions." This is not to say that a poet cannot employ abstract words, nor that all poems have to be about physical things. Much of T. S. Eliot's *Four Quartets* is concerned with time, eternity, history, language, reality, and other things that cannot be physically handled. But Eliot, however high he may soar for a larger view, keeps returning to earth. He makes us aware of *things.*

Marianne Moore   (1887–1972)*

SILENCE   1924

My father used to say,
"Superior people never make long visits,
have to be shown Longfellow's grave
or the glass flowers at Harvard.
Self-reliant like the cat—   5
that takes its prey to privacy,
the mouse's limp tail hanging like a shoelace from its mouth—

they sometimes enjoy solitude,
and can be robbed of speech
by speech which has delighted them.   10
The deepest feeling always shows itself in silence;
not in silence, but restraint."
Nor was he insincere in saying, "Make my house your inn."
Inns are not residences.

QUESTIONS

1. Almost all of "Silence" consists of quotation. What are some possible reasons why the speaker prefers using another person's words?
2. What are the words the father uses to describe people he admires?
3. The poem makes an important distinction between two similar words (lines 13–14). Explain the distinction Moore implies.
4. Why is "Silence" an appropriate title for this poem?

Henry Taylor   (b. 1942)

RIDING A ONE-EYED HORSE   1975

One side of his world is always missing.
You may give it a casual wave of the hand
or rub it with your shoulder as you pass,
but nothing on his blind side ever happens.

Hundreds of trees slip past him into darkness,   5
drifting into a hollow hemisphere
whose sounds you will have to try to explain.
Your legs will tell him not to be afraid

if you learn never to lie. Do not forget
to turn his head and let what comes come seen: 10
he will jump the fences he has to if you swing
toward them from the side that he can see

and hold his good eye straight. The heavy dark
will stay beside you always; let him learn
to lean against it. It will steady him   15
and see you safely through diminished fields.

QUESTION

Do you read this poem as a fable in which the horse stands for something, or as a set of in-structions for riding a one-eyed horse?

Robert Graves   (1895–1985)*
Down, Wanton, Down!   1933

Down, wanton, down! Have you no shame
That at the whisper of Love's name,
Or Beauty's, presto! up you raise
Your angry head and stand at gaze?

Poor bombard-captain, sworn to reach   5
The ravelin and effect a breach—
Indifferent what you storm or why,
So be that in the breach you die!

Love may be blind, but Love at least
Knows what is man and what mere beast;   10
Or Beauty wayward, but requires
More delicacy from her squires.

Tell me, my witless, whose one boast
Could be your staunchness at the post,
When were you made a man of parts   15
To think fine and profess the arts?

Will many-gifted Beauty come
Bowing to your bald rule of thumb,
Or Love swear loyalty to your crown?
Be gone, have done! Down, wanton, down!   20

DOWN, WANTON, DOWN! 5 *bombard-captain:* officer in charge of a bombard, an early type of cannon
that hurled stones. 6 *ravelin:* fortification with two faces that meet in a protruding angle. *effect a
breach:* break an opening through (a fortification). 15 *man of parts:* man of talent or ability.

QUESTIONS

1. How do you define a *wanton?*
2. What wanton does the poet address?
3. Explain the comparison drawn in the second stanza.
4. In line 14, how many meanings do you find in *staunchness at the post?*
5. Explain any other puns you find in lines 15–19.
6. Do you take this to be a cynical poem making fun of Love and Beauty, or is Graves
   making fun of stupid, animal lust?

Barbara Howes   (1914–1996)
Looking Up at Leaves   1966

No one need feel alone looking up at leaves.
There are such depths to them, withdrawal, welcome,
A fragile tumult on the way to sky.

This great trunk holds apart two hemispheres
We lie between. . . . Like water lilies   5
Leaves fall, rise, waver, echoing
On their blue pool, whispering under the sun;
While in this shade, under our hands the brown
Tough roots seek down, lily roots searching
Down through their pool of earth to an equal depth.   10
Constant as water lilies we lie still,
Our breathing like the lapping of pond water,
Balanced between reflection and reflection.

QUESTIONS

1. How can a *tumult* be *fragile* (see line 3)?
2. What does Howes mean when she says the tree's trunk holds apart two *hemispheres?* Is the word being used literally or figuratively?
3. Does the last line have more than one literal meaning?

John Donne   (1572–1631)*

BATTER MY HEART,   (ABOUT 1610)
THREE-PERSONED GOD, FOR YOU

Batter my heart, three-personed God, for You
As yet but knock, breathe, shine, and seek to mend.
That I may rise and stand, o'erthrow me, and bend
Your force to break, blow, burn, and make me new.
I, like an usurped town to another due,   5
Labor to admit You, but Oh! to no end.
Reason, Your viceroy in me, me should defend,
But is captived, and proves weak or untrue.
Yet dearly I love You, and would be lovèd fain,
But am betrothed unto Your enemy;   10
Divorce me, untie or break that knot again;
Take me to You, imprison me, for I,
Except You enthrall me, never shall be free,
Nor ever chaste, except You ravish me.

QUESTIONS

1. In the last line of this sonnet, to what does Donne compare the onslaught of God's love? Do you think the poem is weakened by the poet's comparing a spiritual experience to something so grossly carnal? Discuss.
2. Explain the seeming contradiction in the last line: in what sense can a ravished person be *chaste?* Explain the seeming contradictions in lines 3–4 and 12–13: how can a person thrown down and destroyed be enabled to *rise and stand;* an imprisoned person be *free?*

3. In lines 5–6 the speaker compares himself to a *usurped town* trying to throw off its conqueror by admitting an army of liberation. Who is the "usurper" in this comparison?
4. Explain the comparison of *Reason* to a *viceroy* (lines 7–8).
5. Sum up in your own words the message of Donne's poem. In stating its theme, did you have to read the poem for literal meanings, figurative comparisons, or both?

THE VALUE OF A DICTIONARY

> *Use the dictionary. It's better than the critics.*
> —Elizabeth Bishop to her students

If a poet troubles to seek out the best words available, the least we can do is to find out what the words mean. The dictionary is a firm ally in reading poems; if the poems are more than a century old, it is indispensable. Meanings change. When the Elizabethan poet George Gascoigne wrote, "O Abraham's brats, O brood of blessed seed," the word *brats* implied neither irritation nor contempt. When in the seventeenth century Andrew Marvell imagined two lovers' "vegetable love," he referred to a vegetative or growing love, not one resembling a lettuce. And when King George III called a building an "awful artificial spectacle," he was not condemning it but praising it as an awe-inspiring work of art.

In reading poetry, there is nothing to be done about this inevitable tendency of language except to watch out for it. If you suspect that a word has shifted in meaning over the years, most standard desk dictionaries will be helpful, an unabridged dictionary more helpful yet, and most helpful of all the *Oxford English Dictionary* (*OED*), which gives, for each definition, successive examples of the word's written use through the past thousand years. You need not feel a grim obligation to keep interrupting a poem in order to rummage in the dictionary; but if the poem is worth reading very closely, you may wish any aid you can find.

One of the valuable services of poetry is to recall for us the concrete, physical sense that certain words once had, but since have lost. As the English critic H. Coombes has remarked in *Literature and Criticism*,

> We use a word like *powerful* without feeling that it is really "powerfull." We do not seem today to taste the full flavor of words as we feel that Falstaff (and Shakespeare, and probably his audience) tasted them when he was applauding the virtues of "good sherrissack," which makes the brain "apprehensive, quick, forgetive, full of nimble, fiery, and delectable shapes." And being less aware of the life and substantiality of words, we are probably less aware of the things . . . that these words stand for.

"Every word which is used to express a moral or intellectual fact," said Emerson in his study *Nature*, "if traced to its root, is found to be borrowed from some material appearance. *Right* means straight; *wrong* means twisted. *Spirit* primarily means wind; *transgression*, the crossing of a line; *supercilious*, the raising of

an eyebrow." Browse in a dictionary and you will discover such original con-
cretenesses. These are revealed in your dictionary's etymologies, or brief notes on
the derivation of words, given in most dictionaries near the beginning of an
entry on a word; in some dictionaries, at the end of the entry. Look up *squirrel*,
for instance, and you will find it comes from two Greek words meaning "shadow-
tail." For another example of a common word that originally contained a poetic
metaphor, look up the origin of *daisy*.

EXPERIMENT: *Seeing Words' Origins*

Much of the effect of the following poem depends upon our awareness of the precision with
which the poet has selected his words. We can better see this by knowing their derivations.
For instance, *potpourri* comes from French: *pot* plus *pourri*. What do these words mean? (If
you do not know French, look up the etymology of the word in a dictionary.) Look up the
definitions and etymologies of *revenance, circumstance, inspiration, conceptual, commotion,
cordial*, and *azure*; and try to state the meanings these words have in Wilbur's poem.

Richard Wilbur   (b. 1921)*

IN THE ELEGY SEASON   1950

Haze, char, and the weather of All Souls':
A giant absence mopes upon the trees:
Leaves cast in casual potpourris
Whisper their scents from pits and cellar-holes.

Or brewed in gulleys, steeped in wells, they spend   5
In chilly steam their last aromas, yield
From shallow hells a revenance of field
And orchard air. And now the envious mind

Which could not hold the summer in my head
While bounded by that blazing circumstance   10
Parades these barrens in a golden trance,
Remembering the wealthy season dead,

And by an autumn inspiration makes
A summer all its own. Green boughs arise
Through all the boundless backward of the eyes,   15
And the soul bathes in warm conceptual lakes.

Less proud than this, my body leans an ear
Past cold and colder weather after wings'
Soft commotion, the sudden race of springs,
The goddess' tread heard on the dayward stair,   20

Longs for the brush of the freighted air, for smells
Of grass and cordial lilac, for the sight
Of green leaves building into the light
And azure water hoisting out of wells.

An **allusion** is an indirect reference to any person, place, or thing—fictitious, historical, or actual. Sometimes, to understand an allusion in a poem, we
have to find out something we didn't know before. But usually the poet asks of us
only common knowledge. When, in his poem "To Helen" (page 1096), Edgar
Allan Poe refers to "the glory that was Greece / And the grandeur that was
Rome," he assumes that we have heard of those places. He also expects that we
will understand his allusion to the cultural achievements of those ancient nations and perhaps even catch the subtle contrast between those two similar
words *glory* and *grandeur*, with its suggestion that, for all its merits, Roman civilization was also more pompous than Greek.

Allusions not only enrich the meaning of a poem, they also save space. In
"The Love Song of J. Alfred Prufrock" (page 1059), T. S. Eliot, by giving a brief
introductory quotation from the speech of a damned soul in Dante's *Inferno*, is
able to suggest that his poem will be the confession of a soul in torment, who
sees no chance of escape.

Often in reading a poem you will meet a name you don't recognize, on
which the meaning of a line (or perhaps a whole poem) seems to depend. In this
book, most such unfamiliar references and allusions are glossed or footnoted, but
when you venture out on your own in reading poems, you may find yourself
needlessly perplexed unless you look up such names, the way you look up any
other words. Unless the name is one that the poet made up, you will probably
find it in one of the larger desk dictionaries, such as *Webster's New Collegiate Dictionary, The American Heritage Dictionary,* or *Webster's II.* If you don't solve your
problem there, try an encyclopedia, a world atlas, *The New Century Cyclopedia of
Names,* or *Brewer's Dictionary of Phrase & Fable.*

Some allusions are quotations from other poems. In R. S. Gwynn's "1-800,"
the narrator describes an insomniac watching late-night infomercials:

Credit cards out, pencil and notepad handy,
    The insomniac sinks deeply in his chair,
Begging swift needles in his glass of brandy
    To knit once more the raveled sleeve of care,
As with control, remotely, in one hand he
    Summons bright visions from the midnight air:

In addition to some witty wordplay, like the pun on *remote control,* Gwynn borrows a famous line from Shakespeare's *Macbeth,* "Sleep that knits up the raveled
sleeve of care," to describe his unsnoozing protagonist. (*To ravel* means the same
as *to unravel*—to loosen up or disentangle.) Why quote Shakespeare in a poem
about watching TV commercials? Partly it is just one poet's delight in repeating
another poet's verbal home-runs, but well-chosen allusions also pack an extra

wallop of meaning into a poem. The line that Gwynn borrows comes from Macbeth's description of a mysterious voice he claims to have heard after murdering Duncan. The voice prophesied that "Macbeth shall sleep no more." Alluding to Shakespeare's line, therefore, Gwynn can summon up all sorts of dark, nocturnal associations that he then turns to satiric ends.

EXERCISE: *Catching Allusions*

From your knowledge, supplemented by a dictionary or other reference work if need be, explain the allusions in the following poems.

J. V. Cunningham   (1911–1985)*
FRIEND, ON THIS SCAFFOLD   1960
THOMAS MORE LIES DEAD

Friend, on this scaffold Thomas More lies dead
Who would not cut the Body from the Head.

David R. Axelrod   (b. 1943)
THE DEAD HAVE NO RESPECT   1995

When she died he
had her decked
out better than she'd
looked in life, only to
have her run away with   5
some sailor they
called Charon.

Kelly Cherry   (b. 1940)
ADVICE TO A FRIEND WHO PAINTS   1975

Consider shy Cezanne,
the lay of the land he loved,
its dumbstruck vanity, polite and brute.
The bather in his sketchy suit.
The skull upon the mute pull of cloth.   5
In your taxing and tearing, tugging at art,
consider shy Cezanne.
His blushing apples.
His love of man.

How do you account for the odd combination of images that occur in lines 4–8? What possible connection do a bather, a skull, and an apple share in common?

Henry Wadsworth Longfellow   (1807–1882)

AFTERMATH   1873

When the summer fields are mown,
When the birds are fledged and flown,
    And the dry leaves strew the path;
With the falling of the snow,
With the cawing of the crow,   5
Once again the fields we mow
    And gather in the aftermath.

Not the sweet, new grass with flowers
In this harvesting of ours;
    Not the upland clover bloom;   10
But the rowen mixed with weeds,
Tangled tufts from marsh and meads,
Where the poppy drops its seeds
    In the silence and the gloom.

QUESTIONS

1. How does the etymology and meaning of *aftermath* help explain this poem? (Look the word up in your dictionary.)
2. What is the meaning of *fledged* (line 2) and *rowen* (line 11)?
3. Once you understand the literal meaning of the poem, do you think that Longfellow intended any further significance to it?

John Clare   (1793–1864)

MOUSE'S NEST   (ABOUT 1835)

I found a ball of grass among the hay
And progged it as I passed and went away;
And when I looked I fancied something stirred,
And turned again and hoped to catch the bird—
When out an old mouse bolted in the wheats   5
With all her young ones hanging at her teats;
She looked so odd and so grotesque to me,
I ran and wondered what the thing could be,
And pushed the knapweed bunches where I stood;
Then the mouse hurried from the craking° brood.   *crying*   10

The young ones squeaked, and as I went away
She found her nest again among the hay.
The water o'er the pebbles scarce could run
And broad old cesspools glittered in the sun.

QUESTIONS

1. "To prog" (*progged*, line 2) means "to poke about for food, to forage." In what ways does this word fit more exactly here than *prodded, touched,* or *searched?*
2. Is *craking* (line 10) better than *crying?* Which word better fits the poem? Why?
3. What connections do you find between the last two lines and the rest of the poem? To what are water that *scarce could run* and *broad old cesspools* (lines 13 and 14) likened?

WORD CHOICE AND WORD ORDER

Even if Samuel Johnson's famous *Dictionary* of 1755 had been as thick as Webster's unabridged, an eighteenth-century poet searching through it for words to use would have had a narrower choice. For in English literature of the **neoclassical period** or **Augustan age**—that period from about 1660 into the late eighteenth century—many poets subscribed to a belief in **poetic diction:** "A system of words," said Dr. Johnson, "refined from the grossness of domestic use." The system admitted into a serious poem only certain words and subjects, excluding others as violations of **decorum** (propriety). Accordingly, such common words as *rat, cheese, big, sneeze,* and *elbow,* although admissible to satire, were thought inconsistent with the loftiness of tragedy, epic, ode, and elegy. Dr. Johnson's biographer, James Boswell, tells how a poet writing an epic reconsidered the word "rats" and instead wrote "the whiskered vermin race." Johnson himself objected to Lady Macbeth's allusion to her "keen knife," saying that "we do not immediately conceive that any crime of importance is to be committed with a knife; or who does not, at last, from the long habit of connecting a knife with sordid offices, feel aversion rather than terror?" Probably Johnson was here the victim of his age, and Shakespeare was right, but Johnson in one of his assumptions was right too: there are inappropriate words as well as appropriate ones.

Neoclassical poets chose their classical models more often from Roman writers than from Greek, as their diction suggests by the frequency of Latin derivatives. For example, a *net,* according to Dr. Johnson's dictionary, is "any thing reticulated or decussated, at equal distances, with interstices between the intersections." In company with Latinate words often appeared fixed combinations of adjective and noun ("finny prey" for "fish"), poetic names (a song to a lady named Molly might rechristen her Parthenia), and allusions to classical mythology. Neoclassical poetic diction was evidently being abused when, instead of saying "uncork the bottle," a poet could write,

Apply thine engine to the spongy door,
Set *Bacchus* from his glassy prison free,

in some bad lines ridiculed by Alexander Pope in *Peri Bathous, or, Of the Art of Sinking in Poetry*.

Not all poetic diction is excess baggage. To a reader who knew at first hand both living sheep and the pastoral poems of Virgil—as most readers nowadays do not—such a fixed phrase as "the fleecy care," which seems stilted to us, conveyed pleasurable associations. But "fleecy care" was more than a highfalutin way of saying "sheep"; as one scholar has pointed out, "when they wished, our poets could say 'sheep' as clearly and as often as anybody el..e. In the first place, 'fleecy' drew attention to wool, and demanded the appropriate visual image of sheep; for aural imagery the poets would refer to 'the bleating kind'; it all depended upon what was happening in the poem."[2]

Other poets have found some special kind of poetic language valuable: Old English poets, with their standard figures of speech ("whale-road" for the sea, "ring-giver" for a ruler); makers of folk ballads who, no less than neoclassicists, love fixed epithet-noun combinations ("milk-white steed," "blood-red wine," "steel-driving man"); and Edmund Spenser, whose example made popular the adjective ending in -*y* (*fleecy, grassy, milky*).

When Wordsworth, in his Preface to *Lyrical Ballads*, asserted that "the language really spoken by men," especially by humble rustics, is plainer, more emphatic, and conveys "elementary feelings . . . in a state of greater simplicity," he was, in effect, advocating a new poetic diction. Wordsworth's ideas invited freshness into English poetry and, by admitting words that neoclassical poets would have called "low" ("His poor old *ankles* swell"), helped rid poets of the fear of being thought foolish for mentioning a commonplace.

This theory of the superiority of rural diction was, as Coleridge pointed out, hard to adhere to, and, in practice, Wordsworth was occasionally to write a language as Latinate and citified as these lines on yew trees:

Huge trunks!—and each particular trunk a growth
Of intertwisted fibers serpentine
Up-coiling, and inveterately convolved . . .

Language so Latinate sounds pedantic to us, especially the phrase *inveterately convolved*. In fact, some poets, notably Gerard Manley Hopkins, have subscribed to the view that English words derived from Anglo-Saxon (Old English) have more force and flavor than their Latin equivalents. *Kingly*, one may feel, has more power than *regal*. One argument for this view is that so many words of Old English origin—*man, wife, child, house, eat, drink, sleep*—are basic to our living speech. It may be true that a language closer to Old English is particularly fit for

---

[2]Bonamy Dobrée, *English Literature in the Early Eighteenth Century, 1700–1740* (New York: Oxford UP, 1959) 161.

rendering abstract notions concretely—as does the memorable title of a medieval work of piety, the *Ayenbite of Inwit* ("again-bite of inner wisdom" or "remorse of conscience"). And yet this view, if accepted at all, must be accepted with reservations. Some words of Latin origin carry meanings both precise and physical. In the King James Bible is the admonition, "See then that ye walk circumspectly, not as fools, but as wise" (Ephesians 5:15). To be *circumspect* (a word from two Latin roots meaning "to look" and "around") is to be watchful on all sides—a meaning altogether lost in a modernized wording of the passage once printed on a subway poster for a Bible society: "Be careful how you live, not thoughtlessly but thoughtfully."

When E. E. Cummings begins a poem, "mr youse needn't be so spry / concernin questions arty," we recognize another kind of diction available to poetry: **vulgate** (speech not much affected by schooling). Handbooks of grammar sometimes distinguish various **levels of diction.** A sort of ladder is imagined, on whose rungs words, phrases, and sentences may be ranked in an ascending order of formality, from the curses of an illiterate thug to the commencement-day address of a doctor of divinity. These levels range from vulgate through **colloquial** (the casual conversation or informal writing of literate people) and **general English** (most literate speech and writing, more studied than colloquial but not pretentious), up to **formal English** (the impersonal language of educated persons, usually only written, possibly spoken on dignified occasions). Recently, however, lexicographers have been shunning such labels. The designation *colloquial* has been expelled (*bounced* would be colloquial; *trun out*, vulgate) from *Webster's Third New International Dictionary* on the grounds that "it is impossible to know whether a word out of context is colloquial or not" and that the diction of Americans nowadays is more fluid than the labels suggest. Aware that we are being unscientific, we may find the labels useful. They may help roughly to describe what happens when, as in the following poem, a poet shifts from one level of usage to another. This poem employs, incidentally, a colloquial device throughout: omitting the subjects of sentences. In keeping the characters straight, it may be helpful to fill in the speaker for each *said* and for the verbs *saw* and *ducked* (lines 9 and 10).

Josephine Miles (1911–1985)

REASON 1955

Said, Pull her up a bit will you, Mac, I want to unload there.
Said, Pull her up my rear end, first come first serve.
Said, Give her the gun, Bud, he needs a taste of his own bumper.
Then the usher came out and got into the act:

Said, Pull her up, pull her up a bit, we need this space, sir. 5
Said, For God's sake, is this still a free country or what?
You go back and take care of Gary Cooper's horse
And leave me handle my own car.

Saw them unloading the lame old lady,
Ducked out under the wheel and gave her an elbow,   10
Said, All you needed to do was just explain;
Reason, Reason is my middle name.

Language on more than one level enlivens this miniature comedy; the vulgate of the resentful driver ("Pull her up my rear end," "leave me handle my own car") and the colloquial of the bystander ("Give her the gun"). There is also a contrast in formality between the old lady's driver, who says "Mac," and the usher, who says "sir." These varied levels of language distinguish the speakers in the poem from one another.

The diction of "Reason" is that of standard American speech. At present, most poetry in English avoids elaborate literary expressions such as "fleecy care" in favor of more colloquial language. In many English-speaking areas, like Scotland, there has even been a movement to write poems in regional dialects. (A **dialect** is a particular variety of language spoken by an identifiable regional group or social class of persons.) Dialect poets frequently try to capture the freshness and authenticity of the language spoken in their immediate locale. Most Americans know at least part of one Scottish dialect poem by heart—"Auld Lang Syne," the song commonly sung as the clock strikes twelve on New Year's Eve. Although Robert Burns wrote most of the song's stanzas, the poet claimed to have copied down the famous opening stanza, below, from an old man he heard singing. *Auld* is the Scots word for "old"; *lang syne* means "long since." How differently the lines would seem if they were standard English.

Should auld acquaintance be forgot,
And never brought to mind?
Should auld acquaintance be forgot
And days of auld lang syne?
And days of auld lang syne, my dear,
And days of auld lang syne,
Should auld acquaintance be forgot,
And days of auld lang syne?

Not only the poet's choice of words makes a poem seem more formal, or less, but also the way the words are arranged into sentences. Compare these lines,

Jack and Jill went up the hill
To fetch a pail of water.
Jack fell down and broke his crown
And Jill came tumbling after.

with Milton's account of a more significant downfall:

Earth trembled from her entrails, as again
In pangs, and Nature gave a second groan;
Sky loured, and, muttering thunder, some sad drops

Wept at completing of the mortal sin
Original; while Adam took no thought
Eating his fill, nor Eve to iterate
Her former trespass feared, the more to soothe
Him with her loved society, that now
As with new wine intoxicated both
They swim in mirth, and fancy that they feel
Divinity within them breeding wings
Wherewith to scorn the Earth.

Not all the words in Milton's lines are bookish: indeed, many of them can be found in nursery rimes. What helps, besides diction, to distinguish this account of the Biblical fall from "Jack and Jill" is that Milton's nonstop sentence seems further removed from usual speech in its length (83 words), in its complexity (subordinate clauses), and in its word order ("with new wine intoxicated both" rather than "both intoxicated with new wine"). Should we think less (or more highly) of Milton for choosing a style so elaborate and formal? No judgment need be passed: both Mother Goose and the author of *Paradise Lost* use language appropriate to their purposes.

Among languages, English is by no means the most flexible. English words must be used in fairly definite and inviolable patterns, and whoever departs too far from them will not be understood. In the sentence "Cain slew Abel," if you change the word order, you change the meaning: "Abel slew Cain." Such inflexibility was not true of Latin, in which a poet could lay down words in almost any sequence and, because their endings (inflections) showed what parts of speech they were, could trust that no reader would mistake a subject for an object or a noun for an adjective. (E. E. Cummings has striven, in certain of his poems, for the freedom of Latin. One such poem, "anyone lived in a pretty how town," appears on page 718.)

The rigidity of English word order invites the poet to defy it and to achieve unusual effects by inverting it. It is customary in English to place adjective in front of noun (*a blue mantle, new pastures*). But an unusual emphasis is achieved when Milton ends "Lycidas" by reversing the pattern:

At last he rose, and twitched his mantle blue:
Tomorrow to fresh woods, and pastures new.

Perhaps the inversion in *mantle blue* gives more prominence to the color associated with heaven (and in "Lycidas," heaven is of prime importance). Perhaps the inversion in *pastures new*, stressing the *new*, heightens the sense of a rebirth.

Coleridge offered two "homely definitions of prose and poetry; that is, *prose*: words in their best order; *poetry*: the best words in the best order." If all goes well, a poet may fasten the right word into the right place, and the result may be—as T. S. Eliot said in "Little Gidding"—a "complete consort dancing together."

Emma Lee Warrior   (b. 1941)

How I Came to Have a Man's Name   1988

It's a good thing Dad deserted Mom
and all us kids for a cousin's wiles,
cause then we learned from Grampa
how to pray to the Sun, the Moon and Stars.

Before a January dawn, under a moondog sky,   5
Yellow Dust hitched up a team to a strawfilled sleigh.
Snow squeaked against the runners
in reply to the crisp crackling cottonwoods.
They bundled up bravely in buffalo robes,
their figures pronounced by the white of night;   10
the still distance of the Wolf Trail° greeted them,   *Milky Way*
and Ipisowahs,° the boy child of Natosi,°   *morning star; the sun*
and Kokomiikiisom° watched their hurry.   *the moon*
My momma's body was bent with pain.
Otohkostskaksin° sensed the Morning Star's   *Yellow Dust*   15
presence and so he beseeched him:

"Aayo, Ipisowahs, you see us now,
pitiful creatures.
We are thankful there is no wind.
We are thankful for your light.   20
Guide us safely to our destination.
May my daughter give birth in a warm place.
May her baby be a boy; may he have your name.
May he be fortunate because of your name.
May he live long and be happy.   25
Bestow your name upon him, Ipisowahs.
His name will be Ipisowahs.
Aayo, help us, we are pitiful."

And Ipisowahs led them that icy night
through the Old Man River Valley   30
and out onto the frozen prairie.
They rushed to the hospital
where my mother pushed me into this world
and nobody bothered to change my name.

How I Came to Have a Man's Name. The words glossed in the margin of the poem are the poet's
translations from the Blackfoot language.

Questions

1. What do the words from the Blackfoot language contribute to this poem? (Suggestion: Try reading them aloud as best you can.)

2. If the unborn child was to be named Ipisowahs, "morning star," then why do you
   suppose the poet signs herself Emma Lee Warrior?

Thomas Hardy (1840–1928)*

THE RUINED MAID   1901

"O 'Melia, my dear, this does everything crown!
Who could have supposed I should meet you in Town?
And whence such fair garments, such prosperi-ty?"—
"O didn't you know I'd been ruined?" said she.

—"You left us in tatters, without shoes or socks,   5
Tired of digging potatoes, and spudding up docks°;   *spading up dockweed*
And now you've gay bracelets and bright feathers three!"—
"Yes: that's how we dress when we're ruined," said she.

—"At home in the barton° you said 'thee' and 'thou,'   *farmyard*
And 'thik oon,' and 'theäs oon,' and 't'other'; but now   10
Your talking quite fits 'ee for high compa-ny!"—
"Some polish is gained with one's ruin," said she.

—"Your hands were like paws then, your face blue and bleak
But now I'm bewitched by your delicate cheek,
And your little gloves fit as on any la-dy!"—   15
"We never do work when we're ruined," said she.

—"You used to call home-life a hag-ridden dream,
And you'd sigh, and you'd sock°; but at present you seem   *groan*
To know not of megrims° or melancho-ly!"—   *blues*
"True. One's pretty lively when ruined," said she.   20

—"I wish I had feathers, a fine sweeping gown,
And a delicate face, and could strut about Town!"—
"My dear—a raw country girl, such as you be,
Cannot quite expect that. You ain't ruined," said she.

QUESTIONS

1. Where does this dialogue take place? Who are the two speakers?
2. Comment on Hardy's use of the word *ruined*. What is the conventional meaning of
   the word when applied to a woman? As 'Melia applies it to herself what is its
   meaning?
3. Sum up the attitude of each speaker toward the other. What details of the new
   'Melia does the first speaker most dwell upon? Would you expect Hardy to be so impressed by all these details, or is there, between his view of the characters and their
   view of themselves, any hint of an ironic discrepancy?
4. In losing her country dialect (*thik oon* and *theäs oon* for *this one* and *that one*), 'Melia
   is presumed to have gained in sophistication. What does Hardy suggest by her *ain't*
   in the last line?

Richard Eberhart   (b. 1904)

THE FURY OF AERIAL BOMBARDMENT   1947

You would think the fury of aerial bombardment
Would rouse God to relent; the infinite spaces
Are still silent. He looks on shock-pried faces.
History, even, does not know what is meant.

You would feel that after so many centuries   5
God would give man to repent; yet he can kill
As Cain could, but with multitudinous will,
No farther advanced than in his ancient furies.

Was man made stupid to see his own stupidity?
Is God by definition indifferent, beyond us all?   10
Is the eternal truth man's fighting soul
Wherein the Beast ravens in its own avidity?

Of Van Wettering I speak, and Averill,
Names on a list, whose faces I do not recall
But they are gone to early death, who late in school   15
Distinguished the belt feed lever from the belt holding pawl.

QUESTIONS

1. As a naval officer during World War II, Richard Eberhart was assigned for a time as
   an instructor in a gunnery school. How has this experience apparently contributed
   to the diction of his poem?
2. In his *Life of John Dryden*, complaining about a description of a sea fight Dryden had
   filled with nautical language, Samuel Johnson argued that technical terms should be
   excluded from poetry. Is this criticism applicable to Eberhart's last line? Can a word
   succeed for us in a poem, even though we may not be able to define it? (For more evidence, see also the technical terms in Henry Reed's "Naming of Parts," page 1121.)
3. Some readers have found a contrast in tone between the first three stanzas of this
   poem and the last stanza. How would you describe this contrast? What does diction
   contribute to it?

Wendy Cope   (b. 1945)*

LONELY HEARTS   1986

Can someone make my simple wish come true?
Male biker seeks female for touring fun.
Do you live in North London? Is it you?

Gay vegetarian whose friends are few,
I'm into music, Shakespeare and the sun,   5
Can someone make my simple wish come true?

Executive in search of something new—
Perhaps bisexual woman, arty, young.
Do you live in North London? Is it you?

Successful, straight and solvent? I am too—
Attractive Jewish lady with a son.
Can someone make my simple wish come true?

I'm Libran, inexperienced and blue—
Need slim non-smoker, under twenty-one.
Do you live in North London? Is it you?

Please write (with photo) to Box 152.
Who knows where it may lead once we've begun?
Can someone make my simple wish come true?
Do you live in North London? Is it you?

10

15

LONELY HEARTS. This poem has a double form: the rhetorical, a series of "lonely heart" personal ads from a newspaper, and metrical, a **villanelle,** a fixed form developed by French courtly poets in imitation of Italian folk song. For other villanelles, see Elizabeth Bishop's "One Art" (page 1039) and Dylan Thomas's "Do not go gentle into that good night" (page 872). In the villanelle, the first and the third lines are repeated in a set pattern throughout the poem.

QUESTIONS

1. What sort of language does Wendy Cope borrow for this poem?
2. The form of the villanelle requires that the poet end each stanza with one of two repeating lines. What special use does the author make of these mandatory repetitions?
3. How many speakers are there in the poem? Does the author's voice ever enter or is the entire poem spoken by individuals in personal ads?
4. The poem seems to begin satirically. Does the poem ever move beyond the critical, mocking tone typical of satire?

FOR REVIEW AND FURTHER STUDY
E. E. Cummings   (1894–1962)*

ANYONE LIVED IN A PRETTY HOW TOWN   1940

anyone lived in a pretty how town
(with up so floating many bells down)
spring summer autumn winter
he sang his didn't he danced his did.

Women and men (both little and small)
cared for anyone not at all
they sowed their isn't they reaped their same
sun moon stars rain

children guessed (but only a few
and down they forgot as up they grew
autumn winter spring summer)
that noone loved him more by more

5

10

when by now and tree by leaf
she laughed his joy she cried his grief
bird by snow and stir by still   15
anyone's any was all to her

someones married their everyones
laughed their cryings and did their dance
(sleep wake hope and then) they
said their nevers they slept their dream   20

stars rain sun moon
(and only the snow can begin to explain
how children are apt to forget to remember
with up so floating many bells down)

one day anyone died i guess   25
(and noone stooped to kiss his face)
busy folk buried them side by side
little by little and was by was

all by all and deep by deep
and more by more they dream their sleep   30
noone and anyone earth by april
wish by spirit and if by yes.

Women and men (both dong and ding)
summer autumn winter spring
reaped their sowing and went their came   35
sun moon stars rain

QUESTIONS

1. Summarize the story told in this poem. Who are the characters?
2. Rearrange the words in the two opening lines into the order you would expect them usually to follow. What effect does Cummings obtain by his unconventional word order?
3. Another of Cummings's strategies is to use one part of speech as if it were another; for instance, in line 4, *didn't* and *did* ordinarily are verbs, but here they are used as nouns. What other words in the poem perform functions other than their expected ones?

Jonathan Holden   (b. 1941)

THE NAMES OF THE RAPIDS   1985

Snaggle-Tooth, Maytag, Taylor Falls—
long before we measured with our eyes
the true size of each monstrosity
its name, downriver, was famous to us.

It lay in wait, something to be slain   5
while our raft, errant, eddied
among glancing pinpricks of sun
and every bend giving way to bend
seemed a last reprieve.
But common terror has a raw taste.   10
It's all banality, as when
you stare straight into a bad cut—
this sense of being slightly more
awake than you might like.
When the raft pitches sideways off   15
a ledge, what you land on is less
than its name. It's a mechanism. None
of the demented expressions
that the fleshly water forms
over that stone profile   20
is more than another collision,
a fleeting logic lost and
forming, now lost in the melee.
When the world is most serious
we approach it with wholly open eyes   25
even as we start the plunge
and the stone explanation.

QUESTION

From the names of the three rapids mentioned in line 1, describe what you think each
one would probably be like.

Robert Herrick   (1591–1674)*

UPON JULIA'S CLOTHES   1648

Whenas in silks my Julia goes,
Then, then, methinks, how sweetly flows
That liquefaction of her clothes.

Next, when I cast mine eyes and see
That brave vibration each way free,   5
O how that glittering taketh me!

QUESTIONS

1. What is the literal meaning of *liquefaction*? Why would Herrick use such an uncommon word when another might mean more or less the same thing?
2. Look up the different meanings of the adjective *brave* in the dictionary. In what
   sense does Herrick use the word in this poem?

EXERCISE: *Different Kinds of English*

Read the following poems and see what kinds of diction and word order you find in them. Which poems are least formal in their language and which most formal? Is there any use of vulgate English? Any dialect? What does each poem achieve that its own kind of English makes possible?

Anonymous   (American oral verse)
CARNATION MILK   (ABOUT 1900?)

Carnation Milk is the best in the land;
Here I sit with a can in my hand—
No tits to pull, no hay to pitch,
You just punch a hole in the son of a bitch.

CARNATION MILK. "This quatrain is imagined as the caption under a picture of a rugged-looking cowboy seated upon a bale of hay," notes William Harmon in his *Oxford Book of American Light Verse* (New York: Oxford UP, 1979). Possibly the first to print this work was David Ogilvy (b. 1911), who quotes it in his *Confessions of an Advertising Man* (New York: Atheneum, 1963).

William Wordsworth   (1770–1850)*
MY HEART LEAPS UP WHEN I BEHOLD   1807

My heart leaps up when I behold
  A rainbow in the sky:
So was it when my life began;
So is it now I am a man;
So be it when I shall grow old,   5
  Or let me die!
The Child is father of the Man;
And I could wish my days to be
Bound each to each by natural piety.

William Wordsworth   (1770–1850)*
MUTABILITY   1822

From low to high doth dissolution climb,
And sink from high to low, along a scale
Of awful notes, whose concord shall not fail;
A musical but melancholy chime,
Which they can hear who meddle not with crime,   5
Nor avarice, nor over-anxious care.
Truth fails not; but her outward forms that bear
The longest date do melt like frosty rime°,   *frozen dew*

That in the morning whitened hill and plain
And is no more; drop like the tower sublime   10
Of yesterday, which royally did wear
His crown of weeds, but could not even sustain
Some casual shout that broke the silent air,
Or the unimaginable touch of Time.

Anonymous

SCOTTSBORO   1936

Paper come out—done strewed de news
Seven po' chillun moan deat' house blues,
Seven po' chillun moanin' deat' house blues.
Seven nappy° heads wit' big shiny eye   *frizzy*
All boun' in jail and framed to die,   5
All boun' in jail and framed to die.

Messin' white woman—snake lyin' tale
Hang and burn and jail wit' no bail.
Dat hang and burn and jail wit' no bail.
Worse ol' crime in white folks' lan'   10
Black skin coverin' po' workin' man,
Black skin coverin' po' workin' man.

Judge and jury—all in de stan'
Lawd, biggety name for same lynchin' ban',
Lawd, biggety name for same lynchin' ban'.   15
White folks and nigger in great co't house
Like cat down cellar wit' nohole mouse.
Like cat down cellar wit' nohole mouse.

SCOTTSBORO. This folk blues, collected by Lawrence Gellert in *Negro Songs of Protest* (New York:
Carl Fischer, Inc., 1936), is a comment on the Scottsboro case. In 1931 nine black youths of Scottsboro, Alabama, were arrested and charged with the rape of two white women. Though eventually,
after several trials, they were found not guilty, some of them at the time this song was composed had
been convicted and sentenced to death.

Lewis Carroll
[Charles Lutwidge Dodgson]   (1832–1898)

JABBERWOCKY   1871

'Twas brillig, and the slithy toves
    Did gyre and gimble in the wabe:
All mimsy were the borogoves,
    And the mome raths outgrabe.

"Beware the Jabberwock, my son!   5
  The jaws that bite, the claws that catch!
Beware the Jubjub bird, and shun
  The frumious Bandersnatch!"

He took his vorpal sword in hand;
  Long time the manxome foe he sought—   10
So rested he by the Tumtum tree
  And stood awhile in thought.

And, as in uffish thought he stood,
  The Jabberwock, with eyes of flame,
Came whiffling through the tulgey wood,   15
  And burbled as it came!

One, two! One, two! And through and through
  The vorpal blade went snicker-snack!
He left it dead, and with its head
  He went galumphing back.   20

"And hast thou slain the Jabberwock?
  Come to my arms, my beamish boy!
O frabjous day! Callooh, Callay!"
  He chortled in his joy.

'Twas brillig, and the slithy toves   25
  Did gyre and gimble in the wabe:
All mimsy were the borogoves,
  And the mome raths outgrabe.

JABBERWOCKY. Fussy about pronunciation, Carroll in his preface to *The Hunting of the Snark* declares: "The first 'o' in 'borogoves' is pronounced like the 'o' in 'borrow.' I have heard people try to
give it the sound of the 'o' in 'worry.' Such is Human Perversity." *Toves*, he adds, rimes with
groves.

QUESTIONS

1. Look up *chortled* (line 24) in your dictionary and find out its definition and
   origin.
2. In *Through the Looking Glass*, Alice seeks the aid of Humpty Dumpty to decipher the
   meaning of this nonsense poem. "*Brillig*," he explains, "means four o'clock in the afternoon—the time when you begin *broiling* things for dinner." Does *brillig* sound like
   any other familiar word?
3. "*Slithy*," the explanation goes on, "means 'lithe and slimy.' 'Lithe' is the same as
   'active.' You see it's like a portmanteau—there are two meanings packed up into one
   word." *Mimsy* is supposed to pack together both "flimsy" and "miserable." In the
   rest of the poem, what other portmanteau—or packed suitcase—words can you
   find?

Lewis Carroll

Lewis Carroll on Writing
HUMPTY DUMPTY EXPLICATES "JABBERWOCKY" 1871

"You seem very clever at explaining words, sir," said Alice. "Would you kindly tell me the meaning of the poem called 'Jabberwocky'?"

"Let's hear it," said Humpty Dumpty. "I can explain all the poems that ever were invented—and a good many that haven't been invented just yet."

This sounded very hopeful, so Alice repeated the first verse:

> "'Twas brillig, and the slithy toves
> Did gyre and gimble in the wabe:
> All mimsy were the borogoves,
> And the mome raths outgrabe."

"That's enough to begin with," Humpty Dumpty interrupted: "there are plenty of hard words there. *'Brillig'* means four o'clock in the afternoon—the time when you begin *broiling* things for dinner."

"That'll do very well," said Alice. "And *'slithy'*?"

"Well, *'slithy'* means 'lithe and slimy.' 'Lithe' is the same as 'active.' You see, it's like a portmanteau—there are two meanings packed up in one word."

"I see it now," Alice remarked thoughtfully. "And what are *'toves'*?"

"Well, *'toves'* are something like badgers—they're something like lizards— and they're something like corkscrews."

"They must be very curious-looking creatures."

"They are that," said Humpty Dumpty, "also they make their nests under sundials—also they live on cheese."

"And what's to *'gyre'* and to *'gimble'*?"

"To *'gyre'* is to go round and round like a gyroscope. To *'gimble'* is to make holes like a gimlet."

"And 'the wabe' is the grass plot round a sundial, I suppose?" said Alice, surprised at her own ingenuity.

"Of course it is. It's called 'wabe,' you know, because it goes a long way before it, and a long way behind it."

"And a long way beyond it on each side," Alice added.

"Exactly so. Well, then, 'mimsy' is flimsy and miserable (there's another portmanteau for you). And a 'borogove' is a thin, shabby-looking bird with its feathers sticking out all round—something like a live mop."

"And then 'mome raths'?" said Alice. "I'm afraid I'm giving you a great deal of trouble."

"Well, a 'rath' is a sort of green pig: but 'mome' I'm not certain about. I think it's short for 'from home'—meaning that they'd lost their way, you know."

"And what does 'outgrabe' mean?"

"Well, 'outgribing' is something between bellowing and whistling, with a kind of sneeze in the middle; however, you'll hear it done, maybe—down in the wood yonder—and when you've once heard it you'll be *quite* content. Who's been repeating all that hard stuff to you?"

"I read it in a book," said Alice.

Through the Looking Glass

HUMPTY DUMPTY EXPLICATES "JABBERWOCKY." This celebrated passage is the origin of the term *portmanteau word,* an artificial word that combines parts of other words to express some combination of their qualities. (*Brunch,* for example, is a meal that combines aspects of both breakfast and lunch.) A portmanteau is a large suitcase that opens up into two separate compartments.

◄━► WRITING CRITICALLY ◄━►

How Much Difference Does a Word Make?

Although a poem may contain images and ideas, it is made up of words. Language is the medium of poetry, and the exact wording of a successful poem is the chief source of its power. Writers labor mightily to shape each word and phrase to create particular expressive effects. Changing a single word sometimes ruins a poem's effect, just as changing one number in a combination lock's sequence makes all the other numbers useless.

Before writing about the language of a poem, recruit your intuition into working with your intellect. As you read the poem, ask yourself if there is some particular word or combination of words that gives you particular pleasure or especially intrigues you. Don't worry about why the word or words impress you. Don't even worry about the meaning. Just underline the word or phrase in your book. Then let your analytical powers go to work. Try to determine what makes this part of the poem so intriguing to you. How does it relate to the other lines? What does it contribute to the effect of the poem? In writing about the poem, let that word or phrase be your key into the poem. Often by understanding how a single key word operates in the context of a poem, we gain a special sense of what the whole poem means.

WRITING ASSIGNMENT

In no more than two pages, analyze how a single word or phrase contributes to a poem's total impact. Begin by choosing from any poem in this chapter a line or two that you particularly like. Then, select a key word or phrase and explore how they help shape the poem's total meaning. As part of your analysis rewrite the line by substituting a synonym in place of a single important word. Discuss what is lost by the substitution. A possible topic might be Robert Herrick's line from "Upon Julia's Clothes," "the liquefaction of her clothes." What does the beautiful but unusual word *liquefaction* add to the poem that a synonym would not? Other interesting poems to analyze include Wendy Cope's "Lonely Hearts," Robert Graves's "Down, Wanton, Down," or William Wordsworth's "Mutability."

FURTHER SUGGESTIONS FOR WRITING

1. Choosing a poem that strikes you as particularly inventive or unusual in its language, such as E. E. Cummings's "anyone lived in a pretty how town" (page 718), or Gerard Manley Hopkins's "The Windhover" (page 1084), or Wendy Cope's "Lonely Hearts" (page 717), write a brief analysis of it. Concentrate on the diction of the poem and word order. For what possible purposes does the poet depart from standard English or incorporate unusual vocabulary? (For pointers on writing about poetry by the method of analysis, see page 1899.)

2. In a short essay, set forth the pleasures of browsing in a dictionary. As you browse, see if you can discover any "found poems."

3. "Printing poetry in dialect, such as 'Scottsboro,' insults the literacy of a people." Think about this critical charge and comment on it.

15 Saying and Suggesting

To write so clearly that they might bring "all things as near the mathematical plainness" as possible—that was the goal of scientists according to Bishop Thomas Sprat, who lived in the seventeenth century. Such an effort would seem bound to fail, because words, unlike numbers, are ambiguous indicators. Although it may have troubled Bishop Sprat, the tendency of a word to have multiplicity of meaning rather than mathematical plainness opens broad avenues to poetry.

Every word has at least one **denotation:** a meaning as defined in a dictionary. But the English language has many a common word with so many denotations that a reader may need to think twice to see what it means in a specific context. The noun *field*, for instance, can denote a piece of ground, a sports arena, the scene of a battle, part of a flag, a profession, and a number system in mathematics. Further, the word can be used as a verb ("he fielded a grounder") or an adjective ("field trip," "field glasses").

A word also has **connotations:** overtones or suggestions of additional meaning that it gains from all the contexts in which we have met it in the past. The word *skeleton,* according to a dictionary, denotes "the bony framework of a human being or other vertebrate animal, which supports the flesh and protects the organs." But by its associations, the word can rouse thoughts of war, of disease and death, or (possibly) of one's plans to go to medical school. Think, too, of the difference between "Old Doc Jones" and "Abner P. Jones, M.D." In the mind's eye, the former appears in his shirtsleeves; the latter has a gold nameplate on his door. That some words denote the same thing but have sharply different connotations is pointed out in this anonymous Victorian jingle:

Here's a little ditty that you really ought to know:
Horses "sweat" and men "perspire," but ladies only "glow."

The terms *druggist, pharmacist,* and *apothecary* all denote the same occupation, but apothecaries lay claim to special distinction.

Poets aren't the only people who care about the connotations of language. Advertisers know that connotations make money. Nowadays many automobile dealers advertise their secondhand cars not as "used" but as "pre-owned," as if fearing that "used car" would connote an old heap with soiled upholstery and mysterious engine troubles that somebody couldn't put up with. "Pre-owned," however, suggests that the previous owner has taken the trouble of breaking in the car for you. Not long ago prune-packers, alarmed by a slump in sales, sponsored a survey to determine the connotations of prunes in the public consciousness. Asked, "What do you think of when you hear the word *prunes?*" most people replied, "dried up," "wrinkled," or "constipated." Dismayed, the packers hired an advertising agency to create a new image for prunes, in hopes of inducing new connotations. Soon, advertisements began to show prunes in brightly colored settings, in the company of bikinied bathing beauties.

In imaginative writing, connotations are as crucial as they are in advertising. Consider this sentence: "A new brand of journalism is being born, or spawned" (Dwight Macdonald writing in *The New York Review of Books*). The last word, by its associations with fish and crustaceans, suggests that this new journalism is scarcely the product of human beings. And what do we make of Romeo's assertion that Juliet "is the sun"? Surely even a lovesick boy cannot mean that his sweetheart is "the incandescent body of gases about which the earth and other planets revolve" (a dictionary definition). He means, of course, that he thrives in her sight, that he feels warm in her presence or even at the thought of her, that she illumines his world and is the center of his universe. Because in the mind of the hearer these and other suggestions are brought into play, Romeo's statement, literally absurd, makes excellent sense.

Here is a famous poem that groups together things with similar connotations: certain ships and their cargoes. (A *quinquireme*, by the way, was an ancient Assyrian vessel propelled by sails and oars.)

John Masefield (1878–1967)
CARGOES 1902

Quinquireme of Nineveh from distant Ophir,
Rowing home to haven in sunny Palestine,
With a cargo of ivory,
And apes and peacocks,
Sandalwood, cedarwood, and sweet white wine. 5

Stately Spanish galleon coming from the Isthmus,
Dipping through the Tropics by the palm-green shores,
With a cargo of diamonds,
Emeralds, amethysts,
Topazes, and cinnamon, and gold moidores°. *Portuguese coins* 10

Dirty British coaster with a salt-caked smoke stack,
Butting through the Channel in the mad March days,
With a cargo of Tyne coal,
Road-rails, pig-lead,
Firewood, iron-ware, and cheap tin trays.   15

To us, as well as to the poet's original readers, the place-names in the first
two stanzas suggest the exotic and faraway. Ophir, a vanished place, may have
been in Arabia; according to the Bible, King Solomon sent there for its celebrated pure gold, also for ivory, apes, peacocks, and other luxury items. (See I
Kings 9–10.) In his final stanza, Masefield groups commonplace things (mostly
heavy and metallic), whose suggestions of crudeness, cheapness, and ugliness he
deliberately contrasts with those of the precious stuffs he has listed earlier. For
British readers, the Tyne is a stodgy and familiar river; the English Channel in
March, choppy and likely to upset a stomach. The quinquireme is *rowing*, the
galleon is *dipping*, but the dirty British freighter is *butting*, aggressively pushing.
Conceivably, the poet could have described firewood and even coal as beautiful,
but evidently he wants them to convey sharply different suggestions here, to go
along with the rest of the coaster's cargo. In drawing such a sharp contrast between past and present, Masefield does more than merely draw up bills-of-lading.
Perhaps he even implies a wry and unfavorable comment upon life in the present
day. His meaning lies not so much in the dictionary definitions of his words
("*moidores*: Portuguese gold coins formerly worth approximately five pounds
sterling") as in their rich and vivid connotations.

William Blake   (1757–1827)*

LONDON   1794

I wander through each chartered street,
Near where the chartered Thames does flow,
And mark in every face I meet
Marks of weakness, marks of woe.

In every cry of every man,   5
In every infant's cry of fear,
In every voice, in every ban,
The mind-forged manacles I hear.

How the chimney-sweeper's cry
Every black'ning church appalls   10
And the hapless soldier's sigh
Runs in blood down palace walls.

But most through midnight streets I hear
How the youthful harlot's curse
Blasts the new born infant's tear   15
And blights with plagues the marriage hearse.

Here are only a few of the possible meanings of three of Blake's words:

chartered (lines 1, 2)

> DENOTATIONS: Established by a charter (a written grant or a certificate of incorporation); leased or hired.
> CONNOTATIONS: Defined, limited, restricted, channeled, mapped, bound by law; bought and sold (like a slave or an inanimate object); Magna Carta; charters given to crown colonies by the King.
> OTHER WORDS IN THE POEM WITH SIMILAR CONNOTATIONS: *Ban*, which can denote (1) a legal prohibition; (2) a churchman's curse or malediction; (3) in medieval times, an order summoning a king's vassals to fight for him. *Manacles*, or shackles, restrain movement. *Chimneysweeper*, *soldier*, and *harlot* are all hirelings.
> INTERPRETATION OF THE LINES: The street has had mapped out for it the direction in which it must go; the Thames has had laid down to it the course it must follow. Street and river are channeled, imprisoned, enslaved (like every inhabitant of London).

black'ning (line 10)

> DENOTATION: Becoming black.
> CONNOTATIONS: The darkening of something once light, the defilement of something once clean, the deepening of guilt, the gathering of darkness at the approach of night.
> OTHER WORDS IN THE POEM WITH SIMILAR CONNOTATIONS: Objects becoming marked or smudged (*marks of weakness, marks of woe* in the faces of passers-by; bloodied walls of a palace; marriage blighted with plagues); the word *appalls* (denoting not only "to overcome with horror" but "to make pale" and also "to cast a pall or shroud over"); *midnight streets*.
> INTERPRETATION OF THE LINE: Literally, every London church grows black from soot and hires a chimney-sweeper (a small boy) to help clean it. But Blake suggests too that by profiting from the suffering of the child laborer, the church is soiling its original purity.

Blasts, blights (lines 15–16)

> DENOTATIONS: Both *blast* and *blight* mean "to cause to wither" or "to ruin and destroy." Both are terms from horticulture. Frost *blasts* a bud and kills it; disease *blights* a growing plant.
> CONNOTATIONS: Sickness and death; gardens shriveled and dying; gusts of wind and the ravages of insects; things blown to pieces or rotted and warped.
> OTHER WORDS IN THE POEM WITH SIMILAR CONNOTATIONS: Faces marked with weakness and woe; the child becomes a chimney-sweep; the

soldier killed by war; blackening church and bloodied palace; young girl turned harlot; wedding carriage transformed into a hearse.

INTERPRETATION OF THE LINES: Literally, the harlot spreads the plague of syphilis, which, carried into marriage, can cause a baby to be born blind. In a larger and more meaningful sense, Blake sees the prostitution of even one young girl corrupting the entire institution of matrimony and endangering every child.

Some of these connotations are more to the point than others; the reader of a poem nearly always has the problem of distinguishing relevant associations from irrelevant ones. We need to read a poem in its entirety and, when a word leaves us in doubt, look for other things in the poem to corroborate or refute what we think it means. Relatively simple and direct in its statement, Blake's account of his stroll through the city at night becomes an indictment of a whole social and religious order. The indictment could hardly be this effective if it were "mathematically plain," its every word restricted to one denotation clearly spelled out.

Wallace Stevens   (1879–1955)*

DISILLUSIONMENT OF TEN O'CLOCK   1923

The houses are haunted
By white night-gowns.
None are green,
Or purple with green rings,
Or green with yellow rings,   5
Or yellow with blue rings.
None of them are strange,
With socks of lace
And beaded ceintures.
People are not going   10
To dream of baboons and periwinkles.
Only, here and there, an old sailor,
Drunk and asleep in his boots,
Catches tigers
In red weather.   15

QUESTIONS

1. What are *beaded ceintures?* What does the phrase suggest?
2. What contrast does Stevens draw between the people who live in these houses and the old sailor? What do the connotations of *white night-gowns* and *sailor* add to this contrast?
3. What is lacking in these people who wear white night-gowns? Why should the poet's view of them be a "disillusionment"?

Gwendolyn Brooks   (b. 1917)*

THE BEAN EATERS   1960

They eat beans mostly, this old yellow pair.
Dinner is a casual affair.
Plain chipware on a plain and creaking wood,
Tin flatware.

Two who are Mostly Good.   5
Two who have lived their day,
But keep on putting on their clothes
And putting things away.

And remembering . . .
Remembering, with tinklings and twinges,   10
As they lean over the beans in their rented back room that is full of
   beads and receipts and dolls and cloths, tobacco crumbs, vases
   and fringes.

QUESTIONS

1. What do we infer about this old couple and their life-style from the details in lines
   1–4 about their diet, dishes, dinner table, and cutlery?
2. In that long last line, what is suggested by the things they have saved and stored?

Richard Snyder   (1925–1986)

A MONGOLOID CHILD HANDLING   1971
SHELLS ON THE BEACH

She turns them over in her slow hands,
as did the sea sending them to her;
broken bits from the mazarine maze,
they are the calmest things on this sand.

The unbroken children splash and shout,   5
rough as surf, gay as their nesting towels.
But she plays soberly with the sea's
small change and hums back to it its slow vowels.

QUESTIONS

1. In what ways is the phrase *the mazarine maze* more valuable to this poem than if the
   poet had said "the deep blue sea"?
2. What is suggested by calling the other children *unbroken?* By saying that their towels
   are *nesting?*
3. How is the child like the sea? How are the other children like the surf? What do the
   differences between sea and surf contribute to Richard Snyder's poem?
4. What is the poet's attitude toward the child? How can you tell?

5. Since 1971, when this poem first appeared, the congenital condition once commonly named *mongolism* has come to be called *Down syndrome*, after the physician who first identified its characteristics. The denotations of *mongolism* and *Down syndrome* are identical. What connotations of the word *mongoloid* seem responsible for the word's fall from favor?

Timothy Steele (b. 1948)*

EPITAPH   1979

Here lies Sir Tact, a diplomatic fellow
Whose silence was not golden, but just yellow.

QUESTIONS

1. To what famous saying does the poet allude?
2. What are the connotations of *golden*? Of *yellow*?

Geoffrey Hill (b. 1932)

MERLIN   1959

I will consider the outnumbering dead:
For they are the husks of what was rich seed.
Now, should they come together to be fed,
They would outstrip the locusts' covering tide.

Arthur, Elaine, Mordred; they are all gone   5
Among the raftered galleries of bone.
By the long barrows of Logres they are made one,
And over their city stands the pinnacled corn.

MERLIN. In medieval legend, Merlin was a powerful magician and a seer, an aide of King Arthur. 5 *Elaine:* in Arthurian romance, the beloved of Sir Launcelot. *Mordred:* Arthur's treacherous nephew by whose hand the king died. 7 *barrows:* earthworks for burial of the dead. *Logres:* name of an ancient British kingdom, according to the twelfth-century historian Geoffrey of Monmouth, who gathered legends of King Arthur.

QUESTIONS

1. What does the title "Merlin" contribute to this poem? Do you prefer to read the poem as though it is Merlin who speaks to us—or the poet?
2. Line 4 alludes to the plague of locusts that God sent upon Egypt (Exodus 10): "For they covered the face of the whole earth, so that the land was darkened . . ." With this allusion in mind, explain the comparison of the dead to locusts.
3. Why are the suggestions inherent in the names of *Arthur, Elaine,* and *Mordred* more valuable to this poem than those we might find in the names of other dead persons called, say, Gus, Tessie, and Butch?

4. Explain the phrase in line 6: *the raftered galleries of bone*.
5. In the last line, what *city* does the poet refer to? Does he mean some particular city, or is he making a comparison?
6. What is interesting in the adjective *pinnacled*? How can it be applied to corn?

Walter de la Mare   (1873–1956)

THE LISTENERS   1912

"Is there anybody there?" said the Traveller,
  Knocking on the moonlit door;
And his horse in the silence champed the grasses
  Of the forest's ferny floor:
And a bird flew up out of the turret,   5
  Above the Traveller's head:
And he smote upon the door again a second time;
  "Is there anybody there?" he said.
But no one descended to the Traveller;
  No head from the leaf-fringed sill   10
Leaned over and looked into his gray eyes,
  Where he stood perplexed and still.
But only a host of phantom listeners
  That dwelt in the lone house then
Stood listening in the quiet of the moonlight   15
  To that voice from the world of men:
Stood thronging the faint moonbeams on the dark stair
  That goes down to the empty hall,
Hearkening in an air stirred and shaken
  By the lonely Traveller's call.   20
And he felt in his heart their strangeness,
  Their stillness answering his cry,
While his horse moved, cropping the dark turf,
  'Neath the starred and leafy sky;
For he suddenly smote on the door, even   25
  Louder, and lifted his head:—
"Tell them I came, and no one answered,
  That I kept my word," he said.
Never the least stir made the listeners,
  Though every word he spake   30
Fell echoing through the shadowiness of the still house
  From the one man left awake:
Ay, they heard his foot upon the stirrup,
  And the sound of iron on stone,
And how the silence surged softly backward,   35
  When the plunging hoofs were gone.

1. Before you had read this poem, what suggestions did its title bring to mind?
2. Now that you have read the poem, what do you make of these "listeners"? Who or what do you imagine them to be?
3. Why is *the moonlit door* (in line 2) a phrase more valuable to this poem than if the poet had written simply "the door"?
4. What does *turret* (in line 5) suggest?
5. Reconstruct some earlier events that might have preceded the Traveller's visit. Who might this Traveller be? Who are the unnamed persons—"them" (line 27)—for whom the Traveller leaves a message? What promise has he kept? (The poet doesn't tell us; we can only guess.)
6. Do you think this poem any the worse for the fact that its setting, characters, and action are so mysterious? What does "The Listeners" gain from not telling us all?

Robert Frost   (1874–1963)*

FIRE AND ICE   1923

Some say the world will end in fire,
Some say in ice.
From what I've tasted of desire
I hold with those who favor fire.
But if it had to perish twice,   5
I think I know enough of hate
To say that for destruction ice
Is also great
And would suffice.

QUESTIONS

1. To whom does Frost refer in line 1? In line 2?
2. What connotations of *fire* and *ice* contribute to the richness of Frost's comparison?

Cynthia Zarin   (b. 1959)

SONG   1993

My heart, my dove, my snail, my sail, my
     milktooth, shadow, sparrow, fingernail,
         flower-cat and blossom-hedge, mandrake

root now put to bed, moonshell, sea-swell,
     manatee, emerald shining back at me,   5
         nutmeg, quince, tea leaf and bone, zither,

cymbal, xylophone; paper, scissors, then
     there's stone—Who doesn't come through the door
         to get home?

What do the images of the poem suggest about the person it addresses? What can we guess about the identity of the person? What can we not know for sure?

Alfred, Lord Tennyson   (1809–1892)*

TEARS, IDLE TEARS   1847

Tears, idle tears, I know not what they mean,
Tears from the depth of some divine despair
Rise in the heart, and gather to the eyes,
In looking on the happy autumn-fields,
And thinking of the days that are no more.   5

Fresh as the first beam glittering on a sail,
That brings our friends up from the underworld,
Sad as the last which reddens over one
That sinks with all we love below the verge;
So sad, so fresh, the days that are no more.   10

Ah, sad and strange as in dark summer dawns
The earliest pipe of half-awakened birds
To dying ears, when unto dying eyes
The casement slowly grows a glimmering square;
So sad, so strange, the days that are no more.   15

Dear as remembered kisses after death,
And sweet as those by hopeless fancy feigned
On lips that are for others; deep as love,
Deep as first love, and wild with all regret;
O Death in Life, the days that are no more!   20

Richard Wilbur   (b. 1921)*

LOVE CALLS US TO THE THINGS OF   1956
THIS WORLD

The eyes open to a cry of pulleys,
And spirited from sleep, the astounded soul
Hangs for a moment bodiless and simple
As false dawn.
           Outside the open window   5
The morning air is all awash with angels.

Some are in bed-sheets, some are in blouses,
Some are in smocks: but truly there they are.
Now they are rising together in calm swells
Of halcyon feeling, filling whatever they wear   10
With the deep joy of their impersonal breathing;

Now they are flying in place, conveying
The terrible speed of their omnipresence, moving
And staying like white water; and now of a sudden
They swoon down into so rapt a quiet   15
That nobody seems to be there.
                              The soul shrinks

From all that it is about to remember,
From the punctual rape of every blessèd day,
And cries,   20
        "Oh, let there be nothing on earth but laundry,
Nothing but rosy hands in the rising steam
And clear dances done in the sight of heaven."

Yet, as the sun acknowledges
With a warm look the world's hunks and colors,   25
The soul descends once more in bitter love
To accept the waking body, saying now
In a changed voice as the man yawns and rises,

"Bring them down from their ruddy gallows;
Let there be clean linen for the backs of thieves;   30
Let lovers go fresh and sweet to be undone,
And the heaviest nuns walk in a pure floating
Of dark habits,
                keeping their difficult balance."

LOVE CALLS US TO THE THINGS OF THIS WORLD. Wilbur claimed that his title was taken from St.
Augustine, but in a recent interview he admitted that neither he nor any critic has ever been able to
locate the quotation again. Whatever its source, however, the title establishes the poem's central
idea that love allows us to return from the divine world of the spirit to the imperfect world of our
everyday lives. Wilbur's own comments on the poem are printed below.

QUESTIONS

1. What are the *angels* in line 6? Why does this metaphor seem appropriate to the situation?
2. What is "the punctual rape of every blessed day?" Who is being raped? Who or what commits the rape? Why would Wilbur choose this particular word with all its violent associations?

3. Who or what does the soul love in line 26, and why is that love bitter?
4. Is it merely obesity that make the nuns' balance "difficult" in the two final lines of the poem? What other "balance" does Wilbur's poem suggest?
5. The soul has two speeches in the poem. How do they differ in tone and imagery?
6. The spiritual world is traditionally considered invisible. What concrete images does Wilbur use to express its special character?

WRITER'S PERSPECTIVE

Richard Wilbur

Richard Wilbur on Writing
CONCERNING "LOVE CALLS US
TO THE THINGS OF THIS WORLD"   1966

If I understand this poem rightly, it has a free and organic rhythm: that is to say, its movement arises naturally from the emotion, and from the things and actions described. At the same time, the lines are metrical and disposed in stanzas. The subject matter is both exalted and vulgar. There is, I should think, sufficient description to satisfy an Imagist, but there is also a certain amount of statement; my hope is that the statement seems to grow inevitably out of the situation described. The language of the poem is at one moment elevated and at the next colloquial or slangy: for example, the imposing word "omnipresence" occurs not far from the undignified word "hunks." A critic would find in this poem certain patterns of sound, but those patterns of sound do not constitute an abstract music; they are meant, at any rate, to be inseparable from what is being said, a subordinate aspect of the poem's meaning.

The title of the poem is a quotation from St. Augustine: "Love Calls Us to the Things of This World." You must imagine the poem as occurring at perhaps seven-thirty in the morning; the scene is a bedroom high up in a city apartment building; outside the bedroom window, the first laundry of the day is being yanked across the sky, and one has been awakened by the squeaking pulleys of the laundry-line.

"On My Own Work"

The Ways a Poem Suggests

If we open the front door and find a friend standing there in hysterical tears, the person does not need to say "I'm miserable." We see that already. In a like manner, poems suggest some messages so clearly through imagery, tone, and diction that they do not need to declare them overtly. Poetry is a special way of speaking that requires a special way of listening. Poetry does not merely speak to the analytical parts of our minds but to the wholeness of our humanity. A good poem invites us to become fully alive and respond with our intuition, imagination, emotions, and intelligence. It even speaks to our physical bodies through sound, rhythm, and sensory imagery.

Since poems speak to us so completely, they often convey their meaning indirectly. An image may express something so clearly that the poem does not need to repeat it explicitly. In this sense, poems operate no differently from daily life.

In writing about a poem, listen carefully to everything it is telling you. Before beginning your essay, jot down a few key observations both about what the poem tells us and what we might want to know but aren't told. Note anything important to the story or situation of the poem that we have to infer for ourselves. When journalists write a news story, they always try to cover the "five W's" in their opening paragraph—*who, what, where, when, why*. These may be worthwhile questions to ask about a poem. If one or more of them is missing, how does that affect our understanding of the poem?

1. *Who?* Who is the speaker or central figure of the poem? (In Blake's "London," for instance, the speaker is also the protagonist who witnesses the hellish horror of the city.)
2. *What?* What is being seen or presented? Does the poem ever suddenly change its subject? (In Stevens's "Disillusionment at Ten O'Clock," for example, there are essentially two scenes—one dull and proper, the other wild and disreputable. What does that obvious shift suggest about Stevens's meaning?)
3. *Where?* Where is the poem set? Does the setting so clearly suggest something important that the rest of the poem does not need to repeat the message. (The setting of Brooks's "The Bean Eaters" speaks volumes about the two people in the poem.)
4. *When?* When does the poem take place? If a poet explicitly states a time of day or time of year, it is very likely that the *when* of the poem is important. (The fact that Stevens's poem takes place at 10:00 P.M. rather than 2:00 A.M. tells us a great deal about the people it describes.)
5. *Why?* If the poem describes some dramatic action but does not tell us *why* it is being performed, perhaps the author wants us to ponder the situation carefully. (De la Mare's "The Listeners" gains extra mystery by leaving us in the dark about the people involved, and Tennyson's

"Tears, Idle Tears" becomes more evocative by not being explicit about why the speaker weeps.)

You don't have to answer all the questions, but it will help to ask them. Remember, it is almost as important to know what a poem isn't telling us as what it does.

WRITING ASSIGNMENT

In a short essay (750–1000 words) explain why the speaker in Alfred, Lord Tennyson's "Tears, Idle Tears" (page 736) is weeping. Although the speaker claims not to know what the tears mean, the poem's language and imagery suggest some compelling reasons. Support your theory with specific examples. Be sure to differentiate between evidence that the poem explicitly provides and where an idea or event is only suggested. Feel free to extrapolate slightly beyond the limits of the poem, but *state clearly* where your interpretation goes beyond the literal meaning of the words and where it sticks closely to the text.

FURTHER SUGGESTIONS FOR WRITING

1. In a short essay, analyze a poem full of words that radiate suggestions. Looking into "Poems for Further Reading" that begins on page 1027 you might consider T. S. Eliot's "The Love Song of J. Alfred Prufrock," John Keats's "To Autumn," Sylvia Plath's "Daddy," or many others. Focus on particular words: explain their connotations and show how these suggestions are part of the poem's meaning. (For guidelines on writing about poetry by the method of analysis, see page 1899.)
2. In a current newspaper or magazine, select an advertisement that tries to surround a product with an aura. A new car, for instance, might be described in terms of some powerful jungle cat ("purring power, ready to spring"). Likely hunting-grounds for such ads are magazines that cater to the affluent (*New Yorker, Vogue,* and others). Clip or photocopy the ad and circle words in it that seem especially suggestive. Then, in an accompanying paper, unfold the suggestions in these words and try to explain the ad's appeal. How is the purpose of connotative language used in advertising copy different from that of such language when used in poetry?

16 Imagery

Ezra Pound (1885–1972)*

IN A STATION OF THE METRO   1916

The apparition of these faces in the crowd;
Petals on a wet, black bough.

Pound said he wrote this poem to convey an experience: emerging one day from a train in the Paris subway (*Métro*), he beheld "suddenly a beautiful face, and then another and another." Originally he had described his impression in a poem thirty lines long. In this final version, each line contains an image, which, like a picture, may take the place of a thousand words.

Though the term **image** suggests a thing seen, when speaking of images in poetry we generally mean *a word or sequence of words that refers to any sensory experience*. Often this experience is a sight (**visual imagery,** as in Pound's poem), but it may be a sound (**auditory imagery**) or a touch (**tactile imagery,** as a perception of roughness or smoothness). It may be an odor or a taste or perhaps a bodily sensation such as pain, the prickling of gooseflesh, the quenching of thirst, or—as in the following brief poem—the perception of something cold.

Taniguchi Buson (1716–1783)*

THE PIERCING CHILL I FEEL   (ABOUT 1760)

The piercing chill I feel:
　my dead wife's comb, in our bedroom,
　　under my heel . . .
　　　—*Translated by Harold G. Henderson*

As in this **haiku** (in Japanese, a poem of about seventeen syllables) an image can convey a flash of understanding. Had he wished, the poet might have spoken of the dead woman, of the contrast between her death and his memory of her, of his feelings toward death in general. But such a discussion would be quite different from the poem he actually wrote. Striking his bare foot against the comb, now cold and motionless but associated with the living wife (perhaps worn in her hair), the widower feels a shock as if he had touched the woman's corpse. A literal, physical sense of death is conveyed; the abstraction "death" is understood through the senses. To render the abstract in concrete terms is what poets often try to do; in this attempt, an image can be valuable.

An image may occur in a single word, a phrase, a sentence, or, as in this case, an entire short poem. To speak of the **imagery** of a poem—all its images taken together—is often more useful than to speak of separate images. To divide Buson's haiku into five images—*chill, wife, comb, bedroom, heel*—is possible, for any noun that refers to a visible object or a sensation is an image, but this is to draw distinctions that in themselves mean little and to disassemble a single experience.

Does an image cause a reader to experience a sense impression? Not quite. Reading the word *petals*, no one literally sees petals; but the occasion is given for imagining them. The image asks to be seen with the mind's eye. And although "In a Station of the Metro" records what Ezra Pound saw, it is of course not necessary for a poet actually to have lived through a sensory experience in order to write of it. Keats may never have seen a newly discovered planet through a telescope, despite the image in his sonnet on Chapman's Homer (page 1091).

It is tempting to think of imagery as mere decoration, particularly when we read Keats, who fills his poems with an abundance of sights, sounds, odors, and tastes. But a successful image is not just a dab of paint or a flashy bauble. When Keats opens "The Eve of St. Agnes" with what have been called the coldest lines in literature, he evokes by a series of images a setting and a mood:

St. Agnes' eve—Ah, bitter chill it was!
The owl, for all his feathers, was a-cold;
The hare limped trembling through the frozen grass,
And silent was the flock in woolly fold:
Numb were the Beadsman's fingers, while he told
His rosary, and while his frosted breath,
Like pious incense from a censer old,
Seemed taking flight for heaven, without a death, . . .

Indeed, some literary critics look for much of the meaning of a poem in its imagery, wherein they expect to see the mind of the poet more truly revealed than in whatever the poet explicitly claims to believe. In his investigation of Wordsworth's "Ode: Intimations of Immortality," the critic Cleanth Brooks devotes his attention to the imagery of light and darkness, which he finds carries on and develops Wordsworth's thought.[1]

[1]"Wordsworth and the Paradox of the Imagination," in *The Well Wrought Urn* (New York: Harcourt, 1956).

Though Shakespeare's Theseus (in *A Midsummer Night's Dream*) accuses poets of being concerned with "airy nothings," poets are usually very much concerned with what is in front of them. This concern is of use to us. Perhaps, as Alan Watts has remarked, Americans are not the materialists they are sometimes accused of being. How could anyone taking a look at an American city think that its inhabitants deeply cherish material things? Involved in our personal hopes and apprehensions, anticipating the future so hard that much of the time we see the present through a film of thought across our eyes, perhaps we need a poet occasionally to remind us that even the coffee we absentmindedly sip comes in (as Yeats put it) a "heavy spillable cup."

T. S. Eliot   (1888–1965)*

THE WINTER EVENING SETTLES DOWN   1917

The winter evening settles down
With smell of steaks in passageways.
Six o'clock.
The burnt-out ends of smoky days.
And now a gusty shower wraps   5
The grimy scraps
Of withered leaves about your feet
And newspapers from vacant lots;
The showers beat
On broken blinds and chimney-pots,   10
And at the corner of the street
A lonely cab-horse steams and stamps.

And then the lighting of the lamps.

QUESTIONS

1. What mood is evoked by the images in Eliot's poem?
2. What kind of city neighborhood has the poet chosen to describe? How can you tell?

Theodore Roethke   (1908–1963)*

ROOT CELLAR   1948

Nothing would sleep in that cellar, dank as a ditch,
Bulbs broke out of boxes hunting for chinks in the dark,
Shoots dangled and drooped,
Lolling obscenely from mildewed crates,
Hung down long yellow evil necks, like tropical snakes.   5
And what a congress of stinks!—

Roots ripe as old bait,
Pulpy stems, rank, silo-rich,
Leaf-mold, manure, lime, piled against slippery planks.
Nothing would give up life: 10
Even the dirt kept breathing a small breath.

QUESTIONS

1. As a boy growing up in Saginaw, Michigan, Theodore Roethke spent much of his
   time in a large commercial greenhouse run by his family. What details in his poem
   show more than a passing acquaintance with growing things?
2. What varieties of image does "Root Cellar" contain? Point out examples.
3. What do you understand to be Roethke's attitude toward the root cellar? Does he
   view it as a disgusting chamber of horrors? Pay special attention to the last two lines.

Elizabeth Bishop   (1911–1979)*
THE FISH   1946

I caught a tremendous fish
and held him beside the boat
half out of water, with my hook
fast in a corner of his mouth.
He didn't fight.   5
He hadn't fought at all.
He hung a grunting weight,
battered and venerable
and homely. Here and there
his brown skin hung in strips   10
like ancient wall-paper,
and its pattern of darker brown
was like wall-paper:
shapes like full-blown roses
stained and lost through age.   15
He was speckled with barnacles,
fine rosettes of lime,
and infested
with tiny white sea-lice,
and underneath two or three   20
rags of green weed hung down.
While his gills were breathing in
the terrible oxygen
—the frightening gills,
fresh and crisp with blood,   25
that can cut so badly—
I thought of the coarse white flesh

packed in like feathers,
the big bones and the little bones,
the dramatic reds and blacks
of his shiny entrails,
and the pink swim-bladder
like a big peony.
I looked into his eyes
which were far larger than mine
but shallower, and yellowed,
the irises backed and packed
with tarnished tinfoil
seen through the lenses
of old scratched isinglass.
They shifted a little, but not
to return my stare.
—It was more like the tipping
of an object toward the light.
I admired his sullen face,
the mechanism of his jaw,
and then I saw
that from his lower lip
—if you could call it a lip—
grim, wet, and weapon-like,
hung five old pieces of fish-line,
or four and a wire leader
with the swivel still attached,
with all their five big hooks
grown firmly in his mouth.
A green line, frayed at the end
where he broke it, two heavier lines,
and a fine black thread
still crimped from the strain and snap
when it broke and he got away.
Like medals with their ribbons
frayed and wavering,
a five-haired beard of wisdom
trailing from his aching jaw.
I stared and stared
and victory filled up
the little rented boat,
from the pool of bilge
where oil had spread a rainbow
around the rusted engine
to the bailer rusted orange,
the sun-cracked thwarts,

30

35

40

45

50

55

60

65

70

the oarlocks on their strings,
the gunnels—until everything
was rainbow, rainbow, rainbow!   75
And I let the fish go.

1. How many abstract words does this poem contain? What proportion of the poem is imagery?
2. What is the speaker's attitude toward the fish? Comment in particular on lines 61–64.
3. What attitude do the images of the rainbow of oil (line 69), the orange bailer (bailing bucket, line 71), the *sun-cracked thwarts* (line 72) convey? Does the poet expect us to feel mournful because the boat is in such sorry condition?
4. What is meant by *rainbow, rainbow, rainbow?*
5. How do these images prepare us for the conclusion? Why does the speaker let the fish go?

Anne Stevenson (b. 1933)*

THE VICTORY   1974

I thought you were my victory
though you cut me like a knife
when I brought you out of my body
into your life.

Tiny antagonist, gory,   5
blue as a bruise. The stains
of your cloud of glory
bled from my veins.

How can you dare, blind thing,
blank insect eyes?
You barb the air. You sting   10
with bladed cries.

Snail! Scary knot of desires!
Hungry snarl! Small son.
Why do I have to love you?
How have you won?   15

QUESTIONS

1. Newborn babies are often described as "little angels" or "bundles of joy." How does the speaker of "The Victory" describe her son?
2. Why does the speaker describe the child as an "antagonist" (line 5)?
3. Why is the poem titled "The Victory"?
4. Why is the infant compared to a knife in both lines 2 and 12?

John Haines   (b. 1924)

WINTER NEWS   1966

They say the wells
are freezing
at Northway where
the cold begins.

Oil tins bang   5
as evening comes on,
and clouds of
steaming breath drift
in the street.

Men go out to feed   10
the stiffening dogs,

the voice of the snowman
calls the white-
haired children home.

QUESTIONS

1. Which of the images in this poem strike you as the most vivid? To which senses do
   Haines's images appeal?
2. Why are the children described as "white-haired"?

Emily Dickinson   (1830–1886)*

A ROUTE OF EVANESCENCE   (1879)

A Route of Evanescence
With a revolving Wheel –
A Resonance of Emerald –
A Rush of Cochineal° –   red dye
And every Blossom on the Bush   5
Adjusts its tumbled Head –
The mail from Tunis, probably,
An easy Morning's Ride –

A ROUTE OF EVANESCENCE.   1 *Evanescence*; ornithologist's term for the luminous sheen of certain
birds' feathers. 7 *Tunis*: capital city of Tunisia, North Africa.

QUESTION

What is the subject of this poem? How can you tell?

Jean Toomer   (1894–1967)

REAPERS   1923

Black reapers with the sound of steel on stones
Are sharpening scythes. I see them place the hones
In their hip-pockets as a thing that's done,
And start their silent swinging, one by one.
Black horses drive a mower through the weeds,   5
And there, a field rat, startled, squealing bleeds,
His belly close to ground. I see the blade,
Blood-stained, continue cutting weeds and shade.

QUESTIONS

1. Imagine the scene Jean Toomer describes. Which particulars most vividly strike the mind's eye?
2. What kind of image is *silent swinging?*
3. Read the poem aloud. Notice especially the effect of the words *sound of steel on stones* and *field rat, startled, squealing bleeds.* What interesting sounds are present in the very words that contain these images?
4. What feelings do you get from this poem as a whole? Would you agree with someone who said, "This poem gives us a sense of happy, carefree life down on the farm, close to nature"? Exactly what in "Reapers" makes you feel the way you do? Besides appealing to our auditory and visual imagination, what do the images contribute?

Gerard Manley Hopkins   (1844–1889)*

PIED BEAUTY   (1877)

Glory be to God for dappled things—
    For skies of couple-color as a brinded° cow;   streaked
        For rose-moles all in stipple upon trout that swim;
Fresh-firecoal chestnut-falls; finches' wings;
    Landscape plotted and pieced—fold, fallow, and plow;   5
        And áll trádes, their gear and tackle and trim°.   equipment

All things counter, original, spare, strange;
    Whatever is fickle, freckled (who know how?)
        With swift, slow; sweet, sour; adazzle, dim;
He fathers-forth whose beauty is past change: 10
            Praise him.

QUESTIONS

1. What does the word *pied* mean? (Hint: what does a Pied Piper look like?)
2. According to Hopkins, what do *skies, cow, trout, ripe chestnuts, finches' wings,* and *landscapes* all have in common? What landscapes can the poet have in mind? (Have you ever seen any *dappled* landscape while looking down from an airplane, or from a mountain or high hill?)
3. What do you make of line 6: what can carpenters' saws and ditch-diggers' spades possibly have in common with the dappled things in lines 2–4?

4. Does Hopkins refer only to contrasts that meet the eye? What other kinds of variation interest him?
5. Try to state in your own words the theme of this poem. How essential to our understanding of this theme are Hopkins's images?

ABOUT HAIKU
Arakida Moritake   (1473–1549)
THE FALLING FLOWER   (EARLY SIXTEENTH CENTURY)

The falling flower
I saw drift back to the branch
Was a butterfly.
> —*Translated by Babette Deutsch*

Haiku means "beginning-verse" in Japanese—perhaps because the form may have originated in a game. Players, given a haiku, were supposed to extend its three lines into a longer poem. Haiku (the word can also be plural) consist mainly of imagery, but as we saw in Buson's lines about the cold comb, their imagery is not always only pictorial; it can also involve any of the five senses. Haiku are so short that they depend upon imagery to trigger associations and responses in the reader. A haiku in Japanese is rimeless; its seventeen syllables are traditionally arranged in three lines, usually following a pattern of five, seven, and five syllables. English haiku frequently ignore such a pattern, being rimed or unrimed as the poet prefers. What English haiku do try to preserve is the powerful way Japanese haiku capture the intensity of a particular moment, usually by linking two concrete images. There is little room for abstract thoughts or general observations. The following attempt, though containing seventeen syllables, is far from haiku in spirit:

Now that our love is gone
I feel within my soul
a nagging distress.

Unlike the author of those lines, haiku poets look out upon a literal world, seldom looking inward to *discuss* their feelings. Japanese haiku tend to be seasonal in subject, but because they are so highly compressed, they usually just *imply* a season: a blossom indicates spring; a crow on a branch, autumn; snow, winter. Not just pretty little sketches of nature (as some Westerners think), haiku assume a view of the universe in which observer and nature are not separated.

Haiku emerged in sixteenth-century Japan and soon developed into a deeply esteemed form. Even today, Japanese soldiers, stockbrokers, scientists, schoolchildren, and even the emperor still find occasion to pen haiku. Soon after the form first captured the attention of Western poets at the end of the nineteenth century, it became immensely influential to modern poets like Ezra Pound, William Carlos Williams, and H. D., as a model for the kind of verse they wanted to write—concise, direct, and imagistic.

The Japanese consider the poems of the "Three Masters"—Basho, Buson, and Issa—to be the pinnacle of the classical haiku. Each poet had his own personality: Basho, the ascetic seeker of Zen enlightenment; Buson, the worldly artist; Issa, the sensitive master of wit and pathos. Here are free translations of poems from each of the "Three Masters."

Matsuo Basho (1644–1694)*

HEAT-LIGHTNING STREAK

Heat-lightning streak—
through darkness pierces
the heron's shriek.

IN THE OLD STONE POOL

In the old stone pool
a frogjump:
splishhhhh.

—*Translations by X. J. Kennedy*

Taniguchi Buson (1716–1783)*

ON THE ONE-TON TEMPLE BELL

On the one-ton temple bell
a moonmoth, folded into sleep,
sits still.

—*Translated by X. J. Kennedy*

I GO

I go,
you stay;
two autumns.

—*Translated by Robert Hass*

Kobayashi Issa (1763–1827)*

ONLY ONE GUY

only one guy and
only one fly trying to
make the guest room do.

—*Translated by Cid Corman*

CRICKET

Cricket, be
careful! I'm rolling
over!

—*Translated by Robert Bly*

If you care to try your hand at haiku-writing, here are a few suggestions: Make every word matter. Include few adjectives, shun needless conjunctions. Set your poem in the present. ("Haiku," said Basho, "is simply what is happening in this place at this moment.") Confine your poem to what can be seen, heard, smelled, tasted, or touched. Mere sensory reports, however, will be meaningless unless they make the reader feel something—as a contemporary American writer points out in this spoof.

Richard Brautigan (1935–1985)

HAIKU AMBULANCE 1968

A piece of green pepper fell
off the wooden salad bowl:
so what?

Here are eight more recent haiku written in English. (Don't expect them all to observe a strict arrangement of seventeen syllables, however.) Haiku, in any language, is an art of few words, many suggestions. A haiku starts us thinking and telling. "So the reader," Raymond Roseliep wrote, "keeps getting on where the poet got off."

After weeks of watching the roof leak
    I fixed it tonight
by moving a single board
    —Gary Snyder

Lying in the field
by night making new
    constellations from old stars
    —Michael B. Stillman

broken bowl
the pieces
still rocking
    —Penny Harter

Born Again
she speaks excitedly
of death
    —Jennifer Brutschy

The green cockleburs
Caught in the thick woolly hair
Of the black boy's head.
    —Richard Wright

Let my snow-tracks lead
on, on. Let them, where they stop
stop. There, in mid-field.
    —Hayden Carruth

THE LAZY MAN'S HAIKU

out in the night
a wheelbarrowful
of moonlight.
    —John Ridland

Making jazz swing in
Seventeen syllables AIN'T
No square poet's job.
    —Etheridge Knight

FOR REVIEW AND FURTHER STUDY

John Keats   (1795–1821)*

BRIGHT STAR! WOULD I WERE STEADFAST AS THOU ART   (1819)

Bright star! would I were steadfast as thou art—
    Not in lone splendor hung aloft the night,
And watching, with eternal lids apart,
    Like nature's patient, sleepless Eremite°   *hermit*
The moving waters at their priest-like task   5
    Of pure ablution round earth's human shores,
Or gazing on the new soft-fallen mask
    Of snow upon the mountains and the moors—
No—yet still steadfast, still unchangeable,
    Pillowed upon my fair love's ripening breast,   10
To feel for ever its soft fall and swell,
    Awake for ever in a sweet unrest,
Still, still to hear her tender-taken breath,
And so live ever—or else swoon to death.

1. Stars are conventional symbols for love and a loved one. (Love, Shakespeare tells us in a sonnet, "is the star to every wandering bark.") In this sonnet, why is it not possible for the star to have this meaning? How does Keats use it?
2. What seems concrete and particular in the speaker's observations?
3. Suppose Keats had said *slow and easy* instead of *tender-taken* in line 13. What would have been lost?

EXPERIMENT: *Writing with Images*

Taking the following poems as examples from which to start rather than as models to be slavishly copied, try to compose a brief poem that consists largely of imagery.

Walt Whitman   (1819–1892)*
THE RUNNER   1867

On a flat road runs the well-train'd runner;
He is lean and sinewy, with muscular legs;
He is thinly clothed—he leans forward as he runs,
With lightly closed fists, and arms partially rais'd.

T. E. Hulme   (1883–1917)
IMAGE   (ABOUT 1910)

Old houses were scaffolding once
                and workmen whistling.

William Carlos Williams   (1883–1963)*
THE GREAT FIGURE   1921

Among the rain
and lights
I saw the figure 5
in gold
on a red   5
firetruck
moving
tense
unheeded
to gong clangs   10
siren howls
and wheels rumbling
through the dark city.

Robert Bly   (b. 1926)*
DRIVING TO TOWN LATE TO MAIL A LETTER   1962

It is a cold and snowy night. The main street is deserted.
The only things moving are swirls of snow.
As I lift the mailbox door, I feel its cold iron.
There is a privacy I love in this snowy night.
Driving around, I will waste more time.   5

Gary Snyder   (b. 1930)
MID-AUGUST AT SOURDOUGH   1959
MOUNTAIN LOOKOUT

Down valley a smoke haze
Three days heat, after five days rain
Pitch glows on the fir-cones
Across rocks and meadows
Swarms of new flies.   5

I cannot remember things I once read
A few friends, but they are in cities.
Drinking cold snow-water from a tin cup
Looking down for miles
Through high still air.   10

MID-AUGUST AT SOURDOUGH MOUNTAIN LOOKOUT. *Sourdough Mountain:* in the state of Washington, where the poet's job at the time was to watch for forest fires.

H. D. [Hilda Doolittle]   (1886–1961)*
HEAT   1916

O wind, rend open the heat,
cut apart the heat,
rend it to tatters.

Fruit cannot drop
through this thick air—   5
fruit cannot fall into heat
that presses up and blunts
the points of pears
and rounds the grapes.

Cut the heat—   10
plough through it,
turning it on either side
of your path.

Louise Glück (b. 1943)*

MOCK ORANGE 1985

It is not the moon, I tell you.
It is these flowers
lighting the yard.

I hate them.
I hate them as I hate sex, 5
the man's mouth
sealing my mouth, the man's
paralyzing body—

and the cry that always escapes,
the low, humiliating 10
premise of union—

In my mind tonight
I hear the question and pursuing answer
fused in one sound
that mounts and mounts and then 15
is split into the old selves,
the tired antagonisms. Do you see?
We were made fools of.
And the scent of mock orange
drifts through the window. 20

How can I rest?
How can I be content
when there is still
that odor in the world?

MOCK ORANGE. The mock orange is a flowering shrub with especially fragrant white blossoms and fruit that resemble those of an orange tree.

Billy Collins (b. 1941)

EMBRACE 1988

You know the parlor trick.
Wrap your arms around your own body
and from the back it looks like
someone is embracing you,
her hands grasping your shirt, 5
her fingernails teasing your neck.

From the front it is another story.
You never looked so alone,
your crossed elbows and screwy grin.
You could be waiting for a tailor   10
to fit you for a straitjacket,
one that would hold you really tight.

Emily Grosholz   (b. 1950)

LETTER FROM GERMANY   1984

Though it is only February, turned
less than a week ago,
and though the latitude is upward here
of Newfoundland's north shore,
Mother, spring is out. It's almost hot,   5
simmering above and underground,
and in my veins! where your blood also runs.
The hazels dangle down
green flowery catkins, and the alders too,
those bushy, water-loving trees,   10
have a like ornament, in purple-red.
Spring is so forward here.
Snowbells swing in garden beds;
the pussy willows that you liked to bring
inside, to force their silver fur,   15
are open in the air;
witch hazel in the formal park,
still leafless, wears a ribbon-petaled bloom
of yellow and pale orange.
Once or twice I've walked through clouds   20
of insects by the river to the east
of town; the ducks are back on the canal
now that the ice is gone, loud and in love.
I wish that I could bring you here
to see this fast, unseasonable spring;   25
I wish that I could write a letter home.
But since a year you are not anywhere,
not even underground,
so that the words I might have written down
I say aloud into the atmosphere   30
of pollen and fresh clouds.
I say the litany of my desires,
and wonder, knowing better, if you hear
through some light-rooted organ of the air.

Stevie Smith (1902–1971)*

NOT WAVING BUT DROWNING   1959

Nobody heard him, the dead man,
But still he lay moaning:
I was much further out than you thought
And not waving but drowning.

Poor chap, he always loved larking   5
And now he's dead
It must have been too cold for him his heart gave way,
They said.

Oh, no no no, it was too cold always
(Still the dead one lay moaning)   10
I was much too far out all my life
And not waving but drowning.

WRITER'S PERSPECTIVE

Ezra Pound

Ezra Pound on Writing   THE IMAGE   1913

An "Image" is that which presents an intellectual and emotional complex in an instant of time. I use the term "complex" rather in the technical sense employed by the newer psychologists, such as Hart, though we might not agree absolutely in our application.

It is the presentation of such a "complex" instantaneously which gives that sense of sudden liberation; that sense of freedom from time limits and space limits; that sense of sudden growth, which we experience in the presence of the greatest works of art.

It is better to present one Image in a lifetime than to produce voluminous works.

All this, however, some may consider open to debate. The immediate necessity is to tabulate A LIST OF DON'TS for those beginning to write verses. I can not put all of them into Mosaic negative.

Use no superfluous word, no adjective which does not reveal something.

Don't use such an expression as "dim lands *of peace.*" It dulls the image. It mixes an abstraction with the concrete. It comes from the writer's not realizing that the natural object is always the *adequate* symbol.

Go in fear of abstractions. Do not retell in mediocre verse what has already been done in good prose. Don't think any intelligent person is gong to be deceived when you try to shirk all the difficulties of the unspeakably difficult art of good prose by chopping your composition into line lengths.

"A Few Don'ts"

WRITING CRITICALLY

Analyzing Images

To help you analyze how the imagery of a poem works, here is a simple exercise: Make a short list of the poem's key images. Be sure to write down the images in the order they appear in the poem, because the sequence of images is often as important as the images themselves. (For example, a poem whose images move from *sunlight* to *darkness* might well signify something different from one that begins with *darkness* and concludes with *sunlight.*) Remember that not all images are visual. Images can draw on any or all of the five senses. In jotting down images, don't omit key adjectives or other qualifying words. Those words are often your best clues to a poem's tone or perspective. (T. E. Hulme's image of "whistling" workmen on page 752, for instance, implies something happier than "sweating" workmen would.)

Let's try this method on a short poem. An initial list of images in Robert Bly's "Driving to Town Late to Mail a Letter" (page 753) might look something like this:

cold and snowy night
deserted main street
mailbox door—cold iron
snowy night (speaker *loves* its privacy)
speaker drives around (to waste time)

Did we forget anything? Yes, the title! Always look to a poem's title for guidance. Bly's title, for instance, contains several crucial images. Let's add them to the top of the list:

driving (to town)
late night
a letter (to be mailed)

Looking at our list, we see how the images provide an outline of the poem's story. We also see how Bly begins the poem without allowing us initially to understand how his speaker views the situation. Is driving to town late on a snowy evening a positive, negative, or neutral experience? By noting where (in line 4) the speaker reveals a subjective response to an image ("There is a privacy I love in this snowy night"), we also begin to grasp the overall emotional structure of the poem. We might also note on our list how the poem begins and ends with the same image (driving), but uses it for different effects at the two places. At the beginning the speaker is driving for the practical purpose of mailing a letter but at the end merely for the pure pleasure of it.

After adding a few notes on our list to capture these insights, we are ready to begin writing our paper. Without realizing it, we have already worked out a rough outline of our paper—all on a single sheet of paper or a few inches of computer screen.

Writing Assignment

Examining any poem in this chapter (or in "Poems for Further Reading" on pages 1027–1164), demonstrate how its imagery helps communicate its general theme. Be specific in noting how each key image contributes to the poem's total effect. Feel free to consult criticism on the poem but make sure to credit any observation you borrow exactly from a critical source. (See Chapter Forty-one, "Writing About a Poem," for advice on both writing process and format guidelines.) Here is an essay written in response to this assignment by Becki Woods, a student of Mark Bernier, at Blinn College in Brenham, Texas.

Elizabeth Bishop's Use of Imagery in "The Fish"

Upon first reading, Elizabeth Bishop's "The Fish" appears to be a simple fishing tale. A close investigation of the imagery in Bishop's highly detailed description, however, reveals a different sort of poem. The real theme of Bishop's poem is a compassion and respect for the fish's lifelong struggle to survive. By carefully and effectively describing the captured fish, his reaction to being caught, and the symbols of his past struggles to stay alive, Bishop creates, through her images of beauty, victory, and survival, something more than a simple tale.

The first four lines of the poem are quite ordinary and factual:

I caught a tremendous fish
and held him beside the boat

half out of water, with my hook

fast in a corner of his mouth.   (1-4)

Except for <u>tremendous</u>, Bishop's persona uses no
exaggerations--unlike most fishing stories--to set up
the situation of catching the fish. The detailed
description begins as the speaker recounts the event
further, noticing something signally important about the
captive fish: "He didn't fight" (5). At this point the
poem begins to seem unusual: most fish stories are about
how ferociously the prey resists being captured. The
speaker also notes that the "battered and venerable /
and homely" fish offered no resistance to being caught
(8-9). The image of the submissive attitude of the fish
is essential to the theme of the poem. It is his "utter
passivity [that] makes [the persona's] detailed scrutiny
possible" (McNally 192).

Once the image of the passive fish has been
established, the speaker begins an examination of the
fish itself, nothing that "Here and there / his brown
skin hung in strips / like ancient wall-paper" (9-11).
By comparing the fish's skin to wallpaper, the persona
creates, as Sybil Estess argues, "implicit suggestions
of both artistry and decay" (713). Images of peeling
wallpaper are instantly brought to mind. The comparison
of the fish's skin and wallpaper, though "helpful in
conveying an accurate notion of the fish's color to
anyone with memories of Victorian parlors and their
yellowed wallpaper . . . is," according to Nancy McNally,
"even more useful in evoking the associations of
deterioration which usually surround such memories" (192).

The fish's faded beauty has been hinted at in the comparison, thereby setting up the detailed imagery that soon follows:

> He was speckled with barnacles,
>
> fine rosettes of lime,
>
> and infested
>
> with tiny white sea-lice,
>
> and underneath two or three
>
> rags of green weed hung down.   (16-20)

The persona sees the fish as he is; the infestations and faults are not left out of the description. Yet, at the same time, the fisher "express[es] what [he] has sensed of the character of the fish" (Estess 714).

Bishop's persona notices "shapes like full-blown roses / stained and lost through age" on the fish's skin (14-15). The persona's perception of the fish's beauty is revealed along with a recognition of its faded beauty, which is best revealed in the description of the fish's being speckled with barnacles and spotted with lime. However, the fisher observes these spots and sees them as rosettes—as objects of beauty, not just ugly brown spots. These images contribute to the persona's recognition of beauty's having become faded beauty.

The poem next turns to a description of the fish's gills. The imagery in "While his gills were breathing in / the terrible oxygen" (22-23) leads "to the very structure of the creature" that is now dying (Hopkins 201). The descriptions of the fish's interior beauty— "the coarse white flesh / packed in like feathers," the colors "of his shiny entrails," and his "pink swim-bladder / like a big peony"--are reminders of the life that seems about to end (27-28, 31-33).

The composite image of the fish's essential beauty--his being alive--is developed further in the description of the five fish hooks that the captive, living fish carries in his lip:

> grim, wet, and weapon-like
>
> hung five old pieces of fish-line
>
> . . . .
>
> with all their five big hooks
>
> grown firmly in his mouth.   (50-51, 54-55)

As if fascinated by them, the persona, observing how the lines must have been broken during struggles to escape, sees the hooks as "medals with their ribbons / frayed and wavering, / a five-haired beard of wisdom / trailing from his aching jaw" (61-64), and the fisher becomes enthralled by re-created images of the fish's fighting desperately for his life on at least five separate occasions--and winning. Crale Hopkins suggests that "[i]n its capability not only for mere existence, but for action, escaping from previous anglers, the fish shares the speaker's humanity" (202), thus revealing the fisher's deepening understanding of how he must now act. The persona has "all along," notes Estess, "describe[d] the fish not just with great detail but with an imaginative empathy for the aquatic creature. In her more-than-objective description, [the fisher] relates what [he] has seen to be both the pride and poverty of the fish" (715). It is at this point that the narrator of this fishing tale has a moment of clarity. Realizing the fish's history and the glory the fish has achieved in escaping previous hookings, the speaker sees everything become, "rainbow, rainbow, rainbow!" (74)-- and then unexpectedly lets the fish go.

Bishop's "The Fish" begins by describing an event that might easily be a conventional story's climax: "I caught a tremendous fish" (1). The poem, however, develops into a highly detailed account of a fisher noticing both the age and the faded beauty of the captive and his present beauty and past glory as well. The fishing tale is not simply a recounting of a capture; it is a gradually unfolding epiphany in which the speaker sees the fish in an entirely new light. The intensity of this encounter between an apparently experienced fisher in a rented boat and battle-hardened fish is delivered through the poet's skillful use of imagery. It is through the description of the capture of an aged fish that Bishop offers her audience her theme of compassion derived from a respect for the struggle for survival.

Works Cited

Bishop, Elizabeth. "The Fish." Literature: An Introduction
    to Fiction, Poetry, and Drama. Ed. X.J. Kennedy and
    Dana Gioia. 7th ed. New York: Longman, 1999. 744-46.
Estess, Sybil P. "Elizabeth Bishop: The Delicate Art of
    Map Making." Southern Review 13 (1977): 713-17.
Hopkins, Crale D. "Inspiration as Theme: Art and Nature
    in the Poetry of Elizabeth Bishop." Arizona
    Quarterly 32 (1976): 200-02.

McNally, Nancy L. "Elizabeth Bishop: The Discipline of
   Description." <u>Twentieth-Century Literature</u> 11
   (1966): 192-94.

FURTHER SUGGESTIONS FOR WRITING

1. Choose, from "Poems for Further Reading" that begins on page 1027, a poem that appeals to you. Then write a brief account of your experience in reading it, paying special notice to its imagery. What images strike you, and why? What do they contribute to the poem as a whole? Poems rich in imagery include Samuel Taylor Coleridge's "Kubla Khan," Robert Frost's "Birches," Charlotte Mew's "The Farmer's Bride," William Carlos Williams's "Spring and All (By the road to the contagious hospital)" and many more.

2. After you have read the haiku and the discussion of haiku-writing in this chapter, write three or four haiku of your own. Then write a brief prose account of your experience in writing them. What, if anything, did you find out?

17 Figures of Speech

WHY SPEAK FIGURATIVELY?

"I will speak daggers to her, but use none," says Hamlet, preparing to confront his mother. His statement makes sense only because we realize that *daggers* is to be taken two ways: literally (denoting sharp, pointed weapons) and nonliterally (referring to something that can be used *like* weapons—namely, words). Reading poetry, we often meet comparisons between two things whose similarity we have never noticed before. When Marianne Moore observes that a fir tree has "an emerald turkey-foot at the top," the result is a pleasure that poetry richly affords: the sudden recognition of likenesses.

A treetop like a turkey-foot, words like daggers—such comparisons are called **figures of speech.** In its broadest definition, a figure of speech may be said to occur whenever a speaker or writer, for the sake of freshness or emphasis, departs from the usual denotations of words. Certainly, when Hamlet says he will speak daggers, no one expects him to release pointed weapons from his lips, for *daggers* is not to be read solely for its denotation. Its connotations—sharp, stabbing, piercing, wounding—also come to mind, and we see ways in which words and daggers work alike. (Words too can hurt: by striking through pretenses, possibly, or by wounding their hearer's self-esteem.) In the statement "A razor is sharper than an ax," there is no departure from the usual denotations of *razor* and *ax,* and no figure of speech results. Both objects are of the same class; the comparison is not offensive to logic. But in "How sharper than a serpent's tooth it is to have a thankless child," the objects—snake's tooth (fang) and ungrateful offspring—are so unlike that no reasonable comparison may be made between them. To find similarity, we attend to the connotations of *serpent's tooth*—biting, piercing, venom, pain—rather than to its denotations. If we are aware of the connotations of *red rose* (beauty, softness, freshness, and so forth), then the line "My love is like a red, red rose" need not call to mind a woman with a scarlet face and a thorny neck.

Figures of speech are not devices to state what is demonstrably untrue. Indeed they often state truths that more literal language cannot communicate; they call attention to such truths; they lend them emphasis.

Alfred, Lord Tennyson   (1809–1892)*

THE EAGLE   1851

He clasps the crag with crooked hands;
Close to the sun in lonely lands,
Ringed with the azure world, he stands.

The wrinkled sea beneath him crawls;
He watches from his mountain walls,   5
And like a thunderbolt he falls.

This brief poem is rich in figurative language. In the first line, the phrase *crooked hands* may surprise us. An eagle does not have hands, we might protest; but the objection would be a quibble, for evidently Tennyson is indicating exactly how an eagle clasps a crag, in the way that human fingers clasp a thing. By implication, too, the eagle is a person. *Close to the sun*, if taken literally, is an absurd exaggeration, the sun being a mean distance of 93,000,000 miles from the earth. For the eagle to be closer to it by the altitude of a mountain is an approach so small as to be insignificant. But figuratively, Tennyson conveys that the eagle stands above the clouds, perhaps silhouetted against the sun, and for the moment belongs to the heavens rather than to the land and sea. The word *ringed* makes a circle of the whole world's horizons and suggests that we see the world from the eagle's height; the *wrinkled sea* becomes an aged, sluggish animal; *mountain walls*, possibly literal, also suggests a fort or castle; and finally the eagle itself is likened to a thunderbolt in speed and in power, perhaps also in that its beak is—like our abstract conception of a lightning bolt—pointed. How much of the poem can be taken literally? Only *he clasps the crag, he stands, he watches, he falls*. The rest is made of figures of speech. The result is that, reading Tennyson's poem, we gain a bird's-eye view of sun, sea, and land—and even of bird. Like imagery, figurative language refers us to the physical world.

William Shakespeare   (1564–1616)*

SHALL I COMPARE THEE TO A   1609
SUMMER'S DAY?

Shall I compare thee to a summer's day?
Thou art more lovely and more temperate.
Rough winds do shake the darling buds of May,
And summer's lease hath all too short a date.
Sometime too hot the eye of heaven shines,   5

And often is his gold complexion dimmed;
And every fair° from fair sometimes declines,   *fair one*
By chance, or nature's changing course, untrimmed.
But thy eternal summer shall not fade,
Nor lose possession of that fair thou ow'st°;   *ownest, have*   10
Nor shall death brag thou wand'rest in his shade,
When in eternal lines to time thou grow'st.
   So long as men can breathe or eyes can see,
   So long lives this, and this gives life to thee.

Howard Moss (1922–1987)

SHALL I COMPARE THEE TO A SUMMER'S DAY?   1976

Who says you're like one of the dog days?
You're nicer. And better.
Even in May, the weather can be gray,
And a summer sub-let doesn't last forever.
Sometimes the sun's too hot;   5
Sometimes it is not.
Who can stay young forever?
People break their necks or just drop dead!
But you? Never!
If there's just one condensed reader left   10
Who can figure out the abridged alphabet,
   After you're dead and gone,
   In this poem you'll live on!

SHALL I COMPARE THEE TO A SUMMER'S DAY? (MOSS). *Dog days:* the hottest days of summer. The ancient Romans believed that the Dog-star, Sirius, added heat to summer months.

QUESTIONS

1. In Howard Moss's streamlined version of Shakespeare, from a series called "Modified Sonnets (Dedicated to adapters, abridgers, digesters, and condensers everywhere)," to what extent does the poet use figurative language? In Shakespeare's original sonnet, how high a proportion of Shakespeare's language is figurative?
2. Compare some of Moss's lines to the corresponding lines in Shakespeare's sonnet. Why is *Even in May, the weather can be gray* less interesting than the original? In the lines on the sun (5–6 in both versions), what has Moss's modification deliberately left out? Why is Shakespeare's seeing death as a braggart memorable? Why aren't you greatly impressed by Moss's last two lines?
3. Can you explain Shakespeare's play on the word *untrimmed* (line 8)? Evidently the word can mean "divested of trimmings," but what other suggestions do you find in it?
4. How would you answer someone who argued, "Maybe Moss's language isn't as good as Shakespeare's, but the meaning is still there. What's wrong with putting Shakespeare into up-to-date words that can be understood by everybody?"

Jon Stallworthy   (b. 1935)

Sindhi Woman   1963

Barefoot through the bazaar,
and with the same undulant grace
as the cloth blown back from her face,
she glides with a stone jar
high on her head   5
and not a ripple in her tread.

Watching her cross erect
stones, garbage, excrement, and crumbs
of glass in the Karachi slums,
I, with my stoop, reflect   10
they stand most straight
who learn to walk beneath a weight.

Sindhi Woman. The Sindhi are the predominantly Moslem people of Sind, a former province of India now in Pakistan. 9 *Karachi*: located on the Arabian Sea, from 1948 to 1959 the capital of Pakistan.

Question

Where in the poem does the most striking figurative language occur? What other figurative language does the poet use?

METAPHOR AND SIMILE

Life, like a dome of many-colored glass,
Stains the white radiance of Eternity.

The first of these lines (from Shelley's "Adonais") is a **simile:** a comparison of two things, indicated by some connective, usually *like, as, than,* or a verb such as *resembles.* A simile expresses a similarity. Still, for a simile to exist, the things compared have to be dissimilar in kind. It is no simile to say, "Your fingers are like mine," it is a literal observation. But to say, "Your fingers are like sausages" is to use a simile. Omit the connective—say, "Your fingers are sausages"—and the result is a **metaphor,** a statement that one thing *is* something else, which, in a literal sense, it is not. In the second of Shelley's lines, it is *assumed* that Eternity is light or radiance, and we have an **implied metaphor,** one that uses neither a connective nor the verb *to be.* Here are examples:

Oh, my love is like a red, red rose.	*Simile*
Oh, my love resembles a red, red rose.	*Simile*
Oh, my love is redder than a rose.	*Simile*
Oh, my love is a red, red rose.	*Metaphor*
Oh, my love has red petals and sharp thorns.	*Implied metaphor*
Oh, I placed my love into a long-stem vase	
And I bandaged my bleeding thumb.	*Implied metaphor*

Often you can tell a metaphor from a simile by much more than just the presence or absence of a connective. In general, a simile refers to only one characteristic that two things have in common, while a metaphor is not plainly limited in the number of resemblances it may indicate. To use the simile "He eats like a pig" is to compare man and animal in one respect: eating habits. But to say "He's a pig" is to use a metaphor that might involve comparisons of appearance and morality as well.

For scientists as well as poets, the making of metaphors is customary. In 1933 George Lemaitre, the Belgian priest and physicist credited with the Big Bang theory of the origin of the universe, conceived of a primal atom that existed before anything else, which expanded and produced everything. And so, he remarked, making a wonderful metaphor, the evolution of the cosmos as it is today "can be compared to a display of fireworks that has just ended." As astrophysicist and poet Alan Lightman has noted, we can't help envisioning scientific discoveries in terms of things we know from daily life—spinning balls, waves in water, pendulums, weights on springs. "We have no other choice," Lightman reasons. "We cannot avoid forming mental pictures when we try to grasp the meaning of our equations, and how can we picture what we have not seen?"[1] In science as well as in poetry, it would seem, metaphors are necessary instruments of understanding.

In everyday speech, simile and metaphor occur frequently. We use metaphors ("She's a doll") and similes ("The tickets are selling like hot-cakes") without being fully conscious of them. If, however, we are aware that words possess literal meanings as well as figurative ones, we do not write *died in the wool* for *dyed in the wool* or *tow the line* for *toe the line*, nor do we use **mixed metaphors** as did the writer who advised, "Water the spark of knowledge and it will bear fruit," or the speaker who urged, "To get ahead, keep your nose to the grindstone, your shoulder to the wheel, your ear to the ground, and your eye on the ball." Perhaps the unintended humor of these statements comes from our seeing that the writer, busy stringing together stale metaphors, was not aware that they had any physical reference.

Unlike a writer who thoughtlessly mixes metaphors, a good poet can join together incongruous things and still keep the reader's respect. In his ballad "Thirty Bob a Week," John Davidson has a British workingman tell how it feels to try to support a large family on small wages:

It's a naked child against a hungry wolf;
　It's playing bowls upon a splitting wreck;
It's walking on a string across a gulf
　With millstones fore-and-aft about your neck;
But the thing is daily done by many and many a one;
　And we fall, face forward, fighting, on the deck.

---

[1]"Physicists' Use of Metaphor," *The American Scholar* (Winter 1989): 99.

Like the man with his nose to the grindstone, Davidson's wage-earner is in an absurd fix; but his balancing act seems far from merely nonsensical. For every one of the poet's comparisons—of workingman to child, to bowler, to tight-rope walker, and to seaman—offers suggestions of a similar kind. All help us see (and imagine) the workingman's hard life: a brave and unyielding struggle against impossible odds.

A poem may make a series of comparisons, like Davidson's, or the whole poem may be one extended comparison:

Emily Dickinson (1830–1886)*

MY LIFE HAD STOOD – A LOADED GUN   (ABOUT 1863)

My Life had stood – a Loaded Gun –
In Corners – till a Day
The Owner passed – identified –
And carried Me away –

And now We roam in Sovreign Woods –   5
And now We hunt the Doe –
And every time I speak for Him –
The Mountains straight reply –

And do I smile, such cordial light
Upon the Valley glow –   10
It is as a Vesuvian face
Had let its pleasure through –

And when at Night – Our good Day done –
I guard My Master's Head –
'Tis better than the Eider-Duck's   15
Deep Pillow – to have shared –

To foe of His – I'm deadly foe –
None stir the second time –
On whom I lay a Yellow Eye –
Or an emphatic Thumb –   20

Though I than He – may longer live
He longer must – than I –
For I have but the power to kill,
Without – the power to die –

How much life metaphors bring to poetry may be seen by comparing two poems by Tennyson and Blake.

Alfred, Lord Tennyson   (1809–1892)*
FLOWER IN THE CRANNIED WALL   1869

Flower in the crannied wall,
I pluck you out of the crannies,
I hold you here, root and all, in my hand,
Little flower—but *if* I could understand
What you are, root and all, and all in all,   5
I should know what God and man is.

How many metaphors does this poem contain? None. Compare it with a briefer poem on a similar theme: the quatrain that begins Blake's "Auguries of Innocence." (We follow here the opinion of W. B. Yeats, who, in editing Blake's poems, thought the lines ought to be printed separately.)

William Blake   (1757–1827)*
TO SEE A WORLD IN A GRAIN   (ABOUT 1803)
OF SAND

To see a world in a grain of sand
And a heaven in a wild flower,
Hold infinity in the palm of your hand
And eternity in an hour.

Set beside Blake's poem, Tennyson's—short though it is—seems lengthy. What contributes to the richness of "To see a world in a grain of sand" is Blake's use of a metaphor in every line. And every metaphor is loaded with suggestion. Our world does indeed resemble a grain of sand: in being round, in being stony, in being one of a myriad (the suggestions go on and on). Like Blake's grain of sand, a metaphor holds much, within a small circumference.

Sylvia Plath   (1932–1963)*
METAPHORS   1960

I'm a riddle in nine syllables,
An elephant, a ponderous house,
A melon strolling on two tendrils.
O red fruit, ivory, fine timbers!
This loaf's big with its yeasty rising.   5
Money's new-minted in this fat purse.
I'm a means, a stage, a cow in calf.
I've eaten a bag of green apples,
Boarded the train there's no getting off.

1. To what central fact do all the metaphors in this poem refer?
2. In the first line, what has the speaker in common with a riddle? Why does she say she has *nine* syllables?

N. Scott Momaday   (b. 1934)

SIMILE   1974

What did we say to each other
that now we are as the deer
who walk in single file
with heads high
with ears forward   5
with eyes watchful
with hooves always placed on firm ground
in whose limbs there is latent flight

QUESTIONS

1. Momaday never tells us what was said. Does this omission keep us from understanding the comparison?
2. The comparison is extended with each detail adding some new twist. Explain the
   implications of the last line.

EXPERIMENT: *Likening*

Write a poem that follows the method of N. Scott Momaday's "Simile," consisting of one
long comparison between two objects. Possible subjects might include: Talking to a loved
one long distance. What you feel like going to a weekend job. Being on a diet. Not being
noticed by someone you love. Winning a lottery.

Ruth Whitman   (b. 1922)

CASTOFF SKIN   1973

She lay in her girlish sleep at ninety-six,
small as a twig.
Pretty good figure

for an old lady, she said to me once.
Then she crawled away, leaving   5
a tiny stretched transparence

behind her. When I kissed her paper cheek
I thought of the snake,
of his quick motion.

1. Explain the central metaphor in "Castoff Skin."
2. What other figures of speech does the poem contain?

Emily Dickinson (1830–1886)*

IT DROPPED SO LOW –   (ABOUT 1863)
IN MY REGARD

It dropped so low – in my Regard –
I heard it hit the Ground –
And go to pieces on the Stones
At bottom of my Mind –

Yet blamed the Fate that flung it – *less*   5
Than I denounced Myself,
For entertaining Plated Wares
Upon My Silver Shelf –

QUESTIONS

1. What is *it?* What two things are compared?
2. How much of the poem develops and amplifies this comparison?

Craig Raine (b. 1944)

A MARTIAN SENDS A POSTCARD HOME   1979

Caxtons are mechanical birds with many wings
and some are treasured for their markings—

they cause the eyes to melt
or the body to shriek without pain.

I have never seen one fly, but   5
sometimes they perch on the hand.

Mist is when the sky is tired of flight
and rests its soft machine on ground:

then the world is dim and bookish
like engravings under tissue paper.   10

Rain is when the earth is television.
It has the property of making colours darker.

Model T is a room with the lock inside—
a key is turned to free the world

for movement, so quick there is a film
to watch for anything missed.

But time is tied to the wrist
or kept in a box, ticking with impatience.

In homes, a haunted apparatus sleeps,
that snores when you pick it up.

If the ghost cries, they carry it
to their lips and soothe it to sleep

with sounds. And yet, they wake it up
deliberately, by tickling with a finger.

Only the young are allowed to suffer
openly. Adults go to a punishment room

with water but nothing to eat.
They lock the door and suffer the noises

alone. No one is exempt
and everyone's pain has a different smell.

At night, when all the colours die,
they hide in pairs

and read about themselves—
in colour, with their eyelids shut.

A MARTIAN SENDS A POSTCARD HOME. The title of this poem literally describes the contents. A Martian briefly describes everyday objects and activities on earth, but the visitor sees them all from an alien perspective. The Martian/author lacks a complete vocabulary and sometimes describes general categories of things with a proper noun (as in Model T in line 13). 1 *Caxtons:* Books since William Caxton (c. 1422–1491) was the first person to print books in England.

QUESTION

Can you recognize *everything* the Martian describes and translate it back into Earth-based English?

EXERCISE: *What Is Similar?*

Each of these quotations contains a simile or a metaphor. In each of these figures of speech, what two things is the poet comparing? Try to state exactly what you understand the two things to have in common: the most striking similarity or similarities that the poet sees.

1.   All the world's a stage,
And all the men and women merely players:
They have their exits and their entrances,
And one man in his time plays many parts,
His acts being seven ages.
            —William Shakespeare, *As You Like It*

2. When the hounds of spring are on winter's traces . . .
   —Algernon Charles Swinburne, "Atalanta in Calydon"

3. . . . the sun gnaws the night's bone
   down through the meat and gristle.
   —John Ridland, "Elegy for My Aunt"

4. Art is long, and Time is fleeting,
   And our hearts, though strong and brave,
   Still, like muffled drums are beating
   Funeral marches to the grave.
   —Longfellow, "A Psalm of Life"

5. "Hope" is the thing with feathers –
   That perches in the soul –
   And sings the tune without the words –
   And never stops – at all –
   —Emily Dickinson, an untitled poem

6. Why should I let the toad *work*
      Squat on my life?
   Can't I use my wit as a pitchfork
      And drive the brute off?
   —Philip Larkin, "Toads"

7. I wear my patience like a light-green dress
   and wear it thin.
   —Emily Grosholz, "Remembering the Ardèche"

8. The drive through town was freeze framed in his mind.
   —Robert McDowell, "The Neighborhood"

9. A new electric fence,
   Its five barbed wires tight
   As a steel-stringed banjo.
   —Van K. Brock, "Driving at Dawn"

10. Spring stirs Gossamer Beynon Schoolmistress like a spoon.
    —Dylan Thomas, *Under Milk Wood*

11. Our headlight caught, as in a flashbulb's flare,
    A pair of hitchhikers.
    —Paul Lake, "Two Hitchhikers"

12. My life seems like those country western songs:
    Some man in black keeps walkin' out the door . . .
    —Dessa Crawford, "With Our Boots On"

OTHER FIGURES

When Shakespeare asks, in a sonnet,

> O! how shall summer's honey breath hold out
> Against the wrackful siege of batt'ring days,

it might seem at first that he mixes metaphors. How can a *breath* confront the battering ram of an invading army? But it is summer's breath and, by giving it to summer, Shakespeare makes the season a man or woman. It is as if the fragrance of summer were the breath within a person's body, and winter were the onslaught of old age.

Such is one instance of **personification:** a figure of speech in which a thing, an animal, or an abstract term (*truth, nature*) is made human. A personification extends throughout this whole short poem:

James Stephens (1882–1950)*
THE WIND
1915

The wind stood up and gave a shout.
He whistled on his fingers and

Kicked the withered leaves about
And thumped the branches with his hand

And said he'd kill and kill and kill,
And so he will and so he will.

The wind is a wild man, and evidently it is not just any autumn breeze but a hurricane or at least a stiff gale. In poems that do not work as well as this one, personification may be employed mechanically. Hollow-eyed personifications walk the works of lesser English poets of the eighteenth century: Coleridge has quoted the beginning of one such neoclassical ode, "Inoculation! heavenly Maid, descend!" It is hard for the contemporary reader to be excited by William Collins's "The Passions, An Ode for Music" (1747), which personifies, stanza by stanza, Fear, Anger, Despair, Hope, Revenge, Pity, Jealousy, Love, Hate, Melancholy, and Cheerfulness, and has them listen to Music, until even "Brown Exercise rejoiced to hear, / And Sport leapt up, and seized his beechen spear." Still, in "Two Sonnets on Fame" John Keats makes an abstraction come alive in seeing Fame as "a wayward girl."

Hand in hand with personification often goes **apostrophe:** a way of addressing someone or something invisible or not ordinarily spoken to. In an apostrophe, a poet (in these examples Wordsworth) may address an inanimate object ("Spade! with which Wilkinson hath tilled his lands"), some dead or absent person ("Milton! thou shouldst be living at this hour"), an abstract thing ("Return, Delights!"), or a spirit ("Thou Soul that art the eternity of thought"). More often than not, the poet uses apostrophe to announce a lofty and serious tone. An "O" may even be put in front of it ("O moon!") since, according to W. D. Snodgrass, every poet has a right to do so at least once in a lifetime. But apostrophe doesn't have to be highfalutin. It is a means of giving life to the inanimate. It is a way of giving body to the intangible, a way of speaking to it person to person, as in the words of a moving American spiritual: "Death, ain't you got no shame?"

Most of us, from time to time, emphasize a point with a statement containing exaggeration: "Faster than greased lightning," "I've told him a thousand times." We speak, then, not literal truth but use a figure of speech called **over-statement** (or **hyperbole**). Poets too, being fond of emphasis, often exaggerate for effect. Instances are Marvell's profession of a love that should grow "Vaster than empires, and more slow" and John Burgon's description of Petra: "A rose-red city, half as old as Time." Overstatement can be used also for humorous purposes, as in a fat woman's boast (from a blues song): "Every time I shake, some skinny gal loses her home."[2] The opposite is **understatement,** implying more than is said. Mark Twain in *Life on the Mississippi* recalls how, as an apprentice steamboat-pilot asleep when supposed to be on watch, he was roused by the pilot and sent clambering to the pilot house: "Mr. Bixby was close behind, commenting." Another example is Robert Frost's line "One could do worse than be a swinger of birches"—the conclusion of a poem that has suggested that to swing on a birch tree is one of the most deeply satisfying activities in the world.

In **metonymy,** the name of a thing is substituted for that of another closely associated with it. For instance, we say "The White House decided," and mean the president did. When John Dyer writes in "Grongar Hill,"

A little rule, a little sway,
A sun beam on a winter's day,
Is all the proud and mighty have
Between the cradle and the grave,

we recognize that *cradle* and *grave* signify birth and death. A kind of metonymy, **synecdoche** is the use of a part of a thing to stand for the whole of it or vice versa. We say "She lent a hand," and mean that she lent her entire presence. Similarly, Milton in "Lycidas" refers to greedy clergymen as "blind mouths." Another kind of metonymy is the **transferred epithet:** a device of emphasis in which the poet attributes some characteristic of a thing to another thing closely associated with it. When Thomas Gray observes that, in the evening pastures, "drowsy tinklings lull the distant folds," he well knows that sheep's bells do not drowse, but sheep do. When Hart Crane, describing the earth as seen from an airplane, speaks of "nimble blue plateaus," he attributes the airplane's motion to the earth.

Paradox occurs in a statement that at first strikes us as self-contradictory but that on reflection makes some sense. "The peasant," said G. K. Chesterton, "lives in a larger world than the globe-trotter." Here, two different meanings of *larger* are contrasted: "greater in spiritual values" versus "greater in miles." Some paradoxical statements, however, are much more than plays on words. In a moving sonnet, the blind John Milton tells how one night he dreamed he could see his dead wife. (See page 1105 for the complete sonnet.)The poem ends in a paradox:

But oh, as to embrace me she inclined,
I waked, she fled, and day brought back my night.

[2]Quoted by Amiri Baraka [LeRoi Jones] in *Blues People* (New York: Morrow, 1963).

What paradoxes do you find in the following poem? For each, explain the sense that underlies the statement.

Chidiock Tichborne (1568?–1586)

ELEGY, WRITTEN WITH HIS OWN HAND   1586
IN THE TOWER BEFORE HIS EXECUTION

My prime of youth is but a frost of cares,
  My feast of joy is but a dish of pain,
My crop of corn is but a field of tares°,   *weeds*
  And all my good is but vain hope of gain:
The day is past, and yet I saw no sun,   5
And now I live, and now my life is done.

My tale was heard, and yet it was not told,
  My fruit is fall'n, and yet my leaves are green,
My youth is spent, and yet I am not old,
  I saw the world, and yet I was not seen: 10
My thread is cut, and yet it is not spun,
And now I live, and now my life is done.

I sought my death, and found it in my womb,
  I looked for life, and saw it was a shade,
I trod the earth, and knew it was my tomb,   15
  And now I die, and now I was but made:
My glass is full, and now my glass is run,
And now I live, and now my life is done.

ELEGY, WRITTEN WITH HIS OWN HAND. Accused of taking part in the Babington Conspiracy, a plot by Roman Catholics against the life of Queen Elizabeth I, eighteen-year-old Chidiock Tichborne was hanged, drawn, and quartered at the Tower of London. That is virtually all we know about him.

Asked to tell the difference between men and women, Samuel Johnson replied, "I can't conceive, madam, can you?" The great dictionary-maker was using a figure of speech known to classical rhetoricians as *paronomasia*, better known to us as a **pun** or play on words. How does a pun operate? It reminds us of another word (or other words) of similar or identical sound but of very different denotation. Although puns at their worst can be mere piddling quibbles, at best they can sharply point to surprising but genuine resemblances. The name of a dentist's country estate, Tooth Acres, is accurate: aching teeth paid for the property. In his novel *Moby-Dick*, Herman Melville takes up questions about whales that had puzzled scientists: for instance, are the whale's spoutings water or gaseous vapor? And when Melville speaks pointedly of the great whale "sprinkling and mistifying the gardens of the deep," we catch his pun, and conclude that the creature both mistifies and mystifies at once.

In poetry, a pun may be facetious, as in Thomas Hood's ballad of "Faithless Nelly Gray":

> Ben Battle was a soldier bold,
>   And used to war's alarms;
> But a cannon-ball took off his legs,
>   So he laid down his arms!

Or it may be serious, as in these lines on war by E. E. Cummings:

> the bigness of cannon
> is skillful,

(*is skillful* becoming *is kill-ful* when read aloud), or perhaps, as in Shakespeare's song in *Cymbeline*, "Fear no more the heat o' th' sun," both facetious and serious at once:

> Golden lads and girls all must,
> As chimney-sweepers, come to dust.

Poets often make puns on images thereby combining the sensory force of imagery with the verbal pleasure of wordplay. Find and explain the punning images in these three poems.

Margaret Atwood   (b. 1939)*

YOU FIT INTO ME   1971

you fit into me
like a hook into an eye

a fish hook
an open eye

John Ashbery   (b. 1927)*

THE CATHEDRAL IS   1979

Slated for demolition

George Herbert   (1593–1633)*

THE PULLEY   1633

  When God at first made man,
Having a glass of blessings standing by—
Let us (said he) pour on him all we can;
Let the world's riches, which dispersèd lie,
  Contract into a span.

5

So strength first made a way,
Then beauty flowed, then wisdom, honor, pleasure:
When almost all was out, God made a stay,
Perceiving that, alone of all His treasure,
    Rest in the bottom lay.   10

    For if I should (said he)
Bestow this jewel also on My creature,
He would adore My gifts instead of Me,
And rest in Nature, not the God of Nature:
    So both should losers be.   15

    Yet let him keep the rest,
But keep them with repining restlessness;
Let him be rich and weary, that at least,
If goodness lead him not, yet weariness
    May toss him to My breast.   20

QUESTIONS

1. What different senses of the word *rest* does Herbert bring into this poem?
2. How do God's words in line 16, *Yet let him keep the rest,* seem paradoxical?
3. What do you feel to be the tone of Herbert's poem? Does the punning make the poem seem comic?
4. Why is the poem called "The Pulley"? What is its implied metaphor?

To sum up: even though figures of speech are not to be taken *only* literally, they refer us to a tangible world. By *personifying* an eagle, Tennyson reminds us that the bird and humankind have certain characteristics in common. Through *metonymy*, a poet can focus our attention on a particular detail in a larger object; through *hyperbole* and *understatement*, make us see the physical actuality in back of words. *Pun* and *paradox* cause us to realize this actuality, too, and probably surprise us enjoyably at the same time. Through *apostrophe*, the poet animates the inanimate and asks it to listen—speaks directly to an immediate god or to the revivified dead. Put to such uses, figures of speech have power. They are more than just ways of playing with words.

Theodore Roethke   (1908–1963)*

I KNEW A WOMAN   1958

I knew a woman, lovely in her bones,
When small birds sighed, she would sigh back at them;
Ah, when she moved, she moved more ways than one:
The shapes a bright container can contain!
Of her choice virtues only gods should speak,   5
Or English poets who grew up on Greek
(I'd have them sing in chorus, cheek to cheek).

How well her wishes went! She stroked my chin,
She taught me Turn, and Counter-turn, and Stand;
She taught me Touch, that undulant white skin;   10
I nibbled meekly from her proffered hand;
She was the sickle; I, poor I, the rake,
Coming behind her for her pretty sake
(But what prodigious mowing we did make).

Love likes a gander, and adores a goose: 15
Her full lips pursed, the errant note to seize;
She played it quick, she played it light and loose;
My eyes, they dazzled at her flowing knees;
Her several parts could keep a pure repose,
Or one hip quiver with a mobile nose   20
(She moved in circles, and those circles moved).

Let seed be grass, and grass turn into hay:
I'm martyr to a motion not my own;
What's freedom for? To know eternity.
I swear she cast a shadow white as stone.   25
But who would count eternity in days?
These old bones live to learn her wanton ways:
(I measure time by how a body sways).

QUESTIONS

1. What outrageous puns do you find in Roethke's poem? Describe the effect of them.
2. What kind of figure of speech occurs in all three lines: *Of her choice virtues only gods should speak; My eyes, they dazzled at her flowing knees; and I swear she cast a shadow white as stone?*
3. What sort of figure is the poet's reference to himself as *old bones?*
4. Do you take *Let seed be grass, and grass turn into hay* as figurative language, or literal statement?
5. If you agree that the tone of this poem is witty and playful, do you think the poet is making fun of the woman? What is his attitude toward her? What part do figures of speech play in communicating it?

FOR REVIEW AND FURTHER STUDY

Robert Frost   (1874–1963)*

THE SILKEN TENT   1942

She is as in a field a silken tent
At midday when a sunny summer breeze
Has dried the dew and all its ropes relent,
So that in guys° it gently sways at ease,   *attachments that steady it*

And its supporting central cedar pole,   5
That is its pinnacle to heavenward
And signifies the sureness of the soul,
Seems to owe naught to any single cord,
But strictly held by none, is loosely bound
By countless silken ties of love and thought   10
To everything on earth the compass round,
And only by one's going slightly taut
In the capriciousness of summer air
Is of the slightest bondage made aware.

QUESTIONS

1. Is Frost's comparison of a woman and tent a simile or a metaphor?
2. What are the ropes or cords?
3. Does the poet convey any sense of this woman's character? What sort of person do you believe her to be?
4. Paraphrase the poem, trying to state its implied meaning. (If you need to be re-freshed about paraphrase, turn back to page 652.) Be sure to include the implications of the last three lines.

Denise Levertov (1923–1997)*

LEAVING FOREVER   1964

He says the waves in the ship's wake
are like stones rolling away.
I don't see it that way.
But I see the mountain turning,
turning away its face as the ship   5
takes us away.

QUESTIONS

1. What do you understand to be the man's feelings about leaving forever? How does the speaker feel? With what two figures of speech does the poet express these con-flicting views?
2. Suppose that this poem had ended in another simile (instead of its three last lines):

> I see the mountain as a suitcase
> left behind on the shore
> as the ship takes us away.

How is Denise Levertov's choice of a figure of speech a much stronger one?

Jane Kenyon (1947–1995)

THE SUITOR   1978

We lie back to back. Curtains
lift and fall,
like the chest of someone sleeping.

Wind moves the leaves of the box elder;
they show their light undersides,
turning all at once
like a school of fish.
Suddenly I understand that I am happy.
For months this feeling
has been coming closer, stopping
for short visits, like a timid suitor.

5

10

QUESTION

In each simile you find in this poem, exactly what is the similarity?

Identify the central figure of speech in the following three short poems.

Robert Frost   (1874–1963)*
THE SECRET SITS   1936

We dance round in a ring and suppose,
But the Secret sits in the middle and knows.

W. S. Merwin   (b. 1927)
SONG OF MAN CHIPPING AN ARROWHEAD   1973

Little children you will all go
but the one you are hiding
will fly

A. R. Ammons   (b. 1926)
COWARD   1975

Bravery runs in my family.

Kay Ryan   (b. 1945)
TURTLE   1994

Who would be a turtle who could help it?
A barely mobile hard roll, a four-oared helmet,
she can ill afford the chances she must take
in rowing toward the grasses that she eats.
Her track is graceless, like dragging
a packing-case places, and almost any slope

5

defeats her modest hopes. Even being practical,
she's often stuck up to the axle on her way
to something edible. With everything optimal,
she skirts the ditch which would convert   10
her shell into a serving dish. She lives
below luck-level, never imagining some lottery
will change her load of pottery to wings.
Her only levity is patience,
the sport of truly chastened things.   15

QUESTION

How many metaphors, similes, or implied metaphors can you spot in this poem?

Robinson Jeffers (1887–1962)*

HANDS   1929

Inside a cave in a narrow canyon near Tassajara
The vault of rock is painted with hands,
A multitude of hands in the twilight, a cloud of men's palms,
       no more,
No other picture. There's no one to say
Whether the brown shy quiet people who are dead intended   5
Religion or magic, or made their tracings
In the idleness of art; but over the division of years these
       careful
Signs-manual are now like a sealed message
Saying: "Look: we also were human; we had hands, not paws.
       All hail
You people with the cleverer hands, our supplanters   10
In the beautiful country; enjoy her a season, her beauty, and
       come down
And be supplanted; for you also are human."

QUESTION

Identify examples of personification and apostrophe in "Hands."

Robert Burns (1759–1796)*

OH, MY LOVE IS LIKE A RED, RED ROSE   (ABOUT 1788)

Oh, my love is like a red, red rose
    That's newly sprung in June;
My love is like the melody
    That's sweetly played in tune.

So fair art thou, my bonny lass,   5
    So deep in love am I;
And I will love thee still, my dear,
    Till a' the seas gang° dry.   °go

Till a' the seas gang dry, my dear,
    And the rocks melt wi' the sun;   10
And I will love thee still, my dear,
    While the sands o' life shall run.

And fare thee weel, my only love!
    And fare thee weel awhile!
And I will come again, my love   15
    Though it were ten thousand mile.

WRITER'S PERSPECTIVE

Robert Frost

Robert Frost on Writing
THE IMPORTANCE OF POETIC METAPHOR   1930

I do not think anybody ever knows the discreet use of metaphors, his own and other peoples, the discreet handling of metaphor, unless he has been properly educated in poetry.

Poetry begins in trivial metaphors, pretty metaphors, "grace" metaphors, and goes on to the profoundest thinking that we have. Poetry provides the one permissible way of saying one thing and meaning another. People say, "why don't you say what you mean?" We never do that, do we, being all of us too much poets. We like to talk in parables and in hints and in indirections—whether from diffidence or some other instinct.

I have wanted in late years to go further and further in making metaphor the whole of thinking. I find someone now and then to agree with me that all thinking, except mathematical thinking, is metaphorical, or all thinking except scientific thinking. The mathematical might be difficult for me to bring in, but the scientific is easy enough.

What I am pointing out is that unless you are at home in the metaphor, un-less you have had your proper poetical education in the metaphor, you are not safe anywhere. Because you are not at ease with figurative values: you don't know the metaphor in its strength and its weakness. You don't know how far you may expect to ride it and when it may break down with you. You are not safe in science; you are not safe in history.

"Education by Poetry"

◄■■▭ WRITING CRITICALLY ▭■◄▬

How Metaphors Enlarge a Poem's Meaning

Poems have the particular power of helping us see one thing by pointing out an-other. One of the most distinctive ways poems manage this feat is by calling a thing by a different name, in other words, by creating a metaphor. Paradoxicaly, by connecting an object to something else, a metaphor can reveal interesting as-pects of the original thing we might either never have noticed or have consid-ered unimportant.

Usually we can see the main point of a good metaphor immediately, but in interpreting a poem, the practical issue sometimes arises on how far to extend a comparison. All readers recognize that metaphors enlarge meaning, but they also know that there is always some limit to the comparison and that in most poems the limit remains unstated. If at the dinner table a big brother calls his kid brother "a pig," he probably does not mean to imply that the child has a snout and a kinky tail. Most metaphors have a finite set of associations—even insults from a big brother.

If you plan an essay on a highly metaphorical poem, it is often useful to ex-amine the key comparison or comparisons in the poem. Jot down the major metaphors (or similes). Under each comparison make a two-column list—one marked "true," the other "false." Now start exploring the connections between the object the poem presents and the thing to which it is being compared. What aspects of the comparison are true? Make this list as long as possible. In the second list write the aspects that the two objects do not truly share; this list soon sets the limits of the metaphorical connections. In poems in which the metaphor is rich and resonant, the "true" list will be much longer than the "false" list. In other poems, ones in which the metaphor is narrowly focused on only limited connections between the two objects, the "false" list will quickly outpace the "true" list. Finally, once you have listed the key comparisons in the poem, see if there is any obvious connection between all the metaphors or similes them-selves. Do they share something in common? Are all of them threatening? Inviting? Nocturnal? Exaggerated? Their similarities, if any, will almost certainly be significant.

Don't spend more than a few minutes on each list. The object is not to list every possible connection but only to determine the general scope of the metaphor and its implications. If the poem has a central metaphor, its scope and function should now be clear.

WRITING ASSIGNMENT

In a short essay (approximately 500 words) create your own extended simile or metaphor. Choose something from your life—perhaps a physical possession like a car or coat, a part of your body like your face or hair, or even a personal memory or emotion—and compare it to something else. You may begin by comparing what you choose to something it resembles physically, but you are free to use any comparison you find meaningful. Extend the metaphor as far as you can. Use hyperbole or understatement, as appropriate, but keep the metaphorical connection true enough for the reader to see and enjoy some connection. Feel free to be humorous. If you borrow a metaphor from some poem in this chapter, make sure you add an original twist of your own.

FURTHER SUGGESTIONS FOR WRITING

1. Freely using your imagination, write a paragraph in which you make as many hyperbolic statements as possible. Then write another version, changing all your exaggeration to understatement. Then, in a concluding paragraph, sum up what this experiment shows you about figurative language. Some possible topics are "The Most Gratifying (or Terrifying) Moment of My Life," "The Job I Almost Landed," "The Person I Most Admire."

2. Choose a short poem rich in figurative language: Sylvia Plath's "Metaphors," say, or Burns's "Oh, my love is like a red, red rose." Rewrite the poem, taking for your model Howard Moss's deliberately bepiddling version of "Shall I compare thee to a summer's day?" Eliminate every figure of speech. Turn the poem into language as flat and unsuggestive as possible. (Just ignore any rime or rhythm in the original.) Then, in a paragraph, indicate lines in your revised version that seem glaringly worsened. In conclusion, sum up what your barbaric rewrite tells you about the nature of poetry.

18 Song

SINGING AND SAYING

Most poems are more memorable than most ordinary speech, and when music is combined with poetry the result can be more memorable still. The differences between speech, poetry, and song may appear if we consider, first of all, this fragment of an imaginary conversation between two lovers:

> Let's not drink; let's just sit here and look at each other. Or put a
> kiss inside my goblet and I won't want anything to drink.

Forgettable language, we might think; but let's try to make it a little more interesting:

> Drink to me only with your eyes, and I'll pledge my love to you with
> my eyes;
> Or leave a kiss within the goblet, that's all I'll want to drink.

The passage is closer to poetry, but still has a distance to go. At least we now have a figure of speech—the metaphor that love is wine, implied in the statement that one lover may salute another by lifting an eye as well as by lifting a goblet. But the sound of the words is not yet especially interesting. Here is another try, by Ben Jonson:

> Drink to me only with thine eyes,
>   And I will pledge with mine;
> Or leave a kiss but in the cup,
>   And I'll not ask for wine.

In these opening lines from Jonson's poem "To Celia," the improvement is noticeable. These lines are poetry; their language has become special. For one thing, the lines rime (with an additional rime sound on *thine*). There is interest, too, in the proximity of the words *kiss* and *cup:* the repetition (or alliteration) of the *k* sound. The rhythm of the lines has become regular; generally every other word (or syllable) is stressed:

> DRINK to me ON-ly WITH thine EYES,
>   And I will PLEDGE with MINE;
> OR LEAVE a KISS but IN the CUP,
>   And I'LL not ASK for WINE.

All these devices of sound and rhythm, together with metaphor, produce a pleasing effect—more pleasing than the effect of "Let's not drink; let's look at each other." But the words became more pleasing still when later set to music:

In this memorable form, the poem is still alive today.

Ben Jonson   (1573?–1637)*

To Celia   1616

Drink to me only with thine eyes,
  And I will pledge with mine;
Or leave a kiss but in the cup,
  And I'll not ask for wine.
The thirst that from the soul doth rise   5
  Doth ask a drink divine;
But might I of Jove's nectar sup,
  I would not change for thine.

I sent thee late a rosy wreath,
  Not so much honoring thee   10
As giving it a hope that there
  It could not withered be.
But thou thereon didst only breathe,
  And sent'st it back to me;
Since when it grows, and smells, I swear,   15
  Not of itself but thee.

A compliment to a lady has rarely been put in language more graceful, more wealthy with interesting sounds. Other figures of speech besides metaphor make them unforgettable: for example, the hyperbolic tributes to the power of the lady's sweet breath, which can start picked roses growing again, and her kisses, which even surpass the nectar of the gods.

This song falls into stanzas—as many poems that resemble songs also do. A **stanza** (Italian for "stopping-place" or "room") is a group of lines whose pattern is repeated throughout the poem. Most songs have more than one stanza. When printed, the stanzas of songs and poems usually are set off from one another by space. When sung, stanzas of songs are indicated by a pause or by the introduction of a refrain, or chorus (a line or lines repeated). The word **verse,** which strictly refers to one line of a poem, is sometimes loosely used to mean a whole stanza: "All join in and sing the second verse!" In speaking of a stanza, whether sung or read, it is customary to indicate by a convenient algebra its **rime scheme,** the order in which rimed words recur. For instance, the rime scheme of this stanza by Herrick is *a b a b;* the first and third lines rime and so do the second and fourth:

> Round, round, the roof doth run;
>   And being ravished thus,
> Come, I will drink a tun
>   To my Propertius.

Refrains are words, phrases, or lines repeated at intervals in a song or song-like poem. A refrain usually follows immediately after a stanza, and when it does, it is called **terminal refrain.** A refrain whose words change slightly with each recurrence is called an **incremental refrain.** Sometimes we also hear an **internal refrain:** one that appears within a stanza, generally in a position that stays fixed throughout a poem. Both internal refrains and terminal refrains are used to great effect in the traditional song "The Cruel Mother":

Anonymous   (TRADITIONAL SCOTTISH BALLAD)

THE CRUEL MOTHER

She sat down below a thorn,
  Fine flowers in the valley,
And there she has her sweet babe born
  And the green leaves they grow rarely.

"Smile na sae° sweet, my bonny babe,"   *so*   5
  Fine flowers in the valley,
"And° ye smile sae sweet, ye'll smile me dead."   *if*
  And the green leaves they grow rarely.

She's taen out her little pen-knife,
   Fine flowers in the valley,   10
And twinned° the sweet babe o' its life,   *severed*
   And the green leaves they grow rarely.

She's howket° a grave by the light of the moon,   *dug*
   Fine flowers in the valley,
And there she's buried her sweet babe in   15
   And the green leaves they grow rarely.

As she was going to the church,
   Fine flowers in the valley,
She saw a sweet babe in the porch
   And the green leaves they grow rarely.   20

"O sweet babe, and thou were mine,"
   Fine flowers in the valley,
"I wad cleed° thee in the silk so fine."   *dress*
   And the green leaves they grow rarely.

"O mother dear, when I was thine,"   25
   Fine flowers in the valley,
"You did na prove to me sae kind."
   And the green leaves they grow rarely.

Taken by themselves, the refrain lines might seem mere pretty nonsense. But interwoven with the story of the murdered child, they form a terrible counterpoint. What do they come to mean? Possibly that Nature keeps going about her chores, unmindful of sin and suffering. The effect is an ironic contrast. Besides, by hearing the refrain over and over and over, we find it hard to forget.

We usually meet poems as words on a page, but songs we generally first encounter as sounds in the air. Consequently, songs tend to be written in language simple enough to be understood on first hearing. But some contemporary songwriters have created songs that require listeners to pay close and repeated attention to their words. Beginning in the 1960s with performers like Bob Dylan, Leonard Cohen, Joni Mitchell, and Frank Zappa, some pop songwriters crafted deliberately challenging songs. More recently, Sting, Kurt Cobain, P. J. Harvey, Beck, and Suzanne Vega have written complex lyrics, often full of strange, dreamlike imagery. To unravel them, a listener may have to play the recording many times, with the treble turned up all the way. Anyone who feels that literary criticism is solely an academic enterprise should listen to high school and college students discuss the lyrics of their favorite songs.

One of the most interesting musical and literary developments of the 1980s was the emergence of **rap,** a form of popular music in which words are recited to a driving rhythmic beat. It differs from mainstream popular music in several ways, but, most interesting in literary terms, rap lyrics are *spoken* rather than sung. In that sense, rap is a form of popular poetry as well as popular music. In

Black English, *rap* means "to talk" ("Let's rap about it"), and in most current rap songs, the lead performer or "M.C." talks or recites, usually at top speed, long, rhythmic, four-stress lines that end in rimes. Although today most rap singers and groups use electronic or sampled backgrounds, rap began on city streets in the game of "signifying," in which two poets aim rimed insults at each other, sometimes accompanying their tirades with a beat made by clapping or finger-snapping. This game also includes boasts made by the players on both sides about their own abilities. Anyone interested in the form will enjoy listening to Run DMC, A Tribe Called Quest, Ice Cube, Dr. Dre, L. L. Cool J, and other performers currently popular. Here, for instance, is a transcription of an early rap lyric by Run DMC that shows a sophisticated understanding of the traditions of English popular poetry.

Run D.M.C. (J. Simmons/D. McDaniels/R. Rubin)
from PETER PIPER   1986

Now Dr. Seuss and Mother Goose both did their thing
But Jam Master's getting loose and D.M.C.'s the king
'Cuz he's the adult entertainer, child educator
Jam Master Jay king of the cross-fader
He's the better of the best, best believe he's the baddest   5
Perfect timing when I'm climbing I'm the rhyming acrobatist
Lotta guts, when he cuts girls move their butts
His name is Jay, here to play, he must be nuts
And on the mix real quick, and I'd like to say
He's not Flash but he's fast and his name is Jay.   10

It goes a one, two, three and . . .
Jay's like King Midas, as I was told,
Everything that he touched turned to gold
He's the greatest of the great get it straight he's great
Claim fame 'cuz his name is known in every state   15
His name is Jay to see him play will make you say
God damn that D.J. made my day
Like the butcher, the baker, the candlestick maker
He's a maker, a breaker, and a title taker
Like the little old lady who lived in a shoe   20
If cuts were kids he would be through
Not lying y'all he's the best I know
And if I lie my nose will grow
Like a little wooden boy named Pinnochio
And you all know how the story go   25
Trix are for kids he plays much gigs
He's the big bad wolf and you're the 3 pigs

He's the big bad wolf in your neighborhood
Not bad meaning bad but bad meaning good . . . There it is!
We're Run D.M.C. got a beef to settle   30
Dee's not Hansel, he's not Gretel
Jay's a winner, not a beginner
His pocket gets fat, others' get thinner
Jump on Jay like cow jumped moon
People chase Jay like dish and spoon   35
And like all fairy tales end
You'll see Jay again my friend, hough!

PETER PIPER. (These lyrics were transcribed from the Run D.M.C. hit.) 2 *Jam Master Jay:* the DJ who
provides beats and scratching in the rap group. 4 *Cross-fader:* scratching device. 10 *Flash:* allusion either to Grandmaster Flash, another DJ, or the comic book superhero Flash; rap critics debate this
point.

Many familiar poems began life as songs, but today, their tunes forgotten,
they survive only in poetry anthologies. Shakespeare studded his plays with
songs, and many of his contemporaries wrote verses to fit existing tunes. Some
poets were themselves musicians (like Thomas Campion), and composed both
words and music. In Shakespeare's day, **madrigals,** short secular songs for three or
more voices arranged in counterpoint, enjoyed great popularity. A madrigal by
an unknown poet, "The Silver Swan," is given on page 803. A madrigal is always
short, usually just one stanza, and rarely exceeds twelve or thirteen lines. Elizabethans loved to sing, and a person was considered a dolt if he or she could not
join in a three-part song. Here is a madrigal from one of Shakespeare's comedies:

William Shakespeare (1564–1616)*

TAKE, O, TAKE THOSE LIPS AWAY   (1604)

Take, O, take those lips away
    That so sweetly were forsworn,
And those eyes, the break of day,
    Lights that do mislead the morn;
But my kisses bring again, bring again,   5
Seals of love, but seal'd in vain, seal'd in vain.

TAKE, O, TAKE THOSE LIPS AWAY. This short song appears in *Measure for Measure.* It is sung by a boy
in Act IV, just as we see Mariana, a deserted lover, for the first time.

Some poets who were not composers printed their work in madrigal books
for others to set to music. In the seventeenth century, however, poetry and song
seem to have fallen away from each other. By the end of the century, much new
poetry, other than songs for plays, was written to be printed and to be silently

read. Poets who wrote popular songs—like Thomas D'Urfey, compiler of the collection *Pills to Purge Melancholy*—were considered somewhat disreputable. With the notable exceptions of John Gay, who took existing popular tunes for *The Beggar's Opera*, and Robert Burns, who rewrote folk songs or made completely new words for them, few important English poets since Campion have been first-rate song-writers.

Occasionally, a poet has learned a thing or two from music. "But for the opera I could never have written *Leaves of Grass*," said Walt Whitman, who loved the Italian art form for its expansiveness. Coleridge, Hardy, Auden, and many others have learned from folk ballads, and T. S. Eliot patterned his thematically repetitive *Four Quartets* after the structure of a quartet in classical music. "Poetry," said Ezra Pound, "begins to atrophy when it gets too far from music." Still, even in the twentieth century, the poet has been more often a corrector of printer's proofs than a tunesmith or performer.

Some people think that to write poems and to travel about singing them, as many rock singer-composers now do, is a return to the venerable tradition of the **troubadours,** minstrels of the late Middle Ages. But there are differences. No doubt the troubadours had to please their patrons, but for better or worse their songs were not affected by a producer's video promotion budget or by the technical resources of a sound studio. Bob Dylan has denied that he is a poet, and Paul Simon once told an interviewer, "If you want poetry read Wallace Stevens." Nevertheless, many rock lyrics have the verbal intensity of poetry. No rock lyric, however, can be judged independently of its musical accompaniment. A song joins words and music; a great song joins them inseparably. Although the words of a great song cannot stand on their own without their music, they are not invalidated as lyrics. Song-writers rarely create their lyrics to be read on the page. If the words seem rich and interesting in themselves, our enjoyment is only increased. Like most poems and songs of the past, most current songs may end in the trash can of time. And yet, certain memorable rimed and rhythmic lines may live on, especially if expressed in stirring music and they have been given wide exposure.

EXERCISE: *Comparing Poem and Song*

Compare the following poem by Edwin Arlington Robinson and a popular song lyric based on it. Notice what Paul Simon had to do to Robinson's original poem in order to make it into a song, and how Simon altered Robinson's conception.

Edwin Arlington Robinson (1869–1935)*

RICHARD CORY   1897

Whenever Richard Cory went down town,
We people on the pavement looked at him:
He was a gentleman from sole to crown,
Clean favored, and imperially slim.

And he was always quietly arrayed,   5
And he was always human when he talked;
But still he fluttered pulses when he said,
"Good-morning," and he glittered when he walked.

And he was rich—yes, richer than a king—
And admirably schooled in every grace: 10
In fine°, we thought that he was everything   *in short*
To make us wish that we were in his place.

So on we worked, and waited for the light,
And went without the meat, and cursed the bread;
And Richard Cory, one calm summer night,   15
Went home and put a bullet through his head.

Paul Simon   (b. 1942)

RICHARD CORY   1966

With Apologies to E. A. Robinson

They say that Richard Cory owns
One half of this old town,
With elliptical connections
To spread his wealth around.
Born into Society,   5
A banker's only child,
He had everything a man could want:
Power, grace and style.

Refrain:

But I, I work in his factory
And I curse the life I'm livin'   10
And I curse my poverty
And I wish that I could be
Oh I wish that I could be
Oh I wish that I could be
Richard Cory.   15

The papers print his picture
Almost everywhere he goes:
Richard Cory at the opera,
Richard Cory at a show
And the rumor of his party   20
And the orgies on his yacht—
Oh he surely must be happy
With everything he's got.   *(Refrain.)*

He freely gave to charity,
He had the common touch, 25
And they were grateful for his patronage
And they thanked him very much,
So my mind was filled with wonder
When the evening headlines read:
   "Richard Cory went home last night 30
   And put a bullet through his head."   *(Refrain.)*

RICHARD CORY by Paul Simon. If possible, listen to the ballad sung by Simon and Garfunkel on *Sounds of Silence* (Columbia recording CL 2469, stereo CS 9269), © 1966 by Paul Simon. Used by permission.

BALLADS

Any narrative song, like Paul Simon's "Richard Cory," may be called a **ballad.** In English, some of the most famous ballads are **folk ballads,** loosely defined as anonymous story-songs transmitted orally before they were ever written down. Sir Walter Scott, a pioneer collector of Scottish folk ballads, drew the ire of an old woman whose songs he had transcribed: "They were made for singing and no' for reading, but ye ha'e broken the charm now and they'll never be sung mair." The old singer had a point. Print freezes songs and tends to hold them fast to a single version. If Scott and others had not written them down, however, many would have been lost.

    In his monumental work *The English and Scottish Popular Ballads* (1882–1898), the American scholar Francis J. Child winnowed out 305 folk ballads he considered authentic—that is, creations of illiterate or semiliterate people who had preserved them orally. Child, who worked by insight as well as by learning, did such a good job of telling the difference between folk ballads and other kinds that later scholars have added only about a dozen ballads to his count. Often called **Child ballads,** his texts include "The Three Ravens," "Sir Patrick Spence," "The Twa Corbies," "Edward," "The Cruel Mother," and many others still on the lips of singers. Here is one of the best-known Child ballads.

Anonymous   (TRADITIONAL SCOTTISH BALLAD)

BONNY BARBARA ALLAN

It was in and about the Martinmas time,
   When the green leaves were afalling,
That Sir John Graeme, in the West Country,
   Fell in love with Barbara Allan.

He sent his men down through the town, 5
   To the place where she was dwelling;
"O haste and come to my master dear,
   Gin° ye be Barbara Allan."   *if*

O hooly°, hooly rose she up,   *slowly*
　　To the place where he was lying,   10
And when she drew the curtain by:
　　"Young man, I think you're dying."

"O it's I'm sick, and very, very sick,
　　And 'tis a' for Barbara Allan."—
"O the better for me ye's never be,   15
　　Tho your heart's blood were aspilling.

"O dinna ye mind°, young man," said she,   *don't you remember*
　　"When ye was in the tavern adrinking,
That ye made the health° gae round and round,   *toasts*
　　And slighted Barbara Allan?"   20

He turned his face unto the wall,
　　And death was with him dealing:
"Adieu, adieu, my dear friends all,
　　And be kind to Barbara Allan."

And slowly, slowly raise she up,   25
　　And slowly, slowly left him,
And sighing said she could not stay,
　　Since death of life had reft him.

She had not gane a mile but twa,
　　When she heard the dead-bell ringing,   30
And every jow° that the dead-bell geid,   *stroke*
　　It cried, "Woe to Barbara Allan!"

"O mother, mother, make my bed!
　　O make it saft and narrow!
Since my love died for me today,   35
　　I'll die for him tomorrow."

BONNY BARBARA ALLAN. 1 *Martinmas:* Saint Martin's day, November 11.

QUESTIONS

1. In any line does the Scottish dialect cause difficulty? If so, try reading the line aloud.
2. Without ever coming out and explicitly calling Barbara hard-hearted, this ballad reveals that she is. In which stanza and by what means is her cruelty demonstrated?
3. At what point does Barbara evidently have a change of heart? Again, how does the poem dramatize this change without explicitly talking about it?
4. In many American versions of this ballad, noble knight John Graeme becomes an ordinary citizen. The gist of the story is the same, but at the end are these further stanzas, incorporated from a different ballad:

They buried Willie in the old churchyard
And Barbara in the choir;
And out of his grave grew a red, red rose,
And out of hers a briar.

They grew and grew to the steeple top
Till they could grow no higher;
And there they locked in a true love's knot,
The red rose round the briar.

Do you think this appendage heightens or weakens the final impact of the story? Can the American ending be defended as an integral part of a new song? Explain.
5. Paraphrase lines 9, 15–16, 22, 25–28. By putting these lines into prose, what has been lost?

As you can see from "Bonny Barbara Allan," in a traditional English or Scottish folk ballad the storyteller speaks of the lives and feelings of others. Even if the pronoun "I" occurs, it rarely has much personality. Characters often exchange dialogue, but no one character speaks all the way through. Events move rapidly, perhaps because some of the dull transitional stanzas have been forgotten. The events themselves, as ballad scholar Albert B. Friedman has said, are frequently "the stuff of tabloid journalism—sensational tales of lust, revenge and domestic crime. Unwed mothers slay their newborn babes; lovers unwilling to marry their pregnant mistresses brutally murder the poor women, for which, without fail, they are justly punished."[1] There are also many ballads of the supernatural ("The Twa Corbies") and of gallant knights ("Sir Patrick Spence"), and there are a few humorous ballads, usually about unhappy marriages.

A favorite pattern of ballad-makers is the so-called **ballad stanza,** four lines rimed *a b c b,* tending to fall into 8, 6, 8, and 6 syllables:

Clerk Saunders and Maid Margaret
Walked owre yon garden green,
And deep and heavy was the love
That fell thir twa between°.   *between those two*

Though not the only possible stanza for a ballad, this easily singable quatrain has continued to attract poets since the Middle Ages. Close kin to the ballad stanza is **common meter,** a stanza found in hymns such as "Amazing Grace," by the eighteenth-century English hymnist John Newton:

Amazing grace! how sweet the sound
That saved a wretch like me!
I once was lost, but now am found,
Was blind, but now I see.

[1]Introduction to *The Viking Book of Folk Ballads of the English-Speaking World,* edited by Albert B. Friedman (New York: Viking, 1956).

Notice that its pattern is that of the ballad stanza except for its *two* pairs of rimes. That all its lines rime is probably a sign of more literate artistry than we usually hear in folk ballads. Another sign of schoolteachers' influence is that Newton's rimes are exact. (Rimes in folk ballads are often rough-and-ready, as if made by ear, rather than polished and exact, as if the riming words had been matched for their similar spellings. In "Barbara Allan," for instance, the hard-hearted lover's name rimes with *afalling, dwelling, aspilling, dealing,* and even with *ringing* and *adrinking.*) That so many hymns were written in common meter may have been due to convenience. If a congregation didn't know the tune to a hymn in common meter, they readily could sing its words to the tune of another such hymn they knew. Besides hymnists, many poets have favored common meter, among them A. E. Housman and Emily Dickinson.

Related to traditional folk ballads but displaying characteristics of their own, **broadside ballads** (so called because they were printed on one sheet of paper) often were set to traditional tunes. Most broadside ballads were an early form of journalism made possible by the development of cheap printing and by the growth of audiences who could read, just barely. Sometimes merely humorous or tear-jerking, often they were rimed accounts of sensational news events. That they were widespread and often scorned in Shakespeare's day is attested by the character of Autolycus in *A Winter's Tale*, an itinerant hawker of ballads about sea monsters and strange pregnancies ("a usurer's wife was brought to bed of twenty money-bags"). Although many broadsides tend to be **doggerel** (verse full of irregularities due not to skill but to incompetence), many excellent poets had their work taken up and peddled in the streets—among them Marvell, Swift, and Byron.

Literary ballads, not meant for singing, are written by sophisticated poets for book-educated readers who enjoy being reminded of folk ballads. Literary ballads imitate certain features of folk ballads: they may tell of dramatic conflicts or of mortals who encounter the supernatural; they may use conventional figures of speech or ballad stanzas. Well-known poems of this kind include Keats's "La Belle Dame Sans Merci," Coleridge's "Rime of the Ancient Mariner," and (in our time) Dudley Randall's "Ballad of Birmingham."

Dudley Randall   (b. 1914)*

BALLAD OF BIRMINGHAM   1966

*(On the Bombing of a Church in
Birmingham, Alabama, 1963)*

"Mother dear, may I go downtown
Instead of out to play,
And march the streets of Birmingham
In a Freedom March today?"

"No, baby, no, you may not go,   5
For the dogs are fierce and wild,
And clubs and hoses, guns and jail
Aren't good for a little child."

"But, mother, I won't be alone.
Other children will go with me,   10
And march the streets of Birmingham
To make our country free."

"No, baby, no, you may not go,
For I fear those guns will fire.
But you may go to church instead   15
And sing in the children's choir."

She has combed and brushed her night-dark hair,
And bathed rose petal sweet,
And drawn white gloves on her small brown hands,
And white shoes on her feet.   20

The mother smiled to know her child
Was in the sacred place,
But that smile was the last smile
To come upon her face.

For when she heard the explosion,   25
Her eyes grew wet and wild.
She raced through the streets of Birmingham
Calling for her child.

She clawed through bits of glass and brick,
Then lifted out a shoe.   30
"O here's the shoe my baby wore,
But, baby, where are you?"

QUESTIONS

1. This poem, about a dynamite blast set off in an African-American church by a racial terrorist (later convicted), delivers a message without preaching. How would you sum up this message, its implied theme?
2. What is ironic in the mother's denying her child permission to take part in a protest march?
3. How does this modern poem resemble a traditional ballad?

EXPERIMENT: *Seeing the Traits of Ballads*

In "Poems for Further Reading" on pages 1027–1164 read the Child ballads "Edward," "The Three Ravens," and "The Twa Corbies" (pages 1029–1030). With these ballads in mind, consider one or more of these modern poems:

W. H. Auden, "As I Walked Out One Evening" (page 1034)
William Jay Smith, "American Primitive" (page 1135)
William Butler Yeats, "Crazy Jane Talks with the Bishop" (page 1161).

What characteristics of folk ballads do you find in them? In what ways do these modern poets depart from the traditions of folk ballads of the Middle Ages?

BLUES

Among the many song forms to have shaped the way poetry is written in English, no recent form has been more influential than the blues. Originally a type of folk music developed by black slaves in the South, **blues** songs have both a distinctive form and tone. They traditionally consist of three-line stanzas in which the first two identical lines are followed by a concluding riming third line.

> To dream of muddy water—trouble is knocking at your door.
> To dream of muddy water—trouble is knocking at your door.
> Your man is sure to leave you and never return no more.

Early blues lyrics almost always spoke of some sadness, pain, or deprivation—often the loss of a loved one. The melancholy tone of the lyrics, however, is not only world-weary but also world-wise. The blues expound the hard-won wisdom of bitter life experience. They frequently create their special mood through down-to-earth, even gritty, imagery drawn from everyday life. Although blues reach back into the nineteenth century, they were not widely known outside African-American communities before 1920 when the first commercial recordings appeared. Their influence on both music and song from that time was rapid and extensive. By 1930 James Weldon Johnson could declare, "It is from the blues that all that may be called American music derives its most distinctive characteristic." Blues have not only become an enduring category of popular music; they have helped shape virtually all the major styles of contemporary pop—jazz, rap, rock, gospel, country, and of course, rhythm-and-blues.

The style and structure of blues have also influenced modern poets. Not only African-American writers like Langston Hughes, Sterling A. Brown, Etheridge Knight, and Sonia Sanchez have written blues poems, but white poets as dissimilar as W. H. Auden, Elizabeth Bishop, Donald Justice, and Sandra McPherson have employed the form. The classic touchstones of the blues, however, remain the early singers like Robert Johnson, Ma Rainey, Blind Lemon Jefferson, Charley Patton, and—perhaps preeminently—Bessie Smith, "the Empress of the Blues." Any form that has fascinated Bishop and Auden as well as B. B. King, Mick Jagger, Tracy Chapman, and Eric Clapton surely deserves special notice. The blues remind us of how closely related song and poetry will always be. Here are the lyrics of one of Bessie Smith's earliest songs, based on a traditional folk blues, followed by a blues-influenced cabaret song written by W. H. Auden (with the composer Benjamin Britten) for a night-club singer.

Bessie Smith (1898?–1937)
with Clarence Williams (1898–1965)

JAILHOUSE BLUES   1923

Thirty days in jail with my back turned to the wall.
Thirty days in jail with my back turned to the wall.
Look here, Mister Jailkeeper, put another gal in my stall.

I don't mind bein' in jail but I got to stay there so long.
I don't mind bein' in jail but I got to stay there so long.   5
Well, ev'ry friend I had has done shook hands and gone.

You better stop your man from ticklin' me under my chin.
You better stop your man from ticklin' me under my chin.
'Cause if he keep on ticklin' I'm sure gonna take him in.

Good mornin' blues, blues how do you do?   10
Good mornin' blues, blues how do you do?
Well, I just come here to have a few words with you.

W. H. Auden (1907–1973)*

FUNERAL BLUES   1940

Stop all the clocks, cut off the telephone,
Prevent the dog from barking with a juicy bone,
Silence the pianos and muffled drum
Bring out the coffin, let the mourners come.

Let aeroplanes circle moaning overhead   5
Scribbling on the sky the message He Is Dead,
Tie crepe bows round the white necks of the public doves,
Let the traffic policemen wear black cotton gloves.

He was my North, my South, my East and West,
My working week and my Sunday rest,   10
My noon, my midnight, my talk, my song;
I thought that love would last for ever: I was wrong.

The stars are not wanted now: put out every one,
Pack up the moon and dismantle the sun,
Pour away the ocean and sweep up the woods;   15
For nothing now can ever come to any good.

QUESTION

What features of the traditional blues does Auden keep in his song? What features does
he discard?

John Lennon (1940–1980)
Paul McCartney (b. 1942)

ELEANOR RIGBY   1966

Ah, look at all the lonely people!
Ah, look at all the lonely people!

Eleanor Rigby
Picks up the rice in the church where a wedding has been,
Lives in a dream,
Waits at the window   5
Wearing the face that she keeps in a jar by the door.
Who is it for?

All the lonely people,
Where do they all come from?
All the lonely people,   10
Where do they all belong?

Father McKenzie,
Writing the words of a sermon that no one will hear,
No one comes near
Look at him working,   15
Darning his socks in the night when there's nobody there.
What does he care?

All the lonely people
Where do they all come from?
All the lonely people   20
Where do they all belong?

Eleanor Rigby
Died in the church and was buried along with her name.
Nobody came.
Father McKenzie,   25
Wiping the dirt from his hands as he walks from the grave,
No one was saved.

All the lonely people,
Where do they all come from?
All the lonely people,   30
Where do they all belong?

Ah, look at all the lonely people!
Ah, look at all the lonely people!

QUESTION

Is there any reason to call this famous song lyric a ballad? Compare it with a traditional ballad, such as "Bonny Barbara Allan." Do you notice any similarity? What are the differences?

Anonymous   (English madrigal)

THE SILVER SWAN,	1612

WHO LIVING HAD NO NOTE

The silver swan, who living had no note,
When death approached unlocked her silent throat;
Leaning her breast against the reedy shore,
Thus sung her first and last, and sung no more.
Farewell, all joys; O death, come close mine eyes;   5
More geese than swans now live, more fools than wise.

QUESTION

This anonymous madrigal was first published in the composer Orlando Gibbons's song-book, *The First Set of Madrigals and Mottets* in 1612. If we did not know the poem's origin, however, what features in it would suggest to us that it was a madrigal?

William Blake   (1757–1827)*

JERUSALEM (FROM *MILTON*)	1804–1810

And did those feet in ancient time
Walk upon England's mountains green?
And was the holy Lamb of God
On England's pleasant pastures seen?

And did the Countenance Divine   5
Shine forth upon our clouded hills?
And was Jerusalem builded here
Among these dark Satanic Mills?

Bring me my Bow of burning gold:
Bring me my Arrows of desire: 10
Bring me my Spear: O clouds unfold!
Bring me my Chariot of fire.

I will not cease from Mental Fight,
Nor shall my Sword sleep in my hand
Till we have built Jerusalem   15
In England's green & pleasant Land.

JERUSALEM. In Blake's book *Milton*, this hymn-like poem is untitled. When the composer Hubert Parry set it to music, at the suggestion of Robert Bridges, in 1916, he titled it "Jerusalem" after its central, visionary image. Originally performed at a "Votes for Women" concert, Parry's hymn has become a famous anthem for progressive causes.

QUESTIONS

1. Who is the unnamed figure Blake presents in lines 1 and 2? What evidence does the poem give elsewhere to help us determine the figure's identity?
2. Does Blake suggest that the historical city of Jerusalem was once actually located in England? What does that city's name suggest about Blake's vision of ancient England?
3. What are the "dark Satanic Mills"? What is their relation to the city of Jerusalem? (Does the date of the poem's publication suggest any additional historical meaning to the phrase?)
4. Why does the speaker want weapons? What sort of warfare does the speaker plan to fight?
5. Most hymns are simple and direct expressions of faith. Blake's hymn is a complex and mysterious poem, and yet it has become immensely popular in England. Do you have any ideas on what attracts so many people to this poem?

WRITER'S PERSPECTIVE

Paul McCartney

Paul McCartney on Writing
CREATING "ELEANOR RIGBY"   1978

Well that ["Eleanor Rigby"] started off with sitting down at the piano and getting the first line of the melody, and playing around with the words. I think it was "Miss Daisy Hawkins" originally; then it was her picking up the rice in a church after a wedding. That's how nearly all our songs start, with the first line just suggesting itself from books or newspapers.

At first I thought it was a young Miss Daisy Hawkins, a bit like "Annabel Lee," but not so sexy; but then I saw I'd said she was picking up the rice in church, so she had to be a cleaner; she had missed the wedding, and she was suddenly lonely. In fact she had missed it all—she was the spinster type.

Jane° was in a play in Bristol then, and I was walking round the streets waiting for her to finish. I didn't really like "Daisy Hawkins"—I wanted a name that was more real. The thought just came: "Eleanor Rigby picks up the rice and lives in a dream"—so there she was. The next thing was Father McKenzie. It was going to be Father McCartney, but then I thought that was a bit of a hang-up for my Dad, being in this lonely song. So we looked through the phone book. That's the beauty of working at random—it does come up perfectly, much better than if you try to think it with your intellect.

Anyway there was Father McKenzie, and he was just as I had imagined him, lonely, darning his socks. We weren't sure if the song was going to go on. In the next verse we thought of a bin man, an old feller going through dustbins; but it got too involved—embarrassing. John and I wondered whether to have Eleanor Rigby and him have a thing going, but we couldn't really see how. When I played it to John we decided to finish it.

That was the point anyway. She didn't make it, she never made it with anyone, she didn't even look as if she was going to.

Beatles in Their Own Words

CREATING "ELEANOR RIGBY." *Jane* refers to Jane Asher, a British actress McCartney was dating at the time of this interview.

◄═══WRITING CRITICALLY◄═══►

Is There a Difference Between Poetry and Song?

Poetry and song were originally one art, and even today the two forms remain closely related. We celebrate the beauty of a poem by praising its "music" just as we compliment a great song lyric by calling it "poetic." And yet a very simple distinction separates the two arts: in a song, the lyrics combine with music to create a collaborative total work, whereas in a poem, the author must create all the effects by words alone.

In analyzing song lyrics as poetry, it is important to separate the words temporarily from their music. Before you transcribe the lyrics onto the page, listen to the song and jot down the three or four moments that affect you most powerfully. After you have transcribed the words, consult your notes and look at the lyrics. Are the effects that moved you in the recorded song still evident in the words alone? Or did they reside mostly in the music? Or did they perhaps originate in some special combination of words and music that is not adequately re-created by the text alone?

A song is no less powerful as a song just because the words don't stand on their own as poetry. A song is meant to be sung—transposing song lyrics onto

the page changes their function. This exercise helps you understand lyrics as poetry, but do not scrutinize them unfairly relative to their original purpose.

WRITING ASSIGNMENT

Write a short paper (750–1000 words) in which you analyze the lyrics of a favorite song.
Discuss what the words alone provide and what they lack in recreating the total power of
the original song. The purpose of the paper is not to justify the song you have chosen as
great poetry (though it may perhaps qualify); rather, it is to examine what parts of the
song's power come solely from the words and what come from the music or performance.
(Don't forget to provide your instructor with an accurate transcription of the song lyrics.)

FURTHER SUGGESTIONS FOR WRITING

1. Write a short study of a lyric (or lyrics) by a recent popular song-writer. Show why
   you believe the song-writer's work deserves the name of poetry.
2. Compare and contrast the English folk ballad "The Three Ravens" with the Scottish
   folk ballad "The Twa Corbies" (both in "Poems for Further Reading").
3. Compare the versions of "Richard Cory" by Edwin Arlington Robinson and by Paul
   Simon. Point out changes Simon apparently made in the poem to render it
   singable. What other changes did he make? How did he alter Robinson's story and
   its characters?
4. After listening to some recent examples of rap (see page 790), compose a short rap
   lyric of your own, one that tells a story.

19 *Sound*

SOUND AS MEANING

Isak Dinesen, in a memoir of her life on a plantation in East Africa, tells how some Kikuyu tribesmen reacted to their first hearing of rimed verse:

> The Natives, who have a strong sense of rhythm, know nothing of verse, or at least did not know anything before the times of the schools, where they were taught hymns. One evening out in the maize-field, where we had been harvesting maize, breaking off the cobs and throwing them on to the ox-carts, to amuse myself, I spoke to the field laborers, who were mostly quite young, in Swahili verse. There was no sense in the verses, they were made for the sake of rime—"Ngumbe na-penda chumbe, Malaya mbaya. Wakamba na-kula mamba." The oxen like salt—whores are bad— The Wakamba eat snakes. It caught the interest of the boys, they formed a ring round me. They were quick to understand that meaning in poetry is of no consequence, and they did not question the thesis of the verse, but waited eagerly for the rime, and laughed at it when it came. I tried to make them themselves find the rime and finish the poem when I had begun it, but they could not, or would not, do that, and turned away their heads. As they had become used to the idea of poetry, they begged: "Speak again. Speak like rain." Why they should feel verse to be like rain I do not know. It must have been, however, an expression of applause, since in Africa rain is always longed for and welcomed.[1]

What the tribesmen had discovered is that poetry, like music, appeals to the ear. However limited it may be in comparison with the sound of an orchestra—or a

---

[1]Isak Dinesen, *Out of Africa* (New York: Random, 1972).

tribal drummer—the sound of words in itself gives pleasure. However, we might doubt Isak Dinesen's assumption that "meaning in poetry is of no consequence." "Hey nonny-nonny" and such nonsense has a place in song lyrics and other poems, and we might take pleasure in hearing rimes in Swahili; but most good poetry has meaningful sound as well as musical sound. Certainly the words of a song have an effect different from that of wordless music: they go along with their music and, by making statements, add more meaning. The French poet Isidore Isou, founder of a literary movement called *lettrisme*, maintained that poems can be written not only in words but in letters (sample lines: *xyl, xyl, / prprali dryl / znglo trpylo pwi*). But the sound of letters alone, without denotation and connotation, has not been enough to make Letterist poems memorable. In the response of the Kikuyu tribesmen, there may have been not only the pleasure of hearing sounds but also the agreeable surprise of finding that things not usually associated had been brought together.

More powerful when in the company of meaning, not apart from it, the sounds of consonants and vowels can contribute greatly to a poem's effect. The sound of *s*, which can suggest the swishing of water, has rarely been used more accurately than in Surrey's line "Calm is the sea, the waves work less and less." When, in a poem, the sound of words working together with meaning pleases mind and ear, the effect is **euphony,** as in the following lines from Tennyson's "Come down, O maid":

> Myriads of rivulets hurrying through the lawn,
> The moan of doves in immemorial elms,
> And murmuring of innumerable bees.

Its opposite is **cacophony:** a harsh, discordant effect. It too is chosen for the sake of meaning. We hear it in Milton's scornful reference in "Lycidas" to corrupt clergymen whose songs "Grate on their scrannel pipes of wretched straw." (Read that line and one of Tennyson's aloud and see which requires lips, teeth, and tongue to do more work.) But note that although Milton's line is harsh in sound, the line (when we meet it in his poem) is pleasing because it is artful. In a famous passage from his *Essay on Criticism*, Pope has illustrated both euphony and cacophony. (Given here as Pope printed it, the passage relies heavily on italics and capital letters, for particular emphasis. If you will read these lines aloud, dwelling a little longer or harder on the words italicized, you will find that Pope has given you very good directions for a meaningful reading.)

Alexander Pope (1688–1744)*

TRUE EASE IN WRITING COMES FROM ART, NOT CHANCE 1711

True Ease in Writing comes from Art, not Chance,
As those move easiest who have learned to dance.
'Tis not enough no Harshness gives Offence,

The *Sound* must seem an *Echo* to the *Sense.*
Soft is the strain when *Zephyr°* gently blows, the west wind 5
And the *smooth Stream* in *smoother Numbers°* flows; metrical rhythm
But when loud Surges lash the sounding Shore,
The *hoarse, rough Verse* should like the *Torrent* roar.
When *Ajax* strives, some Rock's vast Weight to throw,
The Line too *labors,* and the Words move *slow;* 10
Not so, when swift *Camilla* scours the Plain,
Flies o'er th' unbending Corn, and skims along the Main°. expanse (of sea)
Hear how *Timotheus'* varied Lays surprise,
And bid Alternate Passions fall and rise!
While, at each Change, the Son of *Lybian Jove* 15
Now *burns* with Glory, and then *melts* with Love;
Now his *fierce Eyes* with *sparkling Fury* glow;
Now *Sighs* steal out, and *Tears begin to flow:*
Persians and Greeks like *Turns of Nature* found,
And the *World's Victor* stood subdued by *Sound!* 20
The Pow'rs of Music all our Hearts allow;
And what *Timotheus* was, is *Dryden* now.

TRUE EASE IN WRITING COMES FROM ART, NOT CHANCE (*An Essay on Criticism,* lines 362–383). 9 *Ajax:* Greek hero, almost a superman, who in Homer's account of the siege of Troy hurls an enormous rock that momentarily flattens Hector, the Trojan prince (*Iliad* VII, 268–272). 11 *Camilla:* a kind of Amazon or warrior woman of the Volcians, whose speed and lightness of step are praised by the Roman poet Virgil: "She could have skimmed across an unmown grainfield / Without so much as bruising one tender blade; / She could have sped across an ocean's surge / Without so much as wetting her quicksilver soles" (*Aeneid* VII, 808–811). 13 *Timotheus:* favorite musician of Alexander the Great. In "Alexander's Feast, or The Power of Music," John Dryden imagines him: "Timotheus, placed on high / Amid the tuneful choir, / With flying fingers touched the lyre: / The trembling notes ascend the sky, / And heavenly joys inspire." 15 *Lybian Jove:* name for Alexander. A Libyan oracle had declared the king to be the son of the god Zeus Ammon.

Notice the pleasing effect of all the *s* sounds in the lines about the west wind and the stream, and in another meaningful place, the effect of the consonants in *Ajax strives,* a phrase that makes our lips work almost as hard as Ajax throwing the rock.

Is sound identical with meaning in lines such as these? Not quite. In the passage from Tennyson, for instance, the cooing of doves is not *exactly* a moan. As John Crowe Ransom pointed out, the sound would be almost the same but the meaning entirely different in "The murdering of innumerable beeves." While it is true that the consonant sound *sl-* will often begin a word that conveys ideas of wetness and smoothness—*slick, slimy, slippery, slush*—we are so used to hearing it in words that convey nothing of the kind—*slave, slow, sledgehammer*—that it is doubtful whether, all by itself, the sound communicates anything definite. The most beautiful phrase in the English language, according to Dorothy Parker, is *cellar door.* Another wit once nominated, as our most euphonious word, not *sunrise* or *silvery* but *syphilis.*

Relating sound more closely to meaning, the device called **onomatopoeia** is an attempt to represent a thing or action by a word that imitates the sound associated with it: *zoom, whiz, crash, bang, ding-dong, pitter-patter, yakety-yak.* Onomatopoeia is often effective in poetry, as in Emily Dickinson's line about the fly with its "uncertain stumbling Buzz," in which the nasal sounds *n, m, ng* and the sibilants *c, s* help make a droning buzz.

Like the Kikuyu tribesmen, others who care for poetry have discovered in the sound of words something of the refreshment of cool rain. Dylan Thomas, telling how he began to write poetry, said that from early childhood words were to him "as the notes of bells, the sounds of musical instruments, the noises of wind, sea, and rain, the rattle of milkcarts, the clopping of hooves on cobbles, the fingering of branches on the window pane, might be to someone, deaf from birth, who has miraculously found his hearing."[2] For readers, too, the sound of words can have a magical spell, most powerful when it points to meaning. James Weldon Johnson in *God's Trombones* has told of an old-time preacher who began his sermon, "Brothers and sisters, this morning I intend to explain the un-explainable—find out the indefinable—ponder over the imponderable—and un-screw the inscrutable!" The repetition of sound in *unscrew* and *inscrutable* has ap-peal, but the magic of the words is all the greater if they lead us to imagine the mystery of all Creation as an enormous screw that the preacher's mind, like a screw-driver, will loosen. Though the sound of a word or the meaning of a word may have value all by itself, both become more memorable when taken together.

William Butler Yeats (1865–1939)*

WHO GOES WITH FERGUS?   1892

Who will go drive with Fergus now,
And pierce the deep wood's woven shade,
And dance upon the level shore?
Young man, lift up your russet brow,
And lift your tender eyelids, maid,   5
And brood on hopes and fear no more.

And no more turn aside and brood
Upon love's bitter mystery;
For Fergus rules the brazen cars°,   *chariots*
And rules the shadows of the wood,   10
And the white breast of the dim sea
And all dishevelled wandering stars.

WHO GOES WITH FERGUS? *Fergus:* Irish king who gave up his throne to be a wandering poet.

[2]"Notes on the Art of Poetry," *Modern Poetics*, ed. James Scully (New York: McGraw-Hill, 1965).

Questions

1. In what lines do you find euphony?
2. In what line do you find cacophony?
3. How do the sounds of these lines stress what is said in them?

Exercise: *Listening to Meaning*

Read aloud the following brief poems. In the sounds of which particular words are meanings well captured? In which of the poems below do you find onomatopoeia?

John Updike (b. 1932)*

Recital   1963

> ROGER BOBO GIVES
> RECITAL ON TUBA
> — Headline in the Times

Eskimos in Manitoba,
    Barracuda off Aruba,
Cock an ear when Roger Bobo
    Starts to solo on the tuba.

Men of every station—Pooh-Bah,   5
    Nabob, bozo, toff, and hobo—
Cry in unison, "Indubi-
    Tably, there is simply nobo-

Dy who oompahs on the tubo,
Solo, quite like Roger Bubo!"   10

Frances Cornford (1886–1960)

The Watch   1923

I wakened on my hot, hard bed,
Upon the pillow lay my head;
Beneath the pillow I could hear
My little watch was ticking clear.
I thought the throbbing of it went   5
Like my continual discontent.
I thought it said in every tick:
I am so sick, so sick, so sick.
O death, come quick, come quick, come quick,
Come quick, come quick, come quick, come quick!   10

William Wordsworth (1770–1850)*
A Slumber Did My Spirit Seal   1800

A slumber did my spirit seal;
  I had no human fears—
She seemed a thing that could not feel
  The touch of earthly years

No motion has she now, no force;   5
  She neither hears nor sees;
Rolled round in earth's diurnal course,
  With rocks, and stones, and trees.

Emanuel di Pasquale (b. 1943)
Rain   1971

Like a drummer's brush,
the rain hushes the surface of tin porches.

Aphra Behn (1640?–1689)
When maidens are young   1687

When maidens are young, and in their spring,
Of pleasure, of pleasure let 'em take their full swing,
  Full swing, full swing,
And love, and dance, and play, and sing,
For Silvia, believe it, when youth is done,   5
There's nought but hum-drum, hum-drum, hum-drum,
There's nought but hum-drum, hum-drum, hum-drum.

ALLITERATION AND ASSONANCE

Listening to a symphony in which themes are repeated throughout each movement, we enjoy both their recurrence and their variation. We take similar pleasure in the repetition of a phrase or a single chord. Something like this pleasure
is afforded us frequently in poetry.

Analogies between poetry and wordless music, it is true, tend to break down
when carried far, since poetry—to mention a single difference—has denotation.
But like musical compositions, poems have patterns of sounds. Among such patterns long popular in English poetry is **alliteration,** which has been defined as a
succession of similar sounds. Alliteration occurs in the repetition of the same
consonant sound at the beginning of successive words—"round and round the

rugged rocks the ragged rascal ran"—or inside the words, as in Milton's description of the gates of Hell:

> On a sudden open fly
> With impetuous recoil and jarring sound
> The infernal doors, and on their hinges grate
> Harsh thunder, that the lowest bottom shook
> Of Erebus.

The former kind is called **initial alliteration,** the latter **internal alliteration** or **hidden alliteration.** We recognize alliteration by sound, not by spelling: *know* and *nail* alliterate, *know* and *key* do not. In a line by E. E. Cummings, "colossal hoax of clocks and calendars," the sound of *x* within *hoax* alliterates with the *cks* in *clocks.* Incidentally, the letter *r* does not *always* lend itself to cacophony: elsewhere in *Paradise Lost* Milton said that

> Heaven opened wide
> Her ever-during gates, harmonious sound
> On golden hinges moving . . .

By itself, a letter-sound has no particular meaning. This is a truth forgotten by people who would attribute the effectiveness of Milton's lines on the Heavenly Gates to, say, "the mellow *o's* and liquid *l* of *harmonious* and *golden.*" Mellow *o's* and liquid *l's* occur also in the phrase *moldy cold oatmeal,* which may have a quite different effect. Meaning depends on larger units of language than letters of the alphabet.

Poetry formerly contained more alliteration than it usually contains today. In Old English verse, each line was held together by alliteration, a basic pattern still evident in the fourteenth century, as in the following description of the world as a "fair field" in *Piers Plowman:*

> A *f*eir *f*eld *f*ul of *f*olk *f*ond I ther bi-twene,
> Of alle *m*aner of *m*en, the *m*ene and the riche . . .

Most poets nowadays save alliteration for special occasions. They may use it to give emphasis, as Edward Lear does: "Far and few, far and few, / Are the lands where the Jumblies live." With its aid they can point out the relationship between two things placed side by side, as in Pope's line on things of little worth: "The courtier's promises, and sick man's prayers." Alliteration, too, can be a powerful aid to memory. It is hard to forget such tongue twisters as "Peter Piper picked a peck of pickled peppers," or common expressions like "green as grass," "tried and true," and "from stem to stern." In fact, because alliteration directs our attention to something, it had best be used neither thoughtlessly nor merely for decoration, lest it call attention to emptiness. A case in point may be a line by Philip James Bailey, a reaction to a lady's weeping: "I saw, but spared to speak." If the poet chose the word *spared* for any meaningful reason other than that it alliterates with *speak,* the reason is not clear.

As we have seen, to repeat the sound of a consonant is to produce alliteration, but to repeat the sound of a *vowel* is to produce **assonance.** Like alliteration, assonance may occur either initially—"all the *awful auguries*"[3]—or internally—Edmund Spenser's "Her goodly *eyes* like sapphires shining bright, / Her forehead *ivory white* . . ." and it can help make common phrases unforgettable: "eager beaver," "holy smoke." Like alliteration, it slows the reader down and focuses attention.

A. E. Housman (1859–1936)*
EIGHT O'CLOCK   1922

He stood, and heard the steeple
  Sprinkle the quarters on the morning town.
One, two, three, four, to market-place and people
  It tossed them down.

Strapped, noosed, nighing his hour,   5
  He stood and counted them and cursed his luck;
And then the clock collected in the tower
  Its strength, and struck.

QUESTIONS

1. Why does the protagonist in this brief drama curse his luck? What is his situation?
2. For so short a poem, "Eight O'Clock" carries a great weight of alliteration. What patterns of initial alliteration do you find? What patterns of internal alliteration? What effect is created by all this heavy emphasis?

Robert Herrick (1591–1674)*
UPON JULIA'S VOICE   1648

So smooth, so sweet, so silv'ry is thy voice,
As, could they hear, the damned would make no noise,
But listen to thee (walking in thy chamber)
Melting melodious words, to lutes of amber.

UPON JULIA'S VOICE. 4 *amber:* either the fossilized resin from which pipestems are sometimes made today, and which might have inlaid the body of a lute; or an alloy of four parts silver and one part gold.

[3]Some prefer to call the repetition of an initial vowel-sound by the name of alliteration: "apt alliteration's artful aid."

1. Is Julia speaking or singing? How do we know for sure?
2. In what moments in this brief poem does the sound of words especially help convey meaning?
3. Does Herrick's reference to the *damned* (presumably howling from Hell's torments) seem out of place?

Janet Lewis   (b. 1899)

GIRL HELP   1927

Mild and slow and young,
She moves about the room,
And stirs the summer dust
With her wide broom.

In the warm, lofted air,   5
Soft lips together pressed,
Soft wispy hair,
She stops to rest,

And stops to breathe,
Amid the summer hum,   10
The great white lilac bloom
Scented with days to come.

QUESTIONS

1. What assonance and alliteration do you find in this poem? (Suggestion: It may help to read the poem aloud.)
2. In this particular poem, how are these repetitions (or echoes) of sound valuable?

EXERCISE: *Hearing How Sound Helps*

Which of these translations of the same passage from Petrarch do you think is better poetry? Why? What do assonance and alliteration have to do with your preference?

1. Love that liveth and reigneth in my thought,
   That built his seat within my captive breast,
   Clad in the arms wherein with me he fought,
   Oft in my face he doth his banner rest.
   —Henry Howard, Earl of Surrey (1517?–1547)

2. The long love that in my thought doth harbor,
   And in mine heart doth keep his residence,
   Into my face presseth with bold pretense
   And therein campeth, spreading his banner.
   —Sir Thomas Wyatt (1503?–1542)

Try reading aloud as rapidly as possible the following poem by Tennyson. From the difficulties you encounter, you may be able to sense the slowing effect of assonance. Then read the poem aloud a second time, with consideration.

Alfred, Lord Tennyson   (1809–1892)*

THE SPLENDOR FALLS ON CASTLE WALLS   1850

The splendor falls on castle walls
  And snowy summits old in story;
The long light shakes across the lakes,
  And the wild cataract leaps in glory.
Blow, bugle, blow, set the wild echoes flying,   5
Blow, bugle; answer, echoes, dying, dying, dying.

O hark, O hear! how thin and clear,
  And thinner, clearer, farther going!
O sweet and far from cliff and scar°   *jutting rock*
  The horns of Elfland faintly blowing!   10
Blow, let us hear the purple glens replying:
Blow, bugle; answer, echoes, dying, dying, dying.

O love, they die in yon rich sky,
  They faint on hill or field or river;
Our echoes roll from soul to soul,   15
  And grow for ever and for ever.
Blow, bugle, blow, set the wild echoes flying,
And answer, echoes, answer, dying, dying, dying.

RIME

Isak Dinesen's tribesmen, to whom rime was a new phenomenon, recognized at once that rimed language is special language. So do we, for, although much English poetry is unrimed, rime is one means to set poetry apart from ordinary conversation and bring it closer to music. A **rime** (or rhyme), defined most narrowly, occurs when two or more words or phrases contain an identical or similar vowel-sound, usually accented, and the consonant-sounds (if any) that follow the vowel-sound are identical: *hay* and *sleigh, prairie schooner* and *piano tuner*.[4] From these examples it will be seen that rime depends not on spelling but on sound.

---

[4]Some definitions of *rime* would apply the term to the repetition of any identical or similar sound, not only a vowel-sound. In this sense, assonance is a kind of rime; so is alliteration (called **initial rime**).

Excellent rimes surprise. It is all very well that a reader may anticipate which vowel-sound is coming next, for patterns of rime give pleasure by satisfying expectations; but riming becomes dull clunking if, at the end of each line, the reader can predict the word that will end the next. Hearing many a jukebox song for the first time, a listener can do so: *charms* lead to *arms*, *skies above* to *love*. As Alexander Pope observes of the habits of dull rimesters,

> Where'er you find "the cooling western breeze,"
> In the next line it "whispers through the trees";
> If crystal streams "with pleasing murmurs creep,"
> The reader's threatened (not in vain) with "sleep" . . .

But who—given the opening line of this comic poem—could predict the lines that follow?

William Cole (b. 1919)

ON MY BOAT ON LAKE CAYUGA   1985

On my boat on Lake Cayuga
I have a horn that goes "Ay-oogah!"
I'm not the modern kind of creep
Who has a horn that goes "beep beep."

Robert Herrick, in a more subtle poem, made good use of rime to indicate a startling contrast:

> Then while time serves, and we are but decaying,
> Come, my Corinna, come, let's go a-Maying.

Though good rimes seem fresh, not all will startle, and probably few will call to mind things so unlike as *May* and *decay*, *Cayuga* and *Ay-oogah*. Some masters of rime often link words that, taken out of text, might seem common and unevocative. Here are the opening lines of Rachel Hadas's poem, "Three Silences," which describe an infant feeding at a mother's breast:

> Of all the times when not to speak is best,
> mother's and infant's is the easiest,
> the milky mouth still warm against her breast.

Hadas's rime words are not especially memorable in themselves, and yet these lines are—at least in part because they rime so well. The quiet echo of sound at the end of each line reinforces the intimate tone of the mother's moment with her child. Poetic invention may be driven home without rime, but it is rime sometimes that rings the doorbell. Admittedly, some rimes wear thin from too much use. More difficult to use freshly than before the establishment of Tin Pan Alley, rimes such as *moon*, *June*, *croon* seem leaden and to ring true would need an extremely powerful context. *Death* and *breath* are a rime that poets have used with wearisome frequency; another is *birth, earth, mirth*. And yet we cannot exclude these from the diction of poetry, for they might be the very words a poet would need in order to say something new and original. The following brief poem seems fresher than its rimes (if taken out of context) would lead us to expect.

William Blake   (1757–1827)*

THE ANGEL THAT PRESIDED O'ER   (1808–1811)
MY BIRTH

The Angel that presided o'er my birth
Said, "Little creature, formed of Joy and Mirth,
Go love without the help of any thing on earth."

What matters to rime is freshness—not of a word but of the poet's way of seeing.

Good poets, said John Dryden, learn to make their rime "so properly a part of the verse, that it should never mislead the sense, but itself be led and governed by it." The comment may remind us that skillful rime—unlike poor rime—is never a distracting ornament. Like other patterns of sound, rime can help a poet to group ideas, emphasize particular words, and weave a poem together. It can start reverberations between words and can point to connections of meaning.

To have an **exact rime,** sounds following the vowel sound have to be the same: *red* and *bread, wealthily* and *stealthily, walk to her* and *talk to her.* If final consonant sounds are the same but the vowel sounds are different, the result is **slant rime,** also called **near rime, off rime,** or **imperfect rime:** *sun* riming with *bone, moon, rain, green, gone, thin.* By not satisfying the reader's expectation of an exact chime, but instead giving a clunk, a slant rime can help a poet say some things in a particular way. It works especially well for disappointed letdowns, negations, and denials, as in Blake's couplet:

He who the ox to wrath has moved
Shall never be by woman loved.

Many poets have admired the unexpected and arresting effects of slant rime. One of the first poets to explore the possibilities of rhyming consonants in a consistent way was Wilfred Owen, an English soldier in World War I, who wrote his best poems in the thirteen months before being killed in action. Seeking a poetic language strong enough to describe the harsh reality of modern war, Owen experimented with matching consonant sounds in striking ways:

Now men will go content with what we spoiled
Or, discontent, boil bloody, and be spilled,
They will be swift with the swiftness of the tigress.
None will break ranks, though nations trek from progress.
Courage was mine, and I had mystery,

Wisdom was mine, and I had mastery:
To miss the march of this retreating world
Into vain citadels that are not walled.

Consonance, a kind of slant rime, occurs when the rimed words or phrases have the same beginning and ending consonant sounds but a different vowel, as in *chitter* and *chatter*. Owen rimes *spoiled* and *spilled* in this way. Consonance is used in a traditional nonsense poem, "The Cutty Wren": "'O where are you going?' says *Milder* to *Malder*." (W. H. Auden wrote a variation on it that begins, "'O where are you going?' said *reader* to *rider*," thus keeping the consonance.)

End rime, as its name indicates, comes at the ends of lines, **internal rime** within them. Most rime tends to be end rime. Few recent poets have used internal rime so heavily as Wallace Stevens in the beginning of "Bantams in Pine-Woods": "Chieftain Iffucan of Azcan in caftan / Of tan with henna hackles, halt!" (lines also heavy on alliteration). A poet may employ both end rime and internal rime in the same poem, as in Robert Burns's satiric ballad "The Kirk's Alarm":

> Orthodox, Orthodox, wha believe in John Knox,
>   Let me sound an alarm to your conscience:
> There's a heretic blast has been blawn i' the wast°,   *west*
>   "That what is not sense must be nonsense."

Masculine rime is a rime of one-syllable words (*jail, bail*) or (in words of more than one syllable) stressed final syllables: *di-VORCE, re-MORSE,* or *horse, re-MORSE*. **Feminine rime** is a rime of two or more syllables, with stress on a syllable other than the last: *TUR-tle, FER-tile,* or (to take an example from Byron) *in-tel-LECT-u-al, hen-PECKED you all*. Often it lends itself to comic verse, but can occasionally be valuable to serious poems, as in Wordsworth's "Resolution and Independence":

> We poets in our youth begin in gladness,
> But thereof come in the end despondency and madness.

or as in Anne Sexton's seriously witty "Eighteen Days Without You":

> and of course we're not married, we are a pair of scissors
> who come together to cut, without towels saying His. Hers.

Serious poems containing feminine rimes of three syllables have been attempted, notably by Thomas Hood in "The Bridge of Sighs":

> Take her up tenderly,
> Lift her with care;
> Fashioned so slenderly,
> Young, and so fair!

But the pattern is hard to sustain without lapsing into unintended comedy, as in the same poem:

Still, for all slips of hers,
One of Eve's family—
Wipe those poor lips of hers,
Oozing so clammily.

It works better when comedy is wanted:

Hilaire Belloc   (1870–1953)

THE HIPPOPOTAMUS   1896

I shoot the Hippopotamus
  with bullets made of platinum,
Because if I use leaden ones
  his hide is sure to flatten 'em.

In **eye rime,** spellings look alike but pronunciations differ—*rough* and *dough*,
idea and *flea*, *Venus* and *menus*. Strictly speaking, eye rime is not rime at all.

Rime in American poetry suffered a significant fall from favor in the early
1960s. A new generation of poets took for models the open forms of Whitman,
Pound, and William Carlos Williams. Recently, however, young poets have
begun skillfully using rime again in their work. Often called the **New Formalists,** these poets include Julia Alvarez, Annie Finch, R. S. Gwynn, Rachel
Hadas, Mark Jarman, Paul Lake, Charles Martin, Molly Peacock, Gjertrud
Schnackenberg, and Timothy Steele. Their poems often use rime and meter to
present unusual contemporary subjects, but they also sometimes write poems
that recollect, converse, and argue with the poetry of the past. In this poem from
his sequence, "Unholy Sonnets" (whose title alludes to John Donne's famous
"Holy Sonnets," two of which appear on pages 1040 and 1041), Jarman ponders
the great traditional themes of death and immortality.

Mark Jarman   (b. 1952)

UNHOLY SONNET: AFTER THE PRAYING   1997

After the praying, after the hymn-singing,
After the sermon's trenchant commentary
On the world's ills, which make ours secondary,
After communion, after the hand-wringing,
And after peace descends upon us, bringing   5
Our eyes up to regard the sanctuary
And how the light swords through it, and how, scary
In their sheer numbers, motes of dust ride, clinging—
There is, as doctors say about some pain,
Discomfort knowing that despite your prayers,   10
Your listening and rejoicing, your small part

In this communal stab at coming clean,
There is one stubborn remnant of your cares
Intact. There is still murder in your heart.

COMPARE

"Unholy Sonnet" to John Donne's "Batter my heart, three-personed God" on page 704.

QUESTION

How many sound effects can you find in this short poem?

Still, most American poets don't write in rime; some even consider it exhausted. Such a view may be a reaction against the wearing-thin of rimes by overuse or the mechanical and meaningless application of a rime scheme. Yet anyone who listens to children skipping rope in the street, making up rimes to delight themselves as they go along, may doubt that the pleasures of rime are ended; and certainly the practice of Yeats and Emily Dickinson, to name only two, suggests that the possibilities of slant rime may be nearly infinite. If successfully employed, as it has been at times by a majority of English-speaking poets whose work we care to save, rime runs through its poem like a spine: the creature moves by means of it.

William Butler Yeats   (1865–1939)*

LEDA AND THE SWAN   1924

A sudden blow: the great wings beating still
Above the staggering girl, her thighs caressed
By the dark webs, her nape caught in his bill,
He holds her helpless breast upon his breast.

How can those terrified vague fingers push   5
The feathered glory from her loosening thighs?
And how can body, laid in that white rush,
But feel the strange heart beating where it lies?

A shudder in the loins engenders there
The broken wall, the burning roof and tower   10
And Agamemnon dead.
                          Being so caught up,
So mastered by the brute blood of the air,
Did she put on his knowledge with his power
Before the indifferent beak could let her drop?

QUESTIONS

1. According to Greek mythology, the god Zeus in the form of a swan descended upon
   Leda, a Spartan queen. Among Leda's children were Clytemnestra, Agamemnon's

unfaithful wife who conspired in his murder, and Helen, on whose account the Trojan war was fought. What does a knowledge of these allusions contribute to our understanding of the poem's last two lines?

2. The slant rime *up* / *drop* (lines 11, 14) may seem accidental or inept. Is it? Would this poem have ended nearly so well if Yeats had made an exact rime like *up* / *cup* or like *stop* / *drop?*

Gerard Manley Hopkins (1844–1889)*

GOD'S GRANDEUR (1877)

The world is charged with the grandeur of God.
It will flame out, like shining from shook foil;
It gathers to a greatness, like the ooze of oil
Crushed. Why do men then now not reck his rod?
Generations have trod, have trod, have trod;   5
And all is seared with trade; bleared, smeared with toil;
And wears man's smudge and shares man's smell: the soil
Is bare now, nor can foot feel, being shod.

And for all this, nature is never spent;
There lives the dearest freshness deep down things;   10
And though the last lights off the black West went
Oh, morning, at the brown brink eastward, springs—
Because the Holy Ghost over the bent
World broods with warm breast and with ah! bright wings.

GOD'S GRANDEUR. 1 *charged:* as though with electricity. 3–4 *It gathers . . . Crushed:* The grandeur of God will rise and be manifest, as oil rises and collects from crushed olives or grain. 4 *reck his rod:* heed His law. 10 *deep down things:* Tightly packing the poem, Hopkins omits the preposition *in* or *within* before *things.* 11 *last lights . . . went:* When in 1534 Henry VIII broke ties with the Roman Catholic Church and created the Church of England.

QUESTIONS

1. In a letter Hopkins explained *shook foil* (line 2): "I mean foil in its sense of leaf or tinsel. . . . Shaken goldfoil gives off broad glares like sheet lightning and also, and this is true of nothing else, owing to its zigzag dints and creasings and network of small many cornered facets, a sort of fork lightning too." What do you think he meant by the phrase *ooze of oil* (line 3)? Would you call this phrase an example of alliteration?

2. What instances of internal rime does the poem contain? How would you describe their effects?

3. Point out some of the poet's uses of alliteration and assonance. Do you believe that Hopkins perhaps goes too far in his heavy use of devices of sound, or would you defend his practice?

4. Why do you suppose Hopkins, in the last two lines, says *over the bent* / *World* instead of (as we might expect) *bent over the world?* How can the world be bent? Can you make any sense out of this wording, or is Hopkins just trying to get his rime scheme to work out?

Fred Chappell (b. 1936)

NARCISSUS AND ECHO
1985

Shall the water not remember   *Ember*
my hand's slow gesture, tracing above   *of*
its mirror my half-imaginary   *airy*
portrait? My only belonging   *longing;*
is my beauty, which I take   *ache*   5
away and then return, as love   *of*
teasing playfully the one being   *unbeing.*
whose gratitude I treasure   *Is your*
moves me. I live apart   *heart*
from myself, yet cannot   *not*   10
live apart. In the water's tone,   *stone?*
that brilliant silence, a flower   *Hour,*
whispers my name with such slight   *light:*
moment, it seems filament of air,   *fare*
the world become cloudswell.   *well.*   15

NARCISSUS AND ECHO. This poem is an example of **Echo Verse**, a form (which dates back to late classical Greek poetry) in which the final syllables of the lines are repeated back as a reply or commentary, often a punning one. *Narcissus:* a beautiful young man, in Greek mythology, who fell in love with his own reflection in the water of a well. He gradually pined away because he could not reach his love; upon dying, he changed into the flower that bears his name. *Echo:* a nymph who, according to Roman tradition, loved Narcissus. When her love was not returned, she pined away until only her voice was left.

QUESTIONS

1. This poem is a dialogue. What is the relation between the two voices? Does the first voice hear the second?
2. How does the meaning of the poem change if we read the speech of each voice separately?
3. Is the echo technique used in this poem a gimmick? Or does it allow the poet to express something he might not be able to in any other way?

Robert Frost   (1874–1963)*

DESERT PLACES
1936

Snow falling and night falling fast, oh, fast
In a field I looked into going past,
And the ground almost covered smooth in snow,
But a few weeds and stubble showing last.

The woods around it have it—it is theirs.   5
All animals are smothered in their lairs,
I am too absent-spirited to count;
The loneliness includes me unawares.

And lonely as it is, that loneliness
Will be more lonely ere it will be less—   10
A blanker whiteness of benighted snow
With no expression, nothing to express.

They cannot scare me with their empty spaces
Between stars—on stars where no human race is.
I have it in me so much nearer home   15
To scare myself with my own desert places.

QUESTIONS

1. What are these desert places that the speaker finds in himself? (More than one theory is possible. What is yours?)
2. Notice how many times, within the short space of lines 8–10, Frost says *lonely* (or *loneliness*). What other words in the poem contain similar sounds that reinforce these words?
3. In the closing stanza, the feminine rimes *spaces*, *race is*, and *places* might well occur in light or comic verse. Does "Desert Places" leave you laughing? If not, what does it make you feel?

READING AND HEARING POEMS ALOUD

Thomas Moore's "The light that lies in women's eyes"—a line rich in internal rime, alliteration, and assonance—is harder to forget than "The light burning in the gaze of a woman." Effective on the page, Moore's line becomes even more striking when heard aloud. Practice reading poetry aloud—there is no better way to understand a poem than to effectively read it aloud. Developing skill at reading poems aloud will not only deepen your understanding of literature, it will also improve your ability to speak in public.

Before trying to read a poem aloud to other people, understand its meaning as thoroughly as possible. If you know what the poet is saying and the poet's attitude toward it, you will be able to find an appropriate tone of voice and to give each part of the poem a proper emphasis.

Except in the most informal situations and in some class exercises, read a poem to yourself before trying it on an audience. No actor goes before the footlights without first having studied the script, and the language of poems usually demands even more consideration than the language of most contemporary plays. Prepare your reading in advance. Check pronunciations you are not sure of. Underline things to be emphasized.

Read more slowly than you would read aloud from a newspaper. Keep in mind that you are saying something to somebody. Don't race through the poem as if you are eager to get it over with.

Don't lapse into singsong. A poem may have a definite swing, but swing should never be exaggerated at the cost of sense. If you understand what the poem is saying and utter the poem as if you do, the temptation to fall into such a mechanical intonation should not occur. Observe the punctuation, making slight pauses for commas, longer pauses for full stops (periods, question marks, exclamation points).

If the poem is rimed, don't raise your voice and make the rimes stand out unnaturally. They should receive no more volume than other words in the poem, though a faint pause at the end of each line will call the listener's attention to them. This advice is contrary to a school that holds that, if a line does not end in any punctuation, one should not pause but run it together with the line following. The trouble is that, from such a reading, a listener may not be able to identify the rimes; besides, the line, that valuable unit of rhythm, is destroyed.

In some older poems rimes that look like slant rimes may have been exact rimes in their day:

Still so perverse and opposite,
As if they worshiped God for spite.
        —Samuel Butler, *Hudibras* (1663)

Soft yielding minds to water glide away,
And sip, with nymphs, their elemental tea.
        —Alexander Pope, "The Rape of the Lock" (1714)

Tyger! Tyger! burning bright
In the forests of the night,
What immortal hand or eye
Could frame thy fearful symmetry?
        —William Blake, "The Tyger" (1794)

You may wish to establish a consistent policy toward such shifting usage: is it worthwhile to distort current pronunciation for the sake of the rime?

Listening to a poem, especially if it is unfamiliar, calls for concentration. Merciful people seldom read poetry uninterruptedly to anyone for more than a few minutes at a time. Robert Frost, always kind to his audiences, used to intersperse poems with many silences and seemingly casual remarks—shrewdly giving his hearers a chance to rest from their labors and giving his poems a chance to settle in.

If, in first listening to a poem, you don't take in all its meaning, don't be discouraged. With more practice in listening, your attention span and your ability to understand poems read aloud will increase. Incidentally, following the text of poems in a book while hearing them read aloud may increase your comprehension, but it may not necessarily help you to *listen*. At least some of the time, close your book and let your ears make the poems welcome. That way, their sounds may better work for you.

Hearing recordings of poets reading their work can help both your ability to read aloud and your ability to listen. Not all poets read their poems well, but there is much to be relished in both the highly dramatic reading style of a Dylan Thomas and the quiet underplay of a Robert Frost. You need feel no obligation, of course, to imitate the poet's reading of a poem. You have to feel about the poem in your own way, in order to read it with conviction and naturalness.

Even if you don't have an audience, the act of speaking poetry can have its own rewards. Perhaps that is what Yvor Winters meant when he said that, even though poetry was written for "the mind's ear" as well as the physical ear, "yet the mind's ear can be trained only by way of the other, and the matter, practically considered, comes inescapably back to the reading of poetry aloud."[5]

EXERCISE: *Reading for Sound and Meaning*

Read these brief poems aloud. What devices of sound do you find in each of them? Try to explain what sound contributes to the total effect of the poem and how it reinforces what the poet is saying.

Michael Stillman   (b. 1940)
IN MEMORIAM JOHN COLTRANE   1972

Listen to the coal
rolling, rolling through the cold
    steady rain, wheel on

    wheel, listen to the
turning of the wheels this night   5
    black as coal dust, steel

    on steel, listen to
these cars carry coal, listen
    to the coal train roll.

IN MEMORIAM JOHN COLTRANE. John Coltrane (1926–1967) was a saxophonist whose originality, passion, and technical wizardry have had a deep influence on the history of modern jazz.

William Shakespeare   (1564–1616)*
FULL FATHOM FIVE   (ABOUT 1611)
THY FATHER LIES

Full fathom five thy father lies;
    Of his bones are coral made;
Those are pearls that were his eyes:
    Nothing of him that doth fade,

[5]"The Audible Reading of Poetry" (1951), reprinted in *The Function of Criticism* (Denver, Alan Swallow, 1957) 81.

But doth suffer a sea change   5
Into something rich and strange.
Sea nymphs hourly ring his knell:
  Ding-dong.
Hark! now I hear them—*Ding-dong, bell.*

FULL FATHOM FIVE THY FATHER LIES. The spirit Ariel sings this song in *The Tempest* to Ferdinand, prince of Naples, who mistakenly thinks his father is drowned.

A. E. Housman   (1859–1936)*

WITH RUE MY HEART IS LADEN   1896

With rue my heart is laden
  For golden friends I had,
For many a rose-lipt maiden
  And many a lightfoot lad.

By brooks too broad for leaping   5
  The lightfoot boys are laid;
The rose-lipt girls are sleeping
  In fields where roses fade.

T. S. Eliot   (1888–1965)*

VIRGINIA   1934

Red river, red river,
Slow flow heat is silence
No will is still as a river
Still. Will heat move
Only through the mocking-bird   5
Heard once? Still hills
Wait. Gates wait. Purple trees,
White trees, wait, wait,
Delay, decay. Living, living,
Never moving. Ever moving   10
Iron thoughts came with me
And go with me:
Red river, river, river.

VIRGINIA. This poem is one of a series entitled "Landscapes."

T.S. Eliot

T. S. Eliot on Writing   THE MUSIC OF POETRY   1942

I would remind you, first, that the music of poetry is not something which exists apart from the meaning. Otherwise, we could have poetry of great musical beauty which made no sense, and I have never come across such poetry. The apparent exceptions only show a difference of degree: there are poems in which we are moved by the music and take the sense for granted, just as there are poems in which we attend to the sense and are moved by the music without noticing it. Take an apparently extreme example—the nonsense verse of Edward Lear. His non-sense is not vacuity of sense: it is a parody of sense, and that is the sense of it. *The Fumblies* is a poem of adventure, and of nostalgia for the romance of foreign voyage and exploration; *The Yongy-Bongy Bo* and *The Dong with a Luminous Nose* are poems of unrequited passion—"blues" in fact. We enjoy the music, which is of a high order, and we enjoy the feeling of irresponsibility towards the sense. Or take a poem of another type, the *Blue Closet* of William Morris. It is a delightful poem, though I cannot explain what it means and I doubt whether the author could have explained it. It has an effect somewhat like that of a rune or charm, but runes and charms are very practical formulae designed to produce definite results, such as getting a cow out of a bog. But its obvious intention (and I think the author succeeds) is to produce the effect of a dream. It is not necessary, in order to enjoy the poem, to know what the dream means; but human beings have an unshakeable belief that dreams mean something: they used to believe—and many still believe—that dreams disclose the secrets of the future; the orthodox modern faith is that they reveal the secrets—or at least the more horrid secrets—of the past.

· · · ·

So, while poetry attempts to convey something beyond what can be conveyed in prose rhythms, it remains, all the same, one person talking to another; and this is just as true if you sing it, for singing is another way of talking. The immediacy of poetry to conversation is not a matter on which we can lay down exact laws. Every revolution in poetry is apt to be, and sometimes to announce itself to be a return to common speech. . . .

It would be a mistake, however, to assume that all poetry ought to be melodious, or that melody is more than one of the components of the music of words. Some poetry is meant to be sung; most poetry, in modern times, is meant to be spoken—and there are many other things to be spoken of besides the murmur of innumerable bees or the moan of doves in immemorial elms. Dissonance, even cacophony, has its place: just as, in a poem of any length, there must be transitions between passages of greater and less intensity, to give a rhythm of fluctuating emotion essential to the musical structure of the whole; and the passages of less intensity will be, in relation to the level on which the total poem operates, prosaic—so that, in the sense implied by that context, it may be said that no poet can write a poem of amplitude unless he is a master of the prosaic.

"The Music of Poetry"

◄▪▪◘ WRITING CRITICALLY ▪◘►

Is it Possible to Write About Sound?

Sound represents an essential aspect of most poems, but it can be an elusive element to isolate for analysis. Even professional critics often disagree about the sonic effects of particular poems.

The easiest way to write about the sound of a poem is usually to focus your discussion. Rather than trying to explain every possible auditory element a poem possesses, concentrate on a single, clearly defined aspect that strikes you as especially noteworthy. For example, you might demonstrate how elements of sound in a poem emphasize its literal meaning. Don't look for hidden meanings. Simply try to understand how sound helps communicate the poem's main theme. Here you might examine how certain features (e.g. rime, rhythm, meter, alliteration, etc.) add force to the literal meaning of each line. Or, for ironic poems, you might look at how those same elements undercut and change the surface meaning of the poem.

A good way to begin this sort of writing assignment is to make a list of the main auditory elements you find in the poem. Does it contain rime, meter, alliteration, assonance, euphony, cacophony, repetition, or onomatopoeia? Note each striking instance of the relevant elements. (Remember that in such detailed analysis, it often helps to chose a short poem. If you want to discuss a longer work, focus on a short passage from it.) See if you can find a stylistic pattern in the items you list. Does this poet favor alliteration or repetition? (Mark Jarman's "Unholy Sonnet" on page 820, for instance, uses repetition as a key element.) Let your data build up before you force any conclusions on the poem. As your list grows, ideas will probably occur to you that were not apparent earlier.

Writing Assignment

In a short essay, examine how one or two elements of sound strengthen the literal meaning of a short poem. Review the conventional terms for elements of sound found in this chapter (alliteration, assonance, slant rime, euphony, and so on) to make sure you are describing correctly the elements you discuss. Support your argument with specific examples from the poem. Possible topics include "Rime and Repetition in Fred Chappell's 'Echo and Narcissus,'" "Alliteration in Shakespeare's 'Full Fathom Five,'" and "Assonance and Repetition in Tennyson's 'The Splendor Falls on Castle Walls.'"

Further Suggestions for Writing

1. Write about a personal experience with reading poems aloud.
2. Explain why contemporary poets are right (or wrong) to junk rime.
3. Consider the verbal music in W. H. Auden's "As I Walked Out One Evening" (or another selection from "Poems for Further Reading"). Analyze the poem for language with ear-appeal and show how the poem's sound is of a piece with its meaning.

20 *Rhythm*

STRESSES AND PAUSES

Rhythms affect us powerfully. We are lulled by a hammock's sway, awakened by an alarm clock's repeated yammer. Long after we come home from a beach, the rising and falling of waves and tides continue in memory. How powerfully the rhythms of poetry also move us may be felt in folk songs of railroad workers and chain gangs whose words were chanted in time to the lifting and dropping of a sledgehammer, and in verse that marching soldiers shout, putting a stress on every word that coincides with a footfall:

> Your LEFT! TWO! THREE! FOUR!
> Your LEFT! TWO! THREE! FOUR!
> You LEFT your WIFE and TWEN-ty-one KIDS
> And you LEFT! TWO! THREE! FOUR!
> You'll NEV-er get HOME to-NIGHT!

A rhythm is produced by a series of recurrences: the returns and departures of the seasons, the repetitions of an engine's stroke, the beats of the heart. A rhythm may be produced by the recurrence of a sound (the throb of a drum, a telephone's busy-signal), but rhythm and sound are not identical. A totally deaf person at a parade can sense rhythm from the motions of the marchers' arms and feet, from the shaking of the pavement as they tramp. Rhythms inhere in the motions of the moon and stars, even though when they move we hear no sound.

In poetry, several kinds of recurrent *sound* are possible, including (as we saw in the last chapter) rime, alliteration, and assonance. But most often when we speak of the **rhythm** of a poem we mean the recurrence of stresses and pauses in it. When we hear a poem read aloud, stresses and pauses are, of course, part of its sound. It is possible to be aware of rhythms in poems read silently, too.

A **stress** (or **accent**) is a greater amount of force given to one syllable in speaking than is given to another. We favor a stressed syllable with a little more breath and emphasis, with the result that it comes out slightly louder, higher in pitch, or longer in duration than other syllables. In this manner we place a stress on the first syllable of words such as *eagle, impact, open,* and *statue,* and on the second syllable in *cigar, mystique, precise,* and *until.* Each word in English carries at least one stress, except (usually) for the articles *a, an,* and *the,* and one-syllable prepositions: *at, by, for, from, of, to, with.* Even these, however, take a stress once in a while: "Get WITH it!" "You're not THE Dolly Parton?" One word by itself is seldom long enough for us to notice a rhythm in it. Usually a se-quence of at least a few words is needed for stresses to establish their pattern: a line, a passage, a whole poem. Strong rhythms may be seen in most Mother Goose rimes, to which children have been responding for hundreds of years. This rime is for an adult to chant while jogging a child up and down on a knee:

> Here goes my lord
> A trot, a trot, a trot, a trot!
> Here goes my lady
> A canter, a canter, a canter, a canter!
> Here goes my young master
> Jockey-hitch, jockey-hitch, jockey-hitch, jockey-hitch!
> Here goes my young miss
> An amble, an amble, an amble, an amble!
> The footman lags behind to tipple ale and wine
> And goes gallop, a gallop, a gallop, to make up his time.

More than one rhythm occurs in these lines, as the make-believe horse changes pace. How do these rhythms differ? From one line to the next, the interval be-tween stresses lengthens or grows shorter. In "a TROT a TROT a TROT a TROT," the stress falls on every other syllable. But in the middle of the line "A CAN-ter a CAN-ter a CAN-ter a CAN-ter," the stress falls on every third syl-lable. When stresses recur at fixed intervals as in these lines, the result is called a **meter.** The line "A trot a trot a trot a trot" is in **iambic meter,** a succession of al-ternate unstressed and stressed syllables.[1] Of all rhythms in the English language, this one is most familiar; most of our traditional poetry is written in it and ordi-nary speech tends to resemble it.

Stresses embody meanings. Whenever two or more fall side by side, words gain in emphasis. Consider these hard-hitting lines from John Donne, in which accent marks have been placed, dictionary-fashion, to indicate the stressed sylla-bles:

> Bat'ter my heart, three-per'soned God, for You
> As yet but knock, breathe, shine, and seek to mend.
> That I may rise and stand, o'er throw me, and bend
> Your force to break, blow, burn, and make me new.

Unstressed (or **slack**) **syllables** also can direct our attention to what the poet means. In a line containing few stresses and a great many unstressed syllables,

[1] Another kind of meter is possible, in which the intervals between stresses vary. This is **accentual meter,** not often found in contemporary poetry. It is discussed in the second part of this chapter

there can be an effect not of power and force but of hesitation and uncertainty. Yeats asks in "Among School Children" what young mother, if she could see her baby grown to be an old man, would think him:

A com·pen·sa·tion for the pang of his birth

Or the un·cer·tain·ty of his set·ting forth?

When unstressed syllables recur in pairs, the result is a rhythm that trips and bounces, as in Robert Service's rollicking line:

A bunch of the boys were whoop·ing it up in the Ma·la·mute

sa·loon . . .

or in Poe's lines—also light but probably supposed to be serious:

For the moon nev·er beams with·out bring·ing me dreams

Of the beau·ti·ful An·na·bel Lee.

Apart from the words that convey it, the rhythm of a poem has no meaning. There are no essentially sad rhythms, nor any essentially happy ones. But some rhythms enforce certain meanings better than others do. The bouncing rhythm of Service's line seems fitting for an account of a merry night in a Klondike saloon; but it may be distracting when encountered in Poe's wistful elegy.

The special power of poetry comes from allowing us to hear simultaneously every level of meaning in language—denotation and connotation, image and idea, abstract content and physical sound. Since sound stress is one of the ways that the English language most clearly communicates meaning, any regular rhythmic pattern will affect the poem's effect. Poets learn to use rhythms that reinforce the meaning and the tone of a poem. As film directors know, any movie scene's effect can change dramatically if different background music accompanies the images. Master of the suspense film Alfred Hitchcock, for instance, could fill an ordinary scene with tension or terror just by playing nervous, grating music underneath it. We also often notice the powerful effect rhythm has on meaning when an author goes awry and tries to create a particular mood in a manner that seems to pull us in an opposing direction. In Eliza Cook's "Song of the Sea-Weed," for instance, the poet depicts her grim and ghoulish scene in a bouncy ballad meter that makes the tone unintentionally comic:

Many a lip is gaping for drink,
    And madly calling for rain;
And some hot brains are beginning to think
    Of a messmate's opened vein.

EXERCISE: Get with the Beat

In each of the following passages the author has established a strong rhythm. Describe how the rhythm helps establish the tone and meaning of the poem. How does each poem's beat seem appropriate to the tone and subject?

1. I sprang to the stirrup, and Joris and he;
   I galloped, Dirck galloped, we galloped all three;
   "Good speed," cried the watch as the gatebolts undrew;
   "Speed!" echoed the wall to us galloping through.
   Behind shut the postern, the lights sank to rest,
   And into the midnight we galloped abreast.
                        —Robert Browning, from "How They Brought the Good News
                           From Ghent to Aix"

2. I couldn't be cooler, I come from Missoula,
   And I rope and I chew and I ride.
   But I'm a heroin dealer, and I drive a four-wheeler
   With stereo speakers inside.
   My ol' lady Phoebe's out rippin' off C.B.'s
   From the rigs at the Wagon Wheel Bar,
   Near a Montana truck stop and a shit-outta-luck stop
   For a trucker who's driven too far.
                        —Greg Keeler, from "There Ain't No Such Thing as a Montana
                           Cowboy" (a song lyric)

3. Of all the lives I cannot live,
   I have elected one

   to haunt me till the margins give
   and I am left alone

   One life has sounded in my voice
   and made me like a stone—

   one that the falling leaves can sink
   not over, but upon.
                        —Annie Finch, "Dickinson"

4. Oh newsprint moonprint Marilyn!
   Rub ink from a finger
   to make your beauty mark.
                        —Rachel Eisler, from "Marilyn's Nocturne" (a poem about a
                           newspaper photograph of Marilyn Monroe)

5. The master, the swabber, the boatswain, and I,
   The gunner and his mate
   Loved Moll, Meg, and Marian, and Margery,
   But none of us cared for Kate;
   For she had a tongue with a tang
   Would cry to a sailor "go hang!"—
   She loved not the savor of tar nor of pitch
   Yet a tailor might scratch her where'er she did itch;
   Then to sea, boys, and let her go hang!
                        —William Shakespeare, a song from *The Tempest*

Rhythms in poetry are due not only to stresses but also to pauses. "Every nice ear," observed Alexander Pope (*nice* meaning "finely tuned"), "must, I believe, have observed that in any smooth English verse of ten syllables, there is naturally a pause either at the fourth, fifth, or sixth syllable." Such a light but definite pause within a line is called a **cesura** (or **caesura**), "a cutting." More liberally than Pope, we apply the name to any pause in a line of any length, after any word in the line. In studying a poem, we often indicate a cesura by double lines (||). Usually, a cesura will occur at a mark of punctuation, but there can be a cesura even if no punctuation is present. Sometimes you will find it at the end of a phrase or clause or, as in these lines by William Blake, after an internal rime:

> And priests in black gowns || were walking their rounds
> And binding with briars || my joys and desires.

Lines of ten or twelve syllables (as Pope knew) tend to have just one cesura, though sometimes there are more:

> Cover her face: || mine eyes dazzle: || she died young.

Pauses also tend to recur at more prominent places—namely, after each line. At the end of a verse (from *versus*, "a turning"), the reader's eye, before turning to go on to the next line, makes a pause, however brief. If a line ends in a full pause—usually indicated by some mark of punctuation—we call it **end-stopped**. All the lines in this passage from Christopher Marlowe's *Doctor Faustus* (in which Faustus addresses the apparition of Helen of Troy) are end-stopped:

> Was this the face that launch'd a thousand ships,
> And burnt the topless towers of Ilium?
> Sweet Helen, make me immortal with a kiss.
> Her lips suck forth my soul: see, where it flies!
> Come, Helen, come, give me my soul again.
> Here will I dwell, for heaven is in these lips,
> And all is dross that is not Helena.

A line that does not end in punctuation and that therefore is read with only a slight pause after it is called a **run-on line.** Because a run-on line gives us only part of a phrase, clause, or sentence, we have to read on to the line or lines following, in order to complete a thought. All these lines from Robert Browning's "My Last Duchess" are run-on lines:

> . . . Sir, 'twas not
> Her husband's presence only, called that spot
> Of joy into the Duchess' cheek: perhaps
> Frà Pandolf chanced to say "Her mantle laps
> Over my lady's wrist too much," or "Paint
> Must never hope to reproduce the faint
> Half-flush that dies along her throat." Such stuff
> Was courtesy, she thought . . . [2]

A passage in run-on lines has a rhythm different from that of a passage like Marlowe's in end-stopped lines. When emphatic pauses occur in the quotation from Browning, they fall within a line rather than at the end of one. The passage by Marlowe and that by Browning are in lines of the same meter (iambic) and the

---

[2]The complete poem, "My Last Duchess," appears on page 661.

same length (ten syllables). What makes the big difference in their rhythms is the running on, or lack of it.

To sum up: rhythm is recurrence. In poems, it is made of stresses and pauses. The poet can produce it by doing any of several things: making the intervals between stresses fixed or varied, long or short; indicating pauses (cesuras) within lines; end-stopping lines or running them over; writing in short or long lines. Rhythm in itself cannot convey meaning. And yet if a poet's words have meaning, their rhythm must be one with it.

Gwendolyn Brooks (b. 1917)*

WE REAL COOL   1960

> The Pool Players.
> Seven at the Golden Shovel.

We real cool. We
Left school. We

Lurk late. We
Strike straight. We

Sing sin. We
Thin gin. We   5

Jazz June. We
Die soon.

QUESTION

Describe the rhythms of this poem. By what techniques are they produced?

Alfred, Lord Tennyson   (1809–1892)*

BREAK, BREAK, BREAK   (1834)

Break, break, break,
  On thy cold gray stones, O Sea!
And I would that my tongue could utter
  The thoughts that arise in me.

O well for the fisherman's boy,   5
  That he shouts with his sister at play!
O well for the sailor lad,
  That he sings in his boat on the bay!

And the stately ships go on
  To their haven under the hill;
But O for the touch of a vanish'd hand,   10
  And the sound of a voice that is still!

Break, break, break,
  At the foot of thy crags, O Sea!
But the tender grace of a day that is dead   15
  Will never come back to me.

QUESTIONS

1. Read the first line aloud. What effect does it create at the beginning of the poem?
2. Is there a regular rhythmic pattern in this poem? If so, how would you describe it?
3. The speaker claims that his or her thoughts are impossible to utter. Using evidence from the poem, can you describe the speaker's thoughts and feelings?

Ben Jonson   (1573–1637)*

SLOW, SLOW, FRESH FOUNT, KEEP TIME   1600
WITH MY SALT TEARS

Slow, slow, fresh fount, keep time with my salt tears;
  Yet slower yet, oh faintly, gentle springs;
List to the heavy part the music bears,
  Woe weeps out her division° when she sings.   *a part in a song*
    Droop herbs and flowers,   5
    Fall grief in showers;
    Our beauties are not ours;
      Oh, I could still,
Like melting snow upon some craggy hill,
  Drop, drop, drop, drop,   10
Since nature's pride is now a withered daffodil.

SLOW, SLOW, FRESH FOUNT. The nymph Echo sings this lament over the youth Narcissus in Jonson's play *Cynthia's Revels*. In mythology, Nemesis, goddess of vengeance, to punish Narcissus for loving his own beauty, caused him to pine away and then transformed him into a narcissus (another name for a *daffodil*, line 11).

QUESTIONS

1. Read the first line aloud rapidly. Why is it difficult to do so?
2. Which lines rely most heavily on stressed syllables?
3. In general, how would you describe the rhythm of this poem? How is it appropriate to what is said?

Alexander Pope   (1688–1744)*

ATTICUS   1735

How did they fume, and stamp, and roar, and chafe!
And swear, not Addison himself was safe.
  Peace to all such! but were there one whose fires

True genius kindles, and fair fame inspires;
Blest with each talent, and each art to please,   5
And born to write, converse, and live with ease,
Should such a man, too fond to rule alone,
Bear, like the Turk, no brother near the throne,
View him with scornful, yet with jealous eyes,
And hate for arts that caused himself to rise;   10
Damn with faint praise, assent with civil leer,
And, without sneering, teach the rest to sneer;
Willing to wound, and yet afraid to strike,
Just hint a fault, and hesitate dislike;
Alike reserved to blame, or to commend,   15
A timorous foe, and a suspicious friend;
Dreading e'en fools, by flatterers besieged,
And so obliging, that he ne'er obliged;
Like Cato, give his little Senate laws,
And sit attentive to his own applause: 20
While wits and Templars every sentence raise,
And wonder with a foolish face of praise—
Who but must laugh, if such a man there be?
Who would not weep, if Atticus were he?

ATTICUS. In this selection from "An Epistle to Dr. Arbuthnot," Pope has been referring to dull versifiers and their angry reception of his satiric thrusts at them. With *Peace to all such!* (line 3) he turns
to his celebrated portrait of a rival man of letters, Joseph Addison. 19 *Cato:* Roman senator about
whom Addison had written a tragedy. 21 *Templars:* London lawyers who dabbled in literature.

QUESTIONS

1. In these lines—one of the most famous damnations in English poetry—what positive virtues, in Pope's view, does Addison lack?
2. Which lines are end-stopped? What is the effect of these lines upon the rhythm of
this passage? (Suggestion: Read "Atticus" aloud.)

EXERCISE: *Two Kinds of Rhythm*

The following compositions in verse have lines of similar length, yet they differ greatly in
rhythm. Explain how they differ and why.

Sir Thomas Wyatt   (1503?–1542)*

WITH SERVING STILL   (1528–1536)

With serving still°   *continually*
  This have I won,
For my goodwill
  To be undone;

And for redress
   Of all my pain,
Disdainfulness
   I have again°;   *in return*

                                            5

And for reward
   Of all my smart   10
Lo, thus unheard,
   I must depart!

Wherefore all ye
   That after shall
By fortune be,   15
   As I am, thrall,

Example take
   What I have won,
Thus for her sake
   To be undone!   20

Dorothy Parker   (1893–1967)

RÉSUMÉ   1926

Razors pain you;
Rivers are damp;
Acids stain you;
And drugs cause cramp.
Guns aren't lawful;   5
Nooses give;
Gas smells awful;
You might as well live.

METER

To enjoy the rhythms of a poem, no special knowledge of meter is necessary. All you need do is pay attention to stresses and where they fall, and you will perceive the basic pattern, if there is any. However, there is nothing occult about the study of meter. Most people find they can master its essentials in no more time than it takes to learn a complicated game such as chess. If you take the time, you will then have the pleasure of knowing what is happening in the rhythms of many a fine poem, and pleasurable knowledge may even deepen your insight into poetry. The following discussion, then, will be of interest only to those who care to go deeper into **prosody,** the study of metrical structures in poetry.

    Far from being artificial constructions found only in the minds of poets, meters occur in everyday speech and prose. As the following example will show, they may need only a poet to recognize them. The English satirist Max Beerbohm, after contemplating the title page of his first book, took his pen and added two more lines.

Max Beerbohm (1872–1956)

ON THE IMPRINT OF THE FIRST   (1896)
ENGLISH EDITION OF
THE WORKS OF MAX BEERBOHM

"London: JOHN LANE, *The Bodley Head*
  New York: Charles Scribner's Sons."
This plain announcement, nicely read,
  Iambically runs.

In everyday life, nobody speaks or writes in perfect iambic rhythm, except at moments: "a HAM on RYE and HIT the MUStard HARD!" (As we have seen, iambic rhythm consists of a series of syllables alternately unstressed and stressed.) Poets rarely speak in it for long, either—at least, not with absolute consistency. If you read aloud Max Beerbohm's lines, you'll hear an iambic rhythm, but not an unvarying one. And yet all of us speak with a rising and falling of stress *somewhat like* iambic meter. Perhaps, as the poet and scholar John Thompson has maintained, "The iambic metrical pattern has dominated English verse because it provides the best symbolic model of our language."[3]

To make ourselves aware of a meter, we need only listen to a poem, or sound its words to ourselves. If we care to work out exactly what a poet is doing, we *scan* a line or a poem by indicating the stresses in it. **Scansion,** the art of so doing, is not just a matter of pointing to syllables; it is also a matter of listening to a poem and making sense of it. To scan a poem is one way to indicate how to read it aloud; in order to see where stresses fall, you have to see the places where the poet wishes to put emphasis. That is why, when scanning a poem, you may find yourself suddenly understanding it.

An objection might be raised against scanning: isn't it too simple to pretend that all language (and poetry) can be divided neatly into stressed syllables and unstressed syllables? Indeed it is. As the linguist Otto Jespersen has said, "In reality there are infinite gradations of stress, from the most penetrating scream to the faintest whisper."[4] However, the idea in scanning a poem is not to reproduce the sound of a human voice. For that we would do better to buy a tape recorder. To scan a poem, rather, is to make a diagram of the stresses (and absences of stress) we find in it. Various marks are used in scansion; in this book we use ´ for a stressed syllable and ˘ for an unstressed syllable.

There are four common accentual-syllabic meters in English—iambic, anapestic, trochaic, and dactylic. Each is named for its basic **foot** (usually a unit

---

[3]*The Founding of English Metre* (New York: Columbia UP, 1966) 12.
[4]"Notes on Metre," (1933), reprinted in *The Structure of Verse: Modern Essays on Prosody,* ed. Harvey Gross, 2nd ed. (New York: Echo P, 1978).

of two or three syllables that contains one strong stress) or building block. Here are some examples of each meter.

1. **Iambic**—a line made up primarily of **iambs,** an unstressed syllable followed by a stressed syllable, ˘′. The iambic measure is the most common meter in English poetry. Many writers, such as Robert Frost, feel iambs most easily capture the natural rhythms of our speech.

   But soft, | what light | through yon | der win | dow breaks?
   —*William Shakespeare*

   When I | have fears | that I | may cease | to be
   —*John Keats*

   If we | had world | e·nough | and time
   This coy| ness, la | dy, were | no crime
   —*Andrew Marvell*

   My life | had stood – | a load | ed Gun
   —*Emily Dickinson*

2. **Anapestic**—a line made up primarily of **anapests,** two unstressed syllables followed by a stressed syllable, ˘˘′. Anapestic meter resembles iambic but contains an extra unstressed syllable. Totally anapestic lines often start to gallop, so poets sometimes slow them down by substituting an iambic foot (as Poe does in "Annabel Lee").

   The As·syr | ian came down | like a wolf | on the fold
   And his co | horts were gleam | ing in pur| ple and gold.
   And the sheen | of their spears | was like stars | on the sea
   When the blue | wave rolls night | ly on deep | Gal·i·lee.
   —*Lord Byron*

   Now this | is the Law | of the Jun | gle—as old | and as true |
      as the sky
   And the Wolf| that shall keep | it may pros | per, | but the
      wolf | that shall break | it must die.
   —*Rudyard Kipling*

   It was ma | ny and ma| ny a year | a·go
      In a king | dom by | the sea
   That a maid | en there lived | whom you | may know
      By the name | of An | na·bel Lee.
   —*Edgar Allan Poe*

3. **Trochaic**—a line made up primarily of **trochees,** a stressed syllable followed by an unstressed syllable, ′‿. The trochaic meter is often associated with songs, chants, and magic spells in English. Trochees make a strong, emphatic meter that is often very mnemonic. Shakespeare and Blake used trochaic meter to exploit its magical associations. Notice how Blake drops the unstressed syllable at the end of his lines from "The Tyger." (The location of a missing syllable in a metrical foot is usually marked with a caret sign, ˅.)

> Dou·ble, | dou·ble, | toil and | trou·ble
> Fi·re | burn and | caul·dron | bub·ble.
>
> *—Shakespeare*

> Ty·ger, | ty·ger, | burn·ing | bright
> In the | for·est | of the | night ˅
>
> *—William Blake*

> Go and | catch a | fall·ing | star
>
> *—John Donne*

4. **Dactylic**—a line made up primarily of **dactyls,** one stressed syllable followed by two unstressed syllables, ′‿‿. The dactylic meter is less common in English than in classical languages like Greek or Latin. Used carefully, dactylic meter can sound stately, as in Longfellow's *Evangeline,* but it also easily becomes a prancing, propulsive measure and is often used in comic verse. Poets often drop the unstressed syllables at the end of a dactylic line, the omission usually being noted with a caret sign, ˅.

> This is the | for·est pri | me·val. The | mur·mur·ing | pines and the
> | hem·lock
>
> *—Henry Wadsworth Longfellow*

> Take her up | ten·der·ly
> Lift her with | care
> fash·ioned so | slen·der·ly
> young and so | fair.
>
> *—Thomas Hood*

> Puss·y·cat, | puss·y·cat, | where have you | been?
>
> *—Mother Goose*

Iambic and anapestic meters are called **rising** meters because their movement rises from unstressed syllable (or syllables) to stress; trochaic and dactylic meters are called **falling.** In the twentieth century, the bouncing meters—anapestic and dactylic—have been used more often for comic verse than for serious poetry. Called feet, though they contain no unaccented syllables, are the **monosyllabic foot** ($'$) and the **spondee** ($''$). Meters are not ordinarily made up of them; if one were, it would be like the steady impact of nails being hammered into a board— no pleasure to hear or to dance to. But inserted now and then, they can lend emphasis and variety to a meter, as Yeats well knew when he broke up the pre- dominantly iambic rhythm of "Who Goes with Fergus?" (page 810) with the line,

$$\cup \qquad \cup \quad ' \quad ' \quad \cup \quad \cup \quad ' \quad '$$
And the white breast of the dim sea,

in which occur two spondees. Meters are classified also by line lengths: *trochaic monometer,* for instance, is a line one trochee long, as in this anonymous brief comment on microbes:

Adam
Had 'em.

A frequently heard metrical description is **iambic pentameter:** a line of five iambs, a meter especially familiar because it occurs in all blank verse (such as Shakespeare's plays and Milton's *Paradise Lost*), heroic couplets, and sonnets. The commonly used names for line lengths follow:

monometer	one foot
dimeter	two feet
trimeter	three feet
tetrameter	four feet
pentameter	five feet
hexameter	six feet
heptameter	seven feet
octameter	eight feet

Lines of more than eight feet are possible but are rare. They tend to break up into shorter lengths in the listening ear.

When Yeats chose the spondees *white breast* and *dim sea,* he was doing what poets who write in meter do frequently for variety—using a foot other than the expected one. Often such a substitution will be made at the very beginning of a line, as in the third line of this passage from Christopher Marlowe's *Tragical History of Doctor Faustus:*

$$\cup \quad ' \quad \cup \quad ' \quad \cup \quad ' \quad \cup \quad ' \quad \cup \quad '$$
Was this | the face | that launched | a thou | sand ships
$$\cup \quad ' \quad \cup \quad ' \quad \cup \quad ' \quad \cup \quad ' \quad \cup \quad '$$
And burnt | the top | less tow'rs of Il | i·um?
$$' \quad ' \quad \cup \quad ' \quad \cup \cup \quad ' \quad \cup \quad ' \quad \cup \quad '$$
Sweet Hel | en, make | me im·mor | tal with | a kiss.

How, we might wonder, can that last line be called iambic at all? But it is, just as a waltz that includes an extra step or two, or leaves a few steps out, remains a waltz. In the preceding lines the basic iambic pentameter is established, and though in the third line the regularity is varied from, it does not altogether dis- appear. It continues for a while to run on in the reader's mind, where (if the poet does not stay away from it for too long) the meter will be when the poem comes back to it.

Like a basic dance step, a meter is not to be slavishly adhered to. The fun in reading a metrical poem often comes from watching the poet continually departing from perfect regularity, giving a few heel-kicks to display a bit of joy or ingenuity, then easing back into the basic step again. Because meter is orderly and the rhythms of living speech are unruly, poets can play one against the other, in a sort of counterpoint. Robert Frost, a master at pitting a line of iambs against a very natural-sounding and irregular sentence, declared, "I am never more pleased than when I can get these into strained relation. I like to drag and break the intonation across the meter as waves first comb and then break stumbling on a shingle."[5]

Evidently Frost's skilled effects would be lost to a reader who, scanning a Frost poem or reading it aloud, distorted its rhythms to fit the words exactly to the meter. With rare exceptions, a good poem can be read and scanned the way we would speak its sentences if they were ours. This, for example, is an unreal scansion:

> ˘ ´ ˘ ´ ˘ ´ ˘ ´ ˘ ´
> That's my last Duch·ess paint·ed on the wall.

—because no speaker of English would say that sentence in that way. We are likely to stress *That's* and *last*.

Variety in rhythm is not merely desirable in poetry, it is a necessity, and the poem that fails to depart often enough from absolute regularity is in trouble. If the beat of its words slips into a mechanical pattern, the poem marches robot-like right into its grave. Robert Frost told an audience one time that if when writing a poem he found its rhythm becoming monotonous, he knew that the poem was going wrong and that he himself didn't believe what it was saying.

Although in good poetry we seldom meet a very long passage of absolute metrical regularity, we sometimes find (in a line or so) a monotonous rhythm that is effective. Words fall meaningfully in Macbeth's famous statement of world-weariness: "Tomorrow and tomorrow and tomorrow . . ." and in the opening lines of Thomas Gray's "Elegy":

> ˘ ´ ˘ ´ ˘ ´ ˘ ´ ´
> The cur·few tolls the knell of part·ing day,
> ˘ ´ ˘ ´ ´ ´ ˘ ´ ˘ ´
> The low·ing herd wind slow·ly o'er the lea,
> ˘ ´ ˘ ´ ˘ ´ ˘ ´ ˘ ´
> The plow·man home·ward plods his wear·y way,
> ˘ ´ ˘ ´ ˘ ´ ˘ ˘ ˘ ´
> And leaves the world to dark·ness and to me.[6]

Although certain unstressed syllables in these lines seem to call for more emphasis than others—you might, for instance, care to throw a little more weight on the second syllable of *curfew* in the opening line—we can still say that the lines are notably iambic. Their almost unvarying rhythm seems just right to convey the tolling of a bell and the weary setting down of one foot after the other.

[5]Letter to John Cournos in 1914, in *Selected Letters of Robert Frost*, ed. Lawrance Thompson (New York: Holt, 1964) 128.
[6]The complete poem, "Elegy Written in a Country Churchyard," appears on page 999.

Besides the two rising meters (iambic, anapestic) and the two falling meters (trochaic, dactylic), English poets have another valuable meter. It is **accentual meter,** in which the poet does not write in feet (as in the other meters) but instead counts accents (stresses). The idea is to have the same number of stresses in every line. The poet may place them anywhere in the line and may include practically any number of unstressed syllables, which do not count. In "Christabel," for instance, Coleridge keeps four stresses to a line, though the first line has only eight syllables and the last line has eleven:

> There is not wind e·nough to twirl
> The one red leaf, the last of its clan,
> That dan·ces as of·ten as dance it can,
> Hang·ing so light, and hang·ing so high,
> On the top-most twig that looks up at the sky.

The history of accentual meter is long and honorable. Old English poetry was written in a kind of accentual meter, but its line was more rule-bound than Coleridge's: four stresses arranged two on either side of a cesura, plus alliteration of three of the stressed syllables. In "Junk," Richard Wilbur revives the pattern:

> An axe an·gles || from my neigh·bor's ash·can . . .

Many poets, from the authors of Mother Goose rimes to Gerard Manley Hopkins, have sometimes found accentual meters congenial. Recently, accentual meter has enjoyed huge popularity through rap poetry, which usually employs a four-stress line (see page 790 for further discussion of rap).

It has been charged that the importation of Greek names for meters and of the classical notion of feet was an unsuccessful attempt to make a Parthenon out of English wattles. The charge is open to debate, but at least it is certain that Greek names for feet cannot mean to us what they meant to Aristotle. Greek and Latin poetry is measured not by stressed and unstressed syllables, but by long and short vowel sounds. An iamb in classical verse is one short syllable followed by a long syllable. Such a meter constructed on the principle of vowel length is called a **quantitative meter.** Campion's "Rose-cheeked Laura" was an attempt to demonstrate it in English, but probably we enjoy the rhythm of the poem's well-placed stresses whether or not we notice its vowel sounds.

Thomas Campion   (1567–1620)*

ROSE-CHEEKED LAURA, COME   1602

Rose-cheeked Laura, come,
Sing thou smoothly with thy beauty's
Silent music, either other
        Sweetly gracing.

Lovely forms do flow   5
From concent° divinely framèd;   *harmony*
Heav'n is music, and thy beauty's
    Birth is heavenly.

These dull notes we sing
Discords need for helps to grace them;   10
Only beauty purely loving
    Knows no discord,

But still moves delight,
Like clear springs renewed by flowing,
Ever perfect, ever in them-   15
    Selves eternal.

    Although less popular among poets today than formerly, meter endures.
Major poets from Shakespeare through Yeats have fashioned their work by it, and
if we are to read their poems with full enjoyment, we need to be aware of it. To
enjoy metrical poetry—even to write it—you do not have to slice lines into feet;
you do need to recognize when a meter is present in a line, and when the line departs from it. An argument in favor of meter is that it reminds us of body rhythms
such as breathing, walking, the beating of the heart. In an effective metrical
poem, these rhythms cannot be separated from what the poet is saying—or, in the
words of an old jazz song, "It don't mean a thing if you ain't got that swing." As
critic Paul Fussell has put it: "No element of a poem is more basic—and I mean
physical—in its effect upon the reader than the metrical element, and perhaps no
technical triumphs reveal more readily than the metrical the poet's sympathy
with that universal human nature . . . which exists outside his own."[7]

Walter Savage Landor   (1775–1864)

On Seeing a Hair of Lucretia Borgia   (1825)

Borgia, thou once wert almost too august
And high for adoration; now thou'rt dust.
All that remains of thee these plaits unfold,
Calm hair, meandering in pellucid gold.

Questions

1. Who was Lucretia Borgia and when did she live? Because of her reputation, what
   connotations does her name add to Landor's poem?
2. What does *meander* mean? How can a hair meander?
3. Scan the poem, indicating stressed syllables. What is the basic meter of most of the
   poem? What happens to this meter in the last line? Note especially *meandering in
   pel-*. How many light, unstressed syllables are there in a row? Does rhythm in any
   way reinforce what Landor is saying?

[7]*Poetic Meter and Poetic Form* (New York: Random, 1965) 110.

EXERCISE: *Meaningful Variation*

At what place or places in each of these passages does the poet depart from basic iambic meter? How does each departure help underscore the meaning?

1. Shadwell alone of all my sons is he
   Who stands confirmed in full stupidity.
   The rest to some faint meaning make pretense,
   But Shadwell never deviates into sense.
   —John Dryden, "Mac Flecknoe" (speech of Flecknoe, prince of
   Nonsense, referring to Thomas Shadwell, poet and playwright)

2. A needless Alexandrine ends the song
   That, like a wounded snake, drags its slow length along.
   —Alexander Pope, from *An Essay on Criticism*

3. Roll on, thou deep and dark blue Ocean—roll!
   Ten thousand fleets sweep over thee in vain;
   Man marks the earth with ruin—his control
   Stops with the shore; upon the watery plain
   The wrecks are all thy deed, nor doth remain
   A shadow of man's ravage, save his own,
   When, for a moment, like a drop of rain,
   He sinks into thy depths with bubbling groan,
   Without a grave, unknell'd, uncoffin'd, and unknown.
   —George Gordon, Lord Byron, *Childe Harold's Pilgrimage*

4. Half-way up the hill, I see the Past
      Lying beneath me with its sounds and sights,—
   A city in the twilight dim and vast,
      With smoking roofs, soft bells, and gleaming lights,—
   And hear above me on the autumnal blast
      The cataract of Death far thundering from the heights.
   —Henry Wadsworth Longfellow, "Mezzo Cammin"

5. Deer walk upon our mountains, and the quail
   Whistle about us their spontaneous cries;
   Sweet berries ripen in the wilderness;
   And, in the isolation of the sky,
   At evening, casual flocks of pigeons make
   Ambiguous undulations as they sink,
   Downward to darkness, on extended wings.
   —Wallace Stevens, "Sunday Morning"

EXERCISE: *Recognizing Rhythms*

Which of the following poems contain predominant meters? Which poems are not wholly metrical, but are metrical in certain lines? Point out any such lines. What reasons do you see, in such places, for the poet's seeking a metrical effect?

Edna St. Vincent Millay   (1892–1950)*

COUNTING-OUT RHYME   1928

Silver bark of beech, and sallow
Bark of yellow birch and yellow
   Twig of willow.

Stripe of green in moosewood maple,
Color seen in leaf of apple,   5
  Bark of popple.

Wood of popple pale as moonbeam,
Wood of oak for yoke and barn-beam,
  Wood of hornbeam.

Silver bark of beech, and hollow   10
Stem of elder, tall and yellow
  Twig of willow.

A. E. Housman (1859–1936)*

WHEN I WAS ONE-AND-TWENTY   1896

When I was one-and-twenty
  I heard a wise man say,
"Give crowns and pounds and guineas
  But not your heart away;
Give pearls away and rubies   5
  But keep your fancy free."
But I was one-and-twenty,
  No use to talk to me.

When I was one-and-twenty
  I heard him say again,   10
"The heart out of the bosom
  Was never given in vain;
'Tis paid with sighs a plenty
  And sold for endless rue."
And I am two-and-twenty,   15
  And oh, 'tis true, 'tis true.

William Carlos Williams (1883–1963)*

THE DESCENT OF WINTER (SECTION 10/30)   1934

To freight cars in the air

all the slow
    clank, clank
    clank, clank
moving about the treetops   5

the
    wha, wha
of the hoarse whistle

pah, pah, pah
pah, pah, pah, pah, pah
piece and piece
piece and piece
moving still trippingly
through the morningmist

long after the engine
has fought by
and disappeared
in silence
to the left

Walt Whitman   (1819–1892)*

BEAT! BEAT! DRUMS!   (1861)

Beat! beat! drums!—blow! bugles! blow!
Through the windows—through doors—burst like a ruthless force,
Into the solemn church, and scatter the congregation,
Into the school where the scholar is studying;
Leave not the bridegroom quiet—no happiness must he have now
    with his bride,   5
Nor the peaceful farmer any peace, ploughing his field or gathering
    his grain,
So fierce you whirr and pound you drums—so shrill you bugles blow.

Beat! beat! drums!—blow! bugles! blow!
Over the traffic of cities—over the rumble of wheels in the streets;
Are beds prepared for sleepers at night in the houses? no sleepers must
    sleep in those beds,   10
No bargainer's bargains by day—no brokers or speculators—would they
    continue?
Would the talkers be talking? would the singer attempt to sing?
Would the lawyer rise in the court to state his case before the judge?
Then rattle quicker, heavier drums—you bugles wilder blow.

Beat! beat! drums!—blow! bugles! blow!   15
Make no parley—stop for no expostulation,
Mind not the timid—mind not the weeper or prayer,
Mind not the old man beseeching the young man,
Let not the child's voice be heard, nor the mother's entreaties,
Make even the trestles to shake the dead where they lie awaiting the
    hearses.   20
So strong you thump O terrible drums—so loud you bugles blow.

David Mason   (b. 1954)
SONG OF THE POWERS   1996

Mine, said the stone,
mine is the hour.
I crush the scissors,
such is my power.
Stronger than wishes,   5
my power, alone.

Mine, said the paper,
mine are the words
that smother the stone
with imagined birds,   10
reams of them, flown
from the mind of the shaper.

Mine, said the scissors,
mine all the knives
gashing through paper's   15
ethereal lives;
nothing's so proper
as tattering wishes.

As stone crushes scissors,
as paper snuffs stone   20
and scissors cut paper,
all end alone.
So heap up your paper
and scissor your wishes
and uproot the stone   25
from the top of the hill.
They all end alone
as you will, you will.

SONG OF THE POWERS. The three key images of this poem are drawn from the children's game of Scissors, Paper, Stone. In this game each object has a specific power: Scissors cuts paper, paper covers stone, and stone crushes scissors.

Langston Hughes   (1902–1967)*
DREAM BOOGIE   1951

Good morning, daddy!
Ain't you heard
The boogie-woogie rumble
Of a dream deferred?

Listen closely: 5
You'll hear their feet
Beating out and beating out a—

    You think
    It's a happy beat?

Listen to it closely: 10
Ain't you heard
something underneath
like a—

    What did I say?

Sure,   15
I'm happy!
Take it away!

    Hey, pop!
    Re-bop!
    Mop!   20

      Y-e-a-h!

WRITER'S PERSPECTIVE

Gwendolyn Brooks

Gwendolyn Brooks on Writing
HEARING "WE REAL COOL"   1969

STAVROS: How about the seven pool players in the poem "We Real Cool?"

BROOKS: They have no pretensions to any glamor. They are supposedly dropouts, or at least they're in the poolroom when they should be possibly in school, since they're probably young enough or at least those I saw were when I looked in a poolroom, and they. . . . First of all, let me tell you how that's supposed to be said, because there's a reason why I set it out as I did. These are people who are essentially saying, "Kilroy is here. We *are*." But they're a little uncertain of the strength of their identity. The "We"—you're supposed to stop after the "We" and think about *validity*; of course, there's no way for you to tell whether it should be said softly or not, I suppose, but I say it rather softly because I want to represent their basic uncertainty, which they don't bother to question every day, of course.

STAVROS: Are you saying that the form of this poem, then, was determined by the colloquial rhythm you were trying to catch?

BROOKS: No, determined by my feelings about these boys, these young men.

"Interview with George Stavros"

⊶⊷WRITING CRITICALLY⊶⊷

Freeze-Framing the Sound

If you plan to write about the rhythm of a poem, the best way to begin is nearly always by scanning. Although scansion may seem a bit intimidating at first, it is really not difficult; it is just a way of notating how to read the poem aloud. A scansion gives us a freeze-frame of the poem's most important sound patterns. And since stress reinforces meaning, it also helps us understand a poem better. Here is a simple way to get started:

1. Copy down the passage you want to analyze.
2. Mark the syllables on which the main speech stresses fall. (When in doubt, just read the line aloud several different ways and try to detect which way seems most natural.)
3. You might also want to make a few notes in the margin about other things that you notice. Are there rimes? How many syllables in each line? Are there any other recurring patterns of sound worth noting?

A simple scansion of the opening of Tennyson's poem "Break, Break, Break" (on page 836) might look like this in your notes:

Break, break, break	(3 syllables)
On thy cold gray stones, o sea	(7 syllables)/rime
And I would that my tongue could utter	(9 syllables)
The thoughts that arise in me.	(7 syllables)/rime

By now some basic organizing principles of the poem have become clear. The lines are rimed *a b c b*, but they contain an irregular number of syllables. The number of strong stresses, however, seems to be constant, at least in the opening stanza. Now that you have a visual diagram of the poem's sound, the rhythm will be much easier to write about.

WRITING ASSIGNMENT

Analyze the rhythm of a key passage from any poem in this chapter. Discuss how the poem uses rhythm to create certain effects. Incorporate into your analysis a scansion of the passage in question. (Your scansion need not identify every element of the poem's sound, but have it show all the elements you discuss.)

FURTHER SUGGESTIONS FOR WRITING

1. When has a rhythm of any kind (whether in poetry or not) stirred you, picked you up, and carried you along with it? Write an account of your experience.
2. The fact that most contemporary poets have given up meter, in the view of Stanley Kunitz, has made poetry "easier to write, but harder to remember." Why so? Comment on Kunitz's remark, or quarrel with it, in two or three paragraphs.
3. Robert Frost once claimed he tried to make poetry out of the "sound of sense." Writing a friend, Frost discussed his notion that "the simple declarative sentence" in English often contained an abstract sound that helped communicate its meaning. "The best place to get the abstract sound of sense," wrote Frost, "is from voices behind a door that cuts off the words." Ask yourself how these sentences of dialogue would sound without the words in which they are embodied:

> You mean to tell me you can't read?
> I said no such thing.
> Well read then.
> You're not my teacher.

Frost went on to say that "The reader must be at no loss to give his voice the posture proper to the sentence." Thinking about Frost's theory, can you see how it throws any light on one of his poems? In two or three paragraphs, discuss how Frost uses the "simple declarative sentence" as a distinctive rhythmic feature in his poetry.

21 Closed Form

Form, as a general idea, is the design of a thing as a whole, the configuration of all its parts. No poem can escape having some kind of form, whether its lines are as various in length as broomstraws, or all in hexameter. To put this point in another way: if you were to listen to a poem read aloud in a language unknown to you, or if you saw the poem printed in that foreign language, whatever in the poem you could see or hear would be the form of it.[1]

Writing in **closed form,** a poet follows (or finds) some sort of pattern, such as that of a sonnet with its rime scheme and its fourteen lines of iambic pentameter. On a page, poems in closed form tend to look regular and symmetrical, often falling into stanzas that indicate groups of rimes. Along with William Butler Yeats, who held that a successful poem will "come shut with a click, like a closing box," the poet who writes in closed form apparently strives for a kind of perfection—seeking, perhaps, to lodge words so securely in place that no word can be budged without a worsening. For the sake of meaning, though, a competent poet often will depart from a symmetrical pattern. As Robert Frost observed, there is satisfaction to be found in things not mechanically regular: "We enjoy the straight crookedness of a good walking stick."

The poet who writes in **open form** usually seeks no final click. Often, such a poet views the writing of a poem as a process, rather than a quest for an absolute. Free to use white space for emphasis, able to shorten or lengthen lines as the sense seems to require, the poet lets the poem discover its shape as it goes along, moving as water flows downhill, adjusting to its terrain, engulfing obstacles. (Open form will provide the focus of the next chapter.)

---

[1]For a good summary of the uses of the term *form* in criticism of poetry, see the article "Form" by G. N. G. Orsini in *Princeton Encyclopedia of Poetry and Poetics,* 2nd ed., eds. Preminger, Warnke, and Hardison (Princeton: Princeton UP, 1975).

Most poetry of the past is in closed form, exhibiting at least a pattern of rime or meter, but since the early 1960s most American poets have preferred forms that stay open. Lately, the situation has been changing yet again, with closed form reappearing in much recent poetry. Whatever the fashion of the moment, the reader who seeks a wide understanding of poetry of both the present and the past will need to know both the closed and open varieties.

Closed form gives some poems a valuable advantage: it makes them more easily memorable. The **epic** poems of nations—long narratives tracing the adventures of popular heroes: the Greek *Iliad* and *Odyssey*, the French *Song of Roland*, the Spanish *Cid*—tend to occur in patterns of fairly consistent line length or number of stresses because these works were sometimes transmitted orally. Sung to the music of a lyre or chanted to a drumbeat, they may have been easier to memorize because of their patterns. If a singer forgot something, the song would have a noticeable hole in it, so rime or fixed meter probably helped prevent an epic from deteriorating when passed along from one singer to another. It is no coincidence that so many English playwrights of Shakespeare's day favored iambic pentameter. Companies of actors, often called upon to perform a different play daily, could count on a fixed line length to aid their burdened memories.

Some poets complain that closed form is a straitjacket, a limit to free expression. Other poets, however, feel that, like fires held fast in a narrow space, thoughts stated in a tightly binding form may take on a heightened intensity. "Limitation makes for power," according to one contemporary practitioner of closed form, Richard Wilbur; "the strength of the genie comes of his being confined in a bottle." Compelled by some strict pattern to arrange and rearrange words, delete, and exchange them, poets must focus on them the keenest attention. Often they stand a chance of discovering words more meaningful than the ones they started out with. And at times, in obedience to a rime scheme, the poet may be surprised by saying something quite unexpected. With the conscious portion of the mind, the poet may wish to express what seems to be a good idea. But a line ending in *year* must be followed by another ending in *atmosphere, beer, bier, bombardier, cashier, deer, friction-gear, frontier*, or some other rime word that otherwise might not have entered the poem. That is why rime schemes and stanza patterns can be mighty allies and valuable disturbers of the unconscious. As Rolfe Humphries has said about strict form: "It makes you think of better things than you would all by yourself."

FORMAL PATTERNS

The best-known one-line pattern for a poem in English is **blank verse:** unrimed iambic pentameter. (This pattern is not a stanza: stanzas have more than one line.) Most portions of Shakespeare's plays are in blank verse, and so are Milton's *Paradise Lost*, Tennyson's "Ulysses," certain dramatic monologues of Browning and Frost, and thousands of other poems. Here is a poem in blank verse that startles us by dropping out of its pattern in the final line. Keats appears to have written it late in his life to his fiancée Fanny Brawne.

John Keats (1795–1821)*

THIS LIVING HAND, NOW WARM AND CAPABLE   (1819?)

This living hand, now warm and capable
Of earnest grasping, would, if it were cold
And in the icy silence of the tomb,
So haunt thy days and chill thy dreaming nights
That thou wouldst wish thine own heart dry of blood   5
So in my veins red life might stream again,
And thou be conscience-calmed—see here it is—
I hold it towards you.

The **couplet** is a two-line stanza, usually rimed. Its lines often tend to be equal in length, whether short or long. Here are two examples:

Blow,
Snow!

As I in hoary winter's night stood shivering in the snow,
Surprised I was with sudden heat which made my heart to glow.

Actually, any pair of rimed lines that contains a complete thought is called a couplet, even if it is not a stanza, such as the couplet that ends a sonnet by Shakespeare. Unlike other stanzas, couplets are often printed solid, one couplet not separated from the next by white space. This practice is usual in printing the **heroic couplet**—or **closed couplet**—two rimed lines of iambic pentameter, the first ending in a light pause, the second more heavily end-stopped. George Crabbe, in *The Parish Register*, described a shotgun wedding:

Next at our altar stood a luckless pair,
Brought by strong passions and a warrant there:
By long rent cloak, hung loosely, strove the bride,
From every eye, what all perceived, to hide;
While the boy bridegroom, shuffling in his place,
Now hid awhile and then exposed his face.
As shame alternately with anger strove
The brain confused with muddy ale to move,
In haste and stammering he performed his part,
And looked the rage that rankled in his heart.

Though employed by Chaucer, the heroic couplet was named from its later use by Dryden and others in poems, translations of classical epics, and verse plays of epic heroes. It continued in favor through most of the eighteenth century. Much of our pleasure in reading good heroic couplets comes from the seemingly easy precision with which a skilled poet unites statements and strict pattern. In doing so, the poet may place a pair of words, phrases, clauses, or sentences side by side in agreement or similarity, forming a **parallel,** or in contrast and opposition, forming an **antithesis.** The effect is neat. For such skill in manipulating parallels and antitheses, John Denham's lines on the river Thames were much admired:

O could I flow like thee, and make thy stream
My great example, as it is my theme!
Though deep, yet clear; though gentle, yet not dull;
Strong without rage, without o'erflowing full.

These lines were echoed by Pope, ridiculing a poetaster, in two heroic couplets in *The Dunciad:*

Flow, Welsted, flow! like thine inspirer, Beer:
Though stale, not ripe; though thin, yet never clear;
So sweetly mawkish, and so smoothly dull;
Heady, not strong; o'erflowing, though not full.

Reading long poems in so exact a form, one may feel like a spectator at a ping-pong match, unless the poet skillfully keeps varying rhythms. One way of escaping such metronome-like monotony is to keep the cesura (see page 834) shifting about from place to place—now happening early in a line, now happening late—and at times unexpectedly to hurl in a second or third cesura. This skill, among other things, distinguishes the work of Dryden and Pope. If you care to see it in action, try working through Dryden's elegy for Oldham (page 1057) or Pope's acid portrait of Atticus (page 837), noticing where the cesuras fall. You'll find that the pauses skip around with lively variety.

A **tercet** is a group of three lines. If rimed, they usually keep to one rime sound, as in this anonymous English children's jingle:

Julius Caesar,
The Roman geezer,
Squashed his wife with a lemon-squeezer.

(That, by the way, is a great demonstration of surprising and unpredictable rimes.) **Terza rima,** the form Dante employs in *The Divine Comedy,* is made of tercets linked together by the rime scheme *a b a, b c b, c d c, d e d, e f e,* and so on. Harder to do in English than in Italian—with its greater resources of riming words—the form nevertheless has been managed by Shelley in "Ode to the West Wind" (with the aid of some slant rimes):

Make me thy lyre, even as the forest is:
What if my leaves are falling like its own!
The tumult of thy mighty harmonies

Will take from both a deep, autumnal tone,
Sweet though in sadness. Be thou, spirit fierce,
My spirit! Be thou me, impetuous one!

The workhorse of English poetry is the **quatrain,** a stanza consisting of four lines. Quatrains are used in more rimed poems than any other form.

Robert Graves (1895–1985)*

Counting the Beats   1959

You, love, and I,
(He whispers) you and I,
And if no more than only you and I
What care you or I?

Counting the beats,   5
Counting the slow heart beats,
The bleeding to death of time in slow heart beats,
Wakeful they lie.

Cloudless day,
Night, and a cloudless day,   10
Yet the huge storm will burst upon their heads one day
From a bitter sky.

Where shall we be,
(She whispers) where shall we be,
When death strikes home, O where then shall we be   15
Who were you and I?

Not there but here,
(He whispers) only here,
As we are, here, together, now and here,
Always you and I.   20

Counting the beats,
Counting the slow heart beats,
The bleeding to death of time in slow heart beats,
Wakeful they lie.

Question

What elements of sound and rhythm are consistent from stanza to stanza? Do any features change unpredictably from stanza to stanza?

Quatrains come in many line lengths, and sometimes contain lines of varying length, as in the ballad stanza (see page 797). Most often, poets rime the second and fourth lines of quatrains, as in the ballad, but the rimes can occur in any combination the poet chooses. Here are two quatrains from Tennyson's long, elegiac poem, In Memoriam. Tennyson's unusual rime scheme, a b b a, became so celebrated that this pattern is now called the "In Memoriam" stanza:

Be near me when my light is low,
    When the blood creeps, and the nerves prick
    And tingle; and the heart is sick,
And all the wheels of being slow.

Be near me when the sensuous frame
　　Is rack'd with pangs that conquer trust;
　　And Time, a maniac scattering dust,
And Life, a Fury slinging flame.

Longer and more complicated stanzas are, of course, possible, but couplet, tercet, and quatrain have been called the building blocks of our poetry because most longer stanzas are made up of them. What short stanzas does John Donne mortar together to make the longer stanza of his "Song"?

John Donne　(1572–1631)*

SONG　1633

Go and catch a falling star,
　　Get with child a mandrake root,
Tell me where all past years are,
　　Or who cleft the Devil's foot,
Teach me to hear mermaids singing,　　5
　　Or to keep off envy's stinging,
　　　　And find
　　　　What wind
Serves to advance an honest mind.

If thou be'st borne to strange sights,　　10
　　Things invisible to see,
Ride ten thousand days and nights,
　　Till age snow white hairs on thee,
Thou, when thou return'st, wilt tell me
　　All strange wonders that befell thee,　　15
　　　　And swear
　　　　Nowhere
Lives a woman true, and fair.

If thou findst one, let me know,
　　Such a pilgrimage were sweet—　　20
Yet do not, I would not go,
　　Though at next door we might meet;
Though she were true, when you met her,
　　And last, till you write your letter,
　　　　Yet she　　25
　　　　Will be
False, ere I come, to two, or three.

Recently in vogue is a form known as **syllabic verse,** in which the poet establishes a pattern of a certain number of syllables to a line. Either rimed or rimeless but usually stanzaic, syllabic verse has been hailed as a way for poets to escape "the tyranny of the iamb" and discover less conventional rhythms, since, if they take as their line length an *odd* number of syllables, then iambs, being feet of *two* syllables, cannot fit perfectly into it. Offbeat victories have been scored in syllabics by such poets as W. H. Auden, W. D. Snodgrass, Donald Hall, Thom Gunn, and Marianne Moore. A well-known syllabic poem is Dylan Thomas's "Fern Hill" (page 1145). Notice its shape on the page, count the syllables in its lines, and you'll perceive its perfect symmetry. Although like playing a game, the writing of such a poem is apparently more than finger exercise: the discipline can help a poet to sing well, though (with Thomas) singing "in . . . chains like the sea."

Poets who write in demanding forms seem to enjoy taking on an arbitrary task for the fun of it, as ballet dancers do, or weightlifters. Much of our pleasure in reading such poems comes from watching words fall into a shape. It is the pleasure of seeing any hard thing done skillfully—a leap executed in a dance, a basketball swished through a basket. Still, to be excellent, a poem needs more than skill; and to enjoy a poem it isn't always necessary for the reader to be aware of the skill that went into it. Unknowingly, the editors of *The New Yorker* once printed an **acrostic**—a poem in which the initial letter of each line, read downward, spells out a word or words—that named (and insulted) a well-known anthologist. Evidently, besides being ingenious, the acrostic was a printable poem. In the Old Testament book of Lamentations, profoundly moving songs tell of the sufferings of the Jews after the destruction of Jerusalem. Four of the songs are written as an alphabetical acrostic, every stanza beginning with a letter of the Hebrew alphabet. However ingenious, such sublime poetry cannot be dismissed as merely witty; nor can it be charged that a poet who writes in such a form does not express deep feeling.

Phillis Levin   (b. 1954)

Brief Bio   1995

Bearer of no news
Under the sun, except
The spring, I quicken
Time, drawing you to see
Earth's lightest pamphlet,   5
Reeling mosaic of rainbow dust,
Filament hinging a new set of wings,
Lord of no land, subject to flowers and wind,
Yesterday born in a palace that hangs by a thread.

Questions

1. What does the poem describe? (How can we know for sure if we have guessed the correct answer to the poem's riddle?)
2. What is the form of the poem?

3. How does the title relate to the rest of the poem?
4. Does the visual shape of the poem on the page suggest any image from the poem itself?

Patterns of sound and rhythm can, however, be striven after in a dull mechanical way, for which reason many poets today think them dangerous. Swinburne, who loved alliterations and tripping meters, had enough detachment to poke fun at his own excessive patterning:

> From the depth of the dreamy decline of the dawn through a
> notable nimbus of nebulous noonshine,
> Pallid and pink as the palm of the flag-flower that flickers with
> fear of the flies as they float,
> Are the looks of our lovers that lustrously lean from a marvel of
> mystic miraculous moonshine,
> These that we feel in the blood of our blushes that thicken and
> threaten with throbs through the throat?

This is bad, but bad deliberately. Viewed mechanically, as so many empty boxes somehow to be filled up, stanzas can impose the most hollow sort of discipline. If any good at all, a poem in a fixed pattern, such as a sonnet, is created not only by the craftsman's chipping away at it, but by the explosion of a sonnet-shaped *idea*.

Ronald Gross (b. 1935)

YIELD   1967

Yield.
No Parking.
Unlawful to Pass.
Wait for Green Light.
Yield.   5

Stop.
Narrow Bridge.
Merging Traffic Ahead.
Yield.

Yield.   10

QUESTIONS

1. This poem by Ronald Gross is a "found poem." After reading it, how would you define **found poetry**?
2. Does "Yield" have a theme? If so, how would you state it?
3. What makes "Yield" mean more than traffic signs ordinarily mean to us?

Ronald Gross, who produces his "found poetry" by arranging prose from such unlikely places as traffic signs and news stories into poem-like lines, has told of making a discovery:

As I worked with labels, tax forms, commercials, contracts, pin-up captions, obituaries, and the like, I soon found myself rediscovering all the traditional verse forms in found materials: ode, sonnet, epigram, haiku, free verse. Such finds made me realize that these forms are not mere artifices, but shapes that language naturally takes when carrying powerful thoughts or feelings.[2]

Though Gross is a playful experimenter, his remark is true of serious poetry. Traditional verse forms like sonnets and haiku aren't a lot of hollow pillowcases for a poet to stuff with verbiage. At best, in the hands of a skilled poet, they can be shapes into which living language seems to fall naturally.

It is fun to see words tumble gracefully into such a shape. Consider, for instance, one famous "found poem," a sentence discovered in a physics textbook: "And so no force, however great, can stretch a cord, however fine, into a horizontal line which shall be absolutely straight."[3] What a good clear sentence containing effective parallels ("however great . . . however fine"), you might say, taking pleasure in it. Yet this plain statement gives extra pleasure if arranged like this:

And so no force, however great,
    Can stretch a cord, however fine,
    Into a horizontal line
Which shall be absolutely straight.

So spaced, in lines that reveal its built-in rimes and rhythms, the sentence would seem one of those "shapes that language naturally takes" that Ronald Gross finds everywhere. (It is possible, of course, that the textbook writer was gleefully planting a quatrain for someone to find; but perhaps it is more likely that he knew much rimed, metrical poetry by heart and couldn't help writing it unconsciously.) Inspired by pop artists who reveal fresh vistas in Brillo boxes and comic strips, found poetry has had a recent flurry of activity. Earlier practitioners include William Carlos Williams, whose long poem *Paterson* quotes historical documents and statistics. Prose, wrote Williams, can be a "laboratory" for poetry: "It throws up jewels which may be cleaned and grouped."

EXPERIMENT: *Finding a Poem*

In a newspaper, magazine, catalogue, textbook, or advertising throwaway, find a sentence or passage that (with a little artistic manipulation on your part) shows promise of becoming a poem. Copy it into lines like poetry, being careful to place what seem to be the most interesting words at the ends of lines to give them greatest emphasis. According to the rules of found poetry, you may excerpt, delete, repeat, and rearrange elements but not

---

[2]"Speaking of Books: Found Poetry," *The New York Times Book Review*, 11 June 1967. See also Gross's *Pop Poems* (New York: Simon, 1967).
[3]William Whewell, *Elementary Treatise on Mechanics* (Cambridge, England, 1819).

add anything. What does this experiment tell you about poetic form? About ordinary prose?

THE SONNET

When we speak, with Ronald Gross, of "traditional verse forms," we usually mean **fixed forms.** If written in a fixed form, a poem inherits from other poems certain familiar elements of structure: an unvarying number of lines, say, or a stanza pattern. In addition, it may display certain **conventions:** expected features such as themes, subjects, attitudes, or figures of speech. In medieval folk ballads a "milk-white steed" is a conventional figure of speech; and if its rider be a cruel and beautiful witch who kidnaps mortals, she is a conventional character. (*Conventional* doesn't necessarily mean uninteresting.)

In the poetry of western Europe and America, the **sonnet** is the fixed form that has attracted for the longest time the largest number of noteworthy practitioners. Originally an Italian form (*sonnetto:* "little song"), the sonnet owes much of its prestige to Petrarch (1304–1374), who wrote in it of his love for the unattainable Laura. So great was the vogue for sonnets in England at the end of the sixteenth century that a gentleman might have been thought a boor if he couldn't turn out a decent one. Not content to adopt merely the sonnet's fourteen-line pattern, English poets also tried on its conventional mask of the tormented lover. They borrowed some of Petrarch's similes (a lover's heart, for instance, is like a storm-tossed boat) and invented others. (If you would like more illustrations of Petrarchan conventions, see Shakespeare's sonnet on page 995.)

Soon after English poets imported the sonnet in the middle of the sixteenth century, they worked out their own rime scheme—one easier for them to follow than Petrarch's, which calls for a greater number of riming words than English can readily provide. (In Italian, according to an exaggerated report, practically everything rimes.) In the following **English sonnet,** sometimes called a **Shakespearean sonnet,** the rimes cohere in four clusters: *a b a b, c d c d, e f e f, g g.* Because a rime scheme tends to shape the poet's statements to it, the English sonnet has three places where the procession of thought is likely to turn in another direction. Within its form, a poet may pursue one idea throughout the three quatrains and then in the couplet end with a surprise.

William Shakespeare   (1564–1616)*

LET ME NOT TO THE MARRIAGE OF TRUE MINDS   1609

Let me not to the marriage of true minds
Admit impediments; love is not love
Which alters when it alteration finds,
Or bends with the remover to remove.

O, no, it is an ever-fixèd mark   5
That looks on tempests and is never shaken;
It is the star to every wand'ring bark,
Whose worth's unknown, although his height be taken.
Love's not Time's fool, though rosy lips and cheeks
Within his bending sickle's compass° come;   *range*   10
Love alters not with his° brief hours and weeks   *Time's*
But bears° it out even to the edge of doom.   *endures*
    If this be error and upon me proved,
    I never writ, nor no man ever loved.

LET ME NOT TO THE MARRIAGE OF TRUE MINDS. 5 *ever-fixèd mark:* a sea-mark like a beacon or a light-house that provides mariners with safe bearings. 7 *the star:* presumably the North Star, which gave sailors the most dependable bearing at sea. 12 *edge of doom:* either the brink of death or—taken more generally—Judgment Day.

Michael Drayton (1563–1631)

SINCE THERE'S NO HELP,   1619
COME LET US KISS AND PART

Since there's no help, come let us kiss and part;
Nay, I have done, you get no more of me,
And I am glad, yea, glad with all my heart
That thus so cleanly I myself can free;
Shake hands for ever, cancel all our vows,   5
And when we meet at any time again,
Be it not seen in either of our brows
That we one jot of former love retain.
Now at the last gasp of Love's latest breath,
When, his pulse failing, Passion speechless lies,   10
When Faith is kneeling by his bed of death,
And Innocence is closing up his eyes,
    Now if thou wouldst, when all have given him over,
    From death to life thou mightst him yet recover.

Less frequently met in English poetry, the **Italian sonnet,** or **Petrarchan sonnet,** follows the rime scheme *a b b a, a b b a* in its first eight lines, the **octave,** and then adds new rime sounds in the last six lines, the **sestet.** The sestet may rime *c d c d c d, c d e c d e, c d c c d c,* or in almost any other variation that doesn't end in a couplet. This organization into two parts sometimes helps arrange the poet's thoughts. In the octave, the poet may state a problem, and then, in the sestet, may offer a resolution. A lover, for example, may lament all octave long that a loved one is neglectful, then in line 9 begin to foresee some outcome: the speaker will die, or accept unhappiness, or trust that the beloved will have a change of heart.

Edna St. Vincent Millay (1892–1950)*

WHAT LIPS MY LIPS HAVE KISSED, AND WHERE, AND WHY

1923

What lips my lips have kissed, and where, and why,
I have forgotten, and what arms have lain
Under my head till morning; but the rain
Is full of ghosts tonight, that tap and sigh
Upon the glass and listen for reply,   5
And in my heart there sits a quiet pain
For unremembered lads that not again
Will turn to me at midnight with a cry.
Thus in the winter stands the lonely tree,
Nor knows what birds have vanished one by one,   10
Yet knows its boughs more silent than before:
I cannot say what loves have come and gone,
I only know that summer sang in me
A little while, that in me sings no more.

In this Italian sonnet, the turn of thought comes at the traditional point—the beginning of the ninth line. Many English-speaking poets, however, feel free to vary its placement. In John Milton's commanding sonnet on his blindness ("When I consider how my light is spent" on page 1106), the turn comes midway through line 8, and no one has ever thought the worse of it for bending the rules.

When we hear the terms *closed form* or *fixed form*, we imagine traditional poetic forms as a series of immutable rules. But, in the hands of the best poets, metrical forms are fluid concepts that change to suit the occasion. Here, for example, is a haunting poem by Robert Frost that simultaneously fulfills the rules of two traditional forms. Is it an innovative sonnet or a poem in terza rima? (See page 857 for a discussion of terza rima.) Frost combined the features of both forms to create a compressed and powerfully lyric poem.

Robert Frost (1874–1963)*

ACQUAINTED WITH THE NIGHT

1928

I have been one acquainted with the night.
I have walked out in rain—and back in rain.
I have outwalked the furthest city light.

I have looked down the saddest city lane.
I have passed by the watchman on his beat   5
And dropped my eyes, unwilling to explain.

I have stood still and stopped the sound of feet
When far away an interrupted cry
Came over houses from another street,

But not to call me back or say good-bye;   10
And further still at an unearthly height,
One luminary clock against the sky

Proclaimed the time was neither wrong nor right
I have been one acquainted with the night.

    "The sonnet," quipped Robert Bly, a contemporary poet-critic, "is where old professors go to die." And certainly in the hands of an unskilled practitioner, the form can seem moribund. Considering the impressive number of powerful sonnets by modern poets such as Yeats, Frost, Auden, Millay, Cummings, Berryman, Lowell, and Heaney, however, the form hardly appears to be exhausted. Like the hero of the popular ballad "Finnegan's Wake," literary forms (though not professors) declared dead have a startling habit of springing up again. No law compels sonnets to adopt an exalted tone, or confines them to an Elizabethan vocabulary. To see some of the surprising shapes contemporary sonnets take, read this selection of four recent examples.

Kim Addonizio   (b. 1954)
FIRST POEM FOR YOU   1994

I like to touch your tattoos in complete
darkness, when I can't see them. I'm sure of
where they are, know by heart the neat
lines of lightning pulsing just above
your nipple, can find, as if by instinct, the blue   5
swirls of water on your shoulder where a serpent
twists, facing a dragon. When I pull you
to me, taking you until we're spent
and quiet on the sheets, I love to kiss
the pictures in your skin. They'll last until   10
you're seared to ashes; whatever persists
or turns to pain between us, they will still
be there. Such permanence is terrifying.
So I touch them in the dark; but touch them, trying.

R. S. Gwynn   (b. 1948)

SCENES FROM THE PLAYROOM   1986

Now Lucy with her family of dolls
Disfigures Mother with an emery board,
While Charles, with match and rubbing alcohol,
Readies the struggling cat, for Chuck is bored.

The young ones pour more ink into the water   5
Through which the latest goldfish gamely swims,
Laughing, pointing at naked, neutered Father.
The toy chest is a Buchenwald of limbs.

Mother is so lovely; Father, so late.
The cook is off, yet dinner must go on.   10
With onions as her only cause for tears
She hacks the red meat from the slippery bone,
Setting the table, where the children wait,
Her grinning babies, clean behind the ears.

QUESTIONS

1. Explain the allusion to Buchenwald in line 8.
2. What do we know about this family and their life-style? What is revealed by the word *latest* (line 6)?
3. What do you think of these children and their parents? What does the poet think of them? By what details is his attitude made clear?

Timothy Steele   (b. 1948)*

SUMMER   1986

Voluptuous in plenty, summer is
Neglectful of the earnest ones who've sought her.
She best resides with what she images:
Lakes windless with profound sun-shafted water;
Dense orchards in which high-grassed heat grows thick;   5
The one-lane country road where, on his knees,
A boy initials soft tar with a stick;
Slow creeks which bear flecked light through depths of trees.

And he alone is summer's who relents
In his poor enterprisings; who can sense,   10
In alleys petal-blown, the wealth of chance;
Or can, supine in a deep meadow, pass
Warm hours beneath a moving sky's expanse,
Chewing the sweetness from long stalks of grass.

1. Define *voluptuous*. How does this word prepare us for the images to follow?
2. How many of the senses does this poem evoke?
3. What would be lost in the impact of line 5 if *dense* were omitted?
4. What images does the poem use to evoke the slow, heavy feeling of summer?

Thomas Carper (b. 1936)

FACTS   1991

It is important that a son should know
His role, and should be told the woman's role,
And know it is effeminate to show
Emotion, or the least lapse of control
That might mean caring for another man—   5
Even a father. "Never say, 'I love
You,'" I was told. If ever tears began
After an argument, he would reprove
Me mockingly: "Only fags cry." The first
Time that he said this to me, I misheard   10
The slangy phrase, but knew my tears were worst
Of possible betrayals. Yet that word
Stays with me, and when my father shall die,
No man will weep because only facts cry.

FACTS. The author, who teaches at the University of Southern Maine, reports that this poem is based on the experience of a student.

QUESTIONS

1. What does the father's language reveal about his attitudes on masculinity?
2. How does the son reveal his attitudes? Does he ever state them directly?
3. This sonnet incorporates an abusive slang term. Would the poem be stronger without the use of this term? Or does the term add something that more acceptable language could not?
4. If this poem discusses differing views of masculinity, what purpose does the title "Facts" serve? Does the title add meaning to the poem or merely distract attention from its real subject?

THE EPIGRAM

Oscar Wilde said that a cynic is "a man who knows the price of everything and the value of nothing." Such a terse, pointed statement is called an epigram. In poetry, however, an **epigram** is a form: "A short poem ending in a witty or ingenious turn of thought, to which the rest of the composition is intended to lead up" (according to the *Oxford English Dictionary*). Often it is a malicious gibe with an unexpected stinger in the final line—perhaps in the very last word:

Alexander Pope   (1688–1744)*

EPIGRAM ENGRAVED ON THE COLLAR   1738
OF A DOG WHICH I GAVE TO HIS ROYAL
HIGHNESS

I am his Highness' dog at Kew;
Pray tell me, sir, whose dog are you?

Cultivated by the Roman poet Martial—for whom the epigram was a short poem, sometimes satiric but not always—this form has been especially favored by English poets who love Latin. Few characteristics of the English epigram seem fixed. Its pattern tends to be brief and rimed, its tone playfully merciless.

Martial   (A.D. 40?–102?)

READERS AND LISTENERS PRAISE   A.D. 90
MY BOOKS

Readers and listeners praise my books;
You swear they're worse than a beginner's.
Who cares? I always plan my dinners
To please the diners, not the cooks.
        —*Translated by R. L. Barth*

Sir John Harrington   (1561?–1612)

OF TREASON   1618

Treason doth never prosper; what's the reason?
For if it prosper, none dare call it treason.

Robert Herrick   (1591–1674)*

MODERATION   1648

In things a moderation keep,
Kings ought to shear, not skin their sheep.

William Blake   (1757–1827)*

HER WHOLE LIFE IS AN EPIGRAM   (1793)

Her whole life is an epigram: smack smooth°, and neatly   *perfectly smooth*
    penned,
Platted° quite neat to catch applause, with a sliding noose   *plaited, woven*
    at the end.

E. E. Cummings   (1894–1962)*

A POLITICIAN   1944

a politician is an arse upon
which everyone has sat except a man

Langston Hughes   (1902–1967)*

PRAYER   1955

Oh, God of dust and rainbows, help us see
That without dust the rainbow would not be.

J. V. Cunningham   (1911–1985)*

THIS HUMANIST WHOM NO BELIEFS   1947
CONSTRAINED

This *Humanist* whom no beliefs constrained
Grew so broad-minded he was scatter-brained.

John Frederick Nims   (b. 1913)*

CONTEMPLATION   1967

"I'm Mark's alone!" you swore. Given cause to doubt you,
I think less of you, dear. But more about you.

Stevie Smith   (1902–1971)*

THIS ENGLISHWOMAN   1937

This Englishwoman is so refined
She has no bosom and no behind.

Thom Gunn   (b. 1929)

JAMESIAN   1992

Their relationship consisted
In discussing if it existed.

Brad Leithauser   (b. 1953)

A VENUS FLYTRAP   1982

The humming fly is turned to carrion.
This vegetable's no vegetarian.

Hilaire Belloc   (1870–1956)

FATIGUE   1923

I'm tired of Love: I'm still more tired of Rhyme.
But Money gives me pleasure all the time.

Wendy Cope   (b. 1945)*

VARIATION ON BELLOC'S "FATIGUE"   1992

I hardly ever tire of love or rhyme—
That's why I'm poor and have a rotten time.

EXPERIMENT: *Expanding an Epigram*

Rewrite any of the preceding epigrams, taking them out of rime and adding a few more
words to them. See if your revisions have nearly the same effect as the originals.

EXERCISE: *Reading for Couplets*

Read all the sonnets by Shakespeare in this book. How do the final couplets of some of
them resemble epigrams? Does this similarity diminish their effect of "seriousness"?

In English the only other fixed form to rival the sonnet and the epigram in
favor is the **limerick:** five anapestic lines usually riming *a a b b a.* The limerick
was made popular by Edward Lear (1812–1888), English painter and author of
such nonsense poems as "The Owl and the Pussycat." Here is a sample, attributed to President Woodrow Wilson (1856–1924):

I sat next to the Duchess at tea;
It was just as I feared it would be:
    Her rumblings abdominal
    Were truly phenomenal
And everyone thought it was me!

EXPERIMENT: *Contriving a Clerihew*

The **clerihew,** a fixed form named for its inventor, Edmund Clerihew Bentley (1875–1956), has straggled behind the limerick in popularity. Here are three examples: how would you define the form and what are its rules? Who or what is its conventional subject matter? Try writing your own example.

> James Watt
> Was the hard-boiled kind of Scot:
> He thought any dream
> Sheer waste of steam.
> —W. H. Auden

> Sir Christopher Wren
> Said, "I am going to dine with some men.
> If anybody calls
> Say I am designing St. Paul's."
> —Edmund Clerihew Bentley

> Etienne de Silhouette
> (It's a good bet)
> Has the shadiest claim
> To fame.
> —Cornelius J. Ter Maat

OTHER FORMS

There are many other verse forms used in English. Some forms, like the villanelle and sestina (discussed below), come from other European literatures. But English has borrowed fixed forms from an astonishing variety of sources. The rubaiyat stanza (see page 972), for instance, comes from Persian poetry; the haiku (see page 749) and tanka originated in Japan. Other borrowed forms include the ghazal (Arabic), pantoum (Malay), and sapphics (Greek). Even blank verse (see page 855), which seems as English as the Royal Family, began as an attempt by Elizabethan poets to copy an Italian eleven syllable line. To conclude this chapter, here are poems in four widely used closed forms—the villanelle, rondeau, triolet, and sestina. Their patterns, which are sometimes called "French forms," have been particularly fascinating to English-language poets because they do not merely require the repetition of rime sounds; instead, they demand more elaborate echoing, involving the repetition of either full words or whole lines of verse. Sometimes difficult to master, these forms can create a powerful musical effect unlike ordinary riming.

Dylan Thomas   (1914–1953)*

DO NOT GO GENTLE INTO THAT   1952
GOOD NIGHT

Do not go gentle into that good night,
Old age should burn and rave at close of day;
Rage, rage against the dying of the light.

Though wise men at their end know dark is right,
Because their words had forked no lightning they
Do not go gentle into that good night.

5

Good men, the last wave by, crying how bright
Their frail deeds might have danced in a green bay,
Rage, rage against the dying of the light.

Wild men who caught and sang the sun in flight,
And learn, too late, they grieved it on its way,
Do not go gentle into that good night.

10

Grave men, near death, who see with blinding sight
Blind eyes could blaze like meteors and be gay,
Rage, rage against the dying of the light.

15

And you, my father, there on the sad height,
Curse, bless, me now with your fierce tears, I pray,
Do not go gentle into that good night.
Rage, rage against the dying of the light.

QUESTIONS

1. "Do not go gentle into that good night" is a **villanelle:** a fixed form originated by French courtly poets of the Middle Ages. What are its rules?
2. Whom does the poem address? What is the speaker saying?
3. Villanelles are sometimes criticized as elaborate exercises in trivial wordplay. How would you defend Thomas's poem against this charge?

Leigh Hunt   (1784–1859)

RONDEAU

1838

Jenny kissed me when we met,
   Jumping from the chair she sat in;
Time, you thief, who love to get
   Sweets into your list, put that in:
Say I'm weary, say I'm sad,
   Say that health and wealth have missed me,
Say I'm growing old, but add,
   Jenny kissed me.

5

QUESTION

The following is a contemporary revision of Hunt's "Rondeau" that yanks open the form of the rimed original:

Jenny kissed me when we met,
jumping from her chair;
Time, you thief, who love to add
sweets into your list, put that in:
say I'm weary, say I'm sad,
say I'm poor and in ill health,
say I'm growing old—but note, too,
Jenny kissed me.

That revised version says approximately the same thing as Hunt's original, doesn't it? Why is it less effective?

Robert Bridges (1844–1930)

TRIOLET   1879

When first we met we did not guess
That Love would prove so hard a master;
Of more than common friendliness
When first we met we did not guess.
Who could foretell this sore distress,   5
This irretrievable disaster
When first we met—We did not guess
That Love would prove so hard a master.

TRIOLET. The **triolet** is a short lyric form borrowed from the French; its two opening lines are repeated according to a set pattern, as Bridges's poem illustrates. The triolet is often used for light verse, but Bridges's poem demonstrates how it can carry heavier emotional loads, if used with sufficient skill.

QUESTION

How do the first two lines change in meaning when they reappear at the end of the poem?

Elizabeth Bishop (1911–1979)*

SESTINA   1965

September rain falls on the house.
In the failing light, the old grandmother
sits in the kitchen with the child
beside the Little Marvel Stove,
reading the jokes from the almanac,   5
laughing and talking to hide her tears.

She thinks that her equinoctial tears
and the rain that beats on the roof of the house
were both foretold by the almanac,
but only known to a grandmother.   10
The iron kettle sings on the stove.
She cuts some bread and says to the child,

It's time for tea now; but the child
is watching the teakettle's small hard tears
dance like mad on the hot black stove,
the way the rain must dance on the house.
Tidying up, the old grandmother
hangs up the clever almanac

on its string. Birdlike, the almanac
hovers half open above the child,
hovers above the old grandmother
and her teacup full of dark brown tears.
She shivers and says she thinks the house
feels chilly, and puts more wood in the stove.

It was to be, says the Marvel Stove.
I know what I know, says the almanac.
With crayons the child draws a rigid house
and a winding pathway. Then the child
puts in a man with buttons like tears
and shows it proudly to the grandmother.

But secretly, while the grandmother
busies herself about the stove,
the little moons fall down like tears
from between the pages of the almanac
into the flower bed the child
has carefully placed in the front of the house.

Time to plant tears, says the almanac.
The grandmother sings to the marvellous stove
and the child draws another inscrutable house.

15

20

25

30

35

SESTINA. As its title indicates, this poem is written in the trickiest of medieval fixed forms, that of the **sestina** (or "song of sixes"), said to have been invented in Provence in the thirteenth century by the troubadour poet Arnaut Daniel. In six six-line stanzas, the poet repeats six end-words (in a pre-scribed order), then reintroduces the six repeated words (in any order) in a closing **envoy** of three lines. Elizabeth Bishop strictly follows the troubadour rules for the order in which the end-words recur. (If you care, you can figure out the formula: in the first stanza, the six words are arranged A B C D E F; in the second, F A E B D C; and so on.) Notable sestinas in English have been written also by Sir Philip Sidney, Algernon Charles Swinburne, and Rudyard Kipling, more recently by Ezra Pound ("Sestina: Altaforte"), by W. H. Auden ("Hearing of Harvests Rotting in the Valleys" and others), and by contemporary poets, among them John Ashbery, Tom Disch, Marilyn Hacker, Michael Heffernan, Donald Justice, Peter Klappert, William Meredith, Howard Nemerov, John Frederick Nims, and Mona Van Duyn.

QUESTIONS

1. A perceptive comment from a student: "Something seems to be going on here that the child doesn't understand. Maybe some terrible loss has happened." Test this guess by reading the poem closely.
2. Then consider this possibility. We don't know that "Sestina" is autobiographical; still, does any information about the poet's early life contribute to your reading of the poem? (See "Lives of the Poets," page 1165.)

3. In the "little moons" that fall from the almanac (line 33), does the poem introduce dream or fantasy, or do you take these to be small round pieces of paper?
4. What is the tone of this poem—the speaker's apparent attitude toward the scene described?
5. In an essay, "The Sestina," in *A Local Habitation* (U of Michigan P, 1985), John Frederick Nims defends the form against an obvious complaint against it:

> A shallow view of the sestina might suggest that the poet writes a stanza, and then is stuck with six words which he has to juggle into the required positions through five more stanzas and an envoy—to the great detriment of what passion and sincerity would have him say. But in a good sestina the poet has six words, six images, six ideas so urgently in his mind that he cannot get away from them; he wants to test them in all possible combinations and come to a conclusion about their relationship.

How well does this description of a good sestina fit "Sestina"?

EXPERIMENT: *Urgent Repetition*

Write a sestina and see what you find out by doing so. (Even if you fail in the attempt, you just might learn something interesting.) To start, pick six words you think are worth repeating six times. This elaborate pattern gives you much help: as John Ashbery has pointed out, writing a sestina is "like riding downhill on a bicycle and having the pedals push your feet." Here is some encouragement from a poet and critic, John Heath-Stubbs: "I have never read a sestina that seemed to me a total failure."

WRITER'S PERSPECTIVE

Robert Graves

Robert Graves on Writing
POETIC INSPIRATION AND POETIC FORM   1956

It is an axiom among poets that if one trusts whole-heartedly to poetic magic, one will be sure to solve any merely verbal problem or else discover that the verbal problem is hiding an imprecision in poetic thought.

I say magic, since the act of composition occurs in a sort of trance, distinguishable from dream only because the critical faculties are not dormant, but on the contrary, more acute than normally. Often a rugger° player is congratulated on having played the smartest game of his life, but regrets that he cannot remember a single incident after the first five minutes, when he got kicked on the head. It is much the same with a poet when he completes a true poem. But often he wakes from the trance too soon and is tempted to solve the remaining problems intellectually. Few self-styled poets have experienced the trance; but all who have, know that to work out a line by an exercise of reason, rather than by a deep-seated belief in miracle, is highly unprofessional conduct. If a trance has been interrupted, it is just too bad. The poem should be left unfinished, in the hope that suddenly, out of the blue, days or months later, it may start stirring again at the back of the mind, when the remaining problems will solve themselves without difficulty.

. . .

It is unprofessional conduct to say: "When next I write a poem I shall use the sonnet form"—because the theme is by definition unforeseeable, and theme chooses metre. A poet should not be conscious of the metrical pattern of a poem he is writing until the first three or four lines have appeared; he may even find himself in the eleventh line of fourteen before realizing that a sonnet is on the way. Besides, metre is only a frame; the atmospheres of two sonnets can be so different that they will not be recognized as having the same form except by a careful count of lines and feet. Theme chooses metre; what is more, theme decides what rhythmic variations should be made on metre. The theory that all poems must be equally rich in sound is an un-English one, borrowed from Virgil. Rainbow-like passages are delightful every now and then, but they match a rare mood of opulence and exaltation which soon fatigues. The riches of *Paradise Lost* fatigue, and even oppress, all but musicians. Rainbows should make their appearances only when the moment has come to disclose the riches of the heart, or soul, or imagination; they testify to passing storms and are short-lived.

"Harp, Anvil, Oar"

On Poetic Inspiration and Poetic Form. *rugger:* rugby.

WRITING CRITICALLY

Turning Points

One possible definition of the sonnet might be: a fourteen-line poem divided into two unequal parts. Italian sonnets divide their parts into the octave and the sestet, while the English sonnet is more lopsided, with a final couplet balanced against the first twelve lines. Some sonnets use less traditional arrangements, but generally poets build sonnets in which the unequal sections strongly contrast in tone, mood, theme, or point of view.

The moment when a sonnet changes its direction is commonly called "the turn." In a Shakespearean sonnet, the turn usually—but not always—comes in the final couplet. In modern sonnets, the turn is often less overt, but identifying the moment when the poem shifts will usually help you better understand both its theme and structure.

But how do you find the moment when a sonnet turns? Study the poem, latch on to the mood and manner of its opening lines. Is the feeling joyful or sad, loving or angry? Read the poem from this opening perspective until you feel it tug strongly in another direction. Sometimes the second part of a sonnet will directly contradict the opening. More often it explains, augments, or qualifies the opening.

WRITING ASSIGNMENT

Using any sonnet in the book, analyze and explain how the two parts of the poem combine to create a total effect neither part could achieve independently. In discussing the sonnet, identify the turning point and paraphrase what each of the poem's two sections say. In addition to the sonnets in this chapter, you might consider any of the following: Elizabeth Barrett Browning's "How Do I Love Thee?" (page 1046); Gerard Manley Hopkins's "The Windhover" (page 1084); John Keats's "When I have fears that I may cease to be" (page 1093); Weldon Kees's "For My Daughter" (page 672); Archibald MacLeish's "The End of the World" (page 1100); John Milton's "When I consider how my light is spent" (page 1106); Wilfred Owen's "Anthem for Doomed Youth" (page 1111); William Shakespeare's "When, in disgrace with Fortune and men's eyes" (page 1130); or William Wordsworth's "Composed upon Westminster Bridge" (page 1158).

FURTHER SUGGESTIONS FOR WRITING

1. William Carlos Williams, in an interview, delivered this blast:

   Forcing twentieth-century America into a sonnet—gosh, how I hate sonnets— is like putting a crab into a square box. You've got to cut his legs off to make him fit. When you get through, you don't have a crab any more.

   In a two-page essay, defend the modern American sonnet against Williams's charge. Or instead, open fire on it, using Williams's view for ammunition. Some sonnets to consider: R. S. Gwynn's "Scenes from the Playroom" (page 867), Julia Alvarez's "The women on my mother's side were known" (page 949), and Archibald MacLeish's "The End of the World" (page 1100).

2. Write an unserious argument for or against the abolition of limericks. Give illustrations of limericks you think worthy of abolition (or preservation).

3. Compare Dylan Thomas's "Do not go gentle into that good night" with Wendy Cope's "Lonely Hearts" (page 717). Discuss how it is possible for the same form to be used to create such different kinds of poems.

22 *Open Form*

Writing in **open form,** a poet seeks to discover a fresh and individual arrangement for words in every poem. Such a poem, generally speaking, has neither a rime scheme nor a basic meter informing the whole of it. Doing without those powerful (some would say hypnotic) elements, the poet who writes in open form relies on other means to engage and to sustain the reader's attention. Novice poets often think that open form looks easy, not nearly so hard as riming everything; but in truth, formally open poems are easy to write only if written carelessly. To compose lines with keen awareness of open form's demands, and of its infinite possibilities, calls for skill: at least as much as that needed to write in meter and rime, if not more. Should the poet succeed, then the discovered arrangement will seem exactly right for what the poem is saying.

Denise Levertov (1923–1997)*

SIX VARIATIONS (PART III)   1961

Shlup, shlup, the dog
as it laps up
water
makes intelligent
music, resting   5
now and then to take breath in irregular
measure.

Open form, in this brief poem, affords Denise Levertov certain advantages. Able to break off a line at whatever point she likes (a privilege not available to the poet writing, say, a conventional sonnet, who has to break off each line after its tenth syllable), she selects her pauses artfully. Line-breaks lend emphasis: a word or phrase at the end of a line takes a little more stress (and receives a little more attention), because the ending of the line compels the reader to make a slight pause, if only for the brief moment it takes to sling back one's eyes (like a typewriter carriage) and fix them on the line following. Slight pauses, then, follow the words and phrases *the dog/laps up/water/intelligent/resting/irregular/measure*—all of these being elements that apparently the poet wishes to call our attention to. (The pause after a line-break also casts a little more weight upon the *first* word or phrase of each succeeding line.) Levertov makes the most of white space—another means of calling attention to things, as any good picture-framer knows. By setting a word all alone on a line (*water/measure*), she makes it stand out more than it would in a line of pentameter. She feels free to include a bit of rime (*Shlup, shlup/up*). She creates rhythms: if you will read aloud the phrases *intelligent/music* and *irregular/measure*, you will sense that in each phrase the arrangement of pauses and stresses is identical. Like the dog's halts to take breath, the lengths of the lines seem naturally irregular. The result is a fusion of meaning and form: indeed, an "intelligent music."

Poetry in open form used to be called **free verse** (from the French **vers libre**), suggesting a kind of verse liberated from the shackles of rime and meter. "Writing free verse," said Robert Frost, who wasn't interested in it, "is like playing tennis with the net down." And yet, as Denise Levertov and many other poets demonstrate, high scores can be made in such an unconventional game, provided it doesn't straggle all over the court. For a successful poem in open form, the term *free verse* seems inaccurate. "Being an art form," said William Carlos Williams, "verse cannot be 'free' in the sense of having *no* limitations or guiding principles."[1] Various substitute names have been suggested: organic poetry, composition by field, raw (as against cooked) poetry, open form poetry. "But what does it matter what you call it?" remark the editors of an anthology called *Naked Poetry*. The best poems of the last thirty years "don't rhyme (usually) and don't move on feet of more or less equal duration (usually). That non-description moves toward the only technical principle they all have in common."[2]

And yet many poems in open form have much more in common than absences and lacks. One positive principle has been Ezra Pound's famous suggestion that poets "compose in the sequence of the musical phrase, not in the sequence of the metronome"—good advice, perhaps, even for poets who write inside fixed forms. In Charles Olson's influential theory of **projective verse,** poets compose by listening to their own breathing. On paper, they indicate the rhythms of a poem by using a little white space or a lot, a slight indentation or a deep one, depending on whether a short pause or a long one is intended. Words can be grouped in clusters on the page (usually no more words than a lungful of

---

[1]"Free Verse," *Princeton Encyclopedia of Poetry and Poetics*, 2nd ed., 1975.
[2]Stephen Berg and Robert Mezey, eds., foreword, *Naked Poetry: Recent American Poetry in Open Forms* (Indianapolis: Bobbs, 1969).

air can accommodate). Heavy cesuras are sometimes shown by breaking a line in two and lowering the second part of it.[3]

To the poet working in open form, no less than to the poet writing a sonnet, line length can be valuable. Walt Whitman, who loved to expand vast sentences for line after line, knew well that an impressive rhythm can accumulate if the poet will keep long lines approximately the same length, causing a pause to recur at about the same interval after every line. Sometimes, too, Whitman repeats the same words at each line's opening. An instance is the masterly sixth section of "When Lilacs Last in the Dooryard Bloom'd," an elegy for Abraham Lincoln:

Coffin that passes through lanes and streets,
Through day and night with the great cloud darkening the land,
With the pomp of the inloop'd flags with the cities draped in
    black,
With the show of the States themselves as of crape-veil'd women
    standing,
With processions long and winding and the flambeaus of the
    night,
With the countless torches lit, with the silent sea of faces and the
    unbared heads,
With the waiting depot, the arriving coffin, and the somber faces,
With dirges through the night, with the thousand voices rising
    strong and solemn,
With all the mournful voices of the dirges pour'd around the
    coffin,
The dim-lit churches and the shuddering organs—where amid
    these you journey,
With the tolling tolling bells' perpetual clang,
Here, coffin that slowly passes,
I give you my sprig of lilac.

There is music in such solemn, operatic arias. Whitman's lines echo another model: the Hebrew **psalms,** or sacred songs, as translated in the King James Version of the Bible. In Psalm 150, repetition also occurs inside of lines:

Praise ye the Lord. Praise God in his sanctuary: praise him in
the firmament of his power.
Praise him for his mighty acts: praise him according to his excellent greatness.
Praise him with the sound of the trumpet: praise him with the
psaltery and harp.
Praise him with the timbrel and dance: praise him with stringed
instruments and organs.

[3]See Olson's essays "Projective Verse" and "Letter to Elaine Feinstein" in *Selected Writings,* edited by Robert Creeley (New York: New Directions, 1966). Olson's letters to Cid Corman are fascinating: *Letters for Origin, 1950–1955,* edited by Albert Glover (New York: Grossman, 1970).

Praise him upon the loud cymbals: praise him upon the high
sounding cymbals.
Let every thing that hath breath praise the Lord. Praise ye the
Lord.

In Biblical Psalms, we are in the presence of (as Robert Lowell has said)
"supreme poems, written when their translators merely intended prose and were
forced by the structure of their originals to write poetry."[4]

Whitman was a more deliberate craftsman than he let his readers think, and
to anyone interested in writing in open form, his work will repay close study. He
knew that repetitions of any kind often make memorable rhythms, as in this passage from "Song of Myself," with every line ending on an -ing word (a stressed
syllable followed by an unstressed syllable):

Here and there with dimes on the eyes walking,
To feed the greed of the belly the brains liberally spooning,
Tickets buying, taking, selling, but in to the feast never once
going,
Many sweating, ploughing, thrashing, and then the chaff for pay-
ment receiving,
A few idly owning, and they the wheat continually claiming.

Much more than simply repetition, of course, went into the music of those
lines—the internal rime *feed, greed,* the use of assonance, the trochees that begin
the third and fourth lines, whether or not they were calculated.

In such classics of open form poetry, sound and rhythm are positive forces.
When speaking a poem in open form, you often may find that it makes a difference for the better if you pause at the end of each line. Try pausing there, however briefly; but don't allow your voice to drop. Read just as you would normally
read a sentence in prose (except for the pauses, of course). Why do the pauses
matter? Open form poetry usually has no meter to lend it rhythm. *Some* lines in
an open form poem, as we have seen in Whitman's "dimes on the eyes" passage,
do fall into metrical feet; sometimes the whole poem does. Usually lacking
meter's aid, however, open form, in order to have more and more noticeable
rhythms, has need of all the recurring pauses it can get. When reading their own
work aloud, open form poets like Robert Creeley and Allen Ginsberg often pause
very definitely at each line break.

Some poems, to be sure, seem more widely open in form than others. A
poet, for instance, may employ rime, but have the rimes recur at various intervals; or perhaps rime lines of various lengths. (See T. S. Eliot's famous "The
Love Song of J. Alfred Prufrock" on page 1059. Is it a closed poem left ajar or an
open poem trying to slam itself?) No law requires a poet to split thoughts into
verse lines at all. Charles Baudelaire, Rainer Maria Rilke, Jorge Luis Borges,

---

[4]"On Freedom in Poetry," in Berg and Mezey, *Naked Poetry.*

Alexander Solzhenitsyn, T. S. Eliot, and many others have written **prose poems,** in which, without caring that eye appeal and some of the rhythm of a line structure may be lost, the poet prints words in a block like a prose paragraph. For an example of a contemporary prose poem, see Carolyn Forché's "The Colonel" on page 891.

"Farewell, stale pale skunky pentameters (the only honest English meter, gloop! gloop!)," Kenneth Koch has exulted, suggesting that it was high time to junk such stale conventions. Many poets who agree with him believe that it is wrong to fit words into any pattern that already exists, and instead believe in letting a poem seek its own shape as it goes along. (Traditionalists might say that that is what all good poems do anyway: sonnets rarely know they are going to be sonnets until the third line has been written. However, there is no doubt that the sonnet form already exists, at least in the back of the head of any poet who has ever read sonnets.) Some open form poets offer a historical motive: they want to reflect the nervous, staccato, disconnected pace of our bumper-to-bumper society. Others see open form as an attempt to suit thoughts and words to a more spontaneous order than the traditional verse forms allow. "Better," says Gary Snyder, quoting from Zen, "the perfect, easy discipline of the swallow's dip and swoop, 'without east or west.'"[5]

At the moment, much exciting new poetry is being written in both open form and closed. Today, many younger poets (labeled New Formalists) have taken up rime and meter and have been writing sonnets, epigrams, and poems in rimed stanzas, giving "pale skunky pentameters" a fresh lease on life.[6]

E. E. Cummings   (1894–1962)*
BUFFALO BILL'S   1923

Buffalo Bill 's
defunct
          who used to
          ride a watersmooth-silver
                                        stallion   5
and break onetwothreefourfive pigeonsjustlikethat
                                        Jesus
he was a handsome man
                    and what i want to know is
how do you like your blueeyed boy   10
Mister Death

[5]"Some Yips & Barks in the Dark," in Berg and Mezey, *Naked Poetry*.
[6]For more samples of recent formal poetry than this book provides, see *Rebel Angels*, ed. by Mark Jarman and David Mason (Brownsville: Story Line, 1996), *The Direction of Poetry*, ed. Robert Richman (Boston: Houghton, 1988), *Ecstatic Occasions, Expedient Forms*, ed. David Lehman (New York: Collier, 1987), and *Strong Measures: Contemporary American Poetry in Traditional Forms*, ed. Philip Dacey and David Jauss (New York: Harper, 1986).

Cummings's poem would look like this if given conventional punctuation and set in a solid block like prose:

> Buffalo Bill's defunct, who used to ride a water-smooth silver stallion and break one, two, three, four, five pigeons just like that. Jesus, he was a handsome man. And what I want to know is: "How do you like your blue-eyed boy, Mister Death?"

If this were done, by what characteristics would it still be recognizable as poetry? But what would be lost?

Emily Dickinson (1830–1886)*

VICTORY COMES LATE (1861)

Victory comes late –
And is held low to freezing lips –
Too rapt with frost
To take it –
How sweet it would have tasted –   5
Just a Drop –
Was God so economical?
His Table's spread too high for Us –
Unless We dine on tiptoe –
Crumbs – fit such little mouths –   10
Cherries – suit Robins –
The Eagle's Golden Breakfast strangles – Them –
God keep His Oath to Sparrows –
Who of little Love – know how to starve –

QUESTIONS

1. In this specimen of poetry in open form, can you see any other places at which the poet might have broken off any of her lines? To place a word last in a line gives it a greater emphasis; she might, for instance, have ended line 12 with *Breakfast* and begun a new line with the word *strangles*. Do you think she knows what she is doing here or does the pattern of this poem seem decided by whim? Discuss.
2. Read the poem aloud. Try pausing for a fraction of a second at every dash. Is there any justification for the poet's unorthodox punctuation?

William Carlos Williams (1883–1963)*

THE DANCE   1944

In Breughel's great picture, The Kermess,
the dancers go round, they go round and
around, the squeal and the blare and the
tweedle of bagpipes, a bugle and fiddles
tipping their bellies (round as the thick-   5

DETAIL. "The Kermess" or "Peasant Dance" by Pieter Breughel the Elder (1520?–1569)

sided glasses whose wash they impound)
their hips and their bellies off balance
to turn them. Kicking and rolling about
the Fair Grounds, swinging their butts, those
shanks must be sound to bear up under such   10
rollicking measures, prance as they dance
in Breughel's great picture, The Kermess.

THE DANCE. Breughel, a Flemish painter known for his scenes of peasant activities, represented in "The Kermess" a celebration on the feast day of a local patron saint.

QUESTIONS

1. Scan this poem and try to describe the effect of its rhythms.
2. Williams, widely admired for his free verse, insisted for many years that what he sought was a form not in the least bit free. What effect does he achieve by ending lines on such weak words as the articles *and* and *the*? By splitting *thick- / sided*? By splitting a prepositional phrase with the break at the end of line 8? By using line breaks to split *those* and *such* from what they modify? What do you think he is trying to convey?
3. Is there any point in his making line 12 a repetition of the opening line?
4. Look at the reproduction of Breughel's painting "The Kermess" (also called "Peasant Dance"). Aware that the rhythms of dancers, the rhythms of a painting, and the rhythms of a poem are not all the same, can you put in your own words what Breughel's dancing figures have in common with Williams's descriptions of them?

5. Compare with "The Dance" another poem that refers to a Breughel painting: W. H. Auden's "Museé des Beaux Arts" on page 1037. What seems to be each poet's main concern: to convey in words a sense of the painting, or to visualize the painting in order to state some theme?

Stephen Crane (1871–1900)
THE HEART   1895

In the desert
I saw a creature, naked, bestial,
Who, squatting upon the ground,
Held his heart in his hands,
And ate of it.   5

I said, "Is it good, friend?"
"It is bitter—bitter," he answered;
"But I like it
Because it is bitter,
And because it is my heart."   10

Walt Whitman (1819–1892)*
CAVALRY CROSSING A FORD   (1865)

A line in long array where they wind betwixt green islands,
They take a serpentine course, their arms flash in the sun—hark to the
        musical clank,
Behold the silvery river, in it the splashing horses loitering stop to drink,
Behold the brown-faced men, each group, each person a picture, the
        negligent rest on the saddles,
Some emerge on the opposite bank, others are just entering the ford—while,   5
Scarlet and blue and snowy white,
The guidon flags flutter gayly in the wind.

QUESTIONS

The following nit-picking questions are intended to help you see exactly what makes these two open form poems by Crane and Whitman so different in their music.

1. What devices of sound occur in Whitman's phrase *silvery river* (line 3)? Where else in his poem do you find these devices?
2. Does Crane use any such devices?
3. In number of syllables, Whitman's poem is almost twice as long as Crane's. Which poem has more pauses in it? (Count pauses at the ends of lines, at marks of punctuation.)

4. Read the two poems aloud. In general, how would you describe the effect of their sounds and rhythms? Is Crane's poem necessarily an inferior poem for having less music?

Wallace Stevens   (1879–1955)*

THIRTEEN WAYS OF LOOKING AT   1923
A BLACKBIRD

I

Among twenty snowy mountains,
The only moving thing
Was the eye of the blackbird.

II

I was of three minds,
Like a tree   5
In which there are three blackbirds.

III

The blackbird whirled in the autumn winds.
It was a small part of the pantomime.

IV

A man and a woman
Are one.   10
A man and a woman and a blackbird
Are one.

V

I do not know which to prefer,
The beauty of inflections
Or the beauty of innuendoes,   15
The blackbird whistling
Or just after.

VI

Icicles filled the long window
With barbaric glass.
The shadow of the blackbird   20
Crossed it, to and fro.
The mood
Traced in the shadow
An indecipherable cause.

VII

O thin men of Haddam,   25
Why do you imagine golden birds?
Do you not see how the blackbird
Walks around the feet
Of the women about you?

VIII

I know noble accents   30
And lucid, inescapable rhythms;
But I know, too,
That the blackbird is involved
In what I know.

IX

When the blackbird flew out of sight,   35
It marked the edge
Of one of many circles.

X

At the sight of blackbirds
Flying in a green light,
Even the bawds of euphony   40
Would cry out sharply.

XI

He rode over Connecticut
In a glass coach.
Once, a fear pierced him,
In that he mistook   45
The shadow of his equipage
For blackbirds.

XII

The river is moving.
The blackbird must be flying.

XIII

It was evening all afternoon.   50
It was snowing
And it was going to snow.
The blackbird sat
In the cedar-limbs.

THIRTEEN WAYS OF LOOKING AT A BLACKBIRD.   25 *Haddam*: This Biblical-sounding name is that of
a town in Connecticut.

QUESTIONS

1. What is the speaker's attitude toward the men of Haddam? What attitude toward
   this world does he suggest they lack? What is implied by calling them *thin* (line
   25)?
2. What do the landscapes of winter contribute to the poem's effectiveness? If Stevens
   had chosen images of summer lawns, what would have been lost?
3. In which sections of the poem does Stevens suggest that a unity exists between
   human being and blackbird, between blackbird and the entire natural world? Can we
   say that Stevens "philosophizes"? What role does imagery play in Stevens's statement of his ideas?
4. What sense can you make of Part X? Make an enlightened guess.
5. Consider any one of the thirteen parts. What patterns of sound and rhythm do you
   find in it? What kind of structure does it have?
6. If the thirteen parts were arranged in some different order, would the poem be just as
   good? Or can we find a justification for its beginning with Part I and ending with
   Part XIII?
7. Does the poem seem an arbitrary combination of thirteen separate poems? Or is
   there any reason to call it a whole?

Gary Gildner   (b. 1938)

FIRST PRACTICE   1969

After the doctor checked to see
we weren't ruptured,
the man with the short cigar took us
under the grade school,
where we went in case of attack   5
or storm, and said
he was Clifford Hill, he was
a man who believed dogs
ate dogs, he had once killed
for his country, and if   10
there were any girls present
for them to leave now.
                 No one
left. OK, he said, he said I take
that to mean you are hungry
men who hate to lose as much   15
as I do. OK. Then
he made two lines of us
facing each other,
and across the way, he said,
is the man you hate most   20
in the world,
and if we are to win
that title I want to see how.
But I don't want to see
any marks when you're dressed,   25
he said. He said, *Now*.

QUESTIONS

1. What do you make of Hill and his world-view?
2. How does the speaker reveal his own view? Why, instead of quoting Hill directly
   ("This is a dog-eat-dog world"), does he call him *a man who believed dogs / ate dogs*
   (lines 8–9)?
3. What effect is made by breaking off and lowering *No one* at the end of line 12?
4. What is gained by having a rime on the poem's last word?
5. For the sake of understanding how right the form of Gildner's poem is for it, imagine
   the poem in meter and a rime scheme, and condensed into two stanzas:

   > Then he made two facing lines of us
   > And he said, Across the way,
   > Of all the men there are in the world
   > Is the man you most want to slay,

And if we are to win that title, he said,   5
I want you to show me how.
But I don't want to see any marks when you're dressed,
He said. Go get him. *Now*.

Why would that rewrite be so unfaithful to what Gildner is saying?
6. How would you answer someone who argued, "This can't be a poem—its subject is ugly and its language isn't beautiful"?

Carolyn Forché   (b. 1950)

THE COLONEL   1982

What you have heard is true. I was in his house. His wife carried a tray of coffee and sugar. His daughter filed her nails, his son went out for the night. There were daily papers, pet dogs, a pistol on the cushion beside him. The moon swung bare on its black cord over the house. On the television was a cop show. It was in English. Broken bottles were embedded in the walls around the house to scoop the kneecaps from a man's legs or cut his hands to lace. On the windows there were gratings like those in liquor stores. We had dinner, rack of lamb, good wine, a gold bell was on the table for calling the maid. The maid brought green mangoes, salt, a type of bread. I was asked how I enjoyed the country. There was a brief commercial in Spanish. His wife took everything away. There was some talk then of how difficult it had become to govern. The parrot said hello on the terrace. The colonel told it to shut up, and pushed himself from the table. My friend said to me with his eyes: say nothing. The colonel returned with a sack used to bring groceries home. He spilled many human ears on the table. They were like dried peach halves. There is no other way to say this. He took one of them in his hands, shook it in our faces, dropped it into a water glass. It came alive there. I am tired of fooling around he said. As for the rights of anyone, tell your people they can go fuck themselves. He swept the ears to the floor with his arm and held the last of his wine in the air. Something for your poetry, no? he said. Some of the ears on the floor caught this scrap of his voice. Some of the ears on the floor were pressed to the ground.

May 1978

QUESTIONS

1. Should we consider "The Colonel" a prose poem or a very short piece of prose? If it is poetry, what features distinguish it from prose? If it should be considered prose, what essential features of poetry does it lack?
2. Forché begins "The Colonel" by saying "What you have heard is true." Who is the *you?* Does she assume a specific person?
3. Should we believe that this story is true? If so, what leads us to believe its veracity?
4. Why does the author end "The Colonel" by giving a date?

VISUAL POETRY

Let's look at a famous poem with a distinctive visible shape. In the seventeenth century, ingenious poets trimmed their lines into the silhouettes of altars and crosses, pillars and pyramids. Here is one. Is it anything more than a demonstration of ingenuity?

George Herbert (1593–1633)*

EASTER WINGS   1633

Lord, who createdst man in wealth and store,
Though foolishly he lost the same,
Decaying more and more
Till he became
Most poor;
With thee
Oh, let me rise
As larks, harmoniously,
And sing this day thy victories;
Then shall the fall further the flight in me.

My tender age in sorrow did begin;
And still with sicknesses and shame
Thou didst so punish sin,
That I became
Most thin.
With thee
Let me combine,
And feel this day thy victory;
For if I imp my wing on thine,
Affliction shall advance the flight in me.

In the next-to-last line, *imp* is a term from falconry meaning to repair the wing of an injured bird by grafting feathers into it.

If we see it merely as a picture, we will have to admit that Herbert's word design does not go far. It renders with difficulty shapes that a sketcher's pencil could set down in a flash, in more detail, more accurately. Was Herbert's effort wasted? It might have been, were there not more to his poem than meets the eye. The mind, too, is engaged by the visual pattern, by the realization that the words *most thin* are given emphasis by their narrow form. Here, visual pattern points out meaning. Heard aloud, too, "Easter Wings" gives further pleasure. Its rimes, its rhythm are perceptible.

Ever since George Herbert's day, poets have continued to experiment with the looks of printed poetry. Notable efforts to entertain the eye are Lewis Carroll's rimed mouse's tail in *Alice in Wonderland;* and the *Calligrammes* of Guillaume Apollinaire, who arranged words in the shapes of a necktie, of the Eiffel Tower, of spears of falling rain. Here is a bird-shaped poem of more recent inspiration than Herbert's. What does its visual form have to do with what the poet is saying?

John Hollander   (b. 1929)

SWAN AND SHADOW   1969

<pre>
                    Dusk
                   Above the
               water hang the
                       loud
                       flies
                      Here
                      O so
                     gray
                     then
                    What   A pale signal will appear
                    When   Soon before its shadow fades
                   Where   Here in this pool of opened eye
                   In us   No Upon us As at the very edges
                of where we take shape in the dark air
                   this object bares its image awakening
                     ripples of recognition that will
                       brush darkness up into light
    even after this bird this hour both drift by atop the perfect sad instant now
                       already passing out of sight
                     toward yet-untroubled reflection
                   this image bears its object darkening
                  into memorial shades Scattered bits of
                   light   No of water Or something across
                   water   Breaking up No Being regathered
                   soon   Yet by then a swan will have
                    gone   Yet out of mind into what
                    vast
                    pale
                    hush
                    of a
                    place
                    past
               sudden dark as
                 if a swan
                    sang
</pre>

A whole poem doesn't need to be such a verbal silhouette, of course, for its appearance on the page to seem meaningful. In some lines of a longer poem, William Carlos Williams has conveyed the way an energetic bellhop (or hotel porter) runs downstairs:

              ta tuck a
                    ta tuck a
                          ta tuck a
                                ta tuck a
                                      ta tuck a

This is not only good onomatopoeia and an accurate description of a rhythm; the steplike appearance of the lines goes together with their meaning.

At least some of our pleasure in silently reading a poem derives from the way it looks upon its page. A poem in an open form can engage the eye with snowfields of white space and thickets of close-set words. A poem in stanzas can please us by its visual symmetry. And, far from being merely decorative, the visual devices of a poem can be meaningful, too. White space—as poets demonstrate who work in open forms—can indicate pauses. If white space entirely surrounds a word or phrase or line, then that portion of the poem obviously takes special emphasis. Typographical devices such as capital letters and italics also can lay stress upon words. In most traditional poems, a capital letter at the beginning of each new line helps indicate the importance the poet places upon line-divisions, whose regular intervals make a rhythm out of pauses. And the poet may be trying to show us that certain lines rime by indenting them.

Some contemporary poets have taken advantage of the computer's ability to mix words and images. They use visual images as integral parts of their poems to explore possibilities beyond traditional prosody. Ezra Pound did similar things in his modernist epic, *The Cantos,* by incorporating Chinese ideograms, musical notations, and marginal notes into the text of the poem. More recently Terry Ehret created a sequence of poems that used ancient Egyptian hieroglyphics to prompt lyric meditations that are half translation and half free association. Here is one section from her poem sequence, "Papyrus." (Note how Ehret uses a hieroglyph, a pictorial character used in ancient Egyptian writing, as the title of her short prose poem.)

Terry Ehret   (b. 1955)

[*from* PAPYRUS]   1992

A lake. A night without moon. Distant memory of what the sun looks like rising. The darkness blows across the water like a wind. Passions that cool with age.

In recent years, a movement called **concrete poetry** has traveled far and wide. Though practitioners of the art disagree over its definition, what most concretists seem to do is make designs out of letters and words. Other concrete poets wield typography like a brush dipped in paint, using such techniques as blow-up, montage, and superimposed elements (the same words printed many times on top of the same impression, so that the result is blurriness). They may even keep words in a usual order, perhaps employing white space as freely as any writer of open form verse. (More freely sometimes—Aram Saroyan has a concrete poem that consists of a page blank except for the word *oxygen*.) Poet Richard Kostelanetz has suggested that a more accurate name for concrete poetry might be "word-imagery." He sees it occupying an area somewhere between conventional poetry and visual art.

Admittedly, some concrete poems mean less than meets the eye. That many pretentious doodlers have taken up concretism may have caused a *Time* writer to sneer: did Joyce Kilmer miss all that much by never having seen a poem lovely as a

```
         t
        ttt
       rrrrr
      rrrrrrr
     eeeeeeeee
        ???
```

Like other structures of language, however, concrete poems evidently can have the effect of poetry, if written by poets. Whether or not it ought to be dubbed "poetry," this art can do what poems traditionally have done: use language in delightful ways that reveal meanings to us.

Dorthi Charles   (b. 1963)
CONCRETE CAT   1971

Questions

1. What does this writer indicate by capitalizing the *a* in *ear?* The *y* in *eye?* The *u* in *mouth?* By using spaces between the letters in the word *tail?*
2. Why is the word *mouse* upside down?
3. What possible pun might be seen in the cat's middle stripe?
4. What is the tone of "Concrete Cat"? How is it made evident?
5. Do these words seem chosen for their connotations or only for their denotations? Would you call this work of art a poem?

Experiment: *Do It Yourself*

Make a concrete poem of your own. If you need inspiration, pick some familiar object or animal and try to find words that look like it. For more ideas, study the typography of a magazine or newspaper; cut out interesting letters and numerals and try pasting them into arrangements. What (if anything) do your experiments tell you about familiar letters and words?

Further Suggestions for Writing

1. Consider whether concrete poetry is a vital new art form or merely visual trivia.
2. Should a poem be illustrated, or is it better left to the mind's eye? Discuss this question in a brief essay. You might care to consider William Blake's illustration for "A Poison Tree" or the illustrations in a collection of poems for children.

Exercise: *Seeing the Logic of Open Form Verse*

Read the following poems in open form silently to yourself, noticing what each poet does with white space, repetitions, line breaks, and indentations. Then read the poems aloud, trying to indicate by slight pauses where lines end and also pausing slightly at any space inside a line. Can you see any reasons for the poet's placing his words in this arrangement rather than in a prose paragraph? Do any of these poets seem to care also about visual effect? (As with other kinds of poetry, there may not be any obvious logical reason for everything that happens in these poems.)

E. E. Cummings   (1894–1962)*

IN JUST-   1923

in Just-
spring   when the world is mud-
luscious the little
lame balloonman

whistles   far   and wee   5

and eddieandbill come
running from marbles and
piracies and it's
spring

when the world is puddle-wonderful   10

the queer
old balloonman whistles
far   and   wee
and bettyandisbel come dancing

from hop-scotch and jump-rope and   15

it's
spring
and
   the

      goat-footed   20

balloonMan   whistles
far
and
wee

Linda Pastan   (b. 1932)*

JUMP CABLING   1984

When our cars   touched
When you lifted the hood   of mine
To see the intimate workings   underneath,
When we were bound   together
By a pulse of pure   energy,   5
When my car like the   princess
In the tale woke with a   start,
I thought why not ride the rest of the way together?

Lucille Clifton   (b. 1936)

HOMAGE TO MY HIPS   1991

these hips are big hips.
they need space to
move around in.
they don't fit into little
petty places, these hips   5
are free hips.
they don't like to be held back.
these hips have never been enslaved,
they go where they want to go
they do what they want to do.   10
these hips are mighty hips.

these hips are magic hips.
i have known them
to put a spell on a man and
spin him like a top!   15

Carole Satyamurti   (b. 1939)

I Shall Paint My Nails Red   1990

Because a bit of colour is a public service.

Because I am proud of my hands.

Because it will remind me I'm a woman.

Because I will look like a survivor.

Because I can admire them in traffic jams.   5

Because my daughter will say ugh.

Because my lover will be surprised.

Because it is quicker than dyeing my hair.

Because it is a ten-minute moratorium.

Because it is reversible.   10

QUESTION

"I Shall Paint My Nails Red" is written in free verse, but the poem has several organizing
principles. How many can you discover?

Alice Fulton   (b. 1952)

WHAT I LIKE   1983

Friend—the face I wallow toward
through a scrimmage of shut faces.
Arms like towropes to haul me home, aide-
memoire, my lost childhood docks, a bottled ark
in harbor. *Friend*—I can't forget   5
how even the word contains an *end*.
We circle each other in a scared bolero,
imagining stratagems: postures and imposters.
Cold convictions keep us solo. I ahem
and hedge my affections. Who'll blow the first kiss,   10
land it like the lifeforces we feel

tickling at each wrist? It should be easy
easy to take your hand, whisper down this distance
labeled hers or his: what I like about you is

QUESTION

Does this poem have an ending? Does it need to have an ending to be a successful poem?

WRITER'S PERSPECTIVE

Walt Whitman

Walt Whitman on Writing
THE POETRY OF THE FUTURE   1876

The poetry of the future, (a phrase open to sharp criticism, and not satisfactory to me, but significant, and I will use it)—the poetry of the future aims at the free expression of emotion, (which means far, far more than appears at first,) and to arouse and initiate, more than to define or finish. Like all modern tendencies, it has direct or indirect reference continually to the reader, to you or me, to the central identity of everything, the mighty Ego. (Byron's was a vehement dash, with plenty of impatient democracy, but lurid and introverted amid all its magnetism; not at all the fitting, lasting song of a grand, secure, free, sunny race.) It is more akin, likewise, to outside life and landscape, (returning mainly to the antique feeling,) real sun and gale, and woods and shores—to the elements themselves—not sitting at ease in parlor or library listening to a good tale of them, told in good rhyme. Character, a feature far above style or polish—a feature not absent at any time, but now first brought to the fore—gives predominant stamp to advancing poetry. . . .

Is there not even now, indeed, an evolution, a departure from the masters? Venerable and unsurpassable after their kind as are the old works, and always unspeakably precious as studies, (for Americans more than any other people,) is it too much to say that by the shifted combinations of the modern mind the whole underlying theory of first-class verse has changed?

Preface to the Centennial Edition of *Leaves of Grass*

Lining Up for Free Verse

"That's not poetry! It's just chopped-up prose." So runs one old-fashioned complaint about free verse. Such criticism may be true of inept poems, but in the best free verse the line endings transform language in ways beyond the possibilities of prose.

To understand the special effect of free verse, start by paying special attention to the line breaks. Look especially at the word at the end of each line, which receives special emphasis by its position. (In prose, we might easily pass over the word since in prose we read sentence by sentence.) Free verse almost always invites us to read more slowly and carefully than we would the same passage printed as prose. Look at how Wallace Stevens's lineation in "Thirteen Ways of Looking at a Blackbird" allows us not only to see but also to savor the implications of the ideas and images.

> I was of three minds,
> Like a tree
> In which there are three blackbirds.

On a purely semantic level, these lines may mean the same as the prose statement, "I was of three minds like a tree in which there are three blackbirds," but Stevens's arrangement into verse adds decisive emphasis at several points. Each of his three lines isolates and presents a separate image (the speaker, the tree, and the blackbirds). The placement of *three* at the same position at the end of the opening and closing line helps us feel the similar nature of the two statements. The short middle line allows us to see the image of the tree before we fully understand why it is parallel to the divided mind—thus adding a touch of suspense not in the prose. Ending each line with a key noun and image also gives the poem a concrete feel not altogether evident in the prose.

Even a short passage like Stevens's three lines suggests how powerfully the visual arrangement and rhythmic emphasis of free verse can amplify and transform the prose meaning of words.

WRITING ASSIGNMENT

Take any free verse poem and retype it as prose (adding conventional prose punctuation and capitalization, if necessary). Then compare the prose version to the original poem and discuss how the two passages differ in tone, rhythm, emphasis, or effect. Also acknowledge in what ways the two texts remain similar. Use any poem from this chapter or consider any of the following: T. S. Eliot's "Journey of the Magi" (page 1057); H. D.'s "Helen" (page 1076); Ezra Pound's "The River Merchant's Wife: a Letter" (page 1118); Theodore Roethke's "Elegy for Jane" (page 1126); Walt Whitman's "I Saw in Louisiana a Live-Oak Growing" (page 1151); William Carlos Williams's "To Waken an Old Lady" (page 1155); or James Wright's "A Blessing" (page 1158).

Further Suggestions for Writing

1. Compare any poem in this chapter or in "Poems for Further Reading" (which begins on page 1027) with a poem in rime and meter. Discuss several key features that they share in common despite their apparent differences in style. Features it might be useful to compare include imagery, tone, figures of speech, and word choice.
2. Is "free verse" totally free? Discuss this question in a short essay, drawing evidence from specific open-form poems that you found interesting.

23 Symbol

The national flag is supposed to bestir our patriotic feelings. When a black cat crosses his path, a superstitious man shivers, foreseeing bad luck. To each of these, by custom, our society expects a standard response. A flag, a black cat crossing one's path—each is a **symbol:** a visible object or action that suggests some further meaning in addition to itself. In literature, a symbol might be the word *flag* or the words *a black cat crossed his path* or every description of flag or cat in an entire novel, story, play, or poem.

A flag and the crossing of a black cat may be called **conventional symbols,** since they can have a conventional or customary effect on us. Conventional symbols are also part of the language of poetry, as we know when we meet the red rose, emblem of love, in a lyric, or the Christian cross in the devotional poems of George Herbert. More often, however, symbols in literature have no conventional, long-established meaning, but particular meanings of their own. In Melville's novel *Moby-Dick*, to take a rich example, whatever we associate with the great white whale is *not* attached unmistakably to white whales by custom. Though Melville tells us that men have long regarded whales with awe and relates Moby Dick to the celebrated fish that swallowed Jonah, the reader's response is to one particular whale, the creature of Herman Melville. Only the experience of reading the novel in its entirety can give Moby Dick his particular meaning.

We should say *meanings,* for as Eudora Welty has observed, it is a good thing Melville made Moby Dick a whale, a creature large enough to contain all that critics have found in him. A symbol in literature, if not conventional, has more than just one meaning. In "The Raven," by Edgar Allan Poe, the appearance of a strange black bird in the narrator's study is sinister; and indeed, if we take the poem seriously, we may even respond with a sympathetic shiver of dread. Does the bird mean death, fate, melancholy, the loss of a loved one, knowledge in the service of evil? All these, perhaps. Like any well-chosen symbol, Poe's raven sets going within the reader an unending train of feelings and associations.

We miss the value of a symbol, however, if we think it can mean absolutely anything we wish. If a poet has any control over our reactions, the poem will guide our responses in a certain direction.

T. S. Eliot (1888–1965)*

THE *Boston Evening Transcript* 1917

The readers of the *Boston Evening Transcript*
Sway in the wind like a field of ripe corn.

When evening quickens faintly in the street,
Wakening the appetites of life in some
And to others bringing the *Boston Evening Transcript*, 5
I mount the steps and ring the bell, turning
Wearily, as one would turn to nod good-bye to La Rochefoucauld,
If the street were time and he at the end of the street,
And I say, "Cousin Harriet, here is the *Boston Evening Transcript*."

The newspaper, whose name Eliot purposely repeats so monotonously, indicates what this poem is about. Now defunct, the *Transcript* covered in detail the slightest activity of Boston's leading families and was noted for the great length of its obituaries. Eliot, then, uses the newspaper as a symbol for an existence of boredom, fatigue *(Wearily)*, petty and unvarying routine (since an evening newspaper, like night, arrives on schedule). The *Transcript* evokes a way of life without zest or passion, for, opposed to people who read it, Eliot sets people who do not: those whose desires revive, not expire, when the working day is through. Suggestions abound in the ironic comparison of the *Transcript's* readers to a cornfield late in summer. To mention only a few: the readers sway because they are sleepy; they vegetate; they are drying up; each makes a rattling sound when turning a page. It is not necessary that we know the remote and similarly disillusioned friend to whom the speaker might nod: La Rochefoucauld, whose cynical *Maxims* entertained Parisian society under Louis XIV (sample: "All of us have enough strength to endure the misfortunes of others"). We understand that the nod is symbolic of an immense weariness of spirit. We know nothing about Cousin Harriet, whom the speaker addresses, but imagine from the greeting she inspires that she is probably a bore.

If Eliot wishes to say that certain Bostonians lead lives of sterile boredom, why does he couch his meaning in symbols? Why doesn't he tell us directly what he means? These questions imply two assumptions not necessarily true: first, that Eliot has a message to impart; second, that he is concealing it. We have reason to think that Eliot did not usually have a message in mind when beginning a poem, for as he once told a critic: "The conscious problems with which one is concerned in the actual writing are more those of a quasi musical nature . . . than of a conscious exposition of ideas." Poets sometimes discover what they have to say while in the act of saying it. And it may be that in his *Transcript* poem, Eliot is saying exactly what he means. By communicating his meaning through symbols instead of statements, he may be choosing the only kind of language appropriate to an idea of great subtlety and complexity. (The paraphrase "Certain Bostonians are bored" hardly begins to describe the poem in all its possible meaning.) And by his use of symbolism, Eliot affords us the pleasure of finding our own entrances to his poem.

This power of suggestion that a symbol contains is, perhaps, its greatest advantage. Sometimes, as in the following poem by Emily Dickinson, a symbol will lead us from a visible object to something too vast to be perceived.

Emily Dickinson (1830–1886)*

THE LIGHTNING IS A YELLOW FORK (ABOUT 1870)

The Lightning is a yellow Fork
From Tables in the sky
By inadvertent fingers dropt
The awful Cutlery

Of mansions never quite disclosed   5
And never quite concealed
The Apparatus of the Dark
To ignorance revealed.

If the lightning is a fork, then whose are the fingers that drop it, the table from which it slips, the household to which it belongs? The poem implies this question without giving an answer. An obvious answer is "God," but can we be sure? We wonder, too, about these partially lighted mansions: if our vision were clearer, what would we behold?[1]

"But how am I supposed to know a symbol when I see one?" The best approach is to read poems closely, taking comfort in the likelihood that it is better not to notice symbols at all than to find significance in every literal stone and

---

[1]In its suggestion of an infinite realm that mortal eyes cannot quite see, but whose nature can be perceived fleetingly through things visible, Emily Dickinson's poem, by coincidence, resembles the work of late-nineteenth-century French poets called **symbolists.** To a symbolist the shirt-tail of Truth is continually seen disappearing around a corner. With their Neoplatonic view of ideal realities existing in a great beyond, whose corresponding symbols are the perceptible cats that bite us and tangible stones we stumble over, French poets such as Charles Baudelaire, Jules Laforgue, and Stéphane Mallarmé were profoundly to affect poets writing in English, notably Yeats (who said a poem "entangles . . . a part of the Divine essence") and Eliot. But we consider in this chapter symbolism as an element in certain poems, not Symbolism, the literary movement.

huge meanings in every thing. In looking for the symbols in a poem, pick out all the references to concrete objects—newspapers, black cats, twisted pins. Consider these with special care. Notice any that the poet emphasizes by detailed description, by repetition, or by placing it at the very beginning or end of the poem. Ask: What is the poem about, what does it add up to? If, when the poem is paraphrased, the paraphrase depends primarily upon the meaning of certain concrete objects, these richly suggestive objects may be the symbols.

There are some things a literary symbol usually is *not*. A symbol is not an abstraction. Such terms as *truth*, *death*, *love*, and *justice* cannot work as symbols (unless personified, as in the traditional figure of Justice holding a scale). Most often, a symbol is something we can see in the mind's eye: a newspaper, a lightning bolt, a gesture of nodding good-bye.

In narratives, a well-developed character who speaks much dialogue and is not the least bit mysterious is usually not a symbol. But watch out for an executioner in a black hood; a character, named for a Biblical prophet, who does little but utter a prophecy; a trio of old women who resemble the Three Fates. (It has been argued, with good reason, that Milton's fully rounded character of Satan in *Paradise Lost* is a symbol embodying evil and human pride, but a narrower definition of symbol is more frequently useful.) A symbol *may* be a part of a person's body (the baleful eye of the murder victim in Poe's story "The Tell-Tale Heart") or a look, a voice, a mannerism.

A symbol usually is not the second term of a metaphor. In the line "The Lightning is a yellow Fork," the symbol is the lightning, not the fork.

Sometimes a symbol addresses a sense other than sight: the sound of a mysterious harp at the end of Chekhov's play *The Cherry Orchard*; or, in William Faulkner's tale "A Rose for Emily," the odor of decay that surrounds the house of the last survivor of a town's leading family—suggesting not only physical dissolution but also the decay of a social order. A symbol is a special kind of image, for it exceeds the usual image in the richness of its connotations. The dead wife's cold comb in the haiku of Buson (discussed on page 741) works symbolically, suggesting among other things the chill of the grave, the contrast between the living and the dead.

Holding a narrower definition than that used in this book, some readers of poetry prefer to say that a symbol is always a concrete object, never an act. They would deny the label "symbol" to Ahab's breaking his tobacco pipe before setting out to pursue Moby Dick (suggesting, perhaps, his determination to allow no pleasure to distract him from the chase) or to any large motion (as Ahab's whole quest). This distinction, while confining, does have the merit of sparing one from seeing all motion to be possibly symbolic. Some would call Ahab's gesture not a symbol but a **symbolic act.**

To sum up: a symbol radiates hints or casts long shadows (to use Henry James's metaphor). We are unable to say it "stands for" or "represents" a meaning. It evokes, it suggests, it manifests. It demands no single necessary interpretation, such as the interpretation a driver gives to a red traffic light. Rather, like Emily Dickinson's lightning bolt, it points toward an indefinite meaning, which may lie in part beyond the reach of words. In a symbol, as Thomas Carlyle said in *Sartor Resartus*, "the Infinite is made to blend with the Finite, to stand visible, and as it were, attainable there."

Thomas Hardy (1840–1928)*

NEUTRAL TONES   1898

We stood by a pond that winter day,
And the sun was white, as though chidden of God,
And a few leaves lay on the starving sod;
    —They had fallen from an ash, and were gray.

Your eyes on me were as eyes that rove   5
Over tedious riddles of years ago;
And some words played between us to and fro
    On which lost the more by our love.

The smile on your mouth was the deadest thing
Alive enough to have strength to die;   10
And a grin of bitterness swept thereby
    Like an ominous bird a-wing. . . .

Since then, keen lessons that love deceives,
And wrings with wrong, have shaped to me
Your face, and the God-curst sun, and a tree,   15
    And a pond edged with grayish leaves.

QUESTIONS

1. Sum up the story told in this poem. In lines 1–12, what is the dramatic situation? What has happened in the interval between the experience related in these lines and the reflection in the last stanza?
2. What meanings do you find in the title?
3. Explain in your own words the metaphor in line 2.
4. What connotations appropriate to this poem does the *ash* (line 4) have, that *oak* or *maple* would lack?
5. What visible objects in the poem function symbolically? What actions or gestures?

If we read of a ship, its captain, its sailors, and the rough seas, and we realize we are reading about a commonwealth and how its rulers and workers keep it going even in difficult times, then we are reading an **allegory.** Closely akin to symbolism, allegory is a description—usually narrative—in which persons, places, and things are employed in a continuous and consistent system of equivalents.

Although more strictly limited in its suggestions than symbolism, allegory need not be thought inferior. Few poems continue to interest readers more than Dante's allegorical *Divine Comedy*. Sublime evidence of the appeal of allegory may be found in Christ's use of the **parable:** a brief narrative—usually allegorical but sometimes not—that teaches a moral.

Matthew 13:24–30
(King James Version, 1611)

THE PARABLE OF THE GOOD SEED

The kingdom of heaven is likened unto a man which sowed good
seed in his field:
But while men slept, his enemy came and sowed tares among the
wheat, and went his way.
But when the blade was sprung up, and brought forth fruit, then
appeared the tares also.
So the servants of the householder came and said unto him, Sir,
didst not thou sow good seed in thy field? From whence then hath
it tares?
He said unto them, An enemy hath done this. The servants said unto
him, Wilt thou then that we go and gather them up? 5
But he said, Nay; lest while ye gather up the tares, ye root up also
the wheat with them.
Let both grow together until the harvest: and in the time of harvest
I will say to the reapers, Gather ye together first the tares, and bind
them in bundles to burn them: but gather the wheat into my barn.

The sower is the Son of man, the field is the world, the good seed are the children of the Kingdom, the tares are the children of the wicked one, the enemy is the devil, the harvest is the end of the world, the reapers are angels. "As therefore the tares are gathered and burned in the fire; so shall it be in the end of this world" (Matthew 13:36–42).

Usually, as in this parable, the meanings of an allegory are plainly labeled or thinly disguised. In John Bunyan's allegorical narrative *The Pilgrim's Progress*, it is clear that the hero Christian, on his journey through places with such pointed names as Vanity Fair, the Valley of the Shadow of Death, and Doubting Castle, is the soul, traveling the road of life on the way toward Heaven. An allegory, when carefully built, is systematic. It makes one principal comparison, the working out of whose details may lead to further comparisons, then still further comparisons: Christian, thrown by Giant Despair into the dungeon of Doubting Castle, escapes by means of a key called Promise. Such a complicated design may take great length to unfold, as in Spenser's *Faerie Queene;* but the method may be seen in a short poem:

George Herbert (1593–1633)*
REDEMPTION   1633

Having been tenant long to a rich Lord,
  Not thriving, I resolvèd to be bold,
And make a suit unto him to afford
  A new small-rented lease and cancel th' old.
In Heaven at his manor I him sought.   5
  They told me there that he was lately gone
About some land which he had dearly bought
  Long since on earth, to take possessiòn.
I straight returned, and knowing his great birth,
  Sought him accordingly in great resorts,   10
  In cities, theaters, gardens, parks, and courts.
At length I heard a ragged noise and mirth
  Of thieves and murderers; there I him espied,
  Who straight "Your suit is granted," said, and died.

QUESTIONS

1. In this allegory, what equivalents does Herbert give each of these terms: *tenant, Lord, not thriving, suit, new lease, old lease, manor, land, dearly bought, take possession, his great birth?*
2. What scene is depicted in the last three lines?

An object in allegory is like a bird whose cage is clearly lettered with its identity—"RAVEN, *Corvus corax;* habitat of specimen, Maine." A symbol, by contrast, is a bird with piercing eyes that mysteriously appears one evening in your library. It is there; you can touch it. But what does it mean? You look at it. It continues to look at you.

John Ciardi (1916–1986)*
MOST LIKE AN ARCH THIS MARRIAGE   1958

Most like an arch—an entrance which upholds
and shores the stone-crush up the air like lace.
Mass made idea, and idea held in place.
A lock in time. Inside half-heaven unfolds.

Most like an arch—two weaknesses that lean
into a strength. Two fallings become firm.
Two joined abeyances become a term
naming the fact that teaches fact to mean.

Not quite that? Not much less. World as it is,
what's strong and separate falters. All I do
at piling stone on stone apart from you
is roofless around nothing. Till we kiss

I am no more than upright and unset.
It is by falling in and in we make
the all-bearing point, for one another's sake,
in faultless failing, raised by our own weight.

QUESTION

Is this poem an allegory or merely a poem with a strong central symbol? (For the definition of allegory, see page 906.)

Whether an object in literature is a symbol, part of an allegory, or no such thing at all, it has at least one sure meaning. Moby Dick is first a whale and the *Boston Evening Transcript* is a newspaper. Besides deriving a multitude of intangible suggestions from the title symbol in Eliot's long poem *The Waste Land*, its readers cannot fail to carry away a sense of the land's physical appearance: a river choked with sandwich papers and cigarette ends, London Bridge "under the brown fog of a winter dawn." A virtue of *The Pilgrim's Progress* is that its walking abstractions are no mere abstractions but are also human: Giant Despair is a henpecked husband. The most vital element of a literary work may pass us by, unless before seeking further depths in a thing, we look to the thing itself.

Emily Dickinson (1830–1886)*

I HEARD A FLY BUZZ—WHEN I DIED   (ABOUT 1862)

I heard a Fly buzz – when I died –
The Stillness in the Room
Was like the Stillness in the Air –
Between the Heaves of Storm –

The Eyes around – had wrung them dry –
And Breaths were gathering firm
For that last Onset – when the King
Be witnessed – in the Room –

I willed my Keepsakes – Signed away
What portion of me be
Assignable – and then it was
There interposed a Fly –

With Blue – uncertain stumbling Buzz –
Between the light – and me –
And then the Windows failed – and then
I could not see to see –

10

15

QUESTIONS

1. Why is the poem written in the past tense? Where is the speaker at present?
2. What do you understand from the repetition of the word *see* in the last line?
3. What does the poet mean by *Eyes around* (line 5), *that last Onset* (line 7), *the King* (line 7), and *What portion of me be / Assignable* (lines 10–11)?
4. In line 13, how can a sound be called *Blue* and *stumbling*?
5. What further meaning might *the Windows* (line 15) suggest, in addition to denoting the windows of the room?
6. What connotations of the word *fly* seem relevant to an account of a death?
7. Summarize your interpretation of the poem. What does the fly mean?

Robert Frost (1874–1963)*

THE ROAD NOT TAKEN   1916

Two roads diverged in a yellow wood,
And sorry I could not travel both
And be one traveler, long I stood
And looked down one as far as I could
To where it bent in the undergrowth;   5

Then took the other, as just as fair,   ?
And having perhaps the better claim,
Because it was grassy and wanted wear;
Though as for that the passing there   ?
Had worn them really about the same,   10

And both that morning equally lay   ?
In leaves no step had trodden black.
Oh, I kept the first for another day!
Yet knowing how way leads on to way,
I doubted if I should ever come back.   15

I shall be telling this with a sigh   ) Future
Somewhere ages and ages hence:) speculation
Two roads diverged in a wood, and I—
I took the one less traveled by,
And that has made all the difference.   Ambiguous'   20
                                        How does he know?

What symbolism do you find in this poem, if any? Back up your claim with evidence.

Christina Rossetti   (1830–1894)

UPHILL   1862

Does the road wind uphill all the way?
   Yes, to the very end.
Will the day's journey take the whole long day?
   From morn to night, my friend.

But is there for the night a resting-place?   5
   A roof for when the slow dark hours begin.
May not the darkness hide it from my face?
   You cannot miss that inn.

Shall I meet other wayfarers at night?
   Those who have gone before.   10
Then must I knock, or call when just in sight?
   They will not keep you standing at that door.

Shall I find comfort, travel-sore and weak?
   Of labor you shall find the sum.
Will there be beds for me and all who seek?   15
   Yea, beds for all who come.

QUESTIONS

1. At what line in reading this poem did you realize that the poet is building an allegory?
2. For what does each thing stand?
3. What does the title of the poem suggest to you?
4. Recast the meaning of line 14, a knotty line, in your own words.
5. Discuss the possible identities of the two speakers—the apprehensive traveler and the character with all the answers. Are they specific individuals? Allegorical figures?
6. Compare "Uphill" with Robert Creeley's "Oh No" (page 681). What striking similarities do you find in these two dissimilar poems?

Gjertrud Schnackenberg   (b. 1953)

SIGNS   1974

Threading the palm, a web of little lines
Spells out the lost money, the heart, the head,
The wagging tongues, the sudden deaths, in signs
We would smooth out, like imprints on a bed,

In signs that can't be helped, geese heading south,   5
In signs read anxiously, like breath that clouds
A mirror held to a barely open mouth,
Like telegrams, the gathering of crowds—

The plane's X in the sky, spelling disaster:
Before the whistle and hit, a tracer flare;   10
Before rubble, a hairline crack in plaster
And a housefly's panicked scribbling on the air.

Questions

1. What are "signs" in this poet's sense of the word?
2. The poem gives a list of signs. What unmistakable meaning does each indicate?
3. Compare Schnackenberg's fly and Emily Dickinson's (page 909). Which insect seems loaded with more suggestions?
4. Can you think of any familiar signs that *aren't* ominous?
5. This poem was written when the poet was a student at Mount Holyoke College. Knowing this fact, do you like it any less, or any more?

For Review and Further Study

Robinson Jeffers   (1887–1962)*

The Beaks of Eagles   1937

An eagle's nest on the head of an old redwood on one of the precipice-
    footed ridges
Above Ventana Creek, that jagged country which nothing but a falling
    meteor will ever plow; no horseman
Will ever ride there, no hunter cross this ridge but the winged ones, no
    one will steal the eggs from this fortress.
The she-eagle is old, her mate was shot long ago, she is now mated
    with a son of hers.
When lightning blasted her nest she built it again on the same tree,
    in the splinters of the thunderbolt.   5
The she-eagle is older than I; she was here when the fires of eighty-five
    raged on these ridges,
She was lately fledged and dared not hunt ahead of them but ate
    scorched meat. The world has changed in her time;
Humanity has multiplied, but not here; men's hopes and thoughts and
    customs have changed, their powers are enlarged,
Their powers and their follies have become fantastic,
The unstable animal never has been changed so rapidly. The motor
    and the plane and the great war have gone over him,   10
And Lenin has lived and Jehovah died: while the mother-eagle

Hunts her same hills, crying the same beautiful and lonely cry and is
    never tired; dreams the same dreams,
And hears at night the rock-slides rattle and thunder in the throats of
    these living mountains.
                  It is good for man
To try all changes, progress and corruption, powers, peace and anguish,
    not to go down the dinosaur's way   15
Until all his capacities have been explored: and it is good for him
To know that his needs and nature are no more changed in fact in ten
    thousand years than the beaks of eagles.

THE BEAKS OF EAGLES. 2 *Ventana Creek:* an isolated creek near Carmel, California. 10 *the great war:*
World War I (1914–1918). 11 *Lenin:* Vladimir Ilyich Lenin (1870–1924), the leader of the Russian
Communist Revolution.

QUESTIONS

1. What does the speaker tell us about the eagle's habitat?
2. What do we know about the age of the eagle? What events have happened in her
   lifetime—both to her and to the outer world?
3. To what other creature is the eagle repeatedly compared?
4. What does the eagle come to symbolize by the end of the poem?
5. Would the meaning of the last line change significantly if the phrase *the beaks of eagles* became merely *eagles?* If so, how would it change?

Sara Teasdale   (1884–1933)

THE FLIGHT   1926

We are two eagles
Flying together,
Under the heavens,
Over the mountains,
Stretched on the wind.   5
Sunlight heartens us,
Blind snow baffles us,
Clouds wheel after us,
Raveled and thinned.

We are like eagles;   10
But when Death harries us,
Human and humbled
When one of us goes,
Let the other follow—
Let the flight be ended,   15
Let the fire blacken,
Let the book close.

1. What do the two eagles experience together? What must they experience separately?
2. In the first stanza, the eagles are a metaphor. In the second stanza, the eagles become a simile. Does this change in the figure of speech have any significance?
3. What new metaphors are introduced in the second stanza?
4. What do the two eagles come to symbolize in this poem?

EXERCISE: *Symbol Hunting*

After you have read each of these poems, decide which description best suits it:

1. The poem has a central symbol.
2. The poem contains no symbolism, but is to be taken literally.

William Carlos Williams (1883–1963)*

POEM   1934

As the cat
climbed over
the top of

the jamcloset
first the right   5
forefoot

carefully
then the hind
stepped down
into the pit of   10
the empty
flowerpot

Ted Kooser (b. 1939)*

CARRIE   1979

"There's never an end to dust
and dusting," my aunt would say
as her rag, like a thunderhead,
scudded across the yellow oak
of her little house. There she lived   5
seventy years with a ball
of compulsion closed in her fist,

and an elbow that creaked and popped
like a branch in a storm. Now dust
is her hands and dust her heart.   10
There is never an end to it.

James Applewhite (b. 1935)

THE STORY OF A DRAWER   1986

Father amazed us waving his pistol
in his story of the station nearly robbed.
The thirty-eight special—blued steel glossy
As cobras—nested near the cash register handle
With foil-pack prophylactics, quarters.   5
We imagined his hand with that blue-black bolt
Of lightening upraised, the drunk punks slinking
For the door while he danced his explosive fist
At ceiling and window. We looked in awe at the thing
Exposed, then slid the drawer shut, were quiet.   10

Lorine Niedecker (1903–1970)*

POPCORN-CAN COVER   (ABOUT 1959)

Popcorn-can cover
screwed to the wall
over a hole
        so the cold
can't mouse in   5

Wallace Stevens (1879–1955)*

ANECDOTE OF THE JAR   1923

I placed a jar in Tennessee,
And round it was, upon a hill.
It made the slovenly wilderness
Surround that hill.

The wilderness rose up to it,   5
And sprawled around, no longer wild.
The jar was round upon the ground
And tall and of a port in air.

It took dominion everywhere.
The jar was gray and bare.   10
It did not give of bird or bush,
Like nothing else in Tennessee.

WRITER'S PERSPECTIVE

William Butler Yeats

William Butler Yeats on Writing POETIC SYMBOLS   1901

Any one who has any experience of any mystical state of the soul knows how there float up in the mind profound symbols, whose meaning, if indeed they do not delude one into the dream that they are meaningless, one does not perhaps understand for years. Nor I think has any one, who has known that experience with any constancy, failed to find some day, in some old book or on some old monument, a strange or intricate image that had floated up before him, and to grow perhaps dizzy with the sudden conviction that our little memories are but a part of some great Memory that renews the world and men's thoughts age after age, and that our thoughts are not, as we suppose, the deep, but a little foam upon the deep.

. . .

It is only by ancient symbols, by symbols that have numberless meanings besides the one or two the writer lays an emphasis upon, or the half-score he knows of, that any highly subjective art can escape from the barrenness and shallowness of a too conscious arrangement, into the abundance and depth of Nature. The poet of essences and pure ideas must seek in the half-lights that glimmer from symbol to symbol as if to the ends of the earth, all that the epic and dramatic poet finds of mystery and shadow in the accidental circumstances of life.

"The Philosophy of Shelley's Poetry"

How to Read a Symbol

A symbol, to use poet John Drury's concise definition, is "an image that radiates meanings." Exactly what those meanings will be, however, often differs from poem to poem. In one poem snow may be a reassuring symbol of sleep and forgetfulness, while in another it becomes a chilling symbol of death. Both meanings easily connect to the natural image of snow, but in each poem, the author has nudged that image in a different direction.

The way a symbol has been used by earlier writers affects the way we grasp the image today. It would be difficult, for example, to put a great white whale in a contemporary poem without summoning up the symbolic association of Melville's Moby Dick. No matter how the poet chooses to handle it, the association will be there as a starting point.

Sometimes a poet gladly adopts the traditional symbolism of an image. In "Go, Lovely Rose" (page 1150) Edmund Waller masterfully employs the image of the rose with all its conventional associations as a symbol of the transience of human beauty. William Butler Yeats believed that poetic symbols acquired their special power by thousands of years of use. Poets, therefore, had to employ symbols consistent with their ancient meanings. Contemporary poets, on the other hand, often enjoy turning traditional symbols upside down. In her poem, "Victory" (page 746), Anne Stevenson presents the newborn child not as a conventional little angel or bundle of joy, but as a frightening, inhuman antagonist.

The same image, therefore, can often convey divergent meanings in different poems—even when the poems are written by contemporaries. Sara Teasdale and Robinson Jeffers, for example, were born only three years apart, and they often published poems in the same journals. Both employed the eagle as the central image of a poem (Teasdale's "The Flight" and Jeffers's "The Beaks of Eagles," pages 913 and 912, respectively), but the image came to symbolize different things in each poem.

When writing about the meaning (or meanings) of a symbol, follow the image through the poem and give it time to establish its own pattern of associations. Don't jump to quick conclusions. If the symbol is a traditional one (the cross, a rose, a reaper and so on), is it being used in the expected way? Or is the poet playing with its associations? And finally, if the image doesn't seem to radiate meanings above and beyond its literal sense, don't feel you have failed as a critic. Not everything is a symbol. As Sigmund Freud once commented about symbol-hunting, "Sometimes a cigar is just a cigar."

WRITING ASSIGNMENT

Compare the use of the eagle as a symbol in Sara Teasdale's "The Flight" and Robinson Jeffers's "The Beaks of Eagles." What does the central image of the eagle suggest in each poem? How does the symbolism differ in each? Are there any meaningful similarities between the two?

FURTHER SUGGESTIONS FOR WRITING

1. Write a paraphrase of Emily Dickinson's "I heard a Fly buzz—when I died." Clarify whatever meanings you find in the fly (and other concrete objects).

2. Discuss the symbolism in a poem in "Poems for Further Reading" (beginning on page 1027). Likely poems to study (among many) are Louise Bogan's "The Dream," T. S. Eliot's "The Love Song of J. Alfred Prufrock," Robert Lowell's "Skunk Hour," Gerard Manley Hopkins's "The Windhover," and Mary Jo Salter's "Welcome to Hiroshima."

3. Take a relatively simple, straightforward poem, such as William Carlos Williams's "This Is Just to Say" (page 700), and write a burlesque critical interpretation of it. Claim to discover symbols that the poem doesn't contain. While running wild with your "reading into" the poem, don't invent anything that you can't somehow support from the text of the poem itself. At the end of your burlesque, sum up in a paragraph what this exercise taught you about how to read poems, or how not to.

24 Myth and Narrative

Poets have long been fond of retelling **myths,** narrowly defined as traditional stories about the exploits of immortal beings. Such stories taken collectively may also be called **myth** or **mythology.** In one of the most celebrated collections of myth ever assembled, the *Metamorphoses,* the Roman poet Ovid told— to take one example from many—how Phaeton, child of the sun god, rashly tried to drive his father's fiery chariot on its daily round, lost control of the horses, and caused disaster both to himself and to the world. Our use of the term *myth* in discussing poetry, then, differs from its use in expressions such as "the myth of communism" and "the myth of democracy." In these examples, myth is used broadly to represent any idea people believe in, whether true or false. Nor do we mean—to take another familiar use of the word—a cock-and-bull story: "Judge Rapp doesn't roast speeders alive; that's just a *myth.*" In the following discussion, *myth* will mean a kind of story—either from ancient or modern sources—whose actions implicitly symbolize some profound truth about human or natural existence.

Traditional myths tell us stories of gods or heroes—their battles, their lives, their loves, and often their suffering—all on a scale of magnificence larger than our life. These exciting stories usually reveal part of a culture's worldview. Myths often try to explain universal natural phenomena, like the phases of the moon or the turning of the seasons. But some myths tell the story of purely local phenomena; one Greek legend, for example, recounts how grief-stricken King Aegeus threw himself into the sea when he mistakenly believed his son, Theseus, had been killed; consequently, the body of water between Greece and Turkey was called the Aegean Sea.

Modern psychologists, like Sigmund Freud and Carl Jung, have been fascinated by myth and legend, since they believe these stories symbolically enact deep truths about human nature. Our myths, psychologists believe, express our wishes, dreams, and nightmares. Whether or not we believe myths, we recognize their psychological power. Even in the first century B.C., Roman poet Ovid did not believe in the literal truth of the legends he so suavely retold; he confessed, "I prate of ancient poets' monstrous lies."

And yet it is characteristic of a myth that it *can* be believed. Throughout history, myths have accompanied religious doctrines and rituals. They have helped sanction or recall the reasons for religious observances. A sublime instance is the New Testament account of the Last Supper. Because of its record of the words of Jesus, "Do this in remembrance of Me," Christians have continued to re-enact the offering and partaking of the body and blood of their Lord, under the appearances of bread and wine. It is essential to recall that, just because a myth narrates the acts of a god, we do not necessarily mean by the term a false or fictitious narrative. When we speak of the "myth of Islam" or "the Christian myth," we do so without implying either belief or disbelief.

Myths can also help sanction customs and institutions other than religious ones. At the same time as the baking of bread was introduced to ancient Greece—one theory goes—the myth of Demeter, goddess of grain, appeared. Demeter was a kindly deity who sent her emissary to teach humankind the valuable art of baking—thus helping to persuade the distrustful that bread was a good thing. Some myths seem designed to divert and regale, not to sanction anything. Such may be the story of the sculptor Pygmalion, who fell in love with the statue he had carved of a beautiful woman; so exquisite was his work, so deep was his feeling, that Aphrodite, the goddess of Love, brought the statue to life. And yet perhaps the story goes deeper than mere diversion: perhaps it is a way of saying that works of art achieve a reality of their own, that love can transform or animate its object.

How does a myth begin? Several theories have been proposed, none universally accepted. One is that a myth is a way to explain some natural phenomenon. Winter comes and the vegetation perishes because Persephone, child of Demeter, must return to the underworld for four months every year. This theory, as classical scholar Edith Hamilton has pointed out, may lead us to think incorrectly that Greek mythology was the creation of a primitive people. Tales of the gods of Mount Olympus may reflect an earlier inheritance, but the Greek myths known to us were transcribed in an era of high civilization. Anthropologists have questioned whether primitive people generally find beauty in the mysteries of nature. Many anthropologists emphasize the practical function of myth; in his influential work of comparative mythology, *The Golden Bough*, Sir James Frazer argued that most myths were originally expressions of human hope that nature would be fertile. Still another theory maintains that many myths began as real events; mythic heroes were real human beings whose deeds have been changed and exaggerated by posterity. Most present-day myth historians would say that different myths probably have different origins.

Poets have many coherent mythologies on which to draw; perhaps those most frequently consulted by British and American poets are the classical, the Christian, the Norse, the Native American, and the folk tales of the American frontier (embodying the deeds of superhuman characters such as Paul Bunyan). Some poets have taken inspiration from other myths as well: T. S. Eliot's *The Waste Land*, for example, is enriched by allusions to Buddhism and to pagan vegetation-cults. Robert Bly borrowed the terrifying Death Goddess of Aztec, Hindu, and Balinese mythology to make her the climactic figure of his long poem, "The Teeth Mother Naked at Last."

A tour through any good art museum will demonstrate how thoroughly myth pervades the painting and sculpture of nearly every civilization. In literature, one evidence of its continuing value to recent poets and storytellers is how frequently ancient myths are retold. Even in modern society, writers often turn to myth when they try to tell stories of deep significance. Mythic structures still touch a powerful and primal part of the human imagination. William Faulkner's story "The Bear" recalls tales of Indian totem animals; John Updike's novel *The Centaur* presents the horse-man Chiron as a modern high school teacher; James Joyce's *Ulysses* retells *The Odyssey* in modern Dublin; Rita Dove's play *The Darker Face of the Earth* retells the story of Oedipus in the slave-era South; Bernard Shaw retells the Pygmalion story in his popular Edwardian social comedy, *Pygmalion*, later the basis of the hit musical *My Fair Lady*; Jean Cocteau's film *Orphée* shows us Eurydice riding to the underworld with an escort of motorcycles. Popular interest in such works may testify to the profound appeal myths continue to hold for us. Like other varieties of poetry, myth is a kind of knowledge, not at odds with scientific knowledge but existing in addition to it.

Robert Frost   (1874–1963)*

NOTHING GOLD CAN STAY   1923

Nature's first green is gold,
Her hardest hue to hold.
Her early leaf's a flower;
But only so an hour.
Then leaf subsides to leaf.   5
So Eden sank to grief,
So dawn goes down to day.
Nothing gold can stay.

QUESTIONS

1. To what myth does this poem allude? Does Frost sound as though he believes in the myth or as though he rejects it?
2. When Frost says, "Nature's first green is gold," he is describing how many leaves first appear as tiny yellow buds and blossoms. But what else does this line imply?
3. What would happen to the poem's meaning if line 6 were omitted?

D. H. Lawrence   (1885–1930)*

BAVARIAN GENTIANS   1932

Not every man has gentians in his house
in soft September, at slow, sad Michaelmas.

Bavarian gentians, big and dark, only dark
darkening the daytime, torch-like with the smoking blueness of Pluto's
    gloom,
ribbed and torch-like, with their blaze of darkness spread blue   5
down flattening into points, flattened under the sweep of white day
torch-flower of the blue-smoking darkness, Pluto's dark-blue daze,
black lamps from the halls of Dis, burning dark blue,
giving off darkness, blue darkness, as Demeter's pale lamps give off light,
lead me then, lead the way.   10

Reach me a gentian, give me a torch!
let me guide myself with the blue, forked torch of this flower
down the darker and darker stairs, where blue is darkened on blueness
even where Persephone goes, just now, from the frosted September
to the sightless realm where darkness is awake upon the dark   15
and Persephone herself is but a voice
or a darkness invisible enfolded in the deeper dark
of the arms Plutonic, and pierced with the passion of dense gloom,
among the splendor of torches of darkness, shedding darkness on the
    lost bride and her groom.

BAVARIAN GENTIANS. 2 *Michaelmas:* The feast of St. Michael (September 29). 4 *Pluto:* Roman
name for Hades, in Greek mythology the ruler of the underworld, who abducted Persephone to be
his bride. Each spring Persephone returns to earth and is welcomed by her mother Demeter, goddess of fruitfulness; each winter she departs again, to dwell with her husband below. 8 *Dis:* Pluto's
realm.

QUESTIONS

1. Read this poem aloud. What devices of sound do you hear in it?
2. What characteristics of gentians appear to remind Lawrence of the story of Persephone? What significance do you attach to the poem's being set in September? How
   does the fact of autumn matter to the gentians and to Persephone?

Thomas Hardy   (1840–1928)*

THE OXEN   1915

Christmas Eve, and twelve of the clock.
    "Now they are all on their knees,"
An elder said as we sat in a flock
    By the embers in hearthside ease.

We pictured the meek mild creatures where   5
    They dwelt in their strawy pen,
Nor did it occur to one of us there
    To doubt they were kneeling then.

So fair a fancy few would weave
    In these years! Yet, I feel,   10
If someone said on Christmas Eve,
    "Come; see the oxen kneel

"In the lonely barton° by yonder coomb°   *farmyard; a hollow*
    Our childhood used to know,"
I should go with him in the gloom,   15
    Hoping it might be so.

THE OXEN. This ancient belief has had wide currency among peasants and farmers of Western Europe. Some also say that on Christmas Eve the beasts can speak.

QUESTIONS

1. What body of myth is Hardy's subject and what are his speaker's attitudes toward it? Perhaps, in Hardy's view, the pious report about oxen is only part of it.
2. Read this poem aloud and notice its sound and imagery. What contrast do you find between the sounds of the first stanza and the sounds of the last stanza? Which words make the difference? What images enforce a contrast in tone between the beginning of the poem and its ending?
3. G. K. Chesterton, writing as a defender of Christian faith, called Hardy's writings "the mutterings of the village atheist." See other poems by Hardy in "Poems for Further Reading." What do you think Chesterton might have meant? Can "The Oxen" be called a hostile mutter?

William Wordsworth (1770–1850)*

THE WORLD IS TOO MUCH WITH US   1807

The world is too much with us; late and soon,
Getting and spending, we lay waste our powers;
Little we see in Nature that is ours;
We have given our hearts away, a sordid boon!
This Sea that bares her bosom to the moon;   5
The winds that will be howling at all hours,
And are up-gathered now like sleeping flowers;
For this, for everything, we are out of tune;
It moves us not. Great God! I'd rather be
A Pagan suckled in a creed outworn;   10
So might I, standing on this pleasant lea,

Have glimpses that would make me less forlorn;
Have sight of Proteus rising from the sea;
Or hear old Triton blow his wreathèd horn.

QUESTIONS

1. In this sonnet by Wordsworth what condition does the poet complain about? To what does he attribute this condition?
2. How does it affect him as an individual?

Louise Bogan (1897–1970)*

MEDUSA   1923

I had come to the house, in a cave of trees,
Facing a sheer sky.
Everything moved,—a bell hung ready to strike,
Sun and reflection wheeled by.

When the bare eyes were before me   5
And the hissing hair,
Held up at a window, seen through a door.
The stiff bald eyes, the serpents on the forehead
Formed in the air.

This is a dead scene forever now.   10
Nothing will ever stir.
The end will never brighten it more than this,
Nor the rain blur.

The water will always fall, and will not fall,
And the tipped bell make no sound.   15
The grass will always be growing for hay
Deep on the ground.

And I shall stand here like a shadow
Under the great balanced day,
My eyes on the yellow dust, that was lifting in the wind,   20
And does not drift away.

MEDUSA. Medusa was one of the Gorgons of Greek mythology. Hideously ugly with snakes for hair, Medusa turned those who looked upon her face into stone.

QUESTIONS

1. Who is the speaker of the poem?
2. Why are the first two stanzas spoken in the past tense while the final three are mainly in the future tense?

3. What is the speaker's attitude toward Medusa? Is there anything surprising about his or her reaction to being transformed into stone?

4. Does Bogan merely dramatize an incident from classical mythology, or does the poem suggest other interpretations?

PERSONAL MYTH

Sometimes poets have been inspired to make up myths of their own, to embody their own visions of life. "I must create a system or be enslaved by another man's," said William Blake, who in his "prophetic books" peopled the cosmos with supernatural beings having names like Los, Urizen, and Vala (side by side with recognizable figures from the Old Testament and New Testament). This kind of system-making probably has advantages and draw-backs. T. S. Eliot, in his essay on Blake, wishes that the author of *The Four Zoas* had accepted traditional myths, and he compares Blake's thinking to a piece of homemade furniture whose construction diverted valuable energy from the writing of poems. Others have found Blake's untraditional cosmos an achievement—notably William Butler Yeats, himself the author of an elaborate personal mythology. Although we need not know all of Yeats's mythology to enjoy his poems, to know of its existence can make a few great poems deeper for us and less difficult.

William Butler Yeats (1865–1939)*

THE SECOND COMING 1921

Turning and turning in the widening gyre°   *spiral*
The falcon cannot hear the falconer;
Things fall apart; the center cannot hold;
Mere anarchy is loosed upon the world,
The blood-dimmed tide is loosed, and everywhere   5
The ceremony of innocence is drowned;
The best lack all conviction, while the worst
Are full of passionate intensity.

Surely some revelation is at hand;
Surely the Second Coming is at hand;   10
The Second Coming! Hardly are those words out
When a vast image out of *Spiritus Mundi*
Troubles my sight: somewhere in sands of the desert
A shape with lion body and the head of a man,
A gaze blank and pitiless as the sun,   15
Is moving its slow thighs, while all about it
Reel shadows of the indignant desert birds.
The darkness drops again; but now I know
That twenty centuries of stony sleep

Were vexed to nightmare by a rocking cradle,   20
And what rough beast, its hour come round at last,
Slouches towards Bethlehem to be born?

What kind of Second Coming does Yeats expect? Evidently it is not to be a
Christian one. Yeats saw human history as governed by the turning of a Great
Wheel, whose phases influence events and determine human personalities—
rather like the signs of the Zodiac in astrology. Every two thousand years comes a
horrendous moment: the Wheel completes a turn; one civilization ends and another begins. Strangely, a new age is always announced by birds and by acts of violence. Thus the Greek-Roman world arrives with the descent of Zeus in swan's
form and the burning of Troy, the Christian era with the descent of the Holy
Spirit—traditionally depicted as a dove—and the Crucifixion. In 1919 when
Yeats wrote "The Second Coming," his Ireland was in the midst of turmoil and
bloodshed; the Western Hemisphere had been severely shaken by World War I.
A new millennium seemed imminent. What sphinxlike, savage deity would next
appear on earth, with birds proclaiming it angrily? Yeats imagines it emerging
from *Spiritus Mundi,* Soul of the World, a collective unconscious from which a
human being (since the individual soul touches it) receives dreams, nightmares,
and racial memories.[1]

It is hard to say whether a poet who discovers a personal myth does so to
have something to live by or to have something to write about. Robert Graves,
who professed his belief in a White Goddess ("Mother of All Living, the ancient
power of love and terror"), declared that he wrote his poetry in a trance, inspired
by his Goddess-Muse.[2] Luckily, we do not have to know a poet's religious affiliation before we can read his or her poems. Perhaps most personal myths that
enter poems are not acts of faith but works of art: stories that resemble traditional mythology.

Dick Allen   (b. 1939)

NIGHT DRIVING   1987

Cold hands on the cold wheel of his car,
Driving from Bridgeport, he watches
The long line of red taillights
Curving before him, remembers
How his father used to say they were cats' eyes   5
Staring back at them, a long line of cats
Watching from the distance—never Fords,

---

[1]Yeats fully explains his system in *A Vision* (1938; reprinted New York: Macmillan, 1956).
[2]See Graves's *The White Goddess,* rev. ed. (New York: Farrar, 1966), or for a terser statement of his
position, see his lecture "The Personal Muse" in *On Poetry: Collected Talks and Essays* (New York:
Doubleday, 1969).

Buicks, Chevrolets, filled with the heads
Of children, lovers, lonely businessmen,
But cats in the darkness. Half asleep,   10
He can believe, or make himself believe
The truth of his father—all the lies
Not really lies: images which make
The world come closer, cats' eyes up ahead.

Questions

1. How does personal myth function in this poem?
2. What suggestions can you find in the poem's title?

James Dickey   (1923–1997)

The Heaven of Animals   1962

Here they are. The soft eyes open.
If they have lived in a wood
It is a wood.
If they have lived on plains
It is grass rolling   5
Under their feet forever.

Having no souls, they have come,
Anyway, beyond their knowing.
Their instincts wholly bloom
And they rise.   10
The soft eyes open.

To match them, the landscape flowers,
Outdoing, desperately
Outdoing what is required:
The richest wood,   15
The deepest field.

For some of these,
It could not be the place
It is, without blood.
These hunt, as they have done,   20
But with claws and teeth grown perfect,

More deadly than they can believe.
They stalk more silently,
And crouch on the limbs of trees,
And their descent   25
Upon the bright backs of their prey

May take years
In a sovereign floating of joy.
And those that are hunted
Know this as their life,   30
Their reward: to walk

Under such trees in full knowledge
Of what is in glory above them,
And to feel no fear,
But acceptance, compliance.   35
Fulfilling themselves without pain

At the cycle's center,
They tremble, they walk
Under the tree,
They fall, they are torn,   40
They rise, they walk again.

Questions

1. In what ways does Dickey's animal heaven resemble the traditional Christian after-life? In what ways does it differ?
2. How does the poem reconcile the carnivores' need to hunt with the well-being of the hunted animals?
3. Does the final stanza of the poem allude to any other part of the Christian mythos?

Myth and Popular Culture

If one can find myths in an art museum, one can also find them abundantly in popular culture. Movies and comic books, for example, are full of myths in modern guise. What is Superman, if not a mythic hero who has adapted himself to modern urban life? Marvel Comics even made the Norse thunder god, Thor, into a superhero, although they initially obliged him, like Clark Kent, to get a job. We also see myths retold on the technicolor screen. Sometimes Hollywood presents the traditional story directly, as in Walt Disney's *Cinderella*; more often the ancient tales acquire contemporary settings, as in another celluloid Cinderella story, *Pretty Woman*. (See how Anne Sexton has retold the Cinderella story from a feminist perspective, later in this chapter, or find a recording of Dana Dane's Brooklyn housing project version of the fairy tale done from a masculine perspective in his underground rap hit "Cinderfella.") George Lucas's *Star Wars* trilogy borrowed the structure of medieval quest legends. In quest stories, young knights pursued their destiny, often by seeking the Holy Grail, the cup Christ used at the Last Supper; in *Star Wars*, Luke Skywalker searched for his own parentage and identity, but his interstellar quest brought him to a surprisingly similar cast of knights, monsters, princesses, and wizards. Medieval Grail romances, which influenced Eliot's *The Waste Land*, also shaped films like *The Fisher King* and *Brazil*. Science fiction also commonly uses myth to novel effect.

Extraterrestrial visitors usually appear as either munificent mythic gods or night-marish demons. Steven Spielberg's *E.T.*, for example, revealed a gentle, Christ-like alien recognized by innocent children, but persecuted by adults. E.T. even healed the sick, fell into a death-like coma, and was resurrected.

It hardly matters whether the popular audience recognizes the literal source of a myth; the viewers intuitively understand the structure of the story and feel its deep imaginative resonance. That is why poets retell these myths; they are powerful sources of collective psychic energy, waiting to be tapped. Just as Holly-wood screenwriters have learned that often the most potent way to use a myth is to disguise it, poets sometimes borrow the forms of popular culture to retell their myths. Here are two contemporary narrative poems that borrow imagery from motion pictures to re-enact stories that not only predate cinema but, most prob-ably, stretch back before the invention of writing itself.

Charles Martin   (b. 1942)

TAKEN UP   1978

Tired of earth, they dwindled on their hill,
Watching and waiting in the moonlight until
The aspens' leaves quite suddenly grew still,

No longer quaking as the disc descended,
That glowing wheel of lights whose coming ended   5
All waiting and watching. When it landed

The ones within it one by one came forth,
Stalking out awkwardly upon the earth,
And those who watched them were confirmed in faith:

Mysterious voyagers from outer space,   10
Attenuated, golden—shreds of lace
Spun into seeds of the sunflower's spinning face—

Light was their speech, spanning mind to mind:
We come here not believing what we find—
Can it be your desire to leave behind   15

The earth, which those called angels bless,
Exchanging amplitude for emptiness?
And in a single voice they answered *Yes,*

Discord of human melodies all blent
To the unearthly strain of their assent.   20
Come then, the Strangers said, and those that were taken, went.

1. What myths does this poem recall?
2. This poem was written about the same time that Steven Spielberg's film *Close En-counters of the Third Kind* (1977) appeared. If you recall the movie, compare its ending with the ending of the poem. Martin had not seen the film before writing "Taken Up." How can we account for the similarity?

Edward Field   (b. 1924)

CURSE OF THE CAT WOMAN   1967

It sometimes happens
that the woman you meet and fall in love with
is of that strange Transylvanian people
with an affinity for cats.

You take her to a restaurant, say, or a show,   5
on an ordinary date, being attracted
by the glitter in her slitty eyes and her catlike walk,
and afterwards of course you take her in your arms
and she turns into a black panther
and bites you to death.   10

Or perhaps you are saved in the nick of time
and she is tormented by the knowledge of her tendency:
That she daren't hug a man
unless she wants to risk clawing him up.

This puts you both in a difficult position—   15
panting lovers who are prevented from touching
not by bars but by circumstance:
You have terrible fights and say cruel things
for having the hots does not give you a sweet temper.

One night you are walking down a dark street   20
And hear the pad-pad of a panther following you,
but when you turn around there are only shadows,
or perhaps one shadow too many.

You approach, calling, "Who's there?"
and it leaps on you.   25
Luckily you have brought along your sword
and you stab it to death.

And before your eyes it turns into the woman you love,
her breast impaled on your sword,
her mouth dribbling blood saying she loved you   30
but couldn't help her tendency.

So death released her from the curse at last,
and you knew from the angelic smile on her dead face
that in spite of a life the devil owned,
love had won, and heaven pardoned her.   35

QUESTIONS

1. This poem parodies a sentimental Hollywood horror film, but it also falls under the film's emotional spell. What details does Field introduce for comic effect? When does he give in to the romantic nature of the story?
2. Is the last stanza just a parody of a slick Hollywood ending or does Field invite us to take his finale seriously, too?

Why do poets retell myths? Why don't they just make up their own stories? First, using myth allows poets to be concise. By alluding to stories that their audiences know, they can draw on powerful associations with just a few words. If someone describes an acquaintance, "He thinks he's James Bond," that one allusion speaks volumes. Likewise, when Robert Frost inserts the single line, "So Eden sank to grief," in "Nothing Gold Can Stay," those five words summon up a wealth of associations. They tie the perishable quality of spring's beauty to the equally transient nature of human youth. They also suggest that everything in the human world is subject to time's ravages, that perfection is impossible for us to maintain just as it was for Adam and Eve.

Second, poets know that many stories fall into familiar mythic patterns, and that the most powerful stories of human existence tend to be the same, generation after generation. Sometimes using an old story allows a writer to describe a new situation in a fresh and surprising way. Novels often try to capture the exact texture of a social situation; they need to present the everyday details to evoke the world in which their characters live. Myths tend to tell their stories more quickly and in more general terms. They give just the essential actions and leave out everything else. Narrative poems also work best when they focus on just the essential elements. Here are two contemporary narrative poems that retell traditional myths to make contemporary interpretations.

A. D. Hope   (b. 1907)

IMPERIAL ADAM   1952

Imperial Adam, naked in the dew,
Felt his brown flanks and found the rib was gone.
Puzzled he turned and saw where, two and two,
The mighty spoor of Jahweh marked the lawn.

Then he remembered through mysterious sleep   5
The surgeon fingers probing at the bone,
The voice so far away, so rich and deep:
"It is not good for him to live alone."

Turning once more he found Man's counterpart
In tender parody breathing at his side.   10
He knew her at first sight, he knew by heart
Her allegory of sense unsatisfied.

The pawpaw drooped its golden breasts above
Less generous than the honey of her flesh;
The innocent sunlight showed the place of love;   15
The dew on its dark hairs winked crisp and fresh.

This plump gourd severed from his virile root,
She promised on the turf of Paradise
Delicious pulp of the forbidden fruit;
Sly as the snake she loosed her sinuous thighs,   20

And waking, smiled up at him from the grass;
Her breasts rose softly and he heard her sigh—
From all the beasts whose pleasant task it was
In Eden to increase and multiply

Adam had learned the jolly deed of kind: 25
He took her in his arms and there and then,
Like the clean beasts, embracing from behind,
Began in joy to found the breed of men.

Then from the spurt of seed within her broke
Her terrible and triumphant female cry,   30
Split upward by the sexual lightning stroke.
It was the beasts now who stood watching by:

The gravid elephant, the calving hind,
The breeding bitch, the she-ape big with young
Were the first gentle midwives of mankind;   35
The teeming lioness rasped her with her tongue;

The proud vicuña nuzzled her as she slept
Lax on the grass; and Adam watching too
Saw how her dumb breasts at their ripening wept,
The great pod of her belly swelled and grew,   40

And saw its water break, and saw, in fear,
Its quaking muscles in the act of birth,
Between her legs a pigmy face appear,
And the first murderer lay upon the earth.

IMPERIAL ADAM. Hope's poem retells the story of Adam and Eve. For the Biblical version, see Genesis 2:18–4:1. 4 *Jahweh:* the Lord of the Old Testament. The Hebrew name of God was written as JHVH, but it was considered too sacred to say aloud. Yahweh and Jehovah are the other most common versions of the vowel-less Hebrew name. 25 *deed of kind:* the act of procreation. This particular expression is usually used to describe the mating of animals. 44 *the first murderer:* Cain, Adam and Eve's first child, who murdered his brother, Abel. See Genesis 4:1–16.

QUESTIONS

1. Why is Adam called "imperial" What empire does he command?
2. What does Hope imply in lines 18–20, when he describes Eve's sexuality?
3. There is no serpent in Hope's version of the Adam and Eve story. And yet by the end of the poem, evil has entered Paradise. What has introduced it?
4. How does the last line of "Imperial Adam" affect the meaning of the poem?

Robert Frost   (1874–1963)*

NEVER AGAIN WOULD BIRDS' SONG   1942
BE THE SAME

He would declare and could himself believe
That the birds there in all the garden round
From having heard the daylong voice of Eve
Had added to their own an oversound,
Her tone of meaning but without the words.   5
Admittedly an eloquence so soft
Could only have had an influence on birds
When call or laughter carried it aloft.
Be that as may be, she was in their song.
Moreover her voice upon their voices crossed   10
Had now persisted in the woods so long
That probably it never would be lost.
Never again would birds' song be the same.
And to do that to birds was why she came.

QUESTIONS

1. Who is *he?*
2. In reading aloud line 9, do you stress *may?* (Do you say "as MAY be" or "as may BE"?) What guide do we have to the poet's wishes here?

3. Which lines does Frost cast mostly or entirely into monosyllables? How would you describe the impact of these lines?

4. In his *Essay on Criticism*, Alexander Pope made fun of poets who wrote mechanically, without wit: "And ten low words oft creep in one dull line." Do you think this criticism is applicable to Frost's lines of monosyllables? Explain.

Anne Sexton   (1928–1974)*

CINDERELLA   1971

You always read about it:
the plumber with twelve children
who wins the Irish Sweepstakes.
From toilets to riches.
That story.   5

Or the nursemaid,
some luscious sweet from Denmark
who captures the oldest son's heart.
From diapers to Dior.
That story.   10

Or a milkman who serves the wealthy,
eggs, cream, butter, yogurt, milk,
the white truck like an ambulance
who goes into real estate
and makes a pile.   15
From homogenized to martinis at lunch.

Or the charwoman
who is on the bus when it cracks up
and collects enough from the insurance.
From mops to Bonwit Teller.   20
That story.

Once
the wife of a rich man was on her deathbed
and she said to her daughter Cinderella:
Be devout. Be good. Then I will smile   25
down from heaven in the seam of a cloud.
The man took another wife who had
two daughters, pretty enough
but with hearts like blackjacks.
Cinderella was their maid.   30
She slept on the sooty hearth each night

and walked around looking like Al Jolson.
Her father brought presents home from town,
jewels and gowns for the other women
but the twig of a tree for Cinderella.   35
She planted that twig on her mother's grave
and it grew to a tree where a white dove sat.
Whenever she wished for anything the dove
would drop it like an egg upon the ground.
The bird is important, my dears, so heed him.   40

Next came the ball, as you all know.
It was a marriage market.
The prince was looking for a wife.
All but Cinderella were preparing
and gussying up for the big event.   45
Cinderella begged to go too.
Her stepmother threw a dish of lentils
into the cinders and said: Pick them
up in an hour and you shall go.
The white dove brought all his friends;   50
all the warm wings of the fatherland came,
and picked up the lentils in a jiffy.
No, Cinderella, said the stepmother,
you have no clothes and cannot dance.
That's the way with stepmothers.   55

Cinderella went to the tree at the grave
and cried forth like a gospel singer:
Mama! Mama! My turtledove,
send me to the prince's ball!
The bird dropped down a golden dress   60
and delicate little gold slippers.
Rather a large package for a simple bird.
So she went. Which is no surprise.
Her stepmother and sisters didn't
recognize her without her cinder face   65
and the prince took her hand on the spot
and danced with no other the whole day.

As nightfall came she thought she'd better
get home. The prince walked her home
and she disappeared into the pigeon house   70
and although the prince took an axe and broke
it open she was gone. Back to her cinders.

These events repeated themselves for three days.
However on the third day the prince
covered the palace steps with cobbler's wax   75
and Cinderella's gold shoe stuck upon it.
Now he would find whom the shoe fit
and find his strange dancing girl for keeps.
He went to their house and the two sisters
were delighted because they had lovely feet.   80
The eldest went into a room to try the slipper on
but her big toe got in the way so she simply
sliced it off and put on the slipper.
The prince rode away with her until the white dove
told him to look at the blood pouring forth.   85
That is the way with amputations.
They don't just heal up like a wish.
The other sister cut off her heel
but the blood told as blood will.
The prince was getting tired.   90
He began to feel like a shoe salesman.
But he gave it one last try.
This time Cinderella fit into the shoe
like a love letter into its envelope.

At the wedding ceremony   95
the two sisters came to curry favor
and the white dove pecked their eyes out.
Two hollow spots were left
like soup spoons.

Cinderella and the prince   100
lived, they say, happily ever after,
like two dolls in a museum case
never bothered by diapers or dust,
never arguing over the timing of an egg,
never telling the same story twice,   105
never getting a middle-aged spread,
their darling smiles pasted on for eternity.
Regular Bobbsey Twins.
That story.

QUESTIONS

1. Most of Sexton's "Cinderella" straightforwardly retells a version of the famous fairy
   tale. But in the beginning and ending of the poem, how does Sexton change the
   story?

2. How does Sexton's refrain of "That story" alter the meaning of the episodes it describes? What is the tone of this poem (the poet's attitude toward her material)?
3. What does Sexton's final stanza suggest about the way fairy tales usually end?

WRITER'S PERSPECTIVE

Anne Sexton

Anne Sexton on Writing TRANSFORMING FAIRY TALES   1970

[*To Paul Brooks*]
                                                October 14, 1970

Dear Paul,
    I wanted to let some time elapse before I answered you so that I could think
carefully about what you had to say. I've written seventeen "Transformations."
My goal was twenty, but I may have to make do with seventeen. Seventeen
would be a nice book anyway, but I will wait a couple of months and see what
comes. I am in the process of typing up the manuscript to submit to you.
    But back to your comments. I realize that the "Transformations" are a depar-
ture from my usual style. I would say that they lack the intensity and perhaps
some of the confessional force of my previous work. I wrote them because I had
to . . . because I wanted to . . . because it made me happy. I would want to publish them for the same reason. I would like my readers to see this side of me, and
it is not in every case the lighter side. Some of the poems are grim. In fact I don't
know how to typify them except to agree that I have made them very contemporary. It would further be a lie to say that they weren't about me, because they are
just as much about me as my other poetry.
    I look at my work in stages, and each new book is a kind of growth and
reaching outward and as always backward. Perhaps the critics will be unhappy
with this book and some of my readers maybe will not like it either. I feel I will
gain new readers and critics who have always disliked my work (and too true, the
critics are not always kind to me) may come around. I have found the people I've

shown them to apathetic in some cases and wildly excited in others. It often depends on their own feelings about Grimms' fairy tales.

[*To Kurt Vonnegut, Jr.*]

November 17, 1970

Dear Kurt,

I meant to write you a postcard before your dentist appointment, but I was away at the time I should have sent it. Sorry. Your graph for "Cinderella" is right over my desk.

The enclosed manuscript is of my new book of poems. I've taken Grimms' Fairy Tales and "Transformed" them into something all of my own. The better books of fairy tales have introductions telling the value of these old fables. I feel my *Transformations* needs an introduction telling of the value of my (one could say) rape of them. Maybe that's an incorrect phrase. I do something very modern to them (have you ever tried to describe your own work? I find I am tongue-tied). They are small, funny and horrifying. Without quite meaning to I have joined the black humorists. I don't know if you know my other work, but humor was never a very prominent feature . . . terror, deformity, madness and torture were my bag. But this little universe of Grimm is not that far away. I think they end up being as wholly personal as my most intimate poems, in a different language, a different rhythm, but coming strangely, for all their story sound, from as deep a place.

Anne Sexton: A Self-Portrait in Letters

TRANSFORMING FAIRY TALES. *Paul Brooks:* Sexton's editor at Houghton Mifflin. He initially had reservations about Sexton's fairy tale poems. *Transformations:* title of Sexton's 1971 volume of poems which contained "Cinderella." *Kurt Vonnegut, Jr.:* popular author of *Cat's Cradle* (1963) and other novels.

◄■■❑WRITING CRITICALLY❑■■►

Demystifying Myth

Myth often seems like an intimidating term. Asked to consider the mythic aspects of a poem, we often begin to worry about how well we remember the original story. Sometimes the version of the myth that we remember from a book or movie seems different from the story being referred to. Or one we have never before encountered feels oddly familiar. Myths often appear elusive because they are stories that lend themselves to adaptation. Two Greek versions of the same story will almost always differ widely in detail: new episodes appear, minor characters change names or vanish. What usually remains fixed, however, is the basic pattern. Orpheus always descends to the Underworld but is never able to rescue his beloved Eurydice. Superhuman Hercules inevitably goes mad and slaughters his wife and sons. Oedipus is always doomed to kill his father and unwittingly marry his widowed mother.

If the artistry of myth is in the details of the tale, the deeper psychological meaning is contained in its permanent underlying structure. In writing about myth, therefore, try to find the underlying pattern of the narrative in question.

Does the basic shape of the poem's story seem familiar? Does that story have some recognizable source in myth or legend? If the poem has no obvious narrative line, does its movement call to mind other stories? In "Cinderella" (page 934) Anne Sexton deliberately reminds us of the mythic patterns of her material ("the plumber with twelve children / who wins the Irish Sweepstakes. / From toilets to riches. / That story.") Although not all poems are conventional narratives, and few authors delight in leaving as many clues as Sexton, most authors do insert some luminous clues in their poems. Why? They want readers to hear the echoes of their sources, because writers understand the resonance of myth. "So Eden sank to grief," confides Frost in "Nothing Gold Can Stay," to let readers know that the poem is not only about spring. His reference to Eden encourages us to see the poem as a universal narrative rather than merely elegant natural description.

Once you have linked the poem to its mythic source, notice what new details the author has added. What do they tell us about his or her attitude toward the original source? Are important elements of the original discarded? What does their absence suggest about the author's primary focus? You can refresh your memory of the original myth by looking it up in a reference work such as *Brewer's Dictionary of Phrase and Fable*, but the essential thing is to recognize the basic narrative underlying the poem and to see how it shapes the new work's meaning. For a helpful overview of how critics analyze myth in literature, see the section "Mythological Criticism," page 1951 in Chapter Forty-four, "Critical Approaches to Literature."

WRITING ASSIGNMENT

Provide a close reading of any poem from this book that uses a traditional myth or legend. In the course of your analysis, demonstrate how the author borrows or changes certain details of the myth to emphasize his or her meaning. In addition to the poems in this chapter, some selections to consider include: Margaret Atwood's "Siren Song," T. S. Eliot's "Journey of the Magi," Anthony Hecht's "Adam," H. D.'s "Helen," William Stafford's "At the Klamath Berry Festival," and William Butler Yeats's "The Magi."

Here is an example of an essay on this assignment written by Heather Burke when she was a sophomore at Wesleyan University in Middletown, Connecticut.

The Bonds Between Love and Hatred

in H.D.'s "Helen"

In her poem "Helen," H.D. examines the close

connection between the emotions of love and hatred as

embodied in the figure of Helen of Troy. Helen was the

cause of the long and bloody Trojan War, and her

homecoming is tainted by the memory of the suffering

this war caused. As in many Imagist poems, the title

is essential to the poem's meaning; it gives the

reader both a specific mythic context and a particular subject. Without the title, it would be virtually impossible to understand the poem fully since Helen's name appears nowhere else in the text. The reader familiar with Greek myth knows that Helen, who was the wife of Menelaus, ran away with Paris. Their adultery provoked the Trojan War, which lasted for ten years and resulted in the destruction of Troy.

What is unusual about the poem is H.D.'s perspective on Helen of Troy. The poem refuses to romanticize Helen's story, but its stark new version is easy for a reader to accept. After suffering so much for the sake of one adulterous woman, how could the Greeks not resent her? Rather than idealizing the situation, H.D. describes the enmity which defiles Helen's homecoming and explores the irony of the hatred which "All Greece" feels for her.

The opening line of the poem sets its tone and introduces its central theme--hatred. Helen's beauty required thousands of men to face death in battle, but it cannot assuage the emotional aftermath of the war. Even though Helen is described as "God's daughter, born of love" (13), all she inspires now is resentment, and the poem explores the ways in which these two emotions are closely related.

In the first stanza, the poet uses the color white, as well as the radiance or luster connected with it, in her description of Helen, and this color will be associated with her throughout the poem: the

> the still eyes in the white face,
>
> the lustre as of olives

where she stands,

and the white hands.   (2-5)

As one of the foundations of agriculture and civilization, the olive was a crucial symbol in Greek culture. Helen's beauty is compared to the "lustre" of this olive. This word presumably refers to the radiance or light which the whiteness of her face reflects, but Helen's identification with this fruit also has an ironic connotation. The olive branch is a traditional symbol of peace, but the woman it is compared to was the cause of a bitter war.

The majority of the imagery in the poem is connected with the color white. H.D. uses white to describe Helen's skin; white would have been seen as the appropriate color for a rich and beautiful woman's skin in pre-twentieth century poetry. This color also has several connotations, all of which operate simultaneously in the poem. The color white has a connection to Helen's paternity; her immortal father Zeus took the form of a white swan when he made love to her mortal mother Leda. At the same time, whiteness suggests a certain chilliness, as with snow or frost. In the third stanza, H.D. makes this suggestion explicit with her use of the phrase "the beauty of cool feet" (14). This image also suggests the barrenness connected with such frigidity. In this sense, it is a very accurate representation of Helen, because in The Odyssey Homer tells us that " . . . the gods had never after granted Helen / a child to bring into the sunlit world / after the first, rose-lipped Hermoine" (4.13-15).

Helen is returned to her rightful husband, but after her adulterous actions, she is unable to bear him any more children. She is a woman who is renowned for exciting passion in legions of men, but that passion is now sterile.

Another traditional connotation of the color white is purity, but this comparison only accentuates Helen's sexual transgressions; she is hardly pure. H.D. emphasizes her lasciviousness through the use of irony. In the third stanza, she refers to Helen as a "maid." A maid is a virgin, but Helen is most definitely not virginal in any sense. In the following line, the poet rhymes "maid" with the word "laid," which refers to the placement of Helen's body on the funeral pyre. This particular word, however, deliberately emphasized by the rhyme, also carries slangy associations with the act of sexual intercourse. This connotation presents another ironic contrast with the word "maid."

The first line of the second stanza is almost identical to that of the first, and again we are reminded of the intense animosity that Helen's presence inspires. This hatred is now made more explicit. The word revile is defined by The American Heritage Dictionary as "to denounce with abusive language" ("Revile"). Helen is a queen, but she is subjected to the insults of her subjects as well as the rest of Greece.

Helen's homecoming is not joyous, but a time of exile and penance. The war is over, but no one, especially Helen, can forget the past. Her memories seem to cause her wanness, which the dictionary defines as "indicating weariness, illness, or unhappiness" ("Wan"). Her face now " . . . grows wan and white, / remembering past enchantments / and past ills" (9-11). The enchantment she remembers is that of Aphrodite, the goddess who lured her from her husband and home to Paris's bed. The "ills" which Helen remembers can be seen as both her sexual offenses and the human losses sustained in the Trojan War. The use of the word ills works in conjunction with the word wan to demonstrate Helen's spiritual sickness; she is plagued by regret.

As the opening of the third stanza shows, the woman who was famous for her beauty and perfection now leaves Greece "unmoved." This opening may not echo the sharpness of those of the first two stanzas, but it picks up on the theme of Helen as a devalued prize. In the eyes of the Greeks, she is not the beauty who called two armies to battle but merely an unfaithful wife for whom many died needlessly.

The final lines of the poem reveal the one condition which could turn the people's hatred into love again. They "could love indeed the maid, / only if she were laid, / white ash amid funereal cypresses" (16-19). The Greeks can only forgive Helen once her body has been burned on the funeral pyre. These disturbing lines illustrate the destructive power of hatred; it can only be conquered by death. These lines also reveal the final significance of the color white. It suggests Helen's death. As Helen's face is pale and white in life, so her ashes will be in death. The flames of the funeral pyre are the only way to purify the flesh which was tainted by the figurative flames of passion. Death is the only way to restore Helen's beauty and make it immortal. While she is alive, her beauty is only a reminder of lost fathers, sons, and brothers. The people of Greece can only despise her while she is living, but they can love and revere the memory of her beauty once she is dead.

Works Cited

H.D. "Helen." Literature: An Introduction to Fiction, Poetry, and Drama. Ed. X.J. Kennedy and Dana Gioia. 7th ed. New York: Longman, 1999. 1076.

Homer. The Odyssey. Trans. Robert Fitzgerald. Garden City: Anchor/Doubleday, 1961.

"Revile." American Heritage Dictionary. New College ed. 1980.

"Wan." American Heritage Dictionary. New College ed. 1980.

FURTHER SUGGESTIONS FOR WRITING

1. Read the original version of either the story of Adam and Eve (the first four chapters of Genesis) or "Cinderella" (in Charles Perrault's *Mother Goose Tales*) and compare it to the corresponding poem in this chapter. Which elements in the myth does the poet change and which does he or she retain?
2. Write an explication of D. H. Lawrence's "Bavarian Gentians" or Thomas Hardy's "The Oxen." (For hints on writing about poetry by the method of explication, see page 1893.)
3. Take any famous myth or fairy tale and retell it to reflect your personal philosophy.

25 *Poetry and Personal Identity*

Only a naive reader assumes that all poems directly reflect the personal experience of their authors. That would be like believing that a TV sitcom actually describes the real family life of its cast. As you will recall if you read "The Person in the Poem" (page 673), poets often speak in voices other than their own. These voices may be borrowed or imaginary. Stevie Smith appropriates the voice of a dead swimmer in her poem, "Not Waving but Drowning" (page 756), and Carter Revard imagines a nonhuman voice in "Birch Canoe" (page 673). Some poets also try to give their personal poems a universal feeling. Edna St. Vincent Millay's emotion-charged sonnet, "Well, I Have Lost You; and I Lost You Fairly" (page 961), describes the end of a difficult love affair with a younger man, but she dramatizes the situation in such a way that it seems deliberately independent of any particular time and place. Even her lover remains shadowy and nameless. No one has ever been able to identify the characters in Shakespeare's sonnets with actual people, but that fact does not diminish our pleasure in them as poems.

And yet there are times when poets try to speak openly in their own voices. What could be a more natural subject for a poet than examining his or her own life? The autobiographical elements in a poem may be indirect, as in Chidiock Tichborne's elegy, written before his execution for treason in 1586 (page 777), or it may form the central subject, as in Sylvia Plath's "Lady Lazarus," which discusses her suicide attempts. In either case, the poem's autobiographical stance affects a reader's response. Although we respond to a poem's formal elements, we cannot also help reacting to what we know about its human origins. To learn that the elegant elegy we have just read was written by an eighteen-year-old boy, who would soon be horribly executed, adds a special poignancy to the poem's content. Likewise, to read Plath's chilling exploration of her death wish, while knowing that within a few months the poet would kill herself, we receive an extra jolt of emotion. In a good autobiographical poem, that shock of veracity adds to the poem's power. In an unsuccessful poem, the autobiographical facts become a substitute for emotions not credibly conveyed by the words themselves.

One literary movement, **Confessional poetry,** has made such frank self-definition its main purpose. As the name implies, Confessional poetry renders personal experience as candidly as possible, even sharing confidences that may violate social conventions or propriety. Confessional poets sometimes shock their readers with admissions of experiences so intimate and painful—adultery, family violence, suicide attempts—that most people would try to suppress them, or at least not proclaim them to the world.

Some Confessional poets, such as Anne Sexton, W. D. Snodgrass, and Robert Lowell, underwent psychoanalysis, and at times their poems sound like patients telling their analysts every detail of their personal lives. For this reason, Confessional poems run the danger of being more interesting to their authors than to their readers. But when a poet successfully frames his or her personal experience so that the reader can feel an extreme emotion from the inside, the result can be powerful. Here is a chilling poem that takes us within the troubled psyche of a poet who contemplates suicide.

Sylvia Plath   (1932–1963)*

LADY LAZARUS   1965

I have done it again.
One year in every ten
I manage it—

A sort of walking miracle, my skin
Bright as a Nazi lampshade,   5
My right foot

A paperweight,
My face a featureless, fine
Jew linen.

Peel off the napkin   10
O my enemy.
Do I terrify?—

The nose, the eye pits, the full set of teeth?
The sour breath
Will vanish in a day.   15

Soon, soon the flesh
The grave cave ate will be
At home on me

And I a smiling woman.
I am only thirty.
And like the cat I have nine times to die.   20

This is Number Three.
What a trash
To annihilate each decade.

What a million filaments. 25
The peanut-crunching crowd
Shoves in to see

Them unwrap me hand and foot—
The big strip tease.
Gentleman, ladies, 30

These are my hands,
My knees.
I may be skin and bone,

Nevertheless, I am the same, identical woman.
The first time it happened I was ten. 35
It was an accident.

The second time I meant
To last it out and not come back at all.
I rocked shut

As a seashell. 40
They had to call and call
And pick the worms off me like sticky pearls.

Dying
Is an art, like everything else.
I do it exceptionally well. 45

I do it so it feels like hell.
I do it so it feels real.
I guess you could say I've a call.

It's easy enough to do it in a cell.
It's easy enough to do it and stay put. 50
It's the theatrical

Comeback in broad day
To the same place, the same face, the same brute
Amused shout:

"A miracle!" 55
That knocks me out.
There is a charge

For the eyeing of my scars, there is a charge
For the hearing of my heart—
It really goes. 60

And there is a charge, a very large charge,
For the word or a touch
Or a bit of blood

Or a piece of my hair or my clothes.
So, so, Herr Doktor.   65
So, Herr Enemy.

I am your opus°,   *work, work of art*
I am your valuable,
The pure gold baby

That melts to a shriek.   70
I turn and burn.
Do not think I underestimate your great concern.

Ash, ash—
You poke and stir.
Flesh, bone, there is nothing there—   75

A cake of soap,
A wedding ring,
A gold filling,

Herr God, Herr Lucifer,
Beware   80
Beware.

Out of the ash
I rise with my red hair.
And I eat men like air.

QUESTIONS

1. Although the poem is openly autobiographical, Plath uses certain symbols to represent herself (Lady Lazarus, a Jew murdered in a concentration camp, a cat with nine
   lives, and so on.). What do these symbols tell us about Plath's attitude toward herself
   and the world around her?
2. In her biography of Plath, *Bitter Fame*, the poet Anne Stevenson says that this poem
   penetrates "the furthest reaches of disdain and rage . . . bereft of all 'normal' human
   feelings." What do you think Stevenson means? Does anything in the poem strike
   you as particularly chilling?
3. The speaker in "Lady Lazarus" says "Dying / Is an art, like everything else" (lines
   43–44). What sense do you make of this metaphor?
4. Does the ending of "Lady Lazarus" imply that the speaker assumes that she will outlive her suicide attempts? Set forth your final understanding of the poem.

Not all autobiographical poetry needs to shock the reader, as Plath overtly
does in "Lady Lazarus." Poets can also try to share the special moments that illuminate their day-to-day lives, as Elizabeth Bishop does in "Filling Station"

(page 1037), when she describes a roadside gas station whose shabby bric-a-brac she saw as symbols of love. But when poets attempt to place their own lives under scrutiny, they face certain difficulties. Honest, thorough self-examination isn't as easy as it might seem. It is one thing to examine oneself in the mirror; it is quite another to sketch what one sees there accurately. Even if we have the skill to describe ourselves in words (or in paint) so that a stranger would recognize the self-portrait, there is the challenge of honesty. Drawing or writing our own self-portrait, most of us yield—often unconsciously—to the temptation of making ourselves a little nobler or better-looking than we really are. The best self-portraits, like Rembrandt's unflattering self-examinations, are usually critical. No one enjoys watching someone else preen in front of a dressing mirror, unless the intention is satiric.

Autobiographical poetry requires a hunger for honest self-examination. Many poets find that, in order to understand themselves and who they are, they must scrutinize more than the self in isolation. Other forces may shape their identities: their ethnic background, their families, their race, their gender, their religion, their economic status, and their age. Aware of these elements, many recent poets have written memorable, personal poems. The Dominican-American poet Julia Alvarez wrote an autobiographical sequence of thirty-three sonnets, as she turned thirty-three. These poems frankly explore her conflicting identities as daughter, sister, divorcee, lover, writer, Dominican, and American. They earn the reader's trust by being open and self-critical. The subject of one sonnet is Alvarez's admission that she is not as beautiful as either her mother or her sister. Reading that admission, we instinctively sympathize with the author.

Julia Alvarez   (b. 1950)

THE WOMEN ON MY MOTHER'S SIDE   1984
WERE KNOWN (FROM "33")

The women on my mother's side were known
for beauty and were given lovely names
passed down for generations. I knew them
as my pretty aunts: Laura, who could turn
any head once, and Ada, whose husband   5
was so devoted he would lay his handkerchief on seats for her and when she rose
thank her; there was Rosa, who got divorced
twice, her dark eyes and thick hair were to blame;
and my mother Julia, who was a catch   10
and looks it in her wedding photographs.
My sister got her looks, I got her name,
and it suits me that between resemblance
and words, I got the right inheritance.

RACE AND ETHNICITY

One of the personal issues Julia Alvarez faces in "33" is her dual identity as Dominican and American. The daughter of immigrants, she was born in New York but spent her childhood in the Dominican Republic. Consequently, self-definition for her has meant resolving the claims of two potentially contradictory cultures. In this sonnet, Alvarez talks about inheriting two kinds of beauty from her mother's side of the family. First, there is the beauty of the flesh, which has been passed onto Alvarez's sister. Second, there is a poetic impulse to create beauty with words, fulfilled by the family names, which Alvarez herself has inherited. Here Alvarez touches on the central issue facing the autobiographical poet— using *words* to embody experience. For a writer, the gift of words is "the right inheritance," even if those words are, for an immigrant poet, sometimes in a different language from that of one's parents. American poetry is rich in immigrant cultures, written both by first-generation writers like Alvarez or John Ciardi, and foreign-born authors like Joseph Brodsky (Russia), Nina Cassian (Romania), Claude McKay (Jamaica), Eamon Grennan (Ireland), Thom Gunn (England), Shirley Geok-lin Lim (Malaysia), Emanuel di Pasquale (Italy), José Emilio Pacheco (Mexico), Herberto Padilla (Cuba), and Derek Walcott (St. Lucia). Some literary immigrants, like the late Russian novelist and poet Vladimir Nabokov, make the difficult transition to writing in English. Others like Cassian or Pacheco continue to write in their native languages. A few like Brodsky write bilingually. Such poetry often reminds us of the multicultural nature of American poetry. Here is a poem by one literary immigrant that raises some important issues of personal identity.

Claude McKay (1890–1948)

AMERICA   1922

Although she feeds me bread of bitterness,
And sinks into my throat her tiger's tooth,
Stealing my breath of life, I will confess
I love this cultured hell that tests my youth.
Her vigor flows like tides into my blood,   5
Giving me strength erect against her hate,
Her bigness sweeps my being like a flood.
Yet, as a rebel fronts a king in state,
I stand within her walls with not a shred
Of terror, malice, not a word of jeer.   10
Darkly I gaze into the days ahead,
And see her might and granite wonders there,
Beneath the touch of Time's unerring hand,
Like priceless treasures sinking in the sand.

1. Is "America" written in a personal or public voice? What specific elements seem personal? What elements seem public?
2. McKay was a black immigrant from Jamaica, but he does not mention either his race or national origin in the poem. Is his personal background important to understanding "America"?
3. "America" is written in a traditional form. How does the poem's form contribute to its impact?

Claude McKay's "America" raises the question of how an author's race and ethnic identity influence the poetry he or she writes. (*Race* usually refers to human traits based on biological descent whereas *ethnic* background assumes the more complex influences of racial, national, cultural, linguistic, and religious characteristics.) In the 1920's, for instance, there was an ongoing discussion among black poets as to whether their poetry should deal specifically with the African-American experience. Did black poetry exist apart from the rest of American poetry or was it, in the words of Robert Hayden, "shaped over some three centuries by social, moral, and literary forces essentially American?" Should black authors primarily address a black audience or should they try to engage a broader literary public? Should black poetry focus on specifically black subjects, forms, and idioms or should it rely mainly on the traditions of English literature? Black poets divided into two camps. Claude McKay and Countee Cullen were among the writers who favored universal themes. (Cullen, for example, insisted he be called a "poet," not a "Negro poet.") Langston Hughes and Jean Toomer were among the "new" poets who believed black poetry must reflect racial themes. They believed, as James Weldon Johnson had once said, that race was "perforce the thing that the American Negro Poet knows best." Writers on both sides of the debate produced excellent poems, but their work has a very different character. Compare McKay's "America" to a recent poem by Rita Dove. Although Dove's poem takes place in Europe, it subtly reflects a lifetime of specifically black American experience.

Rita Dove   (b. 1952)*
POEM IN WHICH I REFUSE CONTEMPLATION   1989

A letter from my mother was waiting:
read in standing, one a.m.,
just arrived at my German mother-in-law

six hours from Paris by car.   5
Our daughter hops on Oma's bed,
happy to be back in a language

she knows. *Hello, all! Your postcard*
came on the nineth—familiar misspelled
words, exclamations. I wish my body

wouldn't cramp and leak; I want to—   10
as my daughter says, pretending to be
"Papa"—pull on boots and go for a long walk

alone. *Your cousin Ronnie in D.C.—*
remember him? —he was the one
a few months younger than you—   15

was strangulated at some chili joint,
your Aunt May is beside herself!
Mom skips to the garden which is

producing—onions, swiss chard,
lettuce, lettuce,lettuce, turnip greens and more lettuce   20
so far! The roses are flurishing.

Haven't I always hated gardening? And German,
with its patient, grunting building blocks,
and for that matter, English, too,

Americanese's chewy twang? *Raccoons*   25
have taken up residence
we were ten *in the crawl space*

but I can't feel his hand *who knows*
anymore *how we'll get them out?*
I'm still standing. Bags to unpack.   30

That's all for now. Take care.

Questions

1. Both "America" and "Poem in Which I Refuse Contemplation" are written in
   the first person. How does the use of the first person voice differ from McKay to
   Dove?
2. What do you learn about the speaker of Dove's poem that you don't learn about the
   speaker of McKay's "America"? Are these details important or trivial to your understanding of Dove's poem?
3. McKay's poem is overtly political. Are there any moments of Dove's poem that make
   subtle political statements?

The debate between ethnicity and universality has echoed among American writers of every racial and religious minority. Today, we find the same issues

being discussed by Arab, Asian, Hispanic, Italian, Jewish, and Native-American authors. There is, ultimately, no one correct answer to the questions of identity, for individual artists need the freedom to pursue their own imaginative vision. But considering the issues of race and ethnicity does help a poet think through the artist's sometimes conflicting responsibilities between group and personal identity. Even in poets who have pursued their individual vision, we often see how unmistakably they write from their racial, social, and cultural background. There may seem to be little overtly Hispanic content in Julia Alvarez's sonnet, but her poem implicitly reflects the close extended family structure of Latin cultures. Alvarez's poem also points out that we inherit our bodies as well as our cultures. Our body represents our genetic inheritance that goes back to the beginning of time. Sometimes a poet's ethnic background becomes part of his or her private mythology. In the following poem, Samuel Menashe talks about how his physical body is the center of his Jewish identity.

Samuel Menashe   (b. 1925)
THE SHRINE WHOSE SHAPE I AM   1961

The shrine whose shape I am
Has a fringe of fire
Flames skirt my skin

There is no Jerusalem but this
Breathed in flesh by shameless love   5
Built high upon the tides of blood
I believe the Prophets and Blake
And like David I bless myself
With all my might

I know many hills were holy once   10
But now in the level lands to live
Zion ground down must become marrow
Thus in my bones I am the King's son
And through death's domain I go
Making my own procession   15

QUESTIONS

1. What does the poem tell you about the race and religion of the author? How is this information conveyed? Point to specific lines.
2. The ancient Jews located the center of Judaism at the Temple of Jerusalem, destroyed by the Romans in 70 A.D. When Menashe declares "There is no Jerusalem but this," what does he mean? What is he specifically referring to?
3. What does this poem imply about the nature of ethnic identity?

Francisco X. Alarcón (b. 1948)

The X in My Name   1993

the poor
signature
of my illiterate
and peasant
self
giving away   5
all rights
in a deceiving
contract for life

Question

What does the speaker imply the X in his name signifies?

Wendy Rose (b. 1948)

For the White Poets   1977
Who Would be Indian

just once
just long enough
to snap up the words
fish-hooked
from our tongues.
You think of us now   5
when you kneel
on the earth,
turn holy
in a temporary tourism
of our souls.   10
With words
you paint your faces.
chew your doeskin,
touch breast to tree
as if sharing a mother   15
were all it takes,
could bring
instant and primal
of knowledge.
You think of us only   20
when your voice
wants for roots,

when you have sat back
on your heels
and become primitive.
You finish your poem
and go back.

25

Questions

1. Who is the speaker of the poem? What is the speaker's attitude toward the persons addressed?
2. What does the speaker mean in line 16 by "sharing a mother?" Who or what is this "mother"?
3. Where do the "white poets" "go back" to in the last line?
4. Why does the speaker believe that "white poets" will always remain outside the American Indian's experience?

Yusef Komunyakaa (b. 1947)

FACING IT

1988

My black face fades,
hiding inside the black granite.
I said I wouldn't,
dammit: No tears.
I'm stone. I'm flesh.   5
My clouded reflection eyes me
like a bird of prey, the profile of night
slanted against morning. I turn
this way—the stone lets me go.
I turn that way—I'm inside   10
the Vietnam Veterans Memorial
again, depending on the light
to make a difference.
I go down the 58,022 names,
half-expecting to find   15
my own in letters like smoke.
I touch the name Andrew Johnson;
I see the booby trap's white flash.
Names shimmer on a woman's blouse
but when she walks away   20
the names stay on the wall.
Brushstrokes flash, a red bird's
wings cutting across my stare.
The sky. A plane in the sky.
A white vet's image floats   25
closer to me, then his pale eyes

look through mine. I'm a window.
He's lost his right arm
inside the stone. In the black mirror
a woman's trying to erase names: 30
No, she's brushing a boy's hair.

QUESTIONS

1. How does the title of "Facing It" relate to the poem? Does it have more than one meaning?
2. The narrator describes the people around him by their reflections on the polished granite rather than by looking at them directly. What does this indirect way of scrutinizing contribute to the poem?
3. This poem comes out of the life experience of a black Vietnam veteran. Is Komunyakaa writing closer to McKay's "universal" method or closer to Toomer's "ethnic" style?

GENDER

In her celebrated study, *You Just Don't Understand: Women and Men in Conversation* (1990), Georgetown University linguist Deborah Tannen explored how men and women use language differently. Tannen compared many everyday conversations between husbands and wives to "cross-cultural communications," as if people from separate worlds lived under the same roof. (Denise Levertov's "Leaving Forever," on page 781, describes the same situation quite vividly.) While analyzing the divergent ways in which women and men converse, Tannen carefully emphasizes that neither linguistic style was superior, only different.

While it would be simplistic to assume that all poems reveal the gender of their authors, many poems do become both richer and clearer when we examine their sexual assumptions. Theodore Roethke's "My Papa's Waltz" (page 668) is hardly a macho poem, but it does reflect the complicated mix of love, authority, and violent horseplay that exists in many father/son relationships. By contrast, Sylvia Plath's "Metaphors" (page 720), which describes her own pregnancy through a series of images, deals with an experience that, by biological definition, only a woman can know first-hand. *Feminist criticism* has shown us how gender influences literary texts in subtler ways. (See page 1959 for a discussion of feminist theory.) The central insight of feminist criticism seems inarguable—our gender does often influence how we speak, write, and interpret language. But that insight need not be intimidating. It can also invite us to bring our whole life experience, as women or men, to reading a poem. It reminds us that poetry, the act of using language with the greatest clarity and specificity, is a means to see the world through the eyes of the opposite sex. Sometimes the messages we get from this exchange aren't pleasant, but at least they may shock us into better understanding.

Anne Stevenson   (b. 1933)*

SOUS-ENTENDU   1969

Don't think

that I don't know
that as you talk to me
the hand of your mind
is inconspicuously   5
taking off my stocking,
moving in resourceful blindness
up along my thigh.

Don't think
that I don't know   10
that you know
everything I say
is a garment.

SOUS-ENTENDU. The title is a French expression for "hidden meaning" or "implication." It describes something left unsaid but assumed to be understood.

QUESTIONS

1. What is left unsaid but assumed to be understood between the two people in this poem?
2. Could this poem have been written by a man? If so, under what circumstances? If not, why not?

Lynne McMahon   (b. 1951)

THE LOST CHILD   1993

Best of all, never to have been—
to stay a thumbnail sketch, rescind
the fetal pole and stop it all,
restitching the nucleic ball
that would divide, divide again,   5
into what you would have been.

Now autumn's here, the yellow clouds
presaging ice, the mallards crowding
past the blinds where blind
men drink and drinking find   10
new fissures in their leather seams.
They are their own imperfect dreams

as we are ours, a monument,
a miniature Pompeii of two retinted
to a smudgy gray,   15
curators of the everyday:
the agency of stone, the stony harrow
of all we did then didn't know.

Never to have been at all.
Repulse the light, unwrite the scrawl   20
of names we would have given you
(for life presumes
another life)—volcano, hunt, catastrophe.
The changeless place you'd rather be.

THE LOST CHILD. 1 *Best of all, never to have been:* the opening line alludes to the Greek dramatist
Sophocles's famous line from *Oedipus at Colonus,* "Not to be born is, past all yearning, best" (translation by Anthony Hecht).

QUESTIONS

1. How has the child in the poem been lost?
2. Who is the *you* in the poem? To whom does the *we* refer?
3. Is the perspective of this poem female in any meaningful sense? Agree or disagree but
   state your reasons.

EXERCISE

Rewrite either of the following poems from the perspective of another gender. Then evaluate in what ways the new poem has changed the original's meaning, and in what ways
the original poem comes through more or less unaltered.

Donald Justice   (b. 1925)*

MEN AT FORTY   1967

Men at forty
Learn to close softly
The doors to rooms they will not be
Coming back to.

At rest on a stair landing,   5
They feel it
Moving beneath them now like the deck of a ship,
Though the swell is gentle.

And deep in mirrors
They rediscover   10
The face of the boy as he practices tying
His father's tie there in secret

And the face of that father,
Still warm with the mystery of lather.
They are more fathers than sons themselves now.   15
Something is filling them, something

That is like the twilight sound
Of the crickets, immense,
Filling the woods at the foot of the slope
Behind their mortgaged houses.   20

Adrienne Rich   (b. 1929)*
WOMEN   1968

My three sisters are sitting
on rocks of black obsidian.
For the first time, in this light, I can see who they are.

My first sister is sewing her costume for the procession.
She is going as the Transparent Lady   5
and all her nerves will be visible.

My second sister is also sewing,
at the seam over her heart which has never healed entirely,
At last, she hopes, this tightness in her chest will ease.

My third sister is gazing   10
at a dark-red crust spreading westward far out on the sea.
Her stockings are torn but she is beautiful.

FOR REVIEW AND FURTHER STUDY

Shirley Geok-lin Lim   (b. 1944)
TO LI PO   1980

I read you in a stranger's tongue,
Brother whose eyes were slanted also.
But you never left to live among
Foreign devils. Seeing the rice you ate grow
In your own backyard, you stayed on narrow   5
Village paths. Only your mind travelled
Easily: east, north, south, and west
Compassed in observation of field
And family. All men were guests
To one who knew traditions, the best   10

Of race. Country man, you believed to be Chinese
No more than a condition of human history.
Yet I cannot speak your tongue with ease,
No longer from China. Your stories
Stir griefs of dispersion and find   15
Me in simplicity of kin.

To Li Po. Li Po, also known as Li T'ai-po (701–62), was one of the great Chinese poets of the T'ang
dynasty.

QUESTION

This poem is about a Chinese poet of the T'ang dynasty, but what does it tell us about the
speaker?

Andrew Hudgins   (b. 1951)

ELEGY FOR MY FATHER, WHO IS NOT DEAD   1991

One day I'll lift the telephone
and be told my father's dead. He's ready.
In the sureness of his faith, he talks
about the world beyond this world
as though his reservations have   5
been made. I think he wants to go,
a little bit—a new desire
to travel building up, an itch
to see fresh worlds. Or older ones.
He thinks that when I follow him   10
he'll wrap me in his arms and laugh,
the way he did when I arrived
on earth. I do not think he's right.
He's ready. I am not. I can't
just say good-bye as cheerfully   15
as if he were embarking on a trip
to make my later trip go well.
I see myself on deck, convinced
his ship's gone down, while he's convinced
I'll see him standing on the dock   20
and waving, shouting, Welcome back.

QUESTIONS

1. The speaker describes his father's view of the afterlife in this poem. What image does
   he use to describe his father's vision of life after death?
2. What metaphor does the poet use to describe his own religious uncertainty?

Judith Ortiz Cofer (b. 1952)

QUINCEAÑERA

1987

My dolls have been put away like dead
children in a chest I will carry
with me when I marry.
I reach under my skirt to feel
a satin slip bought for this day. It is soft   5
as the inside of my thighs. My hair
has been nailed back with my mother's
black hairpins to my skull. Her hands
stretched my eyes open as she twisted
braids into a tight circle at the nape   10
of my neck. I am to wash my own clothes
and sheets from this day on, as if
the fluids of my body were poison, as if
the little trickle of blood I believe
travels from my heart to the world were   15
shameful. Is not the blood of saints and
men in battle beautiful? Do Christ's hands
not bleed into your eyes from His cross?
At night I hear myself growing and wake
to find my hands drifting of their own will   20
to soothe skin stretched tight
over my bones.
I am wound like the guts of a clock,
waiting for each hour to release me.

QUINCEAÑERA. *Quinceañera:* a fifteen-year-old girl's coming-out party in Latin cultures.

QUESTIONS

1. What items and actions are associated with the speaker's new life? What items are put away?
2. What is the speaker waiting to release in the final two lines?
3. If the poem's title were changed to "Fifteen-Year-Old Girl," what would the poem lose in meaning?

Edna St. Vincent Millay (1892–1950)*

WELL, I HAVE LOST YOU; AND I LOST YOU FAIRLY

1931

Well, I have lost you; and I lost you fairly;
In my own way, and with my full consent.
Say what you will, kings in a tumbrel rarely

Went to their deaths more proud than this one went.
Some nights of apprehension and hot weeping   5
I will confess; but that's permitted me;
Day dried my eyes; I was not one for keeping
Rubbed in a cage a wing that would be free.
If I had loved you less or played you slyly
I might have held you for a summer more,   10
But at the cost of words I value highly,
And no such summer as the one before.
Should I outlive this anguish—and men do—
I shall have only good to say of you.

WELL, I HAVE LOST YOU. 3 *Tumbrels*: Farmer's carts that were used during the French Revolution to transport condemned aristocrats to the guillotine.

QUESTIONS

1. We feel we know a great deal about this love affair from Millay's sonnet, but what facts does she not share?
2. Would anything in the text of this sonnet be different if it had been written by a man?

Philip Larkin   (1922–1985)*

AUBADE   1977

I work all day, and get half-drunk at night.
Waking at four to soundless dark, I stare.
In time the curtain-edges will grow light.
Till then I see what's really always there:
Unresting death, a whole day nearer now,   5
Making all thought impossible but how
And where and when I shall myself die.
Arid interrogation: yet the dread
Of dying, and being dead,
Flashes afresh to hold and horrify.   10

The mind blanks at the glare. Not in remorse
—The good not done, the love not given, time
Torn off unused—nor wretchedly because
An only life can take so long to climb
Clear of its wrong beginnings, and may never;   15
But at the total emptiness for ever,
The sure extinction that we travel to

And shall be lost in always. Not to be here,
Not to be anywhere,
And soon; nothing more terrible, nothing more true.   20

This is a special way of being afraid.
No trick dispels. Religion used to try,
That vast moth-eaten musical brocade
Created to pretend we never die,
And specious stuff that says *No rational being*   25
Can fear a thing it will not feel, not seeing
That this is what we fear—no sight, no sound,
No touch or taste or smell, nothing to think with,
Nothing to love or link with,
The anaesthetic from which none come round.   30

And so it stays just on the edge of vision,
A small unfocused blur, a standing chill
That slows each impulse down to indecision.
Most things may never happen: this one will,
And realisation of it rages out   35
In furnace-fear when we are caught without
People or drink. Courage is no good:
It means not scaring others. Being brave
Lets no one off the grave.
Death is no different whined at than withstood.   40

Slowly light strengthens, and the room takes shape.
It stands plain as a wardrobe, what we know,
Have always known, known that we can't escape,
Yet can't accept. One side will have to go.
Meanwhile telephones crouch, getting ready to ring   45
In locked-up offices, and all the uncaring
Intricate rented world begins to rouse.
The sky is white as clay, with no sun.
Work has to be done.
Postmen like doctors go from house to house.   50

Questions

1. Is "Aubade" a Confessional poem? If so, what social taboo does it violate?
2. What embarrassing facts about the narrator does the poem reveal? Do these confessions lead us to trust or distrust him?
3. The narrator says that "Courage is no good" (stanza 4). How might he defend this statement?
4. Would a twenty-year-old reader respond differently to this poem than a seventy-year-old reader? Would a devout Christian respond differently to the poem than an atheist?

Julia Alvarez

Julia Alvarez on Writing
DISCOVERING MY VOICE IN ENGLISH
1996

I remember the night I got my box of twenty-five copies of *Homecoming*. My first book! I had just come home from teaching a late workshop. It was almost midnight, that witching time for ambitious girls with plans. And there it was by my door, a box from Grove publishers. I pushed it indoors, opened it, sat down on it, and read. What had I done? I had gone public with a voice! I was excited, I was scared, I wasn't sure I shouldn't hide my face until all the books out there were sold and forgotten.

Now twelve years later, rereading *Homecoming*, I wonder what all that fuss was about. The confessions of my young woman's voice seem so fresh and tentative—who would they have offended? It pains me, too, that I had no sooner achieved a voice but I wanted to silence her. Even now, three books braver, I think of that young woman so often when I write. I am still she, heart pounding in my chest, wondering, Do I dare?

Where did that young woman's fears come from? Nothing in my Dominican background had prepared me for what I was doing—having a voice, and in English, no less! The only models I had been given by my mother and aunts and the heroines of novels were the homemaking model and the romantic model, both of which I had miserably failed at by age thirty-four.

So you see, what shocked me that midnight was that I heard my own voice loud and clear. And it spooked me. Once I said a little, I could say so much. So I sat on that box, as if to keep the lid on that voice.

But it was too late. I had already set her loose. She had a life of her own, she grew, she gained ground. She went into fiction. And in returning to this book, she had new things to say and little revisions to make.

For instance. In writing *Homecoming*, I can see now how fiercely I was claiming my woman's voice. As I followed my mother cleaning house, washing and ironing clothes, rolling dough, I was using the material of my housebound girl life to claim my woman's legacy. Still, it amazes me how little I dared speak of some of the confusions and complications of that legacy.

. . .

Something else. In trying to find the voice that the speaker of "33" so anxiously searches for, I could not admit the further confusions of my bilingual, bicultural self. Except for "Homecoming," the poem that opened the original book, I did not address my experience as a Dominican-American woman. Indeed, that earlier voice did not even feel permission to do so, as if to call attention to my foreignness would make my readers question my right to write in English.

"Coming Home to Homecoming"

DISCOVERING MY VOICE IN ENGLISH. *Homecoming* is the title of Alvarez's first collection of poems published by Grove Press in 1984. This collection contains the sonnet sequence, "33."

◄═══► WRITING CRITICALLY ◄═══►

Poetic Voice and Personal Identity

When Julia Alvarez describes her fear, excitement, and surprise at seeing her own first book (above) she confides, "What shocked me that midnight was that I heard my own voice loud and clear." Alvarez is not talking about hearing her physical voice, but about recognizing for the first time the specific personality that had emerged from her poems. She was surprised by the ways in which her verbal creation both resembled and differed from her actual self.

When critics discuss poetic voice, they often focus on matters of style—characteristic tone, word choice, figures of speech, and rhythms. An author's *personal* voice, however, encompasses more than style; it also includes characteristic themes and subjects. A recognizable poetic voice usually emerges only when a writer finds the right way of presenting the right subjects.

Finding an authentic voice has long been a central issue among women and minority poets. In exploring their subjects, which often lie outside existing traditions, these writers sometimes need to find innovative forms of expression. Edna St. Vincent Millay, for instance, had to invent a new female voice to write the love poems that made her famous. Although her metrics were traditional, Millay's authoritative tone, self-assured manner, and sexual candor were revolutionary for her time. Sometimes a single word announces a new sort of voice; in Judith Ortiz Cofer's "*Quinceañera*," the title is a Spanish noun for which there is no one-word English equivalent. That one word suggests that we will be hearing a new voice.

When writing about voice in poetry, you will often find it illuminating to consider race, gender, age, ethnicity, and religious belief. Is the poem's perspective shaped by any of those elements of the author's identity? Don't limit the poem's meanings to those categories, but see if considering those concepts helps you understand the work better. Pay special attention to the way the poem's personal perspective is reflected in its formal aspects (imagery, tone, metaphor, and sound). Observing how formal aspects embody the author's special themes and subjects will be central to appreciating his or her voice. For further examination of these issues, you may want to read "Gender Criticism" (page 1959) in Chapter Forty-four, "Critical Approaches to Literature." Although that section discusses only one aspect of identity, the general principles it explores are relevant to the broader questions of how an author's life experience may influence the kinds of poetry he or she creates.

WRITING ASSIGNMENT

Analyze any poem in this chapter from the perspective of an author's race, gender, ethnicity, age, or religious beliefs. Describe how that perspective illuminates the meaning of the poem. Use whatever biographical research you can find, but make sure all of your arguments are specifically based on the poem itself and not merely on biographical data. For examples of similar analyses, see Darryl Pinckney's "On Langston Hughes" (page 1946) and Brett C. Millier's "On Elizabeth Bishop's 'One Art'" (page 1941). Short biographies of many of the poets in this book can be found in Chapter Thirty-one, "Lives of the Poets."

FURTHER SUGGESTIONS FOR WRITING

1. Find another poem in "Poems for Further Reading" in which the poet, like Julia Alvarez, considers his or her own family. Tell in a paragraph or two what the poem reveals about the author.
2. Compare Larkin's "Aubade" with another poem about old age and death, such as William Butler Yeats's "Sailing to Byzantium" (page 991), Frances Cornford's "The Watch" (page 811), William Shakespeare's "That time of year thou mayst in me behold" (page 1129), or Ruth Whitman's "Castoff Skin" (page 771).

26 *Alternatives*

TRANSLATIONS

Poetry, said Robert Frost, is what gets lost in translation. If absolutely true, the comment is bad news for most of us, who have to depend on translations for our only knowledge of great poems in many other languages. However, some translators seem able to save a part of their originals and bring it across the language gap. At times they may even add more poetry of their own, as if to try to compensate for what is lost.

Unlike the writer of an original poem, the translator begins with a meaning that already exists. To convey it, the translator may decide to stick closely to the denotations of the original words or else to depart from them, more or less freely, after something he or she values more. The latter aim is evident in the *Imitations* of Robert Lowell, who said he had been "reckless with literal meaning" and instead had "labored hard to get the tone." Particularly defiant of translation are poems in dialect, uneducated speech, and slang: what can be used for English equivalents? Ezra Pound, in a bold move, translates the song of a Chinese peasant in *The Classic Anthology Defined by Confucius:*

> Yaller bird, let my corn alone,
> Yaller bird, let my crawps alone,
> These folks here won't let me eat,
> I wanna go back whaar I can meet
> the folks I used to know at home,
>> I got a home an' I wanna' git goin'.

Here, it is our purpose to judge a translation not by its fidelity to its original, but by the same standards we apply to any other poem written in English. To do so may be another way to see the difference between appropriate and inappropriate words.

Pablo Neruda (1904–1973)

MUCHOS SOMOS

De tantos hombres que soy,
   que somos,
no puedo encontrar a ninguno:
se me pierden bajo la ropa,
se fueron a otra ciudad.

Cuando todo está preparado
para mostrarme inteligente
el tonto que llevo escondido
se toma la palabra en mi boca.

Otras veces me duermo en medio
de la sociedad distinguida
y cuando busco en mí al valiente,
un cobarde que no conozco
corre a tomar con mi esqueleto
mil deliciosas precauciones.

Cuando arde una casa estimada
en vez del bombero que llamo
se precipita el incendiario
y ése soy yo. No tengo arreglo.
Qué debo hacer para escogerme?
Cómo puedo rehabilitarme?

Todos los libros que leo
celebran héroes refulgentes
siempre seguros de sí mismos:
me muero de envidia por ellos,
y en los films de vientos y balas
me quedo envidiando al jinete,
me quedo admirando al caballo.

Pero cuando pido al intrépido
me sale el viejo perezoso,
y así yo no sé quién soy,
no sé cuántos soy o seremos.
Me gustaría tocar un timbre
y sacar el mí verdadero
porque si yo me necesito
no debo desaparecerme.

Mientras escribo estoy ausente
y cuando vuelvo ya he partido:
voy a ver si a las otras gentes

WE ARE MANY   1958

Of the many men who I am, who
   we are,
I can't find a single one;
they disappear among my clothes,
they've left for another city.

When everything seems to be set   5
to show me off as intelligent,
the fool I always keep hidden
takes over all that I say.

At other times, I'm asleep
among distinguished people,   10
and when I look for my brave self,
a coward unknown to me
rushes to cover my skeleton
with a thousand fine excuses.

When a decent house catches fire,   15
instead of the fireman I summon,
an arsonist bursts on the scene,
and that's me. What can I do?
What can I do to distinguish myself?
How can I pull myself together?   20

All the books I read
are full of dazzling heroes,
always sure of themselves.
I die with envy of them;
and in films full of wind and bullets,   25
I goggle at the cowboys,
I even admire the horses.

But when I call for a hero,
out comes my lazy old self;
so I never know who I am,   30
nor how many I am or will be.
I'd love to be able to touch a bell
and summon the real me,
because if I really need myself,
I mustn't disappear.   35

While I am writing, I'm far away;
and when I come back, I've gone.
I would like to know if others

les pasa lo que a mí me pasa,	go through the same things that I do,
si son tantos como soy yo,	have as many selves as I have, 40
si se parecen a sí mismos	and see themselves similarly;
y cuando lo haya averiguado	and when I've exhausted this problem,
voy a aprender tan bien las cosas	I'm going to study so hard
que para explicar mis problemas	that when I explain myself,
les hablaré de geografía.	I'll be talking geography. 45

—Translated by Alastair Reid*

QUESTIONS

1. Someone who knows Spanish should read the poem aloud to the class. Although it is impossible for a translation fully to capture the resonance of Neruda's Spanish, in what places does the English version most closely approximate it?

2. In line 26, Reid translates Neruda's phrase "me quedo envidiando al jinete" as "I goggle at the cowboys." What does Reid gain or lose with that version? (In Spanish, *jinete* means *horseman* or *rider* but not specifically *cowboy*, which is *vaquero* or even—thanks to Hollywood—*cowboy*.) Neruda once told Reid, "Alastair, don't just translate my poems. I want you to improve them." Is this line an improvement?

3. How many men are in the speaker of the poem? What seems to be their relationship to one another?

EXERCISE: *Comparing Translations*

Which English translation of each of the following poems is the best poetry? The originals may be of interest to some. For those who do not know the foreign language, the editor's line-by-line prose paraphrases may help indicate what the translator had to work with and how much of the translation is the translator's own idea. In which do you find the diction most felicitous? In which do pattern and structure best move as one? What differences in tone are apparent? It is doubtful that any one translation will surpass the others in every detail.

Our verb *translate* is derived from the Latin word *translatus*, the past participle of "to transfer" or "to carry across." The first set of translations try to carry across into English one of the most influential short poems ever written: Horace's ode, which ends with the advice, *carpe diem* ("seize the day"), has left its mark on countless poems. One even sees its imprint on contemporary novels (like Saul Bellow's *Seize the Day*) and films (like *Dead Poets Society*) that echo Horace's command to live in the present moment because no one knows what the future will bring.

Horace (65–8 B.C.)

ODE I (11)   (ABOUT 20 B.C.)

Tu ne quaesieris—scire nefas—quem mihi, quem tibi
finem di dederint, Leuconoe, nec Babylonios
temptaris numeros. Ut melius, quicquid erit, pati!

seu plures hiemes, seu tribuit Iuppiter ultimam,
quae nunc oppositis debilitat pumicibus mare   5
Tyrrhenum. Sapias, vina liques, et spatio brevi
spem longam reseces. Dum loquimur, fugerit invida
aetas: carpe diem, quam minimum credula postero.

ODES I (11). Prose translation: (1,2) Do not ask, Leuconoe—to know is not permitted—what end
the gods have given to you and me, do not (3) consult Babylonian horoscopes. It will be better to endure whatever comes, (4) whether Jupiter grants us more winters or whether this is the last one,
(5) which now against the opposite cliffs wears out (6) the Tuscan sea. Be wise, decant the wine, and
since our space is brief, (7) cut back your far-reaching hope. Even while we talk, envious time has
fled away: (8) seize the day, put little trust in what is to come.

1. Edwin Arlington Robinson,* _Horace to Leuconoe_   1891

I pray you not, Leuconoe, to pore
With unpermitted eyes on what may be
Appointed by the gods for you and me,
Nor on Chaldean figures any more.
'T were infinitely better to implore   5
The present only:—whether Jove decree
More winters yet to come, or whether he
Make even this, whose hard, wave-eaten shore
Shatters the Tuscan seas to-day, the last—
Be wise withal, and rack your wine, nor fill   10
Your bosom with large hopes; for while I sing,
The envious close of time is narrowing;—
So seize the day, or ever it be past,
And let the morrow come for what it will.

2. James Michie   1963

Don't ask (we may not know), Leuconoe,
    What the gods plan for you or me.
        Leave the Chaldees to parse
        The sentence of the stars.

Better to bear the outcome, good or bad,   5
    Whether Jove purposes to add
        Fresh winters to the past
        Or to make this the last

Which now tires out the Tuscan sea and mocks
    Its strength with barricades of rocks.   10
        Be wise, strain clear the wine
        And prune the rambling vine

Of expectation. Life's short. Even while
  We talk Time,' hateful, runs a mile.
    Don't trust tomorrow's bough   15
    For fruit. Pluck this, here, now.

3. John Frederick Nims,* *Horace Coping*   1990

Don't ask—knowing's taboo—what's in the cards, darling, for you, for
    me,
what end heaven intends. Meddle with palm, planet, séance, tea
    leaves?
—rubbish! Shun the occult. Better by far take in your stride what
    comes.
Long life?—possible. Or—? Maybe the gods mean it your last, this grim
winter shaking the shore, booming the surf, wearying wave and rock   5
Well then! Learn to be wise; out with the wine. Knowing the time so
    short,
no grand hopes, do you hear? Now, as we talk, huffishly time goes by.
So take hold of the day. Hugging it close. Nothing beyond is yours.

Questions

1. Which translation seems closest to the literal meaning of the Latin? Does that fidelity help or hinder its impact as a new poem in English?
2. The Nims translation tries to recreate Horace's original meter (Asclepiadean), a measure rarely found in English. Does Nims make this unusual classical meter work naturally in English?
3. If Nims copied a classical meter for his translation, E. A. Robinson used a more familiar English form. What is it?

The second set of translations try to recreate a short lyric by the classical Persian poet Omar Khayyam, the master of the *rubai*, a four-line stanza rimed *a a b a*. This Persian form was introduced in English by Edward FitzGerald (1809–1883) in his hugely popular translation. *The Rubaiyat of Omar Khayyam* (rubaiyat is the plural of rubai). In FitzGerald's Victorian version, Omar Khayyam became one of the most frequently quoted poets in English. Eugene O'Neill borrowed the title of his play *Ah, Wilderness!* from the *Rubaiyat* and expected his audience to catch the allusion. TV buffs may have heard Khayyam's poetry quoted habitually by the SWAT-team commander Howard Hunter on the former TV show *Hill Street Blues*. Here are three poetic translations of a famous rubai. Which qualities of the original does each translation seem to capture?

Omar Khayyam   (1048–1131)

RUBAI   (ABOUT 1100)

Tongi-ye may-e la'l kh'aham o divani
 Sadd-e ramaghi bayad o nesf-e nani
Vangah man o to neshasteh dar virani
 Khoshtar bovad as mamlekat-e soltani.

RUBAI. Prose translation: (1) I want a jug of ruby wine and a book of poems.(2) There must be something to stop my breath from departing, and a half loaf of bread. (3) Then you and I sitting in some deserted ruin (4)Would be sweeter than the realm of a sultan.

1. Edward FitzGerald   1879

A Book of Verses underneath the Bough,
A Jug of Wine, a Loaf of Bread—and Thou
 Beside me singing in the Wilderness—
Oh, Wilderness were Paradise enow°!   *enough*

2. Robert Graves* and Omar Ali-Shah   1968

Should our day's portion be one mancel loaf,
A haunch of mutton and a gourd of wine
Set for us two alone on the wide plain,
No Sultan's bounty could evoke such joy.

3. Dick Davis   1992

I need a bare sufficiency—red wine,
 Some poems, half a loaf on which to dine
With you beside me in some ruined shrine:
 A king's state then is not as sweet as mine!

EXERCISE: *Persian Versions*

Write a rubai of your own on any topic. Some possible subjects include: what you plan to do next weekend to relax; advice to a friend to stop worrying; an invitation to a loved one; a four-line *carpe diem* ode. For your inspiration, here are a few more rubaiyat from Edward FitzGerald's celebrated translation.

> Wake! For the Sun who scattered into flight
> The Stars before him from the Field of Night,
> Drives Night along with them from Heaven, and strikes
> The Sultan's Turret with a Shaft of Light.
>   * * * *
> Come, fill the Cup, and in the Fire of Spring
> Your Winter-garment of Repentence fling:
> The Bird of Time has but a little way
> To flutter—and the Bird is on the Wing.
>   * * * *

Some for the Glories of this World; and some
Sigh for the Prophet's Paradise to come;
    Ah, take the Cash, and let the Credit go,
Nor heed the rumble of a Distant Drum!

                                    * * * *

The Moving Finger writes; and, having writ,
Moves on: nor all your Piety nor Wit
    Shall lure it back to cancel half a Line
Nor all your Tears wash out a Word of it.

                                    * * * *

Ah Love! could you and I with Him conspire
To grasp this sorry Scheme of Things entire,
    Would we not shatter it to bits—and then
Remould it nearer to the Heart's desire.

Octavio Paz   (1914–1998)

| CON LOS OJOS CERRADOS | WITH OUR EYES SHUT | 1968 |

Con los ojos cerrados   With your eyes shut
Te iluminas por dentro   You light up from within
Eres la piedra ciega   You are blind stone

Noche a noche te labro   Night by night I carve you
Con los ojos cerrados   With my eyes shut   5
Eres la piedra franca   You are clear stone

Nos volvemos inmensos   We become immense
Solo por conocernos   Just knowing each other
Con los ojos cerrados   With our eyes shut
                                    —Translated by John Felstiner

PARODY

In a **parody,** one writer imitates another writer or another work, for the purpose
of poking fun. Parody is a favorite medium for child poets, as shown in this jingle
made up by children on the streets of Edinburgh.

Anonymous

WE FOUR LADS FROM LIVERPOOL ARE   (ABOUT 1963)

We four lads from Liverpool are—
Paul in a taxi, John in a car,
George on a scooter, tootin' his hooter,
Following Ringo Starr.

Skillfully written, parody can be a devastating form of literary criticism. Rather than merely flinging abuse, the wise parodist imitates with understanding, even with sympathy. The many crude parodies of T. S. Eliot's difficult poem *The Waste Land* show parodists mocking what they cannot fathom, with the result that, instead of illuminating the original, they belittle it (and themselves). Good parodists have an ear for the sounds and rhythms of their originals, as does James Camp, who echoes Walt Whitman's stately "Out of the Cradle Endlessly Rocking" in his line "Out of the crock endlessly ladling" (what a weary teacher feels he is doing). Parody can be aimed at poems good or bad; yet there are poems of such splendor and dignity that no parodist seems able to touch them without looking like a small dog defiling a cathedral, and others so illiterate that good parody would be squandered on them. Sometimes parodies are even an odd form of flattery; poets poke fun at poems they simply can't get out of their head any other way except by rewriting, as in these three parodies of the *Rubaiyat of Omar Khayyam* by Wendy Cope. For devastating comic effect, Cope sets her contemporary versions of Khayyam in down-at-the-heels contemporary London.

Wendy Cope   (b. 1945)*

FROM *From* STRUGNELL'S *Rubáiyát*   1986

(11)

Here with a Bag of Crisps beneath the Bough,
A Can of Beer, a Radio—and Thou
Beside me half-asleep in Brockwell Park
And Brockwell Park is Paradise enow.

(12)

Some Men to everlasting Bliss aspire,
Their Lives, Auditions for the heavenly Choir;
Oh, use your Credit Card and waive the Rest—
Brave Music of a distant Amplifier!

(51)

The Moving Telex writes and having writ
Moves on; nor all thy Therapy nor Wit
Shall lure it back to cancel half a line
Nor Daz nor Bold wash out a Word of it.

Hugh Kingsmill
[Hugh Kingsmill Lunn] (1889–1949)

WHAT, STILL ALIVE AT   (ABOUT 1920)
TWENTY-TWO?

What, still alive at twenty-two,
A clean, upstanding chap like you?
Sure, if your throat 'tis hard to slit,
Slit your girl's, and swing for it.

Like enough, you won't be glad   5
When they come to hang you, lad:
But bacon's not the only thing
That's cured by hanging from a string.

So, when the spilt ink of the night
Spreads o'er the blotting-pad of light,   10
Lads whose job is still to do
Shall whet their knives, and think of you.

QUESTIONS

1. A. E. Housman considered this the best of many parodies of his poetry. Read his
   poems in this book, particularly "Eight O'Clock" (page 814), "When I was one-and-
   twenty" (page 848), and "To an Athlete Dying Young" (page 1085). What characteristics of theme, form, and language does Hugh Kingsmill's parody convey?
2. What does Kingsmill exaggerate?

Bruce Bennett (b. 1940)

THE LADY SPEAKS AGAIN   1992

"I lift my lamp beside the golden door."
More golden now than ever; don't ask why.
Just list your assets, where you can get more,
and who you know. No others need apply.

QUESTIONS

1. Who is the "lady" speaking? What poem is echoed in Bennett's parody?
2. Is Bennett making fun of the original poem (page 1004)? Or is there another object
   for his satire?

EXERCISE Spotting the Originals

In the following parody, what poem or poet is being kidded? Does the parodist seem only
to be having fun, or is he making any critical point?

George Starbuck (1931–1997)

MARGARET ARE YOU DRUG   1966

Cool it Mag.
Sure it's a drag
With all that green flaked out.
Next thing you know they'll be changing the color of bread.

But look, Chick,   5
Why panic?
Sevennyeighty years, we'll *all* be dead.

Roll with it, Kid.
I did.
Give it the old benefit of the doubt.   10

I mean leaves
Schmeaves.
You sure you aint just feeling sorry for yourself?

MARGARET ARE YOU DRUG. This is one of a series of "Translations from the English."

Gene Fehler (b. 1940)

IF RICHARD LOVELACE BECAME   1984
A FREE AGENT

Tell me not, fans, I am unkind
    For saying my good-bye
And leaving your kind cheers behind
    While I to new fans fly.

Now, I will leave without a trace   5
    And choose a rival's field;
For I have viewed the market place
    And seen what it can yield.

Though my disloyalty is such
    That all you fans abhor,   10
It's not that I don't love you much:
    I just love money more.

QUESTIONS

1. After comparing this parody to Richard Lovelace's "To Lucasta" (page 691), list the elements that Fehler keeps from the original and those he adds.
2. What ideals motivate the speaker of Lovelace's poem? What ideals motivate Fehler's free agent?

Alastair Reid

Alastair Reid on Writing TRANSLATING NERUDA 1996

Translating someone's work, poetry in particular, has something about it akin to being possessed, haunted. Translating a poem means not only reading it deeply and deciphering it but clambering about backstage among the props and the scaffolding. I found I could no longer read a poem of Neruda's simply as words on a page without hearing behind them that languid, caressing voice. Most important to me in translating these two writers [Neruda and Borges] was the sound of their voices in my memory, for it very much helped in finding the English appropriate to those voices. I found that if I learned poems of Neruda's by heart I could replay them at odd moments, on buses, at wakeful times in the night, until, at a certain point, the translation would somehow set. The voice was the clue: I felt that all Neruda's poems were fundamentally vocative—spoken poems, poems of direct address—and that Neruda's voice was in a sense the instrument for which he wrote. He once made a tape for me, reading pieces of different poems, in different tones and rhythms. I played it over so many times that I can hear it in my head at will. Two lines of his I used to repeat like a Zen koan, for they seemed to apply particularly to translating:

> in this net it's not just the strings that count
> but also the air that escapes through the meshes.

He often wrote of himself as having many selves, just as he had left behind him several very different poetic manners and voices.

"Neruda and Borges"

◄━▢ WRITING CRITICALLY ▢━►

Parody Is the Sincerest Form of Flattery

When Elizabeth Bishop taught at Harvard, a surprising question appeared on her take-home final exam. She asked students to write parodies of the three poets they had studied during the semester. This assignment was not for a creative writing class, but in her literature course on modern poetry. Bishop believed that in order to write a good parody you had to understand the original poem deeply. W. H. Auden went even further in declaring the value of parody. In designing his ideal college for aspiring poets, he declared that writing parodies would be the only authorized critical exercise in the curriculum.

Before writing a parody, select two or three poems by an author that seem characteristic of his or her style and concerns. Type out or photocopy the poems and then underline phrases or lines that represent the poet's particular sound. You might also make a short list of typical images, words, or even punctuation that the poet frequently uses. Now select one poem and start to imagine it in a different time or setting (as in Gene Fehler's "If Richard Lovelace Became a Free Agent" on page 976). Or conceive of the same ideas spoken by an altogether different person (as in George Starbuck's "Margaret Are You Drug" on page 976). Create a transposition that strikes you as potentially funny but still illuminates some aspect of the original. Try to keep your parody as close to the original poem as possible in terms of length, form, and syntax. You will be surprised by how much strength of expression you'll gain from the poet's line and sentence structure. Finally, have fun. If you don't enjoy your new poem, neither will a reader.

Writing Assignment

Write a parody of any poem in the book. (Remember, it will probably be funnier to your fellow students if it is one you have all studied.) Do your parody in either prose or verse, and make it follow the structure of the original as closely as possible. If you choose to write in verse, stick to the line structure of the original. It may be helpful to choose a model that isn't too difficult to copy (to parody a sonnet would require at least some command of rime and meter). Bring your parody to class and read it aloud.

Further Suggestions for Writing

1. Write your own version of Horace's "Carpe Diem" ode (page 969). Follow the original line by line but reset the poem in your home town (not ancient Tuscany) and address it to your best friend (not long-dead Leuconoe). Advise your friend in your new images to "seize the day."

2. Write a serious poem in the manner of Emily Dickinson, William Carlos Williams, E. E. Cummings, or any other modern poet whose work interests you and which you feel able to imitate. Try to make it good enough to slip into the poet's *Collected Poems* without anyone being the wiser. Read all the poet's poems in this book, or you can consult a larger selection or collection of the poet's work. Though it may be simplest to choose a particular poem as your model, you may echo any number of poems, if you like. Choose a model within the range of your own skill: to imitate a sonnet, for instance, you need to be able to rime and to write in meter. It is probably a good idea to pick a subject or theme characteristic of the poet. This is a difficult project, but if you can do it even fairly well, you will know a great deal more about poetry and your poet.

27 *Evaluating a Poem*

Why do we call some poems "bad"? We are talking not about their moral implications. Rather, we mean that, for one or more of many possible reasons, the poem has failed to move us or to engage our sympathies. Instead, it has made us doubt that the poet is in control of language and vision; perhaps it has aroused our antipathies or unwittingly appealed to our sense of the comic, though the poet is serious. Some poems can be said to succeed despite burdensome faults. But in general such faults are symptoms of deeper malady: some weakness in a poem's basic conception or in the poet's competence.

Nearly always, a bad poem reveals only a dim and distorted awareness of its probable effect on its audience. Perhaps the sound of words may clash with what a poem is saying, as in the jarring last word of this opening line of tender lyric (author unknown, quoted by Richard Wilbur): "Come into the tent, my love, and close the flap." A bad poem usually overshoots or falls short of its mark by the poet's thinking too little or too much. Thinking too much, a poet contrives an excess of ingenuity like that quoted by Alexander Pope in *Peri Bathous, or Of the Art of Sinking in Poetry*: a hounded stag who "Hears his own feet, and thinks they sound like more; / And fears the hind feet will o'ertake the fore." Thinking too little, a poet writes redundantly, as Wordsworth in "The Thorn": "And they had fixed the wedding-day, / The morning that must wed them both."

In a poem that has a rime scheme or a set line length, when all is well, pattern and structure move inseparably with the rest of their poem, the way a tiger's skin and bones move with their tiger. But sometimes, in a poem that fails, the poet evidently has had difficulty in fitting the statements into a formal pattern. English poets have long felt free to invert word order for a special effect (Milton: "ye myrtles brown"), but the poet having trouble keeping to a rime scheme may invert words for no apparent reason but convenience. Needing a rime for *barge* may lead to ending a line with *a police dog large* instead of *a large police dog*. Another sign of trouble is a profusion of adjectives. If a line of iambic pentameter reads, "Her lovely skin, like dear sweet white old silk," we suspect the poet of stuffing the line to make it long enough.

Even great poets write awful poems, and after their deaths, their worst efforts are collected with their masterpieces with no consumer warning labels to inform the reader. Some lines in the canon of celebrated bards make us wonder, "How could they have written this?" Wordsworth, Shelley, Whitman, and Browning are among the great whose failures can be painful, and sometimes an excellent poem will have a bad spot in it. To be unwilling to read them, though, would be as ill advised as to refuse to see Venice just because the Grand Canal is said to contain impurities. The seasoned reader of poetry thinks no less of Tennyson for having written, "Form, Form, Riflemen Form! . . . Look to your butts, and take good aims!" The collected works of a duller poet may contain no such lines of unconscious double meaning, but neither do they contain any poem as good as "Ulysses." If the duller poet never had a spectacular failure, it may be because of failure to take risks. "In poetry," said Ronsard, "the greatest vice is mediocrity."

Often, inept poems fall into familiar categories. At one extreme is the poem written entirely in conventional diction, dimly echoing Shakespeare, Wordsworth, and the Bible, but garbling them. Couched in a rhythm that ticks along like a metronome, this kind of poem shows no sign that its author has ever taken a hard look at anything that can be tasted, handled, and felt. It employs loosely and thoughtlessly the most abstract of words: *love, beauty, life, death, time, eternity*. Littered with old-fashioned contractions (*'tis, o'er, where'er*), it may end in a simple preachment or platitude. George Orwell's complaint against much contemporary writing (not only poetry) is applicable: "As soon as certain topics are raised"—and one thinks of such standard topics for poetry as spring, a first kiss, and stars—"the concrete melts into the abstract and no one seems able to think of turns of speech that are not hackneyed." Writers, Orwell charged, too often make their sentences out of tacked-together phrases "like the sections of a prefabricated hen-house."[1] Versifiers often do likewise.

At the opposite extreme is the poem that displays no acquaintance with poetry of the past but manages, instead, to fabricate its own clichés. Slightly paraphrased, a manuscript once submitted to *The Paris Review* began:

> Vile
>   rottenflush
>
>   o   —screaming—
>   f CORPSEBLOOD!!   ooze
> STRANGLE my
>   eyes . . .
>   HELL's
>   O, ghastly   stench**!!!

[1] George Orwell, "Politics and the English Language," *Shooting an Elephant and Other Essays* (New York: Harcourt, 1945).

At most, such a work has only a private value. The writer has vented personal frustrations upon words, instead of kicking stray dogs. In its way, "Vile Rotten-flush" is as self-indulgent as the oldfangled "first kiss in spring" kind of poem. "I dislike," said John Livingston Lowes, "poems that black your eyes, or put up their mouths to be kissed."

As jewelers tell which of two diamonds is fine by seeing which scratches the other, two poems may be tested by comparing them. This method works only on poems similar in length and kind: an epigram cannot be held up to test an epic. Most poems we meet are neither sheer trash nor obvious masterpieces. Because good diamonds to be proven need softer ones to scratch, in this chapter you will find a few clear-cut gems and a few clinkers.

Anonymous   (English)

O MOON, WHEN I GAZE ON THY   (ABOUT 1900)
BEAUTIFUL FACE

O Moon, when I gaze on thy beautiful face,
Careering along through the boundaries of space,
The thought has often come into my mind
If I ever shall see thy glorious behind.

O MOON. Sir Edmund Gosse, the English critic (1849–1928), offered this quatrain as the work of his servant, but there is reason to suspect him of having written it.

QUESTIONS

1. To what fact of astronomy does the last line refer?
2. Which words seem chosen with too little awareness of their denotations and connotations?
3. Even if you did not know that these lines probably were deliberately bad, how would you argue with someone who maintained that the opening O in the poem was admirable as a bit of concrete poetry?

Grace Treasone

LIFE   (ABOUT 1963)

Life is like a jagged tooth
that cuts into your heart;
fix the tooth and save the root,
and laughs, not tears, will start.

QUESTIONS

1. Try to paraphrase this poem. What is the poet saying?
2. How consistent is the working out of the comparison of life to a tooth?

Stephen Tropp (b. 1930)

MY WIFE IS MY SHIRT   1960

My wife is my shirt
I put my hands through her armpits
slide my head through her mouth
& finally button her blood around my hands

QUESTIONS

1. How consistently is the metaphor elaborated?
2. Why can this metaphor be said to work in exactly the opposite way from a personification?
3. A paraphrase might discover this simile: "My wife is as intimate, familiar, and close to me as the shirt on my back." If this is the idea and the poem is supposed to be a love poem, how precisely is its attitude expressed?

Emily Dickinson (1830–1886)*

A DYING TIGER – MOANED   (ABOUT 1862)
FOR DRINK

A Dying Tiger – moaned for Drink –
I hunted all the Sand –
I caught the Dripping of a Rock
And bore it in my Hand –

His Mighty Balls – in death were thick –   5
But searching – I could see
A Vision on the Retina
Of Water – and of me –

'Twas not my blame – who sped too slow –
'Twas not his blame – who died   10
While I was reaching him –
But 'twas – the fact that He was dead –

QUESTION

How does this poem compare in success with other poems of Emily Dickinson that you know? Justify your opinion by pointing to some of this poem's particulars.

EXERCISE: *Ten Terrible Moments in Poetry*

Here is a small anthology of bad moments in poetry. For what reasons does each selection fail? In which passages do you attribute the failure to inappropriate sound or diction? To awkward word order? To inaccurate metaphor? To excessive overstatement? To forced rime? To monotonous rhythm? To redundancy? To simple-mindedness or excessive ingenuity?

1. Last lines of *Enoch Arden* by Alfred, Lord Tennyson:

   > So passed the strong heroic soul away.
   > And when they buried him, the little port
   > Had seldom seen a costlier funeral.

2. From *Purely Original Verse* (1891) by J. Gordon Coogler (1865–1901), of Columbia, South Carolina:

   > Alas for the South, her books have grown fewer—
   > She never was much given to literature.

3. From "Lines Written to a Friend on the Death of His Brother, Caused by a Railway Train Running Over Him Whilst He Was in a State of Inebriation" by James Henry Powell:

   > Thy mangled corpse upon the rails in frightful shape was found.
   > The ponderous train had killed thee as its heavy wheels went round,
   > And thus in dreadful form thou met'st a drunkard's awful death
   > And I, thy brother, mourn thy fate, and breathe a purer breath.

4. From *Dolce Far Niente* by the American poet Francis Saltus Saltus, who flourished in the 1890s:

   > Her laugh is like sunshine, full of glee,
   > And her sweet breath smells like fresh-made tea.

5. From another gem by Francis Saltus Saltus, "The Spider":

   > Then all thy feculent majesty recalls
   >   The nauseous mustiness of forsaken bowers,
   > The leprous nudity of deserted halls—
   >   The positive nastiness of sullied flowers.
   >
   > And I mark the colours yellow and black
   >   That fresco thy lithe, dictatorial thighs,
   > I dream and wonder on my drunken back
   >   How God could possibly have created flies!

6. From "Song to the Suliotes" by George Gordon, Lord Byron:

   > Up to battle! Sons of Suli
   > Up, and do your duty duly!
   > There the wall—and there the moat is:
   > Bouwah! Bouwah! Suliotes,
   > There is booty—there is beauty!
   > Up my boys and do your duty!

7. From a juvenile poem of John Dryden, "Upon the Death of the Lord Hastings" (a victim of smallpox):

   > Each little pimple had a tear in it,
   > To wail the fault its rising did commit . . .

8. From "The Abbey Mason" by Thomas Hardy:

   > When longer yet dank death had wormed
   > The brain wherein the style had germed
   >
   > From Gloucester church it flew afar—
   > The style called Perpendicular.—

> To Winton and to Westminster
> It ranged, and grew still beautifuller ...

9. A metaphor from "The Crucible of Life" by the once-popular American newspaper poet Edgar A. Guest:

> Sacred and sweet is the joy that must come
> From the furnace of life when you've poured off the scum.

10. From an elegy for Queen Victoria by one of her subjects:

> Dust to dust, and ashes to ashes,
> Into the tomb the Great Queen dashes.

Sentimentality is a failure of writers who seem to feel a great emotion but who fail to give us sufficient grounds for sharing it. The emotion may be an anger greater than its object seems to call for, as in these lines to a girl who caused scandal (the exact nature of her act never being specified): "The gossip in each hall / Will curse your name ... / Go! better cast yourself right down the falls!"[2] Or it may be an enthusiasm quite unwarranted by its subject: in *The Fleece* John Dyer temptingly describes the pleasures of life in a workhouse for the poor. The sentimental poet is especially prone to tenderness. Great tears fill his eyes at a glimpse of an aged grandmother sitting by a hearth. For all the poet knows, she may be the manager of a casino in Las Vegas who would be startled to find herself an object of pity, but the sentimentalist doesn't care to know about the woman herself. She is a general excuse for feeling maudlin. Any other conventional object will serve as well: a faded valentine, the strains of an old song, a baby's cast-off pacifier. An instance of such emotional self-indulgence is "The Old Oaken Bucket," by Samuel Woodworth, a stanza of which goes:

> How sweet from the green, mossy brim to receive it,
>   As, poised on the curb, it inclined to my lips!
> Not a full-flushing goblet could tempt me to leave it,
>   Tho' filled with the nectar that Jupiter sips.
> And now, far removed from the loved habitation,
>   The tear of regret will intrusively swell,
> As fancy reverts to my father's plantation,
>   And sighs for the bucket that hung in the well.

The staleness of the phrasing and imagery (Jove's nectar, *tear of regret*) suggests that the speaker is not even seeing the actual physical bucket, and the tripping

---

[2] Ali. S. Hilmi, "The Preacher's Sermon," *Verse at Random* (Larnaca, Cyprus: Ohanian Press, 1953).

meter of the lines is inappropriate to an expression of tearful regret. Perhaps the poet's nostalgia is genuine. Indeed, as Keith Waldrop has put it, "a bad poem is always sincere." However sincere in their feelings, sentimental poets are insincere in their art—otherwise, wouldn't they trouble to write better poems? Wet-eyed and sighing for a bucket, Woodworth achieves not pathos but **bathos:** a description that can move us to laughter instead of tears.[3] Tears, of course, can be shed for good reason. A piece of sentimentality is not to be confused with a well-wrought poem whose tone is tenderness.

Rod McKuen   (b. 1933)

THOUGHTS ON CAPITAL PUNISHMENT   1954

There ought to be capital punishment for cars
that run over rabbits and drive into dogs
and commit the unspeakable, unpardonable crime
of killing a kitty cat still in his prime.

Purgatory, at the very least   5
                          should await the driver
     driving over a beast.

Those hurrying headlights coming out of the dark
that scatter the scampering squirrels in the park
should await the best jury that one might compose   10
of fatherless chipmunks and husbandless does.

And then found guilty, after too fair a trial
should be caged in a cage with a hyena's smile
or maybe an elephant with an elephant gun
should shoot out his eyes when the verdict is done.   15

There ought to be something, something that's fair
to avenge Mrs. Badger as she waits in her lair
for her husband who lies with his guts spilling out
cause he didn't know what automobiles are about.

[3]*Bathos* in poetry can also mean an abrupt fall from the sublime to the trivial or incongruous. A sample, from Nicholas Rowe's play *The Fair Penitent:* "Is it the voice of thunder, or my father?" Another, from John Close, a minor Victorian: "Around their heads a dazzling halo shone, / No need of mortal robes, or any hat." When, however, such a letdown is used for a *desirable* effect of humor or contrast, it is usually called an **anticlimax:** as in Alexander Pope's lines on the queen's palace, "Here thou, great Anna! whom three realms obey, / Dost sometimes counsel take—and sometimes tea."

Hell on the highway, at the very least   20
        should await the driver
    driving over a beast.

Who kills a man kills a bit of himself
But a cat too is an extension of God.

William Stafford   (1914–1993)*

TRAVELING THROUGH THE DARK   1962

Traveling through the dark I found a deer
dead on the edge of the Wilson River road.
It is usually best to roll them into the canyon:
that road is narrow; to swerve might make more dead.

By glow of the tail-light I stumbled back of the car   5
and stood by the heap, a doe, a recent killing;
she had stiffened already, almost cold.
I dragged her off; she was large in the belly.

My fingers touching her side brought me the reason—
her side was warm; her fawn lay there waiting,   10
alive, still, never to be born.
Beside that mountain road I hesitated.

The car aimed ahead its lowered parking lights;
under the hood purred the steady engine.
I stood in the glare of the warm exhaust turning red;   15
around our group I could hear the wilderness listen.

I thought hard for us all—my only swerving—
then pushed her over the edge into the river.

QUESTIONS

1. Compare these poems by Rod McKuen and William Stafford. How are they similar?
2. Explain Stafford's title. Who are all those traveling through the dark?
3. Comment on McKuen's use of language. Consider especially: *unspeakable, unpardonable crime* (line 3), *kitty cat* (4), *scatter the scampering squirrels* (9), and *cause he didn't know* (19).
4. Compare the meaning of Stafford's last two lines and McKuen's last two. Does either poem have a moral? Can either poem be said to moralize?
5. Which poem might be open to the charge of sentimentality? Why?

EXERCISE: *Fine or Shoddy Tenderness*

Here are five poems to evaluate. Although different in length and style, each deals with the same theme—the untimely death of a small child. Which of the poems do you find sentimental? Which would you defend? In making your judgment, it might help to consider the language of each poem. Do any of them speak in words that seem stale or second-hand? You might also examine the imagery. Do any of the poems demonstrate some fresh or detailed observation of the physical world? In sentimental poems, the world is often described in borrowed, conventional phrases or not at all.

Julia A. Moore   (1847–1920)

LITTLE LIBBY   1876

One more little spirit to Heaven has flown,
  To dwell in that mansion above,
Where dear little angels, together roam,
  In God's everlasting love.

One little flower has withered and died,   5
  A bud nearly ready to bloom,
Its life on earth is marked with pride;
  Oh, sad it should die so soon.

Sweet little Libby, that precious flower
  Was a pride in her parents' home,   10
They miss their little girl *every* hour,
  Those friends that are left to mourn.

Her sweet silvery voice no more is heard
  In the home where she once roamed;
Her place is *vacant* around the hearth,   15
  Where her friends are mourning lone.

They are mourning the loss of a little girl,
  With black eyes and auburn hair,
She was a treasure to them in this world,
  This beautiful child so fair.   20

One morning in April, a short time ago,
  Libby was active and gay;
Her Saviour called her, she had to go,
  E're the close of that pleasant day.

While eating dinner, this dear little child   25
  Was choked on a piece of beef.
Doctors came, tried their skill awhile,
  But none could give relief.

She was ten years of age, I am told,
  And in school stood very high.   30
Her little form now the earth enfolds,
  In her embrace it must ever lie.

Her friends and schoolmates will not forget
    Little Libby that is no more;
She is waiting on the shining step,   35
    To welcome home friends once more.

Frederick Turner   (b. 1943)

ON THE DEATH OF AN INFANT   1988

Latecomer, first to go,
Like the small arctic flower
Between the snow and snow,
The fragrance of an hour.

Dabney Stuart   (b. 1937)

CRIB DEATH   1987

Kisses are for the living.
Even if the terrible breath of the dead
Never rose from the earth's mouth,
Dread of it would turn our heads aside
As relatives at a funeral meet and kiss.   5
Living in such air is what the living have,
Less choice than a stone what's cut into its face.

Terese Svoboda   (b. 1951)

ON MY FIRST SON (AFTER BEN JONSON)   1985

Goodbye, Deng, Spirit-of-the-Air,
my joy was motherlove to bear

his five years in hope and now in
grief as sweet as some great sin.

O that I could still catch and hold   5
him! He would do as he were told.

Not even science could reverse
a simple accident: the curse

of life that will not stick. I say:
here lies all reason for poetry,   10

for whose sake I promise to love no less
the next child who claims my happiness.

COMPARE:

See Ben Jonson's elegy on his first son (page 1089).

Ted Kooser   (b. 1939)*

A Child's Grave Marker   1985

A small block of granite
engraved with her name and the dates
just wasn't quite pretty enough
for this lost little girl
or her parents, who added a lamb   5
cast in plaster of paris,
using the same kind of cake mold
my grandmother had—iron,
heavy and black as a skillet.
The lamb came out coconut-white,   10
and seventy years have proven it
soft in the rain. On this hill,
overlooking a river in Iowa,
it melts in its own sweet time.

In recent years, the belief that poetry cannot be popular has been shaken by practitioners of **cowboy poetry,** verse about life on the range, written by people who know that life at first hand. Usually realistic, riming and metrical, cowboy poetry is designed to be read aloud or recited to audiences such as the large throng that assembles each January at the Cowboy Poetry Gathering in Elko, Nevada. This kind of folk poetry "has its own criteria of good and bad," insists Gibbs Smith, publisher of two best-selling cowboy poetry anthologies; "it has its own rules; its own tradition, and we should respect that."[4] Devotees of cowboy poetry regard the following poem as a classic. Read it and see if you agree.

Wallace McRae   (b. 1936)

Reincarnation   1980

"What does reincarnation mean?"
A cowpoke ast his friend.
His pal replied, "It happens when
Yer life has reached its end.

[4]Quoted by Sara Terry, "Poem on the Range," *Boston Globe Magazine*, Jan. 19, 1992. The anthologies, edited by Hal Cannon, are *Cowboy Poetry: A Gathering* and *New Cowboy Poetry* (Salt Lake City: Gibbs M. Smith, 1985 and 1990).

They comb yer hair, and warsh yer neck,   5
And clean yer fingernails,
And lay you in a padded box
Away from life's travails.

"The box and you goes in a hole,
That's been dug into the ground.   10
Reincarnation starts in when
Yore planted 'neath a mound.
Them clods melt down, just like yer box,
And you who is inside.
And then yore just beginnin's on   15
Yer transformation ride.

"In a while the grass'll grow
Upon yer rendered mound.
Till some day on yer moldered grave
A lonely flower is found.   20
And say a hoss should wander by
And graze upon this flower
That once wuz you, but now's become
Yer vegetative bower.

"The posey that the hoss done ate   25
Up, with his other feed,
Makes bone, and fat, and muscle
Essential to the steed.
But some is left that he can't use
And so it passes through,   30
And finally lays upon the ground.
This thing, that once wuz you.

"Then say, by chance, I wanders by
And sees this upon the ground,
And I ponders, and I wonders at,   35
This object that I found.
I thinks of reincarnation,
Of life, and death, and such,
And come away concludin': Slim,
You ain't changed, all that much."   40

Questions

1. If you were Slim, how would you react to that last line?
2. Discuss this harsh judgment: "This isn't much of a poem. The poet is only playing an elaborate joke on Slim and on the rest of us."
3. In general, do you believe that a poem is any the worse for a lack of total seriousness?
4. Take a close look at the poem's language. Which words or phrases seem unschooled cowboy speech? Which might be criticized as stilted or bookish? How do you account for this discrepancy?

5. Compare the poem's central idea with a similar notion advanced by Shakespeare's *Hamlet, Prince of Denmark*:

> *Hamlet:* A man may fish with the worm that hath eat of a king, and
> eat of the fish that hath fed of that worm.
> *King:* What dost thou mean by this?
> *Hamlet:* Nothing but to show you how a king may go to progress
> through the guts of a beggar.

> (*Hamlet* IV, iii, 27–32)

Notice that Hamlet, like Slim's friend, also puts his listener on the receiving end of an insult. But how might it be claimed that Shakespeare makes a simple idea rich and complicated?

6. Do you agree with Gibbs Smith that we should judge cowboy poetry only by its own rules (not oblige it to live up to standards we might apply to a passage of Shakespeare or a poem by Robert Frost)?

KNOWING EXCELLENCE

How can we tell an excellent poem from any other? To give reasons for excellence in poetry is harder than to give reasons for failure in poetry (so often due to familiar kinds of imprecision and sentimentality). A bad poem tends to be stereotyped, an excellent poem unique. In judging either, we can have no absolute specifications. A poem is not like an electric toaster that an inspector can test by a check-off list. It has to be judged on the basis of what it is trying to be and how well it succeeds in the effort.

To judge a poem, we first have to understand it. At least, we need to understand it *almost* all the way; there is, to be sure, a poem such as Hopkins's "The Windhover" (page 1084), which most readers probably would call excellent even though its meaning is still being debated. Although it is a good idea to give a poem at least a couple of considerate readings before judging it, sometimes our first encounter starts turning into an act of evaluation. Moving along into the poem, becoming more deeply involved in it, we may begin forming an opinion. In general, the more a poem contains for us to understand, the more rewarding we are likely to find it. Of course, an obscure and highly demanding poem is not always to be preferred to a relatively simple one. Difficult poems can be pretentious and incoherent; still, there is something to be said for the poem complicated enough to leave us something to discover on our fifteenth reading (unlike most limericks, which yield their all at a look). Here is such a poem, one not readily fathomed and exhausted.

William Butler Yeats   (1865–1939)*

SAILING TO BYZANTIUM   1927

That is no country for old men. The young
In one another's arms, birds in the trees
—Those dying generations—at their song,

The salmon-falls, the mackerel-crowded seas,
Fish, flesh, or fowl, commend all summer long   5
Whatever is begotten, born, and dies.
Caught in that sensual music all neglect
Monuments of unaging intellect.

An aged man is but a paltry thing,
A tattered coat upon a stick, unless   10
Soul clap its hands and sing, and louder sing
For every tatter in its mortal dress,
Nor is there singing school but studying
Monuments of its own magnificence;
And therefore I have sailed the seas and come   15
To the holy city of Byzantium.

O sages standing in God's holy fire
As in the gold mosaic of a wall,
Come from the holy fire, perne in a gyre°,   *spin down a spiral*
And be the singing-masters of my soul.
Consume my heart away; sick with desire   20
And fastened to a dying animal
It knows not what it is; and gather me
Into the artifice of eternity.

Once out of nature I shall never take   25
My bodily form from any natural thing,
But such a form as Grecian goldsmiths make
Of hammered gold and gold enameling
To keep a drowsy Emperor awake;
Or set upon a golden bough to sing   30
To lords and ladies of Byzantium
Of what is past, or passing, or to come.

SAILING TO BYZANTIUM. Byzantium was the capital of the Byzantine Empire, the city now called Istanbul. Yeats means, though, not merely the physical city. Byzantium is also a name for his conception of paradise.

   Though *salmon-falls* (line 4) suggests Yeats's native Ireland, the poem, as we find out in line 25, is about escaping from the entire natural world. If the poet desires this escape, then probably the *country* mentioned in the opening line is no political nation but the cycle of birth and death in which human beings are trapped; and, indeed, the poet says his heart is "fastened to a dying animal." Imaginary landscapes, it would seem, are merging with the historical Byzantium. Lines 17–18 refer to mosaic images, adornments of the Byzantine cathedral of St. Sophia, in which the figures of saints are inlaid against backgrounds of gold. The clockwork bird of the last stanza is also a reference to something actual. Yeats noted: "I have read somewhere that in the Emperor's palace at Byzantium was a tree made of gold and silver, and artificial birds that sang." This description of the role the poet would seek—that of a changeless, immortal singer—directs us back to the earlier references to music and singing. Taken all together, they point toward the central metaphor of the poem: the craft of poetry can be a kind of singing. One kind of everlasting monument is a great poem. To study masterpieces of poetry is the only "singing school"—the only way to learn to write a poem.

We have no more than skimmed through a few of this poem's suggestions, enough to show that, out of allusion and imagery, Yeats has woven at least one elaborate metaphor. Surely one thing the poem achieves is that, far from merely puzzling us, it makes us aware of relationships between what a person can imagine and the physical world. There is the statement that a human heart is bound to the body that perishes, and yet it is possible to see consciousness for a moment independent of flesh, to sing with joy at the very fact that the body is crumbling away. Much of the power of Yeats's poem comes from the physical terms with which he states the ancient quarrel between body and spirit, body being a "tattered coat upon a stick." There is all the difference in the world between the work of the poet like Yeats whose eye is on the living thing and whose mind is awake and passionate, and that of the slovenly poet whose dull eye and sleepy mind focus on nothing more than some book read hastily long ago. The former writes a poem out of compelling need, the latter as if it seems a nice idea to write something.

Yeats's poem has the three qualities essential to beauty, according to the definition of Thomas Aquinas: wholeness, harmony, and radiance. The poem is all one; its parts move in peace with one another; it shines with emotional intensity. There is an orderly progression going on in it: from the speaker's statement of his discontent with the world of "sensual music," to his statement that he is quitting this world, to his prayer that the sages will take him in, and his vision of future immortality. And the images of the poem relate to one another—*dying generations* (line 3), *dying animal* (line 22), and the undying golden bird (lines 27–32)—to mention just one series of related things. "Sailing to Byzantium" is not the kind of poem that has, in Pope's words, "One simile, that solitary shines / In the dry desert of a thousand lines." Rich in figurative language, Yeats's whole poem develops a metaphor, with further metaphors as its tributaries.

"Sailing to Byzantium" has a theme that matters to us. What human being does not long, at times, to shed timid, imperfect flesh, to live in a state of absolute joy, unperishing? Being human, perhaps we too are stirred by Yeats's prayer: "Consume my heart away, sick with desire / And fastened to a dying animal . . . ." If it is true that in poetry (as Ezra Pound declared) "only emotion endures," then Yeats's poem ought to endure. (If you happen not to feel moved by this poem, try another—but come back to "Sailing to Byzantium" after a while.)

Most excellent poems, it might be argued, contain significant themes, as does "Sailing to Byzantium." But the presence of such a theme is not enough to render a poem excellent. Not theme alone makes an excellent poem, but how well a theme is stated.

Yeats's poem, some would say, is the match for any lyric in our language. Some might call it inferior to an epic (to Milton's *Paradise Lost*, say, or to the

Iliad), but this claim is to lead us into a different argument: whether certain genres are innately better than others. Such an argument usually leads to a dead end. Evidently, *Paradise Lost* has greater range, variety, matter, length, and ambitiousness. But any poem—whether an epic or an epigram—may be judged by how well it fulfills the design it undertakes. God, who created both fleas and whales, pronounced all good. Fleas, like epigrams, have no reason to feel inferior.

EXERCISE: *Two Poems to Compare*

Here are two poems with a similar theme. Which contains more qualities of excellent poetry? Decide whether the other is bad or whether it may be praised for achieving something different.

Arthur Guiterman   (1871–1943)

ON THE VANITY OF EARTHLY GREATNESS   1936

The tusks that clashed in mighty brawls
Of mastodons, are billiard balls.

The sword of Charlemagne the Just
Is ferric oxide, known as rust.

The grizzly bear whose potent hug   5
Was feared by all, is now a rug.

Great Caesar's bust is on the shelf,
And I don't feel so well myself.

Percy Bysshe Shelley   (1792–1822)

OZYMANDIAS   1818

I met a traveler from an antique land
Who said: Two vast and trunkless legs of stone
Stand in the desert. Near them, on the sand,
Half sunk, a shattered visage lies, whose frown,
And wrinkled lip, and sneer of cold command,   5
Tell that its sculptor well those passions read
Which yet survive, stamped on these lifeless things,
The hand that mocked° them and the heart that fed;   *imitated*
And on the pedestal these words appear:
"My name is Ozymandias, king of kings: 10
Look on my works, ye Mighty, and despair!"

Nothing beside remains. Round the decay
Of that colossal wreck, boundless and bare
The lone and level sands stretch far away.

Some excellent poems of the past will remain sealed to us unless we are willing to sympathize with their conventions. Pastoral poetry, for instance—Marlowe's "Passionate Shepherd" and Milton's "Lycidas"—asks us to accept certain conventions and situations that may seem old-fashioned: idle swains, oaten flutes. We are under no grim duty, of course, to admire poems whose conventions do not appeal to us. But there is no point in blaming a poet for playing a particular game or for observing its rules.

Bad poems, of course, can be woven together out of conventions, like patchwork quilts made of old unwanted words. In Shakespeare's England, poets were busily imitating the sonnets of Petrarch, the Italian poet whose praise of his beloved Laura had become well known. The result of their industry was a surplus of Petrarchan **conceits,** or elaborate comparisons (from the Italian *concetto:* concept, bright idea). In the following sonnet, Shakespeare, who at times helped himself generously from the Petrarchan stockpile, pokes fun at poets who thoughtlessly use such handed-down figures of speech.

William Shakespeare (1564–1616)*

MY MISTRESS' EYES ARE NOTHING LIKE THE SUN   1609

My mistress' eyes are nothing like the sun;
Coral is far more red than her lips' red;
If snow be white, why then her breasts are dun;
If hairs be wires, black wires grow on her head.
I have seen roses damasked red and white,   5
But no such roses see I in her cheeks;
And in some perfumes is there more delight
Than in the breath that from my mistress reeks.
I love to hear her speak, yet well I know
That music hath a far more pleasing sound;   10
I grant I never saw a goddess go:
My mistress, when she walks, treads on the ground.
    And yet, by heaven, I think my love as rare
    As any she°, belied with false compare.   *woman*

Contrary to what you might expect, for years after Shakespeare's time, poets continued to write fine poems with Petrarchan conventions.

Thomas Campion   (1567–1620)*

THERE IS A GARDEN IN HER FACE   1617

There is a garden in her face
Where roses and white lilies grow;
   A heav'nly paradise is that place
Wherein all pleasant fruits do flow.
   There cherries grow which none may buy   5
   Till "Cherry-ripe" themselves do cry.

Those cherries fairly do enclose
Of orient pearl a double row,
   Which when her lovely laughter shows,
They look like rose-buds filled with snow;   10
   Yet them nor° peer nor prince can buy,   *neither*
   Till "Cherry-ripe" themselves do cry.

Her eyes like angels watch them still;
Her brows like bended bows do stand,
   Threat'ning with piercing frowns to kill   15
All that attempt, with eye or hand
   Those sacred cherries to come nigh
   Till "Cherry-ripe" themselves do cry.

THERE IS A GARDEN IN HER FACE. 6 *"Cherry-ripe"*: cry of fruit-peddlers in London streets.

QUESTIONS

1. What does Campion's song owe to Petrarchan tradition?
2. What in it strikes you as fresh observation of actual life?
3. Comment in particular on the last stanza. Does the comparison of eyebrows to threatening bowmen seem too silly or far-fetched? What sense do you find in it?
4. Try to describe the tone of this poem. What do you understand, from this portrait of a young girl, to be the poet's feelings?

Modern poets also use conceits. May Swenson has developed an unusual comparison in the following love poem. Do you think that the conceit is successfully employed?

May Swenson   (1913–1989)

FOUR-WORD LINES   1967

Your eyes are just
like bees, and I
feel like a flower.
Their brown power makes
a breeze go over   5

my skin. When your
lashes ride down and
rise like brown bees'
legs, your pronged gaze
makes my eyes gauze.   10
I wish we were
in some shade and
no swarm of other
eyes to know that
I'm a flower breathing   15
bare, laid open to
your bees' warm stare.
I'd let you wade
in me and seize
with your eager brown   20
bees' power a sweet
glistening at my core.

QUESTIONS

1. The language of "Four-Word Lines" is relatively simple and straightforward. In what ways, however, does it differ from the prose you might read in a newspaper or magazine?
2. The poem grows out of two comparisons made at the beginning (lines 1–3). What are the comparisons and where do they lead?
3. A swarm of bees could easily be a threatening image. Why doesn't the speaker find them scary?
4. The poem's title explains its unusual form, but Swenson occasionally sneaks in some other poetic devices. How many rimes can you find hidden in the poem? (*Hint:* not all the rimes are at the end of lines.)
5. In what ways does the imagery of this poem recall that of the Shakespeare and Campion poems? In what ways is it original?
6. Is this a successful poem? Defend or criticize the poem.

Excellent poetry might be easier to recognize if each poet had a fixed position on the slopes of Mount Parnassus, but from one century to the next, the reputations of some poets have taken humiliating slides, or made impressive clambers. We decide for ourselves which poems to call excellent, but readers of the future may reverse our opinions. Most of us no longer would share this popular view of Walt Whitman by one of his contemporaries:

Walt Whitman (1819–1892), by some regarded as a great poet; by others, as no poet at all. Most of his so-called poems are mere catalogues of things, without meter or rime, but in a few more regular poems and in lines here and there he is grandly poetical, as in "O Captain! My Captain!"[5]

[5]J. Willis Westlake, A.M., *Common-school Literature, English and American, with Several Hundred Extracts to be Memorized* (Philadelphia, 1898).

Walt Whitman   (1819–1892)*

O Captain! My Captain!   1865

O Captain! my Captain! our fearful trip is done,
The ship has weather'd every rack, the prize we sought is won,
The port is near, the bells I hear, the people all exulting,
While follow eyes the steady keel, the vessel grim and daring;
   But O heart! heart! heart!   5
     O the bleeding drops of red,
       Where on the deck my Captain lies,
        Fallen cold and dead.

O Captain! my Captain! rise up and hear the bells;
Rise up—for you the flag is flung—for you the bugle trills,   10
For you bouquets and ribbon'd wreaths—for you the shores a-crowding,
For you they call, the swaying mass, their eager faces turning;
   Here Captain! dear father!
     This arm beneath your head!
       It is some dream that on the deck,   15
        You've fallen cold and dead.

My Captain does not answer, his lips are pale and still,
My father does not feel my arm, he has no pulse nor will,
The ship is anchor'd safe and sound, its voyage closed and done,
From fearful trip the victor ship comes in with object won;   20
   Exult O shores, and ring O bells!
     But I with mournful tread,
       Walk the deck my Captain lies,
        Fallen cold and dead.

O Captain! My Captain! Written soon after the death of Abraham Lincoln, this was, in Whitman's lifetime, by far the most popular of his poems.

Questions

1. Compare this with other Whitman poems. In what ways is "O Captain! My Captain!" uncharacteristic of his works? Do you agree with J. Willis Westlake that this is one of the few occasions on which Whitman is "grandly poetical?"
2. Comment on the appropriateness to its subject of the poem's rhythms.
3. Do you find any evidence in this poem that an excellent poet wrote it?

In a sense, all readers of poetry are constantly reexamining the judgments of the past by choosing those poems they care to go on reading. In the end, we have to admit that the critical principles set forth in this chapter are all very well for admiring excellent poetry we already know, but they cannot be carried like a yardstick in the hand, to go out looking for it. As Ezra Pound said in his *ABC of Reading,* "A classic is classic not because it conforms to certain structural rules, or fits certain definitions (of which its author had quite probably never heard). It is classic because of a certain eternal and irrepressible freshness."

The best poems, like "Sailing to Byzantium," may offer a kind of religious experience. In the last decade of the twentieth century, some of us rarely set foot outside an artificial environment. Whizzing down four-lane superhighways, we observe lakes and trees in the distance. In a way our cities are to us as anthills are to ants: no less than anthills, they are "natural" structures. But the "unnatural" world of school or business is, as Wordsworth says, too much with us. Locked in the shells of our ambitions, our self-esteem, we forget our kinship to earth and sea. We fabricate self-justifications. But a great poem shocks us into another order of perception. It points beyond language to something still more essential. It ushers us into an experience so moving and true that we feel (to quote King Lear) "cut to the brain." In bad or indifferent poetry, words are all there is.

Carl Sandburg   (1878–1967)*

FOG   1916

The fog comes
on little cat feet.
It sits looking
over harbor and city
on silent haunches   5
and then moves on.

QUESTION

In lines 15–22 of "The Love Song of J. Alfred Prufrock" (page 1059), T. S. Eliot also likens fog to a cat. Compare Sandburg's lines and Eliot's. Which passage tells us more about fogs and cats?

Thomas Gray   (1716–1771)*

ELEGY WRITTEN IN A COUNTRY   1753
CHURCHYARD

The curfew tolls the knell of parting day,
    The lowing herd wind slowly o'er the lea,
The plowman homeward plods his weary way,
    And leaves the world to darkness and to me.

Now fades the glimmering landscape on the sight,   5
    And all the air a solemn stillness holds,
Save where the beetle wheels his droning flight,
    And drowsy tinklings lull the distant folds;

Save that from yonder ivy-mantled tower
    The moping owl does to the moon complain   10
Of such, as wand'ring near her secret bower,
    Molest her ancient solitary reign.

Beneath those rugged elms, that yew tree's shade,
    Where heaves the turf in many a mold' ring heap,
Each in his narrow cell forever laid,   15
    The rude° forefathers of the hamlet sleep.   *simple, ignorant*

The breezy call of incense-breathing morn,
    The swallow twitt'ring from the straw-built shed,
The cock's shrill clarion, or the echoing horn°,   *fox-hunters' horn*
    No more shall rouse them from their lowly bed.   20

For them no more the blazing hearth shall burn,
    Or busy housewife ply her evening care;
No children run to lisp their sire's return,
    Or climb his knees the envied kiss to share.

Oft did the harvest to their sickle yield,   25
    Their furrow oft the stubborn glebe° has broke;   *turf*
How jocund did they drive their team afield!
    How bowed the woods beneath their sturdy stroke!

Let not Ambition mock their useful toil,
    Their homely joys, and destiny obscure;   30
Nor Grandeur hear with a disdainful smile
    The short and simple annals of the poor.

The boast of heraldry°, the pomp of pow'r,   *noble birth*
    And all that beauty, all that wealth e'er gave,
Awaits alike th' inevitable hour.   35
    The paths of glory lead but to the grave.

Nor you, ye proud, impute to these the fault,
    If Mem'ry o'er their tomb no trophies raise,
Where through the long-drawn aisle and fretted° vault   *inlaid with designs*
    The pealing anthem swells the note of praise.   40

Can storied urn or animated bust
    Back to its mansion call the fleeting breath?
Can Honor's voice provoke the silent dust,
    Or Flatt'ry soothe the dull cold ear of Death?

Perhaps in this neglected spot is laid   45
    Some heart once pregnant with celestial fire;
Hands that the rod of empire might have swayed,
    Or waked to ecstasy the living lyre.

But knowledge to their eyes her ample page
    Rich with the spoils of time did ne'er unroll;
Chill Penury° repressed their noble rage,
    And froze the genial current of the soul.

50

Poverty

Full many a gem of purest ray serene,
    The dark unfathomed caves of ocean bear:
Full many a flower is born to blush unseen,
    And waste its sweetness on the desert air.

55

Some village Hampden, that with dauntless breast
    The little tyrant of his field withstood;
Some mute inglorious Milton here may rest,
    Some Cromwell, guiltless of his country's blood.

60

Th' applause of list'ning senates to command,
    The threats of pain and ruin to despise,
To scatter plenty o'er a smiling land,
    And read their hist'ry in a nation's eyes,

Their lot forbade; nor circumscribed alone
    Their growing virtues, but their crimes confined;
Forbade to wade through slaughter to a throne,
    And shut the gates of mercy on mankind,

65

The struggling pangs of conscious truth to hide,
    To quench the blushes of ingenuous° shame,
Or heap the shrine of Luxury and Pride
    With incense kindled at the Muse's flame.

innocent 70

Far from the madding° crowd's ignoble strife,
    Their sober wishes never learned to stray;
Along the cool sequestered vale of life
    They kept the noiseless tenor° of their way.

frenzied

75

ongoing motion

Yet ev'n these bones from insult to protect
    Some frail memorial still erected nigh,
With uncouth rhymes and shapeless sculpture decked,
    Implores the passing tribute of a sigh.

80

Their name, their years, spelt by th' unlettered Muse,
    The place of fame and elegy supply:
And many a holy text around she strews,
    That teach the rustic moralist to die.

For who to dumb Forgetfulness a prey,
    This pleasing anxious being e'er resigned,
Left the warm precincts of the cheerful day,
    Nor cast one longing ling'ring look behind?

85

On some fond breast the parting soul relies,
  Some pious drops the closing eye requires;   90
Ev'n from the tomb the voice of Nature cries,
  Ev'n in our ashes live their wonted° fires.   *customary*

For thee, who mindful of th' unhonored dead
  Dost in these lines their artless tale relate;
If chance°, by lonely contemplation led,   *if by chance*   95
  Some kindred spirit shall inquire thy fate,

Haply° some hoary-headed swain° may say,   *perhaps; gray-haired shepherd*
  "Oft have we seen him at the peep of dawn
Brushing with hasty steps the dews away
  To meet the sun upon the upland lawn.   100

"There at the foot of yonder nodding beech
  That wreathes its old fantastic roots so high,
His listless length at noontide would he stretch,
  And pore upon the brook that babbles by.

"Hard by yon wood, now smiling as in scorn,   105
  Mutt'ring his wayward fancies he would rove,
Now drooping, woeful wan, like one forlorn,
  Or crazed with care, or crossed in hopeless love.

"One morn I missed him, on the customed hill,
  Along the heath and near his fav'rite tree;
Another came; nor yet beside the rill°,   110
  Nor up the lawn, nor at the wood was he;   *brook*

"The next with dirges due in sad array
  Slow through the churchway path we saw him borne.
Approach and read (for thou canst read) the lay°,   *song or poem* 115
  Graved on the stone beneath yon aged thorn."

The Epitaph

Here rests his head upon the lap of Earth
  A youth to Fortune and to Fame unknown.
Fair Science° frowned not on his humble birth,   *Knowledge*
  And Melancholy marked him for her own.   120

Large was his bounty, and his soul sincere,
  Heav'n did a recompense as largely send:
He gave to Mis'ry all he had, a tear,
  He gained from Heav'n ('twas all he wished) a friend.

No farther seek his merits to disclose,   125
  Or draw his frailties from their dread abode,
(There they alike in trembling hope repose),
  The bosom of His Father and his God.

ELEGY WRITTEN IN A COUNTRY CHURCHYARD. In English poetry, an **elegy** has come to mean a lament or a sadly meditative poem, sometimes written on the occasion of a death. Other elegies in this book include Chidiock Tichborne's "Elegy," A. E. Housman's "To an Athlete Dying Young," and in more recent poetry, "Elegy for Jane" by Theodore Roethke.
41 *storied urn:* vessel holding the ashes of the dead after cremation. *Storied* can mean (1) decorated with scenes; (2) inscribed with a life's story; or (3) celebrated in story or history. *The animated bust* is a lifelike sculpture of the dead, placed on a tomb. 57 *Hampden:* John Hampden (1594–1643), member of Parliament, had resisted illegal taxes on his lands imposed by Charles I. 60 *Cromwell . . . his country's blood:* Gray blames Oliver Cromwell (1599–1658) for strife and tyranny. As general of the armies of Parliament, Cromwell had won the Civil War against Charles I and had signed the king's death warrant. As Lord Protector of England (1653–1658), he had ruled with an iron hand. 71–72 *heap the shrine . . . Muse's flame:* Gray chides mercenary poets who write poems to please their rich, high-living patrons.

QUESTIONS

1. In contrasting the unknown poor buried in this village churchyard and famous men buried in cathedrals (in *fretted vault*, line 39), what is Gray's theme? What do you understand from the line, *The paths of glory lead but to the grave?*
2. Carl J. Weber thinks that Gray's compassion for the village poor anticipates the democratic sympathies of the American Revolution: "Thomas Gray is the pioneer literary spokesman for the Ordinary Man." But another critic, Lyle Glazier, argues that the "Elegy" isn't political at all: that we misread if we think the poet meant "to persuade the poor and obscure that their barren lives are meaningful"; and also misread if we think he meant to assure the privileged classes "in whose ranks Gray was proud to consider himself" that they need not worry about the poor, "who have already all essential riches." How much truth do you find in either of these views?
3. Cite lines and phrases that show Gray's concern for the musical qualities of words.
4. Who is the *youth* of the closing Epitaph? By *thee* (line 93) does Gray mean himself? Does he mean some fictitious poet supposedly writing the "Elegy"—the first-person speaker (line 4)? Does he mean some village stonecutter, a crude poet whose illiterate Muse (line 81) inspired him to compose tombstone epitaphs? Or could the Epitaph possibly refer to Gray's close friend of school and undergraduate days, the promising poet Richard West, who had died in 1742? Which interpretation seems to you the most reasonable? (Does our lack of absolute certainty negate the value of the poem?)
5. Walter Savage Landor called the Epitaph a tin kettle tied to the tail of a noble dog. Do you agree that the Epitaph is inferior to what has gone before it? What is its function in Gray's poem?
6. Many sources for Gray's phrases and motifs have been found in earlier poets: Virgil, Horace, Dante, Milton, and many more. Even if it could be demonstrated that Gray's poem has not one original line in it, would it be possible to dismiss the "Elegy" as a mere rag-bag of borrowings?
7. In the earliest surviving manuscript of Gray's poem, lines 73–76 read:

> No more with Reason and thyself at strife;
> Give anxious cares and endless wishes room
> But through the cool sequester'd vale of Life
> Pursue the silent tenor of thy doom.

In what ways does the final version of those lines seem superior?
8. Gray's "Elegy" has inspired hundreds of imitations, countless parodies, and translations into eighteen or more languages. To what do you attribute the poem's fame? What do you suppose has proved so universally appealing in it?

9. Compare Gray's "Elegy" with Shelley's "Ozymandias" and Arthur Guiterman's "On the Vanity of Earthly Greatness." What do the three poems have in common? How would you rank them in order of excellence?

EXERCISE: *Re-evaluating Popular Classics*

In this exercise you will read two of the most popular American poems of the nineteenth century. In their time, these poems were not only considered classics by serious critics, but thousands of ordinary readers knew them by heart. Recently, however, these two poems have fallen out of critical favor.

Your assignment is to read these poems carefully and make your own personal, tentative evaluation of each poem's merit. Here are some questions you might ask yourself, as you consider each poem:

Do these poems engage your sympathies? Do they stir you and touch your feelings?

What, if anything, might make them memorable? Do they have any vivid images? Any metaphors, understatement, overstatement, or other figures of speech? Do these poems appeal to the ear?

Do the poems exhibit any wild incompetence? Do you find any forced rimes, inappropriate words, or other unintentionally comic features? Can the poems be accused of bathos or sentimentality, or do you trust the poet to report honest feelings?

How well does the poet seem in control of language? Does the poet's language reflect in any detail the physical world we know?

Do these poems seem entirely drawn from other poetry of the past, or do you have a sense that the poet is thinking and feeling on her (or his) own? Does the poet show any evidence of having read other poets' poetry?

What is the poet trying to do in each poem? How successful, in your opinion, is the attempt?

Try setting these poems next to similar poems you know and admire. (You might try comparing Emma Lazarus's "The New Colossus" to Percy Bysshe Shelley's "Ozymandias," found in this chapter; both are sonnets, and their subjects have interesting similarities and contrasts. Or compare Edgar Allan Poe's "Annabel Lee" to John Crowe Ransom's "Bells for John Whiteside's Daughter" or to A. E. Housman's "To an Athlete Dying Young," both found in "Poems for Further Reading").

Are these poems sufficiently rich and interesting to repay more than one reading?

Do you think that these poems still deserve to be considered classics? Or do they no longer speak powerfully to a contemporary audience?

Emma Lazarus   (1849–1887)

THE NEW COLOSSUS   1883

Not like the brazen giant of Greek fame,
With conquering limbs astride from land to land;
Here at our sea-washed, sunset gates shall stand
A mighty woman with a torch, whose flame
Is the imprisoned lightning, and her name   5
Mother of Exiles. From her beacon-hand
Glows world-wide welcome; her mild eyes command
The air-bridged harbor that twin cities frame.
"Keep, ancient lands, your storied pomp!" cries she
With silent lips. "Give me your tired, your poor,   10

Your huddled masses yearning to breathe free,
The wretched refuse of your teeming shore.
Send these, the homeless, tempest-tost to me,
I lift my lamp beside the golden door!"

THE NEW COLOSSUS. In 1883, a committee formed to raise funds to build a pedestal for what would be the largest statue in the world, "Liberty Enlightening the World" by Fréderic-Auguste Bartholdi, which was a gift from the French people to celebrate America's first bicentennial. American authors were asked to donate manuscripts for a fund-raising auction. The young poet Emma Lazarus, whose parents had come to America as immigrants, sent in this sonnet composed for the occasion. When President Grover Cleveland unveiled the Statue of Liberty in October, 1886, Lazarus's sonnet was read at the ceremony. In 1903, the poem was carved on the statue's pedestal. The reference in the opening line to "the brazen giant of Greek fame" refers to the famous Colossus of Rhodes, a huge bronze statue that once stood in the harbor on the Aegean island of Rhodes. Built to commemorate a military victory, the statue was considered one of the so-called Seven Wonders of the World.

Edgar Allan Poe   (1809–1849)*

ANNABEL LEE   1849

It was many and many a year ago,
   In a kingdom by the sea,
That a maiden there lived whom you may know
   By the name of Annabel Lee;
And this maiden she lived with no other thought   5
   Than to love and be loved by me.

I was a child and *she* was a child,
   In this kingdom by the sea,
But we loved with a love that was more than love—
   I and my Annabel Lee—   10
With a love that the wingéd seraphs of Heaven
   Coveted her and me.

And this was the reason that, long ago,
   In this kingdom by the sea,
A wind blew out of a cloud, chilling   15
   My beautiful Annabel Lee;
So that her highborn kinsmen came
   And bore her away from me,
To shut her up in a sepulchre
   In this kingdom by the sea.   20

The angels, not half so happy in Heaven,
   Went envying her and me:—
Yes!—that was the reason (as all men know,
   In this kingdom by the sea)
That the wind came out of the cloud by night,   25
   Chilling and killing my Annabel Lee.

But our love it was stronger by far than the love
   Of those who were older than we—
   Of many far wiser than we—
And neither the angels in Heaven above,   30
   Nor the demons down under the sea,
Can ever dissever my soul from the soul
   Of the beautiful Annabel Lee:—

For the moon never beams, without bringing me dreams
   Of the beautiful Annabel Lee;   35
And the stars never rise, but I feel the bright eyes
   Of the beautiful Annabel Lee:
And so, all the night-tide, I lie down by the side
   Of my darling—my darling—my life and my bride,
   In the sepulchre there by the sea—   40
   In her tomb by the sounding sea.

WRITER'S PERSPECTIVE

Edgar Allan Poe

Edgar Allan Poe on Writing
A LONG POEM DOES NOT EXIST   1848

I hold that a long poem does not exist. I maintain that the phrase, "a long poem," is simply a flat contradiction in terms.

I need scarcely observe that a poem deserves its title only inasmuch as it excites, by elevating the soul. The value of the poem is in the ratio of its elevative excitement. But all excitements are, through a psychal necessity, transient. That degree of excitement which would entitle a poem to be so called at all cannot be sustained throughout a composition of any great length. After the lapse of half an hour, at the very utmost, it flags—fails—a revulsion ensues—and then the poem is in effect, and in fact, no longer such.

                             "The Poetic Principle"

How to Begin Evaluating a Poem

Evaluation is both the easiest and the hardest part of literary criticism. It is easy because we almost always have some immediate reaction to the poem or story we are reading. We like it or dislike it—sometimes passionately so. While that initial, unrehearsed response will often become part of our ultimate judgment, it will usually end up being no more than a departure point. Literary evaluation is also hard because we must balance this subjective response against the need to view the poem in an informed perspective. The question is not merely, does the work please or move us, but how well does it manage the literary tasks it sets out to perform? Not all good performances will necessarily be to our own taste. A good critic is willing both to admire a strong poem that he or she doesn't like and to admit that a personal favorite might not really be all that good.

Fair evaluation is so difficult that many contemporary theorists have declared it impossible. They maintain that some external factor—personal or ideological—will always get in the way of disinterested judgment. Some theorists even say that the very notion of disinterested evaluation is illusory: to judge one work of art better than another is always to impose a set of values upon it. Although the issues raised by these critics are genuine, there are still both theoretical and practical reasons to evaluate literary works. First, some works of art set out very explicit generic expectations of how they wish to be judged. An epigram, for instance, usually seeks to be witty and concise. If it proves tiresome and verbose, it can fairly be said to fail. Second, there is a strong case to be made for the idea that it is also illusory to pretend we can refrain from judging works of art. Since quality is almost always implicitly evaluated, it may be more useful to make those judgments clear and explicit. Finally, there is the practical issue of time. No one can read (or reread) every work ever written. We need open and informed critical guidance on where best to focus our finite attention.

To begin evaluating a poem, first try to understand your own subjective response—don't pretend it doesn't exist. Admit, at least to yourself, whether the poem delights, moves, bores, or annoys you. Then try to determine what the poem seems designed to make you think and feel. Does it belong to some identifiable form or genre? (Is it, for instance, a love sonnet, narrative ballad, satire, or elegy?) How does its performance stack up against the expectations it creates? Considering those questions will give you some larger sense of perspective from which to evaluate the poem.

Next, move on to specific elements in the poem. How well do its language, imagery, symbols, and figures of speech work in communicating its meaning? Are the metaphors or similes effective? Is the imagery fresh and precise? Is the language ever unnecessarily vague or verbose? Does the poem ever fall into clichés or platitudes? (Although there are dozens of such questions to ask, focus on the specific questions that seem relevant to the particular poem. Finally, once you've examined the details of the poem critically, go back and reread it again—preferably aloud. Does the poem seem better or worse than it did initially? Try to rest your final evaluation on your own honest reaction, but make sure you have nourished that personal response with careful critical examination so that your evaluation has grown into an informed judgment. (For further tips on the process of evaluation, read the checklist of critical questions found on page 1004 under "Exercise: Re-evaluating Popular Classics.")

WRITING ASSIGNMENT

Choose a short poem from this book that you particularly enjoy and write a defense of its excellence. In making your case, first set up the terms by which you will judge the poem and then demonstrate why such criteria are appropriate to this particular text. Finally, show specifically how the poem succeeds according to those standards.

FURTHER SUGGESTIONS FOR WRITING

1. Write a brief evaluation of either "The New Colossus" by Emma Lazarus or "Annabel Lee" by Edgar Allan Poe.
2. Concoct the worst poem you can possibly write and, in a brief accompanying essay, recount the difficulties you met and overcame in writing it. Quote, for example, any lines you wrote but had to discard for not being bad enough.
3. In "Poems for Further Reading," which begins on page 1027, find a poem you particularly admire or dislike. In a brief essay (300–500 words), evaluate it. Refer to particulars in the poem to support your opinion of it.

28 *What Is Poetry?*

Robert Francis   (1901–1987)

CATCH   1950

Two boys uncoached are tossing a poem together,
Overhand, underhand, backhand, sleight of hand, every hand,
Teasing with attitudes, latitudes, interludes, altitudes,
High, make him fly off the ground for it, low, make him stoop,
Make him scoop it up, make him as-almost-as-possible miss it,   5
Fast, let him sting from it, now, now fool him slowly,
Anything, everything tricky, risky, nonchalant,
Anything under the sun to outwit the prosy,
Over the tree and the long sweet cadence down,
Over his head, make him scramble to pick up the meaning,   10
And now, like a posy, a pretty one plump in his hands.

As Robert Francis hints in this playful poem, the pitching poet keeps the catching reader alert by creating little difficulties. Reading some of the poems in this book, you have probably felt like the boy or girl on the receiving end: sometimes having to work to make the catch, once in a while encountering a poem that lands with an easy *plump* right in the middle of your understanding.

What, then, is poetry? By now, perhaps, you have formed your own idea, whether or not you can define it. Robert Frost made a try at a definition: "A poem is an idea caught in the act of dawning." Just in case further efforts at definition can be useful, here are a few memorable ones (including, for a second look, some given earlier):

things that are true expressed in words that are beautiful.
        —*Dante*

the art of uniting pleasure with truth by calling imagination to the help
  of reason.
>   —*Samuel Johnson*

the best words in the best order.
>   —*Samuel Taylor Coleridge*

the spontaneous overflow of powerful feelings.
>   —*William Wordsworth*

musical thought.
>   —*Thomas Carlyle*

emotion put into measure.
>   —*Thomas Hardy*

If I feel physically as if the top of my head were taken off, I know that it
  is poetry.
>   —*Emily Dickinson*

speech framed . . . to be heard for its own sake and interest even over
  and above its interest of meaning.
>   —*Gerard Manley Hopkins*

a way of remembering what it would impoverish us to forget.
>   —*Robert Frost*

a revelation in words by means of the words.
>   —*Wallace Stevens*

Poetry is prose bewitched.
>   —*Mina Loy*

not the assertion that something is true, but the making of that truth
  more fully real to us.
>   —*T. S. Eliot*

the clear expression of mixed feelings.
>   —*W. H. Auden*

the body of linguistic constructions that men usually refer to as poems.
>   —*J. V. Cunningham*

hundreds of things coming together at the right moment.
>   —*Elizabeth Bishop*

anything said in such a way, or put on the page in such a way, as to invite from the hearer or the reader a certain kind of attention.
>   —*William Stafford*

Poetry is life distilled.
>   —*Gwendolyn Brooks*

A poem is something that penetrates for an instant into the unconscious.
>   —*Robert Bly*

A poem differs from most prose in several ways. For one, both writer and reader tend to regard it differently. The poet's attitude is something like this: I offer this piece of writing to be read not as prose but as a poem—that is, more perceptively, thoughtfully, and considerately, with more attention to sounds and connotations. This is a great deal to expect, but in return, the reader, too, has a right to certain expectations. Approaching the poem in the anticipation of out-of-the-ordinary knowledge and pleasure, the reader assumes that the poem may use certain enjoyable devices not available to prose: rime, alliteration, meter, and rhythms—definite, various, or emphatic. (The poet may not *always* decide to use these things.) The reader expects the poet to make greater use, perhaps, of resources of meaning such as figurative language, allusion, symbol, and imagery. As readers of prose we might seek no more than meaning: no more than what could be paraphrased without serious loss. Meeting any figurative language or graceful turns of word order, we think them pleasant extras. But in poetry all these "extras" matter as much as the paraphraseable content, if not more. For, when we finish reading a good poem, we cannot explain precisely to ourselves what we have experienced—without repeating, word for word, the language of the poem itself. Archibald MacLeish makes this point memorably in his "Ars Poetica":

A poem should not mean
But be.

"Poetry is to prose as dancing is to walking," remarked Paul Valéry. It is doubtful, however, that anyone can draw an immovable boundary between poetry and prose. Certain prose needs only to be arranged in lines to be seen as poetry—especially prose that conveys strong emotion in vivid, physical imagery and in terse, figurative, rhythmical language. Even in translation the words of Chief Joseph of the Nez Percé tribe, at the moment of his surrender to the U.S. Army in 1877, still move us and are memorable:

Hear me, my warriors, my heart is sick and sad:
Our chiefs are killed,
The old men all are dead,
It is cold and we have no blankets.

The little children freeze to death.

Hear me, my warriors, my heart is sick and sad:
From where the sun now stands I will fight no more forever.

It may be that a poem can point beyond words to something still more essential. Language has its limits, and probably Edgar Allan Poe was the only poet ever to claim he could always find words for whatever he wished to express. For, of all a human being can experience and imagine, words say only part. "Human speech," said Flaubert, who strove after the best of it, "is like a cracked kettle on which we hammer out tunes to make bears dance, when what we long for is the compassion of the stars."

Like Yeats's chestnut-tree in "Among School Children" (which when asked whether it is leaf, blossom, or bole, has no answer), a poem is to be seen not as a confederation of form, rime, image, metaphor, tone, and theme, but as a whole. We study a poem one element at a time because the intellect best comprehends what it can separate. But only our total attention, involving the participation of our blood and marrow, can see all elements in a poem fused, all dancing together. Yeats knew how to make poems and how to read them:

> God guard me from those thoughts men think
> In the mind alone;
> He that sings a lasting song
> Thinks in a marrow-bone.

Throughout this book, we have been working on the assumption that the patient and conscious explication of poems will sharpen unconscious perceptions. We can only hope that it will; the final test lies in whether you care to go on by yourself, reading other poems, finding in them pleasure and enlightenment. Pedagogy must have a stop; so too must the viewing of poems as if their elements fell into chapters. For the total experience of reading a poem surpasses the mind's categories. The wind in the grass, says a proverb, cannot be taken into the house.

29 *Two Poets in Depth*

EMILY DICKINSON

Emily Dickinson (1830–1886) spent virtually all her life in her family home in Amherst, Massachusetts. Her father, Edward Dickinson, was a prominent lawyer who ranked as Amherst's leading citizen. (He even served a term in the U.S. Congress.) Dickinson attended one year of college at Mount Holyoke Female Seminary in South Hadley. She proved to be a good student, but suffering from homesickness and poor health, she did not return for the second year. This brief period of study and a few trips to Boston, Philadelphia, and Washington, D.C., were the only occasions she left home in her fifty-five year life. As the years passed, Dickinson became more reclusive. She stopped attending church (and refused to endorse the orthodox Congregationalist creed). She also spent increasing time alone in her rooms—often writing poems. Dickinson never married, but she had a significant romantic relationship with at least one unidentified man. Although scholars have suggested several likely candidates, the historical object of Dickinson's affections will never be known. What survives unmistakably, however, is the intensely passionate poetry written from these private circumstances. By the end of her life, Dickinson had become a locally famous recluse who rarely left home. She would greet visitors from her own upstairs room—clearly heard but never seen. In 1886 she was buried, according to her own instructions, within sight of the family home. Although Dickinson composed 1775 known poems, she published only seven in her lifetime. She often, however, sent copies of poems to friends in letters, but only after her death would the full extent of her production become known when a cache of manuscripts was discovered in a trunk in the homestead attic—handwritten little booklets of poems sewn together by the poet with needle and thread. From 1890 until mid-twentieth century, nine posthumous collections of her poems were published by friends and relatives, some of whom rewrote her work and changed her idiosyncratic punctuation to make it more conventional. Thomas H. Johnson's three-volume edition of the *Poems* (1955) established a better text. In relatively few and simple forms clearly indebted to the hymns she heard in church, Dickinson succeeded in being a true visionary and a poet of colossal originality.

SUCCESS IS COUNTED SWEETEST (1859)

Success is counted sweetest
By those who ne'er succeed.
To comprehend a nectar
Requires sorest need.

Not one of all the purple Host°   *an army*   5
Who took the Flag today
Can tell the definition
So clear of Victory

As he defeated – dying –
On whose forbidden ear   10
The distant strains of triumph
Burst agonized and clear!

WILD NIGHTS – WILD NIGHTS! (ABOUT 1861)

Wild Nights – Wild Nights!
Were I with thee
Wild Nights should be
Our luxury!   ·

Futile – the Winds –   5
To a Heart in port –
Done with the Compass –
Done with the Chart!

Rowing in Eden –
Ah, the Sea!   10
Might I but moor – Tonight –
In Thee!

I FELT A FUNERAL, IN MY BRAIN (ABOUT 1861)

I felt a Funeral, in my Brain,
And Mourners to and fro
Kept treading – treading – till it seemed
That Sense was breaking through –

And when they all were seated,   5
A Service, like a Drum –
Kept beating – beating – till I thought
My Mind was going numb –

And then I heard them lift a Box
And creak across my Soul   10
With those same Boots of Lead, again,
Then Space – began to toll,

As all the Heavens were a Bell,
And Being, but an Ear,
And I, and Silence, some strange Race   15
Wrecked, solitary, here –

And then a Plank in Reason, broke,
And I dropped down, and down –
And hit a World, at every plunge,
And Finished knowing – then –   20

I'M NOBODY! WHO ARE YOU?   (ABOUT 1861)

I'm Nobody! Who are you?
Are you – Nobody – too?
Then there's a pair of us!
Dont tell! they'd banish us – you know!

How dreary – to be – Somebody!   5
How public – like a Frog –
To tell your name – the livelong June –
To an admiring Bog!

THE SOUL SELECTS HER
OWN SOCIETY   (ABOUT 1862)

The Soul selects her own Society –
Then – shuts the Door –
To her divine Majority –
Present no more –

Unmoved – she notes the Chariots – pausing –   5
At her low Gate –
Unmoved – an Emperor be kneeling
Upon her Mat –

I've known her – from an ample nation –
Choose One –   10
Then – close the Valves of her attention –
Like Stone –

After great pain, a formal feeling comes (1862)

After great pain, a formal feeling comes –
The Nerves sit ceremonious, like Tombs –
The stiff Heart questions was it He, that bore,
And Yesterday, or Centuries before?

The Feet, mechanical, go round –   5
Of Ground, or Air, or Ought –
A Wooden way
Regardless grown,
A Quartz contentment, like a stone –

This is the Hour of Lead –   10
Remembered, if outlived,
As Freezing persons, recollect the Snow –
First – Chill – then Stupor – then the letting go –

I started Early – Took my Dog (about 1862)

I started Early – Took my Dog –
And visited the Sea –
The Mermaids in the Basement
Came out to look at me –

And Frigates – in the Upper Floor   5
Extended Hempen Hands –
Presuming Me to be a Mouse –
Aground – upon the Sands –

But no Man moved Me – till the Tide
Went past my simple Shoe –   10
And past my Apron – and my Belt
And past my Bodice – too –

And made as He would eat me up –
As wholly as a Dew
Upon a Dandelion's Sleeve –   15
And then – I started – too –

And He – He followed – close behind –
I felt His Silver Heel
Upon my Ankle – Then my Shoes
Would overflow with Pearl –   20

Until We met the Solid Town –
No One He seemed to know –
And bowing – with a Mighty look –
At me – The Sea withdrew –

Because I could not stop for Death

(ABOUT 1863)

Because I could not stop for Death –
He kindly stopped for me –
The Carriage held but just Ourselves –
And Immortality.

We slowly drove – He knew no haste   5
And I had put away
My labor and my leisure too,
For His Civility –

We passed the School, where Children strove
At Recess – in the Ring –   10
We passed the Fields of Gazing Grain –
We passed the Setting Sun –

Or rather – He passed Us –
The Dews drew quivering and chill –
For only Gossamer, my Gown –   15
My Tippet° – only Tulle –   *cape*

We passed before a House that seemed
A Swelling of the Ground –
The Roof was scarcely visible –
The Cornice – in the Ground –   20

Since then – 'tis Centuries – and yet
Feels shorter than the Day
I first surmised the Horses Heads
Were toward Eternity –

Some keep the Sabbath going to Church

(PUBLISHED 1864)

Some keep the Sabbath going to Church –
I keep it, staying at Home –
With a Bobolink for a Chorister –
And an Orchard, for a Dome –

Some keep the Sabbath in Surplice –   5
I just wear my Wings –
And instead of tolling the Bell, for Church,
Our little Sexton – sings.

God preaches, a noted Clergyman –
And the sermon is never long,   10
So instead of getting to Heaven, at last –
I'm going, all along.

Tell all the Truth but tell it slant

Tell all the Truth but tell it slant –
Success in Circuit lies
Too bright for our infirm Delight
The Truth's superb surprise
As Lightning to the Children eased   5
With explanation kind
The Truth must dazzle gradually
Or every man be blind –

COMPARE

More poems by Emily Dickinson that are found in this book:

A Dying Tiger – moaned for Drink (page 982)
I heard a Fly buzz – when I died (page 909)
I like to see it lap the Miles (page 671)
It dropped so low – in my Regard (page 772)
The Lightning is a yellow Fork (page 904)
My Life had stood – a Loaded Gun (page 769)
A Route of Evanescence (page 747)
Victory comes late (page 884)

WRITER'S PERSPECTIVE

Emily Dickinson

Emily Dickinson on Writing   RECOGNIZING POETRY   1870

If I read a book [and] it makes my whole body so cold no fire ever can warm me I know *that* is poetry. If I feel physically as if the top of my head were taken off, I know *that* is poetry. These are the only way I know it. Is there any other way.

How do most people live without any thoughts. There are many people in the world (you must have noticed them in the street) How do they live. How do they get strength to put on their clothes in the morning.

When I lost the use of my Eyes it was a comfort to think there were so few real *books* that I could easily find some one to read me all of them.

Truth is such a *rare* thing it is delightful to tell it.

I find ecstasy in living – the mere sense of living is joy enough.

(in conversation with Thomas Wentworth Higginson)

COMPARE

Dickinson's own comments on poetry with Sandra M. Gilbert and Susan Gubar's critical comments on "The Freedom of Emily Dickinson" (page 1962).

LANGSTON HUGHES

Langston Hughes was born in Joplin, Missouri, in 1902. After his parents separated during his early years, he and his mother often lived a life of itinerant poverty, mostly in Kansas. Hughes attended high school in Cleveland where as a senior, he wrote "The Negro Speaks of Rivers." Reluctantly supported by his father, he attended Columbia University for a year before withdrawing. After a series of menial jobs, Hughes became a merchant seaman in 1923 and visited the ports of West Africa. For a time he lived in Paris, Genoa, and Rome, before returning to the United States. The publication of *The Weary Blues* (1926) earned him immediate fame, which he solidified a few months later with his pioneering essay "The Negro Artist and the Racial Mountain." In 1926 he also entered Lincoln University in Pennsylvania from which he graduated in 1929. By then Hughes was already one of the central figures of the Harlem Renaissance, the flowering of African-American arts and literature in the Harlem district of New York City during the 1920s. A strikingly versatile author, Hughes worked in fiction, drama, translation, criticism, opera libretti, memoir, cinema, and songwriting, as well as poetry. He also became a tireless promoter of African-American culture, crisscrossing the United States on speaking tours as well as compiling twenty-eight anthologies of African-American folklore and poetry. His newspaper columns, which often reported conversations with an imaginary Harlem friend named Jesse B. Semple, nicknamed "Simple," attracted an especially large following. During the 1930s Hughes became involved in radical politics and traveled to the Soviet Union, but after World War II, he gradually shifted to mainstream progressive politics. In his last years he became a spokesman for the moderate wing of the civil-rights movement. He died in Harlem in 1967.

THE NEGRO SPEAKS OF RIVERS   1926

I've known rivers:
I've known rivers ancient as the world and older than the flow of
    human blood in human veins.

My soul has grown deep like the rivers.

I bathed in the Euphrates when dawns were young.
I built my hut near the Congo and it lulled me to sleep.   5
I looked upon the Nile and raised the pyramids above it.
I heard the singing of the Mississippi when Abe Lincoln went down to
    New Orleans, and I've seen its muddy bosom turn all golden in the
    sunset.

I've known rivers:
Ancient, dusky rivers.

My soul has grown deep like the rivers.   10

Mother to Son   1922

Well, son, I'll tell you:
Life for me ain't been no crystal stair.
It's had tacks in it,
And splinters,
And boards torn up,   5
And places with no carpet on the floor —
Bare.
But all the time
I'se been a-climbin' on,
And reachin' landin's,   10
And turnin' corners,
And sometimes goin' in the dark
Where there ain't been no light.
So boy, don't you turn back.
Don't you set down on the steps   15
'Cause you finds it's kinder hard.
Don't you fall now—
For I'se still goin', honey,
I'se still climbin',
And life for me ain't been no crystal stair.   20

The Weary Blues   1926

Droning a drowsy syncopated tune,
Rocking back and forth to a mellow croon,
    I heard a Negro play.
Down on Lenox Avenue the other night
By the pale dull pallor of an old gas light   5
    He did a lazy sway. . . .
    He did a lazy sway. . . .
To the tune o' those Weary Blues.
With his ebony hands on each ivory key
He made that poor piano moan with melody.   10
    O Blues!

Swaying to and fro on his rickety stool
He played that sad raggy tune like a musical fool.
 Sweet Blues!
Coming from a black man's soul.   15
 O Blues!
In a deep song voice with a melancholy tone
I heard that Negro sing, that old piano moan—
 "Ain't got nobody in all this world,
  Ain't got nobody but ma self.   20
  I's gwine to quit ma frownin'
  And put ma troubles on the shelf."

Thump, thump, thump, went his foot on the floor.
He played a few chords then he sang some more—
 "I got the Weary Blues   25
  And I can't be satisfied.
  Got the Weary Blues
  And can't be satisfied—
  I ain't happy no mo'
  And I wish that I had died."   30
And far into the night he crooned that tune.
The stars went out and so did the moon.
The singer stopped playing and went to bed
While the Weary Blues echoed through his head.
He slept like a rock or a man that's dead.   35

THE WEARY BLUES. This poem quotes the first blues song Hughes had ever heard, "The Weary Blues," which begins, "I got de weary blues / And I can't be satisfied / . . . I ain't happy no mo' / And I wish that I had died."

I, Too   1926

I, too, sing America.

I am the darker brother.
They send me to eat in the kitchen
When company comes,
But I laugh,   5
And eat well,
And grow strong.

Tomorrow,
I'll be at the table
When company comes.   10
Nobody'll dare
Say to me,
"Eat in the kitchen,"
Then.

Besides,
They'll see how beautiful I am
And be ashamed—

I, too, am America.

Song for a Dark Girl   1927

Way Down South in Dixie
    (Break the heart of me)
They hung my black young lover
    To a cross roads tree.

Way Down South in Dixie   5
    (Bruised body high in air)
I asked the white Lord Jesus
    What was the use of prayer.

Way Down South in Dixie
    (Break the heart of me)
Love is a naked shadow   10
    On a gnarled and naked tree.

Island   1950

Wave of sorrow,
Do not drown me now:

I see the island
Still ahead somehow.

I see the island   5
And its sands are fair:

Wave of sorrow,
Take me there.

Subway Rush Hour   1951

Mingled
breath and smell
so close
mingled
black and white   5
so near
no room for fear.

SLIVER   1951

Cheap little rhymes
A cheap little tune
Are sometimes as dangerous
As a sliver of the moon.
A cheap little tune   5
To cheap little rhymes
Can cut a man's
Throat sometimes.

HARLEM   [DREAM DEFERRED]   1951

What happens to a dream deferred?

　　Does it dry up
　　like a raisin in the sun?
　　Or fester like a sore—
　　And then run?   5
　　Does it stink like rotten meat?
　　Or crust and sugar over—
　　like a syrupy sweet?

　　Maybe it just sags
　　like a heavy load.   10

　　Or does it explode?

HARLEM. This famous poem appeared under two titles in the author's lifetime. Both titles appear above.

THEME FOR ENGLISH B   1951

The instructor said,

　　Go home and write
　　a page tonight.
　　And let that page come out of you—
　　Then, it will be true.   5

I wonder if it's that simple?
I am twenty-two, colored, born in Winston-Salem.
I went to school there, then Durham, then here
to this college on the hill above Harlem.
I am the only colored student in my class.   10
The steps from the hill lead down into Harlem,

through a park, then I cross St. Nicholas,
Eighth Avenue, Seventh, and I come to the Y,
the Harlem Branch Y, where I take the elevator
up to my room, sit down, and write this page: 15

It's not easy to know what is true for you and me
at twenty-two, my age. But I guess I'm what
I feel and see and hear, Harlem, I hear you:
hear you, hear me—we two—you, me, talk on this page.
(I hear New York, too.) Me—who?   20
Well, I like to eat, sleep, drink, and be in love.
I like to work, read, learn, and understand life.
I like a pipe for a Christmas present,
or records—Bessie, bop, or Bach.
I guess being colored doesn't make me not like   25
the same things other folks like who are other races.
So will my page be colored that I write?
Being me, it will not be white.

But it will be
a part of you, instructor.   30
You are white—
yet a part of me, as I am a part of you.
That's American.
Sometimes perhaps you don't want to be a part of me.
Nor do I often want to be a part of you.   35
But we are, that's true!
As I learn from you,
I guess you learn from me—
although you're older—and white—
and somewhat more free.   40

This is my page for English B.

THEME FOR ENGLISH B.   9 *College on the hill above Harlem:* Columbia University where Hughes was
briefly a student. (Please note, however, that this poem is not autobiographical. The young speaker is
a character invented by the middle-aged author.) 24 *Bessie:* Bessie Smith (1898?–1937) was a
popular blues singer often called the "Empress of the Blues." The lyrics to Smith's "Jailhouse Blues"
appear on page 151.

COMPARE

More poems by Langston Hughes that are found in this book:

Dream Boogie (page 850)
Homecoming (page 672)
Prayer (page 870)

Langston Hughes

Langston Hughes on Writing
THE NEGRO ARTIST AND THE RACIAL MOUNTAIN   1926

Most of my own poems are racial in theme and treatment, derived from the life I know. In many of them I try to grasp and hold some of the meanings and rhythms of jazz. I am as sincere as I know how to be in these poems and yet after every reading I answer questions like these from my own people: Do you think Negroes should always write about Negroes? I wish you wouldn't read some of your poems to white folks. How do you find anything interesting in a place like a cabaret? Why do you write about black people? You aren't black. What makes you do so many jazz poems?

But jazz to me is one of the inherent expressions of Negro life in America; the eternal tom-tom beating in the Negro soul—the tom-tom of revolt against weariness in a white world, a world of subway trains, and work, work, work; the tom-tom of joy and laughter, and pain swallowed in a smile. Yet the Philadelphia clubwoman is ashamed to say that her race created it and she does not like me to write about it. The old subconscious "white is best" runs through her mind. Years of study under white teachers, a lifetime of white books, pictures, and papers, and white manners, morals, and Puritan standards made her dislike the spirituals. And now she turns up her nose at jazz and all its manifestations—likewise almost everything else distinctly racial. She doesn't care for the Winold Reiss portraits of Negroes because they are "too Negro." She does not want a true picture of herself from anybody. She wants the artist to flatter her, to make the white world believe that all Negroes are as smug and as near white in soul as she wants to be. But, to my mind, it is the duty of the younger Negro artist, if he accepts any duties at all from outsiders, to change through the force of his art that old whispering "I want to be white," hidden in the aspirations of his people, to "Why should I want to be white? I am a Negro—and beautiful."

So I am ashamed for the black poet who says, "I want to be a poet, not a Negro poet," as though his own racial world were not as interesting as any other world. I am ashamed, too, for the colored artist who runs from the painting of Negro faces to the painting of sunsets after the manner of the academicians because he fears the strange un-whiteness of his own features. An artist must be free to choose what he does, certainly, but he must also never be afraid to do what he might choose.

"The Negro Artist and the Racial Mountain"

COMPARE

Hughes's comments on the African-American artist with Darryl Pinckney's critical observations on Langston Hughes's public identity as a black poet (page 1946).

FOR FURTHER READING

You can study several other poets in depth in this book. The following writers are represented at length and also have short biographies in "Lives of the Poets."

> Robert Frost—14 poems (plus Writer's Perspective)
> William Shakespeare—10 poems
> William Blake—9 poems
> William Butler Yeats—9 poems (plus Writer's Perspective)
> Thomas Hardy—8 poems
> William Carlos Williams—8 poems

See the Index for specific details.

SUGGESTIONS FOR WRITING

1. Focusing on one or two poems, demonstrate how Dickinson's idiosyncratic capitalization and punctuation add special impact to her work.
2. How do the poems by Dickinson in this chapter and elsewhere in the book illustrate her statement (in Writer's Perspective on page 1018) that "I find ecstasy in living—the mere sense of living is joy enough?"
3. Compare and contrast the use of first-person voices in two poems by Langston Hughes (such as "I, Too" and "Theme for English B" or "Mother to Son" and "Island"). In what ways does the speaker's "I" differ in each poem and in what ways is it similar?
4. Discussing a single poem by Hughes, examine how musical forms (such as jazz, blues, or popular song) help shape the effect of the work.

30 *Poems for Further Reading*

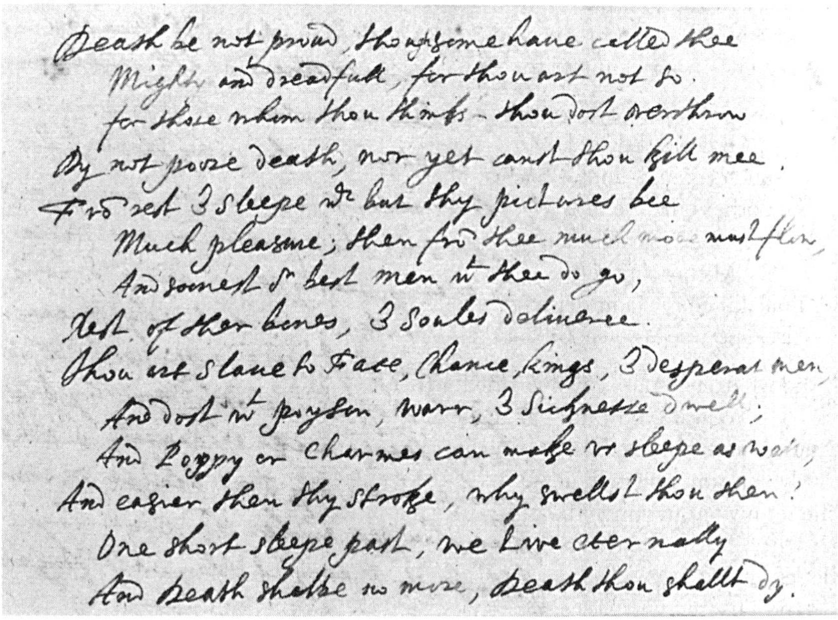
Death be not proud, though some have called thee
Mighty and dreadfull, for thou art not so.
for those whom thou thinkst, thou dost overthrow
Dy not poore death, nor yet canst thou kill mee.
From rest & sleepe wch but thy pictures bee
Much pleasure; then from thee much more must flow,
And soonest our best men wth thee do go,
Rest of their bones, & Soules deliverie.
Thou art slave to Fate, Chance, kings, & desperat men
And dost wth poyson, warr, & Sicknesse dwell;
And Poppy or Charmes can make vs sleepe as well,
And easier then thy stroke, why swellst thou then?
One short sleepe past, we live eternally
And death shalbe no more, death thou shalt dy.

The manuscript of John Donne's sonnet, "Death be not proud"

Anonymous (TRADITIONAL SCOTTISH BALLAD)

EDWARD

"Why dois your brand° sae° drap wi' bluid,   *sword; so*
  Edward, Edward?
Why dois your brand sae drap wi' bluid?
 And why sae sad gang° yee, O?"   *go*
"O, I hae killed my hauke sae guid,   5
  Mither, mither,
O, I hae killed my hauke sae guid,
 And I had nae mair bot° hee, O."   *but*

"Your haukis bluid was nevir sae reid,
  Edward, Edward,
Your haukis bluid was nevir sae reid,   10
 My deir son I tell thee, O."
"O, I hae killed my reid-roan steid,
  Mither, mither,
O, I hae killed my reid-roan steid,   15
 That erst° was sa fair and frie°, O."   *once; free*

"Your steid was auld, and ye hae gat mair,
  Edward, Edward,
Your steid was auld, and ye hae gat mair,
 Sum other dule° ye drie°, O."   *sorrow; suffer* 20
"O, I hae killed my fadir deir,
  Mither, mither,
O, I hae killed my fadir deir,
 Alas, and wae° is mee, O!"   *woe*

"And whatten penance wul ye drie for that,   25
  Edward, Edward?
And whatten penance will ye drie for that?
 My deir son, now tell me, O."
"Ile set my feit in yonder boat,
  Mither, mither,   30
Ile set my feit in yonder boat,
 And Ile fare ovir the sea, O."

"And what wul ye doe wi' your towirs and your ha'° *hall*
  Edward, Edward,
And what wul ye doe wi' your towirs and your ha'   35
 That were sae fair to see, O?"
"Ile let thame stand tul they doun fa',
  Mither, mither,
Ile let thame stand tul they doun fa',
 For here nevir mair maun° I bee, O."   *must* 40

"And what wul ye leive to your bairns° and your wife,   *children*
    Edward, Edward?
And what wul ye leive to your bairns and your wife,
    When ye gang ovir the sea, O?"
"The warldis° room, late° them beg thrae° life,   *world's; let; through*   45
    Mither, mither
The warldis room, late them beg thrae life,
    For thame nevir mair wul I see, O."

"And what wul ye leive to your ain° mither deir,   *own*
    Edward, Edward?   50
And what wul ye leive to your ain mither deir?
    My deir son, now tell me, O."
"The curse of hell frae me sall ye beir,
    Mither, mither,
The curse of hell frae me sall ye beir,   55
    Sic° counseils° ye gave to me, O."   *such; counsel*

COMPARE

"Edward" with a modern ballad such as "Ballad of Birmingham" by Dudley Randall (page 798).

Anonymous   (TRADITIONAL ENGLISH BALLAD)

THE THREE RAVENS

There were three ravens sat on a tree,
    Down a down, hay down, hay down,
There were three ravens sat on a tree,
    With a down,
There were three ravens sat on a tree,   5
They were as black as they might be.
    With a down derry, derry, derry, down, down.

The one of them said to his mate,
"Where shall we our breakfast take?"

"Down in yonder greene field,   10
There lies a knight slain under his shield.

"His hounds they lie down at his feet,
So well they can their master keep.

"His hawks they fly so eagerly,
There's no fowl dare him come nigh."   15

Down there comes a fallow doe,
As great with young as she might go.

She lift up his bloody head,
And kist his wounds that were so red.

She got him up upon her back,   20
And carried him to earthen lake°.   *the grave*

She buried him before the prime°,   *dawn*
She was dead herself ere evensong time.

God send every gentleman
Such hawks, such hounds, and such a leman.°   *lover*   25

THE THREE RAVENS. The lines of refrain are repeated in each stanza. "Perhaps in the folk mind the
doe is the form the soul of a human mistress, now dead, has taken," Albert B. Friedman has suggested
(in *The Viking Book of Folk Ballads*). "Most probably the knight's beloved was understood to be an enchanted woman who was metamorphosed at certain times into an animal." In lines 22 and 23, *prime*
and *evensong* are two of the canonical hours set aside for prayer and worship. Prime is at dawn, evensong at dusk.

Anonymous   (TRADITIONAL SCOTTISH BALLAD)

THE TWA CORBIES

As I was walking all alane,
I heard twa corbies° making a mane°;   *ravens; moan*
The tane° unto the t'other say,   *one*
"Where sall we gang° and dine today?"   *go*

"In behint yon auld fail dyke°,   *turf wall*   5
I wot° there lies a new slain knight;   *know*
And naebody kens° that he lies there,   *knows*
But his hawk, his hound, and lady fair.

"His hound is to the hunting gane,
His hawk to fetch the wild-fowl hame,   10
His lady's ta'en another mate,
So we may mak our dinner sweet.

"Ye'll sit on his white hause-bane°,   *neck bone*
And I'll pike out his bonny blue een;
Wi' ae° lock o' his gowden hair   *one*   15
We'll theek° our nest when it grows bare.   *thatch*

"Mony a one for him makes mane,
But nane sall ken where he is gane;
O'er his white banes, when they are bare,
The wind sall blaw for evermair."   20

THE TWA CORBIES. Sir Walter Scott, the first to print this ballad in his *Minstrelsy of the Scottish
Border* (1802–1803), calls it "rather a counterpart than a copy" of "The Three Ravens." M. J. C.
Hodgart and other scholars think he may have written most of it himself.

Anonymous (ENGLISH LYRIC)

WESTERN WIND
(ABOUT 1500)

Western wind, when wilt thou blow,
The° small rain down can rain?   *(so that) the*
Christ, if my love were in my arms,
And I in my bed again!

COMPARE

"Western Wind" with "The River-Merchant's Wife: a Letter" by Ezra Pound (page 1118).

Anonymous (NAVAJO MOUNTAIN CHANT)

LAST WORDS OF THE PROPHET

Farewell, my younger brother!
From the holy places the gods come for me.
You will never see me again; but when the showers pass and the
    thunders peal,
"There," you will say, "is the voice of my elder brother."
And when the harvest comes, of the beautiful birds and grasshoppers
    you will say,   5
"There is the ordering of my elder brother!"
        —Translated by Washington Matthews

COMPARE

"Last Words of the Prophet" with "At the Klamath Berry Festival" by William Stafford (page 1137).

Matthew Arnold (1822–1888)

DOVER BEACH
1867

The sea is calm tonight.
The tide is full, the moon lies fair
Upon the straits;—on the French coast the light
Gleams and is gone; the cliffs of England stand,
Glimmering and vast, out in the tranquil bay.   5
Come to the window, sweet is the night-air!
Only, from the long line of spray
Where the sea meets the moon-blanched land,
Listen! you hear the grating roar
Of pebbles which the waves draw back, and fling,   10
At their return, up the high strand,

Begin, and cease, and then again begin,
With tremulous cadence slow, and bring
The eternal note of sadness in.

Sophocles long ago   15
Heard it on the Aegean, and it brought
Into his mind the turbid ebb and flow
Of human misery; we
Find also in the sound a thought,
Hearing it by this distant northern sea.   20

The Sea of Faith
Was once, too, at the full, and round earth's shore
Lay like the folds of a bright girdle furled.
But now I only hear
Its melancholy, long, withdrawing roar,   25
Retreating, to the breath
Of the night-wind, down the vast edges drear
And naked shingles° of the world.   *gravel beaches*

Ah, love, let us be true
To one another! for the world, which seems   30
To lie before us like a land of dreams,
So various, so beautiful, so new,
Hath really neither joy, nor love, nor light,
Nor certitude, nor peace, nor help for pain;
And we are here as on a darkling° plain   *darkened or darkening*   35
Swept with confused alarms of struggle and flight,
Where ignorant armies clash by night.

COMPARE

"Dover Beach" with "Hap" by Thomas Hardy (page 1073).

John Ashbery   (b. 1927)*

AT NORTH FARM   1984

Somewhere someone is traveling furiously toward you,
At incredible speed, traveling day and night,
Through blizzards and desert heat, across torrents, through narrow
        passes.
But will he know where to find you,
Recognize you when he sees you,   5
Give you the thing he has for you?

Hardly anything grows here,
Yet the granaries are bursting with meal,
The sacks of meal piled to the rafters.
The streams run with sweetness, fattening fish;   10
Birds darken the sky. Is it enough
That the dish of milk is set out at night,
That we think of him sometimes,
Sometimes and always, with mixed feelings?

COMPARE

"At North Farm" with "Uphill" by Christina Rossetti (page 911).

Margaret Atwood

Margaret Atwood   (b. 1939)*

SIREN SONG   1974

This is the one song everyone
would like to learn: the song
that is irresistible:

the song that forces men
to leap overboard in squadrons   5
even though they see the beached skulls

the song nobody knows
because anyone who has heard it
is dead, and the others can't remember.

Shall I tell you the secret   10
and if I do, will you get me
out of this bird suit?

I don't enjoy it here
squatting on this island
looking picturesque and mythical   15

with these two feathery maniacs,
I don't enjoy singing
this trio, fatal and valuable.

I will tell the secret to you,
to you, only to you.   20
Come closer. This song

is a cry for help: Help me!
Only you, only you can,
you are unique

at last. Alas   25
it is a boring song
but it works every time.

SIREN SONG. In Greek mythology, sirens were half-woman, half-bird nymphs who lured sailors to
their deaths by singing hypnotically beautiful songs.

COMPARE

"Siren Song" with "Her Kind" by Anne Sexton (page 679).

W. H. Auden

W. H. Auden (1907–1973)*

AS I WALKED OUT ONE EVENING   1940

As I walked out one evening,
    Walking down Bristol Street,
The crowds upon the pavement
    Were fields of harvest wheat.

And down by the brimming river
   I heard a lover sing
Under an arch of the railway:
   "Love has no ending.

"I'll love you, dear, I'll love you
   Till China and Africa meet,
And the river jumps over the mountain
   And the salmon sing in the street,

"I'll love you till the ocean
   Is folded and hung up to dry
And the seven stars go squawking
   Like geese about the sky.

"The years shall run like rabbits,
   For in my arms I hold
The Flower of the Ages,
   And the first love of the world."

But all the clocks in the city
   Began to whirr and chime:
"O let not Time deceive you,
   You cannot conquer Time.

"In the burrows of the Nightmare
   Where Justice naked is,
Time watches from the shadow
   And coughs when you would kiss.

"In headaches and in worry
   Vaguely life leaks away,
And Time will have his fancy
   Tomorrow or today.

"Into many a green valley
   Drifts the appalling snow;
Time breaks the threaded dances
   And the diver's brilliant bow.

"O plunge your hands in water,
   Plunge them in up to the wrist;
Stare, stare in the basin
   And wonder what you've missed.

"The glacier knocks in the cupboard,
   The desert sighs in the bed,
And the crack in the teacup opens
   A lane to the land of the dead.

"Where the beggars raffle the banknotes 45
  And the Giant is enchanting to Jack,
And the Lily-white Boy is a Roarer,
  And Jill goes down on her back.

"O look, look in the mirror,
  O look in your distress; 50
Life remains a blessing
  Although you cannot bless.

"O stand, stand at the window
  As the tears scald and start;
You shall love your crooked neighbor 55
  With your crooked heart."

It was late, late in the evening,
  The lovers they were gone;
The clocks had ceased their chiming,
  And the deep river ran on. 60

COMPARE

"As I Walked Out One Evening" with "Dover Beach" by Matthew Arnold (page 1031) and "anyone lived in a pretty how town" by E. E. Cummings (page 718).

"The Fall of Icarus" by Pieter Breughel the Elder (1520?–1569)

W. H. Auden   (1907–1973)*

MUSÉE DES BEAUX ARTS   1940

About suffering they were never wrong,
The Old Masters: how well they understood
Its human position; how it takes place
While someone else is eating or opening a window or just walking
    dully along;
How, when the aged are reverently, passionately waiting   5
For the miraculous birth, there always must be
Children who did not specially want it to happen, skating
On a pond at the edge of the wood:
They never forgot
That even the dreadful martyrdom must run its course   10
Anyhow in a corner, some untidy spot
Where the dogs go on with their doggy life and the torturer's horse
Scratches its innocent behind on a tree.

In Brueghel's *Icarus*, for instance: how everything turns away
Quite leisurely from the disaster; the ploughman may   15
Have heard the splash, the forsaken cry,
But for him it was not an important failure; the sun shone
As it had to on the white legs disappearing into the green
Water; and the expensive delicate ship that must have seen
Something amazing, a boy falling out of the sky,   20
Had somewhere to get to and sailed calmly on.

COMPARE

"Musée des Beaux Arts" with "The Dance" by William Carlos Williams (page 884) and
the painting by Pieter Breughel to which each poem refers.

Elizabeth Bishop   (1911–1979)*

FILLING STATION   1965

Oh, but it is dirty!
—this little filling station,
oil-soaked, oil-permeated
to a disturbing, over-all
black translucency.   5
Be careful with that match!

Father wears a dirty,
oil-soaked monkey suit
that cuts him under the arms,
and several quick and saucy   10
and greasy sons assist him
(it's a family filling station),
all quite thoroughly dirty.

Do they live in the station?
It has a cement porch   15
behind the pumps, and on it
a set of crushed and grease-
impregnated wickerwork;
on the wicker sofa
a dirty dog, quite comfy.   20

Some comic books provide
the only note of color—
of certain color. They lie
upon a big dim doily
draping a taboret°   *stool*   25
(part of the set), beside
a big hirsute begonia.

Why the extraneous plant?
Why the taboret?
Why, oh why, the doily?   30
(Embroidered in daisy stitch
with marguerites, I think,
and heavy with gray crochet.)

Somebody embroidered the doily.
Somebody waters the plant,   35
or oils it, maybe. Somebody
arranges the rows of cans
so that they softly say:
ESSO—SO—SO—SO
to high-strung automobiles.   40
Somebody loves us all.

COMPARE

"Filling Station" with "California Hills in August" by Dana Gioia (page 1068) or "The splendor falls on castle walls" by Alfred, Lord Tennyson (page 816).

Elizabeth Bishop (1911–1979)*

ONE ART   1976

The art of losing isn't hard to master;
so many things seem filled with the intent
to be lost that their loss is no disaster.

Lose something every day. Accept the fluster
of lost door keys, the hour badly spent.   5
The art of losing isn't hard to master.

Then practice losing farther, losing faster:
places, and names, and where it was you meant
to travel. None of these will bring disaster.

I lost my mother's watch. And look! my last, or   10
next-to-last, of three loved houses went.
The art of losing isn't hard to master.

I lost two cities, lovely ones. And, vaster,
some realms I owned, two rivers, a continent.
I miss them, but it wasn't a disaster.   15

—Even losing you (the joking voice, a gesture
I love) I shan't have lied. It's evident
the art of losing's not too hard to master
though it may look like (*Write* it!) like disaster.

COMPARE

"One Art" with "Do not go gentle into that good night" by Dylan Thomas (page 872) and
"Lonely Hearts" by Wendy Cope (page 717).

William Blake   *(1757–1827)*

The Lamb   1789

Little Lamb, who made thee?
  Dost thou know who made thee?
Gave thee life, and bid thee feed
By the stream and o'er the mead;
Gave thee clothing of delight,   5
Softest clothing, wooly, bright;
Gave thee such a tender voice,
Making all the vales rejoice?
  Little Lamb, who made thee?
  Dost thou know who made thee?   10

Little Lamb, I'll tell thee,
  Little Lamb, I'll tell thee:
He is callèd by thy name,
For he calls himself a Lamb.
He is meek, and he is mild;   15
He became a little child.
I a child, and thou a lamb,
We are callèd by his name.
  Little Lamb, God bless thee!
  Little Lamb, God bless thee!   20

COMPARE

"The Lamb" with Blake's "The Tyger."

William Blake   *(1757–1827)*

The Tyger   1794

Tyger! Tyger! burning bright
In the forests of the night,
What immortal hand or eye
Could frame thy fearful symmetry?

In what distant deeps or skies   5
Burnt the fire of thine eyes?
On what wings dare he aspire?
What the hand dare seize the fire?

And what shoulder, and what art,
Could twist the sinews of thy heart?   10
And when thy heart began to beat,
What dread hand? and what dread feet?

What the hammer? what the chain?
In what furnace was thy brain?
What the anvil? what dread grasp   15
Dare its deadly terrors clasp?

When the stars threw down their spears,
And watered heaven with their tears,
Did he smile his work to see?
Did he who made the Lamb make thee?   20

Tyger! Tyger! burning bright
In the forests of the night,
What immortal hand or eye
Dare frame thy fearful symmetry?

COMPARE

"The Tyger" with "The Windhover" by Gerard Manley Hopkins (page 1084) or Blake's
own "The Lamb" (page 1040).

William Blake

William Blake   (1757–1827)*

THE SICK ROSE   1794

O Rose, thou art sick!
The invisible worm
That flies in the night,
In the howling storm,

Has found out thy bed   5
Of crimson joy,
And his dark secret love
Does thy life destroy.

COMPARE

"The Sick Rose" with "Four-Word Lines" by May Swenson (page 996).

Louise Bogan   (1897–1970)*

THE DREAM   1941

O God, in the dream the terrible horse began
To paw at the air, and make for me with his blows.
Fear kept for thirty-five years poured through his mane,
And retribution equally old, or nearly, breathed through his nose.

Coward complete, I lay and wept on the ground   5
When some strong creature appeared, and leapt for the rein.
Another woman, as I lay half in a swound,
Leapt in the air, and clutched at the leather and chain.

Give him, she said, something of yours as a charm.
Throw him, she said, some poor thing you alone claim.   10
No, no, I cried, he hates me; he's out for harm,
And whether I yield or not, it is all the same.

But, like a lion in a legend, when I flung the glove
Pulled from my sweating, my cold right hand,
The terrible beast, that no one may understand,   15
Came to my side, and put down his head in love.

COMPARE

"The Dream" with "Aunt Jennifer's Tigers" by Adrienne Rich (page 657).

Eavan Boland   (b. 1944)

ANOREXIC   1980

Flesh is heretic.
My body is a witch.
I am burning it.

Yes I am torching
her curves and paps and wiles.   5
They scorch in my self denials.

How she meshed my head
in the half-truths
of her fevers

till I renounced   10
milk and honey
and the taste of lunch.

I vomited
her hungers.
Now the bitch is burning.   15

I am starved and curveless.
I am skin and bone.
She has learned her lesson.

Thin as a rib
I turn in sleep.   20
My dreams probe

a claustrophobia
a sensuous enclosure.
How warm it was and wide

once by a warm drum,   25
once by the song of his breath
and in his sleeping side.

Only a little more,
only a few more days
sinless, foodless,   30

I will slip
back into him again
as if I had never been away.

Caged so
I will grow   35
angular and holy

past pain,
keeping his heart
such company

as will make me forget   40
in a small space
the fall

into forked dark,
into python needs
heaving to hips and breasts   45
and lips and heat
and sweat and fat and greed.

COMPARE

"Anorexic" with "Her Kind" by Anne Sexton (page 679).

Emily Brontë
(This is the only surviving group portrait of the three Brontë sisters [front left to right: Anne, Emily, and Charlotte], painted by their brother Branwell.)

Emily Brontë (1818–1848)

LOVE AND FRIENDSHIP (1839)

Love is like the wild rose-briar,
Friendship like the holly-tree—
The holly is dark when the rose-briar blooms
But which will bloom most constantly?

The wild rose-briar is sweet in spring,   5
Its summer blossoms scent the air;
Yet wait till winter comes again
And who will call the wild-briar fair?

COMPARE

"Love and Friendship" with "Since there's no help, come let us kiss and part" by Michael Drayton (page 864).

Gwendolyn Brooks (b. 1917)*

THE MOTHER 1987

Abortions will not let you forget.
You remember the children you got that you did not get,
The damp small pulps with a little or with no hair,
The singers and workers that never handled the air.
You will never neglect or beat   5
Them, or silence or buy with a sweet.
You will never wind up the sucking-thumb
Or scuttle off ghosts that come.
You will never leave them, controlling your luscious sigh,
Return for a snack of them, with gobbling mother-eye.   10

I have heard in the voices of the wind the voices of my dim killed
    children.
I have contracted. I have eased
My dim dears at the breasts they could never suck.
I have said, Sweets, if I sinned, if I seized
Your luck   15
And your lives from your unfinished reach,
If I stole your births and your names,
Your straight baby tears and your games,
Your stilted or lovely loves, your tumults, your marriages, aches, and
    your deaths,
If I poisoned the beginnings of your breaths,   20
Believe that even in my deliberateness I was not deliberate.
Though why should I whine,
Whine that the crime was other than mine?—
Since anyhow you are dead.
Or rather, or instead,   25
You were never made.
But that too, I am afraid,
Is faulty: oh, what shall I say, how is the truth to be said?
You were born, you had body, you died.
It is just that you never giggled or planned or cried.   30

Believe me, I loved you all.
Believe me, I knew you, though faintly, and I loved, I loved you all.

COMPARE

"The Mother" with "Metaphors" by Sylvia Plath (page 770), "The Victory" by Anne
Stevenson (page 746), and "Bells for John Whiteside's Daughter" by John Crowe Ransom
(page 1121).

Gwendolyn Brooks   (b. 1917)*

A STREET IN BRONZEVILLE: 1945
SOUTHEAST CORNER

The School of Beauty's a tavern now.
The Madam is underground.
Out at Lincoln, among the graves
Her own is early found.
Where the thickest, tallest monument   5
Cuts grandly into the air
The Madam lies, contentedly.
Her fortune, too, lies there,
Converted into cool hard steel

And right red velvet lining;
While over her tan impassivity
Shot silk is shining.

COMPARE

"A Street in Bronzeville: Southeast Corner" with "Buffalo Bill 's" by E. E. Cummings
(page 883).

Elizabeth Barrett Browning   (1806–1861)*
GRIEF   1844

I tell you, hopeless grief is passionless;
   That only men incredulous of despair,
   Half-taught in anguish, through the midnight air
Beat upward to God's throne in loud access
Of shrieking and reproach. Full desertness   5
   In souls, as countries, lieth silent-bare
   Under the blanching, vertical eye-glare
Of the absolute Heavens. Deep-hearted man, express
Grief for the Dead in silence like to death:
   Most like a monumental statue set   10
In everlasting watch and moveless woe
Till itself crumble to the dust beneath.
   Touch it: the marble eyelids are not wet—
If it could weep, it could arise and go.

COMPARE

"Grief" with "Tears, Idle Tears" by Alfred, Lord Tennyson (page 736).

Elizabeth Barrett Browning   (1806–1861)*
HOW DO I LOVE THEE?   1850
LET ME COUNT THE WAYS

How do I love thee? Let me count the ways.
I love thee to the depth and breadth and height
My soul can reach, when feeling out of sight
For the ends of being and ideal grace.
I love thee to the level of every day's   5
Most quiet need, by sun and candle-light.
I love thee freely, as men strive for right.
I love thee purely, as they turn from praise.
I love thee with the passion put to use

In my old griefs, and with my childhood's faith.   10
I love thee with a love I seemed to lose
With my lost saints. I love thee with the breath,
Smiles, tears, of all my life; and, if God choose,
I shall but love thee better after death.

COMPARE

"How Do I Love Thee?" with "What lips my lips have kissed" by Edna St. Vincent Millay
(page 865).

Robert Browning   (1812–1889)*

SOLILOQUY OF THE SPANISH CLOISTER   1842

Gr-r-r—there go, my heart's abhorrence!
   Water your damned flower-pots, do!
If hate killed men, Brother Lawrence,
   God's blood, would not mine kill you!
What? your myrtle-bush wants trimming?   5
   Oh, that rose has prior claims—
Needs its leaden vase filled brimming?
   Hell dry you up with its flames!

At the meal we sit together;
   Salve tibi!° I must hear   *Hail to thee!*   10
Wise talk of the kind of weather,
   Sort of season, time of year:
Not a plenteous cork-crop: scarcely
   Dare we hope oak-galls, I doubt;
What's the Latin name for "parsley"?   15
   What's the Greek name for "swine's snout"?

Whew! We'll have our platter burnished,
   Laid with care on our own shelf!
With a fire-new spoon we're furnished,
   And a goblet for ourself,   20
Rinsed like something sacrificial
   Ere 'tis fit to touch our chaps—
Marked with L. for our initial!
   (He-he! There his lily snaps!)

Saint, forsooth! While Brown Dolores   25
   Squats outside the Convent bank
With Sanchicha, telling stories,
   Steeping tresses in the tank,

Blue-black, lustrous, thick like horsehairs,
  —Can't I see his dead eye glow,   30
Bright as 'twere a Barbary corsair's?
  (That is, if he'd let it show!)

When he finishes refection,
  Knife and fork he never lays
Cross-wise, to my recollection,   35
  As I do, in Jesu's praise.
I the Trinity illustrate,
  Drinking watered orange-pulp—
In three sips the Arian frustrate;
  While he drains his at one gulp!   40

Oh, those melons! if he's able
  We're to have a feast; so nice!
One goes to the Abbot's table,
  All of us get each a slice.
How go on your flowers? None double?   45
  Not one fruit-sort can you spy?
Strange!—And I, too, at such trouble,
  Keep them close-nipped on the sly!

There's a great text in Galatians,
  Once you trip on it, entails   50
Twenty-nine distinct damnations,
  One sure, if another fails;
If I trip him just a-dying,
  Sure of heaven as sure can be,
Spin him round and send him flying   55
  Off to hell, a Manichee?

Or, my scrofulous French novel
  On grey paper with blunt type!
Simply glance at it, you grovel
  Hand and foot in Belial's gripe;   60
If I double down its pages
  At the woeful sixteenth print,
When he gathers his greengages,
  Ope a sieve and slip it in't?

Or, there's Satan!—one might venture   65
  Pledge one's soul to him, yet leave
Such a flaw in the indenture
  As he'd miss till, past retrieve,

Blasted lay that rose-acacia
  We're so proud of! *Hy, Zy, Hine*. . . .   70
'St, there's Vespers! *Plena gratia*
  Ave, Virgo!° Gr-r-r—you swine!   *Hail, Virgin, full of grace!*

SOLILOQUY OF THE SPANISH CLOISTER.   *3 Brother Lawrence:* one of the speaker's fellow monks. *31 Barbary corsair:* a pirate operating off the Barbary coast of Africa. *39 Arian:* a follower of Arius, heretic who denied the doctrine of the Trinity. *49 a great text in Galatians:* a difficult verse in this book of the Bible. Brother Lawrence will be damned as a heretic if he wrongly interprets it. *56 Manichee:* another kind of heretic, one who (after the Persian philosopher Mani) sees in the world a constant struggle between good and evil, neither able to win. *60 Belial:* here, not specifically Satan but (as used in the Old Testament) a name for wickedness. *70 Hy, Zy, Hine:* possibly the sound of a bell to announce evening devotions.

COMPARE

"Soliloquy of the Spanish Cloister" with "In Westminster Abbey" by John Betjeman on page 684.

Geoffrey Chaucer (1340?–1400)

YOUR ẎEN TWO WOL (LATE FOURTEENTH CENTURY) SLEE ME SODENLY

Your ẏen° two wol slee° me sodenly;   *eyes; slay*
I may the beautee of hem° not sustene°,   *them; resist*
So woundeth hit thourghout my herte kene.

And but° your word wo! helen° hastily   *unless; heal*
My hertes wounde, while that hit is grene°,   *new* 5
  Your ẏen two wol slee me sodenly;
  I may the beautee of hem not sustene.

Upon my trouthe° I sey you feithfully   *word*
That ye ben of my lyf and deeth the quene;
For with my deeth the trouthe° shal be sene.   *truth* 10
  Your ẏen two wol slee me sodenly;
  I may the beautee of hem not sustene,
    So woundeth it thourghout my herte kene.

YOUR ẎEN TWO WOL SLEE ME SODENLY. This poem is one of a group of three roundels, collectively ti-tled "Merciles Beaute." A **roundel** (or **rondel**) is an English form consisting of 11 lines with 3 stanzas rimed with a refrain. *3 so woundeth . . . kene:* "So deeply does it wound me through the heart."

COMPARE

"Your ẏen two wol slee me sodenly" with "My mistress's eyes are nothing like the sun" by William Shakespeare (page 995) or "Four-Word Lines" by May Swenson (page 996).

G. K. Chesterton (1874–1936)

THE DONKEY

1900

When fishes flew and forests walked
   And figs grew upon thorn,
Some moment when the moon was blood
   Then surely I was born;

With monstrous head and sickening cry   5
   And ears like errant wings,
The devil's walking parody
   On all four-footed things.

The tattered outlaw of the earth,
   Of ancient crooked will;   10
Starve, scourge, deride me: I am dumb,
   I keep my secret still.

Fools! For I also had my hour;
   One far fierce hour and sweet:
There was a shout about my ears,   15
   And palms before my feet.

THE DONKEY. For more details of the donkey's hour of triumph see Matthew 21:1–8.

COMPARE

"The Donkey" with "The Tyger" or "The Lamb," both by William Blake (page 1040).

Samuel Taylor Coleridge (1772–1834)

KUBLA KHAN

(1797–1798)

Or, a Vision in a Dream. A Fragment.

In Xanadu did Kubla Khan
A stately pleasure-dome decree:
Where Alph, the sacred river, ran
Through caverns measureless to man
   Down to a sunless sea.   5
So twice five miles of fertile ground
With walls and towers were girdled round;
And there were gardens bright with sinuous rills,
Where blossomed many an incense-bearing tree;
And here were forests ancient as the hills,   10
Enfolding sunny spots of greenery.

But oh! that deep romantic chasm which slanted
Down the green hill athwart a cedarn cover!
A savage place! as holy and enchanted
As e'er beneath a waning moon was haunted 15
By woman wailing for her demon-lover!
And from this chasm, with ceaseless turmoil seething,
As if this earth in fast thick pants were breathing,
A mighty fountain momently was forced:
Amid whose swift half-intermitted burst 20
Huge fragments vaulted like rebounding hail,
Or chaffy grain beneath the thresher's flail:
And 'mid these dancing rocks at once and ever
It flung up momently the sacred river.
Five miles meandering with a mazy motion 25
Through wood and dale the sacred river ran,
Then reached the caverns measureless to man,
And sank in tumult to a lifeless ocean:
And 'mid this tumult Kubla heard from far
Ancestral voices prophesying war! 30

   The shadow of the dome of pleasure
   Floated midway on the waves;
   Where was heard the mingled measure
   From the fountain and the caves.
It was a miracle of rare device, 35
A sunny pleasure-dome with caves of ice!

   A damsel with a dulcimer
   In a vision once I saw:
   It was an Abyssinian maid,
   And on her dulcimer she played, 40
   Singing of Mount Abora.
   Could I revive within me
   Her symphony and song,
   To such a deep delight 'twould win me,
That with music loud and long, 45
I would build that dome in air,
That sunny dome! those caves of ice!
And all who heard should see them there,
And all should cry, Beware! Beware!
His flashing eyes, his floating hair! 50
Weave a circle round him thrice,
And close your eyes with holy dread,
For he on honey-dew hath fed,
And drunk the milk of Paradise.

KUBLA KHAN. There was an actual Kublai Khan, a thirteenth-century Mongol emperor, and a Chinese city of Xamdu; but Coleridge's dream vision also borrows from travelers's descriptions of such other exotic places as Abyssinia and America. 51 *circle:* a magic circle drawn to keep away evil spirits.

COMPARE

"Kubla Khan" with "Jerusalem" by William Blake (page 803) or "The Dream" by Louise Bogan (page 1042).

E. E. Cummings   (1894–1962)*

SOMEWHERE I HAVE NEVER TRAVELLED,   1931
GLADLY BEYOND

somewhere i have never travelled,gladly beyond
any experience,your eyes have their silence:
in your most frail gesture are things which enclose me,
or which i cannot touch because they are too near

your slightest look easily will unclose me   5
though i have closed myself as fingers,
you open always petal by petal myself as Spring opens
(touching skilfully,mysteriously)her first rose

or if your wish be to close me,i and
my life will shut very beautifully,suddenly,   10
as when the heart of this flower imagines
the snow carefully everywhere descending;

nothing which we are to perceive in this world equals
the power of your intense fragility:whose texture
compels me with the colour of its countries,   15
rendering death and forever with each breathing

(i do not know what it is about you that closes
and opens; only something in me understands
the voice of your eyes is deeper than all roses)
nobody,not even the rain,has such small hands   20

COMPARE

"somewhere i have never travelled,gladly beyond" with "Your ÿen two wol slee me sodenly" by Geoffrey Chaucer (page 1049) or "Elegy for Jane" by Theodore Roethke (page 779).

John Donne (1572–1631)*

DEATH BE NOT PROUD   (ABOUT 1610)

Death be not proud, though some have callèd thee
Mighty and dreadful, for thou art not so;
For those whom thou think'st thou dost overthrow
Die not, poor death, nor yet canst thou kill me.
From rest and sleep, which but thy pictures be,   5
Much pleasure, then from thee much more must flow,
And soonest our best men with thee do go,
Rest of their bones, and soul's delivery.
Thou art slave to fate, chance, kings, and desperate men,
And dost with poison, war, and sickness dwell,   10
And poppy, or charms can make us sleep as well,
And better than thy stroke; why swell'st thou then?
One short sleep past, we wake eternally,
And death shall be no more; death, thou shalt die.

COMPARE

Compare Donne's personification of Death in "Death be not proud" with Emily Dickinson's in "Because I could not stop for Death" (page 1017).

John Donne

John Donne (1572–1631)*

THE FLEA   1633

Mark but this flea, and mark in this
How little that which thou deny'st me is;
It sucked me first, and now sucks thee,
And in this flea our two bloods mingled be;
Thou know'st that this cannot be said   5

A sin, nor shame, nor loss of maidenhead,
   Yet this enjoys before it woo,
   And pampered swells with one blood made of two,
   And this, alas, is more than we would do.

Oh stay, three lives in one flea spare,   10
Where we almost, yea more than married are.
This flea is you and I, and this
Our marriage bed, and marriage temple is;
Though parents grudge, and you, we're met
And cloistered in these living walls of jet.   15
   Though use° make you apt to kill me,   *custom*
   Let not to that, self-murder added be,
   And sacrilege, three sins in killing three.

Cruel and sudden, hast thou since
Purpled thy nail in blood of innocence?   20
Wherein could this flea guilty be,
Except in that drop it sucked from thee?
Yet thou triumph'st, and say'st that thou
Find'st not thyself, nor me, the weaker now;
   'Tis true; then learn how false, fears be;   25
   Just so much honor, when thou yield'st to me,
   Will waste, as this flea's death took life from thee.

COMPARE

"The Flea" with "To His Coy Mistress" by Andrew Marvell (page 1101).

John Donne   (1572–1631)*

A VALEDICTION: FORBIDDING MOURNING   (1611)

As virtuous men pass mildly away,
   And whisper to their souls to go,
Whilst some of their sad friends do say
   The breath goes now, and some say no:

So let us melt, and make no noise,   5
   No tear-floods, nor sigh-tempests move;
'Twere profanation of our joys
   To tell the laity° our love.   *common people*

Moving of th' earth° brings harms and fears;   *earthquake*
   Men reckon what it did and meant;
But trepidation of the spheres,   10
   Though greater far, is innocent°.   *harmless*

Dull sublunary lovers' love
　　(Whose soul is sense) cannot admit
Absence, because it doth remove
　　Those things which elemented° it.　　　　　　　　　　　*constituted*　15

But we, by a love so much refined
　　That ourselves know not what it is,
Inter-assurèd of the mind,
　　Care less, eyes, lips, and hands to miss.　　　　　　　　20

Our two souls, therefore, which are one,
　　Though I must go, endure not yet
A breach, but an expansiòn,
　　Like gold to airy thinness beat.

If they be two, they are two so　　　　　　　　　　　　25
　　As stiff twin compasses are two:
Thy soul, the fixed foot, makes no show
　　To move, but doth, if th' other do.

And though it in the center sit,
　　Yet when the other far doth roam,　　　　　　　　　30
It leans and harkens after it,
　　And grows erect as that comes home.

Such wilt thou be to me, who must,
　　Like th' other foot, obliquely run;
Thy firmness makes my circle just°,　　　　　　　　　*perfect*　35
　　And makes me end where I begun.

A VALEDICTION: FORBIDDING MOURNING. According to Donne's biographer Izaak Walton, Donne's wife received this poem as a gift before the poet departed on a journey to France.　11 *spheres*: in Ptolemaic astronomy, the concentric spheres surrounding the earth. The trepidation or motion of the ninth sphere was thought to change the date of the equinox. 19 *Inter-assurèd of the mind*: each sure in mind that the other is faithful. 24 *gold to airy thinness*: gold is so malleable that, if beaten to the thickness of gold leaf (1/250,000 of one inch), one ounce of gold would cover 250 square feet.

COMPARE

"A Valediction: Forbidding Mourning" with "To Lucasta" by Richard Lovelace (page 691).

Rita Dove (b. 1952)*

DAYSTAR   1986

She wanted a little room for thinking:
but she saw diapers steaming on the line,
a doll slumped behind the door.

So she lugged a chair behind the garage
to sit out the children's naps.   5

Sometimes there were things to watch—
the pinched armor of a vanished cricket,
a floating maple leaf. Other days
she stared until she was assured
when she closed her eyes   10
she'd see only her own vivid blood.

She had an hour, at best, before Liza appeared
pouting from the top of the stairs.
And just *what* was mother doing
out back with the field mice? Why,   15

building a palace. Later
that night when Thomas rolled over and
lurched into her, she would open her eyes
and think of the place that was hers
for an hour—where   20
she was nothing,
pure nothing, in the middle of the day.

COMPARE

"Daystar" with "The Lake Isle of Innisfree" by William Butler Yeats (page 653).

John Dryden   (1631–1700)

To the Memory of Mr. Oldham   1684

Farewell, too little and too lately known,
Whom I began to think and call my own;
For sure our souls were near allied, and thine
Cast in the same poetic mold with mine.
One common note on either lyre did strike,   5
And knaves and fools we both abhorred alike.
To the same goal did both our studies drive:
The last set out the soonest did arrive.
Thus Nissus fell upon the slippery place,
While his young friend performed and won the race.   10
O early ripe! to thy abundant store
What could advancing age have added more?
It might (what Nature never gives the young)
Have taught the numbers° of thy native tongue.   *meters*
But satire needs not those, and wit will shine   15
Through the harsh cadence of a rugged line.
A noble error, and but seldom made,
When poets are by too much force betrayed.
Thy gen'rous fruits, though gathered ere their prime,
Still showed a quickness; and maturing time   20
But mellows what we write to the dull sweets of rhyme.
Once more, hail, and farewell! farewell, thou young
But ah! too short, Marcellus of our tongue!
Thy brows with ivy and with laurels bound;
But fate and gloomy night encompass thee around.   25

To the Memory of Mr. Oldham. John Oldham, poet best remembered for his *Satires upon the Je-suits*, had died at thirty.   9–10 *Nissus; his young friend*: these two close friends, as Virgil tells us in the *Aeneid*, ran a race for the prize of an olive crown. 23 *Marcellus*: had he not died in his twentieth year, he would have succeeded the Roman emperor Augustus. 25 This line echoes the *Aeneid* (VI, 886), in which Marcellus is seen walking under the black cloud of his impending doom.

Compare

"To the Memory of Mr. Oldham" with "Bells for John Whiteside's Daughter" by John Crowe Ransom (page 1121) or "Elegy for Jane" by Theodore Roethke (page 1126).

T. S. Eliot   (1888–1965)*

Journey of the Magi   1927

"A cold coming we had of it,
Just the worst time of the year
For a journey, and such a long journey:

The ways deep and the weather sharp,
The very dead of winter."   5
And the camels galled, sore-footed, refractory,
Lying down in the melting snow.
There were times we regretted
The summer palaces on slopes, the terraces,
And the silken girls bringing sherbet.   10
Then the camel men cursing and grumbling
And running away, and wanting their liquor and women,
And the night-fires going out, and the lack of shelters,
And the cities hostile and the towns unfriendly
And the villages dirty and charging high prices: 15
A hard time we had of it.
At the end we preferred to travel all night,
Sleeping in snatches,
With the voices singing in our ears, saying
That this was all folly.   20

Then at dawn we came down to a temperate valley,
Wet, below the snow line, smelling of vegetation;
With a running stream and a water-mill beating the darkness,
And three trees on the low sky,
And an old white horse galloped away in the meadow.   25
Then we came to a tavern with vine-leaves over the lintel,
Six hands at an open door dicing for pieces of silver,
And feet kicking the empty wine-skins.
But there was no information, and so we continued
And arrived at evening, not a moment too soon   30
Finding the place; it was (you may say) satisfactory.

All this was a long time ago, I remember,
And I would do it again, but set down
This set down
This: were we led all that way for   35
Birth or Death? There was a Birth, certainly,
We had evidence and no doubt. I had seen birth and death,
But had thought they were different; this Birth was
Hard and bitter agony for us, like Death, our death.
We returned to our places, these Kingdoms,   40
But no longer at ease here, in the old dispensation,
With an alien people clutching their gods.
I should be glad of another death.

JOURNEY OF THE MAGI. The story of the Magi, the three wise men who traveled to Bethlehem to behold the baby Jesus, is told in Matthew 2:1–12. That the three were kings is a later tradition.   1-5 A
cold coming . . . winter: Eliot quotes with slight changes from a sermon preached on Christmas day,
1622, by Bishop Lancelot Andrewes. 24 three trees: foreshadowing the three crosses on Calvary (see

Luke 23:32-33). 25 *white horse:* perhaps the steed that carried the conquering Christ in the vision of St. John the Divine (Revelation 19:11–16). 41 *old dispensation:* older, pagan religion about to be displaced by Christianity.

COMPARE

"Journey of the Magi" with "The Magi" by William Butler Yeats (page 1163).

T. S. Eliot

T. S. Eliot (1888–1965)*

THE LOVE SONG OF J. ALFRED PRUFROCK   1917

> *S'io credessi che mia risposta fosse*
> *A persona che mai tornasse al mondo,*
> *Questa fiamma staria senza più scosse.*
> *Ma per ciò che giammai di questo fondo*
> *Non tornò vivo alcun, s'i' odo il vero,*
> *Senza tema d'infamia ti rispondo.*

Let us go then, you and I,
When the evening is spread out against the sky
Like a patient etherized upon a table;
Let us go, through certain half-deserted streets,
The muttering retreats   5
Of restless nights in one-night cheap hotels
And sawdust restaurants with oyster-shells:
Streets that follow like a tedious argument
Of insidious intent
To lead you to an overwhelming question . . .   10
Oh, do not ask, "What is it?"
Let us go and make our visit.

In the room the women come and go
Talking of Michelangelo.

The yellow fog that rubs its back upon the window-panes,   15
The yellow smoke that rubs its muzzle on the window-panes,
Licked its tongue into the corners of the evening,
Lingered upon the pools that stand in drains,
Let fall upon its back the soot that falls from chimneys,
Slipped by the terrace, made a sudden leap,   20
And seeing that it was a soft October night,
Curled once about the house, and fell asleep.

And indeed there will be time
For the yellow smoke that slides along the street
Rubbing its back upon the window-panes;   25
There will be time, there will be time
To prepare a face to meet the faces that you meet;
There will be time to murder and create,
And time for all the works and days of hands
That lift and drop a question on your plate;   30
Time for you and time for me,
And time yet for a hundred indecisions,
And for a hundred visions and revisions,
Before the taking of a toast and tea.

In the room the women come and go   35
Talking of Michelangelo.

And indeed there will be time
To wonder, "Do I dare?" and, "Do I dare?"
Time to turn back and descend the stair,
With a bald spot in the middle of my hair—   40
(They will say: "How his hair is growing thin!")
My morning coat, my collar mounting firmly to the chin,
My necktie rich and modest, but asserted by a simple pin—
(They will say: "But how his arms and legs are thin!")
Do I dare   45
Disturb the universe?
In a minute there is time
For decisions and revisions which a minute will reverse.

For I have known them all already, known them all—
Have known the evenings, mornings, afternoons,   50
I have measured out my life with coffee spoons;
I know the voices dying with a dying fall
Beneath the music from a farther room.
    So how should I presume?

And I have known the eyes already, known them all—   55
The eyes that fix you in a formulated phrase,
And when I am formulated, sprawling on a pin,
When I am pinned and wriggling on the wall,
Then how should I begin
To spit out all the butt-ends of my days and ways?   60
    And how should I presume?

And I have known the arms already, known them all—
Arms that are braceleted and white and bare
(But in the lamplight, downed with light brown hair!)
Is it perfume from a dress   65
That makes me so digress?
Arms that lie along a table, or wrap about a shawl.
    And should I then presume?
    And how should I begin?
    . . . . .
Shall I say, I have gone at dusk through narrow streets   70
And watched the smoke that rises from the pipes
Of lonely men in shirt-sleeves, leaning out of windows? . . .

I should have been a pair of ragged claws
Scuttling across the floors of silent seas.
    . . . . .
And the afternoon, the evening, sleeps so peacefully!   75
Smoothed by long fingers,
Asleep . . . tired . . . or it malingers,
Stretched on the floor, here beside you and me.
Should I, after tea and cakes and ices,
Have the strength to force the moment to its crisis?   80
But though I have wept and fasted, wept and prayed,
Though I have seen my head (grown slightly bald) brought in upon a
    platter,
I am no prophet—and here's no great matter;
I have seen the moment of my greatness flicker,
And I have seen the eternal Footman hold my coat, and snicker,   85
And in short, I was afraid.

And would it have been worth it, after all,
After the cups, the marmalade, the tea,
Among the porcelain, among some talk of you and me,
Would it have been worth while,   90
To have bitten off the matter with a smile,
To have squeezed the universe into a ball
To roll it towards some overwhelming question,
To say: "I am Lazarus, come from the dead,
Come back to tell you all, I shall tell you all"—   95

If one, settling a pillow by her head,
    Should say: "That is not what I meant at all.
    That is not it, at all."

And would it have been worth it, after all,
Would it have been worth while,   100
After the sunsets and the dooryards and the sprinkled streets,
After the novels, after the teacups, after the skirts that trail along the
    floor—
And this, and so much more?—
It is impossible to say just what I mean!
But as if a magic lantern threw the nerves in patterns on a screen: 105
Would it have been worth while
If one, settling a pillow or throwing off a shawl,
And turning toward the window, should say:
    "That is not it at all,
    That is not what I meant, at all."   110
   . . . . .

No! I am not Prince Hamlet, nor was meant to be;
Am an attendant lord, one that will do
To swell a progress, start a scene or two,
Advise the prince; no doubt, an easy tool,
Deferential, glad to be of use,   115
Politic, cautious, and meticulous;
Full of high sentence, but a bit obtuse;
At times, indeed, almost ridiculous—
Almost, at times, the Fool.

I grow old . . . I grow old . . .   120
I shall wear the bottoms of my trousers rolled.

Shall I part my hair behind? Do I dare to eat a peach?
I shall wear white flannel trousers, and walk upon the beach.
I have heard the mermaids singing, each to each.

I do not think that they will sing to me.   125

I have seen them riding seaward on the waves
Combing the white hair of the waves blown back
When the wind blows the water white and black.

We have lingered in the chambers of the sea
By sea-girls wreathed with seaweed red and brown   130
Till human voices wake us, and we drown.

THE LOVE SONG OF J. ALFRED PRUFROCK. The epigraph, from Dante's *Inferno*, is the speech of one dead and damned, who thinks that his hearer also is going to remain in Hell. Count Guido da Montefeltro, whose sin has been to give false counsel after a corrupt prelate had offered him prior absolution and whose punishment is to be wrapped in a constantly burning flame, offers to tell Dante his story: "If I thought my reply were to someone who could ever return to the world, this flame would waver no more. But since, I'm told, nobody ever escapes from this pit, I'll tell you without fear of ill fame." 29 *works and days*: title of a poem by Hesiod (eighth century B.C.), depicting his life as a hard-working Greek farmer and exhorting his brother to be like him. 82 *head . . . platter*: like that of John the Baptist, prophet and praiser of chastity, whom King Herod beheaded at the demand of Herodias, his unlawfully wedded wife (see Mark 6:17–28). 92–93 *squeezed . . . To roll it*: an echo from Marvell's "To His Coy Mistress," lines 41–42 (see page 451). 94 *Lazarus*: probably the Lazarus whom Jesus called forth from the tomb (John 11:1–44), but possibly the beggar seen in Heaven by the rich man in Hell (Luke 16:19–25).

COMPARE

"The Love Song of J. Alfred Prufrock" with "Acquainted With the Night" by Robert Frost (page 865).

Louise Erdrich   (b. 1954)

INDIAN BOARDING SCHOOL: 1984
THE RUNAWAYS

Home's the place we head for in our sleep.
Boxcars stumbling north in dreams
don't wait for us. We catch them on the run.
The rails, old lacerations that we love,
shoot parallel across the face and break   5
just under Turtle Mountains. Riding scars
you can't get lost. Home is the place they cross.

The lame guard strikes a match and makes the dark
less tolerant. We watch through cracks in boards
as the land starts rolling, rolling till it hurts   10
to be here, cold in regulation clothes.
We know the sheriff's waiting at midrun
to take us back. His car is dumb and warm.
The highway doesn't rock, it only hums
like a wing of long insults. The worn-down welts   15
of ancient punishments lead back and forth.

All runaways wear dresses, long green ones,
the color you would think shame was. We scrub
the sidewalks down because it's shameful work.
Our brushes cut the stone in watered arcs   20
and in the soak frail outlines shiver clear

a moment, things us kids pressed on the dark
face before it hardened, pale, remembering
delicate old injuries, the spines of names and leaves.

INDIAN BOARDING SCHOOL: THE RUNAWAYS. 6. *Turtle Mountains:* in North Dakota and Manitoba.
The poet, of German and Native American descent, belongs to the Turtle Mountain Band of the
Chippewa.

COMPARE

"Indian Boarding School: The Runaways" with "How I Came to Have a Man's Name" by
Emma Lee Warrior (page 715).

Robert Frost   (1874–1963)*

BIRCHES   1916

When I see birches bend to left and right
Across the lines of straighter darker trees,
I like to think some boy's been swinging them.
But swinging doesn't bend them down to stay
As ice storms do. Often you must have seen them   5
Loaded with ice a sunny winter morning
After a rain. They click upon themselves
As the breeze rises, and turn many-colored
As the stir cracks and crazes their enamel.
Soon the sun's warmth makes them shed crystal shells   10
Shattering and avalanching on the snow crust—
Such heaps of broken glass to sweep away
You'd think the inner dome of heaven had fallen.
They are dragged to the withered bracken by the load,
And they seem not to break; though once they are bowed   15
So low for long, they never right themselves:
You may see their trunks arching in the woods
Years afterwards, trailing their leaves on the ground
Like girls on hands and knees that throw their hair
Before them over their heads to dry in the sun.   20
But I was going to say when Truth broke in
With all her matter of fact about the ice storm
I should prefer to have some boy bend them
As he went out and in to fetch the cows—
Some boy too far from town to learn baseball,   25
Whose only play was what he found himself,
Summer or winter, and could play alone.
One by one he subdued his father's trees
By riding them down over and over again

Until he took the stiffness out of them,   30
And not one but hung limp, not one was left
For him to conquer. He learned all there was
To learn about not launching out too soon
And so not carrying the tree away
Clear to the ground. He always kept his poise   35
To the top branches, climbing carefully
With the same pains you use to fill a cup
Up to the brim, and even above the brim.
Then he flung outward, feet first, with a swish,
Kicking his way down through the air to the ground.   40
So was I once myself a swinger of birches.
And so I dream of going back to be.
It's when I'm weary of considerations,
And life is too much like a pathless wood
Where your face burns and tickles with the cobwebs   45
Broken across it, and one eye is weeping
From a twig's having lashed across it open.
I'd like to get away from earth awhile
And then come back to it and begin over.
May no fate willfully misunderstand me   50
And half grant what I wish and snatch me away
Not to return. Earth's the right place for love:
I don't know where it's likely to go better.
I'd like to go by climbing a birch tree,
And climb black branches up a snow-white trunk   55
Toward heaven, till the tree could bear no more,
But dipped its top and set me down again.
That would be good both going and coming back.
One could do worse than be a swinger of birches.

COMPARE

"Birches" with "Sailing to Byzantium" by William Butler Yeats (page 991).

Robert Frost   (1874–1963)*

MENDING WALL   1914

Something there is that doesn't love a wall,
That sends the frozen-ground-swell under it,
And spills the upper boulders in the sun;
And makes gaps even two can pass abreast.
The work of hunters is another thing: 5

I have come after them and made repair
Where they have left not one stone on a stone,
But they would have the rabbit out of hiding,
To please the yelping dogs. The gaps I mean,
No one has seen them made or heard them made, 10
But at spring mending-time we find them there.
I let my neighbor know beyond the hill;
And on a day we meet to walk the line
And set the wall between us once again.
We keep the wall between us as we go. 15
To each the boulders that have fallen to each.
And some are loaves and some so nearly balls
We have to use a spell to make them balance:
"Stay where you are until our backs are turned!"
We wear our fingers rough with handling them. 20
Oh, just another kind of outdoor game,
One on a side. It comes to little more:
There where it is we do not need the wall:
He is all pine and I am apple orchard.
My apple trees will never get across 25
And eat the cones under his pines, I tell him.
He only says, "Good fences make good neighbors."
Spring is the mischief in me, and I wonder
If I could put a notion in his head:
"Why do they make good neighbors? Isn't it 30
Where there are cows? But here there are no cows.
Before I built a wall I'd ask to know
What I was walling in or walling out,
And to whom I was like to give offence.
Something there is that doesn't love a wall, 35
That wants it down." I could say "Elves" to him,
But it's not elves exactly, and I'd rather
He said it for himself. I see him there
Bringing a stone grasped firmly by the top
In each hand, like an old-stone savage armed. 40
He moves in darkness as it seems to me,
Not of woods only and the shade of trees.
He will not go behind his father's saying,
And he likes having thought of it so well
He says again, "Good fences make good neighbors." 45

COMPARE

"Mending Wall" with "Digging" by Seamus Heaney (page 1077).

Robert Frost (1874–1963)*

Stopping by Woods on a Snowy Evening   1923

Whose woods these are I think I know.
His house is in the village though;
He will not see me stopping here
To watch his woods fill up with snow.

My little horse must think it queer   5
To stop without a farmhouse near
Between the woods and frozen lake
The darkest evening of the year.

He gives his harness bells a shake
To ask if there is some mistake.   10
The only other sound's the sweep
Of easy wind and downy flake.

The woods are lovely, dark and deep,
But I have promises to keep,
And miles to go before I sleep,   15
And miles to go before I sleep.

Compare

"Stopping by Woods on a Snowy Evening" with "Desert Places" by Robert Frost (page 823).

Allen Ginsberg (1926–1997)

A Supermarket in California   1956

   What thoughts I have of you tonight, Walt Whitman, for I walked down the sidestreets under the trees with a headache self-conscious looking at the full moon.
   In my hungry fatigue, and shopping for images, I went into the neon fruit supermarket, dreaming of your enumerations!
   What peaches and what penumbras! Whole families shopping at night! Aisles full of husbands! Wives in the avocados, babies in the tomatoes!—and you, García Lorca, what were you doing down by the watermelons?

   I saw you, Walt Whitman, childless, lonely old grubber, poking among the meats in the refrigerator and eyeing the grocery boys.
   I heard you asking questions of each: Who killed the pork chops? What price bananas? Are you my Angel?   5

I wandered in and out of the brilliant stacks of cans following you,
and followed in my imagination by the store detective.
We strode down the open corridors together in our solitary fancy
tasting artichokes, possessing every frozen delicacy, and never passing
the cashier.

Where are we going, Walt Whitman? The doors close in an hour.
Which way does your beard point tonight?
(I touch your book and dream of our odyssey in the supermarket and
feel absurd.)
Will we walk all night through solitary streets? The trees add shade
to shade, lights out in the houses, we'll both be lonely.   10
Will we stroll dreaming of the lost America of love past blue auto-
mobiles in driveways, home to our silent cottage?
Ah, dear father, graybeard, lonely old courage-teacher, what
America did you have when Charon quit poling his ferry and you got
out on a smoking bank and stood watching the boat disappear on the
black waters of Lethe?

A Supermarket in California. *2 enumerations:* many of Whitman's poems contain lists of observed details. 3 *García Lorca:* modern Spanish poet who wrote an "Ode to Walt Whitman" in his
booklength sequence *Poet in New York.* 12 *Charon . . . Lethe:* Is the poet confusing two underworld
rivers? Charon, in Greek and Roman mythology, is the boatman who ferries the souls of the dead
across the River Styx. The River Lethe also flows through Hades, and a drink of its waters makes the
dead lose their painful memories of loved ones they have left behind.

Compare

"A Supermarket in California" with Walt Whitman's "To a Locomotive in Winter" (page
670) and "I Saw in Louisiana a Live-Oak Growing" (page 1151).

Dana Gioia (b. 1950)

California Hills in August   1982

I can imagine someone who found
these fields unbearable, who climbed
the hillside in the heat, cursing the dust,
cracking the brittle weeds underfoot,
wishing a few more trees for shade.   5

An Easterner especially, who would scorn
the meagerness of summer, the dry
twisted shapes of black elm,
scrub oak, and chaparral—a landscape
August has already drained of green.   10

One who would hurry over the clinging
thistle, foxtail, golden poppy,
knowing everything was just a weed,
unable to conceive that these trees
and sparse brown bushes were alive.   15

And hate the bright stillness of the noon,
without wind, without motion,
the only other living thing
a hawk, hungry for prey, suspended
in the blinding, sunlit blue.   20

And yet how gentle it seems to someone
raised in a landscape short of rain—
the skyline of a hill broken by no more
trees than one can count, the grass,
the empty sky, the wish for water.   25

COMPARE

"California Hills in August" with "To see a world in a grain of sand" by William Blake
(page 770).

Donald Hall (b. 1928)

NAMES OF HORSES   1978

All winter your brute shoulders strained against collars, padding
and steerhide over the ash hames, to haul
sledges of cordwood for drying through spring and summer,
for the Glenwood stove next winter, and for the simmering range.

In April you pulled cartloads of manure to spread on the fields,   5
dark manure of Holsteins, and knobs of your own clustered with oats.
All summer you mowed the grass in meadow and hayfield, the mowing
     machine
clacketing beside you, while the sun walked high in the morning;

and after noon's heat, you pulled a clawed rake through the same acres,
gathering stacks, and dragged the wagon from stack to stack,   10
and the built hayrack back, uphill to the chaffy barn,
three loads of hay a day from standing grass in the morning.

Sundays you trotted the two miles to church with the light load
of a leather quartertop buggy, and grazed in the sound of hymns.
Generation on generation, your neck rubbed the windowsill   15
of the stall, smoothing the wood as the sea smooths glass.

When you were old and lame, when your shoulders hurt bending to
    graze,
one October the man, who fed you and kept you, and harnessed you
    every morning,
led you through corn stubble to sandy ground above Eagle Pond,
and dug a hole beside you where you stood shuddering in your skin,   20

and lay the shotgun's muzzle in the boneless hollow behind your ear,
and fired the slug into your brain, and felled you into your grave,
shoveling sand to cover you, setting goldenrod upright above you,
where by next summer a dent in the ground made your monument.

For a hundred and fifty years, in the pasture of dead horses,   25
roots of pine trees pushed through the pale curves of your ribs,
yellow blossoms flourished above you in autumn, and in winter
frost heaved your bones in the ground—old toilers, soil makers:

O Roger, Mackerel, Riley, Ned, Nellie, Chester, Lady Ghost.

COMPARE

"Names of Horses" with "The Bull Calf" by Irving Layton (page 1096).

Thomas Hardy   (1840–1928)*

THE CONVERGENCE OF THE TWAIN   1912

Lines on the Loss of the "Titanic"

I

In a solitude of the sea
Deep from human vanity,
And the Pride of Life that planned her, stilly couches she.

II

Steel chambers, late the pyres
Of her salamandrine fires,
Cold currents thrid°, and turn to rhythmic tidal lyres.   5   *thread*

III

Over the mirrors meant
To glass the opulent
The sea-worm crawls—grotesque, slimed, dumb, indifferent.

IV

Jewels in joy designed   10
    To ravish the sensuous mind
Lie lightless, all their sparkles bleared and black and blind.

V

Dim moon-eyed fishes near
    Gaze at the gilded gear
And query: "What does this vaingloriousness down here?" . . .   15

VI

Well: while was fashioning
    This creature of cleaving wing,
The Immanent Will that stirs and urges everything

VII

Prepared a sinister mate
    For her—so gaily great—   20
A Shape of Ice, for the time far and dissociate.

VIII

And as the smart ship grew
    In stature, grace, and hue,
In shadowy silent distance grew the Iceberg too.

IX

Alien they seemed to be: 25
    No mortal eye could see
The intimate welding of their later history,

X

Or sign that they were bent
    By paths coincident
On being anon twin halves of one august event,   30

XI

Till the Spinner of the Years
    Said "Now!" And each one hears,
And consummation comes, and jars two hemispheres.

THE CONVERGENCE OF THE TWAIN. The luxury liner *Titanic*, supposedly unsinkable, went down in 1912 after striking an iceberg on its first Atlantic voyage.   5 *salamandrine*: like the salamander, a lizard that supposedly thrives in fires, or like a spirit of the same name that inhabits fire (according to alchemists).

COMPARE

"The Convergence of the Twain" with "Titanic" by David R. Slavitt (page 1132).

Thomas Hardy

Thomas Hardy   (1840–1928)*

DURING WIND AND RAIN   1917

They sing their dearest songs—
He, she, all of them—yea,
Treble and tenor and bass,
   And one to play;
With the candles mooning each face   5
   Ah, no; the years O!
How the sick leaves reel down in throngs!

They clear the creeping moss—
Elders and juniors—aye,
Making the pathways neat   10
   And the garden gay;
And they build a shady seat. . . .
   Ah, no; the years, the years;
See, the white storm-birds wing across!

They are blithely breakfasting all—
Men and maidens—yea,
Under the summer tree,
   With a glimpse of the bay,
While pet fowl come to the knee. . . .
    Ah, no! the years O!   20
And the rotten rose is ripped from the wall.

They change to a high new house,
He, she, all of them—aye,
Clocks and carpets and chairs
   On the lawn all day,   25
And brightest things that are theirs. . . .
    Ah, no; the years, the years;
Down their carved names the rain-drop plows.

COMPARE

"During Wind and Rain" with "anyone lived in a pretty how town" by E. E. Cummings
(page 718).

Thomas Hardy   (1840–1928)*

HAP   1866

If but some vengeful god would call to me
From up the sky, and laugh: "Thou suffering thing,
Know that thy sorrow is my ecstasy,
That thy love's loss is my hate's profiting!"

Then would I bear it, clench myself, and die,   5
Steeled by the sense of ire unmerited;
Half-eased in that a Powerfuller than I
Had willed and meted me the tears I shed.

But not so. How arrives it joy lies slain,
And why unblooms the best hope ever sown?   10
—Crass Casualty obstructs the sun and rain,
And dicing Time for gladness casts a moan . . .
These purblind Doomsters had as readily strown
Blisses about my pilgrimage as pain.

COMPARE

"Hap" with the Roman poet Horace's *carpe diem* ode on pages 969–971. Choose any of
the three translations there of Horace or use the literal translation provided below the
original Latin.

Thomas Hardy (1840–1928)*

In Church 1914

"And now to God the Father," he ends,
And his voice thrills up to the topmost tiles:
Each listener chokes as he bows and bends,
And emotion pervades the crowded aisles.
Then the preacher glides to the vestry-door,   5
And shuts it, and thinks he is seen no more.

The door swings softly ajar meanwhile,
And a pupil of his in the Bible class,
Who adores him as one without gloss or guile
Sees her idol stand with a satisfied smile   10
And re-enact at the vestry-glass

Each pulpit gesture in deft dumb-show
That had moved the congregation so.

Compare

"In Church" with "In Westminster Abbey" by John Betjeman (page 684).

Robert Hayden (1913–1980)*

Those Winter Sundays 1962

Sundays too my father got up early
and put his clothes on in the blueblack cold,
then with cracked hands that ached
from labor in the weekday weather made
banked fires blaze. No one ever thanked him.   5

I'd wake and hear the cold splintering, breaking.
When the rooms were warm, he'd call,
and slowly I would rise and dress,
fearing the chronic angers of that house,

Speaking indifferently to him,   10
who had driven out the cold
and polished my good shoes as well.
What did I know, what did I know
of love's austere and lonely offices?

Compare

"Those Winter Sundays" with "My Father's Martial Art" by Stephen Shu-ning Liu (page 1098) and "Daddy" by Sylvia Plath (page 1114).

Robert Hayden (1913–1980)*

THE WHIPPING   1970

The old woman across the way
   is whipping the boy again
and shouting to the neighborhood
   her goodness and his wrongs.

Wildly he crashes through elephant ears,   5
   pleads in dusty zinnias,
while she in spite of crippling fat
   pursues and corners him.

She strikes and strikes the shrilly circling
   boy till the stick breaks   10
in her hand. His tears are rainy weather
   to woundlike memories:

My head gripped in bony vise
   of knees, the writhing struggle
to wrench free, the blows, the fear   15
   worse than blows that hateful

Words could bring, the face that I
   no longer knew or loved. . . .
Well, it is over now, it is over
   and the boy sobs in his room,   20

And the woman leans muttering against
   a tree, exhausted, purged—
avenged in part for lifelong hidings
   she has had to bear.

COMPARE

"The Whipping" with "Piano" by D. H. Lawrence (page 656).

H. D. (Hilda Doolittle)

H. D. [Hilda Doolittle]   (1886–1961)*

HELEN   1924

All Greece hates
the still eyes in the white face,
the lustre as of olives
where she stands,
and the white hands.   5

All Greece reviles
the wan face when she smiles,
hating it deeper still
when it grows wan and white,
remembering past enchantments   10
and past ills.

Greece sees unmoved,
God's daughter, born of love,
the beauty of cool feet
and slenderest knees,   15
could love indeed the maid,
only if she were laid,
white ash amid funereal cypresses.

HELEN. In Greek mythology, Helen, most beautiful of all women, was the daughter of a mortal, Leda, by the god Zeus. Her kidnapping set off the long and devastating Trojan War. While married to Menelaus, king of the Greek city-state of Sparta, Helen was carried off by Paris, prince of Troy. Menelaus and his brother Agamemnon raised an army, besieged Troy for ten years, and eventually recaptured her. One episode of the Trojan War is related in the *Iliad*, Homer's epic poem, composed before 700 B.C.

It shall all come true.
Know that it was for you
That all things were begun."

Adam, my child, my son,
Thus spoke Our Father in heaven   10
To his first, fabled child,
The father of us all.
And I, your father, tell
The words over again
As innumerable men   15
From ancient times have done.

Tell them again in pain,
And to the empty air.
Where you are men speak
A different mother tongue.   20
Will you forget our games,
Our hide-and-seek and song?
Child, it will be long
Before I see you again.

Adam, there will be   25
Many hard hours,
As an old poem says,
Hours of loneliness.
I cannot ease them for you;
They are our common lot.   30
During them, like as not,
You will dream of me.

When you are crouched away
In a strange clothes closet
Hiding from one who's "It"   35
And the dark crowds in,
Do not be afraid—
O, if you can, believe
In a father's love
That you shall know some day.   40

Think of the summer rain
Or seedpearls of the mist;
Seeing the beaded leaf,
Try to remember me.
From far away   45
I send my blessing out
To circle the great globe.
It shall reach you yet.

ADAM. According to Genesis 2:6–7, God created Adam, the first man, from the dust of the earth; Adam is also the name of Anthony Hecht's first son. *Epigraph: "Hath the rain a father . . . ?"*: These words are spoken to Job by the voice of God in Job 38:28.

COMPARE

Anthony Hecht's "Adam" with A. D. Hope's "Imperial Adam" (page 931).

George Herbert

George Herbert (1593–1633)*

LOVE   1633

Love bade me welcome; yet my soul drew back,
    Guilty of dust and sin.
But quick-eyed Love, observing me grow slack
    From my first entrance in,
Drew nearer to me, sweetly questioning   5
    If I lacked anything.

"A guest," I answered, "worthy to be here";
    Love said, "You shall be he."
"I, the unkind, ungrateful? Ah, my dear,
    I cannot look on Thee."   10
Love took my hand, and smiling did reply,
    "Who made the eyes but I?"

"Truth, Lord, but I have marred them; let my shame
    Go where it doth deserve."
"And know you not," says Love, "who bore the blame?"   15
    "My dear, then I will serve."
"You must sit down," says Love, "and taste My meat."
    So I did sit and eat.

COMPARE

"Love" with "Batter my heart, three-personed God" by John Donne (page 704).

Robert Herrick   (1591–1674)*

To the Virgins, to Make Much of Time   1648

Gather ye rose-buds while ye may,
   Old Time is still a-flying;
And this same flower that smiles today,
   Tomorrow will be dying.

The glorious lamp of heaven, the sun,   5
   The higher he's a-getting,
The sooner will his race be run,
   And nearer he's to setting.

That age is best which is the first,
   When youth and blood are warmer;   10
But being spent, the worse, and worst
   Times still succeed the former.

Then be not coy, but use your time,
   And while ye may, go marry;
For having lost but once your prime,   15
   You may for ever tarry.

Compare

"To the Virgins, to Make Much of Time" with "To His Coy Mistress" by Andrew Marvell (page 1101) and "Go, Lovely Rose" by Edmund Waller (page 1150).

Garrett Hongo

Garrett Hongo   (b. 1951)

The Cadence of Silk   1988

When I lived in Seattle, I loved watching
the Sonics play basketball; something
about that array of trained and energetic

bodies set in motion to attack a more
sluggish, less physically intelligent opponent   5
appealed to me, taught me about cadence
and play, the offguard breaking free
before the rebound, "releasing," as is said
in the parlance of the game, getting to
the center's downcourt pass and streaking   10
to the basket for a scoopshot layup
off the glass, all in rhythm, all in
perfect declensions of action, smooth
and strenuous as Gorgiasian rhetoric.
I was hooked on the undulant ballet   15
of the pattern offense, on the set play
back-door under the basket, and, at times,
even on the auctioneer's pace and elocution
of the play-by-play man. Now I watch
the Lakers, having returned to Los Angeles   20
some years ago, love them even more than
the Seattle team, long since broken up and aging.
The Lakers are incomparable, numerous
options for any situation, their players
the league's quickest, most intelligent,   25
and, it is my opinion, frankly, the most *cool*.
Few bruisers, they are sleek as arctic seals,
especially the small forward
as he dodges through the key, away from
the ball, rubbing off his man on the screen,   30
setting for his shot. Then, slick as spit,
comes the ball from the point guard,
and my man goes up, cradling the ball
in his right hand like a waiter balancing
a tray piled with champagne in stemmed glasses,   35
cocking his arm and bringing the ball
back behind his ear, pumping, letting fly then
as he jumps, popcorn-like, in the corner,
while the ball, launched, slung dextrously
with a slight backspin, slashes through   40
the basket's silk net with a small,
sonorous splash of completion.

THE CADENCE OF SILK.   14 *Gorgiasian rhetoric*: art of persuasive speaking as practiced by Gorgias (485?–380? B.C.), Greek Sophist philosopher, who argued that nothing exists.

COMPARE

"The Cadence of Silk" with "Ex-Basketball Player" by John Updike (page 1147).

Gerard Manley Hopkins   (1844–1889)*

SPRING AND FALL   (1880)

To a young child

Márgarét, áre you grieving
Over Goldengrove unleaving°   *shedding its leaves*
Leáves, líke the things of man, you
With your fresh thoughts care for, can you?
Áh! ás the heart grows older   5
It will come to such sights colder
By and by, nor spare a sigh
Though worlds of wanwood leafmeal lie;
And yet you *will* weep and know why.
Now no matter, child, the name: 10
Sórrow's spríngs áre the same.
Nor mouth had, no nor mind, expressed
What heart heard of, ghost° guessed: *spirit*
It ís the blight man was born for,
It is Margaret you mourn for.   15

COMPARE

"Spring and Fall" with "Margaret Are You Drug" by George Starbuck (page 976).

Gerard Manley Hopkins

Gerard Manley Hopkins   (1844–1889)*

THOU ART INDEED JUST, LORD,   (1889)
IF I CONTEND

*Justus quidem tu es, Domine, si disputem tecum: verumtamen justa loquar
ad te: Quare via impiorum prosperatur? & c.*

Thou art indeed just, Lord, if I contend
With thee; but, sir, so what I plead is just.
Why do sinners' ways prosper? and why must
Disappointment all I endeavor end?
Wert thou my enemy, O thou my friend,   5
How wouldst thou worse, I wonder than thou dost
Defeat, thwart me? Oh, the sots and thralls of lust
Do in spare hours more thrive than I that spend,

Sir, life upon thy cause. See, banks and brakes°   *ferny marshes*
Now, leavèd how thick! lacèd they are again   10
With fretty chervil°, look, and fresh wind shakes   *wild herb*

Them; birds build—but not I build; no, but strain,
Time's eunuch, and not breed one work that wakes.
Mine, O thou lord of life, send my roots rain.

THOU ART INDEED JUST, LORD, IF I CONTEND. In the first two sentences of this poem, Hopkins translates the Latin quotation from the Vulgate Bible (Jeremiah 12:1).

COMPARE

"Thou art indeed just, Lord . . ." with "When I consider how my light is spent" by John
Milton (page 1106) or with "Hap" by Thomas Hardy (page 1073).

Gerard Manley Hopkins   (1844–1889)*

THE WINDHOVER   (1877)

To Christ Our Lord

I caught this morning morning's minion, king-
    dom of daylight's dauphin, dapple-dawn-drawn Falcon, in his riding
    Of the rolling level underneath him steady air, and striding
High there, how he rung upon the rein of a wimpling wing
In his ecstasy! then off, off forth on swing,   5
    As a skate's heel sweeps smooth on a bow-bend: the hurl and gliding
    Rebuffed the big wind. My heart in hiding
Stirred for a bird, —the achieve of, the mastery of the thing!

Brute beauty and valor and act, oh, air, pride, plume, here
    Buckle! AND the fire that breaks from thee then, a billion   10
Times told lovelier, more dangerous, O my chevalier!

    No wonder of it: shéer plód makes plow down sillion°   *furrow*
Shine, and blue-bleak embers, ah my dear,
    Fall, gall themselves, and gash gold-vermilion.

THE WINDHOVER. A windhover is a kestrel, or small falcon, so called because it can hover upon the
wind.   4 *rung . . . wing*: A horse is "rung upon the rein" when its trainer holds the end of a long rein

and has the horse circle him. The possible meanings of *wimpling* include: (1) curving; (2) pleated, arranged in many little folds one on top of another; (3) rippling or undulating like the surface of a flowing stream.

COMPARE

"The Windhover" with "Batter my heart, three-personed God" by John Donne (page 704) and "Easter Wings" by George Herbert (page 892).

A. E. Housman   (1859–1936)*

LOVELIEST OF TREES, THE CHERRY NOW   1896

Loveliest of trees, the cherry now
Is hung with bloom along the bough,
And stands about the woodland ride°   *path*
Wearing white for Eastertide.

Now, of my threescore years and ten,   5
Twenty will not come again,
And take from seventy springs a score,
It only leaves me fifty more.

And since to look at things in bloom
Fifty springs are little room,   10
About the woodlands I will go
To see the cherry hung with snow.

COMPARE

"Loveliest of trees, the cherry now" with "To the Virgins, to Make Much of Time" by Robert Herrick (page 1081) and "Spring and Fall" by Gerard Manley Hopkins (page 1083).

A. E. Housman   (1859–1936)*

TO AN ATHLETE DYING YOUNG   1896

The time you won your town the race
We chaired you through the market-place;
Man and boy stood cheering by,
And home we brought you shoulder-high.

Today, the road all runners come,   5
Shoulder-high we bring you home,
And set you at your threshold down,
Townsman of a stiller town.

Smart lad, to slip betimes away
From fields where glory does not stay,   10
And early though the laurel grows
It withers quicker than the rose.

Eyes the shady night has shut
Cannot see the record cut,
And silence sounds no worse than cheers   15
After earth has stopped the ears.

Now you will not swell the rout
Of lads that wore their honors out,
Runners whom renown outran
And the name died before the man.   20

So set, before its echoes fade,
The fleet foot on the sill of shade,
And hold to the low lintel up
The still-defended challenge-cup.

And round that early-laureled head   25
Will flock to gaze the strengthless dead,
And find unwithered on its curls
The garland briefer than a girl's.

COMPARE

"To an Athlete Dying Young" with "Ex-Basketball Player" by John Updike (page 1147).

Randall Jarrell

Randall Jarrell   (1914–1965)*
THE DEATH OF THE BALL TURRET GUNNER   1945

From my mother's sleep I fell into the State
And I hunched in its belly till my wet fur froze.
Six miles from earth, loosed from its dream of life,
I woke to black flak and the nightmare fighters.
When I died they washed me out of the turret with a hose.

THE DEATH OF THE BALL TURRET GUNNER. Jarrell has written: "A ball turret was a plexiglass sphere set into the belly of a B-17 or B-24, and inhabited by two .50 caliber machine-guns and one man, a short small man. When this gunner tracked with his machine-guns a fighter attacking his bomber from below, he revolved with the turret; hunched in his little sphere, he looked like the fetus in the womb. The fighters which attacked him were armed with cannon firing explosive shells. The hose was a steam hose."

COMPARE

"The Death of the Ball Turret Gunner" with "Dulce et Decorum Est" by Wilfred Owen (page 691).

Randall Jarrell   (1914–1965)*

NEXT DAY   1965

Moving from Cheer to Joy, from Joy to All,
I take a box
And add it to my wild rice, my Cornish game hens.
The slacked or shorted, basketed, identical
Food-gathering flocks   5
Are selves I overlook. Wisdom, said William James,

Is learning what to overlook. And I am wise
If that is wisdom.
Yet somehow, as I buy All from these shelves
And the boy takes it to my station wagon,   10
What I've become
Troubles me even if I shut my eyes.

When I was young and miserable and pretty
And poor, I'd wish
What all girls wish: to have a husband,   15
A house and children. Now that I'm old, my wish
Is womanish:
That the boy putting groceries in my car

See me. It bewilders me he doesn't see me.
For so many years   20
I was good enough to eat: the world looked at me
And its mouth watered. How often they have undressed me,
The eyes of strangers!
And, holding their flesh within my flesh, their vile

Imaginings within my imagining,   25
I too have taken
The chance of life. Now the boy pats my dog
And we start home. Now I am good.
The last mistaken,
Ecstatic, accidental bliss, the blind   30

Happiness that, bursting, leaves upon the palm
Some soap and water—
It was so long ago, back in some Gay
Twenties, Nineties, I don't know . . . Today I miss
My lovely daughter   35
Away at school, my sons away at school,

My husband away at work—I wish for them.
The dog, the maid,
And I go through the sure unvarying days
At home in them. As I look at my life,   40
I am afraid
Only that it will change, as I am changing:

I am afraid, this morning, of my face.
It looks at me
From the rear-view mirror, with the eyes I hate,   45
The smile I hate. Its plain, lined look
Of gray discovery
Repeats to me: "You're old." That's all, I'm old.

And yet I'm afraid, as I was at the funeral
I went to yesterday.   50
My friend's cold made-up face, granite among its flowers,
Her undressed, operated-on, dressed body
Were my face and body.
As I think of her I hear her telling me.

How young I seem; I *am* exceptional;   55
I think of all I have.
But really no one is exceptional,
No one has anything, I'm anybody,
I stand beside my grave
Confused with my life, that is commonplace and solitary.   60

NEXT DAY. 1 *Cheer to Joy, from Joy to All*: the capitalized words are the brand names of household soaps and detergents. Jarrell puns ironically on their names. 6 *William James*: the American philosopher and psychologist (and brother of novelist Henry James) who lived from 1842 to 1910.

COMPARE

"Next Day" to "A Supermarket in California" by Allen Ginsberg (page 1067).

Robinson Jeffers (1887–1962)*

TO THE STONE-CUTTERS   1925

Stone-cutters fighting time with marble, you foredefeated
Challengers of oblivion
Eat cynical earnings, knowing rock splits, records fall down,

The square-limbed Roman letters
Scale in the thaws, wear in the rain. The poet as well   5
Builds his monument mockingly;
For man will be blotted out, the blithe earth die, the brave sun
Die blind, his heart blackening:
Yet stones have stood for a thousand years, and pained thoughts found
The honey peace in old poems.   10

COMPARE

"To the Stone-cutters" with "Not marble nor the gilded monuments" by William Shakespeare (page 1128).

Ben Jonson   (1573?–1637)*

ON MY FIRST DAUGHTER   1616

Here lies to each her parents' ruth°,   *sorrow*
Mary, the daughter of their youth;
Yet all heaven's gifts being heaven's due,
It makes the father less to rue.
At six months' end, she parted hence   5
With safety of her innocence;
Whose soul heaven's Queen (whose name she bears)
In comfort of her mother's tears,
Hath plac'd amongst her virgin-train:
Where, while that sever'd doth remain,   10
This grave partakes the fleshly birth.
Which cover lightly, gentle earth.

On My First Daughter.   7 *heaven's Queen:* the Virgin Mary.

COMPARE

"On My First Daughter" with Jonson's "On My First Son" (printed below).

Ben Jonson   (1573?–1637)*

ON MY FIRST SON   (1603)

Farewell, thou child of my right hand, and joy.
My sin was too much hope of thee, loved boy;
Seven years thou wert lent to me, and I thee pay,
Exacted by thy fate, on the just day.
Oh, could I lose all father° now. For why   *fatherhood*   5
Will man lament the state he should envỳ?—
To have so soon 'scaped world's and flesh's rage,

And, if no other misery, yet age.
Rest in soft peace, and asked, say, "Here doth lie
Ben Jonson his best piece of poetry,"   10
For whose sake henceforth all his vows be such
As what he loves may never like° too much.   *thrive*

ON MY FIRST SON.   1 *child of my right hand:* Jonson's son was named Benjamin; this phrase translates the Hebrew name. 4 *the just day:* the very day. The boy had died on his seventh birthday. 10 *poetry:* Jonson uses the word *poetry* here reflecting its Greek root *poiesis,* which means *creation.*

COMPARE

"On My First Son" with the five poems on the deaths of children on pages 987–989.

Donald Justice   (b. 1925)*

ON THE DEATH OF FRIENDS   1960
IN CHILDHOOD

We shall not ever meet them bearded in heaven,
Nor sunning themselves among the bald of hell;
If anywhere, in the deserted schoolyard at twilight,
Forming a ring, perhaps, or joining hands
In games whose very names we have forgotten.   5
Come, memory, let us seek them there in the shadows.

COMPARE

"On the Death of Friends in Childhood" and "With rue my heart is laden" by A. E. Housman (page 827).

John Keats   (1795–1821)*

ODE ON A GRECIAN URN   1820

Thou still unravished bride of quietness,
    Thou foster-child of silence and slow time,
Sylvan historian, who canst thus express
    A flowery tale more sweetly than our rhyme:
What leaf-fringed legend haunts about thy shape   5
    Of deities or mortals, or of both,
        In Tempe or the dales of Arcady?
    What men or gods are these? What maidens loth?
What mad pursuit? What struggle to escape?
        What pipes and timbrels? What wild ecstasy?   10

Heard melodies are sweet, but those unheard
 Are sweeter; therefore, ye soft pipes, play on;
Not to the sensual° ear, but, more endeared,   *physical*
 Pipe to the spirit ditties of no tone:
Fair youth, beneath the trees, thou canst not leave   15
  Thy song, nor ever can those trees be bare;
   Bold Lover, never, never canst thou kiss,
Though winning near the goal—yet, do not grieve;
  She cannot fade, though thou hast not thy bliss,
   For ever wilt thou love, and she be fair!   20

Ah, happy, happy boughs! that cannot shed
 Your leaves, nor ever bid the Spring adieu;
And, happy melodist, unwearièd,
 For ever piping songs for ever new;
More happy love! more happy, happy love!   25
  For ever warm and still to be enjoyed,
   For ever panting, and for ever young;
All breathing human passion far above,
  That leaves a heart high-sorrowful and cloyed,
   A burning forehead, and a parching tongue.   30

Who are these coming to the sacrifice?
 To what green altar, O mysterious priest,
Lead'st thou that heifer lowing at the skies,
 And all her silken flanks with garlands drest?
What little town by river or sea shore,   35
 Or mountain-built with peaceful citadel,
  Is emptied of this folk, this pious morn?
And, little town, the streets for evermore
 Will silent be; and not a soul to tell
  Why thou art desolate, can e'er return.   40

O Attic shape! Fair attitude! with brede°   *design*
 Of marble men and maidens overwrought,
With forest branches and the trodden weed;
 Thou, silent form, dost tease us out of thought
As doth Eternity: Cold Pastoral!   45
  When old age shall this generation waste,
   Thou shalt remain, in midst of other woe
  Than ours, a friend to man, to whom thou say'st,
Beauty is truth, truth beauty,—that is all
  Ye know on earth, and all ye need to know.   50

ODE ON A GRECIAN URN. *7 Tempe, dales of Arcady:* valleys in Greece. *41 Attic:* Athenian, possessing a classical simplicity and grace. *49–50:* if Keats had put the urn's words in quotation marks,
critics might have been spared much ink. Does the urn say just "beauty is truth, truth beauty," or does
its statement take in the whole of the last two lines?

COMPARE

"Ode on a Grecian Urn" with "Musée des Beaux Arts" by W. H. Auden (page 1037) and "Long-legged Fly" by William Butler Yeats (page 1162).

John Keats (1795–1821)*

ON FIRST LOOKING INTO CHAPMAN'S HOMER

1816

Much have I traveled in the realms of gold,
　And many goodly states and kingdoms seen;
　Round many western islands have I been
Which bards in fealty to Apollo hold.
Oft of one wide expanse had I been told   5
　That deep-browed Homer ruled as his demesne°,   *domain*
　Yet did I never breathe its pure serene
Till I heard Chapman speak out loud and bold.
Then felt I like some watcher of the skies
　When a new planet swims into his ken;   10
Or like stout Cortez when with eagle eyes
　He stared at the Pacific—and all his men
Looked at each other with a wild surmise—
　Silent, upon a peak in Darien.

ON FIRST LOOKING INTO CHAPMAN'S HOMER. When one evening in October 1816 Keats's friend and former teacher Cowden Clarke introduced the young poet to George Chapman's vigorous Elizabethan translations of the *Iliad* and the *Odyssey*, Keats stayed up all night reading and discussing them in high excitement; then went home at dawn to compose this sonnet, which Clarke received at his breakfast table. 4 *fealty:* in feudalism, the loyalty of a vassal to his lord; *Apollo:* classical god of poetic inspiration. 11 *stout Cortez:* the best-known boner in English poetry. (What Spanish explorer *was* the first European to view the Pacific?) 14 *Darien:* old name for the Isthmus of Panama.

COMPARE

"On First Looking into Chapman's Homer" with "The Master" by Frederick Morgan (page 1108) and "To the Stone-cutters" by Robinson Jeffers (page 1088).

John Keats

John Keats   (1795–1821)*

WHEN I HAVE FEARS THAT I MAY CEASE TO BE   (1818)

When I have fears that I may cease to be
   Before my pen has gleaned my teeming brain,
Before high-pilèd books, in charact'ry°,   *written language*
   Hold like rich garners° the full-ripened grain;   *storehouses*
When I behold, upon the night's starred face,   5
   Huge cloudy symbols of a high romance,
And think that I may never live to trace
   Their shadows with the magic hand of chance;
And when I feel, fair creature of an hour,
   That I shall never look upon thee more,   10
Never have relish in the fairy° power   *supernatural*
   Of unreflecting love—then on the shore
Of the wide world I stand alone, and think
   Till love and fame to nothingness do sink.

WHEN I HAVE FEARS THAT I MAY CEASE TO BE.   12 *unreflecting*: thoughtless and spontaneous, rather than deliberate.

COMPARE

"When I have fears that I may cease to be" with any of the three translations of Horace's *Carpe Diem* ode (pages 970–971) or Philip Larkin's "Aubade" (page 962).

John Keats   (1795–1821)*

TO AUTUMN   1820

I

Season of mists and mellow fruitfulness,
   Close bosom-friend of the maturing sun;

Conspiring with him how to load and bless
　　With fruit the vines that round the thatch-eaves run;
To bend with apples the mossed cottage-trees,
　　And fill all fruit with ripeness to the core;
　　　To swell the gourd, and plump the hazel shells
With a sweet kernel; to set budding more,
And still more, later flowers for the bees,
　　Until they think warm days will never cease,
　　　For Summer has o'er-brimmed their clammy cells.

II

Who hath not seen thee oft amid thy store?
　　Sometimes whoever seeks abroad may find
Thee sitting careless on a granary floor,
　　Thy hair soft-lifted by the winnowing wind;
Or on a half-reaped furrow sound asleep,
　　Drowsed with the fume of poppies, while thy hook°   sickle
　　　Spares the next swath and all its twinèd flowers:
And sometimes like a gleaner thou dost keep
　　Steady thy laden head across a brook;
　　Or by a cider-press, with patient look,
　　　Thou watchest the last oozings hours by hours.

III

Where are the songs of Spring? Ay, where are they?
　　Think not of them, thou hast thy music too,—
While barrèd clouds bloom the soft-dying day,
　　And touch the stubble-plains with rosy hue;
Then in a wailful choir the small gnats mourn
　　Among the river sallows°, borne aloft   willows
　　　Or sinking as the light wind lives or dies;
And full-grown lambs loud bleat from hilly bourn;
Hedge-crickets sing; and now with treble soft
The red-breast whistles from a garden-croft°   garden plot
　　And gathering swallows twitter in the skies.

5

10

15

20

25

30

ODE TO AUTUMN   12 *thee:* Autumn personified. 15 *Thy hair . . . winnowing wind:* Autumn's hair is a
billowing cloud of straw. In winnowing, whole blades of grain were laid on a granary floor and beaten
with wooden flails, then the beaten mass was tossed in a blanket until the yellow straw (or *chaff*)
drifted away on the air, leaving kernels of grain. 30 *bourn:* perhaps meaning a brook. In current English, the word is a cousin of burn, as in the first line of Gerard Manley Hopkins's "Inversnaid"; but in
archaic English, which Keats sometimes liked, a *bourn* can also be a boundary, or a destination. What
possible meaning makes most sense to you?

COMPARE

"To Autumn" with "In the Elegy Season" by Richard Wilbur (page 706).

Philip Larkin

Philip Larkin (1922–1985)*

HOME IS SO SAD   1964

Home is so sad. It stays as it was left,
Shaped to the comfort of the last to go
As if to win them back. Instead, bereft
Of anyone to please, it withers so,
Having no heart to put aside the theft   5

And turn again to what it started as,
A joyous shot at how things ought to be,
Long fallen wide. You can see how it was:
Look at the pictures and the cutlery.
The music in the piano stool. That vase.   10

COMPARE

"Home is so Sad" with "Dark house, by which once more I stand" by Alfred, Lord Tennyson (page 1142) and "Piano" by D. H. Lawrence (page 656).

Philip Larkin (1922–1985)*

POETRY OF DEPARTURES   1955

Sometimes you hear, fifth-hand,
As epitaph:
*He chucked up everything
And just cleared off,*

And always the voice will sound
Certain you approve
This audacious, purifying,
Elemental move.

And they are right, I think.
We all hate home
And having to be there:
I detest my room,
Its specially-chosen junk,
The good books, the good bed,
And my life, in perfect order:
So to hear it said

He walked out on the whole crowd
Leaves me flushed and stirred,
Like *Then she undid her dress*
Or *Take that you bastard;*
Surely I can, if he did?
And that helps me stay
Sober and industrious.
But I'd go today,

Yes, swagger the nut-strewn roads,
Crouch in the fo'c'sle
Stubbly with goodness, if
It weren't so artificial,
Such a deliberate step backwards
To create an object:
Books; china; a life
Reprehensibly perfect.

COMPARE

"Poetry of Departures" with "I started Early – Took my Dog" by Emily Dickinson (page 1016).

Irving Layton   (b. 1912)

THE BULL CALF   1959

The thing could barely stand. Yet taken
from his mother and the barn smells
he still impressed with his pride,
with the promise of sovereignty in the way
his head moved to take us in.
The fierce sunlight tugging the maize from the ground

licked at his shapely flanks.
He was too young for all that pride.
I thought of the deposed Richard II.

"No money in bull calves," Freeman had said.   10
The visiting clergyman rubbed the nostrils
now snuffing pathetically at the windless day.
"A pity," he sighed.
My gaze slipped off his hat toward the empty sky
that circled over the black knot of men,   15
over us and the calf waiting for the first blow.

Struck,
the bull calf drew in his thin forelegs
as if gathering strength for a mad rush . . .
tottered . . . raised his darkening eyes to us,   20
and I saw we were at the far end
of his frightened look, growing smaller and smaller
till we were only the ponderous mallet
that flicked his bleeding ear
and pushed him over on his side, stiffly,   25
like a block of wood.

Below the hill's crest
the river snuffled on the improvised beach.
We dug a deep pit and threw the dead calf into it.
It made a wet sound, a sepulchral gurgle,   30
as the warm sides bulged and flattened.
Settled, the bull calf lay as if asleep,
one foreleg over the other,
bereft of pride and so beautiful now,
without movement, perfectly still in the cool pit,   35
I turned away and wept.

COMPARE:

"The Bull Calf" with "Names of Horses" by Donald Hall (page 1069).

Philip Levine   (b. 1928)

ANIMALS ARE PASSING FROM OUR LIVES   1968

It's wonderful how I jog
on four honed-down ivory toes
my massive buttocks slipping
like oiled parts with each light step.

I'm to market. I can smell   5
the sour, grooved block, I can smell
the blade that opens the hole
and the pudgy white fingers

that shake out the intestines
like a hankie. In my dreams   10
the snouts drool on the marble,
suffering children, suffering flies,

suffering the consumers
who won't meet their steady eyes
for fear they could see. The boy   15
who drives me along believes

that any moment I'll fall
on my side and drum my toes
like a typewriter or squeal
and shit like a new housewife   20

discovering television,
or that I'll turn like a beast
cleverly to hook his teeth
with my teeth. No. Not this pig.

COMPARE

"Animals Are Passing from Our Lives" with "Butcher Shop" by Charles Simic (page 1131).

Stephen Shu-ning Liu   (b. 1930)

My Father's Martial Art   1982

When he came home Mother said he looked
like a monk and stank of green fungus.
At the fireside he told us about life
at the monastery: his rock pillow,
his cold bath, his steel-bar lifting   5
and his wood-chopping. He didn't see
a woman for three winters, on Mountain O Mei.

"My Master was both light and heavy.
He skipped over treetops like a squirrel.
Once he stood on a chair, one foot tied   10
to a rope. We four pulled; we couldn't
move him a bit. His kicks could split
a cedar's trunk."

I saw Father break into a pumpkin
with his fingers. I saw him drop a hawk
with bamboo arrows. He rose before dawn, filled
our backyard with a harsh sound *hah, hah, hah:*
there was his Black Dragon Sweep, his Crane Stand,
his Mantis Walk, his Tiger Leap, his Cobra Coil . . .
Infrequently he taught me tricks and made me
fight the best of all the village boys.

From a busy street I brood over high cliffs
on O Mei, where my father and his Master sit:
shadows spread across their faces as the smog
between us deepens into a funeral pyre.

But don't retreat into night, my father.
Come down from the cliffs. Come
with a single Black Dragon Sweep and hush
this oncoming traffic with your *hah, hah, hah.*

COMPARE

"My Father's Martial Art" with "Those Winter Sundays" by Robert Hayden (page 1074) and "Red Rooster, Yellow Sky" by Amy Uyematsu (page 1148).

Robert Lowell   (1917–1977)

SKUNK HOUR   1959

For Elizabeth Bishop

Nautilus Island's hermit
heiress still lives through winters in her Spartan cottage;
her sheep still graze above the sea.
Her son's a bishop. Her farmer
is first selectman in our village;
she's in her dotage.

Thirsting for
the hierarchic privacy
of Queen Victoria's century,
she buys up all
the eyesores facing her shore,
and lets them fall.

The season's ill—
we've lost our summer millionaire,
who seemed to leap from an L. L. Bean

catalogue. His nine-knot yawl
was auctioned off to lobstermen.
A red fox stain covers Blue Hill.

And now our fairy
decorator brightens his shop for fall;   20
his fishnet's filled with orange cork,
orange, his cobbler's bench and awl;
there is no money in his work,
he'd rather marry.

One dark night,   25
my Tudor Ford climbed the hill's skull;
I watched for love-cars. Lights turned down,
they lay together, hull to hull,
where the graveyard shelves on the town. . . .
My mind's not right.   30

A car radio bleats,
"Love, O careless Love . . . ." I hear
my ill-spirit sob in each blood cell,
as if my hand were at its throat. . . .
I myself am hell;   35
nobody's here—

only skunks, that search
in the moonlight for a bite to eat.
They march on their soles up Main Street:
white stripes, moonstruck eyes' red fire   40
under the chalk-dry and spar spire
of the Trinitarian Church.

I stand on top
of our back steps and breathe the rich air—
a mother skunk with her column of kittens swills the garbage pail.   45
She jabs her wedge-head in a cup
of sour cream, drops her ostrich tail,
and will not scare.

COMPARE

"Skunk Hour" with "Desert Places" by Robert Frost (page 823).

Archibald MacLeish   (1892–1982)

THE END OF THE WORLD   1926

Quite unexpectedly as Vasserot
The armless ambidextrian was lighting
A match between his great and second toe,

And Ralph the lion was engaged in biting
The neck of Madame Sossman while the drum   5
Pointed, and Teeny was about to cough
In waltz-time swinging Jocko by the thumb—
Quite unexpectedly the top blew off:

And there, there overhead, there, there hung over
Those thousands of white faces, those dazed eyes,   10
There in the starless dark the poise, the hover,
There with vast wings across the canceled skies,
There in the sudden blackness the black pall
Of nothing, nothing, nothing—nothing at all.

COMPARE

"The End of the World" with "Fire and Ice" by Robert Frost (page 735) and "The Second Coming" by William Butler Yeats (page 925).

Andrew Marvell   (1621–1678)

To His Coy Mistress   1681

Had we but world enough and time,
This coyness°, lady, were no crime.   *modesty, reluctance*
We would sit down and think which way
To walk, and pass our long love's day.
Thou by the Indian Ganges' side   5
Should'st rubies find; I by the tide
Of Humber would complain°. I would   *sing sad songs*
Love you ten years before the Flood,
And you should, if you please, refuse
Till the conversion of the Jews.   10
My vegetable° love should grow   *vegetative, flourishing*
Vaster than empires, and more slow.
An hundred years should go to praise
Thine eyes, and on thy forehead gaze,
Two hundred to adore each breast,   15
But thirty thousand to the rest.
An age at least to every part,
And the last age should show your heart.
For, lady, you deserve this state°,   *pomp, ceremony*
Nor would I love at lower rate.   20
    But at my back I always hear
Time's wingèd chariot hurrying near,
And yonder all before us lie
Deserts of vast eternity.
Thy beauty shall no more be found,   25

Nor in thy marble vault shall sound
My echoing song; then worms shall try
That long preserved virginity,
And your quaint honor turn to dust,
And into ashes all my lust.   30
The grave's a fine and private place,
But none, I think, do there embrace.
    Now therefore, while the youthful hue
Sits on thy skin like morning glew°   *glow*
And while thy willing soul transpires   35
At every pore with instant° fires,   *eager*
Now let us sport us while we may;
And now, like amorous birds of prey,
Rather at once our time devour
Than languish in his slow-chapped° power.   *slow-jawed* 40
Let us roll all our strength and all
Our sweetness up into one ball
And tear our pleasures with rough strife
Thorough° the iron gates of life.   *through*
Thus, though we cannot make our sun   45
Stand still, yet we will make him run.

To His Coy Mistress. 7 *Humber:* a river that flows by Marvell's town of Hull (on the side of the world opposite from the Ganges). 10 *conversion of the Jews:* an event that, according to St. John the Divine, is to take place just before the end of the world. 35 *transpires:* exudes, as a membrane lets fluid or vapor pass through it.

COMPARE

"To His Coy Mistress" with "To the Virgins, to Make Much of Time" by Robert Herrick (page 1081).

James Merrill (1926–1995)

CHARLES ON FIRE   1966

Another evening we sprawled about discussing
Appearances. And it was the consensus
That while uncommon physical good looks
Continued to launch one, as before, in life
(Among its vaporous eddies and false calms),   5
Still, as one of us said into his beard,
"Without your intellectual and spiritual
Values, man, you are sunk." No one but squared
The shoulders of his own unloveliness.
Long-suffering Charles, having cooked and served the meal,   10

Now brought out little tumblers finely etched
He filled with amber liquor and then passed.
"Say," said the same young man, "in Paris, France,
They do it this way"—bounding to his feet
And touching a lit match to our host's full glass.   15
A blue flame, gentle, beautiful, came, went
Above the surface. In a hush that fell
We heard the vessel crack. The contents drained
As who should step down from a crystal coach.
Steward of spirits, Charles's glistening hand   20
All at once gloved itself in eeriness.
The moment passed. He made two quick sweeps and
Was flesh again. "It couldn't matter less,"
He said, but with a shocked, unconscious glance
Into the mirror. Finding nothing changed,   25
He filled a fresh glass and sank down among us.

COMPARE

"Charles on Fire" with "Recuerdo" by Edna St. Vincent Millay (page 1104).

Charlotte Mew   (1869–1928)

THE FARMER'S BRIDE   1916

Three Summers since I chose a maid,
Too young maybe—but more's to do
At harvest-time than bide and woo.
    When us was wed she turned afraid
Of love and me and all things human;   5
Like the shut of a winter's day.
Her smile went out, and 'twasn't a woman—
    More like a little frightened fay°.   *elf*
        One night, in the Fall, she runned away.

"Out 'mong the sheep, her be," they said,   10
'Should properly have been abed;
But sure enough she wasn't there
Lying awake with her wide brown stare.
So over seven-care field and up-along across the down
    We chased her, flying like a hare   15
Before our lanterns. To Church-Town
    All in a shiver and a scare
We caught her, fetched her home at last
    And turned the key upon her, fast.

She does the work about the house   20
As well as most, but like a mouse:
    Happy enough to chat and play
    With birds and rabbits and such as they,
    So long as men-folk keep away.
"Not near, not near!" her eyes beseech   25
When one of us comes within reach.
    The women say that beasts in stall
    Look round like children at her call.
    I've hardly heard her speak at all.

Shy as a leveret°, swift as he,   hare   30
Straight and slight as a young larch tree,
Sweet as the first wild violets, she,
To her wild self. But what to me?

The short days shorten and the oaks are brown,
    The blue smoke rises to the low gray sky,   35
One leaf in the still air falls slowly down,
    A magpie's spotted feathers lie
On the black earth spread white with rime°,   frost
The berries redden up to Christmas-time.
    What's Christmas-time without there be   40
    Some other in the house than we!

    She sleeps up in the attic there
    Alone, poor maid. 'Tis but a stair
Betwixt us. Oh! my God! the down,
    The soft young down of her, the brown,   45
The brown of her—her eyes, her hair, her hair!

COMPARE

"The Farmer's Bride" with "Cinderella" by Anne Sexton (page 934).

Edna St. Vincent Millay (1892–1950)*

RECUERDO   1920

We were very tired, we were very merry—
We had gone back and forth all night on the ferry.
It was bare and bright, and smelled like a stable—
But we looked into a fire, we leaned across a table,
We lay on a hill-top underneath the moon;   5
And the whistles kept blowing, and the dawn came soon.

We were very tired, we were very merry—
We had gone back and forth all night on the ferry;
And you ate an apple, and I ate a pear,
From a dozen of each we had bought somewhere;   10
And the sky went wan, and the wind came cold,
And the sun rose dripping, a bucketful of gold.

We were very tired, we were very merry,
We had gone back and forth all night on the ferry.
We hailed, "Good morrow, mother!" to a shawl-covered head,   15
And bought a morning paper, which neither of us read;
And she wept, "God bless you!" for the apples and pears,
And we gave her all our money but our subway fares.

RECUERDO. The Spanish title means "a recollection" or "a memory."

COMPARE

"Recuerdo" with "A Blessing" by James Wright (page 1158).

John Milton   (1608–1674)*

METHOUGHT I SAW MY LATE   (1658?)
ESPOUSÈD SAINT

Methought I saw my late espousèd saint
  Brought to me like Alcestis from the grave,
  Whom Jove's great son to her glad husband gave,
  Rescued from Death by force, though pale and faint.
Mine, as whom washed from spot of child-bed taint   5
  Purification in the Old Law did save,
  And such, as yet once more I trust to have
  Full sight of her in heaven without restraint,
Came vested all in white, pure as her mind.
  Her face was veiled; yet to my fancied sight   10
  Love, sweetness, goodness, in her person shined
So clear as in no face with more delight.
  But O, as to embrace me she inclined,
  I waked, she fled, and day brought back my night.

METHOUGHT I SAW MY LATE ESPOUSÈD SAINT. Often titled "On His Dead Wife," this sonnet probably commemorates Milton's second wife, Katherine Woodcock. Since Milton had been blind for several years before they married, it is very likely that he never saw her face—a situation that adds special poignancy to the dream the poem describes.   1 *saint:* since his late wife is now in heaven, she is a saint. 2 *Alcestis:* in Greek legend, Hercules, the son of Jove, brings Alcestis back from the underworld to be reunited with her husband. 6 *Purification in the Old Law:* the Old Testament commands certain rituals to purify women after childbirth.

COMPARE

"Methought I saw my late espousèd saint" with "Funeral Blues" by W. H. Auden (page 801), "Annabel Lee" by Edgar Allan Poe (page 1005), or "On My First Daughter" by Ben Jonson (page 1089).

John Milton   (1608–1674)*

WHEN I CONSIDER HOW MY LIGHT IS SPENT   (1655?)

When I consider how my light is spent,
  Ere half my days in this dark world and wide,
  And that one talent which is death to hide
Lodged with me useless, though my soul more bent
To serve therewith my Maker, and present   5
  My true account, lest He returning chide;
  "Doth God exact day-labor, light denied?"
I fondly° ask. But Patience, to prevent   *foolishly*
That murmur, soon replies, "God doth not need
  Either man's work or His own gifts. Who best   10
  Bear His mild yoke, they serve Him best. His state
Is kingly: thousands at His bidding speed,
  And post o'er land and ocean without rest;
  They also serve who only stand and wait."

WHEN I CONSIDER HOW MY LIGHT IS SPENT.   *1 my light is spent:* Milton had become blind. *3 that one talent:* For Jesus's parable of the talents (measures of money), see Matthew 25:14–30.

COMPARE

"When I consider how my light is spent" with "Thou art indeed just, Lord, if I contend" by Gerard Manley Hopkins (page 1083).

Marianne Moore

Marianne Moore   (1887–1972)*

THE MIND IS AN ENCHANTING THING   1944

is an enchanted thing
   like the glaze on a

katydid-wing
>subdivided by sun
>>till the nettings are legion.
Like Gieseking playing Scarlatti;

like the apteryx-awl
>as a beak, or the
kiwi's rain-shawl
>>of haired feathers, the mind
>>feeling its way as though blind,
walks along with its eyes on the ground.

It has memory's ear
>that can hear without
having to hear.
>>Like the gyroscope's fall,
>>truly unequivocal
because trued by regnant certainty,

it is a power of
>strong enchantment. It
is like the dove-
>>neck animated by
>>sun; it is memory's eye;
it's conscientious inconsistency.

It tears off the veil; tears
>the temptation, the
mist the heart wears,
>>from its eyes,—if the heart
>>has a face; it takes apart
dejection. It's fire in the dove-neck's

iridescence; in the
>inconsistencies
of Scarlatti.
>>Unconfusion submits
>>its confusion to proof; it's
not a Herod's oath that cannot change.

5

10

15

20

25

30

35

THE MIND IS AN ENCHANTING THING. 6 *Gieseking . . . Scarlatti:* Walter Gieseking (1895–1956), German pianist, was a celebrated performer of the difficult sonatas of Italian composer Domenico Scarlatti (1685–1757). 7 *apteryx-awl:* awl-shaped beak of the apteryx, one of the kiwi family. (An awl is a pointed tool for piercing wood or leather.) 36 *Herod's oath:* probably King Herod's order condemning to death all infants in Bethlehem (Matthew 2:1–16). In one medieval English version of the Herod story, a pageant play, the king causes the death of his own child by refusing to withdraw his command. This allusion may also refer to Herod's oath to give Salome anything she wanted. When she asked for the head of John the Baptist on a platter, Herod reluctantly granted her gruesome wish. (See Matthew 14:5–12.)

COMPARE

"The Mind is an Enchanting Thing" with "On First Looking into Chapman's Homer" by
John Keats (page 1092).

Frederick Morgan (b. 1922)

THE MASTER   1982

When Han Kan was summoned
to the imperial capital
it was suggested he sit at the feet of
the illustrious senior court painter
to learn from him the refinements of the art.   5

"No, thank you," he replied,
"I shall apprentice myself to the stables."

And he installed himself and his brushes amid the dung and the flies,
and studied the horses—their bodies' keen alertness—
eye-sparkle of one, another's sensitive stance,   10
the way a third moved graceful in his bulk—
and painted at last the emperor's favorite,
the charger named "Nightshining White,"

whose likeness after centuries still dazzles.

COMPARE

"The Master" with "To Li Po" by Shirley Geok-lin Lim (page 959).

Howard Nemerov (1920–1991)

THE WAR IN THE AIR   1987

For a saving grace, we didn't see our dead,
Who rarely bothered coming home to die
But simply stayed away out there
In the clean war, the war in the air.

Seldom the ghosts came back bearing their tales   5
Of hitting the earth, the incompressible sea,
But stayed up there in the relative wind,
Shades fading in the mind,

Who had no graves but only epitaphs
Where never so many spoke for never so few: 10
Per ardua, said the partisans of Mars,
Per aspera, to the stars.

That was the good war, the war we won
As if there were no death, for goodness' sake,
With the help of the losers we left out there   15
In the air, in the empty air.

COMPARE

"The War in the Air" with "The Death of the Ball Turret Gunner" by Randall Jarrell
(page 1086) and "The Fury of Aerial Bombardment" by Richard Eberhart (page 717).

Lorine Niedecker

Lorine Niedecker   (1903–1970)*

SORROW MOVES IN WIDE WAVES   (ABOUT 1950)

Sorrow moves in wide waves,
   it passes, lets us be.
It uses us, we use it,
   it's blind while we see.

Consciousness is illimitable,   5
   too good to forsake
tho what we feel be misery
   and we know will break.

Old Mother turns blue and from us,
   "Don't let my head drop to the earth.
I'm blind and deaf." Death from the heart,   10
   a thimble in her purse.

"It's a long day since last night.
   Give me space. I need
floors. Wash the floors, Lorine!   15
   Wash clothes! Weed!"

COMPARE

"Sorrow Moves in Wide Waves" with "Grief" by Elizabeth Barrett Browning (page 1046).

Naomi Shihab Nye (b. 1952)

FAMOUS   1982

The river is famous to the fish.

The loud voice is famous to silence,
which knew it would inherit the earth
before anybody said so.

The cat sleeping on the fence is famous to the birds   5
watching him from the birdhouse.

The tear is famous, briefly, to the cheek.

The idea you carry close to your bosom
is famous to your bosom.

The boot is famous to the earth,   10
more famous than the dress shoe,
which is famous only to floors.

The bent photograph is famous to the one who carries it
and not at all famous to the one who is pictured.

I want to be famous to shuffling men   15
who smile while crossing streets,
sticky children in grocery lines,
famous as the one who smiled back.

I want to be famous in the way a pulley is famous,
or a buttonhole, not because it did anything spectacular,   20
but because it never forgot what it could do.

COMPARE

"Famous" with "I Shall Paint My Nails Red" by Carole Satyamurti (page 898).

Sharon Olds   (b. 1942)*

THE ONE GIRL AT THE BOYS' PARTY   1983

When I take my girl to the swimming party
I set her down among the boys. They tower and
bristle, she stands there smooth and sleek,
her math scores unfolding in the air around her.
They will strip to their suits, her body hard and   5
indivisible as a prime number,
they'll plunge in the deep end, she'll subtract
her height from ten feet, divide it into
hundreds of gallons of water, the numbers
bouncing in her mind like molecules of chlorine   10
in the bright blue pool. When they climb out,
her ponytail will hang its pencil lead
down her back, her narrow silk suit
with hamburgers and french fries printed on it
will glisten in the brilliant air, and they will   15
see her sweet face, solemn and
sealed, a factor of one, and she will
see their eyes, two each,
their legs, two each, and the curves of their sexes,
one each, and in her head she'll be doing her   20
wild multiplying, as the drops
sparkle and fall to the power of a thousand from her body.

COMPARE

"The One Girl at the Boys' Party" with "My Papa's Waltz" by Theodore Roethke (page 668).

Wilfred Owen   (1893–1918)*

ANTHEM FOR DOOMED YOUTH   (1917?)

What passing-bells for these who die as cattle?
    Only the monstrous anger of the guns.
    Only the stuttering rifles' rapid rattle
Can patter out their hasty orisons.

No mockeries now for them; no prayers nor bells,   5
    Nor any voice of mourning save the choirs,—
The shrill, demented choirs of wailing shells;
    And bugles calling for them from sad shires°.   *counties*

What candles may be held to speed them all?
    Not in the hands of boys, but in their eyes   10
    Shall shine the holy glimmers of good-byes.
The pallor of girls' brows shall be their pall;
Their flowers the tenderness of patient minds,
And each slow dusk a drawing-down of blinds.

COMPARE

"Anthem for Doomed Youth" with "Facing It" by Yusef Komunyakaa (page 955).

Linda Pastan

Linda Pastan   (b. 1932)*

ETHICS   1980

In ethics class so many years ago
our teacher asked this question every fall:
if there were a fire in a museum
which would you save, a Rembrandt painting
or an old woman who hadn't many   5
years left anyhow? Restless on hard chairs
caring little for pictures or old age
we'd opt one year for life, the next for art
and always half-heartedly. Sometimes
the woman borrowed my grandmother's face   10
leaving her usual kitchen to wander
some drafty, half imagined museum.
One year, feeling clever, I replied
why not let the woman decide herself?
Linda, the teacher would report, eschews   15

the burdens of responsibility.
This fall in a real museum I stand
before a real Rembrandt, old woman,
or nearly so, myself. The colors
within this frame are darker than autumn,   20
darker even than winter—the browns of earth,
though earth's most radiant elements burn
through the canvas. I know now that woman
and painting and season are almost one
and all beyond saving by children.   25

COMPARE

"Ethics" with "Welcome to Hiroshima" by Mary Jo Salter (page 1127).

Robert Phillips   (b. 1938)

RUNNING ON EMPTY   1981

As a teenager I would drive Father's
Chevrolet cross-county, given me

reluctantly: "Always keep the tank
half full, boy, half full, ya hear?"

The fuel gauge dipping, dipping   5
toward Empty, hitting Empty, then

—thrilling!—'way below Empty,
myself driving cross-county

mile after mile, faster and faster,
all night long, this crazy kid driving   10

the earth's rolling surface,
against all laws, defying chemistry,

rules, and time, riding on nothing
but fumes, pushing luck harder

than anyone pushed before, the wind   15
screaming past like the Furies . . .

I stranded myself only once, a white
night with no gas station open, ninety miles

from nowhere. Panicked for a while,
at standstill, myself stalled.   20

At dawn the car and I both refilled. But,
Father, I am running on empty still.

RUNNING ON EMPTY.   16 *Furies:* In Greek mythology, deities who pursue and torment evildoers.

"Running on Empty" with "Those Winter Sundays" by Robert Hayden (page 1074) and "My Papa's Waltz" by Theodore Roethke (page 668).

Sylvia Plath

Sylvia Plath   (1932–1963)*

DADDY   1965

You do not do, you do not do
Any more, black shoe
In which I have lived like a foot
For thirty years, poor and white,
Barely daring to breathe or Achoo.   5

Daddy, I have had to kill you.
You died before I had time—
Marble-heavy, a bag full of God,
Ghastly statue with one grey toe
Big as a Frisco seal   10

And a head in the freakish Atlantic
Where it pours bean green over blue
In the waters off beautiful Nauset.
I used to pray to recover you.
Ach, du.   15

In the German tongue, in the Polish town
Scraped flat by the roller
Of wars, wars, wars.
But the name of the town is common.
My Polack friend   20

Says there are a dozen or two.
So I never could tell where you
Put your foot, your root,

I never could talk to you.
The tongue stuck in my jaw.   25

It stuck in a barb wire snare.
Ich, ich, ich, ich,
I could hardly speak.
I thought every German was you.
And the language obscene   30

An engine, an engine
Chuffing me off like a Jew.
A Jew to Dachau, Auschwitz, Belsen.
I began to talk like a Jew.
I think I may well be a Jew.   35

The snows of the Tyrol, the clear beer of Vienna
Are not very pure or true.
With my gypsy ancestress and my weird luck
And my Taroc pack and my Taroc pack
I may be a bit of a Jew.   40

I have always been scared of *you*,
With your Luftwaffe, your gobbledygoo.
And your neat moustache
And your Aryan eye, bright blue.
Panzer-man, panzer-man, O You—   45

Not God but a swastika
So black no sky could squeak through.
Every woman adores a Fascist,
The boot in the face, the brute
Brute heart of a brute like you.   50

You stand at the blackboard, daddy,
In the picture I have of you,
A cleft in your chin instead of your foot
But no less a devil for that, no not
Any less the black man who   55

Bit my pretty red heart in two.
I was ten when they buried you.
At twenty I tried to die
And get back, back, back to you.
I thought even the bones would do.   60

But they pulled me out of the sack,
And they stuck me together with glue.
And then I knew what to do.
I made a model of you,
A man in black with a Meinkampf look   65

And a love of the rack and the screw.
And I said I do, I do.
So daddy, I'm finally through.
The black telephone's off at the root,
The voices just can't worm through. 70

If I've killed one man, I've killed two—
The vampire who said he was you
And drank my blood for a year,
Seven years, if you want to know.
Daddy, you can lie back now. 75

There's a stake in your fat black heart
And the villagers never liked you.
They are dancing and stamping on you.
They always *knew* it was you.
Daddy, daddy, you bastard, I'm through. 80

DADDY. Introducing this poem in a reading, Sylvia Plath remarked:

> The poem is spoken by a girl with an Electra complex. Her father died while she thought
> he was God. Her case is complicated by the fact that her father was also a Nazi and her
> mother very possibly part Jewish. In the daughter the two strains marry and paralyze each
> other—she has to act out the awful little allegory before she is free of it.

(Quoted by A. Alvarez, *Beyond All This Fiddle*, New York, 1971.)

In some details "Daddy" is autobiography: the poet's father, Otto Plath, a German, had come to the
United States from Grabow, Poland. He had died following amputation of a gangrened foot and leg,
when Sylvia was eight years old. Politically, Otto Plath was a Republican, not a Nazi; but was apparently a somewhat domineering head of the household. (See the recollections of the poet's mother,
Aurelia Schober Plath, in her edition of *Letters Home* by Sylvia Plath, New York, 1975.)

15 *Ach, du*: Oh, you. 27 *Ich, ich, ich, ich*: I, I, I, I. 51 *blackboard*: Otto Plath had been a professor of biology at Boston University. 65 *Meinkampf*: Adolf Hitler entitled his autobiography *Mein Kampf* ("My
Struggle").

COMPARE

"Daddy" with "American Primitive" by William Jay Smith (page 1135).

Edgar Allan Poe   (1809–1849)*

TO HELEN   1831

Helen, thy beauty is to me
  Like those Nicean barks of yore,
That gently, o'er a perfumed sea,
  The weary, way-worn wanderer bore
  To his own native shore. 5

On desperate seas long wont to roam,
    Thy hyacinth hair, thy classic face,
Thy Naiad airs have brought me home
    To the glory that was Greece
And the grandeur that was Rome.   10

Lo! in yon brilliant window-niche
    How statue-like I see thee stand!
    The agate lamp within thy hand,
Ah! Psyche, from the regions which
    Are Holy Land!   15

COMPARE

"To Helen" with "Helen" by H. D. (page 1076).

Alexander Pope   (1688–1744)*

A LITTLE LEARNING IS A DANG'ROUS   1711
THING (FROM AN ESSAY ON CRITICISM)

    A *little Learning* is a dang'rous Thing;
Drink deep, or taste not the *Pierian* Spring:
There *shallow Draughts* intoxicate the Brain,
And drinking *largely* sobers us again.
Fir'd at first Sight with what the *Muse* imparts,   5
In *fearless Youth* we tempt the Heights of Arts,
While from the bounded *Level* of our Mind,
Short Views we take, nor see the *Lengths behind*,
But *more advanc'd*, behold with strange Surprize
New, distant Scenes of *endless* Science rise!   10
So pleas'd at first, the towring *Alps* we try,
Mount o'er the Vales, and seem to tread the Sky;
Th' Eternal Snows appear already past,
And the first *Clouds* and *Mountains* seem the last:
But *those attain'd*, we tremble to survey   15
The growing Labours of the lengthen'd Way,
Th' *increasing* Prospect *tires* our wandring Eyes,
Hills peep o'er Hills, and *Alps* on *Alps* arise!

A LITTLE LEARNING IS A DANG'ROUS THING.   2 *Pierian Spring*: the spring of the Muses.

COMPARE

"A little Learning is a dang'rous Thing" with "The Writer" by Richard Wilbur (page 1152).

Ezra Pound   (1885–1972)*

THE GARRET   1915

Come, let us pity those who are better off than we are.
Come, my friend, and remember
    that the rich have butlers and no friends,
And we have friends and no butlers.
Come, let us pity the married and the unmarried.   5

Dawn enters with little feet
    like a gilded Pavlova,
And I am near my desire.
Nor has life in it aught better
Than this hour of clear coolness,   10
    the hour of waking together.

THE GARRET.   7. *Pavlova:* Anna Pavlova (1885–1931) was a celebrated Russian ballerina.

COMPARE

"The Garret" with "Recuerdo" by Edna St. Vincent Millay (page 1104).

Ezra Pound   (1885–1972)*

THE RIVER-MERCHANT'S WIFE: A LETTER   1915

While my hair was still cut straight across my forehead
I played about the front gate, pulling flowers.
You came by on bamboo stilts, playing horse,
You walked about my seat, playing with blue plums.
And we went on living in the village of Chokan: 5
Two small people, without dislike or suspicion.

At fourteen I married My Lord you.
I never laughed, being bashful.
Lowering my head, I looked at the wall.
Called to, a thousand times, I never looked back.   10

At fifteen I stopped scowling,
I desired my dust to be mingled with yours
Forever and forever and forever.
Why should I climb the lookout?

At sixteen you departed,   15
You went into far Ku-to-yen, by the river of swirling eddies,
And you have been gone five months.
The monkeys make sorrowful noise overhead.

You dragged your feet when you went out.
By the gate now, the moss is grown, the different mosses,   20
Too deep to clear them away!
The leaves fall early this autumn, in wind.
The paired butterflies are already yellow with August
Over the grass in the West garden;
They hurt me. I grow older.   25
If you are coming down through the narrows of the river Kiang,
Please let me know before hand,
And I will come out to meet you
      As far as Cho-fu-sa.

THE RIVER-MERCHANT'S WIFE: A LETTER. A free translation from the Chinese poet Li Po (eighth century).

COMPARE

"The River-Merchant's Wife: a Letter" with "To Li Po" by Shirley Geok-lin Lim (page 959) or "A Valediction: Forbidding Mourning" by John Donne (page 1054).

Wyatt Prunty

Wyatt Prunty   (b. 1947)

THE STARLINGS   1989

Not what they were but how they moved.
As if migration answered their cries,
Though no one call had meaning past
Its echo in another call.
They swept through trees like leaves blown back,   5
Like divinations ushered from before,
So many dividing against one breath . . .
The stillness, bluffed flights, the gliding down.

Above their sweeping fans, a hawk
Circled patiently, but they were thousands.
What he counted never counted him . . .
So many lifting, lighting.
                         And then they were gone.

But what they left they changed, the land
A silent dun without their cries,
Which, briefly, made the way the trees
Unfolded upward to the sky
Seem more than one place, more than one gathering
That in departing raised itself
As if some mute necessity
Had called its children not home but away.

10

15

20

COMPARE

"The Starlings" with Wordsworth's "I Wandered Lonely as a Cloud" (page 676).

Dudley Randall

Dudley Randall   (b. 1914)*

A DIFFERENT IMAGE   1968

The age
requires this task:
create
a different image;
re-animate
the mask.

5

Shatter the icons of slavery and fear.
Replace
the leer
of the minstrel's burnt-cork face
with a proud, serene
and classic bronze of Benin.

10

COMPARE

"A Different Image" with Langston Hughes's "The Negro Speaks of Rivers" on page 1019.

John Crowe Ransom   (1888–1974)

BELLS FOR JOHN WHITESIDE'S DAUGHTER   1924

There was such speed in her little body,
And such lightness in her footfall,
It is no wonder her brown study
Astonishes us all.

Her wars were bruited in our high window.   5
We looked among orchard trees and beyond,
Where she took arms against her shadow,
Or harried unto the pond

The lazy geese, like a snow cloud
Dripping their snow on the green grass,   10
Tricking and stopping, sleepy and proud,
Who cried in goose, Alas,

For the tireless heart within the little
Lady with rod that made them rise
From their noon apple-dreams, and scuttle   15
Goose-fashion under the skies!

But now go the bells, and we are ready;
In one house we are sternly stopped
To say we are vexed at her brown study,
Lying so primly propped.   20

COMPARE

"Bells for John Whiteside's Daughter" with "Elegy for Jane" by Theodore Roethke (page 1126).

Henry Reed   (1914–1986)

NAMING OF PARTS   1946

Today we have naming of parts. Yesterday,
We had daily cleaning. And tomorrow morning,
We shall have what to do after firing. But today,
Today we have naming of parts. Japonica
Glistens like coral in all of the neighboring gardens,   5
          And today we have naming of parts.

This is the lower sling swivel. And this
Is the upper sling swivel, whose use you will see,
When you are given your slings. And this is the piling swivel,
Which in your case you have not got. The branches   10
Hold in the gardens their silent, eloquent gestures,
        Which in our case we have not got.

This is the safety-catch, which is always released
With an easy flick of the thumb. And please do not let me
See anyone using his finger. You can do it quite easy   15
If you have any strength in your thumb. The blossoms
Are fragile and motionless, never letting anyone see
        Any of them using their finger.

And this you can see is the bolt. The purpose of this
Is to open the breech, as you see. We can slide it   20
Rapidly backwards and forwards: we call this
Easing the spring. And rapidly backwards and forwards
The early bees are assaulting and fumbling the flowers:
        They call it easing the Spring.

They call it easing the Spring: it is perfectly easy   25
If you have any strength in your thumb: like the bolt,
And the breech, and the cocking-piece, and the point of balance,
Which in our case we have not got; and the almond-blossom
Silent in all of the gardens and the bees going backwards and forwards,
        For today we have naming of parts.   30

COMPARE

"Naming of Parts" with "The Fury of Aerial Bombardment" by Richard Eberhart (page 717).

Alastair Reid   (b. 1926)*

SPEAKING A FOREIGN LANGUAGE   1963

How clumsy on the tongue, these acquired idioms,
after the innuendos of our own. How far
we are from foreigners, what faith
we rest in one sentence, hoping a smile will follow
on the appropriate face, always wallowing   5
between what we long to say and what we can,
trusting the phrase is suitable to the occasion,
the accent passable, the smile real,
always asking the traveller's fearful question—
what is being lost in translation?   10

Something, to be sure. And yet, to hear
the stumbling of foreign friends, how little we care
for the wreckage of word or tense. How endearing they are,

and how our speech reaches out, like a helping hand,
or limps in sympathy. Easy to understand,   15
through the tangle of language, the heart behind
groping toward us, to make the translation of
syntax into love.

COMPARE

"Speaking a Foreign Language" with "To Li Po" by Shirley Geok-lin Lim (page 959).

Adrienne Rich   (b. 1929)*

PEELING ONIONS   1963

Only to have a grief
equal to all these tears!

There's not a sob in my chest.
Dry-hearted as Peer Gynt
I pare away, no hero,   5
merely a cook.

Crying was labor, once
when I'd good cause.
Walking, I felt my eyes like wounds
raw in my head,   10
so postal-clerks, I thought, must stare.
A dog's look, a cat's, burnt to my brain—
yet all that stayed
stuffed in my lungs like smog.

These old tears in the chopping-bowl.   15

PEELING ONIONS.   4 *Peer Gynt*: Peer Gynt is the title character of Henrik Ibsen's 1867 play. In the
play's last act, Gynt has returned to Norway as an old man. Peeling away the layers of an onion, he
imagines that each one represents a stage of his life. He then discovers there is nothing at the core of
the onion—only separate layers.

COMPARE

"Peeling Onions" with "Tears, Idle Tears" by Alfred, Lord Tennyson (page 736).

Adrienne Rich   (b. 1929)*

POWER   1978

Living   in the earth-deposits   of our history

Today a backhoe divulged   out of a crumbling flank of earth
one bottle   amber   perfect   a hundred-year-old
cure for fever   or melancholy   a tonic
for living on this earth   in the winters of this climate   5

Today I was reading about Marie Curie:
she must have known she suffered   from radiation sickness
her body bombarded for years   by the element
she had purified
It seems she denied to the end   10
the source of the cataracts on her eyes
the cracked and suppurating skin   of her finger-ends
till she could no longer hold   a test-tube or a pencil

She died   a famous woman   denying
her wounds   15
denying
her wounds   came   from the same source as her power

POWER. 6 *Marie Curie:* the Polish scientist (1867–1934) who helped discover polonium and radium. She was the first person to win two Nobel Prizes.

COMPARE

"Power" with "Ethics" by Linda Pastan (page 1112).

Edwin Arlington Robinson

Edwin Arlington Robinson   (1869–1935)*

MINIVER CHEEVY   1910

Miniver Cheevy, child of scorn,
   Grew lean while he assailed the seasons;
He wept that he was ever born,
   And he had reasons.

Miniver loved the days of old   5
    When swords were bright and steeds were prancing;
The vision of a warrior bold
    Would set him dancing.

Miniver sighed for what was not,
    And dreamed, and rested from his labors;   10
He dreamed of Thebes and Camelot,
    And Priam's neighbors.

Miniver mourned the ripe renown
    That made so many a name so fragrant;
He mourned Romance, now on the town,   15
    And Art, a vagrant.

Miniver loved the Medici,
    Albeit he had never seen one;
He would have sinned incessantly
    Could he have been one.   20

Miniver cursed the commonplace
    And eyed a khaki suit with loathing;
He missed the medieval grace
    Of iron clothing.

Miniver scorned the gold he sought,   25
    But sore annoyed was he without it;
Miniver thought, and thought, and thought,
    And thought about it.

Miniver Cheevy, born too late,
    Scratched his head and kept on thinking;   30
Miniver coughed, and called it fate,
    And kept on drinking.

MINIVER CHEEVY. 11 *Thebes*: a city in ancient Greece and the setting of many famous Greek myths; *Camelot*: the legendary site of King Arthur's Court. 12 *Priam*: the last king of Troy, his "neighbors" would have included Helen of Troy, Aeneas, and other famous figures. 17 *the Medici*: the ruling family of Florence during the high Renaissance, the Medici were renowned patrons of the arts.

COMPARE

"Miniver Cheevy" with "Ulysses" by Alfred, Lord Tennyson (page 1143).

Theodore Roethke   (1908–1963)*

ELEGY FOR JANE   1953

My Student, Thrown by a Horse

I remember the neckcurls, limp and damp as tendrils;
And her quick look, a sidelong pickerel smile;
And how, once startled into talk, the light syllables leaped for her,
And she balanced in the delight of her thought,
A wren, happy, tail into the wind,   5
Her song trembling the twigs and small branches.
The shade sang with her;
The leaves, their whispers turned to kissing;
And the mold sang in the bleached valleys under the rose.

Oh, when she was sad, she cast herself down into such a pure depth,   10
Even a father could not find her:
Scraping her cheek against straw;
Stirring the clearest water.

My sparrow, you are not here,
Waiting like a fern, making a spiny shadow.   15
The sides of wet stones cannot console me,
Nor the moss, wound with the last light.

If only I could nudge you from this sleep,
My maimed darling, my skittery pigeon.
Over this damp grave I speak the words of my love: 20
I, with no rights in this matter,
Neither father nor lover.

COMPARE

"Elegy for Jane" with "Bells for John Whiteside's Daughter" by John Crowe Ransom (page 1121).

Mary Jo Salter   (b. 1954)

WELCOME TO HIROSHIMA   1984

is what you first see, stepping off the train:
a billboard brought to you in living English
by Toshiba Electric. While a channel
silent in the TV of the brain

projects those flickering re-runs of a cloud   5
that brims its risen columnful like beer
and, spilling over, hangs its foamy head,
you feel a thirst for history: what year

it started to be safe to breathe the air,
and when to drink the blood and scum afloat   10
on the Ohta River. But no, the water's clear,
they pour it for your morning cup of tea

in one of the countless sunny coffee shops
whose plastic dioramas advertise
mutations of cuisine behind the glass: 15
a pancake sandwich; a pizza someone tops

with a maraschino cherry. Passing by
the Peace Park's floral hypocenter (where
how bravely, or with what mistaken cheer,
humanity erased its own erasure),   20

you enter the memorial museum
and through more glass are served, as on a dish
of blistered grass, three mannequins. Like gloves
a mother clips to coatsleeves, strings of flesh

hang from their fingertips; or as if tied   25
to recall a duty for us, *Reverence*
the dead whose mourners too shall soon be dead,
but all commemoration's swallowed up

in questions of bad taste, how re-created
horror mocks the grim original, 30
and thinking at last *They should have left it all*
you stop. This is the wristwatch of a child.

Jammed on the moment's impact, resolute
to communicate some message, although mute,
it gestures with its hands at eight-fifteen 35
and eight-fifteen and eight-fifteen again

while tables of statistics on the wall
update the news by calling on a roll
of tape, death gummed on death, and in the case
adjacent, an exhibit under glass 40

is glass itself: a shard the bomb slammed in
a woman's arm at eight-fifteen, but some
three decades on—as if to make it plain
hope's only as renewable as pain,

and as if all the unsung 45
debasements of the past may one day come
rising to the surface once again—
worked its filthy way out like a tongue.

COMPARE

"Welcome to Hiroshima" with "Ethics" by Linda Pastan (page 1112) and "Ballad of Birmingham" by Dudley Randall (page 798).

William Shakespeare

William Shakespeare   (1564–1616)*

NOT MARBLE NOR THE GILDED MONUMENTS   1609

Not marble, nor the gilded monuments
Of princes, shall outlive this powerful rhyme;
But you shall shine more bright in these contents
Than unswept stone, besmeared with sluttish time.

William Shakespeare   (1564–1616)*

WHEN ICICLES HANG BY THE WALL   1598

When icicles hang by the wall,
   And Dick the shepherd blows his nail,
And Tom bears logs into the hall,
   And milk comes frozen home in pail,
When blood is nipped and ways° be foul,   *roads*   5
   Then nightly sings the staring owl:
        "Tu-whit, to-who!"
        A merry note,
While greasy Joan doth keel° the pot.   *cool (as by skimming or stirring)*

When all aloud the wind doth blow,   10
   And coughing drowns the parson's saw°,   *old saw, platitude*
And birds sit brooding in the snow,
   And Marian's nose looks red and raw,
When roasted crabs° hiss in the bowl,   *crab apples*
   Then nightly sings the staring owl: 15
        "Tu-whit, to-who!"
        A merry note,
While greasy Joan doth keel the pot.

COMPARE

"When icicles hang by the wall" with "Winter News" by John Haines (page 747).

Charles Simic   (b. 1938)

BUTCHER SHOP   1971

Sometimes walking late at night
I stop before a closed butcher shop.
There is a single light in the store
Like the light in which the convict digs his tunnel.

An apron hangs on the hook: 5
The blood on it smeared into a map
Of the great continents of blood,
The great rivers and oceans of blood.

There are knives that glitter like altars
In a dark church   10
Where they bring the cripple and the imbecile
To be healed.

There's a wooden block where bones are broken,
Scraped clean—a river dried to its bed
Where I am fed,   15
Where deep in the night I hear a voice.

COMPARE

"Butcher Shop" with "Animals Are Passing from Our Lives" by Philip Levine (page 1097).

David R. Slavitt   (b. 1935)

TITANIC   1983

Who does not love the *Titanic*?
If they sold passage tomorrow for that same crossing,
who would not buy?

To go down . . . We all go down, mostly
alone. But with crowds of people, friends, servants,   5
well fed, with music, with lights! Ah!

And the world, shocked, mourns, as it ought to do
and almost never does. There will be the books and movies
to remind our grandchildren who we were
and how we died, and give them a good cry.   10

Not so bad, after all. The cold
water is anaesthetic and very quick.
The cries on all sides must be a comfort.

We all go: only a few, first-class.

COMPARE

"Titanic" with "The Convergence of the Twain" by Thomas Hardy (page 1070).

Christopher Smart   (1722–1771)

FOR I WILL CONSIDER MY CAT JEOFFRY   (1759–1763)

For I will consider my Cat Jeoffry.
For he is the servant of the Living God, duly and daily serving him.
For at the first glance of the glory of God in the East he worships in his
    way.
For is this done by wreathing his body seven times round with elegant
    quickness.
For then he leaps up to catch the musk°, which is the   catnip
    blessing of God upon his prayer.   5
For he rolls upon prank to work it in.
For having done duty and received blessing he begins to consider
    himself.

For this he performs in ten degrees.

For first he looks upon his fore-paws to see if they are clean.

For secondly he kicks up behind to clear away there.   10

For thirdly he works it upon stretch° with   *he works his muscles, stretching*
    the fore-paws extended.

For fourthly he sharpens his paws by wood.

For fifthly he washes himself.

For sixthly he rolls upon wash.

For seventhly he fleas himself, that he may not be interrupted

    upon the beat.°   *his patrol*   15

For eighthly he rubs himself against a post.

For ninthly he looks up for his instructions.

For tenthly he goes in quest of food.

For having considered God and himself he will consider his neighbor.

For if he meets another cat he will kiss her in kindness.   20

For when he takes his prey he plays with it to give it a chance.

For one mouse in seven escapes by his dallying.

For when his day's work is done his business more properly begins.

For he keeps the Lord's watch in the night against the Adversary.

For he counteracts the powers of darkness by his electrical skin

    and glaring eyes.   25

For he counteracts the Devil, who is death, by brisking about the life.

For in his morning orisons he loves the sun and the sun loves him.

For he is of the tribe of Tiger.

For the Cherub Cat is a term of the Angel Tiger.

For he has the subtlety and hissing of a serpent, which in goodness he

    suppresses.   30

For he will not do destruction if he is well-fed, neither will he spit

    without provocation.

For he purrs in thankfulness when God tells him he's a good Cat.

For he is an instrument for the children to learn benevolence upon.

For every house is incomplete without him, and a blessing is lacking in

    the spirit.

For the Lord commanded Moses concerning the cats at the departure of the

    Children of Israel from Egypt.   35

For every family had one cat at least in the bag.

For the English cats are the best in Europe.

For he is the cleanest in the use of his fore-paws of any quadruped.

For the dexterity of his defense is an instance of the love of God to him

    exceedingly.

For he is the quickest to his mark of any creature.   40

For he is tenacious of his point.

For he is a mixture of gravity and waggery.
For he knows that God is his Savior.
For there is nothing sweeter than his peace when at rest.
For there is nothing brisker than his life when in motion.   45
For he is of the Lord's poor, and so indeed is he called by benevolence
    perpetually—Poor Jeoffry! poor Jeoffry! the rat has bit thy throat.
For I bless the name of the Lord Jesus that Jeoffry is better.
For the divine spirit comes about his body to sustain it in complete cat.
For his tongue is exceeding pure so that it has in purity what it wants
    in music.
For he is docile and can learn certain things.   50
For he can sit up with gravity which is patience upon approbation.
For he can fetch and carry, which is patience in employment.
For he can jump over a stick which is patience upon proof positive.
For he can spraggle upon waggle at the word of command.
For he can jump from an eminence into his master's bosom.   55
For he can catch the cork and toss it again.
For he is hated by the hypocrite and miser.
For the former is afraid of detection.
For the latter refuses the charge.
For he camels his back to bear the first notion of business.   60
For he is good to think on, if a man would express himself neatly.
For he made a great figure in Egypt for his signal services.
For he killed the Icneumon-rat, very pernicious by land.
For his ears are so acute that they sting again.
For from this proceeds the passing quickness of his attention.   65
For by stroking of him I have found out electricity.
For I perceived God's light about him both wax and fire.
For the electrical fire is the spiritual substance which God sends from
    heaven to sustain the bodies both of man and beast.
For God has blessed him in the variety of his movements.
For, though he cannot fly, he is an excellent clamberer.   70
For his motions upon the face of the earth are more than any other
    quadruped.
For he can tread to all the measures upon the music.
For he can swim for life.
For he can creep.

For I will consider my Cat Jeoffry. This is a self-contained extract from Smart's long poem *Lord commanded Moses concerning the cats*: No such command is mentioned in Scripture.   54 *spraggle upon waggle*: W. F. Stead, in his edition of Smart's poem, suggests that this means Jeoffry will sprawl when his master waggles a finger or a stick. 59 *the charge*: perhaps the cost of feeding a cat.

COMPARE

"For I will consider my Cat Jeoffry" with "The Lamb" and "The Tyger" by William Blake (page 1040).

William Jay Smith (b. 1918)

AMERICAN PRIMITIVE   1953

Look at him there in his stovepipe hat,
His high-top shoes, and his handsome collar;
Only my Daddy could look like that,
And I love my Daddy like he loves his Dollar.

The screen door bangs, and it sounds so funny—   5
There he is in a shower of gold;
His pockets are stuffed with folding money,
His lips are blue, and his hands feel cold.

He hangs in the hall by his black cravat,
The ladies faint, and the children holler: 10
Only my Daddy could look like that,
And I love my Daddy like he loves his Dollar.

COMPARE

"American Primitive" with "Daddy" by Sylvia Plath (page 1114).

W. D. Snodgrass (b. 1926)

DISPOSAL   1970

The unworn long gown, meant for dances
She would have scarcely dared attend,
Is fobbed off on a friend—
Who can't help wondering if it's spoiled
But thinks, well, she can take her chances.   5

We roll her spoons up like old plans
Or failed securities, seal their case,
Then lay them back. One lace
Nightthing lies in the chest, unsoiled
By wear, untouched by human hands.   10

We don't dare burn those canceled patterns
And markdowns that she actually wore,
Yet who do we know so poor
They'd take them? Spared all need, all passion,
Saved from loss, she lies boxed in satins.   15

Like a pair of party shoes
That seemed to never find a taker;
We send back to its maker
A life somehow gone out of fashion
But still too good to use.   20

COMPARE

"Disposal" with "Eleanor Rigby" by John Lennon and Paul McCartney (page 802).

Cathy Song

Cathy Song   (b. 1955)

STAMP COLLECTING   1988

The poorest countries
have the prettiest stamps
as if impracticality were a major export
shipped with the bananas, t-shirts, and coconuts.
Take Tonga, where the tourists,   5
expecting a dramatic waterfall replete with birdcalls,
are taken to see the island's peculiar mystery:
hanging bats with collapsible wings
like black umbrellas swing upside down from fruit trees.
The Tongan stamp is a fruit.   10

The banana stamp is scalloped like a butter-varnished seashell.
The pineapple resembles a volcano, a spout of green on top,
and the papaya, a tarnished goat skull.

They look impressive,
these stamps of countries without a thing to sell   15
except for what is scraped, uprooted and hulled
from their mule-scratched hills.
They believe in postcards,
in portraits of progress: the new dam;
a team of young native doctors   20
wearing stethoscopes like exotic ornaments;
the recently constructed "Facultad de Medicina,"
a building as lack-lustre as an American motel.

The stamps of others are predictable.
Lucky is the country that possesses indigenous beauty.   25
Say a tiger or a queen.
The Japanese can display to the world
their blossoms: a spray of pink on green.
Like pollen, they drift, airborne.
But pity the country that is bleak and stark.   30

Beauty and whimsey are discouraged as indiscreet.
Unbreakable as their climate, a monument of ice,
they issue serious statements, commemorating
factories, tramways and aeroplanes;
athletes marbled into statues.   35
They turn their noses upon the world, these countries,
and offer this: an unrelenting procession
of a grim, historic profile.

COMPARE

"Stamp Collecting" with Derek Walcott's "The Virgins" on page 1149.

William Stafford   (1914–1993)*

AT THE KLAMATH BERRY FESTIVAL   1966

The war chief danced the old way—
the eagle wing he held before his mouth—
and when he turned the boom-boom
stopped. He took two steps. A sociologist
was there; the Scout troop danced.   5
I envied him the places where he had not been.

The boom began again. Outside he heard
the stick game, and the Blackfoot gamblers
arguing at poker under lanterns.
Still-moccasined and bashful, holding   10
the eagle wing before his mouth,
listening and listening, he danced after others stopped.

He took two steps, the boom caught up,
the mountains rose, the still deep river
slid but never broke its quiet.   15
I looked back when I left:
he took two steps, he took two steps,
past the sociologist.

AT THE KLAMATH BERRY FESTIVAL. The Klamath Indians have a reservation at the base of the Cascade Range in southern Oregon.

COMPARE

"At the Klamath Berry Festival" with "Last Words of the Prophet" from the Navajo Mountain Chant (page 1031) and "Hands" by Robinson Jeffers (page 783).

Wallace Stevens

Wallace Stevens   (1879–1955)*

PETER QUINCE AT THE CLAVIER   1923

I

Just as my fingers on these keys
Make music, so the selfsame sounds
On my spirit make a music, too.

Music is feeling, then, not sound;
And thus it is that what I feel,
Here in this room, desiring you,

Thinking of your blue-shadowed silk,
Is music. It is like the strain
Waked in the elders by Susanna.

Of a green evening, clear and warm,
She bathed in her still garden, while
The red-eyed elders watching, felt

The basses of their beings throb
In witching chords, and their thin blood
Pulse pizzicati of Hosanna.

II

In the green water, clear and warm,
Susanna lay.
She searched
The touch of springs,

And found
Concealed imaginings.
She sighed,
For so much melody.

Upon the bank, she stood
In the cool
Of spent emotions.
She felt, among the leaves,
The dew
Of old devotions.

She walked upon the grass,
Still quavering.
The winds were like her maids,
On timid feet,
Fetching her woven scarves,
Yet wavering.

A breath upon her hand
Muted the night.
She turned—
A cymbal crashed,
And roaring horns.

III

Soon, with a noise like tambourines,
Came her attendant Byzantines.
They wondered why Susanna cried
Against the elders by her side;

And as they whispered, the refrain   45
Was like a willow swept by rain.

Anon, their lamps' uplifted flame
Revealed Susanna and her shame.

And then, the simpering Byzantines
Fled, with a noise like tambourines.   50

IV

Beauty is momentary in the mind—
The fitful tracing of a portal;
But in the flesh it is immortal.

The body dies; the body's beauty lives.
So evenings die, in their green going,   55
A wave, interminably flowing.
So gardens die, their meek breath scenting
The cowl of winter, done repenting.
So maidens die, to the auroral
Celebration of a maiden's choral.   60

Susanna's music touched the bawdy strings
Of those white elders; but, escaping,
Left only Death's ironic scraping.
Now, in its immortality, it plays
On the clear viol of her memory,   65
And makes a constant sacrament of praise.

PETER QUINCE AT THE CLAVIER. In Shakespeare's *Midsummer Night's Dream*, Peter Quince is a clownish carpenter who stages a mock-tragic play. In The Book of Susanna in the Apocrypha, two lustful elders who covet Susanna, a virtuous married woman, hide in her garden, spy on her as she bathes, then threaten to make false accusations against her unless she submits to them. When she refuses, they cry out, and her servants come running. All ends well when the prophet Daniel cross-examines the elders and proves them liars.   15 *pizzicati:* thin notes made by plucking a stringed instrument.   42 *Byzantines:* Susanna's maidservants.

COMPARE

"Peter Quince at the Clavier" with "Ode on a Grecian Urn" by John Keats (page 1090) or "Sailing to Byzantium" by William Butler Yeats (page 991).

Wallace Stevens   (1879–1955)*

THE EMPEROR OF ICE-CREAM   1923

Call the roller of big cigars,
The muscular one, and bid him whip
In kitchen cups concupiscent curds.
Let the wenches dawdle in such dress
As they are used to wear, and let the boys   5
Bring flowers in last month's newspapers.
Let be be finale of seem.
The only emperor is the emperor of ice-cream.

Take from the dresser of deal,
Lacking the three glass knobs, that sheet   10
On which she embroidered fantails once
And spread it so as to cover her face.
If her horny feet protrude, they come
To show how cold she is, and dumb.
Let the lamp affix its beam.   15
The only emperor is the emperor of ice-cream.

THE EMPEROR OF ICE-CREAM.   9 *deal:* fir or pine wood used to make cheap furniture.

COMPARE

"The Emperor of Ice-Cream" with "This living hand, now warm and capable" by John Keats (page 856) and "A Slumber Did My Spirit Seal" by William Wordsworth (page 812).

Ruth Stone   (b. 1915)

SECOND HAND COAT   1982

I feel
in her pockets; she wore nice cotton gloves,
kept a handkerchief box, washed her undies,
ate at the Holiday Inn, had a basement freezer,
belonged to a bridge club.   5
I think when I wake in the morning
that I have turned into her.
She hangs in the hall downstairs,
a shadow with pulled threads.
I slip her over my arms, skin of a matron.   10

Where are you? I say to myself, to the orphaned body,
and her coat says,
Get your purse, have you got your keys?

COMPARE

"Second Hand Coat" with "Home is so Sad" by Philip Larkin (page 1095).

Jonathan Swift   (1667–1745)

A DESCRIPTION OF THE MORNING   1711

Now hardly here and there an hackney-coach°,   *horse-drawn cab*
Appearing, showed the ruddy morn's approach.
Now Betty from her master's bed had flown
And softly stole to discompose her own.
The slipshod 'prentice from his master's door   5
Had pared the dirt, and sprinkled round the floor.
Now Moll had whirled her mop with dextrous airs,
Prepared to scrub the entry and the stairs.
The youth with broomy stumps began to trace
The kennel°-edge, where wheels had worn the place.   *gutter* 10
The small-coal man was heard with cadence deep
Till drowned in shriller notes of chimneysweep,
Duns° at his lordship's gate began to meet,   *bill-collectors*
And Brickdust Moll had screamed through half the street.
The turnkey° now his flock returning sees,   *jailkeeper* 15
Duly let out a-nights to steal for fees;
The watchful bailiffs° take their silent stands;   *constables*
And schoolboys lag with satchels in their hands.

A DESCRIPTION OF THE MORNING.   9 *youth with broomy stumps:* a young man sweeping the gutter's
edge with worn-out brooms, looking for old nails fallen from wagonwheels, which were valuable. 14
Brickdust Moll: woman selling brickdust to be used for scouring.

COMPARE

"A Description of the Morning" with "London" by William Blake (page 729).

Alfred, Lord Tennyson   (1809–1892)*

DARK HOUSE, BY WHICH ONCE   1850
MORE I STAND

Dark house, by which once more I stand
   Here in the long unlovely street,
   Doors, where my heart was used to beat
So quickly, waiting for a hand,

A hand that can be clasped no more— 5
   Behold me, for I cannot sleep,
   And like a guilty thing I creep
At earliest morning to the door.

He is not here; but far away
   The noise of life begins again, 10
   And ghastly through the drizzling rain
On the bald street breaks the blank day.

DARK HOUSE. This poem is one part of the series *In Memoriam,* an elegy for Tennyson's friend Arthur
Henry Hallam.

COMPARE

"Dark house, by which once more I stand" with "The piercing chill I feel" by Taniguchi
Buson (page 741) and "Home is so Sad" by Philip Larkin (page 1095).

Alfred, Lord Tennyson

Alfred, Lord Tennyson   (1809–1892)*

ULYSSES   (1833)

It little profits that an idle king,
By this still hearth, among these barren crags,
Matched with an agèd wife, I mete and dole
Unequal laws unto a savage race
That hoard, and sleep, and feed, and know not me. 5
I cannot rest from travel; I will drink
Life to the lees. All times I have enjoyed
Greatly, have suffered greatly, both with those
That loved me, and alone; on shore, and when
Through scudding drifts the rainy Hyades 10
Vexed the dim sea. I am become a name;

For always roaming with a hungry heart
Much have I seen and known—cities of men
And manners, climates, councils, governments,
Myself not least, but honored of them all— 15
And drunk delight of battle with my peers,
Far on the ringing plains of windy Troy.
I am a part of all that I have met;
Yet all experience is an arch wherethrough
Gleams that untraveled world whose margin fades 20
Forever and forever when I move.
How dull it is to pause, to make an end,
To rust unburnished, not to shine in use!
As though to breathe were life! Life piled on life
Were all too little, and of one to me 25
Little remains; but every hour is saved
From that eternal silence, something more,
A bringer of new things; and vile it were
For some three suns to store and hoard myself,
And this grey spirit yearning in desire 30
To follow knowledge like a sinking star,
Beyond the utmost bound of human thought.
    This is my son, mine own Telemachus,
To whom I leave the scepter and the isle—
Well-loved of me, discerning to fulfill 35
This labor, by slow prudence to make mild
A rugged people, and through soft degrees
Subdue them to the useful and the good.
Most blameless is he, centered in the sphere
Of common duties, decent not to fail 40
In offices of tenderness, and pay
Meet adoration to my household gods,
When I am gone. He works his work, I mine.
    There lies the port; the vessel puffs her sail;
There gloom the dark, broad seas. My mariners, 45
Souls that have toiled, and wrought, and thought with me—
That ever with a frolic welcome took
The thunder and the sunshine, and opposed
Free hearts, free foreheads—you and I are old;
Old age hath yet his honor and his toil. 50
Death closes all; but something ere the end,
Some work of noble note, may yet be done,
Not unbecoming men that strove with Gods.
The lights begin to twinkle from the rocks;

The long day wanes; the low moon climbs; the deep   55
Moans round with many voices. Come, my friends,
'Tis not too late to seek a newer world.
Push off, and sitting well in order smite
The sounding furrows; for my purpose holds
To sail beyond the sunset, and the baths   60
Of all the western stars, until I die.
It may be that the gulfs will wash us down;
It may be we shall touch the Happy Isles,
And see the great Achilles, whom we knew.
Though much is taken, much abides; and though   65
We are not now that strength which in old days
Moved earth and heaven, that which we are, we are—
One equal temper of heroic hearts,
Made weak by time and fate, but strong in will
To strive, to seek, to find, and not to yield.   70

ULYSSES. 10 *Hyades:* daughters of Atlas, who were transformed into a group of stars. Their rising with the sun was thought to be a sign of rain. 63 *Happy Isles:* Elysium, a paradise believed to be attainable by sailing west.

COMPARE

"Ulysses" with "Sir Patrick Spence" (page 658).

Dylan Thomas   (1914–1953)*

FERN HILL   1946

Now as I was young and easy under the apple boughs
About the lilting house and happy as the grass was green,
          The night above the dingle° starry,   *wooded valley*
              Time let me hail and climb
              Golden in the heydays of his eyes,   5
And honored among wagons I was prince of the apple towns
And once below a time I lordly had the trees and leaves
              Trail with daisies and barley
              Down the rivers of the windfall light.

And as I was green and carefree, famous among the barns   10
About the happy yard and singing as the farm was home,
              In the sun that is young once only,
                  Time let me play and be

Golden in the mercy of his means,
And green and golden I was huntsman and herdsman, the calves   15
Sang to my horn, the foxes on the hills barked clear and cold,
        And the sabbath rang slowly
        In the pebbles of the holy streams.

All the sun long it was running, it was lovely, the hay
Fields high as the house, the tunes from the chimneys, it was air   20
        And playing, lovely and watery
        And fire green as grass.
        And nightly under the simple stars
As I rode to sleep the owls were bearing the farm away,
All the moon long I heard, blessed among stables, the nightjars   25
        Flying with the ricks, and the horses
        Flashing into the dark.

And then to awake, and the farm, like a wanderer white
With the dew, come back, the cock on his shoulder: it was all
        Shining, it was Adam and maiden,   30
        The sky gathered again
        And the sun grew round that very day.
So it must have been after the birth of the simple light
In the first, spinning place, the spellbound horses walking warm
        Out of the whinnying green stable   35
        On to the fields of praise.

And honored among foxes and pheasants by the gay house
Under the new made clouds and happy as the heart was long,
        In the sun born over and over,
            I ran my heedless ways,   40
        My wishes raced through the house high hay
And nothing I cared, at my sky blue trades, that time allows
In all his tuneful turning so few and such morning songs
        Before the children green and golden
        Follow him out of grace,   45

Nothing I cared, in the lamb white days, that time would take me
Up to the swallow thronged loft by the shadow of my hand,
        In the moon that is always rising,
            Nor that riding to sleep
        I should hear him fly with the high fields   50
And wake to the farm forever fled from the childless land.
Oh as I was young and easy in the mercy of his means,
        Time held me green and dying
        Though I sang in my chains like the sea.

COMPARE

"Fern Hill" with "in Just-" by E. E. Cummings (page 896) and "The World Is Too Much with Us" by William Wordsworth (page 923).

John Updike (b. 1932)*

EX-BASKETBALL PLAYER   1958

Pearl Avenue runs past the high-school lot,
Bends with the trolley tracks, and stops, cut off
Before it has a chance to go two blocks,
At Colonel McComsky Plaza. Berth's Garage
Is on the corner facing west, and there,   5
Most days, you'll find Flick Webb, who helps Berth out.

Flick stands tall among the idiot pumps—
Five on a side, the old bubble-head style,
Their rubber elbows hanging loose and low.
One's nostrils are two S's, and his eyes   10
An E and O. And one is squat, without
A head at all—more of a football type.

Once Flick played for the high-school team, the Wizards.
He was good: in fact, the best. In '46
He bucketed three hundred ninety points,   15
A county record still. The ball loved Flick.
I saw him rack up thirty-eight or forty
In one home game. His hands were like wild birds.

He never learned a trade, he just sells gas,
Checks oil, and changes flats. Once in a while,   20
As a gag, he dribbles an inner tube,
But most of us remember anyway.
His hands are fine and nervous on the lug wrench.
It makes no difference to the lug wrench, though.

Off work, he hangs around Mae's luncheonette.   25
Grease-gray and kind of coiled, he plays pinball,
Smokes those thin cigars, nurses lemon phosphates.
Flick seldom says a word to Mae, just nods
Beyond her face toward bright applauding tiers
Of Necco Wafers, Nibs, and Juju Beads.   30

COMPARE

"Ex-Basketball Player" with "The Cadence of Silk" by Garrett Hongo (page 1081) and "To an Athlete Dying Young" by A. E. Housman (page 1085).

Amy Uyematsu   (b. 1956)

RED ROOSTER, YELLOW SKY   1992

The grandmother who never spoke
brought me this card from Japan
drawn in a child's hand:
just rooster, sun, and sky.
Under a red sun   5
the rooster's red body
splits in two uneven parts,
each sturdy black foot
holding its own weight.
It was the year of the rooster   10
when I was still ten,
learning to stand myself upright—
my own sky rising yellow
like new, uncut lemons.

COMPARE

"Red Rooster, Yellow Sky" with "My Father's Martial Art" by Stephen Shu-ning Liu
(page 1098).

Mona Van Duyn   (b. 1921)

EARTH TREMORS FELT IN MISSOURI   1964

The quake last night was nothing personal,
you told me this morning. I think one always wonders,
unless, of course, something is visible: tremors
that take us, private and willy-nilly, are usual.

But the earth said last night that what I feel,   5
you feel; what secretly moves you, moves me.
One small, sensuous catastrophe
makes inklings letters, spelled in a worldly tremble.

The earth, with others on it, turns in its course
as we turn toward each other, less than ourselves, gross,   10
mindless, more than we were. Pebbles, we swell
to planets, nearing the universal roll,
in our conceit even comprehending the sun,
whose bright ordeal leaves cool men woebegone.

COMPARE

"Earth Tremors Felt in Missouri" with "Most Like an Arch This Marriage" by John Ciardi
(page 908).

Derek Walcott

Derek Walcott   (b. 1930)

THE VIRGINS   1976

Down the dead streets of sun-stoned Frederiksted,
the first free port to die for tourism,
strolling at funeral pace, I am reminded
of life not lost to the American dream;
but my small-islander's simplicities   5
can't better our new empire's civilized
exchange of cameras, watches, perfumes, brandies
for the good life, so cheaply underpriced
that only the crime rate is on the rise

in streets blighted with sun, stone arches   10
and plazas blown dry by the hysteria
of rumour. A condominium drowns
in vacancy; its bargains are dusted,
but only a jewelled housefly drones
over the bargains. The roulettes spin   15
rustily to the wind—the vigorous trade
that every morning would begin afresh
by revving up green water round the pierhead
heading for where the banks of silver thresh.

THE VIRGINS. The title of this poem refers to the Virgin Islands, a group of 100 small islands in the
Caribbean.   1 *Frederiksted:* the biggest seaport in St. Croix, the largest of the American Virgin Islands. 2 *free port:* a port city where goods can be bought and sold without paying customs taxes. 5
small-islander's: Walcott was born on St. Lucia, another island in the West Indies. 16 *trade:* trade
winds.

COMPARE

"The Virgins" with "London" by William Blake (page 729).

Edmund Waller   (1606–1687)

GO, LOVELY ROSE   1645

    Go, lovely rose,
Tell her that wastes her time and me
    That now she knows,
When I resemble° her to thee,   *compare*
How sweet and fair she seems to be.   5

    Tell her that's young
And shuns to have her graces spied,
    That hadst thou sprung
In deserts where no men abide,
Thou must have uncommended died.   10

    Small is the worth
Of beauty from the light retired:
    Bid her come forth,
Suffer herself to be desired,
And not blush so to be admired.   15

    Then die, that she
The common fate of all things rare
    May read in thee,
How small a part of time they share
That are so wondrous sweet and fair.   20

COMPARE

"Go, Lovely Rose" with "To the Virgins, to Make Much of Time" by Robert Herrick (page 1081) and "To His Coy Mistress" by Andrew Marvell (page 1101).

Walt Whitman   (1819–1892)*

A Noiseless Patient Spider   (1876)

A noiseless patient spider,
I mark'd where on a little promontory it stood isolated,
Mark'd how to explore the vacant vast surrounding,
It launch'd forth filament, filament, filament, out of itself,
Ever unreeling them, ever tirelessly speeding them.   5
And you O my soul where you stand,
Surrounded, detached, in measureless oceans of space,
Ceaselessly musing, venturing, throwing, seeking the spheres to
　　connect them,
Till the bridge you will need be form'd, till the ductile anchor hold,
Till the gossamer thread you fling catch somewhere, O my soul.   10

COMPARE

"A Noiseless Patient Spider" with "Ulysses" by Alfred, Lord Tennyson (page 1143) or "The Eagle" by Alfred, Lord Tennyson (page 765).

Walt Whitman

Walt Whitman   (1819–1892)*

I Saw in Louisiana a Live-Oak Growing   1867

I saw in Louisiana a live-oak growing,
All alone stood it and the moss hung down from the branches,
Without any companion it grew there uttering joyous leaves of dark
　　green,

And its look, rude, unbending, lusty, made me think of myself,
But I wonder'd how it could utter joyous leaves standing alone there
    without its friend near, for I knew I could not,   5
And I broke off a twig with a certain number of leaves upon it, and
    twined around it a little moss,
And brought it away, and I have placed it in sight in my room,
It is not needed to remind me as of my own dear friends,
(For I believe lately I think of little else than of them,)
Yet it remains to me a curious token, it makes me think of manly love;   10
For all that, and though the live-oak glistens there in Louisiana solitary
    in a wide flat space,
Uttering joyous leaves all its life without a friend a lover near,
I know very well I could not.

COMPARE

"I Saw in Louisiana a Live-Oak Growing" with "A Supermarket in California" by Allen Ginsberg (page 1067).

Richard Wilbur   (b. 1921)*

THE WRITER   1976

In her room at the prow of the house
Where light breaks, and the windows are tossed with linden,
My daughter is writing a story.

I pause in the stairwell, hearing
From her shut door a commotion of typewriter-keys   5
Like a chain hauled over a gunwale.

Young as she is, the stuff
Of her life is a great cargo, and some of it heavy:
I wish her a lucky passage.

But now it is she who pauses,   10
As if to reject my thought and its easy figure.
A stillness greatens, in which

The whole house seems to be thinking,
And then she is at it again with a bunched clamor
Of strokes, and again is silent.   15

I remember the dazed starling
Which was trapped in that very room, two years ago;
How we stole in, lifted a sash

And retreated, not to affright it;
And how for a helpless hour, through the crack of the door,   20
We watched the sleek, wild, dark

And iridescent creature
Batter against the brilliance, drop like a glove
To the hard floor, or the desk-top.

And wait then, humped and bloody,   25
For the wits to try it again; and how our spirits
Rose when, suddenly sure,

It lifted off from a chair-back,
Beating a smooth course for the right window
And clearing the sill of the world.   30

It is always a matter, my darling,
Of life or death, as I had forgotten. I wish
What I wished you before, but harder.

COMPARE

"The Writer" with "Digging" by Seamus Heaney (page 1077).

Miller Williams

Miller Williams (b. 1930)
THINKING ABOUT BILL, DEAD OF AIDS   1989

We did not know the first thing about
how blood surrenders to even the smallest threat
when old allergies turn inside out,

the body rescinding all its normal orders
to all defenders of flesh, betraying the head,   5
pulling its guards back from all its borders.

Thinking of friends afraid to shake your hand,
we think of your hand shaking, your mouth set,
your eyes drained of any reprimand.

Loving, we kissed you, partly to persuade   10
both you and us, seeing what eyes had said,
that we were loving and were not afraid.

If we had had more, we would have given more.
As it was we stood next to your bed,
stopping, though, to set our smiles at the door.   15

Not because we were less sure at the last.
Only because, not knowing anything yet,
we didn't know what look would hurt you least.

COMPARE

"Thinking About Bill, Dead of AIDS" with "To the Memory of Mr. Oldham" by John
Dryden (page 1057).

William Carlos Williams (1883–1963)*

SPRING AND ALL   1923

By the road to the contagious hospital
under the surge of the blue
mottled clouds driven from the
northeast—a cold wind. Beyond, the
waste of broad, muddy fields   5
brown with dried weeds, standing and fallen

patches of standing water
the scattering of tall trees

All along the road the reddish
purplish, forked, upstanding, twiggy   10
stuff of bushes and small trees
with dead, brown leaves under them
leafless vines—

Lifeless in appearance, sluggish
dazed spring approaches—   15

They enter the new world naked,
cold, uncertain of all
save that they enter. All about them
the cold, familiar wind—

Now the grass, tomorrow 20
the stiff curl of wildcarrot leaf
One by one objects are defined—
It quickens: clarity, outline of leaf

But now the stark dignity of
entrance—Still, the profound change 25
has come upon them: rooted, they
grip down and begin to awaken

COMPARE

"Spring and All" with "in Just-" by E. E. Cummings (page 896) and "Root Cellar" by
Theodore Roethke (page 743).

William Carlos Williams

William Carlos Williams   (1883–1963)*

To Waken an Old Lady   1921

Old age is
a flight of small
cheeping birds
skimming
bare trees 5
above a snow glaze.

Gaining and failing
they are buffeted
by a dark wind—
But what?
On harsh weedstalks
the flock has rested,
the snow
is covered with broken
seedhusks
and the wind tempered
by a shrill
piping of plenty.

10

15

COMPARE

"To Waken an Old Lady" with "Castoff Skin" by Ruth Whitman (page 771).

Yvor Winters (1900–1968)

AT THE SAN FRANCISCO AIRPORT   1960

To My Daughter, 1954

This is the terminal: the light
Gives perfect vision, false and hard;
The metal glitters, deep and bright.
Great planes are waiting in the yard—
They are already in the night.

5

And you are here beside me, small,
Contained and fragile, and intent
On things that I but half recall—
Yet going whither you are bent.
I am the past, and that is all.

10

But you and I in part are one:
The frightened brain, the nervous will,
The knowledge of what must be done,
The passion to acquire the skill
To face that which you dare not shun.

15

The rain of matter upon sense
Destroys me momently. The score:
There comes what will come. The expense
Is what one thought, and something more—
One's being and intelligence.

20

This is the terminal, the break.
Beyond this point, on lines of air,
You take the way that you must take;
And I remain in light and stare—   25
In light, and nothing else, awake.

COMPARE

"At the San Francisco Airport" with "Do not go gentle into that good night" by Dylan
Thomas (page 872).

William Wordsworth

William Wordsworth   (1770–1850)*

COMPOSED UPON WESTMINSTER BRIDGE   1807

Earth has not anything to show more fair:
Dull would he be of soul who could pass by
A sight so touching in its majesty:
This City now doth, like a garment, wear
The beauty of the morning; silent, bare,   5
Ships, towers, domes, theatres, and temples lie
Open unto the fields, and to the sky;
All bright and glittering in the smokeless air.
Never did sun more beautifully steep
In his first splendor, valley, rock, or hill;   10
Ne'er saw I, never felt, a calm so deep!
The river glideth at his own sweet will:
Dear God! the very houses seem asleep;
And all that mighty heart is lying still!

COMPARE

"Composed upon Westminster Bridge" with "London" by William Blake (page 729).

James Wright

James Wright (1927–1980)*

A BLESSING   1961

Just off the highway to Rochester, Minnesota,
Twilight bounds softly forth on the grass.
And the eyes of those two Indian ponies
Darken with kindness.
They have come gladly out of the willows   5
To welcome my friend and me.
We step over the barbed wire into the pasture
Where they have been grazing all day, alone.
They ripple tensely, they can hardly contain their happiness
That we have come.   10
They bow shyly as wet swans. They love each other.
There is no loneliness like theirs.
At home once more,
They begin munching the young tufts of spring in the darkness.
I would like to hold the slenderer one in my arms,   15
For she has walked over to me
And nuzzled my left hand.
She is black and white,
Her mane falls wild on her forehead,
And the light breeze moves me to caress her long ear   20
That is delicate as the skin over a girl's wrist.
Suddenly I realize

That if I stepped out of my body I would break
Into blossom.

COMPARE

"A Blessing" with "God's Grandeur" by Gerard Manley Hopkins (page 822).

James Wright   (1927–1980)*
AUTUMN BEGINS IN MARTINS FERRY, OHIO   1963

In the Shreve High football stadium,
I think of Polacks nursing long beers in Tiltonsville,
And gray faces of Negroes in the blast furnace at Benwood,
And the ruptured night watchman of Wheeling Steel,
Dreaming of heroes.   5

All the proud fathers are ashamed to go home.
Their women cluck like starved pullets,
Dying for love.

Therefore,
Their sons grow suicidally beautiful   10
At the beginning of October,
And gallop terribly against each other's bodies.

COMPARE

"Autumn Begins in Martin's Ferry, Ohio" with "First Practice" by Gary Gildner (page 890) and "Ex-Basketball Player" by John Updike (page 1147).

Mary Sidney Wroth   (1587?–1623?)
IN THIS STRANGE LABYRINTH   1621

In this strange labyrinth how shall I turn?
Ways are on all sides while the way I miss:
If to the right hand, there in love I burn;
Let me go forward, therein danger is;
If to the left, suspicion hinders bliss,   5
Let me turn back, shame cries I ought return
Nor faint though crosses with my fortunes kiss.
Stand still is harder, although sure to mourn;
Thus let me take the right, or left hand way;
Go forward, or stand still, or back retire;   10

I must these doubts endure without allay
Or help, but travail find for my best hire;
Yet that which most my troubled sense doth move
Is to leave all, and take the thread of love.

IN THIS STRANGE LABYRINTH. This sonnet comes from Wroth's *Urania* (1621), the first significant sonnet sequence by a woman. Wroth was the niece of Sir Philip Sidney and the countess of Pembroke. The *Labyrinth* of the title was the maze built by Minos to trap the young men and women sacrificed to the Minotaur. King Minos's daughter, Ariadne, saved her beloved Theseus by giving him a skein of thread to guide his way through the Labyrinth. (See the final line of the sonnet.)

COMPARE

"In this strange labyrinth" with "Let me not to the marriage of true minds" by William Shakespeare (page 863).

Sir Thomas Wyatt   (1503?–1542)*

THEY FLEE FROM ME THAT   (ABOUT 1535)
SOMETIME DID ME SEKË

They flee from me that sometime did me sekë
   With naked fotë° stalking in my chamber.   *foot*
I have seen them gentle, tame and mekë
    That now are wild, and do not remember
    That sometime they put themself in danger   5
To take bread at my hand; and now they range
Busily seeking with a continual change.

Thankèd be fortune, it hath been otherwise
   Twenty times better; but once in speciàll,
In thin array, after a pleasant guise,   10
    When her loose gown from her shoulders did fall,
    And she me caught in her armës long and small,
Therëwith all sweetly did me kiss,
And softly said, *Dear heart, how like you this?*

It was no dremë: I lay broadë waking.   15
   But all is turned thorough° my gentleness   *through*
Into a strangë fashion of forsaking;
    And I have leave to go of her goodness,
    And she also to use newfangleness°.   *to seek novelty*
But since that I so kindëly am served   20
I would fain knowë what she hath deserved.

THEY FLEE FROM ME THAT SOMETIME DID ME SEKË. Some latter-day critics have called Sir Thomas Wyatt a careless poet because some of his lines appear faltering and metrically inconsistent; others have thought he knew what he was doing. It is uncertain whether the final *e*'s in English spelling were still pronounced in Wyatt's day as they were in Chaucer's, but if they were, perhaps Wyatt has been unjustly blamed. In this text, spellings have been modernized except in words where the final *e* would make a difference in rhythm. To sense how it matters, try reading the poem aloud leaving out the *e*'s and then putting them in wherever indicated. Sound them like the *a* in *sofa*.   20 *kindëly:* according to my kind (or hers); that is, as befits the nature of man (or woman). Perhaps there is also irony here, and the word means "unkindly."

COMPARE

"They flee from me that sometimes did me sekë" with "When, in disgrace with Fortune and men's eyes" by William Shakespeare (page 1129).

William Butler Yeats

William Butler Yeats   (1865–1939)*

CRAZY JANE TALKS WITH THE BISHOP   1933

I met the Bishop on the road
And much said he and I.
"Those breasts are flat and fallen now,
Those veins must soon be dry;
Live in a heavenly mansion,   5
Not in some foul sty."

"Fair and foul are near of kin,
And fair needs foul," I cried.
"My friends are gone, but that's a truth
Nor° grave nor bed denied,   *neither*   10
Learned in bodily lowliness
And in the heart's pride.

"A woman can be proud and stiff
When on love intent;
But Love has pitched his mansion in   15
The place of excrement;
For nothing can be sole or whole
That has not been rent."

COMPARE

"Crazy Jane Talks with the Bishop" with "The Flea" by John Donne (page 1053) or
"Down, Wanton, Down!" by Robert Graves (page 703).

William Butler Yeats   (1865–1939)*

LONG-LEGGED FLY   1940

That civilization may not sink,
Its great battle lost,
Quiet the dog, tether the pony
To a distant post;
Our master Caesar is in the tent   5
Where the maps are spread,
His eyes fixed upon nothing,
A hand under his head.

Like a long-legged fly upon the stream
His mind moves upon silence.   10

That the topless towers be burnt
And men recall that face,
Move most gently if move you must
In this lonely place.
She thinks, part woman, three parts a child,   15
That nobody looks; her feet
Practice a tinker shuffle
Picked up on the street.

Like a long-legged fly upon the stream
Her mind moves upon silence.   20

That girls at puberty may find
The first Adam in their thought,
Shut the door of the Pope's chapel,
Keep those children out.
There on that scaffolding reclines   25
Michael Angelo.
With no more sound than the mice make
His hand moves to and fro.

Like a long-legged fly upon the stream
His mind moves upon silence.   30

LONG-LEGGED FLY. This "fly" is the fresh-water insect also known as the water strider.   11 *topless*
towers: of Troy, burned by the Greeks. Yeats echoes the description of Helen of Troy (whose ab-
duction started the war) given in Christopher Marlowe's play *The Tragical History of Doctor*
Faustus: "Was this the face that launched a thousand ships, / And burnt the topless towers of
Ilium?" 23 *the Pope's chapel:* Michelangelo had to lie on his back to paint upon the ceiling of the
Sistine Chapel his celebrated frescoes depicting the creation, fall, and final judgment of humankind.

COMPARE

"Long-legged Fly" with "Helen" by H. D. (page 1076).

William Butler Yeats   (1865–1939)*
THE MAGI   1914

Now as at all times I can see in the mind's eye,
In their stiff, painted clothes, the pale unsatisfied ones
Appear and disappear in the blue depth of the sky
With all their ancient faces like rain-beaten stones,
And all their helms of silver hovering side by side,   5
And all their eyes still fixed, hoping to find once more,
Being by Calvary's turbulence unsatisfied,
The uncontrollable mystery on the bestial floor.

COMPARE:

"The Magi" with "Journey of the Magi" by T. S. Eliot (page 1057).

William Butler Yeats   (1865–1939)*
WHEN YOU ARE OLD   1893

When you are old and grey and full of sleep,
And nodding by the fire, take down this book,
And slowly read, and dream of the soft look
Your eyes had once, and of their shadows deep;

How many loved your moments of glad grace,   5
And loved your beauty with love false or true,
But one man loved the pilgrim soul in you,
And loved the sorrows of your changing face;

And bending down beside the glowing bars,
Murmur, a little sadly, how Love fled

10

And paced upon the mountains overhead
And hid his face amid a crowd of stars.

COMPARE

"When You Are Old" with "Not marble nor the gilded monuments" by William Shakespeare (page 1128).

31 Lives of the Poets

Here you will find a brief biographical note for each poet represented in the book by more than one selection. There is also a note for Thomas Gray, author of the long poem "Elegy in a Country Churchyard."

John Ashbery

John Ashbery, born in Rochester, New York, in 1927, was educated at Deerfield Academy, Harvard, and Columbia. In 1960 he became an art critic in Paris for the *New York Herald Tribune*, and from 1966 to 1972 served as executive editor of the magazine *Art News* in New York. His first full collection of poetry, *Some Trees* (1956), was chosen by W. H. Auden for publication in the Yale Series of Younger Poets; his *Self-Portrait in a Convex Mirror* (1976) garnered praise and three leading literary prizes, and sold well for a book of serious poetry. Ashbery has written plays and a novel (with James Schuyler), *A Nest of Ninnies* (1969). He now lives in New York

and teaches part time in the writing program at Brooklyn College. Some critics have speculated that Ashbery's experience as an art critic has tinged his poetry: that he performs in words what an abstract expressionist performs on canvas in oils. His work can annoy readers who expect poems to make clear statements to be taken in only one way; others think him the foremost living American poet and major heir to the tradition of Wallace Stevens—that is, to the art of suggesting rather than depicting, of arranging words primarily for their own sake.

Margaret Atwood

Margaret Atwood, born in Ottawa in 1939, is a staunchly Canadian poet, short story writer, and novelist whose literary reputation has extended well beyond the borders of her native country. She published her first book of poems, *Double Persephone*, in 1962, the same year she was graduated from the University of Toronto. She went on to earn a master's degree at Radcliffe and to study Victorian fantasy at Harvard. She has advanced her country's cultural identity by publishing *Survival* (1972), a book about Canadian literature, and has edited *The Oxford Book of Canadian Verse* (1982). Her fiction and poetry, at once comic and grim, often deal with alienation and the destructive nature of human relationships. Her recent novel *Cat's Eye* (1989), won attention on both sides of the Canadian border. The cream of her poetry has been skimmed in *Selected Poems* (1976) and *Selected Poems II* (1987).

W. H. Auden

Wystan Hugh Auden (1907–1973), born in York, England, as a young man in the 1930s became the acknowledged spokesman for a generation of English poets that included Stephen Spender, C. Day Lewis, Christopher Isherwood, and Louis MacNeice. His early work was characterized by blithe wit, a Marxist outlook, and a knowledge of Freudian psychology; in later life, he professed Christianity and (in his views of poetry) increasing conservatism. In 1939 Auden emigrated to America, and in 1946 became a United States citizen. A prolific editor, anthologist, and translator of poetry, he collaborated on verse plays, travel memoirs, and (with his longtime friend Chester Kallman) librettos for operas, including Igor Stravinsky's *The Rake's Progress* (1951). He wrote influential criticism, notably that collected in *The Dyer's Hand* (1962).

Auden divided his last years among England, Italy, Austria, and New York.

Matsuo Basho

Matsuo Basho (1644–1694) was born in Ueno, about thirty miles southwest of Kyoto, which was then the imperial capital of Japan. Basho's father was a samurai-class farmer with considerable land. Basho began writing poetry in adolescence, and he worked variously as a teacher, a waterworks official, and possibly even as a ninja spy. He eventually shaved his head and became a lay monk. In 1689 he and a friend took a five-month journey across Japan in which they covered 1233 miles by foot. *Narrow Road to the Far North*, his account of that trip (written in both verse and prose), is one of the classics of Japanese literature.

Elizabeth Bishop

Elizabeth Bishop (1911–1979) was born in Worcester, Massachusetts. After her father died (in her first year) and her mother was stricken with mental illness, she lived until age six with her grandmother in a coastal village in Nova Scotia. A sufferer from asthma, she received scant elementary schooling, but she read widely and deeply at home. At sixteen she entered Walnut Hill, a boarding school, and later graduated from Vassar. Her undergraduate poems won her the friendship of the poet Marianne Moore, who persuaded her not to go on to medical school, but instead to write. Fond of travel and flower-filled climates, Bishop lived for nine years in

Key West, Florida, then for fifteen years in Brazil, dividing her time between the mountains and Rio de Janeiro. In 1966 she returned to the United States to teach: first at the University of Washington, then at Harvard from 1969 until 1977, when she retired. Most of her sparely disciplined work is contained in two volumes: *Complete Poems 1927–1979* (1983) and *Collected Prose* (1984). Her sharp-eyed poems, full of vivid images and apt metaphors, have affected the work of other poets, among them her friends Randall Jarrell and Robert Lowell.

Marriage of Heaven and Hell (1790), and *Jerusalem* (1804–20). In these later works, out of his readings in alchemy, the Bible, and the works of Plato and Swedenborg, Blake derived support for his lifelong hatred of scientific rationalism and created his own mythology, complete with devils and deities. A sympathizer with both American and French revolutions, Blake was once accused of sedition, but the charges were dismissed. In his lifetime, Wordsworth and Coleridge were among the few admirers of his short lyrics; his "Prophetic Books" have had to wait until our century for compassionate readers.

William Blake

William Blake (1757–1827), poet, painter, and visionary, was born in the Soho district of London and early in life was apprenticed to an engraver. Becoming a skilled craftsman, he earned his living illustrating books, among them Dante's *Divine Comedy*, Milton's poems, and the Book of Job. A remarkable and original graphic artist whose only formal training came from a few months at the Royal Academy, Blake published his own poems, engraving them in a careful script embellished with hand-colored illustrations and decorations. His wife Catherine Boucher, whom he taught to read and write, shared his visions and helped him do the coloring. *Songs of Innocence* (1789) and *Songs of Experience* (1794), brief lyrics written from a child's point of view, are easy to enjoy; but anyone deeply interested in Blake copes also with the longer, more demanding "Prophetic Books," among them *The Book of Thel* (1789), *The*

Robert Bly

Robert Bly was born on a farm in Madison, Minnesota, in 1926, and continued to live there for most of his life. He was graduated from Harvard, where he began studies in mathematics before deciding to devote his life to poetry. Rather than teaching, Bly has preferred to support himself and his family by giving poetry readings and by translating books and poems from Scandinavian and other languages. In 1958 he launched a poetry magazine, *The Fifties* (later renamed, as decades went by, *The Sixties* and *The Seventies*). In it he spoofed academic critics, urged American poets to open their work to dream and surrealism, and introduced in translation the work of important poets of Europe and Latin America. Bly has vitally influenced the work of James Wright, Donald Hall, and many younger poets. His readings, in which he sometimes chants and dons primitive masks, have drawn throngs. In the 1960s he organized (with David Ray) American Writers Against the Vietnam War, and over the years has championed many causes, usually pacifist and antinuclear. Lately he has been leading retreats for men, trying to help them understand their male natures. In 1990, Bly's *Iron John*, a book on contemporary male identity, became a national best-seller.

Louise Bogan

Louise Bogan (1897–1970) was born in Maine to parents of Irish descent. She spent her early years in several New England mill towns. Although she won a scholarship to Radcliffe, she left college to marry an army officer. Her husband's sudden death in 1920 left her alone with a small daughter. She boldly moved to Manhattan and began a literary career. Publishing her first book, *Body of This Death*, in 1923, Bogan developed an austere but emotional style of formal lyric that she continued to use until her final collection, *The Blue Estuaries*, in 1968. For nearly forty years Bogan reviewed poetry for *The New Yorker*. Underappreciated in their own time, Bogan's quiet poems have steadily risen in critical esteem since her death.

Gwendolyn Brooks

Gwendolyn Brooks, born in 1917 in Topeka, Kansas, moved early in life to Chicago's South Side, whose people she has commemorated in her poetry and in a novel, *Maud Martha* (1953). Recipient of the Pulitzer Prize for poetry in 1950, for *Annie Allen*, Brooks has long been recognized as a leading

voice in modern American letters. She has combined several teaching positions with raising two children. Since 1967, when she took part in a conference for black writers at Fisk University and was impressed with young black poets' views, she has increasingly been an activist, teaching teenage black writers in Chicago and addressing her work especially to black audiences. Instead of continuing to publish with a mainstream New York publishing house, she switched her work to Broadside, a small literary press in Detroit founded by black poet Dudley Randall. Her memoir *Report from Part One* (1972) discusses her altered outlook. In 1985 she was named Consultant in Poetry to the Library of Congress. Her goals in life, she has declared, are "to be clean of heart, clear of mind, and claiming of what is right and just."

Elizabeth Barrett Browning

Elizabeth Barrett (1806–1861) was born in a large country house outside Durham, England. The eldest of twelve children, she was raised in a close, affectionate family ruled by her possessive father. Ill health kept her at home as an adult, but she nonetheless achieved literary fame and corresponded with many famous writers. The day after she met one correspondent, Robert Browning, in 1845, he sent her a declaration of love, which she insisted he withdraw if he ever wanted to visit again. Gradually, however, she fell in love with her devoted visitor, but the affair was conducted in secret, since her father had forbidden his children to marry. In 1846 she and Browning eloped to Italy where the couple lived happily until her death in 1861. When William Wordsworth died in 1850, Mrs. Browning was considered for the office of poet laureate (which eventually went to Tennyson). She was the most highly regarded woman poet of the nineteenth century, and her work was immensely popular with both critics and general readers.

Robert Browning

Robert Browning (1812–1889), born in a suburb of London, was educated mainly in his father's six-thousand-volume library. With *Pauline* (1833), he began to print his poetry. After the death of his wife Elizabeth Barrett Browning, with whom he had lived in Italy, he returned to England to become (Henry James wrote) an "accomplished, saturated, sane, sound man of the London world." There, as he neared sixty, he enjoyed late but loud applause and the adulation of the Browning Society: faithful readers whose local groups met over their teacups to explicate him. Readers have most greatly favored Browning's story-poems in a form he perfected, the dramatic monologue—such as "My Last Duchess" and "Soliloquy of the Spanish Cloister"—in which he brings to life persons from the past (some of them famous), has them speak their inmost thoughts and reveal their characters. His masterpiece, *The Ring and the Book* (1868–69), is a long narrative poem in twelve monologues, based on a seventeenth-century Roman murder trial. Browning also wrote several plays, among them *A Blot in the 'Scutcheon* (1842). Through the praise and emulation of his later admirers

Ezra Pound and T. S. Eliot, Browning has profoundly affected modern poetry. A formal experimenter, he speaks to us in energetic, punchy words—and like many later poets he introduces learning into his poems without apology. More important, Browning is among the great yea-sayers in English poetry: an affirmer and celebrant of life.

Robert Burns

Robert Burns (1759–1796), the preeminent poet of Scotland, was born in a two-room farm cottage in Alloway, a hamlet on the River Doon, the son of a farmer who worked himself to death. For most of his days Burns too struggled to farm poor soil. Though his schooling lasted only three years, he eagerly read Shakespeare and Pope as a boy and let poetry pour from his own pen. Only in 1786, when he felt he needed money to emigrate to Jamaica, did he publish his *Poems, Chiefly in the Scottish Dialect*, depicting Scottish rural life with warm humor, tender compassion, and rugged exuberance. The book scored an immediate hit and Burns remained in Scotland for the rest of his days. After Edinburgh's stylish society, which had lionized him for a time, let him drop, he returned to his plough, married Jean Armour (who earlier had borne him two sets of twins), and continued to farm until 1791, when he retired to the easier life of a tax official. But worn from toil, hardship, and poverty, Burns died at thirty-seven. Among his legacies are songs, such as "Flow Gently, Sweet Afton," "Comin' Through the Rye," and a song still heard in this country each New Year's eve, "Auld Lang

Syne." Like Hugh MacDiarmid, Burns wrote poetry in both standard English and Scots dialect—in the latter whenever, as in "The Jolly Beggars" and "Address to the Unco Guid," he expressed defiantly unconventional views.

Taniguchi Buson

Taniguchi Buson (1716–1783) was born on the outskirts of Osaka. Little is known about his childhood, but as a young man he went to Edo (later called Tokyo) to study both painting and poetry. He soon became a celebrated painter as well as one of the "Three Masters" of the classic haiku. Buson studied Buddhism for many years and might have considered becoming a priest. At forty-five, a prosperous artist, he married Tomo, who was also a poet. He lived a comfortable later life as an artist and teacher.

Thomas Campion

Thomas Campion (1567–1620), Elizabethan courtier, physician, musician, and poet, was the author of several books of solo songs with lute accompaniment, much admired for their masterly unity of words and music. In 1602 Campion wrote a tract, *Observations in the Art of English Poesy*, in which he argued in favor of writing quantitative verse in English, after the example of the ancient Greek and Latin poets. "Rose-cheeked Laura" was apparently written to illustrate his theories. In the same tract, he opposed the writing of any more poetry in rime and traditional English meters—in which, however, he excelled.

Wendy Cope

Wendy Cope was born in Kent, England in 1945. Her father, who was nearly sixty when she was born, was a poetry enthusiast of Victorian sensibilities, who often recited Tennyson and Fitzgerald's *Rubaiyat* to the family. After leaving school, she became a primary school music teacher. Cope claims she "forgot about poetry for more than ten years." Her father's death in 1971, however, triggered a depression that eventually led her to seek psychological help. As she regained her self-esteem, Cope began reading poetry again and soon started writing. She first gained notice for her brilliant parodies of famous poems (which include a retelling of T. S. Eliot's *The Waste Land* in five limericks), but gradually her bittersweet and incisive love poems have become equally prized. Her two collections, *Making Cocoa for Kingsley Amis* (1986) and *Serious Concerns* (1992), have become bestsellers in England.

E. E. Cummings

Edward Estlin Cummings (1894–1962) was born in Cambridge, Massachusetts, the son of a minister. As a young man at Harvard, he studied Greek and Latin. In World War I, while serving as an ambulance driver, he was mistakenly arrested and confined to a French prison—an experience that gave rise to a novel filled with vivid portraits of his fellow prisoners, *The Enormous Room* (1922). Off and on throughout the 1920s, Cummings lived in Paris. In *Eimi* (1933) he scathingly and satirically reported on a trip to the Soviet Union. Although many of his lyric poems revel in typographical experiment, in theme and sentiment they are often more conventional than they appear. Besides poetry Cummings wrote essays, plays including *Him* (1927) and *Santa Claus* (1946), and the ballet *Tom* (1935), and produced substantial work as a painter and a graphic artist. Throughout his career, he upheld simple themes: love is good, pomp is silly, one individual is worth a thousand faceless societies.

J. V. Cunningham

James Vincent Cunningham (1911–1985) was born in Maryland, but spent his early life in Montana. A Shakespeare scholar with a Stanford Ph.D., Cunningham taught English at Brandeis for many years (1953–80) and for eight years served as chairman of the department. A reader of Latin and Greek, he became the modern master of the terse, pithy English verse epigram in the classical manner. All his poems have a similar brevity, firm control, and a cold, hardboiled manner. "Poetry is what looks like poetry, what sounds like poetry," he stated. "It is metrical composition." His relatively slim *Collected Poems and Epigrams* (1971) gathers most of his work in verse; his *Collected Essays* (1976), most of his work in prose, including an earlier study, *Woe and Wonder: The Emotional Effect of Shakespearean Tragedy.* In a late critical work, *Dickinson: Lyric and Legend* (1980), Cunningham took a withering look at the bard of Amherst.

Emily Dickinson

See biographical note on page 1013.

John Donne

John Donne (1572–1631), English poet and divine, wrote his subtle, worldly love lyrics as a young man in the court of Queen Elizabeth I. At the time, he came to be known in London as (wrote his contemporary, Richard Baker) "a great visitor of ladies, a great frequenter of plays, a great writer of conceited verses." The poems of his *Songs and Sonnets* were first circulated in manuscript, for in his lifetime Donne printed little. When in 1601 he married without the consent of his bride's father, he was dismissed from his secretarial post at court. For several years he endured poverty. His longer poems, *The First Anniversary* and *The Second Anniversary* (1611, 1612), suffused with gloom, see the order of the universe shaken by science and doubt. In 1615 Donne—apparently with some reluctance, for he had been raised a Catholic—became a priest of the Anglican church. From 1621 until he died he was dean of St. Paul's Cathedral in London, where he preached sermons known for their eloquence. His "Holy Sonnets" date from later life. Almost forgotten for two centuries, Donne's work has had much influence in our time. H. J. C. Grierson brought out a great scholarly edition of it in 1912; shortly thereafter it was championed by T. S. Eliot.

Rita Dove

Rita Dove was born in Akron, Ohio, in 1952. Her parents put a strong emphasis on education, and Dove began writing plays, stories, and poems at an early age. Chosen as one of the nation's 100 top high school seniors, she visited the White House in 1970 as a Presidential Scholar. She matriculated at Miami University in Oxford, Ohio, before spending a year studying in West Germany and then attending the Iowa Writers' Workshop. *The Yellow House*, her first full-length book of poems, appeared in 1980, and was followed by six books in the next ten years, including *Thomas and Beulah* (1986) which won the Pulitzer Prize. In 1993 Dove became the first African-American to serve as U.S. Poet Laureate. Her verse tragedy, *The Darker Face of the Earth*, premiered in 1996 at the Oregon Shakespeare Festival. Dove is currently a professor at the University of Virginia.

T. S. Eliot

Thomas Stearns Eliot (1888–1965) was born of a New England family who had moved to St. Louis. After study at Harvard, Eliot emigrated to London, became a bank clerk and later an influential editor for the publishing house of Faber. In 1927 he became a British citizen and joined the Church of England. During the fire bombings of London in World War II, he served as an air raid warden. Although Eliot strove to keep his private life private, a recent biographer, Peter Ackroyd in *T. S. Eliot* (1984), throws light upon his troubled early marriage. Early poems such as "The Love Song of J. Alfred Prufrock" (1917) and *The Waste Land* (1922), an allusive and seemingly disconnected complaint about the sterility of contemporary city life, enormously influenced young poets. Eliot was mainly responsible for bringing French Symbolism into English poetry, and as a critic he helped revive interest in John Donne and other Metaphysical poets. In an early essay, "Tradition and the Individual Talent" (1919), he finds a necessary continuity in Western civilization. *Four Quartets*, completed in 1943, was Eliot's last major work of poetry: an attempt to structure a long thematic poem like a work of music. In later years he devoted himself to writing verse plays for the London stage; the best received was *The Cocktail Party* (1950), in which Alec Guinness played a psychiatrist. In 1948 Eliot received the Nobel Prize in literature.

Robert Frost

Robert Frost (1874–1963), though born in San Francisco, came to be popularly known as a spokesman of rural New England. In periods of farming, teaching school, and raising chickens and writing for poultry journals, Frost struggled until his late thirties to support his family and to publish his poems, with little success. Moving to England to write and farm in 1912–15, he had his first book published in London: *A Boy's Will* (1913). Returning to America, he settled in New Hampshire, later teaching for many years (in a casual way) at Amherst College in Massachusetts. Audiences responded warmly to the poet's public readings; he was awarded four Pulitzer Prizes. In his later years the white-haired Frost became a sort of elder statesman and poet laureate of the John F. Kennedy administration: invited to read a poem at President Kennedy's inauguration, and dispatched to Russia as a cultural emissary. Frost is sometimes admired for putting colloquial Yankee speech into poetry—and he did, but more essentially he mastered the art of laying conversational American speech along a metrical line. In a three-volume biography (1966–76), Lawrance Thompson made Frost out to be an overweening egotist who tormented his family, and we are only now coming around again to seeing him as more than that.

Louise Glück

Louise Glück was born in New York City in 1943. She attended Sarah Lawrence College and Columbia University. She has taught writing at a dozen colleges and universities, but since 1984, she has been on the faculty of Williams College in Williamstown, Massachusetts. Although her debut volume, *Firstborn* (1968), was well received, it was Glück's second collection, *The House on Marshland* (1975), that first attracted broad critical attention. Glück's poetry usually strikes an odd but alluring balance between its intimate emotional content and its terse, restrained, imagistic style. She won the National Book Critics Circle Prize for *The Triumph of Achilles* in 1985 and the Pulitzer Prize for *The Wild Iris* in 1992. Her slim but provocative collection of essays, *Proofs & Theories*, appeared in 1994.

Robert Graves

Robert von Ranke Graves (1895–1985), one of the most prolifically talented writers of the twentieth century, was born in Wimbledon, England. His father, Alfred Perceval Graves, was a popular poet. During World War I,

Graves enlisted in the Royal Welsh Fusiliers, a unit that saw ferocious combat. Wounded and mistakenly declared dead, Graves was demobilized with shell-shock. His youthful autobiography, *Goodbye to All That* (1929), ranks as the classic British memoir of the First World War, and its stark accounts of the despair and brutality of trench warfare is still shocking today. Moving to Majorca, Spain, in 1929, Graves wrote a series of best-selling historical novels, most famously *I, Claudius,* and *Claudius the God* (both 1934). He later wrote an influential study of poetic mythology, *The White Goddess* (1948), which claims the matriarchal Moon Goddess as the true source of poetic inspiration. Graves's vast poetic output covers many subjects, but he is best remembered as a love poet, an area in which he has few modern equals.

Thomas Gray

Thomas Gray (1716–1771), author of the most often quoted poem in English, was born in London into a middle-class home (his father was a scrivener, his mother kept a hat shop). He was the only one of twelve children to survive infancy. He attended Eton and later Cambridge University, where he studied for four years but did not take a degree. After a tour of Europe with his schoolmate Horace Walpole (the first Gothic novelist) and a short sojourn with his mother in the village of Stoke Poges, Gray returned to Cambridge to spend the rest of his life in seclusion as a sort of perpetual graduate student. He stayed around the university so long and became so widely learned in architecture, heraldry, botany, Greek, Old Norse, and other matters that in 1768, at fifty-two, he was appointed Regius Professor of History. So retiring was Gray that he first published his "Elegy in a Country Churchyard" anonymously— and only when friends browbeat him into printing it. He seems to have suffered from a constitutional lack of energy. He dreaded being known, and when the post of poet laureate was offered him, he rejected it. A dilettante, Gray considered himself an amateur in whatever he did. Poetry was only one of his interests, but in his "Elegy" and his Pindaric odes "The Bard" and "The Progress of Poesy," he spurred English poetry to break away from neoclassicism and move toward plainer speech, more various forms, infatuation with the colorful, primitive Old English past, and love of nature and countryside. Gray is buried in Stoke Poges, in the churchyard for which we remember him.

Thomas Hardy

Thomas Hardy (1840–1928) was both a major Victorian novelist and a great poet of the twentieth century. After his novel *Jude the Obscure* (1896) was trounced by critics who objected to its dismal morbidity, Hardy, who by then had made a modest fortune from his fiction, switched exclusively to his first love, poetry. Hardy was born in the English county of Dorsetshire ("Wessex" in his fiction and poetry), and as a young man worked as an architect. Determined to be a novelist, he first won success with *Far from the Madding Crowd* (1874), followed by *The Return of the Native* (1878), *The Mayor of Casterbridge* (1886), and his

masterpiece *Tess of the D'Urbervilles* (1891). After the death of his first wife Emma, with whom he appears to have had a rather cold and troubled relationship, Hardy was inspired to write a great spate of love poems in her memory. In old age he wrote a two-volume autobiography and charged his second wife, Florence, to publish it after his death under her own name. In both fiction and poetry, Hardy's view of the universe is somber: God appears to have forgotten us, and happiness usually arrives too late. *The Dynasts* (1903–08), a long epic poem, makes amused gods sneer down on the Napoleonic wars. Many modern poets have credited Hardy with teaching them a good deal, probably about irony and the use of spoken language, among them W. H. Auden, Philip Larkin, Dylan Thomas, and W. D. Snodgrass.

Robert Hayden

Robert Hayden (1913–1980) was born in Detroit, Michigan. He attended Detroit City College (now called Wayne State University) and the University of Michigan where he studied with W. H. Auden. In 1946, he began teaching at Fisk University in pre-Civil Rights era Nashville, where Hayden, an African-American, experienced racial segregation for the first time. Although he lived in Nashville until 1968, he eventually sent his wife and daughter to New York where schools were integrated. In 1941, Hayden became a convert to the Baha'i faith, a universalist religion that emphasizes charity, tolerance, and equality; his poetry reflects the compassionate moral courage of that creed. Hayden edited the influential 1967 anthology, *Kaleidoscope: Poems by American Negro Poets*. In 1976, he was appointed the Consultant in Poetry at the Library of Congress, the first African-American to hold that influential office.

H. D. (Hilda Doolittle)

Hilda Doolittle (1886–1961), daugter of a Moravian mother and a professor of mathematics and astronomy, spent her first eight years in Bethlehem, Pennsylvania. At Bryn Mawr, she failed English and suffered a nervous collapse. By 1911, she had become a confirmed expatriate, living in London. At one time she was engaged to Ezra Pound, who submitted her early poems to Harriet Monroe's magazine *Poetry* and signed them "H. D. Imagiste." In 1913, she married poet and translator Richard Aldington, and in 1916 published *Sea Change*, her first book of poems. During World War I, H. D. went through a marital breakup and a number of misfortunes recalled in her novel *Palimpsest* (1926). Alone and in poor health, she was rescued by Winifred Ellerman, a writer signing herself Bryher, who adopted the poet's daughter by Cecil Gray and befriended H. D. for life. During 1933 and 1934, H. D. was a patient of Sigmund Freud, an experience she recalls in *Tribute to Freud* (1956). After World War II, the poet moved to Switzerland. Her last works of poetry were epic-long: *Trilogy* (1944–46) and the dramatic monologue *Helen in Egypt* (1961). Her earlier poems are available in *Collected Poems 1912–1944* (1983), edited by Louis L. Martz. In 1960, back in the United States for the last time, H. D. was given the American Academy of Arts and Letters Award of Merit for Poetry.

Seamus Heaney

Seamus Heaney, the best-known living Irish poet, was born on a farm in County Derry, Northern Ireland, in 1939. He taught at Queens University, Belfast, before leaving Northern Ireland in 1972 to make his home in Dublin. A guest lecturer at the University of California in Berkeley during the 1971–1972 academic year, he now divides his time between Dublin and America, where he teaches at Harvard. Among his recent books of verse are *Station Island* (1985), *The Haw Lantern* (1987), and *The Spirit Level* (1996). Rich with images of love and loss, Heaney's poetry draws inventively on the history of Ireland and the Irish from ancient times to the violent present. In 1985, he became the first Irish poet since W. B. Yeats to win the Nobel Prize in literature.

George Herbert

George Herbert (1593–1633), English devotional poet, the son of an aristocratic family, began writing poems as an undergraduate at Cambridge University. After dabbling for a time in worldly affairs, he entered the priesthood of the Church of England, to live out his days in a country parish. Herbert's poems have many references to music; according to his contemporary John Aubrey, he "had a very good hand on the lute, and set [to music] his own lyrics and sacred poems." Herbert did not publish his poems in his lifetime, but after his death friends collected them in *The Temple* (1633). The book is said to have stimulated Henry Vaughan to follow in Herbert's footsteps as a poet. Herbert makes the religious experience personal, definite, and familiar. For his use of startling "metaphysical" figures of speech, he has been compared with John Donne; but a rare sweetness and plain-spokenness make him unique among poets in English.

Robert Herrick

Robert Herrick (1591–1674), after serving as a goldsmith's apprentice, entered Cambridge University at twenty-two, then considered a late age. For nine years he seems to have lived in London, consorting with a group of poets and wits whose chief was Ben Jonson. In 1629 he became parish priest in Dean Prior, in rural Devonshire, where he lived out his days, sometimes chafing about the boorishness of his parishioners. When in 1647 the Puritans temporarily ousted him from his pulpit, Herrick returned to London. There at fifty-six he brought out his first book, *Noble Numbers* (1647), pious poems; then reprinted them together with five times as many sportive, secular poems in *Hesperides* (1648). Unluckily, the books came too late to cause a stir, Herrick's early fame as a poet having withered and the vogue for chiseled classical lyrics having gone by. Like his master Jonson, Herrick writes songlike poems inspired by Greek and Latin pastoral (or shepherd-and-shepherdess) poetry. We go to him not for profound ideas, but for fresh, tough speech and resonant music. Herrick, who remained a bachelor clergyman, probably imagined the mistresses he praised. He declared in *Hesperides*, "To his book's end this last line he'd have placed: / Jocund his Muse was, but his life was chaste."

Gerard Manley Hopkins

Gerard Manley Hopkins (1844–1889), born in Essex, England, was, like Emily Dickinson, a major poet not known until our century. At twenty, a student at Oxford, he was converted to Roman Catholicism and received into that church by Cardinal Newman. Ordained a Jesuit, Hopkins at first served as parish priest and teacher in working-class sections of large cities (London, Glasgow, Liverpool, Manchester), where poverty and suffering distressed him. But his sermons were reportedly so strange (in one, he likened the church to a cow we milk and whose moo we follow) that his superiors removed him from public view, making him Professor of Greek at University College, Dublin. He died of typhoid fever at forty-four. Nearly thirty years after Hopkins's death, his friend Robert Bridges published his *Poems* (1918), having thought them too demanding for earlier readers. That much of Hopkins's work sounds odd to us may be due to the poet's admiration for Old English, with its gutsy monosyllables, and for Welsh poetry, rich in patterns of sound. Hopkins developed his own theory of versification: "sprung rhythm"—in brief, a kind of accentual verse. Though on entering the priesthood he had renounced poetry, he welcomed the suggestion of a superior that he contribute to a Jesuit magazine a poem on the drowning of five Franciscan nuns. The result, "The Wreck of the *Deutschland*," received a rejection slip. This challenging poem has been called "the dragon guarding the door to Hopkins's poetry," but most readers have gone in by the back door of his more quickly accessible nature poems. In these, the sensuous world bursts forth in irrepressible testimony to its Maker's glory.

A. E. Housman

A. E. Housman (1859–1936), English poet and professor of Latin, was born in a village in rural Shropshire, England. Although as a student at Oxford he distinguished himself as a promising scholar of the classics, he failed his exams, apparently because of some inner crisis precipitated by his love for a fellow male student. Determined to overcome this setback, Housman, while working as a clerk in the British Patent Office, at night wrote scholarly articles. Within ten years these academic writings, bristling with cold sarcasms and scathing put-downs of rival scholars, had won him such high repute that he was invited to be Professor of Latin at the University of London. Later he stepped up to Cambridge University, to spend the rest of his days living a retiring academic life befitting his shy temperament. Though Housman published only two slim collections of poems—the instantly and enormously popular *A Shropshire Lad* (1898) and the conclusively titled *Last Poems* (1922)—his place as a minor master of the English lyric

seems unshakable. Like many Latin poets he admired, he insists in well-turned lines that life is short and comes to a bad end.

Langston Hughes

See biographical note on page 1019.

Kobayashi Issa

Issa (1763–1827) was born Yataro Kobayashi in Kashiwabara, a mountain village in central Japan. His father was an educated farmer; his mother died when he was only two years old, and he was raised by his grandmother. At fifteen he became an apprentice in Edo (now Tokyo). His father, who loved poetry, supported his writing. On his father's death, however, Issa's relatives disputed the will. The settlement required the poet to share the family house with his wrangling clan—by dividing it down the middle. His final years were scarred by the deaths of his first wife and infant children. The poet's pen name, Issa, means "cup of tea."

Randall Jarrell

Randall Jarrell (1914–1965) was born in Nashville, Tennessee, and served as a private in the army air force in World War II, an experience that gave rise to several of his best early poems. Much of his life was spent in academe. At Vanderbilt, a psychology major, he studied literature with poet-critic John Crowe Ransom, who changed the direction of Jarrell's career. When Ransom moved to Kenyon College,

Jarrell followed as an English instructor. At Kenyon, he formed another lifelong friendship: with a student who was to become a distinguished poet, Robert Lowell. Later Jarrell taught at the University of Texas, Sarah Lawrence, Princeton, Illinois, and for many years (1947–65) at the Woman's College of the University of North Carolina (now the U.N.C., Greensboro). His one novel, *Pictures from an Institution* (1954), is a satire set on a campus. As poetry editor for *The Nation* in the mid-1940s, Jarrell drew attention for his witty, astute, outspoken reviews of poetry. *Poetry and the Age* (1953) includes especially brilliant essays on Robert Frost and Wallace Stevens. Jarrell, who loved the German language, translated Goethe's *Faust* (Part I) and some of the Grimm fairy tales. In later years he wrote four books for children (with beautiful drawings by Maurice Sendak) including *The Bat Poet* (1964) and the posthumous *Fly by Night* (1976).

Robinson Jeffers

John Robinson Jeffers (1887–1962) was born in Pittsburgh, Pennsylvania, but had part of his early education in European boarding schools. In 1903, Jeffers's family moved to Southern California where Jeffers entered Occidental College. Graduating at 19, Jeffers studied medicine, forestry, and literature on a graduate level before devoting his life to poetry. In 1906, he met Una Kuster, who was married to an attorney. Their tempestuous love affair eventually led—in 1913—to their marriage. In 1914 the couple visited Carmel, California, and Jeffers knew that it was his "inevitable place"—he would spend his remaining fifty-eight years there. With the help of a local stonemason, Jeffers built his own house on the edge of the Pacific, quarrying stone from the beach. Jeffers's poetry reflects the closeness to nature that made up his daily life. His philosophy of "inhumanism" refused to put mankind above the rest of nature; he demanded that humanity see itself as part of the vast interdependent reality of nature—a message that has made his poetry esteemed by environmentalists. Jeffers's Tor House in Carmel is now a national historic monument.

Ben Jonson

Ben Jonson (1573?–1637), posthumous son of a Scottish minister, was a native Londoner. As a boy he received a firm grounding in Latin and Greek at Westminster School, but instead of enrolling in a university, took up bricklaying, then served as a soldier in Flanders. Home from the wars, he married and became an actor and playwright in London. Although a coolly rational classicist by persuasion, Jonson seems to have been an outspoken hothead, given to quarrels and brawls. In 1598 he killed a fellow actor in a duel and escaped the gallows only by claiming an ancient law that forbade hanging anyone who could read. From about 1606, Jonson frequented the Mermaid Tavern in London's Fleet Street, a favorite hangout of writers and actors. There, on the first Friday of each month, he presided over famed literary discussions; according to one report, his friend Shakespeare would take part at times and match wits with him. Later changing pubs (to the Devil and St. Dunstan), Jonson and his circle became known as the "Tribe of Ben"; Thomas Carew and Robert Herrick were younger members. Later Jonson became the leading writer of masks, elaborate plays with music and dancing produced at court. As a poet Jonson, in his precise Latinate lyrics, odes, and epigrams, helped get rid of worn-out Petrarchan conventions (those Shakespeare mocks in "My mistress' eyes are nothing like the sun"). As a playwright, he excelled; his comedies, especially *Volpone, or The Fox* (1606) and *The Alchemist* (1610), are among the crown jewels of the English stage.

Donald Justice

Donald Justice was born in Miami, Florida, in 1925. He attended public schools, hoping at first to become a composer, but gradually his interests turned toward literature. After graduating from the University of Miami in 1945, he did graduate work at both the University of North Carolina and Stanford University before finishing a Ph.D. from the University of Iowa. Having spent four decades as a professor of creative writing, Justice is widely regarded as the most influential poetry teacher of his generation. His presence in the Iowa Writers' Workshops from 1957–1982 helped build it into national prominence. (He later taught at the University of Florida in Gainesville.) Justice's first book, *The Summer Anniversaries* (1960), won the Lamont Award, and virtually every other prominent poetry prize has followed, most notably the Pulitzer and Bollingen Prizes. Justice is currently retired in Iowa City. His

New and Selected Poems was published in 1995.

John Keats

John Keats (1795–1821), son of a London stable keeper, studied to become a physician and served as a surgeon's apprentice before deciding on poetry as a career. In 1817 he published his first book, *Poems*, including "On First Looking into Chapman's Homer." Despite critics' hostility to his narrative poem *Endymion* (1818), Keats persisted. In 1818 he fell in love with sixteen-year-old Fanny Brawne, but, stricken with tuberculosis, he postponed plans for marriage. In 1820, shortly after publication of his third and last book, Keats went to Italy in hopes of regaining his health, but his poetry soon slowed to a stop. In the following year, at twenty-five, he died in Rome and was buried there beneath the epitaph he wrote for himself: "Here lies one whose name was writ in water." His name, however, has continued to endure. No English poet wrote poems richer in sensuous imagery (as in his great odes, among them "Ode on Melancholy" and "To Autumn"), nor quite so beautifully reimagined the Middle Ages (in poems such as "La Belle Dame sans Merci" and "The Eve of St. Agnes"). He wrote several of the finest sonnets in the language, an unfinished epic of great interest, *Hyperion*, hilarious light verse, and scores of superb letters.

Ted Kooser

Ted Kooser, born in Ames, Iowa, in 1939, attended Iowa State University and then received a master's degree at the University of Nebraska in Lincoln. After teaching high school for one year, Kooser took a job in the insurance industry in 1965 and has remained there since. Kooser's career, like his employment, has been unusual for an American poet. Although his early work gained little attention, his short, understated poems—many published by small presses—gradually attracted a growing following. Kooser's poems are unmistakable. Brief, imagistic, and accessible, they usually describe a small everyday scene from American life in the Great Plains states, but midway there is almost always some unexpected but magical turn of imagination. Kooser lives on a small farm in Garland, Nebraska.

Philip Larkin

Philip Larkin (1922–1985), born in Coventry, England, has been called the most influential British poet since World War II. After studies at Oxford, he drifted into being a librarian, and for many years was head librarian for the University of Hull. Early in his career Larkin wrote two novels, *Jill* (1946) and *A Girl in Winter* (1947). He also reviewed jazz recordings for a London newspaper. A self-declared foe of modernism in music, art, and literature, he published only four slim volumes of poems, traditional in form. The earliest collection was heavily indebted to Yeats: *The North Ship* (1945, reissued in 1966 with a preface making fun of it). With *The Less Deceived* (1955), Larkin hit his characteristic stride, writing most of the poems in the voice of a tough-minded, disillusioned, self-deprecating man facing a dreary urban landscape of quiet frus-

tration. This voice drew an immediate response from readers in postwar England.

D. H. Lawrence

David Herbert Lawrence (1885–1930) was born in Nottinghamshire, England, child of a coalminer and a schoolteacher who hated her husband's toil and vowed that her son should escape it. He took up fiction writing, attaining early success. During World War I, Lawrence and his wife were unjustly suspected of treason (he because of his pacifism, she because of her aristocratic German birth). After the armistice they left England and, seeking a climate healthier for Lawrence, who suffered from tuberculosis, wandered in Italy, France, Australia, Mexico, and the American Southwest. Lawrence is an impassioned spokesman for our unconscious, instinctive natures, which we moderns (he argues) have neglected in favor of our overweening intellects. In *Lady Chatterley's Lover* (1928), he strove to restore explicit sexuality to English fiction. The book, which today seems tame and repetitious, was long banned in Britain and the United States. Deeper Lawrence novels include *Sons and Lovers* (1913), a veiled account of his breaking away from his fiercely possessive mother; *The Rainbow* (1915); *Women in Love* (1921); and *The Plumed Serpent* (1926), about a revival of pagan religion in Mexico. Besides fiction, Lawrence left a rich legacy of poetry, essays, criticism (*Studies in Classic American Literature*, 1923, is especially shrewd and funny), and travel writing. Lawrence exerted deep influence on others, both by the message in his work and by his personal magnetism.

Denise Levertov

Denise Levertov (1923–1997) was born in Essex, England, daughter of a Welsh mother and a Russian Jewish-born priest of the Anglican church. She was educated at home, reading in her father's library. She served as a nurse in World War II. In 1947 she married an American novelist, Mitchell Goodman, and in the following year came to the United States. Her first book, published in England, had observed traditional poetic conventions (including rime and meter), but in America she discovered the work of William Carlos Williams and other open-form poets, and began to write in a different, freer mode. With Robert Creeley and others of the Black Mountain group, she exerted much influence among younger poets. Her critical essays have been collected in *The Poet in the World* (1973) and *Light up the Cave* (1981). Levertov was a tireless political activist, prominent in peace movements of the 1960s, 1970s, and 1980s.

Edna St. Vincent Millay

Edna St. Vincent Millay (1892–1950), born in Rockland, Maine, was the eldest of three daughters. When she was twelve, her father deserted the family. At twenty, she had already published "Renascence," one of her most celebrated poems. In 1917, she was graduated from Vassar College and settled in Greenwich Village, where she be-

came as famous for her vivacious personality, her bohemian life-style, her acting and playwriting, and her feminism, as for her verse. Even as she wrote *The Harp Weaver*, a serious volume of verse that won her a Pulitzer Prize in 1923, Millay did hack writing to pay her bills. Among other work for which she is known are verse dramas such as *Aria da Capo* (1920) and the sonnet cycle *Fatal Interview* (1931). In 1923, she married Eugen Jan Boissevain, Dutch businessman and widower of feminist Inez Milholland. In 1927, Millay's political activism expressed itself in poems about Sacco and Vanzetti, two anarchists accused of murder, and involved her in an unsuccessful campaign to prevent their execution. Though she kept writing poetry well into the 1940s and received several honorary degrees, her reputation waned. Darkened by a nervous breakdown in 1944, she was troubled by a growing sense that the public had deserted her. Millay's life ended with a heart attack at the age of fifty-eight.

John Milton

John Milton (1608–1674), author of *Paradise Lost*, the greatest English epic, was born in London, the son of a scrivener who composed music. His mother early began schooling him to be a minister. He studied zealously. As he later recalled: "From my twelfth year I scarcely ever went to bed before midnight, which was the first cause of injury to my eyes." After he received his B.A. from Cambridge University in 1629, his father supported him through eight years of further study. "Lycidas" (1638), a poem of this period, shows his deepening seriousness about religion and his growing resentment of corruptions in the church, which were to lead him to the Puritan cause. Milton wrote much prose in the service of causes. In *Areopagitica* (1644), he argues for freedom of the press and opposes the strict censorship that had been imposed by Parliament. His unhappy marriage to Mary Powell led him to write tracts in favor of divorce. When Oliver Cromwell and the Puritans ousted King Charles and declared England a commonwealth, Milton's writings were remembered, and earned him a post as Cromwell's foreign secretary. His eyesight strained by years of hard study, Milton went blind and had to dictate his correspondence (in Latin) to clerks, one of whom was fellow poet Andrew Marvell. With the Restoration of Charles II in 1660, Milton's world came crashing down. In retirement, at last he turned to a project he had planned as a young man: his major heroic poem, *Paradise Lost* (1667), about Satan's rebellion and the Fall of Adam and Eve. This epic was followed by *Paradise Regained* (1671) and a verse drama modeled on a Greek tragedy, *Samson Agonistes* (1671).

Marianne Moore

Marianne Moore (1887–1972), whose poems earned praise from fellow poets as dissimilar as William Carlos Williams and T. S. Eliot, was born in Kirkwood, Missouri, a suburb of St. Louis. Her father abandoned the family in 1894, and Moore moved to Pennsylvania. In 1909, she was graduated from Bryn Mawr, where a classmate was the poet H.D. For a time,

Moore taught business courses at the U.S. Indian School in Carlisle, Pennsylvania, where the athlete Jim Thorpe was among her students. By 1915, her poems—witty, satirical, intellectual, disruptive, and innovative—had begun to appear in *Poetry* magazine. Until her mother died in 1947, Moore, a dutiful daughter, lived with her in Brooklyn, supporting herself by a series of conventional jobs. From 1925 to 1929 she edited *The Dial*, a literary magazine in whose pages she published many of the best poets of her day. Besides poems, Moore wrote essays, reviews, and translations including *The Fables of La Fontaine* (1945). For her *Collected Poems* (1951), she won a Pulitzer Prize, the Bollingen Prize, and a National Book Award; her *Complete Poems* appeared in 1967. Late in life, Moore became a media figure for her fondness for the Brooklyn Dodgers and her penchant for three-cornered hats. She stayed in Brooklyn, writing and rewriting, through an active and vigorous old age.

Lorine Niedecker

Lorine Niedecker (1903–1970) spent nearly all her life on Blackhawk Island near Fort Atkinson, Wisconsin, where her father worked as a carp fisherman. After two years at Beloit College, she returned home to care for her ailing mother. Following a brief marriage in 1928, Niedecker held jobs as proofreader, librarian's helper, and cleaning worker in a hospital. After her marriage in 1963 she lived in Milwaukee, but on her husband's retirement the couple moved into a house they had built by the Rock River, and the poet returned to her native grounds. Although she lived an outwardly quiet life remote from publishing centers, Niedecker read widely and maintained a vigorous life of the mind. In the early 1930s she struck up a correspondence with poet and teacher Louis Zukofsky, who encouraged her poetry. In the 1950s poet Cid Corman printed her work in his avant garde little magazine *Origin*. During her lifetime she published sparingly, but *From This Condensery: The Complete Writing of Lorine Niedecker* (1985) contains a large body of poems, as well as critical essays, experimental prose, and five radio plays. Her life and work are the subject of Kristine Thatcher's play *Niedecker*, given an off-Broadway production in 1989.

John Frederick Nims

John Frederick Nims, born in 1913 in Muskegon, Michigan, has had a distinguished career as poet and translator, teacher and editor. He has taught at Florida, Illinois (Urbana and Chicago), Missouri, Notre Dame, Toronto, and other universities, and has held visiting professorships at Harvard and in Florence, Milan, and Madrid. The poems in his first book *The Iron Pastoral* (1947) deal wittily with jukeboxes, penny arcades, poolrooms, and other features of the contemporary scene. In *Of Flesh and Bone* (1967) Nims shows his mastery of the epigram. His *Selected Poems* appeared in 1982. A translator of poetry from languages as varied as classical Greek, Catalan, and Galician, Nims has splendidly rendered into English *The Poems of St. John of the Cross* (1959, revised edition 1968). For several years

(1978–85) he was editor of *Poetry* magazine. He is the author of an introduction to poetry, *Western Wind*, and editor of *The Harper Anthology of Poetry* (1981).

Sharon Olds

Sharon Olds was born in San Francisco in 1942 and attended Stanford University. After graduation in 1964, she moved East and eventually took a Ph.D. from Columbia University in 1972. Her first collection of poems, *Satan Says* (1980), was well received, but her second volume, *The Dead and the Living* (1984), scored a major critical success by winning both the Lamont Award and National Book Critics Circle Award. Olds's work often graphically depicts the passions, joys, and pain of family life. She currently teaches at New York University.

Wilfred Owen

Wilfred Owen (1893–1918) was, like A. E. Housman, a native of Shropshire, England. He attended London University and for a time served as lay assistant to a minister, helping the sick and poor. In 1916, during World War I, he enlisted in the British army, became a company commander, and in less than two years wrote all his famous antiwar poems of life in the trenches. The army seems suddenly to have changed Owen from a competent minor poet with little to say into a powerful voice of pacifism. At age twenty-five, while trying to get his men across a canal under enemy fire on the French front, he was killed in action only a week before the war ended. Though Owen published only four poems, after his death a collection of his work was edited by another front-line war poet, Siegfried Sassoon (1920). Owen is preeminent among English poets who wrote of that conflict, and the reputation of his work has continued to grow.

Linda Pastan

Linda Pastan was born Linda Olenik in New York in 1932. After her graduation from Radcliffe, she took two Master's degrees, at Simmons (M.L.S.) and Brandeis (M.A.). She married in 1953 and has a daughter and two sons. Her first book, *A Perfect Circle of the Sun* (1971), established her as an up-and-comer; *Selected Poems* appeared in 1979, confirming her accomplishment. Her subtle, often powerful poems are exceptionally clear and accessible.

Sylvia Plath

Sylvia Plath (1932–1963), one of the most remarkable poets in English of the past half-century, was born in Boston, the daughter of German immigrants who both taught at Boston University. The death of her father when the poet was eight came as a trauma from which she seems never quite to have recovered. As a scholarship-winning student at Smith College, Plath revealed early promise, and her work received early publication. Like Esther Greenwood, protagonist of her one novel *The Bell Jar* (1963), Plath won a student contest that sent her to work in New York for a national magazine, and struggled with a year-long siege of mental illness for which she underwent shock treatments. Returning to Smith, she was

graduated with top honors. Later she studied at Cambridge University in England, where she met and in 1956 married the poet Ted Hughes. Estranged from her husband, she committed suicide in London, leaving two children and, in manuscript, the intense, powerful poems that went into her posthumous, highly acclaimed collection, *Ariel* (1965).

Edgar Allan Poe

Edgar Allan Poe (1809–1849) was born in Boston, the son of itinerant actors. Poe lost his father in 1810 and his mother the next year. Taken in by a well-to-do Richmond merchant, Poe was given an excellent education, but he eventually dropped out of both the University of Virginia and West Point. Poe became a celebrated journalist, and he edited major journals such as *Southern Literary Messenger, Burton's Gentleman's Magazine,* and *Broadway Journal,* to which he contributed stories, poems, articles, and reviews. Poe's romantic idealism, argumentative personality, heavy drinking, and difficult personal life, however, kept him from achieving financial security. After the death of his wife in 1847, Poe began drinking more heavily and his mental and physical health deteriorated. He was only forty years old when he died in Baltimore on October 7, 1849. The exact circumstances of his death have never adequately been explained.

Alexander Pope

Alexander Pope (1688–1744), the leading English poet of the early eighteenth century, was born in London, son of a Roman Catholic linen merchant. A sickly, stunted, pockmarked child, he suffered from weak health and continual exhaustion throughout his life, and was said to have worn padded clothes to disguise his misshapen frame. Pope excelled early as a poet, composing his *Pastorals* (1709) at age sixteen. His rimed translations of the *Iliad* (1720) and the *Odyssey* (1725–26) and his edition of Shakespeare (1725), bestsellers in their day, made him independently wealthy, and he was able to buy an estate at Twickenham and live in style. Pope did not write an epic, but instead translated epics and wrote great mock epics: *The Rape of the Lock* (1714), in which he voices compassion for women transformed into wives, and *The Dunciad* (1728–43), in which he mocks his many literary enemies. He was a master satirist and splendid craftsman of the heroic couplet. Romantic critics generally think him no poet at all, but G. K. Chesterton remarked, "If Pope be not a poet, then who is?"

Ezra Pound

Ezra Pound (1885–1972), among the most influential (and still controversial) modern poets, was born in Hailey, Idaho. He readied himself for a teaching career, but when in 1907 he lost his job at Wabash College for sheltering a penniless prostitute, he left America. Settling in England and later in Paris, he wielded influence on the work of T. S. Eliot, whose long poem *The Waste Land* he edited; W. B. Yeats, whom he served as secretary and critic; and James Joyce. Pound was perpetually championing writers then unknown, like Robert Frost. In 1924 Pound settled permanently in Italy, where he came to admire Mussolini's economic policies. During World War II he made broadcasts to America by Italian radio, deemed treasonous. When American armed forces arrested him in 1944, Pound spent three weeks in a cage in an army camp in Pisa. Flown to the United States to stand trial, he was declared incompetent and for twelve years was confined in St. Elizabeth's in Washington, a hospital for the criminally insane. In 1958, at the intervention of Robert Frost, Archibald MacLeish, and other old friends, he was pronounced incurable and allowed to return to Italy to spend his last, increasingly silent years. In his prime, Pound was a swaggeringly confident critic, a berater of smugness and mediocrity, a delectable humorist. Among his lasting books are *Personae* (enlarged edition, 1949), short poems; his *ABC of Reading* (1934), an introduction to poetry; and *Literary Essays* (1954). His *Cantos*, a vast poem woven of historical themes published in installments over forty years, Pound never finished. He was a great translator of poetry from Italian, Provençal, Chinese, and other languages. Pare away his delusions, and a remarkable human being and splendid poet remains.

Dudley Randall

Dudley Randall was born in 1914 in Washington, D.C. He was graduated from Wayne State University and the University of Michigan, and has worked as librarian and poet-in-residence at the University of Detroit. A pioneer in the modern movement to publish the work of black writers, Randall founded what has been called the most influential small publishing house in America, Broadside Press. He also edited an important anthology, *The Black Poets* (1971). Randall's *A Litany of Friends: New and Selected Poems* was published in 1981.

Alastair Reid

Alastair Reid was born in Whithorn, Scotland, in 1926. His college work at St. Andrews was interrupted by service in the Royal Navy during World War II, but he eventually graduated with a degree in classics. After teaching a few years in America, Reid began to spend part of each year in Majorca with Robert Graves with whom he collaborated on translations and an opera libretto. Soon Reid became one of the most admired translators of Spanish-language poetry—his versions of the poetry of Pablo Neruda and Jorge Luis Borges are particularly noteworthy. His own poetry, collected in *Weatherings* (1978), is rich and arresting. For years Reid wrote for *The New Yorker*. Married twice, he has one son. He currently lives in the Dominican Republic.

Adrienne Rich

Adrienne Rich was born in Baltimore in 1929. Since the selection of her first volume by W. H. Auden for the Yale Series of Younger Poets in 1951, her work has continually broken new ground, moving from closed forms to feminist poetics and radical politics. Her earlier poems are collected in *The*

Fact of a Doorframe (1984). More recent volumes include *Time's Power* (1989), *An Atlas of the Difficult World* (1991), and *Dark Fields of the Republic* (1995). Her prose works include *On Lies, Secrets, and Silence* (1979), *Blood, Bread, and Poetry* (1986), and *What is Found There* (1993). Her work has received many awards—most notably the Ruth Lilly Prize, the Lambda Literary Award, the Poets' Prize, The Lenore Marshall/Nation Award, and the Dorothea Tanning Prize.

Edwin Arlington Robinson

Edwin Arlington Robinson (1869–1935) was raised in Gardiner, Maine, the model for Tilbury Town, the setting for many of his poems. After a stint at Harvard, Robinson moved to New York City. Initially, he published three books, but slowly sank into poverty and alcoholism. In 1902 President Theodore Roosevelt discovered Robinson's work and obtained for him a government position with virtually no duties. Robinson used this fortunate intercession to embark on a series of literary projects, and he gradually became the most widely esteemed American poet of the early twentieth century. He won the Pulitzer Prize three times in seven years, and his long poem *Tristram* (1927) became a best-seller. Although Robinson's work has suffered from critical neglect in recent years, he remains an important American poet. His austere style, penetrating psychology, and bitter realism represent a turning point in American poetry from nineteenth century romanticism to the threshold of modernism. His work decisively influenced the poetry of Robert Frost.

Theodore Roethke

Theodore Roethke (1908–1963) was born in Saginaw, Michigan, where his family ran a large greenhouse. (No poet seems wealthier in his knowledge of vegetation.) He went to the University of Michigan and (for a year) to Harvard. As a young poet teaching college at a time when creative writing teachers without Ph.D.s were suspect, Roethke held impermanent jobs before coming to rest at the University of Washington in Seattle. There, from 1947 until his death, he was an influential teacher of poetry and poetry writing; among his students were Carolyn Kizer, David Wagoner, and James Wright. Roethke was a large, heavyset man light on his feet (he once coached varsity tennis at Lafayette), and would sometimes prepare for a poetry reading by pacing the stage like an athlete warming up. His poetry developed from rather conventional and imitative lyrics through a phase of disconnected stream of consciousness into (at the end) a meditative poetry reminiscent in its open lines of Walt Whitman's.

Anne Sexton

Anne Sexton (1928–1974) was born in Newton, Massachusetts to an old and prominent New England family. She attended boarding school and finishing school, but never went on to college. In 1948 she eloped with Alfred Sexton (always known as "Kayo" to his wife and family). Beautiful, elegant, and commanding, Sexton dreamed of becoming a model, but shortly after the birth of her second daughter, she suffered the first of many nervous breakdowns. Her fragile mental health would take her in and out of hospitals for the rest of her life. After seeing a television program on "How to Write a Sonnet" in 1956, Sexton began composing poetry (encouraged by her psychiatrist). Dedicating herself to writing, Sexton made astonishing progress and soon published her work in leading journals like *The Hudson Review* and *The New Yorker*. Her strongly emotional and confessional poems earned her wide acclaim, and her third volume, *Live or Die* (1967), won the Pulitzer Prize. Fame, however, could not assuage the pain of her troubled psyche or the increasing disorder of her personal life. In October of 1974, Sexton committed suicide. She was only 45 years old.

William Shakespeare

William Shakespeare (1564–1616), the supreme writer of English, was born, baptized, and buried in the market town of Stratford-on-Avon, eighty miles from London. Son of a glovemaker and merchant who was high bailiff (or mayor) of the town, he probably attended grammar school and learned to read Latin authors in the original. At eighteen he married Anne Hathaway, twenty-six, by whom he had three children, including twins. By 1592 he had become well known and envied as an actor and playwright in London. From 1594 until he retired, he belonged to the same theatrical company, the Lord Chamberlain's Men (later renamed the King's Men in honor of their patron, James I), for whom he wrote thirty-six plays—some of them, such as *Hamlet* and *King Lear*, profound re-workings of old plays. As an actor, Shakespeare is believed to have played supporting roles, such as Hamlet's father's ghost. The company prospered, moved into the Globe in 1599, and in 1608 bought the fashionable Black-friars as well; Shakespeare owned an interest in both theaters. When plagues shut down the theaters from 1592 to 1594, Shakespeare turned to poetry; his great Sonnets (published only in 1609) probably date from the 1590s. Plays were regarded as enter-tainments of little literary merit, like comic books today, and Shakespeare did not bother to supervise their publi-cation. He did, however, carefully see through press his sonnets and the nar-rative poems *Venus and Adonis* (1593) and *The Rape of Lucrece* (1594).

Stevie Smith

Stevie Smith (1902–1971), was born in Hull, Yorkshire, christened Flo-rence Margaret Smith. Being wiry and short, she acquired her nickname from a popular jockey, Stevie Donahue. For more than sixty years, beginning at age three, Smith lived with her aunt in Palmers Green, a suburb of London, and worked for thirty years as a pub-lisher's secretary. Of her three novels, *Novel on Yellow Paper* (1936) is the best known. Her poetry readings, in public and on BBC radio, widened her audience. *Collected Poems* (1976) is il-lustrated with her own witty, slapdash, and rakishly charming drawings. *Me Again: Uncollected Writings* (1982) contains poems, stories, essays, and a play for radio. In the film, *Stevie* (1978), based on a stage play by Hugh Whitemore, Glenda Jackson plays the poet with keen empathy.

William Stafford

William Stafford (1914–1993) was born in Hutchinson, Kansas, gradu-ated from the University of Kansas and later took a doctorate at the Uni-versity of Iowa. During World War II he was interned as a conscientious ob-jector, an experience he recalls in his prose memoir *Down in My Heart* (1947). For many years he taught at Lewis and Clark College in Portland, Oregon, and in 1970–71 he served as Consultant in Poetry for the Library of Congress. *Traveling Through the Dark* (1962) won the National Book Award, and in 1977 Stafford published a large volume of his collected poems, *Stories That Could Be True*. In much of his work he traced the landscapes of the Midwest and of the Pacific North-west, where he long lived. He de-scribed his poetry as "much like talk, with some enhancement." Shortly be-fore his death in 1993, Stafford was chosen in a national poll of American writers as the poet most highly re-garded by his peers.

Timothy Steele

Timothy Steele was born in Bur-lington, Vermont in 1948. He did his undergraduate work at Stanford. After taking his doctorate in English at Brandeis, where he studied with J. V. Cunningham, Steele returned to Cali-fornia, where he has taught ever since. His first book of poems, *Uncertainties at Rest*, appeared in 1979 and has been followed by two other collections. His study, *Missing Measures: Modern Poetry and the Revolt Against Meter* (1990), has been one of the most influential books of literary history of recent years. Steele writes exclusively in traditional forms. His work is characterized by a Yankee reticence and a precise but understated style that holds considerable power within these strict limits. He currently teaches at California State University, Los Angeles.

James Stephens

James Stephens (1882–1950), born in Dublin, Ireland, was a famous member of the Irish Literary Renaissance, a movement early in the century that included William Butler Yeats and the playwrights Lady Gregory, J. M. Synge, and Sean O'Casey. As a young man Stephens took a job as a typist in a lawyer's office, where access to a typewriter started him writing fantastic fiction, some of it based on Irish folklore, such as his most popular novel, *The Crock of Gold* (1912). Other imaginative novels followed, including *The Demi-Gods* (1914) and *Deirdre* (1923). *Irish Fairy Tales* (1920) retells classic legends for young readers. Although best remembered for such books, Stephens was a considerable poet as well. His first collection appeared in 1909, and in 1926 he published his *Collected Poems*. Some of his poems are actually free translations from the Irish: "A Glass of Beer," for instance, is a version of a poem by Dáibhí Ó Bruadair (about 1625–98).

Wallace Stevens

Wallace Stevens (1879–1955) was born in Reading, Pennsylvania; his father was a successful lawyer; his mother, a former schoolteacher. As a special student at Harvard, he became president of the student literary magazine, the *Harvard Advocate*, but he did not want a liberal arts degree. Instead,

he became a lawyer in New York City, and in 1916 joined the legal staff of the Hartford Accident and Indemnity Company. In 1936 he was elected a vice-president. Stevens, who would write poems in his head while walking to work and then dictate them to his secretary, was a leading expert on surety claims. Once asked how he was able to combine poetry and insurance, he replied that the two occupations had an element in common: "calculated risk." As a young man in New York, Stevens made lasting friendships with poets Marianne Moore and William Carlos Williams, but he did not seek literary society. Though his poems are full of references to Europe and remote places, his only travels were annual vacation trips to Key West. He printed his early poems in *Poetry* magazine, but did not publish a book until *Harmonium* appeared in 1923, when he was forty-four. Living quietly in Hartford, Connecticut, Stevens sought to discover order in a chaotic world with his subtle and exotic imagination. His critical essays, collected in *The Necessary Angel* (1951), and his *Letters* (1966), edited by his daughter Holly Stevens, reveal a penetrating, philosophic mind. His *Collected Poems* (1954), published on his seventy-fifth birthday, garnered major prizes and belated recognition for Stevens as a major American poet.

Anne Stevenson

Anne Stevenson is the quintessential trans-Atlantic poet. Born in England in 1933 of American parents, she was educated in the U.S. After graduating from the University of Michigan, she returned to England. She has taught in both countries and now lives in

Durham, North Carolina. Combining two cultures in her background, Stevenson has also combined the careers of scholar and poet. In 1966, she published the first full-length study of Elizabeth Bishop, and, in 1989, she released *Bitter Fame: A Life of Sylvia Plath*, a controversial but authoritative biography. Stevenson's *Collected Poems* appeared in 1996. Including poems from her ten previous books of verse, this substantial volume confirmed her position as a major contemporary poet.

Alfred, Lord Tennyson

Alfred, Lord Tennyson (1809–1892), was born Alfred Tennyson in Lincolnshire, England, the son of an alcoholic rural minister. When Queen Victoria made him a baron in 1883 (at seventy-five), he added the "Lord" to his byline. A precocious poet, Tennyson began writing verse at five, and when still in his teens collaborated with his brother Charles on *Poems by Two Brothers* (1827). As a student at Cambridge, he was unusual: he kept a snake for a pet, won a medal for poetry, and went home without taking a degree. But in college he made influential friendships, especially that of Arthur Hallam, whose death in 1833 inspired Tennyson's *In Memoriam* (1850), the elegiac sequence that contains "Dark house by which once more I stand." The year 1850 was a banner one for Tennyson in other ways: he at last felt prosperous enough to marry Emily Sellwood, who had remained engaged to him for fourteen years, and Queen Victoria named him poet laureate, in which capacity he served for four decades, writing poems for state

occasions. Between 1859 and 1888 Tennyson completed *Idylls of the King*, a twelve-part narrative poem of Arthur and his Round Table. In his mid-sixties he wrote several plays. A spokesman for the Victorian age and its militant colonialism, Tennyson is still respected as a poet of varied assets, including an excellent ear.

Dylan Thomas

Dylan Thomas (1914–1953) was born in the coastal town of Swansea, Wales, the son of a teacher of English. Much of Thomas's life was a bitter struggle to support his wife and children, a struggle intensified by fondness for spending freely. Lacking a university education, Thomas found most paying literary work barred to him in Britain, although late in life he received many assignments to write film and radio scripts. A resonant reader-aloud of poetry, he made broadcasts for BBC radio and undertook several immensely popular reading tours of America, preceded by a reputation for heavy drinking and gustatorial lovemaking. He died in a hospital in New York City after drinking a procession of straight whiskeys, apparently courting the end. Thomas wrote not only poems (in the early ones he brought surrealism into English poetry), he also wrote remarkable stories and a "play for voices," *Under Milk Wood* (1954), based on memories of his home town in Wales.

John Updike

John Updike, born in Shillington, Pennsylvania, in 1932, is primarily regarded as a novelist. But his first book was verse, *The Carpentered Hen*

(1954), from which we take "Ex-Basketball Player"; and ever since, he has continued to produce verse both light and serious. He received his B.A. from Harvard, then went to Oxford to study drawing and fine art. From 1955 to 1957 he worked on the staff of *The New Yorker*. Though he left the magazine to write full-time, he has continued to supply it with bright stories and searching book reviews. Hardly a fall goes by without a new Updike novel. *The Witches of Eastwick* (1984) was made into a successful motion picture. His *Collected Poems* were published in 1993.

Walt Whitman

Walt Whitman (1819–1892) was born on Long Island, son of an impoverished farmer. He spent his early years as a school teacher, a temperance propagandist, a carpenter, a printer, and a newspaper editor on the Brooklyn *Eagle*. He began writing poetry in youth, sometimes declaiming his lines above the crash of waves on New York beaches. Apparently he was also inspired to write wide, spacious, confident lines by attending performances of Italian opera. His self-published *Leaves of Grass* (1855) won praise from Ralph Waldo Emerson and gained Whitman readers in England. For the rest of his life, he kept revising and enlarging it, ceasing with a ninth or "deathbed edition" in 1891–92. Americans at first were slow to accept Whitman's unconventionally open verse forms, his sexual frankness, and his gregarious egoism. The poet of boundless faith in American democracy, Whitman tempered his vision by his experiences as a volunteer hospital nurse during the Civil War (described in his poems *Drum-Taps* and his wartime letters). After the war, he held secretarial jobs to support himself, and lost one such job when his employer's scandalized eye fell upon the *Leaves*. In old age, a semi-invalid after a stroke, Whitman made his home in Camden, New Jersey. Before he died he saw his work finally winning respect and worldwide acceptance. Whitman's influence on later American poetry has been profound, both by the example of his open forms and by his bold encompassing of subject matter that had formerly been considered unpoetic. (In "Song of the Exposition," read aloud at an industrial show in New York, the poet exclaims of his Muse: "She's here, install'd amid the kitchen ware!")

Richard Wilbur

Richard Wilbur, born in 1921 in New York City, was graduated from Amherst College, then served in the army in World War II. He has taught English at Harvard, Wellesley, Wesleyan, and Smith. With his first two collections, *The Beautiful Changes* (1947) and *Ceremony* (1950), Wilbur acquired a high reputation for a poetry of sensitivity, wit, grace, and command of traditional forms. Besides writing poetry, for which he has received many prizes, including two Pulitzer Prizes and a National Book Award, Wilbur has edited the poetry of Shakespeare and Poe. He has written song lyrics for *Candide*, a Broadway musical by Lillian Hellman and Leonard Bernstein (1956); *Loudmouse*, a story for children (1963); and *Responses*, literary criticism (1976); and he has translated plays of Molière and Racine into wonderfully skillful English verse. He divides his time between Cummington, Massachusetts, where he has a home adjacent to an apple orchard, and Key West, Florida. In 1987 he was named United States Poet Laureate by the Library of Congress. His *New and Collected Poems* (1988) gathers most of his original work in poetry.

William Carlos Williams

William Carlos Williams (1883–1963) was born in Rutherford, New Jersey, where he remained in later life as a practicing pediatrician. While taking his M.D. degree at the University of Pennsylvania, he made friends with the poets Ezra Pound and H. D. (Hilda Doolittle). Surprisingly prolific for a busy doctor, Williams wrote (besides poetry) novels and short stories, plays, criticism, and essays in history (*In the American Grain,* 1939). He kept a fliptop desk in his office and between patients would haul out his typewriter and dash off poems. His encouragement of younger poets, among them Allen Ginsberg (whose doctor he was when Ginsberg was a baby), and the long-sustained example of his formally open poetry made him an appealing father figure to the generation of the Beat poets and the Black Mountain poets—Ginsberg, Gary Snyder, and Robert Creeley. But he also had great influence on Robert Lowell, and on a whole younger generation of American poets in our day. Williams believed in truthtelling about ordinary life, championed plain speech "out of the mouths of Polish mothers," and insisted that there can be "no ideas but in things." Combining poetry with prose (including documents and statistics), his long poem in five parts, *Paterson* (1946–58) explores the past, present, and future of the New Jersey industrial city near which Williams lived for most of his days.

William Wordsworth

William Wordsworth (1770–1850) was born in England's Lake District, whose landscapes and people were to inform many of his poems. As a young man he visited France, sympathized with the Revolution, and met a young Frenchwoman who bore him a child. The Reign of Terror prevented him from returning to France, and he and Annette Vallon never married. With his sister Dorothy (1771–1855), his lifelong intellectual companion and the author of remarkable journals, he settled in Dorsetshire. Later they moved to Grasmere, in the Lake District, where Wordsworth lived the rest of his life. In 1798 his friendship with Samuel Taylor Coleridge resulted in their joint publication of *Lyrical Ballads,* a book credited with introducing Romanticism to English poetry. (Wordsworth contributed "Tintern Abbey" and other poems.) To the second edition of 1800, Wordsworth supplied a preface calling for a poetry written "in the real language of men." Time brought him a small official job, a marriage, a swing from left to right in his political sentiments, and appointment as poet laureate. Although he kept on writing, readers have generally preferred his earlier poems. *The Prelude,* a long poem-memoir completed in 1805, did not appear until after the poet's death. One of the most original of writers, Wordsworth—especially for his poems of nature and simple rustics—occupies a popular place in English poetry, much like that of Robert Frost in America.

James Wright

James Wright (1927–1980) was born in Martins Ferry, Ohio. After taking his doctorate at the University of Washington, where he studied with Theodore Roethke, he taught at the University of Minnesota, Macalester College, and Hunter College in New York. His first book, *A Green Wall* (1957), in the Yale Series of Younger Poets, established him as a traditional formalist of great skill. With Robert Bly, by whom he was persuaded to branch out of traditional forms, he translated the poems of Cesar Valejo, Pablo Neruda, and George Trakl. In 1972 he received the Pulitzer Prize for his *Collected Poems*. Wright was a memorable teacher, a great quoter of poetry from memory, and a fine critic. "I try and say how I love my country and how I despise the way it is treated," he declared. "I try and speak of the beauty and again of the ugliness in the lives of the poor and neglected."

Sir Thomas Wyatt

Sir Thomas Wyatt (1503?–1542) was both poet and man of action: diplomat, soldier, and courtier. He was born in his father's castle in Kent, England, and as a boy he was sent to court. In 1516 he entered St. John's College, Cambridge. Wyatt twice saw the inside

of prison when he slipped from the favor of King Henry VIII. He is thought to have been a lover of Anne Boleyn, later the King's wife, a fact that perhaps affects some of his remarkable love lyrics. A prominent man in Tudor England, Wyatt carried out diplomatic missions, served as ambassador to Spain, was a member of Parliament and the king's privy council, and was Commander of the Fleet. Wyatt's mission to Italy in 1527 had great consequence for English poetry, for he brought back knowledge of the works of Petrarch and other Italian love poets. In imitation of them, Wyatt wrote some of the first sonnets in our language—also lyrics, rondels, satires, and psalms.

William Butler Yeats

William Butler Yeats (1865–1939), poet and playwright, an Irishman of English ancestry, was born in Dublin, the son of painter John Butler Yeats. For a time he studied art himself and was irregularly schooled in Dublin and in London. Early in life Yeats sought to transform Irish folklore and legend into mellifluous poems. He overcame shyness to take an active part in cataclysmic events: he became involved in the movement for an Irish nation (partly drawn into it by his unrequited love for Maud Gonne, a crusading nationalist) and in founding the Irish Literary Theatre (1898) and the Irish National Theatre, which in 1904 moved to the renowned Abbey Theatre in Dublin. Dublin audiences were difficult: in 1899 they jeered Yeats's first play, *The Countess Cathleen*, for portraying a woman who, defying the church, sells her soul to the devil to buy bread for starving peasants. Eventually Yeats retired from the fray, to write plays given in drawing rooms, like *Purgatory*. After the establishment of the Irish Free State, Yeats served as a senator (1922–28). His lifelong interest in the occult culminated in his writing of *A Vision* (1937), a view of history as governed by the phases of the moon; Yeats believed the book inspired by spirit masters who dictated communications to his wife, Georgie Hyde-Lees. Had Yeats stopped writing in 1900, he would be remembered as an outstanding minor Victorian. Instead, he went on to become one of the most influential poets of the twentieth century.

DRAMA

In all ages the drama, through its portrayal of the acting and suffering spirit of man, has been more closely allied than any other art to his deeper thoughts concerning his nature and his destiny.

—Ludwig Lewisohn, *The Modern Drama*

Unlike a short story or a novel, a **play** is a work of storytelling in which actors represent the characters. In another essential, a play differs from a work of fiction: it is addressed not to readers but to spectators.

To be part of an audience in a theater is an experience far different from reading a story in solitude. Expectant as the house lights dim and the curtain rises, we become members of a community. The responses of people around us affect our own responses. We, too, contribute to the community's response whenever we laugh, sigh, applaud, murmur in surprise, or catch our breath in excitement. In contrast, when we watch a movie alone by means of a videocassette recorder—say, a slapstick comedy— we probably laugh less often than if we were watching the same film in a theater, surrounded by a roaring crowd. Of course, no one is spilling popcorn down the back of our necks. Each kind of theatrical experience, to be sure, has its advantages.

A theater of live actors has another advantage: a sensitive give-and-take between actors and audience. Such rapport, of course, depends on the actors being skilled and the audience being perceptive. Although professional actors may try to give a top-class performance on all occasions, it is natural for them to feel more keenly inspired by a lively, appreciative audience than by a dull, lethargic one. No doubt a large turnout of spectators also helps draw the best from performers on stage: the *Othello* you get may be somewhat less inspired if you are part of an audience that may be counted on the fingers of one hand. At any rate, as veteran playgoers well know, something unique and wonderful can happen when good actors and a good audience respond to each other.

In another sense, a play is more than actors and audience. Like a short story or a poem, a play is a work of art made of words. The playwright devoted thought and care and skill to the selection and arrangement of language. Watching a play, of course, we do not notice the playwright standing between us and the characters.[1] If the play is absorbing, it flows before our eyes. In a silent reading, the usual play consists mainly of **dialogue**,[2] exchanges of speech, punctuated by stage directions. In performance, though, stage directions vanish. And although the thoughtful efforts of perhaps a hundred people—actors, director, producer, stage designer, costumer, makeup artist, technicians—may have gone into a production, a successful play makes us forget its artifice. We may even forget that the play is literature, for its gestures, facial expressions, bodily stances, lighting, and special effects are as much a part of it as the playwright's written words. Even though words are not all there is to a living play, they are its bones. And the whole play, the finished production, is the total of whatever transpires on stage.

The sense of immediacy we derive from **drama** is suggested by the root of the word. *Drama* means "action" or "deed" (from the Greek *dran*, "to do"). We use *drama* as a synonym for *plays*, but the word has several meanings. Sometimes it refers to one play ("a stirring drama"); or to the work of a playwright, or **dramatist** ("Ibsen's drama"); or perhaps to a body of plays written in a particular time or place ("Elizabethan drama," "French drama of the seventeenth century"). In yet another familiar sense, *drama* often means events that elicit high excitement: "A real-life drama," a news story might begin, "was enacted today before lunchtime crowds in downtown Manhattan as fire fighters battled to free two children trapped on the sixteenth floor of a burning building." In this sense, whatever is "dramatic" implies suspense, tension, or conflict. Plays, as we shall see, frequently contain such "dramatic" chains of events; and yet, if we expect all plays to be crackling with suspense or conflict, we may be disappointed. "Good drama," said critic George Jean Nathan, "is anything that interests an intelligently emotional group of persons assembled together in an illuminated hall."

In partaking of the nature of ritual—something to be repeated in front of an audience on a special occasion—drama is akin to a festival (whether a religious festival or a rock festival) or a church service. Twice in the history of Europe, drama has sprung forth as a part of worship: when in ancient Greece, plays were performed on feast days; and when in the Christian church of the Middle Ages, a play was introduced as an adjunct to the Easter mass with the enactment of the meeting between the three Marys and the angel at Jesus' empty tomb. Evidently, something in drama remains constant over the years—something as old, perhaps, as the deepest desires and highest aspirations of humanity.

---

[1] The word *playwright*, by the way, invites misspelling. Notice that it is not *playwrite*. The suffix *-wright* (from Old English) means "one who makes"—such as a *boatwright*, a worker in a trade.

[2] Not all plays employ dialogue. There is also **pantomime**—generally, a play without words (sometimes also called a **dumb show**). Originally, in ancient Rome, a pantomime meant an actor who single-handedly played all the parts. An eminent modern pantomime (or **mime**) is French stage and screen actor Marcel Marceau.

32 *Reading a Play*

Most plays are written not to be read in books but to be performed. Finding plays in a literature anthology, the student may well ask: Isn't there something wrong with the idea of reading plays on the printed page? Isn't that a perversion of their nature?

True, plays are meant to be seen on stage, but equally true, reading a play may afford advantages. One is that it is better to know some masterpieces by reading them than never to know them at all. Even if you live in a large city with many theaters, even if you attend a college with many theatrical productions, to succeed in your lifetime in witnessing, say, all the plays of Shakespeare might well be impossible. In print, they are as near to hand as a book on a shelf, ready to be enacted (if you like) on the stage of the mind.

After all, a play is literature before it comes alive in a theater, and it might be argued that when we read an unfamiliar play, we meet it in the same form in which it first appears to its actors and its director. If a play is rich and complex or if it dates from the remote past and contains difficulties of language and allusion, to read it on the page enables us to study it at our leisure and return to the parts that demand greater scrutiny.

Let us admit, by the way, that some plays, whatever the intentions of their authors, are destined to be read more often than they are acted. Such a play is sometimes called a **closet drama**—*closet* meaning "a small, private room." Percy Bysshe Shelley's neo-Shakespearean tragedy *The Cenci* (1819) has seldom escaped from its closet, even though Shelley tried without luck to have it performed on the London stage. Perhaps too rich in talk to please an audience or too sparse in opportunities for actors to use their bodies, such works nevertheless may lead long, respectable lives on their own, solely as literature.

But even if a play may be seen in a theater, sometimes to read it in print may be our way of knowing it as the author wrote it in its entirety. Far from regarding Shakespeare's words as holy writ, producers of *Hamlet*, *King Lear*, *Othello*, and other masterpieces often leave out whole speeches and scenes, or shorten them. Besides, the nature of the play, as far as you can tell from a stage production, may depend upon decisions of the director. Shall Othello dress as a Renaissance Moor or as a jet-setting contemporary? Every actor who plays Iago in *Othello* makes his own interpretation of this knotty character. Some see Iago as a figure of pure evil; others, as a madman; still others, as a suffering human being consumed by hatred, jealousy, and pride. What do you think Shakespeare meant? You can always read the play and decide for yourself. If every stage production of a play is a fresh interpretation, so, too, is every reader's reading of it.

Some readers, when silently reading a play to themselves, try to visualize a stage, imagining the characters in costume and under lights. If such a reader is an actor or a director and is reading the play with an eye toward staging it, then that reader may try to imagine every detail of a possible production, even shades of makeup and the loudness of sound effects. But the nonprofessional reader, who regards the play as literature, need not attempt such exhaustive imagining. Although some readers find it enjoyable to imagine the play taking place upon a stage, others prefer to imagine the people and events that the play brings vividly to mind. Sympathetically following the tangled life of Nora in *A Doll's House* by Henrik Ibsen, we forget that we are reading printed stage directions and instead find ourselves in the presence of human conflict. Thus regarded, a play becomes a form of storytelling, and the playwright's instructions to the actors and the director become a conventional mode of narrative that we accept much as we accept the methods of a novel or short story. If we read *A Doll's House* caring more about Nora's fate than the imagined appearance of an actress portraying her, we speed through an ordinary passage such as this (from a scene in which Nora's husband hears the approach of an unwanted caller, Dr. Rank):

> Helmer (*with quiet irritation*): Oh, what does he want now? (*Aloud.*) Hold on.
> (*Goes and opens the door.*) Oh, how nice that you didn't just pass us by!

We read the passage, if the story absorbs us, as though we were reading a novel whose author, employing the conventional devices for recording speech in fiction, might have written:

> "Oh, what does he want now?" said Helmer under his breath, in annoyance. Aloud, he called, "Hold on." Then he walked to the door and opened it and greeted Rank with all the cheer he could muster—"Oh, how nice that you didn't just pass us by!"

Such is the power of an excellent play to make us ignore the playwright's artistry that it becomes a window through which the reader's gaze, given focus, encompasses more than language and typography and beholds a scene of imagined life.

Most plays, whether seen in a theater or in print, employ *some* **conventions:** customary methods of presenting an action, usual and recognizable devices that an audience is willing to accept. In reading a great play from the past, such as *Oedipus the King* or *Othello*, it will help if we know some of the conventions of the classical Greek theater or the Elizabethan theater. When in *Oedipus the King* we encounter a character called the Chorus, it may be useful to be aware that this is a group of citizens who stand to one side of the action, conversing with the principal character and commenting. In *Othello*, when the sinister Iago, left on stage alone, begins to speak (at the end of Act II, Scene I), we recognize the conventional device of a **soliloquy,** a dramatic monologue in which we seem to overhear the character's inmost thoughts uttered aloud. Like conventions in poetry, such familiar methods of staging a story afford us a happy shock of recognition. Often, as in these examples, they are ways of making clear to us exactly what the playwright would have us know.

A PLAY IN ITS ELEMENTS

When we read a play on the printed page and find ourselves swept forward by the motion of its story, we need not wonder how—and of what ingredients—the playwright put it together. Still, to analyze the structure of a play is one way to understand and appreciate a playwright's art. Analysis is complicated, however, because in an excellent play the elements (including plot, theme, and characters) do not stand in isolation. Often, deeds clearly follow from the kinds of people the characters are, and from those deeds it is left to the reader to infer the **theme** of the play—the general point or truth about human beings that may be drawn from it. Perhaps the most meaningful way to study the elements of a play (and certainly the most enjoyable) is to consider a play in its entirety.

Here is a short, famous one-act play worth reading for the boldness of its elements—and for its own sake. *Trifles* tells the story of a murder. As you will discover, the "trifles" mentioned in its title are not of trifling stature. In reading the play, you will probably find yourself imagining what you might see on stage if you were in a theater. You may also care to imagine what took place in the lives of the characters before the curtain rose. All this imagining may sound like a tall order, but don't worry. Just read the play for enjoyment the first time through, and then we will consider what makes it effective.

Susan Glaspell

TRIFLES
1916

Susan Glaspell (1882–1948) grew up in her native Davenport, Iowa, daughter of a grain dealer. After four years at Drake University and a reporting job in Des Moines, she settled in New York's Greenwich Village. In 1915, with her husband George Cram Cook, a theatrical director, she founded the Provincetown Players, the first influential noncommercial theater troupe in America. Summers, in a makeshift playhouse on a Cape Cod pier, the Players staged the earliest plays of Eugene O'Neill and works by John Reed, Edna St. Vincent Millay, and Glaspell herself. (Later transplanting the company to New York, Glaspell and Cook renamed it the Playwrights' Theater.) Glaspell wrote several still-remembered plays, among them a pioneering work of feminist drama, The Verge *(1921), and the Pulitzer Prize-winning* Alison's House *(1930), about the family of a reclusive poet like Emily Dickinson who, after her death, squabble over the right to publish her poems. First widely known for her fiction with an Iowa background, Glaspell wrote ten novels, including* Fidelity *(1915) and* The Morning Is Near Us *(1939). Shortly after writing the play* Trifles, *she rewrote it as a short story, "A Jury of Her Peers."*

Characters

George Henderson, county attorney
Henry Peters, sheriff
Lewis Hale, a neighboring farmer
Mrs. Peters
Mrs. Hale

Scene. The kitchen in the now abandoned farmhouse of John Wright, a gloomy kitchen, and left without having been put in order—unwashed pans under the sink, a loaf of bread outside the breadbox, a dish towel on the table—other signs of incompleted work. At the rear the outer door opens and the Sheriff comes in followed by the County Attorney and Hale. The Sheriff and Hale are men in middle life, the County Attorney is a young man; all are much bundled up and go at once to the stove. They are followed by two women—the Sheriff's wife first; she is a slight wiry woman, a thin nervous face. Mrs. Hale is larger and would ordinarily be called more comfortable looking, but she is disturbed now and looks fearfully about as she enters. The women have come in slowly, and stand close together near the door.

County Attorney: [Rubbing his hands.] This feels good. Come up to the fire, ladies.
Mrs. Peters: [After taking a step forward.] I'm not—cold.
Sheriff: [Unbuttoning his overcoat and stepping away from the stove as if to mark the beginning of official business.] Now, Mr. Hale, before we move things about, you explain to Mr. Henderson just what you saw when you came here yesterday morning.
County Attorney: By the way, has anything been moved? Are things just as you left them yesterday?
Sheriff: [Looking about.] It's just the same. When it dropped below zero last night I thought I'd better send Frank out this morning to make a fire for us—no use getting pneumonia with a big case on, but I told him not to touch anything except the stove—and you know Frank.
County Attorney: Somebody should have been left here yesterday.
Sheriff: Oh—yesterday. When I had to send Frank to Morris Center for that man who went crazy—I want you to know I had my hands full yesterday, I knew you could get back from Omaha by today and as long as I went over everything here myself—
County Attorney: Well, Mr. Hale, tell just what happened when you came here yesterday morning.
Hale: Harry and I had started to town with a load of potatoes. We came along the road from my place and as I got here I said, "I'm going to see if I can't get John Wright to go in with me on a party telephone." I spoke to Wright about it once before and he put me off, saying folks talked too much anyway, and all he asked was peace and quiet—I guess you know about how much he talked himself; but I thought maybe if I went to the house and talked about

it before his wife, though I said to Harry that I didn't know as what his wife wanted made much difference to John—

County Attorney: Let's talk about that later, Mr. Hale. I do want to talk about that, but tell now just what happened when you got to the house.

Hale: I didn't hear or see anything; I knocked at the door, and still it was all quiet inside. I knew they must be up, it was past eight o'clock. So I knocked again, and I thought I heard somebody say, "Come in." I wasn't sure, I'm not sure yet, but I opened the door—this door [Indicating the door by which the two women are still standing] and there in that rocker—[Pointing to it] sat Mrs. Wright.

[They all look at the rocker.]

County Attorney: What—was she doing?

Hale: She was rockin' back and forth. She had her apron in her hand and was kind of—pleating it.

County Attorney: And how did she—look?

Hale: Well, she looked queer.

County Attorney: How do you mean—queer?

Hale: Well, as if she didn't know what she was going to do next. And kind of done up.

County Attorney: How did she seem to feel about your coming?

Hale: Why, I don't think she minded—one way or other. She didn't pay much attention. I said, "How do, Mrs. Wright, it's cold, ain't it?" And she said, "Is it?"—and went on kind of pleating at her apron. Well, I was surprised; she didn't ask me to come up to the stove, or to set down, but just sat there, not even looking at me, so I said, "I want to see John." And then she—laughed. I guess you would call it a laugh. I thought of Harry and the team outside, so I said a little sharp: "Can't I see John?" "No," she says, kind o' dull like. "Ain't he home?" says I. "Yes," says she, "he's home." "Then why can't I see him?" I asked her, out of patience. "'Cause he's dead," says she. "Dead?" says I. She just nodded her head, not getting a bit excited, but rockin' back and forth. "Why—where is he?" says I, not knowing what to say. She just pointed upstairs—like that [Himself pointing to the room above.] I got up, with the idea of going up there. I walked from there to here—then I says, "Why, what did he die of?" "He died of a rope round his neck," says she, and just went on pleatin' at her apron. Well, I went out and called Harry. I thought I might—need help. We went upstairs and there he was lyin'—

County Attorney: I think I'd rather have you go into that upstairs, where you can point it all out. Just go on now with the rest of the story.

Hale: Well, my first thought was to get that rope off. It looked . . . [Stops, his face twitches] . . . but Harry, he went up to him, and he said, "No, he's dead all right, and we'd better not touch anything." So we went back down stairs. She was still sitting that same way. "Has anybody been notified?" I asked. "No," says she, unconcerned. "Who did this, Mrs. Wright?" said Harry. He said it businesslike—and she stopped pleatin' of her apron. "I don't know," she says. "You don't know?" says Harry. "No," says she. "Weren't you sleepin' in the bed with him?" says Harry. "Yes," says she, "but I was on the inside." "Somebody slipped a rope round his neck and strangled him and you didn't wake up?" says Harry. "I didn't wake up," she said after him. We must 'a looked as if we didn't see how that could be, for after a minute she said, "I sleep sound." Harry was going to ask her more questions but I said maybe we ought to let her tell her story first to the coroner, or the sheriff, so Harry went fast as he could to Rivers' place, where there's a telephone.

County Attorney: And what did Mrs. Wright do when she knew that you had gone for the coroner?

Hale: She moved from that chair to this one over here [*Pointing to a small chair in the corner*] and just sat there with her hands held together and looking down. I got a feeling that I ought to make some conversation, so I said I had come in to see if John wanted to put in a telephone, and at that she started to laugh, and then she stopped and looked at me—scared. [*The County Attorney, who has had his notebook out, makes a note.*] I dunno, maybe it wasn't scared. I wouldn't like to say it was. Soon Harry got back, and then Dr. Lloyd came, and you, Mr. Peters, and so I guess that's all I know that you don't.

County Attorney: [*Looking around.*] I guess we'll go upstairs first—and then out to the barn and around there. [*To the Sheriff*] You're convinced that there was nothing important here—nothing that would point to any motive.

Sheriff: Nothing here but kitchen things.

[*The County Attorney, after again looking around the kitchen, opens the door of a cupboard closet. He gets up on a chair and looks on a shelf. Pulls his hand away, sticky.*]

County Attorney: Here's a nice mess.

[*The women draw nearer.*]

Mrs. Peters: [*To the other woman.*] Oh, her fruit; it did freeze. [*To the County Attorney*] She worried about that when it turned so cold. She said the fire'd go out and her jars would break.

Sheriff: Well, can you beat the women! Held for murder and worryin' about her preserves.

County Attorney: I guess before we're through she may have something more serious than preserves to worry about.

Hale: Well, women are used to worrying over trifles.

[*The two women move a little closer together.*]

County Attorney: [*With the gallantry of a young politician.*] And yet, for all their worries, what would we do without the ladies? [*The women do not unbend. He goes to the sink, takes a dipperful of water from the pail and pouring it into a basin, washes his hands. Starts to wipe them on the roller towel, turns it for a cleaner place.*] Dirty towels! [*Kicks his foot against the pans under the sink.*] Not much of a housekeeper, would you say, ladies?

Mrs. Hale: [*Stiffly.*] There's a great deal of work to be done on a farm.

County Attorney: To be sure. And yet [With a little bow to her] I know there are some Dickson county farmhouses which do not have such roller towels.

[He gives it a pull to expose its full length again.]

Mrs. Hale: Those towels get dirty awful quick. Men's hands aren't always as clean as they might be.

County Attorney: Ah, loyal to your sex, I see. But you and Mrs. Wright were neighbors. I suppose you were friends, too.

Mrs. Hale: [Shaking her head.] I've not seen much of her of late years. I've not been in this house—it's more than a year.

County Attorney: And why was that? You didn't like her?

Mrs. Hale: I liked her all well enough. Farmers' wives have their hands full, Mr. Henderson. And then—

County Attorney: Yes—?

Mrs. Hale: [Looking about.] It never seemed a very cheerful place.

County Attorney: No—it's not cheerful. I shouldn't say she had the home-making instinct.

Mrs. Hale: Well, I don't know as Wright had, either.

County Attorney: You mean that they didn't get on very well?

Mrs. Hale: No, I don't mean anything. But I don't think a place'd be any cheer-fuller for John Wright's being in it.

County Attorney: I'd like to talk more of that a little later. I want to get the lay of things upstairs now.

[He goes to the left, where three steps lead to a stair door.]

Sheriff: I suppose anything Mrs. Peters does'll be all right. She was to take in some clothes for her, you know, and a few little things. We left in such a hurry yesterday.

County Attorney: Yes, but I would like to see what you take, Mrs. Peters, and keep an eye out for anything that might be of use to us.

Mrs. Peters: Yes, Mr. Henderson.

[The women listen to the men's steps on the stairs, then look about the kitchen.]

Mrs. Hale: I'd hate to have men coming into my kitchen, snooping around and criticizing.

[She arranges the pans under sink which the County Attorney had shoved out of place.]

Mrs. Peters: Of course it's no more than their duty.

Mrs. Hale: Duty's all right, but I guess that deputy sheriff that came out to make the fire might have got a little of this on. [Gives the roller towel a pull.] Wish I'd thought of that sooner. Seems mean to talk about her for not having things slicked up when she had to come away in such a hurry.

Mrs. Peters: [Who has gone to a small table in the left rear corner of the room, and lifted one end of a towel that covers a pan.] She had bread set.

[Stands still.]

Mrs. Hale: [Eyes fixed on a loaf of bread beside the breadbox, which is on a low shelf at the other side of the room. Moves slowly toward it.] She was going to put this in there. [Picks up loaf, then abruptly drops it. In a manner of returning to familiar things.] It's a shame about her fruit. I wonder if it's all gone. [Gets up on the chair and looks.] I think there's some here that's all right, Mrs. Peters. Yes—here; [Holding it toward the window] this is cherries, too. [Looking again.] I declare I believe that's the only one. [Gets down, bottle in her hand. Goes to the sink and wipes it off on the outside.] She'll feel awful bad after all her hard work in the hot weather. I remember the afternoon I put up my cherries last summer.

[She puts the bottle on the big kitchen table, center of the room. With a sigh, is about to sit down in the rocking-chair. Before she is seated realizes what chair it is; with a slow look at it, steps back. The chair which she has touched rocks back and forth.]

Mrs. Peters: Well, I must get those things from the front room closet. [She goes to the door at the right, but after looking into the other room, steps back.] You coming with me, Mrs. Hale? You could help me carry them.

[They go in the other room; reappear, Mrs. Peters carrying a dress and skirt, Mrs. Hale following with a pair of shoes.]

Mrs. Peters: My, it's cold in there.

[She puts the clothes on the big table, and hurries to the stove.]

Mrs. Hale: [Examining her skirt.] Wright was close. I think maybe that's why she kept so much to herself. She didn't even belong to the Ladies Aid. I suppose she felt she couldn't do her part, and then you don't enjoy things when you feel shabby. She used to wear pretty clothes and be lively, when she was Minnie Foster, one of the town girls singing in the choir. But that—oh, that was thirty years ago. This all you was to take in?

Mrs. Peters: She said she wanted an apron. Funny thing to want, for there isn't much to get you dirty in jail, goodness knows. But I suppose just to make her feel more natural. She said they was in the top drawer in this cupboard. Yes, here. And then her little shawl that always hung behind the door. [Opens stair door and looks.] Yes, here it is.

[Quickly shuts door leading upstairs.]

Mrs. Hale: [Abruptly moving toward her.] Mrs. Peters?
Mrs. Peters: Yes, Mrs. Hale?
Mrs. Hale: Do you think she did it?
Mrs. Peters: [In a frightened voice.] Oh, I don't know.
Mrs. Hale: Well, I don't think she did. Asking for an apron and her little shawl. Worrying about her fruit.
Mrs. Peters: [Starts to speak, glances up, where footsteps are heard in the room above. In a low voice.] Mr. Peters says it looks bad for her. Mr. Henderson is awful sarcastic in a speech and he'll make fun of her sayin' she didn't wake up.

Mrs. Hale: Well, I guess John Wright didn't wake when they was slipping that rope under his neck.

Mrs. Peters: No, it's strange. It must have been done awful crafty and still. They say it was such a—funny way to kill a man, rigging it all up like that.

Mrs. Hale: That's just what Mr. Hale said. There was a gun in the house. He says that's what he can't understand.

Mrs. Peters: Mr. Henderson said coming out that what was needed for the case was a motive; something to show anger, or—sudden feeling.

Mrs. Hale: [Who is standing by the table.] Well, I don't see any signs of anger around here. [She puts her hand on the dish towel which lies on the table, stands looking down at table, one half of which is clean, the other half messy.] It's wiped to here. [Makes a move as if to finish work, then turns and looks at loaf of bread outside the breadbox. Drops towel. In that voice of coming back to familiar things.] Wonder how they are finding things upstairs. I hope she had it a little more red-up° up there. You know, it seems kind of sneaking. Locking her up in town and then coming out here and trying to get her own house to turn against her!

Mrs. Peters: But Mrs. Hale, the law is the law.

Mrs. Hale: I s'pose 'tis. [Unbuttoning her coat.] Better loosen up your things, Mrs. Peters. You won't feel them when you go out.

[Mrs. Peters takes off her fur tippet, goes to hang it on hook at back of room, stands looking at the under part of the small corner table.]

Mrs. Peters: She was piecing a quilt.

[She brings the large sewing basket and they look at the bright pieces.]

Mrs. Hale: It's a log cabin pattern. Pretty, isn't it? I wonder if she was goin' to quilt it or just knot it?

[Footsteps have been heard coming down the stairs. The Sheriff enters followed by Hale and the County Attorney.]

Sheriff: They wonder if she was going to quilt it or just knot it!

[The men laugh; the women look abashed.]

County Attorney: [Rubbing his hands over the stove.] Frank's fire didn't do much up there, did it? Well, let's go out to the barn and get that cleared up.

[The men go outside.]

Mrs. Hale: [Resentfully.] I don't know as there's anything so strange, our takin' up our time with little things while we're waiting for them to get the evidence. [She sits down at the big table smoothing out a block with decision.] I don't see as it's anything to laugh about.

---

red-up: (slang) readied up, ready to be seen.

Mrs. Peters: [*Apologetically.*] Of course they've got awful important things on their minds.

[*Pulls up a chair and joins Mrs. Hale at the table.*]

Mrs. Hale: [*Examining another block.*] Mrs. Peters, look at this one. Here, this is the one she was working on, and look at the sewing! All the rest of it has been so nice and even. And look at this! It's all over the place! Why, it looks as if she didn't know what she was about!

[*After she has said this they look at each, then start to glance back at the door. After an instant Mrs. Hale has pulled at a knot and ripped the sewing.*]

Mrs. Peters: Oh, what are you doing, Mrs. Hale?

Mrs. Hale: [*Mildly.*] Just pulling out a stitch or two that's not sewed very good. [*Threading a needle.*] Bad sewing always made me fidgety.

Mrs. Peters: [*Nervously.*] I don't think we ought to touch things.

Mrs. Hale: I'll just finish up this end. [*Suddenly stopping and leaning forward.*] Mrs. Peters?

Mrs. Peters: Yes, Mrs. Hale?

Mrs. Hale: What do you suppose she was so nervous about?

Mrs. Peters: Oh—I don't know. I don't know as she was nervous. I sometimes sew awful queer when I'm just tired. [*Mrs. Hale starts to say something, looks at Mrs. Peters, then goes on sewing.*] Well, I must get these things wrapped up. They may be through sooner than we think. [*Putting apron and other things together.*] I wonder where I can find a piece of paper, and string.

Mrs. Hale: In that cupboard, maybe.

Mrs. Peters: [*Looking in cupboard.*] Why, here's a birdcage. [*Holds it up.*] Did she have a bird, Mrs. Hale?

Mrs. Hale: Why, I don't know whether she did or not—I've not been here for so long. There was a man around last year selling canaries cheap, but I don't know as she took one; maybe she did. She used to sing real pretty herself.

Mrs. Peters: [*Glancing around.*] Seems funny to think of a bird here. But she must have had one, or why would she have a cage? I wonder what happened to it.

Mrs. Hale: I s'pose maybe the cat got it.

Mrs. Peters: No, she didn't have a cat. She's got that feeling some people have about cats—being afraid of them. My cat got in her room and she was real upset and asked me to take it out.

Mrs. Hale: My sister Bessie was like that. Queer, ain't it?

Mrs. Peters: [*Examining the cage.*] Why, look at this door. It's broke. One hinge is pulled apart.

Mrs. Hale: [*Looking too.*] Looks as if someone must have been rough with it.

Mrs. Peters: Why, yes.

[*She brings the cage forward and puts it on the table.*]

Mrs. Hale: I wish if they're going to find any evidence they'd be about it. I don't like this place.

Mrs. *Peters:* But I'm awful glad you came with me, Mrs. Hale. It would be lonesome for me sitting here alone.

Mrs. *Hale:* It would, wouldn't it? [*Dropping her sewing.*] But I tell you what I do wish, Mrs. Peters. I wish I had come over sometimes when *she* was here. I—[*Looking around the room.*]—wish I had.

Mrs. *Peters:* But of course you were awful busy, Mrs. Hale—your house and your children.

Mrs. *Hale:* I could've come. I stayed away because it weren't cheerful—and that's why I ought to have come. I—I've never liked this place. Maybe because it's down in a hollow and you don't see the road. I dunno what it is but it's a lonesome place and always was. I wish I had come over to see Minnie Foster sometimes. I can see now—

[*Shakes her head.*]

Mrs. *Peters:* Well, you mustn't reproach yourself, Mrs. Hale. Somehow we just don't see how it is with other folks until—something comes up.

Mrs. *Hale:* Not having children makes less work—but it makes a quiet house, and Wright out to work all day, and no company when he did come in. Did you know John Wright, Mrs. Peters?

Mrs. *Peters:* Not to know him; I've seen him in town. They say he was a good man.

Mrs. *Hale:* Yes—good; he didn't drink, and kept his word as well as most, I guess, and paid his debts. But he was a hard man, Mrs. Peters. Just to pass the time of day with him—[*Shivers.*] Like a raw wind that gets to the bone. [*Pauses, her eye falling on the cage.*] I should think she would'a wanted a bird. But what do you suppose went with it?

Mrs. *Peters:* I don't know, unless it got sick and died.

[*She reaches over and swings the broken door, swings it again. Both women watch it.*]

Mrs. *Hale:* You weren't raised round here, were you? [*Mrs. Peters shakes her head.*] You didn't know—her?

Mrs. *Peters:* Not till they brought her yesterday.

Mrs. *Hale:* She—come to think of it, she was kind of like a bird herself—real sweet and pretty, but kind of timid and—fluttery. How—she—did—change. [*Silence; then as if struck by a happy thought and relieved to get back to everyday things.*] Tell you what, Mrs. Peters, why don't you take the quilt in with you? It might take up her mind.

Mrs. *Peters:* Why, I think that's a real nice idea, Mrs. Hale. There couldn't possibly be any objection to it, could there? Now, just what would I take? I wonder if her patches are in here—and her things.

[*They look in the sewing basket.*]

Mrs. *Hale:* Here's some red. I expect this has got sewing things in it. [*Brings out a fancy box.*] What a pretty box. Looks like something somebody would give you. Maybe her scissors are in here. [*Opens box. Suddenly puts her hand to her*

nose.] Why—[Mrs. Peters bends nearer, then turns her face away.] There's
something wrapped up in this piece of silk.

Mrs. Peters: Why, this isn't her scissors.

Mrs. Hale: [Lifting the silk.] Oh, Mrs. Peters—it's—

[Mrs. Peters bends closer.]

Mrs. Peters: It's the bird.

Mrs. Hale: [Jumping up.] But, Mrs. Peters—look at it! Its neck! Look at its neck!
It's all—other side too.

Mrs. Peters: Somebody—wrung—its—neck.

[Their eyes meet. A look of growing comprehension, of horror. Steps are heard
outside. Mrs. Hale slips box under quilt pieces, and sinks into her chair. Enter
Sheriff and County Attorney. Mrs. Peters rises.]

County Attorney: [As one turning from serious things to little pleasantries.] Well,
ladies, have you decided whether she was going to quilt it or knot it?

Mrs. Peters: We think she was going to—knot it.

County Attorney: Well, that's interesting, I'm sure. [Seeing the birdcage.] Has the
bird flown?

Mrs. Hale: [Putting more quilt pieces over the box.] We think the—cat got it.

County Attorney: [Preoccupied.] Is there a cat?

[Mrs. Hale glances in a quick covert way at Mrs. Peters.]

Mrs. Peters: Well, not now. They're superstitious, you know. They leave.

County Attorney: [To Sheriff Peters, continuing an interrupted conversation.] No
sign at all of anyone having come from the outside. Their own rope. Now
let's go up again and go over it piece by piece. [They start upstairs.] It would
have to have been someone who knew just the—

[Mrs. Peters sits down. The two women sit there not looking at one another, but
as if peering into something and at the same time holding back. When they talk
now it is in the manner of feeling their way over strange ground, as if afraid of
what they are saying, but as if they cannot help saying it.]

Mrs. Hale: She liked the bird. She was going to bury it in that pretty box.

Mrs. Peters: [In a whisper.] When I was a girl—my kitten—there was a boy took
a hatchet, and before my eyes—and before I could get there—[Covers her
face an instant.] If they hadn't held me back I would have—[Catches herself,
looks upstairs where steps are heard, falters weakly]—hurt him.

Mrs. Hale: [With a slow look around her.] I wonder how it would seem never to
have had any children around. [Pause.] No, Wright wouldn't like the bird—
a thing that sang. She used to sing. He killed that, too.

Mrs. Peters: [Moving uneasily.] We don't know who killed the bird.

Mrs. Hale: I knew John Wright.

Mrs. Peters: It was an awful thing was done in this house that night, Mrs. Hale.
Killing a man while he slept, slipping a rope around his neck that choked
the life out of him.

Mrs. Hale: His neck. Choked the life out of him.

[*Her hand goes out and rests on the birdcage.*]

Mrs. Peters: [*With rising voice.*] We don't know who killed him. We don't *know.*

Mrs. Hale: [*Her own feeling not interrupted.*] If there'd been years and years of nothing, then a bird to sing to you, it would be awful—still, after the bird was still.

Mrs. Peters: [*Something within her speaking.*] I know what stillness is. When we homesteaded in Dakota, and my first baby died—after he was two years old, and me with no other then—

Mrs. Hale: [*Moving.*] How soon do you suppose they'll be through looking for the evidence?

Mrs. Peters: I know what stillness is. [*Pulling herself back.*] The law has got to punish crime, Mrs. Hale.

Mrs. Hale: [*Not as if answering that.*] I wish you'd seen Minnie Foster when she wore a white dress with blue ribbons and stood up there in the choir and sang. [*A look around the room.*] Oh, I *wish* I'd come over here once in a while! That was a crime! That was a crime! Who's going to punish that?

Mrs. Peters: [*Looking upstairs.*] We mustn't—take on.

Mrs. Hale: I might have known she needed help! I know how things can be— for women. I tell you, it's queer, Mrs. Peters. We live close together and we live far apart. We all go through the same things—it's all just a different kind of the same thing. [*Brushes her eyes; noticing the bottle of fruit, reaches out for it.*] If I was you I wouldn't tell her her fruit was gone. Tell her it *ain't.* Tell her it's all right. Take this in to prove it to her. She—she may never know whether it was broke or not.

Mrs. Peters: [*Takes the bottle, looks about for something to wrap it in; takes petticoat from the clothes brought from the other room, very nervously begins winding this around the bottle. In a false voice.*] My, it's a good thing the men couldn't hear us. Wouldn't they just laugh! Getting all stirred up over a little thing like a—dead canary. As if that could have anything to do with—with— wouldn't they *laugh!*

[*The men are heard coming down stairs.*]

Mrs. Hale: [*Under her breath.*] Maybe they would—maybe they wouldn't.

County Attorney: No, Peters, it's all perfectly clear except a reason for doing it. But you know juries when it comes to women. If there was some definite thing. Something to show—something to make a story about—a thing that would connect up with this strange way of doing it—

[*The women's eyes meet for an instant. Enter Hale from outer door.*]

Hale: Well, I've got the team around. Pretty cold out there.

County Attorney: I'm going to stay here a while by myself. [*To the Sheriff.*] You can send Frank out for me, can't you? I want to go over everything. I'm not satisfied that we can't do better.

Sheriff: Do you want to see what Mrs. Peters is going to take in?

[*The County Attorney goes to the table, picks up the apron, laughs.*]

County Attorney: Oh, I guess they're not very dangerous things the ladies have picked out. [*Moves a few things about, disturbing the quilt pieces which cover the box. Steps back.*] No, Mrs. Peters doesn't need supervising. For that matter, a sheriff's wife is married to the law. Ever think of it that way, Mrs. Peters?

Mrs. Peters: Not—just that way.

Sheriff: [*Chuckling.*] Married to the law. [*Moves toward the other room.*] I just want you to come in here a minute, George. We ought to take a look at these windows.

County Attorney: [*Scoffingly.*] Oh, windows!

Sheriff: We'll be right out, Mr. Hale.

[*Hale goes outside. The Sheriff follows the County Attorney into the other room. Then Mrs. Hale rises, hands tight together, looking intensely at Mrs. Peters, whose eyes make a slow turn, finally meeting Mrs. Hale's. A moment Mrs. Hale holds her, then her own eyes point the way to where the box is concealed. Suddenly Mrs. Peters throws back quilt pieces and tries to put the box in the bag she is wearing. It is too big. She opens box, starts to take bird out, cannot touch it, goes to pieces, stands there helpless. Sound of a knob turning in the other room. Mrs. Hale snatches the box and puts it in the pocket of her big coat. Enter County Attorney and Sheriff.*]

County Attorney: [*Facetiously.*] Well, Henry, at least we found out that she was not going to quilt it. She was going to—what is it you call it, ladies?

Mrs. Hale: [*Her hand against her pocket.*] We call it—knot it, Mr. Henderson.

CURTAIN

QUESTIONS

1. What attitudes toward women do the Sheriff and the County Attorney express? How do Mrs. Hale and Mrs. Peters react to these sentiments?
2. Why does the County Attorney care so much about discovering a motive for the killing?
3. What does Glaspell show us about the position of women in this early twentieth-century community?
4. What do we learn about the married life of the Wrights? By what means is this knowledge revealed to us?
5. What is the setting of this play, and how does it help us to understand Mrs. Wright's deed?
6. What do you infer from the wildly stitched block in Minnie's quilt? Why does Mrs. Hale rip out the crazy stitches?
7. What is so suggestive in the ruined birdcage and the dead canary wrapped in silk? What do these objects have to do with Minnie Foster Wright? What similarity do you notice between the way the canary died and John Wright's own death?
8. What thoughts and memories confirm Mrs. Peters and Mrs. Hale in their decision to help Minnie beat the murder rap?
9. In what places does Mrs. Peters show that she is trying to be a loyal, law-abiding sheriff's wife? How do she and Mrs. Hale differ in background and temperament?
10. What ironies does the play contain? Comment on Mrs. Hale's closing speech: "We call it—knot it, Mr. Henderson." Why is that little hesitation before "knot it" such a meaningful pause?

11. Point out some moments in the play when the playwright gives us to understand much without needing a spoken word.
12. How would you sum up the play's major theme?
13. How does this play, first produced in 1916, show its age? In what ways does it seem still remarkably new?
14. "*Trifles* is a lousy mystery. All the action took place before the curtain went up. Almost in the beginning, on the third page, we find out 'who done it.' So there isn't really much reason for us to sit through the rest of the play." Discuss this view.

Some plays endure, perhaps because (among other reasons) actors take pleasure in performing them. *Trifles* is such a play: a showcase for the skills of its two principals. While the men importantly bumble about, trying to discover a motive, Mrs. Peters and Mrs. Hale solve the case right under their dull noses. The two players in these leading roles face a challenging task: to show both characters growing onstage before us. Discovering a secret that binds them, the two must realize painful truths in their own lives, become aware of all they have in common with Minnie Wright, and gradually resolve to side with the accused against the men. That *Trifles* has lately enjoyed a revival of attention may reflect its evident feminist views, its convincing portrait of two women forced reluctantly to make a moral judgment and to make a defiant move.

Some critics say that the essence of drama is conflict. Evidently, Glaspell's play is rich in this essential, even though its most violent conflict—the war between John and Minnie Wright—takes place earlier, off scene. Right away, when the menfolk barge through the door into the warm room, letting the women trail in after them; right away, when the sheriff makes fun of Minnie for worrying about "trifles" and the county attorney (that slick politician) starts crudely trying to flatter the "ladies," we sense a conflict between officious, self-important men and the women they expect to wait on them. What is the play's *theme*? Surely the title points to it: Women, who men say worry over trifles, can find in those little things large meanings.

Like a carefully constructed traditional short story, *Trifles* has a **plot,** a term sometimes taken to mean whatever happens in a story, but more exactly referring to the unique arrangement of events that the author has made. (For more about plot in a story, see Chapter One.) If Glaspell had elected to tell the story of John and Minnie Wright in chronological order, the sequence in which events took place in time, she might have written a much longer play, opening perhaps with a scene of Minnie's buying her canary and John's cold complaint, "That damned bird keeps twittering all day long!" She might have included scenes showing John strangling the canary and swearing when it beaks him; the Wrights in their loveless bed while Minnie knots her noose; and farmer Hale's entrance after the murder, with Minnie rocking. Only at the end would she have shown us what happened after the crime. That arrangement of events would have made for a quite different play than the short, tight one Glaspell wrote. By telling of events in retrospect, by having the women detectives piece together what happened, Glaspell leads us to focus not only on the murder but, more importantly, on the developing bond between the two women and their growing compassion for the accused.

If *Trifles* may be said to have a **protagonist,** a leading character—a word we usually save for the primary figure of a larger and more eventful play such as *Othello* or *Death of a Salesman*—then you would call the two women dual protagonists. Both act in unison to make the plot unfold. Or you could argue that Mrs. Hale, because she destroys the wild stitching in the quilt; because she finds the dead canary; because she invents a cat to catch the bird (thus deceiving the county attorney); and because in the end when Mrs. Peters helplessly "goes to pieces" it is she who takes the initiative and seizes the evidence, deserves to be called the protagonist. More than anyone else in the play, you could claim, the more decisive Mrs. Hale makes things happen.

A vital part in most plays is an **exposition,** the part in which we first meet the characters, learn what happened before the curtain rose, and find out what is happening now. For a one-act play, *Trifles* has a fairly long exposition, extending from the opening of the kitchen door through the end of farmer Hale's story. Clearly, this substantial exposition is necessary to set the situation and to fill in the facts of the crime. By comparison, Shakespeare's far longer *Tragedy of Richard III* begins almost abruptly, with its protagonist, a duke who yearns to be king, summing up history in an opening speech and revealing his evil character: "And therefore, since I cannot prove a lover . . . I am determined to prove a villain." But Glaspell, too, knows her craft. In the exposition, we are given a **foreshadowing** (or hint of what is to come) in Hale's dry remark, "I didn't know as what his wife wanted made much difference to John." The remark announces the play's theme that men often ignore women's feelings, and it hints at Minnie Wright's motive, later to be revealed. The county attorney, failing to pick up a valuable clue, tables the discussion. (Still another foreshadowing occurs in Mrs. Hale's ripping out the wild, panicky stitches in Minnie's quilt. In the end, Mrs. Hale will make a similar final move to conceal the evidence.)

With the county attorney's speech to the sheriff, "You're convinced that there was nothing important here—nothing that would point to any motive," we begin to understand what he seeks. As he will make even clearer later, the attorney needs a motive in order to convict the accused wife of murder in the first degree. Will Minnie's motive in killing her husband be discovered? Through the first two-thirds of *Trifles*, this is the play's **dramatic question.** Whether or not we state such a question in our minds (and it is doubtful that we do), our interest quickens as we sense that here is a problem to be solved, an uncertainty to be dissipated. When Mrs. Hale and Mrs. Peters find the dead canary with the twisted neck, the question is answered. We know that Minnie killed John to repay him for his act of gross cruelty. The playwright, however, now raises a *new* dramatic question. Having discovered Minnie's motive, will the women reveal it to the lawmen? Alternatively (if you care to phrase the new question differently), what will they do with the incriminating evidence? We keep reading, or stay clamped to our theater seats, because we want that question answered. We share the women's secret now, and we want to see what they will do with it.

Tightly packed, the one-act *Trifles* contains but one plot: the story of how two women discover evidence that might hang another woman and then hide it. Some plays, usually longer ones, may be more complicated. They may contain a **double plot** (or **subplot**), a secondary arrangement of incidents, involving not the protagonist but someone less important. In Henrik Ibsen's *A Doll's House*, the main plot involves a woman and her husband; they are joined by a second couple, whose fortunes we also follow with interest and whose futures pose another dramatic question.

Step by step, *Trifles* builds to a **climax:** a moment, usually coming late in a play, when tension reaches its greatest height. At such a moment, we sense that the play's dramatic question (or its final dramatic question, if the writer has posed more than one) is about to be answered. In *Trifles* this climax occurs when Mrs. Peters finds herself torn between her desire to save Minnie and her duty to the law. "It was an awful thing was done in this house that night," she reminds herself in one speech, suggesting that Minnie deserves to be punished; then in the next speech she insists, "We don't know who killed him. We don't *know*." Shortly after that, in one speech she voices two warring attitudes. Remembering the loss of her first child, she sympathizes with Minnie: "I know what stillness is." But in her next breath she recalls once more her duty to be a loyal sheriff's wife: "The law has got to punish crime, Mrs. Hale." For a moment, she is placed in conflict with Mrs. Hale, who knew Minnie personally. The two now stand on the edge of a fateful brink. Which way will they decide?[1]

From this moment of climax, the play, like its protagonist (or if you like, protagonists), will make a final move. Mrs. Peters takes her stand. Mrs. Hale, too, decides. She owes Minnie something to make up for her own "crime"—her failure to visit the desperate woman. The plot now charges ahead to its outcome or **resolution,** also called the **conclusion** or **dénouement** (French for "untying of a knot"). The two women act: they scoop up the damaging evidence. Seconds before the very end, Glaspell heightens the **suspense,** our enjoyable anxiety, by making Mrs. Peters fumble with the incriminating box as the sheriff and the county attorney draw near. Mrs. Hale's swift grab for the evidence saves the day and presumably saves Minnie's life. The sound of the doorknob turning in the next room, as the lawmen return, is a small but effective bit of **stage business**—any nonverbal action that engages the attention of an audience. Earlier, when Mrs. Hale almost sits down in Minnie's place, the empty chair that ominously starts rocking is another brilliant piece of stage business. Not only does it give us something interesting to watch, but it also gives us something to think about.

Some critics maintain that events in a plot can be arranged in the outline of a pyramid.[2] In this view, a play begins with a **rising action,** that part of the story (including the exposition) in which events start moving toward a climax. After the climax, the story tapers off in a **falling action,** that is, the subsequent events, including a resolution. In a tragedy, this falling action usually is recognizable: the protagonist's fortunes proceed downhill to an inexorable end.

Some plays indeed have demonstrable pyramids. In *Trifles,* we might claim that in the first two-thirds of the play a rising action builds in intensity. It proceeds through each main incident: the finding of the crazily stitched quilt, Mrs. Hale's ripping out the evidence, the discovery of the bird cage, then the bird itself, and Mrs. Hale's concealing it. At the climax, the peak of the pyramid, the two women seem about to clash as Mrs. Peters wavers uncertainly. The action then falls to a swift resolution. If you outlined that pyramid on paper, however, it would look lopsided—a

---

[1]You will sometimes hear *climax* used in a different sense to mean any **crisis**—that is, a moment of tension when one or another outcome is possible. What *crisis* means will be easy to remember if you think of a crisis in medicine: the turning point in a disease when it becomes clear that a patient will either die or recover. In talking about plays, you will probably find both *crisis* and *climax* useful. You can say that a play has more than one crisis, perhaps several. In such a play, the last and most decisive crisis is the climax. A play has only one climax.

[2]The metaphor of a play as a pyramid was invented by German critic Gustav Freytag, in his *Techniques of the Drama,* 1904, reprint ed. (New York: Arno, 1968).

long rise and a short, steep fall. The pyramid metaphor seems more meaningfully to fit longer plays, among them some classic tragedies. Try it on *Oedipus the King* or, for an even neater fit, on Shakespeare's *Julius Caesar*—an unusual play in that its climax, the assassination of Caesar, occurs exactly in the middle (Act III, Scene 1), right where a good pyramid's point ought to be. Nevertheless, in most other plays, it is hard to find a symmetrical pyramid. (For a demonstration of another, quite different way to outline *Trifles*, see "Writing a Card Report" on page 1916.)

Because its action occurs all at one time and in one place, *Trifles* happens to observe the **unities,** certain principles of good drama laid down by Italian literary critics in the sixteenth century. Interpreting the theories of Aristotle as binding laws, these critics set down three basic principles: a good play, they maintained, should display unity of *action*, unity of *time*, and unity of *place*. In practical terms, this theory maintained that a play must represent a single series of interrelated actions that take place within twenty-four hours in a single location. Furthermore, they insisted, to have true unity of action, a play had to be entirely serious or entirely funny. Mixing tragic and comic elements was not allowed. That Glaspell consciously strove to obey those critics is doubtful and certainly many great plays, like Shakespeare's *Othello*, defy such arbitrary rules. Still, it is at least arguable that some of the power of *Trifles* (or Sophocles' *Oedipus the King*) comes from the intensity of the playwright's concentration on what happens in one place, in one short expanse of time.

Brief though it is, *Trifles* has main elements you will find in much longer, more complicated plays. It even has **symbols,** things that hint at large meanings, for example, the broken bird cage and the dead canary, both suggesting the music and the joy that John Wright stifled in Minnie and the terrible stillness that followed his killing the one thing she loved. Perhaps the lone remaining jar of cherries, too, radiates suggestions: it is the one bright, cheerful thing poor Minnie has to show for a whole summer of toil. Symbols in drama may be as big as a house—the home in Ibsen's *A Doll's House*, for instance—or they may appear to be trifles. In Glaspell's rich art, such trifles aren't trifling at all.[3]

Tragedy and Comedy

By **tragedy,** generally speaking, we mean a play that portrays a conflict between human beings and some superior, overwhelming force. It ends sorrowfully and disastrously, and this outcome seems inevitable. Few spectators of *Oedipus the King* wonder how the play will turn out or wish for a happy ending. "In a tragedy," French playwright Jean Anouilh has remarked, "nothing is in doubt and everyone's destiny is known. . . . Tragedy is restful, and the reason is that hope, that foul, deceitful thing, has no part in it. There isn't any hope. You're trapped. The whole sky has fallen on you, and all you can do about it is shout."[4]

Many of our ideas of tragedy go back to ancient Athens; the plays of the Greek dramatists Sophocles, Aeschylus, and Euripides exemplify the art of tragedy. In the

[3]Plays can also contain symbolic characters (generally flat ones such as a prophet who croaks, "Beware the ides of March"), symbolic settings, and symbolic gestures. For more about symbolism, see Chapters Seven and Twenty-three.
[4]Preface to *Antigonê*, translated by Louis Galantière (New York: Random, 1946).

fourth century B.C., the philosopher Aristotle described Sophocles' *Oedipus the King* and other tragedies he had seen, analyzing their elements and trying to account for their power over our emotions. Aristotle's observations will make more sense after you read *Oedipus the King*, so let us save discussion of them for the next chapter. For now, to understand something of the nature of tragedy, we suggest you begin by reading not a classic Greek tragedy but a gripping modern tragedy by the Irish poet and playwright John Millington Synge.

The people of Synge's play are simple fisherfolk who live in the Aran Islands, outposts of barren rock washed by the stormy North Atlantic. They are speakers of Gaelic, the old Irish language. Living in their midst, Synge studied their plain, colorful speech and tried to convey a sense of it in the English of this play. Notice how slowly and quietly the tragedy begins. Gradually, disturbing facts fit into place until we know the whole story of a family that has long struggled with the sea, a dangerous and demanding friend, a relentless enemy.

John Millington Synge

RIDERS TO THE SEA°   1904

John Millington Synge (pronounced "Sing," 1871–1909), a leading figure in the Irish literary revival at the turn of this century, was born near Dublin, where he died. After graduation from Dublin's Trinity College, he studied music in Germany, Italy, and France. In 1899 he struck up a friendship with poet and playwright William Butler Yeats, who advised him to go to the Aran Islands off Ireland's west coast, listen to the spoken language, and observe the life of the islanders. For Synge, this advice bore fruit in his plays, The Shadow of the Glen *(1903) and* Riders to the Sea *(1904), and in a book of impressions,* The Aran Islands *(1907). When first performed at the Abbey Theater in Dublin in 1907, Synge's dark comedy* The Playboy of

John Millington Synge

the Western World *caused a riot. Some in the audience objected to its unflattering, satiric view of rural Irishmen. Later its Irish-American audiences rioted in Boston, Philadelphia, and New York. A considerable poet as well as a playwright, Synge struggled for years against lymphatic sarcoma, a disease that curtailed his life. His unfinished tragedy,* Deirdre of the Sorrows, *was produced after his death.*

Riders to the Sea: The title alludes to a well-known Bible story. After Moses opens a corridor in the sea for the children of Israel to pass through, he obeys the Lord and lets the waters "come again upon the Egyptians, upon their chariots, and upon their horsemen." Then he and the Israelites "sing unto the Lord, for he has triumphed gloriously: the horse and his rider hath he thrown into the sea" (Exodus 14:21–31, 15:1–5).

Characters

Maurya, an old woman
Bartley, her son
Cathleen, her daughter
Nora, a younger daughter
Men and Women

Scene. *An Island off the West of Ireland.*
Cottage kitchen, with nets, oil-skins, spinning-wheel, some new boards standing by the wall, etc. Cathleen, a girl of about twenty, finishes kneading cake, and puts it down in the pot-oven by the fire; then wipes her hands, and begins to spin at the wheel. Nora, a young girl, puts her head in at the door.

Nora (in a low voice): Where is she?
Cathleen: She's lying down, God help her, and may be sleeping, if she's able.

    Nora comes in softly, and takes a bundle from under her shawl.

Cathleen (spinning the wheel rapidly): What is it you have?
Nora: The young priest is after bringing them.° It's a shirt and a plain stocking were got off a drowned man in Donegal.

    Cathleen stops her wheel with a sudden movement, and leans out to listen.

Nora: We're to find out if it's Michael's they are, some time herself will be down looking by the sea.
Cathleen: How would they be Michael's, Nora? How would he go the length of that way to the far north?
Nora: The young priest says he's known the like of it. "If it's Michael's they are," says he, "you can tell yourself he's got a clean burial by the grace of God, and if they're not his, let no one say a word about them, for she'll be getting her death," says he, "with crying and lamenting."

    The door which Nora half-closed is blown open by a gust of wind.

Cathleen (looking out anxiously): Did you ask him would he stop Bartley going this day with the horses to the Galway fair?
Nora: "I won't stop him," says he, "but let you not be afraid. Herself does be saying prayers half through the night, and the Almighty God won't leave her destitute," says he, "with no son living."
Cathleen: Is the sea bad by the white rocks, Nora?
Nora: Middling bad, God help us. There's a great roaring in the west, and it's worse it'll be getting when the tide's turned to the wind.

    She goes over to the table with the bundle.

---

is after bringing them: has just brought them.

Shall I open it now?

Cathleen: Maybe she'd wake up on us, and come in before we'd done. (*Coming to the table.*) It's a long time we'll be, and the two of us crying.

Nora (*goes to the inner door and listens*): She's moving about on the bed. She'll be coming in a minute.

Cathleen: Give me the ladder, and I'll put them up in the turf-loft, the way she won't know of them at all, and maybe when the tide turns she'll be going down to see would he be floating from the east.

They put the ladder against the gable of the chimney; Cathleen goes up a few steps and hides the bundle in the turf-loft. Maurya comes from the inner room.

Maurya (*looking up at Cathleen and speaking querulously*): Isn't it turf enough you have for this day and evening?

Cathleen: There's a cake baking at the fire for a short space (*throwing down the turf*) and Bartley will want it when the tide turns if he goes to Connemara.

Nora picks up the turf and puts it round the pot-oven.

Maurya (*sitting down on a stool at the fire*): He won't go this day with the wind rising from the south and west. He won't go this day, for the young priest will stop him surely.

Nora: He'll not stop him, mother, and I heard Eamon Simon and Stephen Pheety and Colum Shawn saying he would go.

Maurya: Where is he itself?

Nora: He went down to see would there be another boat sailing in the week, and I'm thinking it won't be long till he's here now, for the tide's turning at the green head, and the hooker's° tacking from the east.

Cathleen: I hear some one passing the big stones.

Nora (*looking out*): He's coming now, and he in a hurry.

Bartley (*comes in and looks round the room. Speaking sadly and quietly*): Where is the bit of new rope, Cathleen, was bought in Connemara?

Cathleen (*coming down*): Give it to him, Nora; it's on a nail by the white boards. I hung it up this morning, for the pig with the black feet was eating it.

Nora (*giving him a rope*): Is that it, Bartley?

Maurya: You'd do right to leave that rope, Bartley, hanging by the boards. (*Bartley takes the rope.*) It will be wanting in this place. I'm telling you, if Michael is washed up to-morrow morning, or the next morning, or any morning in the week, for it's a deep grave we'll make him by the grace of God.

Bartley (*beginning to work with the rope*): I've no halter the way I can ride down on the mare, and I must go now quickly. This is the one boat going for two weeks or beyond it, and the fair will be a good fair for horses I heard them saying below.

---

hooker: a one-masted fishing boat.

Maurya: It's a hard thing they'll be saying below if the body is washed up and there's no man in it to make the coffin, and I after giving a big price for the finest white boards you'd find in Connemara.

She looks round at the boards.

Bartley: How would it be washed up, and we after looking each day for nine days, and a strong wind blowing a while back from the west and south?

Maurya: If it wasn't found itself, that wind is raising the sea, and there was a star up against the moon, and it rising in the night. If it was a hundred horses, or a thousand horses you had itself, what is the price of a thousand horses against a son where there is one son only?

Bartley (working at the halter, to Cathleen): Let you go down each day, and see the sheep aren't jumping in on the rye, and if the jobber comes you can sell the pig with the black feet if there is a good price going.

Maurya: How would the like of her get a good price for a pig?

Bartley (to Cathleen): If the west wind holds with the last bit of the moon let you and Nora get up weed enough for another cock for the kelp.° It's hard set we'll be from this day with no one in it but one man to work.

Maurya: It's hard set we'll be surely the day you're drownd'd with the rest. What way will I live and the girls with me, and I an old woman looking for the grave?

Bartley lays down the halter, takes off his old coat, and puts on a newer one of the same flannel.

Bartley (to Nora): Is she coming to the pier?

Nora (looking out): She's passing the green head and letting fall her sails.

Bartley (getting his purse and tobacco): I'll have half an hour to go down, and you'll see me coming again in two days, or in three days, or maybe in four days if the wind is bad.

Maurya (turning round to the fire, and putting her shawl over her head): Isn't it a hard and cruel man won't hear a word from an old woman, and she holding him from the sea?

Cathleen: It's the life of a young man to be going on the sea, and who would listen to an old woman with one thing and she saying it over?

Bartley (taking the halter): I must go now quickly. I'll ride down on the red mare, and the gray pony'll run behind me. . . . The blessing of God on you.

He goes out.

Maurya (crying out as he is in the door): He's gone now, God spare us, and we'll not see him again. He's gone now, and when the black night is falling I'll have no son left me in the world.

Cathleen: Why wouldn't you give him your blessing and he looking round in the door? Isn't it sorrow enough is on every one in this house without your

---

another cock for the kelp: another pile of seaweed. The islanders harvest the weed to fertilize their sparse, rocky soil.

sending him out with an unlucky word behind him, and a hard word in his ear?

Maurya takes up the tongs and begins raking the fire aimlessly without looking round.

Nora (*turning towards her*): You're taking away the turf from the cake.

Cathleen (*crying out*): The Son of God forgive us, Nora, we're after forgetting his bit of bread.

She comes over to the fire.

Nora: And it's destroyed he'll be going till dark night, and he after eating nothing since the sun went up.

Cathleen (*turning the cake out of the oven*): It's destroyed he'll be, surely. There's no sense left on any person in a house where an old woman will be talking for ever.

Maurya sways herself on her stool.

Cathleen (*cutting off some of the bread and rolling it in a cloth; to Maurya*): Let you go down now to the spring well and give him this and he passing. You'll see him then and the dark word will be broken, and you can say "God speed you," the way he'll be easy in his mind.

Maurya (*taking the bread*): Will I be in it as soon as himself?

Cathleen: If you go now quickly.

Maurya (*standing up unsteadily*): It's hard set I am to walk.

Cathleen (*looking at her anxiously*): Give her the stick, Nora, or maybe she'll slip on the big stones.

Nora: What stick?

Cathleen: The stick Michael brought from Connemara.

Maurya (*taking a stick Nora gives her*): In the big world the old people do be leaving things after them for their sons and children, but in this place it is the young men do be leaving things behind for them that do be old.

She goes out slowly. Nora goes over to the ladder.

Cathleen: Wait, Nora, maybe she'd turn back quickly. She's that sorry, God help her, you wouldn't know the thing she'd do.

Nora: Is she gone around by the bush?

Cathleen (*looking out*): She's gone now. Throw it down quickly, for the Lord knows when she'll be out of it again.

Nora (*getting the bundle from the loft*): The young priest said he'd be passing to-morrow, and we might go down and speak to him below if it's Michael's they are surely.

Cathleen (*taking the bundle*): Did he say what way they were found?

Nora (*coming down*): "There were two men," says he, "and they rowing round with poteen before the cocks crowed,° and the oar of one of them caught the body, and they passing the black cliffs of the north."

---

rowing round with poteen . . . crowed: transporting moonshine whiskey under cover of darkness.

Cathleen (*trying to open the bundle*): Give me a knife, Nora, the strings perished with the salt water, and there's a black knot on it you wouldn't loosen in a week.

Nora (*giving her a knife*): I've heard tell it was a long way to Donegal.

Cathleen (*cutting the string*): It is surely. There was a man in here a while ago—the man sold us that knife—and he said if you set off walking from the rock beyond, it would be seven days you'd be in Donegal.

Nora: And what time would a man take, and he floating?

Cathleen opens the bundle and takes out a bit of a stocking. They look at them eagerly.

Cathleen (*in a low voice*): The Lord spare us, Nora! Isn't it a queer hard thing to say if it's his they are surely?

Nora: I'll get his shirt off the hook the way we can put the one flannel on the other. (*She looks through some clothes hanging in the corner.*) It's not with them, Cathleen, and where will it be?

Cathleen: I'm thinking Bartley put it on him in the morning, for his own shirt was heavy with the salt in it. (*Pointing to the corner.*) There's a bit of a sleeve was of the same stuff. Give me that and it will do.

Nora brings it to her and they compare the flannel.

Cathleen: It's the same stuff, Nora; but if it is itself aren't there great rolls of it in the shops of Galway, and isn't it many another man may have a shirt of it as well as Michael himself?

Nora (*who has taken up the stocking and counted the stitches, crying out*): It's Michael, Cathleen, it's Michael; God spare his soul, and what will herself say when she hears this story, and Bartley on the sea?

Cathleen (*taking the stocking*): It's a plain stocking.

Nora: It's the second one of the third pair I knitted, and I put up three score stitches, and I dropped four of them.

Cathleen (*counts the stitches*): It's that number is in it. (*Crying out.*) Ah, Nora, isn't it a bitter thing to think of him floating that way to the far north, and no one to keen° him but the black hags that do be flying on the sea?

Nora (*swinging herself round, and throwing out her arms on the clothes*): And isn't it a pitiful thing when there is nothing left of a man who was a great rower and fisher, but a bit of an old shirt and a plain stocking?

Cathleen (*after an instant*): Tell me is herself coming, Nora? I hear a little sound on the path.

Nora (*looking out*): She is, Cathleen. She's coming up to the door.

Cathleen: Put these things away before she'll come in. Maybe it's easier she'll be after giving her blessing to Bartley, and we won't let on we've heard anything the time he's on the sea.

Nora (*helping Cathleen to close the bundle*): We'll put them here in the corner.

keen: weep and wail.

They put them into a hole in the chimney corner. Cathleen goes back to the spinning-wheel.

Nora: Will she see it was crying I was?

Cathleen: Keep your back to the door the way the light'll not be on you.

Nora sits down at the chimney corner, with her back to the door. Maurya comes in very slowly, without looking at the girls, and goes over to her stool at the other side of the fire. The cloth with the bread is still in her hand. The girls look at each other, and Nora points to the bundle of bread.

Cathleen (*after spinning for a moment*): You didn't give him his bit of bread?

Maurya begins to keen softly, without turning round.

Cathleen: Did you see him riding down?

Maurya goes on keening.

Cathleen (*a little impatiently*): God forgive you; isn't it a better thing to raise your voice and tell what you seen, than to be making lamentation for a thing that's done? Did you see Bartley, I'm saying to you.

Maurya (*with a weak voice*): My heart's broken from this day.

Cathleen (*as before*): Did you see Bartley?

Maurya: I seen the fearfulest thing.

Cathleen (*leaves her wheel and looks out*): God forgive you; he's riding the mare now over the green head, and the gray pony behind him.

Maurya (*starts, so that her shawl falls back from her head and shows her white tossed hair. With a frightened voice*): The gray pony behind him.

Cathleen (*coming to the fire*): What is it ails you, at all?

Maurya (*speaking very slowly*): I've seen the fearfulest thing any person has seen, since the day Bride Dara seen the dead man with the child in his arms.

Cathleen and Nora: Uah.°

They crouch down in front of the old woman at the fire.

Nora: Tell us what it is you seen.

Maurya: I went down to the spring well, and I stood there saying a prayer to myself. Then Bartley came along, and he riding on the red mare with the gray pony behind him. (*She puts up her hands, as if to hide something from her eyes.*) The Son of God spare us, Nora!

Cathleen: What is it you seen?

Maurya: I seen Michael himself.

Cathleen (*speaking softly*): You did not Mother; it wasn't Michael you seen, for his body is after being found in the far north, and he's got a clean burial by the grace of God.

Uah: exclamation of horror and surprise.

Maurya (*a little defiantly*): I'm after seeing him this day, and he riding and galloping. Bartley came first on the red mare; and I tried to say "God speed
you," but something choked the words in my throat. He went by quickly;
and "the blessing of God on you," says he, and I could say nothing. I looked
up then, and I crying, at the gray pony, and there was Michael upon it—
with fine clothes on him, and new shoes on his feet.

Cathleen (*begins to keen*): It's destroyed we are from this day. It's destroyed,
surely.

Nora: Didn't the young priest say the Almighty God wouldn't leave her destitute with no son living?

Maurya (*in a low voice, but clearly*): It's little the like of him knows of the sea. . . .
Bartley will be lost now, and let you call in Eamon and make me a good
coffin out of the white boards, for I won't live after them. I've had a husband, and a husband's father, and six sons in this house—six fine men,
though it was a hard birth I had with every one of them and they coming to
the world—and some of them were found and some of them were not found,
but they're gone now the lot of them. . . . There were Stephen, and Shawn,
were lost in the great wind, and found after in the Bay of Gregory of the
Golden Mouth, and carried up the two of them on the one plank, and in by
that door.

*She pauses for a moment, the girls start as if they heard something through the door
that is half open behind them.*

Nora (*in a whisper*): Did you hear that, Cathleen? Did you hear a noise in the
north-east?

Cathleen (*in a whisper*): There's some one after crying out by the seashore.

Maurya (*continues without hearing anything*): There was Sheamus and his father,
and his own father again, were lost in a dark night, and not a stick or sign
was seen of them when the sun went up. There was Patch after was drowned
out of a curagh° that turned over. I was sitting here with Bartley, and he a
baby, lying on my two knees, and I seen two women, and three women, and
four women coming in, and they crossing themselves, and not saying a
word. I looked out then, and there were men coming after them, and they
holding a thing in the half of a red sail, and water dripping out of it—it was
a dry day, Nora—and leaving a track to the door.

*She pauses again with her hand stretched out towards the door. It opens softly and
old women begin to come in, crossing themselves on the threshold, and kneeling
down in front of the stage with red petticoats over their heads.*

Maurya (*half in a dream, to Cathleen*): Is it Patch, or Michael, or what is it at all?

Cathleen: Michael is after being found in the far north, and when he is found
there how could he be here in this place?

curagh: a canvas-bottomed boat.

Maurya: There does be a power of young men floating round in the sea, and what way would they know if it was Michael they had, or another man like him, for when a man is nine days in the sea, and the wind blowing, it's hard set his own mother would be to say what man was it.

Cathleen: It's Michael, God spare him, for they're after sending us a bit of his clothes from the far north.

She reaches out and hands Maurya the clothes that belonged to Michael. Maurya stands up slowly and takes them in her hand. Nora looks out.

Nora: They're carrying a thing among them and there's water dripping out of it and leaving a track by the big stones.

Cathleen (*in a whisper to the women who have come in*): Is it Bartley it is?

One of the Women: It is surely, God rest his soul.

Two younger women come in and pull out the table. Then men carry in the body of Bartley, laid on a plank, with a bit of sail over it, and lay it on the table.

Cathleen (*to the women, as they are doing so*): What way was he drowned?

One of the Women: The gray pony knocked him into the sea, and he was washed out where there is a great surf on the white rocks.

Maurya has gone over and knelt down at the head of the table. The women are keening softly and swaying themselves with a slow movement. Cathleen and Nora kneel at the other end of the table. The men kneel near the door.

Maurya (*raising her head and speaking as if she did not see the people around her*): They're all gone now, and there isn't anything more the sea can do to me. . . . I'll have no call now to be up crying and praying when the wind breaks from the south and you can hear the surf is in the east, and the surf is in the west, making a great stir with the two noises, and they hitting one on the other. I'll have no call now to be going down and getting Holy Water in the dark nights after Samhain,° and I won't care what way the sea is when the other women will be keening. (*To Nora*) Give me the Holy Water, Nora, there's a small cup still on the dresser.

Nora gives it to her.

Maurya (*drops Michael's clothes across Bartley's feet, and sprinkles the Holy Water over him.*): It isn't that I haven't prayed for you, Bartley, to the Almighty God. It isn't that I haven't said prayers in the dark night till you wouldn't know what I'ld be saying; but it's a great rest I'll have now, and it's time surely. It's a great rest I'll have now, and great sleeping in the long nights after Samhain, if it's only a bit of wet flour we do have to eat, and maybe a fish that would be stinking.

She kneels down again, crossing herself, and saying prayers under her breath.

Samhain: All Saints' Day.

Cathleen (*to an old man*): Maybe yourself and Eamon would make a coffin when the sun rises. We have fine white boards herself bought, God help her, thinking Michael would be found, and I have a new cake you can eat while you'll be working.

The Old Man (*looking at the boards*): Are there nails with them?

Cathleen: There are not, Colum; we didn't think of the nails.

Another Man: It's a great wonder she wouldn't think of the nails, and all the coffins she's been made already.

Cathleen: It's getting old she is, and broken.

> *Maurya stands up again very slowly and spreads out the pieces of Michael's clothes beside the body, sprinkling them with the last of the Holy Water.*

Nora (*in a whisper to Cathleen*): She's quiet now and easy; but the day Michael was drowned you could hear her crying out from this to the spring well. It's fonder she was of Michael, and would any one have thought that?

Cathleen (*slowly and clearly*): An old woman will be soon tired with anything she will do, and isn't it nine days herself is after crying and keening, and making great sorrow in the house?

Maurya (*puts the empty cup mouth downwards on the table, and lays her hands together on Bartley's feet*): They're all together this time, and the end is come. May the Almighty God have mercy on Bartley's soul, and on Michael's soul, and on the souls of Sheamus and Patch, and Stephen and Shawn (*bending her head*); and may He have mercy on my soul, Nora, and on the soul of every one is left living in the world.

> *She pauses, and the keen rises a little more loudly from the women, then sinks away.*

Maurya (*continuing*): Michael has a clean burial in the far north, by the grace of the Almighty God. Bartley will have a fine coffin out of the white boards, and a deep grave surely. What more can we want than that? No man at all can be living for ever, and we must be satisfied.

> *She kneels down again and the curtain falls slowly.*

QUESTIONS

1. What is the situation at the start of *Riders to the Sea*? What motivates Cathleen and Nora to hide Michael's clothes from their mother?
2. What suggestions of deeper meaning do you find in the abruptness with which Cathleen stops her spinning wheel at Nora's mention of the clothes that have been found? in the gust of wind that opens the half-closed door?
3. What motivates the priest not to interfere with Bartley's plan to take the horses to the Galway fair? Why does his mother want him to stay home? How do Cathleen, Nora, and Bartley react to their mother's request?
4. What does Maurya see when she goes to the spring well to give Bartley his bread? What is there about her account of it that makes Cathleen say, "It's destroyed we are from this day. It's destroyed, surely"?
5. How does Bartley die? At what moment is his death foreshadowed?

6. Do you agree with Cathleen's observation at the end of the play that Maurya is "broken"? Explain.
7. Does *Riders to the Sea* have any protagonist? If so, what character has this central role?

Comedy, from the Greek *komos,* "a revel," is thought to have originated in festivities to celebrate spring, ritual performances in praise of Dionysus, god of fertility and wine. In drama, comedy may be broadly defined as whatever makes us laugh. A comedy may be a name for one entire play, or we may say that there is comedy in only part of a play—as in a comic character or a comic situation.

The best-known traditional emblem of drama—a pair of masks, one sorrowful (representing tragedy) and one smiling (representing comedy)—suggests that tragedy and comedy, although opposites, are close relatives. Often, comedy shows people getting into trouble through error or weakness; in this respect it is akin to tragedy. An important difference between comedy and tragedy lies in the attitude toward human failing that is expected of us. When a main character in a comedy suffers from overweening pride, as does Oedipus, or if he fails to recognize that his bride-to-be is actually his mother, we laugh—something we would never do in watching a competent performance of *Oedipus the King.*

Many theories have been propounded to explain why we laugh; most of these notions fall into a few familiar types. One school, exemplified by French philosopher Henri Bergson, sees laughter as a form of ridicule, implying a feeling of disinterested superiority; all jokes are *on* somebody. Bergson suggests that laughter springs from situations in which we sense a conflict between some mechanical or rigid pattern of behavior and our sense of a more natural or "organic" kind of behavior that is possible.[5] An example occurs in Buster Keaton's comic film *The Boat.* Having launched a little boat that springs a leak, Keaton rigidly goes down with it, with frozen face. (The more natural and organic thing to do would be to swim for shore.) Other thinkers view laughter as our response to expectations fulfilled or to expectations set up but then suddenly frustrated. Some hold it to be the expression of our delight in seeing our suppressed urges acted out (as when a comedian hurls an egg at a pompous stuffed shirt); some, to be our defensive reaction to a painful and disturbing truth.

Derisive humor is basic to **satiric comedy,** in which human weakness or folly is ridiculed from a vantage point of supposedly enlightened superiority. Satiric comedy may be coolly malicious and gently biting, but it tends to be critical of people, their manners, and their morals. It is at least as old as the comedies of Aristophanes, who thrived in the fifth century B.C. In *Lysistrata,* the satirist shows how the women of two warring cities speedily halt a war by agreeing to deny themselves to their husbands. (The satirist's target is men so proud that they go to war rather than make the slightest concession.)

Comedy is often divided into two varieties—"high" and "low." **High comedy** relies more on wit and wordplay than on physical action for its humor. It tries to address the audience's intelligence by pointing out the pretension and hypocrisy of human behavior. High comedy also generally avoids derisive humor. Jokes about physical appearances would, for example, be avoided. One technique it employs to appeal to a so-

[5]See Bergson's essay "Le Rire" (1990), translated as "Laughter" in *Comedy,* ed. Wylie Sypher (New York: Anchor, 1956).

phisticated, verbal audience is use of the **epigram,** a brief and witty statement that memorably expresses some truth, large or small. Oscar Wilde's plays like *The Importance of Being Earnest* (1895) and *Lady Windermere's Fan* (1892) sparkle with such brilliant epigrams as: "I can resist everything except temptation"; "Experience is the name everyone gives to their mistakes"; "There is only one thing worse than being talked about, and that is not being talked about." A type of high comedy is the **comedy of manners,** a witty satire set in elite or fashionable society. The comedy of manners was especially popular in the **Restoration period** (the period after 1660 when Charles II, restored to the English throne, reopened the London playhouse, which had been closed by the Puritans who considered theater immoral). The great Restoration playwrights like William Congreve and George Farquhar especially excelled at comedies of manners. In the twentieth century splendid comedies of manners continue to be written. Bernard Shaw's *Pygmalion* (1913), which eventually became the musical *My Fair Lady,* contrasts life in the streets of London with that in aristocratic drawing rooms. Contemporary playwrights like Tom Stoppard, Michael Frayn, Tina Howe, and the late Joe Orton have all created memorable comedies of manners.

Low comedy explores the opposite extreme of humor. It places greater emphasis on physical action and visual gags, and its verbal jokes do not require much intellect to appreciate (as in Groucho Marx's pithy put-down to his brother Chico, "You have the brain of a five-year-old, and I bet he was glad to get rid of it!"). Low comedy does not avoid derisive humor; rather it revels in making fun of whatever will get a good laugh. Drunkenness, stupidity, lust, senility, trickery, insult, and clumsiness are inexhaustible staples for this style of comedy. Although it is all too easy for critics to dismiss low comedy, like high comedy it also serves a valuable purpose in satirizing human failings. Shakespeare indulged in coarse humor in some of his noblest plays. Low comedy is usually the preferred style of popular culture, and it has inspired many incisive satires on modern life—from the classic films of Laurel and Hardy and the Marx Brothers to the weekly TV antics of *Monty Python's Flying Circus* and Matt Groening's *The Simpsons.*

Low comedy includes several distinct types. One is the **burlesque,** a broadly humorous parody or travesty of another play or kind of play. (In the United States, *burlesque* is something else: a once-popular form of show business featuring stripteases interspersed with bits of ribald low comedy.) Another valuable type of low comedy is the **farce,** a broadly humorous play whose action is usually fast-moving and improbable. The farce is a descendant of the Italian *commedia dell'arte* ("artistic comedy") of the late Renaissance, a kind of theater developed by comedians who traveled from town to town, regaling crowds at country fairs and in marketplaces. This popular art featured familiar stock characters in masks or whiteface: Harlequin, a clown; Columbine, his peppery sweetheart; and Pantaloon, a doddering duffer. Lately making a comeback, the more modern farces of French playwright Georges Feydeau (1862–1891) are practically all plot, with only the flattest of characters, mindless ninnies who play frantic games of hide-and-seek in order to deceive their spouses. **Slapstick comedy** (such as that of the Three Stooges) is a kind of farce. Featuring pratfalls, pie throwing, fisticuffs, and other violent action, it takes its name from a circus clown's device—a bat with two boards that loudly clap together when one clown swats another.

Romantic comedy, another traditional sort of comedy, is subtler. Its main characters are generally lovers, and its plot unfolds their ultimately successful strivings to be united. Unlike satiric comedy, romantic comedy portrays its characters not with withering contempt but with kindly indulgence. It may take place in the everyday world, or perhaps in some never-never land, such as the forest of Arden in Shakespeare's *As You Like It.*

Here is a short contemporary comedy by one of America's most ingenious playwrights.

David Ives

SURE THING

1988

David Ives (b. 1950) grew up on the South Side of Chicago. He attended Catholic schools before entering Northwestern University. Later Ives studied at the Yale Drama School—"a blissful time for me," he recalls, "in spite of the fact that there is slush on the ground in New Haven 238 days a year." Ives received his first professional production in Los Angeles at the age of twenty-one "at America's smallest, and possibly worst theater, in a storefront that had a pillar dead center in the middle of the stage." He continued writing for the theater while working as an editor at Foreign Affairs, and gradually achieved a reputation in theatrical circles for his wildly original and brilliantly written short comic plays. His public breakthrough came in 1993 with the New

David Ives

York staging of All in the Timing, which presented six short comedies, including Sure Thing. This production earned ecstatic reviews and a busy box office. In the 1995–96 season, All in the Timing was the most widely performed play in America (except for the works of Shakespeare). Ives followed with Don Juan in Chicago (1994) and Ancient History (1996). In 1997 a second group of one-act comedies, Mere Mortals, was produced with great success in New York City. Ives also writes short stories and screenplays for both motion pictures and television. He lives in New York City.

Characters

Betty
Bill

Scene. A café.
Betty, a woman in her late twenties, is reading at a café table. An empty chair is opposite her. Bill, same age, enters.

Bill: Excuse me. Is this chair taken?
Betty: Excuse me?
Bill: Is this taken?
Betty: Yes it is.
Bill: Oh. Sorry.
Betty: Sure thing.

(*A bell rings softly.*)

Bill: Excuse me. Is this chair taken?
Betty: Excuse me?
Bill: Is this taken?
Betty: No, but I'm expecting somebody in a minute.
Bill: Oh. Thanks anyway.
Betty: Sure thing.

(*A bell rings softly.*)

Bill: Excuse me. Is this chair taken?
Betty: No, but I'm expecting somebody very shortly.
Bill: Would you mind if I sit here till he or she or it comes?
Betty (*glances at her watch*): They do seem to be pretty late. . . .
Bill: You never know who you might be turning down.
Betty: Sorry. Nice try, though.
Bill: Sure thing.

(*Bell.*)

Is this seat taken?
Betty: No it's not.
Bill: Would you mind if I sit here?
Betty: Yes I would.
Bill: Oh.

(*Bell.*)

Is this chair taken?
Betty: No it's not.
Bill: Would you mind if I sit here?
Betty: No. Go ahead.
Bill: Thanks. (*He sits. She continues reading.*) Everyplace else seems to be taken.
Betty: Mm-hm.
Bill: Great place.
Betty: Mm-hm.
Bill: What's the book?
Betty: I just wanted to read in quiet, if you don't mind.
Bill: No. Sure thing.

(*Bell.*)

Bill: Everyplace else seems to be taken.

Betty: Mm-hm.

Bill: Great place for reading.

Betty: Yes, I like it.

Bill: What's the book?

Betty: *The Sound and the Fury.*

Bill: Oh. Hemingway.

(*Bell.*)

What's the book?

Betty: *The Sound and the Fury.*

Bill: Oh. Faulkner.

Betty: Have you read it?

Bill: Not . . . actually. I've sure read *about* it, though. It's supposed to be great.

Betty: It is great.

Bill: I hear it's great. (*Small pause.*) Waiter?

(*Bell.*)

What's the book?

Betty: *The Sound and the Fury.*

Bill: Oh. Faulkner.

Betty: Have you read it?

Bill: I'm a Mets fan, myself.

(*Bell.*)

Betty: Have you read it?

Bill: Yeah, I read it in college.

Betty: Where was college?

Bill: I went to Oral Roberts University.

(*Bell.*)

Betty: Where was college?

Bill: I was lying. I never really went to college. I just like to party.

(*Bell.*)

Betty: Where was college?

Bill: Harvard.

Betty: Do you like Faulkner?

Bill: I love Faulkner. I spent a whole winter reading him once.

Betty: I've just started.

Bill: I was so excited after ten pages that I went out and bought everything else he wrote. One of the greatest reading experiences of my life. I mean, all that incredible psychological understanding. Page after page of gorgeous prose. His profound grasp of the mystery of time and human existence. The smells of the earth . . . What do you think?

Betty: I think it's pretty boring.

(*Bell.*)

Bill: What's the book?

Betty: *The Sound and the Fury.*

Bill: Oh! Faulkner!

Betty: Do you like Faulkner?

Bill: I love Faulkner.

Betty: He's incredible.

Bill: I spent a whole winter reading him once.

Betty: I was so excited after ten pages that I went out and bought everything else he wrote.

Bill: All that incredible psychological understanding.

Betty: And the prose is so gorgeous.

Bill: And the way he's grasped the mystery of time—

Betty: —and human existence. I can't believe I've waited this long to read him.

Bill: You never know. You might not have liked him before.

Betty: That's true.

Bill: You might not have been ready for him. You have to hit these things at the right moment or it's no good.

Betty: That's happened to me.

Bill: It's all in the timing. (*Small pause.*) My name's Bill, by the way.

Betty: I'm Betty.

Bill: Hi.

Betty: Hi. (*Small pause.*)

Bill: Yes I thought reading Faulkner was . . . a great experience.

Betty: Yes. (*Small pause.*)

Bill: *The Sound and the Fury* . . . (*Another small pause.*)

Betty: Well. Onwards and upwards. (*She goes back to her book.*)

Bill: Waiter—?

(*Bell.*)

You have to hit these things at the right moment or it's no good.

Betty: That's happened to me.

Bill: It's all in the timing. My name's Bill, by the way.

Betty: I'm Betty.

Bill: Hi.

Betty: Hi.

Bill: Do you come in here a lot?

Betty: Actually I'm just in town for two days from Pakistan.

Bill: Oh. Pakistan.

(*Bell.*)

My name's Bill, by the way.

Betty: I'm Betty.

Bill: Hi.

Betty: Hi.

Bill: Do you come in here a lot?

Betty: Every once in a while. Do you?

Bill: Not so much anymore. Not as much as I used to. Before my nervous break-down.

(*Bell.*)

Do you come in here a lot?
Betty: Why are you asking?
Bill: Just interested.
Betty: Are you really interested, or do you just want to pick me up?
Bill: No, I'm really interested.
Betty: Why would you be interested in whether I come in here a lot?
Bill: I'm just . . . getting acquainted.
Betty: Maybe you're only interested for the sake of making small talk long enough to ask me back to your place to listen to some music, or because you've just rented this great tape for your VCR, or because you've got some terrific unknown Django Reinhardt record, only all you really want to do is fuck—which you won't do very well—after which you'll go into the bath-room and pee very loudly, then pad into the kitchen and get yourself a beer from the refrigerator without asking me whether I'd like anything, and then you'll proceed to lie back down beside me and confess that you've got a girl-friend named Stephanie who's away at medical school in Belgium for a year, and that you've been involved with her—*off and on*—in what you'll call a very "intricate" relationship, for the past *seven* YEARS. None of which *inter-ests* me, mister!
Bill: Okay.

(*Bell.*)

Do you come in here a lot?
Betty: Every other day, I think.
Bill: I come in here quite a lot and I don't remember seeing you.
Betty: I guess we must be on different schedules.
Bill: Missed connections.
Betty: Yes. Different time zones.
Bill: Amazing how you can live right next door to somebody in this town and never even know it.
Betty: I know.
Bill: City life.
Betty: It's crazy.
Bill: We probably pass each other in the street every day. Right in front of this place, probably.
Betty: Yep.
Bill (*looks around*): Well the waiters here sure seem to be in some different time zone. I can't seem to locate one anywhere. . . . Waiter! (*He looks back.*) So what do you—(*He sees that she's gone back to her book.*)
Betty: I beg pardon?
Bill: Nothing. Sorry.

(*Bell.*)

Betty: I guess we must be on different schedules.

Bill: Missed connections.

Betty: Yes. Different time zones.

Bill: Amazing how you can live right next door to somebody in this town and never even know it.

Betty: I know.

Bill: City life.

Betty: It's crazy.

Bill: You weren't waiting for somebody when I came in, were you?

Betty: Actually I was.

Bill: Oh. Boyfriend?

Betty: Sort of.

Bill: What's a sort-of boyfriend?

Betty: My husband.

Bill: Ah-ha.

(*Bell.*)

You weren't waiting for somebody when I came in, were you?

Betty: Actually I was.

Bill: Oh. Boyfriend?

Betty: Sort of.

Bill: What's a sort-of boyfriend?

Betty: We were meeting here to break up.

Bill: Mm-hm . . .

(*Bell.*)

What's a sort-of boyfriend?

Betty: My lover. Here she comes right now!

(*Bell.*)

Bill: You weren't waiting for somebody when I came in, were you?

Betty: No, just reading.

Bill: Sort of a sad occupation for a Friday night, isn't it? Reading here, all by yourself?

Betty: Do you think so?

Bill: Well sure. I mean, what's a good-looking woman like you doing out alone on a Friday night?

Betty: Trying to keep away from lines like that.

Bill: No, listen—

(*Bell.*)

You weren't waiting for somebody when I came in, were you?

Betty: No, just reading.

Bill: Sort of a sad occupation for a Friday night, isn't it? Reading here all by yourself?

Betty: I guess it is, in a way.

Bill: What's a good-looking woman like you doing out alone on a Friday night anyway? No offense, but . . .

Betty: I'm out alone on a Friday night for the first time in a very long time.

Bill: Oh.

Betty: You see, I just recently ended a relationship.

Bill: Oh.

Betty: Of rather long standing.

Bill: I'm sorry. (*Small pause.*) Well listen, since reading by yourself *is* such a sad occupation for a Friday night, would you like to go elsewhere?

Betty: No . . .

Bill: Do something else?

Betty: No thanks.

Bill: I was headed out to the movies in a while anyway.

Betty: I don't think so.

Bill: Big chance to let Faulkner catch his breath. All those long sentences get him pretty tired.

Betty: Thanks anyway.

Bill: Okay.

Betty: I appreciate the invitation.

Bill: Sure thing.

(*Bell.*)

You weren't waiting for somebody when I came in, were you?

Betty: No, just reading.

Bill: Sort of a sad occupation for a Friday night, isn't it? Reading here all by yourself?

Betty: I guess I was trying to think of it as existentially romantic. You know— cappuccino, great literature, rainy night . . .

Bill: That only works in Paris. We *could* hop the late plane to Paris. Get on a Concorde. Find a café . . .

Betty: I'm a little short on plane fare tonight.

Bill: Darn it, so am I.

Betty: To tell you the truth, I was headed to the movies after I finished this section. Would you like to come along? Since you can't locate a waiter?

Bill: That's a very nice offer, but . . .

Betty: Uh-huh. Girlfriend?

Bill: Two, actually. One of them's pregnant, and Stephanie—

(*Bell.*)

Betty: Girlfriend?

Bill: No, I don't have a girlfriend. Not if you mean the castrating bitch I dumped last night.

(*Bell.*)

Betty: Girlfriend?

Bill: Sort of. Sort of.

Betty: What's a sort-of girlfriend?
Bill: My mother.

   (*Bell.*)

I just ended a relationship, actually.
Betty: Oh.
Bill: Of rather long standing.
Betty: I'm sorry to hear it.
Bill: This is my first night out alone in a long time. I feel a little bit at sea, to tell you the truth.
Betty: So you didn't stop to talk because you're a Moonie, or you have some weird political affiliation—?
Bill: Nope. Straight-down-the-ticket Republican.

   (*Bell.*)

Straight-down-the-ticket Democrat.

   (*Bell.*)

Can I tell you something about politics?

   (*Bell.*)

I like to think of myself as a citizen of the universe.

   (*Bell.*)

I'm unaffiliated.
Betty: That's a relief. So am I.
Bill: I vote my beliefs.
Betty: Labels are not important.
Bill: Labels are not important, exactly. Take me, for example. I mean, what does it matter if I had a two-point at—

   (*Bell.*)

three-point at—

   (*Bell.*)

four-point at college? Or if I did come from Pittsburgh—

   (*Bell.*)

Cleveland—

   (*Bell.*)

Westchester County?
Betty: Sure.
Bill: I believe that a man is what he is.

   (*Bell.*)

A person is what he is.

(*Bell.*)

A person is . . . what they are.

Betty: I think so too.

Bill: So what if I admire Trotsky?

(*Bell.*)

So what if I once had a total-body liposuction?

(*Bell.*)

So what if I don't have a penis?

(*Bell.*)

So what if I spent a year in the Peace Corps? I was acting on my convictions.

Betty: Sure.

Bill: You just can't hang a sign on a person.

Betty: Absolutely. I'll bet you're a Scorpio.

(*Many bells ring.*)

Listen, I was headed to the movies after I finished this section. Would you
  like to come along?

Bill: That sounds like fun. What's playing?

Betty: A couple of the really early Woody Allen movies.

Bill: Oh.

Betty: You don't like Woody Allen?

Bill: Sure. I like Woody Allen.

Betty: But you're not crazy about Woody Allen.

Bill: Those early ones kind of get on my nerves.

Betty: Uh-huh.

(*Bell.*)

Bill: Y'know I was headed to the—

Betty (*simultaneously*): I was thinking about—

Bill: I'm sorry.

Betty: No, go ahead.

Bill: I was going to say that I was headed to the movies in a little while, and . . .

Betty: So was I.

Bill: The Woody Allen festival?

Betty: Just up the street.

Bill: Do you like the early ones?

Betty: I think anybody who doesn't ought to be run off the planet.

Bill: How many times have you seen *Bananas?*

Betty: Eight times.

Bill: Twelve. So are you still interested? (*Long pause.*)

Betty: Do you like Entenmann's crumb cake . . . ?

Bill: Last night I went out at two in the morning to get one. Did you have an Etch-a-Sketch as a child?

Betty: Yes! And do you like Brussels sprouts? (*Pause.*)

Bill: No, I think they're disgusting.

Betty: They *are* disgusting!

Bill: Do you still believe in marriage in spite of current sentiments against it?

Betty: Yes.

Bill: And children?

Betty: Three of them.

Bill: Two girls and a boy.

Betty: Harvard, Vassar, and Brown.

Bill: And will you love me?

Betty: Yes.

Bill: And cherish me forever?

Betty: Yes.

Bill: Do you still want to go to the movies?

Betty: Sure thing.

Bill and Betty (*together*): *Waiter!*

BLACKOUT

QUESTIONS

1. Ives originally planned to set *Sure Thing* at a bus stop. What does its current setting in a café suggest about the characters?
2. What happens on stage when the bell rings?
3. Who is the protagonist? What does the protagonist want?
4. Does the play have a dramatic question?
5. When does the climax of the play occur?
6. Is *Sure Thing* a romantic comedy or a farce? (See pages 1226–27 for definitions of these types of comedy.)
7. "*Sure Thing* was not a funny play because it isn't realistic. Conversations just don't happen this way." Discuss that opinion. Do you agree or disagree?

Here is another contemporary comedy by one of America's master humorists, Garrison Keillor. Retelling an ancient story in a thoroughly up-to-the-minute manner, Keillor mixes old and new with amusing results. Before beginning this comic sketch, you might want to read (or, for most students, reread) "The Parable of the Prodigal Son" found on page 207. One can appreciate Keillor's humor without having read the original, but, as with any parody, it is funniest to those who know the original.

PRODIGAL SON

1991

Garrison Keillor (b. 1942) was born in Anoka, Minnesota. His parents were members of the Plymouth Brethren, a strict fundamentalist sect that forbade many types of entertainment. But their members, Keillor recalls, were "wonderful storytellers, and the purpose of their stories was to imbue us with compassion." While at the University of Minnesota he worked at the campus radio station. Later Keillor worked for Minnesota Public Radio, where in 1974 he created and is still host of A Prairie Home Companion, a weekly live radio variety show that features music, comedy, and storytelling. The centerpiece of each show is Keillor's weekly monologue, "News from Lake Wobegon," a fictional account of the happenings of a small Min-

Garrison Keillor

nesota town "that time forgot and the decades cannot improve." Keillor populates his imaginary hometown with a cast of memorable individuals and local businesses (like Bob's Bank, whose motto is "Neither a borrower nor lender be"). Keillor's gentle satire pokes fun at the absurdities and pathos of small-town life. As A Prairie Home Companion grew in popularity (it was eventually broadcast by two hundred stations), Keillor began publishing his monologues and stories. His first collection of stories and comic pieces, Happy to Be Here, appeared in 1982, followed by the best-selling novel Lake Wobegon Days in 1985. He has produced a steady stream of novels and short stories, including We Are Still Married (1989), WLT: A Radio Romance (1991), and Wobegone Boy (1997). Now a celebrated fiction writer, Keillor remains best known for his ingenious use of live radio, including the comic sketch. Prodigal Son is an example of Keillor's radio drama, which tells its story entirely through voices and sound effects.

Characters

Narrator
Dad
Dwight
Wally
Wise and foolish virgins
Loose companions
Bimbo
Publican
Farmer
Samaritan

Narrator: A happy day, a sunny street, you're young and in love and life is good and you're on your way to lunch, when suddenly a cold shadow falls and (*Loathsome laugh.*) you feel a cold slimy hand touch your face. (*Worse laugh.*) And it's your own hand. (*Worst laugh.*) That's evil. Where does evil come from? Whose fault is it? The American Council of Remorse—a non-profit organization working for greater contrition on the part of people who do terrible things—brings you: The Prodigal Son.

(*Theme.*)

Dad: I run a feed-lot operation here in Judea, fattening feeder calves for the Jerusalem market, in partnership with my two sons: my prodigal son, Wally, and my older son, Dwight. One morning about two years ago, I came down to breakfast and—no Wally. Morning, Dwight.

Dwight: (*Sitting at table, reading newspaper.*) Morning.

Dad: You see your brother this morning?

Dwight: In bed.

Dad: I promised Harry Shepherd I'd be over to his place by seven-thirty. He's got a lost sheep out on the mountain wild and steep.

Dwight: Says here that fatted calves are down one and three-quarter shekels on the Damascus market, Dad. Makes me wonder if maybe *lean* calves wouldn't have a higher profit margin, and then we could spend more time in the vineyard—Dad, are you listening to me?

Dad: I'm worried about your brother.

Dwight: We can't afford to stand still, Dad. Look at the Stewarts—they're buying up land left and right! You've got to move ahead or you lose ground. . . .

Wally: (*Thickly.*) Morning, Dad. Morning, Dwight. (*He sits down, groans, puts his head in his hands.*)

Dad: You look a little peaked, son.

Wally: I donno—it's some kind of morning sickness, Dad. I feel real good at night and then I wake up and hurt all over.

Dwight: I noticed a couple empty wineskins behind the fig tree this morning.

Wally: I dropped them and they spilled! Honest!

Dad: Where were you taking them?

Wally: I was putting them outside! Wine's got to breathe, you know. And so do I, Dad. I've got a real breathing problem here. I'm worried about my health, Dad. I read an article the other day in *Assyrian Digest* that says bad feelings may be environmental. I donno. Maybe I need to get away for a while, Dad. Get my head straight. Work out some things.

Dad: Well, if that's how you feel, I guess I . . .

Wally: I was thinking I'd sort of take my share of the farm and head for a far country for a while until I get back on my feet, headwise, and then come back a brand-new guy.

Dwight: Dad, could we discuss this?

(*Theme.*)

Narrator: And not many days after, the younger son gathered his inheritance together, and took his journey into a far country. . . .

Wally: (*Walking.*)

I'm walkin' . . . to a far-out land.
I'm talkin' . . . got cash in hand.
I'm hot now . . . don't you understand. (*Yokel voices offstage.*)

You're lookin' at a brand-new man.

(*Foolish virgins° enter, harnessed together, led by a wise virgin.*)

Hey! Who's this?
Hey. What's shakin', babes?

Wise: I'm taking these five foolish virgins home, mister. We were supposed to be
at a wedding an hour ago, but they're low on oil. You see an oil station that
way?

Wally: Hey, they don't look foolish to me. They look like kinda fun people. Tell
you what, they can come with me. I'll buy them oil. My treat.

Wise: Sorry, mister. I've got to look after these virgins myself. They take a lot of
supervision. You gotta watch 'em pretty close so they don't bunch up and
walk up each other's backs.

(*Crash.*)

Wally: Whoops—dropped your lamp, huh? Good thing it *didn't* have oil in it.
Well, 'bye! Don't do anything I wouldn't do.

We're movin' . . . down the ole highway.
We're improvin' . . . every day.
We're groovin' . . . and we're okay.

Narrator: And he took his journey into a far country, and there wasted his substance in riotous living. . . . (*Enter Loose Companions, dancing, drinking,
feasting, whooping. Bimbo on Wally's arm.*)

Wally: Take it off! Take it all off! Go for it! Put it on and take it off again!
(*To audience.*) Hey, you Pharisees, loosen up—
(*To pianist.*) Hey, you know "Hey, Judea"?

Bimbo: You're such a wonderful, vital person.

Wally: (*To "Hey Jude."*)

Hey, Judea—you're a real great place.
You're the best spot in the Bi-i-i-ible. . . .
You're right there by Canaan and Galilee,
You're family, you're tribal.
Hey, publican! Another round of wine for my pals! Put it on my tab!
Phhhh! Blaaaaghhhhh! What is this??? Lite wine?

Foolish virgins: in Matthew 25:2–12, Jesus tells a parable of five foolish maidens who forgot to bring
oil for their lamps at a wedding and five wise maidens who brought oil. The five foolish virgins must
go out to buy oil and miss the bridegroom's arrival.

Publican: You don't like it?

Wally: Give it to some virgins—and bring me your best.

Publican: I'll give you a jar to take with you—it's closing time. Time to lock up, Mr. Wally.

Wally: Hey! I'll pay. Let's party!

Bimbo: Oh, Wally! You're so joyful! So many persons with a farm background, they don't know how to let go and have a good time.

Wally: Not me, Wanda! Life is a feast if you know where to find it.

Publican: Here's your bill, Mr. Wally.

Bimbo: That's so beautiful: "Life is a feast." So many people—they place such restrictions on themselves. (*He reads bill, page after page, then searches his pockets and brings out a few coins.*) You have a better sense of who you are. You have that rare quality of trusting yourself. Believing in festivity, not negativity. In a smile, not denial. Sure, rules are good for people who need 'em. But you prefer freedom. You have this tremendous—this great—It's not a structured thing. You know? Your energy is so focused. Like a locust.

Wally: That's the last of my money. That's all I have left. Amazing.

Publican: You all right? You need a ride home?

Wally: No.

Bimbo: Wally—listen. It's been great. Three of the best weeks of my life. Bye.

(*The Bimbo, the Publican, and the Loose Companions leave, one by one.*)

Narrator: And when he had spent all, there arose across a mighty famine in that land, and he began to be in want. And he went and lived with a farmer who sent him into his fields to feed swine.

Farmer: You ever feed swine before?

Wally: No, but I fed calves. You just dump the husks and swill down in front of them, right?

Farmer: Lot more to it than that. Usually we require swine feeders to have at least four years of professional experience. But tell you what—I'll put you in my internship program.

Wally: What does it pay?

Farmer: Pay! I'm offering you a chance to learn the swine business from the mud up.

Wally: So, you mean I'll sleep out here and eat with the pigs?

Farmer: You want it or not?

Wally: Fine. Just want to get it clear in my own mind, that's all. C'mon, hogs. Sooo-eyyy! C'mon, piggy, piggy, piggy.

Narrator: And when he came to himself, he said:

Wally: How many hired servants of my father's have bread enough and to spare, and I perish with hunger! I will arise and go to my father, and will say unto him: "Father, I have sinned against heaven and before thee, and am no more worthy to be called thy son: make me as one of thy hired servants."

No, that doesn't sound good.

I will arise and go to my father and will say unto him, "Father, it was a great learning experience, and now I'm back, looking for an entry-level position"—No. I will arise and go to my father and will say unto him, "Hi, Dad, how you been? Oh, I'm fine. Had a good trip. Say, you got anything to eat around here?"

Narrator: And he arose and came to his father.

Wally: I'm ruined . . . I lost my goods.

So I'm goin' back to my roots.

Samaritan:° (*Enters and latches on to him.*) Here, let me help you!

Wally: Hey! Let go!

Samaritan: Easy. Everything's going to be all right. I'll bind up your wounds here—

Wally: I don't have any wounds! Let go!

Samaritan: Easy.

Wally: Let go!

Samaritan: You sure I can't help?

Wally: Yes! Let go!

Samaritan: Sure you're okay?

Wally: Yes! Let go.

Samaritan: Okay. 'Bye. (*He leaves, reluctantly.*)

Wally: Boy, sometimes those Samaritans won't take no for an answer.

Narrator: And when he was yet a great way off, his father saw him, and had compassion on him, and ran, and fell on his neck, and kissed him. . . .

Dad: Wally! Son! Oh, Wally! (*He shouts offstage.*) Bring some clothes! And a ring! And some shoes! And not those running shoes! The dress shoes! And make that two rings!

(*Offstage clamor.*)

Wally: I spent all the money, Dad.

Dad: And bring the fatted calf—let's eat and be merry! My son who was dead is alive again; he was lost and now he is found. Amazing!

Wally: Mind if I invite some friends too?

(*The Foolish Virgins enter, roped together.*)

I met them on the road. They're okay people once you get to know them.

Dad: More rings! More shoes! Another fatted calf! You look good. You look like you've lost weight.

Wally: I've been on a high-husk diet.

Dad: Dwight! Look who's here! It's Wally!

Dwight: (*Enters reluctantly.*) Hi. Nice to see you. (*His Dad turns to Wally, and Dwight shakes both his fists and sticks out his tongue and makes a vulgar gesture.*)

Dad: We're having veal tonight, Dwight! Wally's home.

Samaritan: in the parable of the Good Samaritan (Luke 10: 30–37), a compassionate Samaritan comes across a man beaten up by thieves, binds his wounds, and takes him to an inn to recover.

Wally: I'm going to go get some of that calf, Dad. Be right back.

Dwight: Dad, I don't want this to sound negative in any way, but—how many years have I been working here?

Dad: All your life.

Dwight: Have I ever disobeyed you, Dad?

Dad: Never.

Dwight: And have you ever given *me* a fatted calf and thrown a big party for me and *my* friends?

Dad: No, but, son—

Dwight: But the minute this *bozo* comes hoofing it home—this leaker—

Dad: But your brother was dead and he's alive again! He was lost and now he's found!

Dwight: I don't think you're hearing what I'm saying, Dad. You never ran up to me and hugged me—I'd just like to point that out.

Dad: I'm not a hugger, I guess.

Wally: (*Enters, mouth full.*) Have some calf, you guys. That fat won't keep, you know. Sure is good fatted calf, Dad. Sure beats husks. (*Off.*) Care for another piece, you virgins?

Dwight: Ever stop to think who *fatted* that calf, Wally? That was our best calf, Dad. The *best* one. (*The others slowly leave, talking among themselves.*) Try to think how I feel. I'm hoeing corn all day, come in bone-tired, there's my brother smelling of pig manure, and they got the beer on ice and *my calf* on the barbecue! And MY RING on his hand! My *ring!* You promised it to me, but oh no—can't give it to the son who's worked his tail off for thirty years, oh no, gotta give it to the weasel who comes dragging his butt in the door— Oh great—Wonderful, Dad. Terrific.

Maybe I'll go sleep with the pigs, seeing as you go for that. See ya later, Wally. Help yourself to the rest of my stuff—clothes, jewels, shekels, just take what you want. Take my room. Don't worry about me. I'll be in the pigpen.

(*He leaves. Offstage sounds: A stove being kicked, muttered curses, pots and pans being thrown, dishes broken.*)

QUESTIONS

1. Divide this play into elements. How much of the play is *exposition?* Who is the *protagonist?* What is the *climax* of the play, the moment when the tension is at its height?

2. Comedy usually portrays human failings. What weaknesses does Wally have? Do Dad and Dwight also have weaknesses?

3. Does Keillor change any important elements of the plot from the original parable? ("The Parable of the Prodigal Son" is found on page 207.) If so, what part or parts of the plot does he alter?

4. How does Keillor turn this famous parable into a comedy? What elements of setting, characterization, or tone does he shift to get his comic effects?

5. Is Keillor's parody disrespectful of the original parable? Or does he explore the same theme in a different way? Is it possible for a comedy to pursue the same themes as a more earnest work?

6. How can this play be considered a comedy if Dwight is so unhappy at the end?

Susan Glaspell

Susan Glaspell on Drama   CREATING *Trifles*   1927

We went to the theater, and for the most part we came away wishing we had gone somewhere else. Those were the days when Broadway flourished almost unchallenged. Plays, like magazine stories, were patterned. They might be pretty good within themselves, seldom did they open out to—where it surprised or thrilled your spirit to follow. They didn't ask much of *you*, those plays. Having paid for your seat, the thing was all done for you, and your mind came out where it went in, only tireder. An audience, Jig° said, had imagination. What was this "Broadway," which could make a thing as interesting as life into a thing as dull as a Broadway play?

There was a meeting at the Liberal Club—Eddie Goodman, Phil Moeller, Ida Rauh, the Boni brothers, exciting talk about starting a theater.

. . .

He [Jig] wrote a letter to the people who had seen the plays, asking if they cared to become associate members of the Provincetown Players. The purpose was to give American playwrights of sincere purpose a chance to work out their ideas in freedom, to give all who worked with the plays their opportunity as artists. Were they interested in this? One dollar for the three remaining bills.

The response paid for seats and stage, and for sets. A production need not cost a lot of money, Jig would say. The most expensive set at the Wharf Theater° cost thirteen dollars. There were sets at the Provincetown Playhouse which cost little more. . . .

"Now, Susan," he [Jig] said to me, briskly, "I have announced a play of yours for the next bill."

Creating *Trifles. Jig:* the nickname of George Cram Cook (1873–1924), Glaspell's husband, who was the central founder and director of the Provincetown Players, perhaps the most influential theater company in the history of American drama. *Wharf Theater:* the makeshift theater that Cook created from an old fishhouse at the end of a Provincetown wharf.

"But I have no play!"

"Then you will have to sit down to-morrow and begin one."

I protested. I did not know how to write a play. I had never "studied it."

"Nonsense," said Jig. "You've got a stage, haven't you?"

So I went out on the wharf, sat alone on one of our wooden benches without a back, and looked a long time at that bare little stage. After a time the stage became a kitchen—a kitchen there all by itself. I saw just where the stove was, the table, and the steps going upstairs. Then the door at the back opened, and people all bundled up came in—two or three men, I wasn't sure which, but sure enough about the two women, who hung back, reluctant to enter that kitchen. When I was a newspaper reporter out in Iowa, I was sent down-state to do a murder trial, and I never forgot going into the kitchen of a woman locked up in town. I had meant to do it as a short story, but the stage took it for its own, so I hurried in from the wharf to write down what I had seen. Whenever I got stuck, I would run across the street to the old wharf, sit in that leaning little theater under which the sea sounded, until the play was ready to continue. Sometimes things written in my room would not form on the stage, and I must go home and cross them out. "What playwrights need is a stage," said Jig, "their own stage."

Ten days after the director said he had announced my play, there was a reading at Mary Heaton Vorse's. I was late to the meeting, home revising the play. But when I got there the crowd liked "Trifles," and voted to put it in rehearsal next day.

The Road to the Temple

━━◯ WRITING CRITICALLY ◯━━

Conflict Resolution

A good play almost always presents a **conflict.** One or more characters want to accomplish something, but another person or thing stands in their way. The central action of the play is how those two opposing forces resolve the conflict.

Reading a play, you will understand it better if you can identify the central dramatic conflict. Who is the protagonist? What does he or she want? Who opposes the protagonist? If you can answer those basic questions, the overall design of the plot will usually become obvious. Remember that many full-length plays (or films) have a double plot (or subplot). In such a case, there will be a secondary set of characters with their own conflicts.

To begin writing about a play, you might start by listing the major characters. (It usually suffices to list only the three or four most important people.) Then after each name, write down what that character wants most at the beginning of the play. If you can't figure out a single, compelling motive for each character, write down several things that they want. You can decide later what motive is most important.

Now look at the list, and decide what character is the protagonist, or hero. What does he or she want, and who opposes that ambition? Then notice how the motivations of the other characters fit into the central conflict.

Select any short play in this chapter, and write a brief essay identifying the protagonist, central conflict, and dramatic question.

Here is a paper by Tara Mazzucca, a student of Beverly Schneller at Millersville University, that examines and compares the protagonists and dramatic question of two short plays by Susan Glaspell.

Outside Trifles

Susan Glaspell was one of America's first feminist playwrights. A founder of the non-commercial Provincetown Players, she used this experimental company to present plays that realistically explored the lives of women. I would like to examine and compare two of Glaspell's early one-act plays, Trifles (1916) and The Outside (1917). I will discuss how they present women who are forced to survive in a world where men make most of the rules.

Both plays focus on female protagonists, and both realistically present the emotional hardships these women endure in their daily lives. Both plays had contemporary settings; they take place in the early twentieth century. Both plays present women who are isolated from society--Mrs. Wright in Trifles and the two protagonists of The Outside. And in both plays a pair of female characters work together to solve the central dramatic question.

In Trifles Glaspell ironically places two wives, one married to a farmer and the other to the sheriff, at the scene of a mysterious murder case. The play takes place entirely in familiar territory for women in the early 1900s--a kitchen. The kitchen becomes a symbol for the game of hot and cold that the characters unwittingly play. In the kitchen where it is hot, the women find all the clues necessary to solve the case. Meanwhile the men search the rest of the cold house and find nothing to suggest a motive for the crime.

The two wives soon recognize the story behind the murder by observing small details in the house. They see clues in what the men pass over as mere trifles. When the women mention the ruined fruit preserves in the kitchen, Mr. Hale dismisses the potential importance of housekeeping details and comments, "Well, women are used to worrying over trifles" (1202). The two women, however, understand that small things can affect a person deeply.

The two women also recognize the importance of singing in Mrs. Wright's life. Singing was something she was known for when she was younger, only to have it taken away from her when she married John Wright. Doing housework alone all day in silence, Mrs. Wright became a different person. The stress of loneliness and depression finally got to Mrs. Wright. She bought a canary for company and enjoyment. She loved the singing bird, but her husband killed it. In desperation the woman decided to live without her husband.

Mrs. Hale and Mrs. Peters instinctively understand Mrs. Wright's worries. Their perspective give them an advantage over their male counterparts. The women must work together, because if they did not, each would break under the pressure of the cold treatment they receive from their husbands-- break like the glass canned fruit Mrs. Wright stores away in her cabinet.

The plot of The Outside is relatively simple. The widowed Mrs. Patrick lives in a remote building that was once a life-saving station. Mrs. Patrick employs another widow, Allie Mayo, to help her with housekeeping. They lead lives of almost total isolation. One day three life-savers bring in the body of a drowned sailor and attempt unsuccessfully to revive him. Mrs. Patrick is furious that they have used her house as a rescue station and demands that they leave. Her behavior so upsets the usually silent Allie that the servant confronts Mrs. Patrick with a passionate speech about the futility of renouncing life.

Allie also keeps to herself from grief. As a girl, she was talkative, but after her young husband vanished at sea, she resolved never to say an unnecessary word. Now twenty years later, she is notorious for her silence. The two women share a common grief of having lost the husbands they loved. Losing a husband changed each woman. Allie chose silence. Mrs. Patrick left society.

When the men bring the drowned young man into the former life-saving station, the incident upsets Mrs. Patrick, and she explodes with anger. This incident disturbs Allie in a different way. She realizes how isolated they have become. She knows that if they do not change, they will die without anyone caring. Deeply disturbed, Allie breaks her silence and argues with her employer. Mrs. Patrick initially resists Allie's remarks because she still has not come to terms with life without her husband. Allie resembles Mrs. Wright in Trifles. Both women keep quiet for years and do what they're told, until they reach a breaking point. A critical event forces each of them to take dramatic action. Allie violently argues with her employer; Mrs. Wright decides to murder her husband.

Mrs. Hale and Mrs. Peters resemble Mrs. Patrick from The Outside. Throughout the play Mrs. Hale and Mrs. Peters try to understand why Mrs. Wright killed her husband. In the end, they recognize that their lives have much in common with that of the murderer. Their actions show their confusion about their own values. They do things that hinder the sheriff's investigation to protect an oppressed woman. First, Mrs. Hale rips out Mrs. Wright's erratic stitching so the men will not notice her nervous condition. Second, Mrs. Peters, who is--ironically--the sheriff's wife, hides the strangled bird from her husband and the other men. The women see a new side of Mrs. Wright's marriage and sympathize with her pathetic situation. By the end of The Outside Mrs. Patrick also sees a new side of Allie. Allie's outburst forces Mrs. Patrick to consider changing her life and reconsider her ideas.

Mrs. Patrick of The Outside and Mrs. Wright of Trifles are also alike because they are now isolated from the world they used to enjoy. One stopped living because of a harsh husband, the other because of a dead husband. Mrs. Hale and Allie also resemble one another because they both waited too late to understand the depression of their neighbor or living companion. In Trifles, Mrs. Hale decides to help her neighbor even though it means protecting a criminal. Allie speaks truthfully even though it might jeopardize her job. In the end, the actions Allie and Mrs. Hale take are helpful. The men never find a motive for the murder. Mrs. Patrick finally considers changing her way of life in The Outside. In the end each woman has found something new inside of her.

Mrs. Hale and Mrs. Peters both realize the secret they must keep to protect Mrs. Wright. They also realize the injustices women go through to be accepted in society. Mrs. Hale says:

I might have known she needed help! I know how
things can be--for women. I tell you, it's queer,
Mrs. Peters. We live close together and we live far
apart. We all go through the same things--it's all
just a different kind of the same thing. (1209)

In The Outside, the women don't feel socially oppressed
by men, but they cannot define their lives except in
relation to their husbands. When they become widows, they
lose their reason to live. Allie realizes that their grief
has gone too far. She finds her voice to say that life must
be lived. Mrs. Patrick listens enough to feel uncertainty
about her life of loneliness and isolation. Each play deals
with death and its effects on the survivors.

A major difference between the two plays is found in
the way the central female characters treat one another. In
Trifles the women work together to solve the mystery, but in
The Outside the women clash and refuse to help one another.
Glaspell did not have only one idealized image of female
behavior. She realized that different women behave
differently. Each play presents different ways women in the
early twentieth century used to survive in a man's world.
Trapped in the trifles of everyday life, many women felt as
if they were living on the outside of the world.

Works Cited

Glaspell, Susan. The Outside. A Century of Plays by American
    Women. Ed. Rachel France. New York: Rosen, 1979. 48-54.
Glaspell, Susan. Trifles. Literature: An Introduction to
    Fiction, Poetry, and Drama. Ed. X.J. Kennedy and Dana
    Gioia. 7th ed. New York: Longman, 1999. 1199-210.

Further Suggestions for Writing

1. Write an account of the *Trifles* case—the discovery of the murder and the arrest of Mrs. Wright—as a newspaper might have reported it. Then, in a separate paragraph or two, sum up the important facts that a reporter couldn't know, but that Susan Glaspell makes clear to us.

2. Write an essay in praise of the language spoken by the characters in *Riders to the Sea*. Arrive at some generalizations about it. (One suggestion is to turn back to Chapter Seventeen to refresh your acquaintance with metaphors and other figures of speech.)

3. Write an essay titled "Comedy on Campus" or "Comedy in Everyday Life." This essay might depend on what you have lately observed, heard reported in conversation, or noticed in current news media. Give an array of examples.

4. Write an alternate version of *Sure Thing* in which you present a couple in a different setting—a fast-food restaurant, a school library, or a mall. Change the dialogue and the characters to reflect the new setting.

5. Write an analysis of Keillor's *Prodigal Son* in relation to its source in the Gospel of Luke. (The original parable is printed on page 207, and the sources for two other parables are cited in footnotes to Keillor's text.) Examine how Keillor uses comedy to dramatize the same themes as the original parables. You should also note any moments where you think Keillor departs from the moral spirit of the original parables.

6. What particular human follies does Keillor satirize in *Prodigal Son?* Write a short essay in which you note and discuss the particular shortcomings of at least three characters.

33 The Theater of Sophocles

For a citizen of Athens in the fifth century B.C. when the surviving classical Greek tragedies originated, a play was a religious occasion. Plays were given at the Lenaea, or feast of the winepress, in January; or during the Great Dionysia, the feast of Dionysus, god of wine and crops, in the spring. So well did the Athenians love contests that at the spring festival each playwright was to present—in competition—three tragedies on successive days, the last tragedy to be followed by a short comedy of a special sort. The comedy was a **satyr play,** a parody of a mythic story, with a chorus of actors playing *satyrs*, creatures half goat or horse, half man.

Seated in the open air, in a hillside amphitheater, as many as fourteen thousand spectators could watch a performance that must have somewhat resembled an opera or a modern musical. The audience, arranged in rows, looked out across a rounded **orchestra,** or dancing place, where the chorus of fifteen (the number was fixed by Sophocles) sang passages of lyric poetry and executed dance movements. (It is also possible that actors and chorus sometimes shared the orchestra.) The modern custom of dividing a play into acts and scenes may have originated in these song and dance interludes. Besides providing stage business, the chorus had a function in telling the story. In the plays of Sophocles, for example, they converse with the main character and sometimes comment on the action, offering words of warning and other unwanted advice. As they *physically* stand between the audience and principal actors, the members of the chorus serve as intermediaries who seem to voice the spectators' reactions.

Behind the orchestra stood the actors, in front of a stage house, or **skene** (the source of our word *scene*). Originally, the *skene* was a dressing room; later it is believed to have borne a painted backdrop. Directly behind the *skene*, a **colonnade,** or row of pillars, provided (according to one scholarly guess) a ready-made set for a palace. (This is a rough description of the Athenian theater of Dionysus; several other Greek cities had theaters, each unique in details.)

In the plays of Aeschylus in the early fifth century B.C., no more than two actors occupied the stage at any time. Sophocles, in the midcentury, increased the number

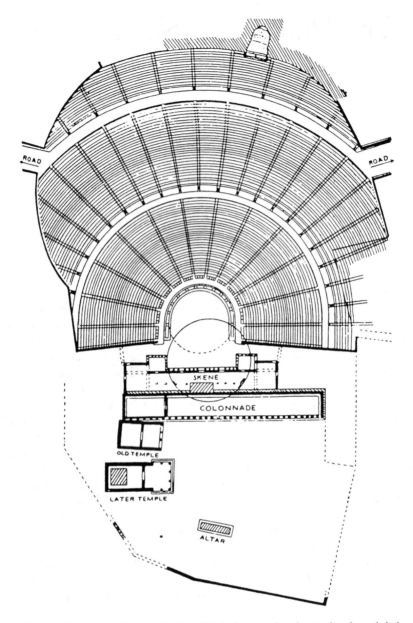

The theater of Dionysus at Athens in the time of Sophocles; a modern drawing based on scholarly guess-work. From R. C. Flickinger, The Greek Theater and Its Drama (1918).

to three, making situations of greater complexity possible. Still later in the century, in the time of Euripides (last of the trio of supreme Greek tragic dramatists), the *skene* supported a hook and pulley by which actors who played gods could be lowered or lifted—hence the Latin phrase **deus ex machina** ("god out of the machine") for any means of bringing a play quickly to a resolution.

What did the actors look like? They wore **masks** (*personae*, the source of our word *person*, "a thing through which sound comes"); some of these masks had exaggerated mouthpieces, probably designed to project speech across the open air. From certain conventional masks the spectators recognized familiar types: the old graybeard, the young soldier, the beautiful girl (women's parts were played by male actors). Perhaps in order to gain in dignity, actors in the Greek theater eventually came to wear the **cothurnus,** or buskin, a high, thick-soled elevator shoe. All this equipment must have given the actors a slightly inhuman appearance, but we may infer that the spectators accepted such conventions as easily as opera lovers accept an opera's natural artifice.

On a Great Dionysia feast day in about the year 430 B.C., not long after Athens had survived a devastating plague, the audience turned out to watch a tragedy by Sophocles, set in the city of Thebes at the moment of another terrible plague. This timely play was *Oedipus the King* ("King Clubfoot," the title given the play by later scholars—the Greek title was *Oedipus Tyrannos,* "Clubfoot the Tyrant"). It was an old story, briefly told in Homer's *Odyssey,* and presumably the audience was familiar with it. They would have known the history of Oedipus who, because a prophecy had foretold that he would grow up to slay his father, had been taken out into the wilderness to perish. They would have known that before being left to die his feet had been pinned together, causing his clubfoot; and they would have known that later, adopted by King Polybus and grown to maturity, Oedipus won the throne of Thebes as a reward for ridding the city of the Sphinx, a winged, woman-headed lion. All comers to the Sphinx were asked a riddle, and failure to solve it meant death: "What goes on four legs in the morning, two at noon, and three at evening?" Oedipus correctly answered, "Man" (because as a baby he crawls on all fours, then as a man he walks erect, then as an old man he uses a cane). Chagrined, the Sphinx leaped from her rocky perch and dashed herself to death.

Sophocles

Oedipus the King

425 B.C.?

Translated by Dudley Fitts and Robert Fitzgerald

Sophocles (496?–406 B.C.), tragic dramatist, priest, for a time one of ten Athenian generals, was among three great ancient Greek writers of tragedy. (The other two were his contemporaries: Aeschylus, his senior, and Euripides, his junior.) Sophocles won his first victory in the Athenian spring drama competition in 468 B.C., when a tragedy he had written defeated a tragedy by Aeschylus. He went on to win many prizes, writing more than 120 plays, of which only seven have survived in their entirety—Ajax, Antigonê, Oedipus the King, Electra, Phil- octetes, The Trachinian Women, and Oedipus at Colonus. (Of the lost plays, about a thousand fragments remain.) In his long life, Sophocles saw Greece rise to supremacy over the Persian Empire. He enjoyed the favor of the statesman Pericles, who, making peace with enemy Sparta, ruled Athens during a Golden Age (461–429 B.C.), during which the Parthenon was built and music, art, drama, and philosophy flourished. The playwright lived on to see his native city-state in decline, its strength drained by the disastrous Peloponnesian War. His last play, Oedipus at Colonus, set twenty years after the events of Oedipus the King, shows the former king in old age, ragged and blind, cast into exile by his sons, but still accompanied by his faithful daughter Antigonê. It was written when Sophocles was nearly ninety. Oedipus the King is believed to have been first produced in 425 B.C., five years after plague had broken out in Athens.

Sophocles

Characters°

Oedipus
A Priest
Creon
Teiresias
Iocastê
Messenger
Shepherd of Laïos
Second Messenger
Chorus of Theban Elders

Characters: Some of these names are usually Anglicized: Jocasta, Laius. In this version, the translators prefer spelling names more nearly like the Greek.

1254   THE THEATER OF SOPHOCLES

Laurence Olivier in Oedipus Rex.

Scene: *Before the palace of Oedipus, King of Thebes. A central door and two lateral doors open onto a platform which runs the length of the façade. On the platform, right and left, are altars; and three steps lead down into the "orchestra," or chorus-ground. At the beginning of the action these steps are crowded by suppliants° who have brought branches and chaplets of olive leaves and who lie in various attitudes of despair. Oedipus enters.*

PROLOGUE°

Oedipus: My children, generations of the living
    In the line of Kadmos,° nursed at his ancient hearth:
    Why have you strewn yourself before these altars
    In supplication, with your boughs and garlands?
    The breath of incense rises from the city   5
    With a sound of prayer and lamentation.
                                 Children,
    I would not have you speak through messengers,
    And therefore I have come myself to hear you—
    I, Oedipus, who bear the famous name.
    (*To a Priest.*) You, there, since you are eldest in the company,   10
    Speak for them all, tell me what preys upon you,
    Whether you come in dread, or crave some blessing:
    Tell me, and never doubt that I will help you
    In every way I can; I should be heartless
    Were I not moved to find you suppliant here.   15

suppliants: persons who come to ask some favor of the king.   *Prologue:* portion of the play containing the exposition.   2 *line of Kadmos:* according to legend the city of Thebes, where the play takes place, had been founded by the hero Cadmus.

Priest: Great Oedipus, O powerful King of Thebes!
    You see how all the ages of our people
    Cling to your altar steps: here are boys
    Who can barely stand alone, and here are priests
    By weight of age, as I am a priest of God,   20
    And young men chosen from those yet unmarried;
    As for the others, all that multitude,
    They wait with olive chaplets in the squares,
    At the two shrines of Pallas,° and where Apollo°
    Speaks in the glowing embers.
                    Your own eyes   25
    Must tell you: Thebes is tossed on a murdering sea
    And can not lift her head from the death surge.
    A rust consumes the buds and fruits of the earth;
    The herds are sick; children die unborn,
    And labor is vain. The god of plague and pyre   30
    Raids like detestable lightning through the city,
    And all the house of Kadmos is laid waste,
    All emptied, and all darkened: Death alone
    Battens upon the misery of Thebes.

    You are not one of the immortal gods, we know;   35
    Yet we have come to you to make our prayer
    As to the man surest in mortal ways
    And wisest in the ways of God. You saved us
    From the Sphinx, that flinty singer, and the tribute
    We paid to her so long; yet you were never   40
    Better informed than we, nor could we teach you:
    It was some god breathed in you to set us free.

    Therefore, O mighty King, we turn to you:
    Find us our safety, find us a remedy,
    Whether by counsel of the gods or men.   45
    A king of wisdom tested in the past
    Can act in a time of troubles, and act well.
    Noblest of men, restore
    Life to your city! Think how all men call you
    Liberator for your triumph long ago;   50
    Ah, when your years of kingship are remembered,
    Let them not say *We rose, but later fell*—
    Keep the State from going down in the storm!
    Once, years ago, with happy augury,
    You brought us fortune; be the same again!   55

---

24 *Pallas:* title for Athena, goddess of wisdom.   24 *Apollo:* god of music, poetry, and prophecy. At his shrine near Thebes, the ashes of fires were used to divine the future.

No man questions your power to rule the land:
But rule over men, not over a dead city!
Ships are only hulls, citadels are nothing,
When no life moves in the empty passageways.
Oedipus: Poor children! You may be sure I know   60
  All that you longed for in your coming here.
  I know that you are deathly sick; and yet,
  Sick as you are, not one is as sick as I.
  Each of you suffers in himself alone
  His anguish, not another's; but my spirit   65
  Groans for the city, for myself, for you.

  I was not sleeping, you are not waking me.
  No, I have been in tears for a long while
  And in my restless thought walked many ways.
  In all my search, I found one helpful course,   70
  And that I have taken: I have sent Creon,
  Son of Menoikeus, brother of the Queen,
  To Delphi, Apollo's place of revelation,°
  To learn there, if he can,
  What act or pledge of mine may save the city.   75
  I have counted the days, and now, this very day,
  I am troubled, for he has overstayed his time.
  What is he doing? He has been gone too long.
  Yet whenever he comes back, I should do ill
  To scant whatever duty God reveals.   80
Priest: It is a timely promise. At this instant
  They tell me Creon is here.
Oedipus: O Lord Apollo!
  May his news be fair as his face is radiant!
Priest: It could not be otherwise: he is crowned with bay,
  The chaplet is thick with berries.
Oedipus: We shall soon know;   85
  He is near enough to hear us now.

  Enter Creon.

                          O Prince:
  Brother: son of Menoikeus:
  What answer do you bring us from the god?
Creon: A strong one. I can tell you, great afflictions
  Will turn out well, if they are taken well.   90
Oedipus: What was the oracle? These vague words

---

73 *Delphi . . . revelation:* In the temple of Delphi at the foot of Mount Parnassus, a priestess of
Dionysos, while in an ecstatic trance, would speak the wine god's words. Such a priestess was called
an *oracle;* the word can also mean "a message from the god."

Leave me still hanging between hope and fear.
Creon: Is it your pleasure to hear me with all these
    Gathered around us? I am prepared to speak,
    But should we not go in?
Oedipus: Let them all hear it   95
    It is for them I suffer, more than for myself.
Creon: Then I will tell you what I heard at Delphi.

    In plain words
    The god commands us to expel from the land of Thebes
    An old defilement we are sheltering.   100
    It is a deathly thing, beyond cure.
    We must not let it feed upon us longer.
Oedipus: What defilement? How shall we rid ourselves of it?
Creon: By exile or death, blood for blood. It was
    Murder that brought the plague-wind on the city.   105
Oedipus: Murder of whom? Surely the god has named him?
Creon: My lord: long ago Laïos was our king,
    Before you came to govern us.
Oedipus: I know;
    I learned of him from others; I never saw him.
Creon: He was murdered; and Apollo commands us now   110
    To take revenge upon whoever killed him.
Oedipus: Upon whom? Where are they? Where shall we find a clue
    To solve that crime, after so many years?
Creon: Here in this land, he said.
                  If we make enquiry,
    We may touch things that otherwise escape us.   115
Oedipus: Tell me: Was Laïos murdered in his house,
    Or in the fields, or in some foreign country?
Creon: He said he planned to make a pilgrimage.
    He did not come home again.
Oedipus: And was there no one,
    No witness, no companion, to tell what happened?   120
Creon: They were all killed but one, and he got away
    So frightened that he could remember one thing only.
Oedipus: What was that one thing? One may be the key
    To everything, if we resolve to use it.
Creon: He said that a band of highwaymen attacked them,   125
    Outnumbered them, and overwhelmed the King.
Oedipus: Strange, that a highwayman should be so daring—
    Unless some faction here bribed him to do it.
Creon: We thought of that. But after Laïos' death
    New troubles arose and we had no avenger.   130
Oedipus: What troubles could prevent your hunting down the killers?
Creon: The riddling Sphinx's song

Made us deaf to all mysteries but her own.
Oedipus: Then once more I must bring what is dark to light. 135
It is most fitting that Apollo shows,
As you do, this compunction for the dead.
You shall see how I stand by you, as I should,
To avenge the city and the city's god,
And not as though it were for some distant friend,
But for my own sake, to be rid of evil. 140
Whoever killed King Laïos might—who knows?—
Decide at any moment to kill me as well.
By avenging the murdered king I protect myself.

Come, then, my children: leave the altar steps,
Lift up your olive boughs!
                    One of you go 145
And summon the people of Kadmos to gather here.
I will do all that I can; you may tell them that.

Exit a Page.

So, with the help of God,
We shall be saved—or else indeed we are lost.
Priest: Let us rise, children. It was for this we came, 150
And now the King has promised it himself.
Phoibos° has sent us an oracle; may he descend
Himself to save us and drive out the plague.

Exeunt Oedipus and Creon into the palace by the central door. The Priest and the Suppliants disperse right and left. After a short pause the Chorus enters the orchestra.

PÁRODOS°

Strophe° 1

Chorus: What is God singing in his profound
    Delphi of gold and shadow?
What oracle for Thebes, the sunwhipped city?

Fear unjoints me, the roots of my heart tremble.

Now I remember, O Healer, your power, and wonder: 5
Will you send doom like a sudden cloud, or weave it
Like nightfall of the past?

Speak, speak to us, issue of holy sound:
Dearest to our expectancy: be tender!

152 *Phoibos:* the sun god Phoebus Apollo.   *Párodos:* part to be sung by the chorus on first entering. A *strophe* (according to theory) was sung while the chorus danced from stage right to stage left.

Let me pray to Athenê, the immortal daughter of Zeus,   10
And to Artemis her sister
Who keeps her famous throne in the market ring,
And to Apollo, bowman at the far butts of heaven—

O gods, descend! Like three streams leap against
The fires of our grief, the fires of darkness;   15
Be swift to bring us rest!

As in the old time from the brilliant house
Of air you stepped to save us, come again!

Strophe 2

Now our afflictions have no end,
Now all our stricken host lies down   20
And no man fights off death with his mind;

The noble plowland bears no grain,
And groaning mothers can not bear—

See, how our lives like birds take wing,
Like sparks that fly when a fire soars,   25
To the shore of the god of evening.

Antistrophe 2

The plague burns on, it is pitiless,
Though pallid children laden with death
Lie unwept in the stony ways,

And old gray women by every path   30
Flock to the strand about the altars

There to strike their breasts and cry
Worship of Phoibos in wailing prayers:
Be kind, God's golden child!

Strophe 3

There are no swords in this attack by fire,   35
No shields, but we are ringed with cries.

Send the besieger plunging from our homes
Into the vast sea-room of the Atlantic
Or into the waves that foam eastward of Thrace—

For the day ravages what the night spares—   40

Destroy our enemy, lord of the thunder!
Let him be riven by lightning from heaven!

Antistrophe 3

Phoibos Apollo, stretch the sun's bowstring,

An *antistrophe* was sung while the chorus danced back again across the stage, from left to right.

That golden cord, until it sing for us,
Flashing arrows in heaven!
                    Artemis, Huntress,   45
Race with flaring lights upon our mountains!

O scarlet god, O golden-banded brow,
O Theban Bacchos in a storm of Maenads,°

Enter Oedipus, center.

Whirl upon Death, that all the Undying hate!
Come with blinding torches, come in joy!   50

SCENE I

Oedipus: Is this your prayer? It may be answered. Come,
   Listen to me, act as the crisis demands,
   And you shall have relief from all these evils.

   Until now I was a stranger to this tale,
   As I had been a stranger to the crime.   5
   Could I track down the murderer without a clue?
   But now, friends,
   As one who became a citizen after the murder,
   I make this proclamation to all Thebans:

   If any man knows by whose hand Laïos, son of Labdakos,   10
   Met his death, I direct that man to tell me everything,
   No matter what he fears for having so long withheld it.
   Let it stand as promised that no further trouble
   Will come to him, but he may leave the land in safety.

   Moreover: If anyone knows the murderer to be foreign,   15
   Let him not keep silent: he shall have his reward from me.
   However, if he does conceal it; if any man
   Fearing for his friend or for himself disobeys this edict,
   Hear what I propose to do:

   I solemnly forbid the people of this country,   20
   Where power and throne are mine, ever to receive that man
   Or speak to him, no matter who he is, or let him
   Join in sacrifice, lustration, or in prayer.
   I decree that he be driven from every house,
   Being, as he is, corruption itself to us: the Delphic   25
   Voice of Zeus has pronounced this revelation.

48 *Bacchos . . . Maenads:* god of wine with his attendant girl revelers.

Thus I associate myself with the oracle
And take the side of the murdered king.

As for the criminal, I pray to God—
Whether it be a lurking thief, or one of a number—   30
I pray that that man's life be consumed in evil and wretchedness.
And as for me, this curse applies no less
If it should turn out that the culprit is my guest here,
Sharing my hearth.
                                    You have heard the penalty.
I lay it on you now to attend to this   35
For my sake, for Apollo's, for the sick
Sterile city that heaven has abandoned.
Suppose the oracle had given you no command:
Should this defilement go uncleansed for ever?
You should have found the murderer: your king,   40
A noble king, had been destroyed!
                                    Now I,
Having the power that he held before me,
Having his bed, begetting children there
Upon his wife, as he would have, had he lived—
Their son would have been my children's brother,   45
If Laïos had had luck in fatherhood!
(But surely ill luck rushed upon his reign)—
I say I take the son's part, just as though
I were his son, to press the fight for him
And see it won! I'll find the hand that brought   50
Death to Labdakos' and Polydoros' child,
Heir of Kadmos' and Agenor's line.
And as for those who fail me,
May the gods deny them the fruit of the earth,
Fruit of the womb, and may they rot utterly!   55
Let them be wretched as we are wretched, and worse!

For you, for loyal Thebans, and for all
Who find my actions right, I pray the favor
Of justice, and of all the immortal gods.
Choragos°: Since I am under oath, my lord, I swear   60
     I did not do the murder, I can not name
     The murderer. Might not the oracle
     That has ordained the search tell where to find him?
Oedipus: An honest question. But no man in the world
     Can make the gods do more than the gods will.   65
Choragos: There is one last expedient—
Oedipus: Tell me what it is.

60 Choragos: spokesperson for the chorus.

Though it seem slight, you must not hold it back.

Choragos: A lord clairvoyant to the lord Apollo,
    As we all know, is the skilled Teiresias.
    One might learn much about this from him, Oedipus.   70

Oedipus: I am not wasting time:
    Creon spoke of this, and I have sent for him—
    Twice, in fact; it is strange that he is not here.

Choragos: The other matter—that old report—seems useless.

Oedipus: Tell me. I am interested in all reports.   75

Choragos: The King was said to have been killed by highwaymen.

Oedipus: I know. But we have no witnesses to that.

Choragos: If the killer can feel a particle of dread,
    Your curse will bring him out of hiding!

Oedipus: No.
    The man who dared that act will fear no curse.   80

Enter the blind seer Teiresias, led by a Page.

Choragos: But there is one man who may detect the criminal.
    This is Teiresias, this is the holy prophet
    In whom, alone of all men, truth was born.

Oedipus: Teiresias: seer: student of mysteries,
    Of all that's taught and all that no man tells,   85
    Secrets of Heaven and secrets of the earth:
    Blind though you are, you know the city lies
    Sick with plague; and from this plague, my lord,
    We find that you alone can guard or save us.

    Possibly you did not hear the messengers?   90
    Apollo, when we sent to him,
    Sent us back word that this great pestilence
    Would lift, but only if we established clearly
    The identity of those who murdered Laïos.
    They must be killed or exiled.

                      Can you use   95
    Birdflight or any art of divination
    To purify yourself, and Thebes, and me
    From this contagion? We are in your hands.
    There is no fairer duty
    Than that of helping others in distress.   100

Teiresias: How dreadful knowledge of the truth can be
    When there's no help in truth! I knew this well,
    But made myself forget. I should not have come.

Oedipus: What is troubling you? Why are your eyes so cold?

Teiresias: Let me go home. Bear your own fate, and I'll   105
    Bear mine. It is better so: trust what I say.

Oedipus: What you say is ungracious and unhelpful

To your native country. Do not refuse to speak.

Teiresias: When it comes to speech, your own is neither temperate
    Nor opportune. I wish to be more prudent.   110

Oedipus: In God's name, we all beg you—

Teiresias: You are all ignorant.
    No; I will never tell you what I know.
    Now it is my misery; then, it would be yours.

Oedipus: What! You do know something, and will not tell us?
    You would betray us all and wreck the State?   115

Teiresias: I do not intend to torture myself, or you.
    Why persist in asking? You will not persuade me.

Oedipus: What a wicked old man you are! You'd try a stone's
    Patience! Out with it! Have you no feeling at all?

Teiresias: You call me unfeeling. If you could only see   120
    The nature of your own feelings . . .

Oedipus: Why,
    Who would not feel as I do? Who could endure
    Your arrogance toward the city?

Teiresias: What does it matter!
    Whether I speak or not; it is bound to come.

Oedipus: Then, if "it" is bound to come, you are bound to tell me.   125

Teiresias: No, I will not go on. Rage as you please.

Oedipus: Rage? Why not!
             And I'll tell you what I think:
    You planned it, you had it done, you all but
    Killed him with your own hands: if you had eyes,
    I'd say the crime was yours, and yours alone.   130

Teiresias: So? I charge you, then,
    Abide by the proclamation you have made:
    From this day forth
    Never speak again to these men or to me;
    You yourself are the pollution of this country.   135

Oedipus: You dare say that! Can you possibly think you have
    Some way of going free, after such insolence?

Teiresias: I have gone free. It is the truth sustains me.

Oedipus: Who taught you shamelessness? It was not your craft.

Teiresias: You did. You made me speak. I did not want to.   140

Oedipus: Speak what? Let me hear it again more clearly.

Teiresias: Was it not clear before? Are you tempting me?

Oedipus: I did not understand it. Say it again.

Teiresias: I say that you are the murderer whom you seek.

Oedipus: Now twice you have spat out infamy. You'll pay for it!   145

Teiresias: Would you care for more? Do you wish to be really angry?

Oedipus: Say what you will. Whatever you say is worthless.

Teiresias: I say you live in hideous shame with those
    Most dear to you. You can not see the evil.

Oedipus: It seems you can go on mouthing like this for ever. 150
Teiresias: I can, if there is power in truth.
Oedipus: There is:
    But not for you, not for you,
    You sightless, witless, senseless, mad old man!
Teiresias: You are the madman. There is no one here
    Who will not curse you soon, as you curse me. 155
Oedipus: You child of endless night! You can not hurt me
    Or any other man who sees the sun.
Teiresias: True: it is not from me your fate will come.
    That lies within Apollo's competence,
    As it is his concern.
Oedipus: Tell me: 160
    Are you speaking for Creon, or for yourself?
Teiresias: Creon is no threat. You weave your own doom.
Oedipus: Wealth, power, craft of statesmanship!
    Kingly position, everywhere admired!
    What savage envy is stored up against these, 165
    If Creon, whom I trusted, Creon my friend,
    For this great office which the city once
    Put in my hands unsought—if for this power
    Creon desires in secret to destroy me!

    He has brought this decrepit fortune-teller, this 170
    Collector of dirty pennies, this prophet fraud—
    Why, he is no more clairvoyant than I am!
                   Tell us:
    Has your mystic mummery ever approached the truth?
    When that hellcat the Sphinx was performing here,
    What help were you to these people? 175
    Her magic was not for the first man who came along:
    It demanded a real exorcist. Your birds—
    What good were they? or the gods, for the matter of that?
    But I came by,
    Oedipus, the simple man, who knows nothing— 180
    I thought it out for myself, no birds helped me!
    And this is the man you think you can destroy,
    That you may be close to Creon when he's king!
    Well, you and your friend Creon, it seems to me,
    Will suffer most. If you were not an old man, 185
    You would have paid already for your plot.
Choragos: We can not see that his words or yours
    Have been spoken except in anger, Oedipus,
    And of anger we have no need. How can God's will
    Be accomplished best? That is what most concerns us. 190
Teiresias: You are a king. But where argument's concerned

I am your man, as much a king as you.
I am not your servant, but Apollo's.
I have no need of Creon to speak for me.

Listen to me. You mock my blindness, do you?   195
But I say that you, with both your eyes, are blind:
You can not see the wretchedness of your life,
Nor in whose house you live, no, nor with whom.
Who are your father and mother? Can you tell me?
You do not even know the blind wrongs   200
That you have done them, on earth and in the world below.
But the double lash of your parents' curse will whip you
Out of this land some day, with only night
Upon your precious eyes.
Your cries then—where will they not be heard?   205
What fastness of Kithairon will not echo them?
And that bridal-descant of yours—you'll know it then,
The song they sang when you came here to Thebes
And found your misguided berthing.
All this, and more, that you can not guess at now,   210
Will bring you to yourself among your children.

Be angry, then. Curse Creon. Curse my words.
I tell you, no man that walks upon the earth
Shall be rooted out more horribly than you.
Oedipus: Am I to bear this from him?—Damnation   215
    Take you! Out of this place! Out of my sight!
Teiresias: I would not have come at all if you had not asked me.
Oedipus: Could I have told that you'd talk nonsense, that
    You'd come here to make a fool of yourself, and of me?
Teiresias: A fool? Your parents thought me sane enough.   220
Oedipus: My parents again!—Wait: who were my parents?
Teiresias: This day will give you a father, and break your heart.
Oedipus: Your infantile riddles! Your damned abracadabra!
Teiresias: You were a great man once at solving riddles.
Oedipus: Mock me with that if you like; you will find it true.   225
Teiresias: It was true enough. It brought about your ruin.
Oedipus: But if it saved this town?
Teiresias (to the Page):   Boy, give me your hand.
Oedipus: Yes, boy; lead him away.
                            —While you are here
    We can do nothing. Go; leave us in peace.
Teiresias: I will go when I have said what I have to say.   230
    How can you hurt me? And I tell you again:
    The man you have been looking for all this time,
    The damned man, the murderer of Laïos,

That man is in Thebes. To your mind he is foreignborn,
But it will soon be shown that he is a Theban,   235
A revelation that will fail to please.
                                A blind man,
Who has his eyes now; a penniless man, who is rich now;
And he will go tapping the strange earth with his staff;
To the children with whom he lives now he will be
Brother and father—the very same; to her   240
Who bore him, son and husband—the very same
Who came to his father's bed, wet with his father's blood.

Enough. Go think that over.
If later you find error in what I have said,
You may say that I have no skill in prophecy.   245

Exit Teiresias, led by his Page. Oedipus goes into the palace.

ODE° I

Strophe 1

Chorus: The Delphic stone of prophecies
       Remembers ancient regicide
       And a still bloody hand.
       That killer's hour of flight has come.
       He must be stronger than riderless   5
       Coursers of untiring wind,
       For the son of Zeus° armed with his father's thunder
       Leaps in lightning after him;
       And the Furies° follow him, the sad Furies.

Antistrophe 1

Holy Parnassos' peak of snow   10
Flashes and blinds that secret man,
That all shall hunt him down:
Though he may roam the forest shade
Like a bull gone wild from pasture
To rage through glooms of stone.   15
Doom comes down on him; flight will not avail him;
For the world's heart calls him desolate,
And the immortal Furies follow, for ever follow.

Strophe 2

But now a wilder thing is heard
From the old man skilled at hearing Fate in the wingbeat of a bird.   20
Bewildered as a blown bird, my soul hovers and can not find

Ode: a choral song. Here again (as in the *párados*), *strophe* and *antistrophe* probably indicate the
movements of a dance.   7 *son of Zeus:* Apollo.   9 *Furies:* three horrific female spirits whose task was
to seek out and punish evildoers.

Foothold in this debate, or any reason or rest of mind.
But no man ever brought—none can bring
Proof of strife between Thebes' royal house,
Labdakos' line,° and the son of Polybos;°   25
And never until now has any man brought word
Of Laïos' dark death staining Oedipus the King.

Antistrophe 2

Divine Zeus and Apollo hold
Perfect intelligence alone of all tales ever told;
And well though this diviner works, he works in his own night;   30
No man can judge that rough unknown or trust in second sight,
For wisdom changes hands among the wise.
Shall I believe my great lord criminal
At a raging word that a blind old man let fall?
I saw him, when the carrion woman faced him of old,   35
Prove his heroic mind! These evil words are lies.

SCENE II

Creon: Men of Thebes:
   I am told that heavy accusations
   Have been brought against me by King Oedipus.

   I am not the kind of man to bear this tamely.

   If in these present difficulties   5
   He holds me accountable for any harm to him
   Through anything I have said or done—why, then,
   I do not value life in this dishonor.

   It is not as though this rumor touched upon
   Some private indiscretion. The matter is grave.   10
   The fact is that I am being called disloyal
   To the State, to my fellow citizens, to my friends.
Choragos: He may have spoken in anger, not from his mind.
Creon: But did you not hear him say I was the one
   Who seduced the old prophet into lying?   15
Choragos: The thing was said; I do not know how seriously.
Creon: But you were watching him! Were his eyes steady?
   Did he look like a man in his right mind?
Choragos: I do not know.
   I can not judge the behavior of great men.
   But here is the King himself.

25 *Labdakos' line:* descendants of Laïos (true father of Oedipus, although the chorus does not know
it).   25 *Polybos:* king who adopted the child Oedipus.

Enter Oedipus.

Oedipus:	So you dared come back.	20

Why? How brazen of you to come to my house,
You murderer!
                Do you think I do not know
That you plotted to kill me, plotted to steal my throne?
Tell me, in God's name: am I coward, a fool,
That you should dream you could accomplish this?   25
A fool who could not see your slippery game?
A coward, not to fight back when I saw it?
You are the fool, Creon, are you not? hoping
Without support or friends to get a throne?
Thrones may be won or bought: you could do neither.   30
Creon: Now listen to me. You have talked; let me talk, too.
    You can not judge unless you know the facts.
Oedipus: You speak well: there is one fact; but I find it hard
    To learn from the deadliest enemy I have.
Creon: That above all I must dispute with you.   35
Oedipus: That above all I will not hear you deny.
Creon: If you think there is anything good in being stubborn
    Against all reason, then I say you are wrong.
Oedipus: If you think a man can sin against his own kind
    And not be punished for it, I say you are mad.   40
Creon: I agree. But tell me: what have I done to you?
Oedipus: You advised me to send for that wizard, did you not?
Creon: I did. I should do it again.
Oedipus: Very well. Now tell me:
    How long has it been since Laïos—
Creon: What of Laïos?
Oedipus: Since he vanished in that onset by the road?   45
Creon: It was long ago, a long time.
Oedipus: And this prophet,
    Was he practicing here then?
Creon: He was; and with honor, as now.
Oedipus: Did he speak of me at that time?
Creon: He never did;
    At least, not when I was present.
Oedipus: But . . . the enquiry?
    I suppose you held one?
Creon: We did, but we learned nothing.   50
Oedipus: Why did the prophet not speak against me then?
Creon: I do not know; and I am the kind of man
    Who holds his tongue when he has no facts to go on.
Oedipus: There's one fact that you know, and you could tell it.
Creon: What fact is that? If I know it, you shall have it.   55

Oedipus: If he were not involved with you, he could not say
    That it was I who murdered Laïos.
Creon: If he says that, you are the one that knows it!—
    But now it is my turn to question you.
Oedipus: Put your questions. I am no murderer.   60
Creon: First then: You married my sister?
Oedipus: I married your sister.
Creon: And you rule the kingdom equally with her?
Oedipus: Everything that she wants she has from me.
Creon: And I am the third, equal to both of you?
Oedipus: That is why I call you a bad friend.   65
Creon: No. Reason it out, as I have done.
    Think of this first: Would any sane man prefer
    Power, with all a king's anxieties,
    To that same power and the grace of sleep?
    Certainly not I.   70
    I have never longed for the king's power—only his rights.
    Would any wise man differ from me in this?
    As matters stand, I have my way in everything
    With your consent, and no responsibilities.
    If I were king, I should be a slave to policy.   75

    How could I desire a scepter more
    Than what is now mine—untroubled influence?
    No, I have not gone mad; I need no honors,
    Except those with the perquisites I have now.
    I am welcome everywhere; every man salutes me,   80
    And those who want your favor seek my ear,
    Since I know how to manage what they ask.
    Should I exchange this ease for that anxiety?
    Besides, no sober mind is treasonable.
    I hate anarchy   85
    And never would deal with any man who likes it.

    Test what I have said. Go to the priestess
    At Delphi, ask if I quoted her correctly.
    And as for this other thing: if I am found
    Guilty of treason with Teiresias,   90
    Then sentence me to death! You have my word
    It is a sentence I should cast my vote for—
    But not without evidence!
                    You do wrong
    When you take good men for bad, bad men for good.
    A true friend thrown aside—why, life itself   95
    Is not more precious!
                In time you will know this well:
    For time, and time alone, will show the just man,

Though scoundrels are discovered in a day.

Choragos: This is well said, and a prudent man would ponder it.
Judgments too quickly formed are dangerous.   100

Oedipus: But is he not quick in his duplicity?
And shall I not be quick to parry him?
Would you have me stand still, hold my peace, and let
This man win everything, through my inaction?

Creon: And you want—what is it, then? To banish me?   105

Oedipus: No, not exile. It is your death I want,
So that all the world may see what treason means.

Creon: You will persist, then? You will not believe me?

Oedipus: How can I believe you?

Creon: Then you are a fool.

Oedipus: To save myself?

Creon: In justice, think of me.   110

Oedipus: You are evil incarnate.

Creon: But suppose that you are wrong?

Oedipus: Still I must rule.

Creon: But not if you rule badly.

Oedipus: O city, city!

Creon: It is my city, too!

Choragos: Now, my lords, be still. I see the Queen,
Iocastê, coming from her palace chambers;   115
And it is time she came, for the sake of you both.
This dreadful quarrel can be resolved through her.

Enter Iocastê.

Iocastê: Poor foolish men, what wicked din is this?
With Thebes sick to death, is it not shameful
That you should rake some private quarrel up?   120
(*To Oedipus.*) Come into the house.

                                  —And you, Creon, go now:
Let us have no more of this tumult over nothing.

Creon: Nothing? No, sister: what your husband plans for me
Is one of two great evils: exile or death.

Oedipus: He is right.

                          Why, woman, I have caught him squarely   125
Plotting against my life.

Creon: No! Let me die
Accurst if ever I have wished you harm!

Iocastê: Ah, believe it, Oedipus!
In the name of the gods, respect this oath of his
For my sake, for the sake of these people here!   130

                                                          Strophe 1

Choragos: Open your mind to her, my lord. Be ruled by her, I beg you!

Oedipus: What would you have me do?

Choragos: Respect Creon's word. He has never spoken like a fool,
    And now he has sworn an oath.

Oedipus: You know what you ask?

Choragos: I do.

Oedipus: Speak on, then.

Choragos: A friend so sworn should not be baited so,   135
    In blind malice, and without final proof.

Oedipus: You are aware, I hope, that what you say
    Means death for me, or exile at the least.

                                    Strophe 2

Choragos: No, I swear by Helios, first in Heaven!
      May I die friendless and accurst,   140
The worst of deaths, if ever I meant that!
    It is the withering fields
      That hurt my sick heart:
Must we bear all these ills,
      And now your bad blood as well?   145

Oedipus: Then let him go. And let me die, if I must,
    Or be driven by him in shame from the land of Thebes.
    It is your unhappiness, and not his talk,
    That touches me.
               As for him—
    Wherever he goes, hatred will follow him.   150

Creon: Ugly in yielding, as you were ugly in rage!
    Natures like yours chiefly torment themselves.

Oedipus: Can you not go? Can you not leave me?

Creon: I can.
    You do not know me; but the city knows me,
    And in its eyes I am just, if not in yours.   155

    Exit Creon.

                               Antistrophe 1

Choragos: Lady Iocastê, did you not ask the King to go to his chambers?

Iocastê: First tell me what has happened.

Choragos: There was suspicion without evidence; yet it rankled
    As even false charges will.

Iocastê: On both sides?

Choragos: On both.

Iocastê: But what was said?

Choragos: Oh let it rest, let it be done with!   160
    Have we not suffered enough?

Oedipus: You see to what your decency has brought you:
    You have made difficulties where my heart saw none.

                             Antistrophe 2

Choragos: Oedipus, it is not once only I have told you—
      You must know I should count myself unwise   165

To the point of madness, should I now forsake you—
You, under whose hand,
   In the storm of another time,
Our dear land sailed out free.
   But now stand fast at the helm!   170

Iocastê: In God's name, Oedipus, inform your wife as well:
   Why are you so set in this hard anger?
Oedipus: I will tell you, for none of these men deserves
   My confidence as you do. It is Creon's work,
   His treachery, his plotting against me.   175
Iocastê: Go on, if you can make this clear to me.
Oedipus: He charges me with the murder of Laïos.
Iocastê: Has he some knowledge? Or does he speak from hearsay?
Oedipus: He would not commit himself to such a charge,
   But he has brought in that damnable soothsayer   180
   To tell his story.
Iocastê: Set your mind at rest.
   If it is a question of soothsayers, I tell you
   That you will find no man whose craft gives knowledge
   Of the unknowable.
              Here is my proof:

An oracle was reported to Laïos once   185
(I will not say from Phoibos himself, but from
His appointed ministers, at any rate)
That his doom would be death at the hands of his own son—
His son, born of his flesh and of mine!

Now, you remember the story: Laïos was killed   190
By marauding strangers where three highways meet;
But his child had not been three days in this world
Before the King had pierced the baby's ankles
And left him to die on a lonely mountainside.

Thus, Apollo never caused that child   195
To kill his father, and it was not Laïos' fate
To die at the hands of his son, as he had feared.
This is what prophets and prophecies are worth!
Have no dread of them.
             It is God himself
Who can show us what he wills, in his own way.   200
Oedipus: How strange a shadowy memory crossed my mind,
   Just now while you were speaking; it chilled my heart.
Iocastê: What do you mean? What memory do you speak of?
Oedipus: If I understand you, Laïos was killed
   At a place where three roads meet.
Iocastê: So it was said;   205

We have no later story.

Oedipus: Where did it happen?

Iocastê: Phokis, it is called: at a place where the Theban Way
    Divides into the roads toward Delphi and Daulia.

Oedipus: When?

Iocastê: We had the news not long before you came
    And proved the right to your succession here.   210

Oedipus: Ah, what net has God been weaving for me?

Iocastê: Oedipus! Why does this trouble you?

Oedipus: Do not ask me yet.
    First, tell me how Laïos looked, and tell me
    How old he was.

Iocastê: He was tall, his hair just touched
    With white; his form was not unlike your own.   215

Oedipus: I think that I myself may be accurst
    By my own ignorant edict.

Iocastê: You speak strangely.
    It makes me tremble to look at you, my King.

Oedipus: I am not sure that the blind man can not see.
    But I should know better if you were to tell me—   220

Iocastê: Anything—though I dread to hear you ask it.

Oedipus: Was the King lightly escorted, or did he ride
    With a large company, as a ruler should?

Iocastê: There were five men with him in all: one was a herald,
    And a single chariot, which he was driving.   225

Oedipus: Alas, that makes it plain enough!
                          But who—
    Who told you how it happened?

Iocastê: A household servant,
    The only one to escape.

Oedipus: And is he still
    A servant of ours?

Iocastê: No; for when he came back at last
    And found you enthroned in the place of the dead king,   230
    He came to me, touched my hand with his, and begged
    That I would send him away to the frontier district
    Where only the shepherds go—
    As far away from the city as I could send him.
    I granted his prayer; for although the man was a slave,   235
    He had earned more than this favor at my hands.

Oedipus: Can he be called back quickly?

Iocastê: Easily.
    But why?

Oedipus: I have taken too much upon myself
    Without enquiry; therefore I wish to consult him.

Iocastê: Then he shall come.

But am I not one also
To whom you might confide these fears of yours?
Oedipus: That is your right; it will not be denied you,
Now least of all; for I have reached a pitch
Of wild foreboding. Is there anyone
To whom I should sooner speak?

Polybos of Corinth is my father.
My mother is a Dorian: Meropê.
I grew up chief among the men of Corinth
Until a strange thing happened—
Not worth my passion, it may be, but strange.

At a feast, a drunken man maundering in his cups
Cries out that I am not my father's son!

I contained myself that night, though I felt anger
And a sinking heart. The next day I visited
My father and mother, and questioned them. They stormed,
Calling it all the slanderous rant of a fool;
And this relieved me. Yet the suspicion
Remained always aching in my mind;
I knew there was talk; I could not rest;
And finally, saying nothing to my parents,
I went to the shrine at Delphi.
The god dismissed my question without reply;
He spoke of other things.
                          Some were clear,
Full of wretchedness, dreadful, unbearable:
As, that I should lie with my own mother, breed
Children from whom all men would turn their eyes;
And that I should be my father's murderer.

I heard all this, and fled. And from that day
Corinth to me was only in the stars
Descending in that quarter of the sky,
As I wandered farther and farther on my way
To a land where I should never see the evil
Sung by the oracle. And I came to this country
Where, so you say, King Laïos was killed.

I will tell you all that happened there, my lady.

There were three highways
Coming together at a place I passed;
And there a herald came towards me, and a chariot
Drawn by horses, with a man such as you describe
Seated in it. The groom leading the horses
Forced me off the road at his lord's command;

But as this charioteer lurched over towards me
I struck him in my rage. The old man saw me
And brought his double goad down upon my head
As I came abreast.
                           He was paid back, and more!   285
Swinging my club in this right hand I knocked him
Out of his car, and he rolled on the ground.
                                                        I killed him.

I killed them all.
Now if that stranger and Laïos were—kin,
Where is a man more miserable than I?   290
More hated by the gods? Citizen and alien alike
Must never shelter me or speak to me—
I must be shunned by all.
                           And I myself
Pronounced this malediction upon myself!

Think of it: I have touched you with these hands,   295
These hands that killed your husband. What defilement!

Am I all evil, then? It must be so,
Since I must flee from Thebes, yet never again
See my own countrymen, my own country,
For fear of joining my mother in marriage   300
And killing Polybos, my father.
                                        Ah,
If I was created so, born to this fate,
Who could deny the savagery of God?

O holy majesty of heavenly powers!
May I never see that day! Never!   305
Rather let me vanish from the race of men
Than know the abomination destined me!
Choragos: We too, my lord, have felt dismay at this.
    But there is hope: you have yet to hear the shepherd.
Oedipus: Indeed, I fear no other hope is left me.   310
Iocastê: What do you hope from him when he comes?
Oedipus: This much:
    If his account of the murder tallies with yours,
    Then I am cleared.
Iocastê: What was it that I said
    Of such importance?
Oedipus: Why, "marauders," you said,
    Killed the King, according to this man's story.   315
    If he maintains that still, if there were several,
    Clearly the guilt is not mine: I was alone.
    But if he says one man, singlehanded, did it,

Then the evidence all points to me.

Iocastê: You may be sure that he said there were several;   320
    And can he call back that story now? He can not.
    The whole city heard it as plainly as I.
    But suppose he alters some detail of it:
    He can not ever show that Laïos' death
    Fulfilled the oracle: for Apollo said   325
    My child was doomed to kill him; and my child—
    Poor baby!—it was my child that died first.

    No. From now on, where oracles are concerned,
    I would not waste a second thought on any.

Oedipus: You may be right.
                            But come: let someone go   330
    For the shepherd at once. This matter must be settled.

Iocastê: I will send for him.
    I would not wish to cross you in anything,
    And surely not in this.—Let us go in.

    Exeunt into the palace.

ODE II

Chorus: Let me be reverent in the ways of right,   *Strophe 1*
    Lowly the paths I journey on;
    Let all my words and actions keep
    The laws of the pure universe
    From highest Heaven handed down.   5
    For Heaven is their bright nurse,
    Those generations of the realms of light;
    Ah, never of mortal kind were they begot,
    Nor are they slaves of memory, lost in sleep:
    Their Father is greater than Time, and ages not.   10

                                                                            Antistrophe 1

    The tyrant is a child of Pride
    Who drinks from his great sickening cup
    Recklessness and vanity,
    Until from his high crest headlong
    He plummets to the dust of hope.   15
    That strong man is not strong.
    But let no fair ambition be denied;
    May God protect the wrestler for the State
    In government, in comely policy,
    Who will fear God, and on His ordinance wait.   20

                                                                            Strophe 2

    Haughtiness and the high hand of disdain
    Tempt and outrage God's holy law;

And any mortal who dares hold
No immortal Power in awe
Will be caught up in a net of pain: 25
The price for which his levity is sold.
Let each man take due earnings, then,
And keep his hands from holy things,
And from blasphemy stand apart—
Else the crackling blast of heaven   30
Blows on his head, and on his desperate heart;
Though fools will honor impious men,
In their cities no tragic poet sings.

Antistrophe 2

Shall we lose faith in Delphi's obscurities,
We who have heard the world's core   35
Discredited, and the sacred wood
Of Zeus at Elis praised no more?
The deeds and the strange prophecies
Must make a pattern yet to be understood.
Zeus, if indeed you are lord of all,   40
Throned in light over night and day,
Mirror this in your endless mind:
Our masters call the oracle
Words on the wind, and the Delphic vision blind!
Their hearts no longer know Apollo,   45
And reverence for the gods has died away.

SCENE III

Enter Iocastê.

Iocastê: Princes of Thebes, it has occurred to me
To visit the altars of the gods, bearing
These branches as a suppliant, and this incense.
Our King is not himself: his noble soul
Is overwrought with fantasies of dread,   5
Else he would consider
The new prophecies in the light of the old.
He will listen to any voice that speaks disaster,
And my advice goes for nothing.

She approaches the altar, right.

                    To you, then, Apollo,
Lycean lord, since you are nearest, I turn in prayer.
Receive these offerings, and grant us deliverance   10
From defilement. Our hearts are heavy with fear

When we see our leader distracted, as helpless sailors
Are terrified by the confusion of their helmsman.

Enter Messenger.

Messenger: Friends, no doubt you can direct me: 15
  Where shall I find the house of Oedipus,
  Or, better still, where is the King himself?
Choragos: It is this very place, stranger; he is inside.
  This is his wife and mother of his children.
Messenger: I wish her happiness in a happy house,   20
  Blest in all the fulfillment of her marriage.
Iocastê: I wish as much for you: your courtesy
  Deserves a like good fortune. But now, tell me:
  Why have you come? What have you to say to us?
Messenger: Good news, my lady, for your house and your husband.   25
Iocastê: What news? Who sent you here?
Messenger: I am from Corinth.
  The news I bring ought to mean joy for you,
  Though it may be you will find some grief in it.
Iocastê: What is it? How can it touch us in both ways?
Messenger: The word is that the people of the Isthmus   30
  Intend to call Oedipus to be their king.
Iocastê: But old King Polybos—is he not reigning still?
Messenger: No. Death holds him in his sepulchre.
Iocastê: What are you saying? Polybos is dead?
Messenger: If I am not telling the truth, may I die myself.   35
Iocastê (to a Maidservant): Go in, go quickly; tell this to your master.

  O riddlers of God's will, where are you now!
  This was the man whom Oedipus, long ago,
  Feared so, fled so, in dread of destroying him—
  But it was another fate by which he died.   40

  Enter Oedipus, center.

Oedipus: Dearest Iocastê, why have you sent for me?
Iocastê: Listen to what this man says, and then tell me
  What has become of the solemn prophecies.
Oedipus: Who is this man? What is his news for me?
Iocastê: He has come from Corinth to announce your father's death! 45
Oedipus: Is it true, stranger? Tell me in your own words.
Messenger: I can not say it more clearly: the King is dead.
Oedipus: Was it by treason? Or by an attack of illness?
Messenger: A little thing brings old men to their rest.
Oedipus: It was sickness, then?
Messenger: Yes, and his many years.   50

Oedipus: Ah!
Why should a man respect the Pythian hearth,° or
Give heed to the birds that jangle above his head?
They prophesied that I should kill Polybos,
Kill my own father; but he is dead and buried,   55
And I am here—I never touched him, never,
Unless he died of grief for my departure,
And thus, in a sense, through me. No. Polybos
Has packed the oracles off with him underground.
They are empty words.

Iocastê: Had I not told you so?   60

Oedipus: You had; it was my faint heart that betrayed me.

Iocastê: From now on never think of those things again.

Oedipus: And yet—must I not fear my mother's bed?

Iocastê: Why should anyone in this world be afraid,
Since Fate rules us and nothing can be foreseen?   65
A man should live only for the present day.

Have no more fear of sleeping with your mother:
How many men, in dreams, have lain with their mothers!
No reasonable man is troubled by such things.

Oedipus: That is true; only—   70
If only my mother were not still alive!
But she is alive. I can not help my dread.

Iocastê: Yet this news of your father's death is wonderful.

Oedipus: Wonderful. But I fear the living woman.

Messenger: Tell me, who is this woman that you fear?   75

Oedipus: It is Meropê, man; the wife of King Polybos.

Messenger: Meropê? Why should you be afraid of her?

Oedipus: An oracle of the gods, a dreadful saying.

Messenger: Can you tell me about it or are you sworn to silence?

Oedipus: I can tell you, and I will.   80
Apollo said through his prophet that I was the man
Who should marry his own mother, shed his father's blood
With his own hands. And so, for all these years
I have kept clear of Corinth, and no harm has come—
Though it would have been sweet to see my parents again.   85

Messenger: And is this the fear that drove you out of Corinth?

Oedipus: Would you have me kill my father?

Messenger: As for that
You must be reassured by the news I gave you.

Oedipus: If you could reassure me, I would reward you.

Messenger: I had that in mind, I will confess: I thought   90
I could count on you when you returned to Corinth.

---

52 *Pythian hearth:* the shrine at Delphi, whose priestess was famous for her prophecies.

Oedipus: No: I will never go near my parents again.
Messenger: Ah, son, you still do not know what you are doing—
Oedipus: What do you mean? In the name of God tell me!
Messenger: —If these are your reasons for not going home.   95
Oedipus: I tell you, I fear the oracle may come true.
Messenger: And guilt may come upon you through your parents?
Oedipus: That is the dread that is always in my heart.
Messenger: Can you not see that all your fears are groundless?
Oedipus: How can you say that? They are my parents, surely?   100
Messenger: Polybos was not your father.
Oedipus: Not my father?
Messenger: No more your father than the man speaking to you.
Oedipus: But you are nothing to me!
Messenger: Neither was he.
Oedipus: Then why did he call me son?
Messenger: I will tell you:
      Long ago he had you from my hands, as a gift.   105
Oedipus: Then how could he love me so, if I was not his?
Messenger: He had no children, and his heart turned to you.
Oedipus: What of you? Did you buy me? Did you find me by chance?
Messenger: I came upon you in the crooked pass of Kithairon.
Oedipus: And what were you doing there?
Messenger: Tending my flocks.   110
Oedipus: A wandering shepherd?
Messenger: But your savior, son, that day.
Oedipus: From what did you save me?
Messenger: Your ankles should tell you that.
Oedipus: Ah, stranger, why do you speak of that childhood pain?
Messenger: I cut the bonds that tied your ankles together.
Oedipus: I have had the mark as long as I can remember.   115
Messenger: That was why you were given the name you bear.
Oedipus: God! Was it my father or my mother who did it?
      Tell me!
Messenger: I do not know. The man who gave you to me
      Can tell you better than I.   120
Oedipus: It was not you that found me, but another?
Messenger: It was another shepherd gave you to me.
Oedipus: Who was he? Can you tell me who he was?
Messenger: I think he was said to be one of Laïos' people.
Oedipus: You mean the Laïos who was king here years ago?   125
Messenger: Yes; King Laïos; and the man was one of his herdsmen.
Oedipus: Is he still alive? Can I see him?
Messenger: These men here
      Know best about such things.
Oedipus: Does anyone here
      Know this shepherd that he is talking about?

Have you seen him in the fields, or in the town?   130
If you have, tell me. It is time things were made plain.
Choragos: I think the man he means is that same shepherd
      You have already asked to see. Iocastê perhaps
      Could tell you something.
Oedipus: Do you know anything
      About him, Lady? Is he the man we have summoned?   135
      Is that the man this shepherd means?
Iocastê: Why think of him?
      Forget this herdsman. Forget it all.
      This talk is a waste of time.
Oedipus: How can you say that,
      When the clues to my true birth are in my hands?
Iocastê: For God's love, let us have no more questioning!   140
      Is your life nothing to you?
      My own is pain enough for me to bear.
Oedipus: You need not worry. Suppose my mother a slave,
      And born of slaves: no baseness can touch you.
Iocastê: Listen to me, I beg you: do not do this thing!   145
Oedipus: I will not listen; the truth must be made known.
Iocastê: Everything that I say is for your own good!
Oedipus: My own good
      Snaps my patience, then; I want none of it.
Iocastê: You are fatally wrong! May you never learn who you are!
Oedipus: Go, one of you, and bring the shepherd here.   150
      Let us leave this woman to brag of her royal name.
Iocastê: Ah, miserable!
      That is the only word I have for you now.
      That is the only word I can ever have.

      Exit into the palace.

Choragos: Why has she left us, Oedipus? Why has she gone   155
      In such a passion of sorrow? I fear this silence:
      Something dreadful may come of it.
Oedipus: Let it come!
      However base my birth, I must know about it.
      The Queen, like a woman, is perhaps ashamed
      To think of my low origin. But I   160
      Am a child of Luck; I can not be dishonored.
      Luck is my mother; the passing months, my brothers,
      Have seen me rich and poor.
                              If this is so,
      How could I wish that I were someone else?
      How could I not be glad to know my birth?   165

ODE III

Chorus: If ever the coming time were known
    To my heart's pondering,
    Kithairon, now by Heaven I see the torches
    At the festival of the next full moon,
    And see the dance, and hear the choir sing   5
    A grace to your gentle shade:
    Mountain where Oedipus was found,
    O mountain guard of a noble race!
    May the god who heals us lend his aid,
    And let that glory come to pass   10
    For our king's cradling-ground.

    Of the nymphs that flower beyond the years,
    Who bore you, royal child,
    To Pan of the hills or the timberline Apollo,
    Cold in delight where the upland clears,   15
    Or Hermês for whom Kyllenê's° heights are piled?
    Or flushed as evening cloud,
    Great Dionysos, roamer of mountains,
    He—was it he who found you there,
    And caught you up in his own proud   20
    Arms from the sweet god-ravisher
    Who laughed by the Muses' fountains?

SCENE IV

Oedipus: Sirs: though I do not know the man,
    I think I see him coming, this shepherd we want:
    He is old, like our friend here, and the men
    Bringing him seem to be servants of my house.
    But you can tell, if you have ever seen him.   5

    Enter Shepherd escorted by servants.

Choragos: I know him, he was Laïos' man. You can trust him.
Oedipus: Tell me first, you from Corinth: is this the shepherd
    We were discussing?
Messenger: This is the very man.
Oedipus (to Shepherd): Come here. No, look at me. You must answer

---

16 *Kyllenê:* a sacred mountain, birthplace of Hermês, the deities' messenger. The chorus assumes that the mountain was created in order to afford him birth.

Everything I ask.—You belonged to Laïos?   10

Shepherd: Yes: born his slave, brought up in his house.

Oedipus: Tell me: what kind of work did you do for him?

Shepherd: I was a shepherd of his, most of my life.

Oedipus: Where mainly did you go for pasturage?

Shepherd: Sometimes Kithairon, sometimes the hills near-by.   15

Oedipus: Do you remember ever seeing this man out there?

Shepherd: What would he be doing there? This man?

Oedipus: This man standing here. Have you ever seen him before?

Shepherd: No. At least, not to my recollection.

Messenger: And that is not strange, my lord. But I'll refresh   20
     His memory: he must remember when we two
     Spent three whole seasons together, March to September,
     On Kithairon or thereabouts. He had two flocks;
     I had one. Each autumn I'd drive mine home
     And he would go back with his to Laïos' sheepfold.—   25
     Is this not true, just as I have described it?

Shepherd: True, yes; but it was all so long ago.

Messenger: Well, then: do you remember, back in those days
     That you gave me a baby boy to bring up as my own?

Shepherd: What if I did? What are you trying to say?   30

Messenger: King Oedipus was once that little child.

Shepherd: Damn you, hold your tongue!

Oedipus: No more of that!
     It is your tongue needs watching, not this man's.

Shepherd: My King, my Master, what is it I have done wrong?

Oedipus: You have not answered his question about the boy.   35

Shepherd: He does not know . . . He is only making trouble . . .

Oedipus: Come, speak plainly, or it will go hard with you.

Shepherd: In God's name, do not torture an old man!

Oedipus: Come here, one of you; bind his arms behind him.

Shepherd: Unhappy king! What more do you wish to learn?   40

Oedipus: Did you give this man the child he speaks of?

Shepherd: I did.
     And I would to God I had died that very day.

Oedipus: You will die now unless you speak the truth.

Shepherd: Yet if I speak the truth, I am worse than dead.

Oedipus: Very well; since you insist upon delaying—   45

Shepherd: No! I have told you already that I gave him the boy.

Oedipus: Where did you get him? From your house? From somewhere else?

Shepherd: Not from mine, no. A man gave him to me.

Oedipus: Is that man here? Do you know whose slave he was?

Shepherd: For God's love, my King, do not ask me any more!   50

Oedipus: You are a dead man if I have to ask you again.

Shepherd: Then . . . Then the child was from the palace of Laïos.

Oedipus: A slave child? or a child of his own line?

Shepherd: Ah, I am on the brink of dreadful speech!

Oedipus: And I of dreadful hearing. Yet I must hear.   55

Shepherd: If you must be told, then . . .

                                    They said it was Laïos' child;

   But it is your wife who can tell you about that.

Oedipus: My wife!—Did she give it to you?

Shepherd: My lord, she did.

Oedipus: Do you know why?

Shepherd: I was told to get rid of it.

Oedipus: An unspeakable mother!

Shepherd: There had been prophecies . . .   60

Oedipus: Tell me.

Shepherd: It was said that the boy would kill his own father.

Oedipus: Then why did you give him over to this old man?

Shepherd: I pitied the baby, my King,

   And I thought that this man would take him far away   65

   To his own country.

                  He saved him—but for what a fate!

   For if you are what this man says you are,

   No man living is more wretched than Oedipus.

Oedipus: Ah God!

   It was true!

          All the prophecies!

                   —Now,   70

   O Light, may I look on you for the last time!

   I, Oedipus,

   Oedipus, damned in his birth, in his marriage damned,

   Damned in the blood he shed with his own hand!

He rushes into the palace.

ODE IV

Strophe 1

Chorus: Alas for the seed of men.

   What measure shall I give these generations

   That breathe on the void and are void

   And exist and do not exist?

   Who bears more weight of joy   5

   Than mass of sunlight shifting in images,

   Or who shall make his thought stay on

   That down time drifts away?

   Your splendor is all fallen.

   O naked brow of wrath and tears,   10

   O change of Oedipus!

I who saw your days call no man blest—
Your great days like ghosts gone.

Antistrophe 1

That mind was a strong bow.

Deep, how deep you drew it then, hard archer,   15
At a dim fearful range,
And brought dear glory down!

You overcame the stranger—
The virgin with her hooking lion claws—
And though death sang, stood like a tower   20
To make pale Thebes take heart.

Fortress against our sorrow!

True king, giver of laws,
Majestic Oedipus!
No prince in Thebes had ever such renown,   25
No prince won such grace of power.

Strophe 2

And now of all men ever known
Most pitiful is this man's story:
His fortunes are most changed, his state
Fallen to a low slave's   30
Ground under bitter fate.

O Oedipus, most royal one!
The great door that expelled you to the light
Gave at night—ah, gave night to your glory:
As to the father, to the fathering son.   35

All understood too late.

How could that queen whom Laïos won,
The garden that he harrowed at his height,
Be silent when that act was done?

Antistrophe 2

But all eyes fail before time's eye,   40
All actions come to justice there.
Though never willed, though far down the deep past,
Your bed, your dread sirings,
Are brought to book at last.

Child by Laïos doomed to die,   45
Then doomed to lose that fortunate little death,
Would God you never took breath in this air
That with my wailing lips I take to cry:

For I weep the world's outcast.

I was blind, and now I can tell why: 50
Asleep, for you had given ease of breath
To Thebes, while the false years went by.

ÉXODOS°

Enter, from the palace, Second Messenger.

Second Messenger: Elders of Thebes, most honored in this land,
　　What horrors are yours to see and hear, what weight
　　Of sorrow to be endured, if, true to your birth,
　　You venerate the line of Labdakos!
　　I think neither Istros nor Phasis, those great rivers,   5
　　Could purify this place of the corruption
　　It shelters now, or soon must bring to light—
　　Evil not done unconsciously, but willed.

　　The greatest griefs are those we cause ourselves.
Choragos: Surely, friend, we have grief enough already;   10
　　What new sorrow do you mean?
Second Messenger: 　　　　　　　　The Queen is dead.
Choragos: Iocastê? Dead? But at whose hand?
Second Messenger: 　　　　　　　　Her own.
　　The full horror of what happened, you can not know,
　　For you did not see it; but I, who did, will tell you
　　As clearly as I can how she met her death.   15

　　When she had left us,
　　In passionate silence, passing through the court,
　　She ran to her apartment in the house,
　　Her hair clutched by the fingers of both hands.
　　She closed the doors behind her; then, by that bed   20
　　Where long ago the fatal son was conceived—
　　That son who should bring about his father's death—
　　We heard her call upon Laïos, dead so many years,
　　And heard her wail for the double fruit of her marriage,
　　A husband by her husband, children by her child.   25

　　Exactly how she died I do not know:
　　For Oedipus burst in moaning and would not let us
　　Keep vigil to the end: it was by him
　　As he stormed about the room that our eyes were caught.
　　From one to another of us he went, begging a sword,   30
　　Cursing the wife who was not his wife, the mother
　　Whose womb had carried his own children and himself.
　　I do not know: it was none of us aided him,

Éxodos: final scene, containing the resolution.

But surely one of the gods was in control!
For with a dreadful cry   35
He hurled his weight, as though wrenched out of himself,
At the twin doors: the bolts gave, and he rushed in.
And there we saw her hanging, her body swaying
From the cruel cord she had noosed about her neck.
A great sob broke from him, heartbreaking to hear,   40
As he loosed the rope and lowered her to the ground.

I would blot out from my mind what happened next!
For the King ripped from her gown the golden brooches
That were her ornament, and raised them, and plunged them down
Straight into his own eyeballs, crying, "No more,   45
No more shall you look on the misery about me,
The horrors of my own doing! Too long you have known
The faces of those whom I should never have seen,
Too long been blind to those for whom I was searching!
From this hour, go in darkness!" And as he spoke,   50
He struck at his eyes—not once, but many times;
And the blood spattered his beard,
Bursting from his ruined sockets like red hail.

So from the unhappiness of two this evil has sprung,
A curse on the man and woman alike. The old   55
Happiness of the house of Labdakos
Was happiness enough: where is it today?
It is all wailing and ruin, disgrace, death—all
The misery of mankind that has a name—
And it is wholly and for ever theirs.   60
Choragos: Is he in agony still? Is there no rest for him?
Second Messenger: He is calling for someone to lead him to the gates
So that all the children of Kadmos may look upon
His father's murderer, his mother's—no,
I can not say it!
               And then he will leave Thebes,   65
Self-exiled, in order that the curse
Which he himself pronounced may depart from the house.
He is weak, and there is none to lead him,
So terrible is his suffering.
               But you will see:
Look, the doors are opening; in a moment   70
You will see a thing that would crush a heart of stone.

The central door is opened; Oedipus, blinded, is led in.

Choragos: Dreadful indeed for men to see.
Never have my own eyes
Looked on a sight so full of fear.

Oedipus! 75
What madness came upon you, what daemon
Leaped on your life with heavier
Punishment than a mortal man can bear?
No: I can not even
Look at you, poor ruined one. 80
And I would speak, question, ponder,
If I were able. No.
You make me shudder.

Oedipus: God. God.
Is there a sorrow greater? 85
Where shall I find harbor in this world?
My voice is hurled far on a dark wind.
What has God done to me?

Choragos: Too terrible to think of, or to see.

Strophe 1

Oedipus: O cloud of night, 90
Never to be turned away: night coming on,
I can not tell how: night like a shroud!

My fair winds brought me here.
                    Oh God. Again
The pain of the spikes where I had sight,
The flooding pain 95
Of memory, never to be gouged out.

Choragos: This is not strange.
You suffer it all twice over, remorse in pain,
Pain in remorse.

Antistrophe 1

Oedipus: Ah dear friend 100
Are you faithful even yet, you alone?
Are you still standing near me, will you stay here,
Patient, to care for the blind?
                    The blind man!
Yet even blind I know who it is attends me,
By the voice's tone— 105
Though my new darkness hide the comforter.

Choragos: Oh fearful act!
What god was it drove you to rake black
Night across your eyes?

Strophe 2

Oedipus: Apollo. Apollo. Dear 110
Children, the god was Apollo.
He brought my sick, sick fate upon me.
But the blinding hand was my own!
How could I bear to see

When all my sight was horror everywhere?   115
Choragos: Everywhere; that is true.
Oedipus: And now what is left?
    Images? Love? A greeting even,
    Sweet to the senses? Is there anything?
    Ah, no, friends: lead me away.   120
    Lead me away from Thebes.
                   Lead the great wreck
    And hell of Oedipus, whom the gods hate.
Choragos: Your fate is clear, you are not blind to that.
    Would God you had never found it out!

Antistrophe 2

Oedipus: Death take the man who unbound   125
    My feet on that hillside
    And delivered me from death to life! What life?
    If only I had died,
    This weight of monstrous doom
    Could not have dragged me and my darlings down.   130
Choragos: I would have wished the same.
Oedipus: Oh never to have come here
    With my father's blood upon me! Never
    To have been the man they call his mother's husband!
    Oh accurst! Oh child of evil,   135
    To have entered that wretched bed—
                  the selfsame one!
    More primal than sin itself, this fell to me.
Choragos: I do not know how I can answer you.
    You were better dead than alive and blind.
Oedipus: Do not counsel me any more. This punishment   140
    That I have laid upon myself is just.
    If I had eyes,
    I do not know how I could bear the sight
    Of my father, when I came to the house of Death,
    Or my mother: for I have sinned against them both   145
    So vilely that I could not make my peace
    By strangling my own life.
               Or do you think my children,
    Born as they were born, would be sweet to my eyes?
    Ah never, never! Nor this town with its high walls,
    Nor the holy images of the gods.
               For I,   150
    Thrice miserable!—Oedipus, noblest of all the line
    Of Kadmos, have condemned myself to enjoy
    These things no more, by my own malediction
    Expelling that man whom the gods declared
    To be a defilement in the house of Laïos.   155

After exposing the rankness of my own guilt,
How could I look men frankly in the eyes?
No, I swear it,
If I could have stifled my hearing at its source,
I would have done it and made all this body   160
A tight cell of misery, blank to light and sound:
So I should have been safe in a dark agony
Beyond all recollection.
                   Ah Kithairon!
Why did you shelter me? When I was cast upon you,
Why did I not die? Then I should never   165
Have shown the world my execrable birth.

Ah Polybos! Corinth, city that I believed
The ancient seat of my ancestors: how fair
I seemed, your child! And all the while this evil
Was cancerous within me!
                  For I am sick   170
In my daily life, sick in my origin.

O three roads, dark ravine, woodland and way
Where three roads met: you, drinking my father's blood,
My own blood, spilled by my own hand: can you remember
The unspeakable things I did there, and the things   175
I went on from there to do?
                O marriage, marriage!
The act that engendered me, and again the act
Performed by the son in the same bed—
                   Ah, the net
Of incest, mingling fathers, brothers, sons,
With brides, wives, mothers: the last evil   180
That can be known by men: no tongue can say
How evil!
       No. For the love of God, conceal me
Somewhere far from Thebes; or kill me; or hurl me
Into the sea, away from men's eyes for ever.

Come, lead me. You need not fear to touch me.   185
Of all men, I alone can bear this guilt.

Enter Creon.

Choragos: We are not the ones to decide; but Creon here
    May fitly judge of what you ask. He only
    Is left to protect the city in your place.
Oedipus: Alas, how can I speak to him? What right have I   190
    To beg his courtesy whom I have deeply wronged?
Creon: I have not come to mock you, Oedipus,
    Or to reproach you, either.

(*To Attendants.*)   —You, standing there:
If you have lost all respect for man's dignity,
At least respect the flame of Lord Helios: 195
Do not allow this pollution to show itself
Openly here, an affront to the earth
And Heaven's rain and the light of day. No, take him
Into the house as quickly as you can.
For it is proper   200
That only the close kindred see his grief.
Oedipus: I pray you in God's name, since your courtesy
Ignores my dark expectation, visiting
With mercy this man of all men most execrable:
Give me what I ask—for your good, not for mine.   205
Creon: And what is it that you would have me do?
Oedipus: Drive me out of this country as quickly as may be
To a place where no human voice can ever greet me.
Creon: I should have done that before now—only,
God's will had not been wholly revealed to me.   210
Oedipus: But his command is plain: the parricide
Must be destroyed. I am that evil man.
Creon: That is the sense of it, yes; but as things are,
We had best discover clearly what is to be done.
Oedipus: You would learn more about a man like me?   215
Creon: You are ready now to listen to the god.
Oedipus: I will listen. But it is to you
That I must turn for help. I beg you, hear me.

The woman in there—
Give her whatever funeral you think proper: 220
She is your sister.
                —But let me go, Creon!
Let me purge my father's Thebes of the pollution
Of my living here, and go out to the wild hills,
To Kithairon, that has won such fame with me,
The tomb my mother and father appointed for me,   225
And let me die there, as they willed I should.
And yet I know
Death will not ever come to me through sickness
Or in any natural way: I have been preserved
For some unthinkable fate. But let that be.   230

As for my sons, you need not care for them.
They are men, they will find some way to live.
But my poor daughters, who have shared my table,
Who never before have been parted from their father—
Take care of them, Creon; do this for me.   235
And will you let me touch them with my hands

A last time, and let us weep together?
Be kind, my lord,
Great prince, be kind!
                    Could I but touch them,
They would be mine again, as when I had my eyes.   240

Enter Antigonê and Ismene, attended.

Ah, God!
Is it my dearest children I hear weeping?
Has Creon pitied me and sent my daughters?
Creon: Yes, Oedipus: I knew that they were dear to you
   In the old days, and know you must love them still.   245
Oedipus: May God bless you for this—and be a friendlier
   Guardian to you than he has been to me!

Children, where are you?
Come quickly to my hands: they are your brother's—
Hands that have brought your father's once clear eyes   250
To this way of seeing—
                    Ah dearest ones,
I had neither sight nor knowledge then, your father
By the woman who was the source of his own life!
And I weep for you—having no strength to see you—,
I weep for you when I think of the bitterness   255
That men will visit upon you all your lives.
What homes, what festivals can you attend
Without being forced to depart again in tears?
And when you come to marriageable age,
Where is the man, my daughters, who would dare   260
Risk the bane that lies on all my children?
Is there any evil wanting? Your father killed
His father; sowed the womb of her who bore him;
Engendered you at the fount of his own existence!
That is what they will say of you.
                          Then, whom   265
Can you ever marry? There are no bridegrooms for you,
And your lives must wither away in sterile dreaming.

O Creon, son of Menoikeus!
You are the only father my daughters have,
Since we, their parents, are both of us gone for ever.   270
They are your own blood: you will not let them
Fall into beggary and loneliness;
You will keep them from the miseries that are mine!
Take pity on them; see, they are only children,
Friendless except for you. Promise me this,   275
Great Prince, and give me your hand in token of it.

Creon clasps his right hand.

Children:
I could say much, if you could understand me,
But as it is, I have only this prayer for you:
Live where you can, be as happy as you can—   280
Happier, please God, than God has made your father!
Creon: Enough. You have wept enough. Now go within.
Oedipus: I must; but it is hard.
Creon: Time eases all things.
Oedipus: But you must promise—
Creon: Say what you desire.
Oedipus: Send me from Thebes!
Creon: God grant that I may!   285
Oedipus: But since God hates me . . .
Creon: No, he will grant your wish.
Oedipus: You promise?
Creon: I can not speak beyond my knowledge.
Oedipus: Then lead me in.
Creon: Come now, and leave your children.
Oedipus: No! Do not take them from me!
Creon: Think no longer
That you are in command here, but rather think   290
How, when you were, you served your own destruction.

Exeunt into the house all but the Chorus; the Choragos chants directly to the audience.

Choragos: Men of Thebes: look upon Oedipus.

This is the king who solved the famous riddle
And towered up, most powerful of men.
No mortal eyes but looked on him with envy,   295
Yet in the end ruin swept over him.

Let every man in mankind's frailty
Consider his last day; and let none
Presume on his good fortune until he find
Life, at his death, a memory without pain.   300

QUESTIONS

1. How explicitly does the prophet Teiresias reveal the guilt of Oedipus? Does it seem to you stupidity on the part of Oedipus or a defect in Sophocles' play that the king takes so long to recognize his guilt and to admit to it?
2. How does Oedipus exhibit weakness of character? Point to lines that reveal him as imperfectly noble in his words, deeds, or treatment of others.
3. "Oedipus is punished not for any fault in himself, but for his ignorance. Not knowing his family history, unable to recognize his parents on sight, he is blameless; and in slaying his

father and marrying his mother, he behaves as any sensible person might behave in the same circumstances." Do you agree with this interpretation?

4. Besides the predictions of Teiresias, what other foreshadowings of the shepherd's revelation does the play contain?
5. Consider the character of Iocastê. Is she a "flat" character—a generalized queen figure—or an individual with distinctive traits of personality? Point to speeches or details in the play to back up your opinion.
6. Do the choral interludes merely interrupt the play with wordy poetry? Other than providing song, dance, and variety, do they have any value to the telling of the story?
7. What is dramatic irony? Besides the example given on page 681, what other instances of dramatic irony do you find in *Oedipus the King*? What do they contribute to the effectiveness of the play?
8. In the drama of Sophocles, violence and bloodshed take place offstage; thus, the suicide of Iocastê is only reported to us. Nor do we witness Oedipus' removal of his eyes; this horror is only given in the report by the second messenger. Of what advantage or disadvantage to the play is this limitation?
9. For what reason does Oedipus blind himself? What meaning, if any, do you find in his choice of a surgical instrument?
10. What are your feelings toward him as the play ends?
11. Read the famous interpretation of this play offered by Sigmund Freud (page 1948). How well does Freud explain why the play moves you?
12. With what attitude toward the gods does the play leave you? By inflicting a plague upon Thebes, by causing barrenness, by cursing both the people and their king, do the gods seem cruel, unjust, or tyrannical? Does the play show any reverence toward them?
13. Does this play end in total gloom?

ARISTOTLE'S CONCEPT OF TRAGEDY

> Tragedy is an imitation of an action of high importance, complete and of some amplitude; in language enhanced by distinct and varying beauties; acted not narrated; by means of pity and fear effecting its purgation of these emotions.
>
> —Aristotle, *Poetics*, Chapter VI

Aristotle's famous definition of tragedy, constructed in the fourth century B.C., is the testimony of one who probably saw many classical tragedies performed. In making his observations, Aristotle does not seem to be laying down laws for what a tragedy ought to be. More likely, he is drawing—from tragedies he has seen or read—a general description of them.

Aristotle observes that the protagonist, the hero or chief character of a tragedy, is a person of "high estate," apparently a king or queen or other member of a royal family. In thus being as keenly interested as contemporary dramatists in the private lives of the powerful, Greek dramatists need not be accused of snobbery. It is the nature of tragedy that the protagonist must fall from power and from happiness; his high estate gives him a place of dignity to fall from and perhaps makes his fall seem all the more a calamity in that it involves an entire nation or people. Nor is the protagonist extraordinary merely in his position in society. Oedipus is not only a king but also a noble soul who suffers profoundly and who employs splendid speech to express his suffering.

The tragic hero, however, is not a superman; he is fallible. The hero's downfall is the result, as Aristotle said, of his **hamartia:** his error or transgression or (as some translators would have it) his flaw or weakness of character. The notion that a tragic hero has such a **tragic flaw** has often been attributed to Aristotle, but it is by no means clear that Aristotle meant just that. According to this interpretation, every tragic hero has some fatal weakness, some moral Achilles' heel, that brings him to a bad end. In some classical tragedies, his transgression is a weakness the Greeks called **hubris**—extreme pride, leading to overconfidence.

Whatever Aristotle had in mind, however, many later critics find value in the idea of the tragic flaw. In this view, the downfall of a hero follows from his very nature. Whatever view we take—whether we find the hero's sufferings due to a flaw of character or to an error of judgment—we will probably find that his downfall results from acts for which he himself is responsible. In a Greek tragedy, the hero is a character amply capable of making choices—capable, too, of accepting the consequences.

It may be useful to take another look at Aristotle's definition of *tragedy,* with which we began. By **purgation** (or **katharsis**), did the ancient theorist mean that after witnessing a tragedy we feel relief, having released our pent-up emotions? Or did he mean that our feelings are purified, refined into something more ennobling? Scholars continue to argue. Whatever his exact meaning, clearly Aristotle implies that after witnessing a tragedy we feel better, not worse—not depressed, but somehow elated. We take a kind of pleasure in the spectacle of a noble man being abased, but surely this pleasure is a legitimate one. For tragedy, Edith Hamilton wrote, affects us as "pain transmuted into exaltation by the alchemy of poetry."[1]

Aristotle, in describing the workings of this inexorable force in *Oedipus the King,* uses terms that later critics have found valuable. One is **recognition,** or discovery (*anagnorisis*): the revelation of some fact not known before or some person's true identity. Oedipus makes such a discovery: he recognizes that he himself was the child whom his mother had given over to be destroyed. Such a recognition also occurs in Shakespeare's *Macbeth* when Macduff reveals himself to have been "from his mother's womb / Untimely ripped," thus disclosing a double meaning in the witches' prophecy that Macbeth could be harmed by "none of woman born," and sweeping aside Macbeth's last shred of belief that he is infallible. Modern critics have taken the term to mean also the terrible enlightenment that accompanies such a recognition. "To see things plain—that is *anagnorisis*," Clifford Leech observes, "and it is the ultimate experience we shall have if we have leisure at the point of death. . . . It is what tragedy ultimately is about: the realization of the unthinkable."[2]

Having made his discovery, Oedipus suffers a reversal in his fortunes; he goes off into exile, blinded and dethroned. Such a fall from happiness seems intrinsic to tragedy, but we should know that Aristotle has a more particular meaning for his term **reversal** (*peripeteia,* Anglicized as **peripety**). He means an action that turns out to have the opposite effect from the one its doer had intended. One of his illustrations of such an ironic reversal is from *Oedipus the King.* The first messenger intends to cheer Oedipus with the partially good news that, contrary to the prophecy that Oedipus would kill his father, his father has died of old age. The reversal is in the fact

---

[1]"The Idea of Tragedy," *The Greek Way to Western Civilization* (New York: Norton, 1942).
[2]*Tragedy* (London: Methuen, 1969) 65.

that, when the messenger further reveals that old Polybos was Oedipus' father only by adoption, the king, instead of having his fears allayed, is stirred to new dread.

We are not altogether sorry, perhaps, to see an arrogant man such as Oedipus humbled, and yet it is difficult not to feel that the punishment of Oedipus is greater than he deserves. Possibly this feeling is what Aristotle meant in his observation that a tragedy arouses our pity and our fear—our compassion for Oedipus and our terror as we sense the remorselessness of a universe in which a man is doomed. Notice, however, that at the end of the play Oedipus does not curse God and die. Although such a complex play is open to many interpretations, it is probably safe to say that the play is not a bitter complaint against the universe. At last, Oedipus accepts the divine will, prays for blessings upon his children, and prepares to endure his exile—fallen from high estate but uplifted in moral dignity.

WRITER'S PERSPECTIVE

Aristotle

Aristotle on Drama   DEFINING TRAGEDY   330 B.C.?

TRANSLATED BY L. J. POTTS

Tragedy is an imitation of an action of high importance, complete and of some amplitude; in language enhanced by distinct and varying beauties; acted not narrated; by means of pity and fear effecting its purgation of these emotions. By the beauties enhancing the language I mean rhythm and melody; by "distinct and varying" I mean that some are produced by meter alone, and others at another time by melody.

· · ·

What will produce the tragic effect? Since, then, tragedy, to be at its finest, requires a complex, not a simple, structure, and its structure should also imitate fearful and pitiful events (for that is the peculiarity of this sort of imitation), it is clear: first, that decent people must not be shown passing from good fortune to misfortune (for that is not fearful or pitiful but disgusting); again, vicious people must not be shown passing from misfortune to good fortune (for that is the most untragic situation possible—it has none of the requisites, it is neither humane, nor pitiful, nor fearful); nor again should an utterly evil man fall from good fortune into misfortune (for though a plot of that kind would be humane, it would not induce pity or fear—pity is induced by undeserved misfortune, and fear by the misfortunes of normal people, so that this situation will be neither pitiful nor fearful). So we are left with the man between these extremes: that is to say, the kind of man who neither is distinguished for excellence and virtue, nor comes to grief on account of baseness and vice, but on account of some error; a man of great reputation and prosperity, like Oedipus and Thyestes and conspicuous people of such families as theirs. So, to be well formed, a fable must be single rather than (as some say) double—there must be no change from misfortune to good fortune, but only the opposite, from good fortune to misfortune; the cause must not be vice, but a great error; and the man must be either of the type specified or better, rather than worse. This is borne out by the practice of poets; at first they picked a fable at random and made an inventory of its contents, but now the finest tragedies are plotted, and concern a few families—for example, the tragedies about Alcmeon, Oedipus, Orestes, Meleager, Thyestes, Telephus, and any others whose lives were attended by terrible experiences or doings.

This is the plot that will produce the technically finest tragedy. Those critics are therefore wrong who censure Euripides on this very ground—because he does this in his tragedies, and many of them end in misfortune; for it is, as I have said, the right thing to do. This is clearly demonstrated on the stage in the competitions, where such plays, if they succeed, are the most tragic, and Euripides, even if he is inefficient in every other respect, still shows himself the most tragic of our poets. The next best plot, which is said by some people to be the best, is the tragedy with a double plot, like the *Odyssey*, ending in one way for the better people and in the opposite way for the worse. But it is the weakness of theatrical performances that gives priority to this kind; when poets write what the audience would like to happen, they are in leading strings.° This is not the pleasure proper to tragedy, but rather to comedy, where the greatest enemies in the fable, say Orestes and Aegisthus, make friends and go off at the end, and nobody is killed by anybody.

The pity and fear can be brought about by the *mise en scène*;° but they can also come from the mere plotting of the incidents, which is preferable, and better poetry. For, without seeing anything, the fable ought to have been so plotted that if one heard the bare facts, the chain of circumstances would make one shudder and pity. That would happen to any one who heard the fable of the *Oedipus*. To produce this effect by the *mise en scène* is less artistic and puts one at the mercy of the technician; and those who use it not to frighten but merely to startle have lost touch with tragedy altogether. We should not try to get all sorts of pleasure from tragedy, but the particular tragic pleasure. And clearly, since this pleasure coming from pity and fear has to be produced by imitation, it is by his handling of the incidents that the poet must create it.

---

in leading strings: each is led, by a string, wherever the audience wills. *mise en scène:* arrangement of actors and scenery.

And in the characterization, as in the plotting of the incidents, the aim should always be either necessity or probability: so that they say or do such things as it is necessary or probable that they would, being what they are; and that for this to follow that is either necessary or probable. (Thus it is clear that the untying of the fable should follow on the circumstances of the fable itself, and not be done *ex machina*, as it is in the *Medea*, or in Book Two of the *Iliad*. But the *deus ex machina*° should be used for matters outside the drama—either things that happened before and that man could not know, or future events that need to be announced prophetically; for we allow the gods to see everything. As for extravagant incidents, there should be none in the story, or if there are they should be kept outside the tragedy, as is the one in the *Oedipus* of Sophocles.)

Since tragedy is an imitation of people above the normal, we must be like good portrait-painters, who follow the original model closely, but refine on it; in the same way the poet, in imitating people whose character is choleric or phlegmatic, and so forth, must keep them as they are and at the same time make them attractive. So Homer made Achilles noble, as well as a pattern of obstinacy.

Poetics, VI, XIII–XV

◄▬▭ WRITING CRITICALLY ▭▬►

Some Things Change, Some Things Don't

Reading an ancient work of literature, like Sophocles' *Oedipus the King* or *Antigonê*, a modern student will often have two contradictory reactions. On the one hand, the student will note how differently people thought, spoke, and conducted themselves in the ancient world. The past will seem in many respects like an alien world. On the other hand, the student will recognize how many things about humanity remain constant across the ages. These presumably mythic characters are recognizably human.

Writing about a classical tragedy, you should stay alert to both impulses. Be open to the play's universal appeal, but never forget its foreignness. Understand in specific detail the basic beliefs and values that the characters hold that are different from your own. How do those elements influence the actions and motivations of the characters?

In making notes for your paper, jot down something about each major character that seems odd or exotic to you. Don't worry about being too basic. They don't represent your finished essay, just a starting place. Furthermore, no one will see the notes but you. You might observe, for example, that Oedipus and Iocastê both believe in the power of prophecy. They also believe that Apollo and the gods would punish the city with a plague for an unsolved crime committed twenty years earlier. These are certainly not mainstream modern beliefs.

You do not need to understand the historical origins or cultural context of the differences you note. You can safely leave those things to scholars. What you want to

---

deus ex machina: "god out of the machine," or an arbitrary way of concluding a play. For a discussion of this term see page 1253.

observe are the differences themselves—at least a few important ones—so that you don't automatically make modern assumptions about the characters. Keeping those differences in mind will give you greater insight into the characters.

WRITING ASSIGNMENT

Write a brief personality profile (two or three pages) of any major character in *Oedipus the King* or in Sophocles' *Antigonê*. Describe the character's age, social position, family background, personality, and beliefs. What is his or her major motivation in the play? In what ways does the character resemble his or her modern equivalent? In what way do they differ?

FURTHER SUGGESTIONS FOR WRITING

1. Suppose you face the task of directing and producing a new stage production of *Oedipus the King*. Decide how you would go about it. Would you use masks? How would you render the chorus? Would you set the play in contemporary North America? Justify your decisions by referring to the play itself.

2. Write a brief comment on the play under the title, "Does Sophocles' Oedipus Have an Oedipus Complex?" Consider psychiatrist Sigmund Freud's famous observations (quoted on page 1948). Your comment can be either serious or light.

3. Compare the version of *Oedipus the King* given in this book with a different English translation of the play. You might use, for instance, any of the versions by Gilbert Murray, J. T. Sheppard, and H. D. F. Kitto; by Paul Roche (in a Signet paperback); by William Butler Yeats (in his *Collected Plays*); by David Grene (University of Chicago Press, 1942); or by Stephen Berg and Diskin Clay (Oxford UP, 1978). Point to significant differences between the two texts. What decisions did the translators have to make? Which version do you prefer? Why?

4. Read *Antigonê* (in "Plays for Further Reading"), and in a brief essay demonstrate its relationship to *Oedipus the King*.

5. John Millington Synge's *Riders to the Sea* has been called the closest approximation to a Greek tragedy in English. Does Synge's play resemble a tragedy of Sophocles in any ways? How does it noticeably differ?

34 *The Theater of Shakespeare*

Compared with the technical resources of a theater of today, those of a London public theater in the time of Queen Elizabeth I seem hopelessly limited. Plays had to be performed by daylight, and scenery had to be kept simple: a table, a chair, a throne, perhaps an artificial tree or two to suggest a forest. But these limitations were, in a sense, advantages. What the theater of today can spell out for us realistically, with massive scenery and electric lighting, Elizabethan playgoers had to imagine and the playwright had to make vivid for them by means of language. Not having a lighting technician to work a panel, Shakespeare had to indicate the dawn by having Horatio, in *Hamlet,* say in a speech rich in metaphor and descriptive detail:

> But look, the morn in russet mantle clad
> Walks o'er the dew of yon high eastward hill.

And yet the theater of Shakespeare was not bare, for the playwright did have *some* valuable technical resources. Costumes could be elaborate, and apparently some costumes conveyed recognized meanings: one theater manager's inventory included "a robe for to go invisible in." There could be musical accompaniment and sound effects such as gunpowder explosions and the beating of a pan to simulate thunder.

The stage itself was remarkably versatile. At its back were doors for exits and entrances and a curtained booth or alcove useful for hiding inside. Above the stage was a higher acting area—perhaps a porch or balcony—useful for a Juliet to stand upon and for a Romeo to raise his eyes to. In the stage floor was a trapdoor leading to a "hell" or cellar, especially useful for ghosts or devils who had to appear or disappear. The stage itself was a rectangular platform that projected into a yard enclosed by three-storied galleries.

The building was round or octagonal. In *Henry V,* Shakespeare calls it a "wooden O." The audience sat in these galleries or else stood in the yard in front of the stage and at its sides. A roof or awning protected the stage and the high-priced gallery seats, but in a sudden rain, the *groundlings,* who paid a penny to stand in the yard, must have been dampened.

Built by the theatrical company to which Shakespeare belonged, the Globe, most celebrated of Elizabethan theaters, was not in the city of London itself but on the south bank of the Thames River. This location had been chosen because earlier, in 1574, public plays had been banished from the city by an ordinance that blamed them for "corruptions of youth and other enormities" (such as providing opportunities for prostitutes and purse cutters).

A playwright had to please all members of the audience, not only the mannered and educated. This obligation may help to explain the wide range of matter and tone in an Elizabethan play: passages of subtle poetry, of deep philosophy, of coarse bawdry; scenes of sensational violence and of quiet psychological conflict (not that most members of the audience did not enjoy all these elements). Because he was an actor as well as a playwright, Shakespeare well knew what his company could do and what his audience wanted. In devising a play, he could write a part to take advantage of some actor's specific skills, or he could avoid straining the company's resources (some of his plays have few female parts, perhaps because of a shortage of competent boy actors). The company might offer as many as thirty plays in a season, customarily changing the program daily. The actors thus had to hold many parts in their heads, which may account for Elizabethan playwrights' fondness for blank verse. Lines of fixed length were easier for actors to commit to memory.

The Tragedy of Othello, here offered for study, may be (if you are fortunate) new to you. It is seldom taught in high school, for it is ablaze with passion and violence. Even if you already know the play, we trust that you (like your instructor and your editors) still have much more to learn from it. Following his usual practice, Shakespeare based the play on a story he had appropriated—from a tale, "Of the Unfaithfulness of Husbands and Wives," by a sixteenth-century Italian writer, Giraldi Cinthio. As he could not help but do, Shakespeare freely transformed his source material. In the original tale, the heroine Disdemona (whose name Shakespeare so hugely improved) is beaten to death with a stocking full of sand—a shoddier death than the bard imagined for her.

The newly reconstructed Globe Theatre in today's London—built as an exact replica of the original theater.

Surely no character in literature can touch us more than Desdemona; no character can shock and disgust us more than Iago. Between these two extremes stands Othello, a black man of courage and dignity—and yet human, capable of being fooled, a pushover for bad advice. Besides breathing life into these characters and a host of others, Shakespeare—as brilliant a writer as any the world has known—enables them to speak poetry. Sometimes, this poetry seems splendid and rich in imagery; at other times, quiet and understated. Always, it seems to grow naturally from the nature of Shakespeare's characters and from their situations. *The Tragedy of Othello* has never ceased to grip readers and beholders alike. It is a safe bet that it will tri-

James Earl Jones as Othello

umphantly live as long as fathers dislike whomever their daughters marry, as long as husbands suspect their wives of cheating, as long as blacks remember slavery, and as long as the ambitious court favor and the jealous work deceit. The play may well make sense as long as public officials connive behind smiling faces, and it may even endure as long as the world makes room for the kind, the true, the beautiful—the blessed pure in heart.

William Shakespeare

THE TRAGEDY OF OTHELLO, THE MOOR OF VENICE · 1604?

EDITED BY DAVID BEVINGTON

William Shakespeare (1564–1616), the supreme writer of English, was born, baptized, and buried in the market town of Stratford-on-Avon, eighty miles from London. Son of a glove maker and merchant who was high bailiff (or mayor) of the town, he probably attended grammar school and learned to read Latin authors in the original. At eighteen he married Anne Hathaway, twenty-six, by whom he had three children, including twins. By 1592 he had become well known and envied as an actor and playwright in London. From 1594 until he retired, he belonged to the same theatrical company, the Lord Chamberlain's Men (later renamed the King's Men in honor of their patron, James I), for whom he wrote thirty-six plays—some of them, such as

William Shakespeare

Hamlet *and* King Lear, *profound reworkings of old plays. As an actor, Shakespeare is believed to have played supporting roles, such as Hamlet's father's ghost. The company pros-*

pered, moved into the Globe in 1599, and in 1608 bought the fashionable Blackfriars as well; Shakespeare owned an interest in both theaters. When plagues shut down the theaters from 1592 to 1594, Shakespeare turned to story poems; his great Sonnets (published only in 1609) probably also date from the 1590s. Plays were regarded as entertainments of little literary merit, like comic books today, and Shakespeare did not bother to supervise their publication. After The Tempest (1611), the last play entirely from his hand, he retired to Stratford, where since 1597 he had owned the second largest house in town. Most critics agree that when he wrote Othello, about 1604, Shakespeare was at the height of his powers.

Characters

Othello, the Moor
Brabantio, [a senator,] father to Desdemona
Cassio, an honorable lieutenant [to Othello]
Iago, [Othello's ancient,] a villain
Roderigo, a gulled gentleman
Duke of Venice
Senators [of Venice]
Montano, governor of Cyprus
Gentlemen of Cyprus
Lodovico and Gratiano, [kinsmen to Brabantio,] two noble Venetians
Sailors
Clown
Desdemona, [daughter to Brabantio and] wife to Othello
Emilia, wife to Iago
Bianca, a courtesan [and mistress to Cassio]
[A Messenger
A Herald
A Musician
Servants, Attendants, Officers, Senators, Musicians, Gentlemen]

[Scene: Venice; a seaport in Cyprus]

ACT I

Scene I [Venice. A Street.]

 Enter Roderigo and Iago.

Roderigo: Tush, never tell me!° I take it much unkindly

NOTE ON THE TEXT: This text of Othello is based on that of the First Folio, or large collection, of Shakespeare's plays (1623). But there are many differences between the Folio text and that of the play's first printing in the Quarto, or small volume, of 1621 (eighteen or nineteen years after the play's first performance). Some readings from the Quarto are included. For the reader's convenienc some material has been added by the editor, David Bevington (some indications of scene, some stage directions). Such additions are enclosed in brackets. Mr. Bevington's text and notes were prepared for his book, The Complete Works of Shakespeare, 4th ed. (New York: HarperCollins, 1992).

1 *never tell me* (An expression of incredulity, like "tell me another one.")

That thou, Iago, who hast had my purse
As if the strings were thine, shouldst know of this.°
Iago: 'Sblood,° but you'll not hear me.
　　If ever I did dream of such a matter,　　　　　　　　　　　　　5
　　Abhor me.
Roderigo: Thou toldst me thou didst hold him in thy hate.
Iago: Despise me
　　If I do not. Three great ones of the city,
　　In personal suit to make me his lieutenant,　　　　　　　　　10
　　Off-capped to him;° and by the faith of man,
　　I know my price, I am worth no worse a place.
　　But he, as loving his own pride and purposes,
　　Evades them with a bombast circumstance°
　　Horribly stuffed with epithets of war,°　　　　　　　　　　　15
　　And, in conclusion,
　　Nonsuits° my mediators. For, "Certes,"° says he,
　　"I have already chose my officer."
　　And what was he?
　　Forsooth, a great arithmetician,°　　　　　　　　　　　　　20
　　One Michael Cassio, a Florentine,
　　A fellow almost damned in a fair wife,°
　　That never set a squadron in the field
　　Nor the division of a battle° knows
　　More than a spinster°—unless the bookish theoric,°　　　　　25
　　Wherein the togaed° consuls° can propose°
　　As masterly as he. Mere prattle without practice
　　Is all his soldiership. But he, sir, had th' election;
　　And I, of whom his° eyes had seen the proof
　　At Rhodes, at Cyprus, and on other grounds　　　　　　　　30
　　Christened° and heathen, must be beleed and calmed°
　　By debitor and creditor.° This countercaster,°
　　He, in good time,° must his lieutenant be,
　　And I—God bless the mark!°—his Moorship's ancient.°

---

3 *this* i.e., Desdemona's elopement　4 *'Sblood* by His (Christ's) blood　11 *him* i.e., Othello　14 *bombast circumstance* wordy evasion. (Bombast is cotton padding.)　15 *epithets of war* military expressions　17 *Nonsuits* rejects the petition of.　*Certes* certainly　20 *arithmetician* i.e., a man whose military knowledge is merely theoretical, based on books of tactics　22 *A . . . wife* (Cassio does not seem to be married, but his counterpart in Shakespeare's source does have a woman in his house. See also Act IV, Scene i, line 127.)　24 *division of a battle* disposition of a military unit　25 *a spinster* i.e., a housewife, one whose regular occupation is spinning.　*theoric* theory　26 *togaed* wearing the toga.　*consuls* counselors, senators.　*propose* discuss　29 *his* i.e., Othello's　31 *Christened* Christian.　*beleed and calmed* left to leeward without wind, becalmed. (A sailing metaphor.)　32 *debitor and creditor* (A name for a system of bookkeeping, here used as a contemptuous nickname for Cassio.)　*countercaster* i.e., bookkeeper, one who tallies with *counters*, or "metal disks." (Said contemptuously.)　33 *in good time* opportunely, i.e., forsooth　34 *God bless the mark* (Perhaps originally a formula to ward off evil; here an expression of impatience.)　*ancie* standard-bearer, ensign

Roderigo: By heaven, I rather would have been his hangman.°   35
Iago: Why, there's no remedy. 'Tis the curse of service;
    Preferment° goes by letter and affection,°
    And not by old gradation,° where each second
    Stood heir to th' first. Now, sir, be judge yourself
    Whether I in any just term° am affined°   40
    To love the Moor.
Roderigo: I would not follow him then.
Iago: O sir, content you.°
    I follow him to serve my turn upon him.
    We cannot all be masters, nor all masters   45
    Cannot be truly° followed. You shall mark
    Many a duteous and knee-crooking knave
    That, doting on his own obsequious bondage,
    Wears out his time, much like his master's ass,
    For naught but provender, and when he's old, cashiered.°   50
    Whip me° such honest knaves. Others there are
    Who, trimmed in forms and visages of duty,°
    Keep yet their hearts attending on themselves,
    And, throwing but shows of service on their lords,
    Do well thrive by them, and when they have lined their coats,°   55
    Do themselves homage.° These fellows have some soul,
    And such a one do I profess myself. For, sir,
    It is as sure as you are Roderigo,
    Were I the Moor I would not be Iago.°
    In following him, I follow but myself—   60
    Heaven is my judge, not I for love and duty,
    But seeming so for my peculiar° end.
    For when my outward action doth demonstrate
    The native° act and figure° of my heart
    In compliment extern,° 'tis not long after   65
    But I will wear my heart upon my sleeve
    For daws° to peck at. I am not what I am.°
Roderigo: What a full° fortune does the thick-lips° owe°
    If he can carry 't thus!°

---

35 *his hangman* the executioner of him   37 *Preferment* promotion.   *letter and affection* personal influence and favoritism   38 *old gradation* step-by-step seniority, the traditional way   40 *term* respect.
affined bound   43 *content you* don't you worry about that   46 *truly* faithfully   50 *cashiered* dismissed
from service   51 *Whip me* whip, as far as I'm concerned   52 *trimmed . . . duty* dressed up in the mere
form and show of dutifulness   55 *lined their coats* i.e., stuffed their purses   56 *Do themselves homage*
i.e., attend to self-interest solely   59 *Were . . . Iago* i.e., if I were able to assume command, I certainly would not choose to remain a subordinate, or, I would keep a suspicious eye on a flattering subordinate   62 *peculiar* particular, personal   64 *native* innate.   *figure* shape, intent   65 *compliment*
extern outward show. (Conforming in this case to the inner workings and intention of the heart.)
67 *daws* small crowlike birds, proverbially stupid and avaricious.   *I am not what I am* i.e., I am not
one who wears his heart on his sleeve   68 *full* swelling.   *thick-lips* (Elizabethans often applied the
term "Moor" to Negroes.)   *owe* own   69 *carry 't thus* carry this off

Iago: Call up her father.
    Rouse him, make after him, poison his delight,   70
    Proclaim him in the streets; incense her kinsmen,
    And, though he in a fertile climate dwell,
    Plague him with flies.° Though that his joy be joy,°
    Yet throw such changes of vexation° on 't
    As it may° lose some color.°   75
Roderigo: Here is her father's house. I'll call aloud.
Iago: Do, with like timorous° accent and dire yell
    As when, by night and negligence,° the fire
    Is spied in populous cities.
Roderigo: What ho, Brabantio! Signor Brabantio, ho!   80
Iago: Awake! What ho, Brabantio! Thieves, thieves, thieves!
    Look to your house, your daughter, and your bags!
    Thieves, thieves!

    Brabantio [enters] above [at a window].°

Brabantio: What is the reason of this terrible summons?
    What is the matter° there?   85
Roderigo: Signor, is all your family within?
Iago: Are your doors locked?
Brabantio: Why, wherefore ask you this?
Iago: Zounds,° sir, you're robbed. For shame, put on your gown!
    Your heart is burst; you have lost half your soul.
    Even now, now, very now, an old black ram   90
    Is tupping° your white ewe. Arise, arise!
    Awake the snorting° citizens with the bell,
    Or else the devil° will make a grandsire of you.
    Arise, I say!
Brabantio: What, have you lost your wits?
Roderigo: Most reverend signor, do you know my voice?   95
Brabantio: Not I. What are you?
Roderigo: My name is Roderigo.
Brabantio: The worser welcome.
    I have charged thee not to haunt about my doors.
    In honest plainness thou hast heard me say   100
    My daughter is not for thee; and now, in madness,
    Being full of supper and distempering° drafts,

72–73 *though . . . flies* though he seems prosperous and happy now, vex him with misery   73 *Though . . . be joy* although he seems fortunate and happy. (Repeats the idea of line 72.)   74 *changes of vexation* vexing changes   75 *As it may* that may cause it to.   *some color* some of its fresh gloss   77 *timorous* frightening   78 *and negligence* i.e., by negligence   83 s.d. *at a window* (This stage direction, from the Quarto, probably calls for an appearance on the gallery above and rearstage.)   85 *the matter* your business   88 *Zounds* by His (Christ's) wounds   91 *tupping* covering, copulating with. (Said of sheep.)   92 *snorting* snoring   93 *the devil* (The devil was conventionally pictured as black.)   102 *distempering* intoxicating

Upon malicious bravery° dost thou come
To start° my quiet.

Roderigo: Sir, sir, sir—

Brabantio: But thou must needs be sure   105
My spirits and my place° have in° their power
To make this bitter to thee.

Roderigo: Patience, good sir.

Brabantio: What tell'st thou me of robbing? This is Venice;
My house is not a grange.°

Roderigo: Most grave Brabantio,
In simple° and pure soul I come to you.   110

Iago: Zounds, sir, you are one of those that will not serve God if the devil bid you. Because we come to do you service and you think we are ruffians, you'll have your daughter covered with a Barbary° horse; you'll have your nephews° neigh to you; you'll have coursers° for cousins° and jennets° for germans.°

Brabantio: What profane wretch art thou?   115

Iago: I am one, sir, that comes to tell you your daughter and the Moor are now making the beast with two backs.

Brabantio: Thou art a villain.

Iago: You are—a senator.°

Brabantio: This thou shalt answer.° I know thee, Roderigo.

Roderigo: Sir, I will answer anything. But I beseech you, 120
If't be your pleasure and most wise° consent—
As partly I find it is—that your fair daughter,
At this odd-even° and dull watch o' the night,
Transported with° no worse nor better guard
But with a knave° of common hire, a gondolier,   125
To the gross clasps of a lascivious Moor—
If this be known to you and your allowance°
We then have done you bold and saucy° wrongs.
But if you know not this, my manners tell me
We have your wrong rebuke. Do not believe   130
That, from° the sense of all civility,°
I thus would play and trifle with your reverence.°
Your daughter, if you have not given her leave,
I say again, hath made a gross revolt,

---

103 *Upon malicious bravery* with hostile intent to defy me   104 *start* startle, disrupt   106 *My spirits and my place* my temperament and my authority of office.   *have in* have it in   109 *grange* isolated country house   110 *simple* sincere   113 *Barbary* from northern Africa (and hence associated with Othello).   *nephews* i.e., grandsons   114 *coursers* powerful horses.   *cousins* kinsmen.   *jennets* small Spanish horses.   *germans* near relatives   118 *a senator* (Said with mock politeness, as though the word itself were an insult.)   119 *answer* be held accountable for   121 *wise* well-informed   123 *odd-even* between one day and the next, i.e., about midnight   124 *with* by   125 *But with a knave* than by a low fellow, a servant   127 *allowance* permission   128 *saucy* insolent   131 *from* contrary to.   *civility* good manners, decency   132 *your reverence* the respect due to you

Tying her duty, beauty, wit,° and fortunes   135
In an extravagant° and wheeling° stranger°
Of here and everywhere. Straight° satisfy yourself.
If she be in her chamber or your house,
Let loose on me the justice of the state
For thus deluding you.   140

Brabantio: Strike on the tinder,° ho!
Give me a taper! Call up all my people!
This accident° is not unlike my dream.
Belief of it oppresses me already.
Light, I say, light!   *Exit [above].*

Iago: Farewell, for I must leave you.   145
It seems not meet° nor wholesome to my place°
To be producted°—as, if I stay, I shall—
Against the Moor. For I do know the state,
However this may gall° him with some check,°
Cannot with safety cast° him, for he's embarked°   150
With such loud reason° to the Cyprus wars,
Which even now stands in act,° that, for their souls,°
Another of his fathom° they have none
To lead their business; in which regard,°
Though I do hate him as I do hell pains,   155
Yet for necessity of present life°
I must show out a flag and sign of love,
Which is indeed but sign. That you shall surely find him,
Lead to the Sagittary° the raisèd search,°
And there will I be with him. So farewell.   *Exit.*   160

Enter [below] Brabantio [in his nightgown°] with servants and torches.

Brabantio: It is too true an evil. Gone she is;
And what's to come of my despisèd time°
Is naught but bitterness. Now, Roderigo,
Where didst thou see her?—O unhappy girl!—
With the Moor, sayst thou?—Who would be a father!—   165
How didst thou know 'twas she?—O, she deceives me
Past thought!—What said she to you?—Get more tapers.

---

135 *wit* intelligence   136 *extravagant* expatriate, wandering far from home.   *wheeling* roving about, vagabond.   *stranger* foreigner   137 *Straight* straightway   141 *tinder* charred linen ignited by a spark from flint and steel, used to light torches or *tapers* (lines 142, 167)   143 *accident* occurrence, event 146 *meet* fitting.   *place* position (as ensign)   147 *producted* produced (as a witness)   149 *gall* rub; oppress.   *check* rebuke   150 *cast* dismiss.   *embarked* engaged   151 *loud reason* unanimous shout of confirmation (in the Senate)   152 *stands in act* are going on.   *for their souls* to save themselves 153 *fathom* i.e., ability, depth of experience   154 *in which regard* out of regard for which   156 *life* livelihood   159 *Sagittary* (An inn or house where Othello and Desdemona are staying, named for its sign of Sagittarius, or Centaur.)   *raisèd search* search party roused out of sleep   160 s.d. *nightgown* dressing gown. (This costuming is specified in the Quarto text.)   162 *time* i.e., remainder of life

Raise all my kindred.—Are they married, think you?

Roderigo: Truly, I think they are.

Brabantio: O heaven! How got she out? O treason of the blood!   170
    Fathers, from hence trust not your daughters' minds
    By what you see them act. Is there not charms°
    By which the property° of youth and maidhood
    May be abused?° Have you not read, Roderigo,
    Of some such thing?

Roderigo: Yes, sir, I have indeed.   175

Brabantio: Call up my brother.—O, would you had had her!—
    Some one way, some another.—Do you know
    Where we may apprehend her and the Moor?

Roderigo: I think I can discover° him, if you please
    To get good guard and go along with me.   180

Brabantio: Pray you, lead on. At every house I'll call;
    I may command° at most.—Get weapons, ho!
    And raise some special officers of night.—
    On, good Roderigo. I will deserve° your pains.

    Exeunt.

Scene II [Venice. Another Street, Before Othello's Lodgings.]

Enter Othello, Iago, attendants with torches.

Iago: Though in the trade of war I have slain men,
    Yet do I hold it very stuff° o' the conscience
    To do no contrived° murder. I lack iniquity
    Sometimes to do me service. Nine or ten times
    I had thought t' have yerked° him° here under the ribs.   5

Othello: 'Tis better as it is.

Iago: Nay, but he prated,
    And spoke such scurvy and provoking terms
    Against your honor
    That, with the little godliness I have,
    I did full hard forbear him.° But, I pray you, sir,   10
    Are you fast married? Be assured of this,
    That the magnifico° is much beloved,
    And hath in his effect° a voice potential°
    As double as the Duke's. He will divorce you,
    Or put upon you what restraint or grievance   15

---

172 *charms* spells   173 *property* special quality, nature   174 *abused* deceived   179 *discover* reveal, uncover   182 *command* demand assistance   184 *deserve* show gratitude for   2 *very stuff* essence, basic material (continuing the metaphor of *trade* from line 1)   3 *contrived* premeditated   5 *yerked* stabbed.   *him* i.e., Roderigo   10 *I . . . him* I restrained myself with great difficulty from assaulting him   12 *magnifico* Venetian grandee, i.e., Brabantio   13 *in his effect* at his command.   *potential* powerful

The law, with all his might to enforce it on,
Will give him cable.°

Othello: Let him do his spite.
My services which I have done the seigniory°
Shall out-tongue his complaints. 'Tis yet to know°—
Which, when I know that boasting is an honor,   20
I shall promulgate—I fetch my life and being
From men of royal siege,° and my demerits°
May speak unbonneted° to as proud a fortune
As this that I have reached. For know, Iago,
But that I love the gentle Desdemona,   25
I would not my unhousèd° free condition
Put into circumscription and confine°
For the sea's worth.° But look, what lights come yond?

Enter Cassio [and certain officers°] with torches.

Iago: Those are the raisèd father and his friends.
You were best go in.

Othello: Not I. I must be found.   30
My parts, my title, and my perfect soul°
Shall manifest me rightly. Is it they?

Iago: By Janus,° I think no.

Othello: The servants of the Duke? And my lieutenant?
The goodness of the night upon you, friends!   35
What is the news?

Cassio: The Duke does greet you, General,
And he requires your haste-post-haste appearance
Even on the instant.

Othello: What is the matter,° think you?

Cassio: Something from Cyprus, as I may divine.°
It is a business of some heat.° The galleys   40
Have sent a dozen sequent° messengers
This very night at one another's heels,
And many of the consuls,° raised and met,
Are at the Duke's already. You have been hotly called for;
When, being not at your lodging to be found,   45
The Senate hath sent about° three several° quests

---

17 *cable* i.e., scope   18 *seigniory* Venetian government   19 *yet to know* not yet widely known   22 *siege* i.e., rank. (Literally, a seat used by a person of distinction.)   *demerits* deserts   23 *unbonneted* without removing the hat, i.e., on equal terms (? Or "with hat off," "in all due modesty.")   26 *unhousèd* unconfined, undomesticated   27 *circumscription and confine* restriction and confinement   28 *the sea's worth* all the riches at the bottom of the sea.   s.d. *officers* (The Quarto text calls for "Cassio with lights, officers with torches.")   31 *My . . . soul* my natural gifts, my position or reputation, and my unflawed conscience   33 *Janus* Roman two-faced god of beginnings   38 *matter* business   39 *divine* guess   40 *heat* urgency   41 *sequent* successive   43 *consuls* senators   46 *about* all over the city. *several* separate

To search you out.

Othello: 'Tis well I am found by you.
I will but spend a word here in the house
And go with you.   [*Exit.*]

Cassio: Ancient, what makes° he here?

Iago: Faith, he tonight hath boarded° a land carrack.°   50
If it prove lawful prize,° he's made forever.

Cassio: I do not understand.

Iago: He's married.

Cassio: To who?

    [*Enter Othello.*]

Iago: Marry,° to—Come, Captain, will you go?

Othello: Have with you.°

Cassio: Here comes another troop to seek for you.   55

    Enter Brabantio, Roderigo, with officers and torches.°

Iago: It is Brabantio. General, be advised.°
He comes to bad intent.

Othello: Holla! Stand there!

Roderigo: Signor, it is the Moor.

Brabantio: Down with him, thief!

    [*They draw on both sides.*]

Iago: You, Roderigo! Come, sir, I am for you.

Othello: Keep up° your bright swords, for the dew will rust them.   60
Good signor, you shall more command with years
Than with your weapons.

Brabantio: O thou foul thief, where hast thou stowed my daughter?
Damned as thou art, thou hast enchanted her!
For I'll refer me° to all things of sense,°   65
If she in chains of magic were not bound
Whether a maid so tender, fair, and happy,
So opposite to marriage that she shunned
The wealthy curlèd darlings of our nation,
Would ever have, t' incur a general mock,   70
Run from her guardage° to the sooty bosom
Of such a thing as thou—to fear, not to delight.
Judge me the world if 'tis not gross in sense°

---

49 *makes* does   50 *boarded* gone aboard and seized as an act of piracy (with sexual suggestion).   *carrack* large merchant ship   51 *prize* booty   53 *Marry* (An oath, originally "by the Virgin Mary"; here used with wordplay on *married*.)   54 *Have with you* i.e., let's go   55 s.d. *officers and torches* (The Quarto text calls for "others with lights and weapons.")   56 *be advised* be on your guard   60 *Keep up* keep in the sheath   65 *refer me* submit my case.   *things of sense* commonsense understandings, or, creatures possessing common sense   71 *her guardage* my guardianship of her   73 *gross in sense* obvious

That thou hast practiced on her with foul charms,
Abused her delicate youth with drugs or minerals°   75
That weakens motion.° I'll have 't disputed on;°
'Tis probable and palpable to thinking.
I therefore apprehend and do attach° thee
For an abuser of the world, a practicer
Of arts inhibited° and out of warrant.°—   80
Lay hold upon him! If he do resist,
Subdue him at his peril.
Othello: Hold your hands,
Both you of my inclining° and the rest.
Were it my cue to fight, I should have known it
Without a prompter.—Whither will you that I go   85
To answer this your charge?
Brabantio: To prison, till fit time
Of law and course of direct session°
Call thee to answer.
Othello: What if I do obey?
How may the Duke be therewith satisfied,   90
Whose messengers are here about my side
Upon some present business of the state
To bring me to him?
Officer: 'Tis true, most worthy signor.
The Duke's in council, and your noble self,
I am sure, is sent for.
Brabantio: How? The Duke in council?   95
In this time of the night? Bring him away.°
Mine's not an idle° cause. The Duke himself,
Or any of my brothers of the state,
Cannot but feel this wrong as 'twere their own;
For if such actions may have passage free,°   100
Bondslaves and pagans shall our statesmen be.

Exeunt.

Scene III [Venice. A Council Chamber.]

Enter Duke [and] Senators [and sit at a table, with lights], and Officers.° [The
Duke and Senators are reading dispatches.]

75 *minerals* i.e., poisons   76 *weakens motion* impair the vital faculties.   *disputed on* argued in court by
professional counsel, debated by experts   78 *attach* arrest   80 *arts inhibited* prohibited arts, black
magic.   *out of warrant* illegal   83 *inclining* following, party   88 *course of direct session* regular or specially convened legal proceedings   96 *away* right along   97 *idle* trifling   100 *have passage free* are
allowed to go unchecked   s.d. *Enter . . . Officers* (The Quarto text calls for the Duke and senators to
"sit at a table with lights and attendants.")

Duke: There is no composition° in these news
    That gives them credit.
First Senator: Indeed, they are disproportioned.°
    My letters say a hundred and seven galleys.
Duke: And mine, a hundred forty.
Second Senator: And mine, two hundred.   5
    But though they jump° not on a just° account—
    As in these cases, where the aim° reports
    'Tis oft with difference—yet do they all confirm
    A Turkish fleet, and bearing up to Cyprus.
Duke: Nay, it is possible enough to judgment.   10
    I do not so secure me in the error
    But the main article I do approve°
    In fearful sense.
Sailor (within):   What ho, what ho, what ho!

    Enter Sailor.

Officer: A messenger from the galleys.
Duke: Now, what's the business?   15
Sailor: The Turkish preparation° makes for Rhodes.
    So was I bid report here to the state
    By Signor Angelo.
Duke: How say you by° this change?
First Senator: This cannot be
    By no assay° of reason. 'Tis a pageant°   20
    To keep us in false gaze.° When we consider
    Th' importancy of Cyprus to the Turk,
    And let ourselves again but understand
    That, as it more concerns the Turk than Rhodes,
    So may he with more facile question bear it,°   25
    For that° it stands not in such warlike brace,°
    But altogether lacks th' abilities°
    That Rhodes is dressed in°—if we make thought of this,
    We must not think the Turk is so unskillful°
    To leave that latest° which concerns him first,   30
    Neglecting an attempt of ease and gain
    To wake° and wage° a danger profitless.
Duke: Nay, in all confidence, he's not for Rhodes.
Officer: Here is more news.

---

1 *composition* consistency   3 *disproportioned* inconsistent   6 *jump* agree. *just* exact   7 *the aim* conjecture   11–12 *I do not . . . approve* I do not take such (false) comfort in the discrepancies that I fail to perceive the main point, i.e., that the Turkish fleet is threatening   16 *preparation* fleet prepared for battle   19 *by* about   20 *assay* test. *pageant* mere show   21 *in false gaze* looking the wrong way   25 *So may . . . it* so also he (the Turk) can more easily capture it (Cyprus)   26 *For that* since. *brace* state of defense   27 *abilities* means of self-defense   28 *dressed in* equipped with   29 *unskillful* deficient in judgment   30 *latest* last   32 *wake* stir up. *wage* risk

Enter a Messenger.

Messenger: The Ottomites, reverend and gracious, 35
  Steering with due course toward the isle of Rhodes,
  Have there injointed them° with an after° fleet.
First Senator: Ay, so I thought. How many, as you guess?
Messenger: Of thirty sail; and now they do restem
  Their backward course,° bearing with frank appearance° 40
  Their purposes toward Cyprus. Signor Montano,
  Your trusty and most valiant servitor,°
  With his free duty° recommends° you thus,
  And prays you to believe him.
Duke: 'Tis certain then for Cyprus. 45
  Marcus Luccicos, is not he in town?
First Senator: He's now in Florence.
Duke: Write from us to him, post-post-haste. Dispatch.
First Senator: Here comes Brabantio and the valiant Moor.

  Enter Brabantio, Othello, Cassio, Iago, Roderigo, and officers.

Duke: Valiant Othello, we must straight° employ you 50
  Against the general enemy° Ottoman.
  [*To Brabantio.*] I did not see you; welcome, gentle° signor.
  We lacked your counsel and your help tonight.
Brabantio: So did I yours. Good Your Grace, pardon me;
  Neither my place° nor aught I heard of business 55
  Hath raised me from my bed, nor doth the general care
  Take hold on me, for my particular° grief
  Is of so floodgate° and o'erbearing nature
  That it engluts° and swallows other sorrows
  And it is still itself.°
Duke: Why, what's the matter? 60
Brabantio: My daughter! O, my daughter!
Duke and Senators: Dead?
Brabantio: Ay, to me.
  She is abused,° stol'n from me, and corrupted
  By spells and medicines bought of mountebanks;
  For nature so preposterously to err,
  Being not deficient,° blind, or lame of sense,° 65
  Sans° witchcraft could not.

---

37 *injointed them* joined themselves. *after* second, following 39–40 *restem . . . course* retrace their original course 40 *frank appearance* undisguised intent 42 *servitor* officer under your command 43 *free duty* freely given and loyal service. *recommends* commends himself and reports to 50 *straight* straightway 51 *general enemy* universal enemy to all Christendom 52 *gentle* noble 55 *place* official position 57 *particular* personal 58 *floodgate* i.e., overwhelming (as when floodgates are opened) 59 *engluts* engulfs 60 *is still itself* remains undiminished 62 *abused* deceived 65 *deficient* defective. *lame of sense* deficient in sensory perception 66 *Sans* without

Duke: Whoe'er he be that in this foul proceeding
    Hath thus beguiled your daughter of herself,
    And you of her, the bloody book of law
    You shall yourself read in the bitter letter   70
    After your own sense°—yea, though our proper° son
    Stood in your action.°
Brabantio: Humbly I thank Your Grace.
    Here is the man, this Moor, whom now it seems
    Your special mandate for the state affairs
    Hath hither brought.
All: We are very sorry for 't.   75
Duke [to Othello]: What, in your own part, can you say to this?
Brabantio: Nothing, but this is so.
Othello: Most potent, grave, and reverend signors,
    My very noble and approved° good masters:
    That I have ta'en away this old man's daughter,   80
    It is most true; true, I have married her.
    The very head and front° of my offending
    Hath this extent, no more. Rude° am I in my speech,
    And little blessed with the soft phrase of peace;
    For since these arms of mine had seven years' pith,°   85
    Till now some nine moons wasted,° they have used
    Their dearest° action in the tented field;
    And little of this great world can I speak
    More than pertains to feats of broils and battle,
    And therefore little shall I grace my cause   90
    In speaking for myself. Yet, by your gracious patience,
    I will a round° unvarnished tale deliver
    Of my whole course of love—what drugs, what charms,
    What conjuration, and what mighty magic,
    For such proceeding I am charged withal,°   95
    I won his daughter.
Brabantio: A maiden never bold;
    Of spirit so still and quiet that her motion
    Blushed at herself;° and she, in spite of nature,
    Of years,° of country, credit,° everything,
    To fall in love with what she feared to look on!   100
    It is a judgment maimed and most imperfect

---

71 *After . . . sense* according to your own interpretation. *our proper* my own   72 *Stood . . . action* were under your accusation   79 *approved* proved, esteemed   82 *head and front* height and breadth, entire extent   83 *Rude* unpolished   85 *since . . . pith* i.e., since I was seven. *pith* strength, vigor 86 *Till . . . wasted* until some nine months ago (since when Othello has evidently not been on active duty, but in Venice)   87 *dearest* most valuable   92 *round* plain   95 *withal* with   97–98 *her . . . herself* i.e., she blushed easily at herself. (*Motion* can suggest the impulse of the soul or of the emotions, or physical movement.)   99 *years* i.e., difference in age. *credit* virtuous reputation

That will confess° perfection so could err
Against all rules of nature, and must be driven
To find out practices° of cunning hell
Why this should be. I therefore vouch° again   105
That with some mixtures powerful o'er the blood,°
Or with some dram conjured to this effect,°
He wrought upon her.
Duke: To vouch this is no proof,
Without more wider° and more overt test°
Than these thin habits° and poor likelihoods°   110
Of modern seeming° do prefer° against him.
First Senator: But Othello, speak.
Did you by indirect and forcèd courses°
Subdue and poison this young maid's affections?
Or came it by request and such fair question°   115
As soul to soul affordeth?
Othello: I do beseech you,
Send for the lady to the Sagittary
And let her speak of me before her father.
If you do find me foul in her report,
The trust, the office I do hold of you   120
Not only take away, but let your sentence
Even fall upon my life.
Duke: Fetch Desdemona hither.
Othello: Ancient, conduct them. You best know the place.

[*Exeunt Iago and attendants.*]

And, till she come, as truly as to heaven
I do confess the vices of my blood,°   125
So justly° to your grave ears I'll present
How I did thrive in this fair lady's love,
And she in mine.
Duke: Say it, Othello.
Othello: Her father loved me, oft invited me,   130
Still° questioned me the story of my life
From year to year—the battles, sieges, fortunes
That I have passed.
I ran it through, even from my boyish days
To th' very moment that he bade me tell it,   135

102 *confess* concede (that)   104 *practices* plots   105 *vouch* assert   106 *blood* passions   107 *dram*
. . . *effect* dose made by magical spells to have this effect   109 *more wider* fuller.   *test* testimony
110 *habits* garments, i.e., appearances.   *poor likelihoods* weak inferences   111 *modern seeming* commonplace assumption.   *prefer* bring forth   113 *forcèd courses* means used against her will   115 *question* conversation   125 *blood* passions, human nature   126 *justly* truthfully, accurately   131 *Still*
continually

Wherein I spoke of most disastrous chances,
Of moving accidents° by flood and field,
Of hairbreadth scapes i' th' imminent deadly breach,°
Of being taken by the insolent foe
And sold to slavery, of my redemption thence,   140
And portance° in my travels' history,
Wherein of antres° vast and deserts idle,°
Rough quarries,° rocks, and hills whose heads touch heaven,
It was my hint° to speak—such was my process—
And of the Cannibals that each other eat,   145
The Anthropophagi,° and men whose heads
Do grow beneath their shoulders. These things to hear
Would Desdemona seriously incline;
But still the house affairs would draw her thence,
Which ever as she could with haste dispatch   150
She'd come again, and with a greedy ear
Devour up my discourse. Which I, observing,
Took once a pliant° hour, and found good means
To draw from her a prayer of earnest heart
That I would all my pilgrimage dilate,°   155
Whereof by parcels° she had something heard,
But not intentively.° I did consent,
And often did beguile her of her tears,
When I did speak of some distressful stroke
That my youth suffered. My story being done,   160
She gave me for my pains a world of sighs.
She swore, in faith, 'twas strange, 'twas passing° strange,
'Twas pitiful, 'twas wondrous pitiful.
She wished she had not heard it, yet she wished
That heaven had made her° such a man. She thanked me,   165
And bade me, if I had a friend that loved her,
I should but teach him how to tell my story,
And that would woo her. Upon this hint° I spake.
She loved me for the dangers I had passed,
And I loved her that she did pity them.   170
This only is the witchcraft I have used.
Here comes the lady. Let her witness it.

Enter Desdemona, Iago, [and] attendants.

---

137 *moving accidents* stirring happenings   138 *imminent . . . breach* death-threatening gaps made in a
fortification   141 *portance* conduct   142 *antres* caverns. *idle* barren, desolate   143 *Rough quarries*
rugged rock formations   144 *hint* occasion, opportunity   146 *Anthropophagi* man-eaters. (A term
from Pliny's *Natural History.*)   153 *pliant* well-suiting   155 *dilate* relate in detail   156 *by parcels*
piecemeal   157 *intentively* with full attention, continuously   162 *passing* exceedingly   165 *made her*
created her to be   168 *hint* opportunity. (Othello does not mean that she was dropping hints.)

Duke: I think this tale would win my daughter too.
Good Brabantio,
Take up this mangled matter at the best.° 175
Men do their broken weapons rather use
Than their bare hands.
Brabantio: I pray you, hear her speak.
If she confess that she was half the wooer,
Destruction on my head if my bad blame
Light on the man!—Come hither, gentle mistress. 180
Do you perceive in all this noble company
Where most you owe obedience?
Desdemona: My noble Father,
I do perceive here a divided duty.
To you I am bound for life and education;°
My life and education both do learn° me 185
How to respect you. You are the lord of duty;°
I am hitherto your daughter. But here's my husband,
And so much duty as my mother showed
To you, preferring you before her father,
So much I challenge° that I may profess 190
Due to the Moor my lord.
Brabantio: God be with you! I have done.
Please it Your Grace, on to the state affairs.
I had rather to adopt a child than get° it.
Come hither, Moor. [*He joins the hands of Othello and Desdemona.*] 195
I here do give thee that with all my heart°
Which, but thou hast already, with all my heart°
I would keep from thee.—For your sake,° jewel,
I am glad at soul I have no other child,
For thy escape° would teach me tyranny, 200
To hang clogs° on them.—I have done, my lord.
Duke: Let me speak like yourself,° and lay a sentence°
Which, as a grece° or step, may help these lovers
Into your favor.
When remedies° are past, the griefs are ended 205
By seeing the worst, which late on hopes depended.°
To mourn a mischief° that is past and gone
Is the next° way to draw new mischief on.

---

175 *Take . . . best* make the best of a bad bargain 184 *education* upbringing 185 *learn* teach 186
of duty to whom duty is due 190 *challenge* claim 194 *get* beget 196 *with all my heart* wherein my
whole affection has been engaged 197 *with all my heart* willingly, gladly 198 *For your sake* on your
account 200 *escape* elopement 201 *clogs* (Literally, blocks of wood fastened to the legs of criminals or convicts to inhibit escape.) 202 *like yourself* i.e., as you would, in your proper temper. *lay a
sentence* apply a maxim 203 *grece* step 205 *remedies* hopes of remedy 206 *which . . . depended*
which griefs were sustained until recently by hopeful anticipation 207 *mischief* misfortune, injury
208 *next* nearest

What° cannot be preserved when fortune takes,
Patience her injury a mockery makes.°   210
The robbed that smiles steals something from the thief;
He robs himself that spends a bootless grief.°

Brabantio: So let the Turk of Cyprus us beguile,
We lose it not, so long as we can smile.
He bears the sentence well that nothing bears   215
But the free comfort which from thence he hears,
But he bears both the sentence and the sorrow
That, to pay grief, must of poor patience borrow.°
These sentences, to sugar or to gall,
Being strong on both sides, are equivocal.°   220
But words are words. I never yet did hear
That the bruisèd heart was piercèd through the ear.°
I humbly beseech you, proceed to th' affairs of state.

Duke: The Turk with a most mighty preparation makes for Cyprus. Othello, the
fortitude° of the place is best known to you; and though we have there a   225
substitute° of most allowed° sufficiency, yet opinion, a sovereign mistress of
effects, throws a more safer voice on you.° You must therefore be content to
slubber° the gloss of your new fortunes with this more stubborn° and boisterous expedition.

Othello: The tyrant custom, most grave senators,   230
Hath made the flinty and steel couch of war
My thrice-driven° bed of down. I do agnize°
A natural and prompt alacrity
I find in hardness,° and do undertake
These present wars against the Ottomites.   235
Most humbly therefore bending to your state,°
I crave fit disposition for my wife,
Due reference of place and exhibition,°
With such accommodation° and besort°
As levels° with her breeding.°   240

Duke: Why, at her father's.

Brabantio: I will not have it so.

---

209 *What* whatever   210 *Patience . . . makes* patience laughs at the injury inflicted by fortune (and thus eases the pain)   212 *spends a bootless grief* indulges in unavailing grief   215–218 *He bears . . . borrow* a person well bears out your maxim who can enjoy its platitudinous comfort, free of all genuine sorrow, but anyone whose grief bankrupts his poor patience is left with your saying and his sorrow, too. (*Bears the sentence* also plays on the meaning, "receives judicial sentence.")   219–220 *These . . . equivocal* these fine maxims are equivocal, either sweet or bitter in their application   222 *piercèd . . . ear* i.e., surgically lanced and cured by mere words of advice   225 *fortitude* strength   226 *substitute* deputy. *allowed* acknowledged   226–227 *opinion . . . on you* general opinion, an important determiner of affairs, chooses you as the best man   228 *slubber* soil, sully. *stubborn* harsh, rough   232 *thrice-driven* thrice sifted, winnowed. *agnize* know in myself, acknowledge   234 *hardness* hardship   236 *bending . . . state* bowing or kneeling to your authority   238 *reference . . . exhibition* provision of appropriate place to live and allowance of money   239 *accommodation* suitable provision. *besort* attendance   240 *levels* equals, suits. *breeding* social position, upbringing

Othello: Nor I.

Desdemona: Nor I. I would not there reside,
    To put my father in impatient thoughts
    By being in his eye. Most gracious Duke,
    To my unfolding° lend your prosperous° ear,   245
    And let me find a charter° in your voice,
    T' assist my simpleness.

Duke: What would you, Desdemona?

Desdemona: That I did love the Moor to live with him,
    My downright violence and storm of fortunes°   250
    May trumpet to the world. My heart's subdued
    Even to the very quality of my lord.°
    I saw Othello's visage in his mind,
    And to his honors and his valiant parts°
    Did I my soul and fortunes consecrate.   255
    So that, dear lords, if I be left behind
    A moth° of peace, and he go to the war,
    The rites° for why I love him are bereft me,
    And I a heavy interim shall support
    By his dear° absence. Let me go with him.   260

Othello: Let her have your voice.°
    Vouch with me, heaven, I therefor beg it not
    To please the palate of my appetite,
    Nor to comply with heat°—the young affects°
    In me defunct—and proper° satisfaction,   265
    But to be free° and bounteous to her mind.
    And heaven defend° your good souls that you think°
    I will your serious and great business scant
    When she is with me. No, when light-winged toys
    Of feathered Cupid seel° with wanton dullness   270
    My speculative and officed instruments,°
    That° my disports° corrupt and taint° my business,
    Let huswives make a skillet of my helm,
    And all indign° and base adversities
    Make head° against my estimation!°   275

Duke: Be it as you shall privately determine,

---

245 *unfolding* explanation, proposal. *prosperous* propitious   246 *charter* privilege, authorization
250 *My . . . fortunes* my plain and total breach of social custom, taking my future by storm and dis-
rupting my whole life   251–252 *My heart's . . . lord* my heart is brought wholly into accord with
Othello's virtues; I love him for his virtues   254 *parts* qualities   257 *moth* i.e., one who consumes
merely   258 *rites* rites of love (with a suggestion, too, of "rights," sharing)   260 *dear* (1) heartfelt
(2) costly   261 *voice* consent   264 *heat* sexual passion. *young affects* passions of youth, desires
265 *proper* personal   266 *free* generous   267 *defend* forbid. *think* should think   270 *seel* i.e., make
blind (as in falconry, by sewing up the eyes of the hawk during training)   271 *speculative . . . instruments* eyes and other faculties used in the performance of duty   272 *That* so that. *disports* sexual
pastimes. *taint* impair   274 *indign* unworthy, shameful   275 *Make head* raise an army. *estimation*
reputation

Either for her stay or going. Th' affair cries haste,
And speed must answer it.

A Senator: You must away tonight.

Desdemona: Tonight, my lord?

Duke: This night.

Othello: With all my heart.

Duke: At nine i' the morning here we'll meet again.   280
Othello, leave some officer behind,
And he shall our commission bring to you,
With such things else of quality and respect°
As doth import° you.

Othello: So please Your Grace, my ancient;
A man he is of honesty and trust.   285
To his conveyance I assign my wife,
With what else needful Your Good Grace shall think
To be sent after me.

Duke: Let it be so.
Good night to everyone. [*To Brabantio.*] And, noble signor,
If virtue no delighted° beauty lack,   290
Your son-in-law is far more fair than black.

First Senator: Adieu, brave Moor. Use Desdemona well.

Brabantio: Look to her, Moor, if thou hast eyes to see.
She has deceived her father, and may thee.

            Exeunt [Duke, Brabantio, Cassio, Senators, and officers].

Othello: My life upon her faith! Honest Iago,   295
My Desdemona must I leave to thee.
I prithee, let thy wife attend on her,
And bring them after in the best advantage.°
Come, Desdemona. I have but an hour
Of love, of worldly matters and direction,°   300
To spend with thee. We must obey the time.°

                     Exit [with Desdemona].

Roderigo: Iago—

Iago: What sayst thou, noble heart?

Roderigo: What will I do, think'st thou?

Iago: Why, go to bed and sleep.   305

Roderigo: I will incontinently° drown myself.

Iago: If thou dost, I shall never love thee after. Why, thou silly gentleman?

Roderigo: It is silliness to live when to live is torment; and then have we a pre-
scription° to die when death is our physician.

---

283 *of quality and respect* of importance and relevance   284 *import* concern   290 *delighted* capable of delighting   298 *in . . . advantage* at the most favorable opportunity   300 *direction* instructions   301 *the time* the urgency of the present crisis   306 *incontinently* immediately, without self-restraint 308–309 *prescription* (1) right based on long-established custom (2) doctor's prescription

Iago: O villainous!° I have looked upon the world for four times seven years, 310
    and, since I could distinguish betwixt a benefit and an injury, I never found
    man that knew how to love himself. Ere I would say I would drown myself
    for the love of a guinea hen,° I would change my humanity with a baboon.
Roderigo: What should I do? I confess it is my shame to be so fond,° but it is not
    in my virtue° to amend it. 315
Iago: Virtue? A fig!° 'Tis in ourselves that we are thus or thus. Our bodies are
    our gardens, to the which our wills are gardeners; so that if we will plant net-
    tles or sow lettuce, set hyssop° and weed up thyme, supply it with one
    gender° of herbs or distract it with° many, either to have it sterile with idle-
    ness° or manured with industry—why, the power and corrigible authority° 320
    of this lies in our wills. If the beam° of our lives had not one scale of reason
    to poise° another of sensuality, the blood° and baseness of our natures would
    conduct us to most preposterous conclusions. But we have reason to cool
    our raging motions,° our carnal stings, our unbitted° lusts, whereof I take
    this that you call love to be a sect or scion.° 325
Roderigo: It cannot be.
Iago: It is merely a lust of the blood and a permission of the will. Come, be a
    man. Drown thyself? Drown cats and blind puppies. I have professed me thy
    friend, and I confess me knit to thy deserving with cables of perdurable°
    toughness. I could never better stead° thee than now. Put money in thy 330
    purse. Follow thou the wars; defeat thy favor° with an usurped° beard. I say,
    put money in thy purse. It cannot be long that Desdemona should continue
    her love to the Moor—put money in thy purse—nor he his to her. It was a
    violent commencement in her, and thou shalt see an answerable sequestra-
    tion°—put but money in thy purse. These Moors are changeable in their 335
    wills°—fill thy purse with money. The food that to him now is as luscious as
    locusts° shall be to him shortly as bitter as coloquintida.° She must change
    for youth; when she is sated with his body, she will find the error of her
    choice. She must have change, she must. Therefore put money in thy purse.
    If thou wilt needs damn thyself, do it a more delicate way than drowning. 340
    Make° all the money thou canst. If sanctimony° and a frail vow betwixt an
    erring° barbarian and a supersubtle Venetian be not too hard for my wits
    and all the tribe of hell, thou shalt enjoy her. Therefore make money. A pox

---

310 *villainous* i.e., what perfect nonsense   313 *guinea hen* (A slang term for a prostitute.)   314 *fond* infatuated   315 *virtue* strength, nature   316 *fig* (To give a fig is to thrust the thumb between the first and second fingers in a vulgar and insulting gesture.)   318 *hyssop* an herb of the mint family   319 *gender* kind.   *distract it with* divide it among.   320 *idleness* want of cultivation.   *corrigible authority* power to correct   321 *beam* balance.   322 *poise* counterbalance.   *blood* natural passions   324 *motions* appetites.   *unbitted* unbridled, uncontrolled   325 *sect or scion* cutting or offshoot   329 *perdurable* very durable   330 *stead* assist   331 *defeat thy favor* disguise your face.   *usurped* (The suggestion is that Roderigo is not man enough to have a beard of his own.)   334–335 *an answerable sequestration* a corresponding separation or estrangement   336 *wills* carnal appetites   337 *locusts* fruit of the carob tree (see Matthew 3:4), or perhaps honeysuckle.   *coloquintida* colocynth or bitter apple, a purgative   341 *Make* raise, collect.   *sanctimony* sacred ceremony   342 *erring* wandering, vagabond, unsteady

of drowning thyself! It is clean out of the way.° Seek thou rather to be
hanged in compassing° thy joy than to be drowned and go without her.   345

Roderigo: Wilt thou be fast° to my hopes if I depend on the issue?°

Iago: Thou art sure of me. Go, make money. I have told thee often, and I retell
thee again and again, I hate the Moor. My cause is hearted;° thine hath no
less reason. Let us be conjunctive° in our revenge against him. If thou canst
cuckold him, thou dost thyself a pleasure, me a sport. There are many events   350
in the womb of time which will be delivered. Traverse,° go, provide thy
money. We will have more of this tomorrow. Adieu.

Roderigo: Where shall we meet i' the morning?

Iago: At my lodging.

Roderigo: I'll be with thee betimes.°   [*He starts to leave.*]   355

Iago: Go to, farewell.—Do you hear, Roderigo?

Roderigo: What say you?

Iago: No more of drowning, do you hear?

Roderigo: I am changed.

Iago: Go to, farewell. Put money enough in your purse.   360

Roderigo: I'll sell all my land.   *Exit.*

Iago: Thus do I ever make my fool my purse;
For I mine own gained knowledge should profane
If I would time expend with such a snipe°
But for my sport and profit. I hate the Moor;   365
And it is thought abroad°that twixt my sheets
He's done my office.° I know not if 't be true;
But I, for mere suspicion in that kind,
Will do as if for surety.° He holds me well;°
The better shall my purpose work on him.   370
Cassio's a proper° man. Let me see now:
To get his place and to plume up° my will
In double knavery—How, how?—Let's see:
After some time, to abuse° Othello's ear
That he° is too familiar with his wife.   375
He hath a person and a smooth dispose°
To be suspected, framed to make women false.
The Moor is of a free° and open° nature,
That thinks men honest that but seem to be so,
And will as tenderly° be led by the nose   380
As asses are.

---

344 *clean . . . way* entirely unsuitable as a course of action   *compassing* encompassing, embracing
346 *fast* true.   *issue* (successful) outcome   348 *hearted* fixed in the heart, heartfelt   349 *conjunctive*
united   351 *Traverse* (A military marching term.)   355 *betimes* early   364 *snipe* woodcock, i.e.,
fool   366 *it is thought abroad* it is rumored   367 *my office* i.e., my sexual function as husband   369
do . . . surety act as if on certain knowledge.   *holds me well* regards me favorably   371 *proper* handsome   372 *plume up* put a feather in the cap of, i.e., glorify, gratify   374 *abuse* deceive   375 *he* i.e.,
Cassio   376 *dispose* disposition   378 *free* frank, generous.   *open* unsuspicious   380 *tenderly* readily

I have 't. It is engendered. Hell and night
Must bring this monstrous birth to the world's light.

[*Exit.*]

ACT II

Scene I [A Seaport in Cyprus. An Open Place Near the Quay.]

Enter Montano and two Gentlemen.

Montano: What from the cape can you discern at sea?
First Gentleman: Nothing at all. It is a high-wrought flood.°
    I cannot, twixt the heaven and the main,°
    Descry a sail.
Montano: Methinks the wind hath spoke aloud at land;   5
    A fuller blast ne'er shook our battlements.
    If it hath ruffianed° so upon the sea,
    What ribs of oak, when mountains° melt on them,
    Can hold the mortise?° What shall we hear of this?
Second Gentleman: A segregation° of the Turkish fleet.   10
    For do but stand upon the foaming shore,
    The chidden° billow seems to pelt the clouds;
    The wind-shaked surge, with high and monstrous mane,°
    Seems to cast water on the burning Bear°
    And quench the guards of th' ever-fixèd pole.   15
    I never did like molestation° view
    On the enchafèd° flood.
Montano: If that° the Turkish fleet
    Be not ensheltered and embayed,° they are drowned;
    It is impossible to bear it out.°   20

Enter a [Third] Gentleman.

Third Gentleman: News, lads! Our wars are done.
    The desperate tempest hath so banged the Turks
    That their designment° halts.° A noble ship of Venice
    Hath seen a grievous wreck° and sufferance°
    On most part of their fleet.   25
Montano: How? Is this true?

---

2 *high-wrought flood* very agitated sea   3 *main* ocean (also at line 41)   7 *ruffianed* raged   8 *mountains* i.e., of water   9 *hold the mortise* hold their joints together. (A *mortise* is the socket hollowed out in fitting timbers.)   10 *segregation* dispersal   12 *chidden* i.e., rebuked, repelled (by the shore), and thus shot into the air   13 *monstrous mane* (The surf is like the mane of a wild beast.)   14 *the burning Bear* i.e., the constellation Ursa Minor or the Little Bear, which includes the polestar (and hence regarded as the *guards of th' ever-fixèd pole* in the next line; sometimes the term *guards* is applied to the two "pointers" of the Big Bear or Dipper, which may be intended here.)   16 *like molestation* comparable disturbance   17 *enchafèd* angry   18 *If that* if   19 *embayed* sheltered by a bay   20 *bear it out* survive, weather the storm   23 *designment* design, enterprise. *halts* is lame   24 *wreck* shipwreck. *sufferance* damage, disaster

Third Gentleman: The ship is here put in,
    A Veronesa;° Michael Cassio,
    Lieutenant to the warlike Moor Othello,
    Is come on shore; the Moor himself at sea,   30
    And is in full commission here for Cyprus.
Montano: I am glad on 't. 'Tis a worthy governor.
Third Gentleman: But this same Cassio, though he speak of comfort
    Touching the Turkish loss, yet he looks sadly°
    And prays the Moor be safe, for they were parted   35
    With foul and violent tempest.
Montano: Pray heaven he be,
    For I have served him, and the man commands
    Like a full° soldier. Let's to the seaside, ho!
    As well to see the vessel that's come in
    As to throw out our eyes for brave Othello,   40
    Even till we make the main and th' aerial blue°
    An indistinct regard.°
Third Gentleman: Come, let's do so,
    For every minute is expectancy°
    Of more arrivance.°

    Enter Cassio.

Cassio: Thanks, you the valiant of this warlike isle,   45
    That so approve° the Moor! O, let the heavens
    Give him defense against the elements,
    For I have lost him on a dangerous sea.
Montano: Is he well shipped?
Cassio: His bark is stoutly timbered, and his pilot   50
    Of very expert and approved allowance;°
    Therefore my hopes, not surfeited to death,°
    Stand in bold cure.°
[A cry] within: "A sail, a sail, a sail!"
Cassio: What noise?
A Gentleman: The town is empty. On the brow o' the sea°   55
    Stand ranks of people, and they cry "A sail!"
Cassio: My hopes do shape him for° the governor.

    [A shot within.]

---

28 *Veronesa* i.e., fitted out in Verona for Venetian service, or possibly *Verennessa* (the Folio spelling), i.e., *verrinessa*, a cutter (from *verrinare*, "to cut through")   34 *sadly* gravely   38 *full* perfect   41 *the main . . . blue* the sea and the sky   42 *An indistinct regard* indistinguishable in our view   43 *is expectancy* gives expectation   44 *arrivance* arrival   46 *approve* admire, honor   51 *approved allowance* tested reputation   52 *surfeited to death* i.e., overextended, worn thin through repeated application or delayed fulfillment   53 *in bold cure* in strong hopes of fulfillment   55 *brow o' the sea* cliff-edge   57 *My . . . for* I hope it is

Second Gentleman: They do discharge their shot of courtesy;°
  Our friends at least.
Cassio: I pray you, sir, go forth,
  And give us truth who 'tis that is arrived.   60
Second Gentleman: I shall.   *Exit.*
Montano: But, good Lieutenant, is your general wived?
Cassio: Most fortunately. He hath achieved a maid
  That paragons° description and wild fame,°
  One that excels the quirks° of blazoning° pens,   65
  And in th' essential vesture of creation
  Does tire the enginer.°

  Enter [Second] Gentleman.°

                    How now? Who has put in?°
Second Gentleman: 'Tis one Iago, ancient to the General.
Cassio: He's had most favorable and happy speed.
  Tempests themselves, high seas, and howling winds,   70
  The guttered° rocks and congregated sands—
  Traitors ensteeped° to clog the guiltless keel—
  As° having sense of beauty, do omit°
  Their mortal° natures, letting go safely by
  The divine Desdemona.
Montano: What is she?   75
Cassio: She that I spake of, our great captain's captain,
  Left in the conduct of the bold Iago,
  Whose footing° here anticipates our thoughts
  A sennight's° speed. Great Jove, Othello guard,
  And swell his sail with thine own powerful breath,   80
  That he may bless this bay with his tall° ship,
  Make love's quick pants in Desdemona's arms,
  Give renewed fire to our extincted spirits,
  And bring all Cyprus comfort!

  Enter Desdemona, Iago, Roderigo, and Emilia.

                    O, behold,
  The riches of the ship is come on shore!   85
  You men of Cyprus, let her have your knees.

  [The gentlemen make curtsy to Desdemona.]

  Hail to thee, lady! And the grace of heaven

---

58 *discharge . . . courtesy* fire a salute in token of respect and courtesy   64 *paragons* surpasses.   *wild fame* extravagant report   65 *quirks* witty conceits.   *blazoning* setting forth as though in heraldic language   66–67 *in . . . enginer* in her real, God-given, beauty, (she) defeats any attempt to praise her. *enginer* engineer, i.e., poet, one who devises.   s.d. *Second Gentleman* (So identified in the Quarto text here and in lines 58, 61, 68, and 96; the Folio calls him a gentleman.)   67 *put in* i.e., to harbor   71 *guttered* jagged, trenched   72 *ensteeped* lying under water   73 *As* as if.   *omit* forbear to exercise   74 *mortal* deadly   78 *footing* landing   79 *sennight's* week's   81 *tall* splendid, gallant

Before, behind thee, and on every hand
Enwheel thee round!

Desdemona: I thank you, valiant Cassio.
What tidings can you tell me of my lord?   90

Cassio: He is not yet arrived, nor know I aught
But that he's well and will be shortly here.

Desdemona: O, but I fear—How lost you company?

Cassio: The great contention of the sea and skies
Parted our fellowship.

(Within) "A sail, a sail!" [A shot.]
                        But hark. A sail!   95

Second Gentleman: They give their greeting to the citadel.
This likewise is a friend.

Cassio: See for the news.

[Exit Second Gentleman.]

Good Ancient, you are welcome. [Kissing Emilia.] Welcome, mistress.
Let it not gall your patience, good Iago,
That I extend° my manners; 'tis my breeding°   100
That gives me this bold show of courtesy.

Iago: Sir, would she give you so much of her lips
As of her tongue she oft bestows on me,
You would have enough.

Desdemona: Alas, she has no speech!°   105

Iago: In faith, too much.
I find it still,° when I have list° to sleep.
Marry, before your ladyship, I grant,
She puts her tongue a little in her heart
And chides with thinking.°

Emilia: You have little cause to say so.   110

Iago: Come on, come on. You are pictures out of doors,°
Bells° in your parlors, wildcats in your kitchens,°
Saints° in your injuries, devils being offended,
Players° in your huswifery,° and huswives° in your beds.

Desdemona: O, fie upon thee, slanderer!   115

Iago: Nay, it is true, or else I am a Turk.°
You rise to play, and go to bed to work.

Emilia: You shall not write my praise.

---

100 *extend* give scope to. *breeding* training in the niceties of etiquette 105 *she has no speech* i.e., she's not a chatterbox, as you allege 107 *still* always. *list* desire 110 *with thinking* i.e., in her thoughts only 111 *pictures out of doors* i.e., silent and well-behaved in public 112 *Bells* i.e., jangling, noisy, and brazen. *in your kitchens* i.e., in domestic affairs. (Ladies would not do the cooking.) 113 *Saints* martyrs 114 *Players* idlers, triflers, or deceivers. *huswifery* housekeeping. *huswives* hussies (i.e., women are "busy" in bed, or unduly thrifty in dispensing sexual favors) 116 *a Turk* an infidel, not to be believed

Iago: No, let me not.
Desdemona: What wouldst write of me, if thou shouldst praise me?
Iago: O gentle lady, do not put me to 't,   120
    For I am nothing if not critical.°
Desdemona: Come on, essay.°—There's one gone to the harbor?
Iago: Ay, madam.
Desdemona: I am not merry, but I do beguile
    The thing I am° by seeming otherwise.   125
    Come, how wouldst thou praise me?
Iago: I am about it, but indeed my invention
    Comes from my pate as birdlime° does from frieze°—
    It plucks out brains and all. But my Muse labors,°
    And thus she is delivered: 130
    If she be fair and wise, fairness and wit,
    The one's for use, the other useth it.°
Desdemona: Well praised! How if she be black° and witty?
Iago: If she be black, and thereto have a wit,
    She'll find a white° that shall her blackness fit.°   135
Desdemona: Worse and worse.
Emilia: How if fair and foolish?
Iago: She never yet was foolish that was fair,
    For even her folly° helped her to an heir.°
Desdemona: These are old fond° paradoxes to make fools laugh i' th' alehouse.
    What miserable praise hast thou for her that's foul and foolish?   140
Iago: There's none so foul° and foolish thereunto,°
    But does foul° pranks which fair and wise ones do.
Desdemona: O heavy ignorance! Thou praisest the worst best. But what praise
    couldst thou bestow on a deserving woman indeed, one that, in the au-
    thority of her merit, did justly put on the vouch° of very malice itself?   145
Iago: She that was ever fair, and never proud,
    Had tongue at will, and yet was never loud,
    Never lacked gold and yet went never gay,°
    Fled from her wish, and yet said, "Now I may,"°
    She that being angered, her revenge being nigh,   150
    Bade her wrong stay° and her displeasure fly,
    She that in wisdom never was so frail

---

121 *critical* censorious   122 *essay* try   125 *The thing I am* i.e., my anxious self   128 *birdlime* sticky substance used to catch small birds.   *frieze* coarse woolen cloth   129 *labors* (1) exerts herself (2) prepares to deliver a child (with a following pun on *delivered* in line 130)   132 *The one's . . . it* i.e., her cleverness will make use of her beauty   133 *black* dark-complexioned, brunette   135 *a white* a fair person (with word-play on "wight," a person).   *fit* (with sexual suggestion of mating)   138 *folly* (with added meaning of "lechery, wantonness").   *to an heir* i.e., to bear a child   139 *fond* foolish   141 *foul* ugly.   *thereunto* in addition   142 *foul* sluttish   145 *put . . . vouch* compel the approval   148 *gay* extravagantly clothed   149 *Fled . . . may* avoided temptation where the choice was hers   151 *Bade . . . stay* i.e., resolved to put up with her injury patiently

To change the cod's head for the salmon's tail,°
She that could think and ne'er disclose her mind,
See suitors following and not look behind,   155
She was a wight, if ever such wight were—

Desdemona: To do what?

Iago: To suckle fools° and chronicle small beer.°

Desdemona: O most lame and impotent conclusion! Do not learn of him,
Emilia, though he be thy husband. How say you, Cassio? Is he not a most   160
profane° and liberal° counselor?

Cassio: He speaks home,° madam. You may relish° him more in° the soldier
than in the scholar.

[*Cassio and Desdemona stand together, conversing intimately.*]

Iago [*aside*]: He takes her by the palm. Ay, well said,° whisper. With as little a
web as this will I ensnare as great a fly as Cassio. Ay, smile upon her, do; I   165
will gyve° thee in thine own courtship.° You say true;° 'tis so, indeed. If such
tricks as these strip you out of your lieutenantry, it had been better you had
not kissed your three fingers so oft, which again you are most apt to
play the sir° in. Very good; well kissed! An excellent courtesy! 'Tis so, indeed. Yet again your fingers to your lips? Would they were clyster pipes° for   170
your sake! [*Trumpet within.*] The Moor! I know his trumpet.

Cassio: 'Tis truly so.

Desdemona: Let's meet him and receive him.

Cassio: Lo, where he comes!

Enter Othello and attendants.

Othello: O my fair warrior!

Desdemona: My dear Othello!   175

Othello: It gives me wonder great as my content
To see you here before me. O my soul's joy,
If after every tempest come such calms,
May the winds blow till they have wakened death,
And let the laboring bark climb hills of seas   180
Olympus-high, and duck again as low
As hell's from heaven! If it were now to die,
'Twere now to be most happy, for I fear
My soul hath her content so absolute
That not another comfort like to this   185

---

153 *To . . . tail* i.e., to exchange a lackluster husband for a sexy lover (?) (*Cod's head* is slang for
"penis," and *tail*, for "pudendum.")   158 *suckle fools* breastfeed babies.   *chronicle small beer* i.e., keep
petty household accounts, keep track of trivial matters   161 *profane* irreverent, ribald.   *liberal* licentious, free-spoken   162 *home* right to the target. (A term from fencing.)   *relish* appreciate   *in* in
the character of   164 *well said* well done   166 *gyve* fetter, shackle.   *courtship* courtesy, show of
courtly manners.   *You say true* i.e., that's right, go ahead   169 *the sir* i.e., the fine gentleman   170
clyster pipes tubes used for enemas and douches

Succeeds in unknown fate.°
Desdemona: The heavens forbid
But that our loves and comforts should increase
Even as our days do grow!
Othello: Amen to that, sweet powers!
I cannot speak enough of this content.   190
It stops me here; it is too much of joy.
And this, and this, the greatest discords be

[*They kiss.*]°

That e'er our hearts shall make!
Iago [*aside*]: O, you are well tuned now!
But I'll set down° the pegs that make this music,   195
As honest as I am.°
Othello: Come, let us to the castle.
News, friends! Our wars are done, the Turks are drowned.
How does my old acquaintance of this isle?—
Honey, you shall be well desired° in Cyprus;   200
I have found great love amongst them. O my sweet,
I prattle out of fashion,° and I dote
In mine own comforts.—I prithee, good Iago,
Go to the bay and disembark my coffers.°
Bring thou the master° to the citadel;   205
He is a good one, and his worthiness
Does challenge° much respect.—Come, Desdemona.—
Once more, well met at Cyprus!

Exeunt Othello and Desdemona [and all but Iago and Roderigo].

Iago [*to an attendant*]: Do thou meet me presently at the harbor. [*To Roderigo.*]
Come hither. If thou be'st valiant—as, they say, base men° being in love 210
have then a nobility in their natures more than is native to them—list° me.
The Lieutenant tonight watches on the court of guard.° First, I must tell
thee this: Desdemona is directly in love with him.
Roderigo: With him? Why, 'tis not possible.
Iago: Lay thy finger thus,° and let thy soul be instructed. Mark me with what vi- 215
olence she first loved the Moor, but° for bragging and telling her fantastical
lies. To love him still for prating? Let not thy discreet heart think it. Her eye
must be fed; and what delight shall she have to look on the devil? When the
blood is made dull with the act of sport,° there should be, again to inflame it

---

186 *Succeeds . . . fate* i.e., can follow in the unknown future   192 s.d. *They kiss* (The direction is
from the Quarto.)   195 *set down* loosen (and hence untune the instrument)   196 *As . . . I am* for
all my supposed honesty   200 *desired* welcomed   202 *out of fashion* irrelevantly, incoherently (?)
204 *coffers* chests, baggage   205 *master* ship's captain   207 *challenge* lay claim to, deserve   210 *base
men* even lowly born men   211 *list* listen to   212 *court of guard* guardhouse. (Cassio is in charge of
the watch.)   215 *thus* i.e., on your lips   216 *but* only   219 *the act of sport* sex

and to give satiety a fresh appetite, loveliness in favor,° sympathy° in years, 220
manners, and beauties—all which the Moor is defective in. Now, for want
of these required conveniences,° her delicate tenderness will find itself
abused,° begin to heave the gorge,° disrelish and abhor the Moor. Very na-
ture° will instruct her in it and compel her to some second choice. Now, sir,
this granted—as it is a most pregnant° and unforced position—who stands 225
so eminent in the degree of° this fortune as Cassio does? A knave very voluble,° no further conscionable° than in putting on the mere form of civil
and humane° seeming for the better compassing of his salt° and most hidden
loose affection.° Why, none, why, none. A slipper° and subtle knave, a
finder out of occasions, that has an eye can stamp° and counterfeit advan- 230
tages,° though true advantage never present itself; a devilish knave. Besides,
the knave is handsome, young, and hath all those requisites in him that
folly° and green° minds look after. A pestilent complete knave, and the
woman hath found him° already.

Roderigo: I cannot believe that in her. She's full of most blessed condition.° 235

Iago: Blessed fig's end!° The wine she drinks is made of grapes. If she had been
blessed, she would never have loved the Moor. Blessed pudding!° Didst thou
not see her paddle with the palm of his hand? Didst not mark that?

Roderigo: Yes, that I did; but that was but courtesy.

Iago: Lechery, by this hand. An index° and obscure° prologue to the history of 240
lust and foul thoughts. They met so near with their lips that their breaths
embraced together. Villainous thoughts, Roderigo! When these
mutualities° so marshal the way, hard at hand° comes the master and main
exercise, th' incorporate° conclusion. Pish! But, sir, be you ruled by me. I
have brought you from Venice. Watch you° tonight; for the command, I'll 245
lay 't upon you.° Cassio knows you not. I'll not be far from you. Do you find
some occasion to anger Cassio, either by speaking too loud, or tainting° his
discipline, or from what other course you please, which the time shall more
favorably minister.°

Roderigo: Well. 250

Iago: Sir, he's rash and very sudden in choler,° and haply° may strike at you.
Provoke him that he may, for even out of that will I cause these of Cyprus to
mutiny,° whose qualification° shall come into no true taste° again but by
the displanting of Cassio. So shall you have a shorter journey to your desires

---

220 *favor* appearance. *sympathy* correspondence, similarity 222 *required conveniences* things con-
ducive to sexual compatibility 223 *abused* cheated, revolted. *heave the gorge* experience nausea
224 *Very nature* her very instincts 225 *pregnant* evident, cogent 226 *in . . . of* as next in line for
227 *voluble* facile, glib. *conscionable* conscientious, conscience-bound 228 *humane* polite, courteous. *salt* licentious 229 *affection* passion. *slipper* slippery 230 *an eye can stamp* an eye that can
coin, create 231 *advantages* favorable opportunities 233 *folly* wantonness. *green* immature 234
found him sized him up, perceived his intent 235 *condition* disposition 236 *fig's end* (See Act I,
Scene iii, line 316 for the vulgar gesture of the fig.) 237 *pudding* sausage 240 *index* table of contents. *obscure* (i.e., the *lust and foul thoughts* in line 241 are secret, hidden from view) 243 *mutual-
ities* exchanges, intimacies. *hard at hand* closely following 244 *incorporate* carnal 245 *Watch you*
stand watch 245–246 *for the command . . . you* I'll arrange for you to be appointed, given orders
247 *tainting* disparaging 249 *minister* provide 251 *choler* wrath *haply* perhaps 253 *mutiny* riot.
qualification appeasement. *true taste* i.e., acceptable state

by the means I shall then have to prefer° them, and the impediment most   255
profitably removed, without the which there were no expectation of our
prosperity.

Roderigo: I will do this, if you can bring it to any opportunity.

Iago: I warrant° thee. Meet me by and by° at the citadel. I must fetch his necessaries ashore. Farewell.   260

Roderigo: Adieu.   *Exit.*

Iago: That Cassio loves her, I do well believe 't;
That she loves him, 'tis apt° and of great credit.°
The Moor, howbeit that I endure him not,
Is of a constant, loving, noble nature,   265
And I dare think he'll prove to Desdemona
A most dear husband. Now, I do love her too,
Not out of absolute lust—though peradventure
I stand accountant° for as great a sin—
But partly led to diet° my revenge   270
For that I do suspect the lusty Moor
Hath leaped into my seat, the thought whereof
Doth, like a poisonous mineral, gnaw my innards;
And nothing can or shall content my soul
Till I am evened with him, wife for wife,   275
Or failing so, yet that I put the Moor
At least into a jealousy so strong
That judgment cannot cure. Which thing to do,
If this poor trash of Venice, whom I trace°
For° his quick hunting, stand the putting on,°   280
I'll have our Michael Cassio on the hip,°
Abuse° him to the Moor in the rank garb—°
For I fear Cassio with my nightcap° too—
Make the Moor thank me, love me, and reward me
For making him egregiously an ass   285
And practicing upon° his peace and quiet
Even to madness. 'Tis here, but yet confused.
Knavery's plain face is never seen till used.   *Exit.*

Scene II [Cyprus. A Street.]

Enter Othello's Herald with a proclamation.

Herald: It is Othello's pleasure, our noble and valiant general, that, upon certain
tidings now arrived, importing the mere perdition° of the Turkish fleet,

---

255 *prefer* advance   259 *warrant* assure.   *by and by* immediately   263 *apt* probable.   *credit* credibility   269 *accountant* accountable   270 *diet* feed   279 *trace* i.e., train, or follow (?), or perhaps
trash, a hunting term, meaning to put weights on a hunting dog in order to slow him down   280
to make more eager.   *stand . . . on* respond properly when I incite him to quarrel   281 *on the hip* at
my mercy, where I can throw him. (A wrestling term.)   282 *Abuse* slander.   *rank garb* coarse
manner, gross fashion   283 *with my nightcap* i.e., as a rival in my bed, as one who gives me cuckold's
horns   286 *practicing upon* plotting against   2 *mere perdition* complete destruction

every man put himself into triumph:° some to dance, some to make bonfires, each man to what sport and revels his addiction° leads him. For, besides these beneficial news, it is the celebration of his nuptial. So much was his pleasure should be proclaimed. All offices° are open, and there is full liberty of feasting from this present hour of five till the bell have told eleven. Heaven bless the isle of Cyprus and our noble general Othello!

Exit.

Scene III [Cyprus. The Citadel.]

Enter Othello, Desdemona, Cassio, and attendants.

Othello: Good Michael, look you to the guard tonight.
Let's teach ourselves that honorable stop°
Not to outsport° discretion.
Cassio: Iago hath direction what to do,
But notwithstanding, with my personal eye
Will I look to 't.
Othello: Iago is most honest.
Michael, good night. Tomorrow with your earliest°
Let me have speech with you. [*To Desdemona.*]
                    Come, my dear love,
The purchase made, the fruits are to ensue;
That profit's yet to come 'tween me and you.°—
Good night.

Exit [Othello, with Desdemona and attendants].

Enter Iago.

Cassio: Welcome, Iago. We must to the watch.
Iago: Not this hour,° Lieutenant; 'tis not yet ten o' the clock. Our general cast° us thus early for the love of his Desdemona; who° let us not therefore blame. He hath not yet made wanton the night with her, and she is sport for Jove.
Cassio: She's a most exquisite lady.
Iago: And, I'll warrant her, full of game.
Cassio: Indeed, she's a most fresh and delicate creature.
Iago: What an eye she has! Methinks it sounds a parley° to provocation.
Cassio: An inviting eye, and yet methinks right modest.
Iago: And when she speaks, is it not an alarum° to love?
Cassio: She is indeed perfection.

5

5

10

15

20

---

3 *triumph* public celebration   4 *addiction* inclination   6 *offices* rooms where food and drink are kept   2 *stop* restraint   3 *outsport* celebrate beyond the bounds of   7 *with your earliest* at your earliest convenience   9–10 *The purchase . . . you* i.e., though married, we haven't yet consummated our love   13 *Not this hour* not for an hour yet.   *cast* dismissed   14 *who* i.e., Othello   19 *sounds a parley* calls for a conference, issues an invitation   21 *alarum* signal calling men to arms (continuing the military metaphor of *parley*, line 19)

Iago: Well, happiness to their sheets! Come, Lieutenant, I have a stoup° of wine, and here without° are a brace° of Cyprus gallants that would fain have a measure° to the health of black Othello.   25

Cassio: Not tonight, good Iago. I have very poor and unhappy brains for drinking. I could well wish courtesy would invent some other custom of entertainment.

Iago: O, they are our friends. But one cup! I'll drink for you.°

Cassio: I have drunk but one cup tonight, and that was craftily qualified° too, and behold what innovation° it makes here.° I am unfortunate in the infir-   30
mity and dare not task my weakness with any more.

Iago: What, man? 'Tis a night of revels. The gallants desire it.

Cassio: Where are they?

Iago: Here at the door. I pray you, call them in.

Cassio: I'll do 't, but it dislikes me.°   *Exit.*   35

Iago: If I can fasten but one cup upon him,
       With that which he hath drunk tonight already,
       He'll be as full of quarrel and offense°
       As my young mistress' dog. Now, my sick fool Roderigo,
       Whom love hath turned almost the wrong side out,   40
       To Desdemona hath tonight caroused°
       Potations pottle-deep;° and he's to watch.°
       Three lads of Cyprus—noble swelling° spirits,
       That hold their honors in a wary distance,°
       The very elements° of this warlike isle—   45
       Have I tonight flustered with flowing cups,
       And they watch° too. Now, 'mongst this flock of drunkards
       Am I to put our Cassio in some action
       That may offend the isle.—But here they come.

       Enter Cassio, Montano, and gentlemen; [servants following with wine].

       If consequence do but approve my dream,°   50
       My boat sails freely both with wind and stream.°

Cassio: 'Fore God, they have given me a rouse° already.

Montano: Good faith, a little one; not past a pint, as I am a soldier.

Iago: Some wine, ho! [*He sings.*]
       "And let me the cannikin° clink, clink,   55
       And let me the cannikin clink.
       A soldier's a man,

---

23 *stoup* measure of liquor, two quarts   24 *without* outside.   *brace* pair   24–25 *fain have a measure* gladly drink a toast   28 *for you* in your place. (Iago will do the steady drinking to keep the gallants company while Cassio has only one cup.)   29 *qualified* diluted   30 *innovation* disturbance, insurrection.   *here* i.e., in my head   35 *it dislikes me* i.e., I'm reluctant   38 *offense* readiness to take offense   41 *caroused* drunk off   42 *pottle-deep* to the bottom of the tankard.   *watch* stand watch   43 *swelling* proud   44 *hold . . . distance* i.e., are extremely sensitive of their honor   45 *very elements* typical sort   47 *watch* are members of the guard   50 *If . . . dream* if subsequent events will only substantiate my scheme   51 *stream* current   52 *rouse* full draft of liquor   55 *cannikin* small drinking vessel

O, man's life's but a span;°
Why, then, let a soldier drink."

Some wine, boys!   60
Cassio: 'Fore God, an excellent song.
Iago: I learned it in England, where indeed they are most potent in potting.°
Your Dane, your German, and your swag-bellied Hollander—drink, ho!—
are nothing to your English.
Cassio: Is your Englishman so exquisite in his drinking?   65
Iago: Why, he drinks you,° with facility, your Dane° dead drunk; he sweats not°
to overthrow your Almain;° he gives your Hollander a vomit ere the next
pottle can be filled.
Cassio: To the health of our general!
Montano: I am for it, Lieutenant, and I'll do you justice.°   70
Iago: O sweet England! [*He sings.*]

> "King Stephen was and-a worthy peer,
> His breeches cost him but a crown;
> He held them sixpence all too dear,
> With that he called the tailor lown.°   75
>
> He was a wight of high renown,
> And thou art but of low degree.
> 'Tis pride° that pulls the country down;
> Then take thy auld° cloak about thee."

Some wine, ho!   80
Cassio: 'Fore God, this is a more exquisite song than the other.
Iago: Will you hear 't again?
Cassio: No, for I hold him to be unworthy of his place that does those things.
Well, God's above all; and there be souls must be saved, and there be souls
must not be saved.   85
Iago: It's true, good Lieutenant.
Cassio: For mine own part—no offense to the General, nor any man of
quality°—I hope to be saved.
Iago: And so do I too, Lieutenant.
Cassio: Ay, but, by your leave, not before me; the lieutenant is to be saved be-   90
fore the ancient. Let's have no more of this; let's to our affairs.—God forgive
us our sins!—Gentlemen, let's look to our business. Do not think, gentlemen, I am drunk. This is my ancient; this is my right hand, and this is my
left. I am not drunk now. I can stand well enough, and speak well enough.

---

58 *span* brief span of time. (Compare Psalm 39:6 as rendered in the 1928 Book of Common Prayer:
"Thou hast made my days as it were a span long.")   62 *potting* drinking   66 *drinks you* drinks. *your
Dane* your typical Dane. *sweats not* i.e., need not exert himself   67 *Almain* German   70 *I'll . . .
justice* i.e., I'll drink as much as you   75 *lown* lout, rascal   78 *pride* i.e., extravagance in dress   79
auld old   88 *quality* rank

Gentlemen: Excellent well.

Cassio: Why, very well then; you must not think then that I am drunk.   *Exit.*

Montano: To th' platform, masters. Come, let's set the watch.°

    [Exeunt Gentlemen.]

Iago: You see this fellow that is gone before.
    He's a soldier fit to stand by Caesar
    And give direction; and do but see his vice.   100
    'Tis to his virtue a just equinox,°
    The one as long as th' other. 'Tis pity of him.
    I fear the trust Othello puts him in,
    On some odd time of his infirmity,
    Will shake this island.
Montano: But is he often thus?   105
Iago: 'Tis evermore the prologue to his sleep.
    He'll watch the horologe a double set,°
    If drink rock not his cradle.
Montano: It were well
    The General were put in mind of it.
    Perhaps he sees it not, or his good nature   110
    Prizes the virtue that appears in Cassio
    And looks not on his evils. Is not this true?

    Enter Roderigo.

Iago [aside to him]: How now, Roderigo?
    I pray you, after the Lieutenant; go.   *[Exit Roderigo.]*
Montano: And 'tis great pity that the noble Moor   115
    Should hazard such a place as his own second
    With° one of an engraffed° infirmity.
    It were an honest action to say so
    To the Moor.
Iago: Not I, for this fair island.
    I do love Cassio well and would do much   120
    To cure him of this evil.   *[Cry within: "Help! Help!"]*
               But, hark! What noise?

    Enter Cassio, pursuing° Roderigo.

Cassio: Zounds, you rogue! You rascal!
Montano: What's the matter, Lieutenant?
Cassio: A knave teach me my duty? I'll beat the knave into a twiggen° bottle.

---

97 *set the watch* mount the guard   101 *just equinox* exact counterpart. (*Equinox* is an equal length of days and nights.)   107 *watch . . . set* stay awake twice around the clock or *horologe*   116–117 *hazard . . . With* risk giving such an important position as his second in command to   117 *engraffed* engrafted, inveterate   121 s.d. *pursuing* (The Quarto text reads, "driving in.")   124 *twiggen* wicker-covered. (Cassio vows to assail Roderigo until his skin resembles wickerwork or until he has driven Roderigo through the holes in a wickerwork.)

Roderigo: Beat me?   125
Cassio: Dost thou prate, rogue?   *[He strikes Roderigo.]*
Montano: Nay, good Lieutenant. *[Restraining him.]* I pray you, sir, hold your hand.
Cassio: Let me go, sir, or I'll knock you o'er the mazard.°
Montano: Come, come, you're drunk.
Cassio: Drunk?   *[They fight.]* 130
Iago [aside to Roderigo]: Away, I say. Go out and cry a mutiny.°

    [Exit Roderigo.]

    Nay, good Lieutenant—God's will, gentlemen—
    Help, ho!—Lieutenant—sir—Montano—sir—
    Help, masters!°—Here's a goodly watch indeed!

    [A bell rings.]°

    Who's that which rings the bell?—Diablo,° ho!   135
    The town will rise.° God's will, Lieutenant, hold!
    You'll be ashamed forever.

    Enter Othello and attendants [with weapons].

Othello: What is the matter here?
Montano: Zounds, I bleed still.
    I am hurt to th' death. He dies! *[He thrusts at Cassio.]*
Othello: Hold, for your lives!
Iago: Hold, ho! Lieutenant—sir—Montano—gentlemen—   140
    Have you forgot all sense of place and duty?
    Hold! The General speaks to you. Hold, for shame!
Othello: Why, how now, ho! From whence ariseth this?
    Are we turned Turks, and to ourselves do that
    Which heaven hath forbid the Ottomites?°   145
    For Christian shame, put by this barbarous brawl!
    He that stirs next to carve for° his own rage
    Holds his soul light;° he dies upon his motion.°
    Silence that dreadful bell. It frights the isle
    From her propriety.° What is the matter, masters?   150
    Honest Iago, that looks dead with grieving,
    Speak. Who began this? On thy love, I charge thee.
Iago: I do not know. Friends all but now, even now,
    In quarter° and in terms° like bride and groom

---

128 *mazard* i.e., head. (Literally, a drinking vessel.)   131 *mutiny* riot   134 *masters* sirs.   s.d. *A bell rings* (This direction is from the Quarto, as are *Exit Roderigo* at line 114, *They fight* at line 130, and *with weapons* at line 137.)   135 *Diablo* the devil   136 *rise* grow riotous   144–145 *to ourselves . . . Ottomites* inflict on ourselves the harm that heaven has prevented the Turks from doing (by destroying their fleet)   147 *carve for* i.e., indulge, satisfy with his sword   148 *Holds . . . light* i.e., places little value on his life.   *upon his motion* if he moves   150 *propriety* proper state or condition   154 *In quarter* in friendly conduct, within bounds.   *in terms* on good terms

Devesting them° for bed; and then, but now— 155
  As if some planet had unwitted men—
  Swords out, and tilting one at others' breasts
  In opposition bloody. I cannot speak°
  Any beginning to this peevish odds;°
  And would in action glorious I had lost 160
  Those legs that brought me to a part of it!
Othello: How comes it, Michael, you are thus forgot?°
Cassio: I pray you, pardon me. I cannot speak.
Othello: Worthy Montano, you were wont be° civil;
  The gravity and stillness° of your youth 165
  The world hath noted, and your name is great
  In mouths of wisest censure.° What's the matter
  That you unlace° your reputation thus
  And spend your rich opinion° for the name
  Of a night-brawler? Give me answer to it. 170
Montano: Worthy Othello, I am hurt to danger.
  Your officer, Iago, can inform you—
  While I spare speech, which something° now offends° me—
  Of all that I do know; nor know I aught
  By me that's said or done amiss this night, 175
  Unless self-charity be sometimes a vice,
  And to defend ourselves it be a sin
  When violence assails us.
Othello: Now, by heaven,
  My blood° begins my safer guides° to rule,
  And passion, having my best judgment collied,° 180
  Essays° to lead the way. Zounds, if I stir,
  Or do but lift this arm, the best of you
  Shall sink in my rebuke. Give me to know
  How this foul rout° began, who set it on;
  And he that is approved in° this offense, 185
  Though he had twinned with me, both at a birth,
  Shall lose me. What? In a town of° war
  Yet wild, the people's hearts brim full of fear,
  To manage° private and domestic quarrel?
  In night, and on the court and guard of safety?° 190
  'Tis monstrous. Iago, who began 't?

155 *Devesting them* undressing themselves 158 *speak* explain 159 *peevish odds* childish quarrel
162 *are thus forgot* have forgotten yourself thus 164 *wont be* accustomed to be 165 *stillness* sobriety
167 *censure* judgment 168 *unlace* undo, lay open (as one might loose the strings of a purse containing reputation) 169 *opinion* reputation 173 *something* somewhat. *offends* pains 179 *blood*
passion (of anger). *guides* i.e., reason 180 *collied* darkened 181 *Essays* undertakes 184 *rout* riot
185 *approved in* found guilty of 187 *town of* town garrisoned for 189 *manage* undertake 190 *on
. . . safety* at the main guardhouse or headquarters and on watch

Montano [*to Iago*]: If partially affined,° or leagued in office,°
 Thou dost deliver more or less than truth,
 Thou art no soldier.
Iago: Touch me not so near.
 I had rather have this tongue cut from my mouth   195
 Than it should do offense to Michael Cassio;
 Yet, I persuade myself, to speak the truth
 Shall nothing wrong him. Thus it is, General.
 Montano and myself being in speech,
 There comes a fellow crying out for help,   200
 And Cassio following him with determined sword
 To execute° upon him. Sir, this gentleman

[*indicating Montano*]

 Steps in to Cassio and entreats his pause.°
 Myself the crying fellow did pursue,
 Lest by his clamor—as it so fell out—   205
 The town might fall in fright. He, swift of foot,
 Outran my purpose, and I returned, the rather°
 For that I heard the clink and fall of swords
 And Cassio high in oath, which till tonight
 I ne'er might say before. When I came back—   210
 For this was brief—I found them close together
 At blow and thrust, even as again they were
 When you yourself did part them.
 More of this matter cannot I report.
 But men are men; the best sometimes forget.°   215
 Though Cassio did some little wrong to him,
 As men in rage strike those that wish them best,°
 Yet surely Cassio, I believe, received
 From him that fled some strange indignity,
 Which patience could not pass.°
Othello: I know, Iago,   220
 Thy honesty and love doth mince this matter,
 Making it light to Cassio. Cassio, I love thee,
 But nevermore be officer of mine.

Enter Desdemona, attended.

 Look if my gentle love be not raised up.
 I'll make thee an example.   225
Desdemona: What is the matter, dear?

192 *partially affined* made partial by some personal relationship. *leagued in office* in league as fellow officers 202 *execute* give effect to (his anger) 203 *his pause* him to stop 207 *rather* sooner 215 *forget* forget themselves 217 *those . . . best* i.e., even those who are well disposed 220 *pass* pass over, overlook

Othello: All's well now, sweeting;
   Come away to bed. [*To Montano.*] Sir, for your hurts,
   Myself will be your surgeon.°—Lead him off.

[*Montano is led off.*]

   Iago, look with care about the town
   And silence those whom this vile brawl distracted.   230
   Come, Desdemona. 'Tis the soldiers' life
   To have their balmy slumbers waked with strife.

   Exit [*with all but Iago and Cassio*].

Iago: What, are you hurt, Lieutenant?
Cassio: Ay, past all surgery.
Iago: Marry, God forbid!   235
Cassio: Reputation, reputation, reputation! O, I have lost my reputation! I have
   lost the immortal part of myself, and what remains is bestial. My reputation,
   Iago, my reputation!
Iago: As I am an honest man, I thought you had received some bodily wound;
   there is more sense in that than in reputation. Reputation is an idle and   240
   most false imposition,° oft got without merit and lost without deserving.
   You have lost no reputation at all, unless you repute yourself such a loser.
   What, man, there are more ways to recover° the General again. You are but
   now cast in his mood°—a punishment more in policy° than in malice, even
   so as one would beat his offenseless dog to affright an imperious lion.°   245
   Sue° to him again and he's yours.
Cassio: I will rather sue to be despised than to deceive so good a commander
   with so slight,° so drunken, and so indiscreet an officer. Drunk? And speak
   parrot?° And squabble? Swagger? Swear? And discourse fustian with one's
   own shadow? O thou invisible spirit of wine, if thou hast no name to be   250
   known by, let us call thee devil!
Iago: What was he that you followed with your sword? What had he done to you?
Cassio: I know not.
Iago: Is 't possible?
Cassio: I remember a mass of things, but nothing distinctly; a quarrel, but   255
   nothing wherefore.° O God, that men should put an enemy in their mouths
   to steal away their brains! That we should, with joy, pleasure, revel, and
   applause° transform ourselves into beasts!
Iago: Why, but you are now well enough. How came you thus recovered?

---

228 *be your surgeon* i.e., make sure you receive medical attention   241 *false imposition* thing artificially imposed and of no real value   243 *recover* regain favor with   244 *cast in his mood* dismissed in
a moment of anger. *in policy* done for expediency's sake and as a public gesture   245 *would . . . lion*
i.e., would make an example of a minor offender in order to deter more important and dangerous of-
fenders   246 *Sue* petition   248 *slight* worthless   248–249 *speak parrot* talk nonsense, rant   256
wherefore why   258 *applause* desire for applause

Cassio: It hath pleased the devil drunkenness to give place to the devil wrath. 260
    One unperfectness shows me another, to make me frankly despise myself.

Iago: Come, you are too severe a moraler.° As the time, the place, and the con-
    dition of this country stands, I could heartily wish this had not befallen; but
    since it is as it is, mend it for your own good.

Cassio: I will ask him for my place again; he shall tell me I am a drunkard. Had I 265
    as many mouths as Hydra,° such an answer would stop them all. To be now
    a sensible man, by and by a fool, and presently a beast! O, strange! Every in-
    ordinate cup is unblessed, and the ingredient is a devil.

Iago: Come, come, good wine is a good familiar creature, if it be well used. Ex-
    claim no more against it. And, good Lieutenant, I think you think I love 270
    you.

Cassio: I have well approved° it, sir. I drunk!

Iago: You or any man living may be drunk at a time,° man. I'll tell you what you
    shall do. Our general's wife is now the general—I may say so in this respect,
    for that° he hath devoted and given up himself to the contemplation, mark, 275
    and denotement° of her parts° and graces. Confess yourself freely to her; im-
    portune her help to put you in your place again. She is of so free,° so kind, so
    apt, so blessed a disposition, she holds it a vice in her goodness not to do
    more than she is requested. This broken joint between you and her husband
    entreat her to splinter;° and, my fortunes against any lay° worth naming, 280
    this crack of your love shall grow stronger than it was before.

Cassio: You advise me well.

Iago: I protest,° in the sincerity of love and honest kindness.

Cassio: I think it freely;° and betimes in the morning I will beseech the virtuous
    Desdemona to undertake for me. I am desperate of my fortunes if they 285
    check° me here.

Iago: You are in the right. Good night, Lieutenant. I must to the watch.

Cassio: Good night, honest Iago.   *Exit Cassio.*

Iago: And what's he then that says I play the villain,
    When this advice is free° I give, and honest, 290
    Probal° to thinking, and indeed the course
    To win the Moor again? For 'tis most easy
    Th' inclining° Desdemona to subdue°
    In any honest suit; she's framed as fruitful°
    As the free elements.° And then for her 295
    To win the Moor—were 't to renounce his baptism,
    All seals and symbols of redeemèd sin—

---

262 *moraler* moralizer   266 *Hydra* the Lernaean Hydra, a monster with many heads and the ability
to grow two heads when one was cut off, slain by Hercules as the second of his twelve labors   272
approved proved   273 *at a time* at one time or another   274–275 *in . . . that* in view of this fact, that
275–276 *mark, and denotement* (Both words mean "observation.")   276 *parts* qualities   277 *free* generous   280 *splinter* bind with splints.   *lay* stake, wager   283 *protest* insist, declare   284 *freely* unre-
servedly   286 *check* repulse   290 *free* (1) free from guile (2) freely given   291 *Probal* probable, reasonable   293 *inclining* favorably disposed.   *subdue* persuade   294 *framed as fruitful* created as
generous   295 *free elements* i.e., earth, air, fire, and water, unrestrained and spontaneous

His soul is so enfettered to her love
That she may make, unmake, do what she list,
Even as her appetite° shall play the god   300
With his weak function.° How am I then a villain,
To counsel Cassio to this parallel° course
Directly to his good? Divinity of hell!°
When devils will the blackest sins put on,°
They do suggest° at first with heavenly shows,   305
As I do now. For whiles this honest fool
Plies Desdemona to repair his fortune,
And she for him pleads strongly to the Moor,
I'll pour this pestilence into his ear,
That she repeals him° for her body's lust;   310
And by how much she strives to do him good,
She shall undo her credit with the Moor.
So will I turn her virtue into pitch,°
And out of her own goodness make the net
That shall enmesh them all.

Enter Roderigo.

                                 How now, Roderigo?   315

Roderigo: I do follow here in the chase, not like a hound that hunts, but one that
fills up the cry.° My money is almost spent; I have been tonight exceedingly
well cudgeled; and I think the issue will be I shall have so much° experience
for my pains, and so, with no money at all and a little more wit, return again
to Venice.   320

Iago: How poor are they that have not patience!
What wound did ever heal but by degrees?
Thou know'st we work by wit, and not by witchcraft,
And wit depends on dilatory time.
Does 't not go well? Cassio hath beaten thee,   325
And thou, by that small hurt, hast cashiered° Cassio.
Though other things grow fair against the sun,
Yet fruits that blossom first will first be ripe.°
Content thyself awhile. By the Mass, 'tis morning!
Pleasure and action make the hours seem short.   330
Retire thee; go where thou art billeted.
Away, I say! Thou shalt know more hereafter.
                                                     Exit Roderigo.
Nay, get thee gone.

---

300 *her appetite* her desire, or, perhaps, his desire for her   301 *function* exercise of faculties (weakened by his fondness for her)   302 *parallel* corresponding to these facts and to his best interests   303
Divinity of hell inverted theology of hell (which seduces the soul to its damnation)   304 *put on* further, instigate   305 *suggest* tempt   310 *repeals him* attempts to get him restored   313 *pitch* i.e., (1)
foul blackness (2) a snaring substance   317 *fills up the cry* merely takes part as one of the pack   318
so much just so much and no more   326 *cashiered* dismissed from service   327–328 *Though . . . ripe*
i.e., plans that are well prepared and set expeditiously in motion will soonest ripen into success

Two things are to be done.
My wife must move° for Cassio to her mistress;
I'll set her on;   335
Myself the while to draw the Moor apart
And bring him jump° when he may Cassio find
Soliciting his wife. Ay, that's the way.
Dull not device° by coldness° and delay.   *Exit.*

ACT III

Scene I [Before the Chamber of Othello and Desdemona.]

Enter Cassio [and] Musicians.

Cassio: Masters, play here—I will content your pains°—
 Something that's brief, and bid "Good morrow, General."   [*They play.*]

 [*Enter*] *Clown.*

Clown: Why, masters, have your instruments been in Naples, that they speak i'
 the nose° thus?
A Musician: How, sir, how?   5
Clown: Are these, I pray you, wind instruments?
A Musician: Ay, marry, are they, sir.
Clown: O, thereby hangs a tail.
A Musician: Whereby hangs a tale, sir?
Clown: Marry, sir, by many a wind instrument° that I know. But, masters, here's 10
 money for you. [*He gives money.*] And the General so likes your music that
 he desires you, for love's sake,° to make no more noise with it.
A Musician: Well, sir, we will not.
Clown: If you have any music that may not° be heard, to 't again; but, as they
 say, to hear music the General does not greatly care.   15
A Musician: We have none such, sir.
Clown: Then put up your pipes in your bag, for I'll away.° Go, vanish into air,
 away!   *Exeunt Musicians.*
Cassio: Dost thou hear, mine honest friend?
Clown: No, I hear not your honest friend; I hear you.   20
Cassio: Prithee, keep up° thy quillets.° There's a poor piece of gold for thee. [*He
 gives money.*] If the gentle-woman that attends the General's wife be stirring,

---

334 *move* plead   337 *jump* precisely   339 *device* plot.   *coldness* lack of zeal   1 *content your pains* reward your efforts   3–4 *speak i' the nose* (1) sound nasal (2) sound like one whose nose has been attacked by syphilis. (Naples was popularly supposed to have a high incidence of venereal disease.)
10 *wind instrument* (With a joke on flatulence. The *tail*, line 8, that hangs nearby the *wind instrument*
suggests the penis.)   12 *for love's sake* (1) out of friendship and affection (2) for the sake of lovemaking in Othello's marriage   14 *may not* cannot   17 *I'll away* (Possibly a misprint, or a snatch of
song?)   21 *keep up* do not bring out, do not use.   *quillets* quibbles, puns

tell her there's one Cassio entreats her a little favor of speech.° Wilt thou do
this?

Clown: She is stirring, sir. If she will stir° hither, I shall seem° to notify unto her.   25

Cassio: Do, good my friend.   *Exit Clown.*

Enter Iago.

                        In happy time,° Iago.

Iago: You have not been abed, then?

Cassio: Why, no. The day had broke
      Before we parted. I have made bold, Iago,
      To send in to your wife. My suit to her   30
      Is that she will to virtuous Desdemona
      Procure me some access.

Iago: I'll send her to you presently;
      And I'll devise a means to draw the Moor
      Out of the way, that your converse and business   35
      May be more free.

Cassio: I humbly thank you for 't.   *Exit [Iago].*
                        I never knew
      A Florentine° more kind and honest.

Enter Emilia.

Emilia: Good morrow, good Lieutenant. I am sorry
      For your displeasure;° but all will sure be well.   40
      The General and his wife are talking of it,
      And she speaks for you stoutly.° The Moor replies
      That he you hurt is of great fame° in Cyprus
      And great affinity,° and that in wholesome wisdom
      He might not but refuse you; but he protests° he loves you   45
      And needs no other suitor but his likings
      To take the safest occasion by the front°
      To bring you in again.

Cassio: Yet I beseech you,
      If you think fit, or that it may be done,
      Give me advantage of some brief discourse   50
      With Desdemon alone.

Emilia: Pray you, come in.
                  I will bestow you where you shall have time

To speak your bosom° freely.
Cassio: I am much bound to you.   [*Exeunt.*]

Scene II [The Citadel.]

Enter Othello, Iago, and Gentlemen.

Othello [*giving letters*]: These letters give, Iago, to the pilot,
       And by him do my duties° to the Senate.
       That done, I will be walking on the works;°
       Repair° there to me.
Iago: Well, my good lord, I'll do 't.
Othello: This fortification, gentlemen, shall we see 't?   5
Gentlemen: We'll wait upon° your lordship.   *Exeunt.*

Scene III [The Garden of the Citadel.]

Enter Desdemona, Cassio, and Emilia.

Desdemona: Be thou assured, good Cassio, I will do
       All my abilities in thy behalf.
Emilia: Good madam, do. I warrant it grieves my husband
       As if the cause were his.
Desdemona: O, that's an honest fellow. Do not doubt, Cassio,   5
       But I will have my lord and you again
       As friendly as you were.
Cassio: Bounteous madam,
       Whatever shall become of Michael Cassio,
       He's never anything but your true servant.
Desdemona: I know 't. I thank you. You do love my lord;   10
       You have known him long, and be you well assured
       He shall in strangeness° stand no farther off
       Than in a politic° distance.
Cassio: Ay, but, lady,
       That policy may either last so long,
       Or feed upon such nice and waterish diet,°   15
       Or breed itself so out of circumstance,°
       That, I being absent and my place supplied,°
       My general will forget my love and service.
Desdemona: Do not doubt° that. Before Emilia here
       I give thee warrant° of thy place. Assure thee,   20
       If I do vow a friendship I'll perform it
       To the last article. My lord shall never rest.

---

53 *bosom* inmost thoughts   2 *do my duties* convey my respects   3 *works* breastworks, fortifications
4 *Repair* return, come   6 *wait upon* attend   12 *strangeness* aloofness   13 *politic* required by wise
policy   15 *Or . . . diet* or sustain itself at length upon such trivial and meager technicalities   16
breed . . . circumstance continually renew itself so out of chance events, or yield so few chances for my
being pardoned   17 *supplied* filled by another person   19 *doubt* fear   20 *warrant* guarantee

I'll watch him tame° and talk him out of patience;°
His bed shall seem a school, his board° a shrift;°   25
I'll intermingle everything he does
With Cassio's suit. Therefore be merry, Cassio,
For thy solicitor° shall rather die
Than give thy cause away.°

Enter Othello and Iago [at a distance].

Emilia: Madam, here comes my lord.
Cassio: Madam, I'll take my leave.   30
Desdemona: Why, stay, and hear me speak.
Cassio: Madam, not now. I am very ill at ease,
    Unfit for mine own purposes.
Desdemona: Well, do your discretion.°   *Exit Cassio.*
Iago: Ha? I like not that.   35
Othello: What dost thou say?
Iago: Nothing, my lord; or if—I know not what.
Othello: Was not that Cassio parted from my wife?
Iago: Cassio, my lord? No, sure, I cannot think it,
    That he would steal away so guiltylike,   40
    Seeing you coming.
Othello: I do believe 'twas he.
Desdemona: How now, my lord?
    I have been talking with a suitor here,
    A man that languishes in your displeasure.   45
Othello: Who is 't you mean?
Desdemona: Why, your lieutenant, Cassio. Good my lord,
    If I have any grace or power to move you,
    His present reconciliation take;°
    For if he be not one that truly loves you,   50
    That errs in ignorance and not in cunning,°
    I have no judgment in an honest face.
    I prithee, call him back.
Othello: Went he hence now?
Desdemona: Yes, faith, so humbled   55
    That he hath left part of his grief with me
    To suffer with him. Good love, call him back.
Othello: Not now, sweet Desdemon. Some other time.
Desdemona: But shall 't be shortly?
Othello: The sooner, sweet, for you.   60
Desdemona: Shall 't be tonight at supper?

23 *watch him tame* tame him by keeping him from sleeping. (A term from falconry.) *out of patience*
past his endurance   24 *board* dining table.   *shrift* confessional   27 *solicitor* advocate   28 *away* up
34 *do your discretion* act according to your own discretion   49 *His . . . take* let him be reconciled to
you right away   51 *in cunning* wittingly

Othello: No, not tonight.
Desdemona: Tomorrow dinner,° then?
Othello: I shall not dine at home.
　　I meet the captains at the citadel. 65
Desdemona: Why, then, tomorrow night, or Tuesday morn,
　　On Tuesday noon, or night, on Wednesday morn.
　　I prithee, name the time, but let it not
　　Exceed three days. In faith, he's penitent;
　　And yet his trespass, in our common reason°— 70
　　Save that, they say, the wars must make example
　　Out of her best°—is not almost° a fault
　　T' incur a private check.° When shall he come?
　　Tell me, Othello. I wonder in my soul
　　What you would ask me that I should deny, 75
　　Or stand so mammering on.° What? Michael Cassio,
　　That came a-wooing with you, and so many a time,
　　When I have spoke of you dispraisingly,
　　Hath ta'en your part—to have so much to do
　　To bring him in!° By 'r Lady, I could do much— 80
Othello: Prithee, no more. Let him come when he will;
　　I will deny thee nothing.
Desdemona: Why, this is not a boon.
　　'Tis as I should entreat you wear your gloves,
　　Or feed on nourishing dishes, or keep you warm, 85
　　Or sue to you to do a peculiar° profit
　　To your own person. Nay, when I have a suit
　　Wherein I mean to touch° your love indeed,
　　It shall be full of poise° and difficult weight,
　　And fearful to be granted. 90
Othello: I will deny thee nothing.
　　Whereon,° I do beseech thee, grant me this,
　　To leave me but a little to myself.
Desdemona: Shall I deny you? No. Farewell, my lord.
Othello: Farewell, my Desdemona. I'll come to thee straight.° 95
Desdemona: Emilia, come.—Be as your fancies° teach you;
　　Whate'er you be, I am obedient. 　　　　*Exit [with Emilia].*
Othello: Excellent wretch!° Perdition catch my soul
　　But I do love thee! And when I love thee not,

---

63 *dinner* (The noontime meal.) 70 *common reason* everyday judgments 71–72 *Save . . . best* were it not that, as the saying goes, military discipline requires making an example of the very best men. (Her refers to *wars* as a singular concept.) 72 *not almost* scarcely 73 *private check* even a private reprimand 76 *mammering on* wavering about 80 *bring him in* restore him to favor 86 *peculiar* particular, personal 88 *touch* test 89 *poise* weight, heaviness; or equipoise, delicate balance involving hard choice 92 *Whereon* in return for which 95 *straight* straightway 96 *fancies* inclinations 98 *wretch* (A term of affectionate endearment.)

Chaos is come again.° 100
Iago: My noble lord—
Othello: What dost thou say, Iago?
Iago: Did Michael Cassio, when you wooed my lady,
    Know of your love?
Othello: He did, from first to last. Why dost thou ask? 105
Iago: But for a satisfaction of my thought;
    No further harm.
Othello: Why of thy thought, Iago?
Iago: I did not think he had been acquainted with her.
Othello: O, yes, and went between us very oft.
Iago: Indeed? 110
Othello: Indeed? Ay, indeed. Discern'st thou aught in that?
    Is he not honest?
Iago: Honest, my lord?
Othello: Honest. Ay, honest.
Iago: My lord, for aught I know. 115
Othello: What dost thou think?
Iago: Think, my lord?
Othello: "Think, my lord?" By heaven, thou echo'st me,
    As if there were some monster in thy thought
    Too hideous to be shown. Thou dost mean something. 120
    I heard thee say even now, thou lik'st not that,
    When Cassio left my wife. What didst not like?
    And when I told thee he was of my counsel°
    In my whole course of wooing, thou criedst "Indeed?"
    And didst contract and purse° thy brow together 125
    As if thou then hadst shut up in thy brain
    Some horrible conceit.° If thou dost love me,
    Show me thy thought.
Iago: My lord, you know I love you.
Othello: I think thou dost; 130
    And, for° I know thou'rt full of love and honesty,
    And weigh'st thy words before thou giv'st them breath,
    Therefore these stops° of thine fright me the more;
    For such things in a false disloyal knave
    Are tricks of custom,° but in a man that's just 135
    They're close dilations,° working from the heart
    That passion cannot rule.°

99–100 *And . . . again* i.e., my love for you will last forever, until the end of time when chaos will re-turn. (But with an unconscious, ironic suggestion that, if anything should induce Othello to cease loving Desdemona, the result would be chaos.)　123 *of my counsel* in my confidence　125 *purse* knit　127 *conceit* fancy　131 *for* because　133 *stops* pauses　135 *of custom* customary　136 *close dilations* secret or involuntary expressions or delays　137 *That passion cannot rule* i.e., that are too passionately strong to be restrained (referring to the workings), or, that cannot rule its own passions (referring to the heart).

Iago: For° Michael Cassio,
    I dare be sworn I think that he is honest.
Othello: I think so too.
Iago: Men should be what they seem;
    Or those that be not, would they might seem none!°   140
Othello: Certain, men should be what they seem.
Iago: Why, then, I think Cassio's an honest man.
Othello: Nay, yet there's more in this.
    I prithee, speak to me as to thy thinkings,
    As thou dost ruminate, and give thy worst of thoughts   145
    The worst of words.
Iago: Good my lord, pardon me.
    Though I am bound to every act of duty,
    I am not bound to that° all slaves are free to.°
    Utter my thoughts? Why, say they are vile and false,
    As where's the palace whereinto foul things   150
    Sometimes intrude not? Who has that breast so pure
    But some uncleanly apprehensions
    Keep leets and law days,° and in sessions sit
    With° meditations lawful?°
Othello: Thou dost conspire against thy friend,° Iago,   155
    If thou but think'st him wronged and mak'st his ear
    A stranger to thy thoughts.
Iago: I do beseech you,
    Though I perchance am vicious° in my guess—
    As I confess it is my nature's plague
    To spy into abuses, and oft my jealousy°   160
    Shapes faults that are not—that your wisdom then,°
    From one° that so imperfectly conceits,°
    Would take no notice, nor build yourself a trouble
    Out of his scattering° and unsure observance.
    It were not for your quiet nor your good,   165
    Nor for my manhood, honesty, and wisdom,
    To let you know my thoughts.
Othello: What dost thou mean?
Iago: Good name in man and woman, dear my lord,
    Is the immediate° jewel of their souls.
    Who steals my purse steals trash; 'tis something, nothing;   170
    'Twas mine, 'tis his, and has been slave to thousands;

---

137 *For* as for   140 *none* i.e., not to be men, or not seem to be honest   148 *that* that which.   *free to* free with respect to   153 *Keep leets and law days* i.e., hold court, set up their authority in one's heart. (*Leets* are a kind of manor court; *law days* are the days courts sit in session, or those sessions.)   154 *With* along with.   *lawful* innocent   155 *thy friend* i.e., Othello   158 *vicious* wrong   160 *jealousy* suspicious nature   161 *then* on that account   162 *one* i.e., myself, Iago.   *conceits* judges, conjectures   164 *scattering* random   169 *immediate* essential, most precious

But he that filches from me my good name
Robs me of that which not enriches him
And makes me poor indeed.
Othello: By heaven, I'll know thy thoughts.   175
Iago: You cannot, if° my heart were in your hand,
   Nor shall not, whilst 'tis in my custody.
Othello: Ha?
Iago: O, beware, my lord, of jealousy.
   It is the green-eyed monster which doth mock
   The meat it feeds on.° That cuckold lives in bliss   180
   Who, certain of his fate, loves not his wronger;°
   But O, what damnèd minutes tells° he o'er
   Who dotes, yet doubts, suspects, yet fondly loves!
Othello: O misery!
Iago: Poor and content is rich, and rich enough,°   185
   But riches fineless° is as poor as winter
   To him that ever fears he shall be poor.
   Good God, the souls of all my tribe defend
   From jealousy!
Othello: Why, why is this?   190
   Think'st thou I'd make a life of jealousy,
   To follow still the changes of the moon
   With fresh suspicions?° No! To be once in doubt
   Is once° to be resolved.° Exchange me for a goat
   When I shall turn the business of my soul   195
   To such exsufflicate and blown° surmises
   Matching thy inference.° 'Tis not to make me jealous
   To say my wife is fair, feeds well, loves company,
   Is free of speech, sings, plays, and dances well;
   Where virtue is, these are more virtuous.   200
   Nor from mine own weak merits will I draw
   The smallest fear or doubt of her revolt,°
   For she had eyes, and chose me. No, Iago,
   I'll see before I doubt; when I doubt, prove;
   And on the proof, there is no more but this—   205
   Away at once with love or jealousy.

---

176 *if* even if   179–180 *doth mock . . . on* mocks and torments the heart of its victim, the man who
suffers jealousy   181 *his wronger* i.e., his faithless wife. (The unsuspecting cuckold is spared the
misery of loving his wife only to discover she is cheating on him.)   182 *tells* counts   185 *Poor . . .
enough* to be content with what little one has is the greatest wealth of all. (Proverbial.)   186 *fineless*
boundless   192–193 *To follow . . . suspicions* to be constantly imagining new causes for suspicion,
changing incessantly like the moon   194 *once* once and for all.   *resolved* free of doubt, having settled the matter   196 *exsufflicate and blown* inflated and blown up, rumored about, or, spat out and fly-
blown, hence, loathsome, disgusting   197 *inference* description or allegation   202 *doubt . . . revolt*
fear of her unfaithfulness

Iago: I am glad of this, for now I shall have reason
    To show the love and duty that I bear you
    With franker spirit. Therefore, as I am bound,
    Receive it from me. I speak not yet of proof. 210
    Look to your wife; observe her well with Cassio.
    Wear your eyes thus, not° jealous nor secure.°
    I would not have your free and noble nature,
    Out of self-bounty,° be abused.° Look to 't.
    I know our country disposition well; 215
    In Venice they do let God see the pranks
    They dare not show their husbands; their best conscience
    Is not to leave 't undone, but keep 't unknown.
Othello: Dost thou say so?
Iago: She did deceive her father, marrying you; 220
    And when she seemed to shake and fear your looks,
    She loved them most.
Othello: And so she did.
Iago: Why, go to,° then!
    She that, so young, could give out such a seeming,°
    To seel° her father's eyes up close as oak,°
    He thought 'twas witchcraft! But I am much to blame. 225
    I humbly do beseech you of your pardon
    For too much loving you.
Othello: I am bound° to thee forever.
Iago: I see this hath a little dashed your spirits.
Othello: Not a jot, not a jot.
Iago: I' faith, I fear it has. 230
    I hope you will consider what is spoke
    Comes from my love. But I do see you're moved.
    I am to pray you not to strain my speech
    To grosser issues° nor to larger reach°
    Than to suspicion. 235
Othello: I will not.
Iago: Should you do so, my lord,
    My speech should fall into such vile success°
    Which my thoughts aimed not. Cassio's my worthy friend.
    My lord, I see you're moved.
Othello: No, not much moved. 240
    I do not think but Desdemona's honest.°
Iago: Long live she so! And long live you to think so!

---

212 *not* neither. *secure* free from uncertainty 214 *self-bounty* inherent or natural goodness and generosity. *abused* deceived 222 *go to* (An expression of impatience.) 223 *seeming* false appearance 224 *seel* blind. (A term from falconry.) *oak* (A close-grained wood.) 228 *bound* indebted (but perhaps with ironic sense of "tied") 234 *issues* significances. *reach* meaning, scope 238 *success* effect, result 241 *honest* chaste

Othello: And yet, how nature erring from itself—
Iago: Ay, there's the point! As—to be bold with you—
    Not to affect° many proposèd matches   245
    Of her own clime, complexion, and degree,°
    Whereto we see in all things nature tends—
    Foh! One may smell in such a will° most rank,
    Foul disproportion,° thoughts unnatural.
    But pardon me. I do not in position°   250
    Distinctly speak of her, though I may fear
    Her will, recoiling° to her better° judgment,
    May fall to match you with her country forms°
    And happily° repent.
Othello: Farewell, farewell!
    If more thou dost perceive, let me know more.   255
    Set on thy wife to observe. Leave me, Iago.
Iago [*going*]: My lord, I take my leave.
Othello: Why did I marry? This honest creature doubtless
    Sees and knows more, much more, than he unfolds.
Iago [*returning*]: My Lord, I would I might entreat your honor   260
    To scan° this thing no farther. Leave it to time.
    Although 'tis fit that Cassio have his place—
    For, sure, he fills it up with great ability—
    Yet, if you please to hold him off awhile,
    You shall by that perceive him and his means.°   265
    Note if your lady strain his entertainment°
    With any strong or vehement importunity;
    Much will be seen in that. In the meantime,
    Let me be thought too busy° in my fears—
    As worthy cause I have to fear I am—   270
    And hold her free,° I do beseech your honor.
Othello: Fear not my government.°
Iago: I once more take my leave.   *Exit.*
Othello: This fellow's of exceeding honesty,
    And knows all qualities,° with a learnèd spirit,   275
    Of human dealings. If I do prove her haggard,°
    Though that her jesses° were my dear heartstrings,
    I'd whistle her off and let her down the wind°

---

245 *affect* prefer, desire   246 *clime . . . degree* country, color, and social position   248 *will* sensuality, appetite   249 *disproportion* abnormality   250 *position* argument, proposition   252 *recoiling* reverting. *better* i.e., more natural and reconsidered   253 *fall . . . forms* undertake to compare you with Venetian norms of handsomeness   254 *happily repent* haply repent her marriage   261 *scan* scrutinize   265 *his means* the method he uses (to regain his post)   266 *strain his entertainment* urge his reinstatement   269 *busy* interfering   271 *hold her free* regard her as innocent   272 *government* self-control, conduct   275 *qualities* natures, types   276 *haggard* wild (like a wild female hawk)   277 *jesses* straps fastened around the legs of a trained hawk   278 *I'd . . . wind* i.e., I'd let her go forever. (To release a hawk downwind was to invite it not to return.)

To prey at fortune.° Haply, for° I am black
And have not those soft parts of conversation°
That chamberers° have, or for I am declined   280
Into the vale of years—yet that's not much—
She's gone. I am abused,° and my relief
Must be to loathe her. O curse of marriage,
That we can call these delicate creatures ours   285
And not their appetites! I had rather be a toad
And live upon the vapor of a dungeon
Than keep a corner in the thing I love
For others' uses. Yet, 'tis the plague of great ones;
Prerogatived° are they less than the base.°   290
'Tis destiny unshunnable, like death.
Even then this forkèd° plague is fated to us
When we do quicken.° Look where she comes.

Enter Desdemona and Emilia.

If she be false, O, then heaven mocks itself!
I'll not believe 't.
Desdemona: How now, my dear Othello?   295
Your dinner, and the generous° islanders
By you invited, do attend° your presence.
Othello: I am to blame.
Desdemona: Why do you speak so faintly?
Are you not well?
Othello: I have a pain upon my forehead here.   300
Desdemona: Faith, that's with watching.° 'Twill away again.

[*She offers her handkerchief.*]

Let me but bind it hard, within this hour
It will be well.
Othello: Your napkin° is too little.
Let it alone.° Come, I'll go in with you.

[*He puts the handkerchief from him, and it drops.*]

Desdemona: I am very sorry that you are not well.   305

Exit [with Othello].

---

279 *prey at fortune* fend for herself in the wild.   *Haply, for* perhaps because   280 *soft . . . conversa-tion* pleasing graces of social behavior   281 *chamberers* gallants   283 *abused* deceived   290 *Preroga-tived* privileged (to have honest wives).   *the base* ordinary citizens. (Socially prominent men are es-pecially prone to the unavoidable destiny of being cuckolded and to the public shame that goes with it.)   292 *forkèd* (An allusion to the horns of the cuckold.)   293 *quicken* receive life. (Quicken may also mean to swarm with maggots as the body festers, as in Act IV, Scene ii, line 69, in which case lines 292–293 suggest that *even then*, in death, we are cuckolded by *forkèd* worms.)   296 *generous* noble   297 *attend* await   301 *watching* too little sleep   303 *napkin* handkerchief   304 *Let it alone* i.e., never mind

Emilia [*picking up the handkerchief*]: I am glad I have found this napkin.
This was her first remembrance from the Moor.
My wayward° husband hath a hundred times
Wooed me to steal it, but she so loves the token—
For he conjured her she should ever keep it—   310
That she reserves it evermore about her
To kiss and talk to. I'll have the work ta'en out,°
And give 't Iago. What he will do with it
Heaven knows, not I;
I nothing but to please his fantasy.°   315

    Enter Iago.

Iago: How now? What do you here alone?
Emilia: Do not you chide. I have a thing for you.
Iago: You have a thing for me? It is a common thing°—
Emilia: Ha?
Iago: To have a foolish wife.   320
Emilia: O, is that all? What will you give me now
    For that same handkerchief?
Iago: What handkerchief?
Emilia: What handkerchief?
    Why, that the Moor first gave to Desdemona;   325
    That which so often you did bid me steal.
Iago: Hast stolen it from her?
Emilia: No, faith. She let it drop by negligence,
    And to th' advantage° I, being here, took 't up.
    Look, here 'tis.
Iago: A good wench! Give it me.   330
Emilia: What will you do with 't, that you have been so earnest
    To have me filch it?
Iago [*snatching it*]:   Why, what is that to you?
Emilia: If it be not for some purpose of import,
    Give 't me again. Poor lady, she'll run mad
    When she shall lack° it.
Iago: Be not acknown on 't.°   335
    I have use for it. Go, leave me.   *Exit Emilia.*
    I will in Cassio's lodging lose° this napkin
    And let him find it. Trifles light as air
    Are to the jealous confirmations strong
    As proofs of Holy Writ. This may do something.   340

---

308 *wayward* capricious   312 *work ta'en out* design of the embroidery copied   315 *fantasy* whim
318 *common thing* (With bawdy suggestion; *common* suggests coarseness and availability to all comers,
and *thing* is a slang term for the pudendum.)   329 *to th' advantage* taking the opportunity   335 *lack*
miss.   *Be . . . on't* do not confess knowledge of it   337 *lose* (The Folio spelling, *loose*, is a normal
spelling for "lose," but it may also contain the idea of "let go," "release.")

The Moor already changes with my poison.
Dangerous conceits° are in their natures poisons,
Which at the first are scarce found to distaste,°
But with a little act° upon the blood
Burn like the mines of sulfur.

Enter Othello.

                          I did say so.   345
Look where he comes! Not poppy nor mandragora°
Nor all the drowsy syrups of the world
Shall ever medicine thee to that sweet sleep
Which thou owedst° yesterday.
Othello: Ha, ha, false to me?
Iago: Why, how now, General? No more of that.   350
Othello: Avaunt! Begone! Thou hast set me on the rack.
    I swear 'tis better to be much abused
    Than but to know 't a little.
Iago: How now, my lord?
Othello: What sense had I of her stolen hours of lust?
    I saw 't not, thought it not, it harmed not me.   355
    I slept the next night well, fed well, was free° and merry;
    I found not Cassio's kisses on her lips.
    He that is robbed, not wanting° what is stolen,
    Let him not know 't and he's not robbed at all.
Iago: I am sorry to hear this.   360
Othello: I had been happy if the general camp,
    Pioners° and all, had tasted her sweet body,
    So° I had nothing known. O, now, forever
    Farewell the tranquil mind! Farewell content!
    Farewell the plumèd troops and the big° wars   365
    That makes ambition virtue! O, farewell!
    Farewell the neighing steed and the shrill trump,
    The spirit-stirring drum, th' ear-piercing fife,
    The royal banner, and all quality,°
    Pride,° pomp, and circumstance° of glorious war!   370
    And O, you mortal engines,° whose rude throats
    Th' immortal Jove's dread clamors° counterfeit,
    Farewell! Othello's occupation's gone.
Iago: Is 't possible, my lord?
Othello: Villain, be sure thou prove my love a whore!   375

---

342 *conceits* fancies, ideas   343 *distaste* be distasteful   344 *act* action, working   346 *mandragora* an opiate made of the mandrake root   349 *thou owedst* you did own   356 *free* carefree   358 *wanting* missing   362 *Pioners* diggers of mines, the lowest grade of soldiers   363 *So* provided   365 *big* stately 369 *quality* character, essential nature   370 *Pride* rich display. *circumstance* pageantry   371 *mortal engines* i.e., cannon. (*Mortal* means "deadly.")   372 *Jove's dread clamors* i.e., thunder

Be sure of it. Give me the ocular proof,
Or, by the worth of mine eternal soul,
Thou hadst been better have been born a dog
Than answer my waked wrath!
Iago: Is 't come to this?
Othello: Make me to see 't, or at the least so prove it   380
    That the probation° bear no hinge nor loop
    To hang a doubt on, or woe upon thy life!
Iago: My noble lord—
Othello: If thou dost slander her and torture me,
    Never pray more; abandon all remorse;°   385
    On horror's head horrors accumulate;°
    Do deeds to make heaven weep, all earth amazed;°
    For nothing canst thou to damnation add
    Greater than that.
Iago: O grace! O heaven forgive me!
    Are you a man? Have you a soul or sense?   390
    God b' wi' you; take mine office. O wretched fool,°
    That lov'st to make thine honesty a vice!°
    O monstrous world! Take note, take note, O world,
    To be direct and honest is not safe.
    I thank you for this profit,° and from hence°   395
    I'll love no friend, sith° love breeds such offense.°
Othello: Nay, stay. Thou shouldst be° honest.
Iago: I should be wise, for honesty's a fool
    And loses that° it works for.
Othello: By the world,
    I think my wife be honest and think she is not;   400
    I think that thou art just and think thou art not.
    I'll have some proof. My name, that was as fresh
    As Dian's° visage, is now begrimed and black
    As mine own face. If there be cords, or knives,
    Poison, or fire, or suffocating streams,   405
    I'll not endure it. Would I were satisfied!
Iago: I see, sir, you are eaten up with passion.
    I do repent me that I put it to you.
    You would be satisfied?
Othello: Would? Nay, and I will.
Iago: And may; but how? How satisfied, my lord?   410

---

381 *probation* proof   385 *remorse* pity, penitent hope for salvation   386 *horrors accumulate* add still
more horrors   387 *amazed* confounded with horror   391 *O wretched fool* (Iago addresses himself as a
fool for having carried honesty too far.)   392 *vice* failing, something overdone   395 *profit* profitable
instruction. *hence* henceforth   396 *sith* since. *offense* i.e., harm to the one who offers help and
friendship   397 *Thou shouldst be* it appears that you are. (But Iago replies in the sense of "ought to
be.")   399 *that* what   403 *Dian* Diana, goddess of the moon and of chastity

Would you, the supervisor,° grossly gape on?
Behold her topped?

Othello:　　　　　　　　Death and damnation! O!

Iago:　It were a tedious difficulty, I think,
　To bring them to that prospect. Damn them then,°
　If ever mortal eyes do see them bolster°　　　　　　　　　　415
　More° than their own.° What then? How then?
　What shall I say? Where's satisfaction?
　It is impossible you should see this,
　Were they as prime° as goats, as hot as monkeys,
　As salt° as wolves in pride,° and fools as gross　　　　　　420
　As ignorance made drunk. But yet I say,
　If imputation and strong circumstances°
　Which lead directly to the door of truth
　Will give you satisfaction, you might have 't.

Othello:　Give me a living reason she's disloyal.　　　　　425

Iago:　I do not like the office.
　But sith° I am entered in this cause so far,
　Pricked° to 't by foolish honesty and love,
　I will go on. I lay with Cassio lately,
　And being troubled with a raging tooth　　　　　　　　430
　I could not sleep. There are a kind of men
　So loose of soul that in their sleeps will mutter
　Their affairs. One of this kind is Cassio.
　In sleep I heard him say, "Sweet Desdemona,
　Let us be wary, let us hide our loves!"　　　　　　　　435
　And then, sir, would he grip and wring my hand,
　Cry "O sweet creature!", then kiss me hard,
　As if he plucked up kisses by the roots
　That grew upon my lips; then laid his leg
　Over my thigh, and sighed, and kissed, and then　　　440
　Cried, "Cursèd fate that gave thee to the Moor!"

Othello:　O monstrous! Monstrous!

Iago:　　　　　　　　Nay, this was but his dream.

Othello:　But this denoted a foregone conclusion.°
　'Tis a shrewd doubt,° though it be but a dream.

Iago:　And this may help to thicken other proofs　　　　445
　That do demonstrate thinly.

Othello:　　　　　　　　I'll tear her all to pieces.

Iago:　Nay, but be wise. Yet we see nothing done;

---

411 *supervisor* onlooker　414 *Damn them then* i.e., they would have to be really incorrigible　415
bolster go to bed together, share a bolster　416 *More* other.　*own* own eyes　419 *prime* lustful　420
salt wanton, sensual.　*pride* heat　422 *imputation . . . circumstances* strong circumstantial evidence
427 *sith* since　428 *Pricked* spurred　443 *foregone conclusion* concluded experience or action　444
shrewd doubt suspicious circumstance

She may be honest yet. Tell me but this:
Have you not sometimes seen a handkerchief
Spotted with strawberries° in your wife's hand?   450
Othello: I gave her such a one. 'Twas my first gift.
Iago: I know not that; but such a handkerchief—
    I am sure it was your wife's—did I today
    See Cassio wipe his beard with.
Othello: If it be that—   455
Iago: If it be that, or any that was hers,
    It speaks against her with the other proofs.
Othello: O, that the slave° had forty thousand lives!
    One is too poor, too weak for my revenge.
    Now do I see 'tis true. Look here, Iago,
    All my fond° love thus do I blow to heaven.   460
    'Tis gone.
    Arise, black vengeance, from the hollow hell!
    Yield up, O love, thy crown and hearted° throne
    To tyrannous hate! Swell, bosom, with thy freight,°
    For 'tis of aspics'° tongues!   465
Iago: Yet be content.°
Othello: O, blood, blood, blood!
Iago: Patience, I say. Your mind perhaps may change.
Othello: Never, Iago. Like to the Pontic Sea,°
    Whose icy current and compulsive course   470
    Ne'er feels retiring ebb, but keeps due on
    To the Propontic° and the Hellespont,°
    Even so my bloody thoughts with violent pace
    Shall ne'er look back, ne'er ebb to humble love,
    I that a capable° and wide revenge   475
    Swallow them up. Now, by yond marble° heaven,
    [*Kneeling*] In the due reverence of a sacred vow
    I here engage my words.
Iago: Do not rise yet.
    [*He kneels.*]° Witness, you ever-burning lights above,
    You elements that clip° us round about,   480
    Witness that here Iago doth give up
    The execution° of his wit,° hands, heart,
    To wronged Othello's service. Let him command,

450 *Spotted with strawberries* embroidered with a strawberry pattern   457 *the slave* i.e., Cassio   460 *fond* foolish (but also suggesting "affectionate")   463 *hearted* fixed in the heart   464 *freight* burden   465 *aspics'* venomous serpents'   466 *content* calm   469 *Pontic Sea* Black Sea   472 *Propontic* Sea of Marmara, between the Black Sea and the Aegean.   *Helllespont* Dardanelles, straits where the Sea of Marmara joins with the Aegean   475 *capable* ample, comprehensive   476 *marble* i.e., gleaming like marble and unrelenting   479 s.d. *He kneels* (In the Quarto text, Iago kneels here after Othello has knelt at line 477.)   480 *clip* encompass   482 *execution* exercise, action.   *wit* mind

And to obey shall be in me remorse,°
What bloody business ever.°   [*They rise.*]

Othello: I greet thy love,   485
Not with vain thanks, but with acceptance bounteous,
And will upon the instant put thee to 't.°
Within these three days let me hear thee say
That Cassio's not alive.

Iago: My friend is dead;
'Tis done at your request. But let her live.   490

Othello: Damn her, lewd minx!° O, damn her, damn her!
Come, go with me apart. I will withdraw
To furnish me with some swift means of death
For the fair devil. Now art thou my lieutenant.

Iago: I am your own forever.   *Exeunt.*   495

Scene IV [Before the Citadel.]

Enter Desdemona, Emilia, and Clown.

Desdemona: Do you know, sirrah,° where Lieutenant Cassio lies?°

Clown: I dare not say he lies anywhere.

Desdemona: Why, man?

Clown: He's a soldier, and for me to say a soldier lies, 'tis stabbing.

Desdemona: Go to. Where lodges he?   5

Clown: To tell you where he lodges is to tell you where I lie.

Desdemona: Can anything be made of this?

Clown: I know not where he lodges, and for me to devise a lodging and say he
   lies here, or he lies there, were to lie in mine own throat.°

Desdemona: Can you inquire him out, and be edified by report?   10

Clown: I will catechize the world for him; that is, make questions, and by them
   answer.

Desdemona: Seek him, bid him come hither. Tell him I have moved° my lord on
   his behalf and hope all will be well.

Clown: To do this is within the compass of man's wit, and therefore I will at-   15
   tempt the doing it.   *Exit Clown.*

Desdemona: Where should I lose that handkerchief, Emilia?

Emilia: I know not, madam.

Desdemona: Believe me, I had rather have lost my purse
   Full of crusadoes;° and but my noble Moor
   Is true of mind and made of no such baseness   20
   As jealous creatures are, it were enough

---

484 *remorse* pity (for Othello's wrongs)   485 *ever* soever   487 *to 't* to the proof   491 *minx* wanton
1 *sirrah* (A form of address to an inferior.)   *lies* lodges. (But the Clown makes the obvious pun.)   9
lie . . . throat (1) lie egregiously and deliberately (2) use the windpipe to speak a lie   13 *moved* peti-
tioned   20 *crusadoes* Portuguese gold coins

> To put him to ill thinking.

Emilia: Is he not jealous?

Desdemona: Who, he? I think the sun where he was born

> Drew all such humors° from him.

Emilia: Look where he comes.   25

> *Enter Othello.*

Desdemona: I will not leave him now till Cassio

> Be called to him.—How is 't with you, my lord?

Othello: Well, my good lady. [*Aside.*] O, hardness to dissemble!—

> How do you, Desdemona?

Desdemona: Well, my good lord.

Othello: Give me your hand. [*She gives her hand.*] This hand is moist, my lady.   30

Desdemona: It yet hath felt no age nor known no sorrow.

Othello: This argues° fruitfulness° and liberal° heart.

> Hot, hot, and moist. This hand of yours requires
> A sequester° from liberty, fasting and prayer,
> Much castigation,° exercise devout;°   35
> For here's a young and sweating devil here
> That commonly rebels. 'Tis a good hand,
> A frank° one.

Desdemona: You may indeed say so,

> For 'twas that hand that gave away my heart.

Othello: A liberal hand. The hearts of old gave hands,°   40

> But our new heraldry is hands, not hearts.°

Desdemona: I cannot speak of this. Come now, your promise.

Othello: What promise, chuck?°

Desdemona: I have sent to bid Cassio come speak with you.

Othello: I have a salt and sorry rheum° offends me;   45

> Lend me thy handkerchief.

Desdemona: Here, my lord.   [*She offers a handkerchief.*]

Othello: That which I gave you.

Desdemona: I have it not about me.

Othello: Not?

Desdemona: No, faith, my lord.   50

Othello: That's a fault. That handkerchief

> Did an Egyptian to my mother give.
> She was a charmer,° and could almost read

---

25 *humors* (Refers to the four bodily fluids thought to determine temperament.)   32 *argues* gives evidence of.   *fruitfulness* generosity, amorousness, and fecundity.   *liberal* generous and sexually free   34 *sequester* separation, sequestration   35 *castigation* corrective discipline.   *exercise devout* i.e., prayer, religious meditation, etc.   38 *frank* generous, open (with sexual suggestion)   40 *The hearts . . . hands* i.e., in former times, people would give their hearts when they gave their hands to something   41 *But . . . hearts* i.e., in our decadent times, the joining of hands is no longer a badge to signify the giving of hearts   43 *chuck* (A term of endearment.)   45 *salt . . . rheum* distressful head cold or watering of the eyes   53 *charmer* sorceress

The thoughts of people. She told her, while she kept it
'Twould make her amiable° and subdue my father   55
Entirely to her love, but if she lost it
Or made a gift of it, my father's eye
Should hold her loathèd and his spirits should hunt
After new fancies.° She, dying, gave it me,
And bid me, when my fate would have me wived,   60
To give it her.° I did so; and take heed on 't;
Make it a darling like your precious eye.
To lose 't or give 't away were such perdition°
As nothing else could match.
Desdemona: Is 't possible?
Othello: 'Tis true. There's magic in the web° of it.   65
    A sibyl, that had numbered in the world
    The sun to course two hundred compasses,°
    In her prophetic fury° sewed the work;°
    The worms were hallowed that did breed the silk,
    And it was dyed in mummy° which the skillful   70
    Conserved of° maidens' hearts.
Desdemona: I' faith! Is 't true?
Othello: Most veritable. Therefore look to 't well.
Desdemona: Then would to God that I had never seen 't!
Othello: Ha? Wherefore?
Desdemona: Why do you speak so startingly and rash?°   75
Othello: Is 't lost? Is 't gone? Speak, is 't out o' the way?°
Desdemona: Heaven bless us!
Othello: Say you?
Desdemona: It is not lost; but what an if° it were?
Othello: How?   80
Desdemona: I say it is not lost.
Othello: Fetch 't, let me see 't.
Desdemona: Why, so I can, sir, but I will not now.
    This is a trick to put me from my suit.
    Pray you, let Cassio be received again.
Othello: Fetch me the handkerchief! My mind misgives.   85
Desdemona: Come, come,
    You'll never meet a more sufficient° man.
Othello: The handkerchief!
Desdemona: I pray, talk° me of Cassio.

---

55 *amiable* desirable   59 *fancies* loves   61 *her* i.e., to my wife   63 *perdition* loss   65 *web* fabric, weaving   67 *compasses* annual circlings. (The *sibyl*, or prophetess, was two hundred years old.)   68 *prophetic fury* frenzy of prophetic inspiration.   *work* embroidered pattern   70 *mummy* medicinal or magical preparation drained from mummified bodies   71 *Conserved of* prepared or preserved out of   75 *startingly and rash* disjointedly and impetuously, excitedly   76 *out o' the way* lost, misplaced   79 *an if* if   87 *sufficient* able, complete   88 *talk* talk to

Othello: The handkerchief!
Desdemona: A man that all his time°
    Hath founded his good fortunes on your love,   90
    Shared dangers with you—
Othello: The handkerchief!
Desdemona: I' faith, you are to blame.
Othello: Zounds!   *Exit Othello.*
Emilia: Is not this man jealous?   95
Desdemona: I ne'er saw this before.
    Sure, there's some wonder in this handkerchief.
    I am most unhappy in the loss of it.
Emilia: 'Tis not a year or two shows us a man.°
    They are all but stomachs, and we all but° food;   100
    They eat us hungerly,° and when they are full
    They belch us.

    Enter Iago and Cassio.

                Look you, Cassio and my husband.
Iago [to Cassio]: There is no other way; 'tis she must do 't.
    And, lo, the happiness!° Go and importune her.
Desdemona: How now, good Cassio? What's the news with you?   105
Cassio: Madam, my former suit. I do beseech you
    That by your virtuous° means I may again
    Exist and be a member of his love
    Whom I, with all the office° of my heart,
    Entirely honor. I would not be delayed.   110
    If my offense be of such mortal° kind
    That nor my service past, nor° present sorrows,
    Nor purposed merit in futurity
    Can ransom me into his love again,
    But to know so must be my benefit;°   115
    So shall I clothe me in a forced content,
    And shut myself up in° some other course,
    To fortune's alms.°
Desdemona: Alas, thrice-gentle Cassio,
    My advocation° is not now in tune.
    My lord is not my lord; nor should I know him,   120
    Were he in favor° as in humor° altered.
    So help me every spirit sanctified

---

89 *all his time* throughout his career   99 *'Tis . . . man* i.e., you can't really know a man even in a year
or two of experience (?), or, real men come along seldom (?)   100 *but* nothing but   101 *hungerly*
hungrily   104 *the happiness* in happy time, fortunately met   107 *virtuous* efficacious   109 *office*
loyal service   111 *mortal* fatal   112 *nor . . . nor* neither . . . nor   115 *But . . . benefit* merely to
know that my case is hopeless will have to content me (and will be better than uncertainty)   117
shut . . . in confine myself to   118 *To fortune's alms* throwing myself on the mercy of fortune   119
advocation advocacy   121 *favor* appearance.   *humor* mood

As I have spoken for you all my best
And stood within the blank° of his displeasure
For my free speech! You must awhile be patient.   125
What I can do I will, and more I will
Than for myself I dare. Let that suffice you.
Iago: Is my lord angry?
Emilia: He went hence but now,
And certainly in strange unquietness.
Iago: Can he be angry? I have seen the cannon   130
When it hath blown his ranks into the air,
And like the devil from his very arm
Puffed his own brother—and is he angry?
Something of moment° then. I will go meet him.
There's matter in 't indeed, if he be angry.   135
Desdemona: I prithee, do so.   *Exit [Iago].*
                          Something, sure, of state,°
Either from Venice, or some unhatched practice°
Made demonstrable here in Cyprus to him,
Hath puddled° his clear spirit; and in such cases
Men's natures wrangle with inferior things,   140
Though great ones are their object. 'Tis even so;
For let our finger ache, and it indues°
Our other, healthful members even to a sense
Of pain. Nay, we must think men are not gods,
Nor of them look for such observancy°   145
As fits the bridal.° Beshrew me° much, Emilia,
I was, unhandsome° warrior as I am,
Arraigning his unkindness with° my soul;
But now I find I had suborned the witness,°
And he's indicted falsely.
Emilia: Pray heaven it be   150
State matters, as you think, and no conception
Nor no jealous toy° concerning you.
Desdemona: Alas the day! I never gave him cause.
Emilia: But jealous souls will not be answered so;
They are not ever jealous for the cause,   155
But jealous for° they're jealous. It is a monster
Begot upon itself,° born on itself.
Desdemona: Heaven keep that monster from Othello's mind!

124 *within the blank* within point-blank range. (The *blank* is the center of the target.)   134 *of moment*
of immediate importance, momentous   136 *of state* concerning state affairs   137 *unhatched practice*
as yet unexecuted or undiscovered plot   139 *puddled* muddied   142 *indues* brings to the same condition   145 *observancy* attentiveness   146 *bridal* wedding (when a bridegroom is newly attentive to
his bride). *Beshrew me* (A mild oath.)   147 *unhandsome* insufficient, unskillful   148 *with* before
the bar of   149 *suborned the witness* induced the witness to give false testimony   152 *toy* fancy   156
for because   157 *Begot upon itself* generated solely from itself

Emilia: Lady, amen.

Desdemona: I will go seek him. Cassio, walk hereabout.   160
    If I do find him fit, I'll move your suit
    And seek to effect it to my uttermost.

Cassio: I humbly thank your ladyship.

    Exit [Desdemona with Emilia].

    Enter Bianca.

Bianca: Save° you, friend Cassio!

Cassio: What make° you from home?   165
    How is 't with you, my most fair Bianca?
    I' faith, sweet love, I was coming to your house.

Bianca: And I was going to your lodging, Cassio.
    What, keep a week away? Seven days and nights?
    Eightscore-eight° hours? And lovers' absent hours
    More tedious than the dial° eightscore times?   170
    O weary reckoning!

Cassio: Pardon me, Bianca.
    I have this while with leaden thoughts been pressed;
    But I shall, in a more continuate° time,
    Strike off this score° of absence. Sweet Bianca,

    [giving her Desdemona's handkerchief]

    Take me this work out.°

Bianca: O Cassio, whence came this?   175
    This is some token from a newer friend.°
    To the felt absence now I feel a cause.
    Is 't come to this? Well, well.

Cassio: Go to, woman!
    Throw your vile guesses in the devil's teeth,
    From whence you have them. You are jealous now   180
    That this is from some mistress, some remembrance.
    No, by my faith, Bianca.

Bianca: Why, whose is it?

Cassio: I know not, neither. I found it in my chamber.
    I like the work well. Ere it be demanded°—
    As like° enough it will—I would have it copied.   185
    Take it and do 't, and leave me for this time.

Bianca: Leave you? Wherefore?

Cassio: I do attend here on the General,
    And think it no addition,° nor my wish,

---

164 *Save* God save. *make* do 169 *Eightscore-eight* one hundred sixty-eight, the number of hours in
a week 170 *the dial* a complete revolution of the clock 173 *continuate* uninterrupted 174 *Strike*
. . . score settle this account 175 *Take . . . out* copy this embroidery for me 176 *friend* mistress
184 *demanded* inquired for 185 *like* likely 189 *addition* i.e., addition to my reputation

To have him see me womaned. 190

Bianca: Why, I pray you?

Cassio: Not that I love you not.

Bianca: But that you do not love me.
    I pray you, bring° me on the way a little,
    And say if I shall see you soon at night. 195

Cassio: 'Tis but a little way that I can bring you,
    For I attend here; but I'll see you soon.

Bianca: 'Tis very good. I must be circumstanced.°

Exeunt omnes.

ACT IV

Scene I [Before the Citadel.]

Enter Othello and Iago.

Iago: Will you think so?

Othello: Think so, Iago?

Iago: What,
    To kiss in private?

Othello: An unauthorized kiss!

Iago: Or to be naked with her friend in bed
    An hour or more, not meaning any harm?

Othello: Naked in bed, Iago, and not mean harm? 5
    It is hypocrisy against the devil.
    They that mean virtuously and yet do so,
    The devil their virtue tempts, and they tempt heaven.

Iago: If they do nothing, 'tis a venial° slip.
    But if I give my wife a handkerchief— 10

Othello: What then?

Iago: Why then, 'tis hers, my lord, and being hers,
    She may, I think, bestow 't on any man.

Othello: She is protectress of her honor too.
    May she give that? 15

Iago: Her honor is an essence that's not seen;
    They have it° very oft that have it not.
    But, for the handkerchief—

Othello: By heaven, I would most gladly have forgot it.
    Thou saidst—O, it comes o'er my memory
    As doth the raven o'er the infectious house,° 20
    Boding to all—he had my handkerchief.

---

194 *bring* accompany   198 *be circumstanced* be governed by circumstance, yield to your conditions
9 *venial* pardonable   17 *They have it* i.e., they enjoy a reputation for it   21 *raven . . . house* (Allusion
to the belief that the raven hovered over a house of sickness or infection, such as one visited by the
plague.)

Iago: Ay, what of that?

Othello: That's not so good now.

Iago: What
    If I had said I had seen him do you wrong?
    Or heard him say—as knaves be such abroad,°   25
    Who having, by their own importunate suit,
    Or voluntary dotage° of some mistress,
    Convincèd or supplied° them, cannot choose
    But they must blab—

Othello: Hath he said anything?

Iago: He hath, my lord; but, be you well assured,   30
    No more than he'll unswear.

Othello: What hath he said?

Iago: Faith, that he did—I know not what he did.

Othello: What? What?

Iago: Lie—

Othello: With her?

Iago: With her, on her; what you will.

Othello: Lie with her? Lie on her? We say "lie on her" when they belie° her. Lie   35
    with her? Zounds, that's fulsome.°—Handkerchief—confessions—handker-
    chief!—To confess and be hanged for his labor—first to be hanged and then
    to confess.°—I tremble at it. Nature would not invest herself in such shad-
    owing passion without some instruction.° It is not words° that shakes me
    thus. Pish! Noses, ears, and lips.—Is 't possible?—Confess—handker-   40
    chief!—O devil!

    Falls in a trance.

Iago: Work on,
    My medicine, work! Thus credulous fools are caught,
    And many worthy and chaste dames even thus,
    All guiltless, meet reproach.—What, ho! My lord!   45
    My lord, I say! Othello!

    Enter Cassio.

                How now, Cassio?

Cassio: What's the matter?

Iago: My lord is fall'n into an epilepsy.
    This is his second fit. He had one yesterday.

Cassio: Rub him about the temples.

---

25 *abroad* around about   27 *voluntary dotage* willing infatuation   28 *Convincèd or supplied* seduced or sexually gratified   35 *belie* slander   36 *fulsome* foul   37–38 *first . . . to confess* (Othello reverses the proverbial *confess* and *be hanged*; Cassio is to be given no time to confess before he dies.)   38–39 *Nature . . . instruction* i.e., without some foundation in fact, nature would not have dressed herself in such an overwhelming passion that comes over me now and fills my mind with images, or in such a lifelike fantasy as Cassio had in his dream of lying with Desdemona   39 *words* mere words

Iago: No, forbear.
The lethargy° must have his° quiet course.
If not, he foams at mouth, and by and by
Breaks out to savage madness. Look, he stirs.
Do you withdraw yourself a little while.   55
He will recover straight. When he is gone,
I would on great occasion° speak with you.

[_Exit Cassio._]

How is it, General? Have you not hurt your head?
Othello: Dost thou mock me?°
Iago: I mock you not, by heaven.
Would you would bear your fortune like a man!
Othello: A hornèd man's a monster and a beast.   60
Iago: There's many a beast then in a populous city,
    And many a civil° monster.
Othello: Did he confess it?
Iago: Good sir, be a man.
    Think every bearded fellow that's but yoked°   65
    May draw with you.° There's millions now alive
    That nightly lie in those unproper° beds
    Which they dare swear peculiar.° Your case is better.°
    O, 'tis the spite of hell, the fiend's arch-mock,
    To lip° a wanton in a secure° couch   70
    And to suppose her chaste! No, let me know,
    And knowing what I am,° I know what she shall be.°
Othello: O, thou art wise. 'Tis certain.
Iago: Stand you awhile apart;
    Confine yourself but in a patient list.°   75
    Whilst you were here o'erwhelmèd with your grief—
    A passion most unsuiting such a man—
    Cassio came hither. I shifted him away,°
    And laid good 'scuse upon your ecstasy,°
    Bade him anon return and here speak with me,   80
    The which he promised. Do but encave° yourself
    And mark the fleers,° the gibes, and notable° scorns
    That dwell in every region of his face;
    For I will make him tell the tale anew,

---

51 _lethargy_ coma. _his_ its   56 _on great occasion_ on a matter of great importance   58 _mock me_ (Othello takes Iago's question about hurting his head to be a mocking reference to the cuckold's horns.)
62 _civil_ i.e., dwelling in a city   65 _yoked_ (1) married (2) put into the yoke of infamy and cuckoldry
66 _draw with you_ pull as you do, like oxen who are yoked, i.e., share your fate as cuckold   67 _unproper_ not exclusively their own   68 _peculiar_ private, their own.   _better_ i.e., because you know the truth
70 _lip_ kiss.   _secure_ free from suspicion   72 _what I am_ i.e., a cuckold.   _she shall be_ will happen to her
75 _in . . . list_ within the bounds of patience   78 _shifted him away_ used a dodge to get rid of him   79
ecstasy trance   81 _encave_ conceal   82 _fleers_ sneers.   _notable_ obvious

Where, how, how oft, how long ago, and when
He hath and is again to cope° your wife.
I say, but mark his gesture. Marry, patience!
Or I shall say you're all-in-all in spleen,°
And nothing of a man.

Othello: Dost thou hear, Iago?
I will be found most cunning in my patience;
But—dost thou hear?—most bloody.

Iago: That's not amiss;
But yet keep time° in all. Will you withdraw?

[*Othello stands apart.*]

Now will I question Cassio of Bianca,
A huswife° that by selling her desires
Buys herself bread and clothes. It is a creature
That dotes on Cassio—as 'tis the strumpet's plague
To beguile many and be beguiled by one.
He, when he hears of her, cannot restrain°
From the excess of laughter. Here he comes.

Enter Cassio.

As he shall smile, Othello shall go mad;
And his unbookish° jealousy must conster°
Poor Cassio's smiles, gestures, and light behaviors
Quite in the wrong.—How do you now, Lieutenant?

Cassio: The worser that you give me the addition°
Whose want° even kills me.

Iago: Ply Desdemona well and you are sure on 't.
[*Speaking lower.*] Now, if this suit lay in Bianca's power,
How quickly should you speed!

Cassio [*laughing*]: Alas, poor caitiff!°

Othello [*aside*]: Look how he laughs already!

Iago: I never knew a woman love man so.

Cassio: Alas, poor rogue! I think, i' faith, she loves me.

Othello: Now he denies it faintly, and laughs it out.

Iago: Do you hear, Cassio?

Othello: Now he importunes him
To tell it o'er. Go to!° Well said,° well said.

Iago: She gives it out that you shall marry her.
Do you intend it?

Cassio: Ha, ha, ha!

---

86 *cope* encounter with, have sex with   88 *all-in-all in spleen* utterly governed by passionate impulses
92 *keep time* keep yourself steady (as in music)   94 *huswife* hussy   98 *restrain* refrain   101 *unbookish*
uninstructed.   *conster* construe   104 *addition* title   105 *Whose want* the lack of which   109 *caitiff*
wretch   115 *Go to* (An expression of remonstrance.)   *Well said* well done

Othello: Do you triumph, Roman?° Do you triumph?

Cassio: I marry her? What? A customer?° Prithee, bear some charity to my wit;°   120
do not think it so unwholesome. Ha, ha, ha!

Othello: So, so, so, so! They laugh that win.°

Iago: Faith, the cry° goes that you shall marry her.

Cassio: Prithee, say true.

Iago: I am a very villain else.°   125

Othello: Have you scored me?° Well.

Cassio: This is the monkey's own giving out. She is persuaded I will marry her
out of her own love and flattery,° not out of my promise.

Othello: Iago beckons me.° Now he begins the story.

Cassio: She was here even now; she haunts me in every place. I was the other   130
day talking on the seabank° with certain Venetians, and thither comes the
bauble,° and, by this hand,° she falls me thus about my neck—

[*He embraces Iago.*]

Othello: Crying, "O dear Cassio!" as it were; his gesture imports it.

Cassio: So hangs and lolls and weep upon me, so shakes and pulls me. Ha, ha, ha!

Othello: Now he tells how she plucked him to my chamber. O, I see that nose of   135
yours, but not that dog I shall throw it to.°

Cassio: Well, I must leave her company.

Iago: Before me,° look where she comes.

Enter Bianca [with Othello's handkerchief].

Cassio: 'Tis such another fitchew!° Marry, a perfumed one.—What do you
mean by this haunting of me?   140

Bianca: Let the devil and his dam° haunt you! What did you mean by that same
handkerchief you gave me even now? I was a fine fool to take it. I must take
out the work? A likely piece of work,° that you should find it in your
chamber and know not who left it there! This is some minx's token, and I
must take out the work? There; give it your hobbyhorse.° [*She gives him the*   145
handkerchief.] Wheresoever you had it, I'll take out no work on 't.

Cassio: How now, my sweet Bianca? How now? How now?

Othello: By heaven, that should be° my handkerchief!

Bianca: If you'll come to supper tonight, you may; if you will not, come when
you are next prepared for.°   150

119 *Roman* (The Romans were noted for their *triumphs* or triumphal processions.)   120 *customer* i.e.,
prostitute.   *bear . . . wit* be more charitable to my judgment   122 *They . . . win* i.e., they that laugh
last laugh best   123 *cry* rumor   125 *I . . . else* call me a complete rogue if I'm not telling the truth
126 *scored me* scored off me, beaten me, made up my reckoning, branded me   128 *flattery* self-flat-
tery, self-deception   129 *beckons* signals   131 *seabank* seashore   132 *bauble* plaything   *by this hand*
I make my vow   136 *not . . . to* (Othello imagines himself cutting off Cassio's nose and throwing it
to a dog.)   138 *Before me* i.e., on my soul   139 *'Tis . . . fitchew* what a polecat she is! Just like all the
others. (Polecats were often compared with prostitutes because of their rank smell and presumed
lechery.)   141 *dam* mother   143 *A likely . . . work* a fine story   145 *hobbyhorse* harlot   148 *should
be* must be   149–150 *when . . . for* when I'm ready for you (i.e., never)

Exit.

Iago: After her, after her.

Cassio: Faith, I must. She'll rail in the streets else.

Iago: Will you sup there?

Cassio: Faith, I intend so.

Iago: Well, I may chance to see you, for I would very fain speak with you.   155

Cassio: Prithee, come. Will you?

Iago: Go to.° Say no more.   [*Exit Cassio.*]

Othello [*advancing*]: How shall I murder him, Iago?

Iago: Did you perceive how he laughed at his vice?

Othello: O, Iago!   160

Iago: And did you see the handkerchief?

Othello: Was that mine?

Iago: Yours, by this hand. And to see how he prizes the foolish woman your wife! She gave it him, and he hath given it his whore.

Othello: I would have him nine years a-killing. A fine woman! A fair woman! A   165 sweet woman!

Iago: Nay, you must forget that.

Othello: Ay, let her rot and perish, and be damned tonight, for she shall not live. No, my heart is turned to stone; I strike it, and it hurts my hand. O, the world hath not a sweeter creature! She might lie by an emperor's side and   170 command him tasks.

Iago: Nay, that's not your way.°

Othello: Hang her! I do but say what she is. So delicate with her needle! An admirable musician! O, she will sing the savageness out of a bear. Of so high and plenteous wit and invention!°   175

Iago: She's the worse for all this.

Othello: O, a thousand, a thousand times! And then, of so gentle a condition!°

Iago: Ay, too gentle.°

Othello: Nay, that's certain. But yet the pity of it, Iago! O, Iago, the pity of it, Iago!   180

Iago: If you are so fond° over her iniquity, give her patent° to offend, for if it touch not you it comes near nobody.

Othello: I will chop her into messes.° Cuckold me?

Iago: O, 'tis foul in her.

Othello: With mine officer?   185

Iago: That's fouler.

Othello: Get me some poison, Iago, this night. I'll not expostulate with her, lest her body and beauty unprovide° my mind again. This night, Iago.

Iago: Do it not with poison. Strangle her in her bed, even the bed she hath contaminated.   190

---

157 *Go to* (An expression of remonstrance.)   172 *your way* i.e., the way you should think of her   175 *invention* imagination   177 *gentle a condition* wellborn and well-bred   178 *gentle* generous, yielding (to other men)   181 *fond* foolish.   *patent* license   183 *messes* portions of meat, i.e., bits   188 *unprovide* weaken, render unfit

Othello: Good, good! The justice of it pleases. Very good.

Iago: And for Cassio, let me be his undertaker.° You shall hear more by midnight.

Othello: Excellent good. [*A trumpet within.*] What trumpet is that same?

Iago: I warrant, something from Venice.

> *Enter Lodovico, Desdemona, and attendants.*

'Tis Lodovico. This comes from the Duke.   195
See, your wife's with him.

Lodovico: God save you, worthy General!

Othello: With all my heart,° sir.

Lodovico [*giving him a letter*]: The Duke and the senators of Venice greet you.

Othello: I kiss the instrument of their pleasures.

> [*He opens the letter, and reads.*]

Desdemona: And what's the news, good cousin Lodovico?   200

Iago: I am very glad to see you, signor.
Welcome to Cyprus.

Lodovico: I thank you. How does Lieutenant Cassio?

Iago: Lives, sir.

Desdemona: Cousin, there's fall'n between him and my lord   205
An unkind° breach; but you shall make all well.

Othello: Are you sure of that?

Desdemona: My lord?

Othello [*reads*]: "This fail you not to do, as you will—"

Lodovico: He did not call; he's busy in the paper.   210
Is there division twixt my lord and Cassio?

Desdemona: A most unhappy one. I would do much
T' atone° them, for the love I bear to Cassio.

Othello: Fire and brimstone!

Desdemona: My lord?   215

Othello: Are you wise?

Desdemona: What, is he angry?

Lodovico: Maybe the letter moved him;
For, as I think, they do command him home,
Deputing Cassio in his government.°

Desdemona: By my troth, I am glad on 't.°   220

Othello: Indeed?

Desdemona: My lord?

Othello: I am glad to see you mad.°

Desdemona: Why, sweet Othello—

---

192 *be his undertaker* undertake to dispatch him   197 *With all my heart* i.e., I thank you most heartily
206 *unkind* unnatural, contrary to their natures; hurtful   213 *atone* reconcile   219 *government* office
220 *on 't* of it   223 *I am . . . mad* i.e., I am glad to see that you are insane enough to rejoice in
Cassio's promotion (? Othello bitterly plays on Desdemona's *I am glad.*)

Othello [*striking her*]: Devil!

Desdemona: I have not deserved this.

Lodovico: My lord, this would not be believed in Venice,
     Though I should swear I saw 't. 'Tis very much.°
     Make her amends; she weeps.

Othello: O devil, devil!
     If that the earth could teem° with woman's tears,
     Each drop she falls would prove a crocodile.°
     Out of my sight!

Desdemona: I will not stay to offend you. [*Going.*]

Lodovico: Truly, an obedient lady.
     I do beseech your lordship, call her back.

Othello: Mistress!

Desdemona [*returning*]: My lord?

Othello: What would you with her, sir?°

Lodovico: Who, I, my lord?

Othello: Ay, you did wish that I would make her turn.
     Sir, she can turn, and turn, and yet go on
     And turn again; and she can weep, sir, weep;
     And she's obedient,° as you say, obedient,
     Very obedient.—Proceed you in your tears.—
     Concerning this, sir—O well-painted passion!°—
     I am commanded home.—Get you away;
     I'll send for you anon.—Sir, I obey the mandate
     And will return to Venice.—Hence, avaunt!

[*Exit Desdemona.*]

     Cassio shall have my place. And, sir, tonight
     I do entreat that we may sup together.
     You are welcome, sir, to Cyprus.—Goats and monkeys!°   *Exit.*   250

Lodovico: Is this the noble Moor whom our full Senate
     Call all in all sufficient? Is this the nature
     Whom passion could not shake? Whose solid virtue
     The shot of accident nor dart of chance
     Could neither graze nor pierce?

Iago: He is much changed.

Lodovico: Are his wits safe? Is he not light of brain?

Iago: He's that he is. I may not breathe my censure
     What he might be. If what he might he is not,

230

235

240

245

255

---

228 *very much* too much, outrageous   230 *teem* breed, be impregnated   231 *falls . . . crocodile* (Crocodiles were supposed to weep hypocritical tears for their victims.)   237 *What . . . sir* (Othello implies that Desdemona is pliant and will do a *turn*, lines 239–241, for any man.)   242 *obedient* (With
much the same sexual connotation as *turn* in lines 239–241.)   244 *passion* i.e., grief   250 *Goats and
monkeys* (See Act III, Scene iii, line 419.)

I would to heaven he were!°
Lodovico: What, strike his wife?
Iago: Faith, that was not so well; yet would I knew   260
  That stroke would prove the worst!
Lodovico: Is it his use?°
  Or did the letters work upon his blood°
  And new-create his fault?
Iago: Alas, alas!
  It is not honesty in me to speak
  What I have seen and known. You shall observe him,   265
  And his own courses will denote° him so
  That I may save my speech. Do but go after,
  And mark how he continues.
Lodovico: I am sorry that I am deceived in him.   *Exeunt.*

Scene II [The Citadel.]

Enter Othello and Emilia.

Othello: You have seen nothing then?
Emilia: Nor ever heard, nor ever did suspect.
Othello: Yes, you have seen Cassio and she together.
Emilia: But then I saw no harm, and then I heard
  Each syllable that breath made up between them.   5
Othello: What, did they never whisper?
Emilia: Never, my lord.
Othello: Nor send you out o' the way?
Emilia: Never.
Othello: To fetch her fan, her gloves, her mask, nor nothing?   10
Emilia: Never, my lord.
Othello: That's strange.
Emilia: I durst, my lord, to wager she is honest,
  Lay down my soul at stake.° If you think other,
  Remove your thought; it doth abuse your bosom.°   15
  If any wretch have put this in your head,
  Let heaven requite it with the serpent's curse!°
  For if she be not honest, chaste, and true,
  There's no man happy; the purest of their wives
  Is foul as slander.
Othello: Bid her come hither. Go.   20

257–259 *I may . . . were* i.e., I dare not venture an opinion as to whether he's of unsound mind, as you suggest, but, if he isn't, then it might be better to wish he were in fact insane, since only that could excuse his wild behavior   261 *use* custom   262 *blood* passions   266 *courses will denote* actions will reveal   14 *at stake* as the wager   15 *abuse your bosom* deceive you   17 *the serpent's curse* the curse pronounced by God on the serpent for deceiving Eve, just as some man has done to Othello and Desdemona. (See Genesis 3:14.)

Exit Emilia.

She says enough; yet she's a simple bawd
That cannot say as much.° This° is a subtle whore,
A closet lock and key° of villainous secrets.
And yet she'll kneel and pray; I have seen her do 't.

Enter Desdemona and Emilia.

Desdemona: My lord, what is your will?   25
Othello: Pray you, chuck, come hither.
Desdemona: What is your pleasure?
Othello: Let me see your eyes.
    Look in my face.
Desdemona: What horrible fancy's this?
Othello [to Emilia]: Some of your function,° mistress.   30
    Leave procreants° alone and shut the door;
    Cough or cry "hem" if anybody come.
    Your mystery, your mystery!° Nay, dispatch.

Exit Emilia.

Desdemona [kneeling]: Upon my knees, what doth your speech import?
    I understand a fury in your words,   35
    But not the words.
Othello: Why, what art thou?
Desdemona: Your wife, my lord, your true
    And loyal wife.
Othello: Come, swear it, damn thyself,
    Lest, being like one of heaven,° the devils themselves
    Should fear to seize thee. Therefore be double damned:
    Swear thou art honest.
Desdemona: Heaven doth truly know it.   40
Othello: Heaven truly knows that thou art false as hell.
Desdemona: To whom, my lord? With whom? How am I false?
Othello [weeping]: Ah, Desdemon! Away, away, away!
Desdemona: Alas the heavy day! Why do you weep?
    Am I the motive° of these tears, my lord?   45
    If haply you my father do suspect
    An instrument of this your calling back,
    Lay not your blame on me. If you have lost him,
    I have lost him too.
Othello: Had it pleased heaven

21–22 *she's . . . much* i.e., any procuress or go-between who couldn't make up as plausible a story as
Emilia's would have to be pretty stupid   22 *This* i.e., Desdemona   23 *closet lock and key* i.e., con-
cealer   29 *Some . . . function* i.e., practice your chosen profession, that of bawd (by guarding the
door)   30 *procreants* mating couples   32 *mystery* trade, occupation   38 *being . . . heaven* looking
like an angel   45 *motive* cause

To try me with affliction, had they° rained   50
All kinds of sores and shames on my bare head,
Steeped me in poverty to the very lips,
Given to captivity me and my utmost hopes,
I should have found in some place of my soul
A drop of patience. But, alas, to make me   55
A fixèd figure for the time of scorn°
To point his° slow and moving finger° at!
Yet could I bear that too, well, very well.
But there where I have garnered° up my heart,
Where either I must live or bear no life,   60
The fountain° from the which my current runs
Or else dries up—to be discarded thence!
Or keep it as a cistern° for foul toads
To knot° and gender° in! Turn thy complexion there,°
Patience, thou young and rose-lipped cherubin—   65
Ay, there look grim as hell!°
Desdemona: I hope my noble lord esteems me honest.°
Othello: O, ay, as summer flies are in the shambles,°
That quicken° even with blowing.° O thou weed,
Who art so lovely fair and smell'st so sweet   70
That the sense aches at thee, would thou hadst ne'er been born!
Desdemona: Alas, what ignorant° sin have I committed?
Othello: Was this fair paper, this most goodly book,
Made to write "whore" upon? What committed?
Committed? O thou public commoner!°   75
I should make very forges of my cheeks,
That would to cinders burn up modesty,
Did I but speak thy deeds. What committed?
Heaven stops the nose at it and the moon winks;°
The bawdy° wind, that kisses all it meets,   80
Is hushed within the hollow mine° of earth
And will not hear 't. What committed?
Impudent strumpet!
Desdemona: By heaven, you do me wrong.
Othello: Are not you a strumpet?

---

50 *they* i.e., heavenly powers   56 *time of scorn* i.e., scornful world   57 *his* its.   *slow and moving finger*
i.e., hour hand of the clock, moving so slowly it seems hardly to move at all. (Othello envisages himself as being eternally pointed at by the scornful world as the numbers on a clock are pointed at by
the hour hand.)   59 *garnered* stored   61 *fountain* spring   63 *cistern* cesspool   64 *knot* couple.
gender engender.   *Turn . . . there* change your color, grow pale, at such a sight   65–66 *Patience . . .
hell* (Even Patience, that rose-lipped cherub, will look grim and pale at this spectacle.)   67 *honest*
chaste   68 *shambles* slaughterhouse   69 *quicken* come to life.   *with blowing* i.e., with the puffing up
of something rotten in which maggots are breeding   72 *ignorant sin* sin in ignorance   75 *commoner*
prostitute   79 *winks* closes her eyes. (The moon symbolizes chastity.)   80 *bawdy* kissing one and all
81 *mine* cave (where the winds were thought to dwell)

Desdemona: No, as I am a Christian. 85
   If to preserve this vessel° for my lord
   From any other foul unlawful touch
   Be not to be a strumpet, I am none.
Othello: What, not a whore?
Desdemona: No, as I shall be saved. 90
Othello: Is 't possible?
Desdemona: O, heaven forgive us!
Othello: I cry you mercy,° then.
   I took you for that cunning whore of Venice
   That married with Othello. [*Calling out.*] You, mistress,
   That have the office opposite to Saint Peter 95
   And keep the gate of hell!

   Enter Emilia.

                          You, you, ay, you!
   We have done our course.° There's money for your pains. [*He gives money.*]
   I pray you, turn the key and keep our counsel.   *Exit.*
Emilia: Alas, what does this gentleman conceive?°
   How do you, madam? How do you, my good lady? 100
Desdemona: Faith, half asleep.°
Emilia: Good madam, what's the matter with my lord?
Desdemona: With who?
Emilia: Why, with my lord, madam.
Desdemona: Who is thy lord?
Emilia: He that is yours, sweet lady. 105
Desdemona: I have none. Do not talk to me, Emilia.
   I cannot weep, nor answers have I none
   But what should go by water.° Prithee, tonight
   Lay on my bed my wedding sheets, remember;
   And call thy husband hither. 110
Emilia: Here's a change indeed!   *Exit.*
Desdemona: 'Tis meet I should be used so, very meet.°
   How have I been behaved, that he might stick°
   The small'st opinion° on my least misuse?°

   Enter Iago and Emilia.

Iago: What is your pleasure, madam? How is 't with you? 115
Desdemona: I cannot tell. Those that do teach young babes
   Do it with gentle means and easy tasks.
   He might have chid me so, for, in good faith,

---

86 *vessel* body   92 *cry you mercy* beg your pardon   97 *course* business (with an indecent suggestion
of "trick," turn at sex)   99 *conceive* suppose, think   101 *half asleep* i.e., dazed   108 *go by water* be
expressed by tears   112 *meet* fitting   113 *stick* attach   114 *opinion* censure.   *least misuse* slightest
misconduct

I am a child to chiding.

Iago: What is the matter, lady? 120

Emilia: Alas, Iago, my lord hath so bewhored her,
Thrown such despite and heavy terms upon her,
That true hearts cannot bear it.

Desdemona: Am I that name, Iago?

Iago: What name, fair lady? 125

Desdemona: Such as she said my lord did say I was.

Emilia: He called her whore. A beggar in his drink
Could not have laid such terms upon his callet.°

Iago: Why did he so?

Desdemona [_weeping_]: I do not know. I am sure I am none such. 130

Iago: Do not weep, do not weep. Alas the day!

Emilia: Hath she forsook so many noble matches,
Her father and her country and her friends,
To be called whore? Would it not make one weep?

Desdemona: It is my wretched fortune.

Iago: Beshrew° him for 't! 135
How comes this trick° upon him?

Desdemona: Nay, heaven doth know.

Emilia: I will be hanged if some eternal° villain,
Some busy and insinuating° rogue,
Some cogging,° cozening° slave, to get some office,
Have not devised this slander. I will be hanged else. 140

Iago: Fie, there is no such man. It is impossible.

Desdemona: If any such there be, heaven pardon him!

Emilia: A halter° pardon him! And hell gnaw his bones!
Why should he call her whore? Who keeps her company?
What place? What time? What form?° What likelihood? 145
The Moor's abused by some most villainous knave,
Some base notorious knave, some scurvy fellow.
O heaven, that° such companions° thou'dst unfold,°
And put in every honest hand a whip
To lash the rascals naked through the world 150
Even from the east to th' west!

Iago: Speak within door.°

Emilia: O, fie upon them! Some such squire° he was
That turned your wit the seamy side without°
And made you to suspect me with the Moor.

Iago: You are a fool. Go to.°

---

128 _callet_ whore   135 _Beshrew_ curse   136 _trick_ strange behavior, delusion   137 _eternal_ inveterate
138 _insinuating_ ingratiating, fawning, wheedling   139 _cogging_ cheating.   _cozening_ defrauding   143
halter hangman's noose   145 _form_ appearance, circumstance   148 _that_ would that.   _companions_ fellows.   _unfold_ expose   151 _within door_ i.e., not so loud   152 _squire_ fellow   153 _seamy side without_
wrong side out   155 _Go to_ i.e., that's enough

Desdemona: Alas, Iago,
    What shall I do to win my lord again?
    Good friend, go to him; for, by this light of heaven,
    I know not how I lost him. Here I kneel. [*She kneels.*]
    If e'er my will did trespass 'gainst his love,
    Either in discourse° of thought or actual deed,   160
    Or that° mine eyes, mine ears, or any sense
    Delighted them° in any other form;
    Or that I do not yet,° and ever did,
    And ever will—though he do shake me off
    To beggarly divorcement—love him dearly,   165
    Comfort forswear° me! Unkindness may do much,
    And his unkindness may defeat° my life,
    But never taint my love. I cannot say "whore."
    It does abhor° me now I speak the word;
    To do the act that might the addition° earn   170
    Not the world's mass of vanity° could make me.

    [*She rises.*]

Iago: I pray you, be content. 'Tis but his humor.°
    The business of the state does him offense,
    And he does chide with you.
Desdemona: If 'twere no other—   175
Iago: It is but so, I warrant.   [*Trumpets within.*]
    Hark, how these instruments summon you to supper!
    The messengers of Venice stays the meat.°
    Go in, and weep not. All things shall be well.

    Exeunt Desdemona and Emilia.

    Enter Roderigo.

    How now, Roderigo?   180
Roderigo: I do not find that thou deal'st justly with me.
Iago: What in the contrary?
Roderigo: Every day thou daff'st me° with some device,° Iago, and rather, as it
    seems to me now, keep'st from me all conveniency° than suppliest me with
    the least advantage° of hope. I will indeed no longer endure it, nor am I yet   185
    persuaded to put up° in peace what already I have foolishly suffered.
Iago: Will you hear me, Roderigo?

---

160 *discourse of thought* process of thinking   161 *that* if. (Also in line 163.)   162 *Delighted them* took delight   163 *yet* still   166 *Comfort forswear* may heavenly comfort forsake   167 *defeat* destroy 169 *abhor* (1) fill me with abhorrence (2) make me whorelike   170 *addition* title   171 *vanity* showy splendor   172 *humor* mood   178 *stays the meat* are waiting to dine   183 *thou daff'st me* you put me off. *device* excuse, trick   184 *conveniency* advantage, opportunity   185 *advantage* increase   186 *put up* submit to, tolerate

Roderigo: Faith, I have heard too much, for your words and performances are no kin together.

Iago: You charge me most unjustly.

Roderigo: With naught but truth. I have wasted myself out of my means. The jewels you have had from me to deliver° Desdemona would half have corrupted a votarist.° You have told me she hath received them and returned me expectations and comforts of sudden respect° and acquaintance, but I find none.

Iago: Well, go to, very well.

Roderigo: "Very well"! "Go to"! I cannot go to,° man, nor 'tis not very well. By this hand, I think it is scurvy, and begin to find myself fopped° in it.

Iago: Very well.

Roderigo: I tell you 'tis not very well.° I will make myself known to Desdemona. If she will return me my jewels, I will give over my suit and repent my unlawful solicitation; if not, assure yourself I will seek satisfaction° of you.

Iago: You have said now?°

Roderigo: Ay, and said nothing but what I protest intendment° of doing.

Iago: Why, now I see there's mettle in thee, and even from this instant do build on thee a better opinion than ever before. Give me thy hand, Roderigo. Thou hast taken against me a most just exception; but yet I protest I have dealt most directly in thy affair.

Roderigo: It hath not appeared.

Iago: I grant indeed it hath not appeared, and your suspicion is not without wit and judgment. But, Roderigo, if thou hast that in thee indeed which I have greater reason to believe now than ever—I mean purpose, courage, and valor—this night show it. If thou the next night following enjoy not Desdemona, take me from this world with treachery and devise engines for° my life.

Roderigo: Well, what is it? Is it within reason and compass?

Iago: Sir, there is especial commission come from Venice to depute Cassio in Othello's place.

Roderigo: Is that true? Why, then Othello and Desdemona return again to Venice.

Iago: O, no; he goes into Mauritania and takes away with him the fair Desdemona, unless his abode be lingered here by some accident; wherein none can be so determinate° as the removing of Cassio.

Roderigo: How do you mean, removing of him?

Iago: Why, by making him uncapable of Othello's place—knocking out his brains.

190

195

200

205

210

215

220

225

---

192 *deliver* deliver to   193 *votarist* nun   194 *sudden respect* immediate consideration   197 *I cannot go to* (Roderigo changes Iago's *go to,* an expression urging patience, to *I cannot go to,* "I have no opportunity for success in wooing.")   198 *fopped* fooled, duped   200 *not very well* (Roderigo changes Iago's *very well,* "all right, then," to *not very well,* "not at all good.")   202 *satisfaction* repayment. (The term normally means settling of accounts in a duel.)   203 *You . . . now* have you finished?   204 *intendment* intention   214 *engines for* plots against   223 *determinate* conclusive

Roderigo: And that you would have me to do?

Iago: Ay, if you dare do yourself a profit and a right. He sups tonight with a
harlotry,° and thither will I go to him. He knows not yet of his honorable
fortune. If you will watch his going thence, which I will fashion to fall out° 230
between twelve and one, you may take him at your pleasure. I will be near to
second your attempt, and he shall fall between us. Come, stand not amazed
at it, but go along with me. I will show you such a necessity in his death that
you shall think yourself bound to put it on him. It is now high° suppertime,
and the night grows to waste.° About it. 235

Roderigo: I will hear further reason for this.

Iago: And you shall be satisfied.   *Exeunt.*

Scene III [The Citadel.]

Enter Othello, Lodovico, Desdemona, Emilia, and attendants.

Lodovico: I do beseech you, sir, trouble yourself no further.

Othello: O, pardon me; 'twill do me good to walk.

Lodovico: Madam, good night. I humbly thank your ladyship.

Desdemona: Your honor is most welcome.

Othello: Will you walk, sir?   5
   O, Desdemona!

Desdemona: My lord?

Othello: Get you to bed on th' instant.
   I will be returned forthwith. Dismiss your attendant there. Look
   't be done.

Desdemona: I will, my lord.   10

   Exit [Othello, with Lodovico and attendants].

Emilia: How goes it now? He looks gentler than he did.

Desdemona: He says he will return incontinent,°
   And hath commanded me to go to bed,
   And bid me to dismiss you.

Emilia: Dismiss me?   15

Desdemona: It was his bidding. Therefore, good Emilia,
   Give me my nightly wearing, and adieu.
   We must not now displease him.

Emilia: I would you had never seen him!

Desdemona: So would not I. My love doth so approve him   20
   That even his stubbornness,° his checks,° his frowns—
   Prithee, unpin me—have grace and favor in them.

   [Emilia prepares Desdemona for bed.]

Emilia: I have laid those sheets you bade me on the bed.

229 *harlotry* slut   230 *fall out* occur   234 *high* fully   235 *grows to waste* wastes away   12 *incontinent*
immediately   21 *stubbornness* roughness. *checks* rebukes

Desdemona: All's one.° Good faith, how foolish are our minds!
   If I do die before thee, prithee shroud me   25
   In one of these same sheets.
Emilia: Come, come, you talk.°
Desdemona: My mother had a maid called Barbary.
   She was in love, and he she loved proved mad°
   And did forsake her. She had a song of "Willow."
   An old thing 'twas, but it expressed her fortune,   30
   And she died singing it. That song tonight
   Will not go from my mind; I have much to do
   But to go hang° my head all at one side
   And sing it like poor Barbary. Prithee, dispatch.
Emilia: Shall I go fetch your nightgown?°   35
Desdemona: No, unpin me here.
   This Lodovico is a proper° man.
Emilia: A very handsome man.
Desdemona: He speaks well.
Emilia: I know a lady in Venice would have walked barefoot to Palestine for a   40
   touch of his nether lip.
Desdemona [*singing*]:
                  "The poor soul sat sighing by a sycamore tree,
                  Sing all a green willow;°
                  Her hand on her bosom, her head on her knee,
                  Sing willow, willow, willow.
                  The fresh streams ran by her and murmured her moans;   45
                  Sing willow, willow, willow;
                  Her salt tears fell from her, and softened the stones—"
   Lay by these.
                  [*Singing.*] "Sing willow, willow, willow—"
   Prithee, hie thee.° He'll come anon.°   50
                  [*Singing.*] "Sing all a green willow must be my garland.
                  Let nobody blame him; his scorn I approve—"
   Nay, that's not next.—Hark! Who is 't that knocks?
Emilia: It's the wind.
Desdemona [*singing*]:   55
                  "I called my love false love; but what said he then?
                  Sing willow, willow, willow;
                  If I court more women, you'll couch with more men."
   So, get thee gone. Good night. Mine eyes do itch;

---

24 *All's one* all right. It doesn't really matter   26 *talk* i.e., prattle   28 *mad* wild, i.e., faithless   32–33
I . . . hang I can scarcely keep myself from hanging   35 *nightgown* dressing gown   37 *proper* handsome   43 *willow* (A conventional emblem of disappointed love.)   51 *hie thee* hurry.   *anon* right
away

Doth that bode weeping?

Emilia: 'Tis neither here nor there.   60

Desdemona: I have heard it said so. O, these men, these men!

    Dost thou in conscience think—tell me, Emilia—

    That there be women do abuse° their husbands

    In such gross kind?

Emilia: There be some such, no question.

Desdemona: Wouldst thou do such a deed for all the world?   65

Emilia: Why, would not you?

Desdemona: No, by this heavenly light!

Emilia: Nor I neither by this heavenly light;

    I might do 't as well i' the dark.

Desdemona: Wouldst thou do such a deed for all the world?

Emilia: The world's a huge thing. It is a great price   70

    For a small vice.

Desdemona: Good troth, I think thou wouldst not.

Emilia: By my troth, I think I should, and undo 't when I had done. Marry, I
would not do such a thing for a joint ring,° nor for measures of lawn,° nor
for gowns, petticoats, nor caps, nor any petty exhibition.° But for all the   75
whole world! Uds° pity, who would not make her husband a cuckold to
make him a monarch? I should venture purgatory for 't.

Desdemona: Beshrew me if I would do such a wrong

    For the whole world.

Emilia: Why, the wrong is but a wrong i' the world, and having the world for   80
your labor, 'tis a wrong in your own world, and you might quickly make it
right.

Desdemona: I do not think there is any such woman.

Emilia: Yes, a dozen, and as many

    To th' vantage° as would store° the world they played° for.   85

    But I do think it is their husbands' faults

    If wives do fall. Say that they slack their duties°

    And pour our treasures into foreign laps,°

    Or else break out in peevish jealousies,

    Throwing restraint upon us? Or say they strike us,°   90

    Or scant our former having in despite?°

    Why, we have galls,° and though we have some grace,

    Yet have we some revenge. Let husbands know

    Their wives have sense° like them. They see, and smell,

    And have their palates both for sweet and sour,   95

---

63 _abuse_ deceive   74 _joint ring_ a ring made in separate halves.   _lawn_ fine linen   75 _exhibition_ gift
76 _Uds_ God's   85 _To th' vantage_ in addition, to boot.   _store_ populate.   _played_ (1) gambled (2)
sported sexually   87 _duties_ marital duties   88 _pour . . . laps_ i.e., are unfaithful, give what is rightfully
ours (semen) to other women   90 _Throwing . . . us_ i.e., jealously restricting our freedom to see other
men   91 _scant . . . despite_ reduce our allowance to spite us   92 _have galls_ i.e., are capable of re-
senting injury and insult   94 _sense_ physical sense

As husbands have. What is it that they do
When they change us for others? Is it sport?°
I think it is. And doth affection° breed it?
I think it doth. Is 't frailty that thus errs?
It is so, too. And have not we affections,   100
Desires for sport, and frailty, as men have?
Then let them use us well; else let them know,
The ills we do, their ills instruct us so.
Desdemona: Good night, good night. God me such uses° send
Not to pick bad from bad, but by bad mend!°   105

Exeunt.

Act V

Scene I [A Street in Cyprus.]

Enter Iago and Roderigo.

Iago: Here stand behind this bulk.° Straight will he come.
Wear thy good rapier bare,° and put it home.
Quick, quick! Fear nothing. I'll be at thy elbow.
It makes us or it mars us. Think on that,
And fix most firm thy resolution.   5
Roderigo: Be near at hand. I may miscarry in 't.
Iago: Here, at thy hand. Be bold, and take thy stand.

[*Iago stands aside. Roderigo conceals himself.*]

Roderigo: I have no great devotion to the deed;
And yet he hath given me satisfying reasons.
'Tis but a man gone. Forth, my sword! He dies.   10

[*He draws.*]

Iago: I have rubbed this young quat° almost to the sense,°
And he grows angry. Now, whether he kill Cassio
Or Cassio him, or each do kill the other,
Every way makes my gain. Live Roderigo,°
He calls me to a restitution large   15
Of gold and jewels that I bobbed° from him
As gifts to Desdemona.
It must not be. If Cassio do remain,
He hath a daily beauty in his life

___

97 *sport* sexual pastime   98 *affection* passion   104 *uses* habit, practice   105 *Not . . . mend* i.e., not to learn bad conduct from others' badness (as Emilia has suggested women learn from men), but to mend my ways by perceiving what badness is, making spiritual benefit out of evil and adversity   1 *bulk* framework projecting from the front of a shop   2 *bare* unsheathed   11 *quat* pimple, pustule. *to the sense* to the quick   14 *Live Roderigo* if Roderigo lives   16 *bobbed* swindled

That makes me ugly; and besides, the Moor
May unfold° me to him; there stand I in much peril.
No, he must die. Be 't so. I hear him coming.

Enter Cassio.

Roderigo [*coming forth*]: I know his gait, 'tis he.—Villain, thou diest!

[*He attacks Cassio.*]

Cassio: That thrust had been mine enemy indeed,
But that my coat° is better than thou know'st.   25
I will make proof° of thine.

[*He draws, and wounds Roderigo.*]

Roderigo: O, I am slain!   [*He falls.*]

[*Iago, from behind, wounds Cassio in the leg, and exits.*]

Cassio: I am maimed forever. Help, ho! Murder! Murder!

Enter Othello.

Othello: The voice of Cassio! Iago keeps his word.
Roderigo: O, villain that I am!
Othello: It is even so.   30
Cassio: O, help, ho! Light! A surgeon!
Othello: 'Tis he. O brave Iago, honest and just,
That hast such noble sense of thy friend's wrong!
Thou teachest me. Minion,° your dear lies dead,
And your unblest fate hies.° Strumpet, I come.   35
Forth of° my heart those charms, thine eyes, are blotted;
Thy bed, lust-stained, shall with lust's blood be spotted.   *Exit Othello.*

Enter Lodovico and Gratiano.

Cassio: What ho! No watch? No passage?° Murder! Murder!
Gratiano: 'Tis some mischance. The voice is very direful.
Cassio: O, help!   40
Lodovico: Hark!
Roderigo: O wretched villain!
Lodovico: Two or three groan. 'Tis heavy° night;
These may be counterfeits. Let's think 't unsafe
To come in to° the cry without more help.   45

[*They remain near the entrance.*]

---

21 *unfold* expose   25 *coat* (Possibly a garment of mail under the outer clothing, or simply a tougher coat than Roderigo expected.)   26 *proof* a test   34 *Minion* hussy (i.e., Desdemona)   35 *hies* hastens on   36 *Forth of* from out   38 *passage* people passing by   43 *heavy* thick, dark   45 *come in to* approach

Roderigo: Nobody come? Then shall I bleed to death.

    Enter Iago [in his shirtsleeves, with a light].

Lodovico: Hark!
Gratiano: Here's one comes in his shirt, with light and weapons.
Iago: Who's there? Whose noise is this that cries on° murder?
Lodovico: We do not know.
Iago: Did not you hear a cry?   50
Cassio: Here, here! For heaven's sake, help me!
Iago: What's the matter?

    [He moves toward Cassio.]

Gratiano [to Lodovico]: This is Othello's ancient, as I take it.
Lodovico [to Gratiano]: The same indeed, a very valiant fellow.
Iago [to Cassio]: What° are you here that cry so grievously?
Cassio: Iago? O, I am spoiled,° undone by villains!   55
    Give me some help.
Iago: O me, Lieutenant! What villains have done this?
Cassio: I think that one of them is hereabout,
    And cannot make° away.
Iago: O treacherous villains!

    [To Lodovico and Gratiano.]

    What are you there? Come in, and give some help.   *[They advance.]*   60
Roderigo: O, help me there!
Cassio: That's one of them.
Iago: O murderous slave! O villain!

    [He stabs Roderigo.]

Roderigo: O damned Iago! O inhuman dog!
Iago: Kill men i' the dark?—Where be these bloody thieves?—
    How silent is this town!—Ho! Murder, murder!—   65
    [To Lodovico and Gratiano.] What may you be? Are you of good or evil?
Lodovico: As you shall prove us, praise° us.
Iago: Signor Lodovico?
Lodovico: He, sir.
Iago: I cry you mercy.° Here's Cassio hurt by villains!   70
Gratiano: Cassio?
Iago: How is 't, brother?
Cassio: My leg is cut in two.
Iago: Marry, heaven forbid!
    Light, gentlemen! I'll bind it with my shirt.   75

---

49 *cries on* cries out   54 *What* who (also at lines 60 and 66)   55 *spoiled* ruined, done for   59 *make*
get   67 *praise* appraise   70 *I cry you mercy* I beg your pardon

[He hands them the light, and tends to Cassio's wound.]

    Enter Bianca.

Bianca: What is the matter, ho? Who is 't that cried?
Iago: Who is 't that cried?
Bianca: O my dear Cassio!
    My sweet Cassio! O Cassio, Cassio, Cassio!
Iago: O notable strumpet! Cassio, may you suspect
    Who they should be that have thus mangled you?   80
Cassio: No.
Gratiano: I am sorry to find you thus. I have been to seek you.
Iago: Lend me a garter. *[He applies a tourniquet.]* So.—O, for a chair,°
    To bear him easily hence!
Bianca: Alas, he faints! O Cassio, Cassio, Cassio!   85
Iago: Gentlemen all, I do suspect this trash
    To be a party in this injury.—
    Patience awhile, good Cassio.—Come, come;
    Lend me a light. *[He shines the light on Roderigo.]*
               Know we this face or no?
    Alas, my friend and my dear countryman   90
    Roderigo! No.—Yes, sure.—O heaven! Roderigo!
Gratiano: What, of Venice?
Iago: Even he, sir. Did you know him?
Gratiano: Know him? Ay.
Iago: Signor Gratiano? I cry your gentle° pardon.   95
    These bloody accidents° must excuse my manners
    That so neglected you.
Gratiano: I am glad to see you.
Iago: How do you, Cassio? O, a chair, a chair!
Gratiano: Roderigo!
Iago: He, he, 'tis he. *[A litter is brought in.]* O, that's well said;° the chair.   100
    Some good man bear him carefully from hence;
    I'll fetch the General's surgeon. *[To Bianca.]* For you, mistress,
    Save you your labor.°—He that lies slain here, Cassio,
    Was my dear friend. What malice° was between you?
Cassio: None in the world, nor do I know the man.   105
Iago [to Bianca]: What, look you pale?—O, bear him out o' th' air.°

    [Cassio and Roderigo are borne off.]

    Stay you,° good gentlemen.—Look you pale, mistress?—
    Do you perceive the gastness° of her eye?—

---

83 *chair* litter   95 *gentle* noble   96 *accidents* sudden events   100 *well said* well done   103 *Save . . . labor* i.e., never you mind tending Cassio   104 *malice* enmity   106 *bear . . . air* (Fresh air was thought to be dangerous for a wound.)   107 *Stay you* (Lodovico and Gratiano are evidently about to leave.)   108 *gastness* terror

Nay, if you stare,° we shall hear more anon.—
Behold her well; I pray you, look upon her.   110
Do you see, gentlemen? Nay, guiltiness
Will speak, though tongues were out of use.

[*Enter Emilia.*]

Emilia: 'Las, what's the matter? What's the matter, husband?
Iago: Cassio hath here been set on in the dark
By Roderigo and fellows that are scaped.   115
He's almost slain, and Roderigo dead.
Emilia: Alas, good gentleman! Alas, good Cassio!
Iago: This is the fruits of whoring. Prithee, Emilia,
Go know° of Cassio where he supped tonight.
[*To Bianca.*] What, do you shake at that?   120
Bianca: He supped at my house, but I therefore shake not.
Iago: O, did he so? I charge you go with me.
Emilia: O, fie upon thee, strumpet!
Bianca: I am no strumpet, but of life as honest°
As you that thus abuse me.   125
Emilia: As I? Faugh! Fie upon thee!
Iago: Kind gentlemen, let's go see poor Cassio dressed.°—
Come, mistress, you must tell's another tale.
Emilia, run you to the citadel
And tell my lord and lady what hath happed.—   130
Will you go on afore? [*Aside.*] This is the night
That either makes me or fordoes° me quite.   *Exeunt.*

Scene II [A Bedchamber in the Citadel.]

Enter Othello [with a light], and Desdemona in her bed.°

Othello: It is the cause,° it is the cause, my soul.
Let me not name it to you, you chaste stars!
It is the cause. Yet I'll not shed her blood,
Nor scar that whiter skin of hers than snow,
And smooth as monumental° alabaster.   5
Yet she must die, else she'll betray more men.
Put out the light, and then put out the light.°
If I quench thee, thou flaming minister,°
I can again thy former light restore,

---

109 *stare* (Iago pretends to interpret Bianca's wild looks as an involuntary confession of guilt.)   119
know learn   124 *honest* chaste   127 *Cassio dressed* Cassio's wounds dressed   132 *fordoes* undoes,
ruins   s.d. *in her bed* (Either the curtains are drawn back to reveal the bed in a recessed area backstage, or the bed is "thrust out" onstage as the scene begins.)   1 *cause* i.e., cause of justice, the offense itself, which Othello must correct as an agent of justice   5 *monumental* i.e., used in making
tombs and funeral monuments   7 *the light . . . light* the torch or lamp . . . Desdemona's life   8
flaming minister torch or lamp that serves m

Should I repent me;° but once put out thy light,

Thou cunning'st pattern° of excelling nature,
I know not where is that Promethean heat°
That can thy light relume.° When I have plucked thy rose,
I cannot give it vital growth again;
It needs must wither. I'll smell thee on the tree.

[*He kisses her.*]

O balmy breath, that dost almost persuade
Justice to break her sword! One more, one more.
Be thus when thou art dead, and I will kill thee,
And love thee after. One more, and that's the last.

[*He kisses her.*]

So sweet was ne'er so fatal. I must weep,
But they are cruel° tears. This sorrow's heavenly;
It strikes where it doth love.° She wakes.
Desdemona: Who's there? Othello?
Othello: Ay, Desdemona.
Desdemona: Will you come to bed, my lord?
Othello: Have you prayed tonight, Desdemon?
Desdemona: Ay, my lord.
Othello: If you bethink yourself of any crime°
Unreconciled as yet to heaven and grace,
Solicit° for it straight.°
Desdemona: Alack, my lord, what may you mean by that?
Othello: Well, do it, and be brief. I will walk by.
I would not kill thy unprepared spirit.
No, heaven forfend!° I would not kill thy soul.
Desdemona: Talk you of killing?
Othello: Ay, I do.
Desdemona: Then heaven
Have mercy on me!
Othello: Amen, with all my heart!
Desdemona: If you say so, I hope you will not kill me.
Othello: Humh!
Desdemona: And yet I fear you; for you're fatal then
When your eyes roll so. Why I should fear I know not,
Since guiltiness I know not; but yet I feel I fear.
Othello: Think on thy sins.

10 *repent me* change my mind   11 *Thou . . . pattern* you skillfully wrought perfect example   12 *Promethean heat* divine fire. (Alluding to the theft of fire from heaven by Prometheus.)   13 *relume* rekindle   21 *cruel* unrelenting   22 *It . . . love* (Compare Hebrews 12:6: "For whom the Lord loveth he chasteneth.")   28 *crime* sin   30 *Solicit* petition, pray.   *straight* immediately   34 *forfend* forbid

Desdemona: They are loves I bear to you.°
Othello: Ay, and for that thou diest.
Desdemona: That death's unnatural that kills for loving.
　　Alas, why gnaw you so your nether lip?
　　Some bloody passion shakes your very frame.   45
　　These are portents; but yet I hope, I hope,
　　They do not point on° me.
Othello: Peace, and be still!
Desdemona: I will so. What's the matter?   50
Othello: That handkerchief which I so loved and gave thee
　　Thou gav'st to Cassio.
Desdemona: No, by my life and soul!
　　Send for the man and ask him.
Othello: Sweet soul, take heed, take heed of perjury.
　　Thou art on thy deathbed.   55
Desdemona: Ay, but not yet to die.
Othello: Yes, presently.°
　　Therefore confess thee freely of thy sin;
　　For to deny each article with oath
　　Cannot remove nor choke the strong conception°
　　That I do groan withal.° Thou art to die.   60
Desdemona: Then Lord have mercy on me!
Othello: I say, amen.
Desdemona: And have you mercy too! I never did
　　Offend° you in my life; never loved Cassio
　　But with such general warranty° of heaven
　　As I might love. I never gave him token.   65
Othello: By heaven, I saw my handkerchief in 's hand.
　　O perjured woman! Thou dost stone° my heart,
　　And makes me call what I intend to do
　　A murder, which I thought a sacrifice.
　　I saw the handkerchief.
Desdemona: He found it, then.   70
　　I never gave it him. Send for him hither;
　　Let him confess a truth.
Othello: He hath confessed.
Desdemona: What, my lord?
Othello: That he hath used thee.
Desdemona: How? Unlawfully?
Othello: Ay.
Desdemona: He will not say so.

---

42 *They are . . . you* i.e., if I sinned, it was in loving you more than my father or more than God   48
point on point at, predict what is to happen to   56 *presently* immediately   59 *conception* (1) belief in
your guilt (2) plan in my mind   60 *groan withal* (1) groan at in sorrow (2) as in giving birth   63 *Offend* wrong   64 *warranty* sanction   67 *stone* turn to stone, harden

Othello:	No, his mouth is stopped;	75

Honest Iago hath ta'en order° for 't.

Desdemona: O, my fear interprets. What, is he dead?

Othello: Had all his hairs been lives, my great revenge
    Had stomach for them all.

Desdemona: Alas, he is betrayed and I undone!   [*She weeps.*] 80

Othello: Out, strumpet! Weep'st thou for him to my face?

Desdemona: O, banish me, my lord, but kill me not!

Othello: Down, strumpet!

Desdemona: Kill me tomorrow; let me live tonight!

Othello: Nay, if you strive—   85

Desdemona: But half an hour!

Othello: Being done,° there is no pause.

Desdemona: But while I say one prayer!

Othello: It is too late.

    Smothers her.

Emilia [*at the door*]: My lord, my lord! What, ho! My lord, my lord!

Othello: What noise is this? Not dead? Not yet quite dead?
    I that am cruel am yet merciful;   90
    I would not have thee linger in thy pain.

    [*He dispatches her.*]

                         So, so.

Emilia [*within*]: What, ho! My lord, my lord!

Othello: Who's there?

Emilia [*within*]: O, good my lord, I would speak a word with you!

Othello: Yes, 'tis Emilia.—By and by.—She's dead.   95
    'Tis like° she comes to speak of Cassio's death.—
    The noise was here.° Ha! No more moving?
    Still as the grave. Shall she come in? Were 't good?—
    I think she stirs again. No. What's best to do?
    If she come in, she'll sure speak to my wife.
    My wife! My wife! What wife? I have no wife.   100
    O, insupportable! O heavy hour!
    Methinks it should be now a huge eclipse
    Of sun and moon, and that th' affrighted globe
    Should yawn° at alteration.°

Emilia [*within*]:   I do beseech you
    That I may speak with you, O, good my lord!   105

---

76 *ta'en order* taken measures   86 *Being done* i.e., since justice has begun its relentless course   95 *like* likely that   96 *here* (The Folio's *high* is possible, suggesting that the commotion of the attack on Cassio was loud.)   104 *yawn* gape in amazement, i.e., move in an earthquake. (According to Pliny, earthquakes often happen during eclipses.)   *at alteration* at these cataclysmic events in nature, well suited to express the horror of Desdemona's death

Othello: I had forgot thee. O, come in, Emilia.—
   Soft,° by and by. Let me the curtains draw.—

[*He closes the bed-curtains and opens the door.*]

   Where art thou?

Enter Emilia.

                              What's the matter with thee now?
Emilia: O, my good lord, yonder's foul murders done!
Othello: What, now?   110
Emilia: But now, my lord.
Othello: It is the very error° of the moon;
   She comes more nearer earth than she was wont,
   And makes men mad.
Emilia: Cassio, my lord, hath killed a young Venetian   115
   Called Roderigo.
Othello: Roderigo killed?
   And Cassio killed?
Emilia: No, Cassio is not killed.
Othello: Not Cassio killed? Then murder's out of tune,
   And sweet revenge grows harsh.
Desdemona: O, falsely, falsely murdered!   120
Emilia: O Lord, what cry is that?
Othello: That? What?
Emilia: Out° and alas, that was my lady's voice.

   [*She opens the bed-curtains.*]

   Help, help, ho, help! O lady, speak again!
   Sweet Desdemona! O sweet mistress, speak!   125
Desdemona: A guiltless death I die.
Emilia: O, who hath done this deed?
Desdemona: Nobody; I myself. Farewell.
   Commend me to my kind lord. O, farewell!   [*She dies.*]
Othello: Why, how should she be murdered?
Emilia: Alas, who knows?   130
Othello: You heard her say herself it was not I.
Emilia: She said so. I must needs report the truth.
Othello: She's like a liar gone to burning hell!
   'Twas I that killed her.
Emilia: O, the more angel she,
   And you the blacker devil!   135
Othello: She turned to folly,° and she was a whore.
Emilia: Thou dost belie° her, and thou art a devil.

---

107 *Soft* wait a minute   112 *error* aberration, irregularity   123 *Out* (A cry of dismay, intensifying *alas*.)   136 *folly* i.e., wantonness, fleshly sin   137 *belie* slander

Othello: She was false as water.

Emilia: Thou art rash as fire to say
　　That she was false. O, she was heavenly true!　　　　140

Othello: Cassio did top her. Ask thy husband else.°
　　O, I were damned beneath all depth in hell
　　But that I did proceed upon just grounds
　　To this extremity. Thy husband knew it all.

Emilia: My husband?　　　　145

Othello: Thy husband.

Emilia: That she was false to wedlock?

Othello: Ay, with Cassio. Nay, had she been true,
　　If heaven would make me such another world
　　Of one entire and perfect chrysolite,°　　　　150
　　I'd not have sold her for it.

Emilia: My husband?

Othello: Ay, 'twas he that told me on her first.
　　An honest man he is, and hates the slime
　　That sticks on filthy deeds.　　　　155

Emilia: My husband?

Othello: What needs this iterance,° woman? I say thy husband.

Emilia: O mistress, villainy hath made mocks with° love!
　　My husband say she was false?

Othello:　　　　　　　　　　He, woman;
　　I say thy husband. Dost understand the word?　　　　160
　　My friend, thy husband, honest, honest Iago.

Emilia: If he say so, may his pernicious soul
　　Rot half a grain a day! He lies to th' heart.
　　She was too fond of her most filthy bargain.

Othello: Ha?　　　　　　　　　　　　[He draws.]　165

Emilia: Do thy worst!
　　This deed of thine is no more worthy heaven
　　Than thou wast worthy her.

Othello:　　　　　　　　　　Peace, you were best.°

Emilia: Thou hast not half that power to do me harm
　　As I have to be hurt.° O gull!° O dolt!　　　　170
　　As ignorant as dirt! Thou hast done a deed—
　　I care not for thy sword; I'll make thee known,
　　Though I lost twenty lives.—Help! Help, ho, help!
　　The Moor hath killed my mistress! Murder, murder!

Enter Montano, Gratiano, and Iago.

---

141 *else* i.e., if you don't believe me　150 *chrysolite* precious topaz　157 *iterance* iteration, repetition
158 *made mocks with* derided, made sport of　168 *you were best* it would be best for you　170 *to be
hurt* i.e., to endure hurt.　*gull* dupe

Montano: What is the matter? How now, General?   175
Emilia: O, are you come, Iago? You have done well,
    That men must lay their murders on your neck.
Gratiano: What is the matter?
Emilia [*to Iago*]: Disprove this villain, if thou be'st a man.
    He says thou toldst him that his wife was false.   180
    I know thou didst not; thou'rt not such a villain.
    Speak, for my heart is full.
Iago: I told him what I thought, and told no more
    Than what he found himself was apt° and true.
Emilia: But did you ever tell him she was false?   185
Iago: I did.
Emilia: You told a lie, an odious, damnèd lie!
    Upon my soul, a lie, a wicked lie.
    She false with Cassio? Did you say with Cassio?
Iago: With Cassio, mistress. Go to, charm° your tongue.   190
Emilia: I will not charm my tongue; I am bound to speak.
    My mistress here lies murdered in her bed—
All: O heavens forfend!
Emilia: And your reports have set the murder on.
Othello: Nay, stare not, masters. It is true indeed.   195
Gratiano: 'Tis a strange truth.
Montano: O monstrous act!
Emilia: Villainy, villainy, villainy!
    I think upon 't—I think I smell 't! O villainy!
    I thought so then°—I'll kill myself for grief—
    O villainy, villainy!   200
Iago: What, are you mad? I charge you, get you home.
Emilia: Good gentlemen, let me have leave to speak.
    'Tis proper I obey him, but not now.
    Perchance, Iago, I will ne'er go home.
Othello: O! O! O!   [*Othello falls on the bed.°*]
Emilia: Nay, lay thee down and roar,   205
    For thou hast killed the sweetest innocent
    That e'er did lift up eye.°
Othello [*rising*]:   O, she was foul!
    I scarce did know you, uncle. There lies your niece,
    Whose breath indeed these hands have newly stopped.
    I know this act shows° horrible and grim.   210
Gratiano: Poor Desdemon! I am glad thy father's dead.
    Thy match was mortal to him, and pure grief

---

184 *apt* plausible   190 *charm* keep silent (as though by a magic spell)   199 *then* (Perhaps at Act III, Scene iii, lines 331–332 and Act IV, Scene ii, lines 137–154.)   205 s.d. *Othello . . . bed* (This direction is from the Quarto, as also *He kisses her* at line 19 and *She dies* at line 129.)   207 *lift up eye* i.e., lift her eyes to heaven   210 *shows* looks

Shore his old thread° in twain. Did he live now,
This sight would make him do a desperate turn,°
Yea, curse his better angel from his side, 215
And fall to reprobance.°
Othello: 'Tis pitiful. But yet Iago knows
That she with Cassio hath the act of shame
A thousand times committed. Cassio confessed it;
And she did gratify° his amorous works 220
With that recognizance° and pledge of love
Which I first gave her. I saw it in his hand;
It was a handkerchief, an antique token
My father gave my mother.
Emilia: O God! O heavenly God! 225
Iago: Zounds, hold your peace.
Emilia: 'Twill out, 'twill out! I peace?
No, I will speak as liberal as the north.°
Let heaven and men and devils, let them all,
All, all, cry shame against me, yet I'll speak.
Iago: Be wise, and get you home.
Emilia: I will not.

[*Iago threatens Emilia.*]

Gratiano: Fie 230
Your sword upon a woman?
Emilia: O thou dull Moor! That handkerchief thou speak'st of
I found by fortune and did give my husband;
For often, with a solemn earnestness,
More than indeed belonged° to such a trifle, 235
He begged of me to steal 't.
Iago: Villainous whore!
Emilia: She give it Cassio? No, alas! I found it,
And I did give 't my husband.
Iago: Filth, thou liest!
Emilia: By heaven, I do not, I do not, gentlemen.
O murderous coxcomb!° What should such a fool 240
Do with so good a wife?
Othello: Are there no stones° in heaven
But what serves for the thunder?—Precious° villain!

[*He runs at Iago; Montano disarms Othello. Iago, from behind, stabs Emilia.*°]

213 *Shore . . . thread* sheared the thread of his old age (as Atropos, one of the three Fates, was
thought to do)   214 *turn* deed   216 *reprobance* damnation, i.e., suicide   220 *gratify* reward   221
recognizance token   227 *liberal as the north* freely as the north wind (blows)   235 *belonged* was appropriate   240 *coxcomb* fool. (Addressed to Othello.)   242 *stones* bolts, such as those used for thunder-
bolts   243 *Precious* i.e., arrant, utter.   s.d. *He . . . Emilia* (The Quarto text reads, "The Moor runs at
Iago. Iago kills his wife." The Quarto also specifies the exit of Iago at line 245 and the death of Emilia
at line 260.)

Gratiano: The woman falls! Sure he hath killed his wife.
Emilia: Ay, ay. O, lay me by my mistress' side.   245

    Exit [Iago.]

Gratiano: He's gone, but his wife's killed.
Montano: 'Tis a notorious villain. Take you this weapon,
    Which I have here recovered from the Moor.
    Come, guard the door without. Let him not pass,
    But kill him rather. I'll after that same villain,   250
    For 'tis a damnèd slave.

    Exit [with all but Othello and Emilia, who has been laid by Desdemona's side].

Othello: I am not valiant neither,
    But every puny whipster° gets my sword.
    But why should honor° outlive honesty?°
    Let it go all.
Emilia: What did thy song bode, lady?   255
    Hark, canst thou hear me? I will play the swan,
    And die in music. [*She sings.*] "Willow, willow, willow."
    Moor, she was chaste. She loved thee, cruel Moor.
    So come my soul to bliss as I speak true.
    So speaking as I think, alas, I die.   [*She dies.*]   260
Othello: I have another weapon in this chamber;
    It was a sword of Spain, the ice-brook's temper°—
    O, here it is. [*He finds a sword.*] Uncle, I must come forth.
Gratiano [within]: If thou attempt it, it will cost thee dear.
    Thou hast no weapon, and perforce must suffer.   265
Othello: Look in upon me then and speak with me,
    Or, naked° as I am, I will assault thee.

    [Enter Gratiano.]

Gratiano: What is the matter?
Othello: Behold, I have a weapon;
    A better never did itself sustain
    Upon a soldier's thigh. I have seen the day   270
    That, with this little arm and this good sword,
    I have made my way through more impediments
    Than twenty times your stop.° But O, vain boast!

---

253 *whipster* contemptible fellow (one who is always ready to whip out his sword)   254 *honor* i.e., the bravery for which one enjoys a soldier's reputation.   *honesty* true integrity   262 *the ice-brook's temper* tempered in ice-cold water   267 *naked* unarmed   273 *stop* power (to stop)

Who can control his fate? 'Tis not so now.
Be not afraid, though you do see me weaponed;   275
Here is my journey's end, here is my butt°
And very seamark° of my utmost sail.

[*Gratiano steps back.*]

Do you go back dismayed? 'Tis a lost° fear;
Man but a rush° against Othello's breast
And he retires. Where should Othello go?   280

[*He turns to Desdemona.*]

Now, how dost thou look now? O ill-starred wench!
Pale as thy smock! When we shall meet at compt,°
This look of thine will hurl my soul from heaven,
And fiends will snatch at it. Cold, cold, my girl?
Even like thy chastity. O cursèd, cursèd slave!°   285
Whip me, ye devils,
From the possession of this heavenly sight!
Blow me about in winds! Roast me in sulfur!
Wash me in steep-down gulfs of liquid fire!
O Desdemon! Dead, Desdemon! Dead! O! O!   290

*Enter Lodovico, Cassio [carried in a litter°], Montano, and Iago [prisoner], with
officers.*

Lodovico: Where is this rash and most unfortunate man?
Othello: That's he that was Othello. Here I am.
Lodovico: Where is that viper? Bring the villain forth.

[*Iago is led forward.*]

Othello: I look down towards his feet;° but that's a fable.
If that thou be'st a devil, I cannot kill thee.   295

[*He wounds Iago.*]

Lodovico: Wrench his sword from him.   [*Othello is disarmed.*]
Iago: I bleed, sir, but not killed.
Othello: I am not sorry neither. I'd have thee live,
For in my sense° 'tis happiness to die.

---

276 *butt* goal, limit. (An archery term.)   277 *seamark* beacon (marking his destination or limit)
278 *lost* wasted, unneeded   279 *Man . . . rush* wield no more than a reed   282 *compt* account, judgment day   285 *slave* i.e., Othello himself   290 s.d. *in a litter* (The Quarto specifies that Cassio is "in
a chair.")   294 *towards his feet* i.e., to see if they are cloven, as the devil's are fabled to be   298 *in my
sense* to one who feels as I do

Lodovico: O thou Othello, that was once so good,
Fall'n in the practice° of a cursèd slave,° 300
What shall be said to thee?
Othello: Why, anything.
An honorable murderer, if you will,
For naught I did in hate, but all in honor.
Lodovico: This wretch hath part confessed his villainy.
Did you and he consent° in Cassio's death? 305
Othello: Ay.
Cassio: Dear General, I never gave you cause.
Othello: I do believe it, and I ask your pardon.
Will you, I pray, demand that demi-devil
Why he hath thus ensnared my soul and body? 310
Iago: Demand me nothing. What you know, you know.
From this time forth I never will speak word.
Lodovico: What, not to pray?
Gratiano: Torments° will ope your lips.
Othello: Well, thou dost best. 315
Lodovico: Sir, you shall understand what hath befall'n,
Which, as I think, you know not. Here is a letter
Found in the pocket of the slain Roderigo;
And here another. [*He produces letters.*] The one of them imports
The death of Cassio, to be undertook 320
By Roderigo.
Othello: O villain!
Cassio: Most heathenish and most gross!°
Lodovico [*showing another paper*]: Now here's another discontented° paper
Found in his pocket too. And this, it seems,
Roderigo meant t' have sent this damnèd villain; 325
But that belike° Iago in the interim
Came in and satisfied him.°
Othello: O thou pernicious caitiff!—
How came you, Cassio, by that handkerchief
That was my wife's?
Cassio: I found it in my chamber; 330
And he himself confessed but even now
That there he dropped it for a special purpose
Which wrought to his desire.°
Othello: O fool, fool, fool!
Cassio: There is besides in Roderigo's letter
How he upbraids Iago, that he made him 335
Brave° me upon the watch, whereon it came°

---

300 *in the practice* through the plotting, into the snare.   *slave* villain   305 *consent* agree   314 *Torments* torture   322 *gross* monstrous   323 *discontented* full of discontent   326 *belike* most likely   327 *Came . . . him* interposed and gave him satisfactory explanation   333 *wrought . . . desire* worked out as he wished, fitted in with his plan   336 *Brave* defy.   *whereon it came* whereof it came about

That I was cast;° and even but now he spake,
After long seeming dead, Iago hurt him,
Iago set him on.
Lodovico [*to Othello*]: You must forsake this room and go with us.   340
    Your power and your command is taken off,°
    And Cassio rules in Cyprus. For this slave,
    If there be any cunning cruelty
    That can torment him much and hold him long,°
    It shall be his. You shall close prisoner rest°   345
    Till that the nature of your fault be known
    To the Venetian state.—Come, bring away.
Othello: Soft you;° a word or two before you go.
    I have done the state some service, and they know 't.
    No more of that. I pray you, in your letters,   350
    When you shall these unlucky° deeds relate,
    Speak of me as I am; nothing extenuate,
    Nor set down aught in malice. Then must you speak
    Of one that loved not wisely but too well;
    Of one not easily jealous but, being wrought,°   355
    Perplexed° in the extreme; of one whose hand,
    Like the base Indian,° threw a pearl away
    Richer than all his tribe; of one whose subdued° eyes,
    Albeit unusèd to the melting mood,
    Drops tears as fast as the Arabian trees   360
    Their medicinable gum.° Set you down this;
    And say besides that in Aleppo once,
    Where a malignant and a turbaned Turk
    Beat a Venetian and traduced the state,
    I took by th' throat the circumcisèd dog   365
    And smote him, thus.   [*He stabs himself.*°]
Lodovico: O bloody period!°
Gratiano: All that is spoke is marred.
Othello: I kissed thee ere I killed thee. No way but this,
    Killing myself, to die upon a kiss.   370

    [*He kisses Desdemona and*] *dies.*

Cassio: This did I fear, but thought he had no weapon;
    For he was great of heart.

---

337 *cast* dismissed   341 *taken off* taken away   344 *hold him long* keep him alive a long time (during his torture)   345 *rest* remain   348 *Soft you* one moment   351 *unlucky* unfortunate   355 *wrought* worked upon, worked into a frenzy   356 *Perplexed* distraught   357 *Indian* (This reading from the Quarto pictures an ignorant savage who cannot recognize the value of a precious jewel. The Folio reading, *Iudean* or *Judean*, i.e., infidel or disbeliever, may refer to Herod, who slew Miriamne in a fit of jealousy, or to Judas Iscariot, the betrayer of Christ.)   358 *subdued* i.e., overcome by grief   361 *gum* i.e., myrrh   366 s.d. *He stabs himself* (This direction is in the Quarto text.)   367 *period* termination, conclusion

Lodovico [*to Iago*]:   O Spartan dog,°
    More fell° than anguish, hunger, or the sea!
    Look on the tragic loading of this bed.
    This is thy work. The object poisons sight;   375
    Let it be hid.° Gratiano, keep° the house,

[*The bed curtains are drawn*]

    And seize upon° the fortunes of the Moor,
    For they succeed on° you. [*To Cassio.*] To you, Lord Governor,
    Remains the censure° of this hellish villain,
    The time, the place, the torture. O, enforce it!   380
    Myself will straight aboard, and to the state
    This heavy act with heavy heart relate.   *Exeunt.*

QUESTIONS

ACT I

1. What is Othello's position in society? How is he regarded by those who know him? By his own words, when we first meet him in Scene ii, what traits of character does he manifest?
2. How do you account for Brabantio's dismay on learning of his daughter's marriage, despite the fact that Desdemona has married a man so generally honored and admired?
3. What is Iago's view of human nature? In his fondness for likening men to animals (as in I, i, 49–50; I, i, 90–91; and I, iii, 380–81), what does he tell us about himself?
4. What reasons does Iago give for his hatred of Othello?
5. In Othello's defense before the senators (Scene iii), how does he explain Desdemona's gradual falling in love with him?
6. Is Brabantio's warning to Othello (I, iii, 293–94) an accurate or an inaccurate prophecy?
7. By what strategy does Iago enlist Roderigo in his plot against the Moor? In what lines do we learn Iago's true feelings toward Roderigo?

ACT II

1. What do the Cypriots think of Othello? Do their words (in Scene i) make him seem to us a lesser man or a larger one?
2. What cruelty does Iago display toward Emilia? How well founded is his distrust of his wife's fidelity?
3. In II, iii, 221, Othello speaks of Iago's "honesty and love." How do you account for Othello's being so totally deceived?
4. For what major events does the merrymaking (proclaimed in Scene ii) give opportunity?

ACT III

1. Trace the steps by which Iago rouses Othello to suspicion. Is there anything in Othello's character or circumstances that renders him particularly susceptible to Iago's wiles?

---

372 *Spartan dog* (Spartan dogs were noted for their savagery and silence.)   373 *fell* cruel   376 *Let it be hid* i.e., draw the bed curtains. (No stage direction specifies that the dead are to be carried offstage at the end of the play.) *keep* remain in   377 *seize upon* take legal possession of   378 *succeed on* pass as though by inheritance to   379 *censure* sentencing

2. In III, iv, 49–98, Emilia knows of Desdemona's distress over the lost handkerchief. At this moment, how do you explain her failure to relieve Desdemona's mind? Is Emilia aware of her husband's villainy?

ACT IV

1. In this act, what circumstantial evidence is added to Othello's case against Desdemona?
2. How plausible do you find Bianca's flinging the handkerchief at Cassio just when Othello is looking on? How important is the handkerchief in this play? What does it represent? What suggestions or hints do you find in it?
3. What prevents Othello from being moved by Desdemona's appeal (IV, ii, 33–92)?
4. When Roderigo grows impatient with Iago (IV, ii, 181–202), how does Iago make use of his fellow plotter's discontent?
5. What does the conversation between Emilia and Desdemona (Scene iii) tell us about the nature of each?
6. In this act, what scenes (or speeches) contain memorable dramatic irony?

ACT V

1. Summarize the events that lead to Iago's unmasking.
2. How does Othello's mistaken belief that Cassio is slain (V, i, 27–34) affect the outcome of the play?
3. What is Iago's motive in stabbing Roderigo?
4. In your interpretation of the play, exactly what impels Othello to kill Desdemona? Jealousy? Desire for revenge? Excess idealism? A wish to be a public avenger who punishes, "else she'll betray more men"?
5. What do you understand by Othello's calling himself "one that loved not wisely but too well" (V, ii, 354)?
6. In your view, does Othello's long speech in V, ii, 348–66 succeed in restoring his original dignity and nobility? Do you agree with Cassio (V, ii, 372) that Othello was "great of heart"?

GENERAL QUESTIONS

1. What motivates Iago to carry out his schemes? Do you find him a devil incarnate, a madman, or a rational human being?
2. Whom besides Othello does Iago deceive? What is Desdemona's opinion of him? Emilia's? Cassio's (before Iago is found out)? To what do you attribute Iago's success as a deceiver?
3. How essential to the play is the fact that Othello is a black man, a Moor, and not a native of Venice?
4. In the introduction to his edition of the play in *The Complete Signet Classic Shakespeare*, Alvin Kernan remarks:

> *Othello* is probably the most neatly, the most formally constructed of Shakespeare's plays. Every character is, for example, balanced by another similar or contrasting character. Desdemona is balanced by her opposite, Iago; love and concern for others at one end of the scale, hatred and concern for self at the other.

Besides Desdemona and Iago, what other pairs of characters strike balances?
5. Consider any passage of the play in which there is a shift from verse to prose, or from prose to verse. What is the effect of this shift?

6. Indicate a passage that you consider memorable for its poetry. Does the passage seem introduced for its own sake? Does it in any way advance the action of the play, express theme, or demonstrate character?

7. Does the play contain any tragic *recognition*—as discussed on page 1296, a moment of terrible enlightenment, a "realization of the unthinkable"?

8. Does the downfall of Othello proceed from any flaw in his nature, or is his downfall entirely the work of Iago?

WRITER'S PERSPECTIVE

W. H. Auden

W. H. Auden on Drama IAGO AS A TRIUMPHANT VILLAIN 1962

Any consideration of the *Tragedy of Othello* must be primarily occupied, not with its official hero but with its villain. I cannot think of any other play in which only one character performs personal actions—all the *deeds* are Iago's—and all the others without exception only exhibit behavior. In marrying each other, Othello and Desdemona have performed a deed, but this took place before the play begins. Nor can I think of another play in which the villain is so completely triumphant: everything Iago sets out to do, he accomplishes—(among his goals, I include his self-destruction). Even Cassio, who survives, is maimed for life.

If *Othello* is a tragedy—and one certainly cannot call it a comedy—it is tragic in a peculiar way. In most tragedies the fall of the hero from glory to misery and death is the work, either of the gods, or of his own freely chosen acts, or, more commonly, a mixture of both. But the fall of Othello is the work of another human being; nothing he says or does originates with himself. In consequence we feel pity for him but no respect; our aesthetic respect is reserved for Iago.

Iago is a wicked man. The wicked man, the stage villain, as a subject of serious dramatic interest does not, so far as I know, appear in the drama of western Europe before the Elizabethans. In the mystery plays, the wicked characters, like Satan or Herod, are treated comically, but the theme of the triumphant villain cannot be treated comically because the suffering he inflicts is real.

"The Joker in the Pack"

Breaking the Language Barrier

The basic problem a modern reader faces with Shakespeare is language. Shakespeare's English is now four hundred years old, and it differs in innumerable small ways from contemporary American usage. Although his idiom may at first seem daunting, it is easily mastered if you make the effort. There is only one way to grow comfortable with Shakespeare's language: you must immerse yourself in it—a highly pleasurable undertaking.

There is no substitute for hearing Shakespeare's language in performance. He wrote the plays to be heard as spoken language rather than read silently on the page. Let your ears do the work. After reading the play in this book, listen to a recording of it. (This is also an invaluable and enjoyable way to review a play.) Most school libraries have recordings of all the major plays of Shakespeare. Hearing *Othello* or *Hamlet* recited by an accomplished actor will almost always communicate its meaning to you, as well as familiarize you with the bard's Elizabethan idiom. It will also help to watch the play on videotape, although you will need to read it carefully as well since most films cut sections of the original text. The more time you spend listening, the more quickly you will master the nuances of the language.

Before you write about any Shakespeare play, read the text more than once. The first time through an Elizabethan-era text, you will almost certainly miss many things. As you grow more familiar with Shakespeare's language, you will be able to read it with more complete comprehension. If you choose to write about a particular episode or character, carefully study the speeches and dialogue in question (paying special attention to footnotes) so that you understand each word. You can't write about a text you don't know how to read. In your paper, don't hesitate to bring in what you have learned. Discuss how key words you quote had different meanings in Shakespeare's day.

Enjoy yourself. From Peking to Berlin, Buenos Aires to Oslo, Shakespeare is almost universally acknowledged as the world's greatest playwright, a master entertainer as well as consummate artist. Literature holds few pleasures so consistently delectable.

WRITING ASSIGNMENT

Select any tragedy found in the book (*Othello, Hamlet, Riders to the Sea, Oedipus the King,* or *Antigonê*), and analyze it using Aristotle's definition of the form. Does the play measure up to Aristotle's requirements for a tragedy? In what ways does it meet the definition? In what ways does it depart? (Be sure to state clearly the Aristotelian rules by which drama is to be judged.)

Here is a paper written in response to this assignment by Janet Housden, a student of Melinda Barth at El Camino College.

Othello: Tragedy or Soap Opera?

When we hear the word "tragedy," we usually think of

either a terrible real-life disaster, or a dark and serious

drama filled with pain, suffering, and loss that involves the downfall of a powerful person due to some character flaw or error in judgment. William Shakespeare's Othello is such a drama. Set in Venice and Cyprus during the Renaissance, the play tells the story of Othello, a Moorish general in the Venetian army, who has just married Desdemona, the daughter of a Venetian nobleman. Through the plotting of a jealous villain, Iago, Othello is deceived into believing that Desdemona has been unfaithful to him. He murders her in revenge, only to discover too late how he has been tricked. Overcome by shame and grief, Othello kills himself.

Dealing as it does with jealousy, murder, and suicide, the play is certainly dark, but is Othello a true tragedy? In the fourth century B.C., the Greek philosopher Aristotle proposed a formal definition of tragedy (Kennedy 1295), which only partially fits Othello.

The first characteristic of tragedy identified by Aristotle is that the protagonist is a person of outstanding quality and high social position. While Othello is not of royal birth as are many tragic heroes and heroines, he does occupy a sufficiently high position to satisfy this part of Aristotle's definition. Although Othello is a foreigner and a soldier by trade, he has risen to the rank of general and has married into a noble family, which is quite an accomplishment for an outsider. Furthermore, Othello is generally liked and respected by those around him. He is often described by others as being "noble," "brave," and "valiant." By virtue of his high rank and the respect he commands from others, Othello would appear to possess the high stature commonly given to the tragic hero in order to make his eventual fall seem all the more tragic.

While Othello displays the nobility and high status commonly associated with the tragic hero, he also possesses another, less admirable characteristic, the flaw or character defect shared by all heroes of classical tragedy. In Othello's case, it is a stunning gullibility, combined with a violent temper that once awakened overcomes all reason. These flaws permit Othello to be easily deceived and manipulated by the villainous Iago and make him easy prey for the "green-eyed monster" (3.3.179).

It is because of this tragic flaw, according to Aristotle, that the hero is at least partially to blame for his own downfall. While Othello's "free and open nature, / That thinks men honest that but seem to be so" (1.3.378-79) is not a fault in itself, it does allow Iago to convince the Moor of his wife's infidelity without one shred of concrete evidence. Furthermore, once Othello has been convinced of Desdemona's guilt, he makes up his mind to take vengeance, and that his "bloody thoughts with violent pace / Shall ne'er look back, ne'er ebb to humble love" (3.3.473-74). He thereby renders himself deaf to the voice of reason, and ignoring Desdemona's protestations of innocence, brutally murders her, only to discover too late that he has made a terrible mistake. Although he is goaded into his crime by Iago, who is a master at manipulating people, it is Othello's own character flaws that lead to his horrible misjudgment.

Aristotle's definition also states that the hero's misfortune is not wholly deserved, that the punishment he receives exceeds his crime. Although it is hard to sympathize with a man as cruel as Othello is to the innocent Desdemona, Othello pays an extremely high price for his sin of gullibility. Othello loses everything—his wife, his position, even his life. Even though it's partially his fault, Othello is not entirely to blame, for without Iago's interference it's highly unlikely that things would turn out as they do. Though it seems incredibly stupid on Othello's part, that a man who has travelled the world and commanded armies should be so easily deceived, there is little evidence that Othello has had much experience with civilian society, and although he is "declined / Into the vale of years" (3.3.281-82) Othello has apparently never been married before. By his own admission, "little of this great world can I speak / More than pertains to feats of broils and battle" (1.3.88-89). Furthermore, Othello has no reason to suspect that "honest Iago" is anything but his loyal friend and supporter.

While it is understandable that Othello could be fooled into believing Desdemona unfaithful, the question remains whether his fate is deserved. In addition to his mistake of believing Iago's lies, Othello commits a more serious error: he lets himself be blinded by anger. Worse yet, in deciding to take vengeance, he also makes up his mind not be swayed from his course, even by his love for Desdemona. In fact, he refuses to listen to her at all, "lest her body and beauty unprovide my mind again" (4.1.187-88), therefore denying her the right to defend herself. Because of his rage and unfairness, perhaps Othello deserves his fate more than Aristotle's ideal tragic hero. Othello's punishment does exceed his crime, but just barely.

According to Aristotle, the tragic hero's fall gives the protagonist deeper understanding and self-awareness. Othello departs from Aristotle's model in that Othello apparently learns nothing from his mistakes. He never realizes that he is partly at fault. He sees himself only as an innocent victim and blames his misfortune on fate rather than accepting responsibility for his actions. To be sure, he realizes he has been tricked and deeply regrets his mistake, but he seems to feel that he was justified under the circumstances, "For naught I did in hate, but all in honor" (5.2.303). Othello sees himself not as someone whose bad judgment and worse temper have resulted in the death of an innocent party, but as one who has "loved not wisely but too well" (5.2.354). This failure to grasp the true nature of his error indicates that Othello hasn't learned his lesson.

Neither accepting responsibility nor learning from his mistakes, Othello fails to fulfill yet another of Aristotle's requirements. Since the protagonist usually gains some understanding along with his defeat, classical tragedy conveys a sense of human greatness and of life's unrealized potentialities--a quality totally absent from Othello. Not only does Othello fail to learn from his mistakes, he never really realizes what those mistakes are, and it apparently never crosses his mind that things could have turned out any differently. "Who can control his fate?" Othello asks (5.2.274), and this defeatist attitude, combined with his failure to salvage any wisdom from his defeat, separates Othello from the tragedy defined by Aristotle.

The last part of Aristotle's definition states that viewing the conclusion of a tragedy should result in catharsis for the audience, and that the audience should be left with a feeling of exaltation rather than depression.

Unfortunately, the feeling we are left with after viewing Othello is neither catharsis nor exaltation but rather a feeling of horror, pity, and disgust at the senseless waste of human lives. The deaths of Desdemona and Othello, as well as those of Emilia and Roderigo, serve no purpose whatsoever. They die not in the service of a great cause but because of lies, treachery, jealousy, and spite. Their deaths don't even benefit Iago, who is directly or indirectly responsible for all of them. No lesson is learned, no epiphany is reached, and the audience, instead of experiencing catharsis, is left with its negative feeling unresolved.

Since Othello only partially fits Aristotle's definition of tragedy, it is questionable whether or not it should be classified as one. Though it does involve a great man undone by a defect in his own character, the hero gains neither insight nor understanding from his defeat, and so there can be no inspiration or catharsis for the audience, as there would be in a "true" tragedy. Othello is tragic only in the everyday sense of the word, the way a plane crash or fire is tragic. At least in terms of Aristotle's classic definition, Othello ultimately comes across as more of a melodrama or soap opera than a tragedy.

Works Cited

Kennedy, X.J., and Dana Gioia, eds. Literature: An Introduction to Fiction, Poetry, and Drama. 7th ed. New York: Longman, 1999. 1295-97.

Shakespeare, William. The Tragedy of Othello, The Moor of Venice. Literature: An Introduction to Fiction, Poetry, and Drama. Ed. X.J. Kennedy and Dana Gioia. 7th ed. New York: Longman, 1999. 1303-1400.

FURTHER SUGGESTIONS FOR WRITING

1. Write a defense of Iago.
2. "Never was any play fraught, like this of Othello, with improbabilities," wrote Thomas Rymer in a famous attack (*A Short View of Tragedy*, 1692). Consider Rymer's objections to the play, either answering it or finding evidence to back up Rymer.
3. Suppose yourself a casting director assigned to a film version of *Othello*. What well-known stars would you cast in the principal roles? Write a report justifying your choices. Don't merely discuss the stars and their qualifications; discuss (with specific reference to the play) what Shakespeare appears to call for.
4. Emilia's long speech at the end of Act IV (iii, 84–103) has been called a Renaissance plea for women's liberation. Do you agree? Write a brief, close analysis of this speech. How timely is it?
5. "The downfall of Oedipus is the work of the gods; the downfall of Othello is self-inflicted." Test this comment with reference to the two plays, and report your findings.

35 *The Modern Theater*

REALISM AND NATURALISM

As the twentieth century began, realism in the theaters of Western Europe, England, and America appeared to have won a resounding victory. (**Realism** in drama, like realism in fiction, may be broadly defined as an attempt to reproduce faithfully the surface appearance of life, especially that of ordinary people in everyday situations.) The theater had been slow to admit controversial or unpleasant themes and reluctant to shed its traditional conventions. From Italian playhouses of the sixteenth century, it had inherited the **picture-frame stage:** one that holds the action within a **proscenium arch,** a gateway standing (as the word *proscenium* indicates) "in front of the scenery." This manner of constructing a playhouse in effect divided the actors from their audience; most commercial theaters even today are so constructed. But as the new century began, actors less often declaimed their passions in oratorical style in front of backdrops painted with waterfalls and volcanoes, while stationed exactly at the center of the stage as if to sing "duets meant to bring forth applause" (as Swedish playwright August Strindberg complained). By 1891 even Victorian London had witnessed a production of a play that frankly portrayed a man dying of venereal disease—Henrik Ibsen's *Ghosts.*

In the theater of realism, a room was represented by a **box set**—three walls that joined in two corners and a ceiling that tilted as if seen in perspective—replacing drapery walls that had billowed and doors that had flapped, not slammed. Instead of posing at stage center to deliver key speeches, actors were instructed to speak from wherever the dramatic situation placed them and now and then turn their backs upon the audience. They were to behave as if they lived in a room with the fourth wall sliced away, unaware that they had an audience.

This realistic convention is familiar to us today, not only from realistic plays but also from the typical television soap opera or situation comedy that takes place in such a three-walled room, with every cup and spoon revealed by the camera. However, such realism went against a long tradition. Watching a play by

Sophocles, the spectators, we may safely assume, had to exert their imagination. We do not expect an ancient Greek tragedy literally to represent the lives of ordinary people in everyday situations. On the contrary, a tragedy, according to Aristotle, its leading ancient theorist, represents an "action of supreme importance," an extraordinary moment in the life of a king or queen or other person of high estate. An open-air stage, though Sophocles adorned it with painted scenery, could hardly change day into night as lighting technicians commonly do today or aspire to reproduce in detail a whole palace. Such limitations prevail upon the theater of Shakespeare as well, encouraging the Bard to flesh out his scene with vivid language, making the spectator willing to imagine that the simple stage—the "wooden O"—is a forest, a storm-swept landscape, or a battlefield. In the classic Nō theater of Japan, spectators recognize conventional props. A simple framework is a boat, four posts and a roof are a palace, an actor's fan may be any useful object—a paintbrush, say, or a knife. In such a nonrealistic theater, the playwright, unhampered by stage sets, can shift scenes as rapidly as the audience can imagine.

In the realistic three-walled room, actors could hardly rant (or, Hamlet said, "tear a passion to tatters") without seeming foolish. Another effect of more lifelike direction was to discourage use of such devices as the soliloquy and the **aside** (villain to audience: "Heh! heh! Now she's in my power!"). To encourage actors further to imitate reality, the influential director Constantin Stanislavsky of the Moscow Art Theater developed his famous system to help actors feel at home inside a playwright's characters. One of Stanislavsky's exercises was to have actors search their memories for personal experiences like those of the characters in the play; another was to have the actors act out things a character did *not* do in the play but might do in life. The system enabled Stanislavsky to bring authenticity to his productions of Chekhov's plays and of Maxim Gorky's *The Lower Depths* (1902), a play that showed the tenants in a sordid lodging house drinking themselves to death (and hanging themselves) in surroundings of realistic squalor.

Gorky's play is a masterpiece of **naturalism,** a kind of realism in fiction and drama dealing with the more brutal or unpleasant aspects of reality. As codified by French novelist and playwright Émile Zola, who influenced Ibsen, naturalism viewed a person as a creature whose acts are determined by heredity and environment; Zola urged writers to study their characters' behavior with the detachment of zoologists studying animals.

No sooner had realism and naturalism won the day than a reaction arose. One opposing force was the **Symbolist movement** in the French theater, most influentially expressed by Belgian playwright Maurice Maeterlinck. Like French Symbolist poets Charles Baudelaire and Stéphane Mallarmé, Maeterlinck assumes that the visible world reflects a spirit world we cannot directly perceive. Accordingly, his plays are filled with hints and portents: suggestive objects (jeweled rings, veils, distant candles), mysterious locales (crumbling castles, dim grottoes), vague sounds from afar, and dialogue rich in silences and unfinished sentences. In *The Intruder* (1890), a blind man sees the approach of Death. In *Pelléas and Mélisande* (1892) a typical bit of Symbolist stage business occurs. A small boy stands on his grandfather's shoulders to peer through a high window and speak of wonders invisible to an audience. (For more about symbolism and Symbolists, see Chapters Seven and Twenty-three.)

Elsewhere, others were working along similar lines. In Russia, Anton Chekhov, whose plays on the surface appeared realistic, built some of his best around a symbol (*The Seagull, The Cherry Orchard*). In Ireland, poet William Butler Yeats, who in 1899 had helped found the Irish Dramatic Movement, was himself of a different mind from the realistic playwrights whose work he had helped produce in Dublin's Abbey Theater. Drawing on Irish lore and legend, Yeats wrote (among other plays) "plays for dancers" to be performed in drawing rooms, often in friends' homes, with simple costumes and props, a few masked actors, and a very few musicians. In Sweden, August Strindberg, who earlier had won fame as a naturalist, reversed direction and in *The Dream Play* (1902) and *The Ghost Sonata* (1907) introduced characters who change their identities and, ignoring space and time, move across dreamlike landscapes. In these plays Strindberg anticipated the movement called **expressionism** in German theater after World War I. Delighting in bizarre sets and exaggerated makeup and costuming, expressionist playwrights and producers sought to reflect intense states of emotion and, sometimes, to depict the world through lunatic eyes. A classic example (on film) is *The Cabinet of Dr. Caligari*, made in Berlin in 1919–1920, in which a hypnotist sends forth a subject to murder people. Garbed in jet black, the killer sleepwalks through a town of lopsided houses, twisted streets, and railings that tilt at gravity-defying angles. In expressionist movies and plays, madness is objectified and dreams become realities.

In 1893 Strindberg had complained of producers who represented a kitchen by a drapery painted with pictures of kettles; but by 1900, realistic play production had gone to opposite extremes. In the 1920s the curtain rose upon a Broadway play with a detailed replica of a Schrafft's restaurant, complete to the last fork and folded napkin. (Still, critic George Jean Nathan remarked, no matter how elaborate a stage dinner, the table never seemed to have any butter.) Theaters housed increasingly complicated machines, making it all the easier to present scenes full of realistic detail. Elevators lifted heavy sets swiftly and quietly into place; other sets, at the touch of a button, revolved on giant turntables. Theaters became warehouses for huge ready-made scenery.

Some playwrights fought domination by the painstakingly realistic set. Bertolt Brecht in Germany and Luigi Pirandello in Italy conceived plays to be performed on bare stages—gas pipes and plaster in full view—to remind spectators that they beheld events in a theater, not in the world. In reaction against the traditional picture-frame stage, new kinds of theaters were designed, such as the **arena theater,** or **theater in the round,** in which the audience sits on all four sides of the performing area; and the **flexible theater,** in which the seats are movable. Such theaters usually are not commercial (most of which maintain their traditional picture-frame stages, built decades ago). Rather, the alternative theaters are found in college and civic playhouses, in large cities, in storefronts, and in converted lofts. Proponents of arena staging claim that it brings actors and audience into greater intimacy; opponents, that it keeps the actors artificially circulating like goldfish in a bowl. Perhaps it is safe to say only that some plays lend themselves to being seen head-on in a picture frame; others, to being surrounded.

Henrik Ibsen

A Doll's House

TRANSLATED BY JAMES McFARLANE

Henrik Ibsen (1828–1906) was born in Skien, a seaport in Norway. When he was six, his father's business losses suddenly reduced his wealthy family to poverty. After a brief attempt to study medicine, young Ibsen worked as a stage manager in provincial Bergen; then, becoming known as a playwright, moved to Oslo as artistic director of the National Theater—practical experiences that gained him firm grounding in his craft. Discouraged when his theater failed and the king turned down his plea for a grant to enable him to write, Ibsen left Norway and for twenty-seven years lived in Italy and Germany. There, in his middle years (1879–1891), he wrote most of his famed plays about small-town life, among them

Henrik Ibsen

A Doll's House, Ghosts, An Enemy of the People, The Wild Duck, *and* Hedda Gabler. *Introducing social problems to the stage, these plays aroused storms of controversy. Although best known as a realist, Ibsen early in his career wrote poetic dramas based on Norwegian history and folklore: the tragedy* Brand *(1866) and the powerful, wildly fantastic* Peer Gynt *(1867). He ended as a Symbolist in* John Gabriel Borkman *(1896) and* When We Dead Awaken *(1899), both encompassing huge mountains that heaven-assaulting heroes try to climb. Late in life Ibsen returned to Oslo, honored at last both at home and abroad.*

Characters

Torvald Helmer, a lawyer
Nora, his wife
Dr. Rank
Mrs. Kristine Linde
Nils Krogstad
Anne Marie, the nursemaid
Helene, the maid
The Helmers' three children
A Porter

The action takes place in the Helmers' flat.

ACT I

A pleasant room, tastefully but not expensively furnished. On the back wall, one door on the right leads to the entrance hall, a second door on the left leads to Helmer's study.

A Doll's House. (*Harvard Theatre Collection*)

Between these two doors, a piano. In the middle of the left wall, a door; and downstage from it, a window. Near the window a round table with armchairs and a small sofa. In the right wall, upstage, a door; and on the same wall downstage, a porcelain stove with a couple of armchairs and a rocking chair. Between the stove and the door a small table. Etchings on the walls. A whatnot with china and other small objets d'art; a small bookcase with books in handsome bindings. Carpet on the floor; a fire burns in the stove. A winter's day.

The front door-bell rings in the hall; a moment later, there is the sound of the front door being opened. Nora comes into the room, happily humming to herself. She is dressed in her outdoor things, and is carrying lots of parcels which she then puts down on the table, right. She leaves the door into the hall standing open; a Porter can be seen outside holding a Christmas tree and a basket; he hands them to the Maid who has opened the door for them.

Nora: Hide the Christmas tree away carefully, Helene. The children mustn't see it till this evening when it's decorated. [*To the Porter, taking out her purse.*] How much?

Porter: Fifty öre.

Nora: There's a crown. Keep the change.

[*The Porter thanks her and goes. Nora shuts the door. She continues to laugh qui-etly and happily to herself as she takes off her things. She takes a bag of macaroons out of her pocket and eats one or two; then she walks stealthily across and listens at her husband's door.*]

Nora: Yes, he's in.

[*She begins humming again as she walks over to the table, right.*]

Helmer [*in his study*]: Is that my little sky-lark chirruping out there?
Nora [*busy opening some of the parcels*]: Yes, it is.
Helmer: Is that my little squirrel frisking about?
Nora: Yes!
Helmer: When did my little squirrel get home?
Nora: Just this minute. [*She stuffs the bag of macaroons in her pocket and wipes her mouth.*] Come on out, Torvald, and see what I've bought.
Helmer: I don't want to be disturbed! [*A moment later, he opens the door and looks out, his pen in his hand.*] 'Bought', did you say? All that? Has my little spend-thrift been out squandering money again?
Nora: But, Torvald, surely this year we can spread ourselves just a little. This is the first Christmas we haven't had to go carefully.
Helmer: Ah, but that doesn't mean we can afford to be extravagant, you know.
Nora: Oh yes, Torvald, surely we can afford to be just a little bit extravagant now, can't we? Just a teeny-weeny bit. You are getting quite a good salary now, and you are going to earn lots and lots of money.
Helmer: Yes, after the New Year. But it's going to be three whole months before the first pay cheque comes in.
Nora: Pooh! We can always borrow in the meantime.
Helmer: Nora! [*Crosses to her and takes her playfully by the ear.*] Here we go again, you and your frivolous ideas! Suppose I went and borrowed a thousand crowns today, and you went and spent it all over Christmas, then on New Year's Eve a slate fell and hit me on the head and there I was. . . .
Nora [*putting her hand over his mouth*]: Sh! Don't say such horrid things.
Helmer: Yes, but supposing something like that did happen . . . what then?
Nora: If anything as awful as that did happen, I wouldn't care if I owed anybody anything or not.
Helmer: Yes, but what about the people I'd borrowed from?
Nora: Them? Who cares about them! They are only strangers!
Helmer: Nora, Nora! Just like a woman! Seriously though, Nora, you know what I think about these things. No debts! Never borrow! There's always some-thing inhibited, something unpleasant, about a home built on credit and borrowed money. We two have managed to stick it out so far, and that's the way we'll go on for the little time that remains.
Nora [*walks over to the stove*]: Very well, just as you say, Torvald.
Helmer [*following her*]: There, there! My little singing bird mustn't go drooping her wings, eh? Has it got the sulks, that little squirrel of mine? [*Takes out his wallet.*] Nora, what do you think I've got here?

Nora [*quickly turning round*]: Money!

Helmer: There! [*He hands her some notes*]. Good heavens, I know only too well how Christmas runs away with the housekeeping.

Nora [*counts*]: Ten, twenty, thirty, forty. Oh, thank you, thank you, Torvald! This will see me quite a long way.

Helmer: Yes, it'll have to.

Nora: Yes, yes, I'll see that it does. But come over here, I want to show you all the things I've bought. And so cheap! Look, some new clothes for Ivar . . . and a little sword. There's a horse and a trumpet for Bob. And a doll and a doll's cot for Emmy. They are not very grand but she'll have them all broken before long anyway. And I've got some dress material and some handkerchiefs for the maids. Though, really, dear old Anne Marie should have had something better.

Helmer: And what's in this parcel here?

Nora [*shrieking*]: No, Torvald! You mustn't see that till tonight!

Helmer: All right. But tell me now, what did my little spendthrift fancy for herself?

Nora: For me? Puh, I don't really want anything.

Helmer: Of course you do. Anything reasonable that you think you might like, just tell me.

Nora: Well, I don't really know. As a matter of fact, though, Torvald . . .

Helmer: Well?

Nora [*toying with his coat buttons, and without looking at him*]: If you did want to give me something, you could . . . you could always . . .

Helmer: Well, well, out with it!

Nora [*quickly*]: You could always give me money, Torvald. Only what you think you could spare. And then I could buy myself something with it later on.

Helmer: But Nora. . . .

Nora: Oh, please, Torvald dear! Please! I beg you. Then I'd wrap the money up in some pretty gilt paper and hang it on the Christmas tree. Wouldn't that be fun?

Helmer: What do we call my pretty little pet when it runs away with all the money?

Nora: I know, I know, we call it a spendthrift. But please let's do what I said, Torvald. Then I'll have a bit of time to think about what I need most. Isn't that awfully sensible, now, eh?

Helmer [*smiling*]: Yes, it is indeed—that is, if only you really could hold on to the money I gave you, and really did buy something for yourself with it. But it just gets mixed up with the housekeeping and frittered away on all sorts of useless things, and then I have to dig into my pocket all over again.

Nora: Oh but, Torvald. . . .

Helmer: You can't deny it, Nora dear. [*Puts his arm round her waist.*] My pretty little pet is very sweet, but it runs away with an awful lot of money. It's incredible how expensive it is for a man to keep such a pet.

Nora: For shame! How can you say such a thing? As a matter of fact I save everything I can.

Helmer [*laughs*]: Yes, you are right there. Everything you *can*. But you simply can't.

Nora [*hums and smiles quietly and happily*]: Ah, if you only knew how many expenses the likes of us sky-larks and squirrels have, Torvald!

Helmer: What a funny little one you are! Just like your father. Always on the look-out for money, wherever you can lay your hands on it; but as soon as you've got it, it just seems to slip through your fingers. You never seem to know what you've done with it. Well, one must accept you as you are. It's in the blood. Oh yes, it is, Nora. That sort of thing is hereditary.

Nora: Oh, I only wish I'd inherited a few more of Daddy's qualities.

Helmer: And I wouldn't want my pretty little song-bird to be the least bit different from what she is now. But come to think of it, you look rather . . . rather . . . how shall I put it? . . . rather guilty today. . . .

Nora: Do I?

Helmer: Yes, you do indeed. Look me straight in the eye.

Nora [*looks at him*]: Well?

Helmer [*wagging his finger at her*]: My little sweet-tooth surely didn't forget herself in town today?

Nora: No, whatever makes you think that?

Helmer: She didn't just pop into the confectioner's for a moment?

Nora: No, I assure you, Torvald . . . !

Helmer: Didn't try sampling the preserves?

Nora: No, really I didn't.

Helmer: Didn't go nibbling a macaroon or two?

Nora: No, Torvald, honestly, you must believe me . . . !

Helmer: All right then! It's really just my little joke. . . .

Nora [*crosses to the table*]: I would never dream of doing anything you didn't want me to.

Helmer: Of course not, I know that. And then you've given me your word. . . . [*Crosses to her.*] Well then, Nora dearest, you shall keep your little Christmas secrets. They'll all come out tonight, I dare say, when we light the tree.

Nora: Did you remember to invite Dr. Rank?

Helmer: No. But there's really no need. Of course he'll come and have dinner with us. Anyway, I can ask him when he looks in this morning. I've ordered some good wine. Nora, you can't imagine how I am looking forward to this evening.

Nora: So am I. And won't the children enjoy it, Torvald!

Helmer: Oh, what a glorious feeling it is, knowing you've got a nice, safe job, and a good fat income. Don't you agree? Isn't it wonderful, just thinking about it?

Nora: Oh, it's marvellous!

Helmer: Do you remember last Christmas? Three whole weeks beforehand you shut yourself up every evening till after midnight making flowers for the Christmas tree and all the other splendid things you wanted to surprise us with. Ugh, I never felt so bored in all my life.

Nora: I wasn't the least bit bored.

Helmer [*smiling*]: But it turned out a bit of an anticlimax, Nora.

Nora: Oh, you are not going to tease me about that again! How was I to know the cat would get in and pull everything to bits?

Helmer: No, of course you weren't. Poor little Nora! All you wanted was for us to have a nice time—and it's the thought behind it that counts, after all. All the same, it's a good thing we've seen the back of those lean times.

Nora: Yes, really it's marvellous.

Helmer: Now there's no need for me to sit here all on my own, bored to tears. And you don't have to strain your dear little eyes, and work those dainty little fingers to the bone. . . .

Nora [*clapping her hands*]: No, Torvald, I don't, do I? Not any more. Oh, how marvellous it is to hear that! [*Takes his arm.*] Now I want to tell you how I've been thinking we might arrange things, Torvald. As soon as Christmas is over. . . . [*The door-bell rings in the hall.*] Oh, there's the bell. [*Tidies one or two things in the room.*] It's probably a visitor. What a nuisance!

Helmer: Remember I'm not at home to callers.

Maid [*in the doorway*]: There's a lady to see you, ma'am.

Nora: Show her in, please.

Maid [*to Helmer*]: And the doctor's just arrived, too, sir.

Helmer: Did he go straight into my room?

Maid: Yes, he did, sir.

[*Helmer goes into his study. The Maid shows in Mrs. Linde, who is in travelling clothes, and closes the door after her.*]

Mrs. Linde [*subdued and rather hesitantly*]: How do you do, Nora?

Nora [*uncertainly*]: How do you do?

Mrs. Linde: I'm afraid you don't recognize me.

Nora: No, I don't think I . . . And yet I seem to. . . . [*Bursts out suddenly.*] Why! Kristine! Is it really you?

Mrs. Linde: Yes, it's me.

Nora: Kristine! Fancy not recognizing you again! But how was I to, when . . . [*Gently.*] How you've changed, Kristine!

Mrs. Linde: I dare say I have. In nine . . . ten years. . . .

Nora: Is it so long since we last saw each other? Yes, it must be. Oh, believe me these last eight years have been such a happy time. And now you've come up to town, too? All that long journey in wintertime. That took courage.

Mrs. Linde: I just arrived this morning on the steamer.

Nora: To enjoy yourself over Christmas, of course. How lovely! Oh, we'll have such fun, you'll see. Do take off your things. You are not cold, are you? [*Helps her.*] There now! Now let's sit down here in comfort beside the stove. No, here, you take the armchair, I'll sit here on the rocking chair. [*Takes her hands.*] Ah, now you look a bit more like your old self again. It was just that when I first saw you. . . . But you are a little paler, Kristine . . . and perhaps even a bit thinner!

Mrs. Linde: And much, much older, Nora.

Nora: Yes, perhaps a little older . . . very, very little, not really very much. [*Stops suddenly and looks serious.*] Oh, what a thoughtless creature I am, sitting here chattering on like this! Dear, sweet Kristine, can you forgive me?

Mrs. Linde: What do you mean, Nora?

Nora [*gently*]: Poor Kristine, of course you're a widow now.

Mrs. Linde: Yes, my husband died three years ago.

Nora: Oh, I remember now. I read about it in the papers. Oh, Kristine, believe me I often thought at the time of writing to you. But I kept putting it off, something always seemed to crop up.

Mrs. Linde: My dear Nora, I understand so well.

Nora: No, it wasn't very nice of me, Kristine. Oh, you poor thing, what you must have gone through. And didn't he leave you anything?

Mrs. Linde: No.

Nora: And no children?

Mrs. Linde: No.

Nora: Absolutely nothing?

Mrs. Linde: Nothing at all . . . not even a broken heart to grieve over.

Nora [*looks at her incredulously*]: But, Kristine, is that possible?

Mrs. Linde [*smiles sadly and strokes Nora's hair*]: Oh, it sometimes happens, Nora.

Nora: So utterly alone. How terribly sad that must be for you. I have three lovely children. You can't see them for the moment, because they're out with their nanny. But now you must tell me all about yourself. . . .

Mrs. Linde: No, no, I want to hear about you.

Nora: No, you start. I won't be selfish today. I must think only about your affairs today. But there's just one thing I really must tell you. Have you heard about the great stroke of luck we've had in the last few days?

Mrs. Linde: No. What is it?

Nora: What do you think? My husband has just been made Bank Manager!

Mrs. Linde: Your husband? How splendid!

Nora: Isn't it tremendous! It's not a very steady way of making a living, you know, being a lawyer, especially if he refuses to take on anything that's the least bit shady—which of course is what Torvald does, and I think he's quite right. You can imagine how pleased we are! He starts at the Bank straight after New Year, and he's getting a big salary and lots of commission. From now on we'll be able to live quite differently . . . we'll do just what we want. Oh, Kristine, I'm so happy and relieved. I must say it's lovely to have plenty of money and not have to worry. Isn't it?

Mrs. Linde: Yes. It must be nice to have enough, at any rate.

Nora: No, not just enough, but pots and pots of money.

Mrs. Linde [*smiles*]: Nora, Nora, haven't you learned any sense yet? At school you used to be an awful spendthrift.

Nora: Yes, Torvald still says I am. [*Wags her finger.*] But little Nora isn't as stupid as everybody thinks. Oh, we haven't really been in a position where I could afford to spend a lot of money. We've both had to work.

Mrs. Linde: You too?

Nora: Yes, odd jobs—sewing, crochet-work, embroidery and things like that. [*Casually.*] And one or two other things, besides. I suppose you know that Torvald left the Ministry when we got married. There weren't any prospects of promotion in his department, and of course he needed to earn more money than he had before. But the first year he wore himself out completely. He had to take on all kinds of extra jobs, you know, and he found himself working all hours of the day and night. But he couldn't go on like that; and he became seriously ill. The doctors said it was essential for him to go South.

Mrs. Linde: Yes, I believe you spent a whole year in Italy, didn't you?

Nora: That's right. It wasn't easy to get away, I can tell you. It was just after I'd had Ivar. But of course we had to go. Oh, it was an absolutely marvellous trip. And it saved Torvald's life. But it cost an awful lot of money, Kristine.

Mrs. Linde: That I can well imagine.

Nora: Twelve hundred dollars. Four thousand eight hundred crowns. That's a lot of money, Kristine.

Mrs. Linde: Yes, but in such circumstances, one is very lucky if one has it.

Nora: Well, we got it from Daddy, you see.

Mrs. Linde: Ah, that was it. It was just about then your father died, I believe, wasn't it?

Nora: Yes, Kristine, just about then. And do you know, I couldn't even go and look after him. Here was I expecting Ivar any day. And I also had poor Torvald, gravely ill, on my hands. Dear, kind Daddy! I never saw him again, Kristine. Oh, that's the saddest thing that has happened to me in all my married life.

Mrs. Linde: I know you were very fond of him. But after that you left for Italy?

Nora: Yes, we had the money then, and the doctors said it was urgent. We left a month later.

Mrs. Linde: And your husband came back completely cured?

Nora: Fit as a fiddle!

Mrs. Linde: But . . . what about the doctor?

Nora: How do you mean?

Mrs. Linde: I thought the maid said something about the gentleman who came at the same time as me being a doctor.

Nora: Yes, that was Dr. Rank. But this isn't a professional visit. He's our best friend and he always looks in at least once a day. No, Torvald has never had a day's illness since. And the children are fit and healthy, and so am I. [*Jumps up and claps her hands.*] Oh God, oh God, isn't it marvellous to be alive, and to be happy, Kristine! . . . Oh, but I ought to be ashamed of myself . . . Here I go on talking about nothing but myself. [*She sits on a low stool near Mrs. Linde and lays her arms on her lap.*] Oh, please, you mustn't be angry with me! Tell me, is it really true that you didn't love your husband? What made you marry him, then?

Mrs. Linde: My mother was still alive; she was bedridden and helpless. And then I had my two young brothers to look after as well. I didn't think I would be justified in refusing him.

Nora: No, I dare say you are right. I suppose he was fairly wealthy then?

Mrs. Linde: He was quite well off, I believe. But the business was shaky. When he died, it went all to pieces, and there just wasn't anything left.

Nora: What then?

Mrs. Linde: Well, I had to fend for myself, opening a little shop, running a little school, anything I could turn my hand to. These last three years have been one long relentless drudge. But now it's finished, Nora. My poor dear mother doesn't need me any more, she's passed away. Nor the boys either; they're at work now, they can look after themselves.

Nora: What a relief you must find it. . . .

Mrs. Linde: No, Nora! Just unutterably empty. Nobody to live for any more. [*Stands up restlessly.*] That's why I couldn't stand it any longer being cut off up there. Surely it must be a bit easier here to find something to occupy your mind. If only I could manage to find a steady job of some kind, in an office perhaps. . . .

Nora: But, Kristine, that's terribly exhausting; and you look so worn out even before you start. The best thing for you would be a little holiday at some quiet little resort.

Mrs. Linde [*crosses to the window*]: I haven't any father I can fall back on for the money, Nora.

Nora [*rises*]: Oh, please, you mustn't be angry with me!

Mrs. Linde [*goes to her*]: My dear Nora, you mustn't be angry with me either. That's the worst thing about people in my position, they become so bitter. One has nobody to work for, yet one has to be on the look-out all the time. Life has to go on, and one starts thinking only of oneself. Believe it or not, when you told me the good news about your step up, I was pleased not so much for your sake as for mine.

Nora: How do you mean? Ah, I see. You think Torvald might be able to do something for you.

Mrs. Linde: Yes, that's exactly what I thought.

Nora: And so he shall, Kristine. Just leave things to me. I'll bring it up so cleverly . . . I'll think up something to put him in a good mood. Oh, I do so much want to help you.

Mrs. Linde: It is awfully kind of you, Nora, offering to do all this for me, particularly in your case, where you haven't known much trouble or hardship in your own life.

Nora: When I . . . ? I haven't known much . . . ?

Mrs. Linde [*smiling*]: Well, good heavens, a little bit of sewing to do and a few things like that. What a child you are, Nora!

Nora [*tosses her head and walks across the room*]: I wouldn't be too sure of that, if I were you.

Mrs. Linde: Oh?

Nora: You're just like the rest of them. You all think I'm useless when it comes to anything really serious. . . .

Mrs. Linde: Come, come. . . .

Nora: You think I've never had anything much to contend with in this hard world.

Mrs. Linde: Nora dear, you've only just been telling me all the things you've had to put up with.

Nora: Pooh! They were just trivialities! [*Softly.*] I haven't told you about the really big thing.

Mrs. Linde: What big thing? What do you mean?

Nora: I know you rather tend to look down on me, Kristine. But you shouldn't, you know. You are proud of having worked so hard and so long for your mother.

Mrs. Linde: I'm sure I don't look down on anybody. But it's true what you say: I am both proud and happy when I think of how I was able to make Mother's life a little easier towards the end.

Nora: And you are proud when you think of what you have done for your brothers, too.

Mrs. Linde: I think I have every right to be.

Nora: I think so too. But now I'm going to tell you something, Kristine. I too have something to be proud and happy about.

Mrs. Linde: I don't doubt that. But what is it you mean?

Nora: Not so loud. Imagine if Torvald were to hear! He must never on any account . . . nobody must know about it, Kristine, nobody but you.

Mrs. Linde: But what is it?

Nora: Come over here. [*She pulls her down on the sofa beside her.*] Yes, Kristine, I too have something to be proud and happy about. I was the one who saved Torvald's life.

Mrs. Linde: Saved . . . ? How . . . ?

Nora: I told you about our trip to Italy. Torvald would never have recovered but for that. . . .

Mrs. Linde: Well? Your father gave you what money was necessary. . . .

Nora [*smiles*]: That's what Torvald thinks, and everybody else. But . . .

Mrs. Linde: But . . . ?

Nora: Daddy never gave us a penny. I was the one who raised the money.

Mrs. Linde: You? All that money?

Nora: Twelve hundred dollars. Four thousand eight hundred crowns. What do you say to that!

Mrs. Linde: But, Nora, how was it possible? Had you won a sweepstake or something?

Nora [*contemptuously*]: A sweepstake? Pooh! There would have been nothing to it then.

Mrs. Linde: Where did you get it from, then?

Nora [*hums and smiles secretively*]: H'm, tra-la-la!

Mrs. Linde: Because what you couldn't do was borrow it.

Nora: Oh? Why not?

Mrs. Linde: Well, a wife can't borrow without her husband's consent.

Nora [*tossing her head*]: Ah, but when it happens to be a wife with a bit of a sense for business . . . a wife who knows her way about things, then. . . .

Mrs. Linde: But, Nora, I just don't understand. . . .

Nora: You don't have to. I haven't said I did borrow the money. I might have got it some other way. [*Throws herself back on the sofa.*] I might even have got it from some admirer. Anyone as reasonably attractive as I am. . . .

Mrs. Linde: Don't be so silly!

Nora: Now you must be dying of curiosity, Kristine.

Mrs. Linde: Listen to me now, Nora dear—you haven't done anything rash, have you?

Nora [*sitting up again*]: Is it rash to save your husband's life?

Mrs. Linde: I think it was rash to do anything without telling him. . . .

Nora: But the whole point was that he mustn't know anything. Good heavens, can't you see! He wasn't even supposed to know how desperately ill he was. It was me the doctors came and told his life was in danger, that the only way to save him was to go South for a while. Do you think I didn't try talking him into it first? I began dropping hints about how nice it would be if I could be taken on a little trip abroad, like other young wives. I wept, I pleaded. I told him he ought to show some consideration for my condition, and let me have a bit of my own way. And then I suggested he might take out a loan. But at that he nearly lost his temper, Kristine. He said I was being frivolous, that it was his duty as a husband not to give in to all these whims and fancies of mine—as I do believe he called them. All right, I thought, somehow you've got to be saved. And it was then I found a way. . . .

Mrs. Linde: Did your husband never find out from your father that the money hadn't come from him?

Nora: No, never. It was just about the time Daddy died. I'd intended letting him into the secret and asking him not to give me away. But when he was so ill . . . I'm sorry to say it never became necessary.

Mrs. Linde: And you never confided in your husband?

Nora: Good heavens, how could you ever imagine such a thing! When he's so strict about such matters! Besides, Torvald is a man with a good deal of pride—it would be terribly embarrassing and humiliating for him if he thought he owed anything to me. It would spoil everything between us; this happy home of ours would never be the same again.

Mrs. Linde: Are you never going to tell him?

Nora [*reflectively, half-smiling*]: Oh yes, some day perhaps . . . in many years time, when I'm no longer as pretty as I am now. You mustn't laugh! What I mean of course is when Torvald isn't quite so much in love with me as he is now, when he's lost interest in watching me dance, or get dressed up, or recite. Then it might be a good thing to have something in reserve. . . . [*Breaks off.*] What nonsense! That day will never come. Well, what have you got to say to my big secret, Kristine? Still think I'm not much good for anything? One thing, though, it's meant a lot of worry for me, I can tell you. It hasn't always been easy to meet my obligations when the time came. You know in business there is something called quarterly interest, and other things called instalments, and these are always terribly difficult things to cope with. So what I've had to do is save a little here and there, you see, wherever I could. I couldn't really save anything out of the housekeeping, because Torvald has to live in decent style. I couldn't let the children go about badly dressed either—I felt any money I got for them had to go on them alone. Such sweet little things!

Mrs. Linde: Poor Nora! So it had to come out of your own allowance?

Nora: Of course. After all, I was the one it concerned most. Whenever Torvald gave me money for new clothes and such-like, I never spent more than half. And always I bought the simplest and cheapest things. It's a blessing most things look well on me, so Torvald never noticed anything. But sometimes I did feel it was a bit hard, Kristine, because it is nice to be well dressed, isn't it?

Mrs. Linde: Yes, I suppose it is.

Nora: I have had some other sources of income, of course. Last winter I was lucky enough to get quite a bit of copying to do. So I shut myself up every night and sat and wrote through to the small hours of the morning. Oh, sometimes I was so tired, so tired. But it was tremendous fun all the same, sitting there working and earning money like that. It was almost like being a man.

Mrs. Linde: And how much have you been able to pay off like this?

Nora: Well, I can't tell exactly. It's not easy to know where you are with transactions of this kind, you understand. All I know is I've paid off just as much as I could scrape together. Many's the time I was at my wit's end. [*Smiles.*] Then I used to sit here and pretend that some rich old gentleman had fallen in love with me. . . .

Mrs. Linde: What! What gentleman?

Nora: Oh, rubbish! . . . and that now he had died, and when they opened his will, there in big letters were the words: 'My entire fortune is to be paid over, immediately and in cash, to charming Mrs. Nora Helmer.'

Mrs. Linde: But my dear Nora—who is this man?

Nora: Good heavens, don't you understand? There never was any old gentleman; it was just something I used to sit here pretending, time and time again, when I didn't know where to turn next for money. But it doesn't make very much difference; as far as I'm concerned, the old boy can do what he likes, I'm tired of him; I can't be bothered any more with him or his will. Because now all my worries are over. [*Jumping up.*] Oh God, what a glorious thought, Kristine! No more worries! Just think of being without a care in the world . . . being able to romp with the children, and making the house nice and attractive, and having things just as Torvald likes to have them! And then spring will soon be here, and blue skies. And maybe we can go away somewhere. I might even see something of the sea again. Oh yes! When you're happy, life is a wonderful thing!

[*The door-bell is heard in the hall.*]

Mrs. Linde [gets up]: There's the bell. Perhaps I'd better go.

Nora: No, do stay, please. I don't suppose it's for me; it's probably somebody for Torvald. . . .

Maid [in the doorway]: Excuse me, ma'am, but there's a gentleman here wants to see Mr. Helmer, and I didn't quite know . . . because the Doctor is in there. . . .

Nora: Who is the gentleman?

Krogstad [in the doorway]: It's me, Mrs. Helmer.

[Mrs. Linde starts, then turns away to the window.]

Nora [tense, takes a step towards him and speaks in a low voice]: You? What is it? What do you want to talk to my husband about?

Krogstad: Bank matters . . . in a manner of speaking. I work at the bank, and I hear your husband is to be the new manager. . . .

Nora: So it's . . .

Krogstad: Just routine business matters, Mrs. Helmer. Absolutely nothing else.

Nora: Well then, please go into his study.

[She nods impassively and shuts the hall door behind him; then she walks across and sees to the stove.]

Mrs. Linde: Nora . . . who was that man?

Nora: His name is Krogstad.

Mrs. Linde: So it really was him.

Nora: Do you know the man?

Mrs. Linde: I used to know him . . . a good many years ago. He was a solicitor's clerk in our district for a while.

Nora: Yes, so he was.

Mrs. Linde: How he's changed!

Nora: His marriage wasn't a very happy one, I believe.

Mrs. Linde: He's a widower now, isn't he?

Nora: With a lot of children. There, it'll burn better now.

[She closes the stove door and moves the rocking chair a little to one side.]

Mrs. Linde: He does a certain amount of business on the side, they say?

Nora: Oh? Yes, it's always possible. I just don't know. . . . But let's not think about business . . . it's all so dull.

[Dr. Rank comes in from Helmer's study.]

Dr. Rank [still in the doorway]: No, no, Torvald, I won't intrude. I'll just look in on your wife for a moment. [Shuts the door and notices Mrs. Linde.] Oh, I beg your pardon. I'm afraid I'm intruding here as well.

Nora: No, not at all! [Introduces them.] Dr. Rank . . . Mrs. Linde.

Rank: Ah! A name I've often heard mentioned in this house. I believe I came past you on the stairs as I came in.

Mrs. Linde: I have to take things slowly going upstairs. I find it rather a trial.

Rank: Ah, some little disability somewhere, eh?

Mrs. Linde: Just a bit run down, I think, actually.

Rank: Is that all? Then I suppose you've come to town for a good rest—doing the rounds of the parties?

Mrs. Linde: I have come to look for work.

Rank: Is that supposed to be some kind of sovereign remedy for being run down?

Mrs. Linde: One must live, Doctor.

Rank: Yes, it's generally thought to be necessary.

Nora: Come, come, Dr. Rank. You are quite as keen to live as anybody.

Rank: Quite keen, yes. Miserable as I am, I'm quite ready to let things drag on as long as possible. All my patients are the same. Even those with a moral affliction are no different. As a matter of fact, there's a bad case of that kind in talking with Helmer at this very moment. . . .

Mrs. Linde [softly]: Ah!

Nora: Whom do you mean?

Rank: A person called Krogstad—nobody you would know. He's rotten to the core. But even he began talking about having to *live*, as though it were something terribly important.

Nora: Oh? And what did he want to talk to Torvald about?

Rank: I honestly don't know. All I heard was something about the Bank.

Nora: I didn't know that Krog . . . that this Mr. Krogstad had anything to do with the Bank.

Rank: Oh yes, he's got some kind of job down there. [*To Mrs. Linde.*] I wonder if you've got people in your part of the country too who go rushing round sniffing out cases of moral corruption, and then installing the individuals concerned in nice, well-paid jobs where they can keep them under observation. Sound, decent people have to be content to stay out in the cold.

Mrs. Linde: Yet surely it's the sick who most need to be brought in.

Rank [shrugs his shoulders]: Well, there we have it. It's that attitude that's turning society into a clinic.

[*Nora, lost in her own thoughts, breaks into smothered laughter and claps her hands.*]

Rank: Why are you laughing at that? Do you know in fact what society is?

Nora: What do I care about your silly old society? I was laughing about something quite different . . . something frightfully funny. Tell me, Dr. Rank, are all the people who work at the Bank dependent on Torvald now?

Rank: Is that what you find so frightfully funny?

Nora [smiles and hums]: Never you mind! Never you mind! [*Walks about the room.*] Yes, it really is terribly amusing to think that we . . . that Torvald now has power over so many people. [*She takes the bag out of her pocket.*] Dr. Rank, what about a little macaroon?

Rank: Look at this, eh? Macaroons. I thought they were forbidden here.

Nora: Yes, but these are some Kristine gave me.

Mrs. Linde: What? I . . . ?

Nora: Now, now, you needn't be alarmed. You weren't to know that Torvald had forbidden them. He's worried in case they ruin my teeth, you know. Still . . . what's it matter once in a while! Don't you think so, Dr. Rank? Here! [*She pops a macaroon into his mouth.*] And you too, Kristine. And I shall have one as well; just a little one . . . or two at the most. [*She walks about the room again.*] Really I am so happy. There's just one little thing I'd love to do now.

Rank: What's that?

Nora: Something I'd love to say in front of Torvald.

Rank: Then why can't you?

Nora: No, I daren't. It's not very nice.

Mrs. Linde: Not very nice?

Rank: Well, in that case it might not be wise. But to us, I don't see why. . . . What is this you would love to say in front of Helmer?

Nora: I would simply love to say: 'Damn.'

Rank: Are you mad!

Mrs. Linde: Good gracious, Nora . . . !

Rank: Say it! Here he is!

Nora [*hiding the bag of macaroons*]: Sh! Sh!

[*Helmer comes out of his room, his overcoat over his arm and his hat in his hand.*]

Nora [*going over to him*]: Well, Torvald dear, did you get rid of him?

Helmer: Yes, he's just gone.

Nora: Let me introduce you. This is Kristine, who has just arrived in town. . . .

Helmer: Kristine . . . ? You must forgive me, but I don't think I know . . .

Nora: Mrs. Linde, Torvald dear. Kristine Linde.

Helmer: Ah, indeed. A school-friend of my wife's, presumably.

Mrs. Linde: Yes, we were girls together.

Nora: Fancy, Torvald, she's come all this long way just to have a word with you.

Helmer: How is that?

Mrs. Linde: Well, it wasn't really. . . .

Nora: The thing is, Kristine is terribly clever at office work, and she's frightfully keen on finding a job with some efficient man, so that she can learn even more. . . .

Helmer: Very sensible, Mrs. Linde.

Nora: And then when she heard you'd been made Bank Manager—there was a bit in the paper about it—she set off at once. Torvald please! You *will* try and do something for Kristine, won't you? For my sake?

Helmer: Well, that's not altogether impossible. You are a widow, I presume?

Mrs. Linde: Yes.

Helmer: And you've had some experience in business?

Mrs. Linde: A fair amount.

Helmer: Well, it's quite probable I can find you a job, I think. . . .

Nora [*clapping her hands*]: There, you see!

Helmer: You have come at a fortunate moment, Mrs. Linde. . . .

Mrs. Linde: Oh, how can I ever thank you . . . ?

Helmer: Not a bit. [*He puts on his overcoat.*] But for the present I must ask you to excuse me. . . .

Rank: Wait. I'm coming with you.

[*He fetches his fur coat from the hall and warms it at the stove.*]

Nora: Don't be long, Torvald dear.

Helmer: Not more than an hour, that's all.

Nora: Are you leaving too, Kristine?

Mrs. Linde [*putting on her things*]: Yes, I must go and see if I can't find myself a room.

Helmer: Perhaps we can all walk down the road together.

Nora [*helping her*]: What a nuisance we are so limited for space here. I'm afraid it just isn't possible. . . .

Mrs. Linde: Oh, you mustn't dream of it! Goodbye, Nora dear, and thanks for everything.

Nora: Goodbye for the present. But . . . you'll be coming back this evening, of course. And you too, Dr. Rank? What's that? If you are up to it? Of course you'll be up to it. Just wrap yourself up well.

[*They go out, talking, into the hall; children's voices can be heard on the stairs.*]

Nora: Here they are! Here they are! [*She runs to the front door and opens it. Anne Marie, the nursemaid, enters with the children.*] Come in! Come in! [*She bends down and kisses them.*] Ah! my sweet little darlings. . . . You see them, Kristine? Aren't they lovely!

Rank: Don't stand here chattering in this draught!

Helmer: Come along, Mrs. Linde. The place now becomes unbearable for anybody except mothers.

[*Dr. Rank, Helmer and Mrs. Linde go down the stairs: the Nursemaid comes into the room with the children, then Nora, shutting the door behind her.*]

Nora: How fresh and bright you look! My, what red cheeks you've got! Like apples and roses. [*During the following, the children keep chattering away to her.*] Have you had a nice time? That's splendid. And you gave Emmy and Bob a ride on your sledge? Did you now! Both together! Fancy that! There's a clever boy, Ivar. Oh, let me take her a little while, Anne Marie. There's my sweet little baby-doll! [*She takes the youngest of the children from the nursemaid and dances with her.*] All right, Mummy will dance with Bobby too. What? You've been throwing snowballs? Oh, I wish I'd been there. No, don't bother, Anne Marie, I'll help them off with their things. No, please, let me—I like doing it. You go on in, you look frozen. You'll find some hot coffee on the stove. [*The nursemaid goes into the room, left. Nora takes off the children's coats and hats and throws them down anywhere, while the children all talk at once.*] Really! A great big dog came running after you? But he didn't bite. No, the doggies wouldn't bite my pretty little dollies. You mustn't touch the parcels, Ivar! What are they? Wouldn't you like to know! No, no, that's nasty. Now? Shall we play something? What shall we play? Hide and seek? Yes, let's play hide and seek. Bob can hide first. Me first? All right, let me hide first.

[*She and the children play, laughing and shrieking, in this room and in the adjacent room on the right. Finally Nora hides under the table; the children come rushing in to look for her but cannot find her; they hear her stifled laughter, rush to the table, lift up the tablecloth and find her. Tremendous shouts of delight. She creeps out and pretends to frighten them. More shouts. Meanwhile there has been a knock at the front door, which nobody has heard. The door half opens, and Krogstad can be seen. He waits a little; the game continues.*]

Krogstad: I beg your pardon, Mrs. Helmer. . . .

Nora [*turns with a stifled cry and half jumps up*]: Ah! What do you want?

Krogstad: Excuse me. The front door was standing open. Somebody must have forgotten to shut it. . . .

Nora [*standing up*]: My husband isn't at home, Mr. Krogstad.

Krogstad: I know.

Nora: Well . . . what are you doing here?

Krogstad: I want a word with you.

Nora: With . . . ? [*Quietly, to the children.*] Go to Anne Marie. What? No, the strange man won't do anything to Mummy. When he's gone we'll have another game. [*She leads the children into the room, left, and shuts the door after them; tense and uneasy.*] You want to speak to me?   ,

Krogstad: Yes, I do.

Nora: Today? But it isn't the first of the month yet. . . .

Krogstad: No, it's Christmas Eve. It depends entirely on you what sort of Christmas you have.

Nora: What do you want? Today I can't possibly . . .

Krogstad: Let's not talk about that for the moment. It's something else. You've got a moment to spare?

Nora: Yes, I suppose so, though . . .

Krogstad: Good. I was sitting in Olsen's café, and I saw your husband go down the road . . .

Nora: Did you?

Krogstad: . . . with a lady.

Nora: Well?

Krogstad: May I be so bold as to ask whether that lady was a Mrs. Linde?

Nora: Yes.

Krogstad: Just arrived in town?

Nora: Yes, today.

Krogstad: And she's a good friend of yours?

Nora: Yes, she is. But I can't see . . .

Krogstad: I also knew her once.

Nora: I know.

Krogstad: Oh? So you know all about it. I thought as much. Well, I want to ask you straight: is Mrs. Linde getting a job in the Bank?

Nora: How dare you cross-examine me like this, Mr. Krogstad? You, one of my husband's subordinates? But since you've asked me, I'll tell you. Yes, Mrs. Linde *has* got a job. And I'm the one who got it for her, Mr. Krogstad. Now you know.

Krogstad: So my guess was right.

Nora [*walking up and down*]: Oh, I think I can say that some of us have a little influence now and again. Just because one happens to be a woman, that doesn't mean. . . . People in subordinate positions, ought to take care they don't offend anybody . . . who . . . hm . . .

Krogstad: . . . has influence?

Nora: Exactly.

Krogstad [*changing his tone*]: Mrs. Helmer, will you have the goodness to use your influence on my behalf?

Nora: What? What do you mean?

Krogstad: Will you be so good as to see that I keep my modest little job at the Bank?

Nora: What do you mean? Who wants to take it away from you?

Krogstad: Oh, you needn't try and pretend to me you don't know. I can quite see that this friend of yours isn't particularly anxious to bump up against me. And I can also see now whom I can thank for being given the sack.

Nora: But I assure you. . . .

Krogstad: All right, all right. But to come to the point: there's still time. And I advise you to use your influence to stop it.

Nora: But, Mr. Krogstad, I *have* no influence.

Krogstad: Haven't you? I thought just now you said yourself . . .

Nora: I didn't mean it that way, of course. Me? What makes you think I've got any influence of that kind over my husband?

Krogstad: I know your husband from our student days. I don't suppose he is any more steadfast than other married men.

Nora: You speak disrespectfully of my husband like that and I'll show you the door.

Krogstad: So the lady's got courage.

Nora: I'm not frightened of you any more. After New Year's I'll soon be finished with the whole business.

Krogstad [*controlling himself*]: Listen to me, Mrs. Helmer. If necessary I shall fight for my little job in the Bank as if I were fighting for my life.

Nora: So it seems.

Krogstad: It's not just for the money, that's the last thing I care about. There's something else . . . well, I might as well out with it. You see it's like this. You know as well as anybody that some years ago I got myself mixed up in a bit of trouble.

Nora: I believe I've heard something of the sort.

Krogstad: It never got as far as the courts; but immediately it was as if all paths were barred to me. So I started going in for the sort of business you know about. I had to do something, and I think I can say I haven't been one of the worst. But now I have to get out of it. My sons are growing up; for their sake I must try and win back what respectability I can. That job in the Bank was like the first step on the ladder for me. And now your husband wants to kick me off the ladder again, back into the mud.

Nora: But in God's name, Mr. Krogstad, it's quite beyond my power to help you.

Krogstad: That's because you haven't the will to help me. But I have ways of making you.

Nora: You wouldn't go and tell my husband I owe you money?

Krogstad: Suppose I did tell him?

Nora: It would be a rotten shame. [*Half choking with tears.*] That secret is all my pride and joy—why should he have to hear about it in this nasty, horrid way . . . hear about it from *you.* You would make things horribly unpleasant for me. . . .

Krogstad: Merely unpleasant?

Nora [*vehemently*]: Go on, do it then! It'll be all the worse for you. Because then my husband will see for himself what a bad man you are, and then you certainly won't be able to keep your job.

Krogstad: I asked whether it was only a bit of domestic unpleasantness you were afraid of?

Nora: If my husband gets to know about it, he'll pay off what's owing at once. And then we'd have nothing more to do with you.

Krogstad [*taking a pace towards her*]: Listen, Mrs. Helmer, either you haven't a very good memory, or else you don't understand much about business. I'd better make the position a little bit clearer for you.

Nora: How do you mean?

Krogstad: When your husband was ill, you came to me for the loan of twelve hundred dollars.

Nora: I didn't know of anybody else.

Krogstad: I promised to find you the money. . . .

Nora: And you did find it.

Krogstad: I promised to find you the money on certain conditions. At the time you were so concerned about your husband's illness, and so anxious to get the money for going away with, that I don't think you paid very much attention to all the incidentals. So there is perhaps some point in reminding you of them. Well, I promised to find you the money against an IOU which I drew up for you.

Nora: Yes, and which I signed.

Krogstad: Very good. But below that I added a few lines, by which your father was to stand security. This your father was to sign.

Nora: Was to . . . ? He did sign it.

Krogstad: I had left the date blank. The idea was that your father was to add the date himself when he signed it. Remember?

Nora: Yes, I think. . . .

Krogstad: I then gave you the IOU to post to your father. Wasn't that so?

Nora: Yes.

Krogstad: Which of course you did at once. Because only about five or six days later you brought it back to me with your father's signature. I then paid out the money.

Nora: Well? Haven't I paid the instalments regularly?

Krogstad: Yes, fairly. But . . . coming back to what we were talking about . . . that was a pretty bad period you were going through then, Mrs. Helmer.

Nora: Yes, it was.

Krogstad: Your father was seriously ill, I believe.

Nora: He was very near the end.

Krogstad: And died shortly afterwards?

Nora: Yes.

Krogstad: Tell me, Mrs. Helmer, do you happen to remember which day your father died? The exact date, I mean.

Nora: Daddy died on 29 September.

Krogstad: Quite correct. I made some inquiries. Which brings up a rather curious point [*takes out a paper*] which I simply cannot explain.

Nora: Curious . . . ? I don't know . . .

Krogstad: The curious thing is, Mrs. Helmer, that your father signed this document three days after his death.

Nora: What? I don't understand. . . .

Krogstad: Your father died on 29 September. But look here. Your father has dated his signature 2 October. Isn't that rather curious, Mrs. Helmer? [*Nora remains silent.*] It's also remarkable that the words '2 October' and the year are not in your father's handwriting, but in a handwriting I rather think I recognize. Well, perhaps that could be explained. Your father might have forgotten to date his signature, and then somebody else might have made a guess at the date later, before the fact of your father's death was known. There is nothing wrong in that. What really matters is the signature. And *that* is of course genuine, Mrs. Helmer? It really was your father who wrote his name here?

Nora [*after a moment's silence, throws her head back and looks at him defiantly*]: No, it wasn't. It was me who signed father's name.

Krogstad: Listen to me. I suppose you realize that that is a very dangerous confession?

Nora: Why? You'll soon have all your money back.

Krogstad: Let me ask you a question: why didn't you send that document to your father?

Nora: It was impossible. Daddy was ill. If I'd asked him for his signature, I'd have to tell him what the money was for. Don't you see, when he was as ill as that I couldn't go and tell him that my husband's life was in danger. It was simply impossible.

Krogstad: It would have been better for you if you had abandoned the whole trip.

Nora: No, that was impossible. This was the thing that was to save my husband's life. I couldn't give it up.

Krogstad: But did it never strike you that this was fraudulent . . . ?

Nora: That wouldn't have meant anything to me. Why should I worry about you? I couldn't stand you, not when you insisted on going through with all those cold-blooded formalities, knowing all the time what a critical state my husband was in.

Krogstad: Mrs. Helmer, it's quite clear you still haven't the faintest idea what it is you've committed. But let me tell you, my own offence was no more and no worse than that, and it ruined my entire reputation.

Nora: You? Are you trying to tell me that you once risked everything to save your wife's life?

Krogstad: The law takes no account of motives.

Nora: Then they must be very bad laws.

Krogstad: Bad or not, if I produce this document in court, you'll be condemned according to them.

Nora: I don't believe it. Isn't a daughter entitled to try and save her father from worry and anxiety on his deathbed? Isn't a wife entitled to save her husband's life? I might not know very much about the law, but I feel sure of one thing: it must say somewhere that things like this are allowed. You mean to say you don't know that—you, when it's your job? You must be a rotten lawyer, Mr. Krogstad.

Krogstad: That may be. But when it comes to business transactions—like the sort between us two—perhaps you'll admit I know something about *them*? Good. Now you must please yourself. But I tell you this: if I'm pitched out a second time, you are going to keep me company.

[*He bows and goes out through the hall.*]

Nora [*stands thoughtfully for a moment, then tosses her head*]: Rubbish! He's just trying to scare me. I'm not such a fool as all that. [*Begins gathering up the children's clothes; after a moment she stops.*] Yet . . . ? No, it's impossible! I did it for love, didn't I?

The Children [*in the doorway, left*]: Mummy, the gentleman's just gone out of the gate.

Nora: Yes, I know. But you mustn't say anything to anybody about that gentleman. You hear? Not even to Daddy!

The Children: All right, Mummy. Are you going to play again?

Nora: No, not just now.

The Children: But Mummy, you promised!

Nora: Yes, but I can't just now. Off you go now, I have a lot to do. Off you go, my darlings. [*She herds them carefully into the other room and shuts the door behind them. She sits down on the sofa, picks up her embroidery and works a few stitches, but soon stops.*] No! [*She flings her work down, stands up, goes to the hall door and calls out.*] Helene! Fetch the tree in for me, please. [*She walks across to the table, left, and opens the drawer; again pauses.*] No, really, it's quite impossible!

Maid [*with the Christmas tree*]: Where shall I put it, ma'am?

Nora: On the floor there, in the middle.

Maid: Anything else you want me to bring?

Nora: No, thank you. I've got what I want.

[*The maid has put the tree down and goes out.*]

Nora [*busy decorating the tree*]: Candles here . . . and flowers here—Revolting man! It's all nonsense! There's nothing to worry about. We'll have a lovely Christmas tree. And I'll do anything you want me to, Torvald; I'll sing for you, dance for you. . . .

[*Helmer, with a bundle of documents under his arm, comes in by the hall door.*]

Nora: Ah, back again already?

Helmer: Yes. Anybody been?

Nora: Here? No.

Helmer: That's funny. I just saw Krogstad leave the house.

Nora: Oh? O yes, that's right. Krogstad was here a minute.

Helmer: Nora, I can tell by your face he's been asking you to put a good word in for him.

Nora: Yes.

Helmer: And you were to pretend it was your own idea? You were to keep quiet about his having been here. He asked you to do that as well, didn't he?

Nora: Yes, Torvald. But . . .

Helmer: Nora, Nora, what possessed you to do a thing like that? Talking to a person like him, making him promises? And then on top of everything, to tell me a lie!

Nora: A lie . . . ?

Helmer: Didn't you say that nobody had been here? [*Wagging his finger at her.*] Never again must my little song-bird do a thing like that! Little song-birds must keep their pretty little beaks out of mischief; no chirruping out of tune! [*Puts his arm round her waist.*] Isn't that the way we want things to be? Yes, of course it is. [*Lets her go.*] So let's say no more about it. [*Sits down by the stove.*] Ah, nice and cosy here!

[*He glances through his papers.*]

Nora [*busy with the Christmas tree, after a short pause*]: Torvald!

Helmer: Yes.

Nora: I'm so looking forward to the fancy dress ball at the Stenborgs on Boxing Day.

Helmer: And I'm terribly curious to see what sort of surprise you've got for me.

Nora: Oh, it's too silly.

Helmer: Oh?

Nora: I just can't think of anything suitable. Everything seems so absurd, so pointless.

Helmer: Has my little Nora come to *that* conclusion?

Nora [*behind his chair, her arms on the chairback*]: Are you very busy, Torvald?

Helmer: Oh. . . .

Nora: What are all those papers?

Helmer: Bank matters.

Nora: Already?

Helmer: I have persuaded the retiring manager to give me authority to make any changes in organisation or personnel I think necessary. I have to work on it over the Christmas week. I want everything straight by the New Year.

Nora: So that was why that poor Krogstad. . . .

Helmer: Hm!

Nora [*still leaning against the back of the chair, running her fingers through his hair*]: If you hadn't been so busy, Torvald, I'd have asked you to do me an awfully big favour.

Helmer: Let me hear it. What's it to be?

Nora: Nobody's got such good taste as you. And the thing is I do so want to look my best at the fancy dress ball. Torvald, couldn't you give me some advice and tell me what you think I ought to go as, and how I should arrange my costume?

Helmer: Aha! So my impulsive little woman is asking for somebody to come to her rescue, eh?

Nora: Please, Torvald, I never get anywhere without your help.

Helmer: Very well, I'll think about it. We'll find something.

Nora: That's sweet of you. [*She goes across to the tree again; pause.*] How pretty these red flowers look.—Tell me, was it really something terribly wrong this man Krogstad did?

Helmer: Forgery. Have you any idea what that means?

Nora: Perhaps circumstances left him no choice?

Helmer: Maybe. Or perhaps, like so many others, he just didn't think. I am not so heartless that I would necessarily want to condemn a man for a single mistake like that.

Nora: Oh no, Torvald, of course not!

Helmer: Many a man might be able to redeem himself, if he honestly confessed his guilt and took his punishment.

Nora: Punishment?

Helmer: But that wasn't the way Krogstad chose. He dodged what was due to him by a cunning trick. And that's what has been the cause of his corruption.

Nora: Do you think it would . . . ?

Helmer: Just think how a man with a thing like that on his conscience will always be having to lie and cheat and dissemble; he can never drop the mask, not even with his own wife and children. And the children—*that's* the most terrible part of it, Nora.

Nora: Why?

Helmer: A fog of lies like that in a household, and it spreads disease and infection to every part of it. Every breath the children take in that kind of house is reeking with evil germs.

Nora [*closer behind him*]: Are you sure of that?

Helmer: My dear Nora, as a lawyer I know what I'm talking about. Practically all juvenile delinquents come from homes where the mother is dishonest.

Nora: Why mothers particularly?

Helmer: It's generally traceable to the mothers, but of course fathers can have the same influence. Every lawyer knows that only too well. And yet there's Krogstad been poisoning his own children for years with lies and deceit. That's the reason I call him morally depraved. [*Holds out his hands to her.*] That's why my sweet little Nora must promise me not to try putting in any more good words for him. Shake hands on it. Well? What's this? Give me your hand. There now! That's settled. I assure you I would have found it impossible to work with him. I quite literally feel physically sick in the presence of such people.

Nora [*draws her hand away and walks over to the other side of the Christmas tree*]: How hot it is in here! And I still have such a lot to do.

Helmer [*stands up and collects his papers together*]: Yes, I'd better think of getting some of this read before dinner. I must also think about your costume. And I might even be able to lay my hands on something to wrap in gold paper and hang on the Christmas tree. [*He lays his hand on her head.*] My precious little singing bird.

[*He goes into his study and shuts the door behind him.*]

Nora [*quietly, after a pause*]: Nonsense! It can't be. It's impossible. It *must* be impossible.

Maid [*in the doorway, left*]: The children keep asking so nicely if they can come in and see Mummy.

Nora: No, no, don't let them in! You stay with them, Anne Marie.

Maid: Very well, ma'am.

[*She shuts the door.*]

Nora [*pale with terror*]: Corrupt my children . . . ! Poison my home? [*Short pause; she throws back her head.*] It's not true! It could never, never be true!

ACT II

The same room. In the corner beside the piano stands the Christmas tree, stripped, bedraggled and with its candles burnt out. Nora's outdoor things lie on the sofa. Nora, alone there, walks about restlessly; at last she stops by the sofa and picks up her coat.

Nora [*putting her coat down again*]: Somebody's coming! [*Crosses to the door, listens.*] No, it's nobody. Nobody will come today, of course, Christmas Day— nor tomorrow, either. But perhaps. . . . [*She opens the door and looks out.*] No, nothing in the letter box; quite empty. [*Comes forward.*] Oh, nonsense! He didn't mean it seriously. Things like that *can't* happen. It's impossible. Why, I have three small children.

[*The Nursemaid comes from the room, left, carrying a big cardboard box.*]

Nursemaid: I finally found it, the box with the fancy dress costumes.

Nora: Thank you. Put it on the table, please.

Nursemaid [*does this*]: But I'm afraid they are in an awful mess.

Nora: Oh, if only I could rip them up into a thousand pieces!

Nursemaid: Good heavens, they can be mended all right, with a bit of patience.

Nora: Yes, I'll go over and get Mrs. Linde to help me.

Nursemaid: Out again? In this terrible weather? You'll catch your death of cold, Ma'am.

Nora: Oh, worse things might happen.—How are the children?

Nursemaid: Playing with their Christmas presents, poor little things, but . . .

Nora: Do they keep asking for me?

Nursemaid: They are so used to being with their Mummy.

Nora: Yes, Anne Marie, from now on I can't be with them as often as I was be-fore.

Nursemaid: Ah well, children get used to anything in time.

Nora: Do you think so? Do you think they would forget their Mummy if she went away for good?

Nursemaid: Good gracious—for good?

Nora: Tell me, Anne Marie—I've often wondered—how on earth could you bear to hand your child over to strangers?

Nursemaid: Well, there was nothing else for it when I had to come and nurse my little Nora.

Nora: Yes but . . . how could you *bring* yourself to do it?

Nursemaid: When I had the chance of such a good place? When a poor girl's been in trouble she must make the best of things. Because *he* didn't help, the rotter.

Nora: But your daughter will have forgotten you.

Nursemaid: Oh no, she hasn't. She wrote to me when she got confirmed, and again when she got married.

Nora [putting her arms round her neck]: Dear old Anne Marie, you were a good mother to me when I was little.

Nursemaid: My poor little Nora never had any other mother but me.

Nora: And if my little ones only had you, I know you would. . . . Oh, what am I talking about! [*She opens the box.*] Go in to them. I must . . . Tomorrow I'll let you see how pretty I am going to look.

Nursemaid: Ah, there'll be nobody at the ball as pretty as my Nora.

[*She goes into the room, left.*]

Nora [begins unpacking the box, but soon throws it down]: Oh, if only I dare go out. If only I could be sure nobody would come. And that nothing would happen in the meantime here at home. Rubbish—nobody's going to come. I mustn't think about it. Brush this muff. Pretty gloves, pretty gloves! I'll put it right out of my mind. One, two, three, four, five, six. . . . [*Screams.*] Ah, they are coming. . . . [*She starts towards the door, but stops irresolute. Mrs. Linde comes from the hall, where she has taken off her things.*] Oh, it's you, Kristine. There's nobody else out there, is there? I'm so glad you've come.

Mrs. Linde: I heard you'd been over looking for me.

Nora: Yes, I was just passing. There's something you must help me with. Come and sit beside me on the sofa here. You see, the Stenborgs are having a fancy dress party upstairs tomorrow evening, and now Torvald wants me to go as a Neapolitan fisher lass and dance the tarantella. I learned it in Capri, you know.

Mrs. Linde: Well, well! So you are going to do a party piece?

Nora: Torvald says I should. Look, here's the costume, Torvald had it made for me down there. But it's got all torn and I simply don't know. . . .

Mrs. Linde: We'll soon have that put right. It's only the trimming come away here and there. Got a needle and thread? Ah, here's what we are after.

Nora: It's awfully kind of you.

Mrs. Linde: So you are going to be all dressed up tomorrow, Nora? Tell you what—I'll pop over for a minute to see you in all your finery. But I'm quite forgetting to thank you for the pleasant time we had last night.

Nora [*gets up and walks across the room*]: Somehow I didn't think yesterday was as nice as things generally are.—You should have come to town a little earlier, Kristine.—Yes, Torvald certainly knows how to make things pleasant about the place.

Mrs. Linde: You too, I should say. You are not your father's daughter for nothing. But tell me, is Dr. Rank always as depressed as he was last night?

Nora: No, last night it was rather obvious. He's got something seriously wrong with him, you know. Tuberculosis of the spine, poor fellow. His father was a horrible man, who used to have mistresses and things like that. That's why the son was always ailing, right from being a child.

Mrs. Linde [*lowering her sewing*]: But my dear Nora, how do you come to know about things like that?

Nora [*walking about the room*]: Huh! When you've got three children, you get these visits from . . . women who have had a certain amount of medical training. And you hear all sorts of things from them.

Mrs. Linde [*begins sewing again; short silence*]: Does Dr. Rank call in every day?

Nora: Every single day. He was Torvald's best friend as a boy, and he's a good friend of *mine*, too. Dr. Rank is almost like one of the family.

Mrs. Linde: But tell me—is he really genuine? What I mean is: doesn't he sometimes rather turn on the charm?

Nora: No, on the contrary. What makes you think that?

Mrs. Linde: When you introduced me yesterday, he claimed he'd often heard my name in this house. But afterwards I noticed your husband hadn't the faintest idea who I was. Then how is it that Dr. Rank should. . . .

Nora: Oh yes, it was quite right what he said, Kristine. You see Torvald is so terribly in love with me that he says he wants me all to himself. When we were first married, it even used to make him sort of jealous if I only as much as mentioned any of my old friends from back home. So of course I stopped doing it. But I often talk to Dr. Rank about such things. He likes hearing about them.

Mrs. Linde: Listen, Nora! In lots of ways you are still a child. Now, I'm a good deal older than you, and a bit more experienced. I'll tell you something: I think you ought to give up all this business with Dr. Rank.

Nora: Give up what business?

Mrs. Linde: The whole thing, I should say. Weren't you saying yesterday something about a rich admirer who was to provide you with money. . . .

Nora: One who's never existed, I regret to say. But what of it?

Mrs. Linde: Has Dr. Rank money?

Nora: Yes, he has.

Mrs. Linde: And no dependents?

Nora: No, nobody. But . . . ?

Mrs. Linde: And he comes to the house every day?

Nora: Yes, I told you.

Mrs. Linde: But how can a man of his position want to pester you like this?

Nora: I simply don't understand.

Mrs. Linde: Don't pretend, Nora. Do you think I don't see now who you borrowed the twelve hundred from?

Nora: Are you out of your mind? Do you really think that? A friend of ours who comes here every day? The whole situation would have been absolutely intolerable.

Mrs. Linde: It *really* isn't him?

Nora: No, I give you my word. It would never have occurred to me for one moment. . . . Anyway, he didn't have the money to lend then. He didn't inherit it till later.

Mrs. Linde: Just as well for you, I'd say, my dear Nora.

Nora: No, it would never have occurred to me to ask Dr. Rank. . . . All the same I'm pretty certain if I were to ask him . . .

Mrs. Linde: But of course you won't.

Nora: No, of course not. I can't ever imagine it being necessary. But I'm quite certain if ever I were to mention it to Dr. Rank. . . .

Mrs. Linde: Behind your husband's back?

Nora: I have to get myself out of that other business. That's also behind his back. I *must* get myself out of that.

Mrs. Linde: Yes, that's what I said yesterday. But . . .

Nora [*walking up and down*]: A man's better at coping with these things than a woman. . . .

Mrs. Linde: Your own husband, yes.

Nora: Nonsense! [*Stops.*] When you've paid everything you owe, you do get your IOU back again, don't you?

Mrs. Linde: Of course.

Nora: And you can tear it up into a thousand pieces and burn it—the nasty, filthy thing!

Mrs. Linde [*looking fixedly at her, puts down her sewing and slowly rises*]: Nora, you are hiding something from me.

Nora: Is it so obvious?

Mrs. Linde: Something has happened to you since yesterday morning. Nora, what is it?

Nora [*going towards her*]: Kristine! [*Listens.*] Hush! There's Torvald back. Look, you go and sit in there beside the children for the time being. Torvald can't stand the sight of mending lying about. Get Anne Marie to help you.

Mrs. Linde [*gathering a lot of the things together*]: All right, but I'm not leaving until we have thrashed this thing out.

[*She goes into the room, left; at the same time Helmer comes in from the hall.*]

Nora [*goes to meet him*]: I've been longing for you to be back, Torvald, dear.

Helmer: Was that the dressmaker . . . ?

Nora: No, it was Kristine; she's helping me with my costume. I think it's going to look very nice . . .

Helmer: Wasn't that a good idea of mine, now?

Nora: Wonderful! But wasn't it also nice of me to let you have your way?

Helmer [*taking her under the chin*]: Nice of you—because you let your husband have his way? All right, you little rogue, I know you didn't mean it that way. But I don't want to disturb you. You'll be wanting to try the costume on, I suppose.

Nora: And I dare say you've got work to do?

Helmer: Yes. [*Shows her a bundle of papers.*] Look at this. I've been down at the Bank . . . .

[*He turns to go into his study.*]

Nora: Torvald!

Helmer [*stopping*]: Yes.

Nora: If a little squirrel were to ask ever so nicely . . . ?

Helmer: Well?

Nora: Would you do something for it?

Helmer: Naturally I would first have to know what it is.

Nora: Please, if only you would let it have its way, and do what it wants, it'd scamper about and do all sorts of marvellous tricks.

Helmer: What is it?

Nora: And the pretty little sky-lark would sing all day long. . . .

Helmer: Huh! It does that anyway.

Nora: I'd pretend I was an elfin child and dance a moonlight dance for you, Torvald.

Helmer: Nora—I hope it's not that business you started on this morning?

Nora [*coming closer*]: Yes, it is, Torvald. I implore you!

Helmer: You have the nerve to bring that up again?

Nora: Yes, yes, you *must* listen to me. You must let Krogstad keep his job at the Bank.

Helmer: My dear Nora, I'm giving his job to Mrs. Linde.

Nora: Yes, it's awfully sweet of you. But couldn't you get rid of somebody else in the office instead of Krogstad?

Helmer: This really is the most incredible obstinacy! Just because you go and make some thoughtless promise to put in a good word for him, you expect me . . .

Nora: It's not that, Torvald. It's for your own sake. That man writes in all the nastiest papers, you told me that yourself. He can do you no end of harm. He terrifies me to death. . . .

Helmer: Aha, now I see. It's your memories of what happened before that are frightening you.

Nora: What do you mean?

Helmer: It's your father you are thinking of.

Nora: Yes . . . yes, that's right. You remember all the nasty insinuations those wicked people put in the papers about Daddy? I honestly think they would have had him dismissed if the Ministry hadn't sent you down to investigate, and you hadn't been so kind and helpful.

Helmer: My dear little Nora, there is a considerable difference between your father and me. Your father's professional conduct was not entirely above suspicion. Mine is. And I hope it's going to stay that way as long as I hold this position.

Nora: But nobody knows what some of these evil people are capable of. Things could be so nice and pleasant for us here, in the peace and quiet of our home—you and me and the children, Torvald! That's why I implore you. . . .

Helmer: The more you plead for him, the more impossible you make it for me to keep him on. It's already known down at the Bank that I am going to give Krogstad his notice. If it ever got around that the new manager had been talked over by his wife. . . .

Nora: What of it?

Helmer: Oh, nothing! As long as the little woman gets her own stubborn way . . . ! Do you want me to make myself a laughing stock in the office? . . . Give people the idea that I am susceptible to any kind of outside pressure? You can imagine how soon I'd feel the consequences of that! Anyway, there's one other consideration that makes it impossible to have Krogstad in the Bank as long as I am manager.

Nora: What's that?

Helmer: At a pinch I might have overlooked his past lapses. . . .

Nora: Of course you could, Torvald!

Helmer: And I'm told he's not bad at his job, either. But we knew each other rather well when we were younger. It was one of those rather rash friendships that prove embarrassing in later life. There's no reason why you shouldn't know we were once on terms of some familiarity. And he, in his tactless way, makes no attempt to hide the fact, particularly when other people are present. On the contrary, he thinks he has every right to treat me as an equal, with his 'Torvald this' and 'Torvald that' every time he opens his mouth. I find it extremely irritating, I can tell you. He would make my position at the Bank absolutely intolerable.

Nora: Torvald, surely you aren't serious?

Helmer: Oh? Why not?

Nora: Well, it's all so petty.

Helmer: What's that you say? Petty? Do you think I'm petty?

Nora: No, not at all, Torvald dear! And that's why . . .

Helmer: Doesn't make any difference! . . . You call my motives petty; so I must be petty too. Petty! Indeed! Well, we'll put a stop to that, once and for all. [*He opens the hall door and calls.*] Helene!

Nora: What are you going to do?

Helmer [*searching among his papers*]: Settle things. [*The Maid comes in.*] See this letter? I want you to take it down at once. Get hold of a messenger and get him to deliver it. Quickly. The address is on the outside. There's the money.

Maid: Very good, sir.

[She goes with the letter.]

Helmer [*putting his papers together*]: There now, my stubborn little miss.

Nora [*breathless*]: Torvald . . . what was that letter?

Helmer: Krogstad's notice.

Nora: Get it back, Torvald! There's still time! Oh, Torvald, get it back! Please for my sake, for your sake, for the sake of the children! Listen, Torvald, please! You don't realize what it can do to us.

Helmer: Too late.

Nora: Yes, too late.

Helmer: My dear Nora, I forgive you this anxiety of yours, although it is actually a bit of an insult. Oh, but it is, I tell you! It's hardly flattering to suppose that anything this miserable pen-pusher wrote could frighten *me*! But I forgive you all the same, because it is rather a sweet way of showing how much you love me. [*He takes her in his arms.*] This is how things must be, my own darling Nora. When it comes to the point, I've enough strength and enough courage, believe me, for whatever happens. You'll find I'm man enough to take everything on myself.

Nora [*terrified*]: What do you mean?

Helmer: Everything, I said. . . .

Nora [*in command of herself*]: That is something you shall never, never do.

Helmer: All right, then we'll share it, Nora—as man and wife. That's what we'll do. [*Caressing her.*] Does that make you happy now? There, there, don't look at me with those eyes, like a little frightened dove. The whole thing is sheer imagination.—Why don't you run through the tarantella and try out the tambourine? I'll go into my study and shut both the doors, then I won't hear anything. You can make all the noise you want. [*Turns in the doorway.*] And when Rank comes, tell him where he can find me.

[He nods to her, goes with his papers into his room, and shuts the door behind him.]

Nora [*wild-eyed with terror, stands as though transfixed*]: He's quite capable of doing it! He would do it! No matter what, he'd do it.—No, never in this world! Anything but that! Help? Some way out . . . ? [*The door-bell rings in the hall.*] Dr. Rank . . . ! Anything but that, *anything*! [*She brushes her hands over her face, pulls herself together and opens the door into the hall. Dr. Rank is standing outside hanging up his fur coat. During what follows it begins to grow dark.*] Hello, Dr. Rank. I recognized your ring. Do you mind not going in to Torvald just yet, I think he's busy.

Rank: And you?

[Dr. Rank comes into the room and she closes the door behind him.]

Nora: Oh, you know very well I've always got time for you.

Rank: Thank you. A privilege I shall take advantage of as long as I am able.

Nora: What do you mean—as long as you are able?

Rank: Does that frighten you?

Nora: Well, it's just that it sounds so strange. Is anything likely to happen?

Rank: Only what I have long expected. But I didn't think it would come quite so soon.

Nora [*catching at his arm*]: What have you found out? Dr. Rank, you must tell me!

Rank: I'm slowly sinking. There's nothing to be done about it.

Nora [*with a sigh of relief*]: Oh, it's *you* you're . . . ?

Rank: Who else? No point in deceiving oneself. I am the most wretched of all my patients, Mrs. Helmer. These last few days I've made a careful analysis of my internal economy. Bankrupt! Within a month I shall probably be lying rotting up there in the churchyard.

Nora: Come now, what a ghastly thing to say!

Rank: The whole damned thing is ghastly. But the worst thing is all the ghastliness that has to be gone through first. I only have one more test to make; and when that's done I'll know pretty well when the final disintegration will start. There's something I want to ask you. Helmer is a sensitive soul; he loathes anything that's ugly. I don't want him visiting me. . . .

Nora: But Dr. Rank. . . .

Rank: On no account must he. I won't have it. I'll lock the door on him.—As soon as I'm absolutely certain of the worst, I'll send you my visiting card with a black cross on it. You'll know then the final horrible disintegration has begun.

Nora: Really, you are being quite absurd today. And here was I hoping you would be in a thoroughly good mood.

Rank: With death staring me in the face? Why should I suffer for another man's sins? What justice is there in that? Somewhere, somehow, every single family must be suffering some such cruel retribution. . . .

Nora [*stopping up her ears*]: Rubbish! Do cheer up!

Rank: Yes, really the whole thing's nothing but a huge joke. My poor innocent spine must do penance for my father's gay subaltern life.

Nora [*by the table, left*]: Wasn't he rather partial to asparagus and *pâté de foie gras?*

Rank: Yes, he was. And truffles.

Nora: Truffles, yes. And oysters, too, I believe?

Rank: Yes, oysters, oysters, of course.

Nora: And all the port and champagne that goes with them. It does seem a pity all these delicious things should attack the spine.

Rank: Especially when they attack a poor spine that never had any fun out of them.

Nora: Yes, that is an awful pity.

Rank [*looks at her sharply*]: Hm. . . .

Nora [*after a pause*]: Why did you smile?

Rank: No, it was you who laughed.

Nora: No, it was you who smiled, Dr. Rank!

Rank [*getting up*]: You are a bigger rascal than I thought you were.

Nora: I feel full of mischief today.

Rank: So it seems.

Nora [*putting her hands on his shoulders*]: Dear, dear Dr. Rank, you mustn't go and die on Torvald and me.

Rank: You wouldn't miss me for long. When you are gone, you are soon forgotten.

Nora [*looking at him anxiously*]: Do you think so?

Rank: People make new contacts, then . . .

Nora: Who make new contacts?

Rank: Both you and Helmer will, when I'm gone. You yourself are already well on the way, it seems to me. What was this Mrs. Linde doing here last night?

Nora: Surely you aren't jealous of poor Kristine?

Rank: Yes, I am. She'll be my successor in this house. When I'm done for, I can see this woman. . . .

Nora: Hush! Don't talk so loud, she's in there.

Rank: Today as well? There you are, you see!

Nora: Just to do some sewing on my dress. Good Lord, how absurd you are! [*She sits down on the sofa.*] Now Dr. Rank, cheer up. You'll see tomorrow how nicely I can dance. And you can pretend I'm doing it just for you—and for Torvald as well, of course. [*She takes various things out of the box.*] Come here, Dr. Rank. I want to show you something.

Rank [*sits*]: What is it?

Nora: Look!

Rank: Silk stockings.

Nora: Flesh-coloured! Aren't they lovely! Of course, it's dark here now, but tomorrow. . . . No, no, no, you can only look at the feet. Oh well, you might as well see a bit higher up, too.

Rank: Hm. . . .

Nora: Why are you looking so critical? Don't you think they'll fit?

Rank: I couldn't possibly offer any informed opinion about that.

Nora [*looks at him for a moment*]: Shame on you. [*Hits him lightly across the ear with the stockings.*] Take that! [*Folds them up again.*]

Rank: And what other delights am I to be allowed to see?

Nora: Not another thing. You are too naughty. [*She hums a little and searches among her things.*]

Rank [*after a short pause*]: Sitting here so intimately like this with you, I can't imagine . . . I simply cannot conceive what would have become of me if I had never come to this house.

Nora [*smiles*]: Yes, I rather think you do enjoy coming here.

Rank [*in a low voice, looking fixedly ahead*]: And the thought of having to leave it all . . .

Nora: Nonsense. You aren't leaving.

Rank [*in the same tone*]: . . . without being able to leave behind even the slightest token of gratitude, hardly a fleeting regret even . . . nothing but an empty place to be filled by the first person that comes along.

Nora: Supposing I were to ask you to . . . ? No . . .

Rank: What?

Nora: . . . to show me the extent of your friendship . . .

Rank: Yes?

Nora: I mean . . . to do me a tremendous favour. . . .

Rank: Would you really, for once, give me that pleasure?

Nora: You have no idea what it is.

Rank: All right, tell me.

Nora: No, really I can't, Dr. Rank. It's altogether too much to ask . . . because I need your advice and help as well. . . .

Rank: The more the better. I cannot imagine what you have in mind. But tell me anyway. You do trust me, don't you?

Nora: Yes, I trust you more than anybody I know. You are my best and my most faithful friend. I know that. So I will tell you. Well then, Dr. Rank, there is something you must help me to prevent. You know how deeply, how passionately Torvald is in love with me. He would never hesitate for a moment to sacrifice his life for my sake.

Rank [*bending towards her*]: Nora . . . do you think he's the only one who . . . ?

Nora [*stiffening slightly*]: Who . . . ?

Rank: Who wouldn't gladly give his life for your sake.

Nora [*sadly*]: Oh!

Rank: I swore to myself you would know before I went. I'll never have a better opportunity. Well, Nora! Now you know. And now you know too that you can confide in me as in nobody else.

Nora [*rises and speaks evenly and calmly*]: Let me past.

Rank [*makes way for her, but remains seated*]: Nora. . . .

Nora [*in the hall doorway*]: Helene, bring the lamp in, please. [*Walks over to the stove.*] Oh, my dear Dr. Rank, that really was rather horrid of you.

Rank [*getting up*]: That I have loved you every bit as much as anybody? Is *that* horrid?

Nora: No, but that you had to go and tell me. When it was all so unnecessary. . . .

Rank: What do you mean? Did you know . . . ?

[*The Maid comes in with the lamp, puts it on the table, and goes out again.*]

Rank: Nora . . . Mrs. Helmer . . . I'm asking you if you knew?

Nora: How can I tell whether I did or didn't. I simply can't tell you. . . . Oh, how could you be so clumsy, Dr. Rank! When everything was so nice.

Rank: Anyway, you know now that I'm at your service, body and soul. So you can speak out.

Nora [*looking at him*]: After this?

Rank: I beg you to tell me what it is.

Nora: I can tell you nothing now.

Rank: You must. You can't torment me like this. Give me a chance—I'll do anything that's humanly possible.

Nora: You can do nothing for me now. Actually, I don't really need any help. It's all just my imagination, really it is. Of course! [*She sits down in the rocking chair, looks at him and smiles.*] I must say, you are a nice one, Dr. Rank! Don't you feel ashamed of yourself, now the lamp's been brought in?

Rank: No, not exactly. But perhaps I ought to go—for good?

Nora: No, you mustn't do that. You must keep coming just as you've always done. You know very well Torvald would miss you terribly.

Rank: And *you?*

Nora: I always think it's tremendous fun having you.

Rank: That's exactly what gave me wrong ideas. I just can't puzzle you out. I often used to feel you'd just as soon be with me as with Helmer.

Nora: Well, you see, there are those people you love and those people you'd almost rather *be* with.

Rank: Yes, there's something in that.

Nora: When I was a girl at home, I loved Daddy best, of course. But I also thought it great fun if I could slip into the maids' room. For one thing they never preached at me. And they always talked about such exciting things.

Rank: Aha! So it's their role I've taken over!

Nora [*jumps up and crosses to him*]: Oh, my dear, kind Dr. Rank, I didn't mean that at all. But you can see how it's a bit with Torvald as it was with Daddy. . . .

[*The Maid comes in from the hall.*]

Maid: Please, ma'am . . . !

[*She whispers and hands her a card.*]

Nora [*glances at the card*]: Ah!

[*She puts it in her pocket.*]

Rank: Anything wrong?

Nora: No, no, not at all. It's just . . . it's my new costume. . . .

Rank: How is that? There's your costume in there.

Nora: That one, yes. But this is another one. I've ordered it. Torvald mustn't hear about it. . . .

Rank: Ah, so that's the big secret, is it!

Nora: Yes, that's right. Just go in and see him, will you? He's in the study. Keep him occupied for the time being. . . .

Rank: Don't worry. He shan't escape me.

[*He goes into Helmer's study.*]

Nora [*to the maid*]: Is he waiting in the kitchen?

Maid: Yes, he came up the back stairs. . . .

Nora: But didn't you tell him somebody was here?

Maid: Yes, but it was no good.

Nora: Won't he go?

Maid: No, he won't till he's seen you.

Nora: Let him in, then. But quietly. Helene, you mustn't tell anybody about this. It's a surprise for my husband.

Maid: I understand, ma'am. . . .

[*She goes out.*]

Nora: Here it comes! What I've been dreading! No, no, it can't happen, it *can't* happen.

[*She walks over and bolts Helmer's door. The maid opens the hall door for Krogstad and shuts it again behind him. He is wearing a fur coat, over-shoes, and a fur cap.*]

Nora [*goes towards him*]: Keep your voice down, my husband is at home.

Krogstad: What if he is?

Nora: What do you want with me?

Krogstad: To find out something.

Nora: Hurry, then. What is it?

Krogstad: You know I've been given notice.

Nora: I couldn't prevent it, Mr. Krogstad, I did my utmost for you, but it was no use.

Krogstad: Has your husband so little affection for you? He knows what I can do to you, yet he dares. . . .

Nora: You don't imagine he knows about it!

Krogstad: No, I didn't imagine he did. It didn't seem a bit like my good friend Torvald Helmer to show that much courage. . . .

Nora: Mr. Krogstad, I must ask you to show some respect for my husband.

Krogstad: Oh, sure! All due respect! But since you are so anxious to keep this business quiet, Mrs. Helmer, I take it you now have a rather clearer idea of just what it is you've done, than you had yesterday.

Nora: Clearer than *you* could ever have given me.

Krogstad: Yes, being as I am such a rotten lawyer. . . .

Nora: What do you want with me?

Krogstad: I just wanted to see how things stood, Mrs. Helmer. I've been thinking about you all day. Even a mere money-lender, a hack journalist, a—well, even somebody like me has a bit of what you might call feeling.

Nora: Show it then. Think of my little children.

Krogstad: Did you or your husband think of mine? But what does it matter now? There was just one thing I wanted to say: you needn't take this business too seriously. I shan't start any proceedings, for the present.

Nora: Ah, I knew you wouldn't.

Krogstad: The whole thing can be arranged quite amicably. Nobody need know. Just the three of us.

Nora: My husband must never know.

Krogstad: How can you prevent it? Can you pay off the balance?

Nora: No, not immediately.

Krogstad: Perhaps you've some way of getting hold of the money in the next few days.

Nora: None I want to make use of.

Krogstad: Well, it wouldn't have been very much help to you if you had. Even if you stood there with the cash in your hand and to spare, you still wouldn't get your IOU back from me now.

Nora: What are you going to do with it?

Krogstad: Just keep it—have it in my possession. Nobody who isn't implicated need know about it. So if you are thinking of trying any desperate remedies . . .

Nora: Which I am. . . .

Krogstad: . . . if you happen to be thinking of running away . . .

Nora: Which I am!

Krogstad: . . . or anything worse . . .

Nora: How did you know?

Krogstad: . . . forget it!

Nora: How did you know I was thinking of *that?*

Krogstad: Most of us think of *that,* to begin with. I did, too; but I didn't have the courage. . . .

Nora [*tonelessly*]: I haven't either.

Krogstad [*relieved*]: So you haven't the courage either, eh?

Nora: No, I haven't! I haven't!

Krogstad: It would also be very stupid. There'd only be the first domestic storm to get over. . . . I've got a letter to your husband in my pocket here. . . .

Nora: And it's all in there?

Krogstad: In as tactful a way as possible.

Nora [*quickly*]: He must never read that letter. Tear it up. I'll find the money somehow.

Krogstad: Excuse me, Mrs. Helmer, but I've just told you. . . .

Nora: I'm not talking about the money I owe you. I want to know how much you are demanding from my husband, and I'll get the money.

Krogstad: I want no money from your husband.

Nora: What do you want?

Krogstad: I'll tell you. I want to get on my feet again, Mrs. Helmer; I want to get to the top. And your husband is going to help me. For the last eighteen months I've gone straight; all that time it's been hard going; I was content to work my way up, step by step. Now I'm being kicked out, and I won't stand for being taken back again as an act of charity. I'm going to get to the top, I tell you. I'm going back into that Bank—with a better job. Your husband is going to create a new vacancy, just for me. . . .

Nora: He'll never do that!

Krogstad: He will do it. I know him. He'll do it without so much as a whimper. And once I'm in there with him, you'll see what's what. In less than a year I'll be his right-hand man. It'll be Nils Krogstad, not Torvald Helmer, who'll be running that Bank.

Nora: You'll never live to see that day!

Krogstad: You mean you . . . ?

Nora: Now I have the courage.

Krogstad: You can't frighten me! A precious pampered little thing like you. . . .

Nora: I'll show you! I'll show you!

Krogstad: Under the ice, maybe? Down in the cold, black water? Then being washed up in the spring, bloated, hairless, unrecognizable. . . .

Nora: You can't frighten me.

Krogstad: You can't frighten me, either. People don't do that sort of thing, Mrs. Helmer. There wouldn't be any point to it, anyway, I'd still have him right in my pocket.

Nora: Afterwards? When I'm no longer . . .

Krogstad: Aren't you forgetting that your reputation would then be entirely in my hands? [*Nora stands looking at him, speechless.*] Well, I've warned you. Don't do anything silly. When Helmer gets my letter, I expect to hear from him. And don't forget: it's him who is forcing me off the straight and narrow again, your own husband! That's something I'll never forgive him for. Goodbye, Mrs. Helmer.

[*He goes out through the hall. Nora crosses to the door, opens it slightly, and listens.*]

Nora: He's going. He hasn't left the letter. No, no, that would be impossible! [*Opens the door further and further.*] What's he doing? He's stopped outside. He's not going down the stairs. Has he changed his mind? Is he . . . ? [*A letter falls into the letter-box. Then Krogstad's footsteps are heard receding as he walks downstairs. Nora gives a stifled cry, runs across the room to the sofa table; pause.*] In the letter-box! [*She creeps stealthily across to the hall door.*] There it is! Torvald, Torvald! It's hopeless now!

Mrs. Linde [*comes into the room, left, carrying the costume*]: There, I think that's everything. Shall we try it on?

Nora [*in a low, hoarse voice*]: Kristine, come here.

Mrs. Linde [*throws the dress down on the sofa*]: What's wrong with you? You look upset.

Nora: Come here. Do you see that letter? *There,* look! Through the glass in the letter-box.

Mrs. Linde: Yes, yes, I can see it.

Nora: It's a letter from Krogstad.

Mrs. Linde: Nora! It was Krogstad who lent you the money!

Nora: Yes. And now Torvald will get to know everything.

Mrs. Linde: Believe me, Nora, it's best for you both.

Nora: But there's more to it than that. I forged a signature. . . .

Mrs. Linde: Heavens above!

Nora: Listen, I want to tell you something, Kristine, so you can be my witness.

Mrs. Linde: What do you mean 'witness'? What do you want me to . . . ?

Nora: If I should go mad . . . which might easily happen . . .

Mrs. Linde: Nora!

Nora: Or if anything happened to me . . . which meant I couldn't be here. . . .

Mrs. Linde: Nora, Nora! Are you out of your mind?

Nora: And if somebody else wanted to take it all upon himself, the whole blame, you understand. . . .

Mrs. Linde: Yes, yes. But what makes you think . . . ?

Nora: Then you must testify that it isn't true, Kristine. I'm not out of my mind; I'm quite sane now. And I tell you this: nobody else knew anything, I alone was responsible for the whole thing. Remember that!

Mrs. Linde: I will. But I don't understand a word of it.

Nora: Why should you? You see something miraculous is going to happen.

Mrs. Linde: Something miraculous?

Nora: Yes, a miracle. But something so terrible as well, Kristine—oh, it must *never* happen, not for anything.

Mrs. Linde: I'm going straight over to talk to Krogstad.

Nora: Don't go. He'll only do you harm.

Mrs. Linde: There was a time when he would have done anything for me.

Nora: Him!

Mrs. Linde: Where does he live?

Nora: How do I know . . . ? Wait a minute. [*She feels in her pocket.*] Here's his card. But the letter, the letter . . . !

Helmer [*from his study, knocking on the door*]: Nora!

Nora [*cries out in terror*]: What's that? What do you want?

Helmer: Don't be frightened. We're not coming in. You've locked the door. Are you trying on?

Nora: Yes, yes, I'm trying on. It looks so nice on me, Torvald.

Mrs. Linde [*who has read the card*]: He lives just round the corner.

Nora: It's no use. It's hopeless. The letter is there in the box.

Mrs. Linde: Your husband keeps the key?

Nora: Always.

Mrs. Linde: Krogstad must ask for his letter back unread, he must find some sort of excuse. . . .

Nora: But this is just the time that Torvald generally . . .

Mrs. Linde: Put him off! Go in and keep him busy. I'll be back as soon as I can.

[*She goes out hastily by the hall door. Nora walks over to Helmer's door, opens it and peeps in.*]

Nora: Torvald!

Helmer [*in the study*]: Well, can a man get into his own living-room again now? Come along, Rank, now we'll see . . . [*In the doorway.*] But what's this?

Nora: What, Torvald dear?

Helmer: Rank led me to expect some kind of marvellous transformation.

Rank [*in the doorway*]: That's what I thought too, but I must have been mistaken.

Nora: I'm not showing myself off to anybody before tomorrow.

Helmer: Nora dear, you look tired. You haven't been practising too hard?

Nora: No, I haven't practised at all yet.

Helmer: You'll have to, though.

Nora: Yes, I certainly must, Torvald. But I just can't get anywhere without your help: I've completely forgotten it.

Helmer: We'll soon polish it up.

Nora: Yes, do help me, Torvald. Promise? I'm so nervous. All those people. . . . You must devote yourself exclusively to me this evening. Pens away! Forget all about the office! Promise me, Torvald dear!

Helmer: I promise. This evening I am wholly and entirely at your service . . . helpless little thing that you are. Oh, but while I remember, I'll just look first . . .

[He goes towards the hall door.]

Nora: What do you want out there?
Helmer: Just want to see if there are any letters.
Nora: No, don't, Torvald!
Helmer: Why not?
Nora: Torvald, *please!* There aren't any.
Helmer: Just let me see.

[He starts to go. Nora, at the piano, plays the opening bars of the tarantella.]

Helmer [*at the door, stops*]: Aha!
Nora: I shan't be able to dance tomorrow if I don't rehearse it with you.
Helmer [*walks to her*]: Are you really so nervous, Nora dear?
Nora: Terribly nervous. Let me run through it now. There's still time before supper. Come and sit here and play for me, Torvald dear. Tell me what to do, keep me right—as you always do.
Helmer: Certainly, with pleasure, if that's what you want.

[He sits at the piano. Nora snatches the tambourine out of the box, and also a long gaily-coloured shawl which she drapes round herself; then with a bound she leaps forward.]

Nora [*shouts*]: Now play for me! Now I'll dance!

[Helmer plays and Nora dances; Dr. Rank stands at the piano behind Helmer and looks on.]

Helmer [*playing*]: Not so fast! Not so fast!
Nora: I can't help it.
Helmer: Not so wild, Nora!
Nora: This is how it has to be.
Helmer [*stops*]: No, no, that won't do at all.
Nora [*laughs and swings the tambourine*]: Didn't I tell you?
Rank: Let me play for her.
Helmer [*gets up*]: Yes, do. Then I'll be better able to tell her what to do.

[Rank sits down at the piano and plays. Nora dances more and more wildly. Helmer stands by the stove giving her repeated directions as she dances; she does not seem to hear them. Her hair comes undone and falls about her shoulders; she pays no attention and goes on dancing. Mrs. Linde enters.]

Mrs. Linde [*standing as though spellbound in the doorway*]: Ah . . . !
Nora [*dancing*]: See what fun we are having, Kristine.
Helmer: But my dear darling Nora, you are dancing as though your life depended on it.

Nora: It does.

Helmer: Stop, Rank! This is sheer madness. Stop, I say.

[*Rank stops playing and Nora comes to a sudden halt.*]

Helmer [*crosses to her*]: I would never have believed it. You have forgotten everything I ever taught you.

Nora [*throwing away the tambourine*]: There you are, you see.

Helmer: Well, some more instruction is certainly needed there.

Nora: Yes, you see how necessary it is. You must go on coaching me right up to
the last minute. Promise me, Torvald?

Helmer: You can rely on me.

Nora: You mustn't think about anything else but me until after tomorrow . . .
mustn't open any letters . . . mustn't touch the letter-box.

Helmer: Ah, you are still frightened of what that man might . . .

Nora: Yes, yes, I am.

Helmer: I can see from your face there's already a letter there from him.

Nora: I don't know. I think so. But you mustn't read anything like that now. We
don't want anything horrid coming between us until all this is over.

Rank [*softly to Helmer*]: I shouldn't cross her.

Helmer [*puts his arm round her*]: The child must have her way. But tomorrow
night, when your dance is done. . . .

Nora: Then you are free.

Maid [*in the doorway, right*]: Dinner is served, madam.

Nora: We'll have champagne, Helene.

Maid: Very good, madam.

[*She goes.*]

Helmer: Aha! It's to be quite a banquet, eh?

Nora: With champagne flowing until dawn. [*Shouts.*] And some macaroons, Helene . . . lots of them, for once in a while.

Helmer [*seizing her hands*]: Now, now, not so wild and excitable! Let me see you
being my own little singing bird again.

Nora: Oh yes, I will. And if you'll just go in . . . you, too, Dr. Rank. Kristine, you
must help me to do my hair.

Rank [*softly, as they leave*]: There isn't anything . . . anything as it were, impending, is there?

Helmer: No, not at all, my dear fellow. It's nothing but these childish fears I was
telling you about.

[*They go out to the right.*]

Nora: Well?

Mrs. Linde: He's left town.

Nora: I saw it in your face.

Mrs. Linde: He's coming back tomorrow evening. I left a note for him.

Nora: You shouldn't have done that. You must let things take their course. Because really it's a case for rejoicing, waiting like this for the miracle.

Mrs. Linde: What is it you are waiting for?

Nora: Oh, you wouldn't understand. Go and join the other two. I'll be there in a minute.

[*Mrs. Linde goes into the dining-room. Nora stands for a moment as though to collect herself, then looks at her watch.*]

Nora: Five. Seven hours to midnight. Then twenty-four hours till the next midnight. Then the tarantella will be over. Twenty-four and seven? Thirty-one hours to live.

Helmer [*in the doorway, right*]: What's happened to our little sky-lark?

Nora [*running towards him with open arms*]: Here she is!

ACT III

The same room. The round table has been moved to the centre of the room, and the chairs placed round it. A lamp is burning on the table. The door to the hall stands open. Dance music can be heard coming from the floor above. Mrs. Linde is sitting by the table, idly turning over the pages of a book; she tries to read, but does not seem able to concentrate. Once or twice she listens, tensely, for a sound at the front door.

Mrs. Linde [*looking at her watch*]: Still not here. There isn't much time left. I only hope he hasn't ... [*She listens again.*] Ah, there he is. [*She goes out into the hall, and cautiously opens the front door. Soft footsteps can be heard on the stairs. She whispers.*] Come in. There's nobody here.

Krogstad [*in the doorway*]: I found a note from you at home. What does it all mean?

Mrs. Linde: I had to talk to you.

Krogstad: Oh? And did it have to be here, in this house?

Mrs. Linde: It wasn't possible over at my place, it hasn't a separate entrance. Come in. We are quite alone. The maid's asleep and the Helmers are at a party upstairs.

Krogstad [*comes into the room*]: Well, well! So the Helmers are out dancing tonight! Really?

Mrs. Linde: Yes, why not?

Krogstad: Why not indeed!

Mrs. Linde: Well then, Nils. Let's talk.

Krogstad: Have we two anything more to talk about?

Mrs. Linde: We have a great deal to talk about.

Krogstad: I shouldn't have thought so.

Mrs. Linde: That's because you never really understood me.

Krogstad: What else was there to understand, apart from the old, old story? A heartless woman throws a man over the moment something more profitable offers itself.

Mrs. Linde: Do you really think I'm so heartless? Do you think I found it easy to break it off.

Krogstad: Didn't you?

Mrs. Linde: You didn't really believe that?

Krogstad: If that wasn't the case, why did you write to me as you did?

Mrs. Linde: There was nothing else I could do. If I had to make the break, I felt in duty bound to destroy any feeling that you had for me.

Krogstad [*clenching his hands*]: So that's how it was. And all that . . . was for money!

Mrs. Linde: You mustn't forget I had a helpless mother and two young brothers. We couldn't wait for you, Nils. At that time you hadn't much immediate prospect of anything.

Krogstad: That may be. But you had no right to throw me over for somebody else.

Mrs. Linde: Well, I don't know. Many's the time I've asked myself whether I was justified.

Krogstad [*more quietly*]: When I lost you, it was just as if the ground had slipped away from under my feet. Look at me now: a broken man clinging to the wreck of his life.

Mrs. Linde: Help might be near.

Krogstad: It was near. Then you came along and got in the way.

Mrs. Linde: Quite without knowing, Nils. I only heard today it's you I'm supposed to be replacing at the Bank.

Krogstad: If you say so, I believe you. But now you do know, aren't you going to withdraw?

Mrs. Linde: No, that wouldn't benefit you in the slightest.

Krogstad: Benefit, benefit . . . ! I would do it just the same.

Mrs. Linde: I have learned to go carefully. Life and hard, bitter necessity have taught me that.

Krogstad: And life has taught me not to believe in pretty speeches.

Mrs. Linde: Then life has taught you a very sensible thing. But deeds are something you surely must believe in?

Krogstad: How do you mean?

Mrs. Linde: You said you were like a broken man clinging to the wreck of his life.

Krogstad: And I said it with good reason.

Mrs. Linde: And I am like a broken woman clinging to the wreck of her life. Nobody to care about, and nobody to care for.

Krogstad: It was your own choice.

Mrs. Linde: At the time there was no other choice.

Krogstad: Well, what of it?

Mrs. Linde: Nils, what about us two castaways joining forces.

Krogstad: What's that you say?

Mrs. Linde: Two of us on *one* wreck surely stand a better chance than each on his own.

Krogstad: Kristine!

Mrs. Linde: Why do you suppose I came to town?

Krogstad: You mean, you thought of me?

Mrs. Linde: Without work I couldn't live. All my life I have worked, for as long as I can remember; that has always been my one great joy. But now I'm completely alone in the world, and feeling horribly empty and forlorn. There's no pleasure in working only for yourself. Nils, give me somebody and something to work for.

Krogstad: I don't believe all this. It's only a woman's hysteria, wanting to be all magnanimous and self-sacrificing.

Mrs. Linde: Have you ever known me hysterical before?

Krogstad: Would you really do this? Tell me—do you know all about my past?

Mrs. Linde: Yes.

Krogstad: And you know what people think about me?

Mrs. Linde: Just now you hinted you thought you might have been a different person with me.

Krogstad: I'm convinced I would.

Mrs. Linde: Couldn't it still happen?

Krogstad: Kristine! You know what you are saying, don't you? Yes, you do. I can see you do. Have you really the courage . . . ?

Mrs. Linde: I need someone to mother, and your children need a mother. We two need each other. Nils, I have faith in what, deep down, you are. With you I can face anything.

Krogstad [*seizing her hands*]: Thank you, thank you, Kristine. And I'll soon have everybody looking up to me, or I'll know the reason why. Ah, but I was forgetting. . . .

Mrs. Linde: Hush! The tarantella! You must go!

Krogstad: Why? What is it?

Mrs. Linde: You hear that dance upstairs? When it's finished they'll be coming.

Krogstad: Yes, I'll go. It's too late to do anything. Of course, you know nothing about what steps I've taken against the Helmers.

Mrs. Linde: Yes, Nils, I do know.

Krogstad: Yet you still want to go on. . . .

Mrs. Linde: I know how far a man like you can be driven by despair.

Krogstad: Oh, if only I could undo what I've done!

Mrs. Linde: You still can. Your letter is still there in the box.

Krogstad: Are you sure?

Mrs. Linde: Quite sure. But . . .

Krogstad [*regards her searchingly*]: Is that how things are? You want to save your friend at any price? Tell me straight. Is that it?

Mrs. Linde: When you've sold yourself *once* for other people's sake, you don't do it again.

Krogstad: I shall demand my letter back.

Mrs. Linde: No, no.

Krogstad: Of course I will, I'll wait here till Helmer comes. I'll tell him he has to give me my letter back . . . that it's only about my notice . . . that he mustn't read it. . . .

Mrs. Linde: No, Nils, don't ask for it back.

Krogstad: But wasn't that the very reason you got me here?

Mrs. Linde: Yes, that was my first terrified reaction. But that was yesterday, and it's quite incredible the things I've witnessed in this house in the last twenty-four hours. Helmer must know everything. This unhappy secret must come out. Those two must have the whole thing out between them. All this secrecy and deception, it just can't go on.

Krogstad: Well, if you want to risk it. . . . But one thing I can do, and I'll do it at once. . . .

Mrs. Linde [*listening*]: Hurry! Go, go! The dance has stopped. We aren't safe a moment longer.

Krogstad: I'll wait for you downstairs.

Mrs. Linde: Yes, do. You must see me home.

Krogstad: I've never been so incredibly happy before.

[*He goes out by the front door. The door out into the hall remains standing open.*]

Mrs. Linde [*tidies the room a little and gets her hat and coat ready*]: How things change! How things change! Somebody to work for . . . to live for. A home to bring happiness into. Just let me get down to it. . . . I wish they'd come. . . . [*Listens.*] Ah, there they are. . . . Get my things.

[*She takes her coat and hat. The voices of Helmer and Nora are heard outside. A key is turned and Helmer pushes Nora almost forcibly into the hall. She is dressed in the Italian costume, with a big black shawl over it. He is in evening dress, and over it a black cloak, open.*]

Nora [*still in the doorway, reluctantly*]: No, no, not in here! I want to go back up again. I don't want to leave so early.

Helmer: But my dearest Nora . . .

Nora: Oh, please, Torvald, I beg you. . . . *Please*, just for another hour.

Helmer: Not another minute, Nora my sweet. You remember what we agreed. There now, come along in. You'll catch cold standing there.

[*He leads her, in spite of her resistance, gently but firmly into the room.*]

Mrs. Linde: Good evening.

Nora: Kristine!

Helmer: Why, Mrs. Linde. You here so late?

Mrs. Linde: Yes. You must forgive me but I did so want to see Nora all dressed up.

Nora: Have you been sitting here waiting for me?

Mrs. Linde: Yes, I'm afraid I wasn't in time to catch you before you went upstairs. And I felt I couldn't leave again without seeing you.

Helmer [*removing Nora's shawl*]: Well take a good look at her. I think I can say she's worth looking at. Isn't she lovely, Mrs. Linde?

Mrs. Linde: Yes, I must say. . . .

Helmer: Isn't she quite extraordinarily lovely? That's what everybody at the party thought, too. But she's dreadfully stubborn . . . the sweet little thing! And what shall we do about that? Would you believe it, I nearly had to use force to get her away.

Nora: Oh Torvald, you'll be sorry you didn't let me stay, even for half an hour.

Helmer: You hear that, Mrs. Linde? She dances her tarantella, there's wild applause—which was well deserved, although the performance was perhaps rather realistic . . . I mean, rather more so than was strictly necessary from the artistic point of view. But anyway! The main thing is she was a success, a tremendous success. Was I supposed to let her stay after that? Spoil the effect? No thank you! I took my lovely little Capri girl—my capricious little Capri girl, I might say—by the arm, whisked her once round the room, a curtsey all round, and then—as they say in novels—the beautiful vision vanished. An exit should always be effective, Mrs. Linde. But I just can't get Nora to see that. Phew! It's warm in here. [*He throws his cloak over a chair and opens the door to his study.*] What? It's dark. Oh yes, of course. Excuse me. . . .

[*He goes in and lights a few candles.*]

Nora [*quickly, in a breathless whisper*]: Well?
Mrs. Linde [*softly*]: I've spoken to him.
Nora: And . . . ?
Mrs. Linde: Nora . . . you must tell your husband everything.
Nora [*tonelessly*]: I knew it.
Mrs. Linde: You've got nothing to fear from Krogstad. But you must speak.
Nora: I won't.
Mrs. Linde: Then the letter will.
Nora: Thank you, Kristine. Now I know what's to be done. Hush . . . !
Helmer [*comes in again*]: Well, Mrs. Linde, have you finished admiring her?
Mrs. Linde: Yes. And now I must say good night.
Helmer: Oh, already? Is this yours, this knitting?
Mrs. Linde [*takes it*]: Yes, thank you. I nearly forgot it.
Helmer: So you knit, eh?
Mrs. Linde: Yes.
Helmer: You should embroider instead, you know.
Mrs. Linde: Oh? Why?
Helmer: So much prettier. Watch! You hold the embroidery like this in the left hand, and then you take the needle in the right hand, like this, and you describe a long, graceful curve. Isn't that right?
Mrs. Linde: Yes, I suppose so. . . .
Helmer: Whereas knitting on the other hand just can't help being ugly. Look! Arms pressed into the sides, the knitting needles going up and down—there's something Chinese about it. . . . Ah, that was marvellous champagne they served tonight.
Mrs. Linde: Well, good night, Nora! And stop being so stubborn.
Helmer: Well said, Mrs. Linde!
Mrs. Linde: Good night, Mr. Helmer.
Helmer [*accompanying her to the door*]: Good night, good night! You'll get home all right, I hope? I'd be only too pleased to. . . . But you haven't far to walk. Good night, good night! [*She goes; he shuts the door behind her and comes in again.*] There we are, got rid of her at last. She's a frightful bore, that woman.
Nora: Aren't you very tired, Torvald?

Helmer: Not in the least.

Nora: Not sleepy?

Helmer: Not at all. On the contrary, I feel extremely lively. What about you? Yes, you look quite tired and sleepy.

Nora: Yes, I'm very tired. I just want to fall straight off to sleep.

Helmer: There you are, you see! Wasn't I right in thinking we shouldn't stay any longer.

Nora: Oh, everything you do is right.

Helmer [*kissing her forehead*]: There's my little sky-lark talking common sense. Did you notice how gay Rank was this evening?

Nora: Oh, was he? I didn't get a chance to talk to him.

Helmer: I hardly did either. But it's a long time since I saw him in such a good mood. [*Looks at Nora for a moment or two, then comes nearer her.*] Ah, it's wonderful to be back in our own home again, and quite alone with you. How irresistibly lovely you are, Nora!

Nora: Don't look at me like that, Torvald!

Helmer: Can't I look at my most treasured possession? At all this loveliness that's mine and mine alone, completely and utterly mine.

Nora [*walks round to the other side of the table*]: You mustn't talk to me like that tonight.

Helmer [*following her*]: You still have the tarantella in your blood, I see. And that makes you even more desirable. Listen! The guests are beginning to leave now. [*Softly.*] Nora . . . soon the whole house will be silent.

Nora: I should hope so.

Helmer: Of course you do, don't you, Nora my darling? You know, whenever I'm out at a party with you . . . do you know why I never talk to you very much, why I always stand away from you and only steal a quick glance at you now and then . . . do you know why I do that? It's because I'm pretending we are secretly in love, secretly engaged and nobody suspects there is anything be-tween us.

Nora: Yes, yes. I know your thoughts are always with me, of course.

Helmer: And when it's time to go, and I lay your shawl round those shapely, young shoulders, round the exquisite curve of your neck . . . I pretend that you are my young bride, that we are just leaving our wedding, that I am taking you to our new home for the first time . . . to be alone with you for the first time . . . quite alone with your young and trembling loveliness! All evening I've been longing for you, and nothing else. And as I watched you darting and swaying in the tarantella, my blood was on fire . . . I couldn't bear it any longer . . . and that's why I brought you down here with me so early. . . .

Nora: Go away, Torvald! Please leave me alone. I won't have it.

Helmer: What's this? It's just your little game isn't it, my little Nora. Won't! Won't! Am I not your husband . . . ?

[*There is a knock on the front door.*]

Nora [*startled*]: Listen . . . !

Helmer [*going towards the hall*]: Who's there?

Rank [*outside*]: It's me. Can I come in for a minute?

Helmer [*in a low voice, annoyed*]: Oh, what does he want now? [*Aloud.*] Wait a moment. [*He walks across and opens the door.*] How nice of you to look in on your way out.

Rank: I fancied I heard your voice and I thought I would just look in. [*He takes a quick glance round.*] Ah yes, this dear, familiar old place! How cosy and comfortable you've got things here, you two.

Helmer: You seemed to be having a pretty good time upstairs yourself.

Rank: Capital! Why shouldn't I? Why not make the most of things in this world? At least as much as one can, and for as long as one can. The wine was excellent. . . .

Helmer: Especially the champagne.

Rank: You noticed that too, did you? It's incredible the amount I was able to put away.

Nora: Torvald also drank a lot of champagne this evening.

Rank: Oh?

Nora: Yes, and that always makes him quite merry.

Rank: Well, why shouldn't a man allow himself a jolly evening after a day well spent?

Helmer: Well spent? I'm afraid I can't exactly claim that.

Rank [*clapping him on the shoulder*]: But I can, you see!

Nora: Dr. Rank, am I right in thinking you carried out a certain laboratory test today?

Rank: Exactly.

Helmer: Look at our little Nora talking about laboratory tests!

Nora: And may I congratulate you on the result?

Rank: You may indeed.

Nora: So it was good?

Rank: The best possible, for both doctor and patient—certainty!

Nora [*quickly and searchingly*]: Certainty?

Rank: Absolute certainty. So why shouldn't I allow myself a jolly evening after that?

Nora: Quite right, Dr. Rank.

Helmer: I quite agree. As long as you don't suffer for it in the morning.

Rank: Well, you never get anything for nothing in this life.

Nora: Dr. Rank . . . you are very fond of masquerades, aren't you?

Rank: Yes, when there are plenty of amusing disguises. . . .

Nora: Tell me, what shall we two go as next time?

Helmer: There's frivolity for you . . . thinking about the next time already!

Rank: We two? I'll tell you. You must go as Lady Luck. . . .

Helmer: Yes, but how do you find a costume to suggest *that*?

Rank: Your wife could simply go in her everyday clothes. . . .

Helmer: That was nicely said. But don't you know what you would be?

Rank: Yes, my dear friend, I know exactly what I shall be.

Helmer: Well?

Rank: At the next masquerade, I shall be invisible.

Helmer: That's a funny idea!

Rank: There's a big black cloak . . . haven't you heard of the cloak of invisibility? That comes right down over you, and then nobody can see you.

Helmer [*suppressing a smile*]: Of course, that's right.

Rank: But I'm clean forgetting what I came for. Helmer, give me a cigar, one of the dark Havanas.

Helmer: With the greatest of pleasure.

[*He offers his case.*]

Rank [*takes one and cuts the end off*]: Thanks.

Nora [*strikes a match*]: Let me give you a light.

Rank: Thank you. [*She holds out the match and he lights his cigar.*] And now, goodbye!

Helmer: Goodbye, goodbye, my dear fellow!

Nora: Sleep well, Dr. Rank.

Rank: Thank you for that wish.

Nora: Wish me the same.

Rank: You? All right, if you want me to. . . . Sleep well. And thanks for the light.

[*He nods to them both, and goes.*]

Helmer [*subdued*]: He's had a lot to drink.

Nora [*absently*]: Very likely.

[*Helmer takes a bunch of keys out of his pocket and goes out into the hall.*]

Nora: Torvald . . . what do you want there?

Helmer: I must empty the letter-box, it's quite full. There'll be no room for the papers in the morning. . . .

Nora: Are you going to work tonight?

Helmer: You know very well I'm not. Hello, what's this? Somebody's been at the lock.

Nora: At the lock?

Helmer: Yes, I'm sure of it. Why should that be? I'd hardly have thought the maids . . . ? Here's a broken hair-pin. Nora, it's one of yours. . . .

Nora [*quickly*]: It must have been the children. . . .

Helmer: Then you'd better tell them not to. Ah . . . there . . . I've managed to get it open. [*He takes the things out and shouts into the kitchen.*] Helene! . . . Helene, put the light out in the hall. [*He comes into the room again with the letters in his hand and shuts the hall door.*] Look how it all mounts up. [*Runs through them.*] What's this?

Nora: The letter! Oh no, Torvald, no!

Helmer: Two visiting cards . . . from Dr. Rank.

Nora: From Dr. Rank?

Helmer [*looking at them*]: Dr. Rank, Medical Practitioner. They were on top. He must have put them in as he left.

Nora: Is there anything on them?

Helmer: There's a black cross above his name. Look. What an uncanny idea. It's just as if he were announcing his own death.

Nora: He is.

Helmer: What? What do you know about it? Has he said anything to you?

Nora: Yes. He said when these cards came, he would have taken his last leave of us. He was going to shut himself up and die.

Helmer: Poor fellow! Of course I knew we couldn't keep him with us very long. But so soon. . . . And hiding himself away like a wounded animal.

Nora: When it has to happen, it's best that it should happen without words. Don't you think so, Torvald?

Helmer [*walking up and down*]: He had grown so close to us. I don't think I can imagine him gone. His suffering and his loneliness seemed almost to provide a background of dark cloud to the sunshine of our lives. Well, perhaps it's all for the best. For him at any rate. [*Pauses.*] And maybe for us as well, Nora. Now there's just the two of us. [*Puts his arms round her.*] Oh, my darling wife, I can't hold you close enough. You know, Nora . . . many's the time I wish you were threatened by some terrible danger so I could risk everything, body and soul, for your sake.

Nora [*tears herself free and says firmly and decisively*]: Now you must read your letters, Torvald.

Helmer: No, no, not tonight. I want to be with you, my darling wife.

Nora: Knowing all the time your friend is dying . . . ?

Helmer: You are right. It's been a shock to both of us. This ugly thing has come between us . . . thoughts of death and decay. We must try to free ourselves from it. Until then . . . we shall go our separate ways.

Nora [*her arms round his neck*]: Torvald . . . good night! Good night!

Helmer [*kisses her forehead*]: Goodnight, my little singing bird. Sleep well, Nora, I'll just read through my letters.

[*He takes the letters into his room and shuts the door behind him.*]

Nora [*gropes around her, wild-eyed, seizes Helmer's cloak, wraps it round herself, and whispers quickly, hoarsely, spasmodically*]: Never see him again. Never, never, never. [*Throws her shawl over her head.*] And never see the children again either. Never, never. Oh, that black icy water. Oh, that bottomless . . . ! If only it were all over! He's got it now. Now he's reading it. Oh no, no! Not yet! Torvald, goodbye . . . and my children. . . .

[*She rushes out in the direction of the hall; at the same moment Helmer flings open his door and stands there with an open letter in his hand.*]

Helmer: Nora!

Nora [*shrieks*]: Ah!

Helmer: What is this? Do you know what is in this letter?

Nora: Yes, I know. Let me go! Let me out!

Helmer [*holds her back*]: Where are you going?

Nora [*trying to tear herself free*]: You mustn't try to save me, Torvald!

Helmer [*reels back*]: True! Is it true what he writes? How dreadful! No, no, it can't possibly be true.

Nora: It *is* true. I loved you more than anything else in the world.

Helmer: Don't come to me with a lot of paltry excuses!

Nora [*taking a step towards him*]: Torvald . . . !

Helmer: Miserable woman . . . what is this you have done?

Nora: Let me go. I won't have you taking the blame for me. You mustn't take it on yourself.

Helmer: Stop play-acting! [*Locks the front door.*] You are staying here to give an account of yourself. Do you understand what you have done? Answer me! Do you understand?

Nora [*looking fixedly at him, her face hardening*]: Yes, now I'm really beginning to understand.

Helmer [*walking up and down*]: Oh, what a terrible awakening this is. All these eight years . . . this woman who was my pride and joy . . . a hypocrite, a liar, worse than that, a criminal! Oh, how utterly squalid it all is! Ugh! Ugh! [*Nora remains silent and looks fixedly at him.*] I should have realized something like this would happen. I should have seen it coming. All your father's irresponsible ways. . . . Quiet! All your father's irresponsible ways are coming out in you. No religion, no morals, no sense of duty. . . . Oh, this is my punishment for turning a blind eye to him. It was for your sake I did it, and this is what I get for it.

Nora: Yes, this.

Helmer: Now you have ruined my entire happiness, jeopardized my whole future. It's terrible to think of. Here I am, at the mercy of a thoroughly unscrupulous person; he can do whatever he likes with me, demand anything he wants, order me about just as he chooses . . . and I daren't even whimper. I'm done for, a miserable failure, and it's all the fault of a feather-brained woman!

Nora: When I've left this world behind, you will be free.

Helmer: Oh, stop pretending! Your father was just the same, always ready with fine phrases. What good would it do me if you left this world behind, as you put it? Not the slightest bit of good. He can still let it all come out, if he likes; and if he does, people might even suspect me of being an accomplice in these criminal acts of yours. They might even think I was the one behind it all, that it was I who pushed you into it! And it's you I have to thank for this . . . and when I've taken such good care of you, all our married life. Now do you understand what you have done to me?

Nora [*coldly and calmly*]: Yes.

Helmer: I just can't understand it, it's so incredible. But we must see about putting things right. Take that shawl off. Take it off, I tell you! I must see if I can't find some way or other of appeasing him. The thing must be hushed up at all costs. And as far as you and I are concerned, things must appear to go on exactly as before. But only in the eyes of the world, of course. In other words you'll go on living here; that's understood. But you will not be allowed to bring up the children, I can't trust you with them. . . . Oh, that I should have to say this to the woman I loved so dearly, the woman I still. . . . Well, that must be all over and done with. From now on, there can be no question of happiness. All we can do is save the bits and pieces from the wreck, preserve appearances. . . . [*The front door-bell rings. Helmer gives a start.*] What's that? So late? How terrible, supposing. . . . If he should . . . ? Hide, Nora! Say you are not well.

[*Nora stands motionless. Helmer walks across and opens the door into the hall.*]

Maid [*half dressed, in the hall*]: It's a note for Mrs. Helmer.
Helmer: Give it to me. [*He snatches the note and shuts the door.*] Yes, it's from him. You can't have it. I want to read it myself.
Nora: You read it then.
Helmer [*by the lamp*]: I hardly dare. Perhaps this is the end, for both of us. Well, I must know. [*He opens the note hurriedly, reads a few lines, looks at another enclosed sheet, and gives a cry of joy.*] Nora! [*Nora looks at him inquiringly.*] Nora! I must read it again. Yes, yes, it's true! I am saved! Nora, I am saved!
Nora: And me?
Helmer: You too, of course, we are both saved, you as well as me. Look, he's sent your IOU back. He sends his regrets and apologies for what he has done. . . . His luck has changed. . . . Oh, what does it matter what he says. We are saved, Nora! Nobody can do anything to you now. Oh, Nora, Nora . . . but let's get rid of this disgusting thing first. Let me see. . . . [*He glances at the IOU.*] No, I don't want to see it. I don't want it to be anything but a dream. [*He tears up the IOU and both letters, throws all the pieces into the stove and watches them burn.*] Well, that's the end of that. He said in his note you'd known since Christmas Eve. . . . You must have had three terrible days of it, Nora.
Nora: These three days haven't been easy.
Helmer: The agonies you must have gone through! When the only way out seemed to be. . . . No, let's forget the whole ghastly thing. We can rejoice and say: It's all over! It's all over! Listen to me, Nora! You don't seem to understand: it's all over! Why this grim look on your face? Oh, poor little Nora, of course I understand. You can't bring yourself to believe I've forgiven you. But I have, Nora, I swear it. I forgive you everything. I know you did what you did because you loved me.
Nora: That's true.
Helmer: You loved me as a wife should love her husband. It was simply that you didn't have the experience to judge what was the best way of going about things. But do you think I love you any the less for that; just because you don't know how to act on your own responsibility? No, no, you just lean on me, I shall give you all the advice and guidance you need. I wouldn't be a proper man if I didn't find a woman doubly attractive for being so obviously helpless. You mustn't dwell on the harsh things I said in that first moment of

horror, when I thought everything was going to come crashing down about my ears. I have forgiven you, Nora, I swear it! I have forgiven you!

Nora: Thank you for your forgiveness.

[*She goes out through the door, right.*]

Helmer: No, don't go! [*He looks through the doorway.*] What are you doing in the spare room?

Nora: Taking off this fancy dress.

Helmer [*standing at the open door*]: Yes, do. You try and get some rest, and set your mind at peace again, my frightened little song-bird. Have a good long sleep; you know you are safe and sound under my wing. [*Walks up and down near the door.*] What a nice, cosy little home we have here, Nora! Here you can find refuge. Here I shall hold you like a hunted dove I have rescued unscathed from the cruel talons of the hawk, and calm your poor beating heart. And that will come, gradually, Nora, believe me. Tomorrow you'll see everything quite differently. Soon everything will be just as it was before. You won't need me to keep on telling you I've forgiven you; you'll feel convinced of it in your own heart. You don't really imagine me ever thinking of turning you out, or even of reproaching you? Oh, a real man isn't made that way, you know, Nora. For a man, there's something indescribably moving and very satisfying in knowing that he has forgiven his wife—forgiven her, completely and genuinely, from the depths of his heart. It's as though it made her his property in a double sense: he has, as it were, given her a new life, and she becomes in a way both his wife and at the same time his child. That is how you will seem to me after today, helpless, perplexed little thing that you are. Don't you worry your pretty little head about anything, Nora. Just you be frank with me, and I'll take all the decisions for you. . . . What's this? Not in bed? You've changed your things?

Nora [*in her everyday dress*]: Yes, Torvald, I've changed.

Helmer: What for? It's late.

Nora: I shan't sleep tonight.

Helmer: But my dear Nora. . . .

Nora [*looks at her watch*]: It's not so terribly late. Sit down, Torvald. We two have a lot to talk about.

[*She sits down at one side of the table.*]

Helmer: Nora, what is all this? Why so grim?

Nora: Sit down. It'll take some time. I have a lot to say to you.

Helmer [*sits down at the table opposite her*]: You frighten me, Nora. I don't understand you.

Nora: Exactly. You don't understand me. And I have never understood you, either—until tonight. No, don't interrupt. I just want you to listen to what I have to say. We are going to have things out, Torvald.

Helmer: What do you mean?

Nora: Isn't there anything that strikes you about the way we two are sitting here?

Helmer: What's that?

Nora: We have now been married eight years. Hasn't it struck you this is the first time you and I, man and wife, have had a serious talk together?

Helmer: Depends what you mean by 'serious.'

Nora: Eight whole years—no, more, ever since we first knew each other—and never have we exchanged one serious word about serious things.

Helmer: What did you want me to do? Get you involved in worries that you couldn't possibly help me to bear?

Nora: I'm not talking about worries. I say we've never once sat down together and seriously tried to get to the bottom of anything.

Helmer: But, my dear Nora, would that have been a thing for you?

Nora: That's just it. You have never understood me . . . I've been greatly wronged, Torvald. First by my father, and then by you.

Helmer: What! Us two! The two people who loved you more than anybody?

Nora [*shakes her head*]: You two never loved me. You only thought now nice it was to be in love with me.

Helmer: But, Nora, what's this you are saying?

Nora: It's right, you know, Torvald. At home, Daddy used to tell me what he thought, then I thought the same. And if I thought differently, I kept quiet about it, because he wouldn't have liked it. He used to call me his baby doll, and he played with me as I used to play with my dolls. Then I came to live in your house. . . .

Helmer: What way is that to talk about our marriage?

Nora [*imperturbably*]: What I mean is: I passed out of Daddy's hands into yours. You arranged everything to your tastes, and I acquired the same tastes. Or I pretended to . . . I don't really know . . . I think it was a bit of both, some-times one thing and sometimes the other. When I look back, it seems to me I have been living here like a beggar, from hand to mouth. I lived by doing tricks for you, Torvald. But that's the way you wanted it. You and Daddy did me a great wrong. It's your fault that I've never made anything of my life.

Helmer: Nora, how unreasonable . . . how ungrateful you are! Haven't you been happy here?

Nora: No, never. I thought I was, but I wasn't really.

Helmer: Not . . . not happy!

Nora: No, just gay. And you've always been so kind to me. But our house has never been anything but a play-room. I have been your doll wife, just as at home I was Daddy's doll child. And the children in turn have been my dolls. I thought it was fun when you came and played with me, just as they thought it was fun when I went and played with them. That's been our mar-riage, Torvald.

Helmer: There is some truth in what you say, exaggerated and hysterical though it is. But from now on it will be different. Play-time is over; now comes the time for lessons.

Nora: Whose lessons? Mine or the children's?

Helmer: Both yours and the children's, my dear Nora.

Nora: Ah, Torvald, you are not the man to teach me to be a good wife for you.

Helmer: How can you say that?

Nora: And what sort of qualifications have I to teach the children?

Helmer: Nora!

Nora: Didn't you say yourself, a minute or two ago, that you couldn't trust me with that job.

Helmer: In the heat of the moment! You shouldn't pay any attention to that.

Nora: On the contrary, you were quite right. I'm not up to it. There's another problem needs solving first. I must take steps to educate myself. You are not the man to help me there. That's something I must do on my own. That's why I'm leaving you.

Helmer [jumps up]: What did you say?

Nora: If I'm ever to reach any understanding of myself and the things around me, I must learn to stand alone. That's why I can't stay here with you any longer.

Helmer: Nora! Nora!

Nora: I'm leaving here at once. I dare say Kristine will put me up for tonight. . . .

Helmer: You are out of your mind! I won't let you! I forbid you!

Nora: It's no use forbidding me anything now. I'm taking with me my own personal belongings. I don't want anything of yours, either now or later.

Helmer: This is madness!

Nora: Tomorrow I'm going home—to what used to be my home, I mean. It will be easier for me to find something to do there.

Helmer: Oh, you blind, inexperienced . . .

Nora: I must set about *getting* experience, Torvald.

Helmer: And leave your home, your husband and your children? Don't you care what people will say?

Nora: That's no concern of mine. All I know is that this is necessary for *me*.

Helmer: This is outrageous! You are betraying your most sacred duty.

Nora: And what do you consider to be my most sacred duty?

Helmer: Does it take me to tell you that? Isn't it your duty to your husband and your children?

Nora: I have another duty equally sacred.

Helmer: You have not. What duty might *that* be?

Nora: My duty to myself.

Helmer: First and foremost, you are a wife and mother.

Nora: That I don't believe any more. I believe that first and foremost I am an individual, just as much as you are—or at least I'm going to try to be. I know most people agree with you, Torvald, and that's also what it says in books. But I'm not content any more with what most people say, or with what it says in books. I have to think things out for myself, and get things clear.

Helmer: Surely you are clear about your position in your own home? Haven't you an infallible guide in questions like these? Haven't you your religion?

Nora: Oh, Torvald, I don't really know what religion is.

Helmer: What do you say!

Nora: All I know is what Pastor Hansen said when I was confirmed. He said religion was this, that and the other. When I'm away from all this and on my own, I'll go into that, too. I want to find out whether what Pastor Hansen told me was right—or at least whether it's right for *me*.

Helmer: This is incredible talk from a young woman! But if religion cannot keep you on the right path, let me at least stir your conscience. I suppose you do have some moral sense? Or tell me—perhaps you don't?

Nora: Well, Torvald, that's not easy to say. I simply don't know. I'm really very confused about such things. All I know is my ideas about such things are very different from yours. I've also learnt that the law is different from what I thought; but I simply can't get it into my head that that particular law is right. Apparently a woman has no right to spare her old father on his deathbed, or to save her husband's life, even. I just don't believe it.

Helmer: You are talking like a child. You understand nothing about the society you live in.

Nora: No, I don't. But I shall go into that too. I must try to discover who is right, society or me.

Helmer: You are ill, Nora. You are delirious. I'm half inclined to think you are out of your mind.

Nora: Never have I felt so calm and collected as I do tonight.

Helmer: Calm and collected enough to leave your husband and children?

Nora: Yes.

Helmer: Then only one explanation is possible.

Nora: And that is?

Helmer: You don't love me any more.

Nora: Exactly.

Helmer: Nora! Can you say that!

Nora: I'm desperately sorry, Torvald. Because you have always been so kind to me. But I can't help it. I don't love you any more.

Helmer [*struggling to keep his composure*]: Is that also a 'calm and collected' decision you've made?

Nora: Yes, absolutely calm and collected. That's why I don't want to stay here.

Helmer: And can you also account for how I forfeited your love?

Nora: Yes, very easily. It was tonight, when the miracle didn't happen. It was then I realized you weren't the man I thought you were.

Helmer: Explain yourself more clearly. I don't understand.

Nora: For eight years I have been patiently waiting. Because, heavens, I knew miracles didn't happen every day. Then this devastating business started, and I became absolutely convinced the miracle *would* happen. All the time Krogstad's letter lay there, it never so much as crossed my mind that you would ever submit to that man's conditions. I was absolutely convinced you would say to him: Tell the whole wide world if you like. And when that was done . . .

Helmer: Yes, then what? After I had exposed my own wife to dishonour and shame . . . !

Nora: When that was done, I was absolutely convinced you would come forward and take everything on yourself, and say: I am the guilty one.

Helmer: Nora!

Nora: You mean I'd never let you make such a sacrifice for my sake? Of course not. But what would my story have counted for against yours?—That was the miracle I went in hope and dread of. It was to prevent it that I was ready to end my life.

Helmer: I would gladly toil day and night for you, Nora, enduring all manner of sorrow and distress. But nobody sacrifices his *honour* for the one he loves.

Nora: Hundreds and thousands of women have.

Helmer: Oh, you think and talk like a stupid child.

Nora: All right. But you neither think nor talk like the man I would want to share my life with. When you had got over your fright—and you weren't concerned about me but only about what might happen to you—and when all danger was past, you acted as though nothing had happened. I was your little sky-lark again, your little doll, exactly as before; except you would have to protect it twice as carefully as before, now that it had shown itself to be so weak and fragile. [*Rises.*] Torvald, that was the moment I realised that for eight years I'd been living with a stranger, and had borne him three children. . . . Oh, I can't bear to think about it! I could tear myself to shreds.

Helmer [*sadly*]: I see. I see. There is a tremendous gulf dividing us. But, Nora, is there no way we might bridge it?

Nora: As I am now, I am no wife for you.

Helmer: I still have it in me to change.

Nora: Perhaps . . . if you have your doll taken away.

Helmer: And be separated from you! No, no, Nora, the very thought of it is inconceivable.

Nora [*goes into the room, right*]: All the more reason why it must be done.

[*She comes back with her outdoor things and a small travelling bag which she puts on the chair beside the table.*]

Helmer: Nora, Nora, not now! Wait till the morning.

Nora [*putting on her coat*]: I can't spend the night in a strange man's room.

Helmer: Couldn't we go on living here like brother and sister . . . ?

Nora [*tying on her hat*]: You know very well that wouldn't last. [*She draws the shawl round her.*] Goodbye, Torvald. I don't want to see the children. I know they are in better hands than mine. As I am now, I can never be anything to them.

Helmer: But some day, Nora, some day . . . ?

Nora: How should I know? I've no idea what I might turn out to be.

Helmer: But you are my wife, whatever you are.

Nora: Listen, Torvald, from what I've heard, when a wife leaves her husband's house as I am doing now, he is absolved by law of all responsibility for her. I can at any rate free you from all responsibility. You must not feel in any way bound, any more than I shall. There must be full freedom on both sides. Look, here's your ring back. Give me mine.

Helmer: That too?

Nora: That too.

Helmer: There it is.

Nora: Well, that's the end of that. I'll put the keys down here. The maids know where everything is in the house—better than I do, in fact. Kristine will come in the morning after I've left to pack up the few things I brought with me from home. I want them sent on.

Helmer: The end! Nora, will you never think of me?

Nora: I dare say I'll often think about you and the children and this house.

Helmer: May I write to you, Nora?

Nora: No, never. I won't let you.

Helmer: But surely I can send you . . .

Nora: Nothing, nothing.

Helmer: Can't I help you if ever you need it?

Nora: I said 'no.' I don't accept things from strangers.

Helmer: Nora, can I never be anything more to you than a stranger?

Nora [takes her bag]: Ah, Torvald, only by a miracle of miracles. . . .

Helmer: Name it, this miracle of miracles!

Nora: Both you and I would have to change to the point where. . . . Oh, Torvald, I don't believe in miracles any more.

Helmer: But I *will* believe. Name it! Change to the point where . . . ?

Nora: Where we could make a real marriage of our lives together. Goodbye!

[*She goes out through the hall door.*]

Helmer [sinks down on a chair near the door, and covers his face with his hands]: Nora! Nora! [*He rises and looks round.*] Empty! She's gone! [*With sudden hope.*] The miracle of miracles . . . ?

[*The heavy sound of a door being slammed is heard from below.*]

Questions

Act I

1. From the opening conversation between Helmer and Nora, what are your impressions of him? of her? of their marriage?
2. At what moment in the play do you understand why it is called *A Doll's House?*
3. In what ways does Mrs. Linde provide a contrast for Nora?
4. What in Krogstad's first appearance on stage, and in Dr. Rank's remarks about him, indicates that the bank clerk is a menace?
5. Of what illegal deed is Nora guilty? How does she justify it?
6. When the curtain falls on Act I, what problems now confront Nora?

Act II

1. As Act II opens, what are your feelings on seeing the stripped, ragged Christmas tree? How is it suggestive?
2. What events that soon occur make Nora's situation even more difficult?
3. How does she try to save herself?
4. Why does Nora fling herself into the wild tarantella?

Act III

1. For what possible reasons does Mrs. Linde pledge herself to Krogstad?
2. How does Dr. Rank's announcement of his impending death affect Nora and Helmer?

3. What is Helmer's reaction to learning the truth about Nora's misdeed? Why does he blame Nora's father? What is revealing (of Helmer's own character) in his remark, "From now on, there can be no question of happiness. All we can do is save the bits and pieces from the wreck, preserve appearances. . . ."?
4. When Helmer finds that Krogstad has sent back the note, what is his response? How do you feel toward him?
5. How does the character of Nora develop in this act?
6. How do you interpret her final slamming of the door?

GENERAL QUESTIONS

1. In what ways do you find Nora a victim? In what ways at fault?
2. Try to state the theme of the play. Does it involve women's rights? self-fulfillment?
3. What dramatic question does the play embody? At what moment can this question first be stated?
4. What is the crisis? In what way is this moment or event a "turning point"? (In what new direction does the action turn?)
5. Eric Bentley, in an essay titled "Ibsen, Pro and Con" (*In Search of Theater* [New York: Knopf, 1953]), criticizes the character of Krogstad, calling him "a mere pawn of the plot." He then adds, "When convenient to Ibsen, he is a blackmailer. When inconvenient, he is converted." Do you agree or disagree?
6. Why is the play considered a work of realism? Is there anything in it that does not seem realistic?
7. In what respects does *A Doll's House* seem to apply to life today? Is it in any way dated? Could there be a Nora in North America today?

WRITER'S PERSPECTIVE

George Bernard Shaw

George Bernard Shaw on Drama
IBSEN AND THE FAMILIAR SITUATION

1913

Up to a certain point in the last act, *A Doll's House* is a play that might be turned into a very ordinary French drama by the excision of a few lines, and the substitution of a sentimental happy ending for the famous last scene: indeed the very first thing the theatrical wiseacres did with it was to effect exactly this transformation, with the result that the play thus pithed° had no success and attracted no notice worth mentioning. But at just that point in the last act, the heroine very unexpectedly (by the wiseacres) stops her emotional acting and says: "We must sit down and discuss all this that has been happening between us." And it was by this new technical feature: this addition of a new movement, as musicians would say, to the dramatic form, that *A Doll's House* conquered Europe and founded a new school of dramatic art.

．　．　．

The drama was born of old from the union of two desires: the desire to have a dance and the desire to hear a story. The dance became a rant: the story became a situation. When Ibsen began to make plays, the art of the dramatist had shrunk into the art of contriving a situation. And it was held that the stranger the situation, the better the play. Ibsen saw that, on the contrary, the more familiar the situation, the more interesting the play. Shakespeare had put ourselves on the stage but not our situations. Our uncles seldom murder our fathers, and cannot legally marry our mothers; we do not meet witches; our kings are not as a rule stabbed and succeeded by their stabbers; and when we raise money by bills we do not promise to pay pounds of our flesh. Ibsen supplies the want left by Shakespeare. He gives us not only ourselves, but ourselves in our own situations. The things that happen to his stage figures are things that happen to us. One consequence is that his plays are much more important to us than Shakespeare's. Another is that they are capable both of hurting us cruelly and of filling us with excited hopes of escape from idealistic tyrannies, and with visions of intenser life in the future.

The Quintessence of Ibsenism (second edition)

TRAGICOMEDY AND THE ABSURD

One of the more prominent developments in mid-twentieth-century drama has been the rise of **tragicomedies,** plays that stir us not only to pity and fear (echoing Aristotle's description of the effect of tragedy) but also to laughter. Although tragicomedy is a kind of drama we think distinctively modern, it is by no means a new invention. The term was used (although jokingly) by the Roman writer of comedy Plautus in about 185 B.C.

Since ancient times, playwrights have mingled laughter and tears, defying the neoclassical doctrine that required strict unity of action and tone (discussed on page 1214) and decreed that a play must be entirely comic or entirely tragic. Shakespeare is fond of tragicomic mingling. For example, in *Hamlet* the prince jokes with a grave digger, and in *Antony and Cleopatra* the queen commits suicide with a poisonous asp brought to her by a wise-cracking clown. Likewise, Shakespeare's darker comedies like *Measure for Measure* and *The Merchant of Venice* deal so forcefully with such stark themes (lust, greed, racism, revenge, and cruelty) that they often seem like tragedies until their happy endings. In the tragedies of Shakespeare and others, passages of clownish humor are sometimes called **comic relief,** meaning that the section of

pithed: killed (to pith is to kill an animal by severing its spinal cord).

comedy introduces a sharp contrast in mood. But such passages can do more than provide relief. In *Othello* (III, iv, 1–22) the clown's banter with Desdemona for a moment makes the surrounding tragedy seem, by comparison, more poignant and intense.

No one doubts that *Othello* is a tragedy, but some twentieth-century plays leave us both bemused and confused: should we laugh or cry? One of the most talked-about plays since World War II, Samuel Beckett's *Waiting for Godot,* portrays two clownish tramps who mark time in a wasteland, wistfully looking for a savior who never arrives. Contemporary drama, by the way, has often featured such **antiheroes:** ordinary people, inglorious and inarticulate, who carry on not from bravery but from inertia. (The rise of the antihero in recent fiction is discussed briefly on page 62; those remarks could apply equally well to contemporary drama.) We cannot help laughing, in *Godot,* at the tramps' painful situation; but, turning the idea around, we also feel deeply moved by their ridiculous plight. Perhaps a modern tragicomedy like *Godot* does not show us great souls suffering greatly—as Edith Hamilton has said we observe in a classical tragedy—but Beckett's play nonetheless touches mysteriously on the universal sorrows of human existence.

Perhaps the full effect of such a play takes time to sink in. Contemporary playwright Edward Albee suggests that sometimes the spectator's sense of relief after experiencing pity and fear (Aristotle calls it *katharsis*) may be a delayed reaction: "I don't feel that catharsis in a play necessarily takes place during the course of a play. Often it should take place afterwards."[1] If Albee is right, we may be amused while watching a tragicomedy and then go home and feel deeply stirred by it.

Straddling the fence between tragedy and comedy, the plays of some modern playwrights portray people whose suffering seems ridiculous. These plays belong to the **theater of the absurd:** a general name for a type of play first staged in Paris in the 1950s. "For the modern critical spirit, nothing can be taken entirely seriously, nor entirely lightly," says Eugène Ionesco, one of the movement's leading playwrights. Behind the literary conventions of the theater of the absurd stands a philosophical fear that human existence has no meaning. Every person, such playwrights assume, is a helpless waif alone in a universe full of ridiculous obstacles. In Ionesco's *Amédée* (1953), a couple share an apartment with a gigantic corpse that keeps swelling relentlessly; in his *Rhinoceros* (1958), the human race starts turning into rhinos, except for one man, who remains human and isolated. A favorite theme in the theater of the absurd is that communication between people is impossible. Language is therefore futile. Ionesco's *The Bald Soprano* (1948) accordingly pokes fun at polite social conversation in a scene whose dialogue consists entirely of illogical strings of catchphrases. In *Endgame* (1957) Samuel Beckett dramatizes his vision of mankind's present condition: the main character is blind and paralyzed, and his legless parents live inside two garbage cans. Oddly, the effect of the play isn't total gloom; we leave the theater both amused and bemused by it.[2]

Trends in drama change along with playwrights' convictions, and during the 1970s and 1980s the theater of the absurd no longer seemed the dominant influence

---

[1]"The Art of the Theater," interview, *Paris Review* 39 (1996).
[2]For an excellent study of the theater of the absurd, see Martin Esslin, *The Theater of the Absurd,* revised edition (New York: Overlook, 1973).

on new drama in America. Along with other protests of the 1960s, experimental theater seemed to have spent its force. During the later period most of the critically celebrated new plays were neither absurd nor experimental. David Mamet's *American Buffalo* (1975) realistically portrays three petty thieves in a junk shop as they plot to steal a coin collection. Albert Innaurato's *Gemini* (1977) takes a realistic (and comic) view of family life and sexual awakening in one of Philadelphia's Italian neighborhoods. Beth Henley's 1979 Pulitzer Prize–winning play, *Crimes of the Heart*, presents an eccentric but still believable group of sisters in a small Southern town. The dialogue in all three plays shows high fidelity to ordinary speech. Meanwhile, many of the most influential plays of **feminist theater,** which explores the lives, problems, and occasional triumphs of contemporary women, were also written in a realistic style. Notable success—with both critics and the ticket-buying public—greeted plays such as Marsha Norman's *'Night, Mother* (1983), Tina Howe's *Painting Churches* (1983), and Wendy Wasserstein's *The Heidi Chronicles* (1988).

Some leading critics, among them Richard Gilman, believed that the American theater had entered an era of **new naturalism**.[3] Indeed, many plays of this time subjected the lives of people, especially poor and unhappy people, to a realistic, searching light, showing the forces that shaped them. Sam Shepard in *Buried Child* (1978) explores violence and desperation in a family that dwells on the edge of poverty; while August Wilson, in *Joe Turner's Come and Gone* (1988), convincingly portrays life in a Pittsburgh ghetto lodging house. But if these newly established playwrights sometimes showed life as frankly as did the earlier naturalists, both of the plays just mentioned also contain rich and suggestive symbolism.

More recently, however, experimental drama, greatly influenced by the theater of the absurd, has made a comeback. David Hwang's work (see his one-act play, *The Sound of a Voice*, on page 1762) combines realistic elements with overtly symbolic devices. Caryl Churchill's *Top Girls* (1982) presents a dinner party in which a contemporary woman invites legendary women from history to a restaurant dinner party. Although Churchill's play examines serious political issues, her straightforward treatment of an impossible premise owes much to Ionesco and Albee. Tony Kushner's *Angels in America* (1992) also mixes realism and fantasy to dramatize the plight of AIDS. Shel Silverstein, popular author of children's poetry, wrote a raucous one-man play, *The Devil and Bill Markham* (1991), entirely in rime, about a series of fantastic adventures in hell featuring a hard-drinking gambler and the Prince of Darkness. Silverstein's play is simultaneously experimental in form but traditional in content with its homage to American ballads and tall tales.

Experimental theater continues to exert a strong influence on American drama. Milcha Sanchez-Scott's *The Cuban Swimmer* (page 1781) deftly assimilates several dramatic styles—symbolism, new naturalism, ethnic drama, theater of the absurd—to create a brilliant original work. The work is simultaneously a family drama, a Latin comedy, a religious parable, and a critique of a media-obsessed American culture. The following play is by Edward Albee, probably the most influential living American experimentalist. His idiosyncratic plays seem perpetually fresh and provocative.

---

[3]"Out Goes Aburdism—In Comes the New Naturalism," *The New York Times Book Review* 19 Mar. 1978.

His one-act play, *The Sandbox*, with its dark humor, overt but odd symbolism, and minimalist staging represents a uniquely American version of theater of the absurd.

Edward Albee

THE SANDBOX

1960

Edward Albee (b. 1928) was adopted by millionaire foster parents who gave him his name. As a boy, he was dismissed from Lawrenceville, a preparatory school, and Valley Forge, a military academy, before settling in at Choate School, where he began to write. He started college at Trinity in Hartford, Connecticut, but soon dropped out to become a writer of radio scripts. Living in Greenwich Village for ten years beginning in 1948, he held jobs as an office boy, a record salesman, a bartender, and a Western Union messenger. In 1958, in a three-week burst of energy, he wrote The Zoo Story, *first performed in 1959 in West Berlin and in the following year (to critical acclaim) at the Provincetown Playhouse in New York. Other plays followed, among them* The Death of Bessie Smith *and* The Sandbox *(both in 1960);* The American Dream *(1961);* Who's Afraid of Virginia Woolf? *(1962, later a successful film);* Tiny Alice *(1964);* Malcolm *(which failed on Broadway after a five-day run, 1966);* A Delicate Balance *(which received a Pulitzer Prize, 1966);* Seascape *(1975);* Listening *(1977); and* The Man Who Had Three Arms *(1983). In 1981 he adapted Vladimir Nabokov's* Lolita *for the stage. By the middle of the 1980s, Albee's career seemed to falter. None of his recent plays had enjoyed great success, and he was savaged by many critics. Then in 1994 his new play,* Three Tall Women, *met with immense critical and commercial success. Winning Albee his third Pulitzer Prize, it confirmed his position as one of America's premier dramatists. Albee currently divides his time between New York City and Long Island.*

A BRIEF PLAY, IN MEMORY OF MY GRANDMOTHER (1876–1959)

Players

The Young Man, 25, a good-looking, well-built boy in a bathing suit
Mommy, 55, a well-dressed, imposing woman
Daddy, 60, a small man; gray, thin
Grandma, 86, a tiny, wizened woman with bright eyes
The Musician, no particular age, but young would be nice

Note. When, in the course of the play, Mommy and Daddy call each other by these names, there should be no suggestion of regionalism. These names are of empty affection and point up the pre-senility and vacuity of their characters.

Scene. A bare stage, with only the following: Near the footlights, far stage-right, two simple chairs set side by side, facing the audience; near the footlights, far stage-left, a chair facing stage-right with a music stand before it; farther back, and stage-center, slightly elevated and raked, a large child's sandbox with a toy pail and shovel; the background is the sky, which alters from brightest day to deepest night.

At the beginning, it is brightest day; the Young Man is alone on stage to the rear of the sandbox, and to one side. He is doing calisthenics; he does calisthenics until quite at the very end of the play. These calisthenics, employing the arms only, should suggest the beating and fluttering of wings. The Young Man is, after all, the Angel of Death.

Mommy and Daddy enter from stage-left, Mommy first.

Mommy (*motioning to Daddy*): Well, here we are; this is the beach.

Daddy (*whining*): I'm cold.

Mommy (*dismissing him with a little laugh*): Don't be silly; it's as warm as toast. Look at that nice young man over there: he doesn't think it's cold. (*Waves to the Young Man*) Hello.

Young Man (*with an endearing smile*): Hi!

Mommy (*looking about*): This will do perfectly . . . don't you think so, Daddy? There's sand there . . . and the water beyond. What do you think, Daddy?

Daddy (*vaguely*): Whatever you say, Mommy.

Mommy (*with the same little laugh*): Well, of course . . . whatever I say. Then, it's settled, is it?

Daddy (*shrugs*): She's *your* mother, not mine.

Mommy: I know she's my mother. What do you take me for? (*A pause*) All right, now; let's get on with it. (*She shouts into the wings, stage-left.*) You! Out there! You can come in now. (*The Musician enters, seats himself in the chair, stage-left, places music on the music stand, is ready to play. Mommy nods approvingly.*) Very nice; very nice. Are you ready, Daddy? Let's go get Grandma.

Daddy: Whatever you say, Mommy.

Mommy (*leading the way out, stage-left*): Of course, whatever I say. (*To the Musician*) You can begin now. (*The Musician begins playing; Mommy and Daddy exit; the Musician, all the while playing, nods to the Young Man.*)

Young Man (*with the same endearing smile*): Hi! (*After a moment, Mommy and Daddy re-enter, carrying Grandma. She is borne in by their hands under her armpits; she is quite rigid; her legs are drawn up; her feet do not touch the ground; the expression on her ancient face is that of puzzlement and fear.*)

Daddy: Where do we put her?

Mommy (*the same little laugh*): Wherever I say, of course. Let me see . . . well . . . all right, over there . . . in the sandbox. (*Pause*) Well, what are you waiting for, Daddy? . . . The sandbox! (*Together they carry Grandma over to the sandbox and more or less dump her in.*)

Grandma (*righting herself to a sitting position; her voice a cross between a baby's laugh and cry*): Ahhhhhh! Graaaaa!

Daddy (*dusting himself*): What do we do now?

Mommy (*to the Musician*): You can stop now. (*The Musician stops.*) (*Back to Daddy*) What do you mean, what do we do now? We go over there and sit down, of course. (*To the Young Man*) Hello there.

Young Man (*again smiling*): Hi! (*Mommy and Daddy move to the chairs, stage-right, and sit down. A pause.*)

Grandma (*same as before*): Ahhhhhh! Ah-haaaaaa! Graaaaaa!

Daddy: Do you think . . . do you think she's . . . comfortable?

Mommy (*impatiently*): How would I know?

Daddy (*pause*): What do we do now?

Mommy (*as if remembering*): We . . . wait. We . . . sit here . . . and we wait . . . that's what we do.

Daddy (*after a pause*): Shall we talk to each other?

Mommy (*with that little laugh; picking something off her dress*): Well, you can talk, if you want to . . . if you can think of anything to say . . . if you can think of anything *new.*

Daddy (*thinks*): No . . . I suppose not.

Mommy (*with a triumphant laugh*): Of course not!

Grandma (*banging the toy shovel against the pail*): Haaaaaa! Ah-haaaaaa!

Mommy (*out over the audience*): Be quiet, Grandma . . . just be quiet, and wait. (*Grandma throws a shovelful of sand at Mommy.*) (*Still out over the audience*) She's throwing sand at me! You stop that, Grandma; you stop throwing sand at Mommy! (*To Daddy*) She's throwing sand at me. (*Daddy looks around at Grandma, who screams at him.*)

Grandma: GRAAAAA!

Mommy: Don't look at her. Just . . . sit here . . . be very still . . . and wait. (*To the Musician*) You . . . uh . . . you go ahead and do whatever it is you do. (*The Musician plays. Mommy and Daddy are fixed, staring out beyond the audience. Grandma looks at them, looks at the Musician, looks at the sandbox, throws down the shovel.*)

Grandma: Ah-haaaaaa! Graaaaaa! (*Looks for reaction; gets none. Now . . . directly to the audience*) Honestly! What a way to treat an old woman! Drag her out of the house . . . stick her in a car . . . bring her out here from the city . . . dump her in a pile of sand . . . and leave her here to set. I'm eighty-six years old! I was married when I was seventeen. To a farmer. He died when I was thirty. (*To the Musician*) Will you stop that, please? (*The Musician stops playing.*) I'm a feeble old woman . . . how do you expect anybody to hear me over that peep! peep! peep! (*To herself*) There's no respect around here. (*To the Young Man*) There's no respect around here!

Young Man (*same smile*): Hi!

Grandma (*after a pause, a mild double-take, continues, to the audience*): My husband died when I was thirty (*indicates Mommy*), and I had to raise that big cow over there all by my lonesome. You can imagine what *that was like.* Lordy! (*To the Young Man*) Where'd they get *you?*

Young Man: Oh . . . I've been around for a while.

Grandma: I'll bet you have! Heh, heh, heh. Will you look at you!

Young Man (*flexing his muscles*): Isn't that something? (*Continues his calisthenics*)

Grandma: Boy, oh boy; I'll say. Pretty good.

Young Man (*sweetly*): I'll say.

Grandma: Where ya from?

Young Man: Southern California.

Grandma (*nodding*): Figgers; figgers. What's your name, honey?

Young Man: I don't know . . .

Grandma (*to the audience*): Bright, too!

Young Man: I mean . . . I mean, they haven't given me one yet . . . the studio . . .

Grandma (*giving him the once-over*): You don't say . . . you don't say. Well . . . uh, I've got to talk some more . . . don't you go 'way.

Young Man: Oh, no.

Grandma (*turning her attention back to the audience*): Fine; fine. (*Then, once more, back to the Young Man*) You're . . . you're an actor, hunh?

Young Man (*beaming*): Yes. I am.

Grandma (*to the audience again; shrugs*): I'm smart that way. Anyhow, I had to raise . . . *that* over there all by my lonesome; and what's next to her there . . . that's what she married. Rich? I tell you . . . money, money, money. They took me off the *farm* . . . which was real decent of them . . . and they moved me into the big town house with *them* . . . fixed a nice place for me under the stove . . . gave me an army blanket . . . and my own dish . . . my very own dish! So, what have I got to complain about? Nothing, of course. I'm not complaining. (*She looks up at the sky, shouts to someone off stage.*) Shouldn't it be getting dark now, dear? (*The lights dim; night comes on. The Musician begins to play; it becomes deepest night. There are spotlights on all the players, including the Young Man, who is, of course, continuing his calisthenics.*)

Daddy (*stirring*): It's nighttime.

Mommy: Shhhh. Be still . . . wait.

Daddy (*whining*): It's so hot.

Mommy: Shhhhhh. Be still . . . wait.

Grandma (*to herself*): That's better. Night. (*To the Musician*) Honey, do you play all through this part? (*The Musician nods.*) Well, keep it nice and soft; that's a good boy. (*The Musician nods again; plays softly.*) That's nice. (*There is an off-stage rumble.*)

Daddy (*starting*): What was that?

Mommy (*beginning to weep*): It was nothing.

Daddy: It was . . . it was . . . thunder . . . or a wave breaking . . . or something.

Mommy (*whispering, through her tears*): It was an off-stage rumble . . . and you know what *that* means . . .

Daddy: I forget . . .

Mommy (*barely able to talk*): It means the time has come for poor Grandma . . . and I can't bear it!

Daddy (*vacantly*): I . . . I suppose you've got to be brave.

Grandma (*mocking*): That's right, kid; be brave. You'll bear up; you'll get over it. (*Another off-stage rumble . . . louder.*)

Mommy: Ohhhhhhhhhh . . . poor Grandma . . . poor Grandma . . .

Grandma (*to Mommy*): I'm fine! I'm all right! It hasn't happened yet! (*A violent off-stage rumble. All the lights go out, save the spot on the Young Man; the Musician stops playing.*)

Mommy: Ohhhhhhhhhh . . . Ohhhhhhhhhh . . . (*Silence.*)

Grandma: Don't put the lights up yet . . . I'm not ready; I'm not quite ready. (*Silence*) All right, dear . . . I'm about done. (*The lights come up again, to brightest day; the Musician begins to play. Grandma is discovered, still in the sandbox, lying on her side, propped up on an elbow, half covered, busily shoveling sand over herself.*)

Grandma (*muttering*): I don't know how I'm supposed to do anything with this goddam toy shovel . . .

Daddy: Mommy! It's daylight!

Mommy (*brightly*): So it is! Well! Our long night is over. We must put away our tears, take off our mourning . . . and face the future. It's our duty.

Grandma (*still shoveling; mimicking*): . . . take off our mourning . . . face the future . . . Lordy! (*Mommy and Daddy rise, stretch. Mommy waves to the Young Man.*)

Young Man (*with that smile*): Hi! (*Grandma plays dead.*[!] *Mommy and Daddy go over to look at her; she is a little more than half buried in the sand; the toy shovel is in her hands, which are crossed on her breast.*)

Mommy (*before the sandbox; shaking her head*): Lovely! It's . . . it's hard to be sad . . . she looks . . . so happy. (*With pride and conviction*) It pays to do things well. (*To the Musician*) All right, you can stop now, if you want to. I mean, stay around for a swim, or something; it's all right with us. (*She sighs heavily.*) Well, Daddy . . . off we go.

Daddy: Brave Mommy!

Mommy: Brave Daddy! (*They exit, stage-left.*)

Grandma (*after they leave; lying quite still*): It pays to do things well . . . Boy, oh boy! (*She tries to sit up*) . . . well, kids . . . (*but she finds she can't*) . . . I . . . I can't get up. I . . . I can't move . . . (*The Young Man stops his calisthenics, nods to the Musician, walks over to Grandma, kneels down by the sandbox.*)

Grandma: I . . . can't move . . .

Young Man: Shhhhh . . . be very still . . .

Grandma: I . . . I can't move . . .

Young Man: Uh . . . ma'am; I . . . I have a line here.

Grandma: Oh, I'm sorry, sweetie; you go right ahead.

Young Man: I am . . . uh . . .

Grandma: Take your time, dear.

Young Man (*prepares; delivers the line like a real amateur*): I am the Angel of Death. I am . . . uh . . . I am come for you.

Grandma: What . . . wha . . . (*then, with resignation*) . . . ohhhh . . . ohhhh, I see. (*The Young Man bends over, kisses Grandma gently on the forehead.*)

Grandma (*her eyes closed, her hands folded on her breast again, the shovel between her hands, a sweet smile on her face*): Well . . . that was very nice, dear . . .

Young Man (*still kneeling*): Shhhhh . . . be still . . .

Grandma: What I meant was . . . you did that very well, dear . . .

Young Man (*blushing*): . . . oh . . .

Grandma: No; I mean it. You've got that . . . you've got a quality.

Young Man (*with his endearing smile*): Oh . . . thank you; thank you very much . . . ma'am.

Grandma (*slowly; softly—as the Young Man puts his hands on top of Grandma's*):
You're . . . you're welcome . . . dear.

(*Tableau. The Musician continues to play as the curtain slowly comes down.*)

Questions

1. What is unusual about the names of the characters in *The Sandbox*? How do the names affect our perceptions of the characters?
2. Where does the play take place? What does the presence of the sandbox suggest?
3. Does *The Sandbox* contain any traditional elements of plot structure? Does the play have a climax? If so, where?
4. Describe how Mommy and Daddy treat Grandma. How do they speak to her?
5. Albee tells the audience quite specifically that the Young Man is the Angel of Death. What other occupation does he have?
6. What purpose does the Musician serve in the play? Would *The Sandbox* have the same effect without this character?
7. In your own words, what do you think is the theme of *The Sandbox*? What parts of the play support your opinion?
8. What aspects of the play seem comic? What aspects appear unpleasant?

WRITER'S PERSPECTIVE

Edward Albee

Edward Albee on Drama THE THEATER OF THE ABSURD   1962

What of this theater in which, for example, a legless old couple live out their lives in twin ashcans, surfacing occasionally for food or conversation (Samuel Beckett's *Endgame*); in which a man is seduced, and rather easily, by a girl with three well-formed and functioning noses (Eugène Ionesco's *Jack, or The Submission*); in which, on the same stage, one group of Negro actors is playing at pretending to be Negro (Jean Genêt's *The Blacks*)?

What of this theater? Is it, as it has been accused of being, obscure, sordid, destructive, anti-theater, perverse, and absurd (in the sense of foolish)? Or is it merely, as I have so often heard it put, that, "This sort of stuff is too depressing, too . . . too mixed up; I go to the theater to relax and have a good time"?

I would submit that it is this latter attitude—that the theater is a place to relax and have a good time—in conflict with the purpose of The Theater of the Absurd—which is to make a man face up to the human condition as it really is—that has produced all the brouhaha and the dissent. I would submit that The Theater of the Absurd, in the sense that it is truly the contemporary theater, facing as it does man's condition as it is, is the Realistic theater of our time; and that the supposed Realistic theater—the term used here to mean most of what is done on Broadway—in the sense that it panders to the public need for self-congratulation and reassurance and presents a false picture of ourselves to ourselves, is, with an occasional very lovely exception, really and truly The Theater of the Absurd.

"Which Theater Is the Absurd One?"

◄▬◘ WRITING CRITICALLY ◖▬►

What's So Realistic About Realism?

When you hear the word *realism* used in relation to drama, it often refers to certain ways of writing and performing plays that emerged during the nineteenth century. In drama, realism tries to imitate the texture of everyday life. To understand the conventions of realism, it might help to contrast a play by Henrik Ibsen with one by Sophocles. Ibsen's characters speak in prose not verse. His settings are drawn from contemporary life, not a legendary past. His characters are ordinary middle-class citizens, not kings, queens, and aristocrats.

Those external characteristics are easy to spot, but you should also notice some less obvious ways that plays of the Realist movement often differ from earlier drama. Realist dramatists like Ibsen and Anton Chekhov try to portray the complexity of human psychology—especially motivation—in a detailed, subtle way. In Shakespeare's *Othello*, the villain Iago announces that he wants revenge on the title character because the Moor has reportedly cuckolded him. This far-fetched assertion is never proved—the facts of the play seem to contradict it everywhere else—and Iago never mentions the motivation again. Shakespeare appears less interested in the reason for Iago's villainy than its consequences. Did Iago have an unhappy childhood or a troubled adolescence? These questions do not greatly matter in Renaissance drama, but to Ibsen they become central. The inner lives, memories, and motivations of the characters now play a crucial role in the dramatic action.

Realist drama does not necessarily come any closer than other dramatic style in getting at the truths of human existence. *A Doll's House*, for example, does not provide a more profound picture of psychological struggle than *Oedipus the King*. But Ibsen does offer a more detailed view of his protagonist's inner life and her daily routine.

When writing about the protagonist of a realistic play, try to understand not only the motivation of the main character but also where those motives originated. Is there some key event, for example, in the protagonist's past that influences his or her present behavior? Do the characters around the protagonist understand the deeper motivation, or do they only see its outward effects? You may even want to construct a brief biography of the central character to understand how his or her childhood or early adulthood affects their current situation.

WRITING ASSIGNMENT

Al Capovilla of Folsom Lake Center College has developed an ingenious assignment based on Ibsen's *A Doll's House* that asks you to combine the skills of a literary critic with those of a lawyer. Here is Professor Capovilla's assignment:

> You are the family lawyer for Torvald and Nora Helmer. The couple comes to you with a request. They want you to listen to an account of their domestic problems and recommend whether they should pursue a divorce or try to reconcile.
>
> You listen to both sides of the argument. (You also know everything that is said by every character.)
>
> Now, it is your task to write a short decision. In stating your opinion, provide a clear and organized explanation of your reasoning. Show both sides of the argument. You may employ as evidence anything said or done in the play.
>
> Conclude your paper with your recommendation. What do you recommend under the circumstances—legal divorce or an attempt at reconciliation?

Here is a paper from Professor Capovilla's course written by Carlota Llarena, a student at Folsom Lake Center College.

Helmer vs. Helmer

In reaching a determination of whether Torvald and Nora Helmer should either get divorced or attempt reconciliation, I have carefully considered the events leading to the breakdown of their marriage in order to decide on an amicable solution to their present predicament. In my belief, marriage is a sacred institution--one that should not be taken lightly. Love and happiness in a marriage should be cultivated by the parties. Obstacles are often found throughout marriage, but in order to overcome those obstacles, a husband and wife should share responsibilities, discuss whatever problems arise, and jointly work on finding solutions to those problems. Based on this belief, I recommend that Torvald and Nora Helmer attempt a reconciliation of the marriage.

In reviewing the testimony provided by both parties, I find it true that Torvald has treated Nora in such a manner to make her feel she was considered a child rather than an equal partner. Torvald handled all their finances and solely resolved all their problems. Torvald never discussed any of their household problems with Nora or attempted to seek her advice. In that regard, I believe that Torvald treated Nora in that fashion because he felt Nora was incapable of handling these types of situations. Nora's every need had always been looked after by her father. She grew up with nannies, never had to take responsibility for herself, and never had to work to earn money as money was always given to her.

I find it also true, however, that Nora has always acted as a child. She has the tendency to sulk if matters don't go her way, is happy when rewarded with gifts, hides treats (like macaroons) for herself when they are prohibited, and likes to play games. These characteristics are clearly evident in Nora. There are at least six examples of her child-like behaviors in the testimonies. First, Nora denied nibbling on a macaroon or two (1417) as a child would deny any wrongdoing. Second, Nora thought it would be "fun" to hang the bills [money] in pretty gilt paper on the Christmas tree (1416) as a child would enjoy bright and colorful objects. Third, Nora considered it to be "wonderful fun" to sit and work to earn money "almost like being a man" (1424) as a child would pretend and play-act adult roles. Fourth, Nora was excited when she received a gift of money from Torvald (1416) as a child would be excited when she receives a present. Fifth, Nora enjoyed dreaming of a rich old gentleman falling in love with her (1424) as a child would dream of getting married to a rich man who would take complete care of her. And, finally, Nora would "do anything to please . . . I'll sing for you, dance for you" (1433) as a child would always attempt to please her parents.

Unfortunately, Torvald reinforced Nora's child-like characteristics by calling her names such as "my little lark" (1415), "my squirrel" (1415), "my pretty little pet" (1416), and "my little Nora" (1434). These nicknames seem more appropriate for a child than a grown woman. Torvald has also been very protective of Nora--just as a parent would be protective of a child. Torvald claimed that Nora had "precious eyes" and "fair little delicate hands" which indicates his belief that Nora was a fragile person, one who does not know how to take care of herself. Since Nora was treated in that same manner by her father, she has never experienced life in any other fashion other than that of a child.

As a further review of the testimony presented, I opine that Torvald is not solely to be blamed for the predicament at hand. Nora has allowed Torvald to treat her in this manner during the eight years they were married. She never told Torvald that she wanted to be treated as an adult and as his equal or that she wanted to become more involved with family matters to help determine solutions to problems they may have. Nora was also guilty of not confiding in Torvald or discussing her problems with him. Did Nora discuss with Torvald the need for them to live in Italy for a year (1423)? Did she sit with her husband and discuss issues concerning money to make such a trip to Italy feasible and where the money actually came from (1423)? Did Nora ever tell Torvald the truth that she had "borrowed" the money from Krogstad, how she was repaying "the loan" and what she did to secure that loan (1432)? The answer to all these questions is no! Accordingly, it is quite clear that Nora and Torvald are both equally guilty of not discussing problems and issues with one another.

In summation, Nora and Torvald are equally at fault on the following issues. First, Torvald treated Nora as a child, and Nora allowed herself to be treated in that manner. Second, Torvald never confided in Nora regarding matters concerning the family or their finances. Nora, however, also did not confide in Torvald. Now that these issues and concerns are made known to the parties, the parties may work on resolving their differences, share the responsibility of handling both family and financial matters by discussing them with one another and finding amicable solutions, and cultivate the trust and judgment of one another. Accordingly, it is my ruling that Nora and Torvald attempt reconciling their marriage and forgo divorce as an immediate option. Only if the parties reach an impasse after an honest and sustained attempt at reconciliation would I suggest reconsidering the option of divorce.

Work Cited

Ibsen, Henrik. A Doll's House. Trans. James McFarlane. Literature: An Introduction to Fiction, Poetry, and Drama. Ed. X.J. Kennedy and Dana Gioia. 7th ed. New York: Longman, 1999. 1413-69.

FURTHER SUGGESTIONS FOR WRITING

1. Demonstrate, in a paragraph or two, how Nora in *A Doll's House* resembles or differs from a feminist of today.

2. Placing yourself in the character of Ibsen's Torvald Helmer, write a defense of him and his attitudes as he himself might write it.
3. Choose the play in this chapter that in your opinion might best lend itself to a television production. Then tell your reader how you would go about adapting it. What changes or deletions, if any, would you make? What problems would you expect to meet in transferring it to a different medium?
4. Perform Albee's *The Sandbox* in your classroom. Assign all the roles, including the Musician. (Find a classmate who plays some instrument or, if worse comes to worst, has a portable tape deck.) After you have performed or seen the play, write a short paper on what the experience revealed to you. Did seeing the play change your opinion of it—for better or worse? Did you understand it better, or did it seem more elusive than ever?

36 *Evaluating a Play*

The critic should describe, and not prescribe.
—Eugène Ionesco, *Improvisation*

To **evaluate** a play is to decide whether the play is any good or not and, if it is good, how good it is in relation to other plays of its kind. In the theater, evaluation is usually thought to be the task of the play reviewer (or, with nobler connotations, "drama critic"), ordinarily a person who sees a new play on its first night and who then tells us, in print or over the air, what the play is about, how well it is done, and whether or not we ought to go to see it. Enthroned in an excellent free seat, the drama critic apparently plies a glamorous trade. What fun it must be to whittle a nasty epigram, for example, to be able to observe, as did a critic of a faltering production of *Uncle Tom's Cabin*, that "the Siberian wolf hound was weakly supported."

Unless you find a job on a large city newspaper or radio station, write for a college paper, or broadcast on a campus FM station, the opportunities to be a drama critic today are probably few and strictly limited. Much more significant, for most of us, is the task of evaluating for our own satisfaction. We see a play, a film, or a drama on television, and then we make up our minds about it; we often have to decide whether to recommend it to someone else.

To evaluate new drama isn't easy. (For this discussion, let us define *drama* broadly as including not only plays but also anything that actors perform in the movies or on television, for most of us see more movies and television programs than plays.) By the time we see a production of any kind at least a part of the process of evaluation has already been accomplished for us. To produce a new play, even in an amateur theater, or to produce a new drama for the movies or for television is complicated and involves large sums of money and the efforts of many people. Sifted from a mountain of submitted play scripts, already subjected to long scrutiny and evaluation, a new play or film, whether or not it is of deep interest, arrives with a built-in air of professional competence. It is probably seldom that a dull play written by the producer's relative or friend finds enough financial backers to reach the stage; only on the fictitious Broadway of Mel Brooks's film *The Producers* could there be a musical comedy as awful as *Springtime for Hitler*. Nor do most college and civic theaters afford us much opportunity to see thoroughly inept plays. Usually they give us new productions of *Oedipus the King* or *Pygmalion* or else (if they are less adventurous) new versions of whatever succeeded on Broadway in the recent past.

And so new plays—the few that we do see—are usually, like television drama, somebody's safe investment. More often than not, our powers of evaluation confront only slick, pleasant, and efficient mediocrity. We owe it to ourselves to discriminate. Life is too short and theater tickets too expensive to spend either on the agreeably second-rate. There are too many marvellous plays we might miss.

⊷ WRITING CRITICALLY ⊶

Critical Performance

Here are a few suggestions designed to help you tell the difference between an ordinary, run-of-the-reel product and a work of drama that may offer high reward.

1. Discard any inexorable rules you may have collected that affirm what a drama ought to be. (One such rule states that a tragedy is innately superior to a comedy, no matter how deep a truth a comedy may strike.) Don't expect all plays to "observe the unities"—that is, unfold their events in one day and in one place and keep tragedy and comedy strictly apart. (Shakespeare ignores such rules.) There is no sense in damning a play for lacking "realism." (What if it's an expressionist play or a fantasy?)

2. Instead, watch the play (or read it) alertly, with your mind and your senses open wide. Recall that theaters, such as the classic Greek theater of Sophocles, impose conventions. Do not condemn *Oedipus the King* for the reason one spectator gave: "That damned chorus keeps sticking their noses in!" Do not complain that Hamlet utters soliloquies.

3. Ask yourself whether the characters are fully realized. Do their actions follow from the kinds of persons they are, or does the action seem to impose itself upon them, making the play seem falsely contrived? Does the resolution arrive (as in a satisfying play) because of the nature of the characters, or are the characters saved (or destroyed) merely by some *deus ex machina* or nick-of-time arrival of the Marines?

4. Recognize drama that belongs to a family, for example *a farce, a comedy of manners*, or a **melodrama** (a play in which suspense and physical action are the prime ingredients). Recognizing such a familiar type of drama may help make some things clear to you and may save you from attacking a play for being what it is, in fact, supposed to be. After all, there can be satisfying melodramas, and excellent plays may have melodramatic elements. What is wrong with thrillers is not that they have suspense, but that suspense usually is all they have. Awhirl with furious action, they employ stick-figure characters.

5. If there are symbols, ask how well they belong to their surrounding worlds. Do they help to reveal meaning or merely decorate? In Tennessee

Williams's *The Glass Menagerie*, Laura's collection of figurines is much more than simply ornamental.

6.   Test the play or film for **sentimentality,** the failure of a dramatist, actor, or director who expects from us a greater emotional response than we are given reason to feel. (For further discussions of sentimentality, see pages 248 and 984.)

7.   Decide what it is that you admire or dislike and, for a play, whether it is the play or the production that you admire or dislike. (It is useful to draw this distinction if you are evaluating the play and not the production.)

8.   Ask yourself what the theme is. What does the drama reveal? How far and how deeply does its statement go; how readily can we apply it beyond the play to the human world outside? Be slow, of course, to attribute to the playwright the opinions of the characters.

9.   Don't be afraid of stating your own honest reaction (balanced, of course, by the careful considerations listed above). When the playwright Eugène Ionesco states that a "critic should describe, and not prescribe," he does not restrict the critic from trying accurately to describe his or her own response to the work in question. We cannot truthfully judge a work of art without somehow involving our own reactions—simple or complicated—to the experience of it.

Follow all these steps, and you may find that evaluating plays, movies, and television plays is a richly meaningful activity. It may reveal wisdom and pleasure that had previously bypassed you. It may even help you decide what to watch in the future, how to choose those works of drama that help you to fulfill—not merely to spend—your waking life.

Writing Assignment

Select any play in this book that is available in performance on videotape, CD, LP, or tape cassette. Pretend you are a critic attending the world premiere, and write a 750 to 1,000-word review of the play. In evaluating the play and performance, clearly state your criteria. (For practical hints on writing a review, see "Reviewing a Play" on page 1920.)

Further Suggestions for Writing

1.   Attend a performance of a play, and write a critical review of it. Consider both the play itself and its production. (For advice on reviewing and a sample review, see page 1920.)

2.   Read two celebrated, still much performed plays of the same era, *Death of a Salesman* (1949) and *The Glass Menagerie* (1945), both in "Plays for Further Reading." Then, in an essay of 700 words or more, decide which you consider the finer play. Back up your evaluation by referring to both.

3.   Read the printed text of a modern or contemporary play not included in this book. (If you can see the play on stage or videotape, so much the better.) Then, in an essay of 500 to 750 words, state your considered opinion of it. Among interesting plays to choose from are these:

> *The Zoo Story* by Edward Albee
> *Waiting for Godot* by Samuel Beckett

'Master Harold' and the Boys by Athol Fugard
Hedda Gabler, The Master Builder, or *Peer Gynt* by Henrik Ibsen
The Bald Soprano or *The Chairs* by Eugène Ionesco
Words, Words, Words by David Ives
American Buffalo by David Mamet
'Night, Mother by Marsha Norman
Long Day's Journey into Night by Eugene O'Neill
The Birthday Party or *The Caretaker* by Harold Pinter
Roosters by Milcha Sanchez-Scott
No Exit by Jean-Paul Sartre
for colored girls who have considered suicide / when the rainbow is enuf by
   Ntozake Shange
Major Barbara or *Pygmalion* by George Bernard Shaw
Buried Child or *True West* by Sam Shepard
Rosencrantz and Guildenstern Are Dead by Tom Stoppard
The Heidi Chronicles by Wendy Wasserstein
Fences or *The Piano Lesson* by August Wilson

All the world's a stage,
And all the men and women merely players:
They have their exits and their entrances,
And one man in his time plays many parts,
His acts being seven ages. At first, the infant
Mewling° and puking in the nurse's arms.   *bawling*
Then the whining schoolboy with his satchel
And shining morning face, creeping like snail
Unwilling to school. And then the lover,
Sighing like furnace, with a woeful ballad
Made to his mistress' eyebrow. Then a soldier
Full of strange oaths and bearded like the pard,°   *leopard*
Jealous in honor, sudden and quick in quarrel,
Seeking the bubble reputation
Even in the cannon's mouth. And then the justice,
In fair round belly with good capon lined,
With eyes severe and beard of formal cut,
Full of wise saws° and modern instances;°   *sayings; examples*
And so he plays his part. The sixth age shifts
Into the lean and slippered pantaloon,°   *old man (from Pantalone*
With spectacles on nose and pouch on side;   *in the* commedia dell'arte)
His youthful hose well saved, a world too wide
For his shrunk shank, and his big manly voice
Turning again toward childish treble, pipes
And whistles in his sound. Last scene of all
That ends this strange eventful history
Is second childishness and mere oblivion,
Sans teeth, sans eyes, sans taste, sans everything.
                         —William Shakespeare, *As You Like It*, II, vii

Sophocles

ANTIGONÊ

441 B.C.

TRANSLATED BY DUDLEY FITTS AND ROBERT FITZGERALD

Sophocles (496?–406 B.C.), Athenian dramatist, is the subject of a biographical note on page 1254, preceding his play Oedipus the King. Antigonê *was produced in 441 B.C.;* Oedipus the King, *not until fifteen or sixteen years later. Although written earlier than its companion play,* Antigonê *relates events supposed to have followed long after.*

Characters

Antigonê
Ismenê
Eurydicê
Creon
Haimon
Teiresias
A Sentry
A Messenger
Chorus

Scene: *Before the palace of Creon, King of Thebes. A central double door, and two lateral doors. A platform extends the length of the façade, and from this platform three steps lead down into the "orchestra," or chorus-ground.*

Time: *Dawn of the day after the repulse of the Argive army from the assault on Thebes.*

PROLOGUE°

Antigonê and Ismenê enter from the central door of the palace.

Antigonê: Ismenê, dear sister,
You would think that we had already suffered enough
For the curse on Oedipus:°

Prologue: portion of the play containing the exposition, or explanation of what has gone before and what is now happening.
3 *the curse on Oedipus:* As Sophocles tells in *Oedipus the King*, the King of Thebes discovered that he had lived his life under a curse. Unknowingly, he had slain his father and married his mother. On realizing this terrible truth, Oedipus put out his own eyes and departed into exile. Now, years later, as *Antigonê* opens, Antigonê and Ismenê, daughters of Oedipus, are recalling how their two brothers died. After the abdication of their father, the brothers had ruled Thebes together. But they fell to quarreling. When Eteoclês expelled Polyneicês, the latter returned with an army and attacked the city. The two brothers killed each other in combat, leaving the throne to Creon. The new king of Thebes has buried Eteoclês with full honors, but, calling Polyneicês a traitor, has decreed that his body shall be left to the crows—an especially terrible decree, for a rotting corpse might offend Zeus; bring down plague, blight, and barrenness upon Thebes; and prevent the soul of a dead hero from entering the Elysian Fields, abode of those favored by the gods.

I cannot imagine any grief
That you and I have not gone through. And now— 5
Have they told you of the new decree of our King Creon?
Ismenê: I have heard nothing: I know
That two sisters lost two brothers, a double death
In a single hour; and I know that the Argive army
Fled in the night; but beyond this, nothing. 10
Antigonê: I thought so. And that is why I wanted you
To come out here with me. There is something we must do.
Ismenê: Why do you speak so strangely?
Antigonê: Listen, Ismenê:
Creon buried our brother Eteoclês 15
With military honors, gave him a soldier's funeral,
And it was right that he should; but Polyneicês,
Who fought as bravely and died as miserably,—
They say that Creon has sworn
No one shall bury him, no one mourn for him, 20
But his body must lie in the fields, a sweet treasure
For carrion birds to find as they search for food.
That is what they say, and our good Creon is coming here
To announce it publicly; and the penalty—
Stoning to death in the public square!
                             There it is, 25
And now you can prove what you are:
A true sister, or a traitor to your family.
Ismenê: Antigonê, you are mad! What could I possibly do?
Antigonê: You must decide whether you will help me or not.
Ismenê: I do not understand you. Help you in what? 30
Antigonê: Ismenê, I am going to bury him. Will you come?
Ismenê: Bury him! You have just said the new law forbids it.
Antigonê: He is my brother. And he is your brother, too.
Ismenê: But think of the danger! Think what Creon will do!
Antigonê: Creon is not strong enough to stand in my way. 35
Ismenê: Ah sister!
Oedipus died, everyone hating him
For what his own search brought to light, his eyes
Ripped out by his own hand; and Iocastê died,
His mother and wife at once: she twisted the cords 40
That strangled her life; and our two brothers died,
Each killed by the other's sword. And we are left:
But oh, Antigonê,
Think how much more terrible than these
Our own death would be if we should go against Creon 45
And do what he has forbidden! We are only women,
We cannot fight with men, Antigonê!

The law is strong, we must give in to the law
In this thing, and in worse. I beg the Dead
To forgive me, but I am helpless: I must yield   50
To those in authority. And I think it is dangerous business
To be always meddling.
Antigonê: If that is what you think,
    I should not want you, even if you asked to come.
    You have made your choice, you can be what you want to be.
    But I will bury him; and if I must die,   55
    I say that this crime is holy: I shall lie down
    With him in death, and I shall be as dear
    To him as he to me.
                         It is the dead,
    Not the living, who make the longest demands:
    We die for ever . . .
                         You may do as you like,   60
    Since apparently the laws of the gods mean nothing to you.
Ismenê: They mean a great deal to me; but I have no strength
    To break laws that were made for the public good.
Antigonê: That must be your excuse, I suppose. But as for me,
    I will bury the brother I love.
Ismenê: Antigonê,   65
    I am so afraid for you!
Antigonê: You need not be:
    You have yourself to consider, after all.
Ismenê: But no one must hear of this, you must tell no one!
    I will keep it a secret, I promise!
Antigonê: O tell it! Tell everyone!
    Think how they'll hate you when it all comes out   70
    If they learn that you knew about it all the time!
Ismenê: So fiery! You should be cold with fear.
Antigonê: Perhaps. But I am doing only what I must.
Ismenê: But you can do it? I say that you cannot.
Antigonê: Very well: when my strength gives out, I shall do no more.   75
Ismenê: Impossible things should not be tried at all.
Antigonê: Go away, Ismenê:
    I shall be hating you soon, and the dead will too,
    For your words are hateful. Leave me my foolish plan:
    I am not afraid of the danger; if it means death,   80
    It will not be the worst of deaths—death without honor.
Ismenê: Go then, if you feel that you must.
    You are unwise,
    But a loyal friend indeed to those who love you.

Exit into the palace. Antigonê goes off, left. Enter the Chorus.

PÁRODOS°

Chorus: Now the long blade of the sun, lying
    Level east to west, touches with glory
    Thebes of the Seven Gates. Open, unlidded
    Eye of golden day! O marching light
    Across the eddy and rush of Dircê's stream,°   5
    Striking the white shields of the enemy
    Thrown headlong backward from the blaze of morning!
Choragos:° Polyneicês their commander
    Roused them with windy phrases,
    He the wild eagle screaming   10
    Insults above our land,
    His wings their shields of snow,
    His crest their marshalled helms.

Antistrophe° 1

Chorus: Against our seven gates in a yawning ring
    The famished spears came onward in the night;   15
    But before his jaws were sated with our blood,
    Or pinefire took the garland of our towers,
    He was thrown back; and as he turned, great Thebes—
    No tender victim for his noisy power—
    Rose like a dragon behind him, shouting war.   20
Choragos: For God hates utterly
    The bray of bragging tongues;
    And when he beheld their smiling,
    Their swagger of golden helms,
    The frown of his thunder blasted   25
    Their first man from our walls.

Strophe 2

Chorus: We heard his shout of triumph high in the air
    Turn to a scream; far out in a flaming arc
    He fell with his windy torch, and the earth struck him.
    And others storming in fury no less than his   30
    Found shock of death in the dusty joy of battle.
Choragos: Seven captains at seven gates
    Yielded their clanging arms to the god
    That bends the battle-line and breaks it.
    These two only, brothers in blood,   35
    Face to face in matchless rage,

Párodos: a song sung by the chorus on first entering. Its *strophe* (according to scholarly theory)
was sung while the chorus danced from stage right to stage left: its *antistrophe*, while it danced
back again. Another párodos follows the prologue of *Oedipus the King.*   5 *Dircê's stream:* river
near Thebes.   8 *Choragos:* leader of the Chorus and principal commentator on the play's action.

Mirroring each the other's death,
Clashed in long combat.

Antistrophe 2

Chorus: But now in the beautiful morning of victory
Let Thebes of the many chariots sing for joy!   40
With hearts for dancing we'll take leave of war:
Our temples shall be sweet with hymns of praise,
And the long night shall echo with our chorus.

SCENE I

Choragos: But now at last our new King is coming:
Creon of Thebes, Menoikeus' son.
In this auspicious dawn of his reign
What are the new complexities
That shifting Fate has woven for him?   5
What is his counsel? Why has he summoned
The old men to hear him?

Enter Creon from the palace, center. He addresses the Chorus from the top step.

Creon: Gentlemen: I have the honor to inform you that our Ship of State,
which recent storms have threatened to destroy, has come safely to harbor
at last, guided by the merciful wisdom of Heaven. I have summoned you   10
here this morning because I know that I can depend upon you: your devotion to King Laïos was absolute; you never hesitated in your duty to our late
ruler Oedipus; and when Oedipus died, your loyalty was transferred to his
children. Unfortunately, as you know, his two sons, the princes Eteoclês and
Polyneicês, have killed each other in battle; and I, as the next in blood,   15
have succeeded to the full power of the throne.

I am aware, of course, that no Ruler can expect complete loyalty from
his subjects until he has been tested in office. Nevertheless, I say to you at
the very outset that I have nothing but contempt for the kind of Governor
who is afraid, for whatever reason, to follow the course that he knows is best 20
for the State; and as for the man who sets private friendship above the
public welfare,—I have no use for him, either. I call God to witness that if I
saw my country headed for ruin, I should not be afraid to speak out plainly;
and I need hardly remind you that I would never have any dealings with an
enemy of the people. No one values friendship more highly than I; but we   25
must remember that friends made at the risk of wrecking our Ship are not
real friends at all.

These are my principles, at any rate, and that is why I have made the
following decision concerning the sons of Oedipus: Eteoclês, who died as a
man should die, fighting for his country, is to be buried with full military   30
honors, with all the ceremony that is usual when the greatest heroes die; but
his brother Polyneicês, who broke his exile to come back with fire and sword
against his native city and the shrines of his fathers' gods, whose one idea

was to spill the blood of his blood and sell his own people into slavery—
Polyneicês, I say, is to have no burial: no man is to touch him or say the   35
least prayer for him; he shall lie on the plain, unburied; and the birds and
the scavenging dogs can do with him whatever they like.

　　This is my command, and you can see the wisdom behind it. As long as
I am King, no traitor is going to be honored with the loyal man. But whoever shows by word and deed that he is on the side of the State,—he shall   40
have my respect while he is living, and my reverence when he is dead.

Choragos: If that is your will, Creon son of Menoikeus,
　　You have the right to enforce it: we are yours.
Creon: That is my will. Take care that you do your part.
Choragos: We are old men: let the younger ones carry it out.   45
Creon: I do not mean that: the sentries have been appointed.
Choragos: Then what is it that you would have us do?
Creon: You will give no support to whoever breaks this law.
Choragos: Only a crazy man is in love with death!
Creon: And death it is, yet money talks, and the wisest   50
　　Have sometimes been known to count a few coins too many.

　　Enter Sentry from left.

Sentry: I'll not say that I'm out of breath from running, King, because every time
　　I stopped to think about what I have to tell you, I felt like going back. And
　　all the time a voice kept saying, "You fool, don't you know you're walking
　　straight into trouble?"; and then another voice: "Yes, but if you let some-   55
　　body else get the news to Creon first, it will be even worse than that for
　　you!" But good sense won out, at least I hope it was good sense, and here I
　　am with a story that makes no sense at all; but I'll tell it anyhow, because, as
　　they say, what's going to happen's going to happen and—
Creon: Come to the point. What have you to say?   60
Sentry: I did not do it. I did not see who did it. You must not punish me for what
　　someone else has done.
Creon: A comprehensive defense! More effective, perhaps,
　　If I knew its purpose. Come: what is it?
Sentry: A dreadful thing . . . I don't know how to put it—   65
Creon: Out with it!
Sentry: 　　　　　　　Well, then;
　　The dead man—
　　　　　　Polyneicês—

　　Pause. The Sentry is overcome, fumbles for words. Creon waits impassively.

　　　　　　　　　　out there—
　　　　　　　　　　　　　someone,—
　　New dust on the slimy flesh!

　　Pause. No sign from Creon.

　　Someone has given it burial that way, and
　　Gone . . .   70

Long pause. Creon finally speaks with deadly control.

Creon: And the man who dared do this?
Sentry: I swear I
   Do not know! You must believe me!
                      Listen:
   The ground was dry, not a sign of digging, no,
   Not a wheeltrack in the dust, no trace of anyone.
   It was when they relieved us this morning: and one of them,   75
   The corporal, pointed to it.
                    There it was,
   The strangest—
          Look:
   The body, just mounded over with light dust: you see?
   Not buried really, but as if they'd covered it
   Just enough for the ghost's peace. And no sign   80
   Of dogs or any wild animal that had been there.

   And then what a scene there was! Every man of us
   Accusing the other: we all proved the other man did it,
   We all had proof that we could not have done it.
   We were ready to take hot iron in our hands,   85
   Walk through fire, swear by all the gods,
   It was not I!
   I do not know who it was, but it was not I!

Creon's rage has been mounting steadily, but the Sentry is too intent upon his story to notice it.

   And then, when this came to nothing, someone said
   A thing that silenced us and made us stare   90
   Down at the ground: you had to be told the news,
   And one of us had to do it! We threw the dice,
   And the bad luck fell to me. So here I am,
   No happier to be here than you are to have me:
   Nobody likes the man who brings bad news.   95
Choragos: I have been wondering, King: can it be that the gods have done this?
Creon (*furiously*): Stop!
   Must you doddering wrecks
   Go out of your heads entirely? "The gods"!
   Intolerable!   100
   The gods favor this corpse? Why? How had he served them?
   Tried to loot their temples, burn their images,
   Yes, and the whole State, and its laws with it!
   Is it your senile opinion that the gods love to honor bad men?
   A pious thought!—
                 No, from the very beginning   105
   There have been those who have whispered together,
   Stiff-necked anarchists, putting their heads together,

Scheming against me in alleys. These are the men,
And they have bribed my own guard to do this thing.

(*Sententiously.*) Money!   110
There's nothing in the world so demoralizing as money.
Down go your cities,
Homes gone, men gone, honest hearts corrupted,
Crookedness of all kinds, and all for money!
(*To Sentry.*)   But you—!
I swear by God and by the throne of God,   115
The man who has done this thing shall pay for it!
Find that man, bring him here to me, or your death
Will be the least of your problems: I'll string you up
Alive, and there will be certain ways to make you
Discover your employer before you die;   120
And the process may teach you a lesson you seem to have missed:
The dearest profit is sometimes all too dear:
That depends on the source. Do you understand me?
A fortune won is often misfortune.

Sentry: King, may I speak?
Creon: Your very voice distresses me.   125
Sentry: Are you sure that it is my voice, and not your conscience?
Creon: By God, he wants to analyze me now!
Sentry: It is not what I say, but what has been done, that hurts you.
Creon: You talk too much.
Sentry: Maybe; but I've done nothing.
Creon: Sold your soul for some silver: that's all you've done.   130
Sentry: How dreadful it is when the right judge judges wrong!
Creon: Your figures of speech
        May entertain you now; but unless you bring me the man,
        You will get little profit from them in the end.

        Exit Creon into the palace.

Sentry: "Bring me the man"—!   135
        I'd like nothing better than bringing him the man!
        But bring him or not, you have seen the last of me here.
        At any rate, I am safe!

        Exit Sentry.

ODE I°

Strophe 1

Chorus: Numberless are the world's wonders, but none
        More wonderful than man; the stormgray sea

Ode I: first song sung by the Chorus, who at the same time danced. Here again, as in the
párodos, strophe and *antistrophe* probably divide the song into two movements of the dance:
right-to-left, then left-to-right.

Yields to his prows, the huge crests bear him high;
Earth, holy and inexhaustible, is graven
With shining furrows where his plows have gone   5
Year after year, the timeless labor of stallions.

Antistrophe 1

The lightboned birds and beasts that cling to cover,
The lithe fish lighting their reaches of dim water,
All are taken, tamed in the net of his mind;
The lion on the hill, the wild horse windy-maned,   10
Resign to him; and his blunt yoke has broken
The sultry shoulders of the mountain bull.

Strophe 2

Words also, and thought as rapid as air,
He fashions to his good use; statecraft is his,
And his the skill that deflects the arrows of snow,   15
The spears of winter rain: from every wind
He has made himself secure—from all but one:
In the late wind of death he cannot stand.

Antistrophe 2

O clear intelligence, force beyond all measure!
O fate of man, working both good and evil!   20
When the laws are kept, how proudly his city stands!
When the laws are broken, what of his city then?
Never may the anárchic man find rest at my hearth,
Never be it said that my thoughts are his thoughts.

SCENE II

Re-enter Sentry leading Antigonê.

Choragos: What does this mean? Surely this captive woman
　　Is the Princess, Antigonê. Why should she be taken?
Sentry: Here is the one who did it! We caught her
　　In the very act of burying him.—Where is Creon?
Choragos: Just coming from the house.

　　Enter Creon, center.

Creon:　　　　　　　　　　　　What has happened?   5
　　Why have you come back so soon?
Sentry (expansively):　　　　　　　　O King,
　　A man should never be too sure of anything:
　　I would have sworn
　　That you'd not see me here again: your anger
　　Frightened me so, and the things you threatened me with; 10
　　But how could I tell then
　　That I'd be able to solve the case so soon?

No dice-throwing this time: I was only too glad to come!

Here is this woman. She is the guilty one:
We found her trying to bury him.   15
Take her, then; question her; judge her as you will.
I am through with the whole thing now, and glad of it.
Creon: But this is Antigonê! Why have you brought her here?
Sentry: She was burying him, I tell you!
Creon (severely):   Is this the truth?
Sentry: I saw her with my own eyes. Can I say more?   20
Creon: The details: come, tell me quickly!
Sentry: It was like this:
After those terrible threats of yours, King,
We went back and brushed the dust away from the body.
The flesh was soft by now, and stinking,
So we sat on a hill to windward and kept guard.   25
No napping this time! We kept each other awake.
But nothing happened until the white round sun
Whirled in the center of the round sky over us:
Then, suddenly,
A storm of dust roared up from the earth, and the sky   30
Went out, the plain vanished with all its trees
In the stinging dark. We closed our eyes and endured it.
The whirlwind lasted a long time, but it passed;
And then we looked, and there was Antigonê!
I have seen   35
A mother bird come back to a stripped nest, heard
Her crying bitterly a broken note or two
For the young ones stolen. Just so, when this girl
Found the bare corpse, and all her love's work wasted,
She wept, and cried on heaven to damn the hands   40
That had done this thing.
                                    And then she brought more dust
And sprinkled wine three times for her brother's ghost.

We ran and took her at once. She was not afraid,
Not even when we charged her with what she had done.
She denied nothing.
                              And this was a comfort to me,   45
And some uneasiness: for it is a good thing
To escape from death, but it is no great pleasure
To bring death to a friend.
                                    Yet I always say
There is nothing so comfortable as your own safe skin!
Creon (slowly, dangerously): And you, Antigonê,   50
You with your head hanging,—do you confess this thing?

Antigonê: I do. I deny nothing.
Creon (to Sentry):　　　　　　You may go.

　　Exit Sentry.

　　(*To Antigonê.*) Tell me, tell me briefly:
　　Had you heard my proclamation touching this matter?
Antigonê: It was public. Could I help hearing it?　　　　　　55
Creon: And yet you dared defy the law.
Antigonê:　　　　　　　　　　I dared.
　　It was not God's proclamation. That final Justice
　　That rules the world below makes no such laws.

　　Your edict, King, was strong,
　　But all your strength is weakness itself against　　　　60
　　The immortal unrecorded laws of God.
　　They are not merely now: they were, and shall be,
　　Operative for ever, beyond man utterly.

　　I knew I must die, even without your decree:
　　I am only mortal. And if I must die　　　　　　65
　　Now, before it is my time to die,
　　Surely this is no hardship: can anyone
　　Living, as I live, with evil all about me,
　　Think Death less than a friend? This death of mine
　　Is of no importance; but if I had left my brother　　70
　　Lying in death unburied, I should have suffered.
　　Now I do not.
　　　　　　You smile at me. Ah Creon,
　　Think me a fool, if you like; but it may well be
　　That a fool convicts me of folly.
Choragos: Like father, like daughter: both headstrong, deaf to reason!　75
　　She has never learned to yield:
Creon:　　　　　　　　She has much to learn.
　　The inflexible heart breaks first, the toughest iron
　　Cracks first, and the wildest horses bend their necks
　　At the pull of the smallest curb.
　　　　　　　　　　Pride? In a slave?
　　This girl is guilty of a double insolence,　　　　80
　　Breaking the given laws and boasting of it.
　　Who is the man here,
　　She or I, if this crime goes unpunished?
　　Sister's child, or more than sister's child,
　　Or closer yet in blood—she and her sister　　　85
　　Win bitter death for this!
　　(*To Servants.*)　　　　Go, some of you,
　　Arrest Ismenê. I accuse her equally.
　　Bring her: you will find her sniffling in the house there.

Her mind's a traitor: crimes kept in the dark
Cry for light, and the guardian brain shudders;   90
But how much worse than this
Is brazen boasting of barefaced anarchy!
Antigonê: Creon, what more do you want than my death?
Creon: Nothing.
     That gives me everything.
Antigonê: Then I beg you: kill me.
     This talking is a great weariness: your words   95
     Are distasteful to me, and I am sure that mine
     Seem so to you. And yet they should not seem so:
     I should have praise and honor for what I have done.
     All these men here would praise me
     Were their lips not frozen shut with fear of you.   100
     (*Bitterly.*) Ah the good fortune of kings,
     Licensed to say and do whatever they please!
Creon: You are alone here in that opinion.
Antigonê: No, they are with me. But they keep their tongues in leash.
Creon: Maybe. But you are guilty, and they are not.   105
Antigonê: There is no guilt in reverence for the dead.
Creon: But Eteoclês—was he not your brother too?
Antigonê: My brother too.
Creon: And you insult his memory?
Antigonê (*softly*): The dead man would not say that I insult it.
Creon: He would: for you honor a traitor as much as him.   110
Antigonê: His own brother, traitor or not, and equal in blood.
Creon: He made war on his country. Eteoclês defended it.
Antigonê: Nevertheless, there are honors due all the dead.
Creon: But not the same for the wicked as for the just.
Antigonê: Ah Creon, Creon,   115
     Which of us can say what the gods hold wicked?
Creon: An enemy is an enemy, even dead.
Antigonê: It is my nature to join in love, not hate.
Creon (*finally losing patience*): Go join them, then; if you must have your love,
     Find it in hell!   120
Choragos: But see, Ismenê comes:

Enter Ismenê, guarded.

     Those tears are sisterly, the cloud
     That shadows her eyes rains down gentle sorrow.
Creon: You too, Ismenê,
     Snake in my ordered house, sucking my blood   125
     Stealthily—and all the time I never knew
     That these two sisters were aiming at my throne!

Ismenê,

    Do you confess your share in this crime, or deny it?
    Answer me.

Ismenê: Yes, if she will let me say so. I am guilty.   130

Antigonê (coldly): No, Ismenê. You have no right to say so.
    You would not help me, and I will not have you help me.

Ismenê: But now I know what you meant; and I am here
    To join you, to take my share of punishment.

Antigonê: The dead man and the gods who rule the dead   135
    Know whose act this was. Words are not friends.

Ismenê: Do you refuse me, Antigonê? I want to die with you:
    I too have a duty that I must discharge to the dead.

Antigonê: You shall not lessen my death by sharing it.

Ismenê: What do I care for life when you are dead?   140

Antigonê: Ask Creon. You're always hanging on his opinions.

Ismenê: You are laughing at me. Why, Antigonê?

Antigonê: It's a joyless laughter, Ismenê.

Ismenê: But can I do nothing?

Antigonê: Yes. Save yourself. I shall not envy you.
    There are those who will praise you; I shall have honor, too.   145

Ismenê: But we are equally guilty!

Antigonê: No more, Ismenê.
    You are alive, but I belong to Death.

Creon (to the Chorus): Gentlemen, I beg you to observe these girls:
    One has just now lost her mind; the other,
    It seems, has never had a mind at all.   150

Ismenê: Grief teaches the steadiest minds to waver, King.

Creon: Yours certainly did, when you assumed guilt with the guilty!

Ismenê: But how could I go on living without her?

Creon: You are.
    She is already dead.

Ismenê: But your own son's bride!

Creon: There are places enough for him to push his plow.   155
    I want no wicked women for my sons!

Ismenê: O dearest Haimon, how your father wrongs you!

Creon: I've had enough of your childish talk of marriage!

Choragos: Do you really intend to steal this girl from your son?

Creon: No; Death will do that for me.

Choragos: Then she must die?   160

Creon (ironically): You dazzle me.
                   —But enough of this talk!
    (*To Guards.*) You, there, take them away and guard them well:
    For they are but women, and even brave men run
    When they see Death coming.

    Exeunt Ismenê, Antigonê, and Guards.

ODE II

Chorus: Fortunate is the man who has never tasted God's vengeance!
    Where once the anger of heaven has struck, that house is shaken
    For ever: damnation rises behind each child
    Like a wave cresting out of the black northeast,
    When the long darkness under sea roars up   5
    And bursts drumming death upon the windwhipped sand.

Antistrophe 1

    I have seen this gathering sorrow from time long past
    Loom upon Oedipus' children: generation from generation
    Takes the compulsive rage of the enemy god.
    So lately this last flower of Oedipus' line   10
    Drank the sunlight! but now a passionate word
    And a handful of dust have closed up all its beauty.

Strophe 2

        What mortal arrogance
        Transcends the wrath of Zeus?
    Sleep cannot lull him nor the effortless long months   15
    Of the timeless gods: but he is young for ever,
    And his house is the shining day of high Olympos.
        All that is and shall be,
        And all the past, is his.
    No pride on earth is free of the curse of heaven.   20

Antistrophe 2

        The straying dreams of men
        May bring them ghosts of joy:
    But as they drowse, the waking embers burn them;
    Or they walk with fixed eyes, as blind men walk.
    But the ancient wisdom speaks for our own time: 25
        Fate works most for woe
        With Folly's fairest show.
    Man's little pleasure is the spring of sorrow.

SCENE III

Choragos: But here is Haimon, King, the last of all your sons.
    Is it grief for Antigonê that brings him here,
    And bitterness at being robbed of his bride?

    Enter Haimon.

Creon: We shall soon see, and no need of diviners.

                  —Son,

You have heard my final judgment on that girl: 5
Have you come here hating me, or have you come
With deference and with love, whatever I do?
Haimon: I am your son, father. You are my guide.
You make things clear for me, and I obey you.
No marriage means more to me than your continuing wisdom.   10
Creon: Good. That is the way to behave: subordinate
Everything else, my son, to your father's will.
This is what a man prays for, that he may get
Sons attentive and dutiful in his house,
Each one hating his father's enemies,   15
Honoring his father's friends. But if his sons
Fail him, if they turn out unprofitably,
What has he fathered but trouble for himself
And amusement for the malicious?

                             So you are right
Not to lose your head over this woman.   20
Your pleasure with her would soon grow cold, Haimon,
And then you'd have a hellcat in bed and elsewhere.
Let her find her husband in Hell!
Of all the people in this city, only she
Has had contempt for my law and broken it.   25

Do you want me to show myself weak before the people?
Or to break my sworn word? No, and I will not.
The woman dies.
I suppose she'll plead "family ties." Well, let her.
If I permit my own family to rebel,   30
How shall I earn the world's obedience?
Show me the man who keeps his house in hand,
He's fit for public authority.

                         I'll have no dealings
With law-breakers, critics of the government:
Whoever is chosen to govern should be obeyed—   35
Must be obeyed, in all things, great and small,
Just and unjust! O Haimon,
The man who knows how to obey, and that man only,
Knows how to give commands when the time comes.
You can depend on him, no matter how fast   40
The spears come: he's a good soldier, he'll stick it out.

Anarchy, anarchy! Show me a greater evil!
This is why cities tumble and the great houses rain down,
This is what scatters armies!

No, no: good lives are made so by discipline.   45
We keep the laws then, and the lawmakers,

And no woman shall seduce us. If we must lose,
    Let's lose to a man, at least! Is a woman stronger than we?
Choragos: Unless time has rusted my wits,
    What you say, King, is said with point and dignity.   50
Haimon (boyishly earnest): Father:
    Reason is God's crowning gift to man, and you are right
    To warn me against losing mine. I cannot say—
    I hope that I shall never want to say!—that you
    Have reasoned badly. Yet there are other men   55
    Who can reason, too; and their opinions might be helpful.
    You are not in a position to know everything
    That people say or do, or what they feel:
    Your temper terrifies them—everyone
    Will tell you only what you like to hear.   60
    But I, at any rate, can listen; and I have heard them
    Muttering and whispering in the dark about this girl.
    They say no woman has ever, so unreasonably,
    Died so shameful a death for a generous act:
    "She covered her brother's body. Is this indecent?   65
    She kept him from dogs and vultures. Is this a crime?
    Death?—She should have all the honor that we can give her!"

    This is the way they talk out there in the city.

    You must believe me:
    Nothing is closer to me than your happiness.   70
    What could be closer? Must not any son
    Value his father's fortune as his father does his?
    I beg you, do not be unchangeable:
    Do not believe that you alone can be right.
    The man who thinks that,   75
    The man who maintains that only he has the power
    To reason correctly, the gift to speak, the soul—
    A man like that, when you know him, turns out empty.

    It is not reason never to yield to reason!

    In flood time you can see how some trees bend,   80
    And because they bend, even their twigs are safe,
    While stubborn trees are torn up, roots and all.
    And the same thing happens in sailing:
    Make your sheet fast, never slacken,—and over you go,
    Head over heels and under: and there's your voyage.   85
    Forget you are angry! Let yourself be moved!
    I know I am young; but please let me say this:
    The ideal condition
    Would be, I admit, that men should be right by instinct;
    But since we are all too likely to go astray,   90

The reasonable thing is to learn from those who can teach.
Choragos: You will do well to listen to him, King,
  If what he says is sensible. And you, Haimon,
  Must listen to your father.—Both speak well.
Creon: You consider it right for a man of my years and experience   95
  To go to school to a boy?
Haimon: It is not right,
  If I am wrong. But if I am young, and right,
  What does my age matter?
Creon: You think it right to stand up for an anarchist?
Haimon: Not at all. I pay no respect to criminals.   100
Creon: Then she is not a criminal?
Haimon: The City would deny it, to a man.
Creon: And the City proposes to teach me how to rule?
Haimon: Ah. Who is it that's talking like a boy now?
Creon: My voice is the one voice giving orders in this City!   105
Haimon: It is no City if it takes orders from one voice.
Creon: The State is the King!
Haimon: Yes, if the State is a desert.

  Pause.

Creon: This boy, it seems, has sold out to a woman.
Haimon: If you are a woman: my concern is only for you.
Creon: So? Your "concern"! In a public brawl with your father!   110
Haimon: How about you, in a public brawl with justice?
Creon: With justice, when all that I do is within my rights?
Haimon: You have no right to trample on God's right.
Creon (completely out of control): Fool, adolescent fool! Taken in by a woman!
Haimon: You'll never see me taken in by anything vile.   115
Creon: Every word you say is for her!
Haimon (quietly, darkly):   And for you.
  And for me. And for the gods under the earth.
Creon: You'll never marry her while she lives.
Haimon: Then she must die.—But her death will cause another.
Creon: Another?   120
  Have you lost your senses? Is this an open threat?
Haimon: There is no threat in speaking to emptiness.
Creon: I swear you'll regret this superior tone of yours!
  You are the empty one!
Haimon: If you were not my father,
  I'd say you were perverse.   125
Creon: You girl-struck fool, don't play at words with me!
Haimon: I am sorry. You prefer silence.
Creon: Now, by God—!
  I swear, by all the gods in heaven above us,
  You'll watch it, I swear you shall!

(*To the Servants.*)   Bring her out!
    Bring the woman out! Let her die before his eyes!   130
    Here, this instant, with her bridegroom beside her!
Haimon: Not here, no; she will not die here, King.
    And you will never see my face again.
    Go on raving as long as you've a friend to endure you.

    Exit Haimon.

Choragos: Gone, gone.   135
    Creon, a young man in a rage is dangerous!
Creon: Let him do, or dream to do, more than a man can.
    He shall not save these girls from death.
Choragos: These girls?
    You have sentenced them both?
Creon: No, you are right.
    I will not kill the one whose hands are clean.   140
Choragos: But Antigonê?
Creon (*somberly*):   I will carry her far away
    Out there in the wilderness, and lock her
    Living in a vault of stone. She shall have food,
    As the custom is, to absolve the State of her death.
    And there let her pray to the gods of hell: 145
    They are her only gods:
    Perhaps they will show her an escape from death,
    Or she may learn,
             though late,
    That piety shown the dead is pity in vain.

    Exit Creon.

Ode III

                                          Strophe

Chorus: Love, unconquerable
    Waster of rich men, keeper
    Of warm lights and all-night vigil
    In the soft face of a girl:
    Sea-wanderer, forest-visitor!   5
    Even the pure Immortals cannot escape you,
    And mortal man, in his one day's dusk,
    Trembles before your glory.

                                      Antistrophe

    Surely you swerve upon ruin
    The just man's consenting heart,
    As here you have made bright anger   10
    Strike between father and son—
    And none has conquered but Love!

A girl's glánce wórking the will of heaven:
Pleasure to her alone who mocks us,   15
Merciless Aphroditê.°

SCENE IV

Choragos (*as Antigonê enters guarded*):
    But I can no longer stand in awe of this,
    Nor, seeing what I see, keep back my tears.
    Here is Antigonê, passing to that chamber
    Where all find sleep at last.

Strophe 1

Antigonê: Look upon me, friends, and pity me   5
    Turning back at the night's edge to say
    Good-by to the sun that shines for me no longer;
    Now sleepy Death
    Summons me down to Acheron,° that cold shore:
    There is no bridesong there, nor any music.   10
Chorus: Yet not unpraised, not without a kind of honor,
    You walk at last into the underworld;
    Untouched by sickness, broken by no sword.
    What woman has ever found your way to death?

Antistrophe 1

Antigonê: How often I have heard the story of Niobê,°   15
    Tantalos' wretched daughter, how the stone
    Clung fast about her, ivy-close: and they say
    The rain falls endlessly
    And sifting soft snow; her tears are never done.
    I feel the loneliness of her death in mine.   20
Chorus: But she was born of heaven, and you
    Are woman, woman-born. If her death is yours,
    A mortal woman's, is this not for you
    Glory in our world and in the world beyond?

Strophe 2

Antigonê: You laugh at me. Ah, friends, friends,   25
    Can you not wait until I am dead? O Thebes,
    O men many-charioted, in love with Fortune,
    Dear springs of Dircê, sacred Theban grove,
    Be witnesses for me, denied all pity,
    Unjustly judged! and think a word of love   30
    For her whose path turns

16 *Aphroditê:* goddess of love and beauty.   9 *Acheron:* river in Hades, domain of the dead.
15 *story of Niobê:* in which this mother, when her fourteen children were slain, wept so copi-
ously that she was transformed to a stone on Mount Sipylos. Her tears became the mountain's
streams.

Under dark earth, where there are no more tears.
Chorus: You have passed beyond human daring and come at last
    Into a place of stone where Justice sits.
    I cannot tell   35
    What shape of your father's guilt appears in this.

Antistrophe 2

Antigonê: You have touched it at last: that bridal bed
    Unspeakable, horror of son and mother mingling:
    Their crime, infection of all our family!
    O Oedipus, father and brother!   40
    Your marriage strikes from the grave to murder mine.
    I have been a stranger here in my own land:
    All my life
    The blasphemy of my birth has followed me.
Chorus: Reverence is a virtue, but strength   45
    Lives in established law: that must prevail.
    You have made your choice,
    Your death is the doing of your conscious hand.

Epode°

Antigonê: Then let me go, since all your words are bitter,
    And the very light of the sun is cold to me.   50
    Lead me to my vigil, where I must have
    Neither love nor lamentation; no song, but silence.

    Creon interrupts impatiently.

Creon: If dirges and planned lamentations could put off death,
    Men would be singing for ever.
    (*To the Servants.*)   Take her, go!
    You know your orders: take her to the vault   55
    And leave her alone there. And if she lives or dies,
    That's her affair, not ours: our hands are clean.
Antigonê: O tomb, vaulted bride-bed in eternal rock,
    Soon I shall be with my own again
    Where Persephonê° welcomes the thin ghosts underground: 60
    And I shall see my father again, and you, mother,
    And dearest Polyneicês—
                         dearest indeed
    To me, since it was my hand
    That washed him clean and poured the ritual wine:
    And my reward is death before my time!   65

    And yet, as men's hearts know, I have done no wrong,

---

48 *Epode:* the final section (after the strophe and antistrophe) of a lyric passage; whereas the earlier sections are symmetrical, it takes a different metrical form. 60 *Persephonê:* whom Pluto, god of the underworld, abducted to be his queen. (See D. H. Lawrence's poem "Bavarian Gentians," page 922.)

I have not sinned before God. Or if I have,
I shall know the truth in death. But if the guilt
Lies upon Creon who judged me, then, I pray,
May his punishment equal my own.
Choragos: O passionate heart,   70
Unyielding, tormented still by the same winds!
Creon: Her guards shall have good cause to regret their delaying.
Antigonê: Ah! That voice is like the voice of death!
Creon: I can give you no reason to think you are mistaken.
Antigonê: Thebes, and you my fathers' gods,   75
And rulers of Thebes, you see me now, the last
Unhappy daughter of a line of kings,
Your kings, led away to death. You will remember
What things I suffer, and at what men's hands,
Because I would not transgress the laws of heaven.   80
(*To the Guards, simply.*) Come: let us wait no longer.

Exit Antigonê, left, guarded.

ODE IV

Strophe 1

Chorus: All Danaê's beauty was locked away
In a brazen cell where the sunlight could not come:
A small room still as any grave, enclosed her.
Yet she was a princess too,
And Zeus in a rain of gold poured love upon her.°   5
O child, child,
No power in wealth or war
Or tough sea-blackened ships
Can prevail against untiring Destiny!

Antistrophe 1

And Dryas' son° also, that furious king,   10
Bore the god's prisoning anger for his pride:
Sealed up by Dionysos in deaf stone,
His madness died among echoes.
So at the last he learned what dreadful power
His tongue had mocked: 15
For he had profaned the revels,
And fired the wrath of the nine

1–5 *All Danaê's beauty . . . poured love upon her:* In legend, when an oracle told Acrisius, king of Argos, that his daughter Danaê would bear a son who would grow up to slay him, he locked the princess into a chamber made of bronze, lest any man impregnate her. But Zeus, father of the gods, entered Danaê's prison in a shower of gold. The resultant child, the hero Perseus, was accidentally to fulfill the prophecy by killing Acrisius with an ill-aimed discus throw.
10 *Dryas' son:* King Lycurgus of Thrace, whom Dionysos, god of wine, caused to be stricken with madness.

Implacable Sisters° that love the sound of the flute.

And old men tell a half-remembered tale
Of horror° where a dark ledge splits the sea   20
And a double surf beats on the gráy shóres:
How a king's new woman, sick
With hatred for the queen he had imprisoned,
Ripped out his two sons' eyes with her bloody hands
While grinning Arês° watched the shuttle plunge   25
Four times: four blind wounds crying for revenge,

Crying, tears and blood mingled.—Piteously born,
Those sons whose mother was of heavenly birth!
Her father was the god of the North Wind
And she was cradled by gales,   30
She raced with young colts on the glittering hills
And walked untrammeled in the open light:
But in her marriage deathless Fate found means
To build a tomb like yours for all her joy.

SCENE V

Enter blind Teiresias, led by a boy. The opening speeches of Teiresias should be in singsong contrast to the realistic lines of Creon.

Teiresias: This is the way the blind man comes, Princes, Princes,
    Lockstep, two heads lit by the eyes of one.
Creon: What new thing have you to tell us, old Teiresias?
Teiresias: I have much to tell you: listen to the prophet, Creon.
Creon: I am not aware that I have ever failed to listen.   5
Teiresias: Then you have done wisely, King, and ruled well.
Creon: I admit my debt to you. But what have you to say?
Teiresias: This, Creon: you stand once more on the edge of fate.
Creon: What do you mean? Your words are a kind of dread.
Teiresias: Listen Creon: 10
    I was sitting in my chair of augury, at the place
    Where the birds gather about me. They were all a-chatter,
    As is their habit, when suddenly I heard
    A strange note in their jangling, a scream, a
    Whirring fury; I knew that they were fighting,   15

---

18 *Sisters:* the Muses, nine sister goddesses who presided over poetry and music, arts and sciences.   19–20 *a half-remembered tale of horror:* As the Chorus recalls in the rest of this song, the point of this tale is that being nobly born will not save one from disaster. King Phineas cast off his first wife Cleopatra (not the later Egyptian queen, but the daughter of Boreas, god of the north wind) and imprisoned her in a cave. Out of hatred for Cleopatra, the cruel Eidothea, second wife of the king, blinded her stepsons.   25 *Arês:* god of war, said to gloat over bloodshed.

Tearing each other, dying
In a whirlwind of wings clashing. And I was afraid.
I began the rites of burnt-offering at the altar,
But Hephaistos° failed me: instead of bright flame,
There was only the sputtering slime of the fat thigh-flesh   20
Melting: the entrails dissolved in gray smoke,
The bare bone burst from the welter. And no blaze!

This was a sign from heaven. My boy described it,
Seeing for me as I see for others.

I tell you, Creon, you yourself have brought   25
This new calamity upon us. Our hearths and altars
Are stained with the corruption of dogs and carrion birds
That glut themselves on the corpse of Oedipus' son.
The gods are deaf when we pray to them, their fire
Recoils from our offering, their birds of omen   30
Have no cry of comfort, for they are gorged
With the thick blood of the dead.
                                    O my son,
These are no trifles! Think: all men make mistakes,
But a good man yields when he knows his course is wrong,
And repairs the evil. The only crime is pride.   35

Give in to the dead man, then: do not fight with a corpse—
What glory is it to kill a man who is dead?
Think, I beg you:
It is for your own good that I speak as I do.
You should be able to yield for your own good.   40
Creon: It seems that prophets have made me their especial province.
    All my life long
    I have been a kind of butt for the dull arrows
    Of doddering fortune-tellers!
                        No, Teiresias:
If your birds—if the great eagles of God himself   45
Should carry him stinking bit by bit to heaven,
I would not yield. I am not afraid of pollution:
No man can defile the gods.
                        Do what you will,
Go into business, make money, speculate
In India gold or that synthetic gold from Sardis,   50
Get rich otherwise than by my consent to bury him.
Teiresias, it is a sorry thing when a wise man
Sells his wisdom, lets out his words for hire!
Teiresias: Ah Creon! Is there no man left in the world—

---

19 *Hephaistos*: god of fire.

Creon: To do what?—Come, let's have the aphorism!   55
Teiresias: No man who knows that wisdom outweighs any wealth?
Creon: As surely as bribes are baser than any baseness.
Teiresias: You are sick, Creon! You are deathly sick!
Creon: As you say: it is not my place to challenge a prophet.
Teiresias: Yet you have said my prophecy is for sale.   60
Creon: The generation of prophets has always loved gold.
Teiresias: The generation of kings has always loved brass.
Creon: You forget yourself! You are speaking to your King.
Teiresias: I know it. You are a king because of me.
Creon: You have a certain skill; but you have sold out.   65
Teiresias: King, you will drive me to words that—
Creon: Say them, say them!
     Only remember: I will not pay you for them.
Teiresias: No, you will find them too costly.
Creon: No doubt. Speak:
     Whatever you say, you will not change my will.
Teiresias: Then take this, and take it to heart!   70
     The time is not far off when you shall pay back
     Corpse for corpse, flesh of your own flesh.
     You have thrust the child of this world into living night,
     You have kept from the gods below the child that is theirs:
     The one in a grave before her death, the other,   75
     Dead, denied the grave. This is your crime:
     And the Furies and the dark gods of Hell
     Are swift with terrible punishment for you.

     Do you want to buy me now, Creon?

                                        Not many days,
     And your house will be full of men and women weeping,   80
     And curses will be hurled at you from far
     Cities grieving for sons unburied, left to rot
     Before the walls of Thebes.

     These are my arrows, Creon: they are all for you.

     (*To Boy.*) But come, child: lead me home.   85
     Let him waste his fine anger upon younger men.
     Maybe he will learn at last
     To control a wiser tongue in a better head.

     Exit Teiresias.

Choragos: The old man has gone, King, but his words
     Remain to plague us. I am old, too,   90
     But I cannot remember that he was ever false.
Creon: That is true. . . . It troubles me.
     Oh it is hard to give in! but it is worse

To risk everything for stubborn pride.
Choragos: Creon: take my advice.
Creon: What shall I do?   95
Choragos: Go quickly: free Antigonê from her vault
　　And build a tomb for the body of Polyneicês.
Creon: You would have me do this!
Choragos: Creon, yes!
　　And it must be done at once: God moves
　　Swiftly to cancel the folly of stubborn men.   100
Creon: It is hard to deny the heart! But I
　　Will do it: I will not fight with destiny.
Choragos: You must go yourself, you cannot leave it to others.
Creon: I will go.
　　　　　　—Bring axes, servants:
　　Come with me to the tomb. I buried her, I   105
　　Will set her free.
　　　　　　Oh quickly!
　　My mind misgives—
　　The laws of the gods are mighty, and a man must serve them
　　To the last day of his life!

Exit Creon.

PAEAN°

Strophe 1

Choragos: God of many names
Chorus: O Iacchos
　　　　　　　　　　　son
　　of Kadmeian Sémelê
　　　　　　　　　　O born of the Thunder!
　　Guardian of the West
　　　　　　　　　Regent
　　of Eleusis' plain
　　　　　　　　　O Prince of maenad Thebes
　　and the Dragon Field by rippling Ismenós:°   5

Antistrophe 1

Choragos: God of many names
Chorus: the flame of torches

Paean: a song of praise or prayer, here to Dionysos, god of wine.   1–5 *God of many names . . .*
Dragon Field by rippling Ismenós: Dionysos was also called Iacchos (or, by the Romans, Bacchus).
He was the son of Zeus ("the Thunderer") and of Sémelê, daughter of Kadmos (or Cadmus),
legendary founder of Thebes. "Regent of Eleusis' plain" is another name for Dionysos, honored
in secret rites at Eleusis, a town northwest of Athens. "Prince of maenad Thebes" is yet another: the Maenads were women of Thebes said to worship Dionysos with wild orgiastic rites.
Kadmos, so the story goes, sowed dragon's teeth in a field beside the river Ismenós. Up sprang a
crop of fierce warriors who fought among themselves until only five remained. These victors became the first Thebans.

flares on our hills
                    the nymphs of Iacchos
dance at the spring of Castalia:°
from the vine-close mountain
                              come ah come in ivy:
Evohé evohé!° sings through the streets of Thebes   10

Strophe 2

Choragos: God of many names
Chorus: Iacchos of Thebes
        heavenly Child
                    of Sémelê bride of the Thunderer!
The shadow of plague is upon us:
                                come
with clement feet
                oh come from Parnasos
down the long slopes
                    across the lamenting water   15

Antistrophe 2

Choragos: Iô° Fire! Chorister of the throbbing stars!
    O purest among the voices of the night!
    Thou son of God, blaze for us!
Chorus: Come with choric rapture of circling Maenads
        Who cry *Iô Iacche!*
                    God of many names!   20

ÉXODOS°

Enter Messenger from left.

Messenger: Men of the line of Kadmos, you who live
        Near Amphion's citadel:°
                            I cannot say
Of any condition of human life "This is fixed,
This is clearly good, or bad." Fate raises up,
And Fate casts down the happy and unhappy alike: 5
No man can foretell his Fate.
                            Take the case of Creon:
Creon was happy once, as I count happiness:
Victorious in battle, sole governor of the land,

---

8 *Castalia:* a spring on Mount Parnassus, named for a maiden who drowned herself in it to avoid rape by the god Apollo. She became a nymph, or nature spirit, dwelling in its waters. In the temple of Delphi, at the mountain's foot, priestesses of Dionysos (the "nymphs of Iacchos") used the spring's waters in rites of purification.   10 *Evohé evohé!*: cry of the Maenads in supplicating Dionysos: "Come forth, come forth!"   16 *Iô:* "Hail" or "Praise be to . . ."   *Éxodos:* the final scene, containing the play's resolution.   2 *Amphion's citadel:* a name for Thebes. Amphion, son of Zeus, had built a wall around the city by playing so beautifully on his lyre that the charmed stones leaped into their slots.

Fortunate father of children nobly born.
And now it has all gone from him! Who can say   10
That a man is still alive when his life's joy fails?
He is a walking dead man. Grant him rich,
Let him live like a king in his great house:
If his pleasure is gone, I would not give
So much as the shadow of smoke for all he owns.   15
Choragos: Your words hint at sorrow: what is your news for us?
Messenger: They are dead. The living are guilty of their death.
Choragos: Who is guilty? Who is dead? Speak!
Messenger: Haimon.
Haimon is dead; and the hand that killed him
Is his own hand.
Choragos: His father's? or his own?   20
Messenger: His own, driven mad by the murder his father had done.
Choragos: Teiresias, Teiresias, how clearly you saw it all!
Messenger: This is my news: you must draw what conclusions you can from it.
Choragos: But look: Eurydicê, our Queen:
Has she overheard us?   25

   Enter Eurydicê from the palace, center.

Eurydicê: I have heard something, friends:
As I was unlocking the gate of Pallas'° shrine,
For I needed her help today, I heard a voice
Telling of some new sorrow. And I fainted
There at the temple with all my maidens about me.   30
But speak again: whatever it is, I can bear it:
Grief and I are no strangers.
Messenger: Dearest Lady.
I will tell you plainly all that I have seen.
I shall not try to comfort you: what is the use,
Since comfort could lie only in what is not true?   35
The truth is always best.
                    I went with Creon
To the outer plain where Polyneicês was lying,
No friend to pity him, his body shredded by dogs.
We made our prayers in that place to Hecatê
And Pluto,° that they would be merciful. And we bathed   40
The corpse with holy water, and we brought
Fresh-broken branches to burn what was left of it,
And upon the urn we heaped up a towering barrow
Of the earth of his own land.

---

27 *Pallas:* Pallas Athene, goddess of wisdom, and hence an excellent source of advice.   39–40
Hecatê and Pluto: two fearful divinities—the goddess of witchcraft and sorcery and the king of
Hades, underworld of the dead.

When we were done, we ran
To the vault where Antigonê lay on her couch of stone.   45
One of the servants had gone ahead,
And while he was yet far off he heard a voice
Grieving within the chamber, and he came back
And told Creon. And as the King went closer,
The air was full of wailing, the words lost,   50
And he begged us to make all haste. "Am I a prophet?"
He said, weeping, "And must I walk this road,
The saddest of all that I have gone before?
My son's voice calls me on. Oh quickly, quickly!
Look through the crevice there, and tell me   55
If it is Haimon, or some deception of the gods!"

We obeyed; and in the cavern's farthest corner
We saw her lying:
She had made a noose of her fine linen veil
And hanged herself. Haimon lay beside her,   60
His arms about her waist, lamenting her,
His love lost under ground, crying out
That his father had stolen her away from him.

When Creon saw him the tears rushed to his eyes
And he called to him: "What have you done, child? Speak to me.   65
What are you thinking that makes your eyes so strange?
O my son, my son, I come to you on my knees!"
But Haimon spat in his face. He said not a word,
Staring—
                    And suddenly drew his sword
And lunged. Creon shrank back, the blade missed; and the boy,   70
Desperate against himself, drove it half its length
Into his own side, and fell. And as he died
He gathered Antigonê close in his arms again,
Choking, his blood bright red on her white cheek.
And now he lies dead with the dead, and she is his   75
At last, his bride in the houses of the dead.

Exit Eurydicê into the palace.

Choragos: She has left us without a word. What can this mean?
Messenger: It troubles me, too; yet she knows what is best,
    Her grief is too great for public lamentation,
    And doubtless she has gone to her chamber to weep   80
    For her dead son, leading her maidens in his dirge.
Choragos: It may be so: but I fear this deep silence.

    Pause.

Messenger: I will see what she is doing. I will go in.

Exit Messenger into the palace.

Enter Creon with attendants, bearing Haimon's body.

Choragos: But here is the king himself: oh look at him,
  Bearing his own damnation in his arms.   85
Creon: Nothing you say can touch me any more.
  My own blind heart has brought me
  From darkness to final darkness. Here you see
  The father murdering, the murdered son—
  And all my civic wisdom!   90

  Haimon my son, so young, so young to die,
  I was the fool, not you; and you died for me.
Choragos: That is the truth; but you were late in learning it.
Creon: This truth is hard to bear. Surely a god
  Has crushed me beneath the hugest weight of heaven,   95
  And driven me headlong a barbaric way
  To trample out the thing I held most dear.

  The pains that men will take to come to pain!

Enter Messenger from the palace.

Messenger: The burden you carry in your hands is heavy,
  But it is not all: you will find more in your house.   100
Creon: What burden worse than this shall I find there?
Messenger: The Queen is dead.
Creon: O port of death, deaf world,
  Is there no pity for me? And you, Angel of evil,
  I was dead, and your words are death again.   105
  Is it true, boy? Can it be true?
  Is my wife dead? Has death bred death?
Messenger: You can see for yourself.

The doors are opened and the body of Eurydicê is disclosed within.

Creon: Oh pity!
  All true, all true, and more than I can bear!   110
  O my wife, my son!
Messenger: She stood before the altar, and her heart
  Welcomed the knife her own hand guided,
  And a great cry burst from her lips for Megareus° dead,
  And for Haimon dead, her sons; and her last breath   115
  Was a curse for their father, the murderer of her sons.
  And she fell, and the dark flowed in through her closing eyes.

---

114 *Megareus:* Son of Creon and brother of Haimon, Megareus was slain in the unsuccessful attack upon Thebes.

Creon: O God, I am sick with fear.
　　Are there no swords here? Has no one a blow for me?
Messenger: Her curse is upon you for the deaths of both.　　　　　　　120
Creon: It is right that it should be. I alone am guilty.
　　I know it, and I say it. Lead me in,
　　Quickly, friends.
　　I have neither life nor substance. Lead me in.
Choragos: You are right, if there can be right in so much wrong.　　　125
　　The briefest way is best in a world of sorrow.
Creon: Let it come,
　　Let death come quickly, and be kind to me.
　　I would not ever see the sun again.
Choragos: All that will come when it will; but we, meanwhile,　　　　130
　　Have much to do. Leave the future to itself.
Creon: All my heart was in that prayer!
Choragos: Then do not pray any more: the sky is deaf.
Creon: Lead me away. I have been rash and foolish.
　　I have killed my son and my wife.　　　　　　　　　　　　　　135
　　I look for comfort; my comfort lies here dead.
　　Whatever my hands have touched has come to nothing.
　　Fate has brought all my pride to a thought of dust.

*As Creon is being led into the house, the Choragos advances and speaks directly to the
audience.*

Choragos: There is no happiness where there is no wisdom;
　　No wisdom but in submission to the gods.　　　　　　　　　　140
　　Big words are always punished,
　　And proud men in old age learn to be wise.

Robert Fitzgerald

Robert Fitzgerald on Drama   TRANSLATING SOPHOCLES   1941

The style of Sophocles was smooth. It has been likened by a modern critic to a molten flow of language, fitting and revealing every contour of the meaning, with no words wasted and no words poured on for effect. To approximate such purity I have sought a spare but felicitous manner of speech, not common and not "elevated" either, except by force of natural eloquence. The Greek writer did not disdain plainness when plainness was appropriate—appropriate, that is, both dramatically and within a context of verse very brilliant, mellifluous and powerful. As in every highly inflected language, the Greek order of words was controlled, by its masters, for special purposes of emphasis and even of meaning; and such of these as I have been acute enough to grasp I have tried to bring out by a comparable phrasing or rhythm in English. This I hold to be part of the business of "literal" rendering.

The difficulties involved in translating Greek dialogue are easily tripled when it comes to translating a chorus. Here the ellipses and compressions possible to the inflected idiom are particularly in evidence; and in the chorus, too, the poet concentrates his allusive power. For the modern reader, who has very little "literature" in the sense in which Samuel Johnson° used the term, two out of three allusions in the Greek odes will be meaningless. This is neither surprising nor deplorable. The Roman writer, Ennius,° translating Euripides for a Latin audience two centuries after the Periclean period, found it advisable to omit many place names and to omit or explain many mythological references; and his public had greater reason to be familiar with such things than we have. My handling of this problem has been governed by the general wish to leave nothing in the English that would drive the literate reader to a library.

"Commentary" to Sophocles' The Oedipus Cycle

Samuel Johnson: Johnson (1709–1784) was the great eighteenth century critic, lexicographer, poet, and conversationalist. His definition of *literature* would have referred mostly to the Greek and Latin classics. *Ennius:* Quintus Ennius (239–169 B.C.) was an early Latin epic poet and tragedian. He created Latin versions of the Greek tragic plays, especially those of Euripides.

William Shakespeare

THE TRAGEDY OF HAMLET, PRINCE OF DENMARK 1600?

EDITED BY DAVID BEVINGTON

Kevin Kline as Hamlet

William Shakespeare (1564–1616), whose life is sketched in a note on page 1303, wrote Hamlet *around 1600. The* Hamlet *story first appears in the* Danish History *of the twelfth-century writer Saxo Gramaticus, but the tale is probably even older than that. Saxo's version recounts the murder of the king of Denmark by his wicked brother and the brother's marriage to the widowed queen; then Prince Amlethus, the dead king's son, feigns madness, escapes a plot on his life, and eventually gains revenge. There was an earlier English play (now lost) written in the 1580s. Called* Hamlet, *it was probably written by Thomas Kyd. It is believed that Shakespeare based his own play on it. Although he borrowed his story (as he did the basic plot of* Othello), *Shakespeare made it entirely his own and populated it with some of the most memorable characters in English drama. It is usually assumed that* Hamlet *was the earliest of Shakespeare's four great mature tragedies (being written just before* Othello, King Lear, *and* Macbeth). *If this speculative dating is true,* Hamlet *represented something extraordinarily innovative in world drama, especially in respect to the title character—a deeply intelligent and reflective man compelled by justice and*

Glenn Close as Gertrude

filial duty to avenge his father's murder but simultaneously riddled by self-doubt and moral conscience. In the brooding figure of Hamlet, Shakespeare presented both the prince's inner and exterior life with startling immediacy and mysterious depth. For centuries critics have considered Hamlet *Shakespeare's most philosophical play, yet it does not lack action. Hamlet contains a vengeful ghost, two sorts of madness (one tragically genuine, the other comically feigned), a suicide, sword fights, poisonings, incest, and multiple murders. The play provides both the compelling entertainment beloved of Elizabethan audiences and a tragic meditation on human existence that has haunted readers of every subsequent age.*

Ghost of Hamlet, the former King of Denmark
Claudius, King of Denmark, the former King's brother
Gertrude, Queen of Denmark, widow of the former King and now wife of Claudius
Hamlet, Prince of Denmark, son of the late King and of Gertrude
Polonius, councillor to the King
Laertes, his son
Ophelia, his daughter
Reynaldo, his servant
Horatio, Hamlet's friend and fellow student
Voltimand,
Cornelius,
Rosencrantz,
Guildenstern, } members of the Danish court
Osric,
A Gentleman,
A Lord,
Bernardo,
Francisco, } officers and soldiers on watch
Marcellus,
Fortinbras, Prince of Norway
Captain in his army
Three or Four Players, taking the roles of *Prologue, Player King, Player Queen, and Lucianus*
Two Messengers
First Sailor
Two Clowns, a gravedigger and his companion
Priest
First Ambassador from England
Lords, Soldiers, Attendants, Guards, other Players, Followers of Laertes, other Sailors, another Ambassador or Ambassadors from England

Scene: *Denmark*

ACT I

Scene I [Elsinore Castle. A Guard Platform.]

Enter Bernardo and Francisco, two sentinels, [meeting].

Bernardo: Who's there?
Francisco: Nay, answer me.° Stand and unfold yourself.°
Bernardo: Long live the King!
Francisco: Bernardo?

---

2 *me* (Francisco emphasizes that *he* is the sentry currently on watch.) *unfold yourself* reveal your identity

Bernardo: He.   5

Francisco: You come most carefully upon your hour.

Bernardo: 'Tis now struck twelve. Get thee to bed, Francisco.

Francisco: For this relief much thanks. 'Tis bitter cold,
     And I am sick at heart.

Bernardo: Have you had quiet guard?   10

Francisco: Not a mouse stirring.

Bernardo: Well, good night.
     If you do meet Horatio and Marcellus,
     The rivals° of my watch, bid them make haste.

     Enter Horatio and Marcellus.

Francisco: I think I hear them.—Stand, ho! Who is there?   15

Horatio: Friends to this ground.°

Marcellus: And liegemen to the Dane.°

Francisco: Give° you good night.

Marcellus: O, farewell, honest soldier. Who hath relieved you?

Francisco: Bernardo hath my place. Give you good night.   20

                                                            Exit Francisco.

Marcellus: Holla! Bernardo!

Bernardo: Say, what, is Horatio there?

Horatio: A piece of him.

Bernardo: Welcome, Horatio. Welcome, good Marcellus.

Horatio: What, has this thing appeared again tonight?   25

Bernardo: I have seen nothing.

Marcellus: Horatio says 'tis but our fantasy,°
     And will not let belief take hold of him
     Touching this dreaded sight twice seen of us.
     Therefore I have entreated him along°   30
     With us to watch° the minutes of this night,
     That if again this apparition come
     He may approve° our eyes and speak to it.

Horatio: Tush, tush, 'twill not appear.

Bernardo: Sit down awhile,
     And let us once again assail your ears,   35
     That are so fortified against our story,
     What° we have two nights seen.

Horatio: Well, sit we down,
     And let us hear Bernardo speak of this.

Bernardo: Last night of all,°
     When yond same star that's westward from the pole°   40

---

14 *rivals* partners   16 *ground* country, land   17 *liegemen to the Dane* men sworn to serve the Danish
king   18 *Give* i.e., may God give   27 *fantasy* imagination   30 *along* to come along   31 *watch* keep
watch during   33 *approve* corroborate   37 *What* with what   39 *Last . . . all* i.e., this *very* last night
(Emphatic.)   40 *pole* polestar, north star

Had made his° course t' illume° that part of heaven
Where now it burns, Marcellus and myself,
The bell then beating one—

Enter Ghost.

Marcellus: Peace, break thee off! Look where it comes again!
Bernardo: In the same figure like the King that's dead.   45
Marcellus: Thou art a scholar.° Speak to it, Horatio.
Bernardo: Looks 'a° not like the King? Mark it, Horatio.
Horatio: Most like. It harrows me with fear and wonder.
Bernardo: It would be spoke to.°
Marcellus: Speak to it, Horatio.
Horatio: What are thou that usurp'st° this time of night,   50
    Together with that fair and warlike form
    In which the majesty of buried Denmark°
    Did sometime° march? By heaven, I charge thee, speak!
Marcellus: It is offended.
Bernardo: See, it stalks away.
Horatio: Stay! Speak, speak! I charge thee, speak!   *Exit Ghost.*   55
Marcellus: 'Tis gone and will not answer.
Bernardo: How now, Horatio? You tremble and look pale.
    Is not this something more than fantasy?
    What think you on 't?°
Horatio: Before my God, I might not this believe   60
    Without the sensible° and true avouch°
    Of mine own eyes.
Marcellus: Is it not like the King?
Horatio: As thou art to thyself.
    Such was the very armor he had on
    When he the ambitious Norway° combated.   65
    So frowned he once when, in an angry parle,°
    He smote the sledded° Polacks° on the ice.
    'Tis strange.
Marcellus: Thus twice before, and jump° at this dead hour,
    With martial stalk° hath he gone by our watch.   70
Horatio: In what particular thought to work° I know not,
    But in the gross and scope° of mine opinion
    This bodes some strange eruption to our state.
Marcellus: Good now,° sit down, and tell me, he that knows,

---

41 *his* its. *illume* illuminate   46 *scholar* one learned enough to know how to question a ghost properly   47 *'a* he   49 *It . . . to* (It was commonly believed that a ghost could not speak until spoken
to.)   50 *usurp'st* wrongfully takes over   52 *buried Denmark* the buried King of Denmark   53 *sometime* formerly   59 *on 't* of it   61 *sensible* confirmed by the senses.   *avouch* warrant, evidence
65 *Norway* King of Norway   66 *parle* parley   67 *sledded* traveling on sleds.   *Polacks* Poles   69 *jump*
exactly   70 *stalk* stride   71 *to work* i.e., to collect my thoughts and try to understand this   72 *gross*
and scope general drift   74 *Good now* (An expression denoting entreaty or expostulation.)

Why this same strict and most observant watch   75
So nightly toils° the subject° of the land,
And why such daily cast° of brazen cannon
And foreign mart° for implements of war,
Why such impress° of shipwrights, whose sore task
Does not divide the Sunday from the week.   80
What might be toward,° that this sweaty haste
Doth make the night joint-laborer with the day?
Who is 't that can inform me?
Horatio: That can I;
At least, the whisper goes so. Our last king,
Whose image even but now appeared to us,   85
Was, as you know, by Fortinbras of Norway,
Thereto° pricked° on by a most emulate° pride,
Dared to the combat; in which our valiant Hamlet—
For so this side of our known world° esteemed him—
Did slay this Fortinbras; who by a sealed° compact   90
Well ratified by law and heraldry
Did forfeit, with his life, all those his lands
Which he stood seized° of, to the conqueror;
Against the° which a moiety competent°
Was gagèd° by our king, which had returned°   95
To the inheritance° of Fortinbras
Had he been vanquisher, as, by the same cov'nant°
And carriage of the article designed,°
His fell to Hamlet. Now, sir, young Fortinbras,
Of unimprovèd mettle° hot and full,   100
Hath in the skirts° of Norway here and there
Sharked up° a list° of lawless resolutes°
For food and diet° to some enterprise
That hath a stomach° in 't, which is no other—
As it doth well appear unto our state—   105
But to recover of us, by strong hand
And terms compulsatory, those foresaid lands
So by his father lost. And this, I take it,
Is the main motive of our preparations,

76 *toils* causes to toil. *subject* subjects 77 *cast* casting 78 *mart* buying and selling 79 *impress* impressment, conscription 81 *toward* in preparation 87 *Thereto . . . pride* (Refers to old Fortinbras, not the Danish King.) *pricked on* incited. *emulate* emulous, ambitious 89 *this . . . world* i.e., all Europe, the Western world 90 *sealed* certified, confirmed 93 *seized* possessed 94 *Against the* in return for. *moiety competent* corresponding portion 95 *gagèd* engaged, pledged. *had returned* would have passed 96 *inheritance* possession 97 *cov'nant* i.e., the *sealed compact* of line 90 98 *carriage . . . designed* carrying out of the article or clause drawn up to cover the point 100 *unimprovèd mettle* untried, undisciplined spirits 101 *skirts* outlying regions, outskirts 102 *Sharked up* gathered up, as a shark takes fish. *list* i.e., troop. *resolutes* desperadoes 103 *For food and diet* i.e., they are to serve as *food,* or "means," *to some enterprise;* also they serve in return for the rations they get 104 *stomach* (1) a spirit of daring (2) an appetite that is fed by the *lawless resolutes*

The source of this our watch, and the chief head° 110
Of this posthaste and rummage° in the land.
Bernardo: I think it be no other but e'en so.
Well may it sort° that this portentous figure
Comes armèd through our watch so like the King
That was and is the question° of these wars. 115
Horatio: A mote° it is to trouble the mind's eye.
In the most high and palmy° state of Rome,
A little ere the mightiest Julius fell,
The graves stood tenantless, and the sheeted° dead
Did squeak and gibber in the Roman streets; 120
As° stars with trains° of fire and dews of blood,
Disasters° in the sun; and the moist star°
Upon whose influence Neptune's° empire stands°
Was sick almost to doomsday° with eclipse.
And even the like precurse° of feared events, 125
As harbingers° preceding still° the fates
And prologue to the omen° coming on,
Have heaven and earth together demonstrated
Unto our climatures° and countrymen.

Enter Ghost.

But soft,° behold! Lo, where it comes again! 130
I'll cross° it, though it blast° me. (*It spreads his° arms.*) Stay, illusion!
If thou hast any sound or use of voice,
Speak to me!
If there be any good thing to be done
That may to thee do ease and grace to me, 135
Speak to me!
If thou art privy to° thy country's fate,
Which, happily,° foreknowing may avoid,
O, speak!
Or if thou hast uphoarded in thy life 140
Extorted treasure in the womb of earth,
For which, they say, you spirits oft walk in death,

---

110 *head* source   111 *rummage* bustle, commotion   113 *sort* suit   115 *question* focus of contention   116 *mote* speck of dust   117 *palmy* flourishing   119 *sheeted* shrouded   121 *As* (This abrupt transition suggests that matter is possibly omitted between lines 120 and 121.)   *trains* trails   122 *Disasters* unfavorable signs or aspects.   *moist star* i.e., moon, governing tides   123 *Neptune* god of the sea.   *stands* depends   124 *sick . . . doomsday* (See Matthew 24:29 and Revelation 6:12.)   125 *precurse* heralding, foreshadowing   126 *harbingers* forerunners.   *still* continually   127 *omen* calamitous event   129 *climatures* regions   130 *soft* i.e., enough, break off   131 *cross* stand in its path, confront.   *blast* wither, strike with a curse.   *s.d. his* its   137 *privy to* in on the secret of   138 *happily* haply, perchance

Speak of it! (*The cock crows.*) Stay and speak!—Stop it, Marcellus.
Marcellus: Shall I strike at it with my partisan?°
Horatio: Do, if it will not stand.   [*They strike at it.*]   145
Bernardo: 'Tis here!
Horatio: 'Tis here!   [*Exit Ghost.*]
Marcellus: 'Tis gone.
    We do it wrong, being so majestical,
    To offer it the show of violence,   150
    For it is as the air invulnerable,
    And our vain blows malicious mockery.
Bernardo: It was about to speak when the cock crew.
Horatio: And then it started like a guilty thing
    Upon a fearful summons. I have heard   155
    The cock, that is the trumpet° to the morn,
    Doth with his lofty and shrill-sounding throat
    Awake the god of day, and at his warning,
    Whether in sea or fire, in earth or air,
    Th' extravagant and erring° spirit hies°   160
    To his confine; and of the truth herein
    This present object made probation.°
Marcellus: It faded on the crowing of the cock.
    Some say that ever 'gainst° that season comes
    Wherein our Savior's birth is celebrated,   165
    This bird of dawning singeth all night long,
    And then, they say, no spirit dare stir abroad;
    The nights are wholesome, then no planets strike,°
    No fairy takes,° nor witch hath power to charm,
    So hallowed and so gracious° is that time.   170
Horatio: So have I heard and do in part believe it.
    But, look, the morn in russet mantle clad
    Walks o'er the dew of yon high eastward hill.
    Break we our watch up, and by my advice
    Let us impart what we have seen tonight   175
    Unto young Hamlet; for upon my life,
    This spirit, dumb to us, will speak to him.
    Do you consent we shall acquaint him with it,
    As needful in our loves, fitting our duty?
Marcellus: Let's do 't, I pray, and I this morning know   180
    Where we shall find him most conveniently.
                                                                       Exeunt.

---

144 *partisan* long-handled spear   156 *trumpet* trumpeter   160 *extravagant and erring* wandering beyond bounds. (The words have similar meaning.)   *hies* hastens   162 *probation* proof   164 *'gainst*
just before   168 *strike* destroy by evil influence   169 *takes* bewitches   170 *gracious* full of grace

Scene II [The Castle.]

*Flourish. Enter Claudius, King of Denmark, Gertrude the Queen, [the] Council,
as° Polonius and his son Laertes, Hamlet, cum aliis° [including Voltimand and
Cornelius].*

King: Though yet of Hamlet our° dear brother's death
    The memory be green, and that it us befitted
    To bear our hearts in grief and our whole kingdom
    To be contracted in one brow of woe,
    Yet so far hath discretion fought with nature   5
    That we with wisest sorrow think on him
    Together with remembrance of ourselves.
    Therefore our sometime° sister, now our queen,
    Th' imperial jointress° to this warlike state,
    Have we, as 'twere with a defeated joy—   10
    With an auspicious and a dropping eye,°
    With mirth in funeral and with dirge in marriage,
    In equal scale weighing delight and dole°—
    Taken to wife. Nor have we herein barred
    Your better wisdoms, which have freely gone   15
    With this affair along. For all, our thanks.
    Now follows that you know° young Fortinbras,
    Holding a weak supposal° of our worth,
    Or thinking by our late dear brother's death
    Our state to be disjoint and out of frame,   20
    Co-leaguèd with° this dream of his advantage,°
    He hath not failed to pester us with message
    Importing° the surrender of those lands
    Lost by his father, with all bonds° of law,
    To our most valiant brother. So much for him.   25
    Now for ourself and for this time of meeting.
    Thus much the business is: we have here writ
    To Norway, uncle of young Fortinbras—
    Who, impotent° and bed-rid, scarcely hears
    Of this his nephew's purpose—to suppress   30
    His° further gait° herein, in that the levies,
    The lists, and full proportions are all made

---

s.d. *as* i.e., such as, including.   *cum aliis* with others   1 *our* my. (The royal "we"; also in the following
lines.)   8 *sometime* former   9 *jointress* woman possessing property with her husband   11 *With . . .
eye* with one eye smiling and the other weeping   13 *dole* grief   17 *that you know* what you know already, that; or, that you be informed as follows   18 *weak supposal* low estimate   21 *Co-leaguèd with*
joined to, allied with.   *dream . . . advantage* illusory hope of having the advantage. (His only ally is
this hope.)   23 *Importing* pertaining to   24 *bonds* contracts   29 *impotent* helpless   31 *His* i.e., Fortinbras'.   *gait* proceeding

Out of his subject;° and we here dispatch
You, good Cornelius, and you, Voltimand,
For bearers of this greeting to old Norway,   35
Giving to you no further personal power
To business with the King more than the scope
Of these dilated° articles allow.   [*He gives a paper.*]
Farewell, and let your haste commend your duty.°
Cornelius, Voltimand: In that, and all things, will we show our duty.   40
King: We doubt it nothing.° Heartily farewell.

                        [*Exeunt Voltimand and Cornelius.*]

And now, Laertes, what's the news with you?
You told us of some suit; what is 't, Laertes?
You cannot speak of reason to the Dane°
And lose your voice.° What wouldst thou beg, Laertes,   45
That shall not be my offer, not thy asking?
The head is not more native° to the heart,
The hand more instrumental° to the mouth,
Than is the throne of Denmark to thy father.
What wouldst thou have, Laertes?
Laertes: My dread lord,   50
Your leave and favor° to return to France,
From whence though willingly I came to Denmark
To show my duty in your coronation,
Yet now I must confess, that duty done,
My thoughts and wishes bend again toward France   55
And bow them to your gracious leave and pardon.°
King: Have you your father's leave? What says Polonius?
Polonius: H'ath,° my lord, wrung from me my slow leave
By laborsome petition, and at last
Upon his will I sealed° my hard° consent.   60
I do beseech you, give him leave to go.
King: Take thy fair hour,° Laertes. Time be thine,
And thy best graces spend it at thy will!°
But now, my cousin° Hamlet, and my son—
Hamlet: A little more than kin, and less than kind.°   65

31–33 *in that . . . subject* since the levying of troops and supplies is drawn entirely from the King of
Norway's own subjects   38 *dilated* set out at length   39 *let . . . duty* let your swift obeying of orders,
rather than mere words, express your dutifulness   41 *nothing* not at all   44 *the Dane* the Danish king
45 *lose your voice* waste your speech   47 *native* closely connected, related   48 *instrumental* serviceable
51 *leave and favor* kind permission   56 *bow . . . pardon* entreatingly make a deep bow, asking your
permission to depart   58 *H'ath* he has   60 *sealed* (as if sealing a legal document).   *hard* reluctant
62 *Take thy fair hour* enjoy your time of youth   63 *And . . . will* and may your finest qualities guide
the way you choose to spend your time   64 *cousin* any kin not of the immediate family   65 *A little
. . . kind* i.e., closer than an ordinary nephew (since I am stepson), and yet more separated in natural
feeling (with pun on *kind* meaning "affectionate" and "natural," "lawful." This line is often read as an
aside, but it need not be. The King chooses perhaps not to respond to Hamlet's cryptic and bitter remark.)

King: How is it that the clouds still hang on you?
Hamlet: Not so, my lord. I am too much in the sun.°
Queen: Good Hamlet, cast thy nighted color° off,
    And let thine eye look like a friend on Denmark.°
    Do not forever with thy vailèd lids°   70
    Seek for thy noble father in the dust.
    Thou know'st 'tis common,° all that lives must die,
    Passing through nature to eternity.
Hamlet: Ay, madam, it is common.
Queen: If it be,
    Why seems it so particular° with thee?   75
Hamlet: Seems, madam? Nay, it is. I know not "seems."
    'Tis not alone my inky cloak, good Mother,
    Nor customary° suits of solemn black,
    Nor windy suspiration° of forced breath,
    No, nor the fruitful° river in the eye,   80
    Nor the dejected havior° of the visage,
    Together with all forms, moods,° shapes of grief,
    That can denote me truly. These indeed seem,
    For they are actions that a man might play.
    But I have that within which passes show;   85
    These but the trappings and the suits of woe.
King: 'Tis sweet and commendable in your nature, Hamlet,
    To give these mourning duties to your father.
    But you must know your father lost a father,
    That father lost, lost his, and the survivor bound   90
    In filial obligation for some term
    To do obsequious° sorrow. But to persever°
    In obstinate condolement° is a course
    Of impious stubbornness. 'Tis unmanly grief.
    It shows a will most incorrect to heaven,   95
    A heart unfortified,° a mind impatient,
    An understanding simple° and unschooled.
    For what we know must be and is as common
    As any the most vulgar thing to sense,°
    Why should we in our peevish opposition   100
    Take it to heart? Fie, 'tis a fault to heaven,
    A fault against the dead, a fault to nature,
    To reason most absurd, whose common theme

---

67 *the sun* i.e., the sunshine of the King's royal favor (with pun on *son*)   68 *nighted color* (1) mourning garments of black (2) dark melancholy   69 *Denmark* the King of Denmark   70 *vailèd lids* lowered eyes   72 *common* of universal occurrence. (But Hamlet plays on the sense of "vulgar" in line 74.)   75 *particular* personal   78 *customary* (1) socially conventional (2) habitual with me   79 *suspiration* sighing   80 *fruitful* abundant   81 *havior* expression   82 *moods* outward expression of feeling   92 *obsequious* suited to obsequies or funerals. *persever* persevere   93 *condolement* sorrowing   96 *unfortified* i.e., against adversity   97 *simple* ignorant   99 *As . . . sense* as the most ordinary experience

Is death of fathers, and who still° hath cried,
From the first corpse° till he that died today,   105
"This must be so." We pray you, throw to earth
This unprevailing° woe and think of us
As of a father; for let the world take note,
You are the most immediate° to our throne,
And with no less nobility of love   110
Than that which dearest father bears his son
Do I impart toward° you. For° your intent
In going back to school° in Wittenberg,°
It is most retrograde° to our desire,
And we beseech you bend you° to remain   115
Here in the cheer and comfort of our eye,
Our chiefest courtier, cousin, and our son.
Queen: Let not thy mother lose her prayers, Hamlet.
    I pray thee, stay with us, go not to Wittenberg.
Hamlet: I shall in all my best° obey you, madam.   120
King: Why, 'tis a loving and a fair reply.
    Be as ourself in Denmark. Madam, come.
    This gentle and unforced accord of Hamlet
    Sits smiling to° my heart, in grace° whereof
    No jocund° health that Denmark drinks today   125
    But the great cannon to the clouds shall tell,
    And the King's rouse° the heaven shall bruit again,°
    Respeaking earthly thunder.° Come away.

                            Flourish. Exeunt all but Hamlet.
Hamlet: O, that this too too sullied° flesh would melt,
    Thaw, and resolve itself into a dew!   130
    Or that the Everlasting had not fixed
    His canon° 'gainst self-slaughter! O God, God,
    How weary, stale, flat, and unprofitable
    Seem to me all the uses° of this world!
    Fie on 't, ah fie! 'Tis an unweeded garden   135
    That grows to seed. Things rank and gross in nature
    Possess it merely.° That it should come to this!
    But two months dead—nay, not so much, not two.
    So excellent a king, that was to° this

---

104 *still* always   105 *the first corpse* (Abel's)   107 *unprevailing* unavailing, useless   109 *most imme-diate* next in succession   112 *impart toward* i.e., bestow my affection on.   *For* as for   113 *to school* i.e., to your studies.   *Wittenberg* famous German university founded in 1502   114 *retrograde* con-trary   115 *bend you* incline yourself   120 *in all my best* to the best of my ability   124 *to* i.e., at.   *grace* thanksgiving   125 *jocund* merry   127 *rouse* drinking of a draft of liquor.   *bruit again* loudly echo   128 *thunder* i.e., of trumpet and kettledrum, sounded when the King drinks; see 1.4.8–12   129 *sullied* defiled. (The early quartos read *sallied;* the Folio, *solid.*)   132 *canon* law   134 *all the uses* the whole routine   137 *merely* completely   139 *to* in comparison to

Hyperion° to a satyr,° so loving to my mother   140
That he might not beteem° the winds of heaven
Visit her face too roughly. Heaven and earth,
Must I remember? Why, she would hang on him
As if increase of appetite had grown
By what it fed on, and yet within a month—   145
Let me not think on 't; frailty, thy name is woman!—
A little month, or ere° those shoes were old
With which she followed my poor father's body,
Like Niobe,° all tears, why she, even she—
O God, a beast, that wants discourse of reason,°   150
Would have mourned longer—married with my uncle,
My father's brother, but no more like my father
Than I to Hercules. Within a month,
Ere yet the salt of most unrighteous tears
Had left the flushing in her gallèd° eyes,   155
She married. O, most wicked speed, to post°
With such dexterity to incestuous° sheets!
It is not, nor it cannot come to good.
But break, my heart, for I must hold my tongue.

Enter Horatio, Marcellus, and Bernardo.

Horatio: Hail to your lordship!
Hamlet: I am glad to see you well.   160
    Horatio!—or I do forget myself.
Horatio: The same, my lord, and your poor servant ever.
Hamlet: Sir, my good friend; I'll change that name° with you.
    And what make you from° Wittenberg, Horatio?
    Marcellus.   165
Marcellus: My good lord.
Hamlet: I am very glad to see you. [*To Bernardo.*] Good even, sir.—
    But what in faith make you from Wittenberg?
Horatio: A truant disposition, good my lord.
Hamlet: I would not hear your enemy say so,   170
    Nor shall you do my ear that violence
    To make it truster of your own report
    Against yourself. I know you are no truant.

---

140 *Hyperion* Titan sun-god, father of Helios. *satyr* a lecherous creature of classical mythology, half-human but with a goat's legs, tail, ears, and horns   141 *beteem* allow   147 *or ere* even before   149 *Niobe* Tantalus' daughter, Queen of Thebes, who boasted that she had more sons and daughters than Leto; for this, Apollo and Artemis, children of Leto, slew her fourteen children. She was turned by Zeus into a stone that continually dropped tears.   150 *wants . . . reason* lacks the faculty of reason   155 *gallèd* irritated, inflamed   156 *post* hasten   157 *incestuous* (In Shakespeare's day, the marriage of a man like Claudius to his deceased brother's wife was considered incestuous.)   163 *change that name* i.e., give and receive reciprocally the name of "friend" (rather than talk of "servant")   164 *make you from* are you doing away from

But what is your affair in Elsinore?
We'll teach you to drink deep ere you depart.   175

Horatio: My lord, I came to see your father's funeral.

Hamlet: I prithee, do not mock me, fellow student;
I think it was to see my mother's wedding.

Horatio: Indeed, my lord, it followed hard° upon.

Hamlet: Thrift, thrift, Horatio! The funeral baked meats°   180
Did coldly° furnish forth the marriage tables.
Would I had met my dearest° foe in heaven
Or ever° I had seen that day, Horatio!
My father!—Methinks I see my father.

Horatio: Where, my lord?

Hamlet: In my mind's eye, Horatio.   185

Horatio: I saw him once. 'A° was a goodly king.

Hamlet: 'A was a man. Take him for all in all,
I shall not look upon his like again.

Horatio: My lord, I think I saw him yesternight.

Hamlet: Saw? Who?   190

Horatio: My lord, the King your father.

Hamlet: The King my father?

Horatio: Season your admiration° for a while
With an attent° ear till I may deliver,
Upon the witness of these gentlemen,   195
This marvel to you.

Hamlet: For God's love, let me hear!

Horatio: Two nights together had these gentlemen,
Marcellus and Bernardo, on their watch,
In the dead waste° and middle of the night,
Been thus encountered. A figure like your father,   200
Armèd at point° exactly, cap-à-pie,°
Appears before them, and with solemn march
Goes slow and stately by them. Thrice he walked
By their oppressed and fear-surprisèd eyes
Within his truncheon's° length, whilst they, distilled°   205
Almost to jelly with the act° of fear,
Stand dumb and speak not to him. This to me
In dreadful° secrecy impart they did,
And I with them the third night kept the watch,
Where, as they had delivered, both in time,   210
Form of the thing, each word made true and good,

---

179 *hard* close   180 *baked meats* meat pies   181 *coldly* i.e., as cold leftovers   182 *dearest* closest (and therefore deadliest)   183 *Or ever* before   186 *'A* he   193 *Season your admiration* restrain your astonishment   194 *attent* attentive   199 *dead waste* desolate stillness   201 *at point* correctly in every detail.   *cap-à-pie* from head to foot   205 *truncheon* officer's staff.   *distilled* dissolved   206 *act* action, operation   208 *dreadful* full of dread

The apparition comes. I knew your father;
These hands are not more like.
Hamlet: But where was this?
Marcellus: My lord, upon the platform where we watch.
Hamlet: Did you not speak to it?
Horatio: My lord, I did,   215
But answer made it none. Yet once methought
It lifted up its head and did address
Itself to motion, like as it would speak;°
But even then° the morning cock crew loud,
And at the sound it shrunk in haste away   220
And vanished from our sight.
Hamlet: 'Tis very strange.
Horatio: As I do live, my honored lord, 'tis true,
And we did think it writ down in our duty
To let you know of it.
Hamlet: Indeed, indeed, sirs. But this troubles me.   225
Hold you the watch tonight?
All: We do, my lord.
Hamlet: Armed, say you?
All: Armed, my lord.
Hamlet: From top to toe?
All: My lord, from head to foot.   230
Hamlet: Then saw you not his face?
Horatio: O, yes, my lord, he wore his beaver° up.
Hamlet: What° looked he, frowningly?
Horatio: A countenance more in sorrow than in anger.
Hamlet: Pale or red?   235
Horatio: Nay, very pale.
Hamlet: And fixed his eyes upon you?
Horatio: Most constantly.
Hamlet: I would I had been there.
Horatio: It would have much amazed you.   240
Hamlet: Very like, very like. Stayed it long?
Horatio: While one with moderate haste might tell° a hundred.
Marcellus, Bernardo: Longer, longer.
Horatio: Not when I saw 't.
Hamlet: His beard was grizzled°—no?   245
Horatio: It was, as I have seen it in his life,
A sable silvered.°
Hamlet: I will watch tonight.
Perchance 'twill walk again.

217–218 did . . . speak began to move as though it were about to speak   219 even then at that very instant   232 beaver visor on the helmet   233 What how   242 tell count   245 grizzled gray   247 sable
silvered black mixed with white

Horatio: I warrant° it will.
Hamlet: If it assume my noble father's person,
      I'll speak to it though hell itself should gape   250
      And bid me hold my peace. I pray you all,
      If you have hitherto concealed this sight,
      Let it be tenable° in your silence still,
      And whatsoever else shall hap tonight,
      Give it an understanding but no tongue.   255
      I will requite your loves. So, fare you well.
      Upon the platform twixt eleven and twelve
      I'll visit you.
All: Our duty to your honor.
Hamlet: Your loves, as mine to you. Farewell.

                                        Exeunt [all but Hamlet].

      My father's spirit in arms! All is not well.   260
      I doubt° some foul play. Would the night were come!
      Till then sit still, my soul. Foul deeds will rise,
      Though all the earth o'erwhelm them, to men's eyes.

                                                        Exit.

Scene III [Polonius' Chambers.]

Enter Laertes and Ophelia, his sister.

Laertes: My necessaries are embarked. Farewell.
      And, sister, as the winds give benefit
      And convoy is assistant,° do not sleep
      But let me hear from you.
Ophelia: Do you doubt that?
Laertes: For Hamlet, and the trifling of his favor,   5
      Hold it a fashion and a toy in blood,°
      A violet in the youth of primy° nature,
      Forward,° not permanent, sweet, not lasting,
      The perfume and suppliance° of a minute—
      No more.
Ophelia: No more but so?
Laertes: Think it no more.   10
      For nature crescent° does not grow alone
      In thews° and bulk, but as this temple° waxes
      The inward service of the mind and soul
      Grows wide withal.° Perhaps he loves you now,
      And now no soil° nor cautel° doth besmirch   15

---

248 *warrant* assure you   253 *tenable* held   261 *doubt* suspect   3 *convoy is assistant* means of conveyance are available   6 *toy in blood* passing amorous fancy   7 *primy* in its prime, springtime   8 *Forward* precocious   9 *suppliance* supply, filler   11 *crescent* growing, waxing   12 *thews* bodily strength.   *temple* i.e., body   14 *Grows wide withal* grows along with it   15 *soil* blemish.   *cautel* deceit

The virtue of his will;° but you must fear,
His greatness weighed,° his will is not his own.
For he himself is subject to his birth.
He may not, as unvalued persons do,
Carve° for himself, for on his choice depends   20
The safety and health of this whole state,
And therefore must his choice be circumscribed
Unto the voice and yielding° of that body
Whereof he is the head. Then if he says he loves you,
It fits your wisdom so far to believe it   25
As he in his particular act and place°
May give his saying deed, which is no further
Than the main voice° of Denmark goes withal.°
Then weigh what loss your honor may sustain
If with too credent° ear you list° his songs,   30
Or lose your heart, or your chaste treasure open
To his unmastered importunity.
Fear it, Ophelia, fear it, my dear sister,
And keep you in the rear of your affection,°
Out of the shot and danger of desire.   35
The chariest° maid is prodigal enough
If she unmask° her beauty to the moon.°
Virtue itself scapes not calumnious strokes.
The canker galls° the infants of the spring
Too oft before their buttons° be disclosed,°   40
And in the morn and liquid dew° of youth
Contagious blastments° are most imminent.
Be wary then; best safety lies in fear.
Youth° to itself rebels, though none else near.
Ophelia: I shall the effect of this good lesson keep   45
    As watchman to my heart. But, good my brother,
    Do not, as some ungracious° pastors do,
    Show me the steep and thorny way to heaven,
    Whiles like a puffed° and reckless libertine
    Himself the primrose path of dalliance treads,   50
    And recks° not his own rede.°

    Enter Polonius.

16 *will* desire   17 *His greatness weighed* if you take into account his high position   20 *Carve* i.e.,
choose   23 *voice and yielding* assent, approval   26 *in . . . place* in his particular restricted circumstances   28 *main voice* general assent.   *withal* along with   30 *credent* credulous.   *list* listen to
34 *keep . . . affection* don't advance as far as your affection might lead you. (A military metaphor.)
36 *chariest* most scrupulously modest   37 *If she unmask* if she does no more than show her beauty.
moon (Symbol of chastity.)   39 *canker galls* cankerworm destroys   40 *buttons* buds.   *disclosed*
opened   41 *liquid dew* i.e., time when dew is fresh and bright   42 *blastments* blights   44 *Youth . . .
rebels* youth is inherently rebellious   47 *ungracious* ungodly   49 *puffed* bloated, or swollen with
pride   51 *recks* heeds.   *rede* counsel.

Laertes: O, fear me not.°
   I stay too long. But here my father comes.
   A double° blessing is a double grace;
   Occasion smiles upon a second leave.°
Polonius: Yet here, Laertes? Aboard, aboard, for shame!   55
   The wind sits in the shoulder of your sail,
   And you are stayed for. There—my blessing with thee!
   And these few precepts in thy memory
   Look° thou character.° Give thy thoughts no tongue,
   Nor any unproportioned° thought his° act.   60
   Be thou familiar,° but by no means vulgar.°
   Those friends thou hast, and their adoption tried,°
   Grapple them unto thy soul with hoops of steel,
   But do not dull thy palm° with entertainment
   Of each new-hatched, unfledged courage.° Beware   65
   Of entrance to a quarrel, but being in,
   Bear 't that° th' opposèd may beware of thee.
   Give every man thy ear, but few thy voice;
   Take each man's censure,° but reserve thy judgment.
   Costly thy habit° as thy purse can buy,   70
   But not expressed in fancy;° rich, not gaudy,
   For the apparel oft proclaims the man,
   And they in France of the best rank and station
   Are of a most select and generous chief in that.°
   Neither a borrower nor a lender be,   75
   For loan oft loses both itself and friend,
   And borrowing dulleth edge of husbandry.°
   This above all: to thine own self be true,
   And it must follow, as the night the day,
   Thou canst not then be false to any man.   80
   Farewell. My blessing season° this in thee!
Laertes: Most humbly do I take my leave, my lord.
Polonius: The time invests° you. Go, your servants tend.°
Laertes: Farewell, Ophelia, and remember well
   What I have said to you.   85
Ophelia: 'Tis in my memory locked,
   And you yourself shall keep the key of it.

---

51 *fear me not* don't worry on my account   53 *double* (Laertes has already bid his father good-bye.)
54 *Occasion . . . leave* happy is the circumstance that provides a second leave-taking. The goddess
Occasion, or Opportunity, smiles.)   59 *Look* be sure that.   *character* inscribe   60 *unproportioned*
badly calculated, intemperate.   *his* its   61 *familiar* sociable.   *vulgar* common   62 *and their adoption
tried* and also their suitability for adoption as friends having been tested   64 *dull thy palm* i.e., shake
hands so often as to make the gesture meaningless   65 *courage* young man of spirit   67 *Bear 't that*
manage it so that   69 *censure* opinion, judgment   70 *habit* clothing   71 *fancy* excessive ornament,
decadent fashion   74 *Are . . . that* are of a most refined and well-bred preeminence in choosing what
to wear   77 *husbandry* thrift   81 *season* mature   83 *invests* besieges, presses upon.   *tend* attend, wait

Laertes: Farewell.

Polonius: What is 't, Ophelia, he hath said to you?

Ophelia: So please you, something touching the Lord Hamlet.　　　　90

Polonius: Marry,° well bethought.
　　'Tis told me he hath very oft of late
　　Given private time to you, and you yourself
　　Have of your audience been most free and bounteous.
　　If it be so—as so 'tis put on° me,　　　　95
　　And that in way of caution—I must tell you
　　You do not understand yourself so clearly
　　As it behooves° my daughter and your honor.
　　What is between you? Give me up the truth.

Ophelia: He hath, my lord, of late made many tenders°　　　　100
　　Of his affection to me.

Polonius: Affection? Pooh! You speak like a green girl,
　　Unsifted° in such perilous circumstance.
　　Do you believe his tenders, as you call them?

Ophelia: I do not know, my lord, what I should think.　　　　105

Polonius: Marry, I will teach you. Think yourself a baby
　　That you have ta'en these tenders for true pay
　　Which are not sterling.° Tender° yourself more dearly,
　　Or—not to crack the wind° of the poor phrase,
　　Running it thus—you'll tender me a fool.°　　　　110

Ophelia: My lord, he hath importuned me with love
　　In honorable fashion.°

Polonius: Ay, fashion you may call it. Go to,° go to.

Ophelia: And hath given countenance° to his speech, my lord,
　　With almost all the holy vows of heaven.　　　　115

Polonius: Ay, springes° to catch woodcocks.° I do know,
　　When the blood burns, how prodigal° the soul
　　Lends the tongue vows. These blazes, daughter,
　　Giving more light than heat, extinct in both
　　Even in their promise as it° is a-making,　　　　120
　　You must not take for fire. From this time
　　Be something° scanter of your maiden presence.
　　Set your entreatments° at a higher rate
　　Than a command to parle.° For Lord Hamlet,

---

91 *Marry* i.e., by the Virgin Mary. (A mild oath.)　95 *put on* impressed on, told to　98 *behooves* befits　100 *tenders* offers　103 *Unsifted* i.e., untried　108 *sterling* legal currency.　*Tender* hold, look after, offer　109 *crack the wind* i.e., run it until it is broken-winded　110 *tender me a fool* (1) show yourself to me as a fool (2) show me up as a fool (3) present me with a grand-child. (*Fool* was a term of endearment for a child.)　113 *fashion* mere form, pretense.　*Go to* (An expression of impatience.)　114 *countenance* credit, confirmation　116 *springes* snares.　*woodcocks* birds easily caught; here used to connote gullibility.　117 *prodigal* prodigally　120 *it* i.e., the promise　122 *something* somewhat　123 *entreatments* negotiations for surrender. (A military term.)　124 *parle* discuss terms with the enemy. (Polonius urges his daughter, in the metaphor of military language, not to meet with Hamlet and consider giving in to him merely because he requests an interview.)

Believe so much in him° that he is young,   125
And with a larger tether may he walk
Than may be given you. In few,° Ophelia,
Do not believe his vows, for they are brokers,°
Not of that dye° which their investments° show,
But mere implorators° of unholy suits,   130
Breathing° like sanctified and pious bawds,
The better to beguile. This is for all:°
I would not, in plain terms, from this time forth
Have you so slander° any moment° leisure
As to give words or talk with the Lord Hamlet.   135
Look to 't, I charge you. Come your ways.°
Ophelia: I shall obey, my lord.   *Exeunt.*

Scene IV [The Guard Platform.]

Enter Hamlet, Horatio, and Marcellus.

Hamlet: The air bites shrewdly;° it is very cold.
Horatio: It is a nipping and an eager° air.
Hamlet: What hour now?
Horatio: I think it lacks of° twelve.
Marcellus: No, it is struck.
Horatio: Indeed? I heard it not.
It then draws near the season°   5
Wherein the spirit held his wont° to walk.

A flourish of trumpets, and two pieces° go off [within].

What does this mean, my lord?
Hamlet: The King doth wake° tonight and takes his rouse,°
Keeps wassail,° and the swaggering upspring° reels;°
And as he drains his drafts of Rhenish° down,   10
The kettledrum and trumpet thus bray out
The triumph of his pledge.°
Horatio: Is it a custom?
Hamlet: Ay, marry, is 't,
But to my mind, though I am native here
And to the manner° born, it is a custom   15
More honored in the breach than the observance.°

---

125 *so . . . him* this much concerning him   127 *In few* briefly   128 *brokers* go-between, procurers
129 *dye* color or sort. *investments* clothes. (The vows are not what they seem.)   130 *mere im-*
plorators out and out solicitors   131 *Breathing* speaking   132 *for all* once for all, in sum
134 *slander* abuse, misuse. *moment* moment's   136 *Come your ways* come along   1 *shrewdly*
keenly, sharply   2 *eager* biting   3 *lacks of* is just short of   5 *season* time   6 *held his wont* was accustomed. *s.d. pieces* i.e., of ordnance, cannon   8 *wake* stay awake and hold revel. *takes his rouse*
carouses   9 *wassail* carousal. *upspring* wild German dance. *reels* dances   10 *Rhenish* Rhine wine
12 *The triumph . . . pledge* i.e., his feat in draining the wine in a single draft   15 *manner* custom (of
drinking)   16 *More . . . observance* better neglected than followed

This heavy-headed revel east and west°
Makes us traduced and taxed of° other nations.
They clepe° us drunkards, and with swinish phrase°
Soil our addition;° and indeed it takes   20
From our achievements, though performed at height,°
The pith and marrow of our attribute.°
So, oft it chances in particular men,
That for° some vicious mole of nature° in them,
As in their birth—wherein they are not guilty,   25
Since nature cannot choose his° origin—
By their o'ergrowth of some complexion,°
Oft breaking down the pales° and forts of reason,
Or by some habit that too much o'erleavens°
The form of plausive° manners, that these men,   30
Carrying, I say, the stamp of one defect,
Being nature's livery° or fortune's star,°
His virtues else,° be they as pure as grace,
As infinite as man may undergo,°
Shall in the general censure° take corruption   35
From that particular fault. The dram of evil
Doth all the noble substance often dout
To his own scandal.°

    Enter Ghost.

Horatio: Look, my lord, it comes!
Hamlet: Angels and ministers of grace° defend us!
   Be thou° a spirit of health° or goblin damned,   40
   Bring° with thee airs from heaven or blasts from hell,
   Be thy intents° wicked or charitable,
   Thou com'st in such a questionable° shape
   That I will speak to thee. I'll call thee Hamlet,
   King, father, royal Dane. O, answer me!   45
   Let me not burst in ignorance, but tell
   Why thy canonized° bones, hearsèd° in death,

17 *east and west* i.e., everywhere 18 *taxed of* censured by 19 *clepe* call. *with swinish phrase* i.e., by calling us swine 20 *addition* reputation 21 *at height* outstandingly 22 *The pith . . . attribute* the essence of the reputation that others attribute to us 24 *for* on account of. *mole of nature* natural blemish in one's constitution 26 *his* its 27 *their o'ergrowth . . . complexion* the excessive growth in individuals of some natural trait 28 *pales* palings, fences (as of a fortification) 29 *o'erleavens* induces a change throughout (as yeast works in dough) 30 *plausive* pleasing 32 *nature's livery* sign of one's servitude to nature. *fortune's star* the destiny that chance brings 33 *His virtues else* i.e., the other qualities of *these men* (line 30) 34 *may undergo* can sustain 35 *general censure* general opinion that people have of him 36–38 *The dram . . . scandal* i.e., the small drop of evil blots out or works against the noble substance of the whole and brings it into disrepute. To *dout* is to blot out. (A famous crux.) 39 *ministers of grace* messengers of God 40 *Be thou* whether you are. *spirit of health* good angel 41 *Bring* whether you bring 42 *Be thy intents* whether your intentions are 43 *questionable* inviting question 47 *canonized* buried according to the canons of the church. *hearsèd* coffined

Have burst their cerements;° why the sepulcher
Wherein we saw thee quietly inurned°
Hath oped his ponderous and marble jaws
To cast thee up again. What may this mean,   50
That thou, dead corpse, again in complete steel,°
Revisits thus the glimpses of the moon,°
Making night hideous, and we fools of nature°
So horridly to shake our disposition°   55
With thoughts beyond the reaches of our souls?
Say, why is this? Wherefore? What should we do?

                                         [The Ghost] beckons [Hamlet].

Horatio: It beckons you to go away with it,
  As if it some impartment° did desire
  To you alone.
Marcellus: Look with what courteous action   60
  It wafts you to a more removèd ground.
  But do not go with it.
Horatio: No, by no means.
Hamlet: It will not speak. Then I will follow it.
Horatio: Do not, my lord!
Hamlet: Why, what should be the fear?
  I do not set my life at a pin's fee,°   65
  And for my soul, what can it do to that,
  Being a thing immortal as itself?
  It waves me forth again. I'll follow it.
Horatio: What if it tempt you toward the flood,° my lord,
  Or to the dreadful summit of the cliff   70
  That beetles o'er° his° base into the sea,
  And there assume some other horrible form
  Which might deprive your sovereignty of reason°
  And draw you into madness? Think of it.
  The very place puts toys of desperation,°   75
  Without more motive, into every brain
  That looks so many fathoms to the sea
  And hears it roar beneath.
Hamlet: It wafts me still.—Go on, I'll follow thee.
Marcellus: You shall not go, my lord.   *[They try to stop him.]*
Hamlet: Hold off your hands!   80
Horatio: Be ruled. You shall not go.

---

48 *cerements* grave clothes 49 *inurned* entombed 52 *complete steel* full armor 53 *glimpses of the moon* pale and uncertain moonlight 54 *fools of nature* mere men, limited to natural knowledge and subject to nature 55 *So . . . disposition* to distress our mental composure so violently 59 *impartment* communication 65 *fee* value 69 *flood* sea 71 *beetles o'er* overhangs threateningly (like bushy eyebrows.) 73 *deprive . . . reason* take away the rule of reason over your mind 75 *toys of desperation* fancies of desperate acts, i.e., suicide

Hamlet:　　　　　　　　　　　My fate cries out,°
　　And makes each petty° artery° in this body
　　As hardy as the Nemean lion's° nerve.°
　　Still am I called. Unhand me, gentlemen.
　　By heaven, I'll make a ghost of him that lets° me!　　　　　　　85
　　I say, away!—Go on, I'll follow thee.

　　　　　　　　　　　　　　　　Exeunt Ghost and Hamlet.

Horatio:　He waxes desperate with imagination.
Marcellus:　Let's follow. 'Tis not fit thus to obey him.
Horatio:　Have after.° To what issue° will this come?
Marcellus:　Something is rotten in the state of Denmark.　　　　90
Horatio:　Heaven will direct it.°
Marcellus:　　　　　　　　Nay, let's follow him.　　　*Exeunt.*

Scene V [The Battlements of the Castle.]

Enter Ghost and Hamlet.

Hamlet:　Whither wilt thou lead me? Speak. I'll go no further.
Ghost:　Mark me.
Hamlet:　　　　　I will.
Ghost:　　　　　　　　My hour is almost come,
　　When I to sulfurous and tormenting flames
　　Must render up myself.
Hamlet:　　　　　　　　Alas, poor ghost!
Ghost:　Pity me not, but lend thy serious hearing　　　　　　5
　　To what I shall unfold.
Hamlet:　Speak. I am bound° to hear.
Ghost:　So art thou to revenge, when thou shalt hear.
Hamlet:　What?
Ghost:　I am thy father's spirit,　　　　　　　　　　　　10
　　Doomed for a certain term to walk the night,
　　And for the day confined to fast° in fires,
　　Till the foul crimes° done in my days of nature°
　　Are burnt and purged away. But that° I am forbid
　　To tell the secrets of my prison house,　　　　　　　　15
　　I could a tale unfold whose lightest word
　　Would harrow up° thy soul, freeze thy young blood,
　　Make thy two eyes like stars start from their spheres,°

---

81 My *fate cries out* my destiny summons me　82 *petty* weak.　*artery* (through which the vital spirits were thought to have been conveyed)　83 *Nemean lion* one of the monsters slain by Hercules in his twelve labors.　*nerve* sinew　85 *lets* hinders　89 *Have after* let's go after him.　*issue* outcome　91 *it* i.e., the outcome　7 *bound* (1) ready (2) obligated by duty and fate. (The Ghost, in line 8, answers in the second sense.)　12 *fast* do penance by fasting　13 *crimes* sins.　*of nature* as a mortal　14 *But that* were it not that　17 *harrow up* lacerate, tear　18 *spheres* i.e., eye-sockets, here compared to the orbits or transparent revolving spheres in which, according to Ptolemaic astronomy, the heavenly bodies were fixed

Thy knotted and combinèd locks° to part,
And each particular hair to stand on end   20
Like quills upon the fretful porcupine.
But this eternal blazon° must not be
To ears of flesh and blood. List, list, O, list!
If thou didst ever thy dear father love—
Hamlet: O God!   25
Ghost: Revenge his foul and most unnatural murder.
Hamlet: Murder?
Ghost: Murder most foul, as in the best° it is,
But this most foul, strange, and unnatural.
Hamlet: Haste me to know 't, that I, with wings as swift   30
As meditation or the thoughts of love,
May sweep to my revenge.
Ghost: I find thee apt;
And duller shouldst thou be° than the fat° weed
That roots itself in ease on Lethe° wharf,
Wouldst thou not stir in this. Now, Hamlet, hear.   35
'Tis given out that, sleeping in my orchard,°
A serpent stung me. So the whole ear of Denmark
Is by a forgèd process° of my death
Rankly abused.° But know, thou noble youth,
The serpent that did sting thy father's life   40
Now wears his crown.
Hamlet: O, my prophetic soul! My uncle!
Ghost: Ay, that incestuous, that adulterate° beast,
With witchcraft of his wit, with traitorous gifts°—
O wicked wit and gifts, that have the power   45
So to seduce!—won to his shameful lust
The will of my most seeming-virtuous queen.
O Hamlet, what a falling off was there!
From me, whose love was of that dignity
That it went hand in hand even with the vow°   50
I made to her in marriage, and to decline
Upon a wretch whose natural gifts were poor
To° those of mine!
But virtue, as it° never will be moved,
Though lewdness court it in a shape of heaven,°   55
So lust, though to a radiant angel linked,
Will sate itself in a celestial bed°

---

19 *knotted . . . locks* hair neatly arranged and confined   22 *eternal blazon* revelation of the secrets of
eternity   28 *in the best* even at best   33 *shouldst thou be* you would have to be.   *fat* torpid, lethargic
34 *Lethe* the river of forgetfulness in Hades   36 *orchard* garden   38 *forgèd process* falsified account
39 *abused* deceived   43 *adulterate* adulterous   44 *gifts* (1) talents (2) presents   50 *even with the vow*
with the very vow   53 *To* compared to   54 *virtue, as it* as virtue   55 *shape of heaven* heavenly form
57 *sate . . . bed* cease to find sexual pleasure in a virtuously lawful marriage

And prey on garbage.
But soft, methinks I scent the morning air.
Brief let me be. Sleeping within my orchard,   60
My custom always of the afternoon,
Upon my secure° hour thy uncle stole,
With juice of cursèd hebona° in a vial,
And in the porches of my ears° did pour
The leprous distillment,° whose effect   65
Holds such an enmity with blood of man
That swift as quicksilver it courses through
The natural gates and alleys of the body,
And with a sudden vigor it doth posset°
And curd, like eager° droppings into milk,   70
The thin and wholesome blood. So did it mine,
And a most instant tetter° barked° about,
Most lazar-like,° with vile and loathsome crust,
All my smooth body.
Thus was I, sleeping, by a brother's hand   75
Of life, of crown, of queen at once dispatched,°
Cut off even in the blossom of my sin,
Unhouseled,° disappointed,° unaneled,°
No reckoning° made, but sent to my account
With all my imperfections on my head.   80
O, horrible! O, horrible, most horrible!
If thou hast nature° in thee, bear it not.
Let not the royal bed of Denmark be
A couch for luxury° and damnèd incest.
But, howsoever thou pursues this act,   85
Taint not thy mind nor let thy soul contrive
Against thy mother aught. Leave her to heaven
And to those thorns that in her bosom lodge,
To prick and sting her. Fare thee well at once.
The glowworm shows the matin° to be near,   90
And 'gins to pale his° uneffectual fire.
Adieu, adieu, adieu! Remember me.   [Exit.]
Hamlet: O all you host of heaven! O earth! What else?
         And shall I couple° hell? O, fie! Hold,° hold, my heart,
         And you, my sinews, grow not instant° old,   95

62 *secure* confident, unsuspicious   63 *hebona* a poison. (The word seems to be a form of *ebony*,
though it is thought perhaps to be related to *henbane*, a poison, or to *ebenus*, "yew.")   64 *porches of
my ears* ears as a porch or entrance of the body   65 *leprous distillment* distillation causing leprosylike
disfigurement   69 *posset* coagulate, curdle   70 *eager* sour, acid   72 *tetter* eruption of scabs. *barked*
covered with a rough covering, like bark of a tree   73 *lazar-like* leperlike   76 *dispatched* suddenly de-
prived   78 *Unhouseled* without having received the Sacrament. *disappointed* unready (spiritually)
for the last journey. *unaneled* without having received extreme unction   79 *reckoning* settling of
accounts   82 *nature* i.e., the promptings of a son   84 *luxury* lechery   90 *matin* morning   91 *his* its
94 *couple* add. *Hold* hold together   95 *instant* instantly

But bear me stiffly up. Remember thee?
Ay, thou poor ghost, whiles memory holds a seat
In this distracted globe.° Remember thee?
Yea, from the table° of my memory
I'll wipe away all trivial fond° records,   100
All saws° of books, all forms,° all pressures° past
That youth and observation copied there,
And thy commandment all alone shall live
Within the book and volume of my brain,
Unmixed with baser matter. Yes, by heaven!   105
O most pernicious woman!
O villain, villain, smiling, damnèd villain!
My tables°—meet it is° I set it down
That one may smile, and smile, and be a villain.
At least I am sure it may be so in Denmark.   110

                                              [*Writing.*]

So, uncle, there you are.° Now to my word:
It is "Adieu, adieu! Remember me."
I have sworn 't.

    Enter Horatio and Marcellus.

Horatio: My lord, my lord!
Marcellus: Lord Hamlet!   115
Horatio: Heavens secure him!°
Hamlet: So be it.
Marcellus: Hilo, ho, ho, my lord!
Hamlet: Hillo, ho, ho, boy! Come, bird, come.°
Marcellus: How is 't, my noble lord?   120
Horatio: What news, my lord?
Hamlet: O, wonderful!
Horatio: Good my lord, tell it.
Hamlet: No, you will reveal it.
Horatio: Not I, my lord, by heaven.   125
Marcellus: Nor I, my lord.
Hamlet: How say you, then, would heart of man once° think it?
    But you'll be secret?
Horatio, Marcellus: Ay, by heaven, my lord.
Hamlet: There's never a villain dwelling in all Denmark
    But he's an arrant° knave.   130
Horatio: There needs no ghost, my lord, come from the grave

---

98 *globe* (1) head (2) world   99 *table* tablet, slate   100 *fond* foolish   101 *saws* wise sayings.   *forms* shapes or images copied onto the slate; general ideas.   *pressures* impressions stamped   108 *tables* writing tablets.   *meet it is* it is fitting   111 *there you are* i.e., there, I've written that down against you   116 *secure him* keep him safe   119 *Hillo . . . come* (A falconer's call to a hawk in air. Hamlet mocks the hallooing as though it were a part of hawking.)   127 *once* ever   130 *arrant* thoroughgoing

                    To tell us this.
Hamlet: Why, right, you are in the right.
    And so, without more circumstance° at all,
    I hold it fit that we shake hands and part,
    You as your business and desire shall point you—   135
    For every man hath business and desire,
    Such as it is—and for my own poor part,
    Look you, I'll go pray.
Horatio: These are but wild and whirling words, my lord.
Hamlet: I am sorry they offend you, heartily;   140
    Yes, faith, heartily.
Horatio: There's no offense, my lord.
Hamlet: Yes, by Saint Patrick,° but there is, Horatio,
    And much offense° too. Touching this vision here,
    It is an honest ghost,° that let me tell you.
    For your desire to know what is between us,   145
    O'ermaster 't as you may. And now, good friends,
    As you are friends, scholars, and soldiers,
    Give me one poor request.
Horatio: What is 't, my lord? We will.
Hamlet: Never make known what you have seen tonight.   150
Horatio, Marcellus: My lord, we will not.
Hamlet: Nay, but swear 't.
Horatio: In faith, my lord, not I.°
Marcellus: Nor I, my lord, in faith.
Hamlet: Upon my sword.°   [*He holds out his sword.*]   155
Marcellus: We have sworn, my lord, already.°
Hamlet: Indeed, upon my sword, indeed.
Ghost (*cries under the stage*): Swear.
Hamlet: Ha, ha, boy, sayst thou so? Art thou there, truepenny?°
    Come on, you hear this fellow in the cellarage.   160
    Consent to swear.
Horatio: Propose the oath, my lord.
Hamlet: Never to speak of this that you have seen,
    Swear by my sword.
Ghost [*beneath*]: Swear.   [*They swear.*]°
Hamlet: Hic et ubique?° Then we'll shift our ground.   165

---

133 *circumstance* ceremony, elaboration   142 *Saint Patrick* (The keeper of Purgatory and patron saint of all blunders and confusion.)   143 *offense* (Hamlet deliberately changes Horatio's "no offense taken" to "an offense against all decency.")   144 *an honest ghost* i.e., a real ghost and not an evil spirit   153 *In faith . . . I* i.e., I swear not to tell what I have seen. (Horatio is not refusing to swear.)   155 *sword* i.e., the hilt in the form of a cross   156 *We . . . already* i.e., we swore in faith   159 *truepenny* honest old fellow   164 s.d. *They swear* (Seemingly they swear here, and at lines 170 and 190, as they lay their hands on Hamlet's sword. Triple oaths would have particular force; these three oaths deal with what they have seen, what they have heard, and what they promise about Hamlet's *antic disposition.*)   165 *Hic et ubique* here and everywhere. (Latin.)

Come hither, gentlemen,
And lay your hands again upon my sword.
Swear by my sword
Never to speak of this that you have heard.
Ghost [*beneath*]: Swear by his sword.   [*They swear.*]   170
Hamlet: Well said, old mole. Canst work i' th' earth so fast?
A worthy pioner!°—Once more remove, good friends.

[*He moves again.*]

Horatio: O day and night, but this is wondrous strange!
Hamlet: And therefore as a stranger° give it welcome.
There are more things in heaven and earth, Horatio,   175
Than are dreamt of in your philosophy.°
But come;
Here, as before, never, so help you mercy,°
How strange or odd soe'er I bear myself—
As I perchance hereafter shall think meet   180
To put an antic° disposition on—
That you, at such times seeing me, never shall,
With arms encumbered° thus, or this headshake,
Or by pronouncing of some doubtful phrase
As "Well, we know," or "We could, an if° we would,"   185
Or "If we list° to speak," or "There be, an if they might,"°
Or such ambiguous giving out,° to note°
That you know aught° of me—this do swear,
So grace and mercy at your most need help you.
Ghost [*beneath*]: Swear.   [*They swear.*]   190
Hamlet: Rest, rest, perturbèd spirit! So, gentlemen,
With all my love I do commend me to you;°
And what so poor a man as Hamlet is
May do t' express his love and friending° to you,
God willing, shall not lack.° Let us go in together,   195
And still° your fingers on your lips, I pray.
The time° is out of joint. O cursèd spite°
That ever I was born to set it right!

[*They wait for him to leave first.*]
Nay, come, let's go together.°   *Exeunt.*

---

172 *pioner* foot soldier assigned to dig tunnels and excavations   174 *as a stranger* i.e., needing your
hospitality   176 *your philosophy* this subject called "natural philosophy" or "science" that people
talk about   178 *so help you mercy* as you hope for God's mercy when you are judged   181 *antic* fantastic   183 *encumbered* folded   185 *an if* if   186 *list* wished.   *There . . . might* i.e., there are people
here (we, in fact) who could tell news if we were at liberty to do so   187 *giving out* intimation.
note draw attention to the fact   188 *aught* i.e., something secret   192 *do . . . you* entrust myself to
you   194 *friending* friendliness   195 *lack* be lacking   196 *still* always   197 *The time* the state of affairs.   *spite* i.e., the spite of Fortune   199 *let's go together* (Probably they wait for him to leave first,
but he refuses this ceremoniousness.)

ACT II

Scene I [Polonius' Chambers.]

Enter Old Polonius With His Man [Reynaldo].

Polonius: Give him this money and these notes, Reynaldo.

[*He gives money and papers.*]

Reynaldo: I will, my lord.

Polonius: You shall do marvelous° wisely, good Reynaldo,
    Before you visit him, to make inquire°
    Of his behavior.

Reynaldo: My lord, I did intend it.   5

Polonius: Marry, well said, very well said. Look you, sir,
    Inquire me first what Danskers° are in Paris,
    And how, and who, what means,° and where they keep,°
    What company, at what expense; and finding
    By this encompassment° and drift° of question   10
    That they do know my son, come you more nearer
    Than your particular demands will touch it.°
    Take you,° as 'twere, some distant knowledge of him,
    As thus, "I know his father and his friends,
    And in part him." Do you mark this, Reynaldo?   15

Reynaldo: Ay, very well, my lord.

Polonius: "And in part him, but," you may say, "not well.
    But if 't be he I mean, he's very wild,
    Addicted so and so," and there put on° him
    What forgeries° you please—marry, none so rank°   20
    As may dishonor him, take heed of that,
    But, sir, such wanton,° wild, and usual slips
    As are companions noted and most known
    To youth and liberty.

Reynaldo: As gaming, my lord.   25

Polonius: Ay, or drinking, fencing, swearing,
    Quarreling, drabbing°—you may go so far.

Reynaldo: My lord, that would dishonor him.

Polonius: Faith, no, as you may season° it in the charge.
    You must not put another scandal on him   30
    That he is open to incontinency;°
    That's not my meaning. But breathe his faults so quaintly°
    That they may seem the taints of liberty,°

---

3 *marvelous* marvelously   4 *inquire* inquiry   7 *Danskers* Danes   8 *what means* what wealth (they have). *keep* dwell   10 *encompassment* roundabout talking. *drift* gradual approach or course   11–12 *come . . . it* you will find out more this way than by asking pointed questions (*particular demands*)   13 *Take you* assume, pretend   19 *put on* impute to   20 *forgeries* invented tales. *rank* gross   22 *wanton* sportive, unrestrained   27 *drabbing* whoring   29 *season* temper, soften   31 *incontinency* habitual sexual excess   32 *quaintly* artfully, subtly   33 *taints of liberty* faults resulting from free living

The flash and outbreak of a fiery mind,
A savageness in unreclaimèd blood,   35
Of general assault.°
Reynaldo: But, my good lord—
Polonius: Wherefore should you do this?
Reynaldo: Ay, my lord, I would know that.
Polonius: Marry, sir, here's my drift,   40
    And I believe it is a fetch of warrant.°
    You laying these slight sullies on my son,
    As 'twere a thing a little soiled wi' the working,°
    Mark you,
    Your party in converse,° him you would sound,°   45
    Having ever° seen in the prenominate crimes°
    The youth you breathe° of guilty, be assured
    He closes with you in this consequence:°
    "Good sir," or so, or "friend," or "gentleman,"
    According to the phrase or the addition°   50
    Of man and country.
Reynaldo: Very good, my lord.
Polonius: And then, sir, does 'a this—'a does—
    what was I about to say? By the Mass, I was
    about to say something. Where did I leave?
Reynaldo: At "closes in the consequence."   55
Polonius: At "closes in the consequence," ay, marry.
    He closes thus: "I know the gentleman,
    I saw him yesterday," or "th' other day,"
    Or then, or then, with such or such, "and as you say,
    There was 'a gaming," "there o'ertook in 's rouse,"°   60
    "There falling out° at tennis," or perchance
    "I saw him enter such a house of sale,"
    Videlicet° a brothel, or so forth. See you now,
    Your bait of falsehood takes this carp° of truth;
    And thus do we of wisdom and of reach,°   65
    With windlasses° and with assays of bias,°
    By indirections find directions° out.
    So by my former lecture and advice
    Shall you my son. You have° me, have you not?

35–36 *A savageness . . . assault* a wildness in untamed youth that assails all indiscriminately   41 *fetch of warrant* legitimate trick   43 *soiled wi' the working* soiled by handling while it is being made, i.e., by involvement in the ways of the world   45 *converse* conversation.   *sound* i.e., sound out   46 *Having ever* if he has ever.   *prenominate crimes* before-mentioned offenses   47 *breathe* speak   48 *closes . . . consequence* takes you into his confidence in some fashion, as follows   50 *addition* title   60 *o'ertook in 's rouse* overcome by drink   61 *falling out* quarreling   63 *Videlicet* namely   64 *carp* a fish   65 *reach* capacity, ability   66 *windlasses* i.e., circuitous paths. (Literally, circuits made to head off the game in hunting.)   *assays of bias* attempts through indirection (like the curving path of the bowling ball, which is biased or weighted to one side)   67 *directions* i.e., the way things really are   69 *have* understand

Reynaldo: My lord, I have.
Polonius: God b' wi'° ye; fare ye well.   70
Reynaldo: Good my lord.
Polonius: Observe his inclination in yourself.°
Reynaldo: I shall, my lord.
Polonius: And let him ply his music.
Reynaldo: Well, my lord.   75
Polonius: Farewell.   Exit Reynaldo.

    Enter Ophelia.

                    How now, Ophelia, what's the matter?
Ophelia: O my lord, my lord, I have been so affrighted!
Polonius: With what, i' the name of God?
Ophelia: My lord, as I was sewing in my closet,°
    Lord Hamlet, with his doublet° all unbraced,°   80
    No hat upon his head, his stockings fouled,
    Ungartered, and down-gyvèd° to his ankle,
    Pale as his shirt, his knees knocking each other,
    And with a look so piteous in purport°
    As if he had been loosèd out of hell   85
    To speak of horrors—he comes before me.
Polonius: Mad for thy love?
Ophelia: My lord, I do not know,
    But truly I do fear it.
Polonius: What said he?
Ophelia: He took me by the wrist and held me hard.
    Then goes he to the length of all his arm,   90
    And, with his other hand thus o'er his brow
    He falls to such perusal of my face
    As° 'a would draw it. Long stayed he so.
    At last, a little shaking of mine arm
    And thrice his head thus waving up and down,   95
    He raised a sigh so piteous and profound
    As it did seem to shatter all his bulk°
    And end his being. That done, he lets me go,
    And with his head over his shoulder turned
    He seemed to find his way without his eyes,   100
    For out o' doors he went without their helps,
    And to the last bended their light on me.
Polonius: Come, go with me. I will go seek the King.
    This is the very ecstasy° of love,

---

70 *b' wi'* be with   72 *in yourself* in your own person (as well as by asking questions)   79 *closet* private
chamber   80 *doublet* close-fitting jacket.   *unbraced* unfastened   82 *down-gyvèd* fallen to the ankles
(like gyves or fetters)   84 *in purport* in what it expressed   93 *As* as if (also in line 97)   97 *bulk* body
104 *ecstasy* madness

Whose violent property° fordoes° itself   105
And leads the will to desperate undertakings
As oft as any passion under heaven
That does afflict our natures. I am sorry.
What, have you given him any hard words of late?
Ophelia: No, my good lord, but as you did command   110
I did repel his letters and denied
His access to me.
Polonius: That hath made him mad.
I am sorry that with better heed and judgment
I had not quoted° him. I feared he did but trifle
And meant to wrack° thee. But beshrew my jealousy!°   115
By heaven, it is as proper to our age°
To cast beyond° ourselves in our opinions
As it is common for the younger sort
To lack discretion. Come, go we to the King.
This must be known,° which, being kept close,° might move   120
More grief to hide than hate to utter love.°
Come.   *Exeunt.*

Scene II [The Castle.]

Flourish. Enter King and Queen, Rosencrantz, and Guildenstern [with others].

King: Welcome, dear Rosencrantz and Guildenstern.
Moreover that° we much did long to see you,
The need we have to use you did provoke
Our hasty sending. Something have you heard
Of Hamlet's transformation—so call it,   5
Sith nor° th' exterior nor the inward man
Resembles that° it was. What it should be,
More than his father's death, that thus hath put him
So much from th' understanding of himself,
I cannot dream of. I entreat you both   10
That, being of so young days° brought up with him,
And sith so neighbored to° his youth and havior,°
That you vouchsafe your rest° here in our court
Some little time, so by your companies
To draw him on to pleasures, and to gather   15

---

105 *property* nature. *fordoes* destroys   114 *quoted* observed   115 *wrack* ruin, seduce. *beshrew my jealousy* a plague upon my suspicious nature   116 *proper . . . age* characteristic of us (old) men   117 *cast beyond* overshoot, miscalculate. (A metaphor from hunting.)   120 *known* made known (to the King). *close* secret   120–121 *might . . . love* i.e., might cause more grief (because of what Hamlet might do) by hiding the knowledge of Hamlet's strange behavior to Ophelia than unpleasantness by telling it   2 *Moreover that* besides the fact that   6 *Sith nor* since neither   7 *that* what   11 *of . . . days* from such early youth   12 *And sith so neighbored to* and since you are (or, and since that time you are) intimately acquainted with. *havior* demeanor   13 *vouchsafe your rest* please to stay

So much as from occasion° you may glean,
Whether aught to us unknown afflicts him thus
That, opened,° lies within our remedy.
Queen: Good gentlemen, he hath much talked of you,
And sure I am two men there is not living   20
To whom he more adheres. If it will please you
To show us so much gentry° and good will
As to expend your time with us awhile
For the supply and profit of our hope,°
Your visitation shall receive such thanks   25
As fits a king's remembrance.°
Rosencrantz: Both Your Majesties
Might, by the sovereign power you have of° us,
Put your dread° pleasures more into command
Than to entreaty.
Guildenstern: But we both obey,
And here give up ourselves in the full bent°   30
To lay our service freely at your feet,
To be commanded.
King: Thanks, Rosencrantz and gentle Guildenstern.
Queen: Thanks, Guildenstern and gentle Rosencrantz.
And I beseech you instantly to visit   35
My too much changèd son. Go, some of you,
And bring these gentlemen where Hamlet is.
Guildenstern: Heavens make our presence and our practices°
Pleasant and helpful to him!
Queen: Ay, amen!
          Exeunt Rosencrantz and Guildenstern [*with some attendants*].

          Enter Polonius.

Polonius: Th' ambassadors from Norway, my good lord,   40
Are joyfully returned.
King: Thou still° hast been the father of good news.
Polonius: Have I, my lord? I assure my good liege
I hold° my duty, as° I hold my soul,
Both to my God and to my gracious king;   45
And I do think, or else this brain of mine
Hunts not the trail of policy° so sure
As it hath used to do, that I have found
The very cause of Hamlet's lunacy.

---

16 *occasion* opportunity   18 *opened* being revealed   22 *gentry* courtesy   24 *supply* . . . *hope* aid and
furtherance of what we hope for   26 *As fits* . . . *remembrance* as would be a fitting gift of a king who
rewards true service   27 *of* over   28 *dread* inspiring awe   30 *in* . . . *bent* to the utmost degree of our
capacity. (An archery metaphor.)   38 *practices* doings   42 *still* always   44 *hold* maintain.   *as* as
firmly as   47 *policy* sagacity

King: O, speak of that! That do I long to hear. 50
Polonius: Give first admittance to th' ambassadors.
    My news shall be the fruit° to that great feast.
King: Thyself do grace° to them and bring them in.

[*Exit Polonius.*]

He tells me, my dear Gertrude, he hath found
    The head and source of all your son's distemper. 55
Queen: I doubt° it is no other but the main,°
    His father's death and our o'erhasty marriage.

Enter Ambassadors [*Voltimand and Cornelius, with Polonius*].

King: Well, we shall sift him.°—Welcome, my good friends!
    Say, Voltimand, what from our brother° Norway?
Voltimand: Most fair return of greetings and desires.° 60
    Upon our first,° he sent out to suppress
    His nephew's levies, which to him appeared
    To be a preparation 'gainst the Polack,
    But, better looked into, he truly found
    It was against Your Highness. Whereat grieved 65
    That so his sickness, age, and impotence°
    Was falsely borne in hand,° sends out arrests°
    On Fortinbras, which he, in brief, obeys,
    Receives rebuke from Norway, and in fine°
    Makes vow before his uncle never more 70
    To give th' assay° of arms against Your Majesty.
    Whereon old Norway, overcome with joy,
    Gives him three thousand crowns in annual fee
    And his commission to employ those soldiers,
    So levied as before, against the Polack, 75
    With an entreaty, herein further shown,

[*giving a paper*]

    That it might please you to give quiet pass
    Through your dominions for this enterprise
    On such regards of safety and allowance°
    As therein are set down.
King: It likes° us well, 80
    And at our more considered° time we'll read,
    Answer, and think upon this business.
    Meantime we thank you for your well-took labor.

---

52 *fruit* dessert   53 *grace* honor (punning on *grace* said before a *feast*, line 52)   56 *doubt* fear, suspect.   *main* chief point, principal concern   58 *sift him* question Polonius closely   59 *brother* fellow king   60 *desires* good wishes   61 *Upon our first* at our first words on the business   66 *impotence* helplessness   67 *borne in hand* deluded, taken advantage of.   *arrests* orders to desist   69 *in fine* in conclusion   71 *give th' assay* make trial of strength, challenge   79 *On . . . allowance* i.e., with such considerations for the safety of Denmark and permission for Fortinbras   80 *likes* pleases   81 *considered* suitable for deliberation

Go to your rest; at night we'll feast together.
Most welcome home!   *Exeunt Ambassadors.*
Polonius: This business is well ended.   85
My liege, and madam, to expostulate°
What majesty should be, what duty is,
Why day is day, night night, and time is time,
Were nothing but to waste night, day, and time.
Therefore, since brevity is the soul of wit,°   90
And tediousness the limbs and outward flourishes,
I will be brief. Your noble son is mad.
Mad call I it, for, to define true madness,
What is 't but to be nothing else but mad?
But let that go.
Queen: More matter, with less art.   95
Polonius: Madam, I swear I use no art at all.
That he's mad, 'tis true; 'tis true 'tis pity,
And pity 'tis 'tis true—a foolish figure,°
But farewell it, for I will use no art.
Mad let us grant him, then, and now remains   100
That we find out the cause of this effect,
Or rather say, the cause of this defect,
For this effect defective comes by cause.°
Thus it remains, and the remainder thus.
Perpend.°   105
I have a daughter—have while she is mine—
Who, in her duty and obedience, mark,
Hath given me this. Now gather and surmise.°
[*He reads the letter.*] "To the celestial and my soul's idol, the most beautified
Ophelia"—That's an ill phrase, a vile phrase; "beautified" is a vile phrase.   110
But you shall hear. Thus:

                                                     [*He reads.*]
"In her excellent white bosom,° these,° etc."
Queen: Came this from Hamlet to her?
Polonius: Good madam, stay° awhile, I will be faithful.°

                                                     [*He reads.*]
"Doubt° thou the stars are fire,   115
    Doubt that the sun doth move,
Doubt truth to be a liar,
    But never doubt I love.

---

86 *expostulate* expound, inquire into   90 *wit* sense or judgment   98 *figure* figure of speech   103 *For
. . . cause* i.e., for this defective behavior, this madness, has a cause   105 *Perpend* consider
108 *gather and surmise* draw your own conclusions   112 *In . . . bosom* (The letter is poetically addressed to her heart.)   *these* i.e., the letter   114 *stay* wait.   *faithful* i.e., in reading the letter accurately   115 *Doubt* suspect

O dear Ophelia, I am ill at these numbers.° I have not art to reckon° my
groans. But that I love thee best, O most best, believe it. Adieu. 120
Thine evermore, most dear lady, whilst this machine° is to him, Hamlet."
This in obedience hath my daughter shown me,
And, more above,° hath his solicitings,
As they fell out° by° time, by means, and place,
All given to mine ear.°

King: But how hath she 125
Received his love?
Polonius: What do you think of me?
King: As of a man faithful and honorable.
Polonius: I would fain° prove so. But what might you think,
When I had seen this hot love on the wing—
As I perceived it, I must tell you that, 130
Before my daughter told me—what might you,
Or my dear Majesty your queen here, think,
If I had played the desk or table book,°
Or given my heart a winking,° mute and dumb,
Or looked upon this love with idle sight?° 135
What might you think? No, I went round° to work,
And my young mistress thus I did bespeak:°
"Lord Hamlet is a prince out of thy star;°
This must not be." And then I prescripts° gave her,
That she should lock herself from his resort,° 140
Admit no messengers, receive no tokens.
Which done, she took the fruits of my advice;
And he, repellèd—a short tale to make—
Fell into a sadness, then into a fast,
Thence to a watch,° thence into a weakness, 145
Thence to a lightness,° and by this declension°
Into the madness wherein now he raves,
And all we° mourn for.
King [to the Queen]:   Do you think 'tis this?
Queen: It may be, very like.
Polonius: Hath there been such a time—I would fain know that— 150
That I have positively said "'Tis so,"
When it proved otherwise?
King: Not that I know.

119 ill . . . numbers unskilled at writing verses.   reckon (1) count (2) number metrically, scan
121 machine i.e., body   123 more above moreover   124 fell out occurred.   by according to
125 given . . . ear i.e., told me about   128 fain gladly   133 played . . . table book i.e., remained shut
up, concealing the information   134 given . . . winking closed the eyes of my heart to this   135 with
idle sight complacently or incomprehendingly   136 round roundly, plainly   137 bespeak address
138 out of thy star above your sphere, position   139 prescripts orders   140 his resort his visits
145 watch state of sleeplessness   146 lightness lightheadedness.   declension decline, deterioration
(with a pun on the grammatical sense)   148 all we all of us, or, into everything that we

Polonius: Take this from this,° if this be otherwise.
　　If circumstances lead me, I will find
　　Where truth is hid, though it were hid indeed　　　　　　　　　155
　　Within the center.°
King:　　　　　　　　　How may we try° it further?
Polonius: You know sometimes he walks four hours together
　　Here in the lobby.
Queen:　　　　　　　So he does indeed.
Polonius: At such a time I'll loose° my daughter to him.
　　Be you and I behind an arras° then.　　　　　　　　　　　160
　　Mark the encounter. If he love her not
　　And be not from his reason fall'n thereon,°
　　Let me be no assistant for a state,
　　But keep a farm and carters.°
King:　　　　　　　　　We will try it.

　　Enter Hamlet [reading on a book].

Queen: But look where sadly° the poor wretch comes reading.　　165
Polonius: Away, I do beseech you both, away.
　　I'll board° him presently.° O, give me leave.°
　　　　　　　　　　　Exeunt King and Queen [with attendants].
　　How does my good Lord Hamlet?
Hamlet: Well, God-a-mercy.°
Polonius: Do you know me, my lord?　　　　　　　　　　　　170
Hamlet: Excellent well. You are a fishmonger.°
Polonius: Not I, my lord.
Hamlet: Then I would you were so honest a man.
Polonius: Honest, my lord?
Hamlet: Ay, sir. To be honest, as this world goes, is to be one man picked out of　175
　　ten thousand.
Polonius: That's very true, my lord.
Hamlet: For if the sun breed maggots in a dead dog, being a good kissing
　　carrion°—Have you a daughter?
Polonius: I have, my lord.　　　　　　　　　　　　　　　　180
Hamlet: Let her not walk i' the sun.° Conception° is a blessing, but as your
　　daughter may conceive, friend, look to 't.

---

153 *Take this from this* (The actor probably gestures, indicating that he means his head from his shoulders, or his staff of office or chain from his hands or neck, or something similar.)　156 *center* middle point of the earth (which is also the center of the Ptolemaic universe).　*try* test, judge　159 *loose* (as one might release an animal that is being mated)　160 *arras* hanging, tapestry　162 *thereon* on that account　164 *carters* wagon drivers　165 *sadly* seriously　167 *board* accost.　*presently* at once.　*give me leave* i.e., excuse me, leave me alone. (Said to those he hurries offstage, including the King and Queen.)　169 *God-a-mercy* God have mercy, i.e., thank you　171 *fishmonger* fish merchant　178–179 *a good kissing carrion* i.e., a good piece of flesh for kissing, or for the sun to kiss　181 *i' the sun* in public (with additional implication of the sunshine of princely favors).　*Conception* (1) understanding (2) pregnancy

Polonius [*aside*]: How say you by that? Still harping on my daughter. Yet he knew
    me not at first; 'a° said I was a fishmonger. 'A is far gone. And truly in my
    youth I suffered much extremity for love, very near this. I'll speak to him 185
    again.—What do you read, my lord?
Hamlet: Words, words, words.
Polonius: What is the matter,° my lord?
Hamlet: Between who?
Polonius: I mean, the matter that you read, my lord. 190
Hamlet: Slanders, sir; for the satirical rogue says here that old men have gray
    beards, that their faces are wrinkled, their eyes purging° thick amber° and
    plum-tree gum, and that they have a plentiful lack of wit,° together with
    most weak hams. All which, sir, though I most powerfully and potently be-
    lieve, yet I hold it not honesty° to have it thus set down, for yourself, sir, 195
    shall grow old° as I am, if like a crab you could go backward.
Polonius [*aside*]: Though this be madness, yet there is method in 't.—Will you
    walk out of the air,° my lord?
Hamlet: Into my grave.
Polonius: Indeed, that's out of the air. [*Aside.*] How pregnant° sometimes his 200
    replies are! A happiness° that often madness hits on, which reason and
    sanity could not so prosperously° be delivered of. I will leave him and
    suddenly° contrive the means of meeting between him and my daughter.—
    My honorable lord, I will most humbly take my leave of you.
Hamlet: You cannot, sir, take from me anything that I will more willingly part 205
    withal°—except my life, except my life, except my life.

    Enter Guildenstern and Rosencrantz.

Polonius: Fare you well, my lord.
Hamlet: These tedious old fools!°
Polonius: You go to seek the Lord Hamlet. There he is.
Rosencrantz [*to Polonius*]: God save you, sir! 210
                                       [*Exit Polonius.*]
Guildenstern: My honored lord!
Rosencrantz: My most dear lord!
Hamlet: My excellent good friends! How dost thou, Guildenstern? Ah, Rosen-
    crantz! Good lads, how do you both?
Rosencrantz: As the indifferent° children of the earth. 215
Guildenstern: Happy in that we are not overhappy.
    On Fortune's cap we are not the very button.
Hamlet: Nor the soles of her shoe?

---

184 *'a* he   188 *matter* substance. (But Hamlet plays on the sense of "basis for a dispute.")   192 *purging* discharging. *amber* i.e., resin, like the resinous *plum-tree gum*   193 *wit* understanding   195 *honesty* decency, decorum   196 *old* as old   198 *out of the air* (The open air was considered dangerous for sick people.)   200 *pregnant* quick-witted, full of meaning   201 *happiness* felicity of expression   202 *prosperously* successfully   203 *suddenly* immediately   206 *withal* with   208 *old fools* i.e., old men like Polonius   215 *indifferent* ordinary, at neither extreme of fortune or misfortune

Rosencrantz: Neither, my lord.

Hamlet: Then you live about her waist, or in the middle of her favors?°   220

Guildenstern: Faith, her privates we.°

Hamlet: In the secret parts of Fortune? O, most true, she is a strumpet.° What
    news?

Rosencrantz: None, my lord, but the world's grown honest.

Hamlet: Then is doomsday near. But your news is not true. Let me question   225
    more in particular. What have you, my good friends, deserved at the hands
    of fortune that she sends you to prison hither?

Guildenstern: Prison, my lord?

Hamlet: Denmark's a prison.

Rosencrantz: Then is the world one.   230

Hamlet: A goodly one, in which there are many confines,° wards,° and dun-
    geons, Denmark being one o' the worst.

Rosencrantz: We think not so, my lord.

Hamlet: Why then 'tis none to you, for there is nothing either good or bad but
    thinking makes it so. To me it is a prison.   235

Rosencrantz: Why then, your ambition makes it one. 'Tis too narrow for your
    mind.

Hamlet: O God, I could be bounded in a nutshell and count myself a king of in-
    finite space, were it not that I have bad dreams.

Guildenstern: Which dreams indeed are ambition, for the very substance of the   240
    ambitious° is merely the shadow of a dream.

Hamlet: A dream itself is but a shadow.

Rosencrantz: Truly, and I hold ambition of so airy and light a quality that it is
    but a shadow's shadow.

Hamlet: Then are our beggars bodies,° and our monarchs and outstretched° heroes   245
    the beggars' shadows. Shall we to the court? For, by my fay,° I cannot reason.

Rosencrantz, Guildenstern: We'll wait upon° you.

Hamlet: No such matter. I will not sort° you with the rest of my servants, for, to
    speak to you like an honest man, I am most dreadfully attended.° But, in the
    beaten way° of friendship, what make° you at Elsinore?   250

Rosencrantz: To visit you, my lord, no other occasion.

Hamlet: Beggar that I am, I am even poor in thanks; but I thank you, and sure,
    dear friends, my thanks are too dear a halfpenny.° Were you not sent for? Is

---

220 *favors* i.e., sexual favors   221 *her privates we* i.e., (1) we are sexually intimate with Fortune, the
fickle goddess who bestows her favors indiscriminately (2) we are her private citizens   222 *strumpet*
prostitute. (A common epithet for indiscriminate Fortune; see line 430.)   231 *confines* places of
confinement.   *wards* cells   240–241 *the very . . . ambitious* that seemingly very substantial thing
that the ambitious pursue   245 *bodies* i.e., solid substances rather than shadows (since beggars are
not ambitious).   *outstretched* (1) far-reaching in their ambition (2) elongated as shadows   246 *fay*
faith   247 *wait upon* accompany, attend. (But Hamlet uses the phrase in the sense of providing menial service.)   248 *sort* class, categorize   249 *dreadfully attended* waited upon in slovenly fashion
250 *beaten way* familiar path, tried-and-true course.   *make* do   253 *too dear a halfpenny* (1) too expensive at even a halfpenny, i.e., of little worth (2) too expensive by a halfpenny in return for worthless kindness

it your own inclining? Is it a free° visitation? Come, come, deal justly with
me. Come, come. Nay, speak.   255

Guildenstern: What should we say, my lord?

Hamlet: Anything but to the purpose.° You were sent for, and there is a kind of
confession in your looks which your modesties° have not craft enough to
color.° I know the good King and Queen have sent for you.

Rosencrantz: To what end, my lord?   260

Hamlet: That you must teach me. But let me conjure° you, by the rights of our
fellowship, by the consonancy of our youth,° by the obligation of our ever-
preserved love, and by what more dear a better° prosper could charge° you
withal, be even° and direct with me whether you were sent for or no.

Rosencrantz [aside to Guildenstern]: What say you?   265

Hamlet [aside]: Nay, then, I have an eye of° you.—If you love me, hold not off.°

Guildenstern: My lord, we were sent for.

Hamlet: I will tell you why; so shall my anticipation prevent your discovery,°
and your secrecy to the King and Queen molt no feather.° I have of late—
but wherefore I know not—lost all my mirth, forgone all custom of exer-   270
cises; and indeed it goes so heavily with my disposition that this goodly
frame, the earth, seems to me a sterile promontory; this most excellent
canopy, the air, look you, this brave° o'erhanging firmament, this majestical
roof fretted° with golden fire, why, it appeareth nothing to me but a foul and
pestilent congregation° of vapors. What a piece of work° is a man! How   275
noble in reason, how infinite in faculties, in form and moving how express°
and admirable, in action how like an angel, in apprehension° how like a
god! The beauty of the world, the paragon of animals! And yet, to me, what
is this quintessence° of dust? Man delights not me—no, nor woman neither,
though by your smiling you seem to say so.   280

Rosencrantz: My lord, there was no such stuff in my thoughts.

Hamlet: Why did you laugh, then, when I said man delights not me?

Rosencrantz: To think, my lord, if you delight not in man, what Lenten enter-
tainment° the players shall receive from you. We coted° them on the way,
and hither are they coming to offer you service.   285

Hamlet: He that plays the king shall be welcome; His Majesty shall have
tribute° of° me. The adventurous knight shall use his foil and target,° the

---

254 *free* voluntary   257 *Anything but to the purpose* anything except a straightforward answer. (Said
ironically.)   258 *modesties* sense of shame   259 *color* disguise   261 *conjure* adjure, entreat   262 *the
consonancy of our youth* our closeness in our younger days   263 *better* more skillful.   *charge* urge
264 *even* straight, honest   266 *of* on.   *hold not off* don't hold back   268 *so . . . discovery* in that way
my saying it first will spare you from revealing the truth   269 *molt no feather* i.e., not diminish in the
least   273 *brave* splendid   274 *fretted* adorned (with fretwork, as in a vaulted ceiling)   275 *congregation* mass.   *piece of work* masterpiece   276 *express* well-framed, exact, expressive   277 *apprehension* power of comprehending   279 *quintessence* the fifth essence of ancient philosophy, beyond
earth, water, air, and fire, supposed to be the substance of the heavenly bodies and to be latent i
things   283–284 *Lenten entertainment* meager reception (appropriate to Lent)   284 *coted* overtook
and passed by   287 *tribute* (1) applause (2) homage paid in money.   *of* from.   *foil and target* sword
and shield

lover shall not sigh gratis,° the humorous man° shall end his part in peace,°
the clown shall make those laugh whose lungs are tickle o' the sear,° and the
lady shall say her mind freely, or the blank verse shall halt° for 't. What   290
players are they?

Rosencrantz: Even those you were wont to take such delight in, the tragedians°
of the city.

Hamlet: How chances it they travel? Their residence,° both in reputation and
profit, was better both ways.   295

Rosencrantz: I think their inhibition° comes by the means of the late° innovation.°

Hamlet: Do they hold the same estimation they did when I was in the city? Are
they so followed?

Rosencrantz: No, indeed are they not.

Hamlet: How° comes it? Do they grow rusty?   300

Rosencrantz: Nay, their endeavor keeps° in the wonted° pace. But there is, sir,
an aerie° of children, little eyases,° that cry out on the top of question° and
are most tyrannically° clapped for 't. These are now the fashion, and so
berattle° the common stages°—so they call them—that many wearing rapiers°
are afraid of goose quills° and dare scarce come thither.   305

Hamlet: What, are they children? Who maintains 'em? How are they escoted?°
Will they pursue the quality° no longer than they can sing?° Will they not
say afterwards, if they should grow themselves to common° players—as it is
most like,° if their means are no better°—their writers do them wrong to
make them exclaim against their own succession?°   310

Rosencrantz: Faith, there has been much to-do° on both sides, and the nation
holds it no sin to tar° them to controversy. There was for a while no money
bid for argument unless the poet and the player went to cuffs in the question.°

Hamlet: Is 't possible?

Guildenstern: O, there has been much throwing about of brains.   315

---

288 *gratis* for nothing. *humorous man* eccentric character, dominated by one trait or "humor." *in
peace* i.e., with full license   289 *tickle o' the sear* easy on the trigger, ready to laugh easily. (A *sear* is part
of a gunlock.)   290 *halt* limp   292 *tragedians* actors   294 *residence* remaining in their usual place, i.e.,
in the city   296 *inhibition* formal prohibition (from acting plays in the city). *late* recent. *innovation*
i.e., the new fashion in satirical plays performed by boy actors in the "private" theaters; or possibly a
political uprising; or the strict limitations set on the theaters in London in 1600   300–317 *How* . . .
load too (The passage, omitted from the early quartos, alludes to the so-called War of the Theaters,
1599–1602, the rivalry between the children's companies and the adult actors.)   301 *keeps* continues.
wonted usual   302 *aerie* nest. *eyases* young hawks. *cry . . . question* speak shrilly, dominating the
controversy (in decrying the public theaters)   303 *tyrannically* outrageously   304 *berattle* berate,
clamor against. *common stages* public theaters. *many wearing rapiers* i.e., many men of fashion, afraid
to patronize the common players for fear of being satirized by the poets writing for the boy actors
305 *goose quills* i.e., pens of satirists   306 *escoted* maintained   307 *quality* (acting) profession. *no
longer . . . sing* i.e., only until their voices change   308 *common* regular, adult   309 *like* likely. *if . . .
better* if they find no better way to support themselves   310 *succession* i.e., future careers   311 *to-do*
ado   312 *tar* set on (as dogs)   312–313 *There . . . question* i.e., for a while, no money was offered by
the acting companies to playwrights for the plot to a play unless the satirical poets who wrote for the
boys and the adult actors came to blows in the play itself

WILLIAM SHAKESPEARE: ACT II, SCENE II   **1561**

Hamlet: Do the boys carry it away?°

Rosencrantz: Ay, that they do, my lord—Hercules and his load° too.

Hamlet: It is not very strange; for my uncle is King of Denmark, and those that would make mouths° at him while my father lived give twenty, forty, fifty, a hundred ducats° apiece for his picture in little.° 'Sblood,° there is something 320 in this more than natural, if philosophy° could find it out.

                                 A flourish [of trumpets within].

Guildenstern: There are the players.

Hamlet [to Rosenkrantz and Guildenstern]: Gentlemen, you are welcome to Elsinore. Your hands, come then. Th' appurtenance° of welcome is fashion and ceremony. Let me comply° with you in this garb,° lest my extent° to the 325 players, which, I tell you, must show fairly outwards,° should more appear like entertainment° than yours. You are welcome. But my uncle-father and aunt-mother are deceived.

Guildenstern: In what, my dear lord?

Hamlet: I am but mad north-north-west.° When the wind is southerly I know a 330 hawk° from a handsaw.

    Enter Polonius.

Polonius: Well be with you, gentlemen!

Hamlet: Hark you, Guildenstern, and you too; at each ear a hearer. That great baby you see there is not yet out of his swaddling clouts.°

Rosencrantz: Haply° he is the second time come to them, for they say an old 335 man is twice a child.

Hamlet: I will prophesy he comes to tell me of the players. Mark it.—You say right, sir, o' Monday morning, 'twas then indeed.

Polonius: My lord, I have news to tell you.

Hamlet: My lord, I have news to tell you. When Roscius° was an actor in Rome— 340

Polonius: The actors are come hither, my lord.

Hamlet: Buzz,° buzz!

Polonius: Upon my honor—

Hamlet: Then came each actor on his ass.

Polonius: The best actors in the world, either for tragedy, comedy, history, pas- 345 toral, pastoral-comical, historical-pastoral, tragical-historical, tragical-com-

---

316 *carry it away* i.e., win the day   317 *Hercules . . . load* (Thought to be an allusion to the sign of the Globe Theatre, which was Hercules bearing the world on his shoulders.)   319 *mouths* faces 320 *ducats* gold coins.   *in little* in miniature.   *'Sblood* by God's (Christ's) blood   321 *philosophy* i.e., scientific inquiry   324 *appurtenance* proper accompaniment   325 *comply* observe the formalities of courtesy.   *garb* i.e., manner.   *my extent* that which I extend, i.e., my polite behavior 326–327 *show fairly outwards* show every evidence of cordiality   327 *entertainment* a (warm) reception   330 *north-north-west* just off true north, only partly   331 *hawk, handsaw* i.e., two very different things, though also perhaps meaning a mattock (or *hack*) and a carpenter's cutting tool, respectively; also birds, with a play on *hernshaw*, or heron   334 *swaddling clouts* cloths in which to wrap a newborn baby   335 *Haply* perhaps   340 *Roscius* a famous Roman actor who died in 62 B.C. 342 *Buzz* (An interjection used to denote stale news.)

ical-historical-pastoral, scene individable,° or poem unlimited.° Seneca°
cannot be too heavy, nor Plautus° too light. For the law of writ and the liberty,° these° are the only men.

Hamlet: O Jephthah, judge of Israel,° what a treasure hadst thou! 350

Polonius: What a treasure had he, my lord?

Hamlet: Why,

> "One fair daughter, and no more,
> The which he lovèd passing° well."

Polonius [*aside*]: Still on my daughter. 355

Hamlet: Am I not i' the right, old Jephthah?

Polonius: If you call me Jephthah, my lord, I have a daughter that I love passing
well.

Hamlet: Nay, that follows not.

Polonius: What follows then, my lord? 360

Hamlet: Why,

> "As by lot,° God wot,"°

and then, you know,

> "It came to pass, as most like° it was"—

the first row° of the pious chanson° will show you more, for look where my 365
abridgement° comes.

Enter the Players.

You are welcome, masters; welcome, all. I am glad to see thee well. Welcome, good friends. O, old friend! Why, thy face is valanced° since I saw
thee last. Com'st thou to beard° me in Denmark? What, my young lady° and
mistress! By 'r Lady,° your ladyship is nearer to heaven than when I saw you 370
last, by the altitude of a chopine.° Pray God your voice, like a piece of un-
current° gold, be not cracked within the ring.° Masters, you are all welcome.
We'll e'en to 't° like French falconers, fly at anything we see. We'll have a
speech straight.° Come, give us a taste of your quality.° Come, a passionate
speech. 375

First Player: What speech, my good lord?

Hamlet: I heard thee speak me a speech once, but it was never acted, or if it was,
not above once, for the play, I remember, pleased not the million; 'twas

347 *scene individable* a play observing the unity of place; or perhaps one that is unclassifiable, or performed without intermission.   *poem unlimited* a play disregarding the unities of time and place; one
that is all-inclusive.   *Seneca* writer of Latin tragedies   348 *Plautus* writer of Latin comedy
348–349 *law . . . liberty* dramatic composition both according to the rules and disregarding the
rules   349 *these* i.e., the actors   350 *Jephthah . . . Israel* (Jephthah had to sacrifice his daughter;
see Judges 11. Hamlet goes on to quote from a ballad on the theme.)   354 *passing* surpassingly
362 *lot* chance.   *wot* knows   364 *like* likely, probable   365 *row* stanza.   *chanson* ballad, song
365–366 *my abridgment* something that cuts short my conversation; also, a diversion   368 *valanced*
fringed (with a beard)   369 *beard* confront, challenge (with obvious pun).   *young lady* i.e., boy
playing women's parts   370 *By 'r Lady* by Our Lady   371 *chopine* thick-soled shoe of Italian
fashion   371–372 *uncurrent* not passable as lawful coinage.   *cracked . . . ring* i.e., changed from
adolescent to male voice, no longer suitable for women's roles. (Coins featured rings enclosing the
sovereign's head; if the coin was cracked within this ring, it was unfit for currency.)   373 *e'en to 't*
go at it   374 *straight* at once.   *quality* professional skill

caviar to the general.° But it was—as I received it, and others, whose judgments in such matters cried in the top of° mine—an excellent play, well   380
digested° in the scenes, set down with as much modesty° as cunning.° I remember one said there were no sallets° in the lines to make the matter savory,
nor no matter in the phrase that might indict° the author of affectation, but
called it an honest method, as wholesome as sweet, and by very much more
handsome° than fine.° One speech in 't I chiefly loved: 'twas Aeneas' tale to   385
Dido, and there-about of it especially when he speaks of Priam's slaughter.° If
it live in your memory, begin at this line: let me see, let me see—
"The rugged Pyrrhus,° like th' Hyrcanian beast"°—
'Tis not so. It begins with Pyrrhus:
"The rugged° Pyrrhus, he whose sable° arms,   390
Black as his purpose, did the night resemble
When he lay couchèd° in the ominous horse,°
Hath now this dread and black complexion smeared
With heraldry more dismal.° Head to foot
Now is he total gules,° horridly tricked°   395
With blood of fathers, mothers, daughters, sons,
Baked and impasted° with the parching streets,°
That lend a tyrannous° and a damnèd light
To their lord's° murder. Roasted in wrath and fire,
And thus o'ersizèd° with coagulate gore,   400
With eyes like carbuncles,° the hellish Pyrrhus
Old grandsire Priam seeks."
So proceed you.
Polonius: 'Fore God, my lord, well spoken, with good
accent and good discretion.
First Player: "Anon he finds him   405
Striking too short at Greeks. His antique° sword,
Rebellious to his arm, lies where it falls,
Repugnant° to command. Unequal matched,

379 *caviar to the general* caviar to the multitude, i.e., a choice dish too elegant for coarse tastes
380 *cried in the top of* i.e., spoke with greater authority than   381 *digested* arranged, ordered.   *modesty* moderation, restraint.   *cunning* skill   382 *sallets* i.e., something savory, spicy improprieties
383 *indict* convict   385 *handsome* well-proportioned.   *fine* elaborately ornamented, showy
386 *Priam's slaughter* the slaying of the ruler of Troy, when the Greeks finally took the city
388 *Pyrrhus* a Greek hero in the Trojan War, also known as Neoptolemus, son of Achilles—another
avenging son. *Hyrcanian beast* i.e., tiger. (On the death of Priam, see Virgil, *Aeneid*, 2.506 ff.; compare the whole speech with Marlowe's *Dido Queen of Carthage*, 2.1.214 ff. On the *Hyrcanian tiger*, see
Aeneid, 4.366–367. Hyrcania is on the Caspian Sea.)   390 *rugged* shaggy, savage.   *sable* black (for
reasons of camouflage during the episode of the Trojan horse)   392 *couchèd* concealed.   *ominous
horse* fateful Trojan horse, by which the Greeks gained access to Troy   394 *dismal* ill-omened
395 *total gules* entirely red. (A heraldic term.)   *tricked* spotted and smeared. (Heraldic.)   397 *im-
pasted* crusted, like a thick paste.   *with . . . streets* by the parching heat of the streets (because of the
fires everywhere)   398 *tyrannous* cruel   399 *their lord's* i.e., Priam's   400 *o'ersizèd* covered as with
size or glue   401 *carbuncles* large fiery-red precious stones thought to emit their own light   406 *antique* ancient, long-used   408 *Repugnant* disobedient, resistant

Pyrrhus at Priam drives, in rage strikes wide,
But with the whiff and wind of his fell° sword   410
Th' unnervèd° father falls. Then senseless Ilium,°
Seeming to feel this blow, with flaming top
Stoops to his° base, and with a hideous crash
Takes prisoner Pyrrhus' ear. For, lo! His sword,
Which was declining° on the milky° head   415
Of reverend Priam, seemed i' th' air to stick.
So as a painted° tyrant Pyrrhus stood,
And, like a neutral to his will and matter,°
Did nothing.
But as we often see against° some storm   420
A silence in the heavens, the rack° stand still,
The bold winds speechless, and the orb° below
As hush as death, anon the dreadful thunder
Doth rend the region,° so, after Pyrrhus' pause,
A rousèd vengeance sets him new a-work,   425
And never did the Cyclops'° hammers fall
On Mars's armor forged for proof eterne°
With less remorse° than Pyrrhus' bleeding sword
Now falls on Priam.
Out, out, thou strumpet Fortune! All you gods   430
In general synod° take away her power!
Break all the spokes and fellies° from her wheel,
And bowl the round nave° down the hill of heaven°
As low as to the fiends!"
Polonius: This is too long.   435
Hamlet: It shall to the barber's with your beard.—Prithee, say on. He's
     for a jig° or a tale of bawdry, or he sleeps. Say on; come to Hecuba.°
First Player: "But who, ah woe! had° seen the moblèd° queen"—
Hamlet: "The moblèd queen?"
Polonius: That's good. "Moblèd queen" is good.   440
First Player: "Run barefoot up and down, threat'ning the flames°
     With bisson rheum,° a clout° upon that head
     Where late° the diadem stood, and, for a robe,
     About her lank and all o'erteemèd° loins

---

410 *fell* cruel   411 *unnervèd* strengthless.   *senseless Ilium* inanimate citadel of Troy   413 *his* its
415 *declining* descending.   *milky* white-haired   417 *painted* i.e., painted in a picture   418 *like . . .
matter* i.e., as though suspended between his intention and its fulfillment   420 *against* just before
421 *rack* mass of clouds   422 *orb* globe, earth   424 *region* sky   426 *Cyclops* giant armor makers in
the smithy of Vulcan   427 *proof eterne* eternal resistance to assault   428 *remorse* pity   431 *synod* assembly   432 *fellies* pieces of wood forming the rim of a wheel   433 *nave* hub.   *hill of heaven* Mount
Olympus   437 *jig* comic song and dance often given at the end of a play.   *Hecuba* wife of Priam
438 *who . . . had* anyone who had (also in line 446).   *moblèd* muffled   441 *threat'ning the flames* i.e.,
weeping hard enough to dampen the flames   442 *bisson rheum* blinding tears.   *clout* cloth   443 *late*
lately   444 *all o'erteemèd* utterly worn out with bearing children

A blanket, in the alarm of fear caught up— 445
Who this had seen, with tongue in venom steeped,
'Gainst Fortune's state° would treason have pronounced.°
But if the gods themselves did see her then
When she saw Pyrrhus make malicious sport
In mincing with his sword her husband's limbs, 450
The instant burst of clamor that she made,
Unless things mortal move them not at all,
Would have made milch° the burning eyes of heaven,°
And passion° in the gods."
Polonius: Look whe'er° he has not turned his color and has tears in 's eyes. 455
Prithee, no more.
Hamlet: 'Tis well; I'll have thee speak out the rest of this soon.—Good my lord,
will you see the players well bestowed?° Do you hear, let them be well used,
for they are the abstract° and brief chronicles of the time. After your death
you were better have a bad epitaph than their ill report while you live. 460
Polonius: My lord, I will use them according to their desert.
Hamlet: God's bodikin,° man, much better. Use every man after° his desert, and
who shall scape whipping? Use them after your own honor and dignity. The
less they deserve, the more merit is in your bounty. Take them in.
Polonius: Come, sirs. [*Exit.*] 465
Hamlet: Follow him, friends. We'll hear a play tomorrow. [*As they start to leave,
Hamlet detains the First Player.*] Dost thou hear me, old friend? Can you play
The Murder of Gonzago?
First Player: Ay, my lord.
Hamlet: We'll ha 't° tomorrow night. You could, for a need, study° a speech of some 470
dozen or sixteen lines which I would set down and insert in 't, could you not?
First Player: Ay, my lord.
Hamlet: Very well. Follow that lord, and look you mock him not. (*Exeunt
Players.*)
My good friends, I'll leave you till night. You are welcome to Elsinore.
Rosencrantz: Good my lord! 475

Exeunt [*Rosencrantz and Guildenstern*].

Hamlet: Ay, so, goodbye to you.—Now I am alone.
O, what a rogue and peasant slave am I!
Is it not monstrous that this player here,
But° in a fiction, in a dream of passion,
Could force his soul so to his own conceit° 480

---

447 *state* rule, managing. *pronounced* proclaimed   453 *milch* milky, moist with tears. *burning eyes
of heaven* i.e., heavenly bodies   454 *passion* overpowering emotion   455 *whe'er* whether   458 *bestowed* lodged   459 *abstract* summary account   462 *God's bodikin* by God's (Christ's) little body,
bodykin. (Not to be confused with *bodkin,* "dagger."). *after* according to   470 *ha 't* have it. *study*
memorize   479 *But* merely   480 *force . . . conceit* bring his innermost being so entirely into accord
with his conception (of the role)

That from her working° all his visage wanned,°
Tears in his eyes, distraction in his aspect,°
A broken voice, and his whole function suiting
With forms to his conceit?° And all for nothing!
For Hecuba!   485
What's Hecuba to him, or he to Hecuba,
That he should weep for her? What would he do
Had he the motive and the cue for passion
That I have? He would drown the stage with tears
And cleave the general ear° with horrid° speech,   490
Make mad the guilty and appall° the free,°
Confound the ignorant,° and amaze° indeed
The very faculties of eyes and ears. Yet I,
A dull and muddy-mettled° rascal, peak°
Like John-a-dreams,° unpregnant° of my cause,   495
And can say nothing—no, not for a king
Upon whose property° and most dear life
A damned defeat° was made. Am I a coward?
Who calls me villain? Breaks my pate° across?
Plucks off my beard and blows it in my face?   500
Tweaks me by the nose? Gives me the lie i' the throat°
As deep as to the lungs? Who does me this?
Ha, 'swounds,° I should take it; for it cannot be
But I am pigeon-livered° and lack gall
To make oppression bitter,° or ere this   505
I should ha' fatted all the region kites°
With this slave's offal.° Bloody, bawdy villain!
Remorseless,° treacherous, lecherous, kindless° villain!
O, vengeance!
Why, what an ass am I! This is most brave,°   510
That I, the son of a dear father murdered,
Prompted to my revenge by heaven and hell,
Must like a whore unpack my heart with words
And fall a-cursing, like a very drab,°
A scullion!° Fie upon 't, foh! About,° my brains!   515

481 *from her working* as a result of, or in response to, his soul's activity. *wanned* grew pale 482 *aspect* look, glance 483–484 *his whole . . . conceit* all his bodily powers responding with actions to suit his thought 490 *the general ear* everyone's ear. *horrid* horrible 491 *appall* (Literally, make pale.) *free* innocent 492 *Confound the ignorant* i.e., dumbfound those who know nothing of the crime that has been committed. *amaze* stun 494 *muddy-mettled* dull-spirited. *peak* mope, pine 495 *John-a-dreams* a sleepy, dreaming idler. *unpregnant of* not quickened by 497 *property* i.e., the crown; also character, quality 498 *damned defeat* damnable act of destruction 499 *pate* head 501 *Gives . . . throat* calls me an out-and-out liar 503 *'swounds* by his (Christ's) wounds 504 *pigeon-livered* (The pigeon or dove was popularly supposed to be mild because it secreted no gall.) 505 *bitter* i.e., bitter to me 506 *region kites* kites (birds of prey) of the air 507 *offal* entrails 508 *Remorseless* pitiless. *kindless* unnatural 510 *brave* fine, admirable. (Said ironically.) 514 *drab* whore 515 *scullion* menial kitchen servant (apt to be foul-mouthed). *About* about it, to work

Hum, I have heard
That guilty creatures sitting at a play
Have by the very cunning° of the scene°
Been struck so to the soul that presently°
They have proclaimed their malefactions;   520
For murder, though it have no tongue, will speak
With most miraculous organ. I'll have these players
Play something like the murder of my father
Before mine uncle. I'll observe his looks;
I'll tent° him to the quick.° If 'a do blench,°   525
I know my course. The spirit that I have seen
May be the devil, and the devil hath power
T' assume a pleasing shape; yea, and perhaps,
Out of my weakness and my melancholy,
As he is very potent with such spirits,°   530
Abuses° me to damn me. I'll have grounds
More relative° than this. The play's the thing
Wherein I'll catch the conscience of the King.   *Exit.*

ACT III

Scene I [The Castle.]

Enter King, Queen, Polonius, Ophelia, Rosencrantz, Guildenstern, lords.

King: And can you by no drift of conference°
    Get from him why he puts on this confusion,
    Grating so harshly all his days of quiet
    With turbulent and dangerous lunacy?
Rosencrantz: He does confess he feels himself distracted,   5
    But from what cause 'a will by no means speak.
Guildenstern: Nor do we find him forward° to be sounded,°
    But with a crafty madness keeps aloof
    When we would bring him on to some confession
    Of his true state.
Queen: Did he receive you well?   10
Rosencrantz: Most like a gentleman.
Guildenstern: But with much forcing of his disposition.°
Rosencrantz: Niggard° of question,° but of our demands
    Most free in his reply.
Queen: Did you assay° him

---

518 *cunning* art, skill. *scene* dramatic presentation   519 *presently* at once   525 *tent* probe. *the quick* the tender part of a wound, the core. *blench* quail, flinch   530 *spirits* humors (of melancholy)   531 *Abuses* deludes   532 *relative* cogent, pertinent   1 *drift of conference* directing of conversation   7 *forward* willing. *sounded* questioned   12 *disposition* inclination   13 *Niggard* stingy. *question* conversation   14 *assay* try to win

To any pastime?   15

Rosencrantz: Madam, it so fell out that certain players
    We o'erraught° on the way. Of these we told him,
    And there did seem in him a kind of joy
    To hear of it. They are here about the court,
    And, as I think, they have already order   20
    This night to play before him.

Polonius: 'Tis most true,
    And he beseeched me to entreat Your Majesties
    To hear and see the matter.

King: With all my heart, and it doth much content me
    To hear him so inclined.   25
    Good gentlemen, give him a further edge°
    And drive his purpose into these delights.

Rosencrantz: We shall, my lord.

                              Exeunt Rosencrantz and Guildenstern.

King: Sweet Gertrude, leave us too,
    For we have closely° sent for Hamlet hither,
    That he, as 'twere by accident, may here   30
    Affront° Ophelia.
    Her father and myself, lawful espials,°
    Will so bestow ourselves that seeing, unseen,
    We may of their encounter frankly judge,
    And gather by him, as he is behaved,   35
    If 't be th' affliction of his love or no
    That thus he suffers for.

Queen: I shall obey you.
    And for your part, Ophelia, I do wish
    That your good beauties be the happy cause
    Of Hamlet's wildness. So shall I hope your virtues   40
    Will bring him to his wonted° way again,
    To both your honors.

Ophelia: Madam, I wish it may.

                                      [Exit Queen.]

Polonius: Ophelia, walk you here.—Gracious,° so please you,
    We will bestow° ourselves. [*To Ophelia.*] Read on this book,[*giving her a book*]
    That show of such an exercise° may color°   45
    Your loneliness.° We are oft to blame in this—
    'Tis too much proved°—that with devotion's visage
    And pious action we do sugar o'er

---

17 *o'erraught* overtook   26 *edge* incitement   29 *closely* privately   31 *Affront* confront, meet   32 *espials* spies   41 *wonted* accustomed   43 *Gracious* Your Grace (i.e., the King)   44 *bestow* conceal 45 *exercise* religious exercise. (The book she reads is one of devotion.)   *color* give a plausible appearance to   46 *loneliness* being alone   47 *too much proved* too often shown to be true, too often practiced

The devil himself.

King [*aside*]: O, 'tis too true!   50
How smart a lash that speech doth give my conscience!
The harlot's cheek, beautied with plastering art,
Is not more ugly to° the thing° that helps it
Than is my deed to my most painted word.
O heavy burden!   55

Polonius: I hear him coming. Let's withdraw, my lord.

[*The King and Polonius withdraw.*°]

Enter Hamlet. [*Ophelia pretends to read a book.*]

Hamlet: To be, or not to be, that is the question:
Whether 'tis nobler in the mind to suffer
The slings° and arrows of outrageous fortune,
Or to take arms against a sea of troubles   60
And by opposing end them. To die, to sleep—
No more—and by a sleep to say we end
The heartache and the thousand natural shocks
That flesh is heir to. 'Tis a consummation
Devoutly to be wished. To die, to sleep;   65
To sleep, perchance to dream. Ay, there's the rub,°
For in that sleep of death what dreams may come,
When we have shuffled° off this mortal coil,°
Must give us pause. There's the respect°
That makes calamity of so long life.°   70
For who would bear the whips and scorns of time,
Th' oppressor's wrong, the proud man's contumely,°
The pangs of disprized° love, the law's delay,
The insolence of office,° and the spurns°
That patient merit of th' unworthy takes,°   75
When he himself might his quietus° make
With a bare bodkin?° Who would fardels° bear,
To grunt and sweat under a weary life,
But that the dread of something after death,
The undiscovered country from whose bourn°   80
No traveler returns, puzzles the will,
And makes us rather bear those ills we have
Than fly to others that we know not of?

---

53 *to* compared to. *the thing* i.e., the cosmetic   56 s.d. *withdraw* (The King and Polonius may retire behind an arras. The stage directions specify that they "enter" again near the end of the scene.)
59 *slings* missiles   66 *rub* (Literally, an obstacle in the game of bowls.)   68 *shuffled* sloughed, cast.
coil turmoil   69 *respect* consideration   70 *of . . . life* so long-lived, something we willingly endure
for so long (also suggesting that long life is itself a calamity)   72 *contumely* insolent abuse   73 *dis-
prized* unvalued   74 *office* officialdom.   *spurns* insults   75 *of . . . takes* receives from unworthy
persons   76 *quietus* acquitance; here, death   77 *a bare bodkin* a mere dagger, unsheathed.   *fardels*
burdens   80 *bourn* frontier, boundary

Thus conscience does make cowards of us all;
And thus the native hue° of resolution   85
Is sicklied o'er with the pale cast° of thought,
And enterprises of great pitch° and moment°
With this regard° their currents° turn awry
And lose the name of action.—Soft you° now,
The fair Ophelia. Nymph, in thy orisons°   90
Be all my sins remembered.
Ophelia: Good my lord,
How does your honor for this many a day?
Hamlet: I humbly thank you; well, well, well.
Ophelia: My lord, I have remembrances of yours,
That I have longèd long to redeliver.   95
I pray you, now receive them.   [*She offers tokens.*]
Hamlet: No, not I, I never gave you aught.
Ophelia: My honored lord, you know right well you did,
And with them words of so sweet breath composed
As made the things more rich. Their perfume lost,   100
Take these again, for to the noble mind
Rich gifts wax poor when givers prove unkind.
There, my lord.   [*She gives tokens.*]
Hamlet: Ha, ha! Are you honest?°
Ophelia: My lord?   105
Hamlet: Are you fair?°
Ophelia: What means your lordship?
Hamlet: That if you be honest and fair, your honesty° should admit no
discourse to° your beauty.
Ophelia: Could beauty, my lord, have better commerce° than with honesty?   110
Hamlet: Ay, truly, for the power of beauty will sooner transform honesty from
what it is to a bawd than the force of honesty can translate beauty into his°
likeness. This was sometime° a paradox,° but now the time° gives it proof. I
did love you once.
Ophelia: Indeed, my lord, you made me believe so.   115
Hamlet: You should not have believed me, for virtue cannot so inoculate° our
old stock but we shall relish of it.° I loved you not.
Ophelia: I was the more deceived.
Hamlet: Get thee to a nunnery.° Why wouldst thou be a breeder of sinners? I am
myself indifferent honest,° but yet I could accuse me of such things that it   120

---

85 *native hue* natural color, complexion 86 *cast* tinge, shade of color 87 *pitch* height (as of a
falcon's flight). *moment* importance 88 *regard* respect, consideration. *currents* courses 89 *Soft
you* i.e., wait a minute, gently 90 *orisons* prayers 104 *honest* (1) truthful (2) chaste 106 *fair* (1)
beautiful (2) just, honorable 108 *your honesty* your chastity 109 *discourse to* familiar dealings with
110 *commerce* dealings, intercourse 112 *his* its 113 *sometime* formerly. *a paradox* a view opposite
to commonly held opinion. *the time* the present age 116 *inoculate* graft, be engrafted to 117 *but
. . . it* that we do not still have about us a taste of the old stock, i.e., retain our sinfulness 119 *nunnery* convent (with possibly an awareness that the word was also used derisively to denote a brothel)
120 *indifferent honest* reasonably virtuous

were better my mother had not borne me: I am very proud, revengeful, ambitious, with more offenses at my beck° than I have thoughts to put them in, imagination to give them shape, or time to act them in. What should such fellows as I do crawling between earth and heaven? We are arrant knaves all; believe none of us. Go thy ways to a nunnery. Where's your father? 125

Ophelia: At home, my lord.

Hamlet: Let the doors be shut upon him, that he may play the fool nowhere but in 's own house. Farewell.

Ophelia: O, help him, you sweet heavens!

Hamlet: If thou dost marry, I'll give thee this plague for thy dowry: be thou as 130 chaste as ice, as pure as snow, thou shalt not escape calumny. Get thee to a nunnery, farewell. Or, if thou wilt needs marry, marry a fool, for wise men know well enough what monsters° you° make of them. To a nunnery, go, and quickly too. Farewell.

Ophelia: Heavenly powers, restore him! 135

Hamlet: I have heard of your paintings too, well enough. God hath given you one face, and you make yourselves another. You jig,° you amble,° and you lisp, you nickname God's creatures,° and make your wantonness your ignorance.° Go to, I'll no more on 't;° it hath made me mad. I say we will have no more marriage. Those that are married already—all but one—shall live. 140 The rest shall keep as they are. To a nunnery, go. *Exit.*

Ophelia: O, what a noble mind is here o'erthrown!
The courtier's, soldier's, scholar's, eye, tongue, sword,
Th' expectancy° and rose° of the fair state,
The glass of fashion and the mold of form,° 145
Th' observed of all observers,° quite, quite down!
And I, of ladies most deject and wretched,
That sucked the honey of his music° vows,
Now see that noble and most sovereign reason
Like sweet bells jangled out of tune and harsh, 150
That unmatched form and feature of blown° youth
Blasted° with ecstasy.° O, woe is me,
T' have seen what I have seen, see what I see!

Enter King and Polonius.

King: Love? His affections° do not that way tend;
Nor what he spake, though it lacked form a little, 155
Was not like madness. There's something in his soul

---

122 *beck* command   133 *monsters* (An illusion to the horns of a cuckold.)   *you* i.e., you women 137 *jig* dance.   *amble* move coyly   137–138 *you nickname . . . creatures* i.e., you give trendy names to things in place of their God-given names   138 *make . . . ignorance* i.e., excuse your affectation on the grounds of pretended ignorance   139 *on 't* of it   144 *expectancy* hope.   *rose* ornament   145 *The glass . . . form* the mirror of true self-fashioning and the pattern of courtly behavior 146 *Th' observed . . . observers* i.e., the center of attention and honor in the court   148 *music* musical, sweetly uttered   151 *blown* blooming   152 *Blasted* withered.   *ecstasy* madness   154 *affections* emotions, feelings

O'er which his melancholy sits on brood,°
And I do doubt° the hatch and the disclose°
Will be some danger; which for to prevent,
I have in quick determination   160
Thus set it down:° he shall with speed to England
For the demand of° our neglected tribute.
Haply the seas and countries different
With variable objects° shall expel
This something-settled matter in his heart,°   165
Whereon his brains still° beating puts him thus
From fashion of himself.° What think you on 't?
Polonius: It shall do well. But yet do I believe
The origin and commencement of his grief
Sprung from neglected love.—How now, Ophelia?   170
You need not tell us what Lord Hamlet said;
We heard it all.—My lord, do as you please,
But, if you hold it fit, after the play
Let his queen-mother° all alone entreat him
To show his grief. Let her be round° with him;   175
And I'll be placed, so please you, in the ear
Of all their conference. If she find him not,°
To England send him, or confine him where
Your wisdom best shall think.
King: It shall be so.
Madness in great ones must not unwatched go.   180

                                                  Exeunt.

Scene II [The Castle.]

Enter Hamlet and three of the Players.

Hamlet: Speak the speech, I pray you, as I pronounced it to you, trippingly on
the tongue. But if you mouth it, as many of our players° do, I had as lief° the
town crier spoke my lines. Nor do not saw the air too much with your hand,
thus, but use all gently; for in the very torrent, tempest, and, as I may say,
whirlwind of your passion, you must acquire and beget a temperance that   5
may give it smoothness. O, it offends me to the soul to hear a robustious°
periwig-pated° fellow tear a passion to tatters, to very rags, to split the ears

---

157 *sits on brood* sits like a bird on a nest, about to *hatch* mischief (line 158)   158 *doubt* fear.   *disclose*
disclosure, hatching   161 *set it down* resolved   162 *For . . . of* to demand   164 *variable objects* various sights and surroundings to divert him   165 *This something . . . heart* the strange matter settled in
his heart   166 *still* continually   167 *From . . . himself* out of his natural manner   174 *queen-mother*
queen and mother   175 *round* blunt   177 *find him not* fails to discover what is troubling him   2 *our
players* players nowadays.   *I had as lief* I would just as soon   6 *robustious* violent, boisterous
7 *periwig-pated* wearing a wig

of the groundlings,° who for the most part are capable of° nothing but inex-
plicable dumb shows° and noise. I would have such a fellow whipped for
o'erdoing Termagant.° It out-Herods Herod.° Pray you, avoid it.   10
First Player: I warrant your honor.
Hamlet: Be not too tame neither, but let your own discretion be your tutor. Suit
the action to the word, the word to the action, with this special observance,
that you o'erstep not the modesty° of nature. For anything so o'erdone is
from° the purpose of playing, whose end, both at the first and now, was and   15
is to hold as 't were the mirror up to nature, to show virtue her feature,
scorn° her own image, and the very age and body of the time° his° form and
pressure.° Now this overdone or come tardy off,° though it makes the un-
skillful° laugh, cannot but make the judicious grieve, the censure of the
which one° must in your allowance° o'erweigh a whole theater of others. O,   20
there be players that I have seen play, and heard others praise, and that
highly, not to speak it profanely,° that, neither having th' accent of Chris-
tians° nor the gait of Christian, pagan, nor man,° have so strutted and bel-
lowed that I have thought some of nature's journeymen° had made men and
not made them well, they imitated humanity so abominably.°   25
First Player: I hope we have reformed that indifferently° with us, sir.
Hamlet: O, reform it altogether. And let those that play your clowns speak no
more than is set down for them; for there be of them° that will themselves
laugh, to set on some quantity of barren° spectators to laugh too, though in
the meantime some necessary question of the play be then to be considered.   30
That's villainous, and shows a most pitiful ambition in the fool that uses it.
Go make you ready.   [*Exeunt Players.*]

Enter Polonius, Guildenstern, and Rosencrantz.

How now, my lord, will the King hear this piece of work?
Polonius: And the Queen too, and that presently.°
Hamlet: Bid the players make haste.   [*Exit Polonius.*]   35
Will you two help to hasten them?
Rosencrantz: Ay, my lord.   *Exeunt they two.*
Hamlet: What ho, Horatio!

---

8 *groundlings* spectators who paid least and stood in the yard of the theater.   *capable of* able to understand   9 *dumb shows* mimed performances, often used before Shakespeare's time to precede a play or
each act   10 *Termagant* a supposed deity of the Mohammedans, not found in any English medieval play
but elsewhere portrayed as violent and blustering.   *Herod* Herod of Jewry. (A character in *The Slaughter
of the Innocents* and other cycle plays. The part was played with great noise and fury.)   14 *modesty* restraint, moderation   15 *from* contrary to   17 *scorn* i.e., something foolish and deserving of scorn.   *the
very . . . time* i.e., the present state of affairs.   *his* its   18 *pressure* stamp, impressed character.   *come
tardy off* inadequately done   18–19 *the unskillful* those lacking in judgment   19–20 *the censure . . . one*
the judgment of even one of whom   20 *your allowance* your scale of values   22 *not . . . profanely*
(Hamlet anticipates his idea in lines 24–25 that some men were not made by God at all.)   22–23 *Christians* i.e., ordinary decent folk   23 *nor man* i.e., nor any human being at all   24 *journeymen* laborers
who are not yet masters in their trade   25 *abominably* (Shakespeare's usual spelling, abhominably, suggests a literal though etymologically incorrect meaning, "removed from human nature.")   26 *indifferently* tolerably   28 *of them* some among them   29 *barren* i.e., of wit   34 *presently* at once

Enter Horatio.

Horatio: Here, sweet lord, at your service.
Hamlet: Horatio, thou art e'en as just a man
    As e'er my conversation coped withal.°   40
Horatio: O, my dear lord—
Hamlet: Nay, do not think I flatter,
    For what advancement may I hope from thee
    That no revenue hast but thy good spirits
    To feed and clothe thee? Why should the poor be flattered?
    No, let the candied° tongue lick absurd pomp,   45
    And crook the pregnant° hinges of the knee
    Where thrift° may follow fawning. Dost thou hear?
    Since my dear soul was mistress of her choice
    And could of men distinguish her election,°
    Sh' hath sealed thee° for herself, for thou hast been   50
    As one, in suffering all, that suffers nothing,
    A man that Fortune's buffets and rewards
    Hast ta'en with equal thanks; and blest are those
    Whose blood° and judgment are so well commeddled°
    That they are not a pipe for Fortune's finger   55
    To sound what stop° she please. Give me that man
    That is not passion's slave, and I will wear him
    In my heart's core, ay, in my heart of heart,
    As I do thee.—Something too much of this.—
    There is a play tonight before the King.   60
    One scene of it comes near the circumstance
    Which I have told thee of my father's death.
    I prithee, when thou seest that act afoot,
    Even with the very comment of thy soul°
    Observe my uncle. If his occulted° guilt   65
    Do not itself unkennel° in one speech,
    It is a damnèd° ghost that we have seen,
    And my imaginations are as foul
    As Vulcan's stithy.° Give him heedful note,
    For I mine eyes will rivet to his face,   70
    And after we will both our judgments join
    In censure of his seeming.°
Horatio: Well, my lord.

---

40 *my . . . withal* my dealings encountered   45 *candied* sugared, flattering   46 *pregnant* compliant
47 *thrift* profit   49 *could . . . election* could make distinguishing choices among persons   50 *sealed*
thee (Literally, as one would seal a legal document to mark possession.)   54 *blood* passion. *comme*
dled commingled   56 *stop* hole in a wind instrument for controlling the sound   64 *very . . . soul*
your most penetrating observation and consideration   65 *occulted* hidden   66 *unkennel* (As one
would say of a fox driven from its lair.)   67 *damnèd* in league with Satan   69 *stithy* smithy, place of
stiths (anvils)   72 *censure of his* seeming judgment of his appearance or behavior

If 'a steal aught° the whilst this play is playing
And scape detecting, I will pay the theft.

[*Flourish.*] *Enter trumpets and kettledrums, King,*

Queen, Polonius, Ophelia, [Rosencrantz, Guildenstern, and other lords, with guards carrying torches].

Hamlet: They are coming to the play. I must be idle.° Get you a place.   75

[*The King, Queen, and courtiers sit.*]

King: How fares our cousin° Hamlet?
Hamlet: Excellent, i' faith, of the chameleon's dish:° I eat the air, promise-crammed. You cannot feed capons° so.
King: I have nothing with° this answer, Hamlet. These words are not mine.°
Hamlet: No, nor mine now.° [*To Polonius.*] My lord, you played once i' th' uni-   80
versity, you say?
Polonius: That did I, my lord, and was accounted a good actor.
Hamlet: What did you enact?
Polonius: I did enact Julius Caesar. I was killed i' the Capitol; Brutus killed me.
Hamlet: It was a brute° part° of him to kill so capital a calf° there.—Be the   85
players ready?
Rosencrantz: Ay, my lord. They stay upon° your patience.
Queen: Come hither, my dear Hamlet, sit by me.
Hamlet: No, good Mother, here's metal° more attractive.
Polonius [*to the King*]: O, ho, do you mark that?   90
Hamlet: Lady, shall I lie in your lap?

[*Lying down at Ophelia's feet.*]

Ophelia: No, my lord.
Hamlet: I mean, my head upon your lap?
Ophelia: Ay, my lord.
Hamlet: Do you think I meant country matters?°   95
Ophelia: I think nothing, my lord.
Hamlet: That's a fair thought to lie between maids' legs.
Ophelia: What is, my lord?
Hamlet: Nothing.°

---

73 *If 'a steal aught* if he gets away with anything   75 *idle* (1) unoccupied (2) mad   76 *cousin* i.e., close relative   77 *chameleon's dish* (Chameleons were supposed to feed on air. Hamlet deliberately misinterprets the King's *fares* as "feeds." By his phrase *eat the air*, he also plays on the idea of feeding himself with the promise of succession, of being the *heir*.)   78 *capons* roosters castrated and *crammed* with feed to make them succulent   79 *have . . . with* make nothing of, or gain nothing from. *are not mine* do not respond to what I asked   80 *nor mine now* (Once spoken, words are proverbially no longer the speaker's own—and hence should be uttered warily.)   85 *brute* (The Latin meaning of *brutus*, "stupid," was often used punningly with the name Brutus.) *part* (1) deed (2) role. *calf* fool   87 *stay upon* await   89 *metal* substance that is *attractive*, i.e., magnetic, but with suggestion also of *mettle*, "disposition"   95 *country matters* sexual intercourse (making a bawdy pun on the first syllable of *country*)   99 *Nothing* the figure zero or naught, suggesting the female sexual anatomy. (*Thing* not infrequently has a bawdy connotation of male or female anatomy, and the reference here could be male.)

Ophelia: You are merry, my lord.   100

Hamlet: Who, I?

Ophelia: Ay, my lord.

Hamlet: O God, your only jig maker.° What should a man do but be merry? For
look you how cheerfully my mother looks, and my father died within 's° two
hours.   105

Ophelia: Nay, 'tis twice two months, my lord.

Hamlet: So long? Nay then, let the devil wear black, for I'll have a suit of sables.°
O heavens! Die two months ago, and not forgotten yet? Then there's hope a
great man's memory may outlive his life half a year. But, by'r Lady, 'a must
build churches, then, or else shall 'a suffer not thinking on,° with the hobby-   110
horse, whose epitaph is "For O, for O, the hobbyhorse is forgot."°

The trumpets sound. Dumb show follows.

*Enter a King and a Queen [very lovingly]; the Queen embracing him, and he her.
[She kneels, and makes show of protestation unto him.] He takes her up, and declines his head upon her neck. He lies him down upon a bank of flowers. She,
seeing him asleep, leaves him. Anon comes in another man, takes off his crown,
kisses it, pours poison in the sleeper's ears, and leaves him. The Queen returns,
finds the King dead, makes passionate action. The Poisoner with some three or
four come in again, seem to condole with her. The dead body is carried away. The
Poisoner woos the Queen with gifts; she seems harsh awhile, but in the end accepts
love.*

                                                                                    [*Exeunt players.*]

Ophelia: What means this, my lord?

Hamlet: Marry, this' miching mallico;° it means mischief.

Ophelia: Belike° this show imports the argument° of the play.

   Enter Prologue.

Hamlet: We shall know by this fellow. The players cannot keep counsel;° they'll   115
tell all.

Ophelia: Will 'a tell us what this show meant?

Hamlet: Ay, or any show that you will show him. Be not you° ashamed to show,
he'll not shame to tell you what it means.

---

103 *only jig maker* very best composer of jigs, i.e., pointless merriment. (Hamlet replies sardonically to
Ophelia's observation that he is merry by saying, "If you're looking for someone who is really merry,
you've come to the right person.")   104 *within 's* within this (i.e., these)   107 *suit of sables* garments
trimmed with the fur of the sable and hence suited for a wealthy person, not a mourner (but with a
pun on *sable*, "black," ironically suggesting mourning once again)   110 *suffer . . . on* undergo
oblivion   111 *For . . . forgot* (Verse of a song occurring also in *Love's Labor's Lost*, 3.1.27–28. The
hobbyhorse was a character made up to resemble a horse and rider, appearing in the morris dance and
such May-game sports. This song laments the disappearance of such customs under pressure from the
Puritans.)   113 *this' miching mallico* this is sneaking mischief   114 *Belike* probably.   *argument* plot
115 *counsel* secret   118 *Be not you* provided you are not

Ophelia: You are naught, you are naught.° I'll mark the play.   120
Prologue: For us, and for our tragedy,
    Here stooping° to your clemency,
    We beg your hearing patiently.   [*Exit.*]
Hamlet: Is this a prologue, or the posy of a ring?°
Ophelia: 'Tis brief, my lord.   125
Hamlet: As woman's love.

    Enter [two Players as] King and Queen.

Player King: Full thirty times hath Phoebus' cart° gone round
    Neptune's salt wash° and Tellus'° orbèd ground,
    And thirty dozen moons with borrowed° sheen
    About the world have times twelve thirties been,   130
    Since love our hearts and Hymen° did our hands
    Unite commutual° in most sacred bands.°
Player Queen: So many journeys may the sun and moon
    Make us again count o'er ere love be done!
    But, woe is me, you are so sick of late,   135
    So far from cheer and from your former state,
    That I distrust° you. Yet, though I distrust,
    Discomfort° you, my lord, it nothing° must.
    For women's fear and love hold quantity;°
    In neither aught, or in extremity.°   140
    Now, what my love is, proof° hath made you know,
    And as my love is sized,° my fear is so.
    Where love is great, the littlest doubts are fear;
    Where little fears grow great, great love grows there.
Player King: Faith, I must leave thee, love, and shortly too;   145
    My operant powers° their functions leave to do.°
    And thou shalt live in this fair world behind,°
    Honored, beloved; and haply one as kind
    For husband shalt thou—
Player Queen: O, confound the rest!
    Such love must needs be treason in my breast.   150
    In second husband let me be accurst!
    None° wed the second but who° killed the first.
Hamlet: Wormwood,° wormwood.

---

120 *naught* indecent. (Ophelia is reacting to Hamlet's pointed remarks about not being ashamed to show all.)   122 *stooping* bowing   124 *posy . . . ring* brief motto in verse inscribed in a ring   127 *Phoebus' cart* the sun-god's chariot, making its yearly cycle   128 *salt wash* the sea. *Tellus* goddess of the earth, of the *orbèd ground*   129 *borrowed* i.e., reflected   131 *Hymen* god of matrimony   132 *commutual* mutually. *bands* bonds   137 *distrust* am anxious about   138 *Discomfort* distress. *nothing* not at all   139 *hold quantity* keep proportion with one another   140 *In . . . extremity* i.e., women fear and love either too little or too much, but the two, fear and love, are equal in either case   141 *proof* experience   142 *sized* in size   146 *operant powers* vital functions. *leave to do* cease to perform   147 *behind* after I have gone   152 *None* i.e., let no woman. *but who* except the one who   153 *Wormwood* i.e., how bitter. (Literally, a bitter-tasting plant.)

Player Queen: The instances° that second marriage move°
    Are base respects of thrift,° but none of love. 155
    A second time I kill my husband dead
    When second husband kisses me in bed.
Player King: I do believe you think what now you speak,
    But what we do determine oft we break.
    Purpose is but the slave to memory,° 160
    Of violent birth, but poor validity,°
    Which° now, like fruit unripe, sticks on the tree,
    But fall unshaken when they mellow be.
    Most necessary 'tis that we forget
    To pay ourselves what to ourselves is debt.° 165
    What to ourselves in passion we purpose,
    The passion ending, doth the purpose lose.
    The violence of either grief or joy
    Their own enactures° with themselves destroy.
    Where joy most revels, grief doth most lament; 170
    Grief joys, joy grieves, on slender accident.°
    This world is not for aye,° nor 'tis not strange
    That even our loves should with our fortunes change;
    For 'tis a question left us yet to prove,
    Whether love lead fortune, or else fortune love. 175
    The great man down,° you mark his favorite flies;
    The poor advanced makes friends of enemies.°
    And hitherto° doth love on fortune tend;°
    For who not needs° shall never lack a friend,
    And who in want° a hollow friend doth try° 180
    Directly seasons him° his enemy.
    But, orderly to end where I begun,
    Our wills and fates do so contrary run°
    That our devices still° are overthrown;
    Our thoughts are ours, their ends° none of our own. 185
    So think thou wilt no second husband wed,
    But die thy thoughts when thy first lord is dead.
Player Queen: Nor° earth to me give food, nor heaven light,

---

154 *instances* motives. *move* motivate   155 *base . . . thrift* ignoble considerations of material prosperity   160 *Purpose . . . memory* our good intentions are subject to forgetfulness   161 *validity* strength, durability   162 *Which* i.e., purpose   164–165 *Most . . . debt* it's inevitable that in time we forget the obligations we have imposed on ourselves   169 *enactures* fulfillments   170–171 *Where . . . accident* the capacity for extreme joy and grief go together, and often one extreme is instantly changed into its opposite on the slightest provocation   172 *aye* ever   176 *down* fallen in fortune   177 *The poor . . . enemies* when one of humble station is promoted, you see his enemies suddenly becoming his friends   178 *hitherto* up to this point in the argument, or, to this extent. *tend* attend   179 *who not needs* he who is not in need (of wealth)   180 *who in want* he who, being in need. *try* test (his generosity)   181 *seasons him* ripens him into   183 *Our . . . run* what we want and what we get go so contrarily   184 *devices still* intentions continually   185 *ends* results   188 *Nor* let neither

Sport and repose lock from me day and night,°
To desperation turn my trust and hope,   190
An anchor's cheer° in prison be my scope!°
Each° opposite that blanks° the face of joy
Meet what I would have well and it destroy!
Both here and hence° pursue me lasting strife
If, once a widow, ever I be wife!   195

Hamlet: If she should break it now!

Player King: 'Tis deeply sworn. Sweet, leave me here awhile;
My spirits° grow dull, and fain I would beguile
The tedious day with sleep.

Player Queen: Sleep rock thy brain,
And never come mischance between us twain!   200

                                    [*He sleeps.*] *Exit* [*Player Queen*].

Hamlet: Madam, how like you this play?

Queen: The lady doth protest too much,° methinks.

Hamlet: O, but she'll keep her word.

King: Have you heard the argument?° Is there no offense° in 't?

Hamlet: No, no, they do but jest,° poison in jest. No offense i' the world.   205

King: What do you call the play?

Hamlet: *The Mousetrap.* Marry, how? Tropically.° This play is the image of a
    murder done in Vienna. Gonzago is the Duke's° name, his wife, Baptista.
    You shall see anon. 'Tis a knavish piece of work, but what of that? Your
    Majesty, and we that have free° souls, it touches us not. Let the galled jade°   210
    wince, our withers° are unwrung.°

    Enter Lucianus.

    This is one Lucianus, nephew to the King.

Ophelia: You are as good as a chorus,° my lord.

Hamlet: I could interpret° between you and your love, if I could see the puppets
    dallying.°   215

---

189 *Sport . . . night* may day deny me its pastimes and night its repose   191 *anchor's cheer* anchorite's
or hermit's fare.   *my scope* the extent of my happiness   192–193 *Each . . . destroy* may every adverse
thing that causes the face of joy to turn pale meet and destroy everything that I desire to see prosper.
192 *blanks* causes to blanch or grow pale   194 *hence* in the life hereafter   198 *spirits* vital spirits
202 *doth . . . much* makes too many promises and protestations   204 *argument* plot   204–205 *offense
. . . offense* cause for objection . . . actual injury, crime   205 *jest* make believe   207 *Tropically* figuratively. (The First Quarto reading, *trapically*, suggests a pun on *trap* in *Mousetrap.*)   208 *Duke's* i.e.,
King's. (A slip that may be due to Shakespeare's possible source, the alleged murder of the Duke of
Urbino by Luigi Gonzaga in 1538.)   210 *free* guiltless.   *galled jade* horse whose hide is rubbed by
saddle or harness.   211 *withers* the part between the horse's shoulder blades   *unwrung* not rubbed
sore   213 *chorus* (In many Elizabethan plays, the forthcoming action was explained by an actor
known as the "chorus"; at a puppet show, the actor who spoke the dialogue was known as an "inter-
preter," as indicated by the lines following.)   214 *interpret* (1) ventriloquize the dialogue, as in
puppet show (2) act as pander   214–215 *puppets dallying* (With suggestion of sexual play, continued
in lines 216–218: *keen,* "sexually aroused," *groaning,* "moaning in pregnancy," and *edge,* "sexual desire" or "impetuosity.")

Ophelia: You are keen, my lord, you are keen.°

Hamlet: It would cost you a groaning to take off mine edge.

Ophelia: Still better, and worse.°

Hamlet: So° you mis-take° your husbands. Begin, murderer; leave thy damnable
    faces and begin. Come, the croaking raven doth bellow for revenge.   220

Lucianus: Thoughts black, hands apt, drugs fit, and time agreeing,
    Confederate season,° else° no creature seeing,°
    Thou mixture rank, of midnight weeds collected,
    With Hecate's ban° thrice blasted, thrice infected,
    Thy natural magic and dire property°   225
    On wholesome life usurp immediately.

                          [He pours the poison into the sleeper's ear.]

Hamlet: 'A poison him i' the garden for his estate.° His° name's Gonzago. The
    story is extant, and written in very choice Italian. You shall see anon how
    the murderer gets the love of Gonzago's wife.

                               [Claudius rises.]

Ophelia: The King rises.   230

Hamlet: What, frighted with false fire?°

Queen: How fares my lord?

Polonius: Give o'er the play.

King: Give me some light. Away!

Polonius: Lights, lights, lights!   235

                        Exeunt all but Hamlet and Horatio.

Hamlet: "Why,° let the strucken deer go weep,
        The hart ungallèd° play.
        For some must watch,° while some must sleep;
        Thus runs the world away."°
    Would not this,° sir, and a forest of feathers°—if the rest of my fortunes turn 240
    Turk with° me—with two Provincial roses° on my razed° shoes, get me a fel-
    lowship° in a cry° of players?

Horatio: Half a share.

Hamlet: A whole one, I.

---

216 *keen* sharp, bitter   218 *Still . . . worse* more keen, always *bettering* what other people say with
witty wordplay, but at the same time more offensive   219 *So* even thus (in marriage).   *mis-take* take
falseheartedly and cheat on. (The marriage vows say "for better, for worse.")   222 *Confederate season*
the time and occasion conspiring (to assist the murderer).   *else* otherwise.   *seeing* seeing me   224
Hecate's ban the curse of Hecate, the goddess of witchcraft   225 *dire property* baleful quality   227 *estate* i.e., the kingship.   *His* i.e., the King's   231 *false fire* the blank discharge of a gun loaded with
powder but no shot   236–239 *Why . . . away* (Probably from an old ballad, with allusion to the popular belief that a wounded deer retires to weep and die; compare with *As You Like It*, Act II, Scene i,
lines 33–66.)   237 *ungallèd* unafflicted   238 *watch* remain awake   239 *Thus . . . away* thus the
world goes   240 *this* i.e., the play.   *feathers* (Allusion to the plumes that Elizabethan actors were fond
of wearing.)   240–241 *turn Turk with* turn renegade against, go back on   241 *Provincial roses* rosettes
of ribbon, named for roses grown in a part of France.   *razed* with ornamental slashing.   241–242 *fellowship . . . players* partnership in a theatrical company.   242 *cry* pack (of hounds)

> "For thou dost know, O Damon° dear,   245
> This° realm dismantled° was
> Of Jove himself, and now reigns here
> A very, very—pajock."

Horatio: You might have rhymed.

Hamlet: O good Horatio, I'll take the ghost's word for a thousand pound. Didst   250
perceive?

Horatio: Very well, my lord.

Hamlet: Upon the talk of the poisoning?

Horatio: I did very well note him.

Enter Rosencrantz and Guildenstern.

Hamlet: Aha! Come, some music! Come, the recorders.°   255
> "For if the King like not the comedy,
> Why then, belike, he likes it not, perdy."°

Come, some music.

Guildenstern: Good my lord, vouchsafe me a word with you.

Hamlet: Sir, a whole history.

Guildenstern: The King, sir—   260

Hamlet: Ay, sir, what of him?

Guildenstern: Is in his retirement° marvelous distempered.°

Hamlet: With drink, sir?

Guildenstern: No, my lord, with choler.   265

Hamlet: Your wisdom should show itself more richer to signify this to the doctor, for for me to put him to his purgation° would perhaps plunge him into more choler.°

Guildenstern: Good my lord, put your discourse into some frame° and start° not so wildly from my affair.   270

Hamlet: I am tame, sir. Pronounce.

Guildenstern: The Queen, your mother, in most great affliction of spirit, hath sent me to you.

Hamlet: You are welcome.

Guildenstern: Nay, good my lord, this courtesy is not of the right breed.° If it   275
shall please you to make me a wholesome answer, I will do your mother's commandment; if not, your pardon° and my return shall be the end of my business.

---

245 *Damon* the friend of Pythias, as Horatio is friend of Hamlet; or, a traditional pastoral name   246–248 *This realm . . . pajock* i.e., Jove, representing divine authority and justice, has abandoned this realm to its own devices, leaving in his stead only a peacock or vain pretender to virtue (though the rhyme-word expected in place of *pajock* or "peacock" suggests that the realm is now ruled over by an "ass").   246 *dismantled* stripped, divested   255 *recorders* wind instruments of the flute kind   257 *perdy* (A corruption of the French *par dieu,* "by God.")   263 *retirement* withdrawal to his chambers.   *distempered* out of humor. (But Hamlet deliberately plays on the wider application to any illness of mind or body, especially to drunkenness.)   267 *purgation* (Hamlet hints at something going beyond medical treatment to blood-letting and the extraction of confession.)   268 *choler* anger. (But Hamlet takes the word in its more basic humoral sense of "bilious disorder.")   269 *frame* order.   *start* shy or jump away (like a horse; the opposite of *tame* in line 271)   275 *breed* (1) kind (2) breeding, manners   277 *pardon* permission to depart

Hamlet: Sir, I cannot.

Rosencrantz: What, my lord? 280

Hamlet: Make you a wholesome answer; my wit's diseased. But, sir, such answer as I can make, you shall command, or rather, as you say, my mother. Therefore no more, but to the matter. My mother, you say—

Rosencrantz: Then thus she says: your behavior hath struck her into amazement and admiration.° 285

Hamlet: O wonderful son, that can so stonish a mother! But is there no sequel at the heels of this mother's admiration? Impart.

Rosencrantz: She desires to speak with you in her closet° ere you go to bed.

Hamlet: We shall obey, were she ten times our mother. Have you any further trade with us? 290

Rosencrantz: My lord, you once did love me.

Hamlet: And do still, by these pickers and stealers.°

Rosencrantz: Good my lord, what is your cause of distemper? You do surely bar the door upon your own liberty° if you deny° your griefs to your friend.

Hamlet: Sir, I lack advancement. 295

Rosencrantz: How can that be, when you have the voice of the King himself for your succession in Denmark?

Hamlet: Ay, sir, but "While the grass grows"°—the proverb is something° musty.

Enter the Players° with recorders.

O, the recorders. Let me see one. [*He takes a recorder.*] To withdraw° with you: why do you go about to recover the wind° of me, as if you would drive 300 me into a toil?°

Guildenstern: O, my lord, if my duty be too bold, my love is too unmannerly.°

Hamlet: I do not well understand that.° Will you play upon this pipe?

Guildenstern: My lord, I cannot.

Hamlet: I pray you. 305

Guildenstern: Believe me, I cannot.

Hamlet: I do beseech you.

Guildenstern: I know no touch of it, my lord.

Hamlet: It is as easy as lying. Govern these ventages° with your fingers and thumb, give it breath with your mouth, and it will discourse most eloquent 310 music. Look you, these are the stops.

Guildenstern: But these cannot I command to any utterance of harmony. I have not the skill.

---

285 *admiration* bewilderment   288 *closet* private chamber   292 *pickers and stealers* i.e., hands. (So called from the catechism, "to keep my hands from picking and stealing.")   294 *liberty* i.e., being freed from *distemper,* line 293; but perhaps with a veiled threat as well.   *deny* refuse to share 298 *While . . . grows* (The rest of the proverb is "the silly horse starves"; Hamlet may not live long enough to succeed to the kingdom.)   *something* somewhat.   s.d. *Players* actors   299 *withdraw* speak privately   300 *recover the wind* get to the windward side (thus driving the game into the toil, or "net")   301 *toil* snare   302 *if . . . unmannerly* if I am using an unmannerly boldness, it is my love that occasions it   303 *I . . . that* i.e., I don't understand how genuine love can be unmannerly   309 *ventages* finger-holes or *stops* (line 315) of the recorder

Hamlet: Why, look you now, how unworthy a thing you make of me! You would play upon me, you would seem to know my stops, you would pluck out the 315 heart of my mystery, you would sound° me from my lowest note to the top of my compass,° and there is much music, excellent voice, in this little organ,° yet cannot you make it speak. 'Sblood, do you think I am easier to be played on than a pipe? Call me what instrument you will, though you can fret° me, you cannot play upon me. 320

Enter Polonius.

God bless you, sir!
Polonius: My lord, the Queen would speak with you, and presently.°
Hamlet: Do you see yonder cloud that's almost in shape of a camel?
Polonius: By the Mass and 'tis, like a camel indeed.
Hamlet: Methinks it is like a weasel. 325
Polonius: It is backed like a weasel.
Hamlet: Or like a whale.
Polonius: Very like a whale
Hamlet: Then I will come to my mother by and by.° [*Aside.*] They fool me° to the top of my bent.°—I will come by and by. 330
Polonius: I will say so. [*Exit.*]
Hamlet: "By and by" is easily said. Leave me, friends.

[*Exeunt all but Hamlet.*]

'Tis now the very witching time° of night,
When churchyards yawn and hell itself breathes out
Contagion to this world. Now could I drink hot blood 335
And do such bitter business as the day
Would quake to look on. Soft, now to my mother.
O heart, lose not thy nature!° Let not ever
The soul of Nero° enter this firm bosom.
Let me be cruel, not unnatural; 340
I will speak daggers to her, but use none.
My tongue and soul in this be hypocrites:
How in my words soever° she be shent,°
To give them seals° never my soul consent! *Exit.*

Scene III [The Castle.]

Enter King, Rosencrantz, and Guildenstern.

King: I like him° not, nor stands it safe with us
To let his madness range. Therefore prepare you.

---

316 *sound* (1) fathom (2) produce sound in   317 *compass* range (of voice).   *organ* musical instrument   319 *fret* irritate (with a quibble on *fret*, meaning the piece of wood, gut, or metal that regulates the fingering on an instrument)   322 *presently* at once   329 *by and by* quite soon.   *fool me* trifle with me, humor my fooling   330 *top of my bent* limit of my ability or endurance. (Literally, th extent to which a bow may be bent.)   333 *witching time* time when spells are cast and evil is abroad   338 *nature* natural feeling   339 *Nero* murderer of his mother, Agrippina   343 *How . . . soever* however much by my words.   *shent* rebuked   344 *give them seals* i.e., confirm them with deeds   1 *him* i.e., his behavior

I your commission will forthwith dispatch,°
And he to England shall along with you.
The terms of our estate° may not endure   5
Hazard so near 's as doth hourly grow
Out of his brows.°
Guildenstern: We will ourselves provide.
     Most holy and religious fear° it is
     To keep those many many bodies safe
     That live and feed upon Your Majesty.   10
Rosencrantz: The single and peculiar° life is bound
     With all the strength and armor of the mind
     To keep itself from noyance,° but much more
     That spirit upon whose weal depends and rests
     The lives of many. The cess° of majesty   15
     Dies not alone, but like a gulf° doth draw
     What's near it with it; or it is a massy° wheel
     Fixed on the summit of the highest mount,
     To whose huge spokes ten thousand lesser things
     Are mortised° and adjoined, which, when it falls,°   20
     Each small annexment, petty consequence,°
     Attends° the boisterous ruin. Never alone
     Did the King sigh, but with a general groan.
King: Arm° you, I pray you, to this speedy voyage,
     For we will fetters put about this fear,   25
     Which now goes too free-footed.
Rosencrantz: We will haste us.
                    Exeunt gentlemen [Rosencrantz and Guildenstern].

     Enter Polonius.

Polonius: My lord, he's going to his mother's closet.
     Behind the arras° I'll convey myself
     To hear the process.° I'll warrant she'll tax him home,°
     And, as you said—and wisely was it said—   30
     'Tis meet° that some more audience than a mother,
     Since nature makes them partial, should o'erhear
     The speech, of vantage.° Fare you well, my liege.

---

3 *dispatch* prepare, cause to be drawn up   5 *terms of our estate* circumstances of my royal position
7 *Out of his brows* i.e., from his brain, in the form of plots and threats   8 *religious fear* sacred concern
11 *single and peculiar* individual and private   13 *noyance* harm   15 *cess* decrease, cessation   16 *gulf*
whirlpool   17 *massy* massive   20 *mortised* fastened (as with a fitted joint).   *when it falls* i.e., when it
descends, like the wheel of Fortune, bringing a king down with it   21 *Each . . . consequence* i.e.,
every hanger-on and unimportant person or thing connected with the King   22 *Attends* participates
in   24 *Arm* prepare   28 *arras* screen of tapestry placed around the walls of household apartments.
(On the Elizabethan stage, the arras was presumably over a door or discovery space in the tiring-
house facade.)   29 *process* proceedings.   *tax him home* reprove him severely   31 *meet* fitting   33 *of*
vantage from an advantageous place, or, in addition

I'll call upon you ere you go to bed
And tell you what I know.

King: Thanks, dear my lord.   35

Exit [*Polonius*].

O, my offense is rank! It smells to heaven.
It hath the primal eldest curse° upon 't,
A brother's murder. Pray can I not,
Though inclination be as sharp as will;°
My stronger guilt defeats my strong intent,   40
And like a man to double business bound°
I stand in pause where I shall first begin,
And both neglect. What if this cursèd hand
Were thicker than itself with brother's blood,
Is there not rain enough in the sweet heavens   45
To wash it white as snow? Whereto serves mercy
But to confront the visage of offense?°
And what's in prayer but this twofold force,
To be forestallèd° ere we come to fall,
Or pardoned being down? Then I'll look up.   50
My fault is past. But O, what form of prayer
Can serve my turn? "Forgive me my foul murder"?
That cannot be, since I am still possessed
Of those effects for which I did the murder:
My crown, mine own ambition, and my queen.   55
May one be pardoned and retain th' offense?°
In the corrupted currents° of this world
Offense's gilded hand° may shove° by justice,
And oft 'tis seen the wicked prize° itself
Buys out the law. But 'tis not so above.   60
There° is no shuffling,° there the action lies°
In his° true nature, and we ourselves compelled,
Even to the teeth and forehead° of our faults,
To give in° evidence. What then? What rests?°
Try what repentance can. What can it not?   65
Yet what can it, when one cannot repent?
O wretched state, O bosom black as death,
O limèd° soul that, struggling to be free,

---

37 *the primal eldest curse* the curse of Cain, the first murderer; he killed his brother Abel   39 *Though . . . will* though my desire is as strong as my determination   41 *bound* (1) destined (2) obliged. (The King wants to repent and still enjoy what he has gained.)   46–47 *Whereto . . . offense* what function does mercy serve other than to meet sin face to face?   49 *forestallèd* prevented (from sinning)   56 *th' offense* the thing for which one offended   57 *currents* courses   58 *gilded hand* hand offering gold as a bribe. *shove by* thrust aside   59 *wicked prize* prize won by wickedness   61 *There* i.e., in heaven. *shuffling* escape by trickery. *the action lies* the accusation is made manifest. (A legal metaphor.)   62 *his* its   63 *to the teeth and forehead* face to face, concealing nothing   64 *give in* provide. *rests* remains   68 *limèd* caught as with birdlime, a sticky substance used to ensnare birds

Art more engaged!° Help, angels! Make assay.°
Bow, stubborn knees, and heart with strings of steel,   70
Be soft as sinews of the newborn babe!
All may be well.   *[He kneels.]*

Enter Hamlet.

Hamlet: Now might I do it pat,° now 'a is a-praying;
And now I'll do 't. [*He draws his sword.*] And so 'a goes to heaven,
And so am I revenged. That would be scanned:°   75
A villain kills my father, and for that,
I, his sole son, do this same villain send
To heaven.
Why, this is hire and salary, not revenge.
'A took my father grossly, full of bread,°   80
With all his crimes broad blown,° as flush° as May;
And how his audit° stands who knows save° heaven?
But in our circumstance and course of thought°
'Tis heavy with him. And am I then revenged,
To take him in the purging of his soul,   85
When he is fit and seasoned° for his passage?
No!
Up, sword, and know° thou a more horrid hent.°
                                      [He puts up his sword.]

When he is drunk asleep, or in his rage,°
Or in th' incestuous pleasure of his bed,   90
At game,° a-swearing, or about some act
That has no relish° of salvation in 't—
Then trip him, that his heels may kick at heaven,
And that his soul may be as damned and black
As hell, whereto it goes. My mother stays.°   95
This physic° but prolongs thy sickly days.   *Exit.*
King: My words fly up, my thoughts remain below.
Words without thoughts never to heaven go.   *Exit.*

Scene IV [The Queen's Private Chamber.]

Enter [Queen] Gertrude and Polonius.

Polonius: 'A will come straight. Look you lay home° to him.
Tell him his pranks have been too broad° to bear with,

---

69 *engaged* entangled.   *assay* trial. (Said to himself.)   73 *pat* opportunely   75 *would be scanned* needs to be looked into, or, would be interpreted as follows   80 *grossly, full of bread* i.e., enjoying his worldly pleasures rather than fasting. (See Ezekiel 16:49.)   81 *crimes broad blown* sins in full bloom.   *flush* vigorous   82 *audit* account.   *save* except for   83 *in . . . thought* as we see it from our mortal perspective   86 *seasoned* matured, readied   88 *know . . . hent* await to be grasped by me on a more horrid occasion. *hent* act of seizing   89 *drunk . . . rage* dead drunk, or in a fit of sexual passion   91 *game* gambling   92 *relish* trace, savor   95 *stays* awaits (me)   96 *physic* purging (by prayer), or, Hamlet's postponement of the killing   1 *lay home* thrust to the heart, reprove him soundly   2 *broad* unrestrained

And that Your Grace hath screened and stood between
Much heat° and him. I'll shroud° me even here.
Pray you, be round° with him.   5
Hamlet (within): Mother, Mother, Mother!
Queen: I'll warrant you, fear me not.
 Withdraw, I hear him coming.

           [Polonius hides behind the arras.]

 Enter Hamlet.

Hamlet: Now, Mother, what's the matter?
Queen: Hamlet, thou hast thy father° much offended.   10
Hamlet: Mother, you have my father much offended.
Queen: Come, come, you answer with an idle° tongue.
Hamlet: Go, go, you question with a wicked tongue.
Queen: Why, how now, Hamlet?
Hamlet: What's the matter now?
Queen: Have you forgot me?°
Hamlet: No, by the rood,° not so: 15
 You are the Queen, your husband's brother's wife,
 And—would it were not so!—you are my mother.
Queen: Nay, then, I'll set those to you that can speak.°
Hamlet: Come, come, and sit you down; you shall not budge.
 You go not till I set you up a glass   20
 Where you may see the inmost part of you.
Queen: What wilt thou do? Thou wilt not murder me?
 Help, ho!
Polonius [behind the arras]: What ho! Help!
Hamlet [drawing]: How now? A rat? Dead for a ducat,° dead!   25
       [He thrusts his rapier through the arras.]
Polonius [behind the arras]: O, I am slain!   *[He falls and dies.]*
Queen: O me, what has thou done?
Hamlet: Nay, I know not. Is it the King?
Queen: O, what a rash and bloody deed is this!
Hamlet: A bloody deed—almost as bad, good Mother,
 As kill a king, and marry with his brother.   30
Queen: As kill a king!
Hamlet: Ay, lady, it was my word.
      [He parts the arras and discovers Polonius.]
 Thou wretched, rash, intruding fool, farewell!

---

4 *Much heat* i.e., the King's anger. *shroud* conceal (with ironic fitness to Polonius' imminent death.
The word is only in the First Quarto; the Second Quarto and the Folio read "silence.") 5 *round*
blunt 10 *thy father* i.e., your stepfather, Claudius 12 *idle* foolish 15 *forgot me* i.e., forgotten that I
am your mother. *rood* cross of Christ 18 *speak* i.e., to someone so rude 25 *Dead for a ducat* i.e., I
bet a ducat he's dead; or, a ducat is his life's fee

I took thee for thy better. Take thy fortune.
Thou find'st to be too busy° is some danger.—
Leave wringing of your hands. Peace, sit you down, 35
And let me wring your heart, for so I shall,
If it be made of penetrable stuff,
If damnèd custom° have not brazed° it so
That it be proof° and bulwark against sense.°
Queen: What have I done, that thou dar'st wag thy tongue 40
In noise so rude against me?
Hamlet: Such an act
That blurs the grace and blush of modesty,
Calls virtue hypocrite, takes off the rose
From the fair forehead of an innocent love
And sets a blister° there, makes marriage vows 45
As false as dicers' oaths. O, such a deed
As from the body of contraction° plucks
The very soul, and sweet religion makes°
A rhapsody° of words. Heaven's face does glow
O'er this solidity and compound mass 50
With tristful visage, as against the doom,
Is thought-sick at the act.°
Queen: Ay me, what act,
That roars so loud and thunders in the index?°
Hamlet [showing her two likenesses]: Look here upon this picture, and on this,
The counterfeit presentment° of two brothers. 55
See what a grace was seated on this brow:
Hyperion's° curls, the front° of Jove himself,
An eye like Mars° to threaten and command,
A station° like the herald Mercury°
New-lighted° on a heaven-kissing hill— 60
A combination and a form indeed
Where every god did seem to set his seal°
To give the world assurance of a man.
This was your husband. Look you now what follows:
Here is your husband, like a mildewed ear,° 65
Blasting° his wholesome brother. Have you eyes?
Could you on this fair mountain leave° to feed

---

34 *busy* nosey   38 *damnèd custom* habitual wickedness.   *brazed* brazened, hardened   39 *proof*
armor.   *sense* feeling   45 *sets a blister* i.e., brands as a harlot   47 *contraction* the marriage contract
48 *sweet religion makes* i.e., makes marriage vows   49 *rhapsody* senseless string   49–52 *Heaven's . . .
act* heaven's face blushes at this solid world compounded of the various elements, with sorrowful face
as though the day of doom were near, and is sick with horror at the deed (i.e., Gertrude's marriage)
53 *index* table of contents, prelude or preface   55 *counterfeit presentment* portrayed representation
57 *Hyperion's* the sun-god's.   *front* brow   58 *Mars* god of war   59 *station* manner of standing.
Mercury winged messenger of the gods   60 *New-lighted* newly alighted   62 *set his seal* i.e., affix his
approval   65 *ear* i.e., of grain   66 *Blasting* blighting   67 *leave* cease

And batten° on this moor?° Ha, have you eyes?
You cannot call it love, for at your age
The heyday° in the blood° is tame, it's humble,   70
And waits upon the judgment, and what judgment
Would step from this to this? Sense,° sure, you have,
Else could you not have motion, but sure that sense
Is apoplexed,° for madness would not err,°
Nor sense to ecstasy was ne'er so thralled,   75
But° it reserved some quantity of choice
To serve in such a difference.° What devil was 't
That thus hath cozened° you at hoodman-blind?°
Eyes without feeling, feeling without sight,
Ears without hands or eyes, smelling sans° all,   80
Or but a sickly part of one true sense
Could not so mope.° O shame, where is thy blush?
Rebellious hell,
If thou canst mutine° in a matron's bones,
To flaming youth let virtue be as wax   85
And melt in her own fire.° Proclaim no shame
When the compulsive ardor gives the charge,
Since frost itself as actively doth burn,
And reason panders will.°
Queen: O Hamlet, speak no more!   90
Thou turn'st mine eyes into my very soul,
And there I see such black and grainèd° spots
As will not leave their tinct.°
Hamlet: Nay, but to live
In the rank sweat of an enseamèd° bed,
Stewed° in corruption, honeying and making love   95
Over the nasty sty!
Queen: O, speak to me no more!
These words like daggers enter in my ears.
No more, sweet Hamlet!

---

68 *batten* gorge.   *moor* barren or marshy ground (suggesting also "dark-skinned")   70 *heyday* state of excitement.   *blood* passion   72 *Sense* perception through the five senses (the functions of the middle or sensible soul)   74 *apoplexed* paralyzed. (Hamlet goes on to explain that, without such a paralysis of will, mere madness would not so err, nor would the five senses so enthrall themselves to *ecstasy* or lunacy; even such deranged states of mind would be able to make the obvious choice between Hamlet Senior and Claudius.)   *err* so err   76 *But* but that   77 *To . . . difference* to help in making a choice between two such men   78 *cozened* cheated.   *hoodman-blind* blindman's buff. (In this game, says Hamlet, the devil must have pushed Claudius toward Gertrude while she was blindfolded.)   80 *sans* without   82 *mope* be dazed, act aimlessly   84 *mutine* incite mutiny   85–86 *be as wax . . . fire* melt like a candle or stick of sealing wax held over the candle flame   86–89 *Proclaim . . . will* call it no shameful business when the compelling ardor of youth delivers the attack, i.e., commits lechery, since the *frost* of advanced age burns with as active a fire of lust and reason perverts itself by fomenting lust rather than restraining it   92 *grainèd* dyed in grain, indelible   93 *leave their tinct* surrender their color   94 *enseamèd* saturated in the grease and filth of passionate lovemaking   95 *Stewed* soaked, bathed (with a suggestion of "stew," brothel)

Hamlet: A murderer and a villain,
　A slave that is not twentieth part the tithe°   100
　Of your precedent lord,° a vice° of kings,
　A cutpurse of the empire and the rule,
　That from a shelf the precious diadem stole
　And put it in his pocket!
Queen: No more!   105

　Enter Ghost.

Hamlet: A king of shreds and patches°—
　Save me, and hover o'er me with your wings,
　You heavenly guards! What would your gracious figure?
Queen: Alas, he's mad!
Hamlet: Do you not come your tardy son to chide,   110
　That, lapsed° in time and passion, lets go by
　Th' important° acting of your dread command?
　O, say!
Ghost: Do not forget. This visitation
　Is but to whet thy almost blunted purpose.   115
　But look, amazement° on thy mother sits.
　O, step between her and her fighting soul!
　Conceit° in weakest bodies strongest works.
　Speak to her, Hamlet.
Hamlet: How is it with you, lady?
Queen: Alas, how is 't with you,   120
　That you do bend your eye on vacancy,
　And with th' incorporal° air do hold discourse?
　Forth at your eyes your spirits wildly peep,
　And, as the sleeping soldiers in th' alarm,°
　Your bedded° hair, like life in excrements,°   125
　Start up and stand on end. O gentle son,
　Upon the heat and flame of thy distemper°
　Sprinkle cool patience. Whereon do you look?
Hamlet: On him, on him! Look you how pale he glares!
　His form and cause conjoined,° preaching to stones,   130
　Would make them capable.°—Do not look upon me,
　Lest with this piteous action you convert
　My stern effects.° Then what I have to do

---

100 *tithe* tenth part   101 *precedent lord* former husband.   *vice* buffoon. (A reference to the Vice of the morality plays.)   106 *shreds and patches* i.e., motley, the traditional costume of the clown or fool   111 *lapsed* delaying   112 *important* importunate, urgent   116 *amazement* distraction   118 *Conceit* imagination   122 *incorporal* immaterial   124 *as . . . alarm* like soldiers called out of sleep by an alarm   125 *bedded* laid flat.   *like life in excrements* i.e., as though hair, an outgrowth of the body, had a life of its own. (Hair was thought to be lifeless because it lacks sensation, and so its standing on end would be unnatural and ominous.)   127 *distemper* disorder   130 *His . . . conjoined* his appearance joined to his cause for speaking   131 *capable* receptive   132–133 *convert . . . effects* divert me from my stern duty

Will want true color—tears perchance for blood.°

Queen: To whom do you speak this? 135

Hamlet: Do you see nothing there?

Queen: Nothing at all, yet all that is I see.

Hamlet: Nor did you nothing hear?

Queen: No, nothing but ourselves.

Hamlet: Why, look you there, look how it steals away! 140
    My father, in his habit° as° he lived!
    Look where he goes even now out at the portal!

                                        Exit Ghost.

Queen: This is the very° coinage of your brain.
    This bodiless creation ecstasy
    Is very cunning in.° 145

Hamlet: Ecstasy?
    My pulse as yours doth temperately keep time,
    And makes as healthful music. It is not madness
    That I have uttered. Bring me to the test,
    And I the matter will reword,° which madness 150
    Would gambol° from. Mother, for love of grace,
    Lay not that flattering unction° to your soul
    That not your trespass but my madness speaks.
    It will but skin° and film the ulcerous place,
    Whiles rank corruption, mining° all within, 155
    Infects unseen. Confess yourself to heaven,
    Repent what's past, avoid what is to come,
    And do not spread the compost° on the weeds
    To make them ranker. Forgive me this my virtue;°
    For in the fatness° of these pursy° times 160
    Virtue itself of vice must pardon beg,
    Yea, curb° and woo for leave° to do him good.

Queen: O Hamlet, thou hast cleft my heart in twain.

Hamlet: O, throw away the worser part of it,
    And live the purer with the other half. 165
    Good night. But go not to my uncle's bed;
    Assume a virtue, if you have it not.
    That monster, custom, who all sense doth eat,°
    Of habits devil,° is angel yet in this,
    That to the use of actions fair and good 170

---

134 *want . . . blood* lack plausibility so that (with a play on the normal sense of *color*) I shall shed colorless tears instead of blood   141 *habit* clothes.   *as* as when   143 *very* mere   144–145 *This . . . in* madness is skillful in creating this kind of hallucination   150 *reword* repeat word for word   151 *gambol* skip away   152 *unction* ointment   154 *skin* grow a skin for   155 *mining* working under the surface   158 *compost* manure   159 *this my virtue* my virtuous talk in reproving you   160 *fatness* grossness.   *pursy* flabby, out of shape   162 *curb* bow, bend the knee.   *leave* permission   168 *who . . . eat* which consumes all proper or natural feeling, all sensibility   169 *Of habits devil* devil-like in prompting evil habits

He likewise gives a frock or livery°
That aptly° is put on. Refrain tonight,
And that shall lend a kind of easiness
To the next abstinence; the next more easy;
For use° almost can change the stamp of nature,°   175
And either° . . . the devil, or throw him out
With wondrous potency. Once more, good night;
And when you are desirous to be blest,
I'll blessing beg of you.° For this same lord,

                    [*pointing to Polonius*]   180

I do repent; but heaven hath pleased it so
To punish me with this, and this with me,
That I must be their scourge and minister.°
I will bestow° him, and will answer° well
The death I gave him. So, again, good night.   185
I must be cruel only to be kind.
This° bad begins, and worse remains behind.°
One word more, good lady.
Queen: What shall I do?
Hamlet: Not this by no means that I bid you do:
Let the bloat° king tempt you again to bed,
Pinch wanton° on your cheek, call you his mouse,   190
And let him, for a pair of reechy° kisses,
Or paddling° in your neck with his damned fingers,
Make you to ravel all this matter out°
That I essentially am not in madness,
But mad in craft.° 'Twere good° you let him know,   195
For who that's but a queen, fair, sober, wise,
Would from a paddock,° from a bat, a gib,°
Such dear concernings° hide? Who would do so?
No, in despite of sense and secrecy,°
Unpeg the basket° on the house's top,   200
Let the birds fly, and like the famous ape,°

---

171 *livery* an outer appearance, a customary garb (and hence a predisposition easily assumed in time of stress)   172 *aptly* readily   175 *use* habit.   *the stamp of nature* our inborn traits   176 *And either* (A defective line, usually emended by inserting the word *master* after *either*, following the Fourth Quarto and early editors.)   178–179 *when . . . you* i.e., when you are ready to be penitent and seek God's blessing, I will ask your blessing as a dutiful son should   182 *their scourge and minister* i.e., agent of heavenly retribution. (By *scourge*, Hamlet also suggests that he himself will eventually suffer punishment in the process of fulfilling heaven's will.)   183 *bestow* stow, dispose of.   *answer* account or pay for   186 *This* i.e., the killing of Polonius.   *behind* to come   189 *bloat* bloated   190 *Pinch wanton* i.e., leave his love pinches on your cheeks, branding you as wanton   191 *reechy* dirty, filthy   192 *paddling* fingering amorously   193 *ravel . . . out* unravel, disclose   195 *in craft* by cunning.   *good* (Said sarcastically; also the following eight lines.)   197 *paddock* toad.   *gib* tomcat   198 *dear concernings* important affairs   199 *sense and secrecy* secrecy that common sense requires   200 *Unpeg the basket* open the cage, i.e., let out the secret   201 *famous ape* (In a story now lost.)

To try conclusions,° in the basket creep
And break your own neck down.°
Queen: Be thou assured, if words be made of breath,
And breath of life, I have no life to breathe   205
What thou hast said to me.
Hamlet: I must to England. You know that?
Queen: Alack,
I had forgot. 'Tis so concluded on.
Hamlet: There's letters sealed, and my two schoolfellows,
Whom I will trust as I will adders fanged,   210
They bear the mandate; they must sweep my way
And marshal me to knavery.° Let it work.°
For 'tis the sport to have the enginer°
Hoist with° his own petard,° and 't shall go hard
But I will° delve one yard below their mines°   215
And blow them at the moon. O, 'tis most sweet
When in one line° two crafts° directly meet.
This man shall set me packing.°
I'll lug the guts into the neighbor room.
Mother, good night indeed. This counselor   220
Is now most still, most secret, and most grave,
Who was in life a foolish prating knave.—
Come, sir, to draw toward an end° with you.—
Good night, Mother.

Exeunt [separately, Hamlet dragging in Polonius].

ACT IV

Scene I [The Castle.]

Enter King and Queen,° with Rosencrantz and Guildenstern.

King: There's matter° in these sighs, these profound heaves.°
You must translate; 'tis fit we understand them.

---

202 *try conclusions* test the outcome (in which the ape apparently enters a cage from which birds
have been released and then tries to fly out of the cage as they have done, falling to its death)
203 *down* in the fall: utterly   211–212 *sweep . . . knavery* sweep a path before me and conduct me
to some *knavery* or treachery prepared for me   212 *work* proceed   213 *enginer* maker of military
contrivances   214 *Hoist with* blown up by.   *petard* an explosive used to blow in a door or make a
breach   214–215 *'t shall . . . will* unless luck is against me, I will   215 *mines* tunnels used in warfare to undermine the enemy's emplacements: Hamlet will countermine by going under their mines
217 *in one line* i.e., mines and countermines on a collision course, or the countermines directly
below the mines.   *crafts* acts of guile, plots   218 *set me packing* set me to making schemes, and set
me to lugging (him), and, also, send me off in a hurry   223 *draw . . . end* finish up (with a pun on
draw, "pull")   s.d. *Enter . . . Queen* (Some editors argue that Gertrude never exits in Act III,
Scene iv, and that the scene is continuous here, as suggested in the Folio, but the Second Quarto
marks an entrance for her and at line 35 Claudius speaks of Gertrude's *closet* as though it were elsewhere. A short time has elapsed, during which the King has become aware of her highly wrought
emotional state.)   1 *matter* significance.   *heaves* heavy sighs

Where is your son?

Queen: Bestow this place on us a little while.

[Exeunt Rosencrantz and Guildenstern.]

Ah, mine own lord, what have I seen tonight!   5

King: What, Gertrude? How does Hamlet?

Queen: Mad as the sea and wind when both contend
Which is the mightier. In his lawless fit,
Behind the arras hearing something stir,
Whips out his rapier, cries, "A rat, a rat!"   10
And in this brainish apprehension° kills
The unseen good old man.

King: O heavy° deed!
It had been so with us,° had we been there.
His liberty is full of threats to all—
To you yourself, to us, to everyone.   15
Alas, how shall this bloody deed be answered?°
It will be laid to us, whose providence°
Should have kept short,° restrained, and out of haunt°
This mad young man. But so much was our love,
We would not understand what was most fit,   20
But, like the owner of a foul disease,
To keep it from divulging,° let it feed
Even on the pith of life. Where is he gone?

Queen: To draw apart the body he hath killed,
O'er whom his very madness, like some ore°   25
Among a mineral° of metals base,
Shows itself pure: 'a weeps for what is done.

King: O Gertrude, come away!
The sun no sooner shall the mountains touch
But we will ship him hence, and this vile deed   30
We must with all our majesty and skill
Both countenance° and excuse.—Ho, Guildenstern!

Enter Rosencrantz and Guildenstern.

Friends both, go join you with some further aid.
Hamlet in madness hath Polonius slain,
And from his mother's closet hath he dragged him.   35
Go seek him out, speak fair, and bring the body
Into the chapel. I pray you, haste in this.

[Exeunt Rosencrantz and Guildenstern.]

Come, Gertrude, we'll call up our wisest friends

---

11 *brainish apprehension* headstrong conception   12 *heavy* grievous   13 *us* i.e., me. (The royal "we";
also in line 15.)   16 *answered* explained   17 *providence* foresight   18 *short* i.e., on a short tether.
out of haunt ecluded   22 *divulging* becoming evident   25 *ore* vein of gold   26 *mineral* mine
32 *countenance* put the best face on

And let them know both what we mean to do
And what's untimely done . . . .°   40
Whose whisper o'er the world's diameter,°
As level° as the cannon to his blank,°
Transports his poisoned shot, may miss our name
And hit the woundless° air. O, come away!
My soul is full of discord and dismay.   *Exeunt.*   45

Scene II [The Castle.]

Enter Hamlet.

Hamlet: Safely stowed.
Rosencrantz, Guildenstern (within): Hamlet! Lord Hamlet!
Hamlet: But soft, what noise? Who calls on Hamlet? O, here they come.

Enter Rosencrantz and Guildenstern.

Rosencrantz: What have you done, my lord, with the dead body?
Hamlet: Compounded it with dust, whereto 'tis kin.   5
Rosencrantz: Tell us where 'tis, that we may take it thence
  And bear it to the chapel.
Hamlet: Do not believe it.
Rosencrantz: Believe what?
Hamlet: That I can keep your counsel and not mine own.° Besides, to be de- 10
  manded of° a sponge, what replication° should be made by the son of a king?
Rosencrantz: Take you me for a sponge, my lord?
Hamlet: Ay, sir, that soaks up the King's countenance,° his rewards, his authori-
  ties.° But such officers do the King best service in the end. He keeps them,
  like an ape, an apple, in the corner of his jaw, first mouthed to be last swal- 15
  lowed. When he needs what you have gleaned, it is but squeezing you, and,
  sponge, you shall be dry again.
Rosencrantz: I understand you not, my lord.
Hamlet: I am glad of it. A knavish speech sleeps in° a foolish ear.
Rosencrantz: My lord, you must tell us where the body is and go with us to the 20
  King.
Hamlet: The body is with the King, but the King is not with the body.° The
  King is a thing—

---

40 *And . . . done* (A defective line: conjectures as to the missing words include *So, haply, slander*
[Capell and others]; *For, haply, slander* [Theobald and others]; and *So envious slander* [Jenkins].)   41 *diameter* extent from side to side   42 *As level* with as direct aim. *his blank* its target at point-blank
range   44 *woundless* invulnerable   10 *That . . . own* i.e., that I can follow your advice (by telling
where the body is) and still keep my own secret   10–11 *demanded of* questioned by   11 *replication*
reply   13 *countenance* favor.   13–14 *authorities* delegated power, influence   19 *sleeps in* has no
meaning to   22 *The . . . body* (Perhaps alludes to the legal commonplace of "the king's two bodies,"
which drew a distinction between the sacred office of kingship and the particular mortal who possessed
it at any given time. Hence, although Claudius' body is necessarily a part of him, true kingship is not
contained in it. Similarly, Claudius will have Polonius' body when it is found, but there is no kingship
in this business either.)

Guildenstern: A thing, my lord?

Hamlet: Of nothing.° Bring me to him. Hide fox, and all after!° *Exeunt* [*running*].   25

Scene III [The Castle.]

Enter King, and two or three.

King: I have sent to seek him, and to find the body.
How dangerous is it that this man goes loose!
Yet must not we put the strong law on him.
He's loved of° the distracted° multitude,
Who like not in their judgment, but their eyes,°   5
And where 'tis so, th' offender's scourge° is weighed,°
But never the offense. To bear all smooth and even,°
This sudden sending him away must seem
Deliberate pause.° Diseases desperate grown
By desperate appliance° are relieved,   10
Or not at all.

Enter Rosencrantz, [Guildenstern,] and all the rest.

        How now, what hath befall'n?

Rosencrantz: Where the dead body is bestowed, my lord,
We cannot get from him.

King: But where is he?

Rosencrantz: Without, my lord; guarded, to know your pleasure.

King: Bring him before us.

Rosencrantz: Ho! Bring in the lord.   15

They enter [with Hamlet].

King: Now, Hamlet, where's Polonius?

Hamlet: At supper.

King: At supper? Where?

Hamlet: Not where he eats, but where 'a is eaten. A certain convocation of
politic worms° are e'en° at him. Your worm° is your only emperor for diet.°   20
We fat all creatures else to fat us, and we fat ourselves for maggots. Your fat
king and your lean beggar is but variable service°—two dishes, but to one
table. That's the end.

King: Alas, alas!

Hamlet: A man may fish with the worm that hath eat° of a king, and eat of the 25
    fish that hath fed of that worm.

King: What dost thou mean by this?

Hamlet: Nothing but to show you how a king may go a progress° through the
    guts of a beggar.

King: Where is Polonius? 30

Hamlet: In heaven. Send thither to see. If your messenger find him not there,
    seek him i' th' other place yourself. But if indeed you find him not within
    this month, you shall nose him as you go up the stairs into the lobby.

King [*to some attendants*]: Go seek him there.

Hamlet: 'A will stay till you come. [*Exeunt attendants.*] 35

King: Hamlet, this deed, for thine especial safety—
    Which we do tender,° as we dearly° grieve
    For that which thou hast done—must send thee hence
    With fiery quickness. Therefore prepare thyself.
    The bark° is ready, and the wind at help, 40
    Th' associates tend,° and everything is bent°
    For England.

Hamlet: For England!

King: Ay, Hamlet.

Hamlet: Good. 45

King: So is it, if thou knew'st our purposes.

Hamlet: I see a cherub° that sees them. But come, for England! Farewell, dear
    mother.

King: Thy loving father, Hamlet.

Hamlet: My mother. Father and mother is man and wife, man and wife is one 50
    flesh, and so, my mother. Come, for England! *Exit.*

King: Follow him at foot;° tempt him with speed aboard.
    Delay it not. I'll have him hence tonight.
    Away! For everything is sealed and done
    That else leans on° th' affair. Pray you, make haste. 55
                                    [*Exeunt all but the King.*]
    And, England,° if my love thou hold'st at aught—°
    As my great power thereof may give thee sense,°
    Since yet thy cicatrice° looks raw and red
    After the Danish sword, and thy free awe°
    Pays homage to us—thou mayst not coldly set° 60
    Our sovereign process,° which imports at full,°

---

25 *eat* eaten. (Pronounced *et.*) 28 *progress* royal journey of state 37 *tender* regard, hold dear.
dearly intensely 40 *bark* sailing vessel 41 *tend* wait. *bent* in readiness 47 *cherub* (Cherubim are
angels of knowledge. Hamlet hints that both he and heaven are onto Claudius' tricks.) 52 *at foot*
close behind, at heel 55 *leans on* bears upon, is related to 56 *England* i.e., King of England. *at
aught* at any value 57 *As . . . sense* for so my great power may give you a just appreciation of the importance of valuing my love 58 *cicatrice* scar 59 *free awe* voluntary show of respect 60 *coldly set*
regard with indifference 61 *process* command. *imports at full* conveys specific directions for

By letters congruing° to that effect,
The present° death of Hamlet. Do it, England,
For like the hectic° in my blood he rages,
And thou must cure me. Till I know 'tis done,   65
Howe'er my haps,° my joys were ne'er begun.   *Exit.*

Scene IV [The Coast of Denmark.]

Enter Fortinbras with his army over the stage.

Fortinbras: Go, Captain, from me greet the Danish king.
    Tell him that by his license° Fortinbras
    Craves the conveyance of° a promised march
    Over his kingdom. You know the rendezvous.
    If that His Majesty would aught with us,   5
    We shall express our duty° in his eye;°
    And let him know so.
Captain: I will do 't, my lord.
Fortinbras: Go softly° on. [*Exeunt all but the Captain.*]

    Enter Hamlet, Rosencrantz, [Guildenstern,] etc.

Hamlet: Good sir, whose powers° are these?   10
Captain: They are of Norway, sir.
Hamlet: How purposed, sir, I pray you?
Captain: Against some part of Poland.
Hamlet: Who commands them, sir?
Captain: The nephew to old Norway, Fortinbras.   15
Hamlet: Goes it against the main° of Poland, sir,
    Or for some frontier?
Captain: Truly to speak, and with no addition,°
    We go to gain a little patch of ground
    That hath in it no profit but the name.   20
    To pay° five ducats, five, I would not farm it;°
    Nor will it yield to Norway or the Pole
    A ranker° rate, should it be sold in fee.°
Hamlet: Why, then the Polack never will defend it.
Captain: Yes, it is already garrisoned.   25
Hamlet: Two thousand souls and twenty thousand ducats
    Will not debate the question of this straw.°
    This is th' impostume° of much wealth and peace,
    That inward breaks, and shows no cause without

---

62 *congruing* agreeing   63 *present* immediate   64 *hectic* persistent fever   66 *haps* fortunes   2 *license* permission   3 *the conveyance of* escort during   6 *duty* respect.   *eye* presence   9 *softly* slowly, circumspectly   10 *powers* forces   16 *main* main part   18 *addition* exaggeration   21 *To pay* i.e., for a yearly rental of.   *farm it* take a lease of it   23 *ranker* higher.   *in fee* fee simple, outright   27 *debate . . . straw* settle this trifling matter   28 *impostume* abscess

Why the man dies. I humbly thank you, sir.   30
Captain: God b' wi' you, sir.   [*Exit.*]
Rosencrantz: Will 't please you go, my lord?
Hamlet: I'll be with you straight. Go a little before.

[*Exeunt all except Hamlet.*]

How all occasions do inform against° me
And spur my dull revenge! What is a man,
If his chief good and market of° his time   35
Be but to sleep and feed? A beast, no more.
Sure he that made us with such large discourse,°
Looking before and after,° gave us not
That capability and godlike reason
To fust° in us unused. Now, whether it be   40
Bestial oblivion,° or some craven° scruple
Of thinking too precisely° on th' event—°
A thought which, quartered, hath but one part wisdom
And ever three parts coward—I do not know
Why yet I live to say "This thing's to do,"   45
Sith° I have cause, and will, and strength, and means
To do 't. Examples gross° as earth exhort me:
Witness this army of such mass and charge,°
Led by a delicate and tender° prince,
Whose spirit with divine ambition puffed
Makes mouths° at the invisible event,°   50
Exposing what is mortal and unsure
To all that fortune, death, and danger dare,°
Even for an eggshell. Rightly° to be great
Is not to stir without great argument,   55
But greatly to find quarrel in a straw
When honor's at the stake.° How stand I, then,
That have a father killed, a mother stained,
Excitements of° my reason and my blood,
And let all sleep, while to my shame I see   60
The imminent death of twenty thousand men
That for a fantasy° and trick° of fame
Go to their graves like beds, fight for a plot°

---

33 *inform against* denounce, betray: take shape against   35 *market of* profit of, compensation for
37 *discourse* power of reasoning   38 *Looking before and after* able to review past events and anticipate the future   40 *fust* grow moldy   41 *oblivion* forgetfulness.   *craven* cowardly   42 *precisely*
scrupulously.   *event* outcome   46 *Sith* since   47 *gross* obvious   48 *charge* expense   49 *delicate and
tender* of fine and youthful qualities   51 *Makes mouths* makes scornful faces.   *invisible event* unforeseeable outcome   53 *dare* could do (to him)   54–57 *Rightly . . . stake* true greatness does not normally consist of rushing into action over some trivial provocation: however, when one's honor is involved, even a trifling insult requires that one respond greatly (?)   57 *at the stake* (A metaphor from
gambling or bear-baiting.)   59 *Excitements of* promptings by   62 *fantasy* fanciful caprice, illusion.
trick trifle, deceit   63 *plot* plot of ground

Whereon the numbers cannot try the cause,°
Which is not tomb enough and continent°   65
To hide the slain? O, from this time forth
My thoughts be bloody or be nothing worth!   *Exit.*

Scene V [The Castle.]

Enter Horatio, [Queen] Gertrude, and a Gentleman.

Queen: I will not speak with her.
Gentleman: She is importunate,
    Indeed distract.° Her mood will needs be pitied.
Queen: What would she have?
Gentleman: She speaks much of her father, says she hears
    There's tricks° i' the world, and hems,° and beats her heart,°   5
    Spurns enviously at straws,° speaks things in doubt°
    That carry but half sense. Her speech is nothing,
    Yet the unshapèd use° of it doth move
    The hearers to collection;° they yawn° at it,
    And botch° the words up fit to their own thoughts,   10
    Which,° as her winks and nods and gestures yield° them,
    Indeed would make one think there might be thought,°
    Though nothing sure, yet much unhappily.°
Horatio: 'Twere good she were spoken with, for she may strew
    Dangerous conjectures in ill-breeding° minds.   15
Queen: Let her come in.   [*Exit Gentleman.*]
    [*Aside.*] To my sick soul, as sin's true nature is,
    Each toy° seems prologue to some great amiss.°
    So full of artless jealousy is guilt,
    It spills itself in fearing to be spilt.°   20

Enter Ophelia° [distracted].

Ophelia: Where is the beauteous majesty of Denmark?
Queen: How now, Ophelia?
Ophelia (she sings):
        "How should I your true love know
        From another one?

---

64 *Whereon . . . cause* on which there is insufficient room for the soldiers needed to engage in a military contest   65 *continent* receptacle, container   2 *distract* distracted   5 *tricks* deceptions. *hems* makes "hmm" sounds. *heart* i.e., breast   6 *Spurns . . . straws* kicks spitefully, takes offense at trifles. *in doubt* obscurely   8 *unshapèd use* incoherent manner   9 *collection* inference, a guess at some sort of meaning. *yawn* gape, wonder; grasp. (The Folio reading, *aim,* is possible.)   10 *botch* patch   11 *Which* which words. *yield* deliver, represent   12 *thought* intended   13 *unhappily* unpleasantly near the truth, shrewdly   15 *ill-breeding* prone to suspect the worst and to make mischief   18 *toy* trifle. *amiss* calamity   19–20 *So . . . spilt* guilt is so full of suspicion that it unskillfully betrays itself in fearing betrayal   20 s.d *Enter Ophelia* (In the First Quarto, Ophelia enters, "playing on a lute, and her hair down, singing.")

                        By his cockle hat° and staff,   25
                        And his sandal shoon.°"

Queen: Alas, sweet lady, what imports this song?
Ophelia: Say you? Nay, pray you, mark.
                        "He is dead and gone, lady,   (*Song.*)
                        He is dead and gone;   30
                        At his head a grass-green turf,
                        At his heels a stone.""

        O, ho!

Queen: Nay, but Ophelia—
Ophelia: Pray you, mark. [*Sings.*]   35
                        "White his shroud as the mountain snow"—

        Enter King.

Queen: Alas, look here, my lord.
Ophelia:
                        "Larded° with sweet flowers;   (*Song.*)
                        Which bewept to the ground did not go
                        With true-love showers.°"   40

King: How do you, pretty lady?
Ophelia: Well, God 'ild° you! They say the owl° was a baker's daughter. Lord,
    we know what we are, but know not what we may be. God be at your table!
King: Conceit° upon her father.
Ophelia: Pray let's have no words of this; but when they ask you what it means,   45
    say you this:
                        "Tomorrow is Saint Valentine's day,   (*Song.*)
                        All in the morning betime,°
                        And I a maid at your window,
                        To be your Valentine.   50
                        Then up he rose, and donned his clothes,
                        And dupped° the chamber door,
                        Let in the maid, that out a maid
                        Never departed more."

King: Pretty Ophelia—   55
Ophelia: Indeed, la, without an oath, I'll make an end on 't:
                        "By Gis° and by Saint Charity,
                        Alack, and he for shame!
                        Young men will do 't, if they come to 't;
                        By Cock,° they are to blame.   60

---

25 *cockle hat* hat with cockleshell stuck in it as a sign that the wearer had been a pilgrim to the shrine
of Saint James of Compostella in Spain   26 *shoon* shoes   38 *Larded* decorated   40 *showers* i.e., tears
42 *God 'ild* God yield or reward.   *owl* (Refers to a legend about a baker's daughter who was turned
into an owl for being ungenerous when Jesus begged a loaf of bread.)   44 *Conceit* brooding   48 *be-
time* early   52 *dupped* did up, opened   57 *Gis* Jesus   60 *Cock* (A perversion of "God" in oaths; here
also with a quibble on the slang word for penis.)

Quoth she, 'Before you tumbled me,
You promised me to wed.'"
He answers:
"'So would I ha' done, by yonder sun,
An° thou hadst not come to my bed.'"   65
King: How long hath she been thus?
Ophelia: I hope all will be well. We must be patient, but I cannot choose but
    weep to think they would lay him i' the cold ground. My brother shall know
    of it. And so I thank you for your good counsel. Come, my coach! Good
    night, ladies, good night, sweet ladies, good night, good night.   [*Exit.*]   70
King [*to Horatio*]: Follow her close. Give her good watch, I pray you.
                                                          [*Exit Horatio.*]

O, this is the poison of deep grief; it springs
All from her father's death—and now behold!
O Gertrude, Gertrude,
When sorrows come, they come not single spies,°   75
But in battalions. First, her father slain;
Next, your son gone, and he most violent author
Of his own just remove;° the people muddied,°
Thick and unwholesome in their thoughts and whispers
For good Polonius' death—and we have done but greenly,°   80
In hugger-mugger° to inter him; poor Ophelia
Divided from herself and her fair judgment,
Without the which we are pictures or mere beasts;
Last, and as much containing° as all these,
Her brother is in secret come from France,   85
Feeds on this wonder, keeps himself in clouds°,
And wants° not buzzers° to infect his ear
With pestilent speeches of his father's death,
Wherein necessity,° of matter beggared,°
Will nothing stick our person to arraign   90
In ear and ear.° O my dear Gertrude, this,
Like to a murdering piece,° in many places
Gives me superfluous death.°   *A noise within.*
Queen: Alack, what noise is this?
King: Attend!°   95
Where is my Switzers?° Let them guard the door.

Enter a Messenger.

---

65 An if   75 *spies* scouts sent in advance of the main force   78 *remove* removal.   *muddied* stirred
up, confused   80 *greenly* in an inexperienced way, foolishly   81 *hugger-mugger* secret haste   84 *as
much containing* as full of serious matter   86 *Feeds . . . clouds* feeds his resentment or shocked griev-
ance, holds himself inscrutable and aloof amid all this rumor   87 *wants* lacks.   *buzzers* gossipers, in-
formers   89 *necessity* i.e., the need to invent some plausible explanation.   *of matter beggared* unpro-
vided with facts   90–91 *Will . . . ear* will not hesitate to accuse my (royal) person in everybody's
ears   92 *murdering piece* cannon loaded so as to scatter its shot   93 *Gives . . . death* kills me over and
over   95 *Attend* i.e., guard me   96 *Switzers* Swiss guards, mercenaries

What is the matter?

Messenger: Save yourself, my lord!
The ocean, overpeering of his list,°
Eats not the flats° with more impetuous° haste
Than young Laertes, in a riotous head,° 100
O'erbears your officers. The rabble call him lord,
And, as° the world were now but to begin,
Antiquity forgot, custom not known,
The ratifiers and props of every word,°
They cry, "Choose we! Laertes shall be king!" 105
Caps,° hands, and tongues applaud it to the clouds,
"Laertes shall be king, Laertes king!"

Queen: How cheerfully on the false trail they cry!   *A noise within.*
O, this is counter,° you false Danish dogs!

Enter Laertes with others.

King: The doors are broke. 110
Laertes: Where is this King?—Sirs, stand you all without.
All: No, let's come in.
Laertes: I pray you, give me leave.
All: We will, we will.
Laertes: I thank you. Keep the door. [*Exeunt followers.*]
            O thou vile king, Give me my father! 115
Queen [restraining him]: Calmly, good Laertes.
Laertes: That drop of blood that's calm proclaims me bastard,
Cries cuckold to my father, brands the harlot
Even here, between° the chaste unsmirchèd brow
Of my true mother.
King: What is the cause, Laertes, 120
That thy rebellion looks so giantlike?
Let him go, Gertrude. Do not fear our° person.
There's such divinity doth hedge° a king
That treason can but peep to what it would,°
Acts little of his will.° Tell me, Laertes, 125
Why thou art thus incensed. Let him go, Gertrude.
Speak, man.
Laertes: Where is my father?
King: Dead.

---

98 *overpeering of his list* overflowing its shore, boundary   99 *flats* i.e., flatlands near shore.   *impetuous* violent (perhaps also with the meaning of impiteous [*impitious, Second Quarto*], "pitiless")   100 *head* insurrection   102 *as* as if   104 *The ratifiers . . . word* i.e., *antiquity* (or tradition) and *custom* ought to confirm (*ratify*) and underprop our every word or promise   106 *Caps* (The caps are thrown in the air.)   109 *counter* (A hunting term, meaning to follow the trail in a direction opposite to that which the game has taken.)   119 *between* in the middle of   122 *fear our* fear for my   123 *hedge* protect, as with a surrounding barrier   124 *can . . . would* can only peep furtively, as through a barrier at what it would intend   125 *Acts . . . will* (but) performs little of what it intends

Queen: But not by him.
King: Let him demand his fill.
Laertes: How came he dead? I'll not be juggled with.°
    To hell, allegiance! Vows, to the blackest devil!   130
    Conscience and grace, to the profoundest pit!
    I dare damnation. To this point I stand,°
    That both the worlds I give to negligence,°
    Let come what comes, only I'll be revenged
    Most throughly° for my father.   135
King: Who shall stay you?
Laertes: My will, not all the world's.°
    And for° my means, I'll husband them so well
    They shall go far with little.
King: Good Laertes,
    If you desire to know the certainty   140
    Of your dear father, is 't writ in your revenge
    That, swoopstake,° you will draw both friend and foe,
    Winner and loser?
Laertes: None but his enemies.
King: Will you know them, then?   145
Laertes: To his good friends thus wide I'll ope my arms,
    And like the kind life-rendering pelican°
    Repast° them with my blood.
King: Why, now you speak
    Like a good child and a true gentleman.
    That I am guiltless of your father's death,   150
    And am most sensibly° in grief for it,
    It shall as level° to your judgment 'pear
    As day does to your eye.   *A noise within.*
Laertes: How now, what noise is that?

    Enter Ophelia.

King: Let her come in.
Laertes: O heat, dry up my brains! Tears seven times salt   155
    Burn out the sense and virtue° of mine eye!
    By heaven, thy madness shall be paid with weight°
    Till our scale turn the beam.° O rose of May!
    Dear maid, kind sister, sweet Ophelia!

---

129 *juggled with* cheated, deceived   132 *To . . . stand* I am resolved in this   133 *both . . . negligence*
i.e., both this world and the next are of no consequence to me   135 *throughly* thoroughly   137 *My
will . . . world's* I'll stop (*stay*) when my will is accomplished, not for anyone else's.   138 *for* as for
142 *swoopstake* i.e., indiscriminately. (Literally taking all stakes on the gambling table at once. *Draw*
is also a gambling term meaning "take from.")   147 *pelican* (Refers to the belief that the female pelican fed its young with its own blood.)   148 *Repast* feed   151 *sensibly* feelingly   152 *level* plain
156 *virtue* faculty, power   157 *paid with weight* repaid, avenged equally or more   158 *beam* crossbar
of a balance

O heavens, is 't possible a young maid's wits   160
Should be as mortal as an old man's life?
Nature is fine in° love, and where 'tis fine
It sends some precious instance° of itself
After the thing it loves.°

Ophelia:

        "They bore him barefaced on the bier,   (Song.)   165
        Hey non nonny, nonny, hey nonny,
        And in his grave rained many a tear—"

Fare you well, my dove!

Laertes: Hadst thou thy wits and didst persuade° revenge,
    It could not move thus.   170

Ophelia: You must sing "A-down a-down," and you "call him a-down-a.°" O, how the wheel° becomes it! It is the false steward° that stole his master's daughter.

Laertes: This nothing's more than matter.°

Ophelia: There's rosemary,° that's for remembrance; pray you, love, remember. And there is pansies;° that's for thoughts.   175

Laertes: A document° in madness, thoughts and remembrance fitted.

Ophelia: There's fennel° for you, and columbines.° There's rue° for you, and here's some for me; we may call it herb of grace o' Sundays. You must wear your rue with a difference.° There's a daisy.° I would give you some violets,° but they withered all when my father died. They say 'a made a good end—   180 [*Sings.*]

        "For bonny sweet Robin is all my joy."

Laertes: Thought° and affliction, passion,° hell itself,
    She turns to favor° and to prettiness.

Ophelia:

        "And will 'a not come again?   (Song.)
        And will 'a not come again?   185
        No, no, he is dead.
        Go to thy deathbed,
        He never will come again.

---

162 *fine in* refined by   163 *instance* token   164 *After . . . loves* i.e., into the grave, along with Polonius   169 *persuade* argue cogently for   171 *You . . . a-down a* (Ophelia assigns the singing of refrains, like her own "Hey non nonny," to others present.)   172 *wheel* spinning wheel as accompaniment to the song, or refrain.   *false steward* (The story is unknown.)   173 *This . . . matter* this seeming nonsense is more eloquent than sane utterance   174 *rosemary* (Used as a symbol of remembrance both at weddings and at funerals.)   175 *pansies* (Emblems of love and courtship; perhaps from French *pensées*, "thoughts.")   176 *document* instruction, lesson   177 *fennel* (Emblem of flattery.)   *columbines* (Emblems of unchastity or ingratitude.)   *rue* (Emblem of repentance—a signification that is evident in its popular name, *herb of grace.*)   179 *with a difference* (A device used in heraldry to distinguish one family from another on the coat of arms, here suggesting that Ophelia and the others have different causes of sorrow and repentance; perhaps with a play on *rue* in the sense of "ruth," "pity.")   *daisy* (Emblem of dissembling, faithlessness.)   *violets* (Emblems of faithfulness.)   182 *Thought* melancholy.   *passion* suffering   183 *favor* grace, beauty

"His beard was as white as snow,
All flaxen was his poll.°   190
He is gone, he is gone,
And we cast away moan.
God ha' mercy on his soul!"
And of all Christian souls, I pray God. God b' wi' you.

[*Exit, followed by Gertrude.*]

Laertes: Do you see this, O God?   195
King: Laertes, I must commune with your grief,
    Or you deny me right. Go but apart,
    Make choice of whom° your wisest friends you will,
    And they shall hear and judge twixt you and me.
    If by direct or by collateral hand°   200
    They find us touched,° we will our kingdom give,
    Our crown, our life, and all that we call ours
    To you in satisfaction; but if not,
    Be you content to lend your patience to us,
    And we shall jointly labor with your soul   205
    To give it due content.
Laertes: Let this be so.
    His means of death, his obscure funeral—
    No trophy,° sword, nor hatchment° o'er his bones,
    No noble rite, nor formal ostentation°—
    Cry to be heard, as 'twere from heaven to earth,   210
    That° I must call 't in question.°
King: So you shall,
    And where th' offense is, let the great ax fall.
    I pray you, go with me.   *Exeunt.*

Scene VI [The Castle.]

Enter Horatio and others.

Horatio: What are they that would speak with me?
Gentleman: Seafaring men, sir. They say they have letters for you.
Horatio: Let them come in.   [*Exit Gentleman.*]
    I do not know from what part of the world
    I should be greeted, if not from Lord Hamlet.   5

Enter Sailors.

First Sailor: God bless you, sir.
Horatio: Let him bless thee too.

---

190 *poll* head   198 *whom* whichever of   200 *collateral hand* indirect agency   201 *us touched* be implicated   208 *trophy* memorial.   *hatchment* tablet displaying the armorial bearings of a deceased person   209 *ostentation* ceremony   211 *That* so that.   *call 't in question* demand an explanation

First Sailor: 'A shall, sir, an 't° please him. There's a letter for you, sir—it came
from th' ambassador° that was bound for England—if your name be Horatio,
as I am let to know it is.   [*He gives a letter.*]   10

Horatio [*reads*]: "Horatio, when thou shalt have overlooked° this, give these fellows some means° to the King; they have letters for him. Ere we were two
days old at sea, a pirate of very warlike appointment° gave us chase. Finding
ourselves too slow of sail, we put on a compelled valor, and in the grapple I
boarded them. On the instant they got clear of our ship, so I alone became   15
their prisoner. They have dealt with me like thieves of mercy,° but they
knew what they did: I am to do a good turn for them. Let the King have the
letters I have sent, and repair° thou to me with as much speed as thou
wouldest fly death. I have words to speak in thine ear will make thee dumb,
yet are they much too light for the bore° of the matter. These good fellows   20
will bring thee where I am. Rosencrantz and Guildenstern hold their course
for England. Of them I have much to tell thee. Farewell.

                                     He that thou knowest thine, Hamlet."
Come, I will give you way° for these your letters,
And do 't the speedier that you may direct me   25
To him from whom you brought them.   *Exeunt.*

Scene VII [The Castle.]

Enter King and Laertes.

King: Now must your conscience my acquittance seal,°
    And you must put me in your heart for friend,
    Sith° you have heard, and with a knowing ear,
    That he which hath your noble father slain
    Pursued my life.
Laertes: It well appears. But tell me   5
    Why you proceeded not against these feats°
    So crimeful and so capital° in nature,
    As by your safety, greatness, wisdom, all things else,
    You mainly° were stirred up.
King: O, for two special reasons,   10
    Which may to you perhaps seem much unsinewed,°
    But yet to me they're strong. The Queen his mother
    Lives almost by his looks, and for myself—
    My virtue or my plague, be it either which—
    She is so conjunctive° to my life and soul   15

---

8 *an 't* if it   9 *th' ambassador* (Evidently Hamlet. The sailor is being circumspect.)   11 *overlooked*
looked over   12 *means* means of access   13 *appointment* equipage   16 *thieves of mercy* merciful
thieves   18 *repair* come   20 *bore* caliber, i.e., importance   24 *way* means of access   1 *my acquittance seal* confirm or acknowledge my innocence   3 *Sith* since   6 *feats* acts   7 *capital* punishable by
death   9 *mainly* greatly   11 *unsinewed* weak   15 *conjunctive* closely united. (An astronomical
metaphor.)

That, as the star moves not but in his° sphere,°
I could not but by her. The other motive
Why to a public count° I might not go
Is the great love the general gender° bear him,
Who, dipping all his faults in their affection,   20
Work° like the spring° that turneth wood to stone,
Convert his gyves° to graces, so that my arrows,
Too slightly timbered° for so loud° a wind,
Would have reverted° to my bow again
But not where I had aimed them.   25

Laertes: And so have I a noble father lost,
A sister driven into desperate terms,°
Whose worth, if praises may go back° again,
Stood challenger on mount° of all the age
For her perfections. But my revenge will come.   30

King: Break not your sleeps for that. You must not think
That we are made of stuff so flat and dull
That we can let our beard be shook with danger
And think it pastime. You shortly shall hear more.
I loved your father, and we love ourself;   35
And that, I hope, will teach you to imagine—

Enter a Messenger with letters.

How now? What news?

Messenger: Letters, my lord, from Hamlet:
This to Your Majesty, this to the Queen.

                                                    [*He gives letters.*]

King: From Hamlet? Who brought them?

Messenger: Sailors, my lord, they say. I saw them not.   40
They were given me by Claudio. He received them
Of him that brought them.

King: Laertes, you shall hear them.—
Leave us.   [*Exit Messenger.*]
[*He reads.*] "High and mighty, you shall know I am set naked° on your
kingdom. Tomorrow shall I beg leave to see your kingly eyes, when I shall,   45
first asking your pardon,° thereunto recount the occasion of my sudden and
more strange return.   Hamlet."

---

16 *his* its.   *sphere* one of the hollow spheres in which, according to Ptolemaic astronomy, the planets
were supposed to move   18 *count* account, reckoning, indictment   19 *general gender* common
people   21 *Work* operate, act.   *spring* i.e., a spring with such a concentration of lime that it coats a
piece of wood with limestone, in effect gilding and petrifying it   22 *gyves* fetters (which, gilded by
the people's praise, would look like badges of honor)   23 *slightly timbered* light.   *loud* (suggesting
public outcry on Hamlet's behalf)   24 *reverted* returned   27 *terms* state, condition   28 *go back* i.e.,
recall what she was   29 *on mount* set up on high   44 *naked* destitute, unarmed, without following
46 *pardon* permission

What should this mean? Are all the rest come back? Or is it some abuse,°
and no such thing?°
Laertes: Know you the hand?
King: 'Tis Hamlet's character.° "Naked!"   50
     And in a postscript here he says "alone."
     Can you devise° me?
Laertes: I am lost in it, my lord. But let him come.
     It warms the very sickness in my heart
     That I shall live and tell him to his teeth,   55
     "Thus didst thou.°"
King: If it be so, Laertes—
     As how should it be so? How otherwise?°—
     Will you be ruled by me?
Laertes: Ay, my lord,
     So° you will not o'errule me to a peace.
King: To thine own peace. If he be now returned,   60
     As checking at° his voyage, and that° he means
     No more to undertake it, I will work him
     To an exploit, now ripe in my device,°
     Under the which he shall not choose but fall;
     And for his death no wind of blame shall breathe,   65
     But even his mother shall uncharge the practice°
     And call it accident.
Laertes: My lord, I will be ruled,
     The rather if you could devise it so
     That I might be the organ.°
King: It falls right.
     You have been talked of since your travel much,   70
     And that in Hamlet's hearing, for a quality
     Wherein they say you shine. Your sum of parts°
     Did not together pluck such envy from him
     As did that one, and that, in my regard,
     Of the unworthiest siege.°   75
Laertes: What part is that, my lord?
King: A very ribbon in the cap of youth,
     Yet needful too, for youth no less becomes°
     The light and careless livery that it wears
     Than settled age his sables° and his weeds°   80

---

49 *abuse* deceit. *no such thing* not what it appears   50 *character* handwriting   52 *devise* explain to
56 *Thus didst thou* i.e., here's for what you did to my father   57 *As . . . otherwise* how can this
(Hamlet's return) be true? Yet how otherwise than true (since we have the evidence of his letter)?
59 *So* provided that   61 *checking at* i.e., turning aside from (like a falcon leaving the quarry to fly at a
chance bird). *that if*   63 *device* devising, invention   66 *uncharge the practice* acquit the stratagem
of being a plot   69 *organ* agent, instrument   72 *Your . . . parts* i.e., all your other virtues   75 *un-
worthiest siege* least important rank   78 *no less becomes* is no less suited by   80 *his sables* its rich robes
furred with sable. *weeds* garments

Importing health and graveness.° Two months since
Here was a gentleman of Normandy.
I have seen myself, and served against, the French,
And they can well° on horseback, but this gallant
Had witchcraft in 't; he grew unto his seat,   85
And to such wondrous doing brought his horse
As had he been incorpsed and demi-natured°
With the brave beast. So far he topped° my thought
That I in forgery° of shapes and tricks
Come short of what he did.
Laertes: A Norman was 't?   90
King: A Norman.
Laertes: Upon my life, Lamord.
King: The very same.
Laertes: I know him well. He is the brooch° indeed
And gem of all the nation.
King: He made confession° of you.   95
And gave you such a masterly report
For art and exercise in your defense,°
And for your rapier most especial,
That he cried out 'twould be a sight indeed
If one could match you. Th' escrimers° of their nation,   100
He swore, had neither motion, guard, nor eye
If you opposed them. Sir, this report of his
Did Hamlet so envenom with his envy
That he could nothing do but wish and beg
Your sudden° coming o'er, to play° with you.   105
Now, out of this—
Laertes: What out of this, my lord?
King: Laertes, was your father dear to you?
Or are you like the painting of a sorrow,
A face without a heart?
Laertes: Why ask you this?
King: Not that I think you did not love your father,   110
But that I know love is begun by time,°
And that I see, in passages of proof,°
Time qualifies° the spark and fire of it.
There lives within the very flame of love

---

81 *Importing . . . graveness* signifying a concern for health and dignified prosperity; also, giving an impression of comfortable prosperity   84 *can well* are skilled   87 *As . . . demi-natured* as if he had been of one body and nearly of one nature (like the centaur)   88 *topped* surpassed   89 *forgery* imagining   93 *brooch* ornament   95 *confession* testimonial, admission of superiority   97 *For . . . defense* with respect to your skill and practice with your weapon   100 *escrimers* fencers   105 *sudden* immediate. *play* fence   111 *begun by time* i.e., created by the right circumstance and hence subject to change   112 *passages of proof* actual instances that prove it   113 *qualifies* weakens, moderates

A kind of wick or snuff° that will abate it,   115
And nothing° is at a like goodness still,
For goodness, growing to a pleurisy,°
Dies in his own too much.° That° we would do,
We should do when we would; for this "would" changes
And hath abatements° and delays as many   120
As there are tongues, are hands, are accidents,°
And then this "should" is like a spendthrift sigh,°
That hurts by easing.° But, to the quick o' th' ulcer:°
Hamlet comes back. What would you undertake
To show yourself in deed your father's son   125
More than in words?
Laertes: To cut his throat i' the church.
King: No place, indeed, should murder sanctuarize;°
Revenge should have no bounds. But good Laertes,
Will you do this,° keep close within your chamber.
Hamlet returned shall know you are come home.   130
We'll put on those shall° praise your excellence
And set a double varnish on the fame
The Frenchman gave you, bring you in fine° together,
And wager on your heads. He, being remiss,°
Most generous,° and free from all contriving,   135
Will not peruse the foils, so that with ease,
Or with a little shuffling, you may choose
A sword unbated,° and in a pass of practice°
Requite him for your father.
Laertes: I will do 't,
And for that purpose I'll anoint my sword.   140
I bought an unction° of a mountebank°
So mortal that, but dip a knife in it,
Where it draws blood no cataplasm° so rare,
Collected from all simples° that have virtue°
Under the moon,° can save the thing from death   145
That is but scratched withal. I'll touch my point

---

115 snuff the charred part of a candlewick   116 nothing . . . still nothing remains at a constant
level of perfection   117 pleurisy excess, plethora. (Literally, a chest inflammation.)   118 in . . .
much of its own excess.   That that which   120 abatements diminutions   121 As . . . accidents as
there are tongues to dissuade, hands to prevent, and chance events to intervene   122 spendthrift
sigh (An allusion to the belief that sighs draw blood from the heart.)   123 hurts by easing i.e., cost
the heart blood and wastes precious opportunity even while it affords emotional relief   quick o' th'
ulcer i.e., heart of the matter   127 sanctuarize protect from punishment. (Alludes to the right of
sanctuary with which certain religious places were invested.)   129 Will you do this if you wish to do
this   131 put on those shall arrange for some to   133 in fine finally   134 remiss negligently unsuspicious   135 generous noble-minded   138 unbated not blunted, having no button.   pass of practice
treacherous thrust   141 unction ointment.   mountebank quack doctor   143 cataplasm plaster or
poultice   144 simples herbs.   virtue potency   145 Under the moon i.e., anywhere (with reference
perhaps to the belief that herbs gathered at night had a special power)

With this contagion, that if I gall° him slightly,
It may be death.
King: Let's further think of this,
Weigh what convenience both of time and means
May fit us to our shape.° If this should fail,   150
And that our drift look through our bad performance,°
'Twere better not assayed. Therefore this project
Should have a back or second, that might hold
If this did blast in proof.° Soft, let me see.
We'll make a solemn wager on your cunnings°—   155
I ha 't!
When in your motion you are hot and dry—
As° make your bouts more violent to that end—
And that he calls for drink, I'll have prepared him
A chalice for the nonce,° whereon but sipping,   160
If he by chance escape your venomed stuck,°
Our purpose may hold there. [*A cry within.*] But stay, what noise?

Enter Queen.

Queen: One woe doth tread upon another's heel,
So fast they follow. Your sister's drowned, Laertes.
Laertes: Drowned! O, where?   165
Queen: There is a willow grows askant° the brook,
That shows his hoar leaves° in the glassy stream;
Therewith fantastic garlands did she make
Of crowflowers, nettles, daisies, and long purples,°
That liberal° shepherds give a grosser name,°   170
But our cold° maids do dead men's fingers call them.
There on the pendent° boughs her crownet° weeds
Clamb'ring to hang, an envious sliver° broke,
When down her weedy° trophies and herself
Fell in the weeping brook. Her clothes spread wide,   175
And mermaidlike awhile they bore her up,
Which time she chanted snatches of old lauds,°
As one incapable of° her own distress,
Or like a creature native and endued°
Unto that element. But long it could not be   180

---

147 *gall* graze, wound   150 *shape* part we propose to act   151 *drift . . . performance* intention should
be made visible by our bungling   154 *blast in proof* burst in the test (like a cannon)   155 *cunnings* respective skills   158 *As* i.e., and you should   160 *nonce* occasion   161 *stuck* thrust. (From *stoccado*; a
fencing term.)   166 *askant* aslant   167 *hoar leaves* white or gray undersides of the leaves   169 *long
purples* early purple orchids   170 *liberal* free-spoken.   *a grosser name* (The testicle-resembling tubers
of the orchid, which also in some cases resemble *dead men's fingers*, have earned various slang names
like "dogstones" and "cullions.")   171 *cold* chaste   172 *pendent* overhanging.   *crownet* made into a
chaplet or coronet   173 *envious sliver* malicious branch   174 *weedy* i.e., of plants   177 *lauds* hymns
178 *incapable of* lacking capacity to apprehend   179 *endued* adapted by nature

Till that her garments, heavy with their drink,
Pulled the poor wretch from her melodious lay
To muddy death.
Laertes: Alas, then she is drowned?
Queen: Drowned, drowned.
Laertes: Too much of water hast thou, poor Ophelia,   185
And therefore I forbid my tears. But yet
It is our trick;° nature her custom holds.
Let shame say what it will. [*He weeps.*] When these are gone,
The woman will be out.° Adieu, my lord.
I have a speech of fire that fain would blaze,   190
But that this folly douts° it.   *Exit.*
King: Let's follow, Gertrude.
How much I had to do to calm his rage!
Now fear I this will give it start again;
Therefore let's follow.   *Exeunt.*

ACT V

Scene I [A Churchyard.]

Enter two Clowns° [with spades and mattocks].

First Clown: Is she to be buried in Christian burial, when she willfully seeks her own salvation?°

Second Clown: I tell thee she is; therefore make her grave straight.° The crowner° hath sat on her,° and finds it° Christian burial.

First Clown: How can that be, unless she drowned herself in her own defense?   5

Second Clown: Why, 'tis found so.°

First Clown: It must be *se offendendo*,° it cannot be else. For here lies the point: if I drown myself wittingly, it argues an act, and an act hath three branches—it is to act, to do, and to perform. Argal,° she drowned herself wittingly.   10

Second Clown: Nay, but hear you, goodman° delver—

First Clown: Give me leave. Here lies the water; good. Here stands the man; good. If the man go to this water and drown himself, it is, will he, nill he,° he goes, mark you that. But if the water come to him and drown him, he

187 *It is our trick* i.e., weeping is our natural way (when sad)   188–189 *When . . . out* when my tears are all shed, the woman in me will be expended, satisfied   191 *douts* extinguishes. (The Second Quarto reads "drowns.")   s.d. *Clowns* rustics   2 *salvation* (A blunder for "damnation," or perhaps a suggestion that Ophelia was taking her own shortcut to heaven.)   3 *straight* straightway, immediately. (But with a pun on *strait*, "narrow.")   4 *crowner* coroner.   *sat on her* conducted an inquest on her case.   *finds it* gives his official verdict that her means of death was consistent with   6 *found so* determined so in the coroner's verdict   7 *se offendendo* (A comic mistake for *se defendendo*, a term used in verdicts of justifiable homicide.)   9 *Argal* (Corruption of *ergo*, "therefore.")   11 *goodman* (An honorific title often used with the name of a profession or craft.)   13 *will he, nill he* whether will or no, willy-nilly

drowns not himself. Argal, he that is not guilty of his own death shortens   15
not his own life.

Second Clown: But is this law?

First Clown: Ay, marry, is 't—crowner's quest law.

Second Clown: Will you ha' the truth on 't? If this had not been a gentlewoman,
she should have been buried out o' Christian burial.   20

First Clown: Why, there thou sayst.° And the more pity that great folk should
have countenance° in this world to drown or hang themselves, more than
their even-Christian.° Come, my spade. There is no ancient° gentlemen but
gardeners, ditchers, and grave makers. They hold up° Adam's profession.

Second Clown: Was he a gentleman?   25

First Clown: 'A was the first that ever bore arms.°

Second Clown: Why, he had none.

First Clown: What, art a heathen? How dost thou understand the Scripture?
The Scripture says Adam digged. Could he dig without arms?° I'll put another question to thee. If thou answerest me not to the purpose, confess   30
thyself°—

Second Clown: Go to.

First Clown: What is he that builds stronger than either the mason, the shipwright, or the carpenter?

Second Clown: The gallows maker, for that frame° outlives a thousand tenants.   35

First Clown: I like thy wit well, in good faith. The gallows does well.° But how
does it well? It does well to those that do ill. Now thou dost ill to say the gallows is built stronger than the church. Argal, the gallows may do well to
thee. To 't again, come.

Second Clown: "Who builds stronger than a mason, a shipwright, or a   40
carpenter?"

First Clown: Ay, tell me that, and unyoke.°

Second Clown: Marry, now I can tell.

First Clown: To 't.

Second Clown: Mass,° I cannot tell.   45

Enter Hamlet and Horatio [at a distance].

First Clown: Cudgel thy brains no more about it, for your dull ass will not mend
his pace with beating; and when you are asked this question next, say "a
grave maker." The houses he makes lasts till doomsday. Go get thee in and
fetch me a stoup° of liquor.

[*Exit Second Clown. First Clown digs.*]
Song.

---

21 *there thou sayst,* i.e., that's right   22 *countenance* privilege   23 *even-Christian* fellow Christians.
ancient going back to ancient times   24 *hold up* maintain   26 *bore arms* (To be entitled to bear a
coat of arms would make Adam a gentleman, but as one who bore a spade, our common ancestor was
an ordinary delver in the earth.)   29 *arms* i.e., the arms of the body   30–31 *confess thyself* (The
saying continues, "and be hanged.")   35 *frame* (1) gallows (2) structure   36 *does well* (1) is an apt
answer (2) does a good turn   42 *unyoke* i.e., after this great effort, you may unharness the team of
your wits   45 *Mass* by the Mass   49 *stoup* two-quart measure

> "In youth, when I did love, did love,°
> Methought it was very sweet,
> To contract—O—the time for—a—my behove,°
> O, methought there—a—was nothing—a—meet.°"   50

Hamlet: Has this fellow no feeling of his business, 'a° sings in grave-making?

Horatio: Custom hath made it in him a property of easiness.°   55

Hamlet: 'Tis e'en so. The hand of little employment hath the daintier sense.°

First Clown: *Song.*

> "But age with his stealing steps
> Hath clawed me in his clutch,
> And hath shipped me into the land,°
> As if I had never been such."   60

[*He throws up a skull.*]

Hamlet: That skull had a tongue in it and could sing once. How the knave jowls° it to the ground, as if 'twere Cain's jawbone, that did the first murder! This might be the pate of a politician,° which this ass now o'erreaches,° one that would circumvent God, might it not?

Horatio: It might, my lord.   65

Hamlet: Or of a courtier, which could say, "Good morrow, sweet lord! How dost thou, sweet lord?" This might be my Lord Such-a-one, that praised my Lord Such-a-one's horse when 'a meant to beg it, might it not?

Horatio: Ay, my lord.

Hamlet: Why, e'en so, and now my Lady Worm's, chapless,° and knocked about   70
the mazard° with a sexton's spade. Here's fine revolution,° an° we had the trick to see° 't. Did these bones cost no more the breeding but° to play at loggets° with them? Mine ache to think on 't.

First Clown: *Song.*

> "A pickax and a spade, a spade,
> For and° a shrouding sheet;
> O, a pit of clay for to be made   75
> For such a guest is meet."

[*He throws up another skull.*]

---

50 *In . . . love* (This and the two following stanzas, with nonsensical variations, are from a poem attributed to Lord Vaux and printed in *Tottel's Miscellany,* 1557. The *O* and *a* [for "*ah*"] seemingly are the grunts of the digger.) 52 *To contract . . . behove* i.e., to shorten the time for my own advantage. (Perhaps he means to *prolong* it.) 53 *meet* suitable, i.e., more suitable 54 *'a* that he 55 *property of easiness* something he can do easily and indifferently 56 *daintier sense* more delicate sense of feeling 59 *into the land* i.e., toward my grave (?) (But note the lack of rhyme in *steps, land.*) 62 *jowls* dashes (with a pun on *jowl,* "jawbone") 63 *politician* schemer, plotter. *o'erreaches* circumvents, gets the better of (with a quibble on the literal sense) 70 *chapless* having no lower jaw. 71 *mazard* i.e., head. (Literally, a drinking vessel.) *revolution* turn of Fortune's wheel, change. *an* if 72 *trick to see* knack of seeing. *cost . . . but* involve so little expense and care in upbringing that we may. 73 *loggets* a game in which pieces of hard wood shaped like Indian clubs or bowling pins are thrown to lie as near as possible to a stake 75 *For and* and moreover

Hamlet: There's another. Why may not that be the skull of a lawyer? Where be
his quiddities° now, his quillities,° his cases, his tenures,° and his tricks?
Why does he suffer this mad knave now to knock him about the sconce° 80
with a dirty shovel, and will not tell him of his action of battery?° Hum, this
fellow might be in 's time a great buyer of land, with his statutes, his recognizances,° his fines,° his double° vouchers° his recoveries.° Is this the fine of
his fines and the recovery of his recoveries, to have his fine pate full of fine
dirt?° Will his vouchers vouch him no more of his purchases, and double 85
ones too, than the length and breadth of a pair of indentures?° The very
conveyances° of his lands will scarcely lie in this box,° and must th'
inheritor° himself have no more, ha?

Horatio: Not a jot more, my lord.

Hamlet: Is not parchment made of sheepskins? 90

Horatio: Ay, my lord, and of calves' skins too.

Hamlet: They are sheep and calves which seek out assurance in that.° I will
speak to this fellow.—Whose grave's this, sirrah?°

First Clown: Mine, sir. [*Sings.*]
　　　　"O, pit of clay for to be made 95
　　　　For such a guest is meet."

Hamlet: I think it be thine, indeed, for thou liest in 't.

First Clown: You lie out on 't, sir, and therefore 'tis not yours. For my part, I do
not lie in 't, yet it is mine.

Hamlet: Thou dost lie in 't, to be in 't and say it is thine. 'Tis for the dead, not 100
for the quick;° therefore thou liest.

First Clown: 'Tis a quick lie, sir; 'twill away again from me to you.

Hamlet: What man dost thou dig it for?

First Clown: For no man, sir.

Hamlet: What woman, then? 105

First Clown: For none, neither.

Hamlet: Who is to be buried in 't?

First Clown: One that was a woman, sir, but, rest her soul, she's dead.

Hamlet: How absolute° the knave is! We must speak by the card,° or equivoca-
tion° will undo us. By the Lord, Horatio, this three years I have took° note 110

---

79 *quiddities* subtleties, quibbles. (From Latin *quid*, "a thing.") *quillities* verbal niceties, subtle distinctions. (Variation of *quiddities*.) *tenures* the holding of a piece of property or office, or the conditions or period of such holding 80 *sconce* head 81 *action of battery* lawsuit about physical assault
82–83 *statutes, his recognizances* legal documents guaranteeing a debt by attaching land and property
83 *fines, recoveries* ways of converting entailed estates into "fee simple" or freehold. *double* signed by
two signatories. *vouchers* guarantees of the legality of a title to real estate 83–85 *fine of his fines
. . . fine pate . . . fine dirt* end of his legal maneuvers . . . elegant head . . . minutely sifted dirt
86 *pair of indentures* legal document drawn up in duplicate on a single sheet and then cut apart on a
zigzag line so that each pair was uniquely matched. (Hamlet may refer to two rows of teeth or den-
tures.) 87 *conveyances* deeds. *box* (1) deed box (2) coffin. ("Skull" has been suggested.) 88 *inher-
itor* possessor, owner 92 *assurance in that* safety in legal parchments 93 *sirrah* (A term of address to
inferiors.) 101 *quick* living 109 *absolute* strict, precise. *by the card* i.e., with precision. (Literally,
by the mariner's compass-card, on which the points of the compass were marked.) 109–110 *equivo-
cation* ambiguity in the use of terms 110 *took* taken

of it: the age is grown so picked° that the toe of the peasant comes so near
the heel of the courtier, he galls his kibe.°—How long hast thou been grave
maker?

First Clown: Of all the days i' the year, I came to 't that day that our last king
Hamlet overcame Fortinbras.   115

Hamlet: How long is that since?

First Clown: Cannot you tell that? Every fool can tell that. It was that very day
that young Hamlet was born—he that is mad and sent into England.

Hamlet: Ay, marry, why was he sent into England?

First Clown: Why, because 'a was mad. 'A shall recover his wits there, or if 'a do   120
not, 'tis no great matter there.

Hamlet: Why?

First Clown: 'Twill not be seen in him there. There the men are as mad as he.

Hamlet: How came he mad?

First Clown: Very strangely, they say.   125

Hamlet: How strangely?

First Clown: Faith, e'en with losing his wits.

Hamlet: Upon what ground?°

First Clown: Why, here in Denmark. I have been sexton here, man and boy,
thirty years.   130

Hamlet: How long will a man lie i' th' earth ere he rot?

First Clown: Faith, if 'a be not rotten before 'a die—as we have many pocky°
corpses nowadays, that will scarce hold the laying in°—'a will last you°
some eight year or nine year. A tanner will last you nine year.

Hamlet: Why he more than another?   135

First Clown: Why, sir, his hide is so tanned with his trade that 'a will keep out
water a great while, and your water is a sore° decayer of your whoreson°
dead body. [*He picks up a skull.*] Here's a skull now hath lien you° i' th' earth
three-and-twenty years.

Hamlet: Whose was it?   140

First Clown: A whoreson mad fellow's it was. Whose do you think it was?

Hamlet: Nay, I know not.

First Clown: A pestilence on him for a mad rogue! 'A poured a flagon of
Rhenish° on my head once. This same skull, sir, was, sir, Yorick's skull, the
King's jester.   145

Hamlet: This?

First Clown: E'en that.

Hamlet: Let me see. [*He takes the skull.*] Alas, poor Yorick! I knew him, Horatio,
a fellow of infinite jest, of most excellent fancy. He hath bore° me on his

---

111 *picked* refined, fastidious   112 *galls his kibe* chafes the courtier's chilblain   128 *ground* cause. (But,
in the next line, the gravedigger takes the word in the sense of "land," "country.")   132 *pocky* rotten,
diseased. (Literally, with the pox, or syphilis.)   133 *hold the laying in* hold together long enough to be
interred.   *last you* last. (*You* is used colloquially here and in the following lines.)   137 *sore* i.e., terrible, great.   *whoreson* i.e., vile, scurvy   138 *lien you* lain. (See the note at line 133.)   144 *Rhenish*
Rhine wine   149 *bore* borne

back a thousand times, and now how abhorred in my imagination it is! My   150
gorge rises° at it. Here hung those lips that I have kissed I know not how oft.
Where be your gibes now? Your gambols, your songs, your flashes of merriment that were wont° to set the table on a roar? Not one now, to mock your
own grinning?° Quite chopfallen?° Now get you to my lady's chamber and
tell her, let her paint an inch thick, to this favor° she must come. Make her   155
laugh at that. Prithee, Horatio, tell me one thing.

Horatio: What's that, my lord?

Hamlet: Dost thou think Alexander looked o' this fashion i' th' earth?

Horatio: E'en so.

Hamlet: And smelt so? Pah! [*He throws down the skull.*]   160

Horatio: E'en so, my lord.

Hamlet: To what base uses we may return, Horatio! Why may not imagination
trace the noble dust of Alexander till 'a find it stopping a bunghole?°

Horatio: 'Twere to consider too curiously° to consider so.

Hamlet: No, faith, not a jot, but to follow him thither with modesty° enough,   165
and likelihood to lead it. As thus: Alexander died, Alexander was buried,
Alexander returneth to dust, the dust is earth, of earth we make loam,° and
why of that loam whereto he was converted might they not stop a beer
barrel?

Imperious° Caesar, dead and turned to clay,   170
Might stop a hole to keep the wind away.
O, that that earth which kept the world in awe
Should patch a wall t' expel the winter's flaw!°

*Enter King, Queen, Laertes, and the corpse [of Ophelia, in procession, with
Priest, lords, etc.].*

But soft,° but soft awhile! Here comes the King,
The Queen, the courtiers. Who is this they follow?   175
And with such maimèd° rites? This doth betoken
The corpse they follow did with desperate hand
Fordo° its own life. 'Twas of some estate.°
Couch we° awhile and mark.
          [*He and Horatio conceal themselves. Ophelia's body is taken to the grave.*]

Laertes: What ceremony else?   180

Hamlet [to Horatio]: That is Laertes, a very noble youth. Mark.

Laertes: What ceremony else?

Priest: Her obsequies have been as far enlarged

150–151 *My gorge rises* i.e., I feel nauseated   153 *were wont* used   153–154 *mock your own grinning*
mock at the way your skull seems to be grinning (just as you used to mock at yourself and those who
grinned at you)   154 *chopfallen* (1) lacking the lower jaw (2) dejected   155 *favor* aspect, appearance
163 *bunghole* hole for filling or emptying a cask   164 *curiously* minutely   165 *modesty* plausible moderation   167 *loam* mortar consisting chiefly of moistened clay and straw   170 *Imperious* imperial
173 *flaw* gust of wind   174 *soft* i.e., wait, be careful   176 *maimèd* mutilated, incomplete   178 *Fordo*
destroy.   *estate* rank   179 *Couch we* let's hide, lie low

As we have warranty.° Her death was doubtful,
And but that great command o'ersways the order°   185
She should in ground unsanctified been lodged°
Till the last trumpet. For° charitable prayers,
Shards,° flints, and pebbles should be thrown on her.
Yet here she is allowed her virgin crants,°
Her maiden strewments,° and the bringing home   190
Of bell and burial.°

Laertes: Must there no more be done?

Priest: No more be done.
    We should profane the service of the dead
    To sing a requiem and such rest° to her
    As to peace-parted souls.°

Laertes: Lay her i' th' earth,   195
    And from her fair and unpolluted flesh
    May violets spring! I tell thee, churlish priest,
    A ministering angel shall my sister be
    When thou liest howling.°

Hamlet [to Horatio]:   What, the fair Ophelia!

Queen [scattering flowers]: Sweets to the sweet! Farewell.   200
    I hoped thou shouldst have been my Hamlet's wife.
    I thought thy bride-bed to have decked, sweet maid,
    And not t' have strewed thy grave.

Laertes: O, treble woe
    Fall ten times treble on that cursèd head
    Whose wicked deed thy most ingenious sense°   205
    Deprived thee of! Hold off the earth awhile,
    Till I have caught her once more in mine arms.
                          [*He leaps into the grave and embraces Ophelia.*]
    Now pile your dust upon the quick and dead,
    Till of this flat a mountain you have made
    T' o'ertop old Pelion or the skyish head   210
    Of blue Olympus.°

Hamlet [coming forward]: What is he whose grief
    Bears such an emphasis,° whose phrase of sorrow
    Conjures the wandering stars° and makes them stand
    Like wonder-wounded° hearers? This is I,

---

184 *warranty* i.e., ecclesiastical authority   185 *great . . . order* orders from on high overrule the pre-
scribed procedures   186 *She should . . . lodged* she should have been buried in unsanctified ground
187 *For* in place of   188 *Shards* broken bits of pottery   189 *crants* garlands betokening maidenhood
190 *strewments* flowers strewn on a coffin   190–191 *bringing . . . burial* laying the body to rest, to the
sound of the bell   194 *such rest* i.e., to pray for such rest   195 *peace-parted souls* those who have died
at peace with God   199 *howling* i.e., in hell   205 *ingenious sense* a mind that is quick, alert, of fine
qualities   210–211 *Pelion, Olympus* sacred mountains in the north of Thessaly   212 *emphasis* i.e.,
rhetorical and florid emphasis. (*Phrase* has a similar rhetorical connotation.)   213 *wandering stars*
planets   214 *wonder-wounded* struck with amazement

Hamlet the Dane.°

Laertes [*grappling with him*°]: The devil take thy soul!

Hamlet: Thou pray'st not well.

    I prithee, take thy fingers from my throat,

    For though I am not splenitive° and rash,

    Yet have I in me something dangerous, 220

    Which let thy wisdom fear. Hold off thy hand.

King: Pluck them asunder.

Queen: Hamlet, Hamlet!

All: Gentlemen!

Horatio: Good my lord, be quiet. 225

                         [*Hamlet and Laertes are parted.*]

Hamlet: Why, I will fight with him upon this theme

    Until my eyelids will no longer wag.°

Queen: O my son, what theme?

Hamlet: I loved Ophelia. Forty thousand brothers

    Could not with all their quantity of love 230

    Make up my sum. What wilt thou do for her?

King: O, he is mad, Laertes.

Queen: For love of God, forbear him.°

Hamlet: 'Swounds,° show me what thou'lt do.

    Woo't° weep? Woo't fight? Woo't fast? Woo't tear thyself? 235

    Woo't drink up° eisel?° Eat a crocodile?°

    I'll do 't. Dost come here to whine?

    To outface me with leaping in her grave?

    Be buried quick° with her, and so will I.

    And if thou prate of mountains, let them throw 240

    Millions of acres on us, till our ground,

    Singeing his pate° against the burning zone,°

    Make Ossa° like a wart! Nay, an° thou'lt mouth,°

    I'll rant as well as thou.

Queen: This is mere° madness,

    And thus awhile the fit will work on him; 245

    Anon, as patient as the female dove

---

215 *the Dane* (This title normally signifies the King; see Act I, Scene i, line 17 and note.)   216 s.d. *grappling with him* The testimony of the First Quarto that "*Hamlet leaps in after Laertes*" and the "Elegy on Burbage" ("Oft have I seen him leap into the grave") seem to indicate one way in which this fight was staged; however, the difficulty of fitting two contenders and Ophelia's body into a confined space (probably the trapdoor) suggests to many editors the alternative, that Laertes jumps out of the grave to attack Hamlet.)   219 *splenitive* quick-tempered   227 *wag* move. (A fluttering eyelid is a conventional sign that life has not yet gone.)   233 *forbear him* leave him alone   234 *'Swounds* by His (Christ's) wounds   235 *Woo't* wilt thou   236 *drink up* drink deeply. *eisel* vinegar. *crocodile* (Crocodiles were tough and dangerous, and were supposed to shed hypocritical tears.)   239 *quick* alive   242 *his pate* its head, i.e., top. *burning zone* zone in the celestial sphere containing the sun's orbit, between the tropics of Cancer and Capricorn   243 *Ossa* another mountain in Thessaly. (In their war against the Olympian gods, the giants attempted to heap Ossa on Pelion to scale Olympus.) *an* if. *mouth* i.e., rant   244 *mere* utter

When that her golden couplets° are disclosed,°
His silence will sit drooping.

Hamlet: Hear you, sir.
What is the reason that you use me thus?
I loved you ever. But it is no matter.   250
Let Hercules himself do what he may,
The cat will mew, and dog will have his day.°

Exit Hamlet.

King: I pray thee, good Horatio, wait upon him.

[Exit] Horatio.

[*To Laertes.*] Strengthen your patience in° our last night's speech;
We'll put the matter to the present push.°—   255
Good Gertrude, set some watch over your son.—
This grave shall have a living° monument.
An hour of quiet° shortly shall we see;
Till then, in patience our proceeding be.   *Exeunt.*

Scene II [The Castle.]

Enter Hamlet and Horatio.

Hamlet: So much for this, sir; now shall you see the other.°
You do remember all the circumstance?
Horatio: Remember it, my lord!
Hamlet: Sir, in my heart there was a kind of fighting
That would not let me sleep. Methought I lay   5
Worse than the mutines° in the bilboes.° Rashly,°
And praised be rashness for it—let us know°
Our indiscretion° sometimes serves us well
When our deep plots do pall,° and that should learn° us
There's a divinity that shapes our ends,   10
Rough-hew° them how we will—
Horatio: That is most certain.
Hamlet: Up from my cabin,
My sea-gown° scarfed° about me, in the dark
Groped I to find out them,° had my desire,
Fingered° their packet, and in fine° withdrew   15
To mine own room again, making so bold,

---

247 *golden couplets* two baby pigeons, covered with yellow down. *disclosed* hatched 251–252 *Let
. . . day* i.e., (1) even Hercules couldn't stop Laertes' theatrical rant (2) I, too, will have my turn; i.e.,
despite any blustering attempts at interference, every person will sooner or later do what he or she
must do 254 *in* i.e., by recalling 255 *present push* immediate test 257 *living* lasting. (For Laertes'
private understanding, Claudius also hints that Hamlet's death will serve as such a monument.)
258 *hour of quiet* time free of conflict 1 *see the other* hear the other news 6 *mutines* mutineers. *bilboes* shackles. *Rashly* on impulse. (This adverb goes with lines 12 ff.) 7 *know* acknowledge 8 *indiscretion* lack of foresight and judgment (not an indiscreet act) 9 *pall* fail, falter, go stale. *learn*
teach 11 *Rough-hew* shape roughly 13 *sea-gown* seaman's coat. *scarfed* loosely wrapped 14 *them*
i.e., Rosencrantz and Guildenstern 15 *Fingered* pilfered, pinched. *in fine* finally, in conclusion

My fears forgetting manners, to unseal
Their grand commission; where I found, Horatio—
Ah, royal knavery!—an exact command,
Larded° with many several° sorts of reasons   20
Importing° Denmark's health and England's too,
With, ho! such bugs° and goblins in my life,°
That on the supervise,° no leisure bated,°
No, not to stay° the grinding of the ax,
My head should be struck off.
Horatio: Is 't possible?   25
Hamlet [giving a document]: Here's the commission. Read it at more leisure.
But wilt thou hear now how I did proceed?
Horatio: I beseech you.
Hamlet: Being thus benetted round with villainies—
Ere I could make a prologue to my brains,   30
They had begun the play°—I sat me down,
Devised a new commission, wrote it fair.°
I once did hold it, as our statists° do,
A baseness° to write fair, and labored much
How to forget that learning, but, sir, now   35
It did me yeoman's° service. Wilt thou know
Th' effect° of what I wrote?
Horatio: Ay, good my lord.
Hamlet: An earnest conjuration° from the King,
As England was his faithful tributary,
As love between them like the palm° might flourish,   40
As peace should still° her wheaten garland° wear
And stand a comma° 'tween their amities,
And many suchlike "as"es° of great charge,°
That on the view and knowing of these contents,
Without debatement further more or less,   45
He should those bearers put to sudden death,
Not shriving time° allowed.
Horatio: How was this sealed?
Hamlet: Why, even in that was heaven ordinant.°
I had my father's signet° in my purse,
Which was the model° of that Danish seal;   50

20 *Larded* garnished. *several* different 21 *Importing* relating to 22 *bugs* bugbears, hobgoblins. *in my life* i.e., to be feared if I were allowed to live 23 *supervise* reading. *leisure bated* delay allowed 24 *stay* await 30–31 *Ere . . . play* before I could consciously turn my brain to the matter, it had started working on a plan 32 *fair* in a clear hand 33 *statists* statesmen 34 *baseness* i.e., lower-class trait 36 *yeoman's* i.e., substantial, faithful, loyal 37 *effect* purport 38 *conjuration* entreaty 40 *palm* (An image of health; see Psalm 92:12.) 41 *still* always. *wheaten garland* (Symbolic of fruitful agriculture, of peace and plenty.) 42 *comma* (Indicating continuity, link.) 43 *"as"es* (1) the "whereases" of a formal document (2) asses. *charge* (1) import (2) burden (appropriate to asses) 47 *shriving time* time for confession and absolution 48 *ordinant* directing 49 *signet* small seal 50 *model* replica

Folded the writ° up in the form of th' other,
Subscribed° it, gave 't th' impression,° placed it safely,
The changeling° never known. Now, the next day
Was our sea fight, and what to this was sequent°
Thou knowest already.   55
Horatio: So Guildenstern and Rosencrantz go to 't.
Hamlet: Why, man, they did make love to this employment.
They are not near my conscience. Their defeat°
Does by their own insinuation° grow.
'Tis dangerous when the baser° nature comes   60
Between the pass° and fell° incensed points
Of mighty opposites.°
Horatio: Why, what a king is this!
Hamlet: Does it not, think thee, stand me now upon°—
He that hath killed my king and whored my mother.
Popped in between th' election° and my hopes,   65
Thrown out his angle° for my proper° life,
And with such cozenage°—is 't not perfect conscience
To quit° him with this arm? And is 't not to be damned
To let this canker° of our nature come
In° further evil?   70
Horatio: It must be shortly known to him from England
What is the issue of the business there.
Hamlet: It will be short. The interim is mine.
And a man's life's no more than to say "one."°
But I am very sorry, good Horatio,   75
That to Laertes I forgot myself.
For by the image of my cause I see
The portraiture of his. I'll court his favors.
But, sure, the bravery° of his grief did put me
Into a tow'ring passion.
Horatio: Peace, who comes here?   80

    Enter a Courtier [Osric].

Osric: Your lordship is right welcome back to Denmark.
Hamlet: I humbly thank you, sir. [*To Horatio.*] Dost know this water fly?
Horatio: No, my good lord.

---

51 *writ* writing   52 *Subscribed* signed (with forged signature).   *impression* i.e., with a wax seal
53 *changeling* i.e., substituted letter. (Literally, a fairy child substituted for a human one.)   54 *was
sequent* followed   58 *defeat* destruction   59 *insinuation* intrusive intervention, sticking their
noses in my business   60 *baser* of lower social station   61 *pass* thrust.   *fell* fierce   62 *opposites*
antagonists   63 *stand me now upon* become incumbent on me now   65 *election* (The Danish
monarch was "elected" by a small number of high-ranking electors.)   66 *angle* fishhook.   *proper*
very   67 *cozenage* trickery   68 *quit* requite, pay back   69 *canker* ulcer   69–70 *come in* grow into
74 *a man's . . . "one"* one's whole life occupies such a short time, only as long as it takes to count
to 1   79 *bravery* bravado

Hamlet: Thy state is the more gracious, for 'tis a vice to know him. He hath much land, and fertile. Let a beast be lord of beasts, and his crib° shall stand at the King's mess°. 'Tis a chuff,° but, as I say, spacious in the possession of dirt.   85

Osric: Sweet lord, if your lordship were at leisure, I should impart a thing to you from His Majesty.

Hamlet: I will receive it, sir, with all diligence of spirit. Put your bonnet° to his° right use; 'tis for the head.   90

Osric: I thank your lordship, it is very hot.

Hamlet: No, believe me, 'tis very cold. The wind is northerly.

Osric: It is indifferent° cold, my lord, indeed.

Hamlet: But yet methinks it is very sultry and hot for my complexion.°

Osric: Exceedingly, my lord. It is very sultry, as 'twere—I cannot tell how. My lord, His Majesty bade me signify to you that 'a has laid a great wager on your head. Sir, this is the matter—   95

Hamlet: I beseech you, remember.

[*Hamlet moves him to put on his hat.*]

Osric: Nay, good my lord; for my ease,° in good faith. Sir, here is newly come to court Laertes—believe me, an absolute° gentleman, full of most excellent differences,° of very soft society° and great showing.° Indeed, to speak feelingly° of him, he is the card° or calendar° of gentry,° for you shall find in him the continent of what part a gentleman would see.°   100

Hamlet: Sir, his definement° suffers no perdition° in you,° though I know to divide him inventorially° would dozy° th' arithmetic of memory, and yet but yaw° neither° in respect of° his quick sail. But, in the verity of extolment,° I take him to be a soul of great article,° and his infusion° of such dearth and rareness° as, to make true diction° of him, his semblable° is his mirror and who else would trace° him his umbrage,° nothing more.   105

Osric: Your lordship speaks most infallibly of him.   110

Hamlet: The concernancy,° sir? Why do we wrap the gentleman in our more rawer breath?°

85–86 *Let . . . mess* i.e., if a man, no matter how beastlike, is as rich in livestock and possessions as Osric, he may eat at the King's table   85 *crib* manger   86 *chuff* boor, churl. (The Second Quarto spelling, *chough*, is a variant spelling that also suggests the meaning here of "chattering jackdaw.")   90 *bonnet* any kind of cap or hat.   *his* its   93 *indifferent* somewhat   94 *complexion* temperament   99 *for my ease* (A conventional reply declining the invitation to put his hat back on.)   100 *absolute* perfect   101 *differences* special qualities.   *soft society* agreeable manners.   *great showing* distinguished appearance   101–102 *feelingly* with just perception   102 *card* chart, map.   *calendar* guide.   *gentry* good breeding   103 *the continent . . . see* one who contains in him all the qualities a gentleman would like to see. (A *continent* is that which contains.)   104 *definement* definition. (Hamlet proceeds to mock Osric by throwing his lofty diction back at him.)   *perdition* loss, diminution.   *you* your description   104–105 *divide him inventorially* enumerate his graces.   *dozy* dizzy.   106 *yaw* swing unsteadily off course. (Said of a ship.)   *neither* for all that.   *in respect of* in comparison with.   *in . . . extolment* in true praise (of him)   107 *of great article* one with many articles in his inventory.   *infusion* essence, character infused into him by nature   107–108 *dearth and rareness* rarity   108 *make true diction* speak truly.   *semblable* only true likeness   109 *who . . . trace* any other person who would wish to follow.   *umbrage* shadow   111 *concernancy* import, relevance   112 *rawer breath* unrefined speech that can only come short in praising him

Osric: Sir?

Horatio: Is 't not possible to understand in another tongue?° You will do 't,° sir, really. 115

Hamlet: What imports the nomination of this gentleman?

Osric: Of Laertes?

Horatio [*to Hamlet*]: His purse is empty already; all 's golden words are spent.

Hamlet: Of him, sir.

Osric: I know you are not ignorant— 120

Hamlet: I would you did, sir. Yet in faith if you did, it would not much approve° me. Well, sir?

Osric: You are not ignorant of what excellence Laertes is—

Hamlet: I dare not confess that, lest I should compare with him in excellence. But to know a man well were to know himself.° 125

Osric: I mean, sir, for° his weapon; but in the imputation laid on him by them,° in his meed° he's unfellowed.°

Hamlet: What's his weapon?

Osric: Rapier and dagger.

Hamlet: That's two of his weapons—but well.° 130

Osric: The King, sir, hath wagered with him six Barbary horses, against the which he° has impawned,° as I take it, six French rapiers and poniards,° with their assigns,° as girdle, hangers,° and so.° Three of the carriages,° in faith, are very dear to fancy,° very responsive° to the hilts, most delicate° carriages, and of very liberal conceit.° 135

Hamlet: What call you the carriages?

Horatio [*to Hamlet*]: I knew you must be edified by the margent° ere you had done.

Osric: The carriages, sir, are the hangers.

Hamlet: The phrase would be more germane to the matter if we could carry a cannon by our sides; I would it might be hangers till then. But, on: six Bar- 140 bary horses against six French swords, their assigns, and three liberal—con- ceited carriages; that's the French bet against the Danish. Why is this im- pawned, as you call it?

---

114 *to understand . . . tongue* i.e., for you, Osric, to understand when someone else speaks your lan- guage. (Horatio twits Osric for not being able to understand the kind of flowery speech he himself uses, when Hamlet speaks in such a vein. Alternatively, all this could be said to Hamlet.) *You will do 't* i.e., you can if you try, or, you may well have to try (to speak plainly) 121 *approve* commend 124–125 *I dare . . . himself* I dare not boast of knowing Laertes' excellence lest I seem to imply a comparable excellence in myself. Certainly to know another person well, one must know oneself 126 *for* i.e., with. *imputation . . . them* reputation given him by others 127 *meed* merit. *unfel- lowed* unmatched 130 *but well* but never mind 132 *he* i.e., Laertes. *impawned* staked, wagered. *poniards* daggers 133 *assigns* appurtenances. *hangers* straps on the sword belt (*girdle*), from which the sword hung. *and so* and so on. *carriages* (An affected way of saying *hangers;* literally, gun car- riages.) 134 *dear to fancy* delightful to the fancy. *responsive* corresponding closely, matching or well-adjusted. *delicate* (i.e., in workmanship) 135 *liberal conceit* elaborate design 137 *margent* margin of a book, place for explanatory notes

Osric: The King, sir, hath laid,° sir, that in a dozen passes° between yourself and
    him, he shall not exceed you three hits. He hath laid on twelve for nine,   145
    and it would come to immediate trial, if your lordship would vouchsafe the
    answer.°

Hamlet: How if I answer no?

Osric: I mean, my lord, the opposition of your person in trial.

Hamlet: Sir, I will walk here in the hall. If it please His Majesty, it is the   150
    breathing time° of day with me. Let° the foils be brought, the gentleman
    willing, and the King hold his purpose, I will win for him an I can; if not, I
    will gain nothing but my shame and the odd hits.

Osric: Shall I deliver you° so?

Hamlet: To this effect, sir—after what flourish your nature will.   155

Osric: I commend° my duty to your lordship.

Hamlet: Yours, yours. [*Exit Osric.*] 'A does well to commend it himself; there are
    no tongues else for 's turn.°

Horatio: This lapwing° runs away with the shell on his head.

Hamlet: 'A did comply with his dug° before 'a sucked it. Thus has he—and many   160
    more of the same breed that I know the drossy° age dotes on—only got the
    tune° of the time and, out of an habit of encounter,° a kind of yeasty° collec-
    tion,° which carries them through and through the most fanned and win-
    nowed opinions;° and do° but blow them to their trial, the bubbles are out.°

Enter a Lord.

Lord: My lord, His Majesty commended him to you by young Osric, who brings   165
    back to him that you attend him in the hall. He sends to know if your plea-
    sure hold to play with Laertes, or that you will take longer time.

Hamlet: I am constant to my purposes; they follow the King's pleasure. If his fit-
    ness speaks, mine is ready;° now or whensoever, provided I be so able as
    now.   170

---

144 *laid* wagered. *passes* bouts. (The odds of the betting are hard to explain. Possibly the King bets that Hamlet will win at least five out of twelve, at which point Laertes raises the odds against himself by betting he will win nine.)   146–147 *vouchsafe the answer* be so good as to accept the challenge. (Hamlet deliberately takes the phrase in its literal sense of replying.)   151 *breathing time* exercise period. *Let* i.e., if   154 *deliver you* report what you say   156 *commend* commit to your favor. (A conventional salutation, but Hamlet wryly uses a more literal meaning, "recommend," "praise," in line 157.)   158 *for 's turn* for his purposes, i.e., to do it for him   159 *lapwing* (A proverbial type of youthful forwardness. Also, a bird that draws intruders away from its nest and was thought to run about with its head in the shell when newly hatched; a seeming reference to Osric's hat.)   160 *comply . . . dug* observe ceremonious formality toward his nurse's or mother's teat   161 *drossy* laden with scum and impurities, frivolous   162 *tune* temper, mood, manner of speech. *an habit of encounter* a demeanor in conversing (with courtiers of his own kind). *yeasty* frothy   162–163 *collection* i.e., of current phrases   163–164 *carries . . . opinions* sustains them right through the scrutiny of persons whose opinions are select and refined. (Literally, like grain separated from its chaff. Osric is both t chaff and the bubbly froth on the surface of the liquor that is soon blown away.)   164 *and do* yet do. *blow . . . out* test them by merely blowing on them, and their bubbles burst   168–169 *If . . . ready* if he declares his readiness, my convenience waits on his

Lord: The King and Queen and all are coming down.

Hamlet: In happy time.°

Lord: The Queen desires you to use some gentle entertainment° to Laertes before you fall to play.

Hamlet: She well instructs me.   [*Exit Lord.*]   175

Horatio: You will lose, my lord.

Hamlet: I do not think so. Since he went into France, I have been in continual practice; I shall win at the odds. But thou wouldst not think how ill all's here about my heart; but it is no matter.

Horatio: Nay, good my lord—   180

Hamlet: It is but foolery, but it is such a kind of gaingiving° as would perhaps trouble a woman.

Horatio: If your mind dislike anything, obey it. I will forestall their repair° hither and say you are not fit.

Hamlet: Not a whit, we defy augury. There is special providence in the fall of a   185 sparrow. If it be now, 'tis not to come; if it be not to come, it will be now; if it be not now; yet it will come. The readiness is all. Since no man of aught he leaves knows, what is 't to leave betimes? Let be.°

A table prepared. [Enter] trumpets, drums, and officers with cushions; King, Queen, [Osric,] and all the state; foils, daggers, [and wine borne in;] and Laertes.

King: Come, Hamlet, come and take this hand from me.

                              [*The King puts Laertes' hand into Hamlet's.*]

Hamlet [to Laertes]: Give me your pardon, sir. I have done you wrong,   190
     But pardon 't as you are a gentleman.
     This presence° knows,
     And you must needs have heard, how I am punished°
     With a sore distraction. What I have done
     That might your nature, honor, and exception°   195
     Roughly awake, I here proclaim was madness.
     Was 't Hamlet wronged Laertes? Never Hamlet.
     If Hamlet from himself be ta'en away,
     And when he's not himself does wrong Laertes,
     Then Hamlet does it not, Hamlet denies it.   200
     Who does it, then? His madness. If 't be so,
     Hamlet is of the faction° that is wronged;
     His madness is poor Hamlet's enemy.
     Sir, in this audience
     Let my disclaiming from a purposed evil   205
     Free me so far in your most generous thoughts

---

172 *In happy time* (A phrase of courtesy indicating that the time is convenient.)   173 *entertainment* greeting   181 *gaingiving* misgiving   183 *repair* coming   187–188 *Since . . . Let be* since no one has knowledge of what he is leaving behind, what does an early death matter after all? Enough; don't struggle against it.   192 *presence* royal assembly   193 *punished* afflicted   195 *exception* disapproval 202 *faction* party

That I have° shot my arrow o'er the house
And hurt my brother.

Laertes: I am satisfied in nature,°
Whose motive° in this case should stir me most
To my revenge. But in my terms of honor   210
I stand aloof, and will no reconcilement
Till by some elder masters of known honor
I have a voice° and precedent of peace°
To keep my name ungored.° But till that time
I do receive your offered love like love,   215
And will not wrong it.

Hamlet: I embrace it freely,
And will this brother's wager frankly° play.—
Give us the foils. Come on.

Laertes: Come, one for me.

Hamlet: I'll be your foil,° Laertes. In mine ignorance
Your skill shall, like a star i' the darkest night,   220
Stick fiery off° indeed.

Laertes: You mock me, sir.

Hamlet: No, by this hand.

King: Give them the foils, young Osric. Cousin Hamlet,
You know the wager?

Hamlet: Very well, my lord.
Your Grace has laid the odds o'° the weaker side.   225

King: I do not fear it; I have seen you both.
But since he is bettered,° we have therefore odds.

Laertes: This is too heavy. Let me see another.

                    [He exchanges his foil for another.]

Hamlet: This likes me° well. These foils have all a length?

                    [They prepare to play.]

Osric: Ay, my good lord.   230

King: Set me the stoups of wine upon that table.
If Hamlet give the first or second hit,
Or quit in answer of the third exchange,°
Let all the battlements their ordnance fire.
The King shall drink to Hamlet's better breath,°   235
And in the cup an union° shall he throw

---

207 *That I have as* if I had   208 *in nature* i.e., as to my personal feelings   209 *motive* prompting
213 *voice* authoritative pronouncement.   *of peace* for reconciliation   214 *name ungored* reputation
unwounded   217 *frankly* without ill feeling or the burden of rancor   219 *foil* thin metal background
that sets a jewel off (with pun on the blunted rapier for fencing)   221 *Stick fiery off* stand out brilliantly   225 *laid the odds o'* bet on, backed   227 *is bettered* has improved; is the odds-on favorite.
(Laertes' handicap is the "three hits" specified in line 145.)   229 *likes me* pleases me   233 *Or . . .
exchange* i.e., or requites Laertes in the third bout for having won the first two   235 *better breath* improved vigor   236 *union* pearl. (So called, according to Pliny's *Natural History*, 9, because pearls are
unique, never identical.)

Richer than that which four successive kings
In Denmark's crown have worn. Give me the cups,
And let the kettle° to the trumpet speak,
The trumpet to the cannoneer without, 240
The cannons to the heavens, the heaven to earth,
"Now the King drinks to Hamlet." Come, begin.

Trumpets the while.

And you, the judges, bear a wary eye.
Hamlet: Come on, sir.
Laertes: Come, my lord. [*They play. Hamlet scores a hit.*] 245
Hamlet: One.
Laertes: No.
Hamlet: Judgment.
Osric: A hit, a very palpable hit.

Drum, trumpets, and shot. Flourish.
A piece goes off.

Laertes: Well, again.
King: Stay, give me drink. Hamlet, this pearl is thine. 250
[*He drinks, and throws a pearl in Hamlet's cup.*]
Here's to thy health. Give him the cup.
Hamlet: I'll play this bout first. Set it by awhile.
Come. [*They play.*] Another hit; what say you?
Laertes: A touch, a touch, I do confess 't.
King: Our son shall win.
Queen: He's fat° and scant of breath. 255
Here, Hamlet, take my napkin,° rub thy brows.
The Queen carouses° to thy fortune, Hamlet.
Hamlet: Good madam!
King: Gertrude, do not drink.
Queen: I will, my lord, I pray you pardon me. [*She drinks.*] 260
King [*aside*]: It is the poisoned cup. It is too late.
Hamlet: I dare not drink yet, madam; by and by.
Queen: Come, let me wipe thy face.
Laertes [*to King*]: My lord, I'll hit him now.
King: I do not think 't.
Laertes [*aside*]: And yet it is almost against my conscience. 265
Hamlet: Come, for the third, Laertes. You do but dally.
I pray you, pass° with your best violence;
I am afeard you make a wanton of me.°
Laertes: Say you so? Come on. [*They play.*]
Osric: Nothing neither way. 270
Laertes: Have at you now!

239 *kettle* kettledrum   255 *fat* not physically fit, out of training   256 *napkin* handkerchief
257 *carouses* drinks a toast   267 *pass* thrust   268 *make . . . me* i.e., treat me like a spoiled child,
trifle with me

[*Laertes wounds Hamlet; then, in scuffling, they change rapiers,° and Hamlet*
wounds Laertes.]

King: Part them! They are incensed.
Hamlet: Nay, come, again.   [*The Queen falls.*]
Osric: Look to the Queen there, ho!
Horatio: They bleed on both sides. How is it, my lord?
Osric: How is 't, Laertes?
Laertes: Why, as a woodcock° to mine own springe,° Osric;   275
    I am justly killed with mine own treachery.
Hamlet: How does the Queen?
King: She swoons to see them bleed.
Queen: No, no, the drink, the drink—O my dear Hamlet—
    The drink, the drink! I am poisoned.   [*She dies.*]
Hamlet: O villainy! Ho, let the door be locked!   280
    Treachery! Seek it out.   [*Laertes falls. Exit Osric.*]
Laertes: It is here, Hamlet. Hamlet, thou art slain.
    No med'cine in the world can do thee good;
    In thee there is not half an hour's life.
    The treacherous instrument is in thy hand,   285
    Unbated° and envenomed. The foul practice°
    Hath turned itself on me. Lo, here I lie,
    Never to rise again. Thy mother's poisoned.
    I can no more. The King, the King's to blame.
Hamlet: The point envenomed too? Then, venom, to thy work.   290
                                      [*He stabs the King.*]

All: Treason! Treason!
King: O, yet defend me, friends! I am but hurt.
Hamlet [*forcing the King to drink*]:
    Here, thou incestuous, murderous, damnèd Dane,
    Drink off this potion. Is thy union° here?
    Follow my mother.   [*The King dies.*]
Laertes: He is justly served.   295
    It is a poison tempered° by himself.
    Exchange forgiveness with me, noble Hamlet.
    Mine and my father's death come not upon thee,
    Nor thine on me!   [*He dies.*]
Hamlet: Heaven make thee free of it! I follow thee.   300
    I am dead, Horatio. Wretched Queen, adieu!
    You that look pale and tremble at this chance,°
    That are but mutes° or audience to this act,

---

271 s.d. *in scuffling, they change rapiers* (This stage direction occurs in the Folio. According to a widespread stage tradition, Hamlet receives a scratch, realizes that Laertes' sword is unbated, and accordingly forces an exchange.)   275 *woodcock* a bird, a type of stupidity or as a decoy.   *springe* trap,
snare   286 *Unbated* not blunted with a button.   *practice* plot   294 *union* pearl. (See line 236; with
grim puns on the word's other meanings: marriage, shared death.)   296 *tempered* mixed   302 *chance*
mischance   303 *mutes* silent observers. (Literally, actors with nonspeaking parts.)

Had I but time—as this fell° sergeant,° Death,
Is strict° in his arrest°—O, I could tell you—   305
But let it be. Horatio, I am dead;
Thou livest. Report me and my cause aright
To the unsatisfied.

Horatio: Never believe it.
I am more an antique Roman° than a Dane.
Here's yet some liquor left.

> [*He attempts to drink from the poisoned cup. Hamlet prevents him.*]

Hamlet: As thou'rt a man,   310
Give me the cup! Let go! By heaven, I'll ha 't.
O God, Horatio, what a wounded name,
Things standing thus unknown, shall I leave behind me!
If thou didst ever hold me in thy heart,
Absent thee from felicity awhile,   315
And in this harsh world draw thy breath in pain
To tell my story. *A march afar off* [*and a volley within*]. What warlike noise is
    this?

Enter Osric.

Osric: Young Fortinbras, with conquest come from Poland,
To th' ambassadors of England gives
This warlike volley.

Hamlet: O, I die, Horatio!   320
The potent poison quite o'ercrows° my spirit.
I cannot live to hear the news from England,
But I do prophesy th' election lights
On Fortinbras. He has my dying voice.°
So tell him, with th' occurrents° more and less   325
Which have solicited°—the rest is silence.   [*He dies.*]

Horatio: Now cracks a noble heart. Good night, sweet prince,
And flights of angels sing thee to thy rest!

[*March within.*]

Why does the drum come hither?

Enter Fortinbras, with the [*English*] *Ambassadors* [*with drum, colors, and atten-*
dants].

Fortinbras: Where is this sight?

Horatio: What is it you would see? 330

If aught of woe or wonder, cease your search.

Fortinbras: This quarry° cries on havoc.° O proud Death,

What feast° is toward° in thine eternal cell,

That thou so many princes at a shot

So bloodily hast struck?

First Ambassador: The sight is dismal, 335

And our affairs from England come too late.

The ears are senseless that should give us hearing,

To tell him his commandment is fulfilled,

That Rosencrantz and Guildenstern are dead.

Where should we have our thanks?

Horatio: Not from his° mouth, 340

Had it th' ability of life to thank you.

He never gave commandment for their death.

But since, so jump° upon this bloody question,°

You from the Polack wars, and you from England,

Are here arrived, give order that these bodies 345

High on a stage° be placèd to the view,

And let me speak to th' yet unknowing world

How these things came about. So shall you hear

Of carnal, bloody, and unnatural acts,

Of accidental judgments,° casual° slaughters, 350

Of deaths put on° by cunning and forced cause,°

And, in this upshot, purposes mistook

Fall'n on th' inventors' heads. All this can I

Truly deliver.

Fortinbras: Let us haste to hear it,

And call the noblest to the audience. 355

For me, with sorrow I embrace my fortune.

I have some rights of memory° in this kingdom,

Which now to claim my vantage° doth invite me.

Horatio: Of that I shall have also cause to speak,

And from his mouth whose voice will draw on more.° 360

But let this same be presently° performed,

Even while men's minds are wild, lest more mischance

On° plots and errors happen.

Fortinbras: Let four captains

Bear Hamlet, like a soldier, to the stage,

---

332 *quarry* heap of dead. *cries on havoc* proclaims a general slaughter 333 *feast* i.e., Death feasting on those who have fallen. *toward* in preparation 340 *his* i.e., Claudius' 343 *jump* precisely, immediately. *question* dispute, affair 346 *stage* platform 350 *judgments* retributions. *casual* occurring by chance 351 *put on* instigated. *forced cause* contrivance 357 *of memory* traditional, remembered, unforgotten 358 *vantage* favorable opportunity 360 *voice . . . more* vote will influence still others 361 *presently* immediately 363 *On* on the basis of; on top of

For he was likely, had he been put on,° 365
To have proved most royal; and for his passage,°
The soldiers' music and the rite of war
Speak° loudly for him.
Take up the bodies. Such a sight as this
Becomes the field,° but here shows much amiss. 370
Go bid the soldiers shoot.
     Exeunt [*marching, bearing off the dead bodies; a peal of ordnance is shot off*].

365 *put on* i.e., invested in royal office and so put to the test   366 *passage* i.e., from life to death
368 *Speak* (let them) speak   370 *Becomes the field* suits the field of battle

WRITER'S PERSPECTIVE

Anthony Burgess

Anthony Burgess on Drama
AN ASIAN CULTURE LOOKS AT SHAKESPEARE 1982

Is translation possible? I first found myself asking this question in the Far East, when I was given the task of translating T. S. Eliot's *The Waste Land* into Indonesian. The difficulties began with the first line: "April is the cruellest month . . ." This I rendered as "*Bulan Abril ia-lah bulan yang dzalim sa-kali . . .* " I had to take *dzalim* from Arabic, since Indonesian did not, at that time, seem to possess a word for *cruel*. The term was accepted, but not the notion that a month, as opposed to a person or institution, could be cruel. Moreover, even if a month could be cruel, how—in the tropics where all the months are the same and the concepts of spring and winter do not exist—can one month be crueller than another? When I came to *forgetful snow*—rendered as *thalji berlupa*—I had to borrow a highly poetical word from the Persian, acceptable as a useful descriptive device for the brown skin of the beloved but not known in terms of a climatic reality. And, again, how could this inanimate substance possess the faculty of forgetting? I gave up the task as hopeless. Evidently the imagery of *The Waste Land* does not relate to a universal experience but applies only to the northern hemisphere, with its temperate climate and tradition of spring and fertility rituals.

As a teacher in Malaysia, I had to consider with a mixed group of Malay, Chinese, Indian, and Eurasian students, seasoned with the odd Buginese, Achinese, and Japanese, a piece of representative postwar British fiction. Although the setting of the book is West Africa, I felt that its story was of universal import. It was a novel by Graham Greene called *The Heart of the Matter*—a tragic story about a police officer named Scobie who is a Catholic convert. He is in love with his wife but falls in love with another woman, discovers that he cannot repent of this adultery, makes a sacrilegious communion so that his very Catholic wife will not suspect that a love affair is in progress, then commits suicide in despair, trusting that God will thrust him into the outer darkness and be no longer agonized by the exploits of sinning Scobie. To us this is a tragic situation. To my Muslim students it was extremely funny. One girl said: "Why cannot this Mr. Scobie become a Muslim? Then he can have four wives and there is no problem."

The only author who seemed to have the quality of universal appeal in Malaysia was William Shakespeare. Despite the problems of translating him, there is always an intelligible residue. I remember seeing in a Borneo kampong the film of *Richard III* made by Laurence Olivier, and the illiterate tribe which surrounded me was most appreciative. They knew nothing here of literary history and nothing of the great world outside this jungle clearing. They took this film about mediaeval conspiracy and tyranny to be a kind of newsreel representation of contemporary England. They approved the mediaeval costumes because they resembled their own ceremonial dress. This story of the assassination of innocents, including children, Machiavellian massacre, and the eventual defeat of a tyrant was typical of their own history, even their contemporary experience, and they accepted Shakespeare as a great poet. Eliot would not have registered with them at all. Translation is not a matter of words only; it is a matter of making intelligible a whole culture. Evidently the Elizabethan culture was still primitive enough to survive transportation over much time and space.

Spoken remarks on the "Importance of Translation"

Arthur Miller

DEATH OF A SALESMAN   1949

Certain Private Conversations in Two Acts and a Requiem

Arthur Miller (b. 1915) was born into a lower-income Jewish family in New York's Harlem but grew up in Brooklyn. He studied playwriting at the University of Michigan, later wrote radio scripts, and in World War II worked as a steamfitter. When the New York Drama Critics named his All My Sons *best play of 1947, Miller told an interviewer, "I don't see how you can write anything decent without using as your basis the question of right and wrong." (The play is about a guilty manufacturer of defective aircraft parts.)* Death of a Salesman *(1949) made Miller famous.* The Crucible *(1953), a dramatic indictment of the Salem witch trials, gained him further attention at a time when Senator Joseph Mc-Carthy was conducting loyalty investigations. For a while (1956–1961), Miller was the husband of actress Marilyn Monroe, whom the main character of his* After the Fall *(1964) resembles. Among Miller's other plays are* A View from the Bridge *(1955);* The Price *(1968);* The Creation of the World and Other Businesses *(1972);* Playing for Time *(1980), written for television; and* Broken Glass *(1994). He has written two novels,* Focus *(1945) and* The Misfits *(1960), which he made into a screenplay featuring Monroe.*

Cast

Willy Loman
Linda
Biff
Charley
Uncle Ben
Howard Wagner
Jenny
Happy
Bernard
The Woman
Stanley
Miss Forsythe
Letta

Scene: *The action takes place in Willy Loman's house and yard and in various places he visits in the New York and Boston of today. Throughout the play, in the stage directions, left and right mean stage left and stage right.*

ACT I

A melody is heard, played upon a flute. It is small and fine, telling of grass and trees and the horizon. The curtain rises.

Before us is the Salesman's house. We are aware of towering, angular shapes behind it, surrounding it on all sides. Only the blue light of the sky falls upon the house and forestage; the surrounding area shows an angry glow of orange. As more light appears, we see a solid vault of apartment houses around the small, fragile-seeming home. An air of the dream clings to the place, a dream rising out of reality. The kitchen at center seems actual enough, for there is a kitchen table with three chairs, and a refrigerator. But no other fixtures are seen. At the back of the kitchen there is a draped entrance, which leads to the living room. To the right of the kitchen, on a level raised two feet, is a bedroom furnished only with a brass bedstead and a straight chair. On a shelf over the bed a silver athletic trophy stands. A window opens onto the apartment house at the side.

Behind the kitchen, on a level raised six and a half feet, is the boys' bedroom, at present barely visible. Two beds are dimly seen, and at the back of the room a dormer window. (This bedroom is above the unseen living room.) At the left a stairway curves up to it from the kitchen.

The entire setting is wholly or, in some places, partially transparent. The roof-line of the house is one-dimensional; under and over it we see the apartment buildings. Before the house lies an apron, curving beyond the forestage into the orchestra. This forward area serves as the backyard as well as the locale of all Willy's imaginings and of his city scenes. Whenever the action is in the present the actors observe the imaginary wall-lines, entering the house only through the door at the left. But in the scenes of the past these boundaries are broken, and characters enter or leave a room by stepping "through" a wall onto the forestage.

From the right, Willy Loman, the Salesman, enters, carrying two large sample cases. The flute plays on. He hears but is not aware of it. He is past sixty years of age, dressed quietly. Even as he crosses the stage to the doorway of the house, his exhaustion is apparent. He unlocks the door, comes into the kitchen, and thankfully lets his burden down, feeling the soreness of his palms. A word-sigh escapes his lips—it might be, "Oh, boy, oh, boy." He closes the door, then carries his cases out into the living room, through the draped kitchen doorway.

Linda, his wife, has stirred in her bed at the right. She gets out and puts on a robe, listening. Most often jovial, she has developed an iron repression of her exceptions to Willy's behavior—she more than loves him, she admires him, as though his mercurial nature, his temper, his massive dreams and little cruelties, served her only as sharp reminders of the turbulent longings within him, longings which she shares but lacks the temperament to utter and follow to their end.

Linda (*hearing Willy outside the bedroom, calls with some trepidation*): Willy!
Willy: It's all right. I came back.
Linda: Why? What happened? (*Slight pause.*) Did something happen, Willy?
Willy: No, nothing happened.
Linda: You didn't smash the car, did you?
Willy (*with casual irritation*): I said nothing happened. Didn't you hear me?
Linda: Don't you feel well?
Willy: I am tired to the death. (*The flute has faded away. He sits on the bed beside her, a little numb.*) I couldn't make it. I just couldn't make it, Linda.

Linda (*very carefully, delicately*): Where were you all day? You look terrible.

Willy: I got as far as a little above Yonkers. I stopped for a cup of coffee. Maybe it was the coffee.

Linda: What?

Willy (*after a pause*): I suddenly couldn't drive any more. The car kept going onto the shoulder, y'know?

Linda (*helpfully*): Oh. Maybe it was the steering again. I don't think Angelo knows the Studebaker.

Willy: No, it's me, it's me. Suddenly I realize I'm goin' sixty miles an hour and I don't remember the last five minutes. I'm—I can't seem to—keep my mind to it.

Linda: Maybe it's your glasses. You never went for your new glasses.

Willy: No, I see everything. I came back ten miles an hour. It took me nearly four hours from Yonkers.

Linda (*resigned*): Well, you'll just have to take a rest. Willy, you can't continue this way.

Willy: I just got back from Florida.

Linda: But you didn't rest your mind. Your mind is overactive, and the mind is what counts, dear.

Willy: I'll start out in the morning. Maybe I'll feel better in the morning. (*She is taking off his shoes.*) These goddam arch supports are killing me.

Linda: Take an aspirin. Should I get you an aspirin? It'll soothe you.

Willy (*with wonder*): I was driving along, you understand? And I was fine. I was even observing the scenery. You can imagine, me looking at scenery, on the road every week of my life. But it's so beautiful up there, Linda, the trees are so thick, and the sun is warm. I opened the windshield and just let the warm air bathe over me. And then all of a sudden I'm goin' off the road! I'm tellin' ya, I absolutely forgot I was driving. If I'd've gone the other way over the white line I might've killed somebody. So I went on again—and five minutes later I'm dreamin' again, and I nearly—(*He presses two fingers against his eyes.*) I have such thoughts, I have such strange thoughts.

Linda: Willy, dear. Talk to them again. There's no reason why you can't work in New York.

Willy: They don't need me in New York. I'm the New England man. I'm vital in New England.

Linda: But you're sixty years old. They can't expect you to keep traveling every week.

Willy: I'll have to send a wire to Portland. I'm supposed to see Brown and Morrison tomorrow morning at ten o'clock to show the line. Goddammit, I could sell them! (*He starts putting on his jacket.*)

Linda (*taking the jacket from him*): Why don't you go down to the place tomorrow and tell Howard you've simply got to work in New York? You're too accommodating, dear.

Willy: If old man Wagner was alive I'd a been in charge of New York now! That man was a prince, he was a masterful man. But that boy of his, that Howard, he don't appreciate. When I went north the first time, the Wagner Company didn't know where New England was!

Linda: Why don't you tell those things to Howard, dear?

Willy (encouraged): I will, I definitely will. Is there any cheese?

Linda: I'll make you a sandwich.

Willy: No, go to sleep. I'll take some milk. I'll be up right away. The boys in?

Linda: They're sleeping. Happy took Biff on a date tonight.

Willy (interested): That so?

Linda: It was so nice to see them shaving together, one behind the other, in the bathroom. And going out together. You notice? The whole house smells of shaving lotion.

Willy: Figure it out. Work a lifetime to pay off a house. You finally own it, and there's nobody to live in it.

Linda: Well, dear, life is a casting off. It's always that way.

Willy: No, no, some people—some people accomplish something. Did Biff say anything after I went this morning?

Linda: You shouldn't have criticized him, Willy, especially after he just got off the train. You mustn't lose your temper with him.

Willy: When the hell did I lose my temper? I simply asked him if he was making any money. Is that a criticism?

Linda: But, dear, how could he make any money?

Willy (worried and angered): There's such an undercurrent in him. He became a moody man. Did he apologize when I left this morning?

Linda: He was crestfallen, Willy. You know how he admires you. I think if he finds himself, then you'll both be happier and not fight any more.

Willy: How can he find himself on a farm? Is that a life? A farmhand? In the beginning, when he was young, I thought, well, a young man, it's good for him to tramp around, take a lot of different jobs. But it's more than ten years now and he has yet to make thirty-five dollars a week!

Linda: He's finding himself, Willy.

Willy: Not finding yourself at the age of thirty-four is a disgrace!

Linda: Shh!

Willy: The trouble is he's lazy, goddammit!

Linda: Willy, please!

Willy: Biff is a lazy bum.

Linda: They're sleeping. Get something to eat. Go on down.

Willy: Why did he come home? I would like to know what brought him home.

Linda: I don't know. I think he's still lost, Willy. I think he's very lost.

Willy: Biff Loman is lost. In the greatest country in the world a young man with such—personal attractiveness, gets lost. And such a hard worker. There's one thing about Biff—he's not lazy.

Linda: Never.

Willy (with pity and resolve): I'll see him in the morning. I'll have a nice talk with him. I'll get him a job selling. He could be big in no time. My God! Remember how they used to follow him around in high school? When he smiled at one of them their faces lit up. When he walked down the street . . . (*He loses himself in reminiscences.*)

Linda (*trying to bring him out of it*): Willy, dear, I got a new kind of American-type cheese today. It's whipped.

Willy: Why do you get American when I like Swiss?

Linda: I just thought you'd like a change—

Willy: I don't want a change! I want Swiss cheese. Why am I always being contradicted?

Linda (*with a covering laugh*): I thought it would be a surprise.

Willy: Why don't you open a window in here, for God's sake?

Linda (*with infinite patience*): They're all open, dear.

Willy: The way they boxed us in here. Bricks and windows, windows and bricks.

Linda: We should've bought the land next door.

Willy: The street is lined with cars. There's not a breath of fresh air in the neighborhood. The grass don't grow any more, you can't raise a carrot in the back yard. They should've had a law against apartment houses. Remember those two beautiful elm trees out there? When I and Biff hung the swing between them?

Linda: Yeah, like being a million miles from the city.

Willy: They should've arrested the builder for cutting those down. They massacred the neighborhood. (*Lost.*) More and more I think of those days, Linda. This time of year it was lilac and wisteria. And then the peonies would come out, and the daffodils. What fragrance in this room!

Linda: Well, after all, people had to move somewhere.

Willy: No, there's more people now.

Linda: I don't think there's more people. I think—

Willy: There's more people! That's what's ruining this country! Population is getting out of control. The competition is maddening! Smell the stink from that apartment house! And another on the other side . . . How can they whip cheese?

On Willy's last line, Biff and Happy raise themselves up in their beds, listening.

Linda: Go down, try it. And be quiet.

Willy (*turning to Linda, guiltily*): You're not worried about me, are you, sweetheart?

Biff: What's the matter?

Happy: Listen!

Linda: You've got too much on the ball to worry about.

Willy: You're my foundation and my support, Linda.

Linda: Just try to relax, dear. You make mountains out of molehills.

Willy: I won't fight with him any more. If he wants to go back to Texas, let him go.

Linda: He'll find his way.

Willy: Sure. Certain men just don't get started till later in life. Like Thomas Edison, I think. Or B. F. Goodrich. One of them was deaf. (*He starts for the bedroom doorway.*) I'll put my money on Biff.

Linda: And Willy—if it's warm Sunday we'll drive in the country. And we'll open the windshield, and take lunch.

Willy: No, the windshields don't open on the new cars.

Linda: But you opened it today.

Willy: Me? I didn't. (*He stops.*) Now isn't that peculiar! Isn't that a remarkable—(*He breaks off in amazement and fright as the flute is heard distantly.*)

Linda: What, darling?

Willy: That is the most remarkable thing.

Linda: What, dear?

Willy: I was thinking of the Chevvy. (*Slight pause.*) Nineteen twenty-eight . . . when I had that red Chevvy—(*Breaks off.*) That funny? I coulda sworn I was driving that Chevvy today.

Linda: Well, that's nothing. Something must've reminded you.

Willy: Remarkable. Ts. Remember those days? The way Biff used to simonize that car? The dealer refused to believe there was eighty thousand miles on it. (*He shakes his head.*) Heh! (*To Linda.*) Close your eyes, I'll be right up. (*He walks out of the bedroom.*)

Happy (*to Biff*): Jesus, maybe he smashed up the car again!

Linda (*calling after Willy*): Be careful on the stairs, dear! The cheese is on the middle shelf! (*She turns, goes over to the bed, takes his jacket, and goes out of the bedroom.*)

Light has risen on the boys' room. Unseen, Willy is heard talking to himself, "Eighty thousand miles," and a little laugh. Biff gets out of bed, comes downstage a bit, and stands attentively. Biff is two years older than his brother Happy, well built, but in these days bears a worn air and seems less self-assured. He has succeeded less, and his dreams are stronger and less acceptable than Happy's. Happy is tall, powerfully made. Sexuality is like a visible color on him, or a scent that many women have discovered. He, like his brother, is lost, but in a different way, for he has never allowed himself to turn his face toward defeat and is thus more confused and hardskinned, although seemingly more content.

Happy (*getting out of bed*): He's going to get his license taken away if he keeps that up. I'm getting nervous about him, y'know, Biff?

Biff: His eyes are going.

Happy: No, I've driven with him. He sees all right. He just doesn't keep his mind on it. I drove into the city with him last week. He stops at a green light and then it turns red and he goes. (*He laughs.*)

Biff: Maybe he's color-blind.

Happy: Pop? Why he's got the finest eye for color in the business. You know that.

Biff (*sitting down on his bed*): I'm going to sleep.

Happy: You're not still sour on Dad, are you, Biff?

Biff: He's all right, I guess.

Willy (*underneath them, in the living room*): Yes, sir, eighty thousand miles—eighty-two thousand!

Biff: You smoking?

Happy (*holding out a pack of cigarettes*): Want one?

Biff (*taking a cigarette*): I can never sleep when I smell it.

Willy: What a simonizing job, heh!

Happy (*with deep sentiment*): Funny, Biff, y'know? Us sleeping in here again? The old beds. (*He pats his bed affectionately.*) All the talk that went across those two beds, huh? Our whole lives.

Biff: Yeah. Lotta dreams and plans.

Happy (*with a deep and masculine laugh*): About five hundred women would like to know what was said in this room.

> *They share a soft laugh.*

Biff: Remember that big Betsy something—what the hell was her name—over on Bushwick Avenue?

Happy (*combing his hair*): With the collie dog!

Biff: That's the one. I got you in there, remember?

Happy: Yeah, that was my first time—I think. Boy, there was a pig! (*They laugh, almost crudely.*) You taught me everything I know about women. Don't forget that.

Biff: I bet you forgot how bashful you used to be. Especially with girls.

Happy: Oh, I still am, Biff.

Biff: Oh, go on.

Happy: I just control it, that's all. I think I got less bashful and you got more so. What happened, Biff? Where's the old humor, the old confidence? (*He shakes Biff's knee. Biff gets up and moves restlessly about the room.*) What's the matter?

Biff: Why does Dad mock me all the time?

Happy: He's not mocking you, he—

Biff: Everything I say there's a twist of mockery on his face. I can't get near him.

Happy: He just wants you to make good, that's all. I wanted to talk to you about Dad for a long time, Biff. Something's—happening to him. He—talks to himself.

Biff: I noticed that this morning. But he always mumbled.

Happy: But not so noticeable. It got so embarrassing I sent him to Florida. And you know something? Most of the time he's talking to you.

Biff: What's he say about me?

Happy: I can't make it out.

Biff: What's he say about me?

Happy: I think the fact that you're not settled, that you're still kind of up in the air . . .

Biff: There's one or two other things depressing him, Happy.

Happy: What do you mean?

Biff: Never mind. Just don't lay it all on me.

Happy: But I think if you just got started—I mean—is there any future for you out there?

Biff: I tell ya, Hap, I don't know what the future is. I don't know—what I'm supposed to want.

Happy: What do you mean?

Biff: Well, I spent six or seven years after high school trying to work myself up. Shipping clerk, salesman, business of one kind or another. And it's a measly manner of existence. To get on that subway on the hot mornings in summer. To devote your whole life to keeping stock, or making phone calls, or selling or buying. To suffer fifty weeks of the year for the sake of a two-week vacation, when all you really desire is to be outdoors, with your shirt off. And always to have to get ahead of the next fella. And still—that's how you build a future.

Happy: Well, you really enjoy it on a farm? Are you content out there?

Biff (with rising agitation): Hap, I've had twenty or thirty different kinds of jobs since I left home before the war, and it always turns out the same. I just realized it lately. In Nebraska when I herded cattle, and the Dakotas, and Arizona, and now in Texas. It's why I came home now, I guess, because I realized it. This farm I work on, it's spring there now, see? And they've got about fifteen new colts. There's nothing more inspiring or—beautiful than the sight of a mare and a new colt. And it's cool there now, see? Texas is cool now, and it's spring. And whenever spring comes to where I am, I suddenly get the feeling, my God, I'm not gettin' anywhere! What the hell am I doing, playing around with horses, twenty-eight dollars a week! I'm thirty-four years old, I oughta be makin' my future. That's when I come running home. And now, I get here, and I don't know what to do with myself. (*After a pause.*) I've always made a point of not wasting my life, and everytime I come back here I know that all I've done is to waste my life.

Happy: You're a poet, you know that, Biff? You're a—you're an idealist!

Biff: No, I'm mixed up very bad. Maybe I oughta get married. Maybe I oughta get stuck into something. Maybe that's my trouble. I'm like a boy. I'm not married, I'm not in business, I just—I'm like a boy. Are you content, Hap? You're a success, aren't you? Are you content?

Happy: Hell, no!

Biff: Why? You're making money, aren't you?

Happy (moving about with energy, expressiveness): All I can do now is wait for the merchandise manager to die. And suppose I get to be merchandise manager? He's a good friend of mine, and he just built a terrific estate on Long Island. And he lived there about two months and sold it, and now he's building another one. He can't enjoy it once it's finished. And I know that's just what I would do. I don't know what the hell I'm workin' for. Sometimes I sit in my apartment—all alone. And I think of the rent I'm paying. And it's crazy. But then, it's what I always wanted. My own apartment, a car, and plenty of women. And still, goddammit, I'm lonely.

Biff (with enthusiasm): Listen, why don't you come out West with me?

Happy: You and I, heh?

Biff: Sure, maybe we could buy a ranch. Raise cattle, use our muscles. Men built like we are should be working out in the open.

Happy (avidly): The Loman Brothers, heh?

Biff (with vast affection): Sure, we'd be known all over the counties!

Happy (*enthralled*): That's what I dream about, Biff. Sometimes I want to just rip my clothes off in the middle of the store and outbox that goddam merchandise manager. I mean I can outbox, outrun, and outlift anybody in that store, and I have to take orders from those common, petty sons-of-bitches till I can't stand it any more.

Biff: I'm tellin' you, kid, if you were with me I'd be happy out there.

Happy (*enthused*): See, Biff, everybody around me is so false that I'm constantly lowering my ideals . . .

Biff: Baby, together we'd stand up for one another, we'd have someone to trust.

Happy: If I were around you—

Biff: Hap, the trouble is we weren't brought up to grub for money. I don't know how to do it.

Happy: Neither can I!

Biff: Then let's go!

Happy: The only thing is—what can you make out there?

Biff: But look at your friend. Builds an estate and then hasn't the peace of mind to live in it.

Happy: Yeah, but when he walks into the store the waves part in front of him. That's fifty-two thousand dollars a year coming through the revolving door, and I got more in my pinky finger than he's got in his head.

Biff: Yeah, but you just said—

Happy: I gotta show some of those pompous, self-important executives over there that Hap Loman can make the grade. I want to walk into the store the way he walks in. Then I'll go with you, Biff. We'll be together yet, I swear. But take those two we had tonight. Now weren't they gorgeous creatures?

Biff: Yeah, yeah, most gorgeous I've had in years.

Happy: I get that any time I want, Biff. Whenever I feel disgusted. The only trouble is, it gets like bowling or something. I just keep knockin' them over and it doesn't mean anything. You still run around a lot?

Biff: Naa. I'd like to find a girl—steady, somebody with substance.

Happy: That's what I long for.

Biff: Go on! You'd never come home.

Happy: I would! Somebody with character, with resistance! Like Mom, y'know? You're gonna call me a bastard when I tell you this. That girl Charlotte I was with tonight is engaged to be married in five weeks. (*He tries on his new hat.*)

Biff: No kiddin'!

Happy: Sure, the guy's in line for the vice-presidency of the store. I don't know what gets into me, maybe I just have an overdeveloped sense of competition or something, but I went and ruined her, and furthermore I can't get rid of her. And he's the third executive I've done that to. Isn't that a crummy characteristic? And to top it all, I go to their weddings! (*Indignantly, but laughing.*) Like I'm not supposed to take bribes. Manufacturers offer me a hundred-dollar bill now and then to throw an order their way. You know how honest I am, but it's like this girl, see. I hate myself for it. Because I don't want the girl, and, still, I take it and—I love it!

Biff: Let's go to sleep.

Happy: I guess we didn't settle anything, heh?

Biff: I just got one idea that I think I'm going to try.

Happy: What's that?

Biff: Remember Bill Oliver?

Happy: Sure, Oliver is very big now. You want to work for him again?

Biff: No, but when I quit he said something to me. He put his arm on my shoulder, and he said, "Biff, if you ever need anything, come to me."

Happy: I remember that. That sounds good.

Biff: I think I'll go to see him. If I could get ten thousand or even seven or eight thousand dollars I could buy a beautiful ranch.

Happy: I bet he'd back you. 'Cause he thought highly of you, Biff. I mean, they all do. You're well liked, Biff. That's why I say to come back here, and we both have the apartment. And I'm tellin' you, Biff, any babe you want . . .

Biff: No, with a ranch I could do the work I like and still be something. I just wonder though. I wonder if Oliver still thinks I stole that carton of basketballs.

Happy: Oh, he probably forgot that long ago. It's almost ten years. You're too sensitive. Anyway, he didn't really fire you.

Biff: Well, I think he was going to. I think that's why I quit. I was never sure whether he knew or not. I know he thought the world of me, though. I was the only one he'd let lock up the place.

Willy (below): You gonna wash the engine, Biff?

Happy: Shh!

Biff looks at Happy, who is gazing down, listening. Willy is mumbling in the parlor.

Happy: You hear that?

They listen. Willy laughs warmly.

Biff (growing angry): Doesn't he know Mom can hear that?

Willy: Don't get your sweater dirty, Biff!

A look of pain crosses Biff's face.

Happy: Isn't that terrible? Don't leave again, will you? You'll find a job here. You gotta stick around. I don't know what to do about him, it's getting embarrassing.

Willy: What a simonizing job!

Biff: Mom's hearing that!

Willy: No kiddin', Biff, you got a date? Wonderful!

Happy: Go on to sleep. But talk to him in the morning, will you?

Biff (reluctantly getting into bed): With her in the house. Brother!

Happy (getting into bed): I wish you'd have a good talk with him.

The light on their room begins to fade.

Biff (to himself in bed): That selfish, stupid . . .

Happy: Sh . . . Sleep, Biff.

Their light is out. Well before they have finished speaking, Willy's form is dimly seen below in the darkened kitchen. He opens the refrigerator, searches in there, and takes out a bottle of milk. The apartment houses are fading out, and the entire house and surroundings become covered with leaves. Music insinuates itself as the leaves appear.

Willy: Just wanna be careful with those girls, Biff, that's all. Don't make any promises. No promises of any kind. Because a girl, y'know, they always be-lieve what you tell 'em, and you're very young, Biff, you're too young to be talking seriously to girls.

Light rises on the kitchen. Willy, talking, shuts the refrigerator door and comes downstage to the kitchen table. He pours milk into a glass. He is totally immersed in himself, smiling faintly.

Willy: Too young entirely, Biff. You want to watch your schooling first. Then when you're all set, there'll be plenty of girls for a boy like you. (*He smiles broadly at a kitchen chair.*) That so? The girls pay for you? (*He laughs.*) Boy, you must really be makin' a hit.

Willy is gradually addressing—physically—a point offstage, speaking through the wall of the kitchen, and his voice has been rising in volume to that of a normal con-versation.

Willy: I been wondering why you polish the car so careful. Ha! Don't leave the hubcaps, boys. Get the chamois to the hubcaps. Happy, use newspaper on the windows, it's the easiest thing. Show him how to do it, Biff! You see, Happy? Pad it up, use it like a pad. That's it, that's it, good work. You're doin' all right, Hap. (*He pauses, then nods in approbation for a few seconds, then looks upward.*) Biff, first thing we gotta do when we get time is clip that big branch over the house. Afraid it's gonna fall in a storm and hit the roof. Tell you what. We get a rope and sling her around, and then we climb up there with a couple of saws and take her down. Soon as you finish the car, boys, I wanna see ya. I got a surprise for you, boys.
Biff (offstage): Whatta ya got, Dad?
Willy: No, you finish first. Never leave a job till you're finished—remember that. (*Looking toward the "big trees."*) Biff, up in Albany I saw a beautiful ham-mock. I think I'll buy it next trip, and we'll hang it right between those two elms. Wouldn't that be something? Just swingin' there under those branches. Boy, that would be . . .

Young Biff and Young Happy appear from the direction Willy was addressing. Happy carries rags and a pail of water. Biff, wearing a sweater with a block "S," carries a football.

Biff (pointing in the direction of the car offstage): How's that, Pop, professional?
Willy: Terrific. Terrific job, boys. Good work, Biff.
Happy: Where's the surprise, Pop?

Willy: In the back seat of the car.

Happy: Boy! (*He runs off.*)

Biff: What is it, Dad? Tell me, what'd you buy?

Willy (laughing, cuffs him): Never mind, something I want you to have.

Biff (turns and starts off): What is it, Hap?

Happy (offstage): It's a punching bag!

Biff: Oh, Pop!

Willy: It's got Gene Tunney's signature on it.

Happy runs onstage with a punching bag.

Biff: Gee, how'd you know we wanted a punching bag?

Willy: Well, it's the finest thing for the timing.

Happy (lies down on his back and pedals with his feet): I'm losing weight, you notice, Pop?

Willy (to Happy): Jumping rope is good too.

Biff: Did you see the new football I got?

Willy (examining the ball): Where'd you get a new ball?

Biff: The coach told me to practice my passing.

Willy: That so? And he gave you the ball, heh?

Biff: Well, I borrowed it from the locker room. (*He laughs confidentially.*)

Willy (laughing with him at the theft): I want you to return that.

Happy: I told you he wouldn't like it!

Biff (angrily): Well, I'm bringing it back!

Willy (stopping the incipient argument, to Happy): Sure, he's gotta practice with a regulation ball, doesn't he? (*To Biff.*) Coach'll probably congratulate you on your initiative.

Biff: Oh, he keeps congratulating my initiative all the time, Pop.

Willy: That's because he likes you. If somebody else took that ball there'd be an uproar. So what's the report, boys, what's the report?

Biff: Where'd you go this time, Dad? Gee we were lonesome for you.

Willy (pleased, puts an arm around each boy and they come down to the apron): Lonesome, heh?

Biff: Missed you every minute.

Willy: Don't say? Tell you a secret, boys. Don't breathe it to a soul. Someday I'll have my own business, and I'll never have to leave home any more.

Happy: Like Uncle Charley, heh?

Willy: Bigger than Uncle Charley! Because Charley is not—liked. He's liked, but he's not—well liked.

Biff: Where'd you go this time, Dad?

Willy: Well, I got on the road, and I went north to Providence. Met the Mayor.

Biff: The Mayor of Providence!

Willy: He was sitting in the hotel lobby.

Biff: What'd he say?

Willy: He said, "Morning!" And I said, "You've got a fine city here, Mayor." And then he had coffee with me. And then I went to Waterbury. Waterbury is a fine city. Big clock city, the famous Waterbury clock. Sold a nice bill there. And then Boston—Boston is the cradle of the Revolution. A fine city. And a couple of other towns in Mass., and on to Portland and Bangor and straight home!

Biff: Gee, I'd love to go with you sometime, Dad.

Willy: Soon as summer comes.

Happy: Promise?

Willy: You and Hap and I, and I'll show you all the towns. America is full of beautiful towns and fine, upstanding people. And they know me, boys, they know me up and down New England. The finest people. And when I bring you fellas up, there'll be open sesame for all of us, 'cause one thing, boys: I have friends. I can park my car in any street in New England, and the cops protect it like their own. This summer, heh?

Biff and Happy (together): Yeah! You bet!

Willy: We'll take our bathing suits.

Happy: We'll carry your bags, Pop!

Willy: Oh, won't that be something! Me comin' into the Boston stores with you boys carryin' my bags. What a sensation!

Biff is prancing around, practicing passing the ball.

Willy: You nervous, Biff, about the game?

Biff: Not if you're gonna be there.

Willy: What do they say about you in school, now that they made you captain?

Happy: There's a crowd of girls behind him everytime the classes change.

Biff (taking Willy's hand): This Saturday, Pop, this Saturday—just for you, I'm going to break through for a touchdown.

Happy: You're supposed to pass.

Biff: I'm takin' one play for Pop. You watch me, Pop, and when I take off my helmet, that means I'm breakin' out. Then you watch me crash through that line!

Willy (kisses Biff): Oh, wait'll I tell this in Boston!

Bernard enters in knickers. He is younger than Biff, earnest and loyal, a worried boy.

Bernard: Biff, where are you? You're supposed to study with me today.

Willy: Hey, looka Bernard. What're you lookin' so anemic about, Bernard?

Bernard: He's gotta study, Uncle Willy. He's got Regents next week.

Happy (tauntingly, spinning Bernard around): Let's box, Bernard!

Bernard: Biff! (*He gets away from Happy.*) Listen, Biff, I heard Mr. Birnbaum say that if you don't start studyin' math he's gonna flunk you, and you won't graduate. I heard him!

Willy: You better study with him, Biff. Go ahead now.

Bernard: I heard him!

Biff: Oh, Pop, you didn't see my sneakers! (*He holds up a foot for Willy to look at.*)

Willy: Hey, that's a beautiful job of printing!

Bernard (wiping his glasses): Just because he printed University of Virginia on his sneakers doesn't mean they've got to graduate him, Uncle Willy!

Willy (angrily): What're you talking about? With scholarships to three universities they're gonna flunk him?

Bernard: But I heard Mr. Birnbaum say—

Willy: Don't be a pest, Bernard! (To his boys.) What an anemic!

Bernard: Okay, I'm waiting for you in my house, Biff.

Bernard goes off. The Lomans laugh.

Willy: Bernard is not well liked, is he?

Biff: He's liked, but he's not well liked.

Happy: That's right, Pop.

Willy: That's just what I mean. Bernard can get the best marks in school, y'understand, but when he gets out in the business world, y'understand, you are going to be five times ahead of him. That's why I thank Almighty God you're both built like Adonises. Because the man who makes an appearance in the business world, the man who creates personal interest, is the man who gets ahead. Be liked and you will never want. You take me, for instance. I never have to wait in line to see a buyer. "Willy Loman is here!" That's all they have to know, and I go right through.

Biff: Did you knock them dead, Pop?

Willy: Knocked 'em cold in Providence, slaughtered 'em in Boston.

Happy (on his back, pedaling again): I'm losing weight, you notice, Pop?

Linda enters, as of old, a ribbon in her hair, carrying a basket of washing.

Linda (with youthful energy): Hello, dear!

Willy: Sweetheart!

Linda: How'd the Chevvy run?

Willy: Chevrolet, Linda, is the greatest car every built. (To the boys.) Since when do you let your mother carry wash up the stairs?

Biff: Grab hold there, boy!

Happy: Where to, Mom?

Linda: Hang them up on the line. And you better go down to your friends, Biff. The cellar is full of boys. They don't know what to do with themselves.

Biff: Ah, when Pop comes home they can wait!

Willy (laughs appreciatively): You better go down and tell them what to do, Biff.

Biff: I think I'll have them sweep out the furnace room.

Willy: Good work, Biff.

Biff (goes through wall-line of kitchen to doorway at back and calls down): Fellas! Everybody sweep out the furnace room! I'll be right down!

Voices: All right! Okay, Biff.

Biff: George and Sam and Frank, come out back! We're hangin' up the wash! Come on, Hap, on the double! (He and Happy carry out the basket.)

Linda: The way they obey him!

Willy: Well, that's training, the training. I'm tellin' you, I was sellin' thousands and thousands, but I had to come home.

Linda: Oh, the whole block'll be at that game. Did you sell anything?

Willy: I did five hundred gross in Providence and seven hundred gross in Boston.

Linda: No! Wait a minute, I've got a pencil. (*She pulls pencil and paper out of her apron pocket.*) That makes your commission . . . Two hundred—my God! Two hundred and twelve dollars!

Willy: Well, I didn't figure it yet, but . . .

Linda: How much did you do?

Willy: Well, I—I did—about a hundred and eighty gross in Providence. Well, no—it came to—roughly two hundred gross on the whole trip.

Linda (*without hesitation*): Two hundred gross. That's . . . (*She figures.*)

Willy: The trouble was that three of the stores were half closed for inventory in Boston. Otherwise I woulda broke records.

Linda: Well, it makes seventy dollars and some pennies. That's very good.

Willy: What do we owe?

Linda: Well, on the first there's sixteen dollars on the refrigerator—

Willy: Why sixteen?

Linda: Well, the fan belt broke, so it was a dollar eighty.

Willy: But it's brand new.

Linda: Well, the man said that's the way it is. Till they work themselves in, y'know.

They move through the wall-line into the kitchen.

Willy: I hope we didn't get stuck on that machine.

Linda: They got the biggest ads of any of them.

Willy: I know, it's a fine machine. What else?

Linda: Well, there's nine-sixty for the washing machine. And for the vacuum cleaner there's three and a half due on the fifteenth. Then the roof, you got twenty-one dollars remaining.

Willy: It don't leak, does it?

Linda: No, they did a wonderful job. Then you owe Frank for the carburetor.

Willy: I'm not going to pay that man! That goddam Chevrolet, they ought to prohibit the manufacture of that car!

Linda: Well, you owe him three and a half. And odds and ends, comes to around a hundred and twenty dollars by the fifteenth.

Willy: A hundred and twenty dollars! My God, if business don't pick up I don't know what I'm gonna do!

Linda: Well, next week you'll do better.

Willy: Oh, I'll knock 'em dead next week. I'll go to Hartford. I'm very well liked in Hartford. You know, the trouble is, Linda, people don't seem to take to me.

They move on the forestage.

Linda: Oh, don't be foolish.

Willy: I know it when I walk in. They seem to laugh at me.

Linda: Why? Why would they laugh at you? Don't talk that way, Willy.

Willy moves to the edge of the stage. Linda goes into the kitchen and starts to darn stockings.

Willy: I don't know the reason for it, but they just pass me by. I'm not noticed.

Linda: But you're doing wonderful, dear. You're making seventy to a hundred dollars a week.

Willy: But I gotta be at it ten, twelve hours a day. Other men—I don't know —they do it easier. I don't know why—I can't stop myself—I talk too much. A man oughta come in with a few words. One thing about Charley. He's a man of few words, and they respect him.

Linda: You don't talk too much, you're just lively.

Willy (smiling): Well, I figure, what the hell, life is short, a couple of jokes. (*To himself.*) I joke too much! (*The smile goes.*)

Linda: Why? You're—

Willy: I'm fat. I'm very—foolish to look at, Linda. I didn't tell you, but Christmas time I happened to be calling on F. H. Stewarts, and a salesman I know, as I was going in to see the buyer I heard him say something about —walrus. And I—I cracked him right across the face. I won't take that. I simply will not take that. But they do laugh at me. I know that.

Linda: Darling . . .

Willy: I gotta overcome it. I know I gotta overcome it. I'm not dressing to advantage, maybe.

Linda: Willy, darling, you're the handsomest man in the world—

Willy: Oh, no, Linda.

Linda: To me you are. (*Slight pause.*) The handsomest.

From the darkness is heard the laughter of a woman. Willy doesn't turn to it, but it continues through Linda's lines.

Linda: And the boys, Willy. Few men are idolized by their children the way you are.

Music is heard as behind a scrim, to the left of the house, The Woman, dimly seen, is dressing.

Willy (with great feeling): You're the best there is, Linda, you're a pal, you know that? On the road—on the road I want to grab you sometimes and just kiss the life outa you.

The laughter is loud now, and he moves into a brightening area at the left, where The Woman has come from behind the scrim and is standing, putting on her hat, looking into a "mirror" and laughing.

Willy: 'Cause I get so lonely—especially when business is bad and there's nobody to talk to. I get the feeling that I'll never sell anything again, that I won't make a living for you, or a business, a business for the boys. (*He talks through The Woman's subsiding laughter; The Woman primps at the "mirror."*) There's so much I want to make for—

The Woman: Me? You didn't make me, Willy. I picked you.

Willy (pleased): You picked me?

The Woman (who is quite proper-looking, Willy's age): I did. I've been sitting at that desk watching all the salesmen go by, day in, day out. But you've got such a sense of humor, and we do have such a good time together, don't we?

Willy: Sure, sure. (*He takes her in his arms.*) Why do you have to go now?

The Woman: It's two o'clock . . .

Willy: No, come on in! (*He pulls her.*)

The Woman: . . . my sisters'll be scandalized. When'll you be back?

Willy: Oh, two weeks about. Will you come up again?

The Woman: Sure thing. You do make me laugh. It's good for me. (*She squeezes his arm, kisses him.*) And I think you're a wonderful man.

Willy: You picked me, heh?

The Woman: Sure. Because you're so sweet. And such a kidder.

Willy: Well, I'll see you next time I'm in Boston.

The Woman: I'll put you right through to the buyers.

Willy (*slapping her bottom*): Right. Well, bottoms up!

The Woman (*slaps him gently and laughs*): You just kill me, Willy. (*He suddenly grabs her and kisses her roughly.*) You kill me. And thanks for the stockings. I love a lot of stockings. Well, good night.

Willy: Good night. And keep your pores open!

The Woman: Oh, Willy!

> *The Woman bursts out laughing, and Linda's laughter blends in. The Woman disappears into the dark. Now the area at the kitchen table brightens. Linda is sitting where she was at the kitchen table, but now is mending a pair of silk stockings.*

Linda: You are, Willy. The handsomest man. You've got no reason to feel that—

Willy (*coming out of The Woman's dimming area and going over to Linda*): I'll make it all up to you, Linda, I'll—

Linda: There's nothing to make up, dear. You're doing fine, better than—

Willy (*noticing her mending*): What's that?

Linda: Just mending my stockings. They're so expensive—

Willy (*angrily, taking them from her*): I won't have you mending stockings in this house! Now throw them out!

> *Linda puts the stockings in her pocket.*

Bernard (*entering on the run*): Where is he? If he doesn't study!

Willy (*moving to the forestage, with great agitation*): You'll give him the answers!

Bernard: I do, but I can't on a Regents! That's a state exam! They're liable to arrest me!

Willy: Where is he? I'll whip him, I'll whip him!

Linda: And he'd better give back that football, Willy, it's not nice.

Willy: Biff! Where is he? Why is he taking everything?

Linda: He's too rough with the girls, Willy. All the mothers are afraid of him!

Willy: I'll whip him!

Bernard: He's driving the car without a license!

> *The Woman's laugh is heard.*

Willy: Shut up!

Linda: All the mothers—

Willy: Shut up!

Bernard (backing quietly away and out): Mr. Birnbaum says he's stuck up.

Willy: Get outa here!

Bernard: If he doesn't buckle down he'll flunk math! (*He goes off.*)

Linda: He's right, Willy, you've gotta—

Willy (exploding at her): There's nothing the matter with him! You want him to be a worm like Bernard? He's got spirit, personality . . .

As he speaks, Linda, almost in tears, exits into the living room. Willy is alone in the kitchen, wilting and staring. The leaves are gone. It is night again, and the apartment houses look down from behind.

Willy: Loaded with it. Loaded! What is he stealing? He's giving it back, isn't he? Why is he stealing? What did I tell him? I never in my life told him anything but decent things.

Happy in pajamas has come down the stairs; Willy suddenly becomes aware of Happy's presence.

Happy: Let's go now, come on.

Willy (sitting down at the kitchen table): Huh! Why did she have to wax the floors herself? Everytime she waxes the floors she keels over. She knows that!

Happy: Shh! Take it easy. What brought you back tonight?

Willy: I got an awful scare. Nearly hit a kid in Yonkers. God! Why didn't I go to Alaska with my brother Ben that time! Ben! That man was a genius, that man was success incarnate! What a mistake! He begged me to go.

Happy: Well, there's no use in—

Willy: You guys! There was a man started with the clothes on his back and ended up with diamond mines!

Happy: Boy, someday I'd like to know how he did it.

Willy: What's the mystery? The man knew what he wanted and went out and got it! Walked into a jungle, and comes out, the age of twenty-one, and he's rich! The world is an oyster, but you don't crack it open on a mattress!

Happy: Pop, I told you I'm gonna retire you for life.

Willy: You'll retire me for life on seventy goddam dollars a week? And your women and your car and your apartment, and you'll retire me for life! Christ's sake, I couldn't get past Yonkers today! Where are you guys, where are you? The woods are burning! I can't drive a car!

Charley has appeared in the doorway. He is a large man, slow of speech, laconic, immovable. In all he says, despite what he says, there is pity, and, now, trepidation. He has a robe over his pajamas, slippers on his feet. He enters the kitchen.

Charley: Everything all right?

Happy: Yeah, Charley, everything's . . .

Willy: What's the matter?

Charley: I heard some noise. I thought something happened. Can't we do something about the walls? You sneeze in here, and in my house hats blow off.

Happy: Let's go to bed, Dad. Come on.

Charley signals to Happy to go.

Willy: You go ahead, I'm not tired at the moment.

Happy (*to Willy*): Take it easy, huh? (*He exits.*)

Willy: What're you doin' up?

Charley (*sitting down at the kitchen table opposite Willy*): Couldn't sleep good. I had a heartburn.

Willy: Well, you don't know how to eat.

Charley: I eat with my mouth.

Willy: No, you're ignorant. You gotta know about vitamins and things like that.

Charley: Come on, let's shoot. Tire you out a little.

Willy (*hesitantly*): All right. You got cards?

Charley (*taking a deck from his pocket*): Yeah, I got them. Someplace. What is it with those vitamins?

Willy (*dealing*): They build up your bones. Chemistry.

Charley: Yeah, but there's no bones in a heartburn.

Willy: What are you talkin' about? Do you know the first thing about it?

Charley: Don't get insulted.

Willy: Don't talk about something you don't know anything about.

They are playing. Pause.

Charley: What're you doin' home?

Willy: A little trouble with the car.

Charley: Oh. (*Pause.*) I'd like to take a trip to California.

Willy: Don't say.

Charley: You want a job?

Willy: I got a job, I told you that. (*After a slight pause.*) What the hell are you of-fering me a job for?

Charley: Don't get insulted.

Willy: Don't insult me.

Charley: I don't see no sense in it. You don't have to go on this way.

Willy: I got a good job. (*Slight pause.*) What do you keep comin' in here for?

Charley: You want me to go?

Willy (*after a pause, withering*): I can't understand it. He's going back to Texas again. What the hell is that?

Charley: Let him go.

Willy: I got nothin' to give him, Charley, I'm clean, I'm clean.

Charley: He won't starve. None a them starve. Forget about him.

Willy: Then what have I got to remember?

Charley: You take it too hard. To hell with it. When a deposit bottle is broken you don't get your nickel back.

Willy: That's easy enough for you to say.

Charley: That ain't easy for me to say.

Willy: Did you see the ceiling I put up in the living room?

Charley: Yeah, that's a piece of work. To put up a ceiling is a mystery to me. How do you do it?

Willy: What's the difference?

Charley: Well, talk about it.

Willy: You gonna put up a ceiling?

Charley: How could I put up a ceiling?

Willy: Then what the hell are you bothering me for?

Charley: You're insulted again.

Willy: A man who can't handle tools is not a man. You're disgusting.

Charley: Don't call me disgusting, Willy.

> *Uncle Ben, carrying a valise and an umbrella, enters the forestage from around the right corner of the house. He is a stolid man, in his sixties, with a mustache and an authoritative air. He is utterly certain of his destiny, and there is an aura of far places about him. He enters exactly as Willy speaks.*

Willy: I'm getting awfully tired, Ben.

> *Ben's music is heard. Ben looks around at everything.*

Charley: Good, keep playing; you'll sleep better. Did you call me Ben?

> *Ben looks at his watch.*

Willy: That's funny. For a second there you reminded me of my brother Ben.

Ben: I have only a few minutes. (*He strolls, inspecting the place. Willy and Charley continue playing.*)

Charley: You never heard from him again, heh? Since that time?

Willy: Didn't Linda tell you? Couple of weeks ago we got a letter from his wife in Africa. He died.

Charley: That so.

Ben (*chuckling*): So this is Brooklyn, eh?

Charley: Maybe you're in for some of his money.

Willy: Naa, he had seven sons. There's just one opportunity I had with that man . . .

Ben: I must make a train, William. There are several properties I'm looking at in Alaska.

Willy: Sure, sure! If I'd gone with him to Alaska that time, everything would've been totally different.

Charley: Go on, you'd froze to death up there.

Willy: What're you talking about?

Ben: Opportunity is tremendous in Alaska, William. Surprised you're not up there.

Willy: Sure, tremendous.

Charley: Heh?

Willy: There was the only man I ever met who knew the answers.

Charley: Who?

Ben: How are you all?

Willy (*taking a pot, smiling*): Fine, fine.

Charley: Pretty sharp tonight.

Ben: Is Mother living with you?

Willy: No, she died a long time ago.

Charley: Who?

Ben: That's too bad. Fine specimen of a lady, Mother.

Willy (to Charley): Heh?

Ben: I'd hoped to see the old girl.

Charley: Who died?

Ben: Heard anything from Father, have you?

Willy (unnerved): What do you mean, who died?

Charley (taking a pot): What're you talkin' about?

Ben (looking at his watch): William, it's half-past eight!

Willy (as though to dispel his confusion he angrily stops Charley's hand): That's my build!

Charley: I put the ace—

Willy: If you don't know how to play the game I'm not gonna throw my money away on you!

Charley (rising): It was my ace, for God's sake!

Willy: I'm through, I'm through!

Ben: When did Mother die?

Willy: Long ago. Since the beginning you never knew how to play cards.

Charley (picks up the cards and goes to the door): All right! Next time I'll bring a deck with five aces.

Willy: I don't play that kind of game!

Charley (turning to him): You ought to be ashamed of yourself!

Willy: Yeah?

Charley: Yeah! (He goes out.)

Willy (slamming the door after him): Ignoramus!

Ben (as Willy comes toward him through the wall-line of the kitchen): So you're William.

Willy (shaking Ben's hand): Ben! I've been waiting for you so long! What's the answer? How did you do it?

Ben: Oh, there's a story in that.

Linda enters the forestage, as of old, carrying the wash basket.

Linda: Is this Ben?

Ben (gallantly): How do you do, my dear.

Linda: Where've you been all these years? Willy's always wondered why you—

Willy (pulling Ben away from her impatiently): Where is Dad? Didn't you follow him? How did you get started?

Ben: Well, I don't know how much you remember.

Willy: Well, I was just a baby, of course, only three or four years old—

Ben: Three years and eleven months.

Willy: What a memory, Ben!

Ben: I have many enterprises, William, and I have never kept books.

Willy: I remember I was sitting under the wagon in—was it Nebraska?

Ben: It was South Dakota, and I gave you a bunch of wild flowers.

Willy: I remember you walking away down some open road.

Ben (laughing): I was going to find Father in Alaska.

Willy: Where is he?

Ben: At that age I had a very faulty view of geography, William. I discovered after a few days that I was heading due south, so instead of Alaska, I ended up in Africa.

Linda: Africa!

Willy: The Gold Coast!

Ben: Principally, diamond mines.

Linda: Diamond mines!

Ben: Yes, my dear. But I've only a few minutes—

Willy: No! Boys! Boys! (*Young Biff and Happy appear.*) Listen to this. This is your Uncle Ben, a great man! Tell my boys, Ben!

Ben: Why, boys, when I was seventeen I walked into the jungle, and when I was twenty-one I walked out. (*He laughs.*) And by God I was rich.

Willy (to the boys): You see what I been talking about? The greatest things can happen!

Ben (glancing at his watch): I have an appointment in Ketchikan Tuesday week.

Willy: No, Ben! Please tell about Dad. I want my boys to hear. I want them to know the kind of stock they sprang from. All I remember is a man with a big beard, and I was in Mamma's lap, sitting around a fire, and some kind of high music.

Ben: His flute. He played the flute.

Willy: Sure, the flute, that's right!

New music is heard, a high, rollicking tune.

Ben: Father was a very great and a very wild-hearted man. We would start in Boston, and he'd toss the whole family into the wagon, and then he'd drive the team right across the country; through Ohio, and Indiana, Michigan, Illinois, and all the Western states. And we'd stop in the towns and sell the flutes that he'd made on the way. Great inventor, Father. With one gadget he made more in a week than a man like you could make in a lifetime.

Willy: That's just the way I'm bringing them up, Ben—rugged, well-liked, all-around.

Ben: Yeah? (*To Biff.*) Hit that, boy—hard as you can. (*He pounds his stomach.*)

Biff: Oh, no, sir!

Ben (taking boxing stance): Come on, get to me! (*He laughs.*)

Willy: Go to it, Biff! Go ahead, show him!

Biff: Okay! (*He cocks his fist and starts in.*)

Linda (to Willy): Why must he fight, dear?

Ben (sparring with Biff): Good boy! Good boy!

Willy: How's that, Ben, heh?

Happy: Give him the left, Biff!

Linda: Why are you fighting?

Ben: Good boy! (*Suddenly comes in, trips Biff, and stands over him, the point of his umbrella poised over Biff's eye.*)

Linda: Look out, Biff!

Biff: Gee!

Ben (patting Biff's knee): Never fight fair with a stranger, boy. You'll never get out of the jungle that way. (*Taking Linda's hand and bowing.*) It was an honor and a pleasure to meet you, Linda.

Linda (withdrawing her hand coldly, frightened): Have a nice—trip.

Ben (to Willy): And good luck with your—what do you do?

Willy: Selling.

Ben: Yes. Well . . . (*He raises his hand in farewell to all.*)

Willy: No, Ben, I don't want you to think . . . (*He takes Ben's arm to show him.*) It's Brooklyn, I know, but we hunt too.

Ben: Really, now.

Willy: Oh, sure, there's snakes and rabbits and—that's why I moved out here. Why, Biff can fell any one of these trees in no time! Boys! Go right over to where they're building the apartment house and get some sand. We're gonna rebuild the entire front stoop right now! Watch this, Ben!

Biff: Yes, sir! On the double, Hap!

Happy (as he and Biff run off): I lost weight, Pop, you notice?

Charley enters in knickers, even before the boys are gone.

Charley: Listen, if they steal any more from that building the watchman'll put the cops on them!

Linda (to Willy): Don't let Biff . . .

Ben laughs lustily.

Willy: You shoulda seen the lumber they brought home last week. At least a dozen six-by-tens worth all kinds of money.

Charley: Listen, if that watchman—

Willy: I gave them hell, understand. But I got a couple of fearless characters there.

Charley: Willy, the jails are full of fearless characters.

Ben (clapping Willy on the back, with a laugh at Charley): And the stock exchange, friend!

Willy (joining in Ben's laughter): Where are the rest of your pants?

Charley: My wife bought them.

Willy: Now all you need is a golf club and you can go upstairs and go to sleep. (*To Ben.*) Great athlete! Between him and his son Bernard they can't hammer a nail!

Bernard (rushing in): The watchman's chasing Biff!

Willy (angrily): Shut up! He's not stealing anything!

Linda (alarmed, hurrying off left): Where is he? Biff, dear! (*She exits.*)

Willy (moving toward the left, away from Ben): There's nothing wrong. What's the matter with you?

Ben: Nervy boy. Good!

Willy (laughing): Oh, nerves of iron, that Biff!

Charley: Don't know what it is. My New England man comes back and he's bleedin', they murdered him up there.

Willy: It's contacts, Charley, I got important contacts!

Charley (sarcastically): Glad to hear it, Willy. Come in later, we'll shoot a little casino. I'll take some of your Portland money. (*He laughs at Willy and exits.*)

Willy (turning to Ben): Business is bad, it's murderous. But not for me, of course.

Ben: I'll stop by on my way back to Africa.

Willy (longingly): Can't you stay a few days? You're just what I need, Ben, because I—I have a fine position, but I—well, Dad left when I was such a baby and I never had a chance to talk to him and I still feel—kind of temporary about myself.

Ben: I'll be late for my train.

They are at opposite ends of the stage.

Willy: Ben, my boys—can't we talk? They'd go into the jaws of hell for me, see, but I—

Ben: William, you're being first-rate with your boys. Outstanding, manly chaps!

Willy (hanging on to his words): Oh, Ben, that's good to hear! Because sometimes I'm afraid that I'm not teaching them the right kind of—Ben, how should I teach them?

Ben (giving great weight to each word, and with a certain vicious audacity): William, when I walked into the jungle, I was seventeen. When I walked out I was twenty-one. And, by God, I was rich! (*He goes off into darkness around the right corner of the house.*)

Willy: . . . was rich! That's just the spirit I want to imbue them with! To walk into a jungle! I was right! I was right! I was right!

Ben is gone, but Willy is still speaking to him as Linda, in nightgown and robe, enters the kitchen, glances around for Willy, then goes to the door of the house, looks out and sees him. Comes down to his left. He looks at her.

Linda: Willy, dear? Willy?

Willy: I was right!

Linda: Did you have some cheese? (*He can't answer.*) It's very late, darling. Come to bed, heh?

Willy (looking straight up): Gotta break your neck to see a star in this yard.

Linda: You coming in?

Willy: What ever happened to that diamond watch fob? Remember? When Ben came from Africa that time? Didn't he give me a watch fob with a diamond in it?

Linda: You pawned it, dear. Twelve, thirteen years ago. For Biff's radio correspondence course.

Willy: Gee, that was a beautiful thing. I'll take a walk.

Linda: But you're in your slippers.

Willy (starting to go around the house at the left): I was right! I was! (*Half to Linda, as he goes, shaking his head.*) What a man! There was a man worth talking to. I was right!

Linda (*calling after Willy*): But in your slippers, Willy!

Willy is almost gone when Biff, in his pajamas, comes down the stairs and enters the kitchen.

Biff: What is he doing out there?

Linda: Sh!

Biff: God Almighty, Mom, how long has he been doing this?

Linda: Don't, he'll hear you.

Biff: What the hell is the matter with him?

Linda: It'll pass by morning.

Biff: Shouldn't we do anything?

Linda: Oh, my dear, you should do a lot of things, but there's nothing to do, so go to sleep.

Happy comes down the stairs and sits on the steps.

Happy: I never heard him so loud, Mom.

Linda: Well, come around more often; you'll hear him. (*She sits down at the table and mends the lining of Willy's jacket.*)

Biff: Why didn't you ever write me about this, Mom?

Linda: How would I write to you? For over three months you had no address.

Biff: I was on the move. But you know I thought of you all the time. You know that, don't you, pal?

Linda: I know, dear, I know. But he likes to have a letter. Just to know that there's still a possibility for better things.

Biff: He's not like this all the time, is he?

Linda: It's when you come home he's always the worst.

Biff: When I come home?

Linda: When you write you're coming, he's all smiles, and talks about the future, and—he's just wonderful. And then the closer you seem to come, the more shaky he gets, and then, by the time you get here, he's arguing, and he seems angry at you. I think it's just that maybe he can't bring himself to—to open up to you. Why are you so hateful to each other? Why is that?

Biff (*evasively*): I'm not hateful, Mom.

Linda: But you no sooner come in the door than you're fighting!

Biff: I don't know why. I mean to change. I'm tryin', Mom, you understand?

Linda: Are you home to stay now?

Biff: I don't know. I want to look around, see what's doin'.

Linda: Biff, you can't look around all your life, can you?

Biff: I just can't take hold, Mom. I can't take hold of some kind of a life.

Linda: Biff, a man is not a bird, to come and go with the springtime.

Biff: Your hair . . . (*He touches her hair.*) Your hair got so gray.

Linda: Oh, it's been gray since you were in high school. I just stopped dyeing it, that's all.

Biff: Dye it again, will ya? I don't want my pal looking old. (*He smiles.*)

Linda: You're such a boy! You think you can go away for a year and . . . You've got to get it into your head now that one day you'll knock on this door and there'll be strange people here—

Biff: What are you talking about? You're not even sixty, Mom.

Linda: But what about your father?

Biff (*lamely*): Well, I meant him too.

Happy: He admires Pop.

Linda: Biff dear, if you don't have any feeling for him, then you can't have any feeling for me.

Biff: Sure I can, Mom.

Linda: No. You can't just come to see me, because I love him. (*With a threat, but only a threat, of tears.*) He's the dearest man in the world to me, and I won't have anyone making him feel unwanted and low and blue. You've got to make up your mind now, darling, there's no leeway any more. Either he's your father and you pay him that respect, or else you're not to come here. I know he's not easy to get along with—nobody knows that better than me—but . . .

Willy (*from the left, with a laugh*): Hey, hey, Biffo!

Biff (*starting to go out after Willy*): What the hell is the matter with him? (*Happy stops him.*)

Linda: Don't—don't go near him!

Biff: Stop making excuses for him! He always, always wiped the floor with you. Never had an ounce of respect for you.

Happy: He's always had respect for—

Biff: What the hell do you know about it?

Happy (*surlily*): Just don't call him crazy!

Biff: He's got no character—Charley wouldn't do this. Not in his own house—spewing out that vomit from his mind.

Happy: Charley never had to cope with what he's got to.

Biff: People are worse off than Willy Loman. Believe me, I've seen them!

Linda: Then make Charley your father, Biff. You can't do that, can you? I don't say he's a great man. Willy Loman never made a lot of money. His name was never in the paper. He's not the finest character that ever lived. But he's a human being, and a terrible thing is happening to him. So attention must be paid. He's not to be allowed to fall into his grave like an old dog. Attention, attention must be finally paid to such a person. You called him crazy—

Biff: I didn't mean—

Linda: No, a lot of people think he's lost his—balance. But you don't have to be very smart to know what his trouble is. The man is exhausted.

Happy: Sure!

Linda: A small man can be just as exhausted as a great man. He works for a company thirty-six years this March, opens up unheard-of territories to their trademark, and now in his old age they take his salary away.

Happy (*indignantly*): I didn't know that, Mom!

Linda: You never asked, my dear! Now that you get your spending money someplace else you don't trouble your mind with him.

Happy: But I gave you money last—

Linda: Christmas time, fifty dollars! To fix the hot water it cost ninety-seven fifty! For five weeks he's been on straight commission, like a beginner, an unknown!

Biff: Those ungrateful bastards!

Linda: Are they any worse than his sons? When he brought them business, when he was young, they were glad to see him. But now his old friends, the old buyers that loved him so and always found some order to hand him in a pinch—they're all dead, retired. He used to be able to make six, seven calls a day in Boston. Now he takes his valises out of the car and puts them back and takes them out again and he's exhausted. Instead of walking he talks now. He drives seven hundred miles, and when he gets there no one knows him any more, no one welcomes him. And what goes through a man's mind, driving seven hundred miles home without having earned a cent? Why shouldn't he talk to himself? Why? When he has to go to Charley and borrow fifty dollars a week and pretend to me that it's his pay? How long can that go on? How long? You see what I'm sitting here and waiting for? And you tell me he has no character? The man who never worked a day but for your benefit? When does he get the medal for that? Is this his reward—to turn around at the age of sixty-three and find his sons, who he loved better than his life, one a philandering bum—

Happy: Mom!

Linda: That's all you are, my baby! (*To Biff.*) And you! What happened to the love you had for him? You were such pals! How you used to talk to him on the phone every night! How lonely he was till he could come home to you!

Biff: All right, Mom. I'll live here in my room, and I'll get a job. I'll keep away from him, that's all.

Linda: No, Biff. You can't stay here and fight all the time.

Biff: He threw me out of this house, remember that.

Linda: Why did he do that? I never knew why.

Biff: Because I know he's a fake and he doesn't like anybody around who knows!

Linda: Why a fake? In what way? What do you mean?

Biff: Just don't lay it all at my feet. It's between me and him—that's all I have to say. I'll chip in from now on. He'll settle for half my pay check. He'll be all right. I'm going to bed. (*He starts for the stairs.*)

Linda: He won't be all right.

Biff (*turning on the stairs, furiously*): I hate this city and I'll stay here. Now what do you want?

Linda: He's dying, Biff.

Happy turns quickly to her, shocked.

Biff (*after a pause*): Why is he dying?

Linda: He's been trying to kill himself.

Biff (*with great horror*): How?

Linda: I live from day to day.

Biff: What're you talking about?

Linda: Remember I wrote you that he smashed up the car again? In February?

Biff: Well?

Linda: The insurance inspector came. He said that they have evidence. That all these accidents in the last year—weren't—weren't—accidents.

Happy: How can they tell that? That's a lie.

Linda: It seems there's a woman ... (*She takes a breath as—*)

Biff (*sharply but contained*): What woman?

Linda (*simultaneously*): ... and this woman ...

Linda: What?

Biff: Nothing. Go ahead.

Linda: What did you say?

Biff: Nothing. I just said what woman?

Happy: What about her?

Linda: Well, it seems she was walking down the road and saw his car. She says that he wasn't driving fast at all, and that he didn't skid. She says he came to that little bridge, and then deliberately smashed into the railing, and it was only the shallowness of the water that saved him.

Biff: Oh, no, he probably just fell asleep again.

Linda: I don't think he fell asleep.

Biff: Why not?

Linda: Last month ... (*With great difficulty.*) Oh, boys, it's so hard to say a thing like this! He's just a big stupid man to you, but I tell you there's more good in him than in many other people. (*She chokes, wipes her eyes.*) I was looking for a fuse. The lights blew out, and I went down the cellar. And behind the fuse box—it happened to fall out—was a length of rubber pipe—just short.

Happy: No kidding?

Linda: There's a little attachment on the end of it. I knew right away. And sure enough, on the bottom of the water heater there's a new little nipple on the gas pipe.

Happy (*angrily*): That—jerk.

Biff: Did you have it taken off?

Linda: I'm—I'm ashamed to. How can I mention it to him? Every day I go down and take away that little rubber pipe. But, when he comes home, I put it back where it was. How can I insult him that way? I don't know what to do. I live from day to day, boys. I tell you, I know every thought in his mind. It sounds so old-fashioned and silly, but I tell you he put his whole life into you and you've turned your backs on him. (*She is bent over in the chair, weeping, her face in her hands.*) Biff, I swear to God! Biff, his life is in your hands!

Happy (*to Biff*): How do you like that damned fool!

Biff (*kissing her*): All right, pal, all right. It's all settled now. I've been remiss. I know that, Mom. But now I'll stay, and I swear to you, I'll apply myself. (*Kneeling in front of her, in a fever of self-reproach.*) It's just—you see, Mom, I don't fit in business. Not that I won't try. I'll try, and I'll make good.

Happy: Sure you will. The trouble with you in business was you never tried to please people.

Biff: I know, I—

Happy: Like when you worked for Harrison's. Bob Harrison said you were tops, and then you go and do some damn fool thing like whistling whole songs in the elevator like a comedian.

Biff (against Happy): So what? I like to whistle sometimes.

Happy: You don't raise a guy to a responsible job who whistles in the elevator!

Linda: Well, don't argue about it now.

Happy: Like when you'd go off and swim in the middle of the day instead of taking the line around.

Biff (his resentment rising): Well, don't you run off? You take off sometimes, don't you? On a nice summer day?

Happy: Yeah, but I cover myself!

Linda: Boys!

Happy: If I'm going to take a fade the boss can call any number where I'm supposed to be and they'll swear to him that I just left. I'll tell you something that I hate to say, Biff, but in the business world some of them think you're crazy.

Biff (angered): Screw the business world!

Happy: All right, screw it! Great, but cover yourself!

Linda: Hap! Hap!

Biff: I don't care what they think! They've laughed at Dad for years, and you know why? Because we don't belong in this nut-house of a city! We should be mixing cement on some open plain, or—or carpenters. A carpenter is allowed to whistle!

Willy walks in from the entrance of the house, at left.

Willy: Even your grandfather was better than a carpenter. (*Pause. They watch him.*) You never grew up. Bernard does not whistle in the elevator, I assure you.

Biff (as though to laugh Willy out of it): Yeah, but you do, Pop.

Willy: I never in my life whistled in an elevator! And who in the business world thinks I'm crazy?

Biff: I didn't mean it like that, Pop. Now don't make a whole thing out of it, will ya?

Willy: Go back to the West! Be a carpenter, a cowboy, enjoy yourself!

Linda: Willy, he was just saying—

Willy: I heard what he said!

Happy (trying to quiet Willy): Hey, Pop, come on now . . .

Willy (continuing over Happy's line): They laugh at me, heh? Go to Filene's, go to the Hub, go to Slattery's, Boston. Call out the name Willy Loman and see what happens! Big shot!

Biff: All right, Pop.

Willy: Big!

Biff: All right!

Willy: Why do you always insult me?

Biff: I didn't say a word. (*To Linda.*) Did I say a word?

Linda: He didn't say anything, Willy.

Willy (going to the doorway of the living room): All right, good night, good night.

Linda: Willy, dear, he just decided . . .

Willy (to Biff): If you get tired hanging around tomorrow, paint the ceiling I put up in the living room.

Biff: I'm leaving early tomorrow.

Happy: He's going to see Bill Oliver, Pop.

Willy (interestedly): Oliver? For what?

Biff (with reserve, but trying, trying): He always said he'd stake me. I'd like to go into business, so maybe I can take him up on it.

Linda: Isn't that wonderful?

Willy: Don't interrupt. What's wonderful about it? There's fifty men in the City of New York who'd stake him. *(To Biff.)* Sporting goods?

Biff: I guess so. I know something about it and—

Willy: He knows something about it! You know sporting goods better than Spalding, for God's sake! How much is he giving you?

Biff: I don't know, I didn't even see him yet, but—

Willy: Then what're you talkin' about?

Biff (getting angry): Well, all I said was I'm gonna see him, that's all!

Willy (turning away): Ah, you're counting your chickens again.

Biff (starting left for the stairs): Oh, Jesus, I'm going to sleep!

Willy (calling after him): Don't curse in this house!

Biff (turning): Since when did you get so clean!

Happy (trying to stop them): Wait a . . .

Willy: Don't use that language to me! I won't have it!

Happy (grabbing Biff, shouts): Wait a minute! I got an idea. I got a feasible idea. Come here, Biff, let's talk this over now, let's talk some sense here. When I was down in Florida last time, I thought of a great idea to sell sporting goods. It just came back to me. You and I, Biff—we have a line, the Loman Line. We train a couple of weeks, and put on a couple of exhibitions, see?

Willy: That's an idea!

Happy: Wait! We form two basketball teams, see? Two water-polo teams. We play each other. It's a million dollars' worth of publicity. Two brothers, see? The Loman Brothers. Displays in the Royal Palms—all the hotels. And banners over the ring and the basketball court: "Loman Brothers." Baby, we could sell sporting goods!

Willy: That is a one-million-dollar idea.

Linda: Marvelous!

Biff: I'm in great shape as far as that's concerned.

Happy: And the beauty of it is, Biff, it wouldn't be like a business. We'd be out playin' ball again . . .

Biff (enthused): Yeah, that's . . .

Willy: Million-dollar . . .

Happy: And you wouldn't get fed up with it, Biff. It'd be the family again. There'd be the old honor, and comradeship, and if you wanted to go off for a swim or somethin'—well, you'd do it! Without some smart cooky gettin' up ahead of you!

Willy: Lick the world! You guys together could absolutely lick the civilized world.

Biff: I'll see Oliver tomorrow. Hap, if we could work that out . . .

Linda: Maybe things are beginning to—

Willy (wildly enthused, to Linda): Stop interrupting! *(To Biff.)* But don't wear sport jacket and slacks when you see Oliver.

Biff: No, I'll—

Willy: A business suit, and talk as little as possible, and don't crack any jokes.

Biff: He did like me. Always liked me.

Linda: He loved you!

Willy (to Linda): Will you stop! *(To Biff.)* Walk in very serious. You are not applying for a boy's job. Money is to pass. Be quiet, fine, and serious. Everybody likes a kidder, but nobody lends him money.

Happy: I'll try to get some myself, Biff. I'm sure I can.

Willy: I can see great things for you, kids, I think your troubles are over. But remember, start big and you'll end big. Ask for fifteen. How much you gonna ask for?

Biff: Gee, I don't know—

Willy: And don't say "Gee." "Gee" is a boy's word. A man walking in for fifteen thousand dollars does not say "Gee!"

Biff: Ten, I think, would be top though.

Willy: Don't be so modest. You always started too low. Walk in with a big laugh. Don't look worried. Start off with a couple of your good stories to lighten things up. It's not what you say, it's how you say it—because personality always wins the day.

Linda: Oliver always thought the highest of him—

Willy: Will you let me talk?

Biff: Don't yell at her, Pop, will ya?

Willy (angrily): I was talking, wasn't I?

Biff: I don't like you yelling at her all the time, and I'm tellin' you, that's all.

Willy: What're you, takin' over the house?

Linda: Willy—

Willy (turning on her): Don't take his side all the time, goddammit!

Biff (furiously): Stop yelling at her!

Willy (suddenly pulling on his cheek, beaten down, guilt ridden): Give my best to Bill Oliver—he may remember me. *(He exits through the living room doorway.)*

Linda (her voice subdued): What'd you have to start that for? *(Biff turns away.)* You see how sweet he was as soon as you talked hopefully? *(She goes over to Biff.)* Come up and say good night to him. Don't let him go to bed that way.

Happy: Come on, Biff, let's buck him up.

Linda: Please, dear. Just say good night. It takes so little to make him happy. Come. *(She goes through the living room doorway, calling upstairs from within the living room.)* Your pajamas are hanging in the bathroom. Willy!

Happy (*looking toward where Linda went out*): What a woman! They broke the mold when they made her. You know that, Biff?

Biff: He's off salary. My God, working on commission!

Happy: Well, let's face it: he's no hot-shot selling man. Except that sometimes, you have to admit, he's a sweet personality.

Biff (*deciding*): Lend me ten bucks, will ya? I want to buy some new ties.

Happy: I'll take you to a place I know. Beautiful stuff. Wear one of my striped shirts tomorrow.

Biff: She got gray. Mom got awful old. Gee, I'm gonna go in to Oliver tomorrow and knock him for a—

Happy: Come on up. Tell that to Dad. Let's give him a whirl. Come on.

Biff (*steamed up*): You know, with ten thousand bucks, boy!

Happy (*as they go into the living room*): That's the talk, Biff, that's the first time I've heard the old confidence out of you! (*From within the living room, fading off.*) You're gonna live with me, kid, and any babe you want you just say the word ... (*The last lines are hardly heard. They are mounting the stairs to their parents' bedroom.*)

Linda (*entering her bedroom and addressing Willy, who is in the bathroom. She is straightening the bed for him*): Can you do anything about the shower? It drips.

Willy (*from the bathroom*): All of a sudden everything falls to pieces! Goddam plumbing, oughta be sued, those people. I hardly finished putting it in and the thing ... (*His words rumble off.*)

Linda: I'm just wondering if Oliver will remember him. You think he might?

Willy (*coming out of the bathroom in his pajamas*): Remember him? What's the matter with you, you crazy? If he'd've stayed with Oliver he'd be on top by now! Wait'll Oliver gets a look at him. You don't know the average caliber any more. The average young man today—(*he is getting into bed*)—is got a caliber of zero. Greatest thing in the world for him was to bum around.

Biff and Happy enter the bedroom. Slight pause.

Willy (*stops short, looking at Biff*): Glad to hear it, boy.

Happy: He wanted to say good night to you, sport.

Willy (*to Biff*): Yeah. Knock him dead, boy. What'd you want to tell me?

Biff: Just take it easy, Pop. Good night. (*He turns to go.*)

Willy (*unable to resist*): And if anything falls off the desk while you're talking to him—like a package or something—don't you pick it up. They have office boys for that.

Linda: I'll make a big breakfast—

Willy: Will you let me finish? (*To Biff.*) Tell him you were in the business in the West. Not farm work.

Biff: All right, Dad.

Linda: I think everything—

Willy (*going right through her speech*): And don't undersell yourself. No less than fifteen thousand dollars.

Biff (*unable to bear him*): Okay. Good night, Mom. (*He starts moving.*)

Willy: Because you got a greatness in you, Biff, remember that. You got all kinds a greatness . . . (*He lies back, exhausted. Biff walks out.*)

Linda (*calling after Biff*): Sleep well, darling!

Happy: I'm gonna get married, Mom. I wanted to tell you.

Linda: Go to sleep, dear.

Happy (*going*): I just wanted to tell you.

Willy: Keep up the good work. (*Happy exits.*) God . . . remember that Ebbets Field game? The championship of the city?

Linda: Just rest. Should I sing to you?

Willy: Yeah. Sing to me. (*Linda hums a soft lullaby.*) When that team came out—he was the tallest, remember?

Linda: Oh, yes. And in gold.

> *Biff enters the darkened kitchen, takes a cigarette, and leaves the house. He comes downstage into a golden pool of light. He smokes, staring at the night.*

Willy: Like a young god. Hercules—something like that. And the sun, the sun all around him. Remember how he waved to me? Right up from the field, with the representatives of three colleges standing by? And the buyers I brought, and the cheers when he came out—Loman, Loman, Loman! God Almighty, he'll be great yet. A star like that, magnificent, can never really fade away!

> *The light on Willy is fading. The gas heater begins to glow through the kitchen wall, near the stairs, a blue flame beneath red coils.*

Linda (*timidly*): Willy, dear, what has he got against you?

Willy: I'm so tired. Don't talk any more.

> *Biff slowly returns to the kitchen. He stops, stares toward the heater.*

Linda: Will you ask Howard to let you work in New York?

Willy: First thing in the morning. Everything'll be all right.

> *Biff reaches behind the heater and draws out a length of rubber tubing. He is horrified and turns his head toward Willy's room, still dimly lit, from which the strains of Linda's desperate but monotonous humming rise.*

Willy (*staring through the window into the moonlight*): Gee, look at the moon moving between the buildings!

> *Biff wraps the tubing around his hand and quickly goes up the stairs. Curtain.*

Act II

> *Music is heard, gay and bright. The curtain rises as the music fades away. Willy, in shirt sleeves, is sitting at the kitchen table, sipping coffee, his hat in his lap. Linda is filling his cup when she can.*

Willy: Wonderful coffee. Meal in itself.

Linda: Can I make you some eggs?

Willy: No. Take a breath.

Linda: You look so rested, dear.

Willy: I slept like a dead one. First time in months. Imagine, sleeping till ten on a Tuesday morning. Boys left nice and early, heh?

Linda: They were out of here by eight o'clock.

Willy: Good work!

Linda: It was so thrilling to see them leaving together. I can't get over the shaving lotion in this house.

Willy (smiling): Mmm—

Linda: Biff was very changed this morning. His whole attitude seemed to be hopeful. He couldn't wait to get downtown to see Oliver.

Willy: He's heading for a change. There's no question, there simply are certain men that take longer to get—solidified. How did he dress?

Linda: His blue suit. He's so handsome in that suit. He could be a—anything in that suit!

Willy gets up from the table. Linda holds his jacket for him.

Willy: There's no question, no question at all. Gee, on the way home tonight I'd like to buy some seeds.

Linda (laughing): That'd be wonderful. But not enough sun gets back there. Nothing'll grow any more.

Willy: You wait, kid, before it's all over we're gonna get a little place out in the country, and I'll raise some vegetables, a couple of chickens . . .

Linda: You'll do it yet, dear.

Willy walks out of his jacket. Linda follows him.

Willy: And they'll get married, and come for a weekend. I'd build a little guest house. 'Cause I got so many fine tools, all I'd need would be a little lumber and some peace of mind.

Linda (joyfully): I sewed the lining . . .

Willy: I could build two guest houses, so they'd both come. Did he decide how much he's going to ask Oliver for?

Linda (getting him into the jacket): He didn't mention it, but I imagine ten or fifteen thousand. You going to talk to Howard today?

Willy: Yeah. I'll put it to him straight and simple. He'll just have to take me off the road.

Linda: And Willy, don't forget to ask for a little advance, because we've got the insurance premium. It's the grace period now.

Willy: That's a hundred . . . ?

Linda: A hundred and eight, sixty-eight. Because we're a little short again.

Willy: Why are we short?

Linda: Well, you had the motor job on the car . . .

Willy: That goddam Studebaker!

Linda: And you got one more payment on the refrigerator . . .

Willy: But it just broke again!

Linda: Well, it's old, dear.

Willy: I told you we should've bought a well-advertised machine. Charley bought a General Electric and it's twenty years old and it's still good, that son-of-a-bitch.

Linda: But, Willy—

Willy: Whoever heard of a Hastings refrigerator? Once in my life I would like to own something outright before it's broken! I'm always in a race with the junkyard! I just finished paying for the car and it's on its last legs. The refrigerator consumes belts like a goddam maniac. They time those things. They time them so when you finally paid for them, they're used up.

Linda (buttoning up his jacket as he unbuttons it): All told, about two hundred dollars would carry us, dear. But that includes the last payment on the mortgage. After this payment, Willy, the house belongs to us.

Willy: It's twenty-five years!

Linda: Biff was nine years old when we bought it.

Willy: Well, that's a great thing. To weather a twenty-five year mortgage is—

Linda: It's an accomplishment.

Willy: All the cement, the lumber, the reconstruction I put in this house! There ain't a crack to be found in it any more.

Linda: Well, it served its purpose.

Willy: What purpose? Some stranger'll come along, move in, and that's that. If only Biff would take this house, and raise a family ... (*He starts to go.*) Good-by, I'm late.

Linda (suddenly remembering): Oh, I forgot! You're supposed to meet them for dinner.

Willy: Me?

Linda: At Frank's Chop House on Forty-eighth near Sixth Avenue.

Willy: Is that so! How about you?

Linda: No, just the three of you. They're gonna blow you to a big meal!

Willy: Don't say! Who thought of that?

Linda: Biff came to me this morning, Willy, and he said, "Tell Dad, we want to blow him to a big meal." Be there six o'clock. You and your two boys are going to have dinner.

Willy: Gee whiz! That's really somethin'. I'm gonna knock Howard for a loop, kid. I'll get an advance, and I'll come home with a New York job. Goddammit, now I'm gonna do it!

Linda: Oh, that's the spirit, Willy!

Willy: I will never get behind a wheel the rest of my life!

Linda: It's changing, Willy, I can feel it changing!

Willy: Beyond a question. G'by, I'm late. (*He starts to go again.*)

Linda (calling after him as she runs to the kitchen table for a handkerchief): You got your glasses?

Willy (feels for them, then comes back in): Yeah, yeah, got my glasses.

Linda (giving him the handkerchief): And a handkerchief.

Willy: Yeah, handkerchief.

Linda: And your saccharine?

Willy: Yeah, my saccharine.

Linda: Be careful on the subway stairs.

> *She kisses him, and a silk stocking is seen hanging from her hand. Willy notices it.*

Willy: Will you stop mending stockings? At least while I'm in the house. It gets me nervous. I can't tell you. Please.

> *Linda hides the stocking in her hand as she follows Willy across the forestage in front of the house.*

Linda: Remember, Frank's Chop House.

Willy (*passing the apron*): Maybe beets would grow out there.

Linda (*laughing*) But you tried so many times.

Willy: Yeah. Well, don't work hard today. (*He disappears around the right corner of the house.*)

Linda: Be careful!

> *As Willy vanishes, Linda waves to him. Suddenly the phone rings. She runs across the stage and into the kitchen and lifts it.*

Linda: Hello? Oh, Biff! I'm so glad you called, I just . . . Yes, sure, I just told him. Yes, he'll be there for dinner at six o'clock, I didn't forget. Listen, I was just dying to tell you. You know that little rubber pipe I told you about? That he connected to the gas heater? I finally decided to go down the cellar this morning and take it away and destroy it. But it's gone! Imagine? He took it away himself, it isn't there! (*She listens.*) When? Oh, then you took it. Oh— nothing, it's just that I'd hoped he'd taken it away himself. Oh, I'm not worried, darling, because this morning he left in such high spirits, it was like the old days! I'm not afraid any more. Did Mr. Oliver see you? . . . Well, you wait there then. And make a nice impression on him, darling. Just don't perspire too much before you see him. And have a nice time with Dad. He may have big news too! . . . That's right, a New York job. And be sweet to him tonight, dear. Be loving to him. Because he's only a little boat looking for a harbor. (*She is trembling with sorrow and joy.*) Oh, that's wonderful, Biff, you'll save his life. Thanks, darling. Just put your arm around him when he comes into the restaurant. Give him a smile. That's the boy . . . Good-by, dear. . . . You got your comb? . . . That's fine. Good-by, Biff dear.

> *In the middle of her speech, Howard Wagner, thirty-six, wheels in a small type- writer table on which is a wire-recording machine and proceeds to plug it in. This is on the left forestage. Light slowly fades on Linda as it rises on Howard. Howard is intent on threading the machine and only glances over his shoulder as Willy ap- pears.*

Willy: Pst! Pst!

Howard: Hello, Willy, come in.

Willy: Like to have a little talk with you, Howard.

Howard: Sorry to keep you waiting. I'll be with you in a minute.

Willy: What's that, Howard?

Howard: Didn't you ever see one of these? Wire recorder.

Willy: Oh. Can we talk a minute?

Howard: Records things. Just got delivery yesterday. Been driving me crazy, the most terrific machine I ever saw in my life. I was up all night with it.

Willy: What do you do with it?

Howard: I bought it for dictation, but you can do anything with it. Listen to this. I had it home last night. Listen to what I picked up. The first one is my daughter. Get this. (*He flicks the switch and "Roll out the Barrel" is heard being whistled.*) Listen to that kid whistle.

Willy: That is lifelike, isn't it?

Howard: Seven years old. Get that tone.

Willy: Ts, ts. Like to ask a little favor if you . . .

> The whistling breaks off, and the voice of Howard's Daughter is heard.

His Daughter: "Now you, Daddy."

Howard: She's crazy for me! (*Again the same song is whistled.*) That's me! Ha! (*He winks.*)

Willy: You're very good!

> The whistling breaks off again. The machine runs silent for a moment.

Howard: Sh! Get this now, this is my son.

His Son: "The capital of Alabama is Montgomery; the capital of Arizona is Phoenix; the capital of Arkansas is Little Rock; the capital of California is Sacramento . . ." (*And on, and on.*)

Howard (*holding up five fingers*): Five years old, Willy!

Willy: He'll make an announcer some day!

His Son (*continuing*): "The capital . . ."

Howard: Get that—alphabetical order! (*The machine breaks off suddenly.*) Wait a minute. The maid kicked the plug out.

Willy: It certainly is a—

Howard: Sh, for God's sake!

His son: "It's nine o'clock, Bulova watch time. So I have to go to sleep."

Willy: That really is—

Howard: Wait a minute! The next is my wife.

> They wait.

Howard's Voice: "Go on, say something." (*Pause.*) "Well, you gonna talk?"

His Wife: "I can't think of anything."

Howard's Voice: "Well, talk—it's turning."

His Wife (*shyly, beaten*): "Hello." (*Silence.*) "Oh, Howard, I can't talk into this . . ."

Howard (*snapping the machine off*): That was my wife.

Willy: That is a wonderful machine. Can we—

Howard: I tell you, Willy, I'm gonna take my camera, and my bandsaw, and all my hobbies, and out they go. This is the most fascinating relaxation I ever found.

Willy: I think I'll get one myself.

Howard: Sure, they're only a hundred and a half. You can't do without it. Supposing you wanna hear Jack Benny, see? But you can't be at home at that hour. So you tell the maid to turn the radio on when Jack Benny comes on, and this automatically goes on with the radio . . .

Willy: And when you come home you . . .

Howard: You can come home twelve o'clock, one o'clock, any time you like, and you get yourself a Coke and sit yourself down, throw the switch, and there's Jack Benny's program in the middle of the night!

Willy: I'm definitely going to get one. Because lots of times I'm on the road, and I think to myself, what I must be missing on the radio!

Howard: Don't you have a radio in the car?

Willy: Well, yeah, but who ever thinks of turning it on?

Howard: Say, aren't you supposed to be in Boston?

Willy: That's what I want to talk to you about, Howard. You got a minute?

(*He draws a chair in from the wing.*)

Howard: What happened? What're you doing here?

Willy: Well . . .

Howard: You didn't crack up again, did you?

Willy: Oh, no. No . . .

Howard: Geez, you had me worried there for a minute. What's the trouble?

Willy: Well, to tell you the truth, Howard, I've come to the decision that I'd rather not travel any more.

Howard: Not travel! Well, what'll you do?

Willy: Remember, Christmas time, when you had the party here? You said you'd try to think of some spot for me here in town.

Howard: With us?

Willy: Well, sure.

Howard: Oh, yeah, yeah. I remember. Well, I couldn't think of anything for you, Willy.

Willy: I tell ya, Howard. The kids are all grown up, y'know. I don't need much any more. If I could take home—well, sixty-five dollars a week, I could swing it.

Howard: Yeah, but Willy, see I—

Willy: I tell ya why, Howard. Speaking frankly and between the two of us, y'know—I'm just a little tired.

Howard: Oh, I could understand that, Willy. But you're a road man, Willy, and we do a road business. We've only got a half-dozen salesmen on the floor here.

Willy: God knows, Howard, I never asked a favor of any man. But I was with the firm when your father used to carry you in here in his arms.

Howard: I know that, Willy, but—

Willy: Your father came to me the day you were born and asked me what I thought of the name of Howard, may he rest in peace.

Howard: I appreciate that, Willy, but there just is no spot here for you. If I had a spot I'd slam you right in, but I just don't have a single, solitary spot.

He looks for his lighter. Willy has picked it up and gives it to him. Pause.

Willy (with increasing anger): Howard, all I need to set my table is fifty dollars a week.

Howard: But where am I going to put you, kid?

Willy: Look, it isn't a question of whether I can sell merchandise, is it?

Howard: No, but it's a business, kid, and everybody's gotta pull his own weight.

Willy (desperately): Just let me tell you a story, Howard—

Howard: 'Cause you gotta admit, business is business.

Willy (angrily): Business is definitely business, but just listen for a minute. You don't understand this. When I was a boy—eighteen, nineteen—I was already on the road. And there was a question in my mind as to whether selling had a future for me. Because in those days I had a yearning to go to Alaska. See, there were three gold strikes in one month in Alaska, and I felt like going out. Just for the ride, you might say.

Howard (barely interested): Don't say.

Willy: Oh, yeah, my father lived many years in Alaska. He was an adventurous man. We've got quite a little streak of self-reliance in our family. I thought I'd go out with my older brother and try to locate him, and maybe settle in the North with the old man. And I was almost decided to go, when I met a salesman in the Parker House. His name was Dave Singleman. And he was eighty-four years old, and he'd drummed merchandise in thirty-one states. And old Dave, he'd go up to his room, y'understand, put on his green velvet slippers—I'll never forget—and pick up his phone and call the buyers, and without ever leaving his room, at the age of eighty-four, he made his living. And when I saw that, I realized that selling was the greatest career a man could want. 'Cause what could be more satisfying than to be able to go, at the age of eighty-four, into twenty or thirty different cities, and pick up a phone, and be remembered and loved and helped by so many different people? Do you know? When he died—and by the way he died the death of a salesman, in his green velvet slippers in the smoker of the New York, New Haven and Hartford, going into Boston—when he died, hundreds of salesmen and buyers were at his funeral. Things were sad on a lotta trains for months after that. (*He stands up. Howard has not looked at him.*) In those days there was personality in it, Howard. There was respect, and comradeship, and gratitude in it. Today, it's all cut and dried, and there's no chance for bringing friendship to bear—or personality. You see what I mean? They don't know me any more.

Howard (moving away, to the right): That's just the thing, Willy.

Willy: If I had forty dollars a week—that's all I'd need. Forty dollars, Howard.

Howard: Kid, I can't take blood from a stone, I—

Willy (desperation is on him now): Howard, the year Al Smith was nominated, your father came to me and—

Howard (starting to go off): I've got to see some people, kid.

Willy (*stopping him*): I'm talking about your father! There were promises made across this desk! You mustn't tell me you've got people to see—I put thirty-four years into this firm, Howard, and now I can't pay my insurance! You can't eat the orange and throw the peel away—a man is not a piece of fruit! (*After a pause.*) Now pay attention. Your father—in 1928 I had a big year. I averaged a hundred and seventy dollars a week in commissions.

Howard (*impatiently*): Now, Willy, you never averaged—

Willy (*banging his hand on the desk*): I averaged a hundred and seventy dollars a week in the year of 1928! And your father came to me—or rather, I was in the office here—it was right over this desk—and he put his hand on my shoulder—

Howard (*getting up*): You'll have to excuse me, Willy, I gotta see some people. Pull yourself together. (*Going out.*) I'll be back in a little while.

On Howard's exit, the light on his chair grows very bright and strange.

Willy: Pull yourself together! What the hell did I say to him? My God, I was yelling at him! How could I! (*Willy breaks off, staring at the light, which occupies the chair, animating it. He approaches this chair, standing across the desk from it.*) Frank, Frank, don't you remember what you told me that time? How you put your hand on my shoulder, and Frank ... (*He leans on the desk and as he speaks the dead man's name he accidentally switches on the recorder, and instantly—*)

Howard's Son: "... of New York is Albany. The capital of Ohio is Cincinnati, the capital of Rhode Island is ..." (*The recitation continues.*)

Willy (*leaping away with fright, shouting*): Ha! Howard! Howard! Howard!

Howard (*rushing in*): What happened?

Willy (*pointing at the machine, which continues nasally, childishly, with the capital cities*): Shut it off! Shut it off!

Howard (*pulling the plug out*): Look, Willy ...

Willy (*pressing his hands to his eyes*): I gotta get myself some coffee. I'll get some coffee ...

Willy starts to walk out. Howard stops him.

Howard (*rolling up the cord*): Willy, look ...

Willy: I'll go to Boston.

Howard: Willy, you can't go to Boston for us.

Willy: Why can't I go?

Howard: I don't want you to represent us. I've been meaning to tell you for a long time now.

Willy: Howard, are you firing me?

Howard: I think you need a good long rest, Willy.

Willy: Howard—

Howard: And when you feel better, come back, and we'll see if we can work something out.

Willy: But I gotta earn money, Howard. I'm in no position—

Howard: Where are your sons? Why don't your sons give you a hand?

Willy: They're working on a very big deal.

Howard: This is no time for false pride, Willy. You go to your sons and tell them that you're tired. You've got two great boys, haven't you?

Willy: Oh, no question, no question, but in the meantime . . .

Howard: Then that's that, heh?

Willy: All right, I'll go to Boston tomorrow.

Howard: No, no.

Willy: I can't throw myself on my sons. I'm not a cripple!

Howard: Look, kid, I'm busy this morning.

Willy (grasping Howard's arm): Howard, you've got to let me go to Boston!

Howard (hard, keeping himself under control): I've got a line of people to see this morning. Sit down, take five minutes, and pull yourself together, and then go home, will ya? I need the office, Willy. (*He starts to go, turns, remembering the recorder, starts to push off the table holding the recorder.*) Oh, yeah. Whenever you can this week, stop by and drop off the samples. You'll feel better, Willy, and then come back and we'll talk. Pull yourself together, kid, there's people outside.

Howard exits, pushing the table off left. Willy stares into space, exhausted. Now the music is heard—Ben's music—first distantly, then closer, closer. As Willy speaks, Ben enters from the right. He carries valise and umbrella.

Willy: Oh, Ben, how did you do it? What is the answer? Did you wind up the Alaska deal already?

Ben: Doesn't take much time if you know what you're doing. Just a short business trip. Boarding ship in an hour. Wanted to say good-by.

Willy: Ben, I've got to talk to you.

Ben (glancing at his watch): Haven't the time, William.

Willy (crossing the apron to Ben): Ben, nothing's working out. I don't know what to do.

Ben: Now, look here, William. I've bought timberland in Alaska and I need a man to look after things for me.

Willy: God, timberland! Me and my boys in those grand outdoors!

Ben: You've a new continent at your doorstep, William. Get out of these cities, they're full of talk and time payments and courts of law. Screw on your fists and you can fight for a fortune up there.

Willy: Yes, yes! Linda! Linda!

Linda enters as of old, with the wash.

Linda: Oh, you're back?

Ben: I haven't much time.

Willy: No, wait! Linda, he's got a proposition for me in Alaska.

Linda: But you've got—(*To Ben.*) He's got a beautiful job here.

Willy: But in Alaska, kid, I could—

Linda: You're doing well enough, Willy!

Ben (to Linda): Enough for what, my dear?

Linda (*frightened of Ben and angry at him*): Don't say those things to him! Enough to be happy right here, right now. (*To Willy, while Ben laughs.*) Why must everybody conquer the world? You're well liked, and the boys love you, and someday—(*to Ben*)—why, old man Wagner told him just the other day that if he keeps it up he'll be a member of the firm, didn't he, Willy?

Willy: Sure, sure. I am building something with this firm, Ben, and if a man is building something he must be on the right track, mustn't he?

Ben: What are you building? Lay your hand on it. Where is it?

Willy (*hesitantly*): That's true, Linda, there's nothing.

Linda: Why? (*To Ben.*) There's a man eighty-four years old—

Willy: That's right, Ben, that's right. When I look at that man I say, what is there to worry about?

Ben: Bah!

Willy: It's true, Ben. All he has to do is go into any city, pick up the phone, and he's making his living and you know why?

Ben (*picking up his valise*): I've got to go.

Willy (*holding Ben back*): Look at this boy!

Biff, in his high school sweater, enters carrying suitcase. Happy carries Biff's shoulder guards, gold helmet, and football pants.

Willy: Without a penny to his name, three great universities are begging for him, and from there the sky's the limit, because it's not what you do, Ben. It's who you know and the smile on your face! It's contacts, Ben, contacts! The whole wealth of Alaska passes over the lunch table at the Commodore Hotel, and that's the wonder, the wonder of this country, that a man can end with diamonds here on the basis of being liked! (*He turns to Biff.*) And that's why when you get out on that field today it's important. Because thousands of people will be rooting for you and loving you. (*To Ben, who has again begun to leave.*) And Ben! when he walks into a business office his name will sound out like a bell and all the doors will open to him! I've seen it, Ben, I've seen it a thousand times! You can't feel it with your hand like timber, but it's there!

Ben: Good-by, William.

Willy: Ben, am I right? Don't you think I'm right? I value your advice.

Ben: There's a new continent at your doorstep, William. You could walk out rich. Rich. (*He is gone.*)

Willy: We'll do it here, Ben! You hear me? We're gonna do it here!

Young Bernard rushes in. The gay music of the boys is heard.

Bernard: Oh, gee, I was afraid you left already!

Willy: Why? What time is it?

Bernard: It's half-past one!

Willy: Well, come on, everybody! Ebbets Field next stop! Where's the pennants? (*He rushes through the wall-line of the kitchen and out into the living room.*)

Linda (*to Biff*): Did you pack fresh underwear?

Biff (*who has been limbering up*): I want to go!

Bernard: Biff, I'm carrying your helmet, ain't I?

Happy: No, I'm carrying the helmet.

Bernard: Oh, Biff, you promised me.

Happy: I'm carrying the helmet.

Bernard: How am I going to get in the locker room?

Linda: Let him carry the shoulder guards. (*She puts her coat and hat on in the kitchen.*)

Bernard: Can I, Biff? 'Cause I told everybody I'm going to be in the locker room.

Happy: In Ebbets Field it's the clubhouse.

Bernard: I meant the clubhouse. Biff!

Happy: Biff!

Biff (*grandly, after a slight pause*): Let him carry the shoulder guards.

Happy (*as he gives Bernard the shoulder guards*): Stay close to us now.

Willy rushes in with the pennants.

Willy (*handing them out*): Everybody wave when Biff comes out on the field. (*Happy and Bernard run off.*) You set now, boy?

The music has died away.

Biff: Ready to go, Pop. Every muscle is ready.

Willy (*at the edge of the apron*): You realize what this means?

Biff: That's right, Pop.

Willy (*feeling Biff's muscles*): You're comin' home this afternoon captain of the All-Scholastic Championship Team of the City of New York.

Biff: I got it, Pop. And remember, pal, when I take off my helmet, that touchdown is for you.

Willy: Let's go! (*He is starting out, with his arm around Biff, when Charley enters, as of old, in knickers.*) I got no room for you, Charley.

Charley: Room? For what?

Willy: In the car.

Charley: You goin' for a ride? I wanted to shoot some casino.

Willy (*furiously*): Casino! (*Incredulously.*) Don't you realize what today is?

Linda: Oh, he knows, Willy. He's just kidding you.

Willy: That's nothing to kid about!

Charley: No, Linda, what's goin' on?

Linda: He's playing in Ebbets Field.

Charley: Baseball in this weather?

Willy: Don't talk to him. Come on, come on! (*He is pushing them out.*)

Charley: Wait a minute, didn't you hear the news?

Willy: What?

Charley: Don't you listen to the radio? Ebbets Field just blew up.

Willy: You go to hell! (*Charley laughs. Pushing them out.*) Come on, come on! We're late.

Charley (*as they go*): Knock a homer, Biff, knock a homer!

Willy (the last to leave, turning to Charley): I don't think that was funny, Charley. This is the greatest day of his life.

Charley: Willy, when are you going to grow up?

Willy: Yeah, heh? When this game is over, Charley, you'll be laughing out of the other side of your face. They'll be calling him another Red Grange. Twenty-five thousand a year.

Charley (kidding): Is that so?

Willy: Yeah, that's so.

Charley: Well, then, I'm sorry, Willy. But tell me something.

Willy: What?

Charley: Who is Red Grange?

Willy: Put up your hands. Goddam you, put up your hands!

Charley, chuckling, shakes his head and walks away, around the left corner of the stage. Willy follows him. The music rises to a mocking frenzy.

Willy: Who the hell do you think you are, better than everybody else? You don't know everything, you big, ignorant, stupid . . . Put up your hands!

Light rises, on the right side of the forestage, on a small table in the reception room of Charley's office. Traffic sounds are heard. Bernard, now mature, sits whistling to himself. A pair of tennis rackets and an overnight bag are on the floor beside him.

Willy (offstage): What are you walking away for? Don't walk away! If you're going to say something say it to my face! I know you laugh at me behind my back. You'll laugh out of the other side of your goddam face after this game. Touchdown! Touchdown! Eighty thousand people! Touchdown! Right between the goal posts.

Bernard is a quiet, earnest, but self-assured young man. Willy's voice is coming from right upstage now. Bernard lowers his feet off the table and listens. Jenny, his father's secretary, enters.

Jenny (distressed): Say, Bernard, will you go out in the hall?

Bernard: What is that noise? Who is it?

Jenny: Mr. Loman. He just got off the elevator.

Bernard (getting up): Who's he arguing with?

Jenny: Nobody. There's nobody with him. I can't deal with him any more, and your father gets all upset everytime he comes. I've got a lot of typing to do, and your father's waiting to sign it. Will you see him?

Willy (entering): Touchdown! Touch—(*He sees Jenny.*) Jenny, Jenny, good to see you. How're ya? Workin'? Or still honest?

Jenny: Fine. How've you been feeling?

Willy: Not much any more, Jenny. Ha, ha! (*He is surprised to see the rackets.*)

Bernard: Hello, Uncle Willy.

Willy (almost shocked): Bernard! Well, look who's here! (*He comes quickly, guiltily, to Bernard and warmly shakes his hand.*)

Bernard: How are you? Good to see you.

Willy: What are you doing here?

Bernard: Oh, just stopped by to see Pop. Get off my feet till my train leaves. I'm going to Washington in a few minutes.

Willy: Is he in?

Bernard: Yes, he's in his office with the accountant. Sit down.

Willy (*sitting down*): What're you going to do in Washington?

Bernard: Oh, just a case I've got there, Willy.

Willy: That so? (*indicating the rackets.*) You going to play tennis there?

Bernard: I'm staying with a friend who's got a court.

Willy: Don't say. His own tennis court. Must be fine people, I bet.

Bernard: They are, very nice. Dad tells me Biff's in town.

Willy (*with a big smile*): Yeah, Biff's in. Working on a very big deal, Bernard.

Bernard: What's Biff doing?

Willy: Well, he's been doing very big things in the West. But he decided to establish himself here. Very big. We're having dinner. Did I hear your wife had a boy?

Bernard: That's right. Our second.

Willy: Two boys! What do you know!

Bernard: What kind of deal has Biff got?

Willy: Well, Bill Oliver—very big sporting-goods man—he wants Biff very badly. Called him in from the West. Long distance, carte blanche, special deliveries. Your friends have their own private tennis court?

Bernard: You still with the old firm, Willy?

Willy (*after a pause*): I'm—I'm overjoyed to see how you made the grade, Bernard, overjoyed. It's an encouraging thing to see a young man really—really—Looks very good for Biff—very—(*He breaks off, then.*) Bernard—(*He is so full of emotion, he breaks off again.*)

Bernard: What is it, Willy?

Willy (*small and alone*): What—what's the secret?

Bernard: What secret?

Willy: How—how did you? Why didn't he ever catch on?

Bernard: I wouldn't know that, Willy.

Willy (*confidentially, desperately*): You were his friend, his boyhood friend. There's something I don't understand about it. His life ended after that Ebbets Field game. From the age of seventeen nothing good ever happened to him.

Bernard: He never trained himself for anything.

Willy: But he did, he did. After high school he took so many correspondence courses. Radio mechanics; television; God knows what, and never made the slightest mark.

Bernard (*taking off his glasses*): Willy, do you want to talk candidly?

Willy (*rising, faces Bernard*): I regard you as a very brilliant man, Bernard. I value your advice.

Bernard: Oh, the hell with the advice, Willy. I couldn't advise you. There's just one thing I've always wanted to ask you. When he was supposed to graduate, and the math teacher flunked him—

Willy: Oh, that son-of-a-bitch ruined his life.

Bernard: Yeah, but, Willy, all he had to do was go to summer school and make up that subject.

Willy: That's right, that's right.

Bernard: Did you tell him not to go to summer school?

Willy: Me? I begged him to go. I ordered him to go!

Bernard: Then why wouldn't he go?

Willy: Why? Why! Bernard, that question has been trailing me like a ghost for the last fifteen years. He flunked the subject, and laid down and died like a hammer hit him!

Bernard: Take it easy, kid.

Willy: Let me talk to you—I got nobody to talk to. Bernard, Bernard, was it my fault? Y'see? It keeps going around in my mind, maybe I did something to him. I got nothing to give him.

Bernard: Don't take it so hard.

Willy: Why did he lay down? What is the story there? You were his friend!

Bernard: Willy, I remember, it was June, and our grades came out. And he'd flunked math.

Willy: That son-of-a-bitch!

Bernard: No, it wasn't right then. Biff just got very angry, I remember, and he was ready to enroll in summer school.

Willy (surprised): He was?

Bernard: He wasn't beaten by it at all. But then, Willy, he disappeared from the block for almost a month. And I got the idea that he'd gone up to New England to see you. Did he have a talk with you then?

Willy stares in silence.

Bernard: Willy?

Willy (with a strong edge of resentment in his voice): Yeah, he came to Boston. What about it?

Bernard: Well, just that when he came back—I'll never forget this, it always mystifies me. Because I'd thought so well of Biff, even though he'd always taken advantage of me. I loved him, Willy, y'know? And he came back after that month and took his sneakers—remember those sneakers with "University of Virginia" printed on them? He was so proud of those, wore them every day. And he took them down in the cellar, and burned them up in the furnace. We had a fist fight. It lasted at least half an hour. Just the two of us, punching each other down the cellar, and crying right through it. I've often thought of how strange it was that I knew he'd given up his life. What happened in Boston, Willy?

Willy looks at him as at an intruder.

Bernard: I just bring it up because you asked me.

Willy (angrily): Nothing. What do you mean, "What happened?" What's that got to do with anything?

Bernard: Well, don't get sore.

Willy: What are you trying to do, blame it on me? If a boy lays down is that my fault?

Bernard: Now, Willy, don't get—

Willy: Well, don't—don't talk to me that way! What does that mean, "What happened?"

Charley enters. He is in his vest, and he carries a bottle of bourbon.

Charley: Hey, you're going to miss that train. (*He waves the bottle.*)

Bernard: Yeah, I'm going. (*He takes the bottle.*) Thanks, Pop. (*He picks up his rackets and bag.*) Good-by, Willy, and don't worry about it. You know, "If at first you don't succeed . . ."

Willy: Yes, I believe in that.

Bernard: But sometimes, Willy, it's better for a man just to walk away.

Willy: Walk away?

Bernard: That's right.

Willy: But if you can't walk away?

Bernard (*after a slight pause*): I guess that's when it's tough. (*Extending his hand.*) Good-by, Willy.

Willy (*shaking Bernard's hand*): Good-by, boy.

Charley (*an arm on Bernard's shoulder*): How do you like this kid? Gonna argue a case in front of the Supreme Court.

Bernard (*protesting*): Pop!

Willy (*genuinely shocked, pained, and happy*): No! The Supreme Court!

Bernard: I gotta run. 'By, Dad!

Charley: Knock 'em dead, Bernard!

Bernard goes off.

Willy (*as Charley takes out his wallet*): The Supreme Court! And he didn't even mention it!

Charley (*counting out money on the desk*): He don't have to—he's gonna do it.

Willy: And you never told him what to do, did you? You never took any interest in him.

Charley: My salvation is that I never took any interest in anything. There's some money—fifty dollars. I got an accountant inside.

Willy: Charley, look . . . (*With difficulty.*) I got my insurance to pay. If you can manage it—I need a hundred and ten dollars.

Charley doesn't reply for a moment; merely stops moving.

Willy: I'd draw it from my bank but Linda would know, and I . . .

Charley: Sit down, Willy.

Willy (*moving toward the chair*): I'm keeping an account of everything, remember. I'll pay every penny back. (*He sits.*)

Charley: Now listen to me, Willy.

Willy: I want you to know I appreciate . . .

Charley (*sitting down on the table*): Willy, what're you doin'? What the hell is goin' on in your head?

Willy: Why? I'm simply . . .

Charley: I offered you a job. You can make fifty dollars a week. And I won't send you on the road.

Willy: I've got a job.

Charley: Without pay? What kind of a job is a job without pay? (*He rises.*) Now, look, kid, enough is enough. I'm no genius but I know when I'm being insulted.

Willy: Insulted!

Charley: Why don't you want to work for me?

Willy: What's the matter with you? I've got a job.

Charley: Then what're you walkin' in here every week for?

Willy (getting up): Well, if you don't want me to walk in here—

Charley: I am offering you a job.

Willy: I don't want your goddam job!

Charley: When the hell are you going to grow up?

Willy (furiously): You big ignoramus, if you say that to me again I'll rap you one! I don't care how big you are! (*He's ready to fight.*)

Pause.

Charley (kindly, going to him): How much do you need, Willy?

Willy: Charley, I'm strapped. I'm strapped. I don't know what to do. I was just fired.

Charley: Howard fired you?

Willy: That snotnose. Imagine that? I named him. I named him Howard.

Charley: Willy, when're you gonna realize that them things don't mean anything? You named him Howard, but you can't sell that. The only thing you got in this world is what you can sell. And the funny thing is that you're a salesman, and you don't know that.

Willy: I've always tried to think otherwise, I guess. I always felt that if a man was impressive, and well liked, that nothing—

Charley: Why must everybody like you? Who liked J. P. Morgan? Was he impressive? In a Turkish bath he'd look like a butcher. But with his pockets on he was very well liked. Now listen, Willy, I know you don't like me, and nobody can say I'm in love with you, but I'll give you a job because—just for the hell of it, put it that way. Now what do you say?

Willy: I—I just can't work for you, Charley.

Charley: What're you, jealous of me?

Willy: I can't work for you, that's all, don't ask me why.

Charley (angered, takes out more bills): You been jealous of me all your life, you damned fool! Here, pay your insurance. (*He puts the money in Willy's hand.*)

Willy: I'm keeping strict accounts.

Charley: I've got some work to do. Take care of yourself. And pay your insurance.

Willy (moving to the right): Funny, y'know? After all the highways, and the trains, and the appointments, and the years, you end up worth more dead than alive.

Charley: Willy, nobody's worth nothin' dead. (*After a slight pause.*) Did you hear what I said?

Willy stands still, dreaming.

Charley: Willy!

Willy: Apologize to Bernard for me when you see him. I didn't mean to argue with him. He's a fine boy. They're all fine boys, and they'll end up big—all of them. Someday they'll all play tennis together. Wish me luck, Charley. He saw Bill Oliver today.

Charley: Good luck.

Willy (*on the verge of tears*): Charley, you're the only friend I got. Isn't that a remarkable thing? (*He goes out.*)

Charley: Jesus!

Charley stares after him a moment and follows. All light blacks out. Suddenly raucous music is heard, and a red glow rises behind the screen at right. Stanley, a young waiter, appears, carrying a table, followed by Happy, who is carrying two chairs.

Stanley (*putting the table down*): That's all right, Mr. Loman, I can handle it myself. (*He turns and takes the chairs from Happy and places them at the table.*)

Happy (*glancing around*): Oh, this is better.

Stanley: Sure, in the front there you're in the middle of all kinds a noise. Whenever you got a party, Mr. Loman, you just tell me and I'll put you back here. Y'know, there's a lotta people they don't like it private, because when they go out they like to see a lotta action around them because they're sick and tired to stay in the house by theirself. But I know you, you ain't from Hackensack. You know what I mean?

Happy (*sitting down*): So how's it coming, Stanley?

Stanley: Ah, it's a dog's life. I only wish during the war they'd a took me in the Army. I coulda been dead by now.

Happy: My brother's back, Stanley.

Stanley: Oh, he come back, heh? From the Far West.

Happy: Yeah, big cattle man, my brother, so treat him right. And my father's coming too.

Stanley: Oh, your father too!

Happy: You got a couple of nice lobsters?

Stanley: Hundred per cent, big.

Happy: I want them with the claws.

Stanley: Don't worry, I don't give you no mice. (*Happy laughs.*) How about some wine? It'll put a head on the meal.

Happy: No. You remember, Stanley, that recipe I brought you from overseas? With the champagne in it?

Stanley: Oh, yeah, sure. I still got it tacked up yet in the kitchen. But that'll have to cost a buck apiece anyways.

Happy: That's all right.

Stanley: What'd you, hit a number or somethin'?

Happy: No, it's a little celebration. My brother is—I think he pulled off a big deal today. I think we're going into business together.

Stanley: Great! That's the best for you. Because a family business, you know what I mean?—that's the best.

Happy: That's what I think.

Stanley: 'Cause what's the difference? Somebody steals? It's in the family. Know what I mean? (*Sotto voce.*) Like this bartender here. The boss is goin' crazy what kinda leak he's got in the cash register. You put it in but it don't come out.

Happy (raising his head): Sh!

Stanley: What?

Happy: You notice I wasn't lookin' right or left, was I?

Stanley: No.

Happy: And my eyes are closed.

Stanley: So what's the—?

Happy: Strudel's comin'.

Stanley (catching on, looks around): Ah, no, there's no—

He breaks off as a furred, lavishly dressed Girl enters and sits at the next table. Both follow her with their eyes.

Stanley: Geez, how'd ya know?

Happy: I got radar or something. (*Staring directly at her profile.*) Oooooooo . . . Stanley.

Stanley: I think that's for you, Mr. Loman.

Happy: Look at that mouth. Oh, God. And the binoculars.

Stanley: Geez, you got a life, Mr. Loman.

Happy: Wait on her.

Stanley (going to The Girl's table): Would you like a menu, ma'am?

Girl: I'm expecting someone, but I'd like a—

Happy: Why don't you bring her—excuse me, miss, do you mind? I sell champagne, and I'd like you to try my brand. Bring her a champagne, Stanley.

Girl: That's awfully nice of you.

Happy: Don't mention it. It's all company money. (*He laughs.*)

Girl: That's a charming product to be selling, isn't it?

Happy: Oh, gets to be like everything else. Selling is selling, y'know.

Girl: I suppose.

Happy: You don't happen to sell, do you?

Girl: No, I don't sell.

Happy: Would you object to a compliment from a stranger? You ought to be on a magazine cover.

Girl (looking at him a little archly): I have been.

Stanley comes in with a glass of champagne.

Happy: What'd I say before, Stanley? You see? She's a cover girl.

Stanley: Oh, I could see, I could see.

Happy (to The Girl): What magazine?

Girl: Oh, a lot of them. (*She takes the drink.*) Thank you.

Happy: You know what they say in France, don't you? "Champagne is the drink of the complexion"—Hya, Biff!

Biff has entered and sits with Happy.

Biff: Hello, kid. Sorry I'm late.

Happy: I just got here. Uh, Miss—?

Girl: Forsythe.

Happy: Miss Forsythe, this is my brother.

Biff: Is Dad here?

Happy: His name is Biff. You might've heard of him. Great football player.

Girl: Really? What team?

Happy: Are you familiar with football?

Girl: No, I'm afraid I'm not.

Happy: Biff is quarterback with the New York Giants.

Girl: Well, that is nice, isn't it? (*She drinks.*)

Happy: Good health.

Girl: I'm happy to meet you.

Happy: That's my name. Hap. It's really Harold, but at West Point they called me Happy.

Girl (*now really impressed*): Oh, I see. How do you do? (*She turns her profile.*)

Biff: Isn't Dad coming?

Happy: You want her?

Biff: Oh, I could never make that.

Happy: I remember the time that idea would never come into your head. Where's the old confidence, Biff?

Biff: I just saw Oliver—

Happy: Wait a minute. I've got to see that old confidence again. Do you want her? She's on call.

Biff: Oh, no. (*He turns to look at The Girl.*)

Happy: I'm telling you. Watch this. (*Turning to The Girl.*) Honey? (*She turns to him.*) Are you busy?

Girl: Well, I am . . . but I could make a phone call.

Happy: Do that, will you, honey? And see if you can get a friend. We'll be here for a while. Biff is one of the greatest football players in the country.

Girl (*standing up*): Well, I'm certainly happy to meet you.

Happy: Come back soon.

Girl: I'll try.

Happy: Don't try, honey, try hard.

The Girl exits. Stanley follows, shaking his head in bewildered admiration.

Happy: Isn't that a shame now? A beautiful girl like that? That's why I can't get married. There's not a good woman in a thousand. New York is loaded with them, kid!

Biff: Hap, look—

Happy: I told you she was on call!

Biff (*strangely unnerved*): Cut it out, will ya? I want to say something to you.

Happy: Did you see Oliver?

Biff: I saw him all right. Now look, I want to tell Dad a couple of things and I want you to help me.

Happy: What? Is he going to back you?

Biff: Are you crazy? You're out of your goddam head, you know that?

Happy: Why? What happened?

Biff (*breathlessly*): I did a terrible thing today, Hap. It's been the strangest day I ever went through. I'm all numb, I swear.

Happy: You mean he wouldn't see you?

Biff: Well, I waited six hours for him, see? All day. Kept sending my name in. Even tried to date his secretary so she'd get me to him, but no soap.

Happy: Because you're not showin' the old confidence, Biff. He remembered you, didn't he?

Biff (*stopping Happy with a gesture*): Finally, about five o'clock, he comes out. Didn't remember who I was or anything. I felt like such an idiot, Hap.

Happy: Did you tell him my Florida idea?

Biff: He walked away. I saw him for one minute. I got so mad I could've torn the walls down! How the hell did I ever get the idea I was a salesman there? I even believed myself that I'd been a salesman for him! And then he gave me one look and—I realized what a ridiculous lie my whole life has been! We've been talking in a dream for fifteen years. I was a shipping clerk.

Happy: What'd you do?

Biff (*with great tension and wonder*): Well, he left, see. And the secretary went out. I was all alone in the waiting-room. I don't know what came over me, Hap. The next thing I know I'm in his office—paneled walls, everything. I can't explain it. I—Hap, I took his fountain pen.

Happy: Geez, did he catch you?

Biff: I ran out. I ran down all eleven flights. I ran and ran and ran.

Happy: That was an awful dumb—what'd you do that for?

Biff (*agonized*): I don't know, I just—wanted to take something, I don't know. You gotta help me, Hap. I'm gonna tell Pop.

Happy: You crazy? What for?

Biff: Hap, he's got to understand that I'm not the man somebody lends that kind of money to. He thinks I've been spiting him all these years and it's eating him up.

Happy: That's just it. You tell him something nice.

Biff: I can't.

Happy: Say you got a lunch date with Oliver tomorrow.

Biff: So what do I do tomorrow?

Happy: You leave the house tomorrow and come back at night and say Oliver is thinking it over. And he thinks it over for a couple of weeks, and gradually it fades away and nobody's the worse.

Biff: But it'll go on forever!

Happy: Dad is never so happy as when he's looking forward to something!

Willy enters.

Happy: Hello, scout!

Willy: Gee, I haven't been here in years!

> *Stanley has followed Willy in and sets a chair for him. Stanley starts off but Happy stops him.*

Happy: Stanley!

> *Stanley stands by, waiting for an order.*

Biff (*going to Willy with guilt, as to an invalid*): Sit down, Pop. You want a drink?

Willy: Sure, I don't mind.

Biff: Let's get a load on.

Willy: You look worried.

Biff: N-no. (*To Stanley.*) Scotch all around. Make it doubles.

Stanley: Doubles, right. (*He goes.*)

Willy: You had a couple already, didn't you?

Biff: Just a couple, yeah.

Willy: Well, what happened, boy? (*Nodding affirmatively, with a smile.*) Everything go all right?

Biff (*takes a breath, then reaches out and grasps Willy's hand*): Pal . . . (*He is smiling bravely, and Willy is smiling too.*) I had an experience today.

Happy: Terrific, Pop.

Willy: That so? What happened?

Biff (*high, slightly alcoholic, above the earth*): I'm going to tell you everything from first to last. It's been a strange day. (*Silence. He looks around, composes himself as best he can, but his breath keeps breaking the rhythm of his voice.*) I had to wait quite a while for him, and—

Willy: Oliver?

Biff: Yeah, Oliver. All day, as a matter of cold fact. And a lot of—instances— facts, Pop, facts about my life came back to me. Who was it, Pop? Who ever said I was a salesman with Oliver?

Willy: Well, you were.

Biff: No, Dad, I was a shipping clerk.

Willy: But you were practically—

Biff (*with determination*): Dad, I don't know who said it first, but I was never a salesman for Bill Oliver.

Willy: What're you talking about?

Biff: Let's hold on to the facts tonight, Pop. We're not going to get anywhere bullin' around. I was a shipping clerk.

Willy (*angrily*): All right, now listen to me—

Biff: Why don't you let me finish?

Willy: I'm not interested in stories about the past or any crap of that kind because the woods are burning, boys, you understand? There's a big blaze going on all around. I was fired today.

Biff (*shocked*): How could you be?

Willy: I was fired, and I'm looking for a little good news to tell your mother, because the woman has waited and the woman has suffered. The gist of it is that I haven't got a story left in my head, Biff. So don't give me a lecture about facts and aspects. I am not interested. Now what've you got to say to me?

Stanley enters with three drinks. They wait until he leaves.

Willy: Did you see Oliver?

Biff: Jesus, Dad!

Willy: You mean you didn't go up there?

Happy: Sure he went up there.

Biff: I did. I—saw him. How could they fire you?

Willy (on the edge of his chair): What kind of a welcome did he give you?

Biff: He won't even let you work on commission?

Willy: I'm out! (*Driving.*) So tell me, he gave you a warm welcome?

Happy: Sure, Pop, sure!

Biff (driven): Well, it was kind of—

Willy: I was wondering if he'd remember you. (*To Happy.*) Imagine, man doesn't see him for ten, twelve years and gives him that kind of welcome!

Happy: Damn right!

Biff (trying to return to the offensive): Pop, look—

Willy: You know why he remembered you, don't you? Because you impressed him in those days.

Biff: Let's talk quietly and get this down to the facts, huh?

Willy (as though Biff had been interrupting): Well, what happened? It's great news, Biff. Did he take you into his office or'd you talk in the waiting-room?

Biff: Well, he came in, see, and—

Willy (with a big smile): What'd he say? Betcha he threw his arm around you.

Biff: Well, he kinda—

Willy: He's a fine man. (*To Happy.*) Very hard man to see, y'know.

Happy (agreeing): Oh, I know.

Willy (to Biff): Is that where you had the drinks?

Biff: Yeah, he gave me a couple of—no, no!

Happy (cutting in): He told him my Florida idea.

Willy: Don't interrupt. (*To Biff.*) How'd he react to the Florida idea?

Biff: Dad, will you give me a minute to explain?

Willy: I've been waiting for you to explain since I sat down here! What happened? He took you into his office and what?

Biff: Well—I talked. And—and he listened, see.

Willy: Famous for the way he listens, y'know. What was his answer?

Biff: His answer was—(*He breaks off, suddenly angry.*) Dad, you're not letting me tell you what I want to tell you!

Willy (accusing, angered): You didn't see him, did you?

Biff: I did see him!

Willy: What'd you insult him or something? You insulted him, didn't you?

Biff: Listen, will you let me out of it, will you just let me out of it!

Happy: What the hell!

Willy: Tell me what happened!
Biff (to Happy): I can't talk to him!

> *A single trumpet note jars the ear. The light of green leaves stains the house, which holds the air of night and a dream. Young Bernard enters and knocks on the door of the house.*

Young Bernard (frantically): Mrs. Loman, Mrs. Loman!
Happy: Tell him what happened!
Biff (to Happy): Shut up and leave me alone!
Willy: No, no! You had to go and flunk math!
Biff: What math? What're you talking about?
Young Bernard: Mrs. Loman, Mrs. Loman!

> *Linda appears in the house, as of old.*

Willy (wildly): Math, math, math!
Biff: Take it easy, Pop.
Young Bernard: Mrs. Loman!
Willy (furiously): If you hadn't flunked you'd've been set by now!
Biff: Now, look, I'm gonna tell you what happened, and you're going to listen to me.
Young Bernard: Mrs. Loman!
Biff: I waited six hours—
Happy: What the hell are you saying?
Biff: I kept sending in my name but he wouldn't see me. So finally he . . . (*He continues unheard as light fades low on the restaurant.*)
Young Bernard: Biff flunked math!
Linda: No!
Young Bernard: Birnbaum flunked him! They won't graduate him!
Linda: But they have to. He's gotta go to the university. Where is he? Biff! Biff!
Young Bernard: No, he left. He went to Grand Central.
Linda: Grand—You mean he went to Boston?
Young Bernard: Is Uncle Willy in Boston?
Linda: Oh, maybe Willy can talk to the teacher. Oh, the poor, poor boy!

> *Light on house area snaps out.*

Biff (at the table, now audible, holding up a gold fountain pen): . . . so I'm washed up with Oliver, you understand? Are you listening to me?
Willy (at a loss): Yeah, sure. If you hadn't flunked—
Biff: Flunked what? What're you talking about?
Willy: Don't blame everything on me! I didn't flunk math—you did! What pen?
Happy: That was awful dumb, Biff, a pen like that is worth—
Willy (seeing the pen for the first time): You took Oliver's pen?
Biff (weakening): Dad, I just explained it to you.
Willy: You stole Bill Oliver's fountain pen!
Biff: I didn't exactly steal it! That's just what I've been explaining to you!

Happy: He had it in his hand and just then Oliver walked in, so he got nervous and stuck it in his pocket!

Willy: My God, Biff!

Biff: I never intended to do it, Dad!

Operator's voice: Standish Arms, good evening!

Willy (shouting): I'm not in my room!

Biff (frightened): Dad, what's the matter? (*He and Happy stand up.*)

Operator: Ringing Mr. Loman for you!

Willy: I'm not there, stop it!

Biff (horrified, gets down on one knee before Willy): Dad, I'll make good, I'll make good. (*Willy tries to get to his feet. Biff holds him down.*) Sit down now.

Willy: No, you're no good, you're no good for anything.

Biff: I am, Dad, I'll find something else, you understand? Now don't worry about anything. (*He holds up Willy's face.*) Talk to me, Dad.

Operator: Mr. Loman does not answer. Shall I page him?

Willy (attempting to stand, as though to rush and silence the Operator): No, no, no!

Happy: He'll strike something, Pop.

Willy: No, no . . .

Biff (desperately, standing over Willy): Pop, listen! Listen to me! I'm telling you something good. Oliver talked to his partner about the Florida idea. You listening? He—he talked to his partner, and he came to me . . . I'm to be all right, you hear? Dad, listen to me, he said it was just a question of the amount!

Willy: Then you . . . got it?

Happy: He's gonna be terrific, Pop!

Willy (trying to stand): Then you got it, haven't you? You got it! You got it!

Biff (agonized, holds Willy down): No, no. Look, Pop. I'm supposed to have lunch with them tomorrow. I'm just telling you this so you'll know that I can still make an impression, Pop. And I'll make good somewhere, but I can't go tomorrow, see?

Willy: Why not? You simply—

Biff: But the pen, Pop!

Willy: You give it to him and tell him it was an oversight!

Happy: Sure, have lunch tomorrow!

Biff: I can't say that—

Willy: You were doing a crossword puzzle and accidentally used his pen!

Biff: Listen, kid, I took those balls years ago, now I walk in with his fountain pen? That clinches it, don't you see? I can't face him like that! I'll try elsewhere.

Page's voice: Paging Mr. Loman!

Willy: Don't you want to be anything?

Biff: Pop, how can I go back?

Willy: You don't want to be anything, is that what's behind it?

Biff (now angry at Willy for not crediting his sympathy): Don't take it that way! You think it was easy walking into that office after what I'd done to him? A team of horses couldn't have dragged me back to Bill Oliver!

Willy: Then why'd you go?

Biff: Why did I go? Why did I go? Look at you! Look at what's become of you!

Off left, The Woman laughs.

Willy: Biff, you're going to go to that lunch tomorrow, or—

Biff: I can't go. I've got no appointment!

Happy: Biff, for . . . !

Willy: Are you spiting me?

Biff: Don't take it that way! Goddammit!

Willy (strikes Biff and falters away from the table): You rotten little louse! Are you spiting me?

The Woman: Someone's at the door, Willy!

Biff: I'm no good, can't you see what I am?

Happy (separating them): Hey, you're in a restaurant! Now cut it out, both of you! (*The Girls enter.*) Hello, girls, sit down.

The Woman laughs, off left.

Miss Forsythe: I guess we might as well. This is Letta.

The Woman: Willy, are you going to wake up?

Biff (ignoring Willy): How're ya, miss, sit down. What do you drink?

Miss Forsythe: Letta might not be able to stay long.

Letta: I gotta get up very early tomorrow. I got jury duty. I'm so excited! Were you fellows ever on a jury?

Biff: No, but I been in front of them! (*The Girls laugh.*) This is my father.

Letta: Isn't he cute? Sit down with us, Pop.

Happy: Sit him down, Biff!

Biff (going to him): Come on, slugger, drink us under the table. To hell with it! Come on, sit down, pal.

On Biff's last insistence, Willy is about to sit.

The Woman (now urgently): Willy, are you going to answer the door!

The Woman's call pulls Willy back. He starts right, befuddled.

Biff: Hey, where are you going?

Willy: Open the door.

Biff: The door?

Willy: The washroom . . . the door . . . where's the door?

Biff (leading Willy to the left): Just go straight down.

Willy moves left.

The Woman: Willy, Willy, are you going to get up, get up, get up, get up?

Willy exits left.

Letta: I think it's sweet you bring your daddy along.

Miss Forsythe: Oh, he isn't really your father!

Biff (at left, turning to her resentfully): Miss Forsythe, you've just seen a prince walk by. A fine, troubled prince. A hard-working, unappreciated prince. A pal, you understand? A good companion. Always for his boys.

Letta: That's so sweet.

Happy: Well, girls, what's the program? We're wasting time. Come on, Biff. Gather round. Where would you like to go?

Biff: Why don't you do something for him?

Happy: Me!

Biff: Don't you give a damn for him, Hap?

Happy: What're you talking about? I'm the one who—

Biff: I sense it, you don't give a good goddam about him. (*He takes the rolled-up hose from his pocket and puts it on the table in front of Happy.*) Look what I found in the cellar, for Christ's sake. How can you bear to let it go on?

Happy: Me? Who goes away? Who runs off and—

Biff: Yeah, but he doesn't mean anything to you. You could help him—I can't! Don't you understand what I'm talking about? He's going to kill himself, don't you know that?

Happy: Don't I know it! Me!

Biff: Hap, help him! Jesus . . . Help him . . . Help me, help me, I can't bear to look at his face! (*Ready to weep, he hurries out, up right.*)

Happy (*starting after him*): Where are you going?

Miss Forsythe: What's he so mad about?

Happy: Come on, girls, we'll catch up with him.

Miss Forsythe (*as Happy pushes her out*): Say, I don't like that temper of his!

Happy: He's just a little overstrung, he'll be all right!

Willy (*off left, as The Woman laughs*): Don't answer! Don't answer!

Letta: Don't you want to tell your father—

Happy: No, that's not my father. He's just a guy. Come on, we'll catch Biff, and, honey, we're going to paint this town! Stanley, where's the check? Hey, Stanley!

They exit. Stanley looks toward left.

Stanley (*calling to Happy indignantly*): Mr. Loman! Mr. Loman!

Stanley picks up a chair and follows them off. Knocking is heard off left. The Woman enters, laughing. Willy follows her. She is in a black slip; he is buttoning his shirt. Raw, sensuous music accompanies their speech.

Willy: Will you stop laughing? Will you stop?

The Woman: Aren't you going to answer the door? He'll wake the whole hotel.

Willy: I'm not expecting anybody.

The Woman: Whyn't you have another drink, honey, and stop being so damn self-centered?

Willy: I'm so lonely.

The Woman: You know you ruined me, Willy? From now on, whenever you come to the office, I'll see that you go right through to the buyers. No waiting at my desk any more, Willy. You ruined me.

Willy: That's nice of you to say that.

The Woman: Gee, you are self-centered! Why so sad? You are the saddest self-centeredest soul I ever did see-saw. (*She laughs. He kisses her.*) Come on inside, drummer boy. It's silly to be dressing in the middle of the night. (*As knocking is heard.*) Aren't you going to answer the door?

Willy: They're knocking on the wrong door.

The Woman: But I felt the knocking. And he heard us talking in here. Maybe the hotel's on fire!

Willy (his terror rising): It's a mistake.

The Woman: Then tell him to go away!

Willy: There's nobody there.

The Woman: It's getting on my nerves, Willy. There's somebody standing out there and it's getting on my nerves!

Willy (pushing her away from him): All right, stay in the bathroom here, and don't come out. I think there's a law in Massachusetts about it, so don't come out. It may be that new room clerk. He looked very mean. So don't come out. It's a mistake, there's no fire.

The knocking is heard again. He takes a few steps away from her, and she vanishes into the wing. The light follows him, and now he is facing Young Biff, who carries a suitcase. Biff steps toward him. The music is gone.

Biff: Why didn't you answer?

Willy: Biff! What are you doing in Boston?

Biff: Why didn't you answer? I've been knocking for five minutes, I called you on the phone—

Willy: I just heard you. I was in the bathroom and had the door shut. Did anything happen at home?

Biff: Dad—I let you down.

Willy: What do you mean?

Biff: Dad . . .

Willy: Biffo, what's this about? (*Putting his arm around Biff.*) Come on, let's go downstairs and get you a malted.

Biff: Dad, I flunked math.

Willy: Not for the term?

Biff: The term. I haven't got enough credits to graduate.

Willy: You mean to say Bernard wouldn't give you the answers?

Biff: He did, he tried, but I only got a sixty-one.

Willy: And they wouldn't give you four points?

Biff: Birnbaum refused absolutely. I begged him, Pop, but he won't give me those points. You gotta talk to him before they close the school. Because if he saw the kind of man you are, and you just talked to him in your way, I'm sure he'd come through for me. The class came right before practice, see, and I didn't go enough. Would you talk to him? He'd like you, Pop. You know the way you could talk.

Willy: You're on. We'll drive right back.

Biff: Oh, Dad, good work! I'm sure he'll change it for you!

Willy: Go downstairs and tell the clerk I'm checkin' out. Go right down.

Biff: Yes, Sir! See, the reason he hates me, Pop—one day he was late for class so I got up at the blackboard and imitated him. I crossed my eyes and talked with a lithp.

Willy (laughing): You did? The kids like it?

Biff: They nearly died laughing!

Willy: Yeah? What'd you do?

Biff: The thquare root of thixthy twee is . . . (*Willy bursts out laughing; Biff joins him.*) And in the middle of it he walked in!

Willy laughs and The Woman joins in offstage.

Willy (without hesitating): Hurry downstairs and—

Biff: Somebody in there?

Willy: No, that was next door.

The Woman laughs offstage.

Biff: Somebody got in your bathroom!

Willy: No, it's the next room, there's a party—

The Woman (enters, laughing. She lisps this): Can I come in? There's something in the bathtub, Willy, and it's moving!

Willy looks at Biff, who is staring open-mouthed and horrified at The Woman.

Willy: Ah—you better go back to your room. They must be finished painting by now. They're painting her room so I let her take a shower here. Go back, go back . . . (*He pushes her.*)

The Woman (resisting): But I've got to get dressed, Willy, I can't—

Willy: Get out of here! Go back, go back . . . (*Suddenly striving for the ordinary.*) This is Miss Francis, Biff, she's a buyer. They're painting her room. Go back, Miss Francis, go back . . .

The Woman: But my clothes, I can't go out naked in the hall!

Willy (pushing her offstage): Get outa here! Go back, go back!

Biff slowly sits down on his suitcase as the argument continues offstage.

The Woman: Where's my stockings? You promised me stockings, Willy!

Willy: I have no stockings here!

The Woman: You had two boxes of size nine sheers for me, and I want them!

Willy: Here, for God's sake, will you get outa here!

The Woman (enters holding a box of stockings): I just hope there's nobody in the hall. That's all I hope. (*To Biff.*) Are you football or baseball?

Biff: Football.

The Woman (angry, humiliated): That's me too. G'night. (*She snatches her clothes from Willy, and walks out.*)

Willy (after a pause): Well, better get going. I want to get to the school first thing in the morning. Get my suits out of the closet. I'll get my valise. (*Biff doesn't move.*) What's the matter? (*Biff remains motionless, tears falling.*) She's a buyer. Buys for J. H. Simmons. She lives down the hall—they're painting. You don't imagine—(*He breaks off. After a pause.*) Now listen, pal, she's just a buyer. She sees merchandise in her room and they have to keep it looking just so . . . (*Pause. Assuming command.*) All right, get my suits. (*Biff doesn't move.*) Now stop crying and do as I say. I gave you an order. Biff, I gave you an order! Is that what you do when I give you an order? How dare you cry! (*Putting his arm around Biff.*) Now look, Biff, when you grow up you'll understand about these things. You mustn't—you mustn't overemphasize a thing like this. I'll see Birnbaum first thing in the morning.

Biff: Never mind.

Willy (*getting down beside Biff*): Never mind! He's going to give you those points. I'll see to it.

Biff: He wouldn't listen to you.

Willy: He certainly will listen to me. You need those points for the U. of Virginia.

Biff: I'm not going there.

Willy: Heh? If I can't get him to change that mark you'll make it up in summer school. You've got all summer to—

Biff (*his weeping breaking from him*): Dad . . .

Willy (*infected by it*): Oh, my boy . . .

Biff: Dad . . .

Willy: She's nothing to me, Biff. I was lonely, I was terribly lonely.

Biff: You—you gave her Mama's stockings! (*His tears break through and he rises to go.*)

Willy (*grabbing for Biff*): I gave you an order!

Biff: Don't touch me, you—liar!

Willy: Apologize for that!

Biff: You fake! You phony little fake! (*Overcome, he turns quickly and weeping fully goes out with his suitcase. Willy is left on the floor on his knees.*)

Willy: I gave you an order! Biff, come back here or I'll beat you! Come back here! I'll whip you!

Stanley comes quickly in from the right and stands in front of Willy.

Willy (*shouts at Stanley*): I gave you an order . . .

Stanley: Hey, let's pick it up, pick it up, Mr. Loman. (*He helps Willy to his feet.*) Your boys left with the chippies. They said they'll see you at home.

A second waiter watches some distance away.

Willy: But we were supposed to have dinner together.

Music is heard, Willy's theme.

Stanley: Can you make it?

Willy: I'll—sure, I can make it. (*Suddenly concerned about his clothes.*) Do I—I look all right?

Stanley: Sure, you look all right. (*He flicks a speck off Willy's lapel.*)

Willy: Here—here's a dollar.

Stanley: Oh, your son paid me. It's all right.

Willy (*putting it in Stanley's hand*): No, take it. You're a good boy.

Stanley: Oh, no, you don't have to . . .

Willy: Here—here's some more, I don't need it any more. (*After a slight pause.*) Tell me—is there a seed store in the neighborhood?

Stanley: Seeds? You mean like to plant?

As Willy turns, Stanley slips the money back into his jacket pocket.

Willy: Yes. Carrots, peas . . .

Stanley: Well, there's hardware stores on Sixth Avenue, but it may be too late now.

Willy (anxiously): Oh, I'd better hurry. I've got to get some seeds. (*He starts off to the right.*) I've got to get some seeds, right away. Nothing's planted. I don't have a thing in the ground.

Willy hurries out as the light goes down. Stanley moves over to the right after him, watches him off. The other waiter has been staring at Willy.

Stanley (to the waiter): Well, whatta you looking at?

The waiter picks up the chairs and moves off right. Stanley takes the table and fol-lows him. The light fades on this area. There is a long pause, the sound of the flute coming over. The light gradually rises on the kitchen, which is empty. Happy ap-pears at the door of the house, followed by Biff. Happy is carrying a large bunch of long-stemmed roses. He enters the kitchen, looks around for Linda. Not seeing her, he turns to Biff, who is just outside the house door, and makes a gesture with his hands, indicating "Not here, I guess." He looks into the living room and freezes. Inside, Linda, unseen, is seated, Willy's coat on her lap. She rises omi-nously and quietly and moves toward Happy, who backs up into the kitchen, afraid.

Happy: Hey, what're you doing up? (*Linda says nothing but moves toward him im-placably.*) Where's Pop? (*He keeps backing to the right, and now Linda is in full view in the doorway to the living room.*) Is he sleeping?

Linda: Where were you?

Happy (trying to laugh it off): We met two girls, Mom, very fine types. Here, we brought you some flowers. (*Offering them to her.*) Put them in your room, Ma.

She knocks them to the floor at Biff's feet. He has now come inside and closed the door behind him. She stares at Biff, silent.

Happy: Now what'd you do that for? Mom, I want you to have some flowers—

Linda (cutting Happy off, violently to Biff): Don't you care whether he lives or dies?

Happy (going to the stairs): Come upstairs, Biff.

Biff (with a flare of disgust, to Happy): Go away from me! (*To Linda.*) What do you mean, lives or dies? Nobody's dying around here, pal.

Linda: Get out of my sight! Get out of here!

Biff: I wanna see the boss.

Linda: You're not going near him!

Biff: Where is he? (*He moves into the living room and Linda follows.*)

Linda (*shouting after Biff*): You invite him for dinner. He looks forward to it all day—(*Biff appears in his parents' bedroom, looks around, and exits*)—and then you desert him there. There's no stranger you'd do that to!

Happy: Why? He had a swell time with us. Listen, when I—(*Linda comes back into the kitchen*)—desert him I hope I don't outlive the day!

Linda: Get out of here!

Happy: Now look, Mom . . .

Linda: Did you have to go to women tonight? You and your lousy rotten whores!

Biff re-enters the kitchen.

Happy: Mom, all we did was follow Biff around trying to cheer him up! (*To Biff.*) Boy, what a night you gave me!

Linda: Get out of here, both of you, and don't come back! I don't want you tormenting him anymore. Go on now, get your things together! (*To Biff.*) You can sleep in his apartment. (*She starts to pick up the flowers and stops herself.*) Pick up this stuff, I'm not your maid any more. Pick it up, you bum, you!

Happy turns his back to her in refusal. Biff slowly moves over and gets down on his knees, picking up the flowers.

Linda: You're a pair of animals! Not one, not another living soul would have had the cruelty to walk out on that man in a restaurant!

Biff (*not looking at her*): Is that what he said?

Linda: He didn't have to say anything. He was so humiliated he nearly limped when he came in.

Happy: But, Mom he had a great time with us—

Biff (*cutting him off violently*): Shut up!

Without another word, Happy goes upstairs.

Linda: You! You didn't even go in to see if he was all right!

Biff (*still on the floor in front of Linda, the flowers in his hand; with self-loathing*): No. Didn't. Didn't do a damned thing. How do you like that, heh? Left him babbling in a toilet.

Linda: You louse. You . . .

Biff: Now you hit it on the nose! (*He gets up, throws the flowers in the wastebasket.*) The scum of the earth, and you're looking at him!

Linda: Get out of here!

Biff: I gotta talk to the boss, Mom. Where is he?

Linda: You're not going near him. Get out of this house!

Biff (*with absolute assurance, determination*): No. We're gonna have an abrupt conversation, him and me.

Linda: You're not talking to him!

Hammering is heard from outside the house, off right. Biff turns toward the noise.

Linda (*suddenly pleading*): Will you please leave him alone?

Biff: What's he doing out there?

Linda: He's planting the garden!
Biff (quietly): Now? Oh, my God!

> *Biff moves outside, Linda following. The light dies down on them and comes up on the center of the apron as Willy walks into it. He is carrying a flashlight, a hoe and a handful of seed packets. He raps the top of the hoe sharply to fix it firmly, and then moves to the left, measuring off the distance with his foot. He holds the flashlight to look at the seed packets, reading off the instructions. He is in the blue of night.*

Willy: Carrots . . . quarter-inch apart. Rows . . . one-foot rows. (*He measures it off.*) One foot. (*He puts down a package and measures off.*) Beets. (*He puts down another package and measures again.*) Lettuce. (*He reads the package, puts it down.*) One foot—(*He breaks off as Ben appears at the right and moves slowly down to him.*) What a proposition, ts, ts. Terrific, terrific. 'Cause she's suffered, Ben, the woman has suffered. You understand me? A man can't go out the way he came in, Ben, a man has got to add up to something. You can't, you can't—(*Ben moves toward him as though to interrupt.*) You gotta consider, now. Don't answer so quick. Remember, it's a guaranteed twenty-thousand-dollar proposition. Now look, Ben, I want you to go through the ins and outs of this thing with me. I've got nobody to talk to, Ben, and the woman has suffered, you hear me?

Ben (standing still, considering): What's the proposition?
Willy: It's twenty thousand dollars on the barrelhead. Guaranteed, gilt-edged, you understand?
Ben: You don't want to make a fool of yourself. They might not honor the policy.
Willy: How can they dare refuse? Didn't I work like a coolie to meet every premium on the nose? And now they don't pay off? Impossible!
Ben: It's called a cowardly thing, William.
Willy: Why? Does it take more guts to stand here the rest of my life ringing up a zero?
Ben (yielding): That's a point, William. (*He moves, thinking, turns.*) And twenty thousand—that is something one can feel with the hand, it is there.
Willy (now assured, with rising power): Oh, Ben, that's the whole beauty of it! I see it like a diamond, shining in the dark, hard and rough, that I can pick up and touch in my hand. Not like—like an appointment! This would not be another damned-fool appointment, Ben, and it changes all the aspects. Because he thinks I'm nothing, see, and so he spites me. But the funeral—(*Straightening up.*) Ben, that funeral will be massive! They'll come from Maine, Massachusetts, Vermont, New Hampshire! All the old-timers with the strange license plates—that boy will be thunder-struck, Ben, because he never realized—I am known! Rhode Island, New York, New Jersey—I am known, Ben, and he'll see it with his eyes once and for all. He'll see what I am, Ben! He's in for a shock, that boy!
Ben (coming down to the edge of the garden): He'll call you a coward.
Willy (suddenly fearful): No, that would be terrible.

Ben: Yes. And a damned fool.

Willy: No, no, he mustn't, I won't have that! (*He is broken and desperate.*)

Ben: He'll hate you, William.

The gay music of the boys is heard.

Willy: Oh, Ben, how do we get back to all the great times? Used to be so full of
light, and comradeship, the sleigh-riding in winter, and the ruddiness on his
cheeks. And always some kind of good news coming up, always something
nice coming up ahead. And never even let me carry the valises in the house,
and simonizing, simonizing that little red car! Why, why can't I give him
something and not have him hate me?

Ben: Let me think about it. (*He glances at his watch.*) I still have a little time.
Remarkable proposition, but you've got to be sure you're not making a fool
of yourself.

Ben drifts off upstage and goes out of sight. Biff comes down from the left.

Willy (*suddenly conscious of Biff, turns and looks up at him, then begins picking up the
packages of seeds in confusion*): Where the hell is that seed? (*Indignantly.*)
You can't see nothing out here! They boxed in the whole goddam neighborhood!

Biff: There are people all around here. Don't you realize that?

Willy: I'm busy. Don't bother me.

Biff (*taking the hoe from Willy*): I'm saying good-by to you, Pop. (*Willy looks at
him, silent, unable to move.*) I'm not coming back any more.

Willy: You're not going to see Oliver tomorrow?

Biff: I've got no appointment, Dad.

Willy: He put his arm around you, and you've got no appointment?

Biff: Pop, get this now, will you? Everytime I've left it's been a fight that sent me
out of here. Today I realized something about myself and I tried to explain it
to you and I—I think I'm just not smart enough to make any sense out of it
for you. To hell with whose fault it is or anything like that. (*He takes Willy's
arm.*) Let's just wrap it up, heh? Come on in, we'll tell Mom. (*He gently tries
to pull Willy to the left.*)

Willy (*frozen, immobile, with guilt in his voice*): No, I don't want to see her.

Biff: Come on! (*He pulls again, and Willy tries to pull away.*)

Willy (*highly nervous*): No, no, I don't want to see her.

Biff (*tries to look into Willy's face, as if to find the answer there*): Why don't you
want to see her?

Willy (*more harshly now*): Don't bother me, will you?

Biff: What do you mean, you don't want to see her? You don't want them
calling you yellow, do you? This isn't your fault; it's me, I'm a bum. Now
come inside! (*Willy strains to get away.*) Did you hear what I said to you?

Willy pulls away and quickly goes by himself into the house. Biff follows.

Linda (*to Willy*): Did you plant, dear?

Biff (*at the door, to Linda*): All right, we had it out. I'm going and I'm not writing any more.

Linda (*going to Willy in the kitchen*): I think that's the best way, dear. 'Cause there's no use drawing it out, you'll just never get along.

Willy doesn't respond.

Biff: People ask where I am and what I'm doing, you don't know, and you don't care. That way it'll be off your mind and you can start brightening up again. All right? That clears it, doesn't it? (*Willy is silent, and Biff goes to him.*) You gonna wish me luck, scout? (*He extends his hand.*) What do you say?

Linda: Shake his hand, Willy.

Willy (*turning to her, seething with hurt*): There's no necessity to mention the pen at all, y'know.

Biff (*gently*): I've got no appointment, Dad.

Willy (*erupting fiercely*): He put his arm around . . . ?

Biff: Dad, you're never going to see what I am, so what's the use of arguing? If I strike oil I'll send you a check. Meantime forget I'm alive.

Willy (*to Linda*): Spite, see?

Biff: Shake hands, Dad.

Willy: Not my hand.

Biff: I was hoping not to go this way.

Willy: Well, this is the way you're going. Good-by.

Biff looks at him a moment, then turns sharply and goes to the stairs.

Willy (*stops him with*): May you rot in hell if you leave this house!

Biff (*turning*): Exactly what is it that you want from me?

Willy: I want you to know, on the train, in the mountains, in the valleys, wherever you go, that you cut down your life for spite!

Biff: No, no.

Willy: Spite, spite, is the word of your undoing! And when you're down and out, remember what did it. When you're rotting somewhere beside the railroad tracks, remember, and don't you dare blame it on me!

Biff: I'm not blaming it on you!

Willy: I won't take the rap for this, you hear?

Happy comes down the stairs and stands on the bottom step, watching.

Biff: That's just what I'm telling you!

Willy (*sinking into a chair at the table, with full accusation*): You're trying to put a knife in me—don't think I don't know what you're doing!

Biff: All right, phony! Then let's lay it on the line. (*He whips the rubber tube out of his pocket and puts it on the table.*)

Happy: You crazy—

Linda: Biff! (*She moves to grab the hose, but Biff holds it down with his hand.*)

Biff: Leave it there! Don't move it!

Willy (*not looking at it*): What is that?

Biff: You know goddam well what that is.

Willy (caged, wanting to escape): I never saw that.

Biff: You saw it. The mice didn't bring it into the cellar! What is this supposed to do, make a hero out of you? This supposed to make me sorry for you?

Willy: Never heard of it.

Biff: There'll be no pity for you, you hear? No pity!

Willy (to Linda): You hear the spite!

Biff: No, you're going to hear the truth—what you are and what I am!

Linda: Stop it!

Willy: Spite!

Happy (coming down toward Biff): You cut it now!

Biff (to Happy): The man don't know who we are! The man is gonna know! (*To Willy.*) We never told the truth for ten minutes in this house!

Happy: We always told the truth!

Biff (turning on him): You big blow, are you the assistant buyer? You're one of the two assistants to the assistant, aren't you?

Happy: Well, I'm practically—

Biff: You're practically full of it! We all are! And I'm through with it. (*To Willy.*) Now hear this, Willy, this is me.

Willy: I know you!

Biff: You know why I had no address for three months? I stole a suit in Kansas City and I was in jail. (*To Linda, who is sobbing.*) Stop crying. I'm through with it.

Linda turns away from them, her hands covering her face.

Willy: I suppose that's my fault!

Biff: I stole myself out of every good job since high school!

Willy: And whose fault is that?

Biff: And I never got anywhere because you blew me so full of hot air I could never stand taking orders from anybody! That's whose fault it is!

Willy: I hear that!

Linda: Don't, Biff!

Biff: It's goddam time you heard that! I had to be boss big shot in two weeks, and I'm through with it!

Willy: Then hang yourself! For spite, hang yourself!

Biff: No! Nobody's hanging himself, Willy! I ran down eleven flights with a pen in my hand today. And suddenly I stopped, you hear me? And in the middle of that office building, do you hear this? I stopped in the middle of that building and I saw—the sky. I saw the things that I love in this world. The work and the food and time to sit and smoke. And I looked at the pen and said to myself, what the hell am I grabbing this for? Why am I trying to become what I don't want to be? What am I doing in an office, making a contemptuous, begging fool of myself, when all I want is out there, waiting for me the minute I say I know who I am! Why can't I say that, Willy? (*He tries to make Willy face him, but Willy pulls away and moves to the left.*)

Willy (with hatred, threateningly): The door of your life is wide open!

Biff: Pop! I'm a dime a dozen, and so are you!

Willy (turning on him now in an uncontrolled outburst): I am not a dime a dozen! I am Willy Loman, and you are Biff Loman!

Biff starts for Willy, but is blocked by Happy. In his fury, Biff seems on the verge of attacking his father.

Biff: I am not a leader of men, Willy, and neither are you. You were never anything but a hard-working drummer who landed in the ash can like all the rest of them! I'm one dollar an hour, Willy! I tried seven states and couldn't raise it. A buck an hour! Do you gather my meaning? I'm not bringing home any prizes any more, and you're going to stop waiting for me to bring them home!

Willy (directly to Biff): You vengeful, spiteful mutt!

Biff breaks from Happy. Willy, in fright, starts up the stairs. Biff grabs him.

Biff (at the peak of his fury): Pop, I'm nothing! I'm nothing, Pop. Can't you understand that? There's no spite in it any more. I'm just what I am, that's all.

Biff's fury has spent itself, and he breaks down, sobbing, holding on to Willy, who dumbly fumbles for Biff's face.

Willy (astonished): What're you doing? What're you doing? (*To Linda.*) Why is he crying?

Biff (crying, broken): Will you let me go, for Christ sake? Will you take that phony dream and burn it before something happens? (*Struggling to contain himself, he pulls away and moves to the stairs.*) I'll go in the morning. Put him—put him to bed. (*Exhausted, Biff moves up the stairs to his room.*)

Willy (after a long pause, astonished, elevated): Isn't that remarkable? Biff—he likes me!

Linda: He loves you, Willy!

Happy (deeply moved): Always did, Pop.

Willy: Oh, Biff! (*Staring wildly.*) He cried! Cried to me. (*He is choking with his love, and now cries out his promise.*) That boy—that boy is going to be magnificent!

Ben appears in the light just outside the kitchen.

Ben: Yes, outstanding, with twenty thousand behind him.

Linda (sensing the racing of his mind, fearfully, carefully): Now come to bed, Willy. It's all settled now.

Willy (finding it difficult not to rush out of the house): Yes, we'll sleep. Come on. Go to sleep, Hap.

Ben: And it does take a great kind of man to crack the jungle.

In accents of dread, Ben's idyllic music starts up.

Happy (his arm around Linda): I'm getting married, Pop, don't forget it. I'm changing everything. I'm gonna run that department before the year is up. You'll see, Mom. (*He kisses her.*)

Ben: The jungle is dark but full of diamonds, Willy.

Willy turns, moves, listening to Ben.

Linda: Be good. You're both good boys, just act that way, that's all.

Happy: 'Night, Pop. (*He goes upstairs.*)

Linda (to Willy): Come, dear.

Ben (with greater force): One must go in to fetch a diamond out.

Willy (to Linda, as he moves slowly along the edge of the kitchen, toward the door): I just want to get settled down, Linda. Let me sit alone for a little.

Linda (almost uttering her fear): I want you upstairs.

Willy (taking her in his arms): In a few minutes, Linda. I couldn't sleep right now. Go on, you look awful tired. (*He kisses her.*)

Ben: Not like an appointment at all. A diamond is rough and hard to the touch.

Willy: Go on now, I'll be right up.

Linda: I think this is the only way, Willy.

Willy: Sure, it's the best thing.

Ben: Best thing!

Willy: The only way. Everything is gonna be—go on, kid, get to bed. You look so tired.

Linda: Come right up.

Willy: Two minutes.

Linda goes into the living room, then reappears in her bedroom. Willy moves just outside the kitchen door.

Willy: Loves me. (*Wonderingly.*) Always loved me. Isn't that a remarkable thing? Ben, he'll worship me for it!

Ben (with promise): It's dark there, but full of diamonds.

Willy: Can you imagine that magnificence with twenty thousand dollars in his pocket?

Linda (calling from her room): Willy! Come up!

Willy (calling from the kitchen): Yes! Yes! Coming! It's very smart, you realize that, don't you, sweetheart? Even Ben sees it. I gotta go, baby. 'By! By! (*Going over to Ben, almost dancing.*) Imagine? When the mail comes he'll be ahead of Bernard again!

Ben: A perfect proposition all around.

Willy: Did you see how he cried to me? Oh, if I could kiss him, Ben!

Ben: Time, William, time!

Willy: Oh, Ben, I always knew one way or another we were gonna make it, Biff and I!

Ben (looking at his watch): The boat. We'll be late. (*He moves slowly off into the darkness.*)

Willy (elegiacally, turning to the house): Now when you kick off, boy, I want a seventy-yard boot, and get right down the field under the ball, and when you hit, hit low and hit hard, because it's important, boy. (*He swings around and faces the audience.*) There's all kinds of important people in the stands, and the first thing you know . . . (*Suddenly realizing he is alone.*)

Ben! Ben, where do I . . . ? (*He makes a sudden movement of search.*) Ben, how do I . . . ?

Linda (*calling*): Willy, you coming up?

Willy (*uttering a gasp of fear, whirling about as if to quiet her*): Sh! (*He turns around as if to find his way; sounds, faces, voices, seem to be swarming in upon him and he flicks at them, crying.*) Sh! Sh! (*Suddenly music, faint and high, stops him. It rises in intensity, almost to an unbearable scream. He goes up and down on his toes, and rushes off around the house.*) Shhh!

Linda: Willy?

There is no answer. Linda waits. Biff gets up off his bed. He is still in his clothes. Happy sits up. Biff stands listening.

Linda (*with real fear*): Willy, answer me! Willy!

There is the sound of a car starting and moving away at full speed.

Linda: No!

Biff (*rushing down the stairs*): Pop!

As the car speeds off, the music crashes down in a frenzy of sound, which becomes the soft pulsation of a single cello string. Biff slowly returns to his bedroom. He and Happy gravely don their jackets. Linda slowly walks out of her room. The music has developed into a dead march. The leaves of day are appearing over everything. Charley and Bernard, somberly dressed, appear and knock on the kitchen door. Biff and Happy slowly descend the stairs to the kitchen as Charley and Bernard enter. All stop a moment when Linda, in clothes of mourning, bearing a little bunch of roses, comes through the draped doorway into the kitchen. She goes to Charley and takes his arm. Now all move toward the audience, through the wall-line of the kitchen. At the limit of the apron, Linda lays down the flowers, kneels, and sits back on her heels. All stare down at the grave.

REQUIEM

Charley: It's getting dark, Linda.

Linda doesn't react. She stares at the grave.

Biff: How about it, Mom? Better get some rest, heh? They'll be closing the gate soon.

Linda makes no move. Pause.

Happy (*deeply angered*): He had no right to do that! There was no necessity for it. We would've helped him.

Charley (*grunting*): Hmmm.

Biff: Come along, Mom.

Linda: Why didn't anybody come?

Charley: It was a very nice funeral.

Linda: But where are all the people he knew? Maybe they blame him.

Charley: Naa. It's a rough world, Linda. They wouldn't blame him.

Linda: I can't understand it. At this time especially. First time in thirty-five years we were just about free and clear. He only needed a little salary. He was even finished with the dentist.

Charley: No man only needs a little salary.

Linda: I can't understand it.

Biff: There were a lot of nice days. When he'd come home from a trip; or on Sundays, making the stoop; finishing the cellar; putting on the new porch; when he built the extra bathroom; and put up the garage. You know something, Charley, there's more of him in that front stoop than in all the sales he ever made.

Charley: Yeah. He was a happy man with a batch of cement.

Linda: He was so wonderful with his hands.

Biff: He had the wrong dreams. All, all, wrong.

Happy (almost ready to fight Biff): Don't say that!

Biff: He never knew who he was.

Charley (stopping Happy's movement and reply. To Biff.): Nobody dast blame this man. You don't understand: Willy was a salesman. And for a salesman, there is no rock bottom to the life. He don't put a bolt to a nut, he don't tell you the law or give you medicine. He's a man out there in the blue, riding on a smile and a shoeshine. And when they start not smiling back—that's an earthquake. And then you get yourself a couple of spots on your hat, and you're finished. Nobody dast blame this man. A salesman is got to dream, boy. It comes with the territory.

Biff: Charley, the man didn't know who he was.

Happy (infuriated): Don't say that!

Biff: Why don't you come with me, Happy?

Happy: I'm not licked that easily. I'm staying right in this city, and I'm gonna beat this racket! (*He looks at Biff, his chin set.*) The Loman Brothers!

Biff: I know who I am, kid.

Happy: All right, boy. I'm gonna show you and everybody else that Willy Loman did not die in vain. He had a good dream. It's the only dream you can have—to come out number-one man. He fought it out here, and this is where I'm gonna win it for him.

Biff (with a hopeless glance at Happy, bends toward his mother): Let's go, Mom.

Linda: I'll be with you in a minute. Go on, Charley. (*He hesitates.*) I want to, just for a minute. I never had a chance to say good-by.

Charley moves away, followed by Happy. Biff remains a slight distance up and left of Linda. She sits there, summoning herself. The flute begins, not far away, playing behind her speech.

Linda: Forgive me, dear. I can't cry. I don't know what it is, but I can't cry. I don't understand it. Why did you ever do that? Help me, Willy, I can't cry. It seems to me that you're just on another trip. I keep expecting you. Willy, dear, I can't cry. Why did you do it? I search and search and search, and I can't understand it, Willy. I made the last payment on the house today. Today, dear. And there'll be nobody home. (*A sob rises in her throat.*) We're free and clear. (*Sobbing more fully, released.*) We're free. (*Biff comes slowly toward her.*) We're free . . . We're free . . .

Biff lifts her to her feet and moves out up right with her in his arms. Linda sobs quietly. Bernard and Charley come together and follow them, followed by Happy. Only the music of the flute is left on the darkening stage as over the house the hard towers of the apartment buildings rise into sharp focus, and—

THE CURTAIN FALLS

WRITER'S PERSPECTIVE

Arthur Miller

Arthur Miller on Drama
TRAGEDY AND THE COMMON MAN°   1949

In this age few tragedies are written. It has often been held that the lack is due to a paucity of heroes among us, or else that modern man has had the blood drawn out of his organs of belief by the skepticism of science, and the heroic attack on life cannot feed on an attitude of reserve and circumspection. For one reason or another, we are often held to be below tragedy—or tragedy above us. The inevitable conclusion is, of course, that the tragic mode is archaic, fit only for the very highly placed, the kings or the kingly, and where this admission is not made in so many words it is most often implied.

I believe that the common man is as apt a subject for tragedy in its highest sense as kings were. On the face of it this ought to be obvious in the light of modern psychiatry, which bases its analysis upon classic formulations, such as the Oedipus and Orestes complexes, for instance, which were enacted by royal beings, but which apply to everyone in similar emotional situations.

A complete essay, originally published in *The New York Times.*

More simply, when the question of tragedy in art is not at issue, we never hesitate to attribute to the well-placed and the exalted the very same mental processes as the lowly. And finally, if the exaltation of tragic action were truly a property of the high-bred character alone, it is inconceivable that the mass of mankind should cherish tragedy above all other forms, let alone be capable of understanding it.

As a general rule, to which there may be exceptions unknown to me, I think the tragic feeling is evoked in us when we are in the presence of a character who is ready to lay down his life, if need be, to secure one thing—his sense of personal dignity. From Orestes to Hamlet, Medea to Macbeth, the underlying struggle is that of the individual attempting to gain his "rightful" position in his society.

Sometimes he is one who has been displaced from it, sometimes one who seeks to attain it for the first time, but the fateful wound from which the inevitable events spiral is the wound of indignity, and its dominant force is indignation. Tragedy, then, is the consequence of a man's total compulsion to evaluate himself justly.

In the sense of having been initiated by the hero himself, the tale always reveals what has been called his "tragic flaw," a failing that is not peculiar to grand or elevated characters. Nor is it necessarily a weakness. The flaw, or crack in the character, is really nothing—and need be nothing—but his inherent unwillingness to remain passive in the face of what he conceives to be a challenge to his dignity, his image of his rightful status. Only the passive, only those who accept their lot without active retaliation, are "flawless." Most of us are in that category.

But there are among us today, as there always have been, those who act against the scheme of things that degrades them, and in the process of action, everything we have accepted out of fear or insensitivity or ignorance is shaken before us and examined, and from this total onslaught by an individual against the seemingly stable cosmos surrounding us—from this total examination of the "unchangeable" environment—comes the terror and the fear that is classically associated with tragedy.

More important, from this total questioning of what has been previously unquestioned, we learn. And such a process is not beyond the common man. In revolutions around the world, these past thirty years, he has demonstrated again and again this inner dynamic of all tragedy.

Insistence upon the rank of the tragic hero, or the so-called nobility of his character, is really but a clinging to the outward forms of tragedy. If rank or nobility of character was indispensable, then it would follow that the problems of those with rank were the particular problems of tragedy. But surely the right of one monarch to capture the domain from another no longer raises our passions, nor are our concepts of justice what they were to the mind of an Elizabethan king.

The quality in such plays that does shake us, however, derives from the underlying fear of being displaced, the disaster inherent in being torn away from our chosen image of what and who we are in this world. Among us today this fear is as strong, and perhaps stronger, than it ever was. In fact, it is the common man who knows this fear best.

Now, if it is true that tragedy is the consequence of a man's total compulsion to evaluate himself justly, his destruction in the attempt posits a wrong or an evil in his environment. And this is precisely the morality of tragedy and its lesson. The discovery of the moral law, which is what the enlightenment of tragedy consists of, is not the discovery of some abstract or metaphysical quantity.

The tragic right is a condition of life, a condition in which the human personality is able to flower and realize itself. The wrong is the condition which suppresses man, perverts the flowing out of his love and creative instinct. Tragedy enlightens— and it must, in that it points the heroic finger at the enemy of man's freedom. The thrust for freedom is the quality in tragedy which exalts. The revolutionary questioning of the stable environment is what terrifies. In no way is the common man debarred from such thoughts or such actions.

Seen in this light, our lack of tragedy may be partially accounted for by the turn which modern literature has taken toward the purely psychiatric view of life, or the purely sociological. If all our miseries, our indignities, are born and bred within our minds, then all action, let alone the heroic action, is obviously impossible.

And if society alone is responsible for the cramping of our lives, then the protagonist must needs be so pure and faultless as to force us to deny his validity as a character. From neither of these views can tragedy derive, simply because neither represents a balanced concept of life. Above all else, tragedy requires the finest appreciation by the writer of cause and effect.

No tragedy can therefore come about when its author fears to question absolutely everything, when he regards any institution, habit or custom as being either everlasting, immutable or inevitable. In the tragic view the need of man to wholly realize himself is the only fixed star, and whatever it is that hedges his nature and lowers it is ripe for attack and examination. Which is not to say that tragedy must preach revolution.

The Greeks could probe the very heavenly origin of their ways and return to confirm the rightness of laws. And Job could face God in anger, demanding his right, and end in submission. But for a moment everything is in suspension, nothing is accepted, and in this stretching and tearing apart of the cosmos, in the very action of so doing, the character gains "size," the tragic stature which is spuriously attached to the royal or the high born in our minds. The commonest of men may take on that stature to the extent of his willingness to throw all he has into the contest, the battle to secure his rightful place in his world.

There is a misconception of tragedy with which I have been struck in review after review, and in many conversations with writers and readers alike. It is the idea that tragedy is of necessity allied to pessimism. Even the dictionary says nothing more about the word than that it means a story with a sad or unhappy ending. This impression is so firmly fixed that I almost hesitate to claim that in truth tragedy implies more optimism in its author than does comedy, and that its final result ought to be the reinforcement of the onlooker's brightest opinions of the human animal.

For, if it is true to say that in essence the tragic hero is intent upon claiming his whole due as a personality, and if this struggle must be total and without reservation, then it automatically demonstrates the indestructible will of man to achieve his humanity.

The possibility of victory must be there in tragedy. Where pathos rules, where pathos is finally derived, a character has fought a battle he could not possibly have won. The pathetic is achieved when the protagonist is, by virtue of his witlessness, his insensitivity, or the very air he gives off, incapable of grappling with a much superior force.

Pathos truly is the mode for the pessimist. But tragedy requires a nicer balance between what is possible and what is impossible. And it is curious, although edifying, that the plays we revere, century after century, are the tragedies. In them, and in them alone, lies the belief—optimistic, if you will—in the perfectibility of man.

It is time, I think, that we who are without kings took up this bright thread of our history and followed it to the only place it can possibly lead in our time—the heart and spirit of the average man.

Tennessee Williams

THE GLASS MENAGERIE   1945

Tennessee Williams (1914–1983) was born Thomas Lanier Williams in Columbus, Mississippi, went to high school in St. Louis, and was graduated from the University of Iowa. As an undergraduate, he saw a performance of Ibsen's Ghosts *and determined to be a playwright himself. His family bore a close resemblance to the Wingfields in* The Glass Menagerie: *his mother came from a line of Southern blue bloods (Tennessee pioneers); his sister Rose suffered from incapacitating shyness; and as a young man Williams himself, like Tom, worked at a job he disliked (in a shoe factory where his father worked), wrote poetry, sought refuge in moviegoing, and finally left home to wander and hold odd jobs. He worked as a bellhop in a New Orleans hotel; a teletype operator in Jacksonville, Florida; an usher and a waiter in New York. In 1945* The Glass Menagerie *scored a success on Broadway, winning a Drama Critics Circle award. Two years later Williams received a Pulitzer Prize for* A Streetcar Named Desire, *a grim, powerful study of a woman's illusions and frustrations, set in New Orleans. In 1955, another Pulitzer Prize went to* Cat on a Hot Tin Roof. *Besides other plays, including* Summer and Smoke *(1948),* Sweet Bird of Youth *(1959),* The Night of the Iguana *(1961),* Small Craft Warnings *(1973),* Clothes for a Summer Hotel *(1980), and* A House Not Meant to Stand *(1981), Williams wrote two novels, poetry, essays, short stories, and* Memoirs *(1975).*

> *Nobody, not even the rain, has such small hands.*
> —E. E. Cummings

Characters

Amanda Wingfield, the mother. A little woman of great but confused vitality clinging frantically to another time and place. Her characterization must be carefully created, not copied from type. She is not paranoiac, but her life is paranoia. There is much to admire in Amanda, and as much to love and pity as there is to laugh at. Certainly she has endurance and a kind of heroism, and though her foolishness makes her unwittingly cruel at times, there is tenderness in her slight person.

Left to right: Anthony Ross (Jim), Laurette Taylor (Amanda), Eddie Dowling (Tom), and Julie Hayden (Laura) in the 1945 original production of The Glass Menagerie, *The Playhouse, New York. (New York Public Library, The Billy Rose Theater Collection)*

Laura Wingfield, her daughter. Amanda, having failed to establish contact with reality, continues to live vitally in her illusions, but Laura's situation is even graver. A childhood illness has left her crippled, one leg slightly shorter than the other, and held in a brace. This defect need not be more than suggested on the stage. Stemming from this, Laura's separation increases till she is like a piece of her own glass collection, too exquisitely fragile to move from the shelf.

Tom Wingfield, her son. And the narrator of the play. A poet with a job in a warehouse. His nature is not remorseless, but to escape from a trap he has to act without pity.

Jim O'Connor, the gentleman caller. A nice, ordinary, young man.

Scene. *An alley in St. Louis.*

Part I. *Preparation for a Gentleman Caller.*

Part II. *The Gentleman Calls.*

Time. *Now and the Past.*

Scene I

The Wingfield apartment is in the rear of the building, one of those vast hive-like conglomerations of cellular living-units that flower as warty growths in overcrowded urban centers of lower middle-class population and are symptomatic of the impulse of this largest and fundamentally enslaved section of American society to avoid fluidity and differentiation and to exist and function as one interfused mass of automatism.

The apartment faces an alley and is entered by a fire-escape, a structure whose name is a touch of accidental poetic truth, for all of these huge buildings are always burning with the slow and implacable fires of human desperation. The fire-escape is included in the set—that is, the landing of it and steps descending from it.

The scene is memory and is therefore unrealistic. Memory takes a lot of poetic license. It omits some details; others are exaggerated, according to the emotional value of the articles it touches, for memory is seated predominantly in the heart. The interior is therefore rather dim and poetic.

At the rise of the curtain, the audience is faced with the dark, grim rear wall of the Wingfield tenement. This building, which runs parallel to the footlights, is flanked on both sides by dark, narrow alleys which run into murky canyons of tangled clotheslines, garbage cans, and the sinister latticework of neighboring fire-escapes. It is up and down these side alleys that exterior entrances and exits are made, during the play. At the end of Tom's opening commentary, the dark tenement wall slowly reveals (by means of a transparency) the interior of the ground floor Wingfield apartment.

Downstage is the living room, which also serves as a sleeping room for Laura, the sofa unfolding to make her bed. Upstage, center, and divided by a wide arch or second proscenium with transparent faded portieres (or second curtain), is the dining room. In an old-fashioned what-not in the living room are seen scores of transparent glass animals. A blown-up photograph of the father hangs on the wall of the living room, facing the audience, to the left of the archway. It is the face of a very handsome young man in a doughboy's First World War cap. He is gallantly smiling, ineluctably smiling, as if to say, "I will be smiling forever."

The audience hears and sees the opening scene in the dining room through both the transparent fourth wall of the building and the transparent gauze portieres of the dining room arch. It is during this revealing scene that the fourth wall slowly ascends, out of sight. This transparent exterior wall is not brought down again until the very end of the play, during Tom's final speech.

The narrator is an undisguised convention of the play. He takes whatever license with dramatic convention as is convenient to his purposes.

Tom enters dressed as a merchant sailor from the alley, stage left, and strolls across the front of the stage to the fire-escape. There he stops and lights a cigarette. He addresses the audience.

Tom: Yes, I have tricks in my pocket, I have things up my sleeve. But I am the opposite of a stage magician. He gives you illusion that has the appearance of truth. I give you truth in the pleasant disguise of illusion. To begin with, I turn back time. I reverse it to that quaint period, the thirties, when the huge middle class of America was matriculating in a school for the blind. Their eyes had failed them, or they had failed their eyes, and so they were having their fingers pressed forcibly down on the fiery Braille alphabet of a dissolving economy. In Spain there was revolution. Here there was only shouting and confusion. In Spain there was Guernica. Here there were disturbances of labor, sometimes pretty violent, in otherwise peaceful cities such as Chicago, Cleveland, St. Louis. . . . This is the social background of the play.

(Music.)

The play is memory. Being a memory play, it is dimly lighted, it is sentimental, it is not realistic. In memory everything seems to happen to music. That explains the fiddle in the wings. I am the narrator of the play, and also a character in it. The other characters are my mother, Amanda, my sister, Laura, and a gentleman caller who appears in the final scenes. He is the most realistic character in the play, being an emissary from a world of reality that we were somehow set apart from. But since I have a poet's weakness for symbols, I am using this character also as a symbol; he is the long delayed but always expected something that we live for. There is a fifth character in the play who doesn't appear except in this larger-than-life photograph over the mantel. This is our father who left us a long time ago. He was a telephone man who fell in love with long distances; he gave up his job with the telephone company and skipped the light fantastic out of town. . . . The last we heard of him was a picture post-card from Mazatlan, on the Pacific coast of Mexico, containing a message of two words—"Hello—Good-bye!" and an address. I think the rest of the play will explain itself. . . .

Amanda's voice becomes audible through the portieres.

(Screen Legend: "Où Sont Les Neiges.")°

He divides the portieres and enters the upstage area.

Amanda and Laura are seated at a drop-leaf table. Eating is indicated by gestures without food or utensils. Amanda faces the audience. Tom and Laura are seated in profile.

The interior has lit up softly and through the scrim we see Amanda and Laura seated at the table in the upstage area.

Amanda (calling): Tom?
Tom: Yes, Mother.
Amanda: We can't say grace until you come to the table!
Tom: Coming, Mother. (*He bows slightly and withdraws, reappearing a few moments later in his place at the table.*)

(*Screen Legend . . . Neiges.*"): "Where are the snows (of yesteryear)?" A slide bearing this line by the French poet François Villon is to be projected on a stage wall.

Amanda (*to her son*): Honey, don't *push* with your *fingers*. If you have to push with something, the thing to push with is a crust of bread. And chew—chew! Animals have sections in their stomachs which enable them to digest food without mastication, but human beings are supposed to chew their food before they swallow it down. Eat food leisurely, son, and really enjoy it. A well-cooked meal has lots of delicate flavors that have to be held in the mouth for appreciation. So chew your food and give your salivary glands a chance to function!

Tom deliberately lays his imaginary fork down and pushes his chair back from the table.

Tom: I haven't enjoyed one bite of this dinner because of your constant directions on how to eat it. It's you that makes me rush through meals with your hawk-like attention to every bite I take. Sickening—spoils my appetite—all this discussion of animals' secretion—salivary glands—mastication!

Amanda (*lightly*): Temperament like a Metropolitan star! (*He rises and crosses downstage.*) You're not excused from the table.

Tom: I am getting a cigarette.

Amanda: You smoke too much.

Laura rises.

Laura: I'll bring in the blanc mange.

He remains standing with his cigarette by the portieres during the following.

Amanda (*rising*): No, sister, no, sister—you be the lady this time and I'll be the darky.

Laura: I'm already up.

Amanda: Resume your seat, little sister—I want you to stay fresh and pretty—for gentlemen callers!

Laura: I'm not expecting any gentlemen callers.

Amanda (*crossing out to kitchenette. Airily*): Sometimes they come when they are least expected! Why, I remember one Sunday afternoon in Blue Mountain—(*Enters kitchenette.*)

Tom: I know what's coming!

Laura: Yes. But let her tell it.

Tom: Again?

Laura: She loves to tell it.

Amanda returns with bowl of dessert.

Amanda: One Sunday afternoon in Blue Mountain—your mother received—seventeen!—gentlemen callers! Why, sometimes there weren't chairs enough to accommodate them all. We had to send the nigger over to bring in folding chairs from the parish house.

Tom (*remaining at portieres*): How did you entertain those gentlemen callers?

Amanda: I understood the art of conversation!

Tom: I bet you could talk.

Amanda: Girls in those days *knew* how to talk, I can tell you.

Tom: Yes?

(Image: Amanda As A Girl On A Porch Greeting Callers.)

Amanda: They knew how to entertain their gentlemen callers. It wasn't enough for a girl to be possessed of a pretty face and a graceful figure—although I wasn't slighted in either respect. She also needed to have a nimble wit and a tongue to meet all occasions.

Tom: What did you talk about?

Amanda: Things of importance going on in the world! Never anything coarse or common or vulgar. (*She addresses Tom as though he were seated in the vacant chair at the table though he remains by portieres. He plays this scene as though he held the book.*) My callers were gentlemen—all! Among my callers were some of the most prominent young planters of the Mississippi Delta— planters and sons of planters!

Tom motions for music and a spot of light on Amanda. Her eyes lift, her face glows, her voice becomes rich and elegiac.

(Screen Legend: "Où Sont Les Neiges.")

There was young Champ Laughlin who later became vice-president of the Delta Planters Bank. Hadley Stevenson who was drowned in Moon Lake and left his widow one hundred and fifty thousand in Government bonds. There were the Cutrere brothers, Wesley and Bates. Bates was one of my bright par- ticular beaux! He got in a quarrel with that wild Wainright boy. They shot it out on the floor of Moon Lake Casino. Bates was shot through the stomach. Died in the ambulance on his way to Memphis. His widow was also well-pro- vided for, came into eight or ten thousand acres, that's all. She married him on the rebound—never loved her—carried my picture on him the night he died! And there was that boy that every girl in the Delta had set her cap for! That beautiful, brilliant young Fitzhugh boy from Green County!

Tom: What did he leave his widow?

Amanda: He never married! Gracious, you talk as though all of my old admirers had turned up their toes to the daisies!

Tom: Isn't this the first you mentioned that still survives?

Amanda: That Fitzhugh boy went North and made a fortune—came to be known as the Wolf of Wall Street! He had the Midas touch, whatever he touched turned to gold! And I could have been Mrs. Duncan J. Fitzhugh, mind you! But—I picked your *father!*

Laura (rising): Mother, let me clear the table.

Amanda: No dear, you go in front and study your typewriter chart. Or practice your shorthand a little. Stay fresh and pretty!—It's almost time for our gen- tlemen callers to start arriving. (*She flounces girlishly toward the kitchenette.*) How many do you suppose we're going to entertain this afternoon?

Tom throws down the paper and jumps up with a groan.

Laura (alone in the dining room): I don't believe we're going to receive any, Mother.

Amanda (*reappearing, airily*): What? No one—not one? You must be joking! (*Laura nervously echoes her laugh. She slips in a fugitive manner through the half-open portieres and draws them gently behind her. A shaft of very clear light is thrown on her face against the jaded tapestry of the curtains.*) (**Music: "The Glass Menagerie" Under Faintly.**) (*Lightly.*) Not one gentleman caller? It can't be true! There must be a flood, there must have been a tornado!

Laura: It isn't a flood, it's not a tornado, Mother. I'm just not popular like you were in Blue Mountain. . . . (*Tom utters another groan. Laura glances at him with a faint, apologetic smile. Her voice catching a little.*) Mother's afraid I'm going to be an old maid.

(**The Scene Dims Out With "Glass Menagerie" Music.**)

SCENE II

"Laura, Haven't You Ever Liked Some Boy?"

On the dark stage the screen is lighted with the image of blue roses.

Gradually Laura's figure becomes apparent and the screen goes out.

The music subsides.

Laura is seated in the delicate ivory chair at the small clawfoot table.

She wears a dress of soft violet material for a kimono—her hair tied back from her forehead with a ribbon.

She is washing and polishing her collection of glass.

Amanda appears on the fire-escape steps. At the sound of her ascent, Laura catches her breath, thrusts the bowl of ornaments away and seats herself stiffly before the diagram of the typewriter keyboard as though it held her spellbound. Something has happened to Amanda. It is written in her face as she climbs to the landing: a look that is grim and hopeless and a little absurd.

She has on one of those cheap or imitation velvety-looking cloth coats with imitation fur collar. Her hat is five or six years old, one of those dreadful cloche hats that were worn in the late twenties, and she is clasping an enormous black patent-leather pocketbook with nickel clasp and initials. This is her full-dress outfit, the one she usually wears to the D.A.R.

Before entering she looks through the door.

She purses her lips, opens her eyes wide, rolls them upward and shakes her head.

Then she slowly lets herself in the door. Seeing her mother's expression Laura touches her lips with a nervous gesture.

Laura: Hello, Mother, I was—(*She makes a nervous gesture toward the chart on the wall. Amanda leans against the shut door and stares at Laura with a martyred look.*)

Amanda: Deception? Deception? (*She slowly removes her hat and gloves, continuing the swift suffering stare. She lets the hat and gloves fall on the floor—a bit of acting.*)

Laura (*shakily*): How was the D.A.R. meeting? (*Amanda slowly opens her purse and removes a dainty white handkerchief which she shakes out delicately and delicately touches to her lips and nostrils.*) Didn't you go to the D.A.R. meeting, Mother?

Amanda (*faintly, almost inaudibly*): —No.—No. (*Then more forcibly.*) I did not have the strength—to go to the D.A.R. In fact, I did not have the courage! I wanted to find a hole in the ground and hide myself in it forever! (*She crosses slowly to the wall and removes the diagram of the typewriter keyboard. She holds it in front of her for a second, staring at it sweetly and sorrowfully—then bites her lips and tears it in two pieces.*)

Laura (*faintly*): Why did you do that, Mother? (*Amanda repeats the same procedure with the chart of the Gregg Alphabet.*) Why are you—

Amanda: Why? Why? How old are you, Laura?

Laura: Mother, you know my age.

Amanda: I thought that you were an adult; it seems that I was mistaken. (*She crosses slowly to the sofa and sinks down and stares at Laura.*)

Laura: Please don't stare at me, Mother.

Amanda closes her eyes and lowers her head. Count ten.

Amanda: What are we going to do, what is going to become of us, what is the future?

Count ten.

Laura: Has something happened, Mother? (*Amanda draws a long breath and takes out the handkerchief again. Dabbing process.*) Mother, has—something happened?

Amanda: I'll be all right in a minute. I'm just bewildered—(*count five*)—by life . . .

Laura: Mother, I wish that you would tell me what's happened.

Amanda: As you know, I was supposed to be inducted into my office at the D.A.R. this afternoon. (**Image: A Swarm of Typewriters.**) But I stopped off at Rubicam's Business College to speak to your teachers about your having a cold and ask them what progress they thought you were making down there.

Laura: Oh . . .

Amanda: I went to the typing instructor and introduced myself as your mother. She didn't know who you were. Wingfield, she said. We don't have any such student enrolled at the school! I assured her she did, that you had been going to classes since early in January. "I wonder," she said, "if you could be talking about that terribly shy little girl who dropped out of school after only a few days' attendance?" "No," I said, "Laura, my daughter, has been going to school every day for the past six weeks!" "Excuse me," she said. She took the attendance book out and there was your name, unmistakably printed, and all the dates you were absent until they decided that you had dropped out of school. I still said, "No, there must have been some mistake! There must have been some mix-up in the records!" And she said, "No—I remember her perfectly now. Her hand shook so that she couldn't hit the right keys! The first time we gave a speed-test, she broke down completely— was sick at the stomach and almost had to be carried into the wash-room! After that morning she never showed up any more. We phoned the house but never got any answer"—while I was working at Famous and Barr, I suppose, demonstrating those—Oh! I felt so weak I could barely keep on my feet. I had to sit down while they got me a glass of water! Fifty dollars' tuition, all of our plans—my hopes and ambitions for you—just gone up the spout, just gone up the spout like that. (*Laura draws a long breath and gets awkwardly to her feet. She crosses to the victrola and winds it up.*) What are you doing?

Laura: Oh! (*She releases the handle and returns to her seat.*)

Amanda: Laura, where have you been going when you've gone out pretending that you were going to business college?

Laura: I've just been going out walking.

Amanda: That's not true.

Laura: It is. I just went walking.

Amanda: Walking? Walking? In winter? Deliberately courting pneumonia in that light coat? Where did you walk to, Laura?

Laura: It was the lesser of two evils, Mother. (**Image: Winter Scene In Park.**) I couldn't go back. I—threw up—on the floor!

Amanda: From half past seven till after five every day you mean to tell me you walked around in the park, because you wanted to make me think that you were still going to Rubicam's Business College?

Laura: It wasn't as bad as it sounds. I went inside places to get warmed up.

Amanda: Inside where?

Laura: I went in the art museum and the bird-houses at the Zoo. I visited the penguins every day! Sometimes I did without lunch and went to the movies. Lately I've been spending most of my afternoons in the Jewel-box, that big glass house where they raise the tropical flowers.

Amanda: You did all this to deceive me, just for the deception? (*Laura looks down.*) Why?

Laura: Mother, when you're disappointed, you get that awful suffering look on your face, like the picture of Jesus' mother in the museum!

Amanda: Hush!

Laura: I couldn't face it.

Pause. A whisper of strings.

(**Legend: "The Crust Of Humility."**)

Amanda (*hopelessly fingering the huge pocketbook*): So what are we going to do the rest of our lives? Stay home and watch the parades go by? Amuse ourselves with the glass menagerie, darling? Eternally play those worn-out phonograph records your father left as a painful reminder of him? We won't have a business career—we've given that up because it gave us nervous indigestion! (*Laughs wearily.*) What is there left but dependence all our lives? I know so well what becomes of unmarried women who aren't prepared to occupy a position. I've seen such pitiful cases in the South—barely tolerated spinsters living upon the grudging patronage of sister's husband or brother's wife!—stuck away in some little mouse-trap of a room—encouraged by one in-law to visit another—little birdlike women without any nest—eating the crust of humility all their life! Is that the future that we've mapped out for ourselves? I swear it's the only alternative I can think of! It isn't a very pleasant alternative, is it? Of course—some girls *do marry.* (*Laura twists her hands nervously.*) Haven't you ever liked some boy?

Laura: Yes I liked one once. (*Rises.*) I came across his picture a while ago.

Amanda (*with some interest*): He gave you his picture?

Laura: No, it's in the year-book.

Amanda (*disappointed*): Oh—a high-school boy.

(Screen Image: Jim As A High-School Hero Bearing A Silver Cup.)

Laura: Yes. His name was Jim. (*Laura lifts the heavy annual from the clawfoot table.*) Here he is in *The Pirates of Penzance.*

Amanda (*absently*): The what?

Laura: The operetta the senior class put on. He had a wonderful voice and we sat across the aisle from each other Mondays, Wednesdays, and Fridays in the Aud. Here he is with the silver cup for debating! See his grin?

Amanda (*absently*): He must have had a jolly disposition.

Laura: He used to call me—Blue Roses.

(Image: Blue Roses.)

Amanda: Why did he call you such a name as that?

Laura: When I had that attack of pleurosis—he asked me what was the matter when I came back. I said pleurosis—he thought that I said Blue Roses! So that's what he always called me after that. Whenever he saw me, he'd holler, "Hello, Blue Roses!" I didn't care for the girl he went out with. Emily Meisenbach. Emily was the best-dressed girl at Soldan. She never struck me, though, as being sincere . . . It says in the Personal Section—they're engaged. That's—six years ago! They must be married by now.

Amanda: Girls that aren't cut out for business careers usually wind up married to some nice man. (*Gets up with a spark of revival.*) Sister, that's what you'll do!

Laura utters a startled, doubtful laugh. She reaches quickly for a piece of glass.

Laura: But, Mother—

Amanda: Yes? (*Crossing to phonograph.*)

Laura (*in a tone of frightened apology*): I'm—crippled!

(Image: Screen.)

Amanda: Nonsense! Laura, I've told you never, never to use that word. Why, you're not crippled, you just have a little defect—hardly noticeable, even! When people have some slight disadvantage like that, they cultivate other things to make up for it—develop charm—and vivacity—and—*charm!* That's all you have to do! (*She turns again to the phonograph.*) One thing your father had *plenty of*—was *charm!*

Tom motions to the fiddle in the wings.

(The Scene Fades Out With Music.)

SCENE III

(Legend On The Screen: "After The Fiasco—")

Tom speaks from the fire-escape landing.

Tom: After the fiasco at Rubicam's Business College, the idea of getting a gentleman caller for Laura began to play a more important part in Mother's calculations. It became an obsession. Like some archetype of the universal unconscious, the image of the gentleman caller haunted our small apartment. . . . **(Image: Young Man At Door With Flowers.)** An evening at home rarely passed without some allusion to this image, this spectre, this hope. . . . Even when he wasn't mentioned, his presence hung in Mother's preoccupied look and in my sister's frightened, apologetic manner—hung like a sentence passed upon the Wingfields! Mother was a woman of action as well as words. She began to take logical steps in the planned direction. Late that winter and in the early spring—realizing that extra money would be needed to properly feather the nest and plume the bird—she conducted a vigorous campaign on the telephone, roping in subscribers to one of those magazines for matrons called *The Home-maker's Companion,* the type of journal that features the serialized sublimations of ladies of letters who think in terms of delicate cup-like breasts, slim, tapering waists, rich, creamy thighs, eyes like wood-smoke in autumn, fingers that soothe and caress like strains of music, bodies as powerful as Etruscan sculpture.

(Screen Image: Glamor Magazine Cover.)

Amanda enters with phone on long extension cord. She is spotted in the dim stage.

Amanda: Ida Scott? This is Amanda Wingfield! We *missed* you at the D.A.R. last Monday! I said to myself: She's probably suffering with that sinus condition! How is that sinus condition? Horrors! Heaven have mercy!—You're a Christian martyr, yes, that's what you are, a Christian martyr! Well, I just now happened to notice that your subscription to the *Companion's* about to expire! Yes, it expires with the next issue, honey!—just when that wonderful new serial by Bessie Mae Hopper is getting off to such an exciting start. Oh, honey, it's something that you can't miss! You remember how *Gone With the Wind* took everybody by storm? You simply couldn't go out if you hadn't read it. All everybody *talked* was Scarlett O'Hara. Well, this is a book that critics already compare to *Gone With the Wind*. It's the *Gone With the Wind* of the post-World War generation!—What?—Burning?—Oh, honey, don't let them burn, go take a look in the oven and I'll hold the wire! Heavens—I think she's hung up!

(Dim Out.)

(Legend On Screen: "You Think I'm In Love With Continental Shoemakers?")

Before the stage is lighted, the violent voices of Tom and Amanda are heard. They are quarreling behind the portieres. In front of them stands Laura with clenched hands and panicky expression.

A clear pool of light on her figure throughout this scene.

Tom: What in Christ's name am I—

Amanda (shrilly): Don't you use that—

Tom: Supposed to do!

Amanda: Expression! Not in my—

Tom: Ohhh!

Amanda: Presence! Have you gone out of your senses?

Tom: I have, that's true, *driven* out!

Amanda: What is the matter with you, you—big—big—IDIOT!

Tom: Look—I've got *no thing,* no single thing—

Amanda: Lower your voice!

Tom: In my life here that I can call my OWN! Everything is—

Amanda: Stop that shouting!

Tom: Yesterday you confiscated my books! You had the nerve to—

Amanda: I took that horrible novel back to the library—yes! That hideous book by that insane Mr. Lawrence. (*Tom laughs wildly.*) I cannot control the output of diseased minds or people who cater to them—(*Tom laughs still more wildly.*) BUT I WON'T ALLOW SUCH FILTH BROUGHT INTO MY HOUSE! No, no, no, no, no!

Tom: House, house! Who pays rent on it, who makes a slave of himself to—

Amanda (fairly screeching): Don't you DARE to—

Tom: No, no, I mustn't say things! *I've* got to just—

Amanda: Let me tell you—

Tom: I don't want to hear any more! (*He tears the portieres open. The upstage area is lit with a turgid smoky red glow.*)

Amanda's hair is in metal curlers and she wears a very old bathrobe, much too large for her slight figure, a relic of the faithless Mr. Wingfield.

An upright typewriter and a wild disarray of manuscripts are on the drop-leaf table. The quarrel was probably precipitated by Amanda's interruption of his creative labor. A chair lying overthrown on the floor.

Their gesticulating shadows are cast on the ceiling by the fiery glow.

Amanda: You *will* hear more, you—

Tom: No, I won't hear more, I'm going out!

Amanda: You come right back in—

Tom: Out, out out! Because I'm—

Amanda: Come back here, Tom Wingfield! I'm not through talking to you!

Tom: Oh, go—

Laura (*desperately*): Tom!

Amanda: You're going to listen, and no more insolence from you! I'm at the end of my patience! (*He comes back toward her.*)

Tom: What do you think I'm at? Aren't I supposed to have any patience to reach the end of, Mother? I know, I know. It seems unimportant to you, what I'm *doing*—what *I want* to do—having a little *difference* between them! You don't think that—

Amanda: I think you've been doing things that you're ashamed of. That's why you act like this. I don't believe that you go every night to the movies. Nobody goes to the movies night after night. Nobody in their right minds goes to the movies as often as you pretend to. People don't go to the movies at nearly midnight, and movies don't let out at two A.M. Come in stumbling. Muttering to yourself like a maniac! You get three hours' sleep and then go to work. Oh, I can picture the way you're doing down there. Moping, doping, because you're in no condition.

Tom (*wildly*): No, I'm in no condition!

Amanda: What right have you got to jeopardize your job? Jeopardize the security of us all? How do you think we'd manage if you were—

Tom: Listen! You think I'm crazy *about* the *warehouse*? (*He bends fiercely toward her slight figure.*) You think I'm in love with the Continental Shoemakers? You think I want to spend fifty-five years down there in that—*celotex interior!* with—*fluorescent*—*tubes!* Look! I'd rather somebody picked up a crowbar and battered out my brains—than go back mornings! I *go!* Every time you come in yelling that God damn *"Rise and Shine!"* *"Rise and Shine!"* I say to myself "How *lucky dead* people are!" But I get up. I *go!* For sixty-five dollars a month I give up all that I dream of doing and being *ever!* And you say self—*self's* all I ever think of. Why, listen, if self is what I thought of, Mother, I'd be where he is—GONE! (*Pointing to father's picture.*) As far as the system of transportation reaches! (*He starts past her. She grabs his arm.*) Don't grab at me, Mother!

Amanda: Where are you going?

Tom: I'm going to the *movies!*

Amanda: I don't believe that lie!

Tom (*crouching toward her, overtowering her tiny figure. She backs away, gasping*): I'm going to opium dens! Yes, opium dens, dens of vice and criminals' hangouts, Mother. I've joined the Hogan gang, I'm a hired assassin, I carry a tommy-gun in a violin case! I run a string of cat-houses in the Valley! They call me Killer, Killer Wingfield, I'm leading a double-life, a simple, honest warehouse worker by day, by night a dynamic *czar* of the *underworld*, Mother. I go to gambling casinos, I spin away fortunes on the roulette table! I wear a patch over one eye and a false mustache, sometimes I put on green whiskers. On those occasions they call me—*El Diablo!* Oh, I could tell you things to make you sleepless! My enemies plan to dynamite this place. They're going to blow us all sky-high some night! I'll be glad, very happy, and so will you! You'll go up, up on a broomstick, over Blue Mountain with seventeen gentlemen callers! You ugly—babbling old—*witch*. . . . (*He goes through a series of violent, clumsy movements, seizing his overcoat, lunging to the door, pulling it fiercely open. The women watch him, aghast. His arm catches in the sleeve of the coat as he struggles to pull it on. For a moment he is pinioned by the bulky garment. With an outraged groan he tears the coat off again, splitting the shoulders of it, and hurls it across the room. It strikes against the shelf of Laura's glass collection, there is a tinkle of shattering glass. Laura cries out as if wounded.*)

(Music Legend: "The Glass Menagerie.")

Laura (*shrilly*): My glass!—menagerie. . . . (*She covers her face and turns away.*)

> But Amanda is still stunned and stupefied by the "ugly witch" so that she barely notices this occurrence. Now she recovers her speech.

Amanda (*in an awful voice*): I won't speak to you—until you apologize! (*She crosses through portieres and draws them together behind her. Tom is left with Laura. Laura clings weakly to the mantel with her face averted. Tom stares at her stupidly for a moment. Then he crosses to shelf. Drops awkwardly to his knees to collect the fallen glass, glancing at Laura as if he would speak but couldn't.*)

("The Glass Menagerie" steals in as the Scene Dims Out.)

SCENE IV

The interior is dark. Faint in the alley.

A deep-voiced bell in a church is tolling the hour of five as the scene commences.

Tom appears at the top of the alley. After each solemn boom of the bell in the tower, he shakes a little noise-maker or rattle as if to express the tiny spasm of man in contrast to the sustained power and dignity of the Almighty. This and the unsteadiness of his advance make it evident that he has been drinking.

As he climbs the few steps to the fire-escape landing light steals up inside. Laura appears in night-dress, observing Tom's empty bed in the front room.

Tom fishes in his pockets for the door-key, removing a motley assortment of articles in the search, including a perfect shower of movie-ticket stubs and an empty bottle. At last he finds the key, but just as he is about to insert it, it slips from his fingers. He strikes a match and crouches below the door.

Tom (*bitterly*): One crack—and it falls through!

> (*Laura opens the door.*)

Laura: Tom! Tom, what are you doing?
Tom: Looking for a door-key.

Laura: Where have you been all this time?

Tom: I have been to the movies.

Laura: All this time at the movies?

Tom: There was a very long program. There was a Garbo picture and a Mickey Mouse and a travelogue and a newsreel and a preview of coming attractions. And there was an organ solo and a collection for the milk-fund—simultaneously—which ended up in a terrible fight between a fat lady and an usher!

Laura (*innocently*): Did you have to stay through everything?

Tom: Of course! And, oh, I forgot! There was a big stage show! The headliner on this stage show was Malvolio the Magician. He performed wonderful tricks, many of them, such as pouring water back and forth between pitchers. First it turned to wine and then it turned to beer and then it turned to whiskey. I know it was whiskey it finally turned into because he needed somebody to come up out of the audience to help him, and I came up—both shows! It was Kentucky Straight Bourbon. A very generous fellow, he gave souvenirs. (*He pulls from his back pocket a shimmering rainbow-colored scarf.*) He gave me this. This is his magic scarf. You can have it, Laura. You wave it over a canary cage and you get a bowl of gold-fish. You wave it over the gold-fish bowl and they fly away canaries. . . . But the wonderfullest trick of all was the coffin trick. We nailed him into a coffin and he got out of the coffin without removing one nail. (*He has come inside.*) There is a trick that would come in handy for me—get me out of this 2 by 4 situation! (*Flops onto bed and starts removing shoes.*)

Laura: Tom—Shhh!

Tom: What're you shushing me for?

Laura: You'll wake up Mother.

Tom: Goody, goody! Pay'er back for all those "Rise an' Shines." (*Lies down, groaning.*) You know it don't take much intelligence to get yourself into a nailed-up coffin, Laura. But who in hell ever got himself out of one without removing one nail?

As if in answer, the father's grinning photograph lights up.

(Scene Dims Out.)

Immediately following: The church bell is heard striking six. At the sixth stroke the alarm clock goes off in Amanda's room, and after a few moments we hear her calling: "Rise and Shine! Rise and Shine! Laura, go tell your brother to rise and shine!"

Tom (*sitting up slowly*): I'll rise—but I won't shine.

The light increases.

Amanda: Laura, tell your brother his coffee is ready.

Laura slips into front room.

Laura: Tom! it's nearly seven. Don't make Mother nervous. (*He stares at her stupidly. Beseechingly.*) Tom, speak to Mother this morning. Make up with her, apologize, speak to her!

Tom: She won't to me. It's her that started not speaking.

Laura: If you just say you're sorry she'll start speaking.

Tom: Her not speaking—is that such a tragedy?

Laura: Please—please!

Amanda (calling from kitchenette): Laura, are you going to do what I asked you to do, or do I have to get dressed and go out myself?

Laura: Going, going—soon as I get on my coat! (*She pulls on a shapeless felt hat with nervous, jerky movements, pleadingly glancing at Tom. Rushes awkwardly for coat. The coat is one of Amanda's inaccurately made-over, the sleeves too short for Laura.*) Butter and what else?

Amanda (entering upstage): Just butter. Tell them to charge it.

Laura: Mother, they make such faces when I do that.

Amanda: Sticks and stones may break my bones, but the expression on Mr. Garfinkel's face won't harm us! Tell your brother his coffee is getting cold.

Laura (at door): Do what I asked you, will you, will you, Tom?

He looks sullenly away.

Amanda: Laura, go now or just don't go at all!

Laura (rushing out): Going—going! (*A second later she cries out. Tom springs up and crosses to the door. Amanda rushes anxiously in. Tom opens the door.*)

Tom: Laura?

Laura: I'm all right. I slipped, but I'm all right.

Amanda (peering anxiously after her): If anyone breaks a leg on those fire-escape steps, the landlord ought to be sued for every cent he possesses! (*She shuts door. Remembers she isn't speaking and returns to other room.*)

As Tom enters listlessly for his coffee, she turns her back to him and stands rigidly facing the window on the gloomy gray vault of the areaway. Its light on her face with its aged but childish features is cruelly sharp, satirical as a Daumier print.

(Music Under: "Ave Maria.")

Tom glances sheepishly but sullenly at her averted figure and slumps at the table. The coffee is scalding hot; he sips it and gasps and spits it back in the cup. At his gasp, Amanda catches her breath and half turns. Then catches herself and turns back to window.

Tom blows on his coffee, glancing sidewise at his mother. She clears her throat. Tom clears his. He starts to rise. Sinks back down again, scratches his head, clears his throat again. Amanda coughs. Tom raises his cup in both hands to blow on it, his eyes staring over the rim of it at his mother for several moments. Then he slowly sets the cup down and awkwardly and hesitantly rises from the chair.

Tom (hoarsely): Mother. I—I apologize. Mother. (*Amanda draws a quick, shuddering breath. Her face works grotesquely. She breaks into childlike tears.*) I'm sorry for what I said, for everything that I said, I didn't mean it.

Amanda (sobbingly): My devotion has made me a witch and so I make myself hateful to my children!

Tom: No, you *don't.*

Amanda: I worry so much, don't sleep, it makes me nervous!

Tom (gently): I understand that.

Amanda: I've had to put up a solitary battle all these years. But you're my right-hand bower! Don't fall down, don't fail!

Tom (gently): I try, Mother.

Amanda (with great enthusiasm): Try and you will SUCCEED! (*The notion makes her breathless.*) Why, you—you're just *full* of natural endowments! Both of my children—they're *unusual* children! Don't you think I know it? I'm so—proud! Happy and—feel I've—so much to be thankful for but—Promise me one thing, son!

Tom: What, Mother?

Amanda: Promise, son you'll—never be a drunkard!

Tom (turns to her grinning): I will never be a drunkard, Mother.

Amanda: That's what frightened me so, that you'd be drinking! Eat a bowl of Purina!

Tom: Just coffee, Mother.

Amanda: Shredded wheat biscuit?

Tom: No. No, Mother, just coffee.

Amanda: You can't put in a day's work on an empty stomach. You've got ten minutes—don't gulp! Drinking too-hot liquids makes cancer of the stomach. . . . Put cream in.

Tom: No, thank you.

Amanda: To cool it.

Tom: No! No, thank you, I want it black.

Amanda: I know, but it's not good for you. We have to do all that we can to build ourselves up. In these trying times we live in, all that we have to cling to is—each other. . . . That's why it's so important to—Tom, I—I sent out your sister so I could discuss something with you. If you hadn't spoken I would have spoken to you. (*Sits down.*)

Tom (gently): What is it, Mother, that you want to discuss?

Amanda: Laura!

Tom puts his cup down slowly.

(Legend On Screen: "Laura.")

(Music: "The Glass Menagerie.")

Tom: —Oh.—Laura . . .

Amanda (touching his sleeve): You know how Laura is. So quiet but—still water runs deep! She notices things and I think she—broods about them. (*Tom looks up.*) A few days ago I came in and she was crying.

Tom: What about?

Amanda: You.

Tom: Me?

Amanda: She has an idea that you're not happy here.

Tom: What gave her that idea?

Amanda: What gives her any idea? However, you do act strangely. I—I'm not criticizing, understand *that!* I know your ambitions do not lie in the warehouse, that like everybody in the whole wide world—you've had to—make sacrifices, but—Tom—Tom—life's not easy, it calls for—Spartan endurance! There's so many things in my heart that I cannot describe to you! I've never told you but I—*loved* your father. . . .

Tom (gently): I know that, Mother.

Amanda: And you—when I see you taking after his ways! Staying out late—and—well, you had been drinking the night you were in that—terrifying condition! Laura says that you hate the apartment and that you go out nights to get away from it! Is that true, Tom?

Tom: No. You say there's so much in your heart that you can't describe to me. That's true of me, too. There's so much in my heart that I can't describe to you! So let's respect each other's—

Amanda: But, why—*why,* Tom—are you always so *restless?* Where do you go to, nights?

Tom: I—go to the movies.

Amanda: Why do you go to the movies so much, Tom?

Tom: I go to the movies because—I like adventure. Adventure is something I don't have much of at work, so I go to the movies.

Amanda: But, Tom, you go to the movies *entirely* too *much!*

Tom: I like a lot of adventure.

Amanda looks baffled, then hurt. As the familiar inquisition resumes he becomes hard and impatient again. Amanda slips back into her querulous attitude toward him.

(Image On Screen: Sailing Vessel With Jolly Roger.)

Amanda: Most young men find adventure in their careers.

Tom: Then most young men are not employed in a warehouse.

Amanda: The world is full of young men employed in warehouses and offices and factories.

Tom: Do all of them find adventure in their careers?

Amanda: They do or they do without it! Not everybody has a craze for adventure.

Tom: Man is by instinct a lover, a hunter, a fighter, and none of those instincts are given much play at the warehouse!

Amanda: Man is by instinct! Don't quote instinct to me! Instinct is something that people have got away from! It belongs to animals! Christian adults don't want it!

Tom: What do Christian adults want, then, Mother?

Amanda: Superior things! Things of the mind and the spirit! Only animals have to satisfy instincts! Surely your aims are somewhat higher than theirs! Than monkeys—pigs—

Tom: I reckon they're not.

Amanda: You're joking. However, that isn't what I wanted to discuss.

Tom (rising): I haven't much time.

Amanda (pushing his shoulder): Sit down.

Tom: You want me to punch in red at the warehouse, Mother?

Amanda: You have five minutes. I want to talk about Laura.

(Legend: "Plans And Provisions.")

Tom: All right! What about Laura?

Amanda: We have to be making plans and provisions for her. She's older than you, two years, and nothing has happened. She just drifts along doing nothing. It frightens me terribly how she just drifts along.

Tom: I guess she's the type that people call home girls.

Amanda: There's no such type, and if there is, it's a pity! That is unless the home is hers, with a husband!

Tom: What?

Amanda: Oh, I can see the handwriting on the wall as plain as I see the nose in front of my face! It's terrifying! More and more you remind me of your father! He was out all hours without explanation—Then *left! Goodbye!* And me with the bag to hold. I saw that letter you got from the Merchant Marine. I know what you're dreaming of. I'm not standing here blindfolded. Very well, then. Then *do* it! But not till there's somebody to take your place.

Tom: What do you mean?

Amanda: I mean that as soon as Laura has got somebody to take care of her, married, a home of her own, independent—why, then you'll be free to go wherever you please, on land, on sea, whichever way the wind blows! But until that time you've got to look out for your sister. I don't say me because I'm old and don't matter! I say for your sister because she's young and dependent. I put her in business college—a dismal failure! Frightened her so it made her sick to her stomach. I took her over to the Young People's League at the church. Another fiasco. She spoke to nobody, nobody spoke to her. Now all she does is fool with those pieces of glass and play those worn-out records. What kind of a life is that for a girl to lead!

Tom: What can I do about it?

Amanda: Overcome selfishness! Self, self, self is all that you ever think of! (*Tom springs up and crosses to get his coat. It is ugly and bulky. He pulls on a cap with earmuffs.*) Where is your muffler? Put your wool muffler on! (*He snatches it angrily from the closet and tosses it around his neck and pulls both ends tight.*) Tom! I haven't said what I had in mind to ask you.

Tom: I'm too late to—

Amanda (catching his arms—very importunately. Then shyly): Down at the warehouse, aren't there some—nice young men?

Tom: No!

Amanda: There *must* be—some . . .

Tom: Mother—

Gesture.

Amanda: Find one that's clean-living—doesn't drink and—ask him out for sister!

Tom: What?

Amanda: For *Sister!* To *meet!* Get *acquainted!*

Tom (*stamping to door*): Oh, my go-osh!

Amanda: Will you? (*He opens door. Imploringly.*) Will you? (*He starts down.*) Will you? Will, you, dear?

Tom (*calling back*): YES!

Amanda closes the door hesitantly and with a troubled but faintly hopeful expression.

(Screen Image: Glamor Magazine Cover.)

Spot Amanda at phone.

Amanda: Ella Cartwright? This is Amanda Wingfield! How are you, honey? How is that kidney condition? (*Count five.*) Horrors! (*Count five.*) You're a Christian martyr, yes, honey, that's what you are, a Christian martyr! Well, I just happened to notice in my little red book that your subscription to the *Companion* has just run out! I knew that you wouldn't want to miss out on the wonderful serial starting in this new issue. It's by Bessie Mae Hopper, the first thing she's written since *Honeymoon for Three.* Wasn't that a strange and interesting story? Well, this one is even lovelier, I believe. It has a sophisticated society background. It's all about the horsey set on Long Island!

(Fade Out.)

SCENE V

(Legend On Screen: "Annunciation.") *Fade with music.*

It is early dusk of a spring evening. Supper has just been finished in the Wingfield apartment. Amanda and Laura in light colored dresses are removing dishes from the table, in the upstage area, which is shadowy, their movements formalized almost as a dance or ritual, their moving forms as pale and silent as moths.

Tom, in white shirt and trousers, rises from the table and crosses toward the fire-escape.

Amanda (*as he passes her*): Son, will you do me a favor?

Tom: What?

Amanda: Comb your hair! You look so pretty when your hair is combed! (*Tom slouches on sofa with evening paper. Enormous caption "Franco Triumphs."*) There is only one respect in which I would like you to emulate your father.

Tom: What respect is that?

Amanda: The care he always took of his appearance. He never allowed himself to look untidy. (*He throws down the paper and crosses to fire-escape.*) Where are you going?

Tom: I'm going out to smoke.

Amanda: You smoke too much. A pack a day at fifteen cents a pack. How much would that amount to in a month? Thirty times fifteen is how much, Tom? Figure it out and you will be astounded at what you could save. Enough to give you a night-school course in accounting at Washington U! Just think what a wonderful thing that would be for you, son!

Tom is unmoved by the thought.

Tom: I'd rather smoke. (*He steps out on landing, letting the screen door slam.*)

Amanda (*sharply*): I know! That's the tragedy of it. . . . (*Alone, she turns to look at her husband's picture.*)

(Dance Music: "All The World Is Waiting For The Sunrise.")

Tom (*to the audience*): Across the alley from us was the Paradise Dance Hall. On evenings in spring the windows and doors were open and the music came outdoors. Sometimes the lights were turned out except for a large glass sphere that hung from the ceiling. It would turn slowly about and filter the dusk with delicate rainbow colors. Then the orchestra played a waltz or a tango, something that had a slow and sensuous rhythm. Couples would come outside, to the relative privacy of the alley. You could see them kissing behind ash-pits and telephone poles. This was the compensation for lives that passed like mine, without any change or adventure. Adventure and change were imminent in this year. They were waiting around the corner for all these kids. Suspended in the mist over Berchtesgaden, caught in the folds of Chamberlain's umbrella—In Spain there was Guernica! But here there was only hot swing music and liquor, dance halls, bars, and movies, and sex that hung in the gloom like a chandelier and flooded the world with brief, deceptive rainbows. . . . All the world was waiting for bombardments!

Amanda turns from the picture and comes outside.

Amanda (*sighing*): A fire-escape landing's a poor excuse for a porch. (*She spreads a newspaper on a step and sits down, gracefully and demurely as if she were settling into a swing on a Mississippi veranda.*) What are you looking at?

Tom: The moon.

Amanda: Is there a moon this evening?

Tom: It's rising over Garfinkel's Delicatessen.

Amanda: So it is! A little silver slipper of a moon. Have you made a wish on it yet?

Tom: Um-hum.

Amanda: What did you wish for?

Tom: That's a secret.

Amanda: A secret, huh? Well, I won't tell mine either. I will be just as mysterious as you.

Tom: I bet I can guess what yours is.

Amanda: Is my head so transparent?

Tom: You're not a sphinx.

Amanda: No, I don't have secrets. I'll tell you what I wished for on the moon. Success and happiness for my precious children! I wish for that whenever there's a moon, and when there isn't a moon, I wish for it, too.

Tom: I thought perhaps you wished for a gentleman caller.

Amanda: Why do you say that?

Tom: Don't you remember asking me to fetch one?

Amanda: I remember suggesting that it would be nice for your sister if you brought home some nice young man from the warehouse. I think I've made that suggestion more than once.

Tom: Yes, you have made it repeatedly.

Amanda: Well?

Tom: We are going to have one.

Amanda: What?

Tom: A gentleman caller!

(The Annunciation Is Celebrated With Music.)

Amanda rises.

(Image On Screen: Caller With Bouquet.)

Amanda: You mean you have asked some nice young man to come over?

Tom: Yep. I've asked him to dinner.

Amanda: You really did?

Tom: I did!

Amanda: You did, and did he—*accept?*

Tom: He did!

Amanda: Well, well—well, well! That's—lovely!

Tom: I thought that you would be pleased.

Amanda: It's definite, then?

Tom: Very definite.

Amanda: Soon?

Tom: Very soon.

Amanda: For heaven's sake, stop putting on and tell me some things, will you?

Tom: What things do you want me to tell you?

Amanda: Naturally I would like to know when he's *coming!*

Tom: He's coming tomorrow.

Amanda: Tomorrow?

Tom: Yep. Tomorrow.

Amanda: But, Tom!

Tom: Yes, Mother?

Amanda: Tomorrow gives me no time!

Tom: Time for what?

Amanda: Preparations! Why didn't you phone me at once, as soon as you asked him, the minute that he accepted? Then, don't you see, I could have been getting ready!

Tom: You don't have to make any fuss.

Amanda: Oh, Tom, Tom, Tom, of course I have to make a fuss! I want things nice, not sloppy! Not thrown together. I'll certainly have to do some fast thinking, won't I?

Tom: I don't see why you have to think at all.

Amanda: You just don't know. We can't have a gentleman caller in a pig-sty! All my wedding silver has to be polished, the monogrammed table linen ought to be laundered! The windows have to be washed and fresh curtains put up. And how about clothes? We have to *wear* something, don't we?

Tom: Mother, this boy is no one to make a fuss over!

Amanda: Do you realize he's the first young man we've introduced to your sister? It's terrible, dreadful, disgraceful that poor little sister has never received a single gentleman caller! Tom, come inside! (*She opens the screen door.*)

Tom: What for?

Amanda: I want to ask you some things.

Tom: If you're going to make such a fuss, I'll call it off, I'll tell him not to come.

Amanda: You certainly won't do anything of the kind. Nothing offends people worse than broken engagements. It simply means I'll have to work like a Turk! We won't be brilliant, but we'll pass inspection. Come on inside. (*Tom follows, groaning.*) Sit down.

Tom: Any particular place you would like me to sit?

Amanda: Thank heavens I've got that new sofa! I'm also making payments on a floor lamp I'll have sent out! And put the chintz covers on, they'll brighten things up! Of course I'd hoped to have these walls re-papered. . . . What is the young man's name?

Tom: His name is O'Connor.

Amanda: That, of course, means fish—tomorrow is Friday! I'll have that salmon loaf—with Durkee's dressing! What does he do? He works at the warehouse?

Tom: Of course! How else would I—

Amanda: Tom, he—doesn't drink?

Tom: Why do you ask me that?

Amanda: Your father *did!*

Tom: Don't get started on that!

Amanda: He *does* drink, then?

Tom: Not that I know of!

Amanda: Make sure, be certain! The last thing I want for my daughter's a boy who drinks!

Tom: Aren't you being a little premature? Mr. O'Connor has not yet appeared on the scene!

Amanda: But will tomorrow. To meet your sister, and what do I know about his character? Nothing! Old maids are better off than wives of drunkards!

Tom: Oh, my God!

Amanda: Be still!

Tom (*leaning forward to whisper*): Lots of fellows meet girls whom they don't marry!

Amanda: Oh, talk sensibly, Tom—and don't be sarcastic! (*She has gotten a hair-brush.*)

Tom: What are you doing?

Amanda: I'm brushing that cow-lick down! What is this young man's position at the warehouse?

Tom (*submitting grimly to the brush and the interrogation*): This young man's position is that of a shipping clerk, Mother.

Amanda: Sounds to me like a fairly responsible job, the sort of a job *you* would be in if you just had more *get-up*. What is his salary? Have you got any idea?

Tom: I would judge it to be approximately eighty-five dollars a month.

Amanda: Well—not princely, but—

Tom: Twenty more than I make.

Amanda: Yes, how well I know! But for a family man, eighty-five dollars a month is not much more than you can just get by on. . . .

Tom: Yes, but Mr. O'Connor is not a family man.

Amanda: He might be, mightn't he? Some time in the future?

Tom: I see. Plans and provisions.

Amanda: You are the only young man that I know of who ignores the fact that the future becomes the present, the present the past, and the past turns into everlasting regret if you don't plan for it!

Tom: I will think that over and see what I can make of it!

Amanda: Don't be supercilious with your mother! Tell me some more about this—what do you call him?

Tom: James D. O'Connor. The D. is for Delaney.

Amanda: Irish on *both* sides! *Gracious!* And doesn't drink?

Tom: Shall I call him up and ask him right this minute?

Amanda: The only way to find out about those things is to make discreet inquiries at the proper moment. When I was a girl in Blue Mountain and it was suspected that a young man drank, the girl whose attentions he had been receiving, if any girl *was*, would sometimes speak to the minister of his church, or rather her father would if her father was living, and sort of feel him out on the young man's character. That is the way such things are discreetly handled to keep a young woman from making a tragic mistake!

Tom: Then how did you happen to make a tragic mistake?

Amanda: That innocent look of your father's had everyone fooled! He *smiled*—the world was *enchanted!* No girl can do worse than put herself at the mercy of a handsome appearance! I hope that Mr. O'Connor is not too good-looking.

Tom: No, he's not too good-looking. He's covered with freckles and hasn't too much of a nose.

Amanda: He's not right-down homely, though?

Tom: Not right-down homely. Just medium homely, I'd say.

Amanda: Character's what to look for in a man.

Tom: That's what I've always said, Mother.

Amanda: You've never said anything of the kind and I suspect you would never give it a thought.

Tom: Don't be suspicious of me.

Amanda: At least I hope he's the type that's up and coming.

Tom: I think he really goes in for self-improvement.

Amanda: What reason have you to think so?

Tom: He goes to night school.

Amanda (*beaming*): Splendid! What does he do, I mean study?

Tom: Radio engineering and public speaking!

Amanda: Then he has visions of being advanced in the world! Any young man who studies public speaking is aiming to have an executive job some day! And radio engineering? A thing for the future! Both of these facts are very illuminating. Those are the sort of things that a mother should know concerning any young man who comes to call on her daughter. Seriously or—not.

Tom: One little warning. He doesn't know about Laura. I didn't let on that we had dark ulterior motives. I just said, why don't you come have dinner with us? He said okay and that was the whole conversation.

Amanda: I bet it was! You're eloquent as an oyster. However, he'll know about Laura when he gets here. When he sees how lovely and sweet and pretty she is, he'll thank his lucky stars he was asked to dinner.

Tom: Mother, you mustn't expect too much of Laura.

Amanda: What do you mean?

Tom: Laura seems all those things to you and me because she's ours and we love her. We don't even notice she's crippled any more.

Amanda: Don't say crippled! You know that I never allow that word to be used!

Tom: But face facts, Mother. She is and—that not's all—

Amanda: What do you mean "not all"?

Tom: Laura is very different from other girls.

Amanda: I think the difference is all to her advantage.

Tom: Not quite all—in the eyes of others—strangers—she's terribly shy and lives in a world of her own and those things make her seem a little peculiar to people outside the house.

Amanda: Don't say peculiar.

Tom: Face the facts. She is.

(The Dance-Hall Music Changes To A Tango That Has A Minor And Somewhat Ominous Tone.)

Amanda: In what way is she peculiar—may I ask?

Tom (*gently*): She lives in a world of her own—a world of—little glass ornaments, Mother. . . . (*Gets up. Amanda remains holding brush, looking at him, troubled.*) She plays old phonograph records and—that's about all—(*He glances at himself in the mirror and crosses to door.*)

Amanda (*sharply*): Where are you going?

Tom: I'm going to the movies. (*Out screen door.*)

Amanda: Not to the movies, every night to the movies! (*Follows quickly to screen door.*) I don't believe you always go to the movies! (*He is gone. Amanda looks worriedly after him for a moment. Then vitality and optimism return and she turns from the door. Crossing to portieres.*) Laura! Laura! (*Laura answers from kitchenette.*)

Laura: Yes, Mother.

Amanda: Let those dishes go and come in front! (*Laura appears with dish towel. Gaily.*) Laura, come here and make a wish on the moon!

Laura (*entering*): Moon—moon?

Amanda: A little silver slipper of a moon. Look over your left shoulder, Laura, and make a wish! (*Laura looks faintly puzzled as if called out of sleep. Amanda seizes her shoulders and turns her at an angle by the door.*) Now! Now, darling, wish!

Laura: What shall I wish for, Mother?

Amanda (*her voice trembling and her eyes suddenly filling with tears*): Happiness! Good Fortune!

The violin rises and the stage dims out.

SCENE VI

(Image: High-School Hero.)

Tom: And so the following evening I brought him home to dinner. I had known Jim slightly in high school. In high school Jim was a hero. He had tremendous Irish good nature and vitality with the scrubbed and polished look of white chinaware. He seemed to move in a continual spotlight. He was a star in basketball, captain of the debating club, president of the senior class and the glee club and he sang the male lead in the annual light operas. He was always running or bounding, never just walking. He seemed always at the point of defeating the law of gravity. He was shooting with such velocity through his adolescence that you would logically expect him to arrive at nothing short of the White House by the time he was thirty. But Jim apparently ran into more interference after his graduation from Soldan. His speed had definitely slowed. Six years after he left high school he was holding a job that wasn't much better than mine.

(Image: Clerk.)

He was the only one at the warehouse with whom I was on friendly terms. I was valuable to him as someone who could remember his former glory, who had seen him win basketball games and the silver cup in debating. He knew of my secret practice of retiring to a cabinet of the washroom to work on my poems when business was slack in the warehouse. He called me Shakespeare. And while the other boys in the warehouse regarded me with suspicious hostility, Jim took a humorous attitude toward me. Gradually his attitude affected the others, their hostility wore off and they also began to smile at me as people smile at an oddly fashioned dog who trots across their path at some distance.

I knew that Jim and Laura had known each other at Soldan, and I had heard Laura speak admiringly of his voice. I didn't know if Jim remembered her or not. In high school Laura had been as unobtrusive as Jim had been astonishing. If he did remember Laura, it was not as my sister, for when I asked him to dinner, he grinned and said, "You know, Shakespeare, I never thought of you as having folks!"

He was about to discover that I did. . . .

(Light Up Stage.)

(Legend On Screen: "The Accent Of A Coming Foot.")

Friday evening. It is about five o'clock of a late spring evening which comes "scattering poems in the sky."

A delicate lemony light is in the Wingfield apartment.

Amanda has worked like a Turk in preparation for the gentleman caller. The results are astonishing. The new floor lamp with its rose-silk shade is in place, a colored paper lantern conceals the broken light fixture in the ceiling, new billowing white curtains are at the windows, chintz covers are on chairs and sofa, a pair of new sofa pillows make their initial appearance.

Open boxes and tissue paper are scattered on the floor.

Laura stands in the middle with lifted arms while Amanda crouches before her, adjusting the hem of the new dress, devout and ritualistic. The dress is colored and designed by memory. The arrangement of Laura's hair is changed; it is softer and more becoming. A fragile, unearthly prettiness has come out in Laura: she is like a piece of translucent glass touched by light, given a momentary radiance, not actual, not lasting.

Amanda (impatiently): Why are you trembling?
Laura: Mother, you've made me so nervous!
Amanda: How have I made you nervous?
Laura: By all this fuss! You make it seem so important!
Amanda: I don't understand you, Laura. You couldn't be satisfied with just sitting home, and yet whenever I try to arrange something for you, you seem to resist it. (*She gets up.*) Now take a look at yourself. No, wait! Wait just a moment—I have an idea!
Laura: What is it now?

Amanda produces two powder puffs which she wraps in handkerchiefs and stuffs in Laura's bosom.

Laura: Mother, what are you doing?
Amanda: They call them "Gay Deceivers"!
Laura: I won't wear them!
Amanda: You will!
Laura: Why should I?
Amanda: Because, to be painfully honest, your chest is flat.
Laura: You make it seem like we were setting a trap.
Amanda: All pretty girls are a trap, a pretty trap, and men expect them to be.
(Legend: "A Pretty Trap.") Now look at yourself, young lady. This is the prettiest you will ever be! I've got to fix myself now! You're going to be surprised by your mother's appearance! (*She crosses through portieres, humming gaily.*)

Laura moves slowly to the long mirror and stares solemnly at herself.

A wind blows the white curtains inward in a slow, graceful motion and with a faint, sorrowful sighing.

Amanda (offstage): It isn't dark enough yet. (*She turns slowly before the mirror with a troubled look.*)

(Legend On Screen: "This Is My Sister: Celebrate Her With Strings!" Music.)

Amanda (laughing, off): I'm going to show you something. I'm going to make a spectacular appearance!

Laura: What is it, Mother?

Amanda: Possess your soul in patience—you will see! Something I've resurrected from that old trunk! Styles haven't changed so terribly much after all. . . . (*She parts the portieres.*) Now just look at your mother! (*She wears a girlish frock of yellowed voile with a blue silk sash. She carries a bunch of jonquils—the legend of her youth is nearly revived. Feverishly.*) This is the dress in which I led the cotillion. Won the cakewalk twice at Sunset Hill, wore one spring to the Governor's ball in Jackson! See how I sashayed around the ballroom, Laura? (*She raises her skirt and does a mincing step around the room.*) I wore it on Sundays for my gentlemen callers! I had it on the day I met your father— I had malaria fever all that spring. The change of climate from East Tennessee to the Delta—weakened resistance—I had a little temperature all the time—not enough to be serious—just enough to make me restless and giddy! Invitations poured in—parties all over the Delta!—"Stay in bed," said Mother, "you have fever!"—but I just wouldn't.—I took quinine but kept on going, going!—Evenings, dances!—Afternoons, long, long rides! Picnics—lovely!—So lovely, that country in May.—All lacy with dogwood, literally flooded with jonquils!—That was the spring I had the craze for jonquils. Jonquils became an absolute obsession. Mother said, "Honey, there's no more room for jonquils." And still I kept bringing in more jonquils. Whenever, wherever I saw them, I'd say, "Stop! Stop! I see jonquils!" I made the young men help me gather the jonquils! It was a joke, Amanda and her jonquils! Finally there were no more vases to hold them, every available space was filled with jonquils. No vases to hold them? All right, I'll hold them myself! And then I—(*She stops in front of the picture.*) (**Music.**) met your father! Malaria fever and jonquils and then—this—boy. . . . (*She switches on the rose-colored lamp.*) I hope they get here before it starts to rain. (*She crosses upstage and places the jonquils in bowl on table.*) I gave your brother a little extra change so he and Mr. O'Connor could take the service car home.

Laura (with altered look): What did you say his name was?

Amanda: O'Connor.

Laura: What is his first name?

Amanda: I don't remember. Oh, yes, I do. It was—Jim!

Laura sways slightly and catches hold of a chair.

(Legend On Screen. "Not Jim!")

Laura (faintly): Not—Jim!

Amanda: Yes, that was it, it was Jim! I've never known a Jim that wasn't nice!

(Music: Ominous.)

Laura: Are you sure his name is Jim O'Connor?

Amanda: Yes. Why?

Laura: Is he the one that Tom used to know in high school?

Amanda: He didn't say so. I think he just got to know him at the warehouse.

Laura: There was a Jim O'Connor we both knew in high school—(*Then, with effort.*) If that is the one that Tom is bringing to dinner—you'll have to excuse me, I won't come to the table.

Amanda: What sort of nonsense is this?

Laura: You asked me once if I'd ever liked a boy. Don't you remember I showed you this boy's picture?

Amanda: You mean the boy you showed me in the year-book?

Laura: Yes, that boy.

Amanda: Laura, Laura, were you in love with that boy?

Laura: I don't know, Mother. All I know is I couldn't sit at the table if it was him!

Amanda: It won't be him! It isn't the least bit likely. But whether it is or not, you will come to the table. You will not be excused.

Laura: I'll have to be, Mother.

Amanda: I don't intend to humor your silliness, Laura. I've had too much from you and your brother, both! So just sit down and compose yourself till they come. Tom has forgotten his key so you'll have to let them in, when they arrive.

Laura (panicky): Oh, Mother—*you* answer the door!

Amanda (lightly): I'll be in the kitchen—busy!

Laura: Oh, Mother, please answer the door, don't make me do it!

Amanda (crossing into kitchenette): I've got to fix the dressing for the salmon. Fuss, fuss—silliness!—over a gentleman caller!

Door swings shut. Laura is left alone.

(Legend: "Terror!")

She utters a low moan and turns off the lamp—sits stiffly on the edge of the sofa, knotting her fingers together.

(Legend On Screen: "The Opening Of A Door!")

Tom and Jim appear on the fire-escape steps and climb to landing. Hearing their approach, Laura rises with a panicky gesture. She retreats to the portieres.
The doorbell. Laura catches her breath and touches her throat. Low drums.

Amanda (calling): Laura, sweetheart! The door!

Laura stares at it without moving.

Jim: I think we just beat the rain.

Tom: Uh-huh. (*He rings again, nervously. Jim whistles and fishes for a cigarette.*)

Amanda (*very, very gaily*): Laura, that is your brother and Mr. O'Connor! Will you let them in, darling?

Laura crosses toward kitchenette door.

Laura (*breathlessly*): Mother—you go to the door!

Amanda steps out of kitchenette and stares furiously at Laura. She points imperiously at the door.

Laura: Please, please!

Amanda (*in a fierce whisper*): What is the matter with you, you silly thing?

Laura (*desperately*): Please, you answer it, *please!*

Amanda: I told you I wasn't going to humor you, Laura. Why have you chosen this moment to lose your mind?

Laura: Please, please, please, you go!

Amanda: You'll have to go to the door because I can't!

Laura (*despairingly*): I can't either!

Amanda: Why?

Laura: I'm *sick!*

Amanda: I'm sick, too—of your nonsense! Why can't you and your brother be normal people? Fantastic whims and behavior! (*Tom gives a long ring.*) Preposterous goings on! Can you give me one reason—(*Calls out lyrically.*) COMING! JUST ONE SECOND!—why should you be afraid to open a door? Now you answer it, Laura!

Laura: Oh, oh, oh . . . (*She returns through the portiers. Darts to the victrola and winds it frantically and turns it on.*)

Amanda: Laura Wingfield, you march right to that door!

Laura: Yes—yes, Mother!

A faraway, scratchy rendition of "Dardanella" softens the air and gives her strength to move through it. She slips to the door and draws it cautiously open. Tom enters with the caller, Jim O'Connor.

Tom: Laura, this is Jim. Jim, this is my sister, Laura.

Jim (*stepping inside*): I didn't know that Shakespeare had a sister!

Laura (*retreating stiff and trembling from the door*): How—how do you do?

Jim (*heartily extending his hand*): Okay!

Laura touches it hesitantly with hers.

Jim: Your hand's *cold,* Laura!

Laura: Yes, well—I've been playing the victrola. . . .

Jim: Must have been playing classical music on it! You ought to play a little hot swing music to warm you up!

Laura: Excuse me—I haven't finished playing the victrola. . . .

She turns awkwardly and hurries into the front room. She pauses a second by the victrola. Then catches her breath and darts through the portieres like a frightened deer.

Jim (*grinning*): What was the matter?

Tom: Oh—with Laura? Laura is—terribly shy.

Jim: Shy, huh? It's unusual to meet a shy girl nowadays. I don't believe you ever mentioned you had a sister.

Tom: Well, now you know. I have one. Here is the *Post Dispatch*. You want a piece of it?

Jim: Uh-huh.

Tom: What piece? The comics?

Jim: Sports! (*Glances at it.*) Ole Dizzy Dean is on his bad behavior.

Tom (*disinterest*): Yeah? (*Lights cigarette and crosses back to fire-escape door.*)

Jim: Where are *you* going?

Tom: I'm going out on the terrace.

Jim (*goes after him*): You know, Shakespeare—I'm going to sell you a bill of goods!

Tom: What goods?

Jim: A course I'm taking.

Tom: Huh?

Jim: In public speaking! You and me, we're not the warehouse type.

Tom: Thanks—that's good news. But what has public speaking got to do with it?

Jim: It fits you for—executive positions!

Tom: Awww.

Jim: I tell you it's done a helluva lot for me.

(Image: Executive At Desk.)

Tom: In what respect?

Jim: In every! Ask yourself what is the difference between you an' me and men in the office down front? Brains?—No!—Ability?—No! Then what? Just one little thing—

Tom: What is that one little thing?

Jim: Primarily it amounts to—social poise! Being able to square up to people and hold your own on any social level!

Amanda (*offstage*): Tom?

Tom: Yes, Mother?

Amanda: Is that you and Mr. O'Connor?

Tom: Yes, Mother.

Amanda: Well, you just make yourselves comfortable in there.

Tom: Yes, Mother.

Amanda: Ask Mr. O'Connor if he would like to wash his hands.

Jim: Aw—no—thank you—I took care of that at the warehouse. Tom—

Tom: Yes?

Jim: Mr. Mendoza was speaking to me about you.

Tom: Favorably?

Jim: What do you think?

Tom: Well—

Jim: You're going to be out of a job if you don't wake up.

Tom: I am waking up—

Jim: You show no signs.

Tom: The signs are interior.

(Image On Screen: The Sailing Vessel With Jolly Roger Again.)

Tom: I'm planning to change. (*He leans over the rail speaking with quiet exhilaration. The incandescent marquees and signs of the first-run movie houses light his face from across the alley. He looks like a voyager.*) I'm right at the point of committing myself to a future that doesn't include the warehouse and Mr. Mendoza or even a night-school course in public speaking.

Jim: What are you gassing about?

Tom: I'm tired of the movies.

Jim: Movies!

Tom: Yes, movies! Look at them—(*A wave toward the marvels of Grand Avenue.*) All of those glamorous people—having adventures—hogging it all, gobbling the whole thing up! You know what happens? People go to the *movies* instead of *moving*! Hollywood characters are supposed to have all the adventures for everybody in America, while everybody in America sits in a dark room and watches them have them! Yes, until there's a war. That's when adventure becomes available to the masses! *Everyone's* dish, not only Gable's! Then the people in the dark room come out of the dark room to have some adventures themselves—Goody, goody—It's our turn now, to go to the South Sea Island—to make a safari—to be exotic, far-off—But I'm not patient. I don't want to wait till then. I'm tired of the *movies* and I am *about* to move!

Jim (*incredulously*): Move?

Tom: Yes!

Jim: When?

Tom: Soon!

Jim: Where? Where?

Theme three music seems to answer the question, while Tom thinks it over. He searches among his pockets.

Tom: I'm starting to boil inside. I know I seem dreamy, but inside—well, I'm boiling! Whenever I pick up a shoe, I shudder a little thinking how short life is and what I am doing!—Whatever that means. I know it doesn't mean shoes—except as something to wear on a traveler's feet! (*Finds paper.*) Look—

Jim: What?

Tom: I'm a member.

Jim (*reading*): The Union of Merchant Seamen.

Tom: I paid my dues this month, instead of the light bill.

Jim: You will regret it when they turn the lights off.

Tom: I won't be here.

Jim: How about your mother?

Tom: I'm like my father. The bastard son of a bastard! See how he grins? And he's been absent going on sixteen years!

Jim: You're just talking, you drip. How does your mother feel about it?

Tom: Shhh—Here comes Mother! Mother is not acquainted with my plans!

Amanda (enters portieres): Where are you all?

Tom: On the terrace, Mother.

> *They start inside. She advances to them. Tom is distinctly shocked at her appearance. Even Jim blinks a little. He is making his first contact with girlish Southern vivacity and in spite of the night-school course in public speaking is somewhat thrown off the beam by the unexpected outlay of social charm.*
>
> *Certain responses are attempted by Jim but are swept aside by Amanda's gay laughter and chatter. Tom is embarrassed but after the first shock Jim reacts very warmly. Grins and chuckles, is altogether won over.*

(Image: Amanda As A Girl.)

Amanda (coyly smiling, shaking her girlish ringlets): Well, well, well, so this is Mr. O'Connor. Introductions entirely unnecessary. I've heard so much about you from my boy. I finally said to him, Tom—good gracious!—why don't you bring this paragon to supper? I'd like to meet this nice young man at the warehouse!—Instead of just hearing him sing your praises so much! I don't know why my son is so stand-offish—that's not Southern behavior! Let's sit down and—I think we could stand a little more air in here! Tom, leave the door open. I felt a nice fresh breeze a moment ago. Where has it gone? Mmm, so warm already! And not quite summer, even. We're going to burn up when summer really gets started. However, we're having—we're having a very light supper. I think light things are better fo' this time of year. The same as light clothes are. Light clothes an' light food are what warm weather calls fo'. You know our blood gets so thick during th' winter—it takes a while fo' us to *adjust* ou'selves!—when the season changes . . . It's come so quick this year. I wasn't prepared. All of a sudden—heavens! Already summer!—I ran to the trunk an' pulled out this light dress—Terribly old! Historical almost! But feels so good—so good an' co-ol, y'know. . . .

Tom: Mother—

Amanda: Yes, honey?

Tom: How about—supper?

Amanda: Honey, you go ask Sister if supper is ready! You know that Sister is in full charge of supper! Tell her you hungry boys are waiting for it. *(To Jim.)* Have you met Laura?

Jim: She—

Amanda: Let you in? Oh, good, you've met already! It's rare for a girl as sweet an' pretty as Laura to be domestic! But Laura is, thank heavens, not only pretty but also very domestic. I'm not at all. I never was a bit. I never could make a thing but angel-food cake. Well, in the South we had so many servants. Gone, gone, gone. All vestiges of gracious living! Gone completely! I wasn't prepared for what the future brought me. All of my gentlemen callers were sons of planters and so of course I assumed that I would be married to one and raise my family on a large piece of land with plenty of servants. But man proposes—and woman accepts the proposal!—To vary that old, old saying a little bit—I married no planter! I married a man who worked for the telephone company!—that gallantly smiling gentleman over there! (*Points to the picture.*) A telephone man who—fell in love with long-distance!—Now he travels and I don't even know where!—But what am I going on for about my—tribulations? Tell me yours—I hope you don't have any! Tom?

Tom (*returning*): Yes, Mother?

Amanda: Is supper nearly ready?

Tom: It looks to me like supper is on the table.

Amanda: Let me look—(*She rises prettily and looks through portieres.*) Oh, lovely—But where is Sister?

Tom: Laura is not feeling well and she says that she thinks she'd better not come to the table.

Amanda: What?—Nonsense!—Laura? Oh, Laura!

Laura (*offstage, faintly*): Yes, Mother.

Amanda: You really must come to the table. We won't be seated until you come to the table! Come in, Mr. O'Connor. You sit over there and I'll—Laura? Laura Wingfield! You're keeping us waiting, honey! We can't say grace until you come to the table!

The back door is pushed weakly open and Laura comes in. She is obviously quite faint, her lips trembling, her eyes wide and staring. She moves unsteadily toward the table.

(Legend: "Terror!")

Outside a summer storm is coming abruptly. The white curtains billow inward at the windows and there is a sorrowful murmur and deep blue dusk.
    Laura suddenly stumbles—She catches at a chair with a faint moan.

Tom: Laura!

Amanda: Laura! (*There is a clap of thunder.*) (**Legend: "Ah!"**) (*Despairingly.*) Why, Laura, you *are* sick, darling! Tom, help your sister into the living room, dear! Sit in the living room, Laura—rest on the sofa. Well! (*To the gentleman caller.*) Standing over the hot stove made her ill!—I told her that it was just too warm this evening, but—(*Tom comes back in. Laura is on the sofa.*) Is Laura all right now?

Tom: Yes.

Amanda: What *is* that? Rain? A nice cool rain has come up! (*She gives the gentleman caller a frightened look.*) I think we may—have grace—now ... (*Tom looks at her stupidly.*) Tom, honey—you say grace!

Tom: Oh ... "For these and all thy mercies—" (*They bow their heads, Amanda stealing a nervous glance at Jim. In the living room Laura, stretched on the sofa, clenches her hand to her lips, to hold back a shuddering sob.*) God's Holy Name be praised—

(The Scene Dims Out.)

SCENE VII

(A Souvenir.)

Half an hour later. Dinner is just being finished in the upstage area which is concealed by the drawn portieres.

As the curtain rises Laura is still huddled upon the sofa, her feet drawn under her, her head resting on a pale blue pillow, her eyes wide and mysteriously watchful. The new floor lamp with its shade of rose-colored silk gives a soft, becoming light to her face, bringing out the fragile, unearthly prettiness which usually escapes attention. There is a steady murmur of rain, but it is slackening and stops soon after the scene begins; the air outside becomes pale and luminous as the moon breaks out.

A moment after the curtain rises, the lights in both rooms flicker and go out.

Jim: Hey, there, Mr. Light Bulb!

Amanda laughs nervously.

(Legend: "Suspension Of A Public Service.")

Amanda: Where was Moses when the lights went out? Ha-ha. Do you know the answer to that one, Mr. O'Connor?
Jim: No, Ma'am, what's the answer?
Amanda: In the dark! (*Jim laughs appreciatively.*) Everybody sit still. I'll light the candles. Isn't it lucky we have them on the table? Where's a match? Which of you gentlemen can provide a match?
Jim: Here.
Amanda: Thank you, sir.
Jim: Not at all, Ma'am!
Amanda: I guess the fuse has burnt out. Mr. O'Connor, can you tell a burnt-out fuse? I know I can't and Tom is a total loss when it comes to mechanics. **(Sound: Getting Up: Voices Recede A Little To Kitchenette.)** Oh, be careful you don't bump into something. We don't want our gentleman caller to break his neck. Now wouldn't that be a fine howdy-do?
Jim: Ha-ha! Where is the fuse-box?
Amanda: Right here next to the stove. Can you see anything?
Jim: Just a minute.
Amanda: Isn't electricity a mysterious thing? Wasn't it Benjamin Franklin who tied a key to a kite? We live in such a mysterious universe, don't we? Some people say that science clears up all the mysteries for us. In my opinion it only creates more! Have you found it yet?

Jim: No, Ma'am. All these fuses look okay to me.

Amanda: Tom!

Tom: Yes, Mother?

Amanda: That light bill I gave you several days ago. The one I told you we got the notices about?

Tom: Oh.—Yeah.

(**Legend: "Ha!"**)

Amanda: You didn't neglect to pay it by any chance?

Tom: Why, I—

Amanda: Didn't! I might have known it!

Jim: Shakespeare probably wrote a poem on that light bill, Mrs. Wingfield.

Amanda: I might have known better than to trust him with it! There's such a high price for negligence in this world!

Jim: Maybe the poem will win a ten-dollar prize.

Amanda: We'll just have to spend the remainder of the evening in the nineteenth century, before Mr. Edison made the Mazda lamp!

Jim: Candlelight is my favorite kind of light.

Amanda: That shows you're romantic! But that's no excuse for Tom. Well, we got through dinner. Very considerate of them to let us get through dinner before they plunged us into everlasting darkness, wasn't it, Mr. O'Connor?

Jim: Ha-ha!

Amanda: Tom, as a penalty for your carelessness you can help me with the dishes.

Jim: Let me give you a hand.

Amanda: Indeed you will not!

Jim: I ought to be good for something.

Amanda: Good for something? (*Her tone is rhapsodic.*) You? Why, Mr. O'Connor, nobody, *nobody's* given me this much entertainment in years— as you have!

Jim: Aw, now, Mrs. Wingfield!

Amanda: I'm not exaggerating, not one bit! But Sister is all by her lonesome. You go keep her company in the parlor! I'll give you this lovely old candelabrum that used to be on the altar at the church of the Heavenly Rest. It was melted a little out of shape when the church burnt down. Lightning struck it one spring. Gypsy Jones was holding a revival at the time and he intimated that the church was destroyed because the Episcopalians gave card parties.

Jim: Ha-ha.

Amanda: And how about coaxing Sister to drink a little wine? I think it would be good for her! Can you carry both at once?

Jim: Sure. I'm Superman!

Amanda: Now, Thomas, get into this apron!

The door of kitchenette swings closed on Amanda's gay laughter; the flickering light approaches the portieres.

Laura sits up nervously as he enters. Her speech at first is low and breathless from the almost intolerable strain of being alone with a stranger.

(The Legend: "I Don't Suppose You Remember Me At All!")

In her first speeches in this scene, before Jim's warmth overcomes her paralyzing shyness, Laura's voice is thin and breathless as though she has run up a steep flight of stairs.

Jim's attitude is gently humorous. In playing this scene it should be stressed that while the incident is apparently unimportant, it is to Laura the climax of her secret life.

Jim: Hello, there, Laura.

Laura (faintly): Hello. (*She clears her throat.*)

Jim: How are you feeling now? Better?

Laura: Yes. Yes, thank you.

Jim: This is for you. A little dandelion wine. (*He extends it toward her with extravagant gallantry.*)

Laura: Thank you.

Jim: Drink it—but don't get drunk! (*He laughs heartily. Laura takes the glass uncertainly; laughs shyly.*) Where shall I set the candles?

Laura: Oh—oh, anywhere . . .

Jim: How about here on the floor? Any objections?

Laura: No.

Jim: I'll spread a newspaper under to catch the drippings. I like to sit on the floor. Mind if I do?

Laura: Oh, no.

Jim: Give me a pillow?

Laura: What?

Jim: A pillow!

Laura: Oh . . . (*Hands him one quickly.*)

Jim: How about you? Don't you like to sit on the floor?

Laura: Oh—yes.

Jim: Why don't you, then?

Laura: I—will.

Jim: Take a pillow! (*Laura does. Sits on the other side of the candelabrum. Jim crosses his legs and smiles engagingly at her.*) I can't hardly see you sitting way over there.

Laura: I can—see you.

Jim: I know, but that's not fair, I'm in the limelight. (*Laura moves her pillow closer.*) Good! Now I can see you! Comfortable?

Laura: Yes.

Jim: So am I. Comfortable as a cow. Will you have some gum?

Laura: No, thank you.

Jim: I think that I will indulge, with your permission. (*Musingly unwraps it and holds it up.*) Think of the fortune made by the guy that invented the first piece of chewing gum. Amazing, huh? The Wrigley Building is one of the sights of Chicago.—I saw it summer before last when I went up to the Century of Progress. Did you take in the Century of Progress?

Laura: No, I didn't.

Jim: Well, it was quite a wonderful exposition. What impressed me most was the Hall of Science. Gives you an idea of what the future will be in America, even more wonderful than the present time is! (*Pause. Smiling at her.*) Your brother tells me you're shy. Is that right, Laura?

Laura: I—don't know.

Jim: I judge you to be an old-fashioned type of girl. Well, I think that's pretty good type to be. Hope you don't think I'm being too personal—do you?

Laura (*hastily, out of embarrassment*): I believe I *will* take a piece of gum, if you—don't mind. (*Clearing her throat.*) Mr. O'Connor, have you—kept up with your singing?

Jim: Singing? Me?

Laura: Yes. I remember what a beautiful voice you had.

Jim: When did you hear me sing?

(Voice Offstage In The Pause.)

Voice (*offstage*):

O blow, ye winds, heigh-ho,
A-roving I will go!
I'm off to my love
With a boxing glove—
Ten thousand miles away!

Jim: You say you've heard me sing?

Laura: Oh, yes! Yes, very often . . . I—don't suppose you remember me—at all?

Jim (*smiling doubtfully*): You know I have an idea I've seen you before. I had that idea soon as you opened the door. It seemed almost like I was about to remember your name. But the name that I started to call you—wasn't a name! And so I stopped myself before I said it.

Laura: Wasn't it—Blue Roses?

Jim (*springs up, grinning*): Blue Roses! My gosh, yes—Blue Roses! That's what I had on my tongue when you opened the door! Isn't it funny what tricks your memory plays? I didn't connect you with the high school somehow or other. But that's where it was; it was high school. I didn't even know you were Shakespeare's sister! Gosh, I'm sorry.

Laura: I didn't expect you to. You—barely knew me!

Jim: But we did have a speaking acquaintance, huh?

Laura: Yes, we—spoke to each other.

Jim: When did you recognize me?

Laura: Oh, right away!

Jim: Soon as I came in the door?

Laura: When I heard your name I thought it was probably you. I knew that Tom used to know you a little in high school. So when you came in the door—Well, then I was—sure.

Jim: Why didn't you say something, then?

Laura (breathlessly): I didn't know what to say, I was—too surprised!

Jim: For goodness sakes! You know, this sure is funny!

Laura: Yes! Yes, isn't it, though . . .

Jim: Didn't we have a class in something together?

Laura: Yes, we did.

Jim: What class was that?

Laura: It was—singing—Chorus!

Jim: Aw!

Laura: I sat across the aisle from you in the Aud.

Jim: Aw.

Laura: Mondays, Wednesdays and Fridays.

Jim: Now I remember—you always came in late.

Laura: Yes, it was so hard for me, getting upstairs. I had that brace on my leg—it clumped so loud!

Jim: I never heard any clumping.

Laura (wincing at the recollection): To me it sounded like thunder!

Jim: Well, well, well. I never even noticed.

Laura: And everybody was seated before I came in. I had to walk in front of all those people. My seat was in the back row. I had to go clumping all the way up the aisle with everyone watching!

Jim: You shouldn't have been self-conscious.

Laura: I know, but I was. It was always such a relief when the singing started.

Jim: Aw, yes, I've placed you now! I used to call you Blue Roses. How was it that I got started calling you that?

Laura: I was out of school a little while with pleurosis. When I came back you asked me what was the matter. I said I had pleurosis—you thought I said Blue Roses. That's what you always called me after that!

Jim: I hope you didn't mind.

Laura: Oh, no—I liked it. You see, I wasn't acquainted with many—people. . . .

Jim: As I remember you sort of stuck by yourself.

Laura: I—I—never had much luck at—making friends.

Jim: I don't see why you wouldn't.

Laura: Well, I—started out badly.

Jim: You mean being—

Laura: Yes, it sort of—stood between me—

Jim: You shouldn't have let it!

Laura: I know, but it did, and—

Jim: You were shy with people!

Laura: I tried not to be but never could—

Jim: Overcome it?

Laura: No, I—I never could!

Jim: I guess being shy is something you have to work out of kind of gradually.

Laura (sorrowfully): Yes—I guess it—

Jim: Takes time!

Laura: Yes—

Jim: People are not so dreadful when you know them. That's what you have to remember! And everybody has problems, not just you, but practically everybody has got some problems. You think of yourself as having the only problems, as being the only one who is disappointed. But just look around you and you will see lots of people as disappointed as you are. For instance, I hoped when I was going to high school that I would be further along at this time, six years later, than I am now—You remember that wonderful write-up I had in *The Torch*?

Laura: Yes! (*She rises and crosses to table.*)

Jim: It said I was bound to succeed in anything I went into! (*Laura returns with the annual.*) Holy Jeez! *The Torch!* (*He accepts it reverently. They smile across it with mutual wonder. Laura crouches beside him and they begin to turn through it. Laura's shyness is dissolving in his warmth.*)

Laura: Here you are in *Pirates of Penzance!*

Jim (wistfully): I sang the baritone lead in that operetta.

Laura (rapidly): So—*beautifully!*

Jim (protesting): Aw—

Laura: Yes, yes—beautifully—beautifully!

Jim: You heard me?

Laura: All three times!

Jim: No!

Laura: Yes!

Jim: All three performances?

Laura (looking down): Yes.

Jim: Why?

Laura: I—wanted to ask you to—autograph my program.

Jim: Why didn't you ask me to?

Laura: You were always surrounded by your own friends so much that I never had a chance to.

Jim: You should have just—

Laura: Well, I—thought you might think I was—

Jim: Thought I might think you was—what?

Laura: Oh—

Jim (with reflective relish): I was beleaguered by females in those days.

Laura: You were terribly popular!

Jim: Yeah—

Laura: You had such a—friendly way—

Jim: I was spoiled in high school.

Laura: Everybody—liked you!

Jim: Including you?

Laura: I—yes, I—did, too—(*She gently closes the book in her lap.*)

Jim: Well, well, well!—Give me that program, Laura. (*She hands it to him. He signs it with a flourish.*) There you are—better late than never!

Laura: Oh, I—what a—surprise!

Jim: My signature isn't worth very much right now. But some day—maybe—it will increase in value! Being disappointed is one thing and being discouraged is something else. I am disappointed but I'm not discouraged. I'm twenty-three years old. How old are you?

Laura: I'll be twenty-four in June.

Jim: That's not old age!

Laura: No, but—

Jim: You finished high school?

Laura (with difficulty): I didn't go back.

Jim: You mean you dropped out?

Laura: I made bad grades in my final examinations. (*She rises and replaces the book and the program. Her voice strained.*) How is—Emily Meisenbach getting along?

Jim: Oh, that kraut-head!

Laura: Why do you call her that?

Jim: That's what she was.

Laura: You're not still—going with her?

Jim: I never see her.

Laura: It said in the Personal Section that you were—engaged!

Jim: I know, but I wasn't impressed by that—propaganda!

Laura: It wasn't—the truth?

Jim: Only in Emily's optimistic opinion!

Laura: Oh—

(Legend: "What Have You Done Since High School?")

Jim lights a cigarette and leans indolently back on his elbows smiling at Laura with a warmth and charm which light her inwardly with altar candles. She remains by the table and turns in her hands a piece of glass to cover her tumult.

Jim (after several reflective puffs on a cigarette): What have you done since high school? (*She seems not to hear him.*) Huh? (*Laura looks up.*) I said what have you done since high school, Laura?

Laura: Nothing much.

Jim: You must have been doing something these six long years.

Laura: Yes.

Jim: Well, then, such as what?

Laura: I took a business course at business college—

Jim: How did that work out?

Laura: Well, not very—well—I had to drop out, it gave me—indigestion—

Jim laughs gently.

Jim: What are you doing now?

Laura: I don't do anything—much. Oh, please don't think I sit around doing nothing! My glass collection takes up a good deal of my time. Glass is something you have to take good care of.

Jim: What did you say—about glass?

Laura: Collection I said—I have one—(*She clears her throat and turns away again, acutely shy.*)

Jim (*abruptly*): You know what I judge to be the trouble with you? Inferiority complex! Know what that is? That's what they call it when someone low-rates himself! I understand it because I had it, too. Although my case was not so aggravated as yours seems to be. I had it until I took up public speaking, developed my voice, and learned that I had an aptitude for science. Before that time I never thought of myself as being outstanding in any way whatsoever! Now I've never made a regular study of it, but I have a friend who says I can analyze people better than doctors that make a profession of it. I don't claim that to be necessarily true, but I can sure guess a person's psychology, Laura! (*Takes out his gum.*) Excuse me, Laura. I always take it out when the flavor is gone. I'll use this scrap of paper to wrap it in. I know how it is to get it stuck on a shoe. Yep—that's what I judge to be your principal trouble. A lack of confidence in yourself as a person. You don't have the proper amount of faith in yourself. I'm basing that fact on a number of your remarks and also on certain observations I've made. For instance that clumping you thought was so awful in high school. You say that you even dreaded to walk into class. You see what you did? You dropped out of school, you gave up an education because of a clump, which as far as I know was practically non-existent! A little physical defect is what you have. Hardly noticeable even! Magnified thousands of times by imagination! You know what my strong advice to you is? Think of yourself as *superior* in some way!

Laura: In what way would I think?

Jim: Why, man alive, Laura! Just look about you a little. What do you see? A world full of common people! All of 'em born and all of 'em going to die! Which of them has one-tenth of your good points! Or mine! Or anyone else's, as far as that goes—Gosh! Everybody excels in some one thing. Some in many! (*Unconsciously glances at himself in the mirror.*) All you've got to do is discover in *what*! Take me, for instance. (*He adjusts his tie at the mirror.*) My interest happens to lie in electrodynamics. I'm taking a course in radio engineering at night school, Laura, on top of a fairly responsible job at the warehouse. I'm taking that course and studying public speaking.

Laura: Ohhhh.

Jim: Because I believe in the future of television! (*Turning back to her.*) I wish to be ready to go up right along with it. Therefore I'm planning to get in on the ground floor. In fact, I've already made the right connections and all that remains is for the industry itself to get under way! Full steam—(*His eyes are starry.*) *Knowledge*—Zzzzzp! *Money*—Zzzzzp!—*Power!* That's the cycle democracy is built on! (*His attitude is convincingly dynamic. Laura stares at him, even her shyness eclipsed in her absolute wonder. He suddenly grins.*) I guess you think I think a lot of myself!

Laura: No—o-o-o, I—

Jim: Now how about you? Isn't there something you take more interest in than anything else?

Laura: Well, I do—as I said—have my—glass collection—

A peal of girlish laughter from the kitchen.

Jim: I'm not right sure I know what you're talking about. What kind of glass is it?

Laura: Little articles of it, they're ornaments mostly! Most of them are little animals made out of glass, the tiniest little animals in the world. Mother calls them a glass menagerie! Here's an example of one, if you'd like to see it! This one is one of the oldest. It's nearly thirteen. (*He stretches out his hand.*) (**Music: "The Glass Menagerie."**) Oh, be careful—if you breathe, it breaks!

Jim: I'd better not take it. I'm pretty clumsy with things.

Laura: Go on, I trust you with him! (*Places it in his palm.*) There now—you're holding him gently! Hold him over the light, he loves the light! You see how the light shines through him?

Jim: It sure does shine!

Laura: I shouldn't be partial, but he is my favorite one.

Jim: What kind of a thing is this one supposed to be?

Laura: Haven't you noticed the single horn on his forehead?

Jim: A unicorn, huh?

Laura: Mmm-hmmm!

Jim: Unicorns, aren't they extinct in the modern world?

Laura: I know!

Jim: Poor little fellow, he must feel sort of lonesome.

Laura (*smiling*): Well, if he does he doesn't complain about it. He stays on a shelf with some horses that don't have horns and all of them seem to get along nicely together.

Jim: How do you know?

Laura (*lightly*): I haven't heard any arguments among them!

Jim (*grinning*): No arguments, huh? Well, that's a pretty good sign! Where shall I set him?

Laura: Put him on the table. They all like a change of scenery once in a while!

Jim (*stretching*): Well, well, well, well—Look how big my shadow is when I stretch!

Laura: Oh, oh, yes—it stretches across the ceiling!

Jim (*crossing to door*): I think it's stopped raining. (*Opens fire-escape door.*) Where does the music come from?

Laura: From the Paradise Dance Hall across the alley.

Jim: How about cutting the rug a little, Miss Wingfield?

Laura: Oh, I—

Jim: Or is your program filled up? Let me have a look at it. (*Grasps imaginary card.*) Why, every dance is taken! I'll just have to scratch some out. (**Waltz Music: "La Golondrina."**) Ahhh, a waltz! (*He executes some sweeping turns by himself, then holds his arms toward Laura.*)

Laura (*breathlessly*): I—can't dance!

Jim: There you go, that inferiority stuff!

Laura: I've never danced in my life!

Jim: Come on, try!

Laura: Oh, but I'd step on you!

Jim: I'm not made out of glass.

Laura: How—how—how do we start?

Jim: Just leave it to me. You hold your arms out a little.

Laura: Like this?

Jim: A little bit higher. Right. Now don't tighten up, that's the main thing about it—relax.

Laura (laughing breathlessly): It's hard not to.

Jim: Okay.

Laura: I'm afraid you can't budge me.

Jim: What do you bet I can't? (*He swings her into motion.*)

Laura: Goodness, yes, you can!

Jim: Let yourself go, now, Laura, just let yourself go.

Laura: I'm—

Jim: Come on!

Laura: Trying!

Jim: Not so stiff—Easy does it!

Laura: I know but I'm—

Jim: Loosen th' backbone! There now, that's a lot better.

Laura: Am I?

Jim: Lots, lots better! (*He moves her about the room in a clumsy waltz.*)

Laura: Oh, my!

Jim: Ha-ha!

Laura: Goodness, yes you can!

Jim: Ha-ha-ha! (*They suddenly bump into the table, Jim stops.*) What did we hit on?

Laura: Table.

Jim: Did something fall off it? I think—

Laura: Yes.

Jim: I hope that it wasn't the little glass horse with the horn!

Laura: Yes.

Jim: Aw, aw, aw. Is it broken?

Laura: Now it is just like all the other horses.

Jim: It's lost its—

Laura: Horn! It doesn't matter. Maybe it's a blessing in disguise.

Jim: You'll never forgive me. I bet that that was your favorite piece of glass.

Laura: I don't have favorites much. It's no tragedy, Freckles. Glass breaks so easily. No matter how careful you are. The traffic jars the shelves and things fall off them.

Jim: Still I'm awfully sorry that I was the cause.

Laura (smiling): I'll just imagine he had an operation. The horn was removed to make him feel less—freakish! (*They both laugh.*) Now he will feel more at home with the other horses, the ones that don't have horns . . .

Jim: Ha-ha, that's very funny! (*Suddenly serious.*) I'm glad to see that you have a sense of humor. You know—you're—well—very different! Surprisingly different from anyone else I know! (*His voice becomes soft and hesitant with a genuine feeling.*) Do you mind me telling you that? (*Laura is abashed beyond speech.*) You make me feel sort of—I don't know how to put it! I'm usually pretty good at expressing things, but—This is something that I don't know how to say! (*Laura touches her throat and clears it—turns the broken unicorn in her hands.*) (*Even softer.*) Has anyone ever told you that you were pretty? (**Pause: Music.**) (*Laura looks up slowly, with wonder, and shakes her head.*) Well, you are! In a very different way from anyone else. And all the nicer because of the difference, too. (*His voice becomes low and husky. Laura turns away, nearly faint with the novelty of her emotions.*) I wish you were my sister. I'd teach you to have some confidence in yourself. The different people are not like other people, but being different is nothing to be ashamed of. Because other people are not such wonderful people. They're one hundred times one thousand. You're one times one! They walk all over the earth. You just stay here. They're common as—weeds, but—you—well, you're—*Blue Roses!*

(**Image On Screen: Blue Roses.**)

(**Music Changes.**)

Laura: But blue is wrong for—roses . . .

Jim: It's right for you—You're—pretty!

Laura: In what respect am I pretty?

Jim: In all respects—believe me! Your eyes—your hair—are pretty! Your hands are pretty! (*He catches hold of her hand.*) You think I'm making this up because I'm invited to dinner and have to be nice. Oh, I could do that! I could put on an act for you, Laura, and say lots of things without being very sincere. But this time I am. I'm talking to you sincerely. I happened to notice you had this inferiority complex that keeps you from feeling comfortable with people. Somebody needs to build your confidence up and make you proud instead of shy and turning away and—blushing—Somebody ought to—ought to—*kiss* you, Laura! (*His hand slips slowly up her arm to her shoulder.*) (**Music Swells Tumultuously.**) (*He suddenly turns her about and kisses her on the lips. When he releases her Laura sinks on the sofa with a bright, dazed look. Jim backs away and fishes in his pocket for a cigarette.*) (**Legend On Screen: "Souvenir."**) Stumble-john! (*He lights the cigarette, avoiding her look. There is a peal of girlish laughter from Amanda in the kitchen. Laura slowly raises and opens her hand. It still contains the little broken glass animal. She looks at it with a tender, bewildered expression.*) Stumble-john! I shouldn't have done that—That was way off the beam. You don't smoke, do you? (*She looks up, smiling, not hearing the question. He sits beside her a little gingerly. She looks at him speechlessly—waiting. He coughs decorously and moves a little farther aside as he considers the situation and senses her feelings, dimly, with perturbation. Gently.*) Would you—care for a—mint? (*She doesn't seem to hear him*

but her look grows brighter even.) Peppermint—Life Saver? My pocket's a regular drug store—wherever I go . . . (*He pops a mint in his mouth. Then gulps
and decides to make a clean breast of it. He speaks slowly and gingerly.*) Laura,
you know, if I had a sister like you, I'd do the same thing as Tom, I'd bring
out fellows—introduce her to them. The right type of boys of a type to—
appreciate her. Only—well—he made a mistake about me. Maybe I've got
no call to be saying this. That may not have been the idea in having me
over. But what if it was? There's nothing wrong about that. The only trouble
is that in my case—I'm not in a situation to—do the right thing. I can't take
down your number and say I'll phone. I can't call up next week and—ask for
a date. I thought I had better explain the situation in case you misunderstood it and—hurt your feelings. . . . (*Pause. Slowly, very slowly, Laura's look
changes, her eyes returning slowly from his to the ornament in her palm.*)

Amanda utters another gay laugh in the kitchen.

Laura (*faintly*): You—won't—call again?
Jim: No, Laura, I can't. (*He rises from the sofa.*) As I was just explaining, I've—
got strings on me, Laura, I've—been going steady! I go out all the time with
a girl named Betty. She's a home-girl like you, and Catholic, and Irish, and
in a great many ways we—get along fine. I met her last summer on a moonlight boat trip up the river to Alton, on the *Majestic*. Well—right away from
the start it was—love! (**Legend: Love!**) (*Laura sways slightly forward and
grips the arm of the sofa. He fails to notice, now enrapt in his own comfortable
being.*) Being in love has made a new man of me! (*Leaning stiffly forward,
clutching the arm of the sofa, Laura struggles visibly with her storm. But Jim is
oblivious, she is a long way off.*) The power of love is really pretty tremendous! Love is something that—changes the whole world, Laura! (*The storm
abates a little and Laura leans back. He notices her again.*) It happened that
Betty's aunt took sick, she got a wire and had to go to Centralia. So Tom—
when he asked me to dinner—I naturally just accepted the invitation, not
knowing that you—that he—that I—(*He stops awkwardly.*) Huh—I'm a
stumble-john! (*He flops back on the sofa. The holy candles in the altar of
Laura's face have been snuffed out! There is a look of almost infinite desolation.
Jim glances at her uneasily.*) I wish that you would—say something. (*She bites
her lip which was trembling and then bravely smiles. She opens her hand again on
the broken glass ornament. Then she gently takes his hand and raises it level with
her own. She carefully places the unicorn in the palm of his hand, then pushes his
fingers closed upon it.*) What are you—doing that for? You want me to have
him?—Laura? (*She nods.*) What for?
Laura: A—souvenir . . .

She rises unsteadily and crouches beside the victrola to wind it up.

(**Legend On Screen: "Things Have A Way Of Turning Out So Badly."**)

(**Or Image: "Gentleman Caller Waving Good-bye!—Gaily."**)

At this moment Amanda rushes brightly back in the front room. She bears a pitcher of fruit punch in an old-fashioned cut-glass pitcher and a plate of macaroons. The plate has a gold border and poppies painted on it.

Amanda: Well, well, well! Isn't the air delightful after the shower? I've made you children a little liquid refreshment. (*Turns gaily to the gentleman caller.*) Jim, do you know that song about lemonade?
    "Lemonade, lemonade
    Made in the shade and stirred with a spade—
    Good enough for any old maid!"

Jim (*uneasily*): Ha-ha! No—I never heard it.
Amanda: Why, Laura! You look so serious!
Jim: We were having a serious conversation.
Amanda: Good! Now you're better acquainted!
Jim (*uncertainly*): Ha-ha! Yes.
Amanda: You modern young people are much more serious-minded than my generation. I was so gay as a girl!
Jim: You haven't changed, Mrs. Wingfield.
Amanda: Tonight I'm rejuvenated! The gaiety of the occasion, Mr. O'Connor! (*She tosses her head with a peal of laughter. Spills lemonade.*) Oooo! I'm baptizing myself!
Jim: Here—let me—
Amanda (*setting the pitcher down*): There now. I discovered we had some maraschino cherries. I dumped them in, juice and all!
Jim: You shouldn't have gone to that trouble, Mrs. Wingfield.
Amanda: Trouble, trouble? Why it was loads of fun! Didn't you hear me cutting up in the kitchen? I bet your ears were burning! I told Tom how outdone with him I was for keeping you to himself so long a time! He should have brought you over much, much sooner! Well, now that you've found your way, I want you to be a very frequent caller! Not just occasional but all the time. Oh, we're going to have a lot of gay times together! I see them coming! Mmm, just breathe that air! So fresh, and the moon's so pretty! I'll skip back out—I know where my place is when young folks are having a— serious conversation!
Jim: Oh, don't go out, Mrs. Wingfield. The fact of the matter is I've got to be going.
Amanda: Going, now? You're joking! Why, it's only the shank of the evening, Mr. O'Connor!
Jim: Well, you know how it is.
Amanda: You mean you're a young workingman and have to keep workingmen's hours. We'll let you off early tonight. But only on the condition that next time you stay later. What's the best night for you? Isn't Saturday night the best night for you workingmen?
Jim: I have a couple of time-clocks to punch, Mrs. Wingfield. One at morning, another one at night!
Amanda: My, but you *are* ambitious! You work at night, too?

Jim: No, Ma'am, not work but—Betty! (*He crosses deliberately to pick up his hat. The band at the Paradise Dance Hall goes into a tender waltz.*)

Amanda: Betty? Betty? Who's—Betty? (*There is an ominous cracking sound in the sky.*)

Jim: Oh, just a girl. The girl I go steady with! (*He smiles charmingly. The sky falls.*)

(Legend: "The Sky Falls.")

Amanda (*a long-drawn exhalation*): Ohhhh . . . Is it a serious romance, Mr. O'Connor?

Jim: We're going to be married the second Sunday in June.

Amanda: Ohhhh—how nice! Tom didn't mention that you were engaged to be married.

Jim: The cat's not out of the bag at the warehouse yet. You know how they are. They call you Romeo and stuff like that. (*He stops at the oval mirror to put on his hat. He carefully shapes the brim and the crown to give a discreetly dashing effect.*) It's been a wonderful evening, Mrs. Wingfield. I guess this is what they mean by Southern hospitality.

Amanda: It really wasn't anything at all.

Jim: I hope it don't seem like I'm rushing off. But I promised Betty I'd pick her up at the Wabash depot, an' by the time I get my jalopy down there her train'll be in. Some women are pretty upset if you keep 'em waiting.

Amanda: Yes, I know—The tyranny of women! (*Extends her hand.*) Goodbye, Mr. O'Connor. I wish you luck—and happiness—and success! All three of them, and so does Laura!—Don't you, Laura?

Laura: Yes!

Jim (*taking her hand*): Goodbye, Laura. I'm certainly going to treasure that souvenir. And don't you forget the good advice I gave you. (*Raises his voice to a cheery shout.*) So long, Shakespeare! Thanks again, ladies—Good night!

He grins and ducks jauntily out.

Still bravely grimacing, Amanda closes the door on the gentleman caller. Then she turns back to the room with a puzzled expression. She and Laura don't dare to face each other. Laura crouches beside the victrola to wind it.

Amanda (*faintly*): Things have a way of turning out so badly. I don't believe that I would play the victrola. Well, well—well—Our gentleman caller was engaged to be married! Tom!

Tom (*from back*): Yes, Mother?

Amanda: Come in here a minute. I want to tell you something awfully funny.

Tom (*enters with macaroon and a glass of the lemonade*): Has the gentleman caller gotten away already?

Amanda: The gentleman caller has made an early departure. What a wonderful joke you played on us!

Tom: How do you mean?

Amanda: You didn't mention that he was engaged to be married.

Tom: Jim? Engaged?

Amanda: That's what he just informed us.

Tom: I'll be jiggered! I didn't know about that.

Amanda: That seems very peculiar.

Tom: What's peculiar about it?

Amanda: Didn't you call him your best friend down at the warehouse?

Tom: He is, but how did I know?

Amanda: It seems extremely peculiar that you wouldn't know your best friend was going to be married!

Tom: The warehouse is where I work, not where I know things about people!

Amanda: You don't know things anywhere! You live in a dream; you manufacture illusions! (*He crosses to door.*) Where are you going?

Tom: I'm going to the movies.

Amanda: That's right, now that you've had us make such fools of ourselves. The effort, the preparations, all the expense! The new floor lamp, the rug, the clothes for Laura! All for what? To entertain some other girl's fiancé! Go to the movies, go! Don't think about us, a mother deserted, an unmarried sister who's crippled and has no job! Don't let anything interfere with your selfish pleasure! Just go, go, go—to the movies!

Tom: All right, I will! The more you shout about my selfishness to me the quicker I'll go, and I won't go to the movies!

Amanda: Go, then! Then go to the moon—you selfish dreamer!

Tom smashes his glass on the floor. He plunges out on the fire-escape, slamming the door. Laura screams—cut by door.

 Dance-hall music up. Tom goes to the rail and grips it desperately, lifting his face in the chill white moonlight penetrating the narrow abyss of the alley.

(Legend On Screen: "And So Good-bye . . .")

Tom's closing speech is timed with the interior pantomime. The interior scene is played as though viewed through sound-proof glass. Amanda appears to be making a comforting speech to Laura who is huddled upon the sofa. Now that we cannot hear the mother's speech, her silliness is gone and she has dignity and tragic beauty. Laura's dark hair hides her face until at the end of the speech she lifts it to smile at her mother. Amanda's gestures are slow and graceful, almost dancelike, as she comforts the daughter. At the end of her speech she glances a moment at the father's picture—then withdraws through the portieres. At close of Tom's speech, Laura blows out the candles, ending the play.

Tom: I didn't go to the movies, I went much further—for time is the longest distance between two places—Not long after that I was fired for writing a poem on the lid of a shoe-box. I left Saint Louis. I descended the steps of this fire-escape for a last time and followed, from then on, in my father's footsteps, attempting to find in motion what was lost in space—I traveled around a great deal. The cities swept about me like dead leaves, leaves that were brightly colored but torn away from the branches. I would have stopped, but was pursued by something. It always came upon me unawares, taking me altogether by surprise. Perhaps it was a familiar bit of music. Perhaps it was only a piece of transparent glass. Perhaps I am walking along a street at night, in some strange city, before I have found companions. I pass the lighted window of a shop where perfume is sold. The window is filled with pieces of colored glass, tiny transparent bottles in delicate colors, like bits of a shattered rainbow. Then all at once my sister touches my shoulder. I turn around and look into her eyes . . . Oh, Laura, Laura, I tried to leave you behind me, but I am more faithful than I intended to be! I reach for a cigarette, I cross the street, I run into the movies or a bar, I buy a drink, I speak to the nearest stranger—anything that can blow your candles out! (*Laura bends over the candles.*)—for nowadays the world is lit by lightning! Blow out your candles, Laura—and so good-bye. . . .

She blows the candles out.

(**The Scene Dissolves.**)

WRITER'S PERSPECTIVE

Tennessee Williams

Tennessee Williams on Drama
How to Stage *The Glass Menagerie*   1945

Being a "memory play," *The Glass Menagerie* can be presented with unusual freedom of convention. Because of its considerably delicate or tenuous material, atmospheric touches and subtleties of direction play a particularly important part. Expressionism and all other unconventional techniques in drama have only one valid aim, and that is a closer approach to truth. When a play employs unconventional techniques, it is not, or certainly shouldn't be, trying to escape its responsibility of dealing with reality, or interpreting experience, but is actually or should be attempting to find a closer approach, a more penetrating and vivid expression of things as they are. The straight realistic play with its genuine Frigidaire and authentic ice-cubes, its characters that speak exactly as its audience speaks, corresponds to the academic landscape and has the same virtue of a photographic likeness. Everyone should know nowadays the unimportance of the photographic in art: that truth, life, or reality is an organic thing which the poetic imagination can represent or suggest, in essence, only through transformation, through changing into other forms than those which were merely present in appearance.

These remarks are not meant as a preface only to this particular play. They have to do with a conception of a new, plastic theater which must take the place of the exhausted theater of realistic conventions if the theater is to resume vitality as a part of our culture.

THE SCREEN DEVICE. There is *only one important difference between the original and acting version of the play* and that is the *omission* in the latter of the device which I tentatively included in my *original* script. This device was the use of a screen on which were projected magic-lantern slides bearing images or titles. I do not regret the omission of this device from the present Broadway production. The extraordinary power of Miss Taylor's performance° made it suitable to have the utmost simplicity in the physical production. But I think it may be interesting to some readers to see how this device was conceived. So I am putting it into the published manuscript. These images and legends, projected from behind, were cast on a section of wall between the front-room and dining-room areas, which should be indistinguishable from the rest when not in use.

The purpose of this will probably be apparent. It is to give accent to certain values in each case. Each scene contains a particular point (or several) which is structurally the most important. In an episodic play, such as this, the basic structure or narrative line may be obscured from the audience; the effect may seem fragmentary rather than architectural. This may not be the fault of the play so much as a lack of attention in the audience. The legend or image upon the screen will strengthen the effect of what is merely allusion in the writing and allow the primary point to be made more simply and lightly than if the entire responsibility were on the spoken lines. Aside from this structural value, I think the screen will have a definite emotional appeal, less definable but just as important. An imaginative producer or director may invent many other uses for this device than those indicated in the present script. In fact the possibilities of the device seem much larger to me than the instance of this play can possibly utilize.

THE MUSIC. Another extra-literary accent in this play is provided by the use of music. A single recurring tune, "The Glass Menagerie," is used to give emotional emphasis to suitable passages. This tune is like circus music, not when you are on the grounds or in the immediate vicinity of the parade, but when you are at some distance and very likely thinking of something else. It seems under those circumstances to continue almost interminably and it weaves in and out of your preoccupied consciousness; then it is the lightest, most delicate music in the world and perhaps the saddest. It expresses the surface vivacity of life with the underlying strain of immutable and inexpressible sorrow. When you look at a piece of delicately spun glass you think of two things: how beautiful it is and how easily it can be broken. Both of

---

Miss Taylor's performance: In the original Broadway production of the play in 1945 (see photograph on page 1711), the role of Amanda Wingfield, the mother, was played by veteran actress Laurette Taylor.

those ideas should be woven into the recurring tune, which dips in and out of the play as if it were carried on a wind that changes. It serves as a thread of connection and allusion between the narrator with his separate point in time and space and the subject of his story. Between each episode it returns as reference to the emotion, nostalgia, which is the first condition of the play. It is primarily Laura's music and therefore comes out most clearly when the play focuses upon her and the lovely fragility of glass which is her image.

THE LIGHTING. The lighting in the play is not realistic. In keeping with the atmosphere of memory, the stage is dim. Shafts of light are focused on selected areas or actors, sometimes in contradistinction to what is the apparent center. For instance, in the quarrel scene between Tom and Amanda, in which Laura has no active part, the clearest pool of light is on her figure. This is also true of the supper scene, when her silent figure on the sofa should remain the visual center. The light upon Laura should be distinct from the others, having a peculiar pristine clarity such as light used in early religious portraits of female saints or madonnas. A certain correspondence to light in religious paintings, such as El Greco's, where the figures are radiant in atmosphere that is relatively dusky, could be effectively used throughout the play. (It will also permit a more effective use of the screen.) A free, imaginative use of light can be of enormous value in giving a mobile, plastic quality to plays of a more or less static nature.

The Author's Production Notes to The Glass Menagerie

The theater is one of the most useful and expressive instruments for a country's edification, the barometer that registers its greatness or its decline.
—Federico García Lorca

David Henry Hwang

THE SOUND OF A VOICE   1983

David Henry Hwang (b. 1957) grew up in San Gabriel, California, the son of first-generation Chinese immigrants. Hwang was born into a family of musicians: his mother was a concert pianist, his sister plays cello in a string quartet, and he studied the violin. As a senior at Stanford University, he directed his first play, F. O. B. (1979)—in a dormitory lounge. F. O. B. was later staged at the New York Shakespeare Festival Public Theater and won a 1981 Obie Award. The Sound of a Voice (1983) was also produced at the Public Theater (as part of a double bill with another Hwang one-act play, The House of Sleeping Beauties). Hwang enjoyed his greatest commercial and critical success with M. Butterfly (1988), which won the Tony Award for best play. While some of his plays are realistic in their approach, Hwang has been fascinated by the possibilities of symbolic drama. In The Sound of a Voice, Hwang creates a timeless, placeless scene in which two characters named Man and Woman act out a story reminiscent of a folk legend or a traditional Japanese Nō drama (a type of symbolic aristocratic drama developed in fourteenth-century Japan in which a ghost acts out the struggles of his or her life for a traveler). Hwang's interest in nonrealistic drama has also led him into opera. He collaborated with composer Philip Glass on 1000 Airplanes on the Roof (1988), a science fiction music drama, and The Voyage (1992), an allegorical grand opera that was commissioned by New York's Metropolitan Opera for the cinque-centenary of Christopher Columbus's arrival in America. Among Hwang's recent plays are Face Value (1993) and Golden Child (1997). Hwang currently lives in San Francisco.

Characters

Man, *fifties, Japanese*
Woman, *fifties, Japanese*

Setting. *Woman's house, in a remote corner of the forest.*

Scene I. *Woman pours tea for Man. Man rubs himself, trying to get warm.*

Man: You're very kind to take me in.
Woman: This is a remote corner of the world. Guests are rare.
Man: The tea—you pour it well.
Woman: No.
Man: The sound it makes—in the cup—very soothing.
Woman: That is the tea's skill, not mine. (*She hands the cup to him.*) May I get
    you something else? Rice, perhaps?
Man: No.
Woman: And some vegetables?
Man: No, thank you.
Woman: Fish? (*Pause.*) It is at least two days' walk to the nearest village. I saw
    no horse. You must be very hungry. You would do a great honor to dine with
    me. Guests are rare.
Man: Thank you.
Woman (*Woman gets up, leaves. Man holds the cup in his hands, using it to warm
    himself. He gets up, walks around the room. It is sparsely furnished, drab, except
    for one shelf on which stands a vase of brightly colored flowers. The flowers stand
    out in sharp contrast to the starkness of the room. Slowly, he reaches out towards
    them. He touches them. Quickly, he takes one of the flowers from the vase, hides
    it in his clothes. He returns to where he had sat previously. He waits. Woman re-
    enters. She carries a tray with food.*): Please. Eat. It will give me great pleasure.
Man: This—this is magnificent.
Woman: Eat.
Man: Thank you. (*He motions for Woman to join him.*)
Woman: No, thank you.
Man: This is wonderful. The best I've tasted.
Woman: You are reckless in your flattery. But anything you say, I will enjoy
    hearing. It's not even the words. It's the sound of a voice, the way it moves
    through the air.
Man: How long has it been since you last had a visitor? (*Pause.*)
Woman: I don't know.
Man: Oh?
Woman: I lose track. Perhaps five months ago, perhaps ten years, perhaps yes-
    terday. I don't consider time when there is no voice in the air. It's pointless.
    Time begins with the entrance of a visitor, and ends with his exit.
Man: And in between? You don't keep track of the days? You can't help but no-
    tice—

Woman: Of course I notice.

Man: Oh.

Woman: I notice, but I don't keep track. (*Pause.*) May I bring out more?

Man: More? No. No. This was wonderful.

Woman: I have more.

Man: Really—the best I've had.

Woman: You must be tired. Did you sleep in the forest last night?

Man: Yes.

Woman: Or did you not sleep at all?

Man: I slept.

Woman: Where?

Man: By a waterfall. The sound of the water put me to sleep. It rumbled like the sounds of a city. You see, I can't sleep in too much silence. It scares me. It makes me feel that I have no control over what is about to happen.

Woman: I feel the same way.

Man: But you live here—alone?

Woman: Yes.

Man: It's so quiet here. How can you sleep?

Woman: Tonight, I'll sleep. I'll lie down in the next room, and hear your breathing through the wall, and fall asleep shamelessly. There will be no silence.

Man: You're very kind to let me stay here.

Woman: This is yours. (*She unrolls a mat; there is a beautiful design of a flower on the mat. The flower looks exactly like the flowers in the vase.*)

Man: Did you make it yourself?

Woman: Yes. There is a place to wash outside.

Man: Thank you.

Woman: Goodnight.

Man: Goodnight. (*Man starts to leave.*)

Woman: May I know your name?

Man: No. I mean, I would rather not say. If I gave you a name, it would only be made-up. Why should I deceive you? You are too kind for that.

Woman: Then what should I call you? Perhaps—"Man Who Fears Silence"?

Man: How about, "Man Who Fears Women"?

Woman: That name is much too common.

Man: And you?

Woman: Yokiko.

Man: That's your name?

Woman: It's what you may call me.

Man: Goodnight, Yokiko. You are very kind.

Woman: You are very smart. Goodnight. (*Man exits. Hanako° goes to the mat. She tidies it, brushes it off. She goes to the vase. She picks up the flowers, studies them. She carries them out of the room with her. Man re-enters. He takes off his*

Hanako: The woman.

outer clothing. He glimpses the spot where the vase used to sit. He reaches into his clothing, pulls out the stolen flower. He studies it. He puts it underneath his head as he lies down to sleep, like a pillow. He starts to fall asleep. Suddenly, a start. He picks up his head. He listens.)

Scene II. *Dawn. Man is getting dressed. Woman enters with food.*

Woman: Good morning.
Man: Good morning, Yokiko.
Woman: You weren't planning to leave?
Man: I have quite a distance to travel today.
Woman: Please. (*She offers him food.*)
Man: Thank you.
Woman: May I ask where you're travelling to?
Man: It's far.
Woman: I know this region well.
Man: Oh? Do you leave the house often?
Woman: I used to. I used to travel a great deal. I know the region from those days.
Man: You probably wouldn't know the place I'm headed.
Woman: Why not?
Man: It's new. A new village. It didn't exist in "those days." (*Pause.*)
Woman: I thought you said you wouldn't deceive me.
Man: I didn't. You don't believe me, do you?
Woman: No.
Man: Then I didn't deceive you. I'm travelling. That much is true.
Woman: Are you in such a hurry?
Man: Travelling is a matter of timing. Catching the light. (*Woman exits; Man finishes eating, puts down his bowl. Woman re-enters with the vase of flowers.*) Where did you find those? They don't grow native around these parts, do they?
Woman: No; they've all been brought in. They were brought in by visitors. Such as yourself. They were left here. In my custody.
Man: But—they look so fresh, so alive.
Woman: I take care of them. They remind me of the people and places outside this house.
Man: May I touch them?
Woman: Certainly.
Man: These have just blossomed.
Woman: No; they were in bloom yesterday. If you'd noticed them before, you would know that.
Man: You must have received these very recently. I would guess—within five days.
Woman: I don't know. But I wouldn't trust your estimate. It's all in the amount of care you show to them. I create a world which is outside the realm of what you know.

Man: What do you do?

Woman: I can't explain. Words are too inefficient. It takes hundreds of words to describe a single act of caring. With hundreds of acts, words become irrelevant. (*Pause.*) But perhaps you can stay.

Man: How long?

Woman: As long as you'd like.

Man: Why?

Woman: To see how I care for them.

Man: I *am* tired.

Woman: Rest.

Man: The light?

Woman: It will return.

Scene III. *Man is carrying chopped wood. He is stripped to the waist. Woman enters.*

Woman: You're very kind to do that for me.

Man: I enjoy it, you know. Chopping wood. It's clean. No questions. You take your axe, you stand up the log, you aim—pow!—you either hit it or you don't. Success or failure.

Woman: You seem to have been very successful today.

Man: Why shouldn't I be? It's a beautiful day. I can see to those hills. The trees are cool. The sun is gentle. Ideal. If a man can't be successful on a day like this, he might as well kick the dust up into his own face. (Man *notices* Woman *staring at him.* Man *pats his belly, looks at her.*) Protection from falls.

Woman: What? (Man *pinches his belly, showing some fat.*) Oh. Don't be silly. (Man *begins slapping the fat on his belly to a rhythm.*)

Man: Listen—I can make music—see?—that wasn't always possible. But now— that I've developed this—whenever I need entertainment.

Woman: You shouldn't make fun of your body.

Man: Why not? I saw you. You were staring.

Woman: I wasn't making fun. (Man *inflates his cheeks.*) I was just—stop that!

Man: Then why were you staring?

Woman: I was—

Man: Laughing?

Woman: No.

Man: Well?

Woman: I was—Your body. It's . . . strong. (*Pause.*)

Man: People say that. But they don't know. I've heard that age brings wisdom. That's a laugh. The years don't accumulate here. They accumulate here. (*Pause; he pinches his belly.*) But today is a day to be happy, right? The woods. The sun. Blue. It's a happy day. I'm going to chop wood.

Woman: There's nothing left to chop. Look.

Man: Oh. I guess . . . that's it.

Woman: Sit. Here.

Man: But—

Woman: There's nothing left. (*Man sits; Woman stares at his belly.*) Learn to love it.

Man: Don't be ridiculous.

Woman: Touch it.

Man: It's flabby.

Woman: It's strong.

Man: It's weak.

Woman: And smooth.

Man: Do you mind if I put on my shirt?

Woman: Of course not. Shall I get it for you?

Man: No. No. Just sit there. (*Man starts to put on his shirt. He pauses, studies his body.*) You think it's cute, huh?

Woman: I think you should learn to love it. (*Man pats his belly, talks to it.*)

Man (To belly): You're okay, sir. You hang onto my body like a great horseman.

Woman: Not like that.

Man (Ibid.): You're also faithful. You'll never leave me for another man.

Woman: No.

Man: What do you want me to say? (*Woman walks over to Man. She touches his belly with her hand. They look at each other.*)

Scene IV. *Night. Man is alone. Flowers are gone from stand. Mat is unrolled. Man lies on it, sleeping. Suddenly, he starts. He lifts up his head. He listens. Silence. He goes back to sleep. Another start. He lifts up his head, strains to hear. Slowly, we begin to make out the strains of a single* shakuhachi° *playing a haunting line. It is very soft. He strains to hear it. The instrument slowly fades out. He waits for it to return, but it does not. He takes out the stolen flower. He stares into it.*

Scene V. *Day. Woman is cleaning, while Man relaxes. She is on her hands and knees, scrubbing. She is dressed in a simple outfit, for working. Her hair is tied back. Man is sweating. He has not, however, removed his shirt.*

Man: I heard your playing last night.

Woman: My playing?

Man: Shakuhachi.

Woman: Oh.

Man: You played very softly. I had to strain to hear it. Next time, don't be afraid. Play out. Fully. Clear. It must've been very beautiful, if only I could've heard it clearly. Why don't you play for me sometime?

Woman: I'm very shy about it.

Man: Why?

Woman: I play for my own satisfaction. That's all. It's something I developed on my own. I don't know if it's at all acceptable by outside standards.

Man: Play for me. I'll tell you.

---

shakuhachi: A Japanese bamboo flute.

Woman: No; I'm sure you're too knowledgeable in the arts.

Man: Who? Me?

Woman: You being from the city and all.

Man: I'm ignorant, believe me.

Woman: I'd play, and you'd probably bite your cheek.

Man: Ask me a question about music. Any question. I'll answer incorrectly. I guarantee it.

Woman: Look at this.

Man: What?

Woman: A stain.

Man: Where?

Woman: Here? See? I can't get it out.

Man: Oh. I hadn't noticed it before.

Woman: I notice it every time I clean.

Man: Here. Let me try.

Woman: Thank you.

Man: Ugh. It's tough.

Woman: I know.

Man: How did it get here?

Woman: It's been there as long as I've lived here.

Man: I hardly stand a chance. (*Pause.*) But I'll try. Uh—one—two—three—four! One—two—three—four! See, you set up . . . gotta set up . . . a rhythm—two—three—four. Like fighting! Like battle! One—two—three—four! Used to practice with a rhythm . . . beat . . . battle! Yes! (*The stain starts to fade away.*) Look—it's—yes!—whoo!—there it goes—got the sides—the edges—yes!—fading quick—fading away—ooo—here we come—towards the center—to the heart—two—three—four—slow—slow death—tough—dead! (*Man rolls over in triumphant laughter.*)

Woman: Dead.

Man: I got it! I got it! Whoo! A little rhythm! All it took! Four! Four!

Woman: Thank you.

Man: I didn't think I could do it—but there—it's gone—I did it!

Woman: Yes. You did.

Man: And you—you were great.

Woman: No—I was carried away.

Man: We were a team! You and me!

Woman: I only provided encouragement.

Man: You were great! You were! (*Man grabs Woman. Pause.*)

Woman: It's gone. Thank you. Would you like to hear me play *shakuhachi?*

Man: Yes I would.

Woman: I don't usually play for visitors. It's so . . . . I'm not sure. I developed it—all by myself—in times when I was alone. I heard nothing—no human voice. So I learned to play *shakuhachi*. I tried to make these sounds resemble the human voice. The *shakuhachi* became my weapon. To ward off the air. It kept me from choking on many a silent evening.

Man: I'm here. You can hear my voice.

Woman: Speak again.
Man: I will.

Scene VI. *Night. Man is sleeping. Suddenly, a start. He lifts his head up. He listens. Silence. He strains to hear. The shakuhachi melody rises up once more. This time, however, it becomes louder and more clear than before. He gets up. He cannot tell from what direction the music is coming. He walks around the room, putting his ear to different places in the wall, but he cannot locate the sound. It seems to come from all directions at once, as omnipresent as the air. Slowly, he moves towards the wall with the sliding panel through which the Woman enters and exits. He puts his ear against it, thinking the music may be coming from there. Slowly, he slides the door open just a crack, ever so carefully. He peeks through the crack. As he peeks through, the Upstage wall of the set becomes transparent, and through the scrim, we are able to see what he sees. Woman is Upstage of the scrim. She is tending a room filled with potted and vased flowers of all variety. The lushness and beauty of the room Upstage of the scrim stands out in stark contrast to the barrenness of the main set. She is also transformed. She is a young woman. She is beautiful. She wears a brightly colored kimono. Man observes this scene for a long time. He then slides the door shut. The scrim returns to opaque. The music continues. He returns to his mat. He picks up the stolen flower. It is brown and wilted, dead. He looks at it. The music slowly fades out.*

Scene VII. *Morning. Man is half-dressed. He is practicing sword maneuvers. He practices with the feel of a man whose spirit is willing, but the flesh is inept. He tries to execute deft movements, but is dissatisfied with his efforts. He curses himself, and returns to basic exercises. Suddenly, he feels something buzzing around his neck—a mosquito. He slaps his neck, but misses it. He sees it flying near him. He swipes at it with his sword. He keeps missing. Finally, he thinks he's hit it. He runs over, kneels down to recover the fallen insect. He picks up two halves of a mosquito on two different fingers. Woman enters the room. She looks as she normally does. She is carrying a vase of flowers, which she places on its shelf.*

Man: Look.
Woman: I'm sorry?
Man: Look.
Woman: What? (*He brings over the two halves of mosquito to show her.*)
Man: See?
Woman: Oh.
Man: I hit it—chop!
Woman: These are new forms of target practice?
Man: Huh? Well—yes—in a way.
Woman: You seem to do well at it.
Man: Thank you. For last night. I heard your *shakuhachi*. It was very loud, strong—good tone.
Woman: Did you enjoy it? I wanted you to enjoy it. If you wish, I'll play it for you every night.
Man: Every night!

Woman: If you wish.

Man: No—I don't—I don't want you to treat me like a baby.

Woman: What? I'm not.

Man: Oh, yes. Like a baby. Who you must feed in the middle of the night or he cries. Waaah! Waaah!

Woman: Stop that!

Man: You need your sleep.

Woman: I don't mind getting up for you. (*Pause.*) I would enjoy playing for you. Every night. While you sleep. It will make me feel—like I'm shaping your dreams. I go through long stretches when there is no one in my dreams. It's terrible. During those times, I avoid my bed as much as possible. I paint. I weave. I play *shakuhachi.* I sit on mats and rub powder into my face. Anything to keep from facing a bed with no dreams. It is like sleeping on ice.

Man: What do you dream of now?

Woman: Last night—I dreamt of you. I don't remember what happened. But you were very funny. Not in a mocking way. I wasn't laughing at you. But you made me laugh. And you were very warm. I remember that. (*Pause.*) What do you remember about last night?

Man: Just your playing. That's all. I got up, listened to it, and went back to sleep. (*Man gets up, resumes practicing with his sword.*)

Woman: Another mosquito bothering you?

Man: Just practicing. Ah! Weak! Too weak! I tell you, it wasn't always like this. I'm telling you, there were days when I could chop the fruit from a tree without ever taking my eyes off the ground. (*He continues practicing.*) You ever use one of these?

Woman: I've had to pick one up, yes.

Man: Oh?

Woman: You forget—I live alone—out here—there is . . . not much to sustain me but what I manage to learn myself. It wasn't really a matter of choice.

Man: I used to be very good, you know. Perhaps I can give you some pointers.

Woman: I'd really rather not.

Man: C'mon—a woman like you—you're absolutely right. You need to know how to defend yourself.

Woman: As you wish.

Man: Do you have something to practice with?

Woman: Yes. Excuse me. (*She exits. He practices more. She re-enters with two wooden sticks. He takes one of them.*) Will these do?

Man: Nice. Now, show me what you can do.

Woman: I'm sorry?

Man: Run up and hit me.

Woman: Please.

Man: Go on—I'll block it.

Woman: I feel so . . . undignified.

Man: Go on. (*She hits him playfully with stick.*) Not like that!

Woman: I'll try to be gentle.

Man: What?

Woman: I don't want to hurt you.

Man: You won't—Hit me! (*Woman charges at Man, quickly, deftly. She scores a hit.*) Oh!

Woman: Did I hurt you?

Man: No—you were—let's try that again. (*They square off again. Woman rushes forward. She appears to attempt a strike. He blocks that apparent strike, which turns out to be a feint. She scores.*) Huh?

Woman: Did I hurt you? I'm sorry.

Man: No.

Woman: I hurt you.

Man: No.

Woman: Do you wish to hit me?

Man: No.

Woman: Do you want me to try again?

Man: No.

Woman: Thank you.

Man: Just practice there—by yourself—let me see you run through some maneuvers.

Woman: Must I?

Man: Yes! Go! (*She goes to an open area.*) My greatest strength was always as a teacher. (*Woman executes a series of deft movements. Her whole manner is transformed. Man watches with increasing amazement. Her movements end. She regains her submissive manner.*)

Woman: I'm so embarrassed. My skills—they're so—inappropriate. I look like a man.

Man: Where did you learn that?

Woman: There is much time to practice here.

Man: But you—the techniques.

Woman: I don't know what's fashionable in the outside world. (*Pause.*) Are you unhappy?

Man: No.

Woman: Really?

Man: I'm just . . . surprised.

Woman: You think it's unbecoming for a woman.

Man: No, no. Not at all.

Woman: You want to leave.

Man: No!

Woman: All visitors do. I know. I've met many. They say they'll stay. And they do. For a while. Until they see too much. Or they learn something new. There are boundaries outside of which visitors do not want to see me step. Only who knows what those boundaries are? Not I. They change with every visitor. You have to be careful not to cross them, but you never know where they are. And one day, inevitably, you step outside the lines. The visitor knows. You don't. You didn't know that you'd done anything different. You thought it was just another part of you. The visitor sneaks away. The next day, you learn that you had stepped outside his heart. I'm afraid you've seen too much.

Man: There are stories.

Woman: What?

Man: People talk.

Woman: Where? We're two days from the nearest village.

Man: Word travels.

Woman: What are you talking about?

Man: There are stories about you. I heard them. They say that your visitors never leave this house.

Woman: That's what you heard?

Man: They say you imprison them.

Woman: Then you were a fool to come here.

Man: Listen.

Woman: Me? Listen? You. Look! Where are these prisoners? Have you seen any?

Man: They told me you were very beautiful.

Woman: Then they are blind as well as ignorant.

Man: You are.

Woman: What?

Man: Beautiful.

Woman: Stop that! My skin feels like seaweed.

Man: I didn't realize it at first. I must confess—I didn't. But over these few days—your face has changed for me. The shape of it. The feel of it. The color. All changed. I look at you now, and I'm no longer sure you are the same woman who had poured tea for me just a week ago. And because of that I remembered—how little I know about a face that changes in the night. (*Pause.*) Have you heard those stories?

Woman: I don't listen to old wives' tales.

Man: But have you heard them?

Woman: Yes. I've heard them. From other visitors—young—hotblooded—or old—who came here because they were told great glory was to be had by killing the witch in the woods.

Man: I was told that no man could spend time in this house without falling in love.

Woman: Oh? So why did you come? Did you wager gold that you could come out untouched? The outside world is so flattering to me. And you—are you like the rest? Passion passing through your heart so powerfully that you can't hold onto it?

Man: No! I'm afraid!

Woman: Of what?

Man: Sometimes—when I look into the flowers, I think I hear a voice—from inside—a voice beneath the petals. A human voice.

Woman: What does it say? "Let me out"?

Man: No. Listen. It hums. It hums with the peacefulness of one who is completely imprisoned.

Woman: I understand that if you listen closely enough, you can hear the ocean.

Man: No. Wait. Look at it. See the layers? Each petal—hiding the next. Try and see where they end. You can't. Follow them down, further down, around—and as you come down—faster and faster—the breeze picks up. The breeze becomes a wail. And in that rush of air—in the silent midst of it—you can hear a voice.

Woman (Woman grabs flower from Man.): So, you believe I water and prune my lovers? How can you be so foolish? (*She snaps the flower in half, at the stem. She throws it to the ground.*) Do you come only to leave again? To take a chunk of my heart, then leave with your booty on your belt, like a prize? You say that I imprison hearts in these flowers? Well, bits of my heart are trapped with travellers across this land. I can't even keep track. So kill me. If you came here to destroy a witch, kill me now. I can't stand to have it happen again.

Man: I won't leave you.

Woman: I believe you. (*She looks at the flower that she has broken, bends to pick it up. He touches her. They embrace.*)

Scene VIII. *Day. Woman wears a simple undergarment, over which she is donning a brightly colored kimono, the same one we saw her wearing Upstage of the scrim. Man stands apart.*

Woman: I can't cry. I don't have the capacity. Right from birth, I didn't cry. My mother and father were shocked. They thought they'd given birth to a ghost, a demon. Sometimes I've thought myself that. When great sadness has welled up inside me, I've prayed for a means to release the pain from my body. But my prayers went unanswered. The grief remained inside me. It would sit like water, still. (*Pause; she models her kimono.*) Do you like it?

Man: Yes, it's beautiful.

Woman: I wanted to wear something special today.

Man: It's beautiful. Excuse me. I must practice.

Woman: Shall I get you something?

Man: No.

Woman: Some tea, maybe?

Man: No. (*Man resumes swordplay.*)

Woman: Perhaps later today—perhaps we can go out—just around here. We can look for flowers.

Man: All right.

Woman: We don't have to.

Man: No. Let's.

Woman: I just thought if—

Man: Fine. Where do you want to go?

Woman: There are very few recreational activities around here, I know.

Man: All right. We'll go this afternoon. (*Pause.*)

Woman: Can I get you something?

Man (Turning around.): What?

Woman: You might be—

Man: I'm not hungry or thirsty or cold or hot.

Woman: Then what are you?

Man: Practicing. (*Man resumes practicing; Woman exits. As soon as she exits, he rests. He sits down. He examines his sword. He runs his finger along the edge of it. He takes the tip, runs it against the soft skin under his chin. He places the sword on the ground with the tip pointed directly upwards. He keeps it from falling by placing the tip under his chin. He experiments with different degrees of pressure. Woman re-enters. She sees him in this precarious position. She jerks his head upward; the sword falls.*)

Woman: Don't do that!

Man: What?

Woman: You can hurt yourself!

Man: I was practicing!

Woman: You were playing!

Man: I was practicing!

Woman: It's dangerous.

Man: What do you take me for—a child?

Woman: Sometimes wise men do childish things.

Man: I knew what I was doing!

Woman: It scares me.

Man: Don't be ridiculous. (*He reaches for the sword again.*)

Woman: Don't! Don't do that!

Man: Get back! (*He places the sword back in its previous position, suspended between the floor and his chin, upright.*)

Woman: But—

Man: Sssssh!

Woman: I wish—

Man: Listen to me! The slightest shock, you know—the slightest shock—surprise—it might make me jerk or—something—and then . . . so you must be perfectly still and quiet.

Woman: But I—

Man: Sssssh! (*Silence.*) I learned this exercise from a friend—I can't even remember his name—good swordsman—many years ago. He called it his meditation position. He said, like this, he could feel the line between this world and the others because he rested on it. If he saw something in another world that he liked better, all he would have to do is let his head drop, and he'd be there. Simple. No fuss. One day, they found him with the tip of his sword run clean out the back of his neck. He was smiling. I guess he saw something he liked. Or else he'd fallen asleep.

Woman: Stop that.

Man: Stop what?

Woman: Tormenting me.

Man: I'm not.

Woman: Take it away!

Man: You don't have to watch, you know.

Woman: Do you want to die that way—an accident?

Man: I was doing this before you came in.

Woman: If you do, all you need to do is tell me.

Man: What?

Woman: I can walk right over. Lean on the back of your head.

Man: Don't try to threaten—

Woman: Or jerk your sword up.

Man: Or scare me. You can't threaten—

Woman: I'm not. But if that's what you want.

Man: You can't threaten me. You wouldn't do it.

Woman: Oh?

Man: Then I'd be gone. You wouldn't let me leave that easily.

Woman: Yes, I would.

Man: You'd be alone.

Woman: No. I'd follow you. Forever. (*Pause.*) Now, let's stop this nonsense.

Man: No! I can do what I want! Don't come any closer!

Woman: Then release your sword.

Man: Come any closer and I'll drop my head.

Woman (*Woman slowly approaches Man. She grabs the hilt of the sword. She looks into his eyes. She pulls it out from under his chin.*): There will be no more of this. (*She exits with the sword. He starts to follow her, then stops. He touches under his chin. On his finger, he finds a drop of blood.*)

Scene IX. *Night. Man is leaving the house. He is just about out, when he hears a shakuhachi playing. He looks around, trying to locate the sound. Woman appears in the doorway to the outside. Shakuhachi slowly fades out.*

Woman: It's time for you to go?

Man: Yes. I'm sorry.

Woman: You're just going to sneak out? A thief in the night? A frightened child?

Man: I care about you.

Woman: You express it strangely.

Man: I leave in shame because it is proper. (*Pause.*) I came seeking glory.

Woman: To kill me? You can say it. You'll be surprised at how little I blanche. As if you'd said, "I came for a bowl of rice," or "I came seeking love" or "I came to kill you."

Man: Weakness. All weakness. Too weak to kill you. Too weak to kill myself. Too weak to do anything but sneak away in shame. (*Woman brings out Man's sword.*)

Woman: Were you even planning to leave without this? (*He takes sword.*) Why not stay here?

Man: I can't live with someone who's defeated me.

Woman: I never thought of defeating you. I only wanted to take care of you. To make you happy. Because that made me happy and I was no longer alone.

Man: You defeated me.

Woman: Why do you think that way?

Man: I came here with a purpose. The world was clear. You changed the shape of your face, the shape of my heart—rearranged everything—created a world where I could do nothing.

Woman: I only tried to care for you.

Man: I guess that was all it took. (*Pause.*)

Woman: You still think I'm a witch. Just because old women gossip. You are so cruel. Once you arrived, there were only two possibilities: I would die or you would leave. (*Pause.*) If you believe I'm a witch, then kill me. Rid the province of one more evil.

Man: I can't—

Woman: Why not? If you believe that about me, then it's the right thing to do.

Man: You know I can't.

Woman: Then stay.

Man: Don't try and force me.

Woman: I won't force you to do anything. (*Pause.*) All I wanted was an escape—for both of us. The sound of a human voice—the simplest thing to find, and the hardest to hold onto. This house—my loneliness is etched into the walls. Kill me, but don't leave. Even in death, my spirit would rest here and be comforted by your presence.

Man: Force me to stay.

Woman: I won't. (*Man starts to leave.*) Beware.

Man: What?

Woman: The ground on which you walk is weak. It could give way at any moment. The crevice beneath is dark.

Man: Are you talking about death? I'm ready to die.

Woman: Fear for what is worse than death.

Man: What?

Woman: Falling. Falling through the darkness. Waiting to hit the ground. Picking up speed. Waiting for the ground. Falling faster. Falling alone. Waiting. Falling. Waiting. Falling.

(*Woman wails and runs out through the door to her room. Man stands, confused, not knowing what to do. He starts to follow her, then hesitates, and rushes out the door to the outside. Silence. Slowly, he re-enters from the outside. He looks for her in the main room. He goes slowly towards the panel to her room. He throws down his sword. He opens the panel. He goes inside. He comes out. He unrolls his mat. He sits on it, cross-legged. He looks out into space. He notices near him a shakuhachi. He picks it up. He begins to blow into it. He tries to make sounds. He continues trying through the end of the play. The Upstage scrim lights up. Upstage, we see the Woman. She is young. She is hanging from a rope suspended from the roof. She has hung herself. Around her are scores of vases with flowers in them whose blossoms have been blown off. Only the stems remain in the vases. Around her swirl the thousands of petals from the flowers. They fill the Upstage scrim area like a blizzard of color. Man continues to attempt to play. Lights fade to black.*)

David Henry Hwang

David Henry Hwang on Drama MULTICULTURAL THEATER 1989

INTERVIEWER: How did you begin . . . exploring your [Chinese-American] heritage?

HWANG: A lot of that happened in college. I was in college in the mid-to-late 1970s, and whereas most people seem to associate collegiate life in the seventies with John Travolta, there was at that time a third-world consciousness, a third-world power movement, in the universities, particularly among Hispanics and Asians. The blacks really started it in the late sixties and early seventies, and it took a while to trickle down into the other third-world communities. Asians probably picked it up last. . . . While I was never a very ardent Marxist, I studied the ideas and I was interested in the degree to which we all may have been affected by certain prejudices in the society without having realized it, and to what degree we had incorporated that into our persons by the time we'd reached our early twenties.

The other thing that I think fascinated me about exploring my Chineseness at that time was consistent with my interest in play-writing. I had become very interested in Sam Shepard, particularly in the way in which Shepard likes to create a sort of American mythology. In his case it's the cowboy mythology, but nonetheless it's something that is larger than simply our present-day, fast-food existence. In my context, creating a mythology, creating a past for myself, involved going into Chinese history and Chinese-American history. I think the combination of wanting to delve into those things for artistic reasons and being exposed to an active third-world-consciousness movement was what started to get me interested in my roots when I was in college.

INTERVIEWER: I wonder if there will come a time when the expression "ethnic theater" won't have any meaning.

HWANG: I'm hopeful that there will be a time at some point, but I think it's going to be fifty years or so down the road. The whole idea of being ethnic only applies when it's clear what the dominant culture is. Once it becomes less clear and the culture is acknowledged to be more multicultural, then the idea of what's ethnic becomes irrelevant. I think even today we're starting to see that. The monoethnic theaters—that is, the Asian theaters, the black theaters, the Hispanic theaters—are really useful; they serve a purpose. But I think, if we do our jobs correctly, we will phase out our own need for existence, and the future of theaters will be in multicultural theaters, theaters that do a black play and a Jewish play and a classic and whatever . . .

There are so many people now who can't be labeled. I know a couple in which the man is Japanese and Jewish and the woman is Haitian and Filipino. They have a child, and sociologists have told them that a child of that stock probably hasn't existed before. When someone like that becomes a writer, what do we call him? Do we say he's an Asian writer, or what? As those distinctions become increasingly muddled, the whole notion of what is ethnic as opposed to what is mainstream is going to become more and more difficult to define.

Interview in *Contemporary Authors*

Terrence McNally

ANDRE'S MOTHER   1988

Terrence McNally (b. 1939) was born in St. Petersburg, Florida, but he was raised mostly in Corpus Christi, Texas, where his Irish-Catholic father worked as a beer distributor. After attending Columbia University, McNally worked as a theatrical stage manager, magazine editor, and film critic while writing his first plays. A versatile dramatist, he has written plays, musicals, and screenplays. His screwball comedy The Ritz *(1973) became a popular 1976 film, which McNally himself adapted for the screen. He also rewrote his romantic drama* Frankie and Johnny in the Claire de Lune *(1987) for Gary Marshall's film* Frankie and Johnny *(1991), starring Al Pacino and Michelle Pfeiffer. Other notable McNally plays include* The Lisbon Traviata *(1985);* Lips Together, Teeth Apart *(1991); and* A Perfect Ganesh *(1993). In 1995 his play about the opera singer Maria Callas,* Master Class, *became an international success. His work for television includes an adaptation of John Cheever's "The 5:48" (1980). McNally's television version of Andre's Mother won an Emmy in 1990, but the original stage version—written as one brief and memorable scene—needs no video backup to communicate its troubling message of heartache and loss.*

Characters

Cal, a young man
Arthur, his father
Penny, his sister
Andre's Mother

Time. *Now*
Place. *New York City, Central Park*

Four people—Cal, Arthur, Penny, and Andre's Mother—enter. They are nicely dressed and each carries a white helium-filled balloon on a string.

Cal: You know what's really terrible? I can't think of anything terrific to say. Goodbye. I love you. I'll miss you. And I'm supposed to be so great with words!

Penny: What's that over there?

Arthur: Ask your brother.

Cal: It's a theatre. An outdoor theatre. They do plays there in the summer. Shakespeare's plays. (*To Andre's Mother.*) God, how much he wanted to play Hamlet again. He would have gone to Timbuktu to have another go at that part. The summer he did it in Boston, he was so happy!

Penny: Cal, I don't think she . . . ! It's not the time. Later.

Arthur: Your son was a . . . the Jews have a word for it . . .

Penny (*quietly appalled*): Oh my God!

Arthur: Mensch, I believe it is, and I think I'm using it right. It means warm, solid, the real thing. Correct me if I'm wrong.

Penny: Fine, Dad, fine. Just quit while you're ahead.

Arthur: I won't say he was like a son to me. Even my son isn't always like a son to me. I mean . . . ! In my clumsy way, I'm trying to say how much I liked Andre. And how much he helped me to know my own boy. Cal was always two handsful but Andre and I could talk about anything under the sun. My wife was very fond of him, too.

Penny: Cal, I don't understand about the balloons.

Cal: They represent the soul. When you let go, it means you're letting his soul ascend to Heaven. That you're willing to let go. Breaking the last earthly ties.

Penny: Does the Pope know about this?

Arthur: Penny!

Penny: Andre loved my sense of humor. Listen, you can hear him laughing. (*She lets go of her white balloon.*) So long, you glorious, wonderful, I-know-what-Cal-means-about-words . . . *man!* God forgive me for wishing you were straight every time I laid eyes on you. But if any man was going to have you, I'm glad it was my brother! Look how fast it went up. I bet that means some-thing. Something terrific.

Arthur (*lets his balloon go*): Goodbye. God speed.

Penny: Cal?

Cal: I'm not ready yet.

Penny: Okay. We'll be over there. Come on, Pop, you can buy your little girl a Good Humor.

Arthur: They still make Good Humor?
Penny: Only now they're called Dove Bars and they cost twelve dollars.

(*Penny takes Arthur off. Cal and Andre's Mother stand with their balloons.*)

Cal: I wish I knew what you were thinking. I think it would help me. You know almost nothing about me and I only know what Andre told me about you. I'd always had it in my mind that one day we would be friends, you and me. But if you didn't know about Andre and me . . . If this hadn't happened, I wonder if he would have ever told you. When he was sick, if I asked him once I asked him a thousand times, tell her. She's your mother. She won't mind. But he was so afraid of hurting you and of your disapproval. I don't know which was worse. (*No response. He sighs.*) God, how many of us live in this city because we don't want to hurt our mothers and live in mortal terror of their disapproval. We lose ourselves here. Our lives aren't furtive, just our feelings toward people like you are! A city of fugitives from our parents' scorn or heartbreak. Sometimes he'd seem a little down and I'd say, "What's the matter, babe?" and this funny sweet, sad smile would cross his face and he'd say, "Just a little homesick, Cal, just a little bit." I always accused him of being a country boy just playing at being a hotshot, sophisticated New Yorker. (*He sighs.*)

It's bullshit. It's all bullshit. (*Still no response.*)

Do you remember the comic strip *Little Lulu*? Her mother had no name, she was so remote, so formidable to all the children. She was just Lulu's mother. "Hello, Lulu's Mother," Lulu's friends would say. She was almost anonymous in her remoteness. You remind me of her. Andre's mother. Let me answer the questions you can't ask and then I'll leave you alone and you won't ever have to see me again. Andre died of AIDS. I don't know how he got it. I tested negative. He died bravely. You would have been proud of him. The only thing that frightened him was you. I'll have everything that was his sent to you. I'll pay for it. There isn't much. You should have come up the summer he played Hamlet. He was magnificent. Yes, I'm bitter. I'm bitter I've lost him. I'm bitter what's happening. I'm bitter even now, after all this, I can't reach you. I'm beginning to feel your disapproval and it's making me ill. (*He looks at his balloon.*) Sorry, old friend. I blew it. (*He lets go of the balloon.*)

Good night, sweet prince, and flights of angels sing thee to thy rest! (*Beat.*)

Goodbye, Andre's mother.

(*He goes. Andre's Mother stands alone holding her white balloon. Her lips tremble. She looks on the verge of breaking down. She is about to let go of the balloon when she pulls it down to her. She looks at it awhile before she gently kisses it. She lets go of the balloon. She follows it with her eyes as it rises and rises. The lights are beginning to fade. Andre's Mother's eyes are still on the balloon. The lights fade.*)

Terrence McNally

Terrence McNally on Drama   HOW TO WRITE A PLAY   1995

INTERVIEWER: Could you tell us how you go about writing a play? What is your writing process?

McNALLY: It's very simple, really. You have to go to the typewriter, that's all you have to do. I have a word processor now, and you turn it on and something happens after a while, and that's all writing is to me. If I don't go to the typewriter I don't write. I'm not being facetious. I think it's a very practical thing, and deadlines help a lot. You realize that *Lips Together* opens April twelfth and it's December twelfth and you haven't written a word of the play. I carry them up in my head for a long time. That process is very hard to talk about. It's partially my unconscious. It's usually a year or two before I sit at the typewriter, but people say, "God, you write plays so quickly." Well, I think walking around with things in your head for two years is not exactly quickly. The typing part is pretty quick, if you really know what you're doing in a play. Once I know what my characters are doing, the play just comes very, very easily.

.   .   .

INTERVIEWER: Do you write to discover what you feel about something?

McNALLY: That's not the motive to write something, but I do discover something and how I feel about things while I'm writing a play. But it's not the motive. I don't say, "Well, I'll write a play about suicide so I can see what it would be like to kill myself." Writing a play is not psychotherapy. But I do learn an awful lot about myself, and it makes me more aware of other people. I would like to think that my work is about equal parts autobiographical feeling, imagined feeling, and people I've observed. I've never created a character that I've had no empathy for, and I've never based a character 100 percent on a person I've known in real life. It's a blend, and in the process you learn something about yourself.

Interview with Joy Zinoman
The Playwright's Art: Conversations with Contemporary American Dramatists

Milcha Sanchez-Scott

THE CUBAN SWIMMER   1984

Milcha Sanchez-Scott (b. 1955) was born on the island of Bali. Her father was Colombian. Her mother was Chinese, Indonesian, and Dutch. Her father's work as an agronomist required constant travel, so when the young Sanchez-Scott reached school age, she was placed in a convent boarding school near London where she first learned English. Colombia, however, remained the family's one permanent home. Every Christmas and summer vacation was spent on a ranch in San Marta, Colombia, where four generations of family lived together. When she was fourteen, Sanchez-Scott's family moved to California. After attending the University of San Diego, where she majored in literature and philosophy, she worked at the San Diego Zoo and later at an employment agency in Los Angeles. Her first play, Latina, *premiered in 1980 and won seven Drama-Logue awards.* Dog Lady *and* The Cuban Swimmer *followed in 1984. Sanchez-Scott then went to New York for a year to work with playwright Irene Fornes, in whose theater workshop she developed* Roosters *(1988). Her other plays include* Evening Star *(1989) and* City of Angels. *Sanchez-Scott lives in Southern California.*

Characters

Margarita Suárez, the swimmer
Eduardo Suárez, her father, the coach
Simón Suárez, her brother
Aída Suárez, the mother
Abuela, her grandmother
Voice of Mel Munson
Voice of Mary Beth White
Voice of Radio Operator

Setting. *The Pacific Ocean between San Pedro and Catalina Island.*

Time. *Summer.*

Live conga drums can be used to punctuate the action of the play.

SCENE 1

Pacific Ocean. Midday. On the horizon, in perspective, a small boat enters upstage left, crosses to upstage right, and exits. Pause. Lower on the horizon, the same boat, in larger perspective, enters upstage right, crosses and exits upstage left. Blackout.

Scene from the University of Colorado's production of The Cuban Swimmer. *(Photograph by Richard Devin)*

SCENE 2

Pacific Ocean. Midday. The swimmer, Margarita Suárez, is swimming. On the boat following behind her are her father, Eduardo Suárez, holding a megaphone, and Simón, her brother, sitting on top of the cabin with his shirt off, punk sunglasses on, binoculars hanging on his chest.

Eduardo (Leaning forward, shouting in time to Margarita's swimming.): Uno, dos, uno, dos. Y uno, dos° . . . keep your shoulders parallel to the water.
Simón: I'm gonna take these glasses off and look straight into the sun.

Uno, dos, uno, dos. Y uno, dos: One, two, one, two. And one, two.

Eduardo (*Through megaphone.*): *Muy bien, muy bien*° . . . but punch those arms in, baby.

Simón (*Looking directly at the sun through binoculars.*): Come on, come on, zap me. Show me something. (*He looks behind at the shoreline and ahead at the sea.*) Stop! Stop, *Papi!* Stop!

(*Aída Suárez and Abuela, the swimmer's mother and grandmother, enter running from the back of the boat.*)

Aída and Abuela: Qué? Qué es?°

Aída: Es un shark?°

Eduardo: Eh?

Abuela: Que es un shark *dicen?*°

(*Eduardo blows whistle. Margarita looks up at the boat.*)

Simón: No, *Papi*, no shark, no shark. We've reached the halfway mark.

Abuela (*Looking into the water.*): *A dónde está?*°

Aída: It's not in the water.

Abuela: Oh, no? Oh, no?

Aída: No! *A poco* do you think they're gonna have signs in the water to say you are halfway to Santa Catalina? No. It's done very scientific. *A ver, hijo,*° explain it to your grandma.

Simón: Well, you see, Abuela—(*He points behind.*) There's San Pedro. (*He points ahead.*) And there's Santa Catalina. Looks halfway to me.

(*Abuela shakes her head and is looking back and forth, trying to make the decision, when suddenly the sound of a helicopter is heard.*)

Abuela (*Looking up.*): *Virgencita de la Caridad del Cobre. Qué es eso?*°

(*Sound of helicopter gets closer. Margarita looks up.*)

Margarita: Papi, Papi!

(*A small commotion on the boat, with everybody pointing at the helicopter above. Shadows of the helicopter fall on the boat. Simón looks up at it through binoculars.*)

Papi—qué es? What is it?

Eduardo (*Through megaphone.*): Uh . . . uh . . . uh, *un momentico . . . mi hija.*° . . . Your *papi's* got everything under control, understand? Uh . . . you just keep stroking. And stay . . . uh . . . close to the boat.

Simón: Wow, *Papi!* We're on TV, man! Holy Christ, we're all over the fucking U.S.A.! It's Mel Munson and Mary Beth White!

Aída: Por Dios!° Simón, don't swear. And put on your shirt.

Muy bien, muy bien: Very good, very good.   *Qué? Qué es?:* What? What is it?   *Es un shark?:* Is it a shark?   *Que es un shark dicen?:* Did they say a shark?   *A dónde está?:* Where is it?   *A ver, hijo:* Look here, son.   *Virgencita de la Caridad del Cobre. Qué es eso?:* Virgin of Charity! What is that?   *un momentico . . . mi hija:* Just a second, my daughter.   *Por Dios!:* For God's Sake!

(*Aída fluffs her hair, puts on her sunglasses and waves to the helicopter. Simón leans over the side of the boat and yells to Margarita.*)

Simón: Yo, Margo! You're on TV, man.

Eduardo: Leave your sister alone. Turn on the radio.

Margarita: Papi! Qué está pasando?°

Abuela: Que es la televisión dicen? (*She shakes her head.*) Porque como yo no puedo ver nada sin mis espejuelos.°

(*Abuela rummages through the boat, looking for her glasses. Voices of Mel Munson and Mary Beth White are heard over the boat's radio.*)

Mel's Voice: As we take a closer look at the gallant crew of *La Havana* . . . and there . . . yes, there she is . . . the little Cuban swimmer from Long Beach, California, nineteen-year-old Margarita Suárez. The unknown swimmer is our Cinderella entry . . . a bundle of tenacity, battling her way through the choppy, murky waters of the cold Pacific to reach the Island of Romance . . . Santa Catalina . . . where should she be the first to arrive, two thousand dollars and a gold cup will be waiting for her.

Aída: Doesn't even cover our expenses.

Abuela: Qué dice?

Eduardo: Shhhh!

Mary Beth's Voice: This is really a family effort, Mel, and—

Mel's Voice: Indeed it is. Her trainer, her coach, her mentor, is her father, Eduardo Suárez. Not a swimmer himself, it says here, Mr. Suárez is head usher of the Holy Name Society and the owner-operator of Suárez Treasures of the Sea and Salvage Yard. I guess it's one of those places—

Mary Beth's Voice: If I might interject a fact here, Mel, assisting in this swim is Mrs. Suárez, who is a former Miss Cuba.

Mel's Voice: And a beautiful woman in her own right. Let's try and get a closer look.

(*Helicopter sound gets louder. Margarita, frightened, looks up again.*)

Margarita: Papi!

Eduardo (*Through megaphone.*): Mi hija, don't get nervous . . . it's the press. I'm handling it.

Aída: I see how you're handling it.

Eduardo (*Through megaphone.*): Do you hear? Everything is under control. Get back into your rhythm. Keep your elbows high and kick and kick and kick and kick . . .

Abuela (*Finds her glasses and puts them on.*): Ay sí, es la televisión . . . (*She points to helicopter.*) Qué lindo mira . . . (*She fluffs her hair, gives a big wave.*) Aló América! Viva mi Margarita, viva todo los Cubanos en los Estados Unidos!°

Papi! Qué está pasando?: Dad. What's happening? *Que es la televisión dicen? Porque como yo no puedo ver nada sin mis espejuelos:* Did they say television? Because I can't see without my glasses. *Aló América! Viva mi Margarita, viva todo los Cubanos en los Estados Unidos!:* Hello America! Hurray for my Margarita, hurray for all the Cubans in the United States!

Aída: Ay por Dios, Cecilia, the man didn't come all this way in his helicopter to look at you jumping up and down, making a fool of yourself.

Abuela: I don't care. I'm proud.

Aída: He can't understand you anyway.

Abuela: Viva . . . (*She stops.*) Simón, *cómo se dice viva?*°

Simón: Hurray.

Abuela: Hurray for *mi Margarita* y for all the Cubans living *en* the United States, *y un abrazo* . . . Simón, *abrazo* . . .

Simón: A big hug.

Abuela: Sí, a big hug to all my friends in Miami, Long Beach, Union City, except for my son Carlos, who lives in New York in sin! He lives . . . (*She crosses herself.*) in Brooklyn with a Puerto Rican woman in sin! *No decente* . . .

Simón: Decent.

Abuela: Carlos, *no decente.* This family, *decente.*

Aída: Cecilia, *por Dios.*

Mel's Voice: Look at that enthusiasm. The whole family has turned out to cheer little Margarita on to victory! I hope they won't be too disappointed.

Mary Beth's Voice: She seems to be making good time, Mel.

Mel's Voice: Yes, it takes all kinds to make a race. And it's a testimonial to the all-encompassing fairness . . . the greatness of this, the Wrigley Invitational Women's Swim to Catalina, where among all the professionals there is still room for the amateurs . . . like these, the simple people we see below us on the ragtag *La Havana,* taking their long-shot chance to victory. *Vaya con Dios!*°

(*Helicopter sound fading as family, including Margarita, watch silently. Static as Simón turns radio off. Eduardo walks to bow of boat, looks out on the horizon.*)

Eduardo (*To himself.*): Amateurs.

Aída: Eduardo, that person insulted us. Did you hear, Eduardo? That he called us a simple people in a ragtag boat? Did you hear . . . ?

Abuela (*Clenching her fist at departing helicopter.*): *Mal-Rayo los parta!*°

Simón (*Same gesture.*): Asshole!

(*Aída follows Eduardo as he goes to side of boat and stares at Margarita.*)

Aída: This person comes in his helicopter to insult your wife, your family, your daughter . . .

Margarita (*Pops her head out of the water.*): Papi?

Aída: Do you hear me, Eduardo? I am not simple.

Abuela: Sí.

Aída: I am complicated.

Abuela: Sí, demasiada complicada.

---

cómo se dice viva?: How do you say "viva" [in English]?   *Vaya con Dios!*: Go with God. [God bless you.]   *Mal-Rayo los parta!*: To hell with you!

Aída: Me and my family are not so simple.

Simón: Mom, the guy's an asshole.

Abuela (Shaking her fist at helicopter.): Asshole!

Aída: If my daughter was simple, she would not be in that water swimming.

Margarita: Simple? *Papi* . . . ?

Aída: Ahora, Eduardo, this is what I want you to do. When we get to Santa Catalina, I want you to call the TV station and demand an apology.

Eduardo: Cállete mujer! Aquí mando yo.° I will decide what is to be done.

Margarita: Papi, tell me what's going on.

Eduardo: Do you understand what I am saying to you, Aída?

Simón (Leaning over side of boat, to Margarita.): Yo Margo! You know that Mel Munson guy on TV? He called you a simple amateur and said you didn't have a chance.

Abuela (Leaning directly behind Simón.): Mi hija, insultó a la familia. Desgraciado!

Aída (Leaning in behind Abuela.): He called us peasants! And your father is not doing anything about it. He just knows how to yell at me.

Eduardo (Through megaphone.): Shut up! All of you! Do you want to break her concentration? Is that what you are after? Eh?

(*Abuela, Aída and Simón shrink back. Eduardo paces before them.*)

Swimming is rhythm and concentration. You win a race *aquí.* (*Pointing to his head.*) Now . . . (*To Simón.*) you, take care of the boat, Aída y Mama . . . do something. Anything. Something practical.

(*Abuela and Aída get on knees and pray in Spanish.*)

Hija, give it everything, eh? . . . *por la familia.* Uno . . . dos . . . . You must win.

(*Simón goes into cabin. The prayers continue as lights change to indicate bright sunlight, later in the afternoon.*)

SCENE 3

Tableau for a couple of beats. Eduardo on bow with timer in one hand as he counts strokes per minute. Simón is in the cabin steering, wearing his sunglasses, baseball cap on backward. Abuela and Aída are at the side of the boat, heads down, hands folded, still muttering prayers in Spanish.

Aída and Abuela (Crossing themselves.): En el nombre del Padre, del Hijo y del Espíritu Santo amén.°

Eduardo (Through megaphone.): You're stroking seventy-two!

Simón (Singing.): Mama's stroking, Mama's stroking seventy-two. . . .

Eduardo (Through megaphone.): You comfortable with it?

Simón (Singing.): Seventy-two, seventy-two, seventy-two for you.

Cállete mujer! Aquí mando yo: Quiet! I'm in charge here.   *En el nombre del Padre, del Hijo y del Espíritu Santo amén:* In the name of the Father, the Son, and the Holy Ghost, Amen.

Aída (*Looking at the heavens.*): Ay, Eduardo, *ven acá,*° we should be grateful that *Nuestro Señor*° gave us such a beautiful day.

Abuela (*Crosses herself.*): Sí, *gracias a Dios.*°

Eduardo: She's stroking seventy-two, with no problem (*He throws a kiss to the sky.*) It's a beautiful day to win.

Aída: *Qué hermoso!*° So clear and bright. Not a cloud in the sky. *Mira! Mira!*° Even rainbows on the water . . . a sign from God.

Simón (*Singing.*): Rainbows on the water . . . you in my arms . . .

Abuela and Eduardo (*Looking the wrong way.*): *Dónde?*

Aída (*Pointing toward Margarita.*): There, dancing in front of Margarita, leading her on . . .

Eduardo: Rainbows on . . . Ay coño! It's an oil slick! You . . . you . . . (*To Simón.*) Stop the boat. (*Runs to bow, yelling.*) Margarita! Margarita!

(*On the next stroke, Margarita comes up all covered in black oil.*)

Margarita: Papi! Papi . . . !

(*Everybody goes to the side and stares at Margarita, who stares back. Eduardo freezes.*)

Aída: *Apúrate,*° Eduardo, move . . . what's wrong with you . . . *no me oíste,* get my daughter out of the water.

Eduardo (*Softly.*): We can't touch her. If we touch her, she's disqualified.

Aída: But I'm her mother.

Eduardo: Not even by her own mother. Especially by her own mother. . . . You always want the rules to be different for you, you always want to be the exception. (*To Simón.*) And you . . . you didn't see it, eh? You were playing again?

Simón: Papi, I was watching . . .

Aída (*Interrupting.*): Pues, do something Eduardo. You are the big coach, the monitor.

Simón: Mentor! Mentor!

Eduardo: How can a person think around you? (*He walks off to bow, puts head in hands.*)

Abuela (*Looking over side.*): Mira como todos los little birds are dead. (*She crosses herself.*)

Aída: Their little wings are glued to their sides.

Simón: Christ, this is like the La Brea tar pits.

Aída: They can't move their little wings.

Abuela: Esa niña tiene que *moverse.*°

Simón: Yeah, Margo, you gotta move, man.

(*Abuela and Simón gesture for Margarita to move. Aída gestures for her to swim.*)

---

ven acá: Look here. *Nuestro Señor:* Our father [God]. *Sí, gracias a Dios:* Yes, thanks be to God. *Qué hermoso!:* How beautiful! *Mira!:* look. *Apúrate . . . no me oíste:* Finish this! . . . didn't you hear me? *Esa niña tiene que moverse:* That girl has to move

Abuela: Anda niña, muévete.°

Aída: Swim, *hija,* swim or the *aceite°* will stick to your wings.

Margarita: Papi?

Abuela (Taking megaphone.): Your *papi* say "move it!"

(*Margarita with difficulty starts moving.*)

Abuela, Aída and Simón (Laboriously counting.): Uno, dos . . . uno, dos . . . anda
. . . uno, dos.

Eduardo (Running to take megaphone from Abuela.): Uno, dos . . .

(*Simón races into cabin and starts the engine. Abuela, Aída and Eduardo count together.*)

Simón (Looking ahead.): Papi, it's over there!

Eduardo: Eh?

Simón (Pointing ahead and to the right.): It's getting clearer over there.

Eduardo (Through megaphone.): Now pay attention to me. Go to the right.

(*Simón, Abuela, Aída and Eduardo all lean over side. They point ahead and to the right, except Abuela, who points to the left.*)

Family (Shouting together.): Para yá!° Para yá!

(*Lights go down on boat. A special light on Margarita, swimming through the oil, and on Abuela, watching her.*)

Abuela: Sangre de mi sangre,° you will be another to save us. En Bolondron, where your great-grandmother Luz Suárez was born, they say one day it rained blood. All the people, they run into their houses. They cry, they pray, *pero* your great-grandmother Luz she had *cojones* like a man. She run outside. She look straight at the sky. She shake her fist. And she say to the evil one, "Mira . . . (*Beating her chest.*) coño, Diablo, aquí estoy si me quieres."° And she open her mouth, and she drunk the blood.

BLACKOUT.

Scene 4

Lights up on boat. Aída and Eduardo are on deck watching Margarita swim. We hear the gentle, rhythmic lap, lap, lap of the water, then the sound of inhaling and exhaling as Margarita's breathing becomes louder. Then Margarita's heartbeat is heard, with the lapping of the water and the breathing under it. These sounds continue beneath the dialogue to the end of the scene.

Aída: Dios mío. Look how she moves through the water. . . .

Eduardo: You see, it's very simple. It is a matter of concentration.

Anda niña, muévete: Come on, girl, Move! *aceite:* oil. *Para yá:* over there. *Sangre de mi sangre:* blood of my blood. *Mira . . . coño, Diablo, aquí estoy si me quieres:* Look . . . damn it Devil, here I am if you want me.

Aída: The first time I put her in water she came to life, she grew before my eyes. She moved, she smiled, she loved it more than me. She didn't want my breast any longer. She wanted the water.

Eduardo: And of course, the rhythm. The rhythm takes away the pain and helps the concentration.

(*Pause. Aída and Eduardo watch Margarita.*)

Aída: Is that my child or a seal. . . .

Eduardo: Ah, a seal, the reason for that is that she's keeping her arms very close to her body. She cups her hands, and then she reaches and digs, reaches and digs.

Aída: To think that a daughter of mine. . . .

Eduardo: It's the training, the hours in the water. I used to tie weights around her little wrists and ankles.

Aída: A spirit, an ocean spirit, must have entered my body when I was carrying her.

Eduardo (*To Margarita.*): Your stroke is slowing down.

(*Pause. We hear Margarita's heartbeat with the breathing under, faster now.*)

Aída: Eduardo, that night, the night on the boat . . .

Eduardo: Ah, the night on the boat again . . . the moon was . . .

Aída: The moon was full. We were coming to America. . . . *Qué romantico.*

(*Heartbeat and breathing continue.*)

Eduardo: We were cold, afraid, with no money, and on top of everything, you were hysterical, yelling at me, tearing at me with your nails. (*Opens his shirt, points to the base of his neck.*) Look, I still bear the scars . . . telling me that I didn't know what I was doing . . . saying that we were going to die. . . .

Aída: You took me, you stole me from my home . . . you didn't give me a chance to prepare. You just said we have to go now, now! Now, you said. You didn't let me take anything. I left everything behind. . . . I left everything behind.

Eduardo: Saying that I wasn't good enough, that your father didn't raise you so that I could drown you in the sea.

Aída: You didn't let me say even a good-bye. You took me, you stole me, you tore me from my home.

Eduardo: I took you so we could be married.

Aída: That was in Miami. But that night on the boat, Eduardo. . . . We were not married, that night on the boat.

Eduardo: *No pasó nada!°* Once and for all get it out of your head, it was cold, you hated me, and we were afraid. . . .

Aída: *Mentiroso!°*

Eduardo: A man can't do it when he is afraid.

Aída: Liar! You did it very well.

No pasó nada!: Nothing happened.   *Mentiroso!:* Liar!

Eduardo: I did?

Aída: Sí. Gentle. You were so gentle and then strong . . . my passion for you so deep. Standing next to you . . . I would ache . . . looking at your hands I would forget to breathe, you were irresistible.

Eduardo: I was?

Aída: You took me into your arms, you touched my face with your fingertips . . . you kissed my eyes . . . *la esquina de la boca y* . . .

Eduardo: Sí, Sí, and then . . .

Aída: I look at your face on top of mine, and I see the lights of Havana in your eyes. That's when you seduced me.

Eduardo: Shhh, they're gonna hear you.

(*Lights go down. Special on Aída.*)

Aída: That was the night. A woman doesn't forget those things . . . and later that night was the dream . . . the dream of a big country with fields of fertile land and big, giant things growing. And there by a green, slimy pond I found a giant pea pod and when I opened it, it was full of little, tiny baby frogs.

(*Aída crosses herself as she watches Margarita. We hear louder breathing and heartbeat.*)

Margarita: Santa Teresa. Little Flower of God, pray for me. San Martín de Porres, pray for me. Santa Rosa de Lima, *Virgencita de la Caridad del Cobre,* pray for me. . . . Mother pray for me.

Scene 5

Loud howling of wind is heard, as lights change to indicate unstable weather, fog and mist. Family on deck, braced and huddled against the wind. Simón is at the helm.

Aída: Ay Dios mío, qué viento.°

Eduardo (Through megaphone.): Don't drift out . . . that wind is pushing you out. (*To Simón.*) You! Slow down. Can't you see your sister is drifting out?

Simón: It's the wind, *Papi.*

Aída: Baby, don't go so far. . . .

Abuela (To heaven.): Ay Gran Poder de Dios, quita este maldito viento.°

Simón: Margo! Margo! Stay close to the boat.

Eduardo: Dig in. Dig in hard. . . . Reach down from your guts and dig in.

Abuela (To heaven.): Ay Virgen de la Caridad del Cobre, por lo más tú quieres a pararla.

Aída (Putting her hand out, reaching for Margarita.): Baby, don't go far.

(*Abuela crosses herself. Action freezes. Lights get dimmer, special on Margarita. She keeps swimming, stops, starts again, stops, then, finally exhausted, stops altogether. The boat stops moving.*)

Ay Dios mío, qué viento: Oh my God, what wind!   Ay Gran Poder de Dios, quita este maldito viento: By the great power of God, keep the cursed winds away!

Eduardo: What's going on here? Why are we stopping?

Simón: Papi, she's not moving! Yo Margo!

(*The family all run to the side.*)

Eduardo: Hija! . . . Hijita! You're tired, eh?

Aída: Por supuesto she's tired. I like to see you get in the water, waving your arms and legs from San Pedro to Santa Catalina. A person isn't a machine, a person has to rest.

Simón: Yo, Mama! Cool out, it ain't fucking brain surgery.

Eduardo (*To Simón.*): Shut up, you. (*Louder to Margarita.*) I guess your mother's right for once, huh? . . . I guess you had to stop, eh? . . . Give your brother, the idiot . . . a chance to catch up with you.

Simón (*Clowning like Mortimer Snerd.*): Dum dee dum dee dum ooops, ah shucks . . .

Eduardo: I don't think he's Cuban.

Simón (*Like Ricky Ricardo.*): Oye, Lucy! I'm home! Ba ba lu!

Eduardo (*Joins in clowning, grabbing Simón in a headlock.*): What am I gonna do with this idiot, eh? I don't understand this idiot. He's not like us, Margarita. (*Laughing.*) You think if we put him into your bathing suit with a cap on his head . . . (*He laughs hysterically.*) You think anyone would know . . . huh? Do you think anyone would know? (*Laughs.*)

Simón (*Vamping.*): Ay, *mi amor.* Anybody looking for tits would know.

(*Eduardo slaps Simón across the face, knocking him down. Aída runs to Simón's aid. Abuela holds Eduardo back.*)

Margarita: Mía culpa!° Mía culpa!

Abuela: Qué dices hija?

Margarita: Papi, it's my fault, it's all my fault. . . . I'm so cold, I can't move. . . . I put my face in the water . . . and I hear them whispering . . . laughing at me. . . .

Aída: Who is laughing at you?

Margarita: The fish are all biting me . . . they hate me . . . they whisper about me. She can't swim, they say. She can't glide. She has no grace. . . . Yellow-tails, bonita, tuna, man-o'-war, snub-nose sharks, *los baracudas* . . . they all hate me . . . only the dolphins care . . . and sometimes I hear the whales crying . . . she is lost, she is dead. I'm so numb, I can't feel. *Papi! Papi!* Am I dead?

Eduardo: Vamos, baby, punch those arms in. Come on . . . do you hear me?

Margarita: Papi . . . *Papi* . . . forgive me. . . .

(*All is silent on the boat. Eduardo drops his megaphone, his head bent down in dejection. Abuela, Aída, Simón, all leaning over the side of the boat. Simón slowly walks away.*)

Mía culpa!: It's my fault.

Aída: Mi hija, qué tienes?

Simón: Oh, Christ, don't make her say it. Please don't make her say it.

Abuela: Say what? Qué cosa?

Simón: She wants to quit, can't you see she's had enough?

Abuela: Mira, para eso. Esta niña is turning blue.

Aída: Oyeme, mi hija. Do you want to come out of the water?

Margarita: Papi?

Simón (To Eduardo.): She won't come out until you tell her.

Aída: Eduardo . . . answer your daughter.

Eduardo: Le dije to concentrate . . . concentrate on your rhythm. Then the rhythm would carry her . . . ay, it's a beautiful thing, Aída. It's like yoga, like meditation, the mind over matter . . . the mind controlling the body . . . that's how the great things in the world have been done. I wish you . . . I wish my wife could understand.

Margarita: Papi?

Simón (To Margarita.): Forget him.

Aída (Imploring.): Eduardo, por favor.

Eduardo (Walking in circles.): Why didn't you let her concentrate? Don't you understand, the concentration, the rhythm is everything. But no, you wouldn't listen. (Screaming to the ocean.) Goddamn Cubans, why, God, why do you make us go everywhere with our families? (He goes to back of boat.)

Aída (Opening her arms.): Mi hija, ven, come to Mami. (Rocking.) Your mami knows.

(Abuela has taken the training bottle, puts it in a net. She and Simón lower it to Margarita.)

Simón: Take this. Drink it. (As Margarita drinks, Abuela crosses herself.)

Abuela: Sangre de mi sangre.

(Music comes up softly. Margarita drinks, gives the bottle back, stretches out her arms, as if on a cross. Floats on her back. She begins a graceful backstroke. Lights fade on boat as special lights come up on Margarita. She stops. Slowly turns over and starts to swim, gradually picking up speed. Suddenly as if in pain she stops, tries again, then stops in pain again. She becomes disoriented and falls to the bottom of the sea. Special on Margarita at the bottom of the sea.)

Margarita: Ya no puedo . . . I can't. . . . A person isn't a machine . . . es mi culpa . . . Father forgive me . . . Papi! Papi! One, two. Uno, dos. (Pause.) Papi! A dónde estás? (Pause.) One, two, one, two. Papi! Ay, Papi! Where are you . . . ? Don't leave me. . . . Why don't you answer me? (Pause. She starts to swim, slowly.) Uno, dos, uno, dos. Dig in, dig in. (Stops swimming.) Por favor, Papi! (Starts to swim again.) One, two, one, two. Kick from your hip, kick from your hip. (Stops swimming. Starts to cry.) Oh God, please. . . . (Pause.) Hail Mary, full of grace . . . dig in, dig in . . . the Lord is with thee. . . . (She swims to the rhythm of her Hail Mary.) Hail Mary, full of grace . . . dig in, dig in . . . the Lord is with thee . . . dig in, dig in. . . . Blessed art thou among women. . . . Mami, it hurts. You let go of my hand. I'm lost. . . . And blessed is the fruit of thy womb, now and at the hour of our death. Amen. I don't want to die, I don't want to die.

(*Margarita is still swimming. Blackout. She is gone.*)

SCENE 6

Lights up on boat, we hear radio static. There is a heavy mist. On deck we see only black outline of Abuela with shawl over her head. We hear the voices of Eduardo, Aída, and Radio Operator.

Eduardo's Voice: La Havana! Coming from San Pedro. Over.
Radio Operator's Voice: Right, DT6-6, you say you've lost a swimmer.
Aída's Voice: Our child, our only daughter . . . listen to me. Her name is Margarita Inez Suárez, she is wearing a black one-piece bathing suit cut high in the legs with a white racing stripe down the sides, a white bathing cap with goggles and her whole body covered with a . . . with a . . .
Eduardo's Voice: With lanolin and paraffin.
Aída's Voice: Sí . . . *con lanolin and paraffin.*

(*More radio static. Special on Simón, on the edge of the boat.*)

Simón: Margo! Yo Margo! (*Pause.*) Man don't do this. (*Pause.*) Come on. . . . Come on. . . . (*Pause.*) God, why does everything have to be so hard? (*Pause.*) Stupid. You know you're not supposed to die for this. Stupid. It's his dream and he can't even swim. (*Pause.*) Punch those arms in. Come home. Come home. I'm your little brother. Don't forget what Mama said. You're not supposed to leave me behind. *Vamos,* Margarita, take your little brother, hold his hand tight when you cross the street. He's so little. (*Pause.*) Oh Christ, give us a sign. . . . I know! I know! Margo, I'll send you a message . . . like mental telepathy. I'll hold my breath, close my eyes, and I'll bring you home. (*He takes a deep breath; a few beats.*) This time I'll beep . . . I'll send out sonar signals like a dolphin. (*He imitates dolphin sounds.*)

(*The sound of real dolphins takes over from Simón, then fades into sound of Abuela saying the Hail Mary in Spanish, as full lights come up slowly.*)

SCENE 7

Eduardo coming out of cabin, sobbing, Aída holding him. Simón anxiously scanning the horizon. Abuela looking calmly ahead.

Eduardo: Es mi culpa, sí, es mi culpa.° (*He hits his chest.*)
Aída: Ya, ya viejo.° . . . it was my sin . . . I left my home.

Es mi culpa, sí, es mi culpa: It's my fault, yes, it's my fault. *Ya, ya viejo:* Yes, yes, old man.

Eduardo: Forgive me, forgive me. I've lost our daughter, our sister, our granddaughter, *mi carne, mi sangre, mis ilusiones.°* (*To heaven.*) *Dios mío,* take me
. . . take me, I say . . . Goddammit, take me!

Simón: I'm going in.

Aída and Eduardo: No!

Eduardo (*Grabbing and holding Simón, speaking to heaven.*): God, take me, not my
children. They are my dreams, my illusions . . . and not this one, this one is my
mystery . . . he has my secret dreams. In him are the parts of me I cannot see.

(*Eduardo embraces Simón. Radio static becomes louder.*)

Aída: I . . . I think I see her.

Simón: No, it's just a seal.

Abuela (*Looking out with binoculars.*): Mi nietacita, dónde estás? (*She feels her
heart.*) I don't feel the knife in my heart . . . my little fish is not lost.

(*Radio crackles with static. As lights dim on boat, Voices of Mel and Mary Beth
are heard over the radio.*)

Mel's Voice: Tragedy has marred the face of the Wrigley Invitational Women's
Race to Catalina. The Cuban swimmer, little Margarita Suárez, has report-
edly been lost at sea. Coast Guard and divers are looking for her as we speak.
Yet in spite of this tragedy the race must go on because . . .

Mary Beth's Voice (*Interrupting loudly.*): Mel!

Mel's Voice (*Startled.*): What!

Mary Beth's Voice: Ah . . . excuse me, Mel . . . we have a winner. We've just received word from Catalina that one of the swimmers is just fifty yards from
the breakers . . . it's, oh, it's . . . Margarita Suárez!

(*Special on family in cabin listening to radio.*)

Mel's Voice: What? I thought she died!

(*Special on Margarita, taking off bathing cap, trophy in hand, walking on the water.*)

Mary Beth's Voice: Ahh . . . unless . . . unless this is a tragic . . . No . . . there she
is, Mel. Margarita Suárez! The only one in the race wearing a black bathing
suit cut high in the legs with a racing stripe down the side.

(*Family cheering, embracing.*)

Simón (*Screaming.*): Way to go, Margo!

Mel's Voice: This is indeed a miracle! It's a resurrection! Margarita Suárez, with
a flotilla of boats to meet her, is now walking on the waters, through the
breakers . . . onto the beach, with crowds of people cheering her on. What a
jubilation! This is a miracle!

(*Sound of crowds cheering. Lights and cheering sounds fade.*)

BLACKOUT.

---

mi carne, mi sangre, mis ilusiones: My flesh, my blood, my dreams.

Milcha Sanchez-Scott

Milcha Sanchez-Scott on Drama
WRITING *The Cuban Swimmer*   1989

From these women [recent immigrants Sanchez-Scott met at the employment agency where she worked] I got my material for *Latina*, my first play. I'd never tried to write. I was just collecting stories—for instance, a woman told me her child had died two years previously, and that at the mortuary she had lifted her child and put it across her face to give it a last goodbye. For two years, she said, the whole side of her face and her lips were cold. And being with my cousin again reminded me of the way we say things in Colombia: "Do you remember the summer when all the birds flew into the bedroom?" I was just writing things down.

About this time I was hired by Susan Loewenberg of L.A. Theatre Works to act in a project at the women's prison in Chino. I saw the way Doris Baizley, the writer, had put the women's stories together. When I offered Susan my notes, hoping she could make a piece out of them, she persuaded me to write it myself.

I'd found a channel to get all sorts of things flowing out. I liked controlling my own time, and *making* things—I've always admired architects. Acting seemed very airy to me because I could never take it home and show it to anybody. I had trouble being alone for long periods, but then I would go to the airport or someplace else busy to write. Doris and I used to do things like write under blankets by flashlight, which makes you feel like a little kid with a big secret.

L.A. Theatre Works got a grant and we toured *Latina* up and down the state with ten Latin actresses who were always feuding. We had one who was illegal, and wouldn't perform anyplace she thought Immigration might come, so I had to go on in her place. Then Susan commissioned me to write something else, which turned out to be *Dog Lady* and *Cuban Swimmer*. I saw the long-distance swimmer Diana Nyad on TV and I saw Salazar—the Cuban runner—and started thinking. I wanted to set a play in the water. So I put a family on a boat and a swimmer in the water and said, "Now, *what?*" I happened to be in a church and saw the most beautiful Stations of the

Cross. It struck me as a good outline for anybody undertaking an endeavor—there's all this tripping and falling and rising. So that's what I used.

On New Ground

August Wilson

JOE TURNER'S COME AND GONE°   1988

August Wilson (b. 1945) was the eldest son of a German-American father and an African-American mother. His parents separated early, and the young Wilson was raised on The Hill, a Pittsburgh ghetto neighborhood. Although he quit school in the ninth grade when a teacher accused him of submitting a ghost-written paper, which in truth he had written himself, Wilson continued his education in local libraries, supporting himself by cooking and stock-clerking. In 1968 he co-founded a community troupe, the Black Horizons Theater, staging plays by LeRoi Jones and other militants; later he moved from Pittsburgh to Saint Paul, Minnesota, where at last he saw a play of his own performed. Jitney, his first effort, won him entry to a 1982 playwrights' conference at the Eugene O'Neill Theater Center. There, Lloyd Richards, dean of Yale University School of Drama, took an interest in Wilson's work and offered to produce his plays at Yale. Ma Rainey's Black Bottom was the first to reach Broadway (in 1985), where it ran for ten months and received a prize from the New York Drama Critics Circle. In 1987 Fences, starring Mary Alice and James Paul Jones, won another Critics Circle Award, besides a Tony Award and the Pulitzer Prize for best American play of its year. It set a box office record for a Broadway nonmusical. Joe Turner's Come and Gone has also received high acclaim, and in 1990 his fourth major work, The Piano Lesson, won him a second Pulitzer Prize. His recent plays include Two Trains Running (1992) and Seven Guitars (1995). A published poet, Wilson once told an interviewer, "After writing poetry for twenty-one years, I approach a play the same way. The mental process is poetic: you use metaphor and condense."

Characters

Seth Holly, owner of the boardinghouse
Bertha Holly, his wife
Bynum Walker, a rootworker°
Rutherford Selig, a peddler
Jeremy Furlow, a resident
Herald Loomis, a resident
Zonia Loomis, his daughter
Mattie Campbell, a resident
Reuben Scott, boy who lives next door

Joe Turner's Come and Gone: In Tennessee around the turn of the century, Joe Turner became legendary: a professional bounty hunter, and one who claimed a reward for finding an escaped convict. To increase his profits, Turner impressed not only convicts into a chain gang but innocent men as well.   *rootworker:* a conjure man, or voodoo practitioner.

Molly Cunningham, a resident
Martha Pentecost, Herald Loomis's wife

Setting. *August, 1911. A boardinghouse in Pittsburgh. At right is a kitchen. Two doors open off the kitchen. One leads to the outhouse and Seth's workshop. The other to Seth's and Bertha's bedroom. At left is a parlor. The front door opens into the parlor, which gives access to the stairs leading to the upstairs rooms.*

There is a small outside playing area.

The Play. *It is August in Pittsburgh, 1911. The sun falls out of heaven like a stone. The fires of the steel mill rage with a combined sense of industry and progress. Barges loaded with coal and iron ore trudge up the river to the mill towns that dot the Monongahela and return with fresh, hard, gleaming steel. The city flexes its muscles. Men throw countless bridges across the river, lay roads and carve tunnels through the hills sprouting with houses.*

From the deep and the near South the sons and daughters of newly freed African slaves wander into the city. Isolated, cut off from memory, having forgotten the names of the gods and only guessing at their faces, they arrive dazed and stunned, their heart kicking in their chest with a song worth singing. They arrive carrying Bibles and guitars, their pockets lined with dust and fresh hope, marked men and women seeking to scrape from the narrow, crooked cobbles and the fiery blasts of the coke furnace a way of bludgeoning and shaping the malleable parts of themselves into a new identity as free men of definite and sincere worth.

Foreigners in a strange land, they carry as part and parcel of their baggage a long line of separation and dispersement which informs their sensibilities and marks their conduct as they search for ways to reconnect, to reassemble, to give clear and luminous meaning to the song which is both a wail and a whelp of joy.

ACT I
Scene 1

The lights come up on the kitchen. Bertha busies herself with breakfast preparations. Seth stands looking out the window at Bynum in the yard. Seth is in his early fifties. Born of Northern free parents, a skilled craftsman, and owner of the boardinghouse, he has a stability that none of the other characters have. Bertha is five years his junior. Married for over twenty-five years, she has learned how to negotiate around Seth's apparent orneriness.

Seth (*at the window, laughing*): If that ain't the damndest thing I seen. Look here, Bertha.

Bertha: I done seen Bynum out there with them pigeons before.

Seth: Naw . . . naw . . . look at this. That pigeon flopped out of Bynum's hand and he about to have a fit.

(*Bertha crosses over to the window.*)

He down there on his hands and knees behind that bush looking all over for that pigeon and it on the other side of the yard. See it over there?

Bertha: Come on and get your breakfast and leave that man alone.

Seth: Look at him . . . he still looking. He ain't seen it yet. All that old mumbo jumbo nonsense. I don't know why I put up with it.

Bertha: You don't say nothing when he bless the house.

Seth: I just go along with that 'cause of you. You around here sprinkling salt all over the place . . . got pennies lined up across the threshold . . . all that heebie-jeebie stuff. I just put up with that 'cause of you. I don't pay that kind of stuff no mind. And you going down there to the church and wanna come home and sprinkle salt all over the place.

Bertha: It don't hurt none. I can't say if it help . . . but it don't hurt none.

Seth: Look at him. He done found that pigeon and now he's talking to it.

Bertha: These biscuits be ready in a minute.

Seth: He done drew a big circle with that stick and now he's dancing around. I know he'd better not . . .

(*Seth bolts from the window and rushes to the back door.*)

Hey, Bynum! Don't be hopping around stepping in my vegetables. Hey, Bynum . . . Watch where you stepping!

Bertha: Seth, leave that man alone.

Seth (*coming back into the house*): I don't care how much he be dancing around . . . just don't be stepping in my vegetables. Man got my garden all messed up now . . . planting them weeds out there . . . burying them pigeons and whatnot.

Bertha: Bynum don't bother nobody. He ain't even thinking about your vegetables.

Seth: I know he ain't! That's why he out there stepping on them.

Bertha: What Mr. Johnson say down there?

Seth: I told him if I had the tools I could go out here and find me four or five fellows and open up my own shop instead of working for Mr. Olowski. Get me four or five fellows and teach them how to make pots and pans. One man making ten pots is five men making fifty. He told me he'd think about it.

Bertha: Well, maybe he'll come to see it your way.

Seth: He wanted me to sign over the house to him. You know what I thought of that idea.

Bertha: He'll come to see you're right.

Seth: I'm going up and talk to Sam Green. There's more than one way to skin a cat. I'm going up and talk to him. See if he got more sense than Mr. Johnson. I can't get nowhere working for Mr. Olowski and selling Selig five or six pots on the side. I'm going up and see Sam Green. See if he loan me the money.

(*Seth crosses back to the window.*)

Now he got that cup. He done killed that pigeon and now he's putting its blood in that little cup. I believe he drink that blood.

Bertha: Seth Holly, what is wrong with you this morning? Come on and get your breakfast so you can go to bed. You know Bynum don't be drinking no pigeon blood.

Seth: I don't know what he do.

Bertha: Well, watch him, then. He's gonna dig a little hole and bury that pigeon. Then he's gonna pray over that blood . . . pour it on top . . . mark out his circle and come on into the house.

Seth: That's what he doing . . . he pouring that blood on top.

Bertha: When they gonna put you back working daytime? Told me two months ago he was gonna put you back working daytime.

Seth: That's what Mr. Olowski told me. I got to wait till he say when. He tell me what to do. I don't tell him. Drive me crazy to speculate on the man's wishes when he don't know what he want to do himself.

Bertha: Well, I wish he go ahead and put you back working daytime. This working all hours of the night don't make no sense.

Seth: It don't make no sense for that boy to run out of here and get drunk so they lock him up either.

Bertha: Who? Who they got locked up for being drunk?

Seth: That boy that's staying upstairs . . . Jeremy. I stopped down there on Logan Street on my way home from work and one of the fellows told me about it. Say he seen it when they arrested him.

Bertha: I was wondering why I ain't seen him this morning.

Seth: You know I don't put up with that. I told him when he came . . .

(*Bynum enters from the yard carrying some plants. He is a short, round man in his early sixties. A conjure man, or rootworker, he gives the impression of always being in control of everything. Nothing ever bothers him. He seems to be lost in a world of his own making and to swallow any adversity or interference with his grand design.*)

What you doing bringing them weeds in my house? Out there stepping on my vegetables and now wanna carry them weeds in my house.

Bynum: Morning, Seth. Morning, Sister Bertha.

Seth: Messing up my garden growing them things out there. I ought to go out there and pull up all them weeds.

Bertha: Some gal was by here to see you this morning, Bynum. You was out there in the yard . . . I told her to come back later.

Bynum (to Seth): You look sick. What's the matter, you ain't eating right?

Seth: What if I was sick? You ain't getting near me with none of that stuff.

(*Bertha sets a plate of biscuits on the table.*)

Bynum: My . . . my . . . Bertha, your biscuits getting fatter and fatter.

(*Bynum takes a biscuit and begins to eat.*)

Where Jeremy? I don't see him around this morning. He usually be around riffing and raffing on Saturday morning.

Seth: I know where he at. I know just where he at. They got him down there in the jail. Getting drunk and acting a fool. He down there where he belong with all that foolishness.

Bynum: Mr. Piney's boys got him, huh? They ain't gonna do nothing but hold on to him for a little while. He's gonna be back here hungrier than a mule directly.

Seth: I don't go for all that carrying on and such. This is a respectable house. I don't have no drunkards or fools around here.

Bynum: That boy got a lot of country in him. He ain't been up here but two weeks. It's gonna take a while before he can work that country out of him.

Seth: These niggers coming up here with that old backward country style of living. It's hard enough now without all that ignorant kind of acting. Ever since slavery got over with there ain't been nothing but foolish-acting niggers. Word get out they need men to work in the mill and put in these roads . . . and niggers drop everything and head North looking for freedom. They don't know the white fellows looking too. White fellows coming from all over the world. White fellow come over and in six months got more than what I got. But these niggers keep on coming. Walking . . . riding . . . carrying their Bibles. That boy done carried a guitar all the way from North Carolina. What he gonna find out? What he gonna do with that guitar? This the city.

(There is a knock on the door.)

Niggers coming up here from the backwoods . . . coming up here from the country carrying Bibles and guitars looking for freedom. They got a rude awakening.

(Seth goes to answer the door. Rutherford Selig enters. About Seth's age, he is a thin white man with greasy hair. A peddler, he supplies Seth with the raw materials to make pots and pans which he then peddles door to door in the mill towns along the river. He keeps a list of his customers as they move about and is known in the various communities as the People Finder. He carries squares of sheet metal under his arm.)

Ho! Forgot you was coming today. Come on in.

Bynum: If it ain't Rutherford Selig . . . the People Finder himself.

Selig: What say there, Bynum?

Bynum: I say about my shiny man. You got to tell me something. I done give you my dollar . . . I'm looking to get a report.

Selig: I got eight here, Seth.

Seth (taking the sheet metal): What is this? What you giving me here? What I'm gonna do with this?

Selig: I need some dustpans. Everybody asking me about dustpans.

Seth: Gonna cost you fifteen cents apiece. And ten cents to put a handle on them.

Selig: I'll give you twenty cents apiece with the handles.

Seth: Alright. But I ain't gonna give you but fifteen cents for the sheet metal.

Selig: It's twenty-five cents apiece for the metal. That's what we agreed on.

Seth: This low-grade sheet metal. They ain't worth but a dime. I'm doing you a favor giving you fifteen cents. You know this metal ain't worth no twenty-five cents. Don't come talking that twenty-five cent stuff to me over no low-grade sheet metal.

Selig: Alright, fifteen cents apiece. Just make me some dustpans out of them.

(*Seth exits with the sheet metal out the back door.*)

Bertha: Sit on down there, Selig. Get you a cup of coffee and a biscuit.

Bynum: Where you coming from this time?

Selig: I been upriver. All along the Monongahela. Past Rankin and all up around Little Washington.

Bynum: Did you find anybody?

Selig: I found Sadie Jackson up in Braddock. Her mother's staying down there in Scotchbottom say she hadn't heard from her and she didn't know where she was at. I found her up in Braddock on Enoch Street. She bought a frying pan from me.

Bynum: You around here finding everybody how come you ain't found my shiny man?

Selig: The only shiny man I saw was the Nigras working on the road gang with the sweat glistening on them.

Bynum: Naw, you'd be able to tell this fellow. He shine like new money.

Selig: Well, I done told you I can't find nobody without a name.

Bertha: Here go one of these hot biscuits, Selig.

Bynum: This fellow don't have no name. I call him John 'cause it was up around Johnstown where I seen him. I ain't even so sure he's one special fellow. That shine could pass on to anybody. He could be anybody shining.

Selig: Well, what's he look like besides being shiny? There's lots of shiny Nigras.

Bynum: He's just a man I seen out on the road. He ain't had no special look. Just a man walking toward me on the road. He come up and asked me which way the road went. I told him everything I knew about the road, where it went and all, and he asked me did I have anything to eat 'cause he was hungry. Say he ain't had nothing to eat in three days. Well, I never be out there on the road without a piece of dried meat. Or an orange or an apple. So I give this fellow an orange. He take and eat that orange and told me to come and go along the road a little ways with him, that he had something he wanted to show me. He had a look about him made me wanna go with him, see what he gonna show me.

We walked on a bit and it's getting kind of far from where I met him when it come up on me all of a sudden, we wasn't going the way he had come from, we was going back my way. Since he said he ain't knew nothing about the road, I asked him about this. He say he had a voice inside him telling him which way to go and if I come and go along with him he was gonna show me the Secret of Life. Quite naturally I followed him. A fellow that's gonna show you the Secret of Life ain't to be taken lightly. We get near this bend in the road . . .

(*Seth enters with an assortment of pans.*)

Seth: I got six here, Selig.

Selig: Wait a minute, Seth. Bynum's telling me about the secret of life. Go ahead, Bynum. I wanna hear this.

(*Seth sets the pots down and exits out the back.*)

Bynum: We get near this bend in the road and he told me to hold out my hands. Then he rubbed them together with his and I looked down and see they got blood on them. Told me to take and rub it all over me . . . say that was a way of cleaning myself. Then we went around the bend in that road. Got around that bend and it seem like all of a sudden we ain't in the same place. Turn around that bend and everything look like it was twice as big as it was. The trees and everything bigger than life! Sparrows big as eagles! I turned around to look at this fellow and he had this light coming out of him. I had to cover up my eyes to keep from being blinded. He shining like new money with that light. He shined until all the light seemed like it seeped out of him and then he was gone and I was by myself in this strange place where everything was bigger than life.

I wandered around there looking for that road, trying to find my way back from this big place . . . and I looked over and seen my daddy standing there. He was the same size he always was, except for his hands and his mouth. He had a great big old mouth that look like it took up his whole face and his hands were as big as hams. Look like they was too big to carry around. My daddy called me to him. Said he had been thinking about me and it grieved him to see me in the world carrying other people's songs and not having one of my own. Told me he was gonna show me how to find my song. Then he carried me further into this big place until we come to this ocean. Then he showed me something I ain't got words to tell you. But if you stand to witness it, you done seen something there. I stayed in that place awhile and my daddy taught me the meaning of this thing that I had seen and showed me how to find my song. I asked him about the shiny man and he told me he was the One Who Goes Before and Shows the Way. Said there was lots of shiny men and if I ever saw one again before I died then I would know that my song had been accepted and worked its full power in the world and I could lay down and die a happy man. A man who done left his mark on life. On the way people cling to each other out of the truth they find in themselves. Then he showed me how to get back to the road. I came out where everything was its own size and I had my song. I had the Binding Song. I choose that song because that's what I seen most when I was traveling . . . people walking away and leaving one another. So I takes the power of my song and binds them together.

(*Seth enters from the yard carrying cabbages and tomatoes.*)

Been binding people ever since. That's why they call me Bynum. Just like glue I sticks people together.

Seth: Maybe they ain't supposed to be stuck sometimes. You ever think of that?

Bynum: Oh, I don't do it lightly. It cost me a piece of myself every time I do. I'm a Binder of What Clings. You got to find out if they cling first. You can't bind what don't cling.

Selig: Well, how is that the Secret of Life? I thought you said he was gonna show you the secret of life. That's what I'm waiting to find out.

Bynum: Oh, he showed me alright. But you still got to figure it out. Can't nobody figure it out for you. You got to come to it on your own. That's why I'm looking for the shiny man.

Selig: Well, I'll keep my eye out for him. What you got there, Seth?

Seth: Here go some cabbage and tomatoes. I got some green beans coming in real nice. I'm gonna take and start me a grapevine out there next year. Butera says he gonna give me a piece of his vine and I'm gonna start that out there.

Selig: How many of them pots you got?

Seth: I got six. That's six dollars minus eight on top of fifteen for the sheet metal come to a dollar twenty out the six dollars leave me four dollars and eighty cents.

Selig (counting out the money): There's four dollars . . . and . . . eighty cents.

Seth: How many of them dustpans you want?

Selig: As many as you can make out them sheets.

Seth: You can use that many? I get to cutting on them sheets figuring how to make them dustpans . . . ain't no telling how many I'm liable to come up with.

Selig: I can use them and you can make me some more next time.

Seth: Alright, I'm gonna hold you to that, now.

Selig: Thanks for the biscuit, Bertha.

Bertha: You know you welcome anytime, Selig.

Seth: Which way you heading?

Selig: Going down to Wheeling. All through West Virginia there. I'll be back Saturday. They putting in new roads down that way. Makes traveling easier.

Seth: That's what I hear. All up around here too. Got a fellow staying here working on that road by the Brady Street Bridge.

Selig: Yeah, it's gonna make traveling real nice. Thanks for the cabbage, Seth. I'll see you on Saturday.

(*Selig exits.*)

Seth (to Bynum): Why you wanna start all that nonsense talk with that man? All that shiny man nonsense.

Bynum: You know it ain't no nonsense. Bertha know it ain't no nonsense. I don't know if Selig know or not.

Bertha: Seth, when you get to making them dustpans make me a coffeepot.

Seth: What's the matter with your coffee? Ain't nothing wrong with your coffee. Don't she make some good coffee, Bynum?

Bynum: I ain't worried about the coffee. I know she makes some good biscuits.

Seth: I ain't studying no coffeepot, woman. You heard me tell the man I was gonna cut as many dustpans as them sheets will make . . . and all of a sudden you want a coffeepot.

Bertha: Man, hush up and go on and make me that coffeepot.

(Jeremy enters the front door. About twenty-five, he gives the impression that he has the world in his hand, that he can meet life's challenges head on. He smiles a lot. He is a proficient guitar player, though his spirit has yet to be molded into song.)

Bynum: I hear Mr. Piney's boys had you.

Jeremy: Fined me two dollars for nothing! Ain't done nothing.

Seth: I told you when you come on here everybody know my house. Know these is respectable quarters. I don't put up with no foolishness. Everybody know Seth Holly keep a good house. Was my daddy's house. This house been a decent house for a long time.

Jeremy: I ain't done nothing, Mr. Seth. I stopped by the Workmen's Club and got me a bottle. Me and Roper Lee from Alabama. Had us a half pint. We was fixing to cut that half in two when they came up on us. Asked us if we was working. We told them we was putting in the road over yonder and that it was our payday. They snatched hold of us to get that two dollars. Me and Roper Lee ain't even had a chance to take a drink when they grabbed us.

Seth: I don't go for all that kind of carrying on.

Bertha: Leave the boy alone, Seth. You know the police do that. Figure there's too many people out on the street they take some of them off. You know that.

Seth: I ain't gonna have folks talking.

Bertha: Ain't nobody talking nothing. That's all in your head. You want some grits and biscuits, Jeremy?

Jeremy: Thank you, Miss Bertha. They didn't give us a thing to eat last night. I'll take one of them big bowls if you don't mind.

(There is a knock at the door. Seth goes to answer it. Enter Herald Loomis and his eleven-year-old daughter, Zonia. Herald Loomis is thirty-two years old. He is at times possessed. A man driven not by the hellhounds that seemingly bay at his heels, but by his search for a world that speaks to something about himself. He is unable to harmonize the forces that swirl around him, and seeks to recreate the world into one that contains his image. He wears a hat and a long wool coat.)

Loomis: Me and my daughter looking for a place to stay, mister. You got a sign say you got rooms.

(Seth stares at Loomis, sizing him up.)

Mister, if you ain't got no rooms we can go somewhere else.

Seth: How long you plan on staying?

Loomis: Don't know. Two weeks or more maybe.

Seth: It's two dollars a week for the room. We serve meals twice a day. It's two dollars for room and board. Pay up in advance.

(Loomis reaches into his pocket.)

It's a dollar extra for the girl.

Loomis: The girl sleep in the same room.

Seth: Well, do she eat off the same plate? We serve meals twice a day. That's a dollar extra for food.

Loomis: Ain't got no extra dollar. I was planning on asking your missus if she could help out with the cooking and cleaning and whatnot.

Seth: Her helping out don't put no food on the table. I need that dollar to buy some food.

Loomis: I'll give you fifty cents extra. She don't eat much.

Seth: Okay . . . but fifty cents don't buy but half a portion.

Bertha: Seth, she can help me out. Let her help me out. I can use some help.

Seth: Well, that's two dollars for the week. Pay up in advance. Saturday to Saturday. You wanna stay on then it's two more come Saturday.

(Loomis pays Seth the money.)

Bertha: My name's Bertha. This my husband, Seth. You got Bynum and Jeremy over there.

Loomis: Ain't nobody else live here?

Bertha: They the only ones live here now. People come and go. They the only ones here now. You want a cup of coffee and a biscuit?

Loomis: We done ate this morning.

Bynum: Where you coming from, Mister . . . I didn't get your name.

Loomis: Name's Herald Loomis. This my daughter, Zonia.

Bynum: Where you coming from?

Loomis: Come from all over. Whicheverway the road take us that's the way we go.

Jeremy: If you looking for a job, I'm working putting in that road down there by the bridge. They can't get enough mens. Always looking to take somebody on.

Loomis: I'm looking for a woman named Martha Loomis. That's my wife. Got married legal with the papers and all.

Seth: I don't know nobody named Loomis. I know some Marthas but I don't know no Loomis.

Bynum: You got to see Rutherford Selig if you wanna find somebody. Selig's the People Finder. Rutherford Selig's a first-class People Finder.

Jeremy: What she look like? Maybe I seen her.

Loomis: She a brownskin woman. Got long pretty hair. About five feet from the ground.

Jeremy: I don't know. I might have seen her.

Bynum: You got to see Rutherford Selig. You give him one dollar to get her name on his list . . . and after she get her name on his list Rutherford Selig will go right on out there and find her. I got him looking for somebody for me.

Loomis: You say he find people. How you find him?

Bynum: You just missed him. He's gone downriver now. You got to wait till Saturday. He's gone downriver with his pots and pans. He come to see Seth on Saturdays. You got to wait till then.

Seth: Come on, I'll show you to your room.

(*Seth, Loomis, and Zonia exit up the stairs.*)

Jeremy: Miss Bertha, I'll take that biscuit you was gonna give that fellow, if you don't mind. Say, Mr. Bynum, they got somebody like that around here sure enough? Somebody that find people?

Bynum: Rutherford Selig. He go around selling pots and pans and every house he come to he write down the name and address of whoever lives there. So if you looking for somebody, quite naturally you go and see him ... 'cause he's the only one who know where everybody live at.

Jeremy: I ought to have him look for this old gal I used to know. It be nice to see her again.

Bertha (giving Jeremy a biscuit): Jeremy, today's the day for you to pull them sheets off the bed and set them outside your door. I'll set you out some clean ones.

Bynum: Mr. Piney's boys done ruined your good time last night, Jeremy ... what you planning for tonight?

Jeremy: They got me scared to go out, Mr. Bynum. They might grab me again.

Bynum: You ought to take your guitar and go down to Seefus. Seefus got a gambling place down there on Wylie Avenue. You ought to take your guitar and go down there. They got guitar contest down there.

Jeremy: I don't play no contest, Mr. Bynum. Had one of them white fellows cure me of that. I ain't been nowhere near a contest since.

Bynum: White fellow beat you playing guitar?

Jeremy: Naw, he ain't beat me. I was sitting at home just fixing to sit down and eat when somebody come up to my house and got me. Told me there's a white fellow say he was gonna give a prize to the best guitar player he could find. I take up my guitar and go down there and somebody had gone up and got Bobo Smith and brought him down there. Him and another fellow called Hooter. Old Hooter couldn't play no guitar, he do more hollering than playing, but Bobo could go at it awhile.

This fellow standing there say he the one that was gonna give the prize and me and Bobo started playing for him. Bobo play something and then I'd try to play something better than what he played. Old Hooter, he just holler and bang at the guitar. Man was the worst guitar player I ever seen. So me and Bobo played and after a while I seen where he was getting the attention of this white fellow. He'd play something and while he was playing it he be slapping on the side of the guitar, and that made it sound like he was playing more than he was. So I started doing it too. White fellow ain't knew no difference. He ain't knew as much about guitar playing as Hooter did. After we play awhile, the white fellow called us to him and said he couldn't make up his mind, say all three of us was the best guitar player and we'd have to split the prize between us. Then he give us twenty-five cents. That's eight cents apiece and a penny on the side. That cured me of playing contest to this day.

Bynum: Seefus ain't like that. Seefus give a whole dollar and a drink of whiskey.

Jeremy: What night they be down there?

Bynum: Be down there every night. Music don't know no certain night.

Bertha: You go down to Seefus with them people and you liable to end up in a raid and go to jail sure enough. I don't know why Bynum tell you that.

Bynum: That's where the music at. That's where the people at. The people down there making music and enjoying themselves. Some things is worth taking the chance going to jail about.

Bertha: Jeremy ain't got no business going down there.

Jeremy: They got some women down there, Mr. Bynum?

Bynum: Oh, they got women down there, sure. They got women everywhere. Women be where the men is so they can find each other.

Jeremy: Some of them old gals come out there where we be putting in that road. Hanging around there trying to snatch somebody.

Bynum: How come some of them ain't snatched hold of you?

Jeremy: I don't want them kind. Them desperate kind. Ain't nothing worse than a desperate woman. Tell them you gonna leave them and they get to crying and carrying on. That just make you want to get away quicker. They get to cutting up your clothes and things trying to keep you staying. Desperate women ain't nothing but trouble for a man.

(*Seth enters from the stairs.*)

Seth: Something ain't setting right with that fellow.

Bertha: What's wrong with him? What he say?

Seth: I take him up there and try to talk to him and he ain't for no talking. Say he been traveling . . . coming over from Ohio. Say he a deacon in the church. Say he looking for Martha Pentecost. Talking about that's his wife.

Bertha: How you know it's the same Martha? Could be talking about anybody. Lots of people named Martha.

Seth: You see that little girl? I didn't hook it up till he said it, but that little girl look just like her. Ask Bynum. (*To Bynum.*) Bynum. Don't that little girl look just like Martha Pentecost?

Bertha: I still say he could be talking about anybody.

Seth: The way he described her wasn't no doubt who he was talking about. Described her right down to her toes.

Bertha: What did you tell him?

Seth: I ain't told him nothing. The way that fellow look I wasn't gonna tell him nothing. I don't know what he looking for her for.

Bertha: What else he have to say?

Seth: I told you he wasn't for no talking. I told him where the outhouse was and to keep that gal off the front porch and out of my garden. He asked if you'd mind setting a hot tub for the gal and that was about the gist of it.

Bertha: Well, I wouldn't let it worry me if I was you. Come on get your sleep.

Bynum: He says he looking for Martha and he a deacon in the church.

Seth: That's what he say. Do he look like a deacon to you?

Bertha: He might be, you don't know. Bynum ain't got no special say on whether he a deacon or not.

Seth: Well, if he the deacon I'd sure like to see the preacher.

Bertha: Come on get your sleep. Jeremy, don't forget to set them sheets outside the door like I told you.

(*Bertha exits into the bedroom.*)

Seth: Something ain't setting right with that fellow, Bynum. He's one of them mean-looking niggers look like he done killed somebody gambling over a quarter.

Bynum: He ain't no gambler. Gamblers wear nice shoes. This fellow got on clod-hoppers. He been out there walking up and down them roads.

(*Zonia enters from the stairs and looks around.*)

Bynum: You looking for the back door, sugar? There it is. You can go out there and play. It's alright.

Seth (*showing her the door*): You can go out there and play. Just don't get in my garden. And don't go messing around in my workshed.

(*Seth exits into the bedroom. There is a knock on the door.*)

Jeremy: Somebody at the door.

(*Jeremy goes to answer the door. Enter Mattie Campbell. She is a young woman of twenty-six whose attractiveness is hidden under the weight and concerns of a dissatisfied life. She is a woman in an honest search for love and companionship. She has suffered many defeats in her search, and though not always uncompromising, still believes in the possibility of love.*)

Mattie: I'm looking for a man named Bynum. Lady told me to come back later.

Jeremy: Sure, he here. Mr. Bynum, somebody here to see you.

Bynum: Come to see me, huh?

Mattie: Are you the man they call Bynum? The man folks say can fix things?

Bynum: Depend on what need fixing. I can't make no promises. But I got a powerful song in some matters.

Mattie: Can you fix it so my man come back to me?

Bynum: Come on in . . . have a sit down.

Mattie: You got to help me. I don't know what else to do.

Bynum: Depend on how all the circumstances of the thing come together. How all the pieces fit.

Mattie: I done everything I knowed how to do. You got to make him come back to me.

Bynum: It ain't nothing to make somebody come back. I can fix it so he can't stand to be away from you. I got my roots and powders, I can fix it so wherever he's at this thing will come up on him and he won't be able to sleep for seeing your face. Won't be able to eat for thinking of you.

Mattie: That's what I want. Make him come back.

Bynum: The roots is a powerful thing. I can fix it so one day he'll walk out his front door . . . won't be thinking of nothing. He won't know what it is. All he knows is that a powerful dissatisfaction done set in his bones and can't nothing he do make him feel satisfied. He'll set his foot down on the road and the wind in the trees be talking to him and everywhere he step on the road, that road'll give back your name and something will pull him right up to your doorstep. Now, I can do that. I can take my roots and fix that easy. But maybe he ain't supposed to come back. And if he ain't supposed to come back . . . then he'll be in your bed one morning and it'll come up on him that he's in the wrong place. That he's lost outside of time from his place that he's supposed to be in. Then both of you be lost and trapped outside of life and ain't no way for you to get back into it. 'Cause you lost from yourselves and where the places come together, where you're supposed to be alive, your heart kicking in your chest with a song worth singing.

Mattie: Make him come back to me. Make his feet say my name on the road. I don't care what happens. Make him come back.

Bynum: What's your man's name?

Mattie: He go by Jack Carper. He was born in Alabama then he come to West Texas and find me and we come here. Been here three years before he left. Say I had a curse prayer on me and he started walking down the road and ain't never come back. Somebody told me, say you can fix things like that.

Bynum: He just got up one day, set his feet on the road, and walked away?

Mattie: You got to make him come back, mister.

Bynum: Did he say goodbye?

Mattie: Ain't said nothing. Just started walking. I could see where he disappeared. Didn't look back. Just keep walking. Can't you fix it so he come back? I ain't got no curse prayer on me. I know I ain't.

Bynum: What made him say you had a curse prayer on you?

Mattie: 'Cause the babies died. Me and Jack had two babies. Two little babies that ain't lived two months before they died. He say it's because somebody cursed me not to have babies.

Bynum: He ain't bound to you if the babies died. Look like somebody trying to keep you from being bound up and he's gone on back to whoever it is 'cause he's already bound up to her. Ain't nothing to be done. Somebody else done got a powerful hand in it and ain't nothing to be done to break it. You got to let him go find where he's supposed to be in the world.

Mattie: Jack done gone off and you telling me to forget about him. All my life I been looking for somebody to stop and stay with me. I done already got too many things to forget about. I take Jack Carper's hand and it feel so rough and strong. Seem like he's the strongest man in the world the way he hold me. Like he's bigger than the whole world and can't nothing bad get to me. Even when he act mean sometimes he still make everything seem okay with the world. Like there's part of it that belongs just to you. Now you telling me to forget about him?

Bynum: Jack Carper gone off to where he belong. There's somebody searching for your doorstep right now. Ain't no need you fretting over Jack Carper.

Right now he's a strong thought in your mind. But every time you catch yourself fretting over Jack Carper you push that thought away. You push it out your mind and that thought will get weaker and weaker till you wake up one morning and you won't even be able to call him up on your mind.

(*Bynum gives her a small cloth packet.*)

Take this and sleep with it under your pillow and it'll bring good luck to you. Draw it to you like a magnet. It won't be long before you forget all about Jack Carper.

Mattie: How much . . . do I owe you?

Bynum: Whatever you got there . . . that'll be alright.

(*Mattie hands Bynum two quarters. She crosses to the door.*)

You sleep with that under your pillow and you'll be alright.

(*Mattie opens the door to exit and Jeremy crosses over to her. Bynum overhears the first part of their conversation, then exits out the back.*)

Jeremy: I overheard what you told Mr. Bynum. Had me an old gal did that to me. Woke up one morning and she was gone. Just took off to parts unknown. I woke up that morning and the only thing I could do was look around for my shoes. I woke up and got out of there. Found my shoes and took off. That's the only thing I could think of to do.

Mattie: She ain't said nothing?

Jeremy: I just looked around for my shoes and got out of there.

Mattie: Jack ain't said nothing either. He just walked off.

Jeremy: Some mens do that. Womens too. I ain't gone off looking for her. I just let her go. Figure she had a time to come to herself. Wasn't no use of me standing in the way. Where you from?

Mattie: Texas. I was born in Georgia but I went to Texas with my mama. She dead now. Was picking peaches and fell dead away. I come up here with Jack Carper.

Jeremy: I'm from North Carolina. Down around Raleigh where they got all that tobacco. Been up here about two weeks. I likes it fine except I still got to find me a woman. You got a nice look to you. Look like you have mens standing in your door. Is you got mens standing in your door to get a look at you?

Mattie: I ain't got nobody since Jack left.

Jeremy: A woman like you need a man. Maybe you let me be your man. I got a nice way with the women. That's what they tell me.

Mattie: I don't know. Maybe Jack's coming back.

Jeremy: I'll be your man till he come. A woman can't be by her lonesome. Let me be your man till he come.

Mattie: I just can't go through life piecing myself out to different mens. I need a man who wants to stay with me.

Jeremy: I can't say what's gonna happen. Maybe I'll be the man. I don't know. You wanna go along the road a little ways with me?

Mattie: I don't know. Seem like life say it's gonna be one thing and end up being another. I'm tired of going from man to man.

Jeremy: Life is like you got to take a chance. Everybody got to take a chance. Can't nobody say what's gonna be. Come on . . . take a chance with me and see what the year bring. Maybe you let me come and see you. Where you staying?

Mattie: I got me a room up on Bedford. Me and Jack had a room together.

Jeremy: What's the address? I'll come by and get you tonight and we can go down to Seefus. I'm going down there and play my guitar.

Mattie: You play guitar?

Jeremy: I play guitar like I'm born to it.

Mattie: I live at 1727 Bedford Avenue. I'm gonna find out if you can play guitar like you say.

Jeremy: I plays it sugar, and that ain't all I do. I got a ten-pound hammer and I knows how to drive it down. Good god . . . you ought to hear my hammer ring!

Mattie: Go on with that kind of talk, now. If you gonna come by and get me I got to get home and straighten up for you.

Jeremy: I'll be by at eight o'clock. How's eight o'clock? I'm gonna make you forget all about Jack Carper.

Mattie: Go on, now. I got to get home and fix up for you.

Jeremy: Eight o'clock, sugar.

(*The lights go down in the parlor and come up on the yard outside. Zonia is singing and playing a game.*)

Zonia:

I went downtown
To get my grip
I came back home
Just a pullin' the skiff

I went upstairs
To make my bed
I made a mistake
And I bumped my head
Just a pullin' the skiff

I went downstairs
To milk the cow
I made a mistake
And I milked the sow
Just a pullin' the skiff

Tomorrow, tomorrow
Tomorrow never comes
The marrow the marrow
The marrow in the bone.

(Reuben enters.)

Reuben: Hi.

Zonia: Hi.

Reuben: What's your name?

Zonia: Zonia.

Reuben: What kind of name is that?

Zonia: It's what my daddy named me.

Reuben: My name's Reuben. You staying in Mr. Seth's house?

Zonia: Yeah.

Reuben: That your daddy I seen you with this morning?

Zonia: I don't know. Who you see me with?

Reuben: I saw you with some man had on a great big old coat. And you was walking up to Mr. Seth's house. Had on a hat too.

Zonia: Yeah, that's my daddy.

Reuben: You like Mr. Seth?

Zonia: I ain't see him much.

Reuben: My grandpap say he a great big old windbag. How come you living in Mr. Seth's house? Don't you have no house?

Zonia: We going to find my mother.

Reuben: Where she at?

Zonia: I don't know. We got to find her. We just go all over.

Reuben: Why you got to find her? What happened to her?

Zonia: She ran away.

Reuben: Why she run away?

Zonia: I don't know. My daddy say some man named Joe Turner did something bad to him once and that made her run away.

Reuben: Maybe she coming back and you don't have to go looking for her.

Zonia: We ain't there no more.

Reuben: She could have come back when you wasn't there.

Zonia: My daddy said she ran off and left us so we going looking for her.

Reuben: What he gonna do when he find her?

Zonia: He didn't say. He just say he got to find her.

Reuben: Your daddy say how long you staying in Mr. Seth's house?

Zonia: He don't say much. But we never stay too long nowhere. He say we got to keep moving till we find her.

Reuben: Ain't no kids hardly live around here. I had me a friend but he died. He was the best friend I ever had. Me and Eugene used to keep secrets. I still got his pigeons. He told me to let them go when he died. He say, "Reuben, promise me when I die you'll let my pigeons go." But I keep them to remember him by. I ain't never gonna let them go. Even when I get to be grown up. I'm just always gonna have Eugene's pigeons.

(Pause.)

Mr. Bynum a conjure man. My grandpap scared of him. He don't like me to come over here too much. I'm scared of him too. My grandpap told me not to let him get close enough to where he can reach out his hand and touch me.

Zonia: He don't seem scary to me.

Reuben: He buys pigeons from me . . . and if you get up early in the morning you can see him out in the yard doing something with them pigeons. My grandpap say he kill them. I sold him one yesterday. I don't know what he do with it. I just hope he don't spook me up.

Zonia: Why you sell him pigeons if he's gonna spook you up?

Reuben: I just do like Eugene do. He used to sell Mr. Bynum pigeons. That's how he got to collecting them to sell to Mr. Bynum. Sometime he give me a nickel and sometime he give me a whole dime.

(*Loomis enters from the house.*)

Loomis: Zonia!

Zonia: Sir?

Loomis: What you doing?

Zonia: Nothing.

Loomis: You stay around this house, you hear? I don't want you wandering off nowhere.

Zonia: I ain't wandering off nowhere.

Loomis: Miss Bertha set that hot tub and you getting a good scrubbing. Get scrubbed up good. You ain't been scrubbing.

Zonia: I been scrubbing.

Loomis: Look at you. You growing too fast. Your bones getting bigger everyday. I don't want you getting grown on me. Don't you get grown on me too soon. We gonna find your mamma. She around here somewhere. I can smell her. You stay on around this house now. Don't you go nowhere.

Zonia: Yes, sir.

(*Loomis exits into the house.*)

Reuben: Wow, your daddy's scary!

Zonia: He is not! I don't know what you talking about.

Reuben: He got them mean-looking eyes!

Zonia: My daddy ain't got no mean-looking eyes!

Reuben: Aw, girl, I was just messing with you. You wanna go see Eugene's pigeons? Got a great big coop out the back of my house. Come on, I'll show you.

(*Reuben and Zonia exit as the lights go down.*)

Scene 2

It is Saturday morning, one week later. The lights come up on the kitchen. Bertha is at the stove preparing breakfast while Seth sits at the table.

Seth: Something ain't right about that fellow. I been watching him all week. Something ain't right, I'm telling you.

Bertha: Seth Holly, why don't you hush up about that man this morning?

Seth: I don't like the way he stare at everybody. Don't look at you natural like. He just be staring at you. Like he trying to figure out something about you. Did you see him when he come back in here?

Bertha: That man ain't thinking about you.

Seth: He don't work nowhere. Just go out and come back. Go out and come back.

Bertha: As long as you get your boarding money it ain't your cause about what he do. He don't bother nobody.

Seth: Just go and come back. Going around asking everybody about Martha. Like Henry Allen seen him down at the church last night.

Bertha: The man's allowed to go to church if he want. He say he a deacon. Ain't nothing wrong about him going to church.

Seth: I ain't talking about him going to church. I'm talking about him hanging around *outside* the church.

Bertha: Henry Allen say that?

Seth: Say he be standing around outside the church. Like he be watching it.

Bertha: What on earth he wanna be watching the church for, I wonder?

Seth: That's what I'm trying to figure out. Looks like he fixing to rob it.

Bertha: Seth, now do he look like the kind that would rob the church?

Seth: I ain't saying that. I ain't saying how he look. It's how he do. Anybody liable to do anything as far as I'm concerned. I ain't never thought about how no church robbers look . . . but now that you mention it, I don't see where they look no different than how he look.

Bertha: Herald Loomis ain't the kind of man who would rob no church.

Seth: I ain't even so sure that's his name.

Bertha: Why the man got to lie about his name?

Seth: Anybody can tell anybody anything about what their name is. That's what you call him . . . Herald Loomis. His name is liable to be anything.

Bertha: Well, until he tell me different that's what I'm gonna call him. You just getting yourself all worked up about the man for nothing.

Seth: Talking about Loomis: Martha's name wasn't no Loomis nothing. Martha's name is Pentecost.

Bertha: How you so sure that's her right name? Maybe she changed it.

Seth: Martha's a good Christian woman. This fellow here look like he owe the devil a day's work and he's trying to figure out how he gonna pay him. Martha ain't had a speck of distrust about her the whole time she was living here. They moved the church out there to Rankin and I was sorry to see her go.

Bertha: That's why he be hanging around the church. He looking for her.

Seth: If he looking for her, why don't he go inside and ask? What he doing hanging around outside the church acting sneaky like?

(*Bynum enters from the yard.*)

Bynum: Morning, Seth. Morning, Sister Bertha.

(*Bynum continues through the kitchen and exits up the stairs.*)

Bertha: That's who you should be asking the questions. He been out there in that yard all morning. He was out there before the sun come up. He didn't even come in for breakfast. I don't know what he's doing. He had three of them pigeons line up out there. He dance around till he get tired. He sit down awhile then get up and dance some more. He come through here a little while ago looking like he was mad at the world.

Seth: I don't pay Bynum no mind. He don't spook me up with all that stuff.

Bertha: That's how Martha come to be living here. She come to see Bynum. She come to see him when she first left from down South.

Seth: Martha was living here before Bynum. She ain't come on here when she first left from down there. She come on here after she went back to get her little girl. That's when she come on here.

Bertha: Well, where was Bynum? He was here when she came.

Seth: Bynum ain't come till after her. That boy Hiram was staying up there in Bynum's room.

Bertha: Well, how long Bynum been here?

Seth: Bynum ain't been here no longer than three years. That's what I'm trying to tell you. Martha was staying up there and sewing and cleaning for Doc Goldblum when Bynum came. This the longest he ever been in one place.

Bertha: How you know how long the man been in one place?

Seth: I know Bynum. Bynum ain't no mystery to me. I done seen a hundred niggers like him. He's one of them fellows never could stay in one place. He was wandering all around the country till he got old and settled here. The only thing different about Bynum is he bring all this heebie-jeebie stuff with him.

Bertha: I still say he was staying here when she came. That's why she came . . . to see him.

Seth: You can say what you want. I know the facts of it. She come on here four years ago all heartbroken 'cause she couldn't find her little girl. And Bynum wasn't nowhere around. She got mixed up in that old heebie-jeebie nonsense with him after he came.

Bertha: Well, if she came on before Bynum I don't know where she stayed. 'Cause she stayed up there in Hiram's room. Hiram couldn't get along with Bynum and left out of here owing you two dollars. Now, I know you ain't forgot about that!

Seth: Sure did! You know Hiram ain't paid me that two dollars yet. So that's why he be ducking and hiding when he see me down on Logan Street. You right. Martha did come on after Bynum. I forgot that's why Hiram left.

Bertha: Him and Bynum never could see eye to eye. They always rubbed each other the wrong way. Hiram got to thinking that Bynum was trying to put a fix on him and he moved out. Martha came to see Bynum and ended up taking Hiram's room. Now, I know what I'm talking about. She stayed on here three years till they moved the church.

Seth: She out there in Rankin now. I know where she at. I know where they moved the church to. She right out there in Rankin in that place used to be shoe store. Used to be Wolf's shoe store. They moved to a bigger place and they put that church in there. I know where she at. I know just where she at.

Bertha: Why don't you tell the man? You see he looking for her.

Seth: I ain't gonna tell that man where that woman is! What I wanna do that for? I don't know nothing about that man. I don't know why he looking for her. He might wanna do her a harm. I ain't gonna carry that on my hands. He looking for her, he gonna have to find her for himself. I ain't gonna help him. Now, if he had come and presented himself as a gentleman—the way Martha Pentecost's husband would have done—then I would have told him. But I ain't gonna tell this old wild-eyed mean-looking nigger nothing!

Bertha: Well, why don't you get a ride with Selig and go up there and tell her where he is? See if she wanna see him. If that's her little girl . . . you say Martha was looking for her.

Seth: You know me, Bertha. I don't get mixed up in nobody's business.

(Bynum enters from the stairs.)

Bynum: Morning, Seth. Morning, Bertha. Can I still get some breakfast? Mr. Loomis been down here this morning?

Seth: He done gone out and come back. He up there now. Left out of here early this morning wearing that coat. Hot as it is, the man wanna walk around wearing a big old heavy coat. He come back in here paid me for another week, sat down there waiting on Selig. Got tired of waiting and went on back upstairs.

Bynum: Where's the little girl?

Seth: She out there in the front. Had to chase her and that Reuben off the front porch. She out there somewhere.

Bynum: Look like if Martha was around here he would have found her by now. My guess is she ain't in the city.

Seth: She ain't! I know where she at. I know just where she at. But I ain't gonna tell him. Not the way he look.

Bertha: Here go your coffee, Bynum.

Bynum: He says he gonna get Selig to find her for him.

Seth: Selig can't find her. He talk all that . . . but unless he get lucky and knock on her door he can't find her. That's the only way he find anybody. He got to get lucky. But I know just where she at.

Bertha: Here go some biscuits, Bynum.

Bynum: What else you got over there, Sister Bertha? You got some grits and gravy over there? I could go for some of that this morning.

Bertha (sets a bowl on the table): Seth, come on and help me turn this mattress over. Come on.

Seth: Something ain't right with that fellow, Bynum. I don't like the way he stare at everybody.

Bynum: Mr. Loomis alright, Seth. He just a man got something on his mind. He just got a straightforward mind, that's all.

Seth: What's that fellow that they had around here? Moses, that's Moses Houser. Man went crazy and jumped off the Brady Street Bridge. I told you when I seen him something wasn't right about him. And I'm telling you about this fellow now.

(*There is a knock on the door. Seth goes to answer it. Enter Rutherford Selig.*)

Ho! Come on in, Selig.

Bynum: If it ain't the People Finder himself.

Selig: Bynum, before you start . . . I ain't seen no shiny man now.

Bynum: Who said anything about that? I ain't said nothing about that. I just called you a first-class People Finder.

Selig: How many dustpans you get out of that sheet metal, Seth?

Seth: You walked by them on your way in. They sitting out there on the porch. Got twenty-eight. Got four out of each sheet and made Bertha a coffeepot out the other one. They a little small but they got nice handles.

Selig: That was twenty cents apiece, right? That's what we agreed on.

Seth: That's five dollars and sixty cents. Twenty on top of twenty-eight. How many sheets you bring me?

Selig: I got eight out there. That's a dollar twenty makes me owe you . . .

Seth: Four dollars and forty cents.

Selig (*paying him*): Go on and make me some dustpans. I can use all you can make.

(*Loomis enters from the stairs.*)

Loomis: I been watching for you. He say you find people.

Bynum: Mr. Loomis here wants you to find his wife.

Loomis: He say you find people. Find her for me.

Selig: Well, let see here . . . find somebody, is it?

(*Selig rummages through his pockets. He has several notebooks and he is searching for the right one.*)

Alright now . . . what's the name?

Loomis: Martha Loomis. She my wife. Got married legal with the paper and all.

Selig (*writing*): Martha . . . Loomis. How tall is she?

Loomis: She five feet from the ground.

Selig: Five feet . . . tall. Young or old?

Loomis: She a young woman. Got long pretty hair.

Selig: Young . . . long . . . pretty . . . hair. Where did you last see her?

Loomis: Tennessee. Nearby Memphis.

Selig: When was that?

Loomis: Nineteen hundred and one.

Selig: Nineteen . . . hundred and one. I'll tell you, mister . . . you better off without them. Now you take me . . . old Rutherford Selig could tell you a thing or two about these women. I ain't met one yet I could understand. Now, you take Sally out there. That's all a man needs is a good horse. I say giddup and she go. Say whoa and she stop. I feed her some oats and she carry me wherever I want to go. Ain't had a speck of trouble out of her since I had her. Now, I been married. A long time ago down in Kentucky. I got up one morning and I saw this look on my wife's face. Like way down deep inside her she was wishing I was dead. I walked around that morning and every time I looked at her she had that look on her face. It seem like she knew I could see it on her. Every time I looked at her I got smaller and smaller. Well, I wasn't gonna stay around there and just shrink away. I walked out on the porch and closed the door behind me. When I closed the door she locked it. I went out and bought me a horse. And I ain't been without one since! Martha Loomis, huh? Well, now I'll do the best I can do. That's one dollar.

Loomis (*holding out dollar suspiciously*): How you find her?

Selig: Well now, it ain't no easy job like you think. You can't just go out there and find them like that. There's a lot of little tricks to it. It's not an easy job keeping up with you Nigras the way you move about so. Now you take this woman you looking for . . . this Martha Loomis. She could be anywhere. Time I find her, if you don't keep your eye on her, she'll be gone off someplace else. You'll be thinking she over here and she'll be over there. But like I say there's lot of little tricks to it.

Loomis: You say you find her.

Selig: I can't promise anything but we been finders in my family for a long time. Bringers and finders. My great-granddaddy used to bring Nigras across the ocean on ships. That's wasn't no easy job either. Sometimes the winds would blow so hard you'd think the hand of God was set against the sails. But it set him well in pay and he settled in this new land and found him a wife of good Christian charity with a mind for kids and the like and well . . . here I am, Rutherford Selig. You're in good hands, mister. Me and my daddy have found plenty Nigras. My daddy, rest his soul, used to find runaway slaves for the plantation bosses. He was the best there was at it. Jonas B. Selig. Had him a reputation stretched clean across the country. After Abraham Lincoln give you all Nigras your freedom papers and with you all looking all over for each other . . . we started finding Nigras for Nigras. Of course, it don't pay as much. But the People Finding business ain't so bad.

Loomis (*hands him the dollar*): Find her. Martha Loomis. Find her for me.

Selig: Like I say, I can't promise you anything. I'm going back upriver, and if she's around in them parts I'll find her for you. But I can't promise you anything.

Loomis: When you coming back?

Selig: I'll be back on Saturday. I come and see Seth to pick up my order on Saturday.

Bynum: You going upriver, huh? You going up around my way. I used to go all up through there. Blawknox . . . Clairton. Used to go up to Rankin and take that first righthand road. I wore many a pair of shoes out walking around that way. You'd have thought I was a missionary spreading the gospel the way I wandered all around them parts.

Selig: Okay, Bynum. See you on Saturday.

Seth: Here, let me walk out with you. Help you with them dustpans.

(*Seth and Selig exit out the back. Bertha enters from the stairs carrying a bundle of sheets.*)

Bynum: Herald Loomis got the People Finder looking for Martha.

Bertha: You can call him a People Finder if you want to. I know Rutherford Selig carries people away too. He done carried a whole bunch of them away from here. Folks plan on leaving plan by Selig's timing. They wait till he get ready to go, then they hitch a ride on his wagon. Then he charge folks a dollar to tell them where he took them. Now, that's the truth of Rutherford Selig. This old People Finding business is for the birds. He ain't never found nobody he ain't took away. Herald Loomis, you just wasted your dollar.

(*Bertha exits into the bedroom.*)

Loomis: He say he find her. He say he find her by Saturday. I'm gonna wait till Saturday.

(*The lights fade to black.*)

Scene 3

It is Sunday morning, the next day. The lights come up on the kitchen. Seth sits talking to Bynum. The breakfast dishes have been cleared away.

Seth: They can't see that. Neither one of them can see that. Now, how much sense it take to see that? All you got to do is be able to count. One man making ten pots is five men making fifty pots. But they can't see that. Asked where I'm gonna get my five men. Hell, I can teach anybody how to make a pot. I can teach you. I can take you out there and get you started right now. Inside of two weeks you'd know how to make a pot. All you got to do is want to do it. I can get five men. I ain't worried about getting no five men.

Bertha (calls from the bedroom): Seth. Come on and get ready now. Reverend Gates ain't gonna be holding up his sermon 'cause you sitting out there talking.

Seth: Now, you take the boy, Jeremy. What he gonna do after he put in that road? He can't do nothing but go put in another one somewhere. Now, if he let me show him how to make some pots and pans . . . then he'd have something can't nobody take away from him. After a while he could get his own tools and go off somewhere and make his own pots and pans. Find him somebody to sell them to. Now, Selig can't make no pots and pans. He can sell them but he can't make them. I get me five men with some tools and we'd make him so many pots and pans he'd have to open up a store somewhere. But they can't see that. Neither Mr. Cohen nor Sam Green.

Bertha (calls from the bedroom): Seth . . . time be wasting. Best be getting on.

Seth: I'm coming, woman! (*To Bynum.*) Want me to sign over the house to borrow five hundred dollars. I ain't that big a fool. That's all I got. Sign it over to them and then I won't have nothing.

(*Jeremy enters waving a dollar and carrying his guitar.*)

Jeremy: Look here, Mr. Bynum . . . won me another dollar last night down at Seefus! Me and that Mattie Campbell went down there again and I played contest. Ain't no guitar players down there. Wasn't even no contest. Say, Mr. Seth, I asked Mattie Campbell if she wanna come by and have Sunday dinner with us. Get some fried chicken.

Seth: It's gonna cost you twenty-five cents.

Jeremy: That's alright. I got a whole dollar here. Say Mr. Seth . . . me and Mattie Campbell talked it over last night and she gonna move in with me. If that's alright with you.

Seth: Your business is your business . . . but it's gonna cost her a dollar a week for her board. I can't be feeding nobody for free.

Jeremy: Oh, she know that, Mr. Seth. That's what I told her, say she'd have to pay for her meals.

Seth: You say you got a whole dollar there . . . turn loose that twenty-five cents.

Jeremy: Suppose she move in today, then that make seventy-five cents more, so I'll give you the whole dollar for her now till she gets here.

(Seth pockets the money and exits into the bedroom.)

Bynum: So you and that Mattie Campbell gonna take up together?

Jeremy: I told her she don't need to be by her lonesome, Mr. Bynum. Don't make no sense for both of us to be by our lonesome. So she gonna move in with me.

Bynum: Sometimes you got to be where you supposed to be. Sometimes you can get all mixed up in life and come to the wrong place.

Jeremy: That's just what I told her, Mr. Bynum. It don't make no sense for her to be all mixed up and lonesome. May as well come here and be with me. She a fine woman too. Got them long legs. Knows how to treat a fellow too. Treat you like you wanna be treated.

Bynum: You just can't look at it like that. You got to look at the whole thing. Now, you take a fellow go out there, grab hold to a woman and think he got something 'cause she sweet and soft to the touch. Alright. Touching's part of life. It's in the world like everything else. Touching's nice. It feels good. But you can lay your hand upside a horse or a cat, and that feels good too. What's the difference? When you grab hold to a woman, you got something there. You got a whole world there. You got a way of life kicking up under your hand. That woman can take and make you feel like something. I ain't just talking about in the way of jumping off into bed together and rolling around with each other. Anybody can do that. When you grab hold to that woman and look at the whole thing and see what you got . . . why, she can take and make something out of you. Your mother was a woman. That's enough right there to show you what a woman is. Enough to show you what she can do. She made something out of you. Taught you converse, and all about how to take care of yourself, how to see where you at and where you going tomorrow, how to look out to see what's coming in the way of eating, and what to do with yourself when you get lonesome. That's a mighty thing she did. But you just can't look at a woman to jump off into bed with her. That's a foolish thing to ignore a woman like that.

Jeremy: Oh, I ain't ignoring her, Mr. Bynum. It's hard to ignore a woman got legs like she got.

Bynum: Alright. Let's try it this way. Now, you take a ship. Be out there on the water traveling about. You out there on that ship sailing to and from. And then you see some land. Just like you see a woman walking down the street. You see that land and it don't look like nothing but a line out there on the horizon. That's all it is when you first see it. A line that cross your path out there on the horizon. Now, a smart man know when he see that land, it ain't just a line setting out there. He know that if you get off the water to go take a good look . . . why, there's a whole world right there. A whole world with everything imaginable under the sun. Anything you can think of you can find on that land. Same with a woman. A woman is everything a man need. To a smart man she water and berries. And that's all a man need. That's all he need to live on. You give me some water and berries and if there ain't nothing else I can live a hundred years. See, you just like a man looking at the horizon from a ship. You just seeing a part of it. But it's a blessing when you learn to look at a woman and see in maybe just a few strands of her hair, the way her cheek curves . . . to see in that everything there is out of life to be gotten. It's a blessing to see that. You know you done right and proud by your mother to see that. But you got to learn it. My telling you ain't gonna mean nothing. You got to learn how to come to your own time and place with a woman.

Jeremy: What about your woman, Mr. Bynum? I know you done had some woman.

Bynum: Oh, I got them in memory time. That lasts longer than any of them ever stayed with me.

Jeremy: I had me an old gal one time . . .

(There is a knock on the door, Jeremy goes to answer it. Enter Molly Cunningham. She is about twenty-six, the kind of woman that "could break in on a dollar anywhere she goes." She carries a small cardboard suitcase, and wears a colorful dress of the fashion of the day. Jeremy's heart jumps out of his chest when he sees her.)

Molly: You got any rooms here? I'm looking for a room.

Jeremy: Yeah . . . Mr. Seth got rooms. Sure . . . wait till I get Mr. Seth. (*Calls.*) Mr. Seth! Somebody here to see you! (*To Molly.*) Yeah, Mr. Seth got some rooms. Got one right next to me. This is a nice place to stay, too. My name's Jeremy. What's yours?

(Seth enters dressed in his Sunday clothes.)

Seth: Ho!

Jeremy: This here woman looking for a place to stay. She say you got any rooms.

Molly: Mister, you got any rooms? I seen your sign say you got rooms.

Seth: How long you plan to staying?

Molly: I ain't gonna be here long. I ain't looking for no home or nothing. I'd be in Cincinnati if I hadn't missed my train.

Seth: Rooms cost two dollars a week.

Molly: Two dollars!

Seth: That includes meals. We serve two meals a day. That's breakfast and dinner.

Molly: I hope it ain't on the third floor.

Seth: That's the only one I got. Third floor to the left. That's pay up in advance week to week.

Molly (going into her bosom): I'm gonna pay you for one week. My name's Molly. Molly Cunningham.

Seth: I'm Seth Holly. My wife's name is Bertha. She do the cooking and take care of around here. She got sheets on the bed. Towels twenty-five cents a week extra if you ain't got none. You get breakfast and dinner. We got fried chicken on Sundays.

Molly: That sounds good. Here's two dollars and twenty-five cents. Look here, Mister . . . ?

Seth: Holly. Seth Holly.

Molly: Look here, Mr. Holly. I forgot to tell you. I likes me some company from time to time. I don't like being by myself.

Seth: Your business is your business. I don't meddle in nobody's business. But this is a respectable house. I don't have no riffraff around here. And I don't have no women hauling no men up to their rooms to be making their living. As long as we understand each other then we'll be alright with each other.

Molly: Where's the outhouse?

Seth: Straight through the door over yonder.

Molly: I get my own key to the front door?

Seth: Everybody get their own key. If you come in late just don't be making no whole lot of noise and carrying on. Don't allow no fussing and fighting around here.

Molly: You ain't got to worry about that, mister. Which way you say that outhouse was again?

Seth: Straight through that door over yonder.

(*Molly exits out the back door. Jeremy crosses to watch her.*)

Jeremy: Mr. Bynum, you know what? I think I know what you was talking about now.

(*The lights go down on the scene.*)

Scene 4

The lights come up on the kitchen. It is later the same evening. Mattie and all the residents of the house, except Loomis, sit around the table. They have finished eating and most of the dishes have been cleared.

Molly: That sure was some good chicken.

Jeremy: That's what I'm talking about. Miss Bertha, you sure can fry some chicken. I thought my mama could fry some chicken. But she can't do half as good as you.

Seth: I know it. That's why I married her. She don't know that, though. She think I married her for something else.

Bertha: I ain't studying you, Seth. Did you get your things moved in alright, Mattie?

Mattie: I ain't had that much. Jeremy helped me with what I did have.

Bertha: You'll get to know your way around here. If you have any questions about anything just ask me. You and Molly both. I get along with everybody. You'll find I ain't no trouble to get along with.

Mattie: You need some help with the dishes?

Bertha: I got me a helper. Ain't I, Zonia? Got me a good helper.

Zonia: Yes, ma'am.

Seth: Look at Bynum sitting over there with his belly all poked out. Ain't saying nothing. Sitting over there half asleep. Ho, Bynum!

Bertha: If Bynum ain't saying nothing what you wanna start him up for?

Seth: Ho, Bynum!

Bynum: What you hollering at me for? I ain't doing nothing.

Seth: Come on, we gonna Juba.

Bynum: You know me, I'm always ready to Juba.

Seth: Well, come on, then.

(*Seth pulls out a harmonica and blows a few notes.*)

Come on there, Jeremy. Where's your guitar? Go get your guitar. Bynum says he's ready to Juba.

Jeremy: Don't need no guitar to Juba. Ain't you never Juba without a guitar?

(*Jeremy begins to drum on the table.*)

Seth: It ain't that. I ain't never Juba with one! Figured to try it and see how it worked.

Bynum (*drumming on the table*): You don't need no guitar. Look at Molly sitting over there. She don't know we Juba on Sunday. We gonna show you something tonight. You and Mattie Campbell both. Ain't that right, Seth?

Seth: You said it! Come on, Bertha, leave them dishes be for a while. We gonna Juba.

Bynum: Alright. Let's Juba down!

(*The Juba is reminiscent of the Ring Shouts of the African slaves. It is a call and response dance. Bynum sits at the table and drums. He calls the dance as others clap hands, shuffle and stomp around the table. It should be as African as possible, with the performers working themselves up into a near frenzy. The words can be improvised, but should include some mention of the Holy Ghost. In the middle of the dance Herald Loomis enters.*)

Loomis (*in a rage*): Stop it! Stop!

(*They stop and turn to look at him.*)

You all sitting up here singing about the Holy Ghost. What's so holy about the Holy Ghost? You singing and singing. You think the Holy Ghost coming? You singing for the Holy Ghost to come? What he gonna do, huh? He gonna come with tongues of fire to burn up your woolly heads? You gonna tie onto the Holy Ghost and get burned up? What you got then? Why God got to be so big? Why he got to be bigger than me? How much big is there? How much big do you want?

(*Loomis starts to unzip his pants.*)

Seth: Nigger, you crazy!
Loomis: How much big you want?
Seth: You done plumb lost your mind!

(*Loomis begins to speak in tongues and dance around the kitchen. Seth starts after him.*)

Bertha: Leave him alone, Seth. He ain't in his right mind.
Loomis (*stops suddenly*): You all don't know nothing about me. You don't know what I done seen. Herald Loomis done seen some things he ain't got words to tell you.

(*Loomis starts to walk out the front door and is thrown back and collapses, terror-stricken by his vision. Bynum crawls to him.*)

Bynum: What you done seen, Herald Loomis?
Loomis: I done seen bones rise up out the water. Rise up and walk across the water. Bones walking on top of the water.
Bynum: Tell me about them bones, Herald Loomis. Tell me what you seen.
Loomis: I come to this place . . . to this water that was bigger than the whole world. And I looked out . . . and I seen these bones rise up out the water. Rise up and begin to walk on top of it.
Bynum: Wasn't nothing but bones and they walking on top of the water.
Loomis: Walking without sinking down. Walking on top of the water.
Bynum: Just marching in a line.
Loomis: A whole heap of them. They come up out the water and started marching.
Bynum: Wasn't nothing but bones and they walking on top of the water.
Loomis: One after the other. They just come up out the water and start to walking.
Bynum: They walking on the water without sinking down. They just walking and walking. And then . . . what happened, Herald Loomis?
Loomis: They just walking across the water.
Bynum: What happened, Herald Loomis? What happened to the bones?
Loomis: They just walking across the water . . . and then . . . they sunk down.
Bynum: The bones sunk into the water. They all sunk down.
Loomis: All at one time! They just all fell in the water at one time.
Bynum: Sunk down like anybody else.

Loomis: When they sink down they made a big splash and this here wave come up . . .

Bynum: A big wave, Herald Loomis. A big wave washed over the land.

Loomis: It washed them out of the water and up on the land. Only . . . only . . .

Bynum: Only they ain't bones no more.

Loomis: They got flesh on them! Just like you and me!

Bynum: Everywhere you look the waves is washing them up on the land right on top of one another.

Loomis: They black. Just like you and me. Ain't no difference.

Bynum: Then what happened, Herald Loomis?

Loomis: They ain't moved or nothing. They just laying there.

Bynum: You just laying there. What you waiting on, Herald Loomis?

Loomis: I'm laying there . . . waiting.

Bynum: What you waiting on, Herald Loomis?

Loomis: I'm waiting on the breath to get into my body.

Bynum: The breath coming into you, Herald Loomis. What you gonna do now?

Loomis: The wind's blowing the breath into my body. I can feel it. I'm starting to breathe again.

Bynum: What you gonna do, Herald Loomis?

Loomis: I'm gonna stand up. I got to stand up. I can't lay here no more. All the breath coming into my body and I got to stand up.

Bynum: Everybody's standing up at the same time.

Loomis: The ground's starting to shake. There's a great shaking. The world's busting half in two. The sky's splitting open. I got to stand up.

(*Loomis attempts to stand up.*)

My legs . . . my legs won't stand up!

Bynum: Everybody's standing and walking toward the road. What you gonna do, Herald Loomis?

Loomis: My legs won't stand up.

Bynum: They shaking hands and saying goodbye to each other and walking every whichaway down the road.

Loomis: I got to stand up!

Bynum: They walking around here now. Mens. Just like you and me. Come right up out the water.

Loomis: Got to stand up.

Bynum: They walking, Herald Loomis. They walking around here now.

Loomis: I got to stand up. Get up on the road.

Bynum: Come on, Herald Loomis.

(*Loomis tries to stand up.*)

Loomis: My legs won't stand up! My legs won't stand up!

(*Loomis collapses on the floor as the lights go down to black.*)

Act II
Scene 1

The lights come up on the kitchen. Bertha busies herself with breakfast preparations.
Seth sits at the table.

Seth: I don't care what his problem is! He's leaving here!

Bertha: You can't put the man out and he got that little girl. Where they gonna go then?

Seth: I don't care where he go. Let him go back where he was before he come here. I ain't asked him to come here. I knew when I first looked at him something wasn't right with him. Dragging that little girl around with him. Looking like he be sleeping in the woods somewhere. I knew all along he wasn't right.

Bertha: A fellow get a little drunk he's liable to say or do anything. He ain't done no big harm.

Seth: I just don't have all that carrying on in my house. When he come down here I'm gonna tell him. He got to leave here. My daddy wouldn't stand for it and I ain't gonna stand for it either.

Bertha: Well, if you put him out you have to put Bynum out too. Bynum right there with him.

Seth: If it wasn't for Bynum ain't no telling what would have happened. Bynum talked to that fellow just as nice and calmed him down. If he wasn't here ain't no telling what would have happened. Bynum ain't done nothing but talk to him and kept him calm. Man acting all crazy with that foolishness. Naw, he's leaving here.

Bertha: What you gonna tell him? How you gonna tell him to leave?

Seth: I'm gonna tell him straight out. Keep it nice and simple. Mister, you got to leave here!

(Molly enters from the stairs.)

Molly: Morning.

Bertha: Did you sleep alright in that bed?

Molly: Tired as I was I could have slept anywhere. It's a real nice room, though. This is a nice place.

Seth: I'm sorry you had to put up with all that carrying on last night.

Molly: It don't bother me none. I done seen that kind of stuff before.

Seth: You won't have to see it around here no more.

(Bynum is heard singing offstage.)

I don't put up with all that stuff. When that fellow come down here I'm gonna tell him.

Bynum (singing):
> Soon my work will all be done
> Soon my work will all be done

Soon my work will all be done
I'm going to see the king.

Bynum (*enters*): Morning, Seth. Morning, Sister Bertha. I see we got Molly Cunningham down here at breakfast.

Seth: Bynum, I wanna thank you for talking to that fellow last night and calming him down. If you hadn't been here ain't no telling what might have happened.

Bynum: Mr. Loomis alright, Seth. He just got a little excited.

Seth: Well, he can get excited somewhere else 'cause he leaving here.

(*Mattie enters from the stairs.*)

Bynum: Well, there's Mattie Campbell.

Mattie: Good morning.

Bertha: Sit on down there, Mattie. I got some biscuits be ready in a minute. The coffee's hot.

Mattie: Jeremy gone already?

Bynum: Yeah, he leave out of here early. He got to be there when the sun come up. Most working men got to be there when the sun come up. Everybody but Seth. Seth work at night. Mr. Olowski so busy in his shop he got fellows working at night.

(*Loomis enters from the stairs.*)

Seth: Mr. Loomis, now . . . I don't want no trouble. I keeps me a respectable house here. I don't have no carrying on like what went on last night. This has been a respectable house for a long time. I'm gonna have to ask you to leave.

Loomis: You got my two dollars. That two dollars say we stay till Saturday.

(*Loomis and Seth glare at each other.*)

Seth: Alright. Fair enough. You stay till Saturday. But come Saturday you got to leave here.

Loomis (*continues to glare at Seth. He goes to the door and calls*): Zonia. You stay around this house, you hear? Don't you go anywhere.

(*Loomis exits out the front door.*)

Seth: I knew it when I first seen him. I knew something wasn't right with him.

Bertha: Seth, leave the people alone to eat their breakfast. They don't want to hear that. Go on out there and make some pots and pans. That's the only time you satisfied is when you out there. Go on out there and make some pots and pans and leave them people alone.

Seth: I ain't bothering anybody. I'm just stating the facts. I told you, Bynum.

(*Bertha shoos Seth out the back door and exits into the bedroom.*)

Molly (*to Bynum*): You one of them voo-doo people?

Bynum: I got a power to bind folks if that what you talking about.

Molly: I thought so. The way you talked to that man when he started all that spooky stuff. What you say you had the power to do to people? You ain't the cause of him acting like that, is you?

Bynum: I binds them together. Sometimes I help them find each other.

Molly: How do you do that?

Bynum: With a song. My daddy taught me how to do it.

Molly: That's what they say. Most folks be what they daddy is. I wouldn't want to be like my daddy. Nothing ever set right with him. He tried to make the world over. Carry it around with him everywhere he go. I don't want to be like that. I just take life as it come. I don't be trying to make it over.

(*Pause.*)

Your daddy used to do that too, huh? Make people stay together?

Bynum: My daddy used to heal people. He had the Healing Song. I got the Binding Song.

Molly: My mama used to believe in all that stuff. If she got sick she would have gone and saw your daddy. As long as he didn't make her drink nothing. She wouldn't drink nothing nobody give her. She was always afraid somebody was gonna poison her. How your daddy heal people?

Bynum: With a song. He healed people by singing over them. I seen him do it. He sung over this little white girl when she was sick. They made a big to-do about it. They carried the girl's bed out in the yard and had all her kinfolk standing around. The little girl laying up there in the bed. Doctors standing around can't do nothing to help her. And they had my daddy come up and sing his song. It didn't sound no different than any other song. It was just somebody singing. But the song was its own thing and it come out and took upon this little girl with its power and it healed her.

Molly: That's sure something else. I don't understand that kind of thing. I guess if the doctor couldn't make me well I'd try it. But otherwise I don't wanna be bothered with that kind of thing. It's too spooky.

Bynum: Well, let me get on out here and get to work.

(*Bynum gets up and heads out the back door.*)

Molly: I ain't meant to offend you or nothing. What's your name . . . Bynum? I ain't meant to say nothing to make you feel bad now.

(*Bynum exits out the back door.*)

(*To Mattie.*) I hope he don't feel bad. He's a nice man. I don't wanna hurt nobody's feelings or nothing.

Mattie: I got to go on up to Doc Goldblum's and finish this ironing.

Molly: Now, that's something I don't never wanna do. Iron no clothes. Especially somebody else's. That's what I believe killed my mama. Always ironing and working, doing somebody else's work. Not Molly Cunningham.

Mattie: It's the only job I got. I got to make it someway to fend for myself.

Molly: I thought Jeremy was your man. Ain't he working?

Mattie: We just be keeping company till maybe Jack come back.

Molly: I don't trust none of these men. Jack or nobody else. These men liable to do anything. They wait just until they get one woman tied and locked up with them . . . then they look around to see if they can get another one. Molly don't pay them no mind. One's just as good as the other if you ask me. I ain't never met one that meant nobody no good. You got any babies?

Mattie: I had two for my man, Jack Carper. But they both died.

Molly: That be the best. These men make all these babies, then run off and leave you to take care of them. Talking about they wanna see what's on the other side of the hill. I make sure I don't get no babies. My mama taught me how to do that.

Mattie: Don't make me no mind. That be nice to be a mother.

Molly: Yeah? Well, you go on, then. Molly Cunningham ain't gonna be tied down with no babies. Had me a man one time who I thought had some love in him. Come home one day and he was packing his trunk. Told me the time come when even the best of friends must part. Say he was gonna send me a Special Delivery some old day. I watched him out the window when he carried that trunk out and down to the train station. Said if he was gonna send me a Special Delivery I wasn't gonna be there to get it. I done found out the harder you try to hold onto them, the easier it is for some gal to pull them away. Molly done learned that. That's why I don't trust nobody but the good Lord above, and I don't love nobody but my mama.

Mattie: I got to get on. Doc Goldblum gonna be waiting.

(*Mattie exits out the front door. Seth enters from his workshop with his apron, gloves, goggles, etc. He carries a bucket and crosses to the sink for water.*)

Seth: Everybody gone but you, huh?

Molly: That little shack out there by the outhouse . . . that's where you make them pots and pans and stuff?

Seth: Yeah, that's my workshed. I go out there . . . take these hands and make something out of nothing. Take that metal and bend and twist it whatever way I want. My daddy taught me that. He used to make pots and pans. That's how I learned it.

Molly: I never knew nobody made no pots and pans. My uncle used to shoe horses.

(*Jeremy enters at the front door.*)

Seth: I thought you was working? Ain't you working today?

Jeremy: Naw, they fired me. White fellow come by told me to give him fifty cents if I wanted to keep working. Going around to all the colored making them give him fifty cents to keep hold to their jobs. Them other fellows, they was giving it to him. I kept hold to mine and they fired me.

Seth: Boy, what kind of sense that make? What kind of sense it make to get fired from a job where you making eight dollars a week and all it cost you is fifty cents. That's seven dollars and fifty cents profit! This way you ain't got nothing.

Jeremy: It didn't make no sense to me. I don't make but eight dollars. Why I got to give him fifty cents of it? He go around to all the colored and he got ten dollars extra. That's more than I make for a whole week.

Seth: I see you gonna learn the hard way. You just looking at the facts of it. See, right now, without the job, you ain't got nothing. What you gonna do when you can't keep a roof over your head? Right now, come Saturday, unless you come up with another two dollars, you gonna be out there in the streets. Down up under one of them bridges trying to put some food in your belly and wishing you had given that fellow that fifty cents.

Jeremy: Don't make me no difference. There's a big road out there. I can get my guitar and always find me another place to stay. I ain't planning on staying in one place for too long noway.

Seth: We gonna see if you feel like that come Saturday!

(*Seth exits out the back. Jeremy sees Molly.*)

Jeremy: Molly Cunningham. How you doing today, sugar?

Molly: You can go on back down there tomorrow and go back to work if you want. They won't even know who you is. Won't even know it's you. I had me a fellow did that one time. They just went ahead and signed him up like they never seen him before.

Jeremy: I'm tired of working anyway. I'm glad they fired me. You sure look pretty today.

Molly: Don't come telling me all that pretty stuff. Beauty wanna come in and sit down at your table asking to be fed. I ain't hardly got enough for me.

Jeremy: You know you pretty. Ain't no sense in you saying nothing about that. Why don't you come on and go away with me?

Molly: You tied up with that Mattie Campbell. Now you talking about running away with me.

Jeremy: I was just keeping her company 'cause she lonely. You ain't the lonely kind. You the kind that know what she want and how to get it. I need a woman like you to travel around with. Don't you wanna travel around and look at some places with Jeremy? With a woman like you beside him, a man can make it nice in the world.

Molly: Molly can make it nice by herself too. Molly don't need nobody leave her cold in hand. The world rough enough as it is.

Jeremy: We can make it better together. I got my guitar and I can play. Won me another dollar last night playing guitar. We can go around and I can play at the dances and we can just enjoy life. You can make it by yourself alright, I agrees with that. A woman like you can make it anywhere she go. But you can make it better if you got a man to protect you.

Molly: What places you wanna go around and look at?

Jeremy: All of them! I don't want to miss nothing. I wanna go everywhere and do everything there is to be got out of life. With a woman like you it's like having water and berries. A man got everything he need.

Molly: You got to be doing more than playing that guitar. A dollar a day ain't hardly what Molly got in mind.

Jeremy: I gambles real good. I got a hand for it.
Molly: Molly don't work. And Molly ain't up for sale.
Jeremy: Sure, baby. You ain't got to work with Jeremy.
Molly: There's one more thing.
Jeremy: What's that, sugar?
Molly: Molly ain't going South.

    (*The lights go down on the scene.*)

Scene 2

The lights come up on the parlor. Seth and Bynum sit playing a game of dominoes. Bynum sings to himself.

Bynum (*singing*):

    They tell me Joe Turner's come and gone
    Ohhh Lordy
    They tell me Joe Turner's come and gone
    Ohhh Lordy
    Got my man and gone

    Come with forty links of chain
    Ohhh Lordy
    Come with forty links of chain
    Ohhh Lordy
    Got my man and gone

Seth: Come on and play if you gonna play.
Bynum: I'm gonna play. Soon as I figure out what to do.
Seth: You can't figure out if you wanna play or you wanna sing.
Bynum: Well sir, I'm gonna do a little bit of both.

    (*Playing.*)

    There. What you gonna do now?

    (*Singing.*)

    ' They tell me Joe Turner's come and gone
    Ohhh Lordy
    They tell me Joe Turner's come and gone
    Ohhh Lordy

Seth: Why don't you hush up that noise.
Bynum: That's a song the women sing down around Memphis. The women down there made up that song. I picked it up down there about fifteen years ago.

    (*Loomis enters from the front door.*)

Bynum: Evening, Mr. Loomis.
Seth: Today's Monday, Mr. Loomis. Come Saturday your time is up. We done ate already. My wife roasted up some yams. She got your plate sitting in there on the table. (*To Bynum.*) Whose play is it?

Bynum: Ain't you keeping up with the game? I thought you was a domino player. I just played so it got to be your turn.

(*Loomis goes into the kitchen, where a plate of yams is covered and set on the table. He sits down and begins to eat with his hands.*)

Seth (*plays*): Twenty! Give me twenty! You didn't know I had that ace five. You was trying to play around that. You didn't know I had that lying there for you.

Bynum: You ain't done nothing. I let you have that to get mine.

Seth: Come on and play. You ain't doing nothing but talking. I got a hundred and forty points to your eighty. You ain't doing nothing but talking. Come on and play.

Bynum (*singing*):

They tell me Joe Turner's come and gone
Ohhh Lordy
They tell me Joe Turner's come and gone
Ohhh Lordy
Got my man and gone

He come with forty links of chain
Ohhh Lordy

Loomis: Why you singing that song? Why you singing about Joe Turner?

Bynum: I'm just singing to entertain myself.

Seth: You trying to distract me. That's what you trying to do.

Bynum (*singing*):

Come with forty links of chain
Ohhh Lordy
Come with forty links of chain
Ohhh Lordy

Loomis: I don't like you singing that song, mister!

Seth: Now, I ain't gonna have no more disturbance around here, Herald Loomis. You start any more disturbance and you leavin' here, Saturday or no Saturday.

Bynum: The man ain't causing no disturbance, Seth. He just say he don't like the song.

Seth: Well, we all friendly folk. All neighborly like. Don't have no squabbling around here. Don't have no disturbance. You gonna have to take that someplace else.

Bynum: He just say he don't like the song. I done sung a whole lot of songs people don't like. I respect everybody. He here in the house too. If he don't like the song, I'll sing something else. I know lots of songs. You got "I Belong to the Band," "Don't You Leave Me Here." You got "Praying on the Old Campground," "Keep Your Lamp Trimmed and Burning" . . . I know lots of songs. (*Sings.*)

Boys, I'll be so glad when payday come
Captain, Captain, when payday comes
Gonna catch that Illinois Central
Going to Kankakee

Seth: Why don't you hush up that hollering and come on and play dominoes.

Bynum: You ever been to Johnstown, Herald Loomis? You look like a fellow I seen around there.

Loomis: I don't know no place with that name.

Bynum: That's around where I seen my shiny man. See, you looking for this woman. I'm looking for a shiny man. Seem like everybody looking for something.

Seth: I'm looking for you to come and play these dominoes. That's what I'm looking for.

Bynum: You a farming man, Herald Loomis? You look like you done some farming.

Loomis: Same as everybody. I done farmed some, yeah.

Bynum: I used to work at farming . . . picking cotton. I reckon everybody done picked some cotton.

Seth: I ain't! I ain't never picked no cotton. I was born up here in the North. My daddy was a freedman. I ain't never even seen no cotton!

Bynum: Mr. Loomis done picked some cotton. Ain't you, Herald Loomis? You done picked a bunch of cotton.

Loomis: How you know so much about me? How you know what I done? How much cotton I picked?

Bynum: I can tell from looking at you. My daddy taught me how to do that. Say when you look at a fellow, if you taught yourself to look for it, you can see his song written on him. Tell you what kind of man he is in the world. Now, I can look at you, Mr. Loomis, and see you a man who done forgot his song. Forgot how to sing it. A fellow forget that and he forget who he is. Forget how he's supposed to mark down life. Now, I used to travel all up and down this road and that . . . looking here and there. Searching. Just like you, Mr. Loomis. I didn't know what I was searching for. The only thing I knew was something was keeping me dissatisfied. Something wasn't making my heart smooth and easy. Then one day my daddy gave me a song. That song had a weight to it that was hard to handle. That song was hard to carry. I fought against it. Didn't want to accept that song. I tried to find my daddy to give him back the song. But I found out it wasn't his song. It was my song. It had come from way deep inside me. I looked long back in memory and gathered up pieces and snatches of things to make that song. I was making it up out of myself. And that song helped me on the road. Made it smooth to where my footsteps didn't bite back at me. All the time that song getting bigger and bigger. That song growing with each step of the road. It got so I used all of myself up in the making of that song. Then I was the song in search of itself. That song rattling in my throat and I'm looking for it. See, Mr. Loomis, when a man forgets his song he goes off in search of it . . . till he find out he's got it with him all the time. That's why I can tell you one of Joe Turner's niggers. 'Cause you forgot how to sing your song.

Loomis: You lie! How you see that? I got a mark on me? Joe Turner done marked me to where you can see it? You telling me I'm a marked man. What kind of mark you got on you?

(*Bynum begins singing.*)

Bynum:

They tell me Joe Turner's come and gone
Ohhh Lordy
They tell me Joe Turner's come and gone
Ohhh Lordy
Got my man and gone

Loomis: Had a whole mess of men he catched. Just go out hunting regular like you go out hunting possum. He catch you and go home to his wife and family. Ain't thought about you going home to yours. Joe Turner catched me when my little girl was born. Wasn't nothing but a little baby sucking on her mama's titty when he catched me. Joe Turner catched me in nineteen hundred and one. Kept me seven years until nineteen hundred and eight. Kept everybody seven years. He'd go out hunting and bring back forty men at a time. And keep them seven years.
I was walking down this road in this little town outside of Memphis. Come up on these fellows gambling. I was a deacon in the Abundant Life Church. I stopped to preach to these fellows to see if maybe I could turn some of them from their sinning when Joe Turner, brother of the Governor of the great sovereign state of Tennessee, swooped down on us and grabbed everybody there. Kept us all seven years.
My wife Martha gone from me after Joe Turner catched me. Got out from under Joe Turner on his birthday. Me and forty other men put in our seven years and he let us go on his birthday. I made it back to Henry Thompson's place where me and Martha was sharecropping and Martha's gone. She taken my little girl and left her with her mama and took off North. We been looking for her ever since. That's been going on four years now we been looking. That's the only thing I know to do. I just wanna see her face so I can get me a starting place in the world. The world got to start somewhere. That's what I been looking for. I been wandering a long time in somebody else's world. When I find my wife that be the making of my own.
Bynum: Joe Turner tell why he caught you? You ever asked him that?
Loomis: I ain't never seen Joe Turner. Seen him to where I could touch him. I asked one of them fellows one time why he catch niggers. Asked him what I got he want? Why don't he keep on to himself? Why he got to catch me going down the road by my lonesome? He told me I was worthless. Worthless is something you throw away. Something you don't bother with. I ain't seen him throw me away. Wouldn't even let me stay away when I was by my lonesome. I ain't tried to catch him when he going down the road. So I must got something he want. What I got?
Seth: He just want you to do his work for him. That's all.

Loomis: I can look at him and see where he big and strong enough to do his own work. So it can't be that. He must want something he ain't got.

Bynum: That ain't hard to figure out. What he wanted was your song. He wanted to have that song to be his. He thought by catching you he could learn that song. Every nigger he catch he's looking for the one he can learn that song from. Now he's got you bound up to where you can't sing your own song. Couldn't sing it them seven years 'cause you was afraid he would snatch it from under you. But you still got it. You just forgot how to sing it.

Loomis (to Bynum): I know who you are. You one of them bones people.

(The lights go down to black.)

Scene 3

The lights come up on the kitchen. It is the following morning. Mattie and Bynum sit at the table. Bertha busies herself at the stove.

Bynum: Good luck don't know no special time to come. You sleep with that up under your pillow and good luck can't help but come to you. Sometimes it come and go and you don't even know it's been there.

Bertha: Bynum, why don't you leave that gal alone? She don't wanna be hearing all that. Why don't you go on and get out the way and leave her alone?

Bynum (getting up): Alright, alright. But you mark what I'm saying. It'll draw it to you just like a magnet.

(Bynum exits up the stairs and Loomis enters.)

Bertha: I got some grits here, Mr. Loomis.

(Bertha sets a bowl on the table.)

If I was you, Mattie, I wouldn't go getting all tied up with Bynum in that stuff. That kind of stuff, even if it do work for a while, it don't last. That just get people more mixed up than they is already. And I wouldn't waste my time fretting over Jeremy either. I seen it coming. I seen it when she first come here. She that kind of woman run off with the first man got a dollar to spend on her. Jeremy just young. He don't know what he getting into. That gal don't mean him no good. She's just using him to keep from being by herself. That's the worst use of a man you can have. You ought to be glad to wash him out of your hair. I done seen all kind of men. I done seen them come and go through here. Jeremy ain't had enough to him for you. You need a man who's got some understanding and who willing to work with that understanding to come to the best he can. You got your time coming. You just tries too hard and can't understand why it don't work for you. Trying to figure it out don't do nothing but give you a troubled mind. Don't no man want a woman with a troubled mind.

You get all that trouble off your mind and just when it look like you ain't never gonna find what you want . . . you look up and it's standing right there. That's how I met my Seth. You gonna look up one day and find everything you want standing right in front of you. Been twenty-seven years now since that happened to me. But life ain't no happy-go-lucky time where everything be just like you want it. You got your time coming. You watch what Bertha's saying.

(*Seth enters.*)

Seth: Ho!

Bertha: What you doing come in here so late?

Seth: I was standing down there on Logan Street talking with the fellows. Henry Allen tried to sell me that old piece of horse he got.

(*He sees Loomis.*)

Today's Tuesday, Mr. Loomis.

Bertha (*pulling him toward the bedroom*): Come on in here and leave that man alone to eat his breakfast.

Seth: I ain't bothering nobody. I'm just reminding him what day it is.

(*Seth and Bertha exit into the bedroom.*)

Loomis: That dress got a color to it.

Mattie: Did you really see them things like you said? Them people come up out the ocean?

Loomis: It happened just like that, yeah.

Mattie: I hope you find your wife. It be good for your little girl for you to find her.

Loomis: Got to find her for myself. Find my starting place in the world. Find me a world I can fit in.

Mattie: I ain't never found no place for me to fit. Seem like all I do is start over. It ain't nothing to find no starting place in the world. You just start from where you find yourself.

Loomis: Got to find my wife. That be my starting place.

Mattie: What if you don't find her? What you gonna do then if you don't find her?

Loomis: She out there somewhere. Ain't no such thing as not finding her.

Mattie: How she got lost from you? Jack just walked away from me.

Loomis: Joe Turner split us up. Joe Turner turned the world upside-down. He bound me on to him for seven years.

Mattie: I hope you find her. It be good for you to find her.

Loomis: I been watching you. I been watching you watch me.

Mattie: I was just trying to figure out if you seen things like you said.

Loomis (*getting up*): Come here and let me touch you. I been watching you. You a full woman. A man needs a full woman. Come on and be with me.

Mattie: I ain't got enough for you. You'd use me up too fast.

Loomis: Herald Loomis got a mind seem like you a part of it since I first seen you. It's been a long time since I seen a full woman. I can smell you from here. I know you got Herald Loomis on your mind, can't keep him apart from it. Come on and be with Herald Loomis.

(*Loomis has crossed to Mattie. He touches her awkwardly, gently, tenderly. Inside he howls like a lost wolf pup whose hunger is deep. He goes to touch her but finds he cannot.*)

I done forgot how to touch.

(*The lights fade to black.*)

Scene 4

It is early the next morning. The lights come up on Zonia and Reuben in the yard.

Reuben: Something spooky going on around here. Last night Mr. Bynum was out in the yard singing and talking to the wind . . . and the wind it just be talking back to him. Did you hear it?

Zonia: I heard it. I was scared to get up and look. I thought it was a storm.

Reuben: That wasn't no storm. That was Mr. Bynum. First he say something . . . and the wind it say back to him.

Zonia: I heard it. Was you scared? I was scared.

Reuben: And then this morning . . . I seen Miss Mabel!

Zonia: Who Miss Mabel?

Reuben: Mr. Seth's mother. He got her picture hanging up in the house. She been dead.

Zonia: How you seen her if she been dead?

Reuben: Zonia . . . if I tell you something you promise you won't tell anybody?

Zonia: I promise.

Reuben: It was early this morning . . . I went out to the coop to feed the pigeons. I was down on the ground like this to open up the door to the coop . . . when all of a sudden I seen some feets in front of me. I looked up . . . and there was Miss Mabel standing there.

Zonia: Reuben, you better stop telling that! You ain't seen nobody!

Reuben: Naw, it's the truth. I swear! I seen her just like I see you. Look . . . you can see where she hit me with her cane.

Zonia: Hit you? What she hit you for?

Reuben: She says, "Didn't you promise Eugene something?" Then she hit me with her cane. She say, "Let them pigeons go." Then she hit me again. That's what made them marks.

Zonia: Jeez man . . . get away from me. You done see a haunt!

Reuben: Shhhh. You promised, Zonia!

Zonia: You sure it wasn't Miss Bertha come over there and hit you with her hoe?

Reuben: It wasn't no Miss Bertha. I told you it was Miss Mabel. She was standing right there by the coop. She had this light coming out of her and then she just melted away.

Zonia: What she had on?

Reuben: A white dress. Ain't even had no shoes or nothing. Just had on that white dress and them big hands . . . and that cane she hit me with.

Zonia: How you reckon she knew about the pigeons? You reckon Eugene told her?

Reuben: I don't know. I sure ain't asked her none. She say Eugene was waiting on them pigeons. Say he couldn't go back home till I let them go. I couldn't get the door to the coop open fast enough.

Zonia: Maybe she an angel? From the way you say she look with that white dress. Maybe she an angel.

Reuben: Mean as she was . . . how she gonna be an angel? She used to chase us out her yard and frown up and look evil all the time.

Zonia: That don't mean she can't be no angel 'cause of how she looked and 'cause she wouldn't let no kids play in her yard. It go by if you got any spots on your heart and if you pray and go to church.

Reuben: What about she hit me with her cane? An angel wouldn't hit me with her cane.

Zonia: I don't know. She might. I still say she was an angel.

Reuben: You reckon Eugene the one who sent old Miss Mabel?

Zonia: Why he send her? Why he don't come himself?

Reuben: Figured if he send her maybe that'll make me listen. 'Cause she old.

Zonia: What you think it feel like?

Reuben: What?

Zonia: Being dead.

Reuben: Like being sleep only you don't know nothing and can't move no more.

Zonia: If Miss Mabel can come back . . . then maybe Eugene can come back too.

Reuben: We can go down to the hideout like we used to! He could come back everyday! It be just like he ain't dead.

Zonia: Maybe that ain't right for him to come back. Feel kinda funny to be playing games with a haunt.

Reuben: Yeah . . . what if everybody came back? What if Miss Mabel came back just like she ain't dead? Where you and your daddy gonna sleep then?

Zonia: Maybe they go back at night and don't need no place to sleep.

Reuben: It still don't seem right. I'm sure gonna miss Eugene. He's the bestest friend anybody ever had.

Zonia: My daddy say if you miss somebody too much it can kill you. Say he missed me till it liked to killed him.

Reuben: What if your mama's already dead and all the time you looking for her?

Zonia: Naw, she ain't dead. My daddy say he can smell her.

Reuben: You can't smell nobody that ain't here. Maybe he smelling old Miss Bertha. Maybe Miss Bertha your mama?

Zonia: Naw, she ain't. My mama got long pretty hair and she five feet from the ground!

Reuben: Your daddy say when you leaving?

(*Zonia doesn't respond.*)

Maybe you gonna stay in Mr. Seth's house and don't go looking for your mama no more.

Zonia: He say we got to leave on Saturday.

Reuben: Dag! You just only been here for a little while. Don't seem like nothing ever stay the same.

Zonia: He say he got to find her. Find him a place in the world.

Reuben: He could find him a place in Mr. Seth's house.

Zonia: It don't look like we never gonna find her.

Reuben: Maybe he find her by Saturday then you don't have to go.

Zonia: I don't know.

Reuben: You look like a spider!

Zonia: I ain't no spider!

Reuben: Got them long skinny arms and legs. You look like one of them Black Widows.

Zonia: I ain't no Black Window nothing! My name is Zonia!

Reuben: That's what I'm gonna call you . . . Spider.

Zonia: You can call me that, but I don't have to answer.

Reuben: You know what? I think maybe I be your husband when I grow up.

Zonia: How you know?

Reuben: I ask my grandpap how you know and he say when the moon falls into a girl's eyes that how you know.

Zonia: Did it fall into my eyes?

Reuben: Not that I can tell. Maybe I ain't old enough. Maybe you ain't old enough.

Zonia: So there! I don't know why you telling me that lie!

Reuben: That don't mean nothing 'cause I can't see it. I know it's there. Just the way you look at me sometimes look like the moon might have been in your eyes.

Zonia: That don't mean nothing if you can't see it. You supposed to see it.

Reuben: Shucks, I see it good enough for me. You ever let anybody kiss you?

Zonia: Just my daddy. He kiss me on the cheek.

Reuben: It's better on the lips. Can I kiss you on the lips?

Zonia: I don't know. You ever kiss anybody before?

Reuben: I had a cousin let me kiss her on the lips one time. Can I kiss you?

Zonia: Okay.

(*Reuben kisses her and lays his head against her chest.*)

What you doing?

Reuben: Listening. Your heart singing?

Zonia: It is not.

Reuben: Just beating like a drum. Let's kiss again.

(*They kiss again.*)

Now you mine, Spider. You my girl, okay?

Zonia: Okay.

Reuben: When I get grown, I come looking for you.

Zonia: Okay.

(*The lights fade to black.*)

Scene 5

The lights come up on the kitchen. It is Saturday. Bynum, Loomis, and Zonia sit at the table. Bertha prepares breakfast. Zonia has on a white dress.

Bynum: With all this rain we been having he might have ran into some washed-out roads. If that wagon got stuck in the mud he's liable to be still upriver somewhere. If he's upriver then he ain't coming until tomorrow.

Loomis: Today's Saturday. He say he be here on Saturday.

Bertha: Zonia, you gonna eat your breakfast this morning.

Zonia: Yes, ma'am.

Bertha: I don't know how you expect to get any bigger if you don't eat. I ain't never seen a child that didn't eat. You about as skinny as a bean pole.

(Pause.)

Mr. Loomis, there's a place down on Wylie. Zeke Mayweather got a house down there. You ought to see if he got any rooms.

(Loomis doesn't respond.)

Well, you're welcome to some breakfast before you move on.

(Mattie enters from the stairs.)

Mattie: Good morning.

Bertha: Morning, Mattie. Sit on down there and get you some breakfast.

Bynum: Well, Mattie Campbell, you been sleeping with that up under your pillow like I told you?

Bertha: Bynum, I done told you to leave that gal alone with all that stuff. You around here meddling in other people's lives. She don't want to hear all that. You ain't doing nothing but confusing her with that stuff.

Mattie (to Loomis): You all fixing to move on?

Loomis: Today's Saturday. I'm paid up till Saturday.

Mattie: Where you going to?

Loomis: Gonna find my wife.

Mattie: You going off to another city?

Loomis: We gonna see where the road take us. Ain't no telling where we wind up.

Mattie: Eleven years is a long time. Your wife . . . she might have taken up with someone else. People do that when they get lost from each other.

Loomis: Zonia. Come on, we gonna find your mama.

(Loomis and Zonia cross to the door.)

Mattie (to Zonia): Zonia, Mattie got a ribbon here match your dress. Want Mattie to fix your hair with her ribbon?

(Zonia nods. Mattie ties the ribbon in her hair.)

There . . . it got a color just like your dress. *(To Loomis.)* I hope you find her. I hope you be happy.

Loomis: A man looking for a woman be lucky to find you. You a good woman, Mattie. Keep a good heart.

(*Loomis and Zonia exit.*)

Bertha: I been watching that man for two weeks . . . and that's the closest I come to seeing him act civilized. I don't know what's between you all, Mattie . . . but the only thing that man needs is somebody to make him laugh. That's all you need in the world is love and laughter. That's all anybody needs. To have love in one hand and laughter in the other.

(*Bertha moves about the kitchen as though blessing it and chasing away the huge sadness that seems to envelop it. It is a dance and demonstration of her own magic, her own remedy that is centuries old and to which she is connected by the muscles of her heart and the blood's memory.*)

You hear me, Mattie? I'm talking about laughing. The kind of laugh that comes from way deep inside. To just stand and laugh and let life flow right through you. Just laugh to let yourself know you're alive.

(*She begins to laugh. It is a near-hysterical laughter that is a celebration of life, both its pain and its blessing. Mattie and Bynum join in the laughter. Seth enters from the front door.*)

Seth: Well, I see you all having fun.

(*Seth begins to laugh with them.*)

That Loomis fellow standing up there on the corner watching the house. He standing right up there on Manila Street.

Bertha: Don't you get started on him. The man done left out of here and that's the last I wanna hear of it. You about to drive me crazy with that man.

Seth: I just say he standing up there on the corner. Acting sneaky like he always do. He can stand up there all he want. As long as he don't come back in here.

(*There is a knock on the door. Seth goes to answer it. Enter Martha Loomis [Pentecost]. She is a young woman about twenty-eight. She is dressed as befitting a member of an Evangelist church. Rutherford Selig follows.*)

Seth: Look here, Bertha. It's Martha Pentecost. Come on in, Martha. Who that with you? Oh . . . that's Selig. Come on in, Selig.

Bertha: Come on in, Martha. It's sure good to see you.

Bynum: Rutherford Selig, you a sure enough first-class People Finder!

Selig: She was right out there in Rankin. You take that first righthand road . . . right there at that church on Wooster Street. I started to go right-past and something told me to stop at the church and see if they needed any dustpans.

Seth: Don't she look good, Bertha.

Bertha: Look all nice and healthy.

Martha: Mr. Bynum . . . Selig told me my little girl was here.

Seth: There's some fellow around here say he your husband. Say his name is
    Loomis. Say you his wife.

Martha: Is my little girl with him?

Seth: Yeah, he got a little girl with him. I wasn't gonna tell him where you was.
    Not the way this fellow look. So he got Selig to find you.

Martha: Where they at? They upstairs?

Seth: He was standing right up there on Manila Street. I had to ask him to leave
    'cause of how he was carrying on. He come in here one night—

(*The door opens and Loomis and Zonia enter. Martha and Loomis stare at each
other.*)

Loomis: Hello, Martha.

Martha: Herald . . . Zonia?

Loomis: You ain't waited for me, Martha. I got out the place looking to see your
    face. Seven years I waited to see your face.

Martha: Herald, I been looking for you. I wasn't but two months behind you
    when you went to my mama's and got Zonia. I been looking for you ever
    since.

Loomis: Joe Turner let me loose and I felt all turned around inside. I just wanted
    to see your face to know that the world was still there. Make sure everything
    still in its place so I could reconnect myself together. I got there and you was
    gone, Martha.

Martha: Herald . . .

Loomis: Left my little girl motherless in the world.

Martha: I didn't leave her motherless, Herald. Reverend Tolliver wanted to
    move the church up North 'cause of all the trouble the colored folks was
    having down there. Nobody knew what was gonna happen traveling them
    roads. We didn't even know if we was gonna make it up here or not. I left
    her with my mama so she be safe. That was better than dragging her out on
    the road having to duck and hide from people. Wasn't no telling what was
    gonna happen to us. I didn't leave her motherless in the world. I been
    looking for you.

Loomis: I come up on Henry Thompson's place after seven years of living in
    hell, and all I'm looking to do is see your face.

Martha: Herald, I didn't know if you was ever coming back. They told me Joe
    Turner had you and my whole world split half in two. My whole life shat-
    tered. It was like I had poured it in a cracked jar and it all leaked out the
    bottom. When it go like that there ain't nothing you can do to put it back
    together. You talking about Henry Thompson's place like I'm still gonna be
    working the land by myself. How I'm gonna do that? You wasn't gone but
    two months and Henry Thompson kicked me off his land and I ain't had no
    place to go but to my mama's. I stayed and waited there for five years before
    I woke up one morning and decided that you was dead. Even if you weren't,
    you was dead to me. I wasn't gonna carry you with me no more. So I killed
    you in my heart. I buried you. I mourned you. And then I picked up what

was left and went on to make life without you. I was a young woman with life at my beckon. I couldn't drag you behind me like a sack of cotton.

Loomis: I just been waiting to look on your face to say my goodbye. That goodbye got so big at times, seem like it was gonna swallow me up. Like Jonah in the whale's belly I sat up in that goodbye for three years. That goodbye kept me out on the road searching. Not looking on women in their houses. It kept me bound up to the road. All the time that goodbye swelling up in my chest till I'm about to bust. Now that I see your face I can say my goodbye and make my own world.

(*Loomis takes Zonia's hand and presents her to Martha.*)

Martha . . . here go your daughter. I tried to take care of her. See that she had something to eat. See that she was out of the elements. Whatever I know I tried to teach her. Now she need to learn from her mother whatever you got to teach her. That way she won't be no one-sided person.

(*Loomis stoops to Zonia.*)

Zonia, you go live with your mama. She a good woman. You go on with her and listen to her good. You my daughter and I love you like a daughter. I hope to see you again in the world somewhere. I'll never forget you.

Zonia (throws her arms around Loomis in a panic): I won't get no bigger! My bones won't get no bigger! They won't! I promise! Take me with you till we keep searching and never finding. I won't get no bigger! I promise!

Loomis: Go on and do what I told you now.

Martha (goes to Zonia and comforts her): It's alright, baby. Mama's here. Mama's here. Don't worry. Don't cry.

(*Martha turns to Bynum.*)

Mr. Bynum, I don't know how to thank you. God bless you.

Loomis: It was you! All the time it was you that bind me up! You bound me to the road!

Bynum: I ain't bind you, Herald Loomis. You can't bind what don't cling.

Loomis: Everywhere I go people wanna bind me up. Joe Turner wanna bind me up! Reverend Tolliver wanna bind me up. You wanna bind me up. Everybody wanna bind me up. Well, Joe Turner's come and gone and Herald Loomis ain't for no binding. I ain't gonna let nobody bind me up!

(*Loomis pulls out a knife.*)

Bynum: It wasn't you, Herald Loomis. I ain't bound you. I bound the little girl to her mother. That's who I bound. You binding yourself. You bound onto your song. All you got to do is stand up and sing it, Herald Loomis. It's right there kicking at your throat. All you got to do is sing it. Then you be free.

Martha: Herald . . . look at yourself! Standing there with a knife in your hand. You done gone over to the devil. Come on . . . put down the knife. You got to look to Jesus. Even if you done fell away from the church you can be saved again. The Bible say, "The Lord is my shepherd I shall not want. He maketh me to lie down in green pastures. He leads me beside the still water. He restoreth my soul. He leads me in the path of righteousness for His name's sake. Even though I walk through the shadow of death—"

Loomis: That's just where I be walking!

Martha: "I shall fear no evil. For Thou art with me. Thy rod and thy staff, they comfort me."

Loomis: You can't tell me nothing about no valleys. I done been all across the valleys and the hills and the mountains and the oceans.

Martha: "Thou preparest a table for me in the presence of my enemies."

Loomis: And all I seen was a bunch of niggers dazed out of their woolly heads. And Mr. Jesus Christ standing there in the middle of them, grinning.

Martha: "Thou anointest my head with oil, my cup runneth over."

Loomis: He grin that big old grin . . . and niggers wallowing at his feet.

Martha: "Surely goodness and mercy shall follow me all the days of my life, and I shall dwell in the house of the Lord forever."

Loomis: Great big old white man . . . your Mr. Jesus Christ. Standing there with a whip in one hand and tote board in another, and them niggers swimming in a sea of cotton. And he counting. He tallying up the cotton. "Well, Jeremiah . . . what's the matter, you ain't picked but two hundred pounds of cotton today? Got to put you on half rations." And Jeremiah go back and lay up there on his half rations and talk about what a nice man Mr. Jesus Christ is 'cause he give him salvation after he die. Something wrong here. Something don't fit right!

Martha: You got to open up your heart and have faith, Herald. This world is just a trial for the next. Jesus offers you salvation.

Loomis: I been wading in the water. I been walking all over the River Jordan. But what it get me, huh? I done been baptized with blood of the lamb and the fire of the Holy Ghost. But what I got, huh? I got salvation? My enemies all around me picking the flesh from my bones. I'm choking on my own blood and all you got to give me is salvation?

Martha: You got to be clean, Herald. You got to be washed with the blood of the lamb.

Loomis: Blood make you clean? You clean with blood?

Martha: Jesus bled for you. He's the Lamb of God who takest away the sins of the world.

Loomis: I don't need nobody to bleed for me! I can bleed for myself.

Martha: You got to be something, Herald. You just can't be alive. Life don't mean nothing unless it got a meaning.

Loomis: What kind of meaning you got? What kind of clean you got, woman? You want blood? Blood make you clean? You clean with blood?

(*Loomis slashes himself across the chest. He rubs the blood over his face and comes to a realization.*)

I'm standing! I'm standing. My legs stood up! I'm standing now!

(*Having found his song, the song of self-sufficiency, fully resurrected, cleansed and given breath, free from any encumbrance other than the workings of his own* heart and the bonds of the flesh, having accepted the responsibility for his own presence in the world, he is free to soar above the environs that weighed and pushed his spirit into terrifying contractions.)

Goodbye, Martha.

(*Loomis turns and exits, the knife still in his hands. Mattie looks about the room and rushes out after him.*)

Bynum: Herald Loomis, you shining! You shining like new money!

The lights go down to BLACK.

WRITER'S PERSPECTIVE

August Wilson

August Wilson on Drama   BLACK EXPERIENCE IN AMERICA   1989

INTERVIEWER: Your plays are set in the past—*Joe Turner's Come and Gone* in 1911, *Ma Rainey's Black Bottom* in 1927, *Fences* in the 1950s. Do you ever consider writing about what's happening today?

WILSON: I suspect eventually I will get to that. Right now I enjoy the benefit of the historical perspective. You can look back to a character in 1936, for instance, and you can see him going down a particular path that you know did not work out for that character. Part of what I'm trying to do is to see some of the choices that we as blacks in America have made. Maybe we have made some incorrect choices. By writing about that, you can illuminate the choices.

INTERVIEWER: Give me an example of a choice that you think may have been the wrong one.

WILSON: I think we should have stayed in the South. We attempted to plant what in essence was an emerging culture, a culture that had grown out of our experience of

200 years as slaves in the South. The cities of the urban North have not been hospitable. If we had stayed in the South, we could have strengthened the culture. . . .

INTERVIEWER: One of your characters has said, "Everyone has to find his own song." How do these people find their song?

WILSON: They have it. They just have to realize that, and then they have to learn how to sing it. In that particular case, in *Joe Turner*, the song was the African identity. It was connecting yourself to that and understanding that this is who you are. Then you can go out in the world and sing your song as an African. . . .

INTERVIEWER: But if blacks keep looking for the African in them, if they keep returning spiritually or emotionally to their roots, can they ever come to terms with living in these two worlds? Aren't they always going to be held by the past in a way that is potentially destructive?

WILSON: It's not potentially destructive at all. To say that I am an African, and I can participate in this society as an African, is to say that I don't have to adopt European values, European aesthetics, and European ways of doing things in order to live in the world. We would not be here had we not learned to adapt to American culture. Blacks know more about whites in the white culture and white life than whites know about blacks. We *have* to know because our survival depends on it. White people's survival does not depend on knowing blacks.

· · ·

INTERVIEWER: Don't you grow weary of thinking black, writing black, being asked questions about blacks?

WILSON: How could one grow weary of that? Whites don't get tired of thinking white or being who they are. I'm just who I am. You never transcend who you are. Black is not limiting. There's no idea in the world that is not contained by black life. I could write forever about the black experience in America.

"August Wilson's America,"
Interview with Bill Moyers in *American Theatre*

WRITING

39 *Writing About Literature*

In the study of literature, common sense (poet Gerard Manley Hopkins assures us) is never out of place. For most of a class hour, a professor once rhapsodized about the arrangement of the contents of W. H. Auden's *Collected Poems*. Auden, he claimed, was a master of thematic continuity, who had brilliantly placed the poems in an order that (to the ingenious mind) best complemented each other. Near the end of the hour, his theories were punctured—with a great inaudible pop—when a student, timidly raising a hand, pointed out that Auden had arranged the poems in the book not by theme but in alphabetical order according to the first word of each poem. The professor's jaw dropped: "Why didn't you say that sooner?" The student was apologetic: "I—I was afraid I'd sound too *ordinary*." Don't be afraid to state a conviction, though it seems obvious. Does it matter that you may be repeating something that, once upon a time or even just the other day, has been said before? There are excellent old ideas as well as new.

BEGINNING

Offered a choice of literary works to write about, you probably will do best if you choose what appeals to you. And how to find out what appeals? Whether you plan to write a short paper that requires no research beyond the story or poem or play itself, or a long term paper that will take you to the library, the first stage of your project is reading carefully—and taking notes. To concentrate your attention, one time-honored method is to read with a pencil, marking (if the book is yours) passages that stand out in importance, jotting brief notes in a margin (*"Key symbol—this foreshadows the ending"*; *"Dramatic irony"*; or other possibly useful remarks). In a long story or poem or play, some students asterisk passages that cry for comparison—for instance, all the places in which they find the same theme or symbol. Later, at a glance, they can review the highlights of a work and, when writing a paper about it, quickly refer to evidence. This method shoots holes in a book's resale value, but many find the sacrifice worthwhile. Students who dislike butchering a book prefer to take notes on looseleaf notebook paper, holding one sheet beside a page in the book and giving it the book's page number. Later, in writing a paper, they can place book page and companion note page together again. This method has the advantage of affording a lot of room for note taking; it is a good one for short poems closely packed with complexities.

Note Cards

By far, though, the most popular method of taking notes (after writing on the pages of books) is to write on index cards—the 3×5 kind for brief notes and titles, 5×8 cards for longer notes. Write on one side only; notes on the back of a card usually get overlooked later. Cards are easy to shuffle and, in organizing your material, to deal. To save work, instead of copying out on a card the title and author of a book you're taking a note from, just keep a numbered list of the books you're using. Then, when making a note, you need write only the book's identifying number and page references on the card in order to identify your source.

Photocopying

Now that coin-operated photocopy machines are to be found in all libraries, you no longer need to spend hours copying by hand whole poems and long prose passages. If accuracy is essential (and surely it is) and if a poem or passage is long enough to be worth the small investment, you can lay photocopied material into place in your paper with transparent tape or rubber cement. The latest copyright law permits students and scholars to reproduce a single copy of books and periodicals in this fashion; it does not, however, permit making a dozen or more copies for public sale.

Using Sources

Certain literary works, because they offer intriguing difficulties, have attracted professional critics by the score. On library shelves, great phalanxes of critical books now stand at the side of James Joyce's complex novels *Ulysses* and *Finnegans Wake*, and T. S. Eliot's allusive poem *The Waste Land*. The student who undertakes to study such works seriously is well advised to profit from the critics' labors. Chances are, too, that even in discussing a relatively uncomplicated work, you will want to seek the aid of some critics. If you quote them, quote them exactly, in quotation marks, and give them credit. When employed in any but the most superlative student paper, a brilliant phrase (or even a not-so-brilliant sentence) from a renowned critic is likely to stand out like a golf ball in a garter snake's midriff, and most English instructors are likely to recognize it. If you rip off the critic's words, then go ahead and steal the whole essay, for good critics write in seamless unities. Then, when apprehended, you can exclaim—like the student whose term paper was found to be the work of a well-known scholar—"I've been robbed! That paper cost me fifty dollars!" This student not only cheated his teacher but himself, having got nothing for his college tuition but a little practice in touch typing. Giving proper acknowledgment to words and ideas not your own is both a moral and legal obligation. Take it seriously.

While taking notes on your readings, jot down the title of every book you might refer to in your paper and the page number of any passage you might wish to quote. Even if you summarize a critic's idea in your own words rather than quote, you have to give credit to your source. Nothing is cheaper to give than proper credit. Certainly it's easier to take notes while you read than to have to run back to the library during the final typing.

Choosing an Appropriate Topic

Choose a topic appropriate to the assigned length of your paper. How do you know the probable length of your discussion until you write it? When in doubt, you are better off to define your topic narrowly. Your paper will be stronger if you go deeper into your subject than if you choose some gigantic subject and then find yourself able to touch on most aspects of it only superficially. A thorough explication of a short story is hardly possible in a paper of 250 words. There are, in truth, four-line poems whose surface 250 words might only begin to scratch. A profound topic ("The Character of Shakespeare's Hamlet") might overflow a book, but a more focused topic ("Hamlet's Views of Acting" or "Hamlet's Puns") might result in a manageable term paper. You can narrow and focus a large topic while you work your way into it. A general interest in "Hemingway's Heroes" might lead you, in reading, taking notes, and thinking further, to the narrower topic, "Jake Barnes: Spokesman for Hemingway's Views of War."

Many student writers find it helpful in defining a topic to state an emerging idea for a paper in a provisional **thesis sentence:** a summing-up of the one main idea or argument that the paper will embody. (A thesis sentence is for your own use; you don't necessarily have to implant it in your paper unless your instructor asks for it.) A good statement of a thesis is not just a disembodied subject; it comes with both subject and verb. ("The Downfall of Oedipus Rex" is not yet a complete idea for a paper; "What Caused the Downfall of Oedipus Rex?" is.) "The Isolation of Laura in *The Glass Menagerie*" might be a decent title for a paper, but it isn't a useful thesis because it doesn't indicate what one might say about that isolation (nor what Tennessee Williams is saying about it). It may be obvious that isolation isn't desirable, but a clearer and more workable thesis sentence might be, "In *The Glass Menagerie*, the playwright shows how Laura's isolation leads her to take refuge in a world of dreams."

DISCOVERING AND PLANNING

Writing is not likely to proceed in a straight line. Like thought, it often goes by fits and starts, by charges and retreats and mopping-up operations. All the while you take notes, you discover material to write about; all the while you turn over your topic in your mind, you plan. It is the nature of ideas, those headstrong things, to happen in any order they desire. While you continue to plan, while you write a draft, and while you revise, expect to keep discovering new thoughts—perhaps the best thoughts of all. If you do, be sure to let them in.

Topic in hand (which may get drastically changed as you continue), you begin to sort out your miscellaneous notes, thoughts, and impressions. If you can see that you haven't had enough ideas, you may wish to **brainstorm** or **freewrite**—to set yourself, say, fifteen minutes in which to write down as fast as you can all the ideas on your topic that come into your head, without worrying whether they are going to be useful. (You can look over the results and decide that later.) Write rapidly and uncritically, letting your thoughts tumble onto paper as fast as your pen, typewriter, or computer can capture them. This method will often goad the unconscious into coming up with unexpectedly good ideas; at least you will generate more potentially useful raw material.

Outlining

To outline or not to outline? Unless your topic, by its nature, suggests some obvious way to organize your paper ("An Explication of a Wordsworth Sonnet" might mean simply working through the poem line by line), then some kind of outline will probably help. In high school or other prehistoric times, you perhaps learned how to construct a beautiful outline, laid out with Roman numerals, capital letters, Arabic numerals, and lowercase letters. It was a thing of beauty and symmetry, and it possibly even had something to do with paper writing. But if now you are skeptical of the value of outlining, reflect: not every outline needs to be detailed and elaborate. Some students, of course, find it helpful to outline in detail—particularly if they are planning a long term paper involving several literary works, comparing and contrasting several aspects of them. For a 500-word analysis of a short story's figures of speech, though, all you might need is a simple list of points to make, scribbled down in the order in which you will make them. This order is probably not, of course, the order in which the points first occurred to you. Thoughts, when they first come to mind, can arrive as a confused rabble.

While granting the need for order in a piece of writing, the present writer confesses that he is a reluctant outliner. His tendency (or curse) is to want to keep whatever random thoughts occur to him, to polish his prose right then and there, and finally to try to juggle his disconnected paragraphs into something like logical order. The usual result is that he has large blocks of illogical thought left over. This process is wasteful, and if you can learn to live with an outline, then you belong to the legion of the blessed and will never know the pain of scrapping pages that cost you hours. On the other hand, you will never know the joy of meandering—of bursting into words and surprising yourself. As novelist E. M. Forster remarked, "How do I know what I think until I see what I say?"

An outline, if you use one, is not meant to stand as an achievement in itself. It should—as Ezra Pound said literary criticism ought to do—consume itself and disappear. Here is a once-valuable outline not worth keeping—a very informal one that enabled a student to organize the paper that appears on page 1880, "The Hearer of the Tell-Tale Heart." Before he wrote, the student jotted down the ideas that had occurred to him. Looking them over, he could see that certain ones predominated. Since the aim of his paper was to analyze Poe's story for its point of view, he began with some notes about the narrator of the story. His other leading ideas had emerged as questions: Is the story supposed to be a ghost story or an account of a delusion?

Can we read the whole thing as a nightmare, having no reality outside the narrator's mind? Having seen that his thoughts weren't a totally disconnected jumble, he drew connections. Going down his list, he numbered with the same numbers those ideas that belonged together.

```
 /  1 Killer is mad--can listen in on Hell.

Point  2 He is obsessed with the Evil Eye.
  of
 view  1 He thinks he is sane, we know he's mad.

      Old man rich--a miser?

      Is this a ghost story? NO! Natural explanations

        for the heartbeat:

  4   His mind is playing tricks.

      Hears his own heart (Hoffman's idea).

  3 Maybe the whole story is only his dream?

      Poe must have been crazy too.
```

The numbers now showed him the order in which he planned to take up each of his four chief ideas. Labeling his remarks about the narrator with the number "1," he decided to open his paper with them and to declare at once that they indicated the story's point of view. As you can tell from his finished paper, he discarded two notions that didn't seem to relate to his purpose: the point about the old man's wealth and the speculation (which he realized he couldn't prove) that Poe himself was mad. Having completed this rough outline, he felt encouraged to return to Poe's story and on rereading it noticed a few additional points, which you will find in his paper. His outline didn't tell him exactly what to say at every moment, but it was clear and easy to follow.

DRAFTING AND REVISING

Seated at last or striking some other businesslike stance,[1] you prepare to write, only to find yourself besieged with petty distractions. All of a sudden you remember a friend you had promised to call, some dry cleaning you were supposed to pick up, a neglected Coke (in another room) growing warmer and flatter by the minute. If your paper is to be written, you have only one course of action: collar these thoughts and for the moment banish them.

When first you draft your paper—that is, when you write it out in the rough— you will probably do best to write rapidly. At this early stage, you don't need to be fussy about spelling, grammar, and punctuation. To be sure, those picayune details matter, but you can worry about them later, when you are **editing** (combing through

[1]R. H. Super of the University of Michigan wrote a definitive biography of British poet Walter Savage Landor while standing up, typing on a machine atop a filing cabinet.

your draft repairing grammar, cutting excess words, making small verbal improvements) and **proofreading** (going over your finished paper line by line, checking it for typographical or other mistakes). Right now, it is more important to get your thoughts down on paper in a steady flow than to keep taking time out to check spellings in the dictionary. Forge ahead, and don't be too nastily self-critical. Perhaps when you write your draft, you won't even want to look at all those notes on your reading that you collected so industriously. When you come to a place where a note will fit, you might just insert a reminder to yourself, such as SEE CARD 19 or SEE ARISTOTLE ON COMEDY.

Let us admit that writing about literature is a fussier kind of writing than turning out a narrative essay called, "My Most Exciting Experience." You may need to draft some of your paper slowly and painstakingly. You'll find yourself coping with all sorts of small problems, many of them simple and mechanical. What, for instance, will you call the author whose work you are dealing with? Decide at the outset. Most critics favor the author's last name alone: "Dickinson implies . . ." ("Miss Dickinson" or "Ms. Dickinson" may sound fussily polite; "Emily," too chummy.) Will you include footnotes in your paper, and if so, do you know how they work? (Some pointers on handling the pesky things will come in a few pages.)

Acknowledging Sources

You will want to give credit to any critics who helped you out, and to do so properly is to be painstaking. To paraphrase a critic, you do more than just rearrange the critic's words and phrases; you translate them into language of your own. Suppose you wish to refer to an insight of Randall Jarrell, who comments on the images of spider, flower, and moth in Robert Frost's poem "Design":

> Notice how the *heal-all*, because of its name, is the one flower in all the world picked to be the altar for this Devil's Mass; notice how *holding up* the moth brings something ritual and hieratic, a ghostly, ghastly formality, to this priest and its sacrificial victim.

It would be incorrect to say, without quotation marks:

```
Frost picks the heal-all as the one flower in all

the world to be the altar for this Devil's Mass.

There is a ghostly, ghastly formality to the spider

holding up the moth, like a priest holding a sacrifi-

cial victim.
```

This rewording, although not exactly in Jarrell's language, manages to steal his memorable phrases without giving him credit. Nor is it sufficient just to include Jarrell's essay in the Works Cited list at the end of your paper. If you do, you are still a crook; you merely point to the scene of your crime. What is needed, clearly, is to think through Jarrell's words to the point he is making; and if you want to keep any of his striking phrases (and why not?), put them exactly as he wrote them in quotation marks:

```
As Randall Jarrell points out, Frost portrays the

spider as a kind of priest in a Mass, or Black Mass,

elevating the moth like an object for sacrifice, with

"a ghostly, ghastly formality" (42).
```

To be scrupulous in your acknowledgment, tell where you found your quotation from Jarrell, citing the page reference. (See "Documenting Your Sources," page 1859.)

Using Literary Terminology

One more word of Dutch uncle warning. In this book you are offered a vocabulary with which to discuss literature: a flurry of terms such as *irony*, *symbol*, and *image*, printed in **boldface** when first introduced. In your writing you may decide to enlist a few of these terms. Literary terminology sometimes sounds so impressive that a beginning critic can be tempted to use it indiscriminately. Nothing is less sophisticated or more opaque, however, than too many technical terms thrown together for grandiose effect: "The mythic symbolism of this *archetype* is the *antithesis* of the *dramatic situation*." Far better to choose plain words you're already at ease with. Your instructor has met many a critical term before and is not likely to be impressed by the mere sight of another one. Knowingly selected and placed, a critical term can help sharpen a thought and make it easier to handle. It is less cumbersome, for example, to refer to the *tone* of a story than to have to say, "the way the author makes you feel that she feels about what she is talking about." But the paper writer who declares, "The tone of this poem is full of ironic imagery," fries words to a hash—mixed up and indigestible.

Revision

When you write your first draft, by the way, leave plenty of space between lines and set enormous margins. Then, when later thoughts come to you, you can easily squeeze them in.

Does any writer write with perfection on first try? Some writers have claimed to do so—among them the English novelist Anthony Trollope, who thought it "unmanly" not to write a thought right the first time. Jack Kerouac, leading novelist of the Beat Generation of the 1950s, believed in spontaneous prose. He used to write entire novels on uncut ribbons of teletype paper, thus saving himself the interruption of stopping at the bottom of each page. His specialty, though, was fiction of ecstasy and hallucination, not essays in explication, or comparison and contrast. For most of us, however, good writing is largely a matter of revising—of going back over our first thoughts word by word. Painstaking revision is more than a matter of tidying up grammar and spelling; in the process of reconsidering our words, we sometimes discover fresher and sharper ideas. "Writing and rewriting," says John Updike, "are a constant search for what one is saying."

To achieve effective writing, you must have the courage to be wild. Aware that no reader need see your rough drafts, you can treat them mercilessly—scissor them apart, rearrange their pieces, reassemble them into a stronger order. The art of revising calls for a textbook in itself, but here are a few simple suggestions:

1. Insofar as your deadline allows, be willing to revise as many times as need be.

2. Don't think of revision as the simple chore of fixing up spelling mistakes. That's proofreading, and it comes last. When you revise, be willing to cut and slash, to discover new insights, to move blocks of words around so that they follow in a stronger order. Stand ready to question your whole approach to a work of literature, to entertain the notion of throwing everything you have written into the wastebasket and starting over again.

3. At this stage, you may find it helpful to enlist outside advice—from your instructor, from your roommate or your mate, from any friend who will read your rough draft and give you a reaction. If you can enlist such a willing reader, ask him or her: What isn't clear to you?

4. If you (or your willing reader) should find any places that aren't readily understandable, single them out for rewriting. After all, you don't need to revise a whole draft if only parts of it need work. Try rewriting any troublesome passage or paragraph.

5. Short, skimpy paragraphs of one or two sentences may indicate places that call for more thought or more material. Can you supply them with more evidence, more explanation, more example and illustration?

6. A time-tested method of revising is to lay aside your manuscript for a while, forget about it, and then after a long interval (the Roman poet Horace recommended nine years, but obviously that won't do), go back to it for a fresh look. If you have time, take a nap or a walk, or at least a yawn and a stretch before you take yet another look.

7. When your paper is in a *last* draft—then it's time to edit it. Once you have your ideas in firm shape, you can check those uncertain spellings, look up the agreement of subjects and verbs in a grammar book or handbook, make your pronouns and antecedents agree, cut needless words, pull out a weak word and send in a stronger one. Back when you were drafting, being prematurely fussy about such small things might have frozen you up. But once you feel satisfied that you have made yourself clear, you can be as fussy as you like.

THE FORM OF YOUR FINISHED PAPER

Now that you have smoothed your final draft as fleck-free as you can, your instructor may have specific advice for the form of your finished paper. If none is forthcoming, it is only reasonable to:

1. Choose standard letter-size ($8\frac{1}{2} \times 11$) paper.
2. Give your name, your instructor's name, the course number, and the date at the top of your first page.
3. Leave an inch or more of margin on all four sides of each page and a few inches of blank paper or an additional sheet after your conclusion, so that your instructor can offer comments.
4. Double-space, including quotations and notes. If you handwrite, skip every other ruled line.
5. Give your name and the page number in the top right-hand corner of each page, one-half inch from the top.

And what of titles of works discussed: when do you put them in quotation marks and when do you underline them? One rule of thumb is that titles of works shorter than a book-length rate quotation marks (poems, short stories, articles); but titles of books (including book-length poems such as *The Odyssey*), plays, and periodicals take underlining. (In a manuscript to be set in type, an underline is a signal to the compositor to use *italics*.)

DOCUMENTING YOUR SOURCES

When you quote from other writers, when you borrow their information, or when you summarize or paraphrase their ideas, make sure you give them their due. Document everything you take. Identify the writer by name; cite not only the very book, magazine, newspaper, pamphlet, letter, or other source you are using but also the page or pages you are quoting.

By so doing, you invite your readers to go to your original source and check up on you. Most readers won't bother, of course, but at least your invitation enlists their confidence. Besides, the duty to document keeps you carefully looking at your sources—and so helps keep your writing accurate and responsible. The latest and most efficient way for writers to document their sources is that recommended in the *MLA Handbook for Writers of Research Papers*, 4th ed. (New York: Modern Language Association of America, 1995). In the long run, whether you write a long term paper citing dozens of sources or a short paper citing only three or four, the MLA's advice will save you and your reader time and trouble.

These pointers cannot take the place of the *MLA Handbook* itself, but the gist of the method is this: Begin by listing your sources—all the works from which you're going to quote, summarize, paraphrase, or take information. Later on, when you type up your paper in finished form, you're going to *end* it with a neat copy of this list (once called a *bibliography*, now entitled "Works Cited"). But in writing your paper, every time you refer to one of these works, you need give only enough information to help a reader locate it under "Works Cited." Usually, you can just give (in parentheses) an author's last name and a page citation. If you were writing, for example, a paper on Weldon Kees's sonnet "For My Daughter" and wanted to include an observation from Samuel Maio's book *Creating Another Self*, you would incorporate the information right in the text of your paper, most often at the end of a sentence:

```
One critic has observed that the distinctive tone of

"For My Daughter" depends on Kees's combination of

personal subject matter with an impersonal voice

(Maio 123).
```

If you wanted to cite *two* books or magazine articles by Maio in your paper, how would the reader tell them apart? In your text, condense the title of each book or article into a word or two. Remember that condensed book titles are also underlined, and condensed article titles are still placed within quotation marks:

```
One critic has observed that the distinctive tone of

"For My Daughter" depends on Kees's combination of

personal subject matter with an impersonal voice

(Maio, Creating 123).
```

If you have already mentioned the name of the author in your sentence you need give only the page number when you refer to the source:

```
As Samuel Maio has observed, Kees creates a distinc-

tive tone in this sonnet by combining a personal sub-

ject with an impersonal voice (123).
```

If you wanted to quote more than four lines, you should set it off from the body of your paper. Start a new line; indent one inch (or ten typewriter spaces); type the quote, double-spaced. After the period at the end of the quotation, put the page reference in parentheses. You do not need to use quotation marks.

```
Samuel Maio made an astute observation about the

nature of Kees's distinctive tone:

          Kees has therefore combined a personal

          subject matter with an impersonal voice

          --that is, one that is consistent in its

          tone evenly recording the speaker's

          thoughts without showing any emotional
```

```
                   intensity which might lie behind those

                   thoughts. (123)
```

The beauty of this documentation method is that you don't have to stop the flow of your thought with a detailed footnote identifying your source. At the end of your paper, in your list of works cited, your reader can find a fuller description of your source—in this case, a critical book:

```
     Maio, Samuel. Creating Another Self: Voice in Modern

          American Personal Poetry. Kirksville: Thomas

          Jefferson UP, 1995.
```

Final List of Works Cited

As you write, keep a list of all your sources. Later when you type your paper in finished form, you should include a complete list at the end of all the works you have cited. The *MLA Handbook* provides complete instructions for citing a myriad of different types of sources, from books to online databases. Here is only a partial checklist of how the *Handbook* recommends presenting such a list.

1. Start a new page for the Works Cited list, and continue the page numbering from the body of your paper.
2. Center the title, "Works Cited," one inch from the top of the page.
3. Double-space between all lines (including after the title and between entries).
4. Type each entry beginning at the left-hand margin. If an entry runs longer than a single line, indent following lines one-half inch (or five full spaces if you are using a typewriter) from the left-hand margin.
5. Alphabetize each entry according to the author's last name.
6. Include three sections in each entry: author, title, publication information. You will, however, give slightly different information for a book or a journal article or other references.

For a book cite:
   a. Author's full name as it appears on the title page, last name first.
   b. Book's full title (and subtitle, if it has one, separated by a colon) followed by a period. Remember to underline or italicize the title.
   c. Publication information: city of publication followed by a colon, the name of the publisher followed by a comma, and the year of publication followed by a period.
      (1) *Make your citation of the city of publication brief, but clear.* If the title page lists more than one city, cite only the first. For United States cities, you need not provide the state unless the name of the city alone may be confusing or is unfamiliar. For cities outside the United

States, add a country abbreviation if the city is unfamiliar. For Canadian cities, use the province abbreviation. (Examples: Rome, GA; Leeds, Eng.; Victoria, BC)

(2) *Shorten the publisher's name.* Eliminate articles (*A, An, The*), business abbreviations (*Co., Corp., Inc., Ltd.*), and descriptive words (*Books, House, Press, Publishers*). The exception is a university press, for which you should use the letters *U* (for University) and *P* (for Press). Use only the first listed *surname* of the publisher. Examples below:

Publisher's Name	Proper Citation
Harvard University Press	Harvard UP
University of Chicago Press	U of Chicago P
Farrar, Straus and Giroux, Inc.	Farrar
Alfred A. Knopf, Inc.	Knopf

Final citation for a book should read:

```
Author's last name, First name. Book title.
      Publication city: Publisher, Year.
```

For a journal article cite:

a. Author's name, last name first, followed by a period.
b. Title of the article, followed by a period, all within quotation marks.
c. Publication information: journal title (underlined); volume number; the year of publication in parentheses, followed by a colon; and, finally, the inclusive page numbers of the entire article followed by a period.

```
Author's last name, First name. "Article Title."
      Journal Volume (Year): Pages.
```

If the journal starts the pagination of *each* issue from page one (in contrast to continuous numbering from the previous issue), then you must give both the volume and issue number. For example, if the article you cite appears in volume 5, issue 2 of such a journal, cite it as 5.2.

```
Author's last name, First name. "Article Title."
      Journal Volume.Issue (Year): Pages.
```

For a short paper on Kees's "For My Daughter," a student's Work Cited list might look as follows:

Works Cited

```
Grosholz, Emily. "The Poetry of Memory." Weldon Kees:
      A Critical Introduction. Ed. Jim Elledge.
      Metuchen: Scarecrow, 1985. 46-47.
```

Howard, Ben. "Four Voices." Weldon Kees: A Critical
    Introduction. Ed. Jim Elledge. Metuchen:
    Scarecrow, 1985. 177-79.

Kees, Weldon. The Collected Poems of Weldon Kees. Ed.
    Donald Justice. Lincoln: U Nebraska P, 1975.

Libera, Sharon Meyer. "The Disappearance of Weldon
    Kees." Ploughshares 5.1 (1979): 147-59.

Maio, Samuel. Creating Another Self: Voice in Modern
    American Personal Poetry. Kirksville: Thomas
    Jefferson UP, 1995.

Nelson, Raymond. "The Fitful Life of Weldon Kees."
    American Literary History 1 (1989): 816-52.

Ross, William T. Weldon Kees. Twayne's US Authors
    Ser. 484. Boston: Twayne, 1985.

We have only outlined the current *MLA Handbook* format. You will probably want to consult the *Handbook* itself for complete guidelines.

Footnotes and Endnotes

It's imperative to keep the citations and quotations in your text brief and snappy, lest they hinder the flow of your prose. You may wish to append a note supplying a passage of less important (yet possibly valuable) information or making careful qualifying statements ("On the other hand, not every expert agrees. John Binks finds that poets are often a little magazine's only cash customers; while Molly MacGuire maintains that . . ."). If you want to put in such an aside and suspect that you can't put it in your text without interrupting your paper awkwardly, then cast it into a **footnote** (a note placed at the bottom of a page) or an **endnote** (a note placed at the end of a paper).

How do you drop in such notes? The number of each consecutive note comes (following any punctuation) after the last word of a sentence. So that the number will stand out, roll your typewriter carriage up a click (or order your computer to do a superscript), thus lifting the number slightly above the level of your prose.

as other observers have claimed.[1]

When you come to type the footnote or endnote itself, skip five full character spaces, elevate the number again, skip a space, and proceed. Be certain to include appropriate pagination.

> [1] John Binks, to name only one such observer,
> finds . . .

Although now useful mainly for such asides, footnotes and endnotes are time-honored ways to document *all* sources in a research paper. Indeed, some instructors still prefer them to the new MLA guidelines and urge students to use such notes to indicate every writer cited. Though such notes take more work, they have the advantage of hiding dull data away from your reader's eyes, enabling you to end sentences effectively with only inconspicuous note numbers instead of whimpering parentheses (Glutz-Finnegan, *Lesser Corollary* 1029–30). Besides, in a brief paper containing only one citation or two, to use footnotes or endnotes may be simpler and less showy than to compile a Works Cited list that has only two entries. Once again, always check with your instructor.

Large mindedly, the *MLA Handbook* tolerates the continued use of footnotes and endnotes for documentation. Indeed, it offers advice for their preparation, which is shown here. If you do use footnotes or endnotes to document all your sources, here is how to format them. A note identifying a magazine article looks like this:

> [16] Louise Horton, "Who Reads Small Literary Magazines and What Good Do They Do?" <u>Texas Review</u> 9.1 (1984): 108–09.

Notice that, in notes, the author's first name comes first. (In a list of Works Cited, you proceed differently: you put last name first, so that you can readily arrange your list of authors in easy-to-consult alphabetical order.) A footnote or endnote for a reference to a book (as opposed to a magazine or journal article) looks like this:

> [17] Elizabeth Frank, <u>Louise Bogan: A Portrait</u> (New York: Knopf, 1985) 59–60.

Should you return later to cite another place in Frank's book, you need not repeat all its information. Just write:

> [18] Frank 192.

If in your paper you refer to *two* sources by Elizabeth Frank, give the full title of each in the first note citing it. Then, if you cite it again, use a shortened form of its title:

Your readers should not have to interrupt their reading of your essay to glance down at a note to find out whom you are quoting. It is poor form to write:

> Dylan Thomas's poem "Fern Hill" is a memory of the poet's childhood: of his Aunt Ann Jones's farm, where he spent his holidays. One critic has observed, "Time, which has an art to throw dust on all things, broods over the poem."[1] The farm, indeed, is a lost paradise--a personal garden of Eden.

> ---
> [1] William York Tindall, A Reader's Guide to Dylan Thomas (New York: Noonday, 1962) 268.

That is annoying because the reader has to stop reading and look at the footnote to find out who made that resonant statement about Time's brooding over the poem. A better wording is:

> "Time," as William York Tindall has observed, "which has an art to throw dust on all things, broods over the poem."[1]

Your footnote or endnote should then cite Tindall's book:

> [1] A Reader's Guide to Dylan Thomas (New York: Noonday, 1962) 268.

What to do now but hand in your paper? "And good riddance," you may feel, after such an expenditure of thinking, time, and energy. But a good paper is not only worth submitting, it is worth keeping. If you return to it, after a while, you may find to your surprise that it will preserve and even renew what you have learned.

REFERENCE GUIDE FOR CITATIONS

Here is a comprehensive summary of the types of citations you are likely to need for most student essays. The format follows the current MLA standards for Works Cited lists.

Books

No Author Listed

A Keepsake Anthology of the Fiftieth Anniversary
    Celebration of the Consultantship in Poetry.
    Washington: Library of Congress, 1987.

One Author

Middlebrook, Diane Wood. Anne Sexton: A Biography.
    Boston: Houghton, 1991.

Two or Three Authors

Jarman, Mark, and Robert McDowell. The Reaper:
    Essays. Brownsville, OR: Story Line, 1996.

Four or More Authors

Phillips, Rodney, et al. The Hand of the Poet. New
    York: Rizzoli, 1997.
or
Phillips, Rodney, Susan Benesch, Kenneth Benson, and
    Barbara Bergeron. The Hand of the Poet. New
    York: Rizzoli, 1997.

Two Books by Same Author

Bawer, Bruce. The Aspect of Eternity. St. Paul:
    Graywolf, 1993.
---. Diminishing Fictions: Essays on the Modern
    American Novel and Its Critics. St. Paul:
    Graywolf, 1988.

Corporate Author

Poets & Writers. A Writer's Guide to Copyright. New
York: Poets & Writers, 1979.

Author and Editor

Shakespeare, William. The Sonnets. Ed. G. Blakemore
Evans. Cambridge, Eng.: Cambridge UP,
1996.

One Editor

Monteiro, George, ed. Conversations with Elizabeth
Bishop. Jackson: UP of Mississippi, 1996.

Two Editors

Craig, David, and Janet McCann, eds. Odd Angles of
Heaven: Contemporary Poetry by People of Faith.
Wheaton, IL: Shaw, 1994.

Translation

Chekhov, Anton. Selected Stories. Trans. Ann
Dunnigan. New York: Signet, 1960.

Introduction, Preface, Foreword, or Afterword

Thwaite, Anthony. Preface. Contemporary Poets. Ed.
Thomas Riggs. 6th ed. New York: St. James, 1996.
vii-viii.

Lapham, Lewis. Introduction. Understanding Media: The
Extensions of Man. By Marshall McLuhan.
Cambridge: MIT P, 1994. vi-x.

Work in an Anthology

Allen, Dick. "The Emperor's New Clothes." Poetry
After Modernism. Ed. Robert McDowell.
Brownsville, OR: Story Line, 1991. 71-99.

Translation in an Anthology

Neruda, Pablo. "We Are Many." Trans. Alastair Reid. Literature: An Introduction to Fiction, Poetry, and Drama. Ed. X.J. Kennedy and Dana Gioia. 7th ed. New York: Longman, 1999. 968.

Multivolume Work

Wellek, René. A History of Modern Criticism, 1750-1950. Vol. 7. New Haven: Yale UP, 1991. 8 vols. 1955-92.

Book in a Series

Ross, William T. Weldon Kees. Twayne's US Authors Ser. 484. Boston: Twayne, 1985.

Republished Book

Ellison, Ralph. Invisible Man. 1952. New York: Vintage, 1995.

Revised or Subsequent Editions

Janouch, Gustav. Conversations with Kafka. Trans. Goronwy Rees. Rev. ed. New York: New Directions, 1971.

Reference Books

Signed Article

McPhillips, Robert. "Timothy Steele." The Oxford Companion to Twentieth-Century Poetry in English. Ed. Ian Hamilton. Oxford: Oxford UP, 1994.

Unsigned Encyclopedia Article—Standard Reference Book

"James Dickey." The New Encyclopaedia Britannica: Micropaedia. 15th ed. 1987.

Dictionary Entry

"Design." <u>Merriam-Webster's Collegiate Dictionary</u>.
    10th ed. 1993.

Periodicals

Journal with Continuous Paging

Balée, Susan. "Flannery O'Connor Resurrected." <u>Hudson</u>
    <u>Review</u> 47 (1994): 377-93.

Journal That Pages Each Issues Separately

Salter, Mary Jo. "The Heart Is Slow to Learn." <u>New</u>
    <u>Criterion</u> 10.8 (1992): 23-29.

Signed Magazine Article

Gioia, Dana. "Studying with Miss Bishop." <u>New Yorker</u>.
    5 Sept. 1986: 90-101.

Unsigned Magazine Article

"Fair Strike." <u>New Republic</u>. 16 Feb. 1998: 7-8.

Newspaper Article

Lyall, Sarah. "In Poetry, Ted Hughes Breaks His
    Silence on Sylvia Plath." <u>New York Times</u> 19 Jan.
    1998, natl. ed.: A1+.

Signed Book Review

Harper, John. "Well-Crafted Tales with Tabloid
    Titles." Rev. of <u>Tabloid Dreams</u>, by Robert Olen
    Butler. <u>Orlando Sentinel</u> 15 Dec. 1996: D4.

Unsigned, Untitled Book Review

Rev. of <u>Otherwise: New and Selected Poems</u>, by Jane
    Kenyon. <u>Virginia Quarterly Review</u> 72 (1996): 136.

CD-ROM Reference Works

Periodically Published Information, Collected on CD-ROM

Kakutani, Michiko. "Slogging Surreally in the
Vietnamese Jungle." Rev. of The Things They
Carried, by Tim O'Brien. New York Times 6 Mar.
1990, late ed.: C21. New York Times Ondisc. CD-
ROM. UMI-Proquest. Oct. 1993.

CD-ROM Publication

"Appall." The Oxford English Dictionary. 2nd ed. CD-
ROM. Oxford: Oxford UP, 1992.

Online Databases

Online Scholarly Project

Voice of the Shuttle. Ed. Alan Liu. 3 Mar. 1998. U of
California, Santa Barbara. 12 Mar. 1998
⟨http://humanitas.ucsb.edu/⟩.

Online Reference Database

Britannica Online. Vers. 97. 1.1. Mar. 1997.
Encyclopaedia Britannica. 19 Mar. 1997
⟨http://www.eb.com/⟩.

Online Professional Site

Wallace Stegner Environmental Center. San Francisco
Public Library. 15 Mar. 1998 ⟨http://sfpl.lib.
ca.us/stegner/wallace.html⟩.

Online Book

Whitman, Walt. Leaves of Grass. [1892] 15 Mar. 1998
⟨http://www.bibliomania.com/Poetry/Whitman/Grass/⟩.

Article in Online Scholarly Journal

Hoffman, Tyler B. "Emily Dickinson and the Limit of
War." Emily Dickinson Journal 3.2 (1994). 15
Mar. 1998 ⟨http:/www.colorado.edu/EDIS/journal/
articles/III.2.Hoffman.html⟩.

Article in Online Newspaper

Koehler, Robert. "Latino Perspective Takes Center
Stage." Los Angeles Times Web Site. 31 July
1993. 15 Mar. 1998 ⟨http://www.latimes.com/
HOME/ARCHIVES/⟩.

Article Accessed via Computer Service

Bray, Rosemary L. "Renaissance for a Pioneer of Black
Pride." New York Times 4 Feb. 1990, late ed.,
sec. 2: 7. New York Times Online. Nexis. 1 Mar.
1998.

Article in Online Magazine

Garner, Dwight. "The Salon Interview: Jamaica
Kincaid." Salon 13 Jan. 1996. 1 Mar. 1998
⟨http://www:salonmagazine.com/05/features/
kincaid.html⟩.

Review in Online Newspaper

Hollander, John. "The Fluent Mundo." Rev. of Wallace
Stevens: Collected Poetry and Prose, by Wallace
Stevens. Los Angeles Times Web Site 16 Nov.
1997. 14 Mar. 1998 ⟨http://www.latimes.com/
HOME/ARCHIVES/⟩.

Online Posting

Grossenbacher, Laura. "Comments about the Ending
  Illustration." 4 Sept. 1996. Online posting. The
  Yellow Wallpaper Site. 14 Mar. 1998
  ⟨http://www:cwrl.utexas.edu/~daniel/amlit/
  wallpaper/readcomments.html⟩.

Audio Recordings

Roethke, Theodore. Theodore Roethke Reads His Poetry.
  Audiocassette. Caedmon, 1972.

Film

Hamlet. By William Shakespeare. Dir. Franco
  Zeffirelli. Perf. Mel Gibson, Glenn Close,
  Helena Bonham Carter, Alan Bates, and Paul
  Scofield. Warner, 1991.

Television Program

Moby Dick. By Herman Melville. Dir. Franc Roddam.
  Perf. Patrick Stewart and Gregory Peck. 2
  episodes. USA Network. 16-17 Mar. 1998.

Videocassette

Henry V. By William Shakespeare. Dir. Laurence
  Olivier. Perf. Laurence Olivier. 1944.
  Videocassette. Paramount, 1988.

KEEPING A JOURNAL

The essay is not, of course, the only medium in which you can write your responses to literature. Many instructors ask students to keep a **journal:** a day-to-day account of what they read and how they react to it. A great advantage in keeping a journal is that you can express your thoughts and feelings immediately, before they grow cold. You can set down all your miscellaneous reactions to what you read, whether or not they fit into a paper topic. (If you have to write a paper later on, your journal just might suggest topics galore.) Depending on what your instructor thinks is essential, your journal may take in all your reading for the course, or you may concentrate on the work of some writer or writers, or on one kind of story. As you read, you can jot down anything you notice that you wish to remember. Does a theme in a story or a line of dialogue strike you forcefully? Make a note of it. Does something in the story not make sense? Record your bewilderment. Your journal is personal: a place for you to sound off, to express your feelings. Don't just copy your class notes into it; don't simply quote the stories. Mere length of your entries will not impress your instructor either: try for insights. A paragraph or two will probably suffice to set down your main reactions to most stories. In keeping a journal (a kind of writing primarily for yourself), you don't rewrite; so you need not feel obliged to polish your prose. Your aim is to store information without delay, to wrap words around your reactions and observations.

Keeping a journal will be satisfying only if you keep it up-to-date. Record your feelings and insights while you still have a story freshly in mind. Get weeks behind, and you will have to grind out a journal from scratch, the night before it is due, and the whole project will decay into meaningless drudgery. If you faithfully do a little reading and writing every day or so, you will find yourself keeping track of the life of your mind. When your journal is closed, you will have a lively record not only of the literature you have read but also of your involvement with it.

Robert Wallace (b. 1932)
The Girl Writing Her English Paper   1979

lies on one hip by the fire,
blond, in jeans.

The wreckage of her labor, elegant as Eden
or petals from a tree,
surrounds her—   5

a little farm, smoke rising from the ashtray,
book, notebooks, papers, fields;
a poem's furrows

If the lights were to go out suddenly,
stars would be overhead,   10
the edge of the wood still and dark.

40 *Writing About a Story*

A good discussion of fiction doesn't just toss forth a random lot of impressions. It makes some point about which the writer feels strongly. In order to write a meaningful paper, then, you need something you *want* to say—a meaningful topic. For suggestions on finding such a topic (also some pointers on organizing, writing, revising, and finishing your paper), please see "Writing About Literature," which begins on page 1851. The advice there may be applied to papers on fiction, poetry, and drama. Some methods especially useful for writing about stories are gathered in the present chapter.

Unlike a brief poem or a painting that you can take in with one long glance, a work of fiction—even a short story—may be too complicated to hold all at once in the mind's eye. Before you can write about it, you may need to give it two or more careful readings, and even then, as you begin to think further about it, you will probably have to thumb through it to reread passages. The first time through it is best just to read attentively, open to whatever pleasure and wisdom the story may afford. On second look, you may find it useful to read with pencil in hand, either to mark your personal copy or to take notes to jog your memory. To see the design and meaning of a story need not be a boring chore, any more than it is to land a fighting fish and to study it with admiration.

In this chapter all the discussions and examples refer to Edgar Allan Poe's short story "The Tell-Tale Heart" (page 33). If you haven't already read it, you can do so in only a few minutes, so that the rest of this chapter will make more sense to you.

EXPLICATING

Explication is the patient unfolding of meanings in a work of literature. An explication—that is, an essay that follows this method—proceeds carefully through a story, poem, or play, usually interpreting it line by line—perhaps even word by word. A good explication dwells on details, as well as on larger things. It brings them to the attention of a reader who might have missed them (the reader probably hasn't read so closely as the writer of the explication). Alert and willing to take pains, the writer of such an essay notices anything meaningful that isn't obvious, whether it is a colossal theme suggested by a symbol or a little hint contained in a single word.

To write an honest explication of a story takes time and space, probably too much time and space to devote to a long and complex story unless you are writing a long term paper, an honors thesis, or a dissertation. For example, a thorough explication of Nathaniel Hawthorne's "Young Goodman Brown" would be likely to run much longer than the rich and intriguing short story itself. Ordinarily, explication is best suited dealing with a short passage or section of a story: a key scene, a crucial conversation, a statement of theme, or an opening or closing paragraph. Storytellers who are especially fond of language invite closer attention to their words than others do. Edgar Allan Poe, for one, is a poet sensitive to the rhythms of his sentences and a symbolist whose stories abound in potent suggestions. Here is an explication, by a student, of a short but essential passage in "The Tell-Tale Heart." The passage occurs in the third paragraph of the story, and (to help us follow the explication) the student quotes it in full at the beginning of her paper.

Student's Name

Professor's Name

Course   Name

Date

By Lantern Light: An Explication of a Passage
    in Poe's "The Tell-Tale Heart"

And every night, about midnight, I turned the

latch of his door and opened it--oh, so gently!

And then, when I had made an opening sufficient

for my head, I put in a dark lantern, all closed,

closed, so that no light shone out, and then I

thrust in my head. Oh, you would have laughed to

see how cunningly I thrust it in! I moved it

slowly--very, very slowly, so that I might not

disturb the old man's sleep. It took me an hour

to place my whole head within the opening so far

that I could see him as he lay upon his bed. Ha!--

would a madman have been so wise as this? And

then, when my head was well in the room, I undid

the lantern cautiously--oh, so cautiously--
cautiously (for the hinges creaked)--I undid it
just so much that a single thin ray fell upon the
vulture eye. And this I did for seven long
nights--every night just at midnight--but I found
the eye always closed; and so it was impossible
to do the work; for it was not the old man who
vexed me, but his Evil Eye (par. 3).

Although Poe has suggested in the first lines of his
story that the person who addresses us is insane, it is only
when we come to the speaker's account of his preparations
for murdering the old man that we find his madness fully
revealed. Even more convincingly than his earlier words (for
we might possibly think that someone who claims to hear
things in heaven and hell is a religious mystic), these
preparations reveal him to be mad. What strikes us is that
they are so elaborate and meticulous. A significant detail
is the exactness of his schedule for spying: "every night
just at midnight." The words with which he describes his
motions also convey the most extreme care (and I will
indicate them by underlining): "how wisely I proceeded--with
what caution," "I turned the latch of his door and opened
it--oh, so gently!" "how cunningly I thrust it [my head] in!
I moved it slowly--very, very slowly," "I undid the lantern
cautiously--oh, so cautiously--cautiously." Taking a whole
hour to intrude his head into the room, he asks, "Ha!--would
a madman have been so wise as this?" But of course the word
wise is unconsciously ironic, for clearly it is not wisdom

the speaker displays, but an absurd degree of care, an
almost fiendish ingenuity. Such behavior, I understand, is
typical of certain mental illnesses. All his careful
preparations that he thinks prove him sane only convince us
instead that he is mad.

Obviously his behavior is self-defeating. He wants to
catch the "vulture eye" open, and yet he takes all these
pains not to disturb the old man's sleep. If he behaved
logically, he might go barging into the bedroom with his
lantern ablaze, shouting at the top of his voice. And yet,
if we can see things his way, there is a strange logic to
his reasoning. He regards the eye as a creature in itself,
quite apart from its possessor. "It was not," he says, "the
old man who vexed me, but his Evil Eye." Apparently, to be
inspired to do his deed, the madman needs to behold the
eye--at least, this is my understanding of his remark, "I
found the eye always closed; and so it was impossible to do
the work." Poe's choice of the word work, by the way, is
also revealing. Murder is made to seem a duty or a job; and
anyone who so regards murder is either extremely cold-
blooded, like a hired killer for a gangland assassination,
or else deranged. Besides, the word suggests again the
curious sense of detachment that the speaker feels toward
the owner of the eye.

In still another of his assumptions, the speaker shows
that he is madly logical, or operating on the logic of a
dream. There seems a dreamlike relationship between his dark
lantern "all closed, closed, so that no light shone out,"

and the sleeping victim. When the madman opens his lantern so that it emits a single ray, he is hoping that the eye in the old man's head will be open too, letting out its corresponding gleam. The latch that he turns so gently, too, seems like the eye, whose lid needs to be opened in order for the murderer to go ahead. It is as though the speaker is trying to get the eyelid to lift. By taking such great pains and by going through all this nightly ritual, he is practicing some kind of magic, whose rules are laid down not by our logic, but by the logic of dreams.

Work Cited

Poe, Edgar Allan. "The Tell-Tale Heart." Literature: An Introduction to Fiction, Poetry, and Drama. Ed. X.J. Kennedy and Dana Gioia. 7th ed. New York: Longman, 1999. 33-37.

An unusually well-written paper, "By Lantern Light" cost the student two or three careful revisions. Rather than attempting to say something about *everything* in the passage from Poe, she selects only the details that strike her as most meaningful. In her very first sentence, she briefly shows us how the passage functions in the context of Poe's story: how it clinches our suspicions that the narrator is mad. In writing her paper, the student went by the following rough, simple outline—nothing more than a list of the points she wanted to express:

1. Speaker's extreme care and exactness--typical of some mental illnesses.
2. Speaker doesn't act by usual logic but by a crazy logic.
3. Dreamlike connection between latch and lantern and old man's eye.

As she wrote, she followed her brief list, setting forth her ideas one at a time, one idea to a paragraph. There is a different (and still easier) way to organize an explication: just work through the original passage line by line or sentence by sentence. The danger of this procedure, however, is that you may find yourself falling into a boring singsong: "In the first sentence I noticed . . . ," "In the next sentence . . . ," "Now in the third sentence . . . ," "Finally, in the last paragraph." (If you choose to organize an explication in such a way, then boldly vary your transitions.) Notice that the student who wrote "By Lantern Light" doesn't inch through the passage sentence by sentence but freely takes up its details in an order that seems appropriate to her argument.

In a long critical essay in which we don't adhere to one method all the way through, the method of explication may appear from time to time—as when the critic, in discussing a story, stops to unravel a particularly knotty passage. However, useful as it may be to know how to write an explication of fiction, it is probably still more useful (in most literature courses) to know how to write an analysis.

ANALYZING

Assignment: "Write an **analysis** of a story or novel." What do you do? Following the method of analysis (from the Greek: "breaking up"), you separate a story or novel into its components and then (usually) select one part for close study. One likely topic for an analysis might be "The Character of James Thurber's Mr. Martin" (referring to "The Catbird Seat"), in which the writer would concentrate on showing us Martin's highly individual features and traits of personality. Other typical analyses might be written about, say, "Gothic Elements in a Story by Joyce Carol Oates" (referring to "Where Are You Going, Where Have You Been?") or "The Unidentified Narrator in 'A Rose for Emily.'"

To be sure, no element of a story dwells in isolation from the story's other elements. In "The Tell-Tale Heart," the madness of the leading character apparently makes it necessary to tell the story from a special point of view and probably helps determine the author's choice of theme, setting, symbolism, tone, style, and ironies. But it would be mind-boggling to try to study all those elements simultaneously. For this reason, when we write an analysis, we generally study just one element, though we may suggest—probably at the start of the essay—its relation to the whole story. Indeed, analysis is the method used in this book, in which, chapter by chapter, we have separated fiction into its components of plot, point of view, character, setting, tone and style, and so on. If you have read the discussion on the plot of "Godfather Death" (page 9) or the attempt to state the theme of Hemingway's "A Clean, Well-Lighted Place" (page 176), then you have already read some brief essays in analysis. Here is a student-written analysis of "The Tell-Tale Heart," dealing with just one element—the story's point of view.

Student's Name

Professor's Name

Course Name

Date

The Hearer of the Tell-Tale Heart

Although there are many things we do not know about
the narrator of Edgar Allan Poe's story "The Tell-Tale
Heart"--is he a son? a servant? a companion?--there is one
thing we are sure of from the start. He is mad. In the
opening paragraph, Poe makes the narrator's condition
unmistakable, not only from his excited and worked-up speech
(full of dashes and exclamation points), but also from his
wild claims. He says it is merely some disease which has
sharpened his senses that has made people call him crazy.
Who but a madman, however, would say, "I heard all things in
the heaven and in the earth," and brag how his ear is a kind
of CB radio, listening in on Hell? Such a statement leaves
no doubt that the point of view in the story is an ironic
one.

Because the participating narrator is telling his
story in the first person, some details in the story stand
out more than others. When the narrator goes on to tell how
he watches the old man sleeping, he rivets his attention on
the old man's "vulture eye." When a ray from his lantern
finds the Evil Eye open, he says, "I could see nothing else
of the old man's face or person" (par. 9). Actually, the
reader can see almost nothing else about the old man
anywhere in the rest of the story. All we are told is that
the old man treated the younger man well, and we gather that
the old man was rich, because his house is full of

treasures. We do not have a clear idea of what the old man looks like, though, nor do we know how he talks, for we are not given any of his words. Our knowledge of him is mainly confined to his eye and its effect on the narrator. This confinement gives that symbolic eye a lot of importance in the story. The narrator tells us all we know and directs our attention to parts of it.

This point of view raises an interesting question. Since we are dependent on the narrator for all our information, how do we know the whole story isn't just a nightmare in his demented mind? We have really no way to be sure it isn't, as far as I can see. I assume, however, that there really is a dark shuttered house and an old man and real policemen who start snooping around when screams are heard in the neighborhood, because it is a more memorable story if it is a crazy man's view of reality than if it is all just a terrible dream. But we can't take stock in the madman's interpretation of what happens. Poe keeps putting distances between what the narrator says and what we are supposed to think, apparently. For instance: the narrator has boasted that he is calm and clear in the head, but as soon as he starts trying to explain why he killed the old man, we gather that he is confused, to say the least (par. 2). "I think it was his eye!" the narrator exclaims, as if not quite sure (par. 2). As he goes on to explain how he conducted the murder, we realize that he is a man with a fixed idea working with a patience that is certainly mad, almost diabolical.

Some readers might wonder if "The Tell-Tale Heart" is a story of the supernatural. Is the heartbeat that the narrator hears a ghost come back to haunt him? Here, I think, the point of view is our best guide to what to believe. The simple explanation for the heartbeat is this: it is all in the madman's mind. Perhaps he feels such guilt that he starts hearing things. Another explanation is possible, one suggested by Daniel Hoffman, a critic who has discussed the story: the killer hears the sound of his own heart (227). Hoffman's explanation (which I don't like as well as mine) also is a natural one, and it fits the story as a whole. Back when the narrator first entered the old man's bedroom to kill him, the heartbeat sounded so loud to him that he was afraid the neighbors would hear it too. Evidently they didn't, and so Hoffman may be right in thinking that the sound was only that of his own heart pounding in his ears. Whichever explanation you take, it is a more down-to-earth and reasonable explanation than that (as the narrator believes) the heart is still alive, even though its owner has been cut to pieces. Then, too, the police keep chatting. If they heard the heartbeat, wouldn't they leap to their feet, draw their guns, and look all around the room? As the author has kept showing us in the rest of the story, the narrator's view of things is untrustworthy. You don't kill someone just because you dislike the look in his eye. You don't think that such a murder is funny. For all its Gothic atmosphere of the old dark house with a secret hidden inside, "The Tell-Tale

Heart" is not a ghost story. We have only to see its point of view to know it is a study in abnormal psychology.

Works Cited

Hoffman, Daniel. <u>Poe Poe Poe Poe Poe Poe Poe</u>. New York: Anchor, 1973.

Poe, Edgar Allan. "The Tell-Tale Heart." <u>Literature: An Introduction to Fiction, Poetry, and Drama</u>. Ed. X.J. Kennedy and Dana Gioia. 7th ed. New York: 1999. 33-37.

A temptation in writing an analysis is to include all sorts of insights that the writer proudly wishes to display, even though they aren't related to the main idea. In the preceding essay, the student resists this temptation admirably. In fairly plump and ample paragraphs, he works out his ideas and supports his contentions with specific references to Poe's story. Although his paper is not brilliantly written and contains no insight so fresh as the suggestion (by the writer of the first paper) that the madman's lantern is like the old man's head, still, it is a good brief analysis. By sticking faithfully to his purpose and by confronting the problems he raises ("how do we know the whole story isn't just a nightmare?"), the writer persuades us that he understands not only the story's point of view but also the story in its entirety.

Our analysis so far deals with one element in Poe's story: point of view. In another type of writing assignment, the **card report,** one is asked to analyze a story into its *several* elements. Usually confined to the front and back of one 5- × 8-inch index card (see the next page for an example), such a report is just as challenging to write as an essay, if not more so. To do the job well, you have to see the story in its elements and then specify them succinctly and accurately. Following is a typical card report listing and detailing the essentials of "The Tell-Tale Heart." In this assignment, the student was asked to include:

1. The title of the story and the date of its original publication.
2. The author's name and dates.
3. The name (if any) of the main character, together with a description of that character's dominant traits or features.
4. Other characters in the story, dealt with in the same fashion.
5. A short description of the setting.

(The list continues on page 1886, following sample card report.)

(Student's name)   (Course and section)

<u>Story</u>: "The Tell-Tale, Heart," 1850

<u>Author</u>: Edgar Allan Poe (1809-1849)

<u>Central character</u>: An unnamed younger man whom people call mad, who claims that a nervous disease has greatly sharpened his sense perceptions. He is proud of his own cleverness. <u>Other characters</u>: The old man, whose leading feature is one pale blue, filmed eye; said to be rich, kind, and lovable. Also three policemen, not individually described.

<u>Setting</u>: A shuttered house full of wind, mice, and treasures; pitch dark even in the afternoon.

<u>Narrator</u>: The madman himself.

<u>Events in summary</u>: (1) Dreading one vulturelike eye of the old man he shares a house with, a madman determines to kill its owner. (2) Each night he spies on the sleeping old man, but finding the eye shut, he stays his hand. (3) On the eighth night, finding the eye open, he suffocates its owner beneath the mattress and conceals the dismembered body under the floor of the bedchamber. (4) Entertaining some inquiring police officers in the very room where the body lies hidden, the killer again hears (or thinks he hears) the beat of the victim's heart. (5) Terrified, convinced that the police also hear the heartbeat growing louder, the killer confesses.

<u>Tone</u>: Horror at the events described, skepticism toward the narrator's claims to be sane, detachment from his gaiety and laughter.

Style: Written as if told aloud by a deranged man eager to be believed, the story is punctuated by laughter, interjections ("Hearken!"), nervous halts, and fresh beginnings--indicated by dashes that grow more frequent as the story goes on and the narrator becomes more excited. Poe often relies on general adjectives ("mournful," "hideous," "hellish,") to convey atmosphere; also on exact details (the lantern that emits "a single dim ray, like the thread of a spider").

Irony: The whole story is ironic in its point of view. Presumably the author is not mad, nor does he share the madman's self-admiration. Many of the narrator's statements therefore seem verbal ironies: his account of taking an hour to move his head through the bedroom door.

Theme: Possibly "Murder will out," but I really don't find any theme either stated or clearly implied.

Symbols: The vulture eye, called an Evil Eye (in superstition, one that can implant a curse), perhaps suggesting too the all-seeing eye of God the Father, from whom no guilt can be concealed. The ghostly heartbeat, sound of the victim's coming back to be avenged (or the God who cannot be slain?). Death watches: beetles said to be death omens, whose ticking sound foreshadows the sound of the tell-tale heart "as a watch makes when enveloped in cotton."

Evaluation: Despite the overwrought style (to me slightly comic bookish), a powerful story, admirable for its conclusion and for its memorable portrait of a deranged killer. Poe knows how it is to be mad.

6. The narrator of the story. (To identify him or her is, of course, to define the point of view from which the story is told.)
7. A terse summary of the main events of the story, given in chronological order.
8. A description of the general tone of the story, that is, the author's feelings toward the central character or the main events.
9. Some comments on the style in which the story is written. (Brief illustrative quotations are helpful, insofar as space permits.)
10. Whatever kinds of irony the story contains and what they contribute to the story.
11. The story's main theme in a sentence.
12. Leading symbols (if the story has any), with an educated guess at whatever each symbol suggests.
13. Finally, an evaluation of the story as a whole, concisely setting forth the student's opinion of it. (Some instructors regard this as the most important part of the report, and most students find that, by the time they have so painstakingly separated the ingredients of the story, they have arrived at a definite opinion of it.)

To fit so much on one card may sometimes seem like trying to engrave the Declaration of Independence on the head of a pin. The student who wrote this succinct report had to spoil a few trial cards before he was able to do it. Every word has to count, and making each count is a discipline worthwhile in almost any sort of expository writing. Some students enjoy the challenge. In doing such a report, though you may feel severely limited, you'll probably be surprised at how thoroughly you come to understand a story. Besides, if you care to keep the card for future reference, it won't take much storage room. A longer story, even a novel, may be analyzed in the same way, but insist on taking a second card if you are asked to analyze some especially hefty and complicated novel—say, Leo Tolstoi's panoramic, thousand-page *War and Peace*.

COMPARING AND CONTRASTING

If you were to write on "The Humor of Frank O'Connor's 'First Confession' and Alice Munro's 'How I Met My Husband,'" you would probably employ one or two other methods. You might use **comparison,** placing the two stories side by side and pointing out their similarities, or you might use **contrast,** pointing out their differences. Most of the time, in dealing with a pair of stories, you will find them similar in some ways and different in others, and so you will be using both methods in writing your paper.

No law requires you to devote equal space to each method. You might have to do more contrasting than comparing, or the other way around. If the stories are obviously similar but subtly different, you will probably compare them briefly, listing the similarities and then, at greater length, contrast them by calling attention to their important differences. If, however, the stories at first glance seem as different as peas and polecats yet are in fact closely related, you'll probably spend most of your time comparing them rather than contrasting them. (You might not just compare and contrast but also analyze, in that you might select one element of the stories for your investigation.) Other topics for papers involving two stories might be "The Experience of Coming of Age in James Joyce's 'Araby' and William Faulkner's 'Barn Burning'"; and "Mother and Daughter Relationships in Alice Walker's 'Everyday Use' and Tillie Olsen's 'I Stand Here Ironing.'"

Your paper, of course, will hang together better if you choose a pair of stories that apparently have much in common than if you choose two as unlike as cow and cantaloupe. Before you start writing, think: Do the two stories I've selected throw some light on each other? An essay that likened W. Somerset Maugham's terse, ironic fable "The Appointment in Samarra" with William Faulkner's rich, complex "Barn Burning" just might reveal unexpected similarities. More likely, it would seem strained and pointless.

You can also write an essay in comparison and contrast that deals with just one story. You might consider, for example, the attitudes of the younger waiter and the older waiter in Hemingway's "A Clean, Well-Lighted Place." In Flannery O'Connor's "Revelation," you might contrast Mrs. Turpin's smug view of herself with young Mary Grace's merciless view of her.

If your topic calls for both comparison and contrast and you are dealing with two stories, don't write the first half of your paper all about one story, then pivot and write the second half about the other, never permitting the two to mingle. The result probably would not be a unified essay in contrast and comparison but two separate commentaries yoked together.

One workable way to organize such a paper is to make (before you begin) a brief list of points to look for in each story. Then, as you write, consider each point—first in one story and then in the other. Here is a simple outline for an essay bringing together William Faulkner's "A Rose for Emily" and Flannery O'Connor's "Revelation." The topic is "Two Would-Be Aristocrats: The Characters of Emily Grierson and Mrs. Turpin."

```
1. Character's view of her own innate superiority

   a. Emily Grierson

   b. Mrs. Turpin

2. Author's evaluation of character's moral worth

   a. Emily Grierson

   b. Mrs. Turpin
```

3. Character's ability to change

    a. Emily Grierson

    b. Mrs. Turpin

It is best, however, not to follow such an outline in plodding, mechanical fashion ("Well, now it's time to whip over to Mrs. Turpin again"), lest your readers feel they are watching a back-and-forth tennis match. Some points are bound to interest you more than others, and, when they do, you will want to give them greater emphasis.

SUGGESTIONS FOR WRITING

What kinds of topics are likely to result in papers that will reveal something about works of fiction? Here is a list of typical topics, suitable for papers of various lengths, offered in the hope of stimulating your own ideas. For other topics, see Further Suggestions for Writing at the end of every chapter. For specific advice on finding a topic of your own, see "Discovering and Planning," page 1853.

Topics for Brief Papers (250–500 words)

1. Consider a short story in which the central character has to make a decision or must take some decisive step that will alter the rest of his or her life. Faulkner's "Barn Burning" is one such story; another is Updike's "A & P." As concisely and as thoroughly as you can, explain the nature of the character's decision, the reasons for it, and its probable consequences (as suggested by what the author tells us).

2. Write an informal (rather than a complete) explication of the opening paragraph or first few lines of a story. Show how it prepares us for what will happen. (An alternate topic: take instead a closing paragraph and sum up whatever insight it leaves us with.) Don't feel obliged to deal with everything in the passage, as you would do in writing a more complete explication. Within this suggested word length, limit your discussion to whatever strikes you as most essential.

3. Make a card report (see page 1884) on a short story in "Stories for Further Reading" or one suggested by your instructor. Include all the elements in the report illustrated in this chapter (unless your instructor wishes you to emphasize some element or offers other advice).

4. Show how reading a specific short story caused you to change or modify an attitude or opinion you once had.

5. Just for fun, try writing a different ending to one of the short stories in this anthology. What does this exercise suggest about the wisdom of the author in ending things as done in the original? (Try to keep a sense of the author's style.)

6. Another wild idea: Write a sequel to one of your favorite short stories—or at least the beginning of a sequel, enough to give your reader a sense of it.

7. Argue from your own experience that a character in any story behaves (or doesn't behave) as people behave in life.

Topics for More Extended Papers (600–1,000 words)

1. Choose a short passage (one of, say, three or four sentences) in a story, a passage that interests you. Perhaps it will contain a decisive movement in a plot, a revealing comment on a character, or a statement of the story's major theme. Then write a reasonably thorough explication. As the writer of the paper "By Lantern Light" did (page 1875), go through the passage in some detail, noticing words that especially convey the author's meanings.

2. Write an analysis of a short story, singling out an element such as the author's voice (tone, style, irony), point of view, character, theme, symbolism, or Gothic elements (if the story has any). Try to show how this element functions in the story as a whole. For a typical paper in response to this assignment, see "The Hearer of the Tell-Tale Heart" (page 1880).

3. Analyze a story in which a character experiences some realization or revelation. How does the writer prepare us for the moment of enlightenment? What is the nature of each realization or revelation? How does it affect the character? Stories to consider might include "Miss Brill," "Gimpel the Fool," "Greasy Lake," "Araby," "The Chrysanthemums," "Revelation," and "Sonny's Blues."

4. Explore how humor functions in a story. What is funny? How is humor implied by the story's style or tone? Does humor help set forth a theme or reveal character? Any of the following stories deserves exploration: "A & P," "Gimpel the Fool," "Greasy Lake," "Where I'm Calling From," "Revelation," "First Confession," "Angel Levine," and "The Catbird Seat."

5. For anyone interested in a career in teaching: Explain how you would teach a story, either to an imaginary class or to the class you belong to now. Perhaps you might arrange with your instructor to write about a story your class hasn't read yet; and then, after writing your paper, actually to teach the story in class.

6. See whether you can discover a new Stephen Crane—another journalist who brings literary skill to reporting (as Crane does in "The Open Boat"). In an essay, examine some news story, interview, or feature that you think reads like excellent fiction. Point out whatever elements of good storytelling you find in it. (Is there a plot? lively dialogue? suspense? vivid style? thought-provoking theme? rounded characters, or at least memorable ones? shrewd choice of a point of view?) For such a story, consult your daily newspaper or a weekly news magazine. Supply a clipping or copy of your discovery along with your finished paper.

7. If your daily newspaper lacks literary quality but you'd like to try that last topic, see any of the following books. Each contains some reporting that will show you storytelling art:

> Nora Ephron, *Crazy Salad: Some Things About Women* (New York: Knopf, 1975). Includes a portrait of the first woman umpire and a cutthroat national baking competition.

> Donald Hall, *Life Work* (Boston: Beacon Press, 1993). An inspiring account of the pleasures of working at what one loves, especially good on the joys of writing.

> John Hersey, *Hiroshima* (New York: Knopf, 1946). The first atomic holocaust as seen by six survivors.

> Garrison Keillor, *Lake Wobegon Days* (New York: Viking, 1985). Gentle comic reports of a practically vanished small-town way of life.

> Tracy Kidder, *Among Schoolchildren* (Boston: Houghton, 1989). Close observations of a year in the life of an elementary school teacher.

> Lillian Ross, *Reporting* (New York: Dodd, 1981). Seven classic essays in journalism, among them a profile of Ernest Hemingway.

> Hunter S. Thompson, *The Great Shark Hunt* (New York: Summit, 1979). Reports of politics, sports, and pleasure seeking in the 1960s and 1970s.

> Tom Wolfe, *The Right Stuff* (New York: Farrar, 1979). The story of America's first astronauts.

Topics for Long Papers (1,500 words or more)

1. Selecting a short story from "Stories for Further Reading" in this book or taking one suggested by your instructor, write an informal essay setting forth (as thoroughly as you can) your understanding of it. Point out any difficulties you encountered in first reading the story, for the benefits of other students who might meet the same difficulties. If you find particularly complicated passages, briefly explicate them. An ample statement of the meaning of the story probably will not deal only with plot or only with theme but will also consider how the story is written and structured.

2. Dealing with a single element of fiction, write an analysis of Baldwin's "Sonny's Blues," Kafka's *The Metamorphosis*, or of some other long story that your instructor suggests.

3. Select a short story in which most of the events take place in the physical world (rather than inside some character's mind), and translate it into a one-act play, complete with stage directions. After you have done so, you might present a reading of it with the aid of other members of the class and then perhaps discuss what you had to do to the story to make a play of it.

4. Selecting an author from this book whose work appeals to you, read at least three or four of his or her other stories. Then write an analysis of them, concentrating on an element of fiction that you find present in all.
5. Again going beyond this book if necessary, compare and contrast two writers' handling of a similar theme. Let your essay build to a conclusion in which you state your opinion: which author's expression of theme is deeper or more memorable?

41 *Writing About a Poem*

Assignment: write a paper about a poem. You can approach your paper as a grim duty: any activity can look like a dull obligation. For Don Juan, in Spanish legend, even making love became a chore. But the act of writing, like the act of love, is easier if your feelings take part in it. Write about something you dislike and don't understand, and you not only set yourself the labors of Hercules, but you also guarantee your reader discouragingly hard labor, too.

To write about a poem well, you need first to experience it. It helps to live with the poem for as long as possible; there is little point in trying to encompass the poem in a ten-minute tour of inspection on the night before the paper falls due. However challenging, writing about poetry has immediate rewards. To mention just one, the poem you spend time writing about is going to mean much more to you than poems skimmed over ever do.

Most of the problems you will meet in writing about a poem are the same ones you encounter in writing about a play or a story: finding a topic, organizing your thoughts, writing, revising. For general advice on writing papers about any kind of literature, see the earlier chapter, "Writing About Literature," on page 1851. In a few ways, however, a poem requires a different approach. In this chapter we will deal briefly with some of them and will offer a few papers that students have written. We think you will agree that these papers are interesting, and we assure you that most students can write equally good papers.

Briefer than most stories and plays, lyric poems look easier to write about. They call, however, for your keenest attention. You may find that, before you can discuss a short poem, you will have to read it slowly and painstakingly, with your mind (like your pencil) sharp and ready. Unlike a play or a short story, a lyric poem tends to have very little plot, and perhaps you will find little to say about what happens in it. In order to understand a poem, you'll need to notice elements other than narrative: the connotations or suggestions of its words, surely, and the rhythm of phrases and lines. The subtleties of language are so essential to a poem (and so elusive) that

Robert Frost was moved to say, "Poetry is what gets lost in translation." Once in a while, of course, you'll read a story whose prose abounds in sounds, rhythms, figures of speech, imagery, and other elements you expect of poetry. Certain novels of Herman Melville and William Faulkner contain paragraphs that, if extracted, seem in themselves prose poems—so lively are they in their wordplay, so rich in metaphor. But such writing is exceptional, and the main business of most fiction is to get a story told. An extreme case of a fiction writer who didn't want his prose to sound poetic is Georges Simenon, best known for his mystery novels, who said that whenever he noticed in his manuscript any word or phrase that called attention to itself, he struck it out. This method of writing would never do for a poet, who revels in words and phrases that fix themselves in memory. It is safe to say that, in order to write well about a poem, you have to read it carefully enough to remember at least part of it word for word.

Let's consider three commonly useful approaches to writing about poetry.

EXPLICATING

In an **explication** (literally, "an unfolding") of a poem, a writer explains the entire poem in detail, unraveling any complexities to be found in it. This method is a valuable one in approaching a lyric poem, especially if the poem is rich in complexities (or in suggestions worth rendering explicit). Most poems that you'll ever be asked to explicate are short enough to discuss thoroughly within a limited time; fully to explicate a long and involved work, such as John Milton's epic *Paradise Lost,* might require a lifetime. (To explicate a short passage of Milton's long poem, however, would be a practical and interesting course assignment.)

The writer of an explication tries to examine and unfold all the details in a poem that a sensitive reader might consider. These might include allusions, the denotations or connotations of words, the possible meanings of symbols, the effects of certain sounds and rhythms and formal elements (rime schemes, for instance), the sense of any statements that contain irony, and other particulars. Not intent on ripping a poem to pieces, the author of a useful explication instead tries to show how each part contributes to the whole.

An explication is easy to organize. You can start with the first line of the poem and keep working straight on through. An explication should not be confused with a paraphrase. A paraphrase simply puts the literal meaning of a poem into plain prose sense: it is a sort of translation that might prove helpful in clarifying a poem's main theme. Perhaps in writing an explication you will wish to do some paraphrasing, but an explication (unlike a paraphrase) does not simply restate. It explains a poem, in great detail.

Here, for example, is a famous poem by Robert Frost, followed by a student's concise explication. (The assignment was to explain whatever in "Design" seemed most essential, in not more than 750 words.)

Robert Frost (1874–1963)*

DESIGN

I found a dimpled spider, fat and white,
On a white heal-all, holding up a moth
Like a white piece of rigid satin cloth—
Assorted characters of death and blight
Mixed ready to begin the morning right,   5
Like the ingredients of a witches' broth—
A snow-drop spider, a flower like a froth,
And dead wings carried like a paper kite.

What had that flower to do with being white,
The wayside blue and innocent heal-all?   10
What brought the kindred spider to that height,
Then steered the white moth thither in the night?
What but design of darkness to appall?—
If design govern in a thing so small.

Student's Name

Professor's Name

Course Name

Date

          An Unfolding of Robert Frost's "Design"

    "I always wanted to be very observing," Robert Frost
once told an audience, after reading his poem "Design." Then
he added, "But I have always been afraid of my own
observations" (qtd. in Cook 126-27). What could Frost have
observed that could scare him? Let's examine the poem in
question and see what we discover.

    Starting with the title, "Design," any reader of this
poem will find it full of meaning. As Webster's New
Collegiate Dictionary defines design, the word can denote
among other things a plan, purpose, intention or aim
("Design"). Some arguments for the existence of God (I

remember from Sunday School) are based on the "argument from design": that because the world shows a systematic order, there must be a Designer who made it. But the word design can also mean "a secret or sinister scheme" such as we attribute to a "designing person" ("Design"). As we shall see, Frost's poem incorporates all of these meanings. His poem raises the old philosophic question of whether there a Designer, an evil Designer, or no Designer at all.

Like many other sonnets, "Design" is divided into two parts. The first eight lines draw a picture centering on the spider, who at first seems almost jolly. It is dimpled and fat like a baby, or Santa Claus. The spider stands on a wildflower whose name, heal-all, seems ironic: a heal-all is supposed to cure any disease, but this flower has no power to restore life to the dead moth. (Later, in line ten, we learn that the heal-all used to be blue. Presumably, it has died and become bleached-looking.) In the second line we discover, too, that the spider has hold of another creature, a dead moth. We then see the moth described with an odd simile in line three: "Like a white piece of rigid satin cloth." Suddenly, the moth becomes not a creature but a piece of fabric--lifeless and dead--and yet satin has connotations of beauty. Satin is a luxurious material used in rich formal clothing, such as coronation gowns and brides' dresses. Additionally, there great accuracy in the word: the smooth and slightly plush surface of satin is like the powder-smooth surface of moths' wings. But this "cloth," rigid and white, could be the lining to Dracula's coffin.

In the fifth line an invisible hand enters. The characters are "mixed" like ingredients in an evil potion. Some force doing the mixing is behind the scene. The characters in themselves are innocent enough, but when brought together, their whiteness and look of rigor mortis are overwhelming. There is something diabolical in the spider's feast. The "morning right" echoes the word rite, a ritual--in this case apparently a Black Mass or a Witches' Sabbath. The simile in line seven ("a flower like a froth") is more ambiguous and harder to describe. A froth is white, foamy, and delicate--something found on a brook in the woods or on a beach after a wave recedes. However, in the natural world, froth also can be ugly: the foam on a polluted stream or a rabid dog's mouth. The dualism in nature--its beauty and its horror--is there in that one simile.

So far, the poem has portrayed a small, frozen scene, with the dimpled killer holding its victim as innocently as a boy holds a kite. Already, Frost has hinted that Nature may be, as Radcliffe Squires suggests, "Nothing but an ash-white plain without love or faith or hope, where ignorant appetites cross by chance" (87). Now, in the last six lines of the sonnet, Frost comes out and directly states his theme. What else could bring these deathly pale, stiff things together "but design of darkness to appall?" The question is clearly rhetorical; we are meant to answer, "Yes, there does seem an evil design at work here!" I take the next-to-last line to mean, "What except a design so dark and sinister that we're appalled by it?" "Appall," by the

way, is the second pun in the poem: it sounds like a pall or
shroud. (The derivation of appall, according to Webster's,
is ultimately from a Latin word meaning "to grow pale"--an
interesting word choice for a poem full of white pale images
["Appall"].) Steered carries the suggestion of a steering-
wheel or rudder that some pilot had to control. Like the
word brought, it implies that some invisible force charted
the paths of spider, heal-all, and moth, so that they
arrived together.

Having suggested that the universe is in the hands of
that sinister force (an indifferent God? Fate? the Devil?),
Frost adds a note of doubt. The Bible tells us that "His eye
is on the sparrow," but at the moment the poet doesn't seem
sure. Maybe, he hints, when things in the universe drop
below a certain size, they pass completely out of the
Designer's notice. When creatures are this little, maybe God
doesn't bother to govern them but just lets them run wild.
And possibly the same mindless chance is all that governs
human lives. And because this is even more senseless than
having an angry God intent on punishing us, it is, Frost
suggests, the worst suspicion of all.

Works Cited

"Appall." Webster's Tenth New Collegiate Dictionary. 1993.

Cook, Reginald. Robert Frost: A Living Voice. Amherst: U of
    Massachusetts P, 1974.

"Design." Webster's Tenth New Collegiate Dictionary. 1991.

Frost, Robert. "Design." Collected Poems, Prose and Plays.
New York: Library of America, 1995. 275.

Squires, Radcliffe. The Major Themes of Robert Frost. Ann
Arbor: U of Michigan P, 1963.

This excellent paper, while finding something worth unfolding in every line in Frost's poem, does so without seeming mechanical. Notice that, although the student proceeds sequentially through the poem from the title to the last line, she takes up, when necessary, some points, out of order. In paragraph two, for example, the writer looks ahead to the end of the poem and briefly states the poem's main theme. (She does so in order to relate this theme to the poem's title.) In the third paragraph, she explicates the poem's *later* image of the heal-all, relating it to the first image. She also comments on the form of the poem ("Like many other sonnets"), on its similes and puns, and on its denotations and connotations.

This paper also demonstrates good use of manuscript form, following the *MLA Handbook*, 4th ed. Brief references (in parentheses) tell us where the writer found Frost's remarks and give page numbers for her quotation from a book by Radcliffe Squires. At the end of the paper, a list of Works Cited uses the abbreviations for *University* and *Press* that the *MLA Handbook* recommends.

It might seem that to work through a poem line by line is a mechanical task, and yet there can be genuine excitement in doing so. Randall Jarrell once wrote an explication of "Design" in which he managed to convey just such excitement. See if you can sense Jarrell's joy in writing about the poem.

> Frost's details are so diabolically good that it seems criminal to leave some unremarked; but notice how *dimpled, fat,* and *white* (all but one; all but one) come from our regular description of any baby; notice how the *heal-all,* because of its name, is the one flower in all the world picked to be the altar for this Devil's Mass; notice how *holding up* the moth brings something ritual and hieratic, a ghostly, ghastly formality, to this priest and its sacrificial victim; notice how terrible to the fingers, how full of the stilling rigor of death, that *white piece of rigid satin cloth* is. And *assorted characters of death and blight* is, like so many things in this poem, sharply ambiguous: *a mixed bunch of actors* or *diverse representative signs.* The tone of the phrase *assorted characters of death and blight* is beautifully developed in the ironic Breakfast-Club-calisthenics, Radio-Kitchen heartiness of *mixed ready to begin the morning right* (which assures us, so unreassuringly, that this isn't any sort of Strindberg *Spook Sonata,* but hard fact), and concludes in the *ingredients* of the witches' broth, giving the soup a sort of cuddly shimmer that the cauldron in *Macbeth* never had; the *broth,* even, is brought to life—we realize that witches' broth *is* broth, to be supped with a long spoon.[1]

---

[1] *Poetry and the Age* (New York: Knopf, 1953), 42–43.

Evidently, Jarrell's cultural interests are broad: ranging from August Strindberg's ground-breaking modern play down to *The Breakfast Club* (a once-popular radio program that cheerfully exhorted its listeners to march around their tables). And yet breadth of knowledge, however much it deepens and enriches Jarrell's writing, isn't all that he brings to the reading of poetry. For him an explication isn't a dull plod, but a voyage of discovery. His prose—full of figures of speech (*diabolically good, cuddly shimmer*)—conveys the apparent delight he takes in showing off his findings. Such a joy, of course, can't be acquired deliberately. But it can grow, the more you read and study poetry.

ANALYZING

An **analysis** of a poem, like a news commentator's analysis of a crisis in the Middle East or a chemist's analysis of an unknown fluid, separates its subject into elements, as a means to understanding that subject—to see what composes it. Usually, the writer of such an essay singles out one of these elements for attention: "Imagery of Light and Darkness in Frost's 'Design'"; "The Character of Satan in Milton's *Paradise Lost*."

Like explication, analysis can be particularly useful in dealing with a short poem. Unlike explication (which inches through a poem line by line), analysis often suits a long poem, too, because it allows the writer to discuss just one manageable element in the poem. A good analysis casts intense light upon a poem from one direction. If you care enough about a poem and about some perspective on it—its theme, say, or its symbolism or its singability—writing an analysis can enlighten and give pleasure.

In this book you probably have met a few brief analyses: the discussion of connotations in John Masefield's "Cargoes" (page 729), for instance, or the examination of symbols in T. S. Eliot's "The *Boston Evening Transcript*" (page 903). In fact, most of the discussions in this book are analytic. Temporarily, we have separated the whole art of poetry into elements such as tone, irony, literal meaning, suggestions, imagery, figures of speech, sound, rhythm, and so on. No element of a poem, of course, exists apart from all the other elements. Still, by taking a closer look at particular elements, one at a time, we see them more clearly and can more easily study them.

Long analyses of metrical feet, rime schemes, and indentations tend to make ponderous reading. Such formal and technical elements are perhaps the hardest to discuss engagingly. And yet formal analysis (at least a little of it) can be interesting and illuminating; it can measure the very pulse beat of lines. If you do care about the technical side of poetry, then write about it, by all means. You will probably find it helpful to learn the terms for the various meters, stanzas, fixed forms, and other devices, so that you can summon them to your aid with confidence. Here is a short formal analysis of "Design" by a student who evidently cares for technicalities and finds an interesting way to talk about them. Concentrating on Frost's use of the sonnet form in "Design," the student casts light upon the entire poem.

Student's Name

Professor's Name

Course Name

Date

The Design of Robert Frost's "Design"

For "Design" the sonnet form has at least two advantages. As in most Italian sonnets, the poem's argument falls into two parts. In the octave Robert Frost's persona draws a still-life of a spider, a flower, and a moth; then in the sestet he contemplates the meaning of his still-life. The sestet focuses on a universal: the possible existence of a vindictive deity who causes the spider to catch the moth and, no doubt, also causes--when viewed anthropomorphically --other suffering.

Frost's persona weaves his own little web. The unwary audience is led through the poem's argument from its opening "story" to a point at which something must be made of the story's symbolic significance. Even the rhyme scheme contributes to the poem's successful leading of the audience toward the sestet's theological questioning. The word white ends the first line of the sestet, and the same vowel sound is echoed in the lines that follow. All in all, half of the sonnet's lines end in the "ite" sound, as if to render significant the whiteness--the symbolic innocence--of nature's representation of a greater truth.

A sonnet has a familiar design, and the poem's classical form points to the thematic concern that there seems to be an order to the universe that might be perceived by looking at even seemingly insignificant natural events. The sonnet must follow certain conventions, and nature, though not as readily apprehensible as a poetic form, is apparently governed by a set of laws. There is a ready-made irony in Frost's choosing such an order-driven form to meditate on whether or not there is any order in the universe. However, whether or not his questioning sestet is actually approaching an answer or, indeed, the answer, Frost has approached an order that seems to echo a larger order in his using the sonnet form. An approach through poetic form and substance is itself significant in Frost's own estimation, for Frost argues that what a poet achieves in writing poetry is "a momentary stay against confusion" (777).

Although design clearly governs in this poem--in "this thing so small," the design is not entirely predictable. The poem does start out in the form of an Italian sonnet, relying on only two rhyming sounds. However, unlike an Italian sonnet, one of the octave's rhyming sounds--the "ite"--continues into the sestet. And additionally, "Design" ends in a couplet, much in the manner of the Shakespearean sonnet, which frequently offers, in the final couplet, a summing up of the sonnet's argument. Perhaps not only nature's "story" of the spider, the flower, and the moth but also Frost's poem itself echoes the larger universe. It looks perfectly orderly until the details are given their due.

Work Cited

Frost, Robert. "The Figure a Poem Makes." Collected Poems, Prose and Plays. New York: Library of America, 1995. 776-78.

COMPARING AND CONTRASTING

To write a **comparison** of two poems, you place them side by side and point out their likenesses; to write a **contrast,** you point out their differences. If you wish, you can combine the two methods in the same paper. For example, even though you may emphasize similarities, you may also call attention to significant differences, or vice versa.

Such a paper makes most sense if you pair two poems that have much in common. It would be possible to compare Wallace McRae's comic cowboy poem "Reincarnation" with Thomas Gray's profoundly elegiac "Elegy Written in a Country Churchyard" but comparison would be difficult, perhaps futile. Though both poems are in English and both deal with the themes of death and transfiguration, the two seem hopelessly remote from each other—in diction, tone, complexity, and scope. Your first task, therefore, is to choose two poems that shed light on one another when they are examined together.

Having found a pair of poems that illuminate each other, you then try to demonstrate in your paper further, unsuspected resemblances—not just the ones that are obvious ("'Design' and 'Wing-Spread' are both about bugs"). The interesting resemblances are ones that take thinking to discover. Similarly, you may want to show noteworthy differences—besides those your reader will see without any help.

In comparing two poems, you may be tempted to discuss one of them and be done with it, then spend the latter half of your paper discussing the other. This simple way of organizing an essay can be dangerous if it leads you to keep the two poems in total isolation from each other. The whole idea of such an assignment, of course, is to see what can be learned by comparing the two poems. There is nothing wrong in discussing all of poem A first, then discussing poem B—*if* in discussing B you keep looking back at A. Another procedure is to keep comparing the two poems all the way through your paper—dealing first, let's say, with their themes; then with their central metaphors; and finally, with their respective merits.

More often than not, a comparison is a kind of analysis—a study of a theme common to two poems, for instance, or of two poets' similar fondness for the myth of Eden. You also can evaluate poems by comparing and contrasting them, placing them side by side in order to decide which poet deserves the brighter laurels. Here, for example, is a poem by Abbie Huston Evans, followed by a paper that considers Frost's "Design" and Evans's "Wing-Spread." By comparing and contrasting the two poems for both their language and their themes, this student shows us reasons for his evaluation.

Abbie Huston Evans (1881–1979)

WING-SPREAD   1938

The midge spins out to safety
Through the spider's rope;
But the moth, less lucky,
Has to grope.

Mired in glue-like cable 5
See him foundered swing
By the gap he opened
With his wing,

Dusty web enlacing
All that blue and beryl. 10
In a netted universe
Wing-spread is peril.

Student's Name

Professor's Name

Course Name

Date

"Wing-Spread" Does a Dip

Abbie Huston Evans's "Wing-Spread" is an effective short poem, but it lacks the complexity and depth of Robert Frost's "Design." These two poems were published only two years apart, and both present a murderous spider and an unlucky moth, but Frost's treatment differs from Evans's approach in at least two important ways. First, Frost uses poetic language more evocatively than Evans. Second, "Design" digs more deeply into the situation to uncover a more memorable theme.

If we compare the language of the two poems, we find "Design" is full of words and phrases rich with suggestions. The language of "Wing-Spread," by comparison, seems thinner. Frost's "dimpled spider, fat and white," for example, is certainly a more suggestive description. Actually, Evans does not describe her spider; she just says, "the spider's rope." (Evans does vividly show the spider and moth in action. In Frost's poem, they are already dead and petrified.) In "Design," the spider's dimples show that it is like a chubby little baby. This seems an odd way to look at a spider, but it is more original than Evans's conventional view (although I like her word cable, suggesting that the spider's web is a kind of high-tech food trap). Frost's word-choice--his repetition of white--paints a more striking scene than Evans's slightly vague "All that blue and beryl." Except for her brief personification of the moth in the second stanza, Evans hardly uses any figures of speech, and even this one is not a clear personification-- she simply gives the moth a sex by referring to it as "him." Frost's striking metaphors, similes, and even puns (right, appall), show him, as usual, to be a master of figures of speech. He calls the moth's wings "satin cloth" and "a paper kite;" Evans just refers in line 8 to a moth's wing. As far as the language of the two poems goes, we might as well compare a vase brimming with flowers and a single flower stuck in a vase. In fairness to Evans, I would say that her poem, while lacking complexity, still makes its point effectively. Her poem has powerful sounds: short lines with the riming words coming at us again and again.

In theme, however, "Wing-Spread" seems much more narrow than "Design." The first time I read Evans's poem, all I felt was: Ho hum, the moth's wings were too wide and got stuck. The second time I read it, I realized that she was saying something with a universal application. This message comes out in line 11, in "a netted universe." That metaphorical phrase is the most interesting part of her poem. Netted makes me imagine the universe as being full of nets rigged by someone who is fishing for us. Maybe, like Frost, Evans sees an evil plan operating. She does not, though, investigate it. She says that the midge escapes because it is tiny. On the other hand, things with wide wing-spreads get stuck. Her theme as I read it is, "Be small and inconspicuous if you want to survive," or maybe, "Isn't it too bad that in this world the big beautiful types crack up and die, while the little puny punks keep sailing?" Now, this is a valuable idea. I have often thought that very same thing myself. But Frost's closing note ("If design govern in a thing so small") is really devastating because it raises a huge uncertainty. "Wing-Spread" leaves us with not much besides a moth stuck in a web and a moral. In both language and theme, "Design" climbs to a higher altitude.

Works Cited

Evans, Abbie Huston. "Wing-Spread." Literature: An Introduction to Fiction, Poetry and Drama. Ed. X.J. Kennedy and Dana Gioia. 7th ed. New York: Longman, 1999. 1902.

Frost, Robert. "Design." Collected Poems, Prose and Plays. New York: Library of America, 1995. 275.

HOW TO QUOTE A POEM

When you discuss a short poem, you should usually quote the whole text of the poem at the beginning of your paper, with its lines numbered. Then you can refer to it with ease, and your instructor can follow you without having to juggle a book. Ask your instructor, however, whether he or she prefers the full text to be quoted this way.

Quoted to illustrate some point, memorable lines can add interest to your paper. Good commentators on poetry tend to be apt quoters, helping their readers to experience a word, a phrase, a line, or a passage that otherwise might be neglected. Quoting poetry accurately, however, raises certain difficulties you don't face in quoting prose.

If you are quoting fewer than four lines of poetry, you should transform the line arrangement into prose form, separating each line by a space, diagonal (/), and a space. The diagonal (/) indicates the writer's respect for where the poet's lines begin and end. Do not change the poet's capitalization or punctuation. Be sure to identify the line numbers you are quoting, as follows:

```
The color white preoccupies Frost. The spider is "fat

and white, / On a white heal-all" (1-2), and even the

victim moth is pale, too.
```

There are also lines to think about—important and meaningful units whose shape you will need to preserve. If you are quoting four or more lines, it is good policy to arrange the lines that you are quoting just as they occur in the poem, white space and all, and to identify the line numbers you are quoting. In general, follow these rules:

1. Indent the quotation one inch, or ten spaces, from the left-hand margin.
2. Double-space between the quoted lines.
3. Type the poem exactly as it appears in the original; you do not need to use quotation marks.
4. Cite the line numbers you are quoting in a parenthesis.

```
At the outset, the poet tells us of his discovery of:

            a dimpled spider, fat and white,

      On a white heal-all, holding up a moth

      Like a white piece of rigid satin cloth--

      Assorted characters of death and blight (1-4)

and implies that the small killer is both childlike

and sinister.
```

When you are beginning the quotation in the middle of a line of verse, position your starting word as closely as possible to where it occurs in the poem (as in the above example)—not at the left-hand margin.

If a line you are quoting is too long to fit on one line, you should indent it one-quarter inch, or three spaces, as follows:

```
     What had that flower to do with being
          white,
     The wayside blue and innocent heal-all?
     What brought the kindred spider to that
          height,
     Then steered the white moth thither in the
          night? (9-12)
```

If you omit words from the lines you quote, indicate the omission with an ellipsis (. . .), as in the following example:

```
The color white preoccupies Frost in his description
of the spider "fat and white, / On a white heal-all
. . . / Like a white piece of rigid satin cloth"
(1-3).
```

There's no need for an ellipsis, if the lines you are quoting go right to the end of a sentence in the original, or if it is obvious that only a phrase is being quoted.

```
The speaker says that he "found a dimpled spider,"
and he goes on to portray it as a kite-flying
boy.
```

If you leave out whole lines of verse, indicate the omission by a line of spaced periods about the length of a line of the poem you are quoting.

```
Maybe, she hints, when things in the universe drop
below a certain size, they pass completely out of the
Designer's notice:
          The midge spins out to safety
          Through the spider's rope;

          .  .  .  .  .  .  .  .  .  .  .  .  .

          In a netted universe
          Wing-spread is peril. (1-2, 11-12)
```

Before You Begin

You will probably already have spent considerable time in reading, thinking, and feeling. Having selected your topic, you will have taken a further look at the poem or poems you have chosen, letting further thoughts and feelings come to you. The quality of your paper will depend, above all, upon the quality of your preparation. Now you are ready at last to write.

Try to make the language with which you analyze a poem as fresh and accurate as possible. It is easy to fall into habitual expression—especially to overuse a few convenient words. Mechanical language may tempt you to think of the poem in mechanical terms. Here, for instance, is a plodding discussion of Robert Frost's poem:

```
The symbols Frost uses in "Design" are very suc-

cessful. Frost makes the spider stand for Nature. He

wants us to see nature as blind and cruel. He also

employs good sounds. He uses a lot of i's because he

is trying to make you think of falling rain.
```

What's wrong with this "analysis"? The underscored words are worth questioning here. While understandable, the words *employs* and *uses* seem to lead the writer to see Frost only as a conscious tool-manipulator. To be sure, Frost in a sense "uses" symbols, but did he grab hold of them and lay them into his poem? For all we know, perhaps the symbols arrived quite unbidden and used the poet. To write a good poem, Frost maintained, a poet himself has to be surprised. (How, by the way, can we hope to know what a poet *wants* to do? And there isn't much point in saying that the poet is *trying* to do something. He has already done it, if he has written a good poem.) At least it is likely that Frost didn't plan to fulfill a certain quota of *i*-sounds. Writing his poem, not by following a blueprint but probably by bringing it slowly to the surface of his mind, Frost no doubt had enough to do without trying to engineer the reactions of his possible audience. Like all true symbols, Frost's spider doesn't *stand for* anything. The writer would be closer to the truth to say that the spider *suggests* or *reminds us* of Nature or of certain forces in the natural world. (Symbols just hint; they don't indicate.)

After the student discussed the paper in a conference with his instructor, he rewrote the two sentences:

```
The symbols in Frost's "Design" are highly effective.

The spider, for instance, suggests the blindness and

cruelty of Nature. Frost's word-sounds, too, are part

of the meaning of his poem, for the i's remind the

reader of falling rain.
```

Not every reader of "Design" will hear rain falling, but the student's revision probably comes closer to describing the experience of the poem most of us know.

In writing about poetry, an occasional note of self-doubt can be useful—now and then a *perhaps* or *a possibly* or an *it seems*. Such qualifying expressions may seem timid shilly-shallying, but at least they keep the writer from thinking, "I know all there is to know about this poem."

Facing the showdown with your empty sheaf of paper or blank computer screen, however, you can't worry forever about your critical vocabulary. To do so is to risk the fate of the centipede in a bit of comic verse, who was running along efficiently until someone asked, "Pray, which leg comes after which?" whereupon "He lay distracted in a ditch / Considering how to run." It is a safe bet that your instructor is human. Your main task as a writer is to communicate to another human being your sensitive reading of a poem.

SUGGESTIONS FOR WRITING

Topics for Brief Papers (250–500 words)

1. Write a concise *explication* of a short poem of your choice or one suggested by your instructor. In a paper this brief, you probably won't have room to explain everything in the poem; explain what you think most needs explaining. (An illustration of an explication appears on page 1894.)

2. Write an *analysis* of a short poem that focuses on how one of its key elements shapes its meaning. (An illustration of an analysis appears on page 1900.) For examples, here are a few specific topics:

   Kinds of Irony in Hardy's "The Workbox"

   The Attitude of the Speaker in Marvell's "To His Coy Mistress"

   The Theme of Pastan's "Ethics"

   An Extended Metaphor in Yeats's "Long-legged Fly." (Explain the one main comparison that the poem makes and show how the whole poem makes it. Other likely poems for a paper on extended metaphor: Dickinson's "Because I could not stop for Death," Dove's "Daystar," Frost's "The Silken Tent," Lowell's "Skunk Hour," Rich's "Aunt Jennifer's Tigers," Stevenson's "The Victory.")

   The Rhythms of Plath's "Daddy"

   (To locate any of these poems, see the Index of Authors and Titles.)

3. Select a poem in which the main speaker is a character who for any reason interests you. You might consider, for instance, Betjeman's "In Westminster Abbey," Browning's "Soliloquy of the Spanish Cloister," Dove's "Daystar," or Eliot's "The Love Song of J. Alfred Prufrock." Then write a brief profile of this character, drawing only on what the poem tells you (or reveals). What is the character's approximate age? Situation in life? Attitude toward self? Attitude toward others? General personality? Do you find this character admirable?

4. Although each of these poems tells a story, what happens in the poem isn't necessarily obvious: Cummings's "anyone lived in a pretty how town," Eliot's "The Love Song of J. Alfred Prufrock," Stafford's "At the Klamath Berry Festival," Winters's "At the San Francisco Airport," Wright's "A Blessing." Choose one of these poems, and in a paragraph sum up what you think happens in it. Then in a second paragraph, ask yourself: what, *besides* the element of story, did you consider in order to understand the poem?

5. Think of someone you know (or someone you can imagine) whose attitude toward poetry in general is one of dislike. Suggest a poem for that person to read—a poem that you like—and, addressing your skeptical reader, point out whatever you find to enjoy in it, something that you think the skeptic just might enjoy too.

Topics for More Extensive Papers (600–1,000 words)

1. Write an explication of a poem short enough for you to work through line by line—for instance, Dickinson's "My Life had stood—a Loaded Gun" or MacLeish's "The End of the World." As if offering your reading experience to a friend who hasn't read the poem before, try to point out all the leading difficulties you encountered and set forth in detail your understanding of any lines that contain such difficulties.

2. Write an explication of a longer poem—for instance, Eliot's "The Love Song of J. Alfred Prufrock," Hardy's "The Convergence of the Twain," Plath's "Lady Lazarus," or Stevens's "Peter Quince at the Clavier." Although you will not be able to go through every line of the poem, explain what you think most needs explaining.

3. In this book you will find from five to eighteen poems by each of these poets: Auden, Blake, Dickinson, Donne, Eliot, Frost, Hardy, Hopkins, Housman, Hughes, Keats, Rich, Cummings, Shakespeare, Stevens, Tennyson, Whitman, William Carlos Williams, Wordsworth, and Yeats; and multiple selections for many more. After you read a few poems by a poet who interests you, write an analysis of *more than one* of the poet's poems. To do this, you need to select one characteristic theme (or other element) to deal with—something typical of the poet's work not found only in a single poem. Here are a few specific topics for such an analysis:

    What Angers William Blake? A Look at Three Poems of Protest

    How Emily Dickinson's Lyrics Resemble Hymns

    The Humor of Robert Frost

    Folk Elements in the Poetry of Langston Hughes

    John Keats's Sensuous Imagery

    The Vocabulary of Music in Poems of Wallace Stevens

    Non-free Verse: Patterns of Sound in Three Poems of William Carlos Williams

4. Compare and contrast two poems in order to evaluate them. Which is more satisfying and effective poetry? To make a meaningful comparison, be sure

to choose two poems that genuinely have much in common, perhaps a similar theme or subject. (For an illustration of such a paper, see the one given in this chapter. For suggestions of poems to compare, see "Poems for Further Reading.")

5. Evaluate by the method of comparison two versions of a poem, one an early draft and one a late draft, or perhaps two translations from another language. For parallel versions to work on, see Chapter Twenty-six, "Alternatives."

6. If the previous topic appeals to you, consider this. In 1912, twenty-four years before he published "Design," Robert Frost sent a correspondent this early version:

In White

A dented spider like a snow drop white
On a white Heal-all, holding up a moth
Like a white piece of lifeless satin cloth—
Saw ever curious eye so strange a sight?—
Portent in little, assorted death and blight   5
Like ingredients of a witches' broth?—
The beady spider, the flower like a froth,
And the moth carried like a paper kite.

What had that flower to do with being white,
The blue prunella every child's delight.   10
What brought the kindred spider to that height?
(Make we no thesis of the miller's plight.)
What but design of darkness and of night?
Design, design! Do I use the word aright?

Compare "In White" with "Design." In what respects is the finished poem superior?

Topics for Long Papers (1,500 words or more)

1. Write a line-by-line explication of a poem rich in matters to explain or of a longer poem that offers ample difficulty. While relatively short, Donne's "A Valediction: Forbidding Mourning" or Hopkins's "The Windhover" are poems that will take a good bit of time to explicate. Even a short, apparently simple poem such as Frost's "Stopping by Woods on a Snowy Evening" can provide more than enough to explicate thoughtfully in a longer paper.

2. Write an analysis of the work of one poet (as suggested above, in the third topic for more extensive papers) in which you go beyond this book to read an entire collection of that poet's work.

3. Write an analysis of a certain theme (or other element) that you find in the work of two or more poets. It is probable that in your conclusion you will want to set the poets' work side by side, comparing or contrasting it, and perhaps making some evaluation. Sample topics include:

Langston Hughes, Gwendolyn Brooks, and Dudley Randall as Prophets of Social Change

What It Is to Be a Woman: The Special Knowledge of Sylvia Plath, Anne Sexton, and Adrienne Rich

Popular Culture as Reflected in the Poetry of Wendy Cope, Edward Field, and Charles Martin

4. Select one of the "Writer's Perspectives" that are found at the end of each chapter, and use the ideas it contains to cast light on a poem by the same author. Do Frost's ideas on metaphors seem consistent with his own poetic practice? What sort of personality does the speaker in Julia Alvarez's sonnet (page 949) present? How do Ezra Pound's comments on imagery help us read his poems?

42 *Writing About a Play*

METHODS

How is writing about a play any different from writing about a short story or a poem? Differences will quickly appear if you are writing about a play you have actually seen performed. Although, like a story or a poem, a play in print is usually the work of one person (and it is relatively fixed and changeless), a play on stage may be the joint effort of seventy or eighty people—actors, director, costumers, set designers, and technicians—and in its many details it may change from season to season, or even from night to night. Later in this chapter, you will find some advice on reviewing a performance of a play, as you might do for a class assignment or for publication in, say, a campus newspaper. But in a literature course, for the most part, you will probably write about the plays you quietly read and behold only in the theater of your mind. At least one advantage in writing about a printed play is that you can always go back and reread it, unlike the reviewer who, unless provided with a script, has nothing but memory to rely on.

Before you begin to write, it makes sense to read the *whole* play—not just the dialogue but also everything in italics: descriptions of scenes, instructions to the actors, and other stage directions. This point may seem obvious, but the meaning of a scene, or even of an entire play, may depend on the tone of voice in which an actor is supposed to deliver a line. At the end of *A Doll's House*, for example, we need to pay attention to what Ibsen tells the actor playing Helmer—*"With sudden hope"*—if we are to understand that, when Nora departs, she ignores Helmer's last desperate hope for a reconciliation and slams the door emphatically. And of course there is a resounding meaning in the final stage direction—*"The heavy sound of a door being slammed is heard from below."*

Taking notes on passages you will want to quote or refer to in your paper, you can use a concise method for keeping track of them. If you are reading a play in verse, jot down the numbers of act, scene, and line—for instance: I, ii, 42. Later, when you write, this handy shorthand will save space, and you can use the MLA format to indicate the exact lines you are quoting or referring to:

Iago's hypocrisy, apparent in his famous defense of
his good name (3.3.168-74), is aptly summed up by
Roderigo, who accuses him: "Your words and performances are no kin together" (4.2.188-89).

Any of the methods frequently applied in writing about fiction and poetry—explication, analysis, comparison and contrast—can serve in writing about a play. All
three methods are discussed in "Writing About a Story," and again in "Writing
About a Poem." (For student papers that illustrate explication, see pages 1875 and
1894; analysis, pages 1880 and 1900; comparison and contrast, page 1903.) Here are
a few suggestions for using these methods to write about plays in particular.

A whole play is too much to cover in an ordinary **explication**—a detailed, line-
by-line unfolding of meaning. For example, an explication of *Othello* could take
years. A more reasonable class assignment would be to explicate a single key speech
or passage from a play, such as Iago's description of a "deserving woman" (*Othello*, II,
i, 148–158); or the first chorus in *Oedipus the King*.

If you decide to write an essay by the method of **comparison and contrast** (two
methods, actually, but they usually work together), you might set two plays side by
side and point out their similarities and differences. Again, watch out: do not bite off
more than you can chew. A profound topic—"The Self-Deceptions of Othello and
Oedipus"—might do for a three-hundred-page dissertation, but an essay of a mere
thousand words could treat it only sketchily. Probably the dual methods of comparison and contrast are most useful for a long term paper on a large but finite topic:
"Attitudes Toward Marriage in *A Doll's House* and *Trifles*." In a shorter paper, you
might confine your comparing and contrasting to the same play: "Willy's and Biff's Illusions in *Death of a Salesman*."

For writing about drama, **analysis** (a separation into elements) is an especially
useful method. You can consider just one element in a play, and so your topic tends
to be humanly manageable—"Animal Imagery in Some Speeches from *Othello*," or
"The Theme of Fragility in *The Glass Menagerie*." Not all plays, however, contain
every element you might find in fiction and poetry. Unlike a short story or a novel,
for example, a play does not ordinarily have a narrator. In most plays, the point of
view is that of the audience, who sees the events not through some narrator's eyes
but through its own.[1] Furthermore, though it is usual for a short story to be written in
an all-pervading style, some plays seem written in as many styles as there are speaking
characters. (You might also argue that in Susan Glaspell's *Trifles* both main characters speak the same language.) Traditional poetic devices, such as rime schemes and

---

[1]Point of view in drama is a study in itself; this mere mention grossly simplifies the matter. Some playwrights attempt to govern what the spectator sees, trying to make the stage become the mind of a character. An obvious example is the classic German film *The Cabinet of Dr. Caligari*, in which the scenery is
distorted as though perceived by a lunatic. Some plays contain characters who act as narrators, directly addressing the audience in much the way that first-person narrators in fiction often address the reader. In
Tennessee Williams's *The Glass Menagerie*, Tom Wingfield behaves as such a narrator, introducing scenes,
commenting on the action. The Stage Manager in Thornton Wilder's *Our Town* (1938) actually addresses
the audience directly, but such a character in a play does not alter our angle of vision, our physical point of
view.

metrical patterns, are seldom found in contemporary plays, which tend to sound like ordinary conversation. To be sure, some plays *are* written in poetic forms, for example, the blank verse of the greater portion of *Othello*. Nevertheless, despite whatever some plays may lack, most have more than enough elements for analysis, including characters, themes, tone, irony, imagery, figures of speech, symbols, myths, and conventions.

Ready to begin writing an analysis of a play, you might think at first that one element—the plot—ought to be particularly easy to detach from the rest and write about. But beware. In a good play (as in a good novel or short story), plot and character and theme are likely to be one, not perfectly simple to tell apart. Besides, if in your essay you were to summarize the events in the play and then stop, you wouldn't tell your readers much that they couldn't observe for themselves just by reading the play or by seeing it. In a meaningful, informative analysis, the writer does not merely isolate an element but also shows how it functions within its play and why it is necessary to the whole.

How to Quote a Play

To quote from a play, you should use the same guidelines as for quoting prose or poetry (see the chapters "Writing About Literature" and "Writing About a Poem"). When you are quoting an extended section or dialogue that involves more than one character, set the passage off from the body of your paper using the following format:

1. Indent one inch (or ten spaces).
2. Type the character's names in all capitals, followed by a period.
3. Indent any additional lines in the same character's speech an additional one-quarter inch (or three spaces on a typewriter).
4. Provide a citation reference (and if the play is written in prose, a page number).

Here is an example of that format:

```
The men never find a motive for the murder because,

ironically, they consider all the real clues

"trifles" that don't warrant their attention:

          SHERIFF. Well, can you beat the women!

             Held for murder and worryin' about

             her preserves.

          COUNTY ATTORNEY. I guess before we're

             through she may have something more

             serious than preserves to worry about.

          HALES. Well, women are used to worrying

             over trifles. (1202)
```

If you are quoting a *verse* play, however, the rules for citing poetry should be observed. Be careful to respect the line breaks. For citation references, use the act, scene, and line numbers. This helps readers find your quotation in any edition of the play. Here is an example of a quotation from Shakespeare's *Othello* using the MLA format:

Even before her death, Othello will not confront Desdemona with

his specific suspicions:

> OTHELLO. Think on thy sins.
>
> DESDEMONA.   They are loves I bear to you.
>
> OTHELLO. Ay, and for that thou diest.
>
> DESDEMONA. That death's unnatural that kills for loving.
>
>   Alas, why gnaw you so your nether lip?
>
>   Some bloody passion shakes your very frame.
>
>   These are portents; but yet I hope, I hope,
>
>   They do not point on me. (5.2.42-48)

WRITING A CARD REPORT

Instead of an essay, some instructors like to assign a **card report.** If asked to write a card report on a play, you will find yourself writing a kind of analysis. To do so, you first single out elements of a play and then list them on 5- × 8-inch index cards as concisely as possible. Such an exercise is often assigned in a class studying fiction; and one student's card report on the Edgar Allan Poe story, "The Tell-Tale Heart," appears on page 1884. When you deal with a play, however, you need to include some elements different from those in a short story. And because a full-length play may take more room to summarize than a short story, your instructor may suggest that, if necessary, you take two cards (four sides) for your report. Still, in order to write a good card report, you have to be both brief and specific. Before you start, sort out your impressions of the play and try to decide which characters, scenes, and lines of dialogue are the most important and memorable. Reducing your scattered impressions to essentials, you will have to reexamine what you have read. When you finish, you will know the play much more thoroughly.

Here is an example: a card report on Susan Glaspell's one-act play, *Trifles.* (For the play itself, see page 1199.) By including only the elements that seemed most important, the writer managed to analyze the brief play on the front and back of one card. Still, he managed to work in a few pertinent quotations to give a sense of the play's remarkable language. Although the report does not say everything about Glaspell's little masterpiece, an adequate criticism of the play could hardly be much briefer. For this report, the writer was assigned to include:

1. The playwright's name, nationality, and dates.
2. The title of the play and the date of its first performance.

3. The central character or characters, with a brief description that includes leading traits.
4. Other characters, also described.
5. The scene or scenes and, if the play does not take place in the present, the time of its action.
6. The dramatic question. This question is whatever the play leads us to ask ourselves: some conflict whose outcome we wonder about, some uncertainty to whose resolution we look forward. (For a more detailed discussion of dramatic questions, see page 1212.)
7. A brief summary of the play's principal events, in the order in which the playwright presents them. If you are reporting on a play longer than *Trifles*, you may find it simplest to sum up what happens in each act, perhaps in each scene.
8. The tone of the play, as best you can detect it. Try to describe the playwright's apparent feelings toward the characters or what happens to them.
9. The language spoken in the play: try to describe it. Does any character speak with a choice of words or with figures of speech that strike you as unusual, distinctive, poetic—or maybe dull and drab? Does language indicate a character's background or place of birth? Brief quotations, in what space you have, will be valuable.
10. In a sentence, try to sum up the play's central theme. If you find none, say so. Plays often contain more than one theme. Which of them seems most clearly borne out by the main events?
11. Any symbols you notice and believe to matter. Try to state in a few words what each suggests.
12. A concise evaluation of the play: what did you think of it? (For more suggestions on being a drama critic, see "Evaluating a Play.")

The card report on *Trifles* begins on the following page.

Front of Card

(Student's name)   (Course and section)

Susan Glaspell, American, 1882-1948   <u>Trifles</u>, 1916

<u>Central characters</u>: Mrs. Peters, the sheriff's nervous wife, dutiful but independent, not "married to the law"--whose sorrows make her able to sympathize with a woman accused of murder. Mrs. Hale, who knows the accused; more decisive.

<u>Other characters</u>: The County Attorney, self-important but short-sighted. The Sheriff, a man of only middling intelligence, another sexist. Hale, a farmer, a cautious man. Not seen on stage, two others are central: Minnie (Foster) Wright, the accused, a music lover reduced to near despair by years of grim marriage and isolation; and John Wright, the victim, known for his cruelty.

<u>Scene</u>: The kitchen of a gloomy farmhouse after the arrest of a wife on suspicion of murder; little things left in disarray.

<u>Major dramatic question</u>: Why did Minnie Wright kill her husband? When this question is answered, a new major dramatic question is raised: Will Mrs. Peters and Mrs. Hale cover up incriminating evidence?

<u>Events</u>: In the exposition, Sheriff and C.A., investigating the death of Wright, hear Hale tell how he found the body and a distracted Mrs. Wright. Then (1) C.A. starts looking for a motive. (2) His jeering at Mrs. Wright (and all women) for their concern with "trifles" cause Mrs. Peters and Mrs. Hale to rally to the woman's defense.   [continued on back of card]

[Events, continued] (3) When the two women find evidence that Mrs. Wright had panicked (a patch of wild sewing in a quilt), Mrs. Hale destroys it. (4) Mrs. Peters finds more evidence: a wrecked birdcage. (5) The women find a canary with its neck wrung and realize that Minnie killed her husband in a similar way. (6) The women align themselves with Minnie when Mrs. Peters recalls her own sorrows, and Mrs. Hale decides her own failure to visit Minnie was "a crime." (7) The C.A. unwittingly provides Mrs. Peters with a means to smuggle out the canary. (8) The two women unite to seize the evidence.

Tone: Made clear in the women's dialogue: mingled horror and sadness at what has happened, compassion for a fellow woman, smoldering resentment toward men who crush women.

Language: The plain speech of farm people, with a dash of rural Midwestern slang (red-up for tidy; Hale's remark that the accused was "kind of done up"). Unschooled speech: Mrs. Hale says ain't--and yet her speech rises at moments to simple poetry: "She used to sing. He killed that too." Glaspell hints the self-importance of the County Attorney by his heavy reliance on the first person.

Central theme: Women, in their supposed concern for trifles, see more deeply than men do.

Symbols: The broken birdcage and the dead canary, both suggesting the music and the joy that John Wright stifled in Minnie.

Evaluation: A powerful, successful, realistic play that conveys its theme with great economy--in its views, more than seventy years ahead of its time.

REVIEWING A PLAY

Writing a **play review,** a brief critical account of an actual performance, involves making an evaluation. To do so, you first have to decide what to evaluate: the work of the playwright; the work of the actors, director, and production staff; or the work of both. If the play is some classic of Shakespeare or Ibsen, evidently the more urgent task for a reviewer is not to evaluate the playwright's work but to evaluate the success of the actors, director, and production staff in interpreting it. To be sure, a reviewer's personal feelings toward a play (even a towering classic) may deserve mention. Writing of an Ibsen masterpiece, the critic H. L. Mencken made the memorable comment that, next to being struck down by a taxicab and having his hat smashed, he could think of no worse punishment than going to another production of *Rosmersholm.* However, a newer, less well-known play is probably more in need of evaluation.

To judge a live performance is, in many ways, more of a challenge than to judge a play read in a book. Obviously there is much to consider besides the playwright's script: acting, direction, costumes, sets, lighting, perhaps music, anything else that contributes to one's total experience in the theater. Still, many students find that to write a play review is more stimulating—and even more fun—than most writing assignments. Although the student with experience in acting or in stagecraft may be a more knowing reviewer than the student without such experience, the latter may prove just as capable in responding to a play and in judging it fairly and perceptively.

In the chapter "Evaluating a Play," we assumed that in order to judge a play one has to understand it and be aware of its conventions. (For a list of things to consider in judging a play, see "Writing Critically" on page 1487.) Some plays evoke a strong positive or negative response in the reviewer, either at once or by the time the final curtain tumbles; others need to be pondered. Incidentally, harsh evaluations sometimes tempt a reviewer to flashes of wit. One celebrated flash is Eugene Field's observation of an actor in a production of *Hamlet,* that "he played the king as though he were in constant fear that somebody else was going to play the ace." The comment isn't merely nasty; it implies that Field had closely watched the actor's performance and had discerned what was wrong with it. Readers, of course, have a right to expect that reviewers do not just sneer (or gush praise) but clearly set forth reasons for their feelings.

Reviewing plays is an act with few fixed rules, but a competent critic usually tries to includes at least the following information somewhere in the review:

1. *The basic facts.* Give the play's title and author, the theatrical company producing it, and the theater in which it is performed.
2. *A brief plot summary.* Tell a reader unacquainted with the play what it is generally about.
3. *An evaluation of the chief actors.* Name the actors playing the principal roles, and comment on the quality of their performance.

A good reviewer will, of course, want to go far beyond these few fundamentals. If the play is unfamiliar, it is also helpful to summarize its theme. If the play is familiar and often performed, some comment on the director's whole approach to it may be useful.

Is the production exactly what you'd expect, or are there any fresh and apparently original innovations? If the production is fresh, does it achieve its freshness by violating the play? (The director of one college production of *Othello*—a fresh, but not entirely successful, innovation—emphasized the play's being partly set in Venice by staging it in the campus swimming pool, with actors floating about on barges and a homemade gondola.) Does the play seem firmly directed, so that the actors neither lag nor hurry and so that they speak and gesture not in an awkward, stylized manner, but naturally? Are they well cast? Usually, also, a reviewer pays attention to the costumes, sets, and lighting, if these are noteworthy. And if the reviewer has not been making clear an opinion of the play and its production all along, an opinion will probably come in the concluding paragraph.

For further pointers, read a few professional play reviews in magazines such as *The New Yorker, Time, Newsweek, The New Criterion, American Theatre*, and others; or on the entertainment pages of a metropolitan newspaper. Here is a good, concise review of an amateur production of *Trifles* as it might be written for a college newspaper. It is similar to what your instructor might ask you to write for a course assignment.

Trifles Scores Mixed Success in

Monday Players' Production

Women have come a long way since 1916. At least, that impression was conveyed yesterday when the Monday Players presented Susan Glaspell's classic one-act play *Trifles* in Alpaugh Theater.

At first, in Glaspell's taut story of two subjugated farm women who figure out why a fellow farm woman strangled her husband, Lloyd Fox and Cal Federicci get to strut around. As a small-town sheriff and a county attorney, they lord it over the womenfolk, making sexist remarks about women in general. Fox and Federicci obviously enjoy themselves as the pompous types that Glaspell means them to be.

But of course it is the women with their keen eyes for small details who prove the superior detectives. In the demanding roles of the two Nebraska Miss Marples, Kathy Betts and Ruth Fine cope as best they can with what is asked of them. Fine is especially convincing. As Mrs. Hale, a friend of the wife accused of the murder, she projects a growing sense of independence. Visibly smarting under the verbal lashes of the menfolk, she seems to straighten her spine inch by inch as the play goes on.

Unluckily for Betts, director Alvin Klein seems determined to view Mrs. Peters as a comedian. Though Glaspell's stage directions call the woman "nervous," I doubt she is supposed to be quite so fidgety as Betts makes her. Betts vibrates like a tuning fork every time a new clue turns up, and when obliged to smell a dead canary bird (another clue), you would think she was whiffing a dead hippopotamus. Mrs. Peters, whose sad past includes a lost baby and a kitten some maniac chopped up with a hatchet, is no figure of fun to my mind. Played for laughs, her character fails to grow visibly on stage, as Fine makes Mrs. Hale grow.

Klein, be it said in his favor, makes the quiet action proceed at a brisk pace. Feminists in the audience must have been a little embarrassed, though, by his having Betts and Fine deliver every speech defending women in an extra-loud voice. After all, Glaspell makes her points clear enough just by showing us what she shows. Not everything is overstated, however. As a farmer who found the murder victim, Cal Valdez acts his part with quiet authority.

Despite flaws in its direction, this powerful play still spellbinds an audience. Anna Winterbright's set, seen last week as a background for Dracula and just slightly touched up, provides appropriate gloom.

SUGGESTIONS FOR WRITING

Finding a topic you care to write about is, of course, the most important step toward writing a valuable paper. (For some general advice on topic finding, see page 1853.) The following list of suggestions is not meant to replace your own ideas but to stimulate them.

Topics for Brief Papers (250–500 words)

1. When the curtain comes down on the conclusion of some plays, the audience is left to decide exactly what finally happened. In a short informal essay, state your interpretation of the conclusion of one of these plays: *The Sound of a Voice, Andre's Mother, The Glass Menagerie, Joe Turner's Come and Gone*. Don't just give a plot summary; tell what you think the conclusion means.

2. Sum up the main suggestions you find in one of these meaningful objects (or actions): the handkerchief in *Othello*; the Christmas tree in *A Doll's House* (or Nora's doing a wild tarantella); Willy Loman's planting a garden in *Death of a Salesman*; Laura's collection of figurines in *The Glass Menagerie*.

3. Here is an exercise in being terse. Write a card report on a short, one-scene play (other than *Trifles*), and confine your remarks to both sides of one 5- × 8-inch card. (For further instructions see pages 1916–17.) Possible subjects: *Riders to the Sea, The Sound of a Voice, Andre's Mother*.

4. Review a play you have seen within recent memory and have felt strongly about (for or against). Give your opinion of *either* the performance or the playwright's writing, with reasons for your evaluation.

5. Write an essay entitled "Why I Prefer Plays to Films" (or vice versa). Cite some plays and films to support your argument. (If you have never seen any professional plays, pick some other topic.)

Topics for More Extended Papers (600–1,000 words)

1. From a play you have enjoyed, choose a passage that strikes you as difficult, worth reading closely. Try to pick a passage not longer than about 200 words, or twenty lines. Explicate it, working through it sentence by sentence or line by line. For instance, any of these passages might be considered memorable (and essential to their plays):

   > Oedipus to Teiresias, speech beginning, "Wealth, power, craft of statesmanship" (*Oedipus the King*, Scene 1, 163–86).

   > Iago's soliloquy, "Thus do I ever make my fool my purse" (*Othello*, I, iii, 362–83).

   > Tom Wingfield's opening speech, "Yes, I have tricks in my pocket," through "I think the rest of the play will explain itself. . . ." (*The Glass Menagerie*, Scene I).

2. Take just a single line or sentence from a play—one that stands out for some reason as greatly important. Perhaps it states a theme, reveals a character, or

serves as a crisis (or turning point). Write an essay demonstrating its importance—how it functions, why it is necessary. Some possible lines include:

> Iago to Roderigo: "I am not what I am" (*Othello*, I, i, 67).

> Amanda to Tom: "You live in a dream; you manufacture illusions!" (*The Glass Menagerie*, Scene VII).

> Charley to Biff: "A salesman is got to dream, boy. It comes with the territory" (*Death of a Salesman*, the closing Requiem).

3. Write an essay in analysis, in which you single out an element of a play for examination—character, plot, setting, theme, dramatic irony, tone, language, symbolism, conventions, or any other element. Try to relate this element to the play as a whole. Sample topics: "The Function of Teiresias in *Oedipus the King*," "Imagery of Poison in *Othello*," "Irony in *Antigonê*," "Williams's Use of Magic-Lantern Slides in *The Glass Menagerie*," "The Theme of Success in *Death of a Salesman*," "Magic in *Joe Turner's Come and Gone*."

4. Compare a character, situation, or theme in a play with a similar element in a short story. For instance: women's role in society as seen in *Trifles* and in Tillie Olsen's "I Stand Here Ironing"; "The Ocean as an Opponent in *Riders to the Sea* and Stephen Crane's 'The Open Boat.'" Or compare Garrison Keillor's comic version of "The Prodigal Son" with the original Gospel parable.

5. Imagine a completely different ending for a play you have read, one that especially interests you. Briefly summarize the new resolution you have in mind. Then, looking back over the play's earlier scenes, tell what would happen to the rest of the play if it were to acquire this new ending. What else would need to be changed? What, if anything, does this exercise reveal?

6. In an essay, consider how you would go about staging a play of Shakespeare, Sophocles, or some other classic, in modern dress, with sets representing the world of today. What problems would you face? Can such an attempt ever succeed?

Topics for Long Papers (1,500 words or more)

1. Choosing any of the four works in "Plays for Further Reading" or taking some other modern or contemporary play your instructor suggests, report any difficulties you encountered in reading and responding to it. Explicate any troublesome passages for the benefit of other readers.

2. Compare and contrast two plays—a play in this book and another play by the same author—with attention to one element. For instance: "The Theme of Woman's Independence in Ibsen's *A Doll's House* and *Hedda Gabler*"; "Antirealism in the Stagecraft of Tennessee Williams: *The Glass Menagerie* and *Camino Real*"; or "Christian Symbols and Allusions in Williams's *Menagerie* and *Night of the Iguana*."

3. Compare and contrast in *The Glass Menagerie* and *Death of a Salesman* the elements of dream life and fantasy.

4. For at least a month, keep a journal of your experience in watching drama on stage, on a movie screen, or on television. Make use of any skills you have learned from your reading and study of plays, and try to demonstrate how you have become a more critical and perceptive member of the viewing audience.

5. If you have ever acted or taken part in staging plays, consult with your instructor and see whether you both find that your experience could enable you to write a substantial paper. With the aid of specific recollections, perhaps, you might sum up what you have learned about the nature of drama or about what makes a play effective.

6. Watch a film version of a play, and then read the original as produced on stage. What differences do you find, and how do you account for them? You might, for instance, compare one of the film versions of *Hamlet* with Shakespeare's original, or Ibsen's *A Doll's House* with any of its movie adaptations.

43 *Writing and Researching on the Computer*

Most college students use computers at one stage or another in writing papers for their English classes. Some use the computer only in the final stages of composition. They draft and revise the paper by hand and then type the final draft into a computer to produce a clean copy to turn in. Other students compose directly on the computer. They brainstorm ideas, draft out paragraphs, and revise drafts until they arrive at a final version. Computer use by other students falls somewhere in between. No one approach is intrinsically superior to another, but there are advantages and disadvantages to be aware of in using computers for writing. Knowing them may help you avoid some pitfalls.

Computers almost always produce a better-looking paper than do typewriters. Unless you are a superb typist, you can probably create with a computer a paper that looks "prettier" than one that is handwritten or typed. A computer-done paper usually has perfect margins and neatly printed, uniform characters of type. As computer specialists have been saying since the days of punch-card methods of data processing, however, a computer always works on a GIGO basis: "Garbage In, Garbage Out." A paper done on a computer may look better than one handwritten or erratically typed, but it will ultimately be no better than what is said in it.

WRITING AND REVISING

Computers are known for speed—such and such megahertz, so many megabytes per second, and so on. Most people who can type can keyboard substantially faster than they can write by hand. Thus the computer user may get elusive thoughts down before they escape the mind. Many people find that the computer greatly facilitates freewriting a first draft, but it is important to remember that the first quick draft is only a departure point for the final paper. Any free-written first draft will contain awkwardly connected thoughts and gangling sentences that cannot stand close scrutiny. The computer invites—but does not compel—revision, but wise revision is what makes writing improve.

Most word processing programs let you delete or move great swaths of text faster than you can cross them out and rewrite them with a pencil on a printed page. These programs can make a complete cut-and-paste reorganization of a draft easier. A piece of prose initially written as it popped into the writer's head may more quickly become a logical and coherent exposition of ideas when such techniques are applied. Who wants to get out the scissors and slash the rough draft literally to ribbons or to rewrite the whole text several times, painstakingly reinscribing each word by hand in each revision? Still, the fact that a revision is technically easier with a computer does not ensure that the revision will be sounder. Only a good grasp of writing fundamentals can ensure that. Tinkering endlessly does not improve a text if the tinkerer does not know good writing from bad. In revising your papers, remember that while the computer does a bang-up job of typing, formatting, and printing, you still have to do the critical thinking yourself.

USING SPELL-CHECK PROGRAMS

Most word processing programs have a program to check spelling automatically. These devices make it much easier to proofread, but they will not catch all errors. It is still crucial that you proofread and correct your papers in the old-fashioned way—read them yourself.

The most common type of error that occurs is when the spell-check program approves of a perfectly acceptable word that is incorrect in context. *In* or *it* frequently gets mistyped as *is*, for example, and the spell-check program won't catch the misspelling. Likewise, *the* is often erroneously keyboarded as *he*. This produces memorable spell-check-approved sentences such as, "It Edna St. Vincent Millay's sonnet, we hear he voice of feminist concerns not often found is Modernist poetry." No human reader would ever approve of this pseudosentence, but a computer will.

Another common problem is that the names of most authors, places, and special literary terms are not in most standard spell-check memories. Unfamiliar words will be identified during the spell-check process, but you still must intervene to correct possible errors made during keyboarding. Check all proper nouns carefully, so that Robert Forst, Gwendolyn Broks, or Emily Dickenson don't make unauthorized appearances midway in your otherwise exemplary paper. As the well-known authors Dina Gioia, Dan Goia, Dana Glola, and Dana Gioia advise, always check the spelling of all names.

RESEARCHING ON THE WORLD WIDE WEB

Computers can be an important resource for research. Knowing how to use them for this purpose is a bit like knowing how to use the library. The growth of the World Wide Web has placed within a few mouse clicks huge amounts of information you once might have had to travel great distances to get—including some you might never have found. Consider how much work and time would be involved in trying to view the illustrations of a nineteenth-century edition of a story by Edgar Allan Poe. Yet you can see a photo reproduction of it on file at a Web site maintained by a major research library—without leaving your desk!—if you have your computer hooked up to the World Wide Web and you are a skilled enough Web surfer to find what you want.

Even more than the library, the computer is eclectic rather than selective. You do have to learn to sort through all the electronic information you find and, more importantly, learn how to sort critically. Otherwise, you will end up with material of dubious value rather than useful information. Here is one example. Suppose you are researching the Holocaust in World War II. You use your "search engines" to sniff out material on this topic. You find many excellent resources, but you also find things you should not take at face value. On one hand, you will locate testimonies from the Nuremberg trials; on the other, you will find Neo-Nazi propaganda, masquerading as serious scholarship. If you do not examine all material critically, you might end up making dubious sources as credible as authoritative ones. The easy access of the World Wide Web tends to erase distinctions of credibility and authority since everything comes to you care of the same screen. We used to joke that "It must be true, I read it in the newspaper." Now we quip, "It must be true—I found it on the Internet!" Be vigilant about the *quality* of information you find and use. If you have any questions about the information you find online, ask your instructor for guidance.

The sheer volume of digital information now available in the world is impressive, but it creates the misleading idea that everything one might want to know is available from computers. This is simply not true. Probably *less than 1 percent* of the information available in print has been translated to electronic formats. Much will never be transcribed. Important books that exist only in limited editions from the last century may actually crumble to dust before they are translated to electronic form. On the other hand, some information you need may increasingly be available *only* electronically. Banks discourage the use of live tellers because they cost more to "operate" than machines; similarly, soon you will not be able to use a library catalog made up of drawers full of paper cards. Some scholarly organizations with members in far-flung places could not function without electronic mail to conduct their business and exchange ideas.

Every day new Web sites appear and old ones vanish, but there are always a huge number of literary sites that can help you in your research for a paper. Almost every major American author will either have one or more individual Web sites or else be included within a slightly more general listing.

If your computer has a "search engine" (such Metacrawler), use it to surf the Net. When we queried "famous author homepages" and "famous writer homepages" with Metacrawler, our computer turned up over two hundred sites in less than ten minutes; some popular authors had multiple sites. To give you an idea of how comprehensive the selection can be, here is a sample of over four dozen current home sites of authors, randomly selected from an alphabetized printout.

A. E. Housman	Charlotte Perkins Gilman
Alfred, Lord Tennyson	Coleridge
Allen Ginsberg	Dante
Ambrose Bierce	Derek Walcott
Andrew Marvell	Doris Lessing
Arthur Miller	Dorothy Parker
Borges	Dylan Thomas
Charles Lutwidge Dodgson	E. E. Cummings
(Lewis Carroll)	Edgar Allan Poe (3 sites)

Elizabeth Bishop	Pablo Neruda
Emily Brontë	Percy Bysshe Shelley
Ernest Hemingway	Raymond Carver
Ezra Pound	Rita Dove
Franz Kafka	Robert Browning
Geoffrey Chaucer	Robert Frost
H. D. (Hilda Doolittle)	Robert Herrick
Henrik Ibsen	Shakespeare
Henry Miller	S. T. Coleridge
Jane Austen	Sylvia Plath
John Donne	W. H. Auden
John Keats	Wallace Stevens
John Milton	Walt Whitman
Joyce Carol Oates	Wilfred Owen
Langston Hughes	Willa Cather
Marianne Moore	William Butler Yeats
Nathaniel Hawthorne	William Carlos Williams
Omar Khayyam	Zora Neale Hurston

TWO WAYS TO START RESEARCHING

The Web is a powerful but anarchic research tool. In the case of literature, there are two major ways to approach sifting through the vast amount of information available. One way is simply to type a subject or author's name into a search engine and then explore whatever comes up. Obviously, this approach can be a bit overwhelming. A more narrow search will yield results that are somewhat easier to navigate. For example, entering an author's name will probably give far better results than simply plugging in a broader term such as *modern drama*. (The latter will generate an intimidating number of sites.) On the other hand, if your literary topic is specific enough, such as "versification," you may turn up useful sites quite quickly, such as the electronic journal of that name, the only publication (electronic or otherwise) that is devoted to the subject.

A second way to proceed is to go directly to one of the many Web pages that are devoted to organizing other pages in your area of study. For example, you might try going to a page such as *Voice of the Shuttle* at <http://humanitas/ucsb.edu/>. This site is maintained by Alan Liu, a professor of English at the University of California in Santa Barbara, and gives well-organized access to literally thousands of other Web pages in the humanities. *Voice of the Shuttle* is organized by discipline, period, and subject, and all areas are carefully cross-referenced.

Let's consider a specific example. If your instructor has asked you to write a research paper on a modern American poet and you have chosen Robinson Jeffers, you might begin by typing in his name as the subject of a search. Using this keyword search will turn up several strong options, such as access to the Robinson Jeffers Association homepage and the Tor House Foundation homepage. Both sites provide extensive and reliable information on the author. You have to be selective, however, because the search will also inevitably turn up the posting of poems by people interested in Jeffers and other sites with little or no scholarly value. You can also use hyperlinks to search for information on your topic. If you follow the links at *Voice of the Shuttle*, you will discover that (compared with the keyword search) *Shuttle* page, massive as it is, does not provide much information that is useful for your purposes.

In the end, the best way to use the Web is probably in the preliminary stages of research: building bibliographies, finding out where books and journals are, and ordering materials. It is also useful for learning basic facts, as long as you are careful to make sure that the source with which you're dealing is reliable. It is a mistake—and will remain a mistake—to rely on the Web to provide everything you need to do a thorough job with literary research. The Web is only a tool, and its most useful function is in generating information, not creating knowledge. You are still the one who must master that process, by organizing and studying materials from a wide range of sources, most of which must somehow be filtered carefully through print and all of which require careful judgment on your part.

PLAGIARISM

Finally, a warning: Do not be seduced by the apparent ease of cheating by computer. The World Wide Web may turn up several sites that offer term papers to download. (Just as you can find pornography, political propaganda, and questionable get-rich-quick schemes!) These sites will often want money for what they offer, but some will not, happy just to strike a blow against the "oppressive" insistence of English teachers that students learn to think and write. This is an old game: the fraternity file and the "research-assistance" service have been around far longer than the computer. It may seem easy enough to download a paper, put your name at the head of it, and turn it in for an easy grade. Such papers usually stick out like a sore thumb, however, as any writing teacher can tell you. The style will be wrong, the work will be not be consistent with other work by the same student in any number of ways, and the teacher will sometimes have seen the exact same phony paper before. The ease with which electronic texts are reproduced makes it even more likely that the same paper will appear again and again. The most important thing to remember is that cheating is *wrong*, period.

In the end, then, the computer is just a machine. A wonderful machine, to be sure, but one that always needs an active and alert operator in charge. A computer can help you perform certain tasks more easily. It can help you research a topic. It can even make mental work—thinking things through, putting them in reasonable order, writing clearly and concisely—easier, but it is no substitute for a vital, working mind.

LITERATURE ONLINE

If you want to research a major author found in this book, you will find that the easiest way to begin is to visit the special Web pages created for the seventh edition of *Literature*. They feature several hundred pages of material written specifically to accompany and supplement this anthology. *Kennedy/Gioia Literature Online* provides in-depth biographies, critical overviews, bibliographies, and annotated links to other sources on the Web. It also provides critical articles on major works and substantial casebooks for some authors, consisting of documents, illustrations, background readings, and other relevant research material. To visit *Kennedy/Gioia Literature Online*, point your browser to <http://longman.awl.com/kennedy>.

44 *Critical Approaches to Literature*

> Literary criticism should arise out of a debt of love.
> —George Steiner

Literary criticism is not an abstract, intellectual exercise; it is a natural human response to literature. If a friend informs you she is reading a book you have just finished, it would be odd indeed if you did not begin swapping opinions. Literary criticism is nothing more than discourse—spoken or written—about literature. A student who sits quietly in a morning English class, intimidated by the notion of literary criticism, will spend an hour that evening talking animatedly about the meaning of R.E.M. lyrics or comparing the relative merits of the three *Star Trek* TV series. It is inevitable that people will ponder, discuss, and analyze the works of art that interest them.

The informal criticism of friends talking about literature tends to be casual, unorganized, and subjective. Since Aristotle, however, philosophers, scholars, and writers have tried to create more precise and disciplined ways of discussing literature. Literary critics have borrowed concepts from other disciplines, such as linguistics, psychology, and anthropology, to analyze imaginative literature more perceptively. Some critics have found it useful to work in the abstract area of **literary theory,** criticism that tries to formulate general principles rather than discuss specific texts. Mass media critics, such as newspaper reviewers, usually spend their time evaluating works—telling us which books are worth reading, which plays not to bother seeing. But most serious literary criticism is not primarily evaluative; it assumes we know that *Othello* or *The Metamorphosis* are worth reading. Instead, it is analytical; it tries to help us better understand a literary work.

In the following pages you will find overviews of ten critical approaches to literature. While these ten methods do not exhaust the total possibilities of literary criticism, they represent the most widely used contemporary approaches. Although presented separately, the approaches are not necessarily mutually exclusive; many critics mix methods to suit their needs and interests. For example, a historical critic may use formalist techniques to analyze a poem; a biographical critic will frequently use psychological theories to analyze an author. The summaries neither try to provide a history of each approach, nor do they try to present the latest trends in each school. Their purpose is to give you a practical introduction to each critical method and then provide representative examples of it. If one of these critical methods interests you, why not try to write a class paper using the approach?

FORMALIST CRITICISM

Formalist criticism regards literature as a unique form of human knowledge that needs to be examined on its own terms. "The natural and sensible starting point for work in literary scholarship," René Wellek and Austin Warren wrote in their influential *Theory of Literature*, "is the interpretation and analysis of the works of literature themselves." To a formalist, a poem or story is not primarily a social, historical, or biographical document; it is a literary work that can be understood only by reference to its intrinsic literary features, that is, those elements, found in the text itself. To analyze a poem or story, therefore, the formalist critic focuses on the words of the text rather than facts about the author's life or the historical milieu in which it was written. The critic would pay special attention to the formal features of the text—the style, structure, imagery, tone, and genre. These features, however, are usually not examined in isolation, because formalist critics believe that what gives a literary text its special status as art is how all of its elements work together to create the reader's total experience. As Robert Penn Warren commented, "Poetry does not inhere in any particular element but depends upon the set of relationships, the structure, which we call the poem."

A key method that formalists use to explore the intense relationships within a poem is **close reading,** a careful step-by-step analysis and explication of a text. (For further discussion of explication, see pages 1874 and 1893). The purpose of close reading is to understand how various elements in a literary text work together to shape its effects on the reader. Since formalists believe that the various stylistic and thematic elements of literary work influence each other, these critics insist that form and content cannot be meaningfully separated. The complete interdependence of form and content is what makes a text literary. When we extract a work's theme or paraphrase its meaning, we destroy the aesthetic experience of the work.

When Robert Langbaum examines Robert Browning's "My Last Duchess" he uses several techniques of formalist criticism. First, he places the poem in relation to its literary form, the dramatic monologue. Second, he discusses the dramatic structure of the poem—why the duke tells his story, whom he addresses, and the physical circumstances in which he speaks. Third, Langbaum analyzes how the duke tells his story—his tone, manner, even the order in which he makes his disclosures. Langbaum neither introduces facts about Browning's life into his analysis, nor relates the poem to the historical period or social conditions that produced it. He focuses on the text itself to explain how it produces a complex effect on the reader.

Cleanth Brooks (1906–1994)

The Formalist Critic

1951

Here are some articles of faith I could subscribe to:

That literary criticism is a description and an evaluation of its object.

That the primary concern of criticism is with the problem of unity—the kind of whole which the literary work forms or fails to form, and the relation of the various parts to each other in building up this whole.

That the formal relations in a work of literature may include, but certainly exceed, those of logic.

That in a successful work, form and content cannot be separated.

That form is meaning.

That literature is ultimately metaphorical and symbolic.

That the general and the universal are not seized upon by abstraction, but got at through the concrete and the particular.

That literature is not a surrogate for religion.

That, as Allen Tate says, "specific moral problems" are the subject matter of literature, but that the purpose of literature is not to point a moral.

That the principles of criticism define the area relevant to literary criticism; they do not constitute a method for carrying out the criticism.

. . .

The formalist critic knows as well as anyone that poems and plays and novels are written by men—that they do not somehow happen—and that they are written as expressions of particular personalities and are written from all sorts of motives—for money, from a desire to express oneself, for the sake of a cause, etc. Moreover, the formalist critic knows as well as anyone that literary works are merely potential until they are read—that is, that they are recreated in the minds of actual readers, who vary enormously in their capabilities, their interests, their prejudices, their ideas. But the formalist critic is concerned primarily with the work itself. Speculation on the mental processes of the author takes the critic away from the work into biography and psychology. There is no reason, of course, why he should not turn away into biography and psychology. Such explorations are very much worth making. But they should not be confused with an account of the work. Such studies describe the process of composition, not the structure of the thing composed, and they may be performed quite as validly for the poor work as for the good one. They may be validly performed for any kind of expression—non-literary as well as literary.

"The Formalist Critic"

Michael Clark (b. 1946)

Light and Darkness in "Sonny's Blues"   1985

"Sonny's Blues" by James Baldwin is a sensitive story about the reconciliation of
two brothers, but it is much more than that. It is, in addition, an examination of
the importance of the black heritage and of the central importance of music in
that heritage. Finally, the story probes the central role that art must play in
human existence. To examine all of these facets of human existence is a rather
formidable undertaking in a short story, even in a longish short story such as this
one. Baldwin not only undertakes this task, but he does it superbly. One of the
central ways that Baldwin fuses all of these complex elements is by using a
metaphor of childhood, which is supported by ancillary images of light and darkness. He does the job so well that the story is a *tour de force*, a penetrating study
of American culture.

. . .

Sonny's quest is best described by himself when he writes to the narrator: "I
feel like a man who's been trying to climb up out of some deep, real deep and
funky hole and just saw the sun up there, outside. I got to get outside." Sonny is
a person who finds his life a living hell, but he knows enough to strive for the
"light." As it is chronicled in this story, his quest is for regaining something from
the past—from his own childhood and from the pasts of all who have come before him. The means for doing this is his music, which is consistently portrayed
in terms of light imagery. When Sonny has a discussion with the narrator about
the future, the narrator describes Sonny's face as a mixture of concern and hope:
"[T]he worry, the thoughtfulness, played on it still, the way shadows play on a
face which is staring into the fire." This fire image is reinforced shortly afterward
when the narrator describes Sonny's aspirations once more in terms of light: "[I]t
was as though he were all wrapped up in some cloud, some fire, some vision all
his own." To the narrator and to Isabel's family, the music that Sonny plays is
simply "weird and disordered," but to Sonny, the music is seen in starkly positive
terms: his failure to master the music will mean "death," while success will mean
"life."

The light and dark imagery culminates in the final scene, where the narrator, apparently for the first time, listens to Sonny play the piano. The location
is a Greenwich Village club. Appropriately enough, the narrator is seated "in a
dark corner." In contrast, the stage is dominated by light, which Baldwin reiter-
ates with a succession of images: "light . . . circle of light . . . light . . . flame . . .
light." Although Sonny has a false start, he gradually settles into his playing and
ends the first set with some intensity: "Everything had been burned out of
[Sonny's face], and at the same time, things usually hidden were being burned in,
by the fire and fury of the battle which was occurring in him up there."

The culmination of the set occurs when Creole, the leader of the players,
begins to play "Am I Blue." At this point, "something began to happen." Apparently, the narrator at this time realizes that this music *is* important. The music is

central to the experience of the black experience, and it is described in terms of light imagery:

> Creole began to tell us what the blues were all about. They were not about anything very new. He and his boys up there were keeping it new, at the risk of ruin, destruction, madness, and death, in order to find new ways to make us listen. For, while the tale of how we suffer, and how we are delighted, and how we may triumph is never new, it always must be heard. There isn't any other tale to tell, it's the only light we've got in all this darkness.

"James Baldwin's 'Sonny's Blues': Childhood, Light, and Art"

Robert Langbaum (b. 1924)
On Robert Browning's "My Last Duchess"   1957

When we have said all the objective things about Browning's "My Last Duchess," we will not have arrived at the meaning until we point out what can only be substantiated by an appeal to effect—that moral judgment does not figure importantly in our response to the duke, that we even identify ourselves with him. But how is such an effect produced in a poem about a cruel Italian duke of the Renaissance who out of unreasonable jealousy has had his last duchess put to death, and is now about to contract a second marriage for the sake of dowry? Certainly, no summary or paraphrase would indicate that condemnation is not our principal response. The difference must be laid to form, to that extra quantity which makes the difference in artistic discourse between content and meaning.

The objective fact that the poem is made up entirely of the duke's utterance has of course much to do with the final meaning, and it is important to say that the poem is in form a monologue. But much more remains to be said about the way in which the content is laid out, before we can come near accounting for the whole meaning. It is important that the duke tells the story of his kind and generous last duchess to, of all people, the envoy from his prospective duchess. It is important that he tells his story while showing off to the envoy the artistic merits of a portrait of the last duchess. It is above all important that the duke carries off his outrageous indiscretion, proceeding triumphantly in the end downstairs to conclude arrangements for the dowry. All this is important not only as content but also as form, because it establishes a relation between the duke on the one hand, and the portrait and the envoy on the other, which determines the reader's relation to the duke and therefore to the poem—which determines, in other words, the poem's meaning.

The utter outrageousness of the duke's behavior makes condemnation the least interesting response, certainly not the response that can account for the poem's success. What interests us more than the duke's wickedness is his immense attractiveness. His conviction of matchless superiority, his intelligence and bland amorality, his poise, his taste for art, his manners—high-handed aristocratic manners that break the ordinary rules and assert the duke's superiority when he is being most solicitous of the envoy, waiving their difference of rank ("Nay, we'll go / Together down, sir"); these qualities overwhelm the envoy, causing him apparently to suspend judgment of the duke, for he raises no demur. The reader is no less overwhelmed. We suspend moral judgment because we prefer to participate in the duke's power and freedom, in his hard core of character fiercely loyal to itself. Moral judgment is in fact important as the thing to be suspended, as a measure of the price we pay for the privilege of appreciating to the full this extraordinary man.

It is because the duke determines the arrangement and relative subordination of the parts that the poem means what it does. The duchess's goodness shines through the duke's utterance; he makes no attempt to conceal it, so preoccupied is he with his own standard of judgment and so oblivious of the world's. Thus the duchess's case is subordinated to the duke's, the novelty and complexity of which engages our attention. We are busy trying to understand the man who can combine the connoisseur's pride in the lady's beauty with a pride that caused him to murder the lady rather than tell her in what way she displeased him, for in that

> would be some stooping; and I choose
> Never to stoop.
> [lines 42–3]

The duke's paradoxical nature is fully revealed when, having boasted how at his command the duchess's life was extinguished, he turns back to the portrait to admire of all things its life-likeness:

> There she stands
> As if alive.
> [lines 46–7]

This occurs ten lines from the end, and we might suppose we have by now taken the duke's measure. But the next ten lines produce a series of shocks that outstrip each time our understanding of the duke, and keep us panting after revelation with no opportunity to consolidate our impression of him for moral judgment. For it is at this point that we learn to whom he has been talking; and he goes on to talk about dowry, even allowing himself to murmur the hypocritical assurance that the new bride's self and not the dowry is of course his object. It seems to me that one side of the duke's nature is here stretched as far as it will go; the dazzling figure threatens to decline into paltriness admitting moral judgment, when Browning retrieves it with two brilliant strokes. First, there is the lordly waiving of rank's privilege as the duke and the envoy are about to proceed downstairs, and then there is the perfect all-revealing gesture of the last two and a half lines when the duke stops to show off yet another object in his collection:

> Notice Neptune, though,
> Taming a sea-horse, thought a rarity,
> Which Claus of Innsbruck cast in bronze for me!
> [lines 54–6]

The lines bring all the parts of the poem into final combination, with just the relative values that constitute the poem's meaning. The nobleman does not hurry on his way to business, the connoisseur cannot resist showing off yet another precious object, the possessive egotist counts up his possessions even as he moves toward the acquirement of a new possession, a well-dowered bride; and most important, the last duchess is seen in final perspective. She takes her place as one of a line of objects in an art collection; her sad story becomes the *cicerone's* anecdote° lending piquancy to the portrait. The duke has taken from her what he wants, her beauty, and thrown the life away; and we watch with awe as he proceeds to take what he wants from the envoy and by implication from the new duchess. He carries all before him by sheer force of will so undeflected by ordinary compunctions as even, I think, to call into question—the question rushes into place behind the startling illumination of the last lines, and lingers as the poem's haunting afternote—the duke's sanity.

The Poetry of Experience

BIOGRAPHICAL CRITICISM

Biographical criticism begins with the simple but central insight that literature is written by actual people and that understanding an author's life can help readers more thoroughly comprehend the work. Anyone who reads the biography of a writer quickly sees how much an author's experience shapes—both directly and indirectly—what he or she creates. Reading that biography will also change (and usually deepen) our response to the work. Sometimes even knowing a single important fact illuminates our reading of a poem or story. Learning, for example, that poet Josephine Miles was confined to a wheelchair or that Weldon Kees committed suicide at forty-one will certainly make us pay attention to certain aspects of their poems we might otherwise have missed or considered unimportant. A formalist critic might complain that we would also have noticed those things through careful textual analysis, but biographical information provides the practical assistance of underscoring subtle but important meanings in the poems. Though many literary theorists have assailed biographical criticism on philosophical grounds, the biographical approach to literature has never disappeared because of its obvious practical advantage in illuminating literary texts.

It may be helpful here to make a distinction between biography and biographical criticism. **Biography** is, strictly speaking, a branch of history; it provides a written account of a person's life. To establish and interpret the facts of a poet's life, for instance, a biographer would use all the available information—not just personal documents such as letters and diaries but also the poems for the possible light they might shed on the subject's life. A biographical *critic*, however, is not concerned with recreating the record of an author's life. Biographical criticism focuses on explicating

---

cicerone's *anecdote:* The Duke's tale. (In Italian, a *cicerone* is one who conducts guided tours for sightseers.)

the literary work by using the insight provided by knowledge of the author's life. Quite often, biographical critics, such as Brett C. Millier in her discussion of Elizabeth Bishop's "One Art," will examine the drafts of a poem or story to see both how the work came into being and how it might have been changed from its autobiographical origins.

A reader, however, must use biographical interpretations cautiously. Writers are notorious for revising the facts of their own lives; they often delete embarrassments and invent accomplishments while changing the details of real episodes to improve their literary impact. John Cheever, for example, frequently told reporters about his sunny, privileged youth; after the author's death, his biographer Scott Donaldson discovered a childhood scarred by a distant mother; a failed, alcoholic father; and nagging economic uncertainty. Likewise, Cheever's outwardly successful adulthood was plagued by alcoholism, sexual promiscuity, and family tension. The chilling facts of Cheever's life significantly changed the way critics read his stories. The danger in the case of a famous writer (Sylvia Plath and F. Scott Fitzgerald are two modern examples) is that the life story can overwhelm and eventually distort the work. A savvy biographical critic always remembers to base an interpretation on what is in the text itself; biographical data should amplify the meaning of the text, not drown it out with irrelevant material.

Leslie Fiedler (b. 1917)

THE RELATIONSHIP OF POET AND POEM · 1960

A central dogma of much recent criticism asserts that biographical information is irrelevant to the understanding and evaluation of poems, and that conversely, poems cannot legitimately be used as material for biography. This double contention is part of a larger position which holds that history is history and art is art, and that to talk about one in terms of the other is to court disaster. Insofar as this position rests upon the immortal platitude that it is good to know what one is talking about, it is unexceptionable; insofar as it is a reaction based upon the procedures of pre-Freudian critics, it is hopelessly outdated; and insofar as it depends upon the extreme nominalist definition of a work of art, held by many "formalists" quite unawares, it is metaphysically reprehensible. It has the further inconvenience of being quite unusable in the practical sphere (all of its proponents, in proportion as they are sensitive critics, immediately betray it when speaking of specific works, and particularly of large bodies of work); and, as if that were not enough, it is in blatant contradiction with the assumptions of most serious practicing writers.

That the anti-biographical position was once "useful," whatever its truth, cannot be denied; it was even once, what is considerably rarer in the field of criticism, amusing; but for a long time now it has been threatening to turn into one of those annoying clichés of the intellectually middle-aged, proffered with all the air of a stimulating heresy. The position was born in dual protest against an excess of Romantic criticism and one of "scientific scholarship." Romantic aesthetics appeared bent on dissolving the formally realized "objective" elements in works of art into "expression of personality"; while the "scholars," in revolt against Romantic subjectivity, seemed set on casting out all the more shifty questions of value and *gestalt* as "subjective," and concentrating on the kind of "facts" amenable to scientific verification. Needless to say, it was not the newer psychological sciences that the "scholars" had in mind, but such purer disciplines as physics and biology. It was at this point that it became fashionable to talk about literary study as "research," and graphs and tables began to appear in analyses of works of art.

. . .

The poet's life is the focusing glass through which pass the determinants of the shape of his work: the tradition available to him, his understanding of "kinds," the impact of special experiences (travel, love, etc.). But the poet's life is more than a burning glass; with his work, it makes up his total meaning. I do not intend to say, of course, that some meanings of works of art, satisfactory and as far as they go sufficient, are not available in the single work itself (only a really *bad* work depends for all substantial meaning on a knowledge of the life-style of its author); but a whole body of work will contain larger meanings, and, where it is available, a sense of the life of the writer will raise that meaning to a still higher power. The latter two kinds of meaning fade into each other; for as soon as two works by a single author are considered side by side, one has begun to deal with biography—that is, with an interconnectedness fully explicable only in terms of a personality, inferred or discovered.

One of the essential functions of the poet is the assertion and creation of a personality, in a profounder sense than any nonartist can attain. We ask of the poet a definition of man, at once particular and abstract, stated and acted out. It is impossible to draw a line between the work the poet writes and the work he lives, between the life he lives and the life he writes. And the agile critic, there-fore, must be prepared to move constantly back and forth between life and poem, not in a pointless circle, but in a meaningful spiraling toward the absolute point.

No! in Thunder

Virginia Llewellyn Smith
CHEKHOV'S ATTITUDE TO ROMANTIC LOVE   1973

It has been shown that the theme of love being destroyed by a cruel fate did not always have for Chekhov the appeal of the tragic: that it could also serve him as a good framework on which to build farce. Nor could one claim that the theme of illicit passion found its source in Chekhov's own imagination, let alone expe-rience: Tolstoy's *Anna Karenina*° had been published in the later 1870s, before

---

Anna Karenina: Leo Tolstoy's novel (1875–77) dealt explicitly with an adulterous affair.

any of Chekhov's work. None the less the coincidence of plot and emotion found in "About Love" and "The Lady with the Dog," together with the fact that the theme occupied Chekhov chiefly in the 1890s, has given rise to some speculation as to whether in fact Chekhov's own love-life during those years suffered as one critic puts it from the interference of a *force majeure.*° Since in this period Chekhov's private life is no longer a closed book (although many pages are indecipherable) the search for the romantic heroine becomes more complex. It becomes feasible to try to connect with her image certain women whose relations with Chekhov are at least partially illuminated and illuminating. Of Chekhov's female friends three in particular must now claim our attention.

No other single work of Chekhov's fiction constitutes a more meaningful comment on Chekhov's attitude to women and to love than does "The Lady with the Dog." So many threads of Chekhov's thought and experience appear to have been woven together into this succinct story that it may be regarded as something in the nature of a summary of the entire topic.

Gurov, the hero of the story, may at first appear no more closely identifiable with Chekhov himself than are many other sympathetic male characters in Chekhov's fiction: he has a post in a bank and is a married man with three children. It is because he has this wife and family that his love-affair with Anna Sergeevna leads him into an *impasse*. And the affair itself, involving Gurov's desperate trip to Anna's home town, has no obvious feature in common with anything we know of Chekhov's amorous liaisons.

And yet Chekhov's own attitudes and experience have clearly shaped Gurov's character and fate. The reader is told that Gurov "was not yet forty": Chekhov was thirty-nine when he wrote "The Lady with the Dog." Gurov "was married young" (*ego zhenili rano*): there is a faint implication in the phrase that an element of coercion played some part in his taking this step—a step which Chekhov, when he was young, managed to avoid. As in general with early marriages in Chekhov's fiction, Gurov's has not proved a success. His wife seems "much older than he" and imagines herself to be an intellectual: familiar danger-signals. She is summed-up in three words: "stiff, pompous, dignified" (*pryamaya, vazhnaya, solidnaya*) which epitomize a type of woman (and man) that Chekhov heartily disliked.

Gurov has had, however, liaisons that were, for him, enjoyable—and these we note, were brief: as was Chekhov's liaison with Yavorskaya and indeed, so far as we know, all the sexual relationships that he had before he met Olga Knipper.

"Frequent experience and indeed bitter experience had long since taught [Gurov] that every liaison which to begin with makes such a pleasant change . . . inevitably evolves into a real and extremely complex problem, and the situation eventually becomes a burden." That his friendships with, for instance, Lika and Avilova should evolve into a situation of this kind seems to have been exactly what Chekhov himself feared: he backed out of these friendships as soon as there appeared to be a danger of close involvement.

force majeur: French for an "irresistible force."

Gurov cannot do without the company of women, and yet he describes them as an "inferior breed": his experience of intimacy with women is limited to casual affairs and an unsatisfactory marriage. Chekhov also enjoyed the company of women and had many female friends and admirers: but he failed, or was un-willing, to involve himself deeply or lastingly with them. That in his work he should suggest that women are an inferior breed can be to some extent explained by the limited knowledge of women his self-contained attitude brought him—and perhaps, to some extent, by a sense of guilt concerning his inability to feel involved.

Gurov's behaviour to Anna Sergeevna at the beginning of their love-affair is characterized by an absence of emotional involvement, just such as appears in Chekhov's attitude towards certain women. There is a scene in "The Lady with the Dog" where, after they have been to bed together, Gurov eats a watermelon while Anna Sergeevna weeps over her corruption. It is not difficult to imagine Chekhov doing something similarly prosaic—weeding his garden, perhaps—while Lika poured out her emotional troubles to him.

Gurov's egocentricity is dispelled, however, by the potent influence of love, because Anna Sergeevna turns out to be the ideal type of woman: pitiable, de-fenseless, childlike, capable of offering Gurov an unquestioning love. Love is seen to operate as a force for good: under its influence Gurov feels revulsion for the philistinism of his normal life and associates.

Chekhov wrote "The Lady with the Dog" in Yalta in the autumn of 1899, not long after he and Olga were there together (although they were not, as yet, lovers) and had made the trip back to Moscow together. In the Kokkoz valley, it will be remembered, they apparently agreed to marry: and so by then, we may presume, Chekhov knew what it was to love.

Anton Chekhov and the Lady with the Dog

Brett C. Millier (b. 1958)

ON ELIZABETH BISHOP'S "ONE ART" 1993

Elizabeth Bishop left seventeen drafts of the poem "One Art" among her papers. In the first draft, she lists all the things she's lost in her life—keys, pens, glasses, cities—and then she writes "One might think this would have prepared me / for losing one average-sized not exceptionally / beautiful or dazzlingly intelligent person . . . / But it doesn't seem to have at all. . . ." By the seventeenth draft, nearly every word has been transformed, but most importantly, Bishop discov-ered along the way that there might be a way to master this loss.

One way to read Bishop's modulation between the first and last drafts from "the loss of you is impossible to master" to something like "I am still the master of losing even though losing you looks like a disaster" is that in the writing of such a disciplined, demanding poem as this villanelle ("[*Write* it!]") lies the po-tential mastery of the loss. Working through each of her losses—from the bold, painful catalog of the first draft to the finely-honed and privately meaningful final version—is the way to overcome them or, if not to overcome them, then to see the way in which she might possibly master herself in the face of loss. It is all, perhaps "one art"—writing elegy, mastering loss, mastering grief, self-mastery. Bishop had a precocious familiarity with loss. Her father died before her first birthday, and four years later her mother disappeared into a sanitarium, never to be seen by her daughter again. The losses in the poem are real: time in the form of the "hour badly spent" and, more tellingly for the orphaned Bishop "my mother's watch": the lost houses, in Key West, Petrópolis, and Ouro Prêto, Brazil. The city of Rio de Janeiro and the whole South American continent (where she had lived for nearly two decades) were lost to her with the suicide of her Brazilian companion. And currently, in the fall of 1975, she seemed to have lost her dearest friend and lover, who was trying to end their relationship. But each version of the poem distanced the pain a little more, depersonalized it, moved it away from the tawdry self-pity and "confession" that Bishop disliked in so many of her contemporaries.

Bishop's friends remained for a long time protective of her personal reputation, and unwilling to have her grouped among lesbian poets or even among the other great poets of her generation—Robert Lowell, John Berryman, Theodore Roethke—as they seemed to self-destruct before their readers' eyes. Bishop herself taught them this reticence by keeping her private life to herself, and by investing what "confession" there was in her poems deeply in objects and places, thus deflecting biographical inquiry. In the development of this poem, discretion is both a poetic method, and a part of a process of self-understanding, the seeing of a pattern in her own life.

Adapted by the author from *Elizabeth Bishop: Life and the Memory of It*

HISTORICAL CRITICISM

Historical criticism seeks to understand a literary work by investigating the social, cultural, and intellectual context that produced it—a context that necessarily includes the artist's biography and milieu. Historical critics are less concerned with explaining a work's literary significance for today's readers than with helping us understand the work by re-creating, as nearly as possible, the exact meaning and impact it had on its original audience. A historical reading of a literary work begins by exploring the possible ways in which the meaning of the text has changed over time. The analysis of William Blake's poem "London" for instance, carefully examines how certain words had different connotations for the poem's original readers than they do today. It also explores the probable associations an eighteenth-century English reader would have made with certain images and characters, like the poem's persona, the chimney sweep—a type of exploited child laborer who, fortunately, no longer exists in our society.

Reading ancient literature, no one doubts the value of historical criticism. There have been so many social, cultural, and linguistic changes that some older texts are incomprehensible without scholarly assistance. But historical criticism can even help us better understand modern texts. To return to Weldon Kees's "For My Daughter" for example, we learn a great deal by considering two rudimentary historical facts—

the year in which the poem was first published (1940) and the nationality of its author (American)—and then asking ourselves how this information has shaped the meaning of the poem. In 1940 war had already broken out in Europe, and most Americans realized that their country, still recovering from the Depression, would soon be drawn into it. For a young man like Kees, the future seemed bleak, uncertain, and personally dangerous. Even this simple historical analysis helps explain at least part of the bitter pessimism of Kees's poem, though a psychological critic would rightly insist that Kees's dark personality also played a crucial role. In writing a paper on a poem, you might explore how the time and place of its creation affects its meaning. For a splendid example of how to re-create the historical context of a poem's genesis, read the following account by Hugh Kenner of Ezra Pound's imagistic "In a Station of the Metro."

Hugh Kenner (b. 1923)

IMAGISM   1971

For it was English post-Symbolist verse that Pound's Imagism set out to reform, by deleting its self-indulgences, intensifying its virtues, and elevating the glimpse into the vision. The most famous of all Imagist poems commenced, like any poem by Arthur Symons,° with an accidental glimpse. Ezra Pound, on a visit to Paris in 1911, got out of the Metro at La Concorde, and "saw suddenly a beautiful face, and then another and another, and then a beautiful child's face, and then another beautiful woman, and I tried all that day to find words for what they had meant to me, and I could not find any words that seemed to me worthy, or as lovely as that sudden emotion."

The oft-told story is worth one more retelling. This was just such an experience as Arthur Symons cultivated, bright unexpected glimpses in a dark setting, instantly to melt into the crowd's kaleidoscope. And a poem would not have given Symons any trouble. But Pound by 1911 was already unwilling to write a Symons poem.

He tells us that he first satisfied his mind when he hit on a wholly abstract vision of colors, splotches on darkness like some canvas of Kandinsky's (whose work he had not then seen). This is a most important fact. Satisfaction lay not in preserving the vision, but in devising with mental effort an abstract equivalent for it, reduced, intensified. He next wrote a 30-line poem and destroyed it; after six months he wrote a shorter poem, also destroyed; and after another year, with, as he tells us, the Japanese *hokku* in mind, he arrived at a poem which needs every one of its 20 words, including the six words of its title:

IN A STATION OF THE METRO

The apparition of these faces in the crowd;
Petals on a wet, black bough.

Arthur Symons: Symons (1865–1945) was a British poet who helped introduce French symbolist verse into English. His own verse was often florid and impressionistic.

We need the title so that we can savor that vegetal contrast with the world of machines: this is not any crowd, moreover, but a crowd seen underground, as Odysseus and Orpheus and Koré saw crowds in Hades. And carrying forward the suggestion of wraiths, the word "apparition" detaches these faces from all the crowded faces, and presides over the image that conveys the quality of their separation:

> Petals on a wet, black bough.

Flowers, underground; flowers, out of the sun; flowers seen as if against a natural gleam, the bough's wetness gleaming on its darkness, in this place where wheels turn and nothing grows. The mind is touched, it may be, with a memory of Persephone, as we read of her in the 106th Canto,

> Dis' bride, Queen over Phlegethon,
>   girls faint as mist about her.

—the faces of those girls likewise "apparitions."

What is achieved, though it works by way of the visible, is no picture of the thing glimpsed, in the manner of

> The light of our cigarettes
> Went and came in the gloom.

It is a simile with "like" suppressed: Pound called it an equation, meaning not a redundancy, *a* equals *a*, but a generalization of unexpected exactness. The statements of analytic geometry, he said, "are 'lords' over fact. They are the thrones and dominations that rule over form and recurrence. And in like manner are great works of art lords over fact, over race-long recurrent moods, and over tomorrow." So this tiny poem, drawing on Gauguin and on Japan, on ghosts and on Persephone, on the Underworld and on the Underground, the Metro of Mallarmé's capital and a phrase that names a station of the Metro as it might a station of the Cross, concentrates far more than it need ever specify, and indicates the means of delivering post-Symbolist poetry from its pictorialist impasse. "An 'Image' is that which presents an intellectual and emotional complex in an instant of time": that is the elusive Doctrine of the Image. And, just 20 months later, "The image . . . is a radiant node or cluster; it is what I can, and must perforce, call a VORTEX, from which, and through which, and into which, ideas are constantly rushing." And: "An *image* . . . is real because we know it directly."

The Pound Era

Sally Fitzgerald (b. 1916)

SOUTHERN SOURCES OF "A GOOD MAN IS HARD TO FIND"   1997

The germ of the story, like a number of others, came from the newspapers close to home—in this instance from several newspaper accounts of unrelated matters shortly before she wrote the story, in 1953. The title she found in a local item—

with photograph—concerning a prize-winning performance by a hideously painted-up little girl still in kitten teeth, decked out in ribbons and tutu and sausage curls, singing "A Good Man Is Hard to Find." Beyond the title, there is no connection between the photograph and the events of the short story, but possibly this child served to inspire the awful little granddaughter, June Star, who sasses her way through the action, and does her tap-routine at the barbecue stand of Red Sammy Butts, the fat veteran "with the happy laugh," who is so thoroughly nasty to his wife. Flannery thought well enough of this newspaper photograph and caption to pass them along for my delectation, together with various ads and testimonials for patent medicines and inspirational columns from the local press, and I remember the clipping very clearly. So did she, and she took the nectar from it to make her fictional honey.

About the same time, an article appeared in the Atlanta paper about a small-time robber who called himself "The Misfit," in a self-pitying explanation or excuse for his crimes. A clipping about him and his honorary title turned up among her papers. Obviously, the name he gave himself was the only thing about this man that much interested the author, and certainly he was no match for the towering figure she turned him into. Incidentally, his excuse for his peccadilloes was taken rather literally in the judicial system: he was judged to be of unsound mind and committed to the lunatic asylum—in Milledgeville, the town in which Flannery lived. This news cannot have escaped her notice. By the way, the mental hospital there was once the largest in the world under one roof. Flannery once described Milledgeville as a town of 8,000, of whom 4,000 were locked up.

There was a third element in the inspirational mix for the story, and this was also to be found in the newspapers, in a series of accounts of another criminal "aloose" in the region. The subject was the person of Mr. James Francis ("Three-Gun") Hill, who amassed a record of twenty-six kidnappings in four states, an equal number of robberies, ten car thefts, and a daring rescue of four Florida convicts from a prison gang—all brought off in two fun-filled weeks. The papers at the time were full of these accounts, and the lurid headlines of the day might well have excited a grandmother like the one who is shaking a newspaper at Bailey Boy's bald head and lecturing him on the dangers to be feared on the road to Florida, when the O'Connor story opens.

Mr. Hill was a far more formidable figure than the original self-styled Misfit, and a more vivid one. Newspaper photographs show him to have looked almost exactly as she described the character in her story, complete with metal-rimmed spectacles. There were other details evidently appropriated by Flannery from life, or life as strained through the Atlanta Journal and the Atlanta Constitution: Mr. Hill was proud of his courtly manners, and in one press account called himself a "gentleman-bandit," explaining that he never cussed before ladies. (Readers will remember that Flannery's mass-murderer blushes when Bailey curses his mother for her incautious tongue.) In some accounts, "Three-Gun" Hill had two accomplices, although the fictional Hiram and Bobby Lee seem entirely imagined by O'Connor in their physical aspects and rather subhuman personalities.

The Misfit in O'Connor's story recounts a brush with a "head-doctor," which accords with the fate of both these actual criminals who initially inspired her. "Three-Gun" Hill, too, was committed to an insane asylum in the end, when he pled guilty to the charges against him. He was sent to a hospital in Tennessee, however, and not to Milledgeville, but the author no doubt read about the sentencing, and it may be that the eventual guilty plea suggested to her the beginnings of capitulation, the stirring of life in the Misfit, whom she conceived as a spoiled prophet, on which note her story ends.

"Happy Endings"

Darryl Pinckney (b. 1953)
ON LANGSTON HUGHES   1989

Fierce identification with the sorrows and pleasures of the poor black—"I myself belong to that class"—propelled Hughes toward the voice of the black Everyman. He made a distinction between his lyric and his social poetry, the private and the public. In the best of his social poetry he turned himself into a transmitter of messages and made the "I" a collective "I":

> I've known rivers:
> I've known rivers ancient as the world and older than the flow of
>   human blood in human veins.
>
> My soul has grown deep like the rivers.
>
> I bathed in the Euphrates when dawns were young.
> I built my hut near the Congo and it lulled me to sleep.
> I looked upon the Nile and raised the pyramids above it.
> I heard the singing of the Mississippi when Abe Lincoln went down to
>   New Orleans, and I've seen its muddy bosom turn all golden in the
>   sunset.
>
> ("The Negro Speaks of Rivers")

The medium conveys a singleness of intention: to make the black known. The straightforward, declarative style doesn't call attention to itself. Nothing distracts from forceful statement, as if the shadowy characters Sandburg wrote about in, say, "When Mammy Hums" had at last their chance to come forward and testify. Poems like "Aunt Sue's Stories" reflect the folk ideal of black women as repositories of racial lore. The story told in dramatic monologues like "The Negro Mother" or "Mother to Son" is one of survival—life "ain't been no crystal stair." The emphasis is on the capacity of black people to endure, which is why Hughes's social poetry, though not strictly protest writing, indicts white America, even taunts it with the steady belief that blacks will overcome simply by "keeping on":

> I, too, sing America.
>
> I am the darker brother.
> They send me to the kitchen
> When company comes,

But I laugh,
And eat well,
And grow strong.   ("I, Too")

Whites were not the only ones who could be made uneasy by Hughes's attempts to boldly connect past and future. The use of "black" and the invocation of Africa were defiant gestures back in the days when many blacks described themselves as brown. When Hughes answered Sandburg's "Nigger" ("I am the nigger, / Singer of Songs . . .") with "I am a Negro, / Black as the night is black, / Black like the depths of my Africa" ("Negro") he challenged the black middle class with his absorption in slave heritage.

"Suitcase in Harlem"

PSYCHOLOGICAL CRITICISM

Modern psychology has had an immense effect on both literature and literary criticism. Sigmund Freud's psychoanalytic theories changed our notions of human behavior by exploring new or controversial areas such as wish-fulfillment, sexuality, the unconscious, and repression. Freud also expanded our sense of how language and symbols operate by demonstrating their ability to reflect unconscious fears or desires. Freud admitted that he himself had learned a great deal about psychology from studying literature: Sophocles, Shakespeare, Goethe, and Dostoevsky were as important to the development of his ideas as were his clinical studies. Some of Freud's most influential writing was, in a broad sense, literary criticism, such as his psychoanalytic examination of Sophocles' Oedipus.

This famous section of *The Interpretation of Dreams* (1900) often raises an important question for students: Was Freud implying that Sophocles knew or shared Freud's theories? (Variations of this question can be asked for most critical approaches: Does using a critical approach require that the author under scrutiny believed in it?) The answer is, of course, no; in analyzing Sophocles' Oedipus, Freud paid the classical Greek dramatist the considerable compliment that the playwright had such profound insight into human nature that his characters display the depth and complexity of real people. In focusing on literature, Freud and his disciples like Carl Jung, Ernest Jones, Marie Bonaparte, and Bruno Bettelheim endorse the belief that great literature truthfully reflects life.

Psychological criticism is a diverse category, but it often employs three approaches. First, it investigates the creative process of the artist: What is the nature of literary genius, and how does it relate to normal mental functions? The second major area for psychological criticism is the psychological study of a particular artist. Most modern literary biographies employ psychology to understand their subject's motivations and behavior. One recent book, Diane Middlebrook's controversial *Anne Sexton: A Biography*, actually used tapes of the poet's sessions with her psychiatrist as material for the study. The third common area of psychological criticism is the analysis of fictional characters. Freud's study of Oedipus is the prototype for this approach, which tries to bring modern insights about human behavior into the study of how fictional people act.

Sigmund Freud (1856–1939)

THE DESTINY OF OEDIPUS   1900

TRANSLATED BY JAMES STRACHEY

If *Oedipus the King* moves a modern audience no less than it did the contemporary Greek one, the explanation can only be that its effect does not lie in the
contrast between destiny and human will, but is to be looked for in the particular
nature of the material on which that contrast is exemplified. There must be
something which makes a voice within us ready to recognize the compelling
force of destiny in the *Oedipus,* while we can dismiss as merely arbitrary such dis-
positions as are laid down in *Die Ahnfrau°* or other modern tragedies of destiny.
And a factor of this kind is in fact involved in the story of King Oedipus. His
destiny moves us only because it might have been ours—because the oracle laid
the same curse upon us before our birth as upon him. It is the fate of all of us,
perhaps, to direct our first sexual impulse towards our mother and our first hatred
and our first murderous wish against our father. Our dreams convince us that
that is so. King Oedipus, who slew his father Laius and married his mother Jocasta, merely shows us the fulfillment of our own childhood wishes. But, more
fortunate than he, we have meanwhile succeeded, insofar as we have not become psychoneurotics, in detaching our sexual impulses from our mothers and in
forgetting our jealousy of our fathers. Here is one in whom these primeval wishes
of our childhood have been fulfilled, and we shrink back from him with the
whole force of the repression by which those wishes have since that time been
held down within us. While the poet, as he unravels the past, brings to light the
guilt of Oedipus, he is at the same time compelling us to recognize our own inner
minds, in which those same impulses, though suppressed, are still to be found.
The contrast with which the closing Chorus leaves us confronted—

> look upon Oedipus.

> This is the king who solved the famous riddle
> And towered up, most powerful of men.
> No mortal eyes but looked on him with envy,
> Yet in the end ruin swept over him.

—strikes as a warning at ourselves and our pride, at us who since our childhood
have grown so wise and so mighty in our own eyes. Like Oedipus, we live in ignorance of these wishes, repugnant to morality, which have been forced upon us
by Nature, and after their revelation we may all of us well seek to close our eyes
to the scenes of our childhood.

The Interpretation of Dreams

Die Ahnfrau: "The Foremother," a verse play by Franz Grillparzer (1791–1872), Austrian dramatist
and poet.

Daniel Hoffman (b. 1923)

THE FATHER-FIGURE IN "THE TELL-TALE HEART" 1972

There are no parents in the tales of Edgar Poe, nary a Mum nor a Dad. Instead all is symbol. And what does this total repression of both sonhood and parenthood signify but that to acknowledge such relationships is to venture into territory too dangerous, too terrifying, for specificity. Desire and hatred are alike insatiable and unallayed. But the terrible war of superego upon the id, the endless battle between conscience and impulse, the unsleeping enmity of the self and its Imp of the Perverse—these struggles are enacted and reenacted in Poe's work, but always in disguise.

Take "The Tell-Tale Heart," surely one of his nearly perfect tales. It's only four pages long, a triumph of the art of economy:

> How, then, am I mad? Hearken! and observe how healthily—how calmly I can tell you the whole story.

When a narrator commences in *this* vein, we know him to be mad already. But we also know his author to be sane. For with such precision to portray the methodicalness of a madman is the work not of a madman but of a man who truly understands what it is to be mad. Artistic control is the warrant of auctorial sanity. It is axiomatic in the psychiatric practice of our century that self-knowledge is a necessary condition for the therapeutic process. Never using the language of the modern diagnostician—which was unavailable to him in the first place, and which in any case he didn't need—Poe demonstrates the extent of his self-knowledge in his manipulation of symbolic objects and actions toward ends which his tales embody.

The events are few, the action brief. "I" (in the story) believes himself sane because he is so calm, so methodical, so fully aware and in control of his purpose. Of course his knowledge of that purpose is limited, while his recital thereof endows the reader with a greater knowledge than his own. "The disease," he says right at the start, "had sharpened my senses. . . . Above all was the sense of hearing acute. I heard all things in the heavens and in the earth. I heard many things in hell." Now of whom can this be said but a delusional person? At the same time, mad as he is, this narrator is *the hero of sensibility*. His heightened senses bring close both heaven and hell.

His plot is motiveless. "Object there was none. Passion there was none. I loved the old man. He had never wronged me. He had never given me insult. For his gold I had no desire." The crime he is about to commit will be all the more terrible because apparently gratuitous. But let us not be lulled by this narrator's lack of admitted motive. He may have a motive—one which he cannot admit, even to himself.

Nowhere does this narrator explain what relationship, if any, exists between him and the possessor of the Evil Eye. We do, however, learn from his tale that he and the old man live under the same roof—apparently alone together, for there's no evidence of anyone else's being in the house. Is the young man the old man's servant? Odd that he would not say so. Perhaps the youth is the old man's son. Quite natural that he should not say so. "I loved the old man. He had never wronged me. . . . I was never kinder to the old man than during the whole week before I killed him." Such the aggressive revulsion caused by the old man's Evil Eye!

What can this be all about? The Evil Eye is a belief as old and as dire as any in man's superstitious memory, and it usually signifies the attribution to another of a power wished for by the self. In this particular case there are other vibrations emanating from the vulture-like eye of the benign old man. Insofar as we have warrant—which I think we do—to take him as a father-figure, his Eye becomes the all-seeing surveillance of the child by the father, even by The Father. This surveillance is of course the origin of the child's conscience, the inculcation into his soul of the paternal principles of right and wrong. As such, the old man's eye becomes a ray to be feared. For if the boy deviates ever so little from the strict paths of rectitude, *it will find him out*.

. . .

Could he but rid himself of its all-seeing scrutiny, he would then be free of his subjection to time.

All the more so if the father-figure in this tale be, in one of his aspects, a Father-Figure. As, to an infant, his own natural father doubtless is. As, to the baby Eddie, his foster-father may have been. Perhaps he had even a subliminal memory of his natural father, who so early deserted him, eye and all, to the hard knocks experience held in store. So, the evil in that Evil Eye is likely a mingling of the stem reproaches of conscience with the reminder of his own subjection to time, age, and death.

Poe Poe Poe Poe Poe Poe Poe

Harold Bloom (b. 1930)

POETIC INFLUENCE   1975

Let me reduce my argument to the hopelessly simplistic; poems, I am saying, are neither about "subjects" nor about "themselves." They are necessarily about *other poems*; a poem is a response to a poem, as a poet is a response to a poet, or a person to his parent. Trying to write a poem takes the poet back to the origins of what a poem *first was* for him, and so takes the poet back beyond the pleasure principle to the decisive initial encounter and response that began him. We do not think of W. C. Williams as a Keatsian poet, yet he *began and ended as one*, and his late celebration of his Greeny Flower is another response to Keats's odes. *Only a poet challenges a poet as poet*, and so only a poet makes a poet. To the poet-in-a-poet, a poem is always *the other man*, the precursor, and so a poem is always a person, always the father of one's Second Birth. To live, the poet must *misinterpret* the father, by the crucial act of misprision, which is the rewriting of the father.

But who, what is the poetic father? The voice of the other, of the *daimon,* is always speaking in one; the voice that cannot die because already it has survived death—*the dead poet lives in one.* In the last phase of strong poets, they attempt to join the undying *by living in the dead poets* who are already alive in them. This late Return of the Dead recalls us, as readers, to a recognition of the original motive for the catastrophe of poetic incarnation. Vico, who identified the origins of poetry with the impulse towards divination (to foretell, but also to become a god by fore-telling), implicitly understood (as did Emerson, and Wordsworth) that a poem is written to escape dying. Literally, poems are refusals of mortality. Every poem therefore has two makers: the precursor, and the ephebe's rejected mortality.

A poet, I argue in consequence, is not so much a man speaking to men as a man rebelling against being spoken to by a dead man (the precursor) outra-geously more alive than himself.

A Map of Misreading

MYTHOLOGICAL CRITICISM

Mythological critics look for the recurrent universal patterns underlying most literary works. **Mythological criticism** is an interdisciplinary approach that combines the in-sights of anthropology, psychology, history, and comparative religion. If psycholog-ical criticism examines the artist as an individual, mythological criticism explores the artist's common humanity by tracing how the individual imagination uses myths and symbols common to different cultures and epochs.

A central concept in mythological criticism is the **archetype,** a symbol, char-acter, situation, or image that evokes a deep universal response. The idea of the ar-chetype came into literary criticism from the Swiss psychologist Carl Jung, a lifetime student of myth and religion. Jung believed that all individuals share a "collective unconscious," a set of primal memories common to the human race, existing below each person's conscious mind. Archetypal images (which often relate to experi-encing primordial phenomena like the sun, moon, fire, night, and blood), Jung be-lieved, trigger the collective unconscious. We do not need to accept the literal truth of the collective unconscious, however, to endorse the archetype as a helpful critical concept. The late Northrop Frye defined the archetype in considerably less occult terms as "a symbol, usually an image, which recurs often enough in literature to be recognizable as an element of one's literary experience as a whole."

Identifying archetypal symbols and situations in literary works, mythological critics almost inevitably link the individual text under discussion to a broader context of works that share an underlying pattern. In discussing Shakespeare's *Hamlet,* for in-stance, a mythological critic might relate Shakespeare's Danish prince to other mythic sons avenging the deaths of their fathers, like Orestes from Greek myth or Sigmund of Norse legend; or, in discussing *Othello,* relate the sinister figure of Iago to the devil in traditional Christian belief. Critic Joseph Campbell took such comparisons even fur-ther; his compendious study *The Hero with a Thousand Faces* demonstrates how similar mythic characters appear in virtually every culture on every continent.

Northrop Frye (1912–1991)

MYTHIC ARCHETYPES   1957

We begin our study of archetypes, then, with a world of myth, an abstract or purely literary world of fictional and thematic design, unaffected by canons of plausible adaptation to familiar experience. In terms of narrative, myth is the imitation of actions near or at the conceivable limits of desire. The gods enjoy beautiful women, fight one another with prodigious strength, comfort and assist man, or else watch his miseries from the height of their immortal freedom. The fact that myth operates at the top level of human desire does not mean that it necessarily presents its world as attained or attainable by human beings. . . .

Realism, or the art of verisimilitude, evokes the response "How like that is to what we know!" When what is written is *like* what is known, we have an art of extended or implied simile. And as realism is an art of implicit simile, myth is an art of implicit metaphorical identity. The word "sun-god," with a hyphen used instead of a predicate, is a pure ideogram, in Pound's terminology, or literal metaphor, in ours. In myth we see the structural principles of literature isolated; in realism we see the *same* structural principles (not similar ones) fitting into a context of plausibility. (Similarly in music, a piece by Purcell and a piece by Benjamin Britten may not be in the least *like* each other, but if they are both in D major their tonality will be the same.) The presence of a mythical structure in realistic fiction, however, poses certain technical problems for making it plausible, and the devices used in solving these problems may be given the general name of *displacement*.

Myth, then, is one extreme of literary design; naturalism is the other, and in between lies the whole area of romance, using that term to mean, not the historical mode of the first essay, but the tendency, noted later in the same essay, to displace myth in a human direction and yet, in contrast to "realism," to conventionalize content in an idealized direction. The central principle of displacement is that what can be metaphorically identified in a myth can only be linked in romance by some form of simile: analogy, significant association, incidental accompanying imagery, and the like. In a myth we can have a sun-god or a tree-god; in a romance we may have a person who is significantly associated with the sun or trees.

Anatomy of Criticism

Edmond Volpe (b. 1922)

MYTH IN FAULKNER'S "BARN BURNING"   1964

"Barn Burning" however is not really concerned with class conflict. The story is centered upon Sarty's emotional dilemma. His conflict would not have been altered in any way if the person whose barn Ab burns had been a simple poor farmer, rather than an aristocratic plantation owner. The child's tension, in fact, begins to surface during the hearing in which a simple farmer accuses Ab of burning his barn. The moral antagonists mirrored in Sarty's conflict are not sharecropper and aristocrat. They are the father, Ab Snopes, versus the rest of mankind. Major De Spain is not developed as a character; his house is important to Sarty because it represents a totally new and totally different social and moral entity. Within the context of the society Faulkner is dealing with, the gap between the rich aristocrat and the poor sharecropper provides a viable metaphor for dramatizing the crisis Sarty is undergoing. Ab Snopes is by no means a social crusader. The De Spain manor is Sarty's first contact with a rich man's house, though he can recall, in the short span of his life, at least a dozen times the family had to move because Ab burned barns. Ab does not discriminate between rich and poor. For him there are only two categories: blood kin and "they," into which he lumps all the rest of mankind. Ab's division relates to Sarty's crisis and only by defining precisely the nature of the conflict the boy is undergoing can we determine the moral significance Faulkner sees in it. The clue to Sarty's conflict rests in its resolution.

. . .

The boy's anxiety is created by his awakening sense of his own individuality. Torn between strong emotional attachment to the parent and his growing need to assert his own identity, Sarty's crisis is psychological and his battle is being waged far below the level of his intellectual and moral awareness.

Faulkner makes this clear in the opening scene with imagery that might be described as synesthesia. The real smell of cheese is linked with the smell of the hermetic meat in the tin cans with the scarlet devils on the label that his "intestines believed he smelled coming in intermittent gusts momentary and brief between the other constant one, the smell and sense just a little of fear because mostly of despair and grief, the old fierce pull of blood." The smells below the level of the olfactory sense link the devil image and the blood image to identify the anxiety the father creates in the child's psyche. Tension is created by the blood demanding identification with his father against "*our enemy* he thought in that despair; *ourn! mine and hisn both! He's my father!*" Sarty's conflict is played out in terms of identification, not in moral terms. He does not think of his father as bad, his father's enemies as good.

Ab unjustly accuses Sarty of intending to betray him at the hearing, but he correctly recognizes that his son is moving out of childhood, developing a mind and will of his own and is no longer blindly loyal. In instructing the boy that everyone is the enemy and his loyalty belongs to his blood, Ab's phrasing is revealing: "'Don't you know all they wanted was a chance to get at me because they knew I had them beat?'" Ab does not use the plural "us." It is "I" and "they." Blood loyalty means total identification with Ab, and in the ensuing scenes, Snopes attempts to make his son an extension of himself by taking him to the De Spain house, rise up before dawn to be with him when he returns the rug, accompany him to the hearing against De Spain and finally make him an accomplice in the burning of De Spain's barn.

The moral import of Ab's insistence on blood loyalty is fully developed by the satanic imagery Faulkner introduces in the scene at the mansion. As they go up the drive, Sarty follows his father, seeing the stiff black form against the white plantation house. Traditionally the devil casts no shadow, and Ab's figure appears to the child as having "that impervious quality of something cut ruthlessly from tin, depthless, as though sidewise to the sun it would cast no shadow." The cloven hoof of the devil is suggested by Ab's limp upon which the boy's eyes are fixed as the foot unwaveringly comes down into the manure. Sarty's increasing tension resounds in the magnified echo of the limping foot on the porch boards, "a sound out of all proportion to the displacement of the body it bore, as though it had attained to a sort of vicious and ravening minimum not to be dwarfed by anything." At first Sarty thought the house was impervious to his father, but his burgeoning fear of the threat the father poses is reflected in his vision of Ab becoming magnified and monstrous as the black arm reaches up the white door and Sarty sees "the lifted hand like a curled claw."

The satanic images are projected out of the son's nightmarish vision of his father, but they are reinforced by the comments of the adult narrator. Sarty believes Snopes fought bravely in the Civil War, but Ab, we are told, wore no uniform, gave his fealty to no cause, admitted the authority of no man. He went to war for booty. Ab's ego is so great it creates a centripetal force into which everything must flow or be destroyed. The will-less, abject creature who is his wife symbolizes the power of his will. What Ab had done to his wife, he sets out to do to the emerging will of his son. Ab cannot tolerate any entity that challenges the dominance of his will. By allowing his hog to forage in the farmer's corn and by dirtying and ruining De Spain's rug, he deliberately creates a conflict that requires the assertion of primacy. Fire, the element of the devil, is the weapon for the preservation of his dominance. Ab's rage is not fired by social injustice. It is fired by a pride, like Lucifer's, so absolute it can accept no order beyond its own. In the satanic myth, Lucifer asserts his will against the divine order and is cast out of heaven. The angels who fall with Lucifer become extensions of his will. In the same way, Ab is an outcast and pariah among men. He accepts no order that is not of his blood.

"'Barn Burning': A Definition of Evil"

Maud Bodkin (1875–1967)

LUCIFER IN SHAKESPEARE'S *Othello*   1934

If we attempt to define the devil in psychological terms, regarding him as an archetype, a persistent or recurrent mode of apprehension, we may say that the devil is our tendency to represent in personal form the forces within and without us that threaten our supreme values. When Othello finds those values of confident love, of honor, and pride in soldiership, that made up his purposeful life, falling into ruin, his sense of the devil in all around him becomes acute. Desdemona has become "a fair devil"; he feels "a young and sweating devil" in her hand. The cry "O devil" breaks out among his incoherent words of raving. When Iago's falsehoods are disclosed, and Othello at last, too late, wrenches himself free from the spell of Iago's power over him, his sense of the devil incarnate in Iago's shape before him becomes overwhelming. If those who tell of the devil have failed to describe Iago, they have lied:

> I look down towards his feet; but that's a fable.
> If that thou be'st a devil, I cannot kill thee.

We also, watching or reading the play, experience the archetype. Intellectually aware, as we reflect, of natural forces, within a man himself as well as in society around, that betray or shatter his ideals, we yet feel these forces aptly symbolized for the imagination by such a figure as Iago—a being though personal yet hardly human, concentrated wholly on the hunting to destruction of its destined prey, the proud figure of the hero.

Archetypal Patterns in Poetry

SOCIOLOGICAL CRITICISM

Sociological criticism examines literature in the cultural, economic, and political context in which it is written or received. "Art is not created in a vacuum," critic Wilbur Scott observed, "it is the work not simply of a person, but of an author fixed in time and space, answering a community of which he is an important, because articulate part." Sociological criticism explores the relationships between the artist and society. Sometimes it looks at the sociological status of the author to evaluate how the profession of the writer in a particular milieu affected what was written. Sociological criticism also analyzes the social content of literary works—what cultural, economic or political values a particular text implicitly or explicitly promotes. Finally, sociological criticism examines the role the audience has in shaping literature. A sociological view of Shakespeare, for example, might look at the economic position of Elizabethan playwrights and actors; it might also study the political ideas expressed in the plays or discuss how the nature of an Elizabethan theatrical audience (which was usually all male unless the play was produced at court) helped determine the subject, tone, and language of the plays.

An influential type of sociological criticism has been Marxist criticism, which focuses on the economic and political elements of art. Marxist criticism, like the work of the Hungarian philosopher Georg Lukacs, often explores the ideological content of literature. Whereas a formalist critic would maintain that form and content are inextricably blended, Lukacs believed that content determines form and that therefore, all art is political. Even if a work of art ignores political issues, it makes a political statement, Marxist critics believe, because it endorses the economic and political status quo. Consequently, Marxist criticism is frequently evaluative and judges some literary work better than others on an ideological basis; this tendency can lead to reductive judgment, as when Soviet critics rated Jack London a novelist superior to William Faulkner, Ernest Hemingway, Edith Wharton, and Henry James, because he illustrated the principles of class struggle more clearly. But, as an analytical tool, Marxist criticism, like other sociological methods, can illuminate political and economic dimensions of literature other approaches overlook.

Georg Lukacs (1885–1971)

CONTENT DETERMINES FORM
1962

What determines the style of a given work of art? How does the intention determine the form? (We are concerned here, of course, with the intention realized in the work; it need not coincide with the writer's conscious intention.) The distinctions that concern us are not those between stylistic "techniques" in the formalistic sense. It is the view of the world, the ideology or *Weltanschauung*° underlying a writer's work, that counts. And it is the writer's attempt to reproduce this view of the world which constitutes his "intention" and is the formative principle underlying the style of a given piece of writing. Looked at in this way, style ceases to be a formalistic category. Rather, it is rooted in content; it is the specific form of a specific content.

Content determines form. But there is no content of which Man himself is not the focal point. However various the *données*° of literature (a particular experience, a didactic purpose), the basic question is, and will remain: what is Man?

Here is a point of division: if we put the question in abstract, philosophical terms, leaving aside all formal considerations, we arrive—for the realist school—at the traditional Aristotelian dictum (which was also reached by other than purely aesthetic considerations): Man is *zoon politikon*,° a social animal. The Aristotelian dictum is applicable to all great realistic literature. Achilles and Werther, Oedipus and Tom Jones, Antigone and Anna Karenina: their individual existence—their *Sein an sich*,° in the Hegelian terminology; their "ontological being," as a more fashionable terminology has it—cannot be distinguished from their social and historical environment. Their human significance, their specific individuality cannot be separated from the context in which they were created.

Realism in Our Time

Daniel P. Watkins

MONEY AND LABOR IN "THE ROCKING-HORSE WINNER"
1987

It is a commonplace that D. H. Lawrence's "The Rocking-Horse Winner" is a story about the devastating effect that money can have on a family, and, further, that Lawrence's specific objections in the story are not to money abstractly conceived but to money as it is understood and valued by capitalist culture. This is one of Lawrence's most savage and compact critiques of what he elsewhere calls "the god-damn bourgeoisie" and of individuals who, despite their natural or po-

---

Weltanschauung: German for "world view," an outlook on life. *données*: French for "given"; it means the materials a writer uses to create his or her work or the subject or purpose of a literary work. *zoon politikon*: Greek for "political animal." *Sein an sich*: the German philosopher G. W. F. Hegel's term for "pure existence."

tential goodness, "swallow the culture bait" and hence become victims to the world they (wrongly) believe holds the key to human happiness.

. . .

The class nature of labor under capital is presented symbolically in the story in terms of the adult and non-adult worlds. That is, social reality is controlled by parents whose primary concern is to bring in money sufficient to "the social position which they (have) to keep up." While they have a small income, and while "The father went in to town to some office," they never are really seen to work actively and productively. Rather, they set a tone of need in their world that generates intense and pervasive anxiety, which then is passed down to their children, who interiorize the values and attitudes of the adult world and set about (as best they can) to satisfy the demands of that world. Even when money is produced, however, the demands of the adult world are never fully met, but, quite the reverse, intensify further, so that more labor is necessary. In this context, work is not a means of meeting basic human needs, but rather only a way of producing greater sums of money, and thus it is clearly socially unproductive. Seen from this perspective, it is not important that the parents are not capitalists in the crudest sense (that is, they are not drawn as investors of money); what is important is that they both set the tone (economic scarcity) and determine the values (consumerism) of the world they inhabit, and in addition expropriate the wealth that others produce for their own private consumption.

Young Paul exemplifies vividly the sort of work that arises under capital. Simply put, he is a laborer for his mother, to whom he gives all of his money, only to find that the more he gives the more she needs. It is true, of course, that as a handicapper he invests money, betting on a profitable return on his investment, and that in this sense he is a sort of capitalist; indeed, it is his betting that is the literal sign of the economic relations controlling the world of the story. But at the same time his character is made to carry a much larger symbolic significance, for what he is investing, in real terms, is himself, selling his skills to generate wealth that he is not free to possess, but that is necessary to the maintenance of existing social relations. As his mother touches the money he earns, she uses it not to satisfy family needs—it has little or no *use* value—but to extend her social position and social power, and the process of extension of course is never ending, requiring ever greater sums of money: "There were certain new furnishings, and Paul had a tutor. He was *really* going to Eton, his father's school, in the following autumn. There were flowers in the winter, and a blossoming of the luxury Paul's mother had been used to. And yet the voices in the house, behind the sprays of mimosa and almond-blossom, and from under the piles of iridescent cushions, simply trilled and screamed in a sort of ecstasy: 'There *must* be more money!'" This passage clearly focuses the priority of money over commodity and the relentlessness with which the power associated with money controls even the most personal dimension of life.

The work itself that Paul performs cannot, under such conditions, be personally satisfying, and this is shown powerfully by the sort of work he does. The rocking horse is a brilliant symbol of non-productive labor, for even while it moves it remains stationary: even while Paul is magically (humanly) creative, producing untold wealth for his mother, he does not advance in the least, and in fact becomes increasingly isolated and fearful that even the abilities he now possesses will be taken from him. The labor, which drives him to "a sort of madness," that consumes him to an ever greater degree, leaves him nothing for himself, driving him down a terrible path to emotional and then physical distress. He is never satisfied with what he produces because it in no way relieves the pressure that his world places on him, and thus his anxiety and alienation grow to the point of destroying any sense of real personal worth and removing him literally from all meaningful social exchange, as when he takes his rocking horse to his bedroom and rides alone late into the night trying to find the key to wealth.

"Labor and Religion in D. H. Lawrence's 'The Rocking-Horse Winner'"

Alfred Kazin (1915–1998)

WALT WHITMAN AND ABRAHAM LINCOLN   1984

In Lincoln's lifetime Whitman was the only major writer to describe him with love. Whitman identified Lincoln with himself in the worshipful fashion that became standard after Lincoln's death. That Lincoln was a class issue says a good deal about the prejudices of American society in the East. A leading New Yorker, George Templeton Strong, noted in his diary that while he never disavowed the "lank and hard featured man," Lincoln was "despised and rejected by a third of the community, and only tolerated by the other two-thirds." Whitman the professional man of the people had complicated reasons for loving Lincoln. The uneasiness about him among America's elite was based on the fear that this unknown, untried man, elected without administrative experience (and without a majority) might not be up to his "fearful task."

. . .

Whitman related himself to the popular passion released by war and gave himself to this passion as a political cause. He understood popular opinion in a way that Emerson, Thoreau, and Hawthorne did not attempt to understand it. Emerson said, like any conventional New England clergyman, that the war was holy. He could not speak for the masses who bore the brunt of the war. Whitman was able to get so much out of the war, to create a lasting image of it, because he knew what people were feeling. He was not above the battle like Thoreau and Hawthorne, not suspicious of the majority like his fellow New Yorker Herman Melville, who in "The House-top," the most personal poem in *Battle-Pieces*, denounced the "ship-rats" who had taken over the city in the anti-draft riots of 1863.

Despite Whitman's elusiveness—he made a career out of longings it would have ended that career to fulfill—he genuinely felt at home with soldiers and other "ordinary" people who were inarticulate by the standards of men "from the schools." He was always present, if far from available, presenting the picture of a nobly accessible and social creature. He certainly got on better with omnibus drivers, workingmen, and now "simple" soldiers (especially when they were wounded and open to his ministrations) than he did with "scribblers." By the time Whitman went down after Fredericksburg to look for brother George, the war was becoming a revolution of sorts and Whitman's old radical politics were becoming "the nation." This made him adore Lincoln as the symbol of the nation's unity. An essential quality of Whitman's Civil War "memoranda" is Whitman's libidinous urge to associate himself with the great, growing, ever more powerful federal cause. Whitman's characteristic lifelong urge to join, to combine, to see life as movement, unity, totality, became during the Civil War an actively loving association with the broad masses of the people and *their* war. In his cult of the Civil War, Whitman allies himself with a heroic and creative energy which sees itself spreading out from the people and their representative men, Lincoln and Whitman.

Hawthorne's and Thoreau's horror of America as the Big State did not reflect Whitman's image of the Union. His passion for the "cause" reflected his intense faith in democracy at a juncture when the United States at war represented the revolutionary principle to Marx, the young Ibsen, Mill, Browning, Tolstoy. Whitman's deepest feeling was that his own rise from the city streets, his future as a poet of democracy, was tied up with the Northern armies.

An American Procession

GENDER CRITICISM

Gender criticism examines how sexual identity influences the creation and reception of literary works. Gender studies began with the feminist movement and were influenced by such works as Simone de Beauvoir's *The Second Sex* (1949) and Kate Millett's *Sexual Politics* (1970) as well as sociology, psychology, and anthropology. Feminist critics believe that culture has been so completely dominated by men that literature is full of unexamined "male-produced" assumptions. They see their criticism correcting this imbalance by analyzing and combatting patriarchal attitudes. Feminist criticism has explored how an author's gender influences—consciously or unconsciously—his or her writing. While a formalist critic like Allen Tate emphasized the universality of Emily Dickinson's poetry by demonstrating how powerfully the language, imagery, and myth making of her poems combine to affect a generalized reader, Sandra M. Gilbert, a leading feminist critic, has identified attitudes and assumptions in Dickinson's poetry that she believes are essentially female. Another important theme in feminist criticism is analyzing how sexual identity influences the reader of a text. If Tate's hypothetical reader was deliberately sexless, Gilbert's reader sees a text through the eyes of his or her sex. Finally, feminist critics carefully examine how the images of men and women in imaginative literature reflect or reject the social forces that have historically kept the sexes from achieving total equality.

Recently, gender criticism has expanded beyond its original feminist perspective. Critics have explored the impact of different sexual orientations on literary creation and reception. A men's movement has also emerged in response to feminism. The men's movement does not seek to reject feminism but to rediscover masculine identity in an authentic, contemporary way. Led by poet Robert Bly, the men's movement has paid special attention to interpreting poetry and fables as myths of psychic growth and sexual identity.

Elaine Showalter (b. 1941)

TOWARD A FEMINIST POETICS   1979

Feminist criticism can be divided into two distinct varieties. The first type is concerned with *woman as reader*—with woman as the consumer of male-produced literature, and with the way in which the hypothesis of a female reader changes our apprehension of a given text, awakening us to the significance of its sexual codes. I shall call this kind of analysis the *feminist critique*, and like other kinds of critique it is a historically grounded inquiry which probes the ideological assumptions of literary phenomena. Its subjects include the images and stereotypes of women in literature, the omissions of and misconceptions about women in criticism, and the fissures in male-constructed literary history. It is also concerned with the exploitation and manipulation of the female audience, especially in popular culture and film; and with the analysis of woman-as-sign in semiotic systems. The second type of feminist criticism is concerned with *woman as writer*—with woman as the producer of textual meaning, with the history, themes, genres, and structures of literature by women. Its subjects include the psychodynamics of female creativity; linguistics and the problem of a female language; the trajectory of the individual or collective female literary career; literary history; and, of course, studies of particular writers and works. No term exists in English for such a specialized discourse, and so I have adapted the French term *la gynocritique:* "gynocritics" (although the significance of the male pseudonym in the history of women's writing also suggested the term "georgics").

The feminist critique is essentially political and polemical, with theoretical affiliations to Marxist sociology and aesthetics; gynocritics is more self-contained and experimental, with connections to other modes of new feminist research. In a dialogue between these two positions, Carolyn Heilbrun, the writer, and Catharine Stimpson, editor of the journal *Signs: Women in Culture and Society*, compare the feminist critique to the Old Testament, "looking for the sins and errors of the past," and gynocritics to the New Testament, seeking "the grace of imagination." Both kinds are necessary, they explain, for only the Jeremiahs of the feminist critique can lead us out of the "Egypt of female servitude" to the promised land of the feminist vision. That the discussion makes use of these Biblical metaphors points to the connections between feminist consciousness and conversion narratives which often appear in women's literature; Carolyn Heilbrun comments on her own text, "When I talk about feminist criticism, I am amazed at how high a moral tone I take."

"Toward a Feminist Poetics"

Juliann Fleenor (b. 1942)

Gender and Pathology in "The Yellow Wallpaper" 1983

Although it is not generally known, Gilman wrote at least two other Gothic stories around the same time as "The Yellow Wallpaper." All three were published in the *New England Magazine*. At the time that "The Rocking Chair" and "The Giant Wistaria" were written, Gilman and her young daughter, Katherine, were living in the warmth of Pasadena, separated from her husband, Charles Walter Stetson. Gilman later noted in her papers: "'The Yellow Wallpaper' was written in two days, with the thermometer at one hundred and three in Pasadena, Ca." Her husband was living on the east coast, and, perhaps coincidentally, all three stories appear to be set in a nameless eastern setting, one urban and two rural. All three display similar themes, and all three are evidence that the conflict, central to Gilman's Gothic fiction and later to her autobiography, was a conflict with the mother, with motherhood, and with creation.

In all three stories women are confined within the home; it is their prison, their insane asylum, even their tomb. A sense of the female isolation which Gilman felt, of exclusion from the public world of work and of men, is contained in the anecdote related by Zona Gale in her introduction to Gilman's autobiography. After watching the approach of several locomotives to a train platform in a small town in Wisconsin, Gilman said, "'All that, . . . and women have no part in it. Everything done by men, working together, while women worked on alone within their four walls!'" Female exclusion, women denied the opportunity to work, or their imprisonment behind four walls, led to madness. Her image, interestingly, does not suggest a female subculture of women working together; Gilman was working against her own culture's definition of women, and her primary antagonists were women like her own mother.

Diseased maternity is explicit in Gilman's third Gothic story. The yellow wallpaper symbolizes more than confinement, victimization, and the inability to write. It suggests a disease within the female self. When the narrator peels the wallpaper off, "It sticks horribly and the pattern just enjoys it! All those strangled heads and bulbous eyes and the waddling fungus growths just shriek with derision." This passage describes more than the peeling of wallpaper: the "strangled heads and bulbous eyes and waddling fungus" imply something strange and terrible about birth and death conjoined, about female procreation, and about female physiology. Nature is perverted here, too. The narrator thinks of "old foul, bad yellow things." The smell "creeps all over the house." She finds it "hovering in the dining-room, skulking in the parlor, hiding in the hall, lying in wait for me on the stairs." Finally, "it gets into my hair."

The paper stains the house in a way that suggests the effect of afterbirth. The house, specifically this room, becomes more than a symbol of a repressive society; it represents the physical self of the narrator as well. She is disgusted, perhaps awed, perhaps frightened of her own bodily processes. The story establishes a sense of fear and disgust, the skin crawls and grows clammy with the sense of physiological fear that Ellen Moers refers to as the Female Gothic.

My contention that one of the major themes in the story, punishment for becoming a mother (as well as punishment for being female), is supported by the absence of the child. The child is taken away from the mother, almost in punishment, as was the child in "The Giant Wistaria." This differs from Gilman's experience; she had been told to keep her child with her at all times. In both the story and in Gilman's life, a breakdown occurs directly after the birth of a child. The narrator is confined as if she had committed a crime. Maternity—the creation of a child—is combined with writing—the creation of writing—in a way that suggests they are interrelated and perhaps symbiotic, as are the strange toadstools behind the wallpaper.

The pathological nature of both experiences is not surprising, given the treatment Gilman received, and given the fact that maternity reduced women to mothers and not writers. Childbirth has long been a rite of passage for women. But the question is, where does that passage lead? Becoming a mother leads to a child-like state. The narrator becomes the absent child.

"The Gothic Prism"

Sandra M. Gilbert (b. 1936) and Susan Gubar (b. 1944)

THE FREEDOM OF EMILY DICKINSON   1985

[Emily Dickinson] defined herself as a *woman* writer, reading the works of female precursors with special care, attending to the implications of novels like Charlotte Brontë's *Jane Eyre*, Emily Brontë's *Wuthering Heights*, and George Eliot's *Middlemarch* with the same absorbed delight that characterized her devotion to Elizabeth Barrett Browning's *Aurora Leigh*. Finally, then, the key to her enigmatic identity as a "supposed person" who was called the "Myth of Amherst" may rest, not in investigations of her questionable romance, but in studies of her unquestionably serious reading as well as in analyses of her disquietingly powerful writing. Elliptically phrased, intensely compressed, her poems are more linguistically innovative than any other nineteenth-century verses, with the possible exception of some works by Walt Whitman and Gerard Manley Hopkins, her two most radical male contemporaries. Throughout her largely secret but always brilliant career, moreover, she confronted precisely the questions about the individual and society, time and death, flesh and spirit, that major precursors from Milton to Keats had faced. Dreaming of "Amplitude and Awe," she recorded sometimes vengeful, sometimes mystical visions of social and personal transformation in poems as inventively phrased and imaginatively constructed as any in the English language.

Clearly such accomplishments required not only extraordinary talent but also some measure of freedom. Yet because she was the unmarried daughter of conservative New Englanders, Dickinson was obliged to take on many household tasks; as a nineteenth-century New England wife, she would have had the same number of obligations, if not more. Some of these she performed with pleasure; in 1856, for instance, she was judge of a bread-baking contest, and in 1857 she won a prize in that contest. But as Higginson's "scholar," as a voracious reader and an ambitious writer, Dickinson had to win herself time for "Amplitude and Awe," and it is increasingly clear that she did so through a strategic withdrawal from her ordinary world. A story related by her niece Martha Dickinson Bianchi reveals that the poet herself knew from the first what both the price and the prize might be: on one occasion, said Mrs. Bianchi, Dickinson took her up to the room in which she regularly sequestered herself, and, mimicking locking herself in, "thumb and forefinger closed on an imaginary key," said "with a quick turn of her wrist, 'It's just a turn—and freedom, Matty!'"

In the freedom of her solitary, but not lonely, room, Dickinson may have become what her Amherst neighbors saw as a bewildering "myth." Yet there, too, she created myths of her own. Reading the Brontës and Barrett Browning, studying Transcendentalism and the Bible, she contrived a theology which is powerfully expressed in many of her poems. That it was at its most hopeful a female-centered theology is revealed in verses like those she wrote about the women artists she admired, as well as in more general works like her gravely pantheistic address to the "Sweet Mountains" who "tell me no lie," with its definition of the hills around Amherst as "strong Madonnas" and its description of the writer herself as "The Wayward Nun — beneath the Hill — / Whose service is to You —." As Dickinson's admirer and descendant Adrienne Rich has accurately observed, this passionate poet consistently chose to confront her society—to "have it out"—"on her own premises."

Introduction to Emily Dickinson,
The Norton Anthology of Literature by Women

READER-RESPONSE CRITICISM

Reader-response criticism attempts to describe what happens in the reader's mind while interpreting a text. If traditional criticism assumes that imaginative writing is a creative act, reader-response theory recognizes that reading is also a creative process. Reader-response critics believe that no text provides self-contained meaning; literary texts do not exist independently of readers' interpretations. A text, according to this critical school, is not finished until it is read and interpreted. The practical problem then arises that no two individuals necessarily read a text in exactly the same way. Rather than declare one interpretation correct and the other mistaken, reader-response criticism recognizes the inevitable plurality of readings. Instead of trying to ignore or reconcile the contradictions inherent in this situation, it explores them.

The easiest way to explain reader-response criticism is to relate it to the common experience of rereading a favorite book after many years. Rereading a novel as an adult, for example, that "changed your life" as an adolescent, is often a shocking experience. The book may seem substantially different. The character you remembered liking most now seems less admirable, and another character you disliked now seems more sympathetic. Has the book changed? Very unlikely, but *you* certainly have in the intervening years. Reader-response criticism explores how the different individuals (or classes of individuals) see the same text differently. It emphasizes how religious, cultural, and social values affect readings; it also overlaps with gender criticism in exploring how men and women read the same text with different assumptions.

While reader-response criticism rejects the notion that there can be a single correct reading for a literary text, it doesn't consider all readings permissible. Each text creates limits to its possible interpretations. As Stanley Fish admits in the following critical selection, we cannot arbitrarily place an Eskimo in William Faulkner's story "A Rose for Emily" (though Professor Fish does ingeniously imagine a hypothetical situation where this bizarre interpretation might actually be possible).

Stanley Fish (b. 1938)

An Eskimo "A Rose for Emily" 1980

The fact that it remains easy to think of a reading that most of us would dismiss out of hand does not mean that the text excludes it but that there is as yet no elaborated interpretive procedure for producing that text. . . . Norman Holland's analysis of Faulkner's "A Rose for Emily" is a case in point. Holland is arguing for a kind of psychoanalytic pluralism. The text, he declares, is "at most a matrix of psychological possibilities for its readers," but, he insists, "only some possibilities . . . truly fit the matrix": "One would not say, for example, that a reader of . . . 'A Rose for Emily' who thought the 'tableau' [of Emily and her father in the doorway] described an Eskimo was really responding to the story at all—only pursuing some mysterious inner exploration."

Holland is making two arguments: first, that anyone who proposes an Eskimo reading of "A Rose for Emily" will not find a hearing in the literary community. And that, I think, is right. ("We are right to rule out at least some readings.") His second argument is that the unacceptability of the Eskimo reading is a function of the text, of what he calls its "sharable promptuary," the public "store of structured language" that sets limits to the interpretations the words can accommodate. And that, I think, is wrong. The Eskimo reading is unacceptable because there is at present no interpretive strategy for producing it, no way of "looking" or reading (and remember, all acts of looking or reading are "ways") that would result in the emergence of obviously Eskimo meanings. This does not mean, however, that no such strategy could ever come into play, and it is not difficult to imagine the circumstances under which it would establish itself. One such circumstance would be the discovery of a letter in which Faulkner confides that he has always believed himself to be an Eskimo changeling. (The example is absurd only if one forgets Yeats's *Vision* or Blake's Swedenborgianism° or James Miller's recent elaboration of a homosexual reading of *The Waste Land*.) Imme-

---

Yeats's Vision *or Blake's* Swedenborgianism: Irish poet William Butler Yeats and Swedish mystical writer Emanuel Swedenborg both claimed to have received revelations from the spirit world; some of Swedenborg's ideas are embodied in the long poems of William Blake.

diately the workers in the Faulkner industry would begin to reinterpret the canon in the light of this newly revealed "belief" and the work of reinterpretation would involve the elaboration of a symbolic or allusive system (not unlike mythological or typological criticism) whose application would immediately transform the text into one informed everywhere by Eskimo meanings. It might seem that I am admitting that there is a text to be transformed, but the object of transformation would be the text (or texts) given by whatever interpretive strategies the Eskimo strategy was in the process of dislodging or expanding. The result would be that whereas we now have a Freudian "A Rose for Emily," a mythological "A Rose for Emily," a Christological "A Rose for Emily," a regional "A Rose for Emily," a sociological "A Rose for Emily," a linguistic "A Rose for Emily," we would in addition have an Eskimo "A Rose for Emily," existing in some relation of compatibility or incompatibility with the others.

Again the point is that while there are always mechanisms for ruling out readings, their source is not the text but the presently recognized interpretive strategies for producing the text. It follows, then, that no reading, however outlandish it might appear, is inherently an impossible one.

Is There a Text in This Class?

Robert Scholes (b. 1929)
"How Do We Make a Poem?" 1982

Let us begin with one of the shortest poetic texts in the English language, "Elegy" by W. S. Merwin:

Who would I show it to

One line, one sentence, unpunctuated, but proclaimed an interrogative by its grammar and syntax—what makes it a poem? Certainly without its title it would not be a poem; but neither would the title alone constitute a poetic text. Nor do the two together simply make a poem by themselves. Given the title and the text, the *reader* is encouraged to make a poem. He is not forced to do so, but there is not much else he can do with this material, and certainly nothing else so rewarding. (I will use the masculine pronoun here to refer to the reader, not because all readers are male but because I am, and my hypothetical reader is not a pure construct but an idealized version of myself.)

How do we make a poem out of this text? There are only two things to work on, the title and the question posed by the single, colloquial line. The line is not simply colloquial, it is prosaic; with no words of more than one syllable, concluded by a preposition, it is within the utterance range of every speaker of English. It is, in a sense, completely intelligible. But in another sense it is opaque, mysterious. Its three pronouns—who, I, it—pose problems of reference. Its conditional verb phrase—would . . . show to—poses a problem of situation. The context that would supply the information required to make that simple sentence meaningful as well as intelligible is not there. It must be supplied by the reader.

To make a poem of this text the reader must not only know English, he must know a poetic code as well: the code of the funeral elegy, as practiced in English from the Renaissance to the present time. The "words on the page" do not constitute a poetic "work," complete and self-sufficient, but a "text," a sketch or outline that must be completed by the active participation of a reader equipped with the right sort of information. In this case part of that information consists of an acquaintance with the elegiac tradition: its procedures, assumptions, devices, and values. One needs to know works like Milton's "Lycidas," Shelley's "Adonais," Tennyson's "In Memoriam," Whitman's "When Lilacs Last in the Dooryard Bloomed," Thomas's "Refusal to Mourn the Death by Fire of a Child in London," and so on, in order to "read" this simple poem properly. In fact, it could be argued that the more elegies one can bring to bear on a reading of this one, the better, richer poem this one becomes. I would go even further, suggesting that a knowledge of the critical tradition—of Dr. Johnson's objections to "Lycidas," for instance, or Wordsworth's critique of poetic diction—will also enhance one's reading of this poem. For the poem is, of course, an anti-elegy, a refusal not simply to mourn, but to write a sonorous, eloquent, mournful, but finally acquiescent, accepting—in a word, "elegiac"—poem at all.

Reading the poem involves, then, a special knowledge of its tradition. It also involves a special interpretive skill. The forms of the short, written poem as they have developed in English over the past few centuries can be usefully seen as compressed, truncated, or fragmented imitations of other verbal forms, especially the play, story, public oration, and personal essay. The reasons for this are too complicated for consideration here, but the fact will be apparent to all who reflect upon the matter. Our short poems are almost always elliptical versions of what can easily be conceived of as dramatic, narrative, oratorical, or meditative texts. Often, they are combinations of these and other modes of address. To take an obvious example, the dramatic monologue in the hands of Robert Browning is like a speech from a play (though usually more elongated than most such speeches). But to "read" such a monologue we must imagine the setting, the situation, the context, and so on. The dramatic monologue is "like" a play but gives us less information of certain sorts than a play would, requiring us to provide that information by decoding the clues in the monologue itself in the light of our understanding of the generic model. Most short poems work this way. They require both special knowledge and special skills to be "read."

To understand "Elegy" we must construct a situation out of the clues provided. The "it" in "Who would I show it to" is of course the elegy itself. The "I" is the potential writer of the elegy. The "Who" is the audience for the poem. But the verb phrase "would . . . show to" indicates a condition contrary to fact. Who would I show it to *if* I were to write it? This implies in turn that for the potential elegiac poet there is one person whose appreciation means more than that of all the rest of the potential audience for the poem he might write, and it further implies that the death of this particular person is the one imagined in the poem. If this person were dead, the poet suggests, so would his inspiration be dead. With no one to write for, no poem would be forthcoming. This poem is not only a "refusal to mourn," like that of Dylan Thomas, it is a refusal to elegize. The whole elegiac tradition, like its cousin the funeral oration, turns finally away from mourning toward acceptance, revival, renewal, a return to the concerns of life, symbolized by the very writing of the poem. Life goes on; there *is* an audience; and the mourned person will live through accomplishments, influence, descendants, and also (not least) in the elegiac poem itself. Merwin rejects all that. *If I wrote an elegy for X, the person for whom I have always written, X would not be alive to read it; therefore, there is no reason to write an elegy for the one person in my life who most deserves one; therefore, there is no reason to write any elegy, anymore, ever.* Finally, and of course, this poem called "Elegy" is not an elegy.

Semiotics and Interpretation

Joel Wingard (b. 1946)

FILLING THE GAPS IN *Hamlet*   1996

Hamlet is a long play, one of Shakespeare's longest in terms of lines and scenes (though all his plays are five acts). Like any play on the page and like Shakespeare's especially, it is riddled with gaps. Many of these gaps . . . involve the reader's knowing or unknowing. As you read on through the text, you will fill in some of these gaps easily enough as you find out more through the characters' words and actions. Others will remain open; some that have been identified over the years are still open and always will be, even if one strong reading or another has proposed a way to close them.

One consequence of a reader's identification of gaps in the text is the opportunity to apply consistency building as a reading strategy. As you read, or as you watch a production, you may find yourself trying to explain in some kind of logical or consistent terms why Hamlet does what he does, or why he doesn't do what he's supposed to do—get revenge on Claudius—right away. Indeed the question of Hamlet's "delay" or why he delays exacting revenge has been a significant gap in the text for many readers for the past couple of hundred years, a gap filled in differently by various readers. Many readers also have pondered the question of Hamlet's "madness." After he hears his father's ghost's story in Act 1, Hamlet tells his friend Horatio that he will "put an antic disposition on" in order to disguise his inquiry into what the ghost has told him; in other words, he'll act crazy. But over the years, readers have debated the extent to which Hamlet is in control of his insanity act or whether he goes at least temporarily insane as he plays it out. A reader's decision that Hamlet really *is* mad, for instance, based on the way he behaves in Acts 2–4 and on what other characters say about him, is an instance of consistency building to fill in this gap.

The play affords many opportunities for you to use this reading strategy, but you should also remember before you start to read that consistency building has a complementary reading strategy: what the critic Wolfgang Iser calls "wandering viewpoint." This strategy isn't exactly what it sounds like, so it would probably help if you think of it in contrast to consistency building. If consistency building is filling in gaps or closing down interpretive options as you read (Hamlet delays because he goes insane, for instance), adopting a wandering viewpoint means keeping those gaps or options open not making up your mind as to, for instance, what makes Hamlet tick.

In an academic context, you are used to engaging in consistency building as you read, even if the term itself is new to you, and you are encouraged to practice it for the sake of writing about literature in papers where you have to argue an interpretation. Reading to come up with a consistent interpretation of a complex character or text seems to be the "natural" way of doing things, but of course it is really a learned procedure. If you find *Hamlet* difficult, apart from the language, it may be because you have trouble building a consistent interpretation with such a contradictory character in such a complex play. So it may just take some of that pressure off you to remember that consistency building is an *optional* reading strategy and that you can also read with a wandering viewpoint and leave your interpretive options open.

"Reading and Responding: A Shakespearean Tragedy"

DECONSTRUCTIONIST CRITICISM

Deconstructionist criticism rejects the traditional assumption that language can accurately represent reality. Language, according to deconstructionists, is a fundamentally unstable medium; consequently, literary texts, which are made up of words, have no fixed, single meaning. Deconstructionists insist, according to critic Paul de Man, on "the impossibility of making the actual expression coincide with what has to be expressed, of making the actual signs coincide with what is signified." Since they believe that literature cannot definitively express its subject matter, deconstructionists tend to shift their attention away from *what* is being said to *how* language is being used in a text.

Paradoxically, deconstructionist criticism often resembles formalist criticism; both methods usually involve close reading. But while a formalist usually tries to demonstrate how the diverse elements of a text cohere into meaning, the deconstructionist approach attempts to show how the text "deconstructs," that is, how it can be broken down—by a skeptical critic—into mutually irreconcilable positions. A biographical or historical critic might seek to establish the author's intention as a means to interpreting a literary work, but deconstructionists reject the notion that the critic should endorse the myth of authorial control over language. Deconstructionist critics like Roland Barthes and Michel Foucault have therefore called for "the death of the author," that is, the rejection of the assumption that the author, no matter how ingenious, can fully control the meaning of a text. They have also announced the death of literature as a special category of writing. In their view, poems and novels are merely words on a page that deserve no privileged status as art; all texts are created equal—equally untrustworthy, that is.

Deconstructionists focus on how language is used to achieve power. Since they believe, in the words of critic David Lehman, that "there are no truths, only rival interpretations," deconstructionists try to understand how some "interpretations" come to be regarded as truth. A major goal of deconstruction is to demonstrate how those supposed truths are at best provisional and at worst contradictory.

Deconstruction, as you may have inferred, calls for intellectual subtlety and skill. If you pursue your literary studies beyond the introductory stage, you will want to become more familiar with its assumptions. Deconstruction may strike you as a negative, even destructive, critical approach, and yet its best practitioners are adept at exposing the inadequacy of much conventional criticism. By patient analysis, they can sometimes open up the most familiar text and find unexpected significance.

Roland Barthes (1915–1980)

THE DEATH OF THE AUTHOR   1968

TRANSLATED BY STEPHEN HEATH

Succeeding the Author, the scriptor no longer bears within him passions, humours, feelings, impressions, but rather this immense dictionary from which he draws a writing that can know no halt: life never does more than imitate the book, and the book itself is only a tissue of signs, an imitation that is lost, infinitely deferred.

Once the Author is removed, the claim to decipher a text becomes quite futile. To give a text an Author is to impose a limit on that text, to furnish it with a final signified, to close the writing. Such a conception suits criticism very well, the latter then allotting itself the important task of discovering the Author (or its hypostases: society, history, psyché, liberty) beneath the work: when the Author has been found, the text is "explained"—victory to the critic. Hence there is no surprise in the fact that, historically, the reign of the Author has also been that of the Critic, nor again in the fact that criticism (be it new) is today undermined along with the Author. In the multiplicity of writing, everything is to be *disentangled*, nothing *deciphered*; the structure can be followed, "run" (like the thread of a stocking) at every point and at every level, but there is nothing beneath: the space of writing is to be ranged over, not pierced; writing ceaselessly posits meaning ceaselessly to evaporate it, carrying out a systematic exemption of meaning. In precisely this way literature (it would be better from now on to say *writing*), by refusing to assign a "secret," an ultimate meaning, to the text (and to the world as text), liberates what may be called an anti-theological activity, an activity that is truly revolutionary since to refuse to fix meaning is, in the end, to refuse God and his hypostases— reason, science, law.

"The Death of the Author"

Barbara Johnson (b. 1947)

RIGOROUS UNRELIABILITY   1987

As a critique of a certain Western conception of the nature of signification, deconstruction focuses on the functioning of claim-making and claim-subverting structures within texts. A deconstructive reading is an attempt to show how the conspicuously foregrounded statements in a text are systematically related to discordant signifying elements that the text has thrown into its shadows or margins, an attempt both to recover what is lost and to analyze what happens when a text is read solely in function of intentionality, meaningfulness, and representativity. Deconstruction thus confers a new kind of readability on those elements in a text that readers have traditionally been trained to disregard, overcome, explain away, or edit out—contradictions, obscurities, ambiguities, incoherences, discontinuities, ellipses, interruptions, repetitions, and plays of the signifier. In this sense it involves a reversal of values, a revaluation of the signifying function of everything that, in a signified-based theory of meaning, would constitute "noise." Derrida has chosen to speak of the values involved in this reversal in terms of "speech" and "writing," in which "speech" stands for the privilege accorded to meaning as immediacy, unity, identity, truth, and presence, while "writing" stands for the devalued functions of distance, difference, dissimulation, and deferment.

This transvaluation has a number of consequences for the appreciation of literature. By shifting the attention from intentional meaning to writing as such, deconstruction has enabled readers to become sensitive to a number of recurrent literary topoi° in a new way.

. . .

In addition, by seeing interpretation itself as a fiction-making activity, deconstruction has both reversed and displaced the narrative categories of "showing" and "telling," mimesis and diegesis.° Instead of according moments of textual self-interpretation an authoritative metalinguistic status, deconstruction considers anything the text says about itself to be another fiction, an allegory of the reading process. Hence, the privilege traditionally granted to showing over telling is reversed: "telling" becomes a more sophisticated form of "showing," in which what is "shown" is the breakdown of the show/tell distinction. Far from doing the reader's work for her, the text's self-commentary only gives the reader more to do. Indeed, it is the way in which a text subverts the possibility of any authoritative reading by inscribing the reader's strategies into its own structures that often, for de Man, ends up being constitutive of literature as such.

Deconstructors, therefore, tend to privilege texts that are self-reflexive in interestingly and rigorously unreliable ways. Since self-reflexive texts often explicitly posit themselves as belated or revolutionary with respect to a tradition on which they comment, deconstruction can both reinstate the self-consciously outmoded or overwritten (such as Melville's Pierre°) and canonize the experimental or avant-garde. But because deconstruction has focused on the ways in which the Western white male philosophico-literary tradition subverts itself *from within*, it has often tended to remain within the confines of the established

---

topoi: the plural of the Greek *topos*, for "place"; it means a commonly used literary device. *diegesis*: the main events of a story, the basic plot, as distinct from the narration. *Pierre*: Pierre, or the Ambiguities (1852), a complex novel by Herman Melville, was a failure during the author's lifetime; it was not widely read until the mid-twentieth century.

literary and philosophical canon. . . . If it has questioned the boundary lines of literature, it has done so not with respect to the noncanonical but with respect to the line between literature and philosophy or between literature and criticism. It is as a rethinking of those distinctions that deconstruction most radically displaces certain traditional evaluative assumptions.

A World of Difference

Geoffrey Hartman (b. 1929)
ON WORDSWORTH'S "A SLUMBER DID MY SPIRIT SEAL"   1987

Take Wordsworth's well-known lyric of eight lines, one of the "Lucy" poems, which has been explicated so many times without its meaning being fully determined:

> A slumber did my spirit seal;
>   I had no human fears:
> She seemed a thing that could not feel
>   The touch of earthly years.
>
> No motion has she now, no force;
>   She neither hears nor sees;
> Rolled round in earth's diurnal course,
>   With rocks, and stones, and trees.

It does not matter whether you interpret the second stanza (especially its last line) as tending toward affirmation, or resignation, or a grief verging on bitterness. The tonal assignment of one rather than another possible meaning, to repeat Susanne Langer° on musical form, is curiously open or beside the point. Yet the lyric does not quite support Langer's general position, that "Articulation is its life, but not assertion," because the poem is composed of a series of short and definitive statements, very like assertions. You could still claim that the poem's life is not in the assertions but somewhere else: but where then? What would articulation mean in that case? Articulation is not anti-assertive here; indeed the sense of closure is so strong that it thematizes itself in the very first line.

Nevertheless, is not the harmony or aesthetic effect of the poem greater than this local conciseness; is not the sense of closure broader and deeper than our admiration for a perfect technical construct? The poem is surely something else than a fine box, a well-wrought coffin.

That it is a kind of epitaph is relevant, of course. We recognize, even if genre is not insisted on, that Wordsworth's style is laconic, even lapidary. There may be a mimetic or formal motive related to the ideal of epitaphic poetry. But

---

Susanne Langer: Langer (1895–1985) was an American philosopher who discussed the relationship between aesthetics and artistic form.

the motive may also be, in a precise way, meta-epitaphic. The poem, first of all, marks the closure of a life that has never opened up: Lucy is likened in other poems to a hidden flower or the evening star. Setting overshadows rising, and her mode of existence is inherently inward, westering. I will suppose then, that Wordsworth was at some level giving expression to the traditional epitaphic wish: Let the earth rest lightly on the deceased. If so, his conversion of this epitaphic formula is so complete that to trace the process of conversion might seem gratuitous. The formula, a trite if deeply grounded figure of speech, has been catalyzed out of existence. Here it is formula itself, or better, the adjusted words of the mourner that lie lightly on the girl and everyone who is a mourner.

I come back, then, to the "aesthetic" sense of a burden lifted, rather than denied. A heavy element is made lighter. One may still feel that the term "elation" is inappropriate in this context; yet elation is, as a mood, the very subject of the first stanza. For the mood described is love or desire when it *eternizes* the loved person, when it makes her a star-like being that "could not feel / The touch of earthly years." This *naïve* elation, this spontaneous movement of the spirit upward, is reversed in the downturn or cata-strophe of the second stanza. Yet this stanza does not close out the illusion; it preserves it within the elegaic form. The illusion is elated, in our use of the word: *aufgehoben*° seems the proper term. For the girl is still, and all the more, what she seemed to be: beyond touch, like a star, if the earth in its daily motion is a planetary and erring rather than a fixed star, and if all on this star of earth must partake of its sublunar, mortal, temporal nature.

. . .

To sum up: In Wordsworth's lyric the specific gravity of words is weighed in the balance of each stanza; and this balance is as much a judgment on speech in the context of our mortality as it is a meaningful response to the individual death. At the limit of the medium of words, and close to silence, what has been purged is not concreteness, or the empirical sphere of the emotions—shock, disillusion, trauma, recognition, grief, atonement—what has been purged is a series of flashy schematisms and false or partial mediations: artificial plot, inflated consolatory rhetoric, the coercive absolutes of logic or faith.

"Elation in Hegel and Wordsworth"

CULTURAL STUDIES

Unlike the other critical approaches discussed in this chapter, cultural criticism (or **cultural studies**) does not offer a single way of analyzing literature. No central methodology is associated with cultural studies. Nor is cultural criticism solely, or even mainly, concerned with literary texts in the conventional sense. Instead, the term *cultural studies* refers to a relatively recent interdisciplinary field of academic inquiry. This field borrows methodologies from other approaches to analyze a wide range of cultural products and practice.

Aufgehoben: German for "taken up" or "lifted up," but this term can also mean "canceled" or "nullified." Hartman uses the term for its double meaning.

To understand cultural studies, it helps to know a bit about its origins. In the English-speaking world, the field was first defined at the Centre for Contemporary Cultural Studies of Birmingham University in Great Britain. Founded in 1964, this graduate program tried to expand the range of literary study beyond traditional approaches to canonic literature in order to explore a broader spectrum of historical, cultural, and political issues. The most influential teacher at the Birmingham Centre was Raymond Williams (1921–1983), a Welsh socialist with wide intellectual interests. Williams argued that scholars should not study culture as a canon of great works by individual artists but rather examine it as an evolutionary process that involves the entire society. "We cannot separate literature and art," Williams said, "from other kinds of social practice." The cultural critic, therefore, does not study fixed aesthetic objects as much as dynamic social processes. The critic's challenge is to identify and understand the complex forms and effects of the process of culture.

A Marxist intellectual, Williams called his approach cultural materialism (a reference to the Marxist doctrine of dialectical materialism), but later scholars soon discarded that name for two broader and more neutral terms, cultural criticism and cultural studies. From the start, this interdisciplinary field relied heavily on literary theory, especially Marxist and feminist criticism. It also employed the documentary techniques of historical criticism combined with political analysis focused on issues of social class, race, and gender. (This approach flourished in the United States, where it is called new historicism.) Cultural studies is also deeply antiformalist, since the field concerns itself with investigating the complex relationship among history, politics, and literature. Cultural studies rejects the notion that literature exists in an aesthetic realm separate from ethical and political categories.

A chief goal of cultural studies is to understand the nature of social power as reflected in "texts." For example, if the object of analysis were a sonnet by Shakespeare, the cultural studies adherent might investigate the moral, psychological, and political assumptions reflected in the poem and then deconstruct them to see what individuals, social classes, or gender might benefit from having those assumptions perceived as true. The relevant mission of cultural studies is to identify both the overt and covert values reflected in a cultural practice. The cultural studies critic also tries to trace out and understand the structures of meaning that hold those assumptions in place and give them the appearance of objective representation. Any analytical technique that helps illuminate these issues is employed.

In theory, a cultural studies critic might employ any methodology. In practice, however, he or she will most often borrow concepts from deconstruction, Marxist analysis, gender criticism, race theory, and psychology. Each of these earlier methodologies provides particular analytical tools that cultural critics find useful. What cultural studies borrows from deconstructionism is its emphasis on uncovering conflict, dissent, and contradiction in the works under analysis. Whereas traditional critical approaches often sought to demonstrate the unity of a literary work, cultural studies often seeks to portray social, political, and psychological conflicts it masks. What cultural studies borrows from Marxist analysis is an attention to the ongoing struggle between social classes, each seeking economic (and therefore political) advantage. Cultural studies often asks questions about what social class created a work of art and what class (or classes) served as its audience. Among the many things that cultural studies borrowed from gender criticism and race theory is a concern with social inequality between the sexes and races. It seeks to investigate how these inequities have been reflected in the texts of a historical period or a society. Cultural studies is, above all, a political enterprise that views literary analysis as a means of furthering social justice.

Since cultural studies does not adhere to any single methodology (or even a consistent set of methodologies), it is impossible to characterize the field briefly, because there are exceptions to every generalization offered. What one sees most clearly are characteristic tendencies, especially the commitment to examining issues of class, race, and gender. There is also the insistence on expanding the focus of critical inquiry beyond traditional high literary culture. British cultural studies guru Anthony Easthope can, for example, analyze with equal aplomb Gerard Manley Hopkins's "The Windhover," Edgar Rice Burrough's *Tarzan of the Apes*, a Benson and Hedges's cigarette advertisement, and Sean Connery's eyebrows. Cultural studies is infamous—even among its practitioners—for its habitual use of literary jargon. It is also notorious for its complex intellectual analysis of mundane materials such as Easthope's cigarette ad, which may be interesting in its own right but remote from most readers' literary experience. Some scholars, such as Heather Glen, however, use the principles of cultural studies to provide new social, political, and historical insights on canonic texts such as William Blake's "London." Omnivorous, iconoclastic, and relentlessly analytical, cultural criticism has become a major presence in contemporary literary studies.

Vincent B. Leitch (b. 1944)

POSTSTRUCTURALIST CULTURAL CRITIQUE   1992

Whereas a major goal of New Criticism and much other modern formalistic criticism is aesthetic evaluation of freestanding texts, a primary objective of cultural criticism is cultural critique, which entails investigation and assessment of ruling and oppositional beliefs, categories, practices, and representations, inquiring into the causes, constitutions, and consequences as well as the modes of circulation and consumption of linguistic, social, economic, political, historical, ethical, religious, legal, scientific, philosophical, educational, familial, and aesthetic discourses and institutions. In rendering a judgment on an aesthetic artifact, a New Critic privileges such key things as textual coherence and unity, intricacy and complexity, ambiguity and irony, tension and balance, economy and autonomy, literariness and spatial form. In mounting a critique of a cultural "text," an advocate of poststructuralist cultural criticism evaluates such things as degrees of exclusion and inclusion, of complicity and resistance, of domination and letting-be, of abstraction and situatedness, of violence and tolerance, of monologue and polylogue, of quietism and activism, of sameness and otherness, of oppression and emancipation, of centralization and decentralization. Just as the aforementioned system of evaluative criteria underlies the exegetical and judgmental labor of New Criticism, so too does the above named set of commitments undergird the work of poststructuralist cultural critique.

Given its commitments, poststructuralist cultural criticism is, as I have suggested, suspicious of literary formalism. Specifically, the trouble with New Criticism is its inclination to advocate a combination of quietism and asceticism, connoisseurship and exclusiveness, aestheticism and apoliticism. . . . The monotonous practical effect of New Critical reading is to illustrate the subservience of each textual element to a higher, overarching, economical poetic structure without remainders. What should be evident here is that the project of poststructuralist cultural criticism possesses a set of commitments and criteria that enable it to engage in the enterprise of cultural critique. It should also be evident that the cultural ethicopolitics of this enterprise is best characterized, using current terminology, as "liberal" or "leftist," meaning congruent with certain socialist, anarchist, and libertarian ideals, none of which, incidentally, are necessarily Marxian. Such congruence, derived from extrapolating a generalized stance for poststructuralism, constitutes neither a party platform nor an observable course of practical action; avowed tendencies often account for little in the unfolding of practical engagements.

Cultural Criticism, Literary Theory, Poststructuralism

Mark Bauerlein (b. 1959)

What Is Cultural Studies?   1997

Traditionally, disciplines naturally fell into acknowledged subdivisions, for example, as literary criticism broke up into formalist literary criticism, philological criticism, narratological analysis, and other methodologically distinguished pursuits, all of which remained comfortably within the category "literary criticism." But cultural studies eschews such institutional disjunctions and will not let any straitening adjective precede the "cultural studies" heading. There is no distinct formalist cultural studies or historicist cultural studies, but only cultural studies. (Feminist cultural studies may be one exception.) Cultural studies is a field that will not be parceled out to the available disciplines. It spans culture at large, not this or that institutionally separated element of culture. To guarantee this transcendence of disciplinary institutions, cultural studies must select a name for itself that has no specificity, that has too great an extension to mark off any expedient boundaries for itself. "Cultural studies" serves well because, apart from distinguishing between "physical science" and "cultural analysis," the term provides no indication of where any other boundaries lie.

This is exactly the point. To blur disciplinary boundaries and frustrate the intellectual investments that go along with them is a fundamental motive for cultural studies practice, one that justifies the vagueness of the titular term. This explains why the related label "cultural criticism," so much in vogue in 1988, has declined. The term "criticism" has a narrower extension than does "studies," ruling out some empirical forms of inquiry (like field work) that "studies" admits. "Studies" preserves a methodological openness that "criticism" closes. Since such closures have suspect political intentions behind them, cultural studies maintains its institutional purity by disdaining disciplinary identity and methodological uniformity.

. . .

A single approach will miss too much, will overlook important aspects of culture not perceptible to that particular angle of vision. A multitude of approaches will pick up an insight here and a piece of knowledge there and more of culture will enter into the inquiry. A diversity of methods will match the diversity of culture, thereby sheltering the true nature of culture from the reductive appropriations of formal disciplines.

But how do cultural critics bring all these methods together into a coherent inquiry? Are there any established rules of incorporating "important insights and knowledge" coming out of different methods into a coherent scholarly project of cultural studies? How might a scholar use both phonemic analysis and deconstruction in a single inquiry when deconstructionist arguments call into question the basic premises of phonetics? What scholar has the competence to handle materials from so many disciplines in a rigorous and knowing manner? Does cultural criticism as a "studies" practice offer any transdisciplinary evaluative standards to apply to individual pieces of cultural criticism? If not, if there is no clear methodological procedures or evaluative principles in cultural studies, it is hard to see how one might popularize it, teach it, make it into a recognized scholarly activity. In practical terms, one does not know how to communicate it to others or show students how to do it when it assumes so many different methodological forms. How does one create an academic department out of an outspokenly antidisciplinary practice? What criteria can faculty members jointly invoke when they are trying to make curricular and personnel decisions?

Once again, this is precisely the point. One reason for the generality of the term is to render such institutional questions unanswerable. Cultural studies practice mingles methods from a variety of fields, jumps from one cultural subject matter to another, simultaneously proclaims superiority to other institutionalized inquiries (on a correspondence to culture basis) and renounces its own institutionalization—gestures that strategically forestall disciplinary standards being applied to it. By studying culture in heterogenous ways, by clumping texts, events, persons, objects, and ideologies into a cultural whole (which, cultural critics say, is reality) and bringing a melange of logical argument, speculative propositions, empirical data, and political outlooks to bear upon it, cultural critics invent a new kind of investigation immune to methodological attack.

Literary Criticism: An Autoposy

Heather Glen

The Stance of Observation in William Blake's "London" 1983

In choosing to present his vision of social disaster thus, Blake was engaging with a familiar literary mode. The assumption of a stance of "observation," freely passing judgment on that which is before it, is common to much eighteenth-century literature: "There mark what ills the scholar's life assail".[1] But nowhere is it more prominent than in that which attempts to describe London, a place of bewildering diversity, changing and growing rapidly, in which a new kind of anonymity and alienation was becoming a remarked-upon fact of life. Indeed, it seems that in the literature of London the implications of this state were beginning to become an explicit preoccupation. Thus, Ben Sedgly in 1751:

> No man can take survey of this opulent city, without meeting in his way, many melancholy instances resulting from this consumption of spirituous liquors: poverty, diseases, misery and wickedness, are the daily observations to be made in every part of this great metropolis: whoever passes along the streets, may find numbers of abandoned wretches stretched upon the cold pavement, motionless and insensible, removed only by the charity of passengers from the danger of being crushed by carriages, trampled by horses, or strangled with filth in the common sewers.

"Take survey of," "meeting in his way," "observations to be made," "whoever passes along the streets may find"—the sense throughout is of an anonymous and freely observing stranger, rather than of a member of a society who sees himself as shaped by it and interacting with others within it. Perhaps such a perspective is natural in a documentary work such as Sedgly's. But this sense of the self in the city is central, too, to much of the most powerful imaginative literature of the century, literature which is after all not merely a description of or meditation upon the world, but the recreation of a certain mode of being within it. It is a sense that informs the novels of Defoe: the figures of Roxana and Colonel Jack and Moll Flanders move through the streets from adventure to adventure with a freedom from social constraint which is only possible because of the nature of London life. It is to be found in Gay's *Trivia* and *The Beggar's Opera*; in Boswell's *Journal*; in Johnson's *London*, and even in those of his essays which seem to have nothing to do with London at all:

> He that considers how little he dwells upon the condition of others, will learn how little the attention of others is attracted by himself. While we see multitudes passing before us, of whom perhaps not one appears to deserve our notice, or excites our sympathy, we should remember, that we likewise are lost in the same throng, that eye which happens to glance upon us is turned in a moment on him that follows us, and that the utmost which we can reasonably hope or fear is to fill a vacant hour with prattle, and be forgotten.[2]

Here, the tone is one of judicious moralizing. But the imagery is that of the confusing eighteenth-century London street, in which relations with one's fellow

---

[1] Johnson, "The Vanity of Human Wishes," I. 159. The opening lines of this poem are perhaps the dramatization *par excellence* of this stance: "Let observation with extensive view, / Survey mankind, from China to Peru; / Remark each anxious toil, each eager strife, / And watch the busy scenes of crouded life."
[2] Samuel Johnson, *The Rambler*, 159.

beings involve attracting attention, deserving notice, glancing and turning, even *exciting* sympathy: in which the other is the object of observation rather than one with whom one interacts. And the supposedly free individual who sees those who pass before him as a mighty spectacle is himself "lost in the same throng."

The eighteenth-century London street was not, then, merely a place where suffering and distress could be seen on a hitherto unprecedented scale: it was also a place where that sense of the other as object—often as feeble and wretched object—which Blake exposes in "The Human Abstract" ("we . . . make somebody Poor") was the dominant mode of relationship. And it is a sense which is an ironic point of reference in "London." For this poem begins with a speaker who seems to be a detached observer, who wanders "thro'" the streets of the city and "marks" the sights before him. Yet his is not the lively and distinctive London of Defoe or Gay or Johnson: what he records is not variety, but sameness. To him, both streets and river are simply "charter'd": the different faces which pass all bear the same message, "Marks of weakness, marks of woe." And the tight quatrain with its present indicative tense conveys not flexible responsiveness to constantly changing possibilities, but entrapment. What this speaker sees is fatally linked to the way in which he sees it. In the notebook draft, the second word of the third line was "see": Blake's alteration limits any incipient sense of freedom. The triple beat of "mark"—an active verb materializing into two plural nouns—registers a new consciousness of this "I'"s implication in the world "thro'" which he wanders. What he observes is the objectification of his own activity.

"Mark" is not the only change which Blake made in this stanza. In the notebook draft, the first two lines read:

I wander thro' each dirty street,
Near where the dirty Thames does flow.

The substitution, in the engraved version, of "charter'd," signals a complex process of poetic thought. For "charter'd" in 1793 was a word at the centre of political debate: a word whose accepted meaning of "granted privileges or rights" had been challenged by Paine a year earlier, in a book whose sales had by now reached 200,000:

It is a perversion of terms to say, that a charter gives rights. It operates by a contrary effect, that of taking rights away. Rights are inherently in all the inhabitants; but charters, by annulling those rights in the majority, leave the right by exclusion in the hands of a few . . . all charters have no other than an indirect negative operation. They do not give rights to A, but they make a difference in favour of A by taking away the right of B, and consequently are instruments of injustice.[3]

No contemporary of Blake's could have read the two altered opening lines of his poem as an objective description of the trading organization of the city. Their repetition of "charter'd" forces into prominence the newly, ironically recognized

[3]Paine, *Rights of Man*, ed. Henry Collins (Harmondsworth: Penguin, 1969) 242–43.

sense that the very language of "objective" description may be riddled with ideological significance: that beneath the assurance of polite usage may lurk another, "cheating" meaning. And this sense informs the stanza in a peculiar way. It is as though beneath the polite surface—the observer in London wandering the streets of a city whose "charter'd" organization he notes, as the guidebooks noted its commercial organization, and whose manifestations of distress and depravity he, like hundreds of other eighteenth-century writers, remarks—there is another set of meanings, which are the *reverse* of those such description could customarily bear. They are not meanings private to Blake: and they are meanings which focus in those sound-linked and repeated words, "mark" and "charter'd."

Vision and Disenchantment

Acknowledgments

Literary Acknowledgments

FICTION

Chinua Achebe: "Civil Peace" from *Girls At War and Other Stories* by Chinua Achebe. Copyright © 1972, 1973 by Chinua Achebe. Reprinted by permission of Doubleday, a division of Bantam Doubleday Dell Publishing Group, Inc., and Harold Ober Associates.

James Baldwin: "Sonny's Blues" was originally published in *Partisan Review*. Collected in *Going to Meet the Man* © 1965 by James Baldwin. Copyright renewed. Published by Vintage Books. Reprinted by arrangement with the James Baldwin Estate.

Mark Bauerlein: "What Is Cultural Studies?" excerpted from *Literary Criticism: An Autopsy* by Mark Bauerlein. Copyright © 1997 by the University of Pennsylvania Press. Reprinted by permission.

Jorge Luis Borges: "The Gospel According to Mark" from *Doctor Brodie's Report* by Jorge Luis Borges. Copyright © 1970, 1971, 1972 by Emece Editores, S.A., and Norman Thomas di Giovanni. Reprinted by permission of Dutton Signet, a division of Penguin Books USA, Inc.

T. Coraghessan Boyle: "Greasy Lake." From *Greasy Lake and Other Stories* by T. Coraghessan Boyle. Copyright © 1979, 1981, 1982, 1983, 1984, 1985 by T. Coraghessan Boyle. Reprinted by permission of Viking Penguin, a division of Penguin Books USA, Inc.

Robert Olen Butler: "A Good Scent from a Strange Mountain" from *A Good Scent from a Strange Mountain* by Robert Olen Butler. Copyright © 1992 by Robert Olen Butler. Reprinted by permission of Henry Holt and Company, Inc.

Raymond Carver: "Cathedral" from *Cathedral* by Raymond Carver. Copyright © 1981, 1982, 1983 by Raymond Carver. Reprinted by permission of Alfred A. Knopf, Inc.

John Cheever: "The Five-Forty-Eight." From *The Stories of John Cheever* by John Cheever. Copyright © 1954 by John Cheever. Reprinted by permission of Alfred A. Knopf, Inc.

Anton Chekhov: "The Lady with the Pet Dog" by Anton Chekhov, from *The Portable Chekhov* by Anton Chekhov, edited by Avrahm Yarmolinsky. Copyright 1947, © 1968 by Viking Penguin, Inc. Renewed © 1975 by Avrahm Yarmolinsky. Reprinted by permission of Viking Penguin, a division of Penguin Books USA, Inc.

Sandra Cisneros: "Barbie-Q" from *Woman Hollering Creek*. Copyright © 1991 by Sandra Cisneros. Published by Vintage Books, a division of Random House, Inc., New York, and originally in hardcover by Random House, Inc. Reprinted by permission of Susan Bergholz Literary Services, New York. All rights reserved.

Michael Clark: "James Baldwin's Blues." *CLA Journal* 26 (September, 1982). Reprinted by permission of the *CLA Journal*.

Ralph Ellison: "Battle Royal" from *Invisible Man* by Ralph Ellison. Copyright 1948 by Ralph Ellison. Reprinted by permission of Random House, Inc.

William Faulkner: "A Rose for Emily" from *Collected Stories of William Faulkner* by William Faulkner. Copyright 1930 and renewed 1958 by William Faulkner. "Barn Burning" from *Collected Stories of William Faulkner* by William Faulkner. Copyright 1950 by Random House, Inc. Copyright renewed 1977 by Jill Faulkner Summers. Both stories are reprinted by permission of Random House, Inc.

Stanley Fish: Excerpt from *Is There a Text in This Class?* by Stanley Fish. Cambridge, Mass.: Harvard University Press. Copyright © 1980 by the President and Fellows of Harvard College. Reprinted by permission of the publisher.

Sally Fitzgerald: "Southern Sources of 'A Good Man is Hard to Find'" from "Happy Endings" by Sally Fitzgerald. *Image,* Summer 1997. Reprinted by permission of *Image.*

Juliann Fleenor: "Gender and Pathology in 'The Yellow Wallpaper'" from "The Gothic Prism: Charlotte Perkins Gilman's Gothic Stories and Her Autobiography" in *The Female Gothic* by Juliann Fleenor (Montreal: Eden Press, 1983). Reprinted by permission of the author.

Mavis Gallant: "Across the Bridge" by Mavis Gallant. Copyright © 1993 by Mavis Gallant. Reprinted by permission of Random House, Inc., and McClelland & Stewart, Inc. *The Canadian Publishers.*

Gabriel García Márquez: All pages from "A Very Old Man With Enormous Wings" from *Leaf Storm and Other Stories* by Gabriel García Márquez, translated by Gregory Rabassa. Copyright © 1971 by Gabriel García Márquez. Reprinted by permission of HarperCollins Publishers, Inc.

Nadine Gordimer: "The Defeated" from *The Soft Voice of the Serpent* by Nadine Gordimer. Reprinted by permission of Russell & Volkening as agents for the author. Copyright 1952, renewed © 1980 by Nadine Gordimer.

Jakob and Wilhelm Grimm: "Godfather Death" from *The Juniper Tree and Other Tales by the Brothers Grimm*, translated by Lore Segal and Randall Jarrell with pictures by Maurice Sendak. Translation copyright © 1973 by Lore Segal. Pictures copyright © 1973 by Maurice Sendak. Reprinted by permission of Farrar, Straus & Giroux, Inc.

Ernest Hemingway: "A Clean, Well-Lighted Place." Reprinted with permission of Scribner, a division of Simon & Schuster, from *Winner Take Nothing* by Ernest Hemingway. Copyright 1933 by Charles Scribner's Sons. Copyright renewed © 1961 by Mary Hemingway. Excerpt from "An Afternoon with Hemingway" by Edward Stafford from *Writer's Digest*, 44 (December, 1964) reprinted by permission of *Writer's Digest*.

Daniel Hoffman: "The Father-Figure in 'The Tell-Tale Heart,'" from *Poe Poe Poe Poe Poe Poe Poe*. Baton Rouge: Louisiana State University Press, 1998. Copyright © 1972 by Daniel Hoffman. Reprinted by permission of the author.

Langston Hughes: "On the Road" from *Something in Common* by Langston Hughes. Copyright © 1963 by Langston Hughes. Copyright renewed © 1991 by Arnold Rampersad and Ramona Bass. Reprinted by permission of Hill and Wang, a division of Farrar, Straus & Giroux, Inc.

Zora Neale Hurston: "Sweat" from *Spunk: Selected Short Stories of Zora Neale Hurston*. Copyright © 1985 by Turtle Island Foundation. Reprinted by permission of the author's estate.

Shirley Jackson: *"The Lottery"* from *The Lottery* by Shirley Jackson. Copyright 1948, 1949 by Shirley Jackson. Renewal copyright 1976, 1977 by Laurence Hyman, Barry Hyman, Mrs. Sarah Webster, and Mrs. Joanne Schnurer. Reprinted by permission of Farrar, Straus & Giroux, Inc.

Gish Jen: "In the American Society." Copyright © 1986 by Gish Jen. First published in *Southern Review*. Reprinted by permission of the author from Maxine Groffsky Literary Agency.

Barbara Johnson: "Rigorous Unreliability" from *A World of Difference* by Barbara Johnson. Copyright © 1987. Reprinted by permission of Johns Hopkins University Press.

Franz Kafka: "The Metamorphosis" translated by Willa and Edwin Muir. From *Franz Kafka: The Complete Stories by Franz Kafka*. Copyright 1946, 1947, 1948, 1954, 1958, 1971 by Schocken Books, Pantheon Books, a division of Random House, Inc. Reprinted by permission of the publisher. Excerpt from *Conversations with Kafka* by Gustav Janouch, translated by Goronwy Rees. Copyright © 1968 by S. Fischer Verlag GmbH. Translation copyright © 1971 by S. Fischer Verlag GmbH. Reprinted by permission of New Directions Publishing Corp.

Jamaica Kincaid: "Girl" from *At the Bottom of the River* by Jamaica Kincaid. Copyright © 1978, 1983 by Jamaica Kincaid. Reprinted by permission of Farrar, Straus & Giroux, Inc.

D. H. Lawrence: "The Rocking-Horse Winner" by D. H. Lawrence, copyright 1933 by the Estate of D. H. Lawrence, renewed © 1961 by Angelo Ravagli and C. M. Weekley, Executors of the Estate of Frieda Lawrence, from *Complete Short Stories of D. H. Lawrence* by D. H. Lawrence. Used by permission of Viking Penguin, a division of Penguin Books USA, Inc.

SKY Lee: "The Soong Sisters" from *Bellydancer* by SKY Lee. Press Gang Publishers, 1994. Reprinted by permission of the publisher.

Ursula K. Le Guin: "The Ones Who Walk Away from Omelas." Copyright © 1973 by Ursula K. Le Guin; first appeared in *New Dimensions 3*. Reprinted by permission of the author and the author's agent, Virginia Kidd. "Note on 'The Ones Who Walk Away from Omelas,'" from *The Wind's Twelve Quarters* by Ursula K. Le Guin, Harper & Row, 1975.

Vincent B. Leitch: Excerpt from *Cultural Criticism, Literary Theory, Poststructuralism* by Vincent B. Leitch. Copyright © 1992, Columbia University Press. Reprinted by permission of the publisher.

Doris Lessing: "A Woman on a Roof" from *Stories* by Doris Lessing. Copyright © 1978 by Doris Lessing. Reprinted by permission of Alfred A. Knopf, Inc., and Jonathan Clowes Ltd. on behalf of Doris Lessing.

Virginia Llewellyn Smith: "Chekhov's Attitude to Romantic Love" from *Anton Chekhov and the Lady with the Dog* by Virginia Llewellyn Smith. Copyright © 1973 by Oxford University Press. Reprinted by permission of Oxford University Press.

Ralph Lombreglia: "Jungle Video" from *Men Under Water* by Ralph Lombreglia. Reprinted by permission of Darhansoff & Verrill Agency. "Creating 'Jungle Video'" by Ralph Lombreglia reprinted by permission of Darhansoff & Verrill Agency.

Bernard Malamud: "Angel Levine" from *The Stories of Bernard Malamud*. Copyright © 1950, 1951, 1952, 1954, 1955, 1956, 1958, 1959, 1961, 1963, 1968, 1972, 1973, 1983 by Bernard Malamud. Renewal copyright © 1977, 1979, 1980, 1982, 1983 by Bernard Malamud. All rights reserved. Reprinted by permission of Farrar, Straus & Giroux.

Katherine Mansfield: "Miss Brill" from *The Short Stories of Katherine Mansfield* by Katherine Mansfield. Copyright 1922 by Alfred A. Knopf, Inc., and renewed 1950 by John Middleton Murry. Reprinted by permission of the publisher. Excerpt from January 19, 1921, letter to Richard Murry from *The Letters of Katherine Mansfield*, edited by John Middleton Murry. Reprinted by permission of The Society of Authors as the literary representative of the Estate of Katherine Mansfield.

Bobbie Ann Mason: "Shiloh" from *Shiloh and Other Stories* by Bobbie Ann Mason. Copyright © 1982 by Bobbie Ann Mason. Reprinted by permission of HarperCollins Publishers, Inc.

W. Somerset Maugham: "An Appointment in Samarra" from *Sheppey* by W. Somerset Maugham. Copyright 1933 by W. Somerset Maugham. Reprinted by permission of Doubleday, a division of Bantam Doubleday Dell Publishing Group, Inc., and A.P. Watt Ltd. on behalf of The Royal Literary Fund.

Guy de Maupassant: "The Necklace" from *The Collected*

Novels and Stories of Guy de Maupassant by Guy de Maupassant, translated by E. Boyd. Copyright 1924 and renewed 1952 by Alfred A. Knopf, Inc. Reprinted by permission of the publisher.

Alice Munro: "How I Met My Husband" from *Something I've Been Meaning to Tell You* by Alice Munro. Copyright © 1974 by Alice Munro. Originally published by McGraw Hill Ryerson. Reprinted by permission of the Virginia Barber Literary Agency, Inc. All rights reserved.

Joyce Carol Oates: "Where Are You Going, Where Have You Been?" by Joyce Carol Oates, published in *The Wheel of Love and Other Stories* of 1970, published by Vanguard. Copyright © 1970 by Joyce Carol Oates. Reprinted by permission of John Hawkins & Associates, Inc.

Tim O'Brien: "The Things They Carried" from *The Things They Carried*. Copyright © 1990 by Tim O'Brien. Reprinted by permission of Houghton Mifflin Co./Seymour Lawrence. All rights reserved.

Flannery O'Connor: "A Good Man Is Hard to Find" from *A Good Man Is Hard to Find and Other Stories*. Copyright © 1953 by Flannery O'Connor and renewed 1981 by Regina O'Connor. Reprinted by permission of Harcourt Brace & Company. "Everything that Rises Must Converge" and "Revelation" from *Everything That Rises Must Converge* by Flannery O'Connor. Copyright © 1961, 1965 by the Estate of Mary Flannery O'Connor. Reprinted by permission of Farrar, Straus & Giroux, Inc. Excerpt from "On Her Own Work" and excerpt from "The Grotesque in Southern Fiction" from *Mystery and Manners* by Flannery O'Connor. Copyright © 1967, 1979 by the Estate of Mary Flannery O'Connor. Reprinted by permission of Farrar, Straus & Giroux, Inc.

Frank O'Connor: "First Confession" from *Collected Stories* by Frank O'Connor. Copyright 1951 by Frank O'Connor. Reprinted by permission of Alfred A. Knopf, Inc., and Joan Daves.

Tillie Olsen: "I Stand Here Ironing." Copyright © 1956, 1957, 1960, 1961 by Tillie Olsen. From *Tell Me a Riddle* by Tillie Olsen. Introduction by John Leonard. Reprinted by permission of Delacorte Press/Seymour Lawrence, a division of Bantam Doubleday Dell Publishing Group, Inc.

Katherine Anne Porter: "The Jilting of Granny Weatherall" from *Flowering Judas and Other Stories*. Copyright © 1930 and renewed 1958 by Katherine Anne Porter. Reprinted by permission of Harcourt Brace & Company.

Leslie Marmon Silko: "The Man to Send Rain Clouds." Copyright © 1981 by Leslie Marmon Silko. Reprinted from *Storyteller* by Leslie Marmon Silko, published by Seaver Books, New York, New York.

Isaac Bashevis Singer: "Gimple the Fool" by Isaac Bashevis Singer, translated by Saul Bellow. Copyright © 1953 by The Partisan Review, renewed © 1981 by Isaac Bashevis Singer. From *A Treasury of Yiddish Stories* by Irving Howe and Eliezer Greenberg. "Isaac Bashevis Singer" by Harold Flender, from *Writers At Work, Fifth Series*, by George Plimpton, editor. Introduction by F. du Plessix Gray. Copyright © 1981 by

The Paris Review. Both selections are reprinted by permission of Viking Penguin, a division of Penguin Books USA, Inc.

John Steinbeck: "The Chrysanthemums." Copyright © 1937, renewed © 1965 by John Steinbeck. From *The Long Valley* by John Steinbeck. Reprinted by permission of Viking Penguin, a division of Penguin Books USA, Inc.

Elizabeth Tallent: "No One's a Mystery" from *Time with Children* by Elizabeth Tallent. Copyright © 1987 by Elizabeth Tallent. First printed in *Time with Children*. Reprinted by permission of The Wylie Agency, Inc.

Amy Tan: "A Pair of Tickets." Reprinted by permission of The Putnam Publishing Group from *The Joy Luck Club* by Amy Tan. Copyright © 1989 by Amy Tan. Excerpt from "Mother Tongue" by Amy Tan, copyright © 1989 by Amy Tan. First appeared in "The Threepenny Review." Reprinted by permission of Amy Tan and the Sandra Dijkstra Literary Agency.

James Thurber: "The Catbird Seat." Copyright © 1945 James Thurber. Copyright © 1973 Helen Thurber & Rosemary A. Thurber. From *The Thurber Carnival*, published by HarperCollins. Reprinted by permission.

John Updike: "A & P." From *Pigeon Feathers and Other Stories* by John Updike. Copyright © 1962 by John Updike. Originally appeared in *The New Yorker*. Excerpt from *Picked-Up Pieces* by John Updike. Copyright © 1975 by John Updike. Both selections are reprinted by permission of Alfred A. Knopf, Inc.

Edmond L. Volpe: "'Barn Burning': A Definition of Evil" from *Faulkner, The Unappeased Imagination: A Collection of Critical Essays*, edited by Glen O. Carey.

Kurt Vonnegut: "Harrison Bergeron." From *Welcome to the Monkey House* by Kurt Vonnegut, Jr. Copyright © 1961 by Kurt Vonnegut, Jr. Reprinted by permission of Delacorte Press/Seymour Lawrence, a division of Bantam Doubleday Dell Publishing Group, Inc. "The Themes of Science Fiction" from *Meangin Quarterly*, 30, Autumn 1971.

Alice Walker: "Everyday Use" from *In Love and Trouble: Stories of Black Women* by Alice Walker. Copyright © 1973 by Alice Walker. Reprinted by permission of Harcourt Brace & Company.

Daniel P. Watkins: Excerpt from "Labor and Religion in D. H. Lawrence's 'The Rocking-Horse Winner.'" From *Studies In Short Fiction*, Volume 24, No. 3, Summer, 1987. Reprinted by permission of the author.

Eudora Welty: "A Visit of Charity" from *A Curtain of Green and Other Stories*. Copyright 1941 and renewed 1969 by Eudora Welty. Reprinted by permission of Harcourt Brace and Company.

William Carlos Williams: "The Use of Force" from *William Carlos Williams: The Doctor Stories*. Copyright 1933 by William Carlos Williams. Reprinted by permission of New Directions Publishing Corporation.

POETRY

Kim Addonizio: "First Poem for You." Copyright © 1994 by Kim Addonizio. Reprinted from *The Philosopher's Club* by Kim Addonizio, with the permission of BOA Editions, Ltd., Rochester, NY.

Francisco X. Alarcón: "The X in My Name" from *No Golden Gate for Us* by Francisco X. Alarcón. Copyright © 1993 by Francisco X. Alarcón. Reprinted by permission of Pennywhistle Press, Tesuque, NM 87574.

Dick Allen: "Night Driving" from *Flight and Pursuit, Poems* by Dick Allen. Copyright © 1987 by Dick Allen. Reprinted by permission of Louisiana State University Press.

Julia Alvarez: "33" and "The Women on My Mother's Side Were Known" from "33" in *Homecoming* by Julia Alvarez. Copyright © 1984, 1996 by Julia Alvarez. Published by Plume, an imprint of Dutton Signet, a division of Penguin USA; originally published by Grove Press. Reprinted by permission of Susan Bergholz Literary Services, New York. All rights reserved.

A. R. Ammons: "Coward." Reprinted by permission of the author.

James Applewhite: "The Story of a Drawer" © 1983, 1984, 1985, 1986 by James Applewhite. Reprinted from *Ode to the Chinaberry Tree and Other Poems* by permission of Louisiana State University Press.

John Ashbery: "The Cathedral Is" from *As We Know* by John Ashbery. Copyright © 1979 by John Ashbery. Reprinted by permission of Penguin USA. "At North Farm" from *A Wave* by John Ashbery. Copyright © 1984 by John Ashbery. Originally appeared in *The New Yorker*. Reprinted by permission of Georges Borchardt, Inc.

Margaret Atwood: "Siren Song" from *You Are Happy, Selected Poems 1965–1975*. Copyright © 1976 by Margaret Atwood. Reprinted by permission of Houghton Mifflin Co. and Oxford University Press, Canada. © Margaret Atwood 1990. All rights reserved. "Siren Song" from *Selected Poems 1966–1984* by Margaret Atwood. Copyright © 1990 by Margaret Atwood. Reprinted by permission of Oxford University Press Canada. "you fit into me" from *Power Politics* by Margaret Atwood. Copyright © 1971 by Margaret Atwood. (House of Anansi Press Ltd.). Reprinted by permission.

W. H. Auden: "James Watt" from *Academic Graffiti* by W. H. Auden and F. Sonjuste. Copyright © 1971 by W. H. Auden and F. Sonjuste. "The Unknown Citizen," "Musée des Beaux Arts," "As I Walked Out One Evening," and "Stop All the Clocks" from *W. H. Auden: Collected Poems*. Copyright © 1940 and renewed 1968 by W. H. Auden. Reprinted by permission of Random House, Inc. and Faber and Faber Ltd.

David R. Axelrod: "The Dead Have No Respect" from *The Chi of Poetry*. Reprinted by permission of Birnham Wood Graphics.

Roland Barthes: "The Death of the Author" from *Image/Music/Text* by Roland Barthes, translated by Stephen Heath. English translation © 1977 by Stephen Heath. Reprinted by permission of Hill and Wang, a division of Farrar, Straus & Giroux, Inc., and HarperCollins Publishers Limited.

Max Beerbohm: On the imprint of the first English edition of *The Works of Max Beerbohm*. Final two lines inscribed by Max Beerbohm in a presentation copy of his book. Used by permission of Sir Geoffrey Keynes.

Hilaire Belloc: "The Hippopotamus" from *Cautionary Verses* by Hilaire Belloc. Reprinted by permission of Peters Fraser & Dunlop.

Bruce Bennett: "The Lady Speaks Again" from *Taking Off* by Bruce Bennett (Orchises Press). Copyright © 1992 by Bruce Bennett. Reprinted by permission of the author.

Edmund Clerihew Bentley: "Sir Christopher Wren" from *Clerihews Complete* by E. C. Bentley, © E. C. Bentley. Reprinted by permission of Curtis Brown Ltd., London.

John Betjeman: "In Westminster Abbey" from *Collected Poems*. Reprinted by permission of John Murray (Publishers) Ltd.

Elizabeth Bishop: "The Fish," "Sestina," "Fillling Station," and "One Art" from *The Complete Poems 1927–1979* by Elizabeth Bishop. Copyright © 1979, 1983 by Alice Helen Methfessel. Reprinted by permission of Farrar, Straus & Giroux, Inc.

Harold Bloom: "Poetic Influence" from *A Map of Misreading* by Harold Bloom. Copyright © 1975 by Oxford University Press, Inc. Reprinted by permission.

Robert Bly: "Driving to Town Late to Mail a Letter" from *Silence in the Snow Fields* by Robert Bly (Wesleyan University Press). Copyright © 1959, 1960, 1961, 1962 by Robert Bly. Reprinted by permission of the author.

Louise Bogan: "The Dream" from *The Blue Estuaries* by Louise Bogan. Copyright © 1968 by Louise Bogan. Copyright renewed © 1996 by Ruth Limmer. Reprinted by permission of Farrar, Straus & Giroux, Inc.

Eavan Boland: "Anorexic" from *An Origin Like Water: Collected Poems 1967–1987* by Eavan Boland. Copyright © 1996 by Eavan Boland. Reprinted by permission of W. W. Norton & Company, Inc.

Anne Bradstreet: The Author to Her Book." Reprinted by permission of the publishers from *The Works of Anne Bradstreet*, edited by Jeannine Hensley, Cambridge, Mass.: Harvard University Press. Copyright © 1967 by the President and Fellows of Harvard College.

Richard Brautigan: "Haiku Ambulance" from *The Pill Versus the Springhill Mine Disaster*. Copyright © 1965 by Richard Brautigan. Reprinted by permission of Houghton Mifflin Company. All rights reserved.

Cleanth Brooks: "Excerpts from 'The Formalist Critic.' " Copyright 1951 by Cleanth Brooks. Originally appeared in *The Kenyon Review*. Reprinted by permission of the author.

Gwendolyn Brooks: "The Bean Eaters," "We Real Cool," "Southeast Corner," and "The Mother" from *Blacks* by Gwendolyn Brooks. Reprinted by permission of the author. Excerpt entitled "On 'We Real Cool' " from *Part One* by Gwendolyn Brooks. Reprinted by permission of the author.

Jennifer Brutschy: "Born Again" from *The San Francisco Haiku Anthology*, edited by J. Ball. Reprinted by permission of the author.

Taniguchi Buson: "I go . . ." from *The Essential Haiku* translated by Robert Hass. Copyright © 1994 by Robert Hass. First published by The Ecco Press in 1994. Reprinted by permission of The Ecco Press.

Thomas Carper: "Facts" from *Fiddle Lane* (The Johns

Hopkins University Press, 1991). Reprinted by permission of the publisher.

Hayden Carruth: "Let my snowtracks lead" from *Collected Shorter Poems: 1946–1991*. © 1992 by Hayden Carruth. Reprinted by permission of Copper Canyon Press, P.O. Box 217, Port Townsend, WA 98368.

Charles Causley: "I Saw a Jolly Hunter" from *Collected Poems 1951–1975*. Copyright © 1975 by Charles Causley. Reprinted by permission of Harold Ober Associates Incorporated.

Fred Chappell: "Narcissus and Echo." © 1985 by Fred Chappell. Reprinted from *Poems* by Fred Chappell by permission of Louisiana State University Press.

Kelly Cherry: "Advice to a Friend Who Paints" from *Lovers and Agnostics* by Kelly Cherry. Reprinted by permission of the author.

John Ciardi: "Most Like an Arch This Marriage." Copyright © 1958 by John Ciardi. Reprinted from *Selected Poems* by John Ciardi by permission of The University of Arkansas Press

Lucille Clifton: "homage to my hips" copyright © 1980 by University of Massachusetts Press. Now published in *good woman: poems and a memoir 1969–1980* by BOA Editions Ltd. Reprinted by permission of Curtis Brown, Ltd.

Judith Ortiz Cofer: "Quinceañera" from *Terms of Survival* by Judith Ortiz Cofer. (Houston: Arte Público Press, University of Houston, 1987). Reprinted by permission of Arte Público Press.

Billy Collins: "Embrace" from *The Apple That Astonished Paris*. Copyright © 1988 by Billy Collins. Reprinted by permission of The University of Arkansas Press.

Wendy Cope: "Lonely Hearts" and lines from "From Strugnell's Rubaiyat" from *Making Cocoa for Kingsley Amis* by Wendy Cope. © Wendy Cope 1986. Reprinted by permission of Faber and Faber Ltd. "Variation on Belloc's 'Fatigue'" from *Serious Concerns* by Wendy Cope. © Wendy Cope, 1992. Reprinted by permission of Faber and Faber Ltd.

Cid Corman: Translation of the haiku by Issa from *One Man's Moon: Fifty Haiku* (Gnomon Press, 1984). Reprinted by permission of the publisher and the author.

Frances Cornford: "The Watch" from *Collected Poems* by Frances Cornford. © 1954 Cressett Press, Hutchinson Publishing Group. Reprinted by permission of Random Century Group Ltd. on behalf of the Estate of Frances Cornford.

Robert Creeley: "Oh No" from *Collected Poems of Robert Creeley, 1945–1975*. Copyright © 1983 The Regents of the University of California. Reprinted by permission of the Regents of the University of California and the University of California Press.

Countee Cullen: "For a Lady I Know." Reprinted by permission of GRM Associates, Inc., agents for the Estate of Ida M. Cullen. From the book *Color* by Countee Cullen. Copyright 1925 by Harper & Brothers; copyright renewed 1953 by Ida M. Cullen.

E. E. Cummings: "a politician is an arse upon," "anyone lived in a pretty how town," "Buffalo Bill 's," "in Just-," "somewhere i have never travelled,gladly beyond" from *Complete Poems: 1904–1962* by E. E. Cummings, edited by George J. Firmage. Copyright 1923, 1925, 1926, 1931, 1935, 1938, 1939, 1940, 1944, 1945, 1946, 1947, 1948, 1949, 1950, 1951, 1952, 1953, 1954, 1955, 1956, 1957, 1958, 1959, 1960, 1961, 1962, 1963, 1966, 1967, 1968, 1972, 1973, 1974, 1975, 1976, 1977, 1978, 1980, 1981, 1982, 1983, 1984, 1985, 1986, 1987, 1988, 1989, 1990, 1991 by the Trustees for the E. E. Cummings Trust. Copyright © 1973, 1976, 1978, 1979, 1981, 1983, 1985, 1991 by George James Firmage. Reprinted by permission of Liveright Publishing Corporation.

J. V. Cunningham: "Friend, on this scaffold Thomas More lies dead . . ." from *The Exclusions of a Rhyme* by J. V. Cunningham. Reprinted with the permission of Jessie C. Cunningham and Swallow Press/University of Ohio Press.

H. D.: "Helen" and "Heat" from *Collected Poems* by Hilda Doolittle. Copyright © 1982 by the Estate of Hilda Doolittle. Reprinted by permission of New Directions Publishing Corporation.

Dick Davis: The translation of lines from "The Rubaiyat of Omar Khayyam" is reprinted by permission of the translator, Dick Davis.

Walter de la Mare: "The Listeners" from *The Complete Poems of Walter de la Mare*, 1969 (USA, 1970). Reprinted by permission of The Literary Trustees of Walter de la Mare and the Society of Authors as their representative.

Emanuel di Pasquale. "Rain." Reprinted by permission of the author.

James Dickey: "The Heaven of Animals" from *Poems 1957–1967*. Copyright © 1968 by James Dickey. Reprinted by permission of Simon & Schuster.

Emily Dickinson: "Success is counted sweetest," "Wild Nights – Wild Nights!" "I Felt a Funeral in my Brain," "I'm Nobody! Who are you?" "After great pain, a formal feeling comes," "Some keep the Sabbath going to Church," "Tell all the Truth, but tell it slant," "A Dying Tiger – moaned for Drink," "Because I could not stop for Death," "I heard a Fly buzz – when I died," "I like to see it lap the Miles," "I started Early – Took my Dog," "It dropped so low – in my Regard," "My Life had stood – a Loaded Gun," "The lightning is a yellow Fork," "The Soul selects her own Society" and "Victory comes late" reprinted by permission of the publishers and the Trustees of Amherst College from *The Poems of Emily Dickinson*, Thomas H. Johnson, ed. Cambridge, Mass.: The Belknap Press of Harvard University Press. Copyright © 1951, 1955, 1979, 1983 by the President and Fellows of Harvard College. "My Life had stood – a Loaded Gun" and "After great pain, a formal feeling comes" from *The Complete Poems of Emily Dickinson* by T. H. Johnson. Copyright 1929 by Martha Dickinson Bianchi; copyright © renewed 1957 by Mary L. Hampson. By permission of Little, Brown and Company.

Rita Dove: "Daystar" from *Thomas and Beulah* by Rita Dove. Reprinted by permission of Carnegie Mellon University Press. Copyright © 1986 by Rita Dove.

"Poem in Which I Refuse Contemplation" from *Grace Notes* by Rita Dove. Copyright © 1989 by Rita Dove. Reprinted by permission of the author and W. W. Norton & Company, Inc.

Richard Eberhart: "The Fury of Aerial Bombardment" from *Collected Poems 1930–1986* by Richard Eberhart. Copyright © 1988 by Richard Eberhart. Reprinted by permission of Oxford University Press, Inc.

Edward Field: "Curse of the Cat Woman." Copyright © 1992 by Edward Field. Reprinted from *Counting Myself Lucky: Selected Poems 1963–1992* with the permission of Black Sparrow Press.

Terry Ehret: "Papyrus" from *Lost Body.* © 1992 by Terry Ehret. Reprinted by permission of Copper Canyon Press, P. O. Box 271, Port Townsend, WA 98368.

T. S. Eliot: "The Music of Poetry" from *On Poetry and Poets* by T. S. Eliot. Copyright © 1957 by T. S. Eliot. Copyright © renewed 1985 by Valerie Eliot. Reprinted by permission of Farrar, Straus & Giroux, Inc. and Faber & Faber Ltd. "The Love Song of J. Alfred Prufrock" from *Prufrock and Other Observations.* "The Winter Evening Settles Down" from *Preludes* by T. S. Eliot. "The Boston Evening Transcript" from *Prufrock and Other Observations* by T. S. Eliot. Reprinted by permission of Faber and Faber Ltd. "Virginia" and "Journey of the Magi" from *Collected Poems 1909–1962* by T. S. Eliot. Copyright 1936 by Harcourt Brace & Company, copyright © 1963 by T. S. Eliot. Reprinted by permission of the publishers, Harcourt Brace & Company and Faber and Faber Ltd.

Louise Erdrich: "Indian Boarding School: The Runaways" from *Jacklight Poems* by Louise Erdrich. © 1984 by Louise Erdrich. Reprinted by permission of Henry Holt & Co., Inc.

Abbie Huston Evans: "Wing-Spread." Reprinted from *Collected Poems* by Abbie Huston Evans, by permission of the University of Pittsburgh Press. Copyright 1950 by Abbie Huston Evans.

Gene Fehler: "If Richard Lovelace Became a Free Agent." Reprinted by permission of the author.

Leslie A. Fiedler: "The Relationship of Poet and Poem" from *No! In Thunder* by Leslie A. Fiedler. Copyright © 1960 by Leslie A. Fiedler. Reprinted by permission of Stein & Day, a division of Madison Books, Lanham, MD 20763.

Edward Field: "Curse of the Cat Woman." Copyright © 1992 by Edward Field. Reprinted from *Counting Myself Lucky: Selected Poems 1963–1992* with the permission of Black Sparrow Press.

Carolyn Forché: "The Colonel" from *The Country Between Us* by Carolyn Forché. Copyright © 1980 by Carolyn Forché. Reprinted by permission of HarperCollins Publishers.

Robert Francis: "Catch" from *The Orb Weaver.* Copyright © 1960 by Robert Francis, Wesleyan University Press by permission of University Press of New England.

Robert Frost: "Fire and Ice," "The Silken Tent," "The Secret Sits," "Desert Places," "Never Again Would Birds' Song be the Same," "Acquainted With The Night," "Nothing Gold Can Stay," "Stopping By Woods on a Snowy Evening," and "Design" from *The Poetry of Robert Frost,* edited by Edward Connery Lathem. Copyright 1923, 1928, 1936, 1951 by Robert Frost, © 1964, 1975 by Lesley Frost Ballantine, © 1969 by Henry Holt & Co., Inc. Reprinted by permission of Henry Holt & Co., Inc.

Northrop Frye: "Mythic Archetypes" from *Anatomy of Criticism.* Copyright © 1957, renewed 1985 by Princeton University Press. Reprinted by permission of Princeton University Press.

Alice Fulton: "What I Like" from *Dance Script with Electric Ballerina* (reissued by University of Illinois Press 1996). Copyright © 1983, 1992, 1994, 1995, 1996, 1997 by Alice Fulton.

Tess Gallagher: "I Stop Writing the Poem." Copyright 1992 by Tess Gallagher. Reprinted from *Moon Crossing Bridge* with the permission of Graywolf Press, Saint Paul, Minnesota.

Sandra M. Gilbert and Susan Gubar: "Editors' introduction to Emily Dickinson" from *The Norton Anthology of Literature by Women: The Tradition in English* by Sandra M. Gilbert and Susan Gubar. Copyright © 1985 by Sandra M. Gilbert and Susan Gubar. Reprinted by permission of W. W. Norton & Company, Inc.

Gary Gildner: "First Practice" from *First Practice* by Gary Gildner. Reprinted by permission of the University of Pittsburgh Press. © 1969 the University of Pittsburgh Press.

Allen Ginsberg: "A Supermarket in California" from *Collected Poems 1947–1980 of Allen Ginsberg.* Copyright © 1955, 1980 by Allen Ginsberg. Reprinted by permission of HarperCollins Publishers, Inc.

Dana Gioia: "California Hills in August" from *Daily Horoscope* (Graywolf Press) Copyright © 1986 by Dana Gioia. Originally in *The New Yorker.*

Louise Glück: "Mock Orange" from *The First Four Books of Poems* by Louise Glück. Copyright © 1995 by Louise Glück. Published by The Ecco Press. Reprinted by permission of The Ecco Press. "The Gold Lily" from *The Wild Iris* by Louise Glück. Copyright © 1992 by Louise Glück. Published by The Ecco Press. Reprinted by permission of The Ecco Press.

Robert Graves and Omar Ali-Shah. Lines from *The Rubaiyat of Omar Kahayyam,* translated by Robert Graves and Omar Ali-Shah (Doubleday). Reprinted by permission of Carcanet Press Limited. "Counting the Beats" from *Collected Poems* by Robert Graves. Excerpt from *The Crowning Privilege* by Robert Graves. Reprinted by permission of Curtis Brown, Ltd. Copyright © 1955, Robert Graves, renewed. Copyright © 1967, Robert Graves, renewed. "Down, Wanton, Down!" from *Collected Poems* by Robert Graves. Copyright © 1988 by Robert Graves. Reprinted by permission of Oxford University Press, Inc. and A. P. Watt on behalf of the Estate of Robert Graves.

Emily Grosholz: "Letter from Germany" in *The River Painter.* Copyright © 1984 by Emily Grosholz. Used with permission of the author and the University of Illinois Press.

Ronald Gross: "Yield" from *Pop Poems* by Ronald Gross. Copyright © 1967 by Ronald Gross. Reprinted by permission of Simon & Schuster, Inc.

Arthur Guiterman: "On the Vanity of Earthly Greatness." Copyright © 1936 by E. P. Dutton & Co. Reprinted from *Gaily the Troubadour* by permission of Louise H. Sclove.

Thom Gunn: "Jamesian" from *The Man With Night Sweats*. Copyright © 1994 by Thom Gunn. Reprinted by permission of Farrar, Straus & Giroux, Inc. and Faber and Faber Ltd.

R. S. Gwynn: "Scenes from the Playroom." Reprinted from *The Drive-In: Poems* by R. S. Gwynn, by permission of the University of Missouri Press. Copyright © 1986 by the author.

John Haines: "Winter News" from *Winter News*. Copyright 1966 by John Haines, Wesleyan University Press by permission of University Press of New England.

Donald Hall: "Names of Horses" from *Old and New Poems* by Donald Hall. Copyright © 1990 by Donald Hall. Reprinted by permission of Houghton Mifflin Company. All rights reserved. Originally published in *The New Yorker*.

Penny Harter: "broken bowl" from *In the Broken Curve* by Penny Harter. Copyright © 1984 by Penny Harter. Reprinted by permission of Burnt Lake Press.

Geoffrey Hartman: "On Wordsworth's 'A Slumber Did My Spirit Seal'" from "Elation in Hegel and Wordsworth" in *The Unremarkable Wordsworth* by Geoffrey Hartman. Copyright © 1987 by the University of Minnesota. Reprinted by permission of the University of Minnesota Press.

Robert Hayden: "The Whipping." Copyright © 1966 by Robert Hayden. "Those Winter Sundays." Copyright © 1966 by Robert Hayden from *Collected Poems of Robert Hayden*, Frederick Glaysher, editor. Reprinted by permission of Liveright Publishing Corporation.

Seamus Heaney: "Digging" and "Mother of the Groom" from *Poems 1965–1975* by Seamus Heaney. Copyright © 1980 by Seamus Heaney. Reprinted by permission of Farrar, Straus & Giroux, Inc., and Faber and Faber Ltd.

Anthony Hecht: "Adam" from *Collected Earlier Poems* by Anthony Hecht. Copyright © 1990 by Anthony E. Hecht. Reprinted by permission of Alfred A. Knopf, Inc.

Geoffrey Hill: "Merlin" from *Collected Poems* by Geoffrey Hill. Copyright © 1985 by Geoffrey Hill. Reprinted by permission of Oxford University Press.

Jonathan Holden: "The Names of the Rapids" from *The Names of the Rapids* by Jonathan Holden (Amherst: University of Massachusetts Press, 1985) copyright © 1985 by Jonathan Holden.

John Hollander: "Swan and Shadow" from *Types of Shape* by John Hollander. Copyright © 1969 by John Hollander. Reprinted by permission of the author.

Garrett Hongo: "The Cadence of Silk" from *The River of Heaven* by Garrett Hongo. Copyright © 1981, 1983, 1985, 1986, 1987, 1988 by Garrett Hongo. Reprinted by permission of Alfred A. Knopf, Inc.

A. D. Hope: "Imperial Adam" by A. D. Hope from *Collected Poems*. © 1968 A. D. Hope. Reprinted by permission of Collins/Angus & Robertson Publishers.

Barbara Howes: "Looking up at Leaves" from *Collected Poems* by Barbara Howes. Copyright © 1966 by Barbara Howes. Reprinted by permission of The University of Arkansas Press.

Andrew Hudgins: "Elegy for My Father, Who Is Not Dead" from *The Never-Ending*. Copyright © 1991 by Andrew Hudgins. Reprinted by permission of Houghton Mifflin Company. All rights reserved.

Langston Hughes: "Dream Deferred" from *The Panther and the Lash* by Langston Hughes. Copyright © 1951 by Langston Hughes. Reprinted by permission of Alfred A. Knopf, Inc. "Dream Boogie," "Theme for English B." "Two Somewhat Different Epigrams," "Homecoming," "Mother to Son," "The Weary Blues," "I, Too," "Song for a Dark Girl," "Island," "Subway Rush Hour," "Sliver," from *Collected Poems* by Langston Hughes. Copyright © 1994 by The Estate of Langston Hughes. "The Negro Speaks of Rivers." Copyright 1926 by Alfred A. Knopf, Inc., and renewed 1954 by Langston Hughes from *Selected Poems of Langston Hughes*. Reprinted by permission of Alfred A. Knopf, Inc. "The Negro Artist and the Racial Mountain" (The Nation). Copyright © 1926 by Langston Hughes. Copyright renewed 1980 by George Houston Bass.

Kobayshi Issa: "Cricket." Translated by Robert Bly. Reprinted from *Ten Poems by Issa*, English versions by Robert Bly, Floating Island, 1992. Copyright 1972, 1992 by Robert Bly. Reprinted with his permission.

Mark Jarman: "Unholy Sonnet: After the Praying" reprinted by permission of the author.

Randall Jarrell: "The Death of the Ball Turret Gunner" and "Next Day" from *The Complete Poems* by Randall Jarrell. Copyright © 1969 by Mrs. Randall Jarrell. Reprinted by permission of Farrar, Straus & Giroux, Inc.

Robinson Jeffers: "The Beaks of Eagles" reprinted from *The Collected Poetry of Robinson Jeffers*, Volume Two, 1928–1938, edited by Tim Hunt with the permission of the publishers, Stanford University Press. Copyright © 1938 and renewed 1966 by Donnan Jeffers and Garth Jeffers. Copyright © 1995 by the Board of Trustees of the Leland Stanford Junior University. "Hands." Copyright 1929 and renewed © 1957 by Robinson Jeffers. From *The Selected Poetry of Robinson Jeffers*. Reprinted by permission of Random House, Inc.

Donald Justice: "On the Death of Friends in Childhood" from *The Summer Anniversaries*. Copyright 1981 by Donald Justice. "Men at Forty" from *Night Light*. Copyright 1967 by Donald Justice. Both poems reprinted by permission of the author.

Alfred Kazin: excerpt from *An American Procession*. Reprinted by permission of Alfred A. Knopf, Inc. Copyright © 1984 by Alfred Kazin.

Weldon Kees: "For My Daughter." Reprinted from *The Collected Poems of Weldon Kees*, edited by Donald Justice, by permission of the University of Nebraska Press. Copyright © 1975 by the University of Nebraska Press.

Hugh Kenner: "Imagism" from *The Pound Era* by Hugh Kenner. Copyright © 1971 by Hugh Kenner. Reprinted by permission of the University of California Press.

Jane Kenyon: "The Suitor" from *From Room to Room*. © 1978 by Jane Kenyon. Reprinted courtesy of Alice

James Books, 33 Richdale Avenue, Cambridge, MA 02138.

Hugh Kingsmill: "What, Still Alive at Twenty-Two?" from *The Best of Hugh Kingsmill*. Reprinted by permission of Victor Gollancz Ltd.

Etheridge Knight: "Making Jazz Swing In" from *Strong Measures*. Edited by P. Dacey and D. Jauss (HarperCollins). Reprinted by permission of the author.

Yusef Komunjakaa: "Facing It" from *Dien Kai Dau*. Copyright 1988 by Yusef Komunyakaa, Wesleyan University Press by permission of University Press of New England.

Ted Kooser: "A Child's Grave Marker" from *One World at a Time*, by Ted Kooser. © 1985. Reprinted by permission of the University of Pittsburgh Press. "Carrie" from *Sure Signs, New and Selected Poems*, by Ted Kooser. © 1980. Reprinted by permission of the University of Pittsburgh Press.

Robert Langbaum: "On Robert Browning's 'My Last Duchess' " from *The Poetry of Experience* by Robert Langbaum. Copyright © 1957, 1986 by Robert Langbaum. Reprinted by permission of the publisher, The University of Chicago Press.

Philip Larkin: "Aubade" and "Home is so Sad" from *Collected Poems* by Philip Larkin, edited by Anthony Twaite. Copyright © 1988, 1989 by the Estate of Philip Larkin. Reprinted by permission of Farrar, Straus & Giroux, Inc., and Faber and Faber Ltd. "Poetry of Departures" is reprinted from *The Less Deceived* by Philip Larkin by permission of The Marvell Press, England and Australia. Copyright © The Marvell Press 1955, 1960.

D. H. Lawrence: "Bavarian Gentians" from *The Complete Poems of D. H. Lawrence* by D. H. Lawrence. Copyright © 1964, 1971 by Angelo Ravagli and C. M. Weekley, executors of the Estate of Frieda Lawrence Ravagli. Used by permission of Penguin Books USA.

Irving Layton: "The Bull Calf" from *A Red Carpet for the Sun*. (McClelland & Stewart) Reprinted by permission of the author.

Brad Leithauser: "A Venus Flytrap" from *Odd Carnivore* from *Hundreds of Fireflies* by Brad Leithauser. Copyright © 1982 by Brad Leithauser. Reprinted by permission of Alfred A. Knopf, Inc.

John Lennon/Paul McCartney: "Eleanor Rigby." Words and Music by John Lennon and Paul McCartney. © 1966, renewed 1994 Sony/ATV Songs LLC. Administered by EMI Blackwood Music Inc. (BMI). All rights reserved. International copyright secured. Used by permission.

Denise Levertov: "Leaving Together" and "Six Variations, III" from *Poems 1960–1967* by Denise Levertov. Copyright © 1958, 1963, 1964, 1969 by Denise Levertov Goodman. "Leaving Together" was first published in *Poetry*. Reprinted by permission of New Directions Publishing Corporation.

Phillis Levin: "Brief Bio" from *The Afterimage*. Reprinted by permission of Copper Beech Press.

Philip Levine: "Animals Are Passing from Our Lives." Reprinted from *Not This Pig*. © 1968 by Philip Levine. Wesleyan University Press. By permission of University Press of New England.

Janet Lewis: "Girl Help" from *Poems Old & New, 1918–1978* by Janet Lewis. Reprinted by permission of Ohio University Press/Swallow Press, Athens.

Shirley Geok-lin Lim: "To Li Po" from *Crossing the Peninsula & Other Poems*, Heinemann Education Books (Asia) Ltd. © Shirley Lim 1980. Reprinted by permission of the author.

Robert Lowell: "Skunk Hour" from *Life Studies* by Robert Lowell. Copyright © 1956, 1959 by Robert Lowell. Copyright renewed © 1987 by Harriet Lowell, Sheridan Lowell, and Caroline Lowell. Reprinted by permission of Farrar, Straus & Giroux, Inc.

Georg Lukacs: "Content Determines Form" from *Realism in Our Time*. © 1962 Merlin Press Ltd., © 1964 George Steiner. Reprinted by permission.

Archibald MacLeish: "The End of the World" from *Collected Poems 1917–1982* by Archibald MacLeish. Copyright © 1985 by The Estate of Archibald MacLeish. Reprinted by permission of Houghton Mifflin Co. All rights reserved.

Charles Martin: "Taken Up" from *Room for Error* (University of Georgia Press, 1978). Reprinted by permission of the author.

John Masefield: "Cargoes" from *Poems*. Reprinted by permission of The Society of Authors as the literary representative of the Estate of John Masefield.

David Mason: "Song of the Powers" from *The Country I Remember* by David Mason. Reprinted by permission of Story Line Press. "Song of the Powers" first appeared in *The Sewanee Review*.

Paul McCartney: Extract from "The Beatles in Their Own Words" by Miles. Used by permission of the publisher, Omnibus Press, 8/9 Frith Street, London W1V 5TZ.

Claude McKay: "America" from *Selected Poems of Claude McKay*. Published by Harcourt Brace Jovanovich, 1981. By permission of the Arachives of Claude McKay: Carl Cowl, Administrator.

Rod McKuen: "Thoughts on Capital Punishment" from *Stanyan Street and Other Sorrows* by Rod McKuen. Copyright © 1954, 1960, 1961, 1962, 1963, 1964, 1965, 1966 by Rod McKuen. Reprinted by permission of Random House, Inc.

Lynne McMahon: "The Lost Child" from *Devolution of the Nude* by Lynne McMahon. Reprinted by permission of David R. Godine, Publisher, Inc. Copyright © 1993 by Lynne McMahon.

Wallace D. McRae: "Reincarnation" from *Cowboy Curmudgeon and Other Poems*. Reprinted by permission of the author.

Samuel Menashe: "The Shrine Whose Shape I Am" from *Collected Poems* by Samuel Menashe. Copyright © 1986 by Samuel Menashe. Reprinted by permission of The National Poetry Foundation.

James Merrill: "Charles on Fire" from *Selected Poems 1946–1985* by James Merrill. Copyright © 1992 by James Merrill. Reprinted by permission of Alfred A. Knopf.

W. S. Merwin: "Song of Man Chipping an Arrowhead" from *Writings to an Unfinished Accompaniment* © 1969, 1970, 1971, 1972, 1973 by W. S. Merwin. Reprinted by permission of Georges Borchardt, Inc.

James Michie: Translation of Ode XI, *The Odes of Horace, Book I*. Copyright © 1963 by James Michie. Reprinted by permission of Washington Square Press and Pocket Books, divisions of Simon & Schuster, Inc.

Miles: Extract from *The Beatles in Their Own Words* by Miles. Used by permission of the publisher, Omnibus Press, 8/9 Frith Street, London W1V 5TZ.

Josephine Miles: "Reason" from *Poems 1930–1960* by Josephine Miles. Copyright © 1960 by Indiana University Press. Reprinted by permission.

Edna St. Vincent Millay: "Counting-out Rhyme" and Sonnet XLVII of *Fatal Interview*. Copyright © 1928, 1931, 1955, 1958 by Edna St. Vincent Millay and Norma Millay Ellis. All rights reserved. Reprinted by permission of Elizabeth Barnett, literary executor.

Brett C. Millier: "On Elizabeth Bishop's 'One Art.' " Copyright © 1993 by Brett C. Millier. Used by permission of the author. A fuller treatment of the subject appears in *Elizabeth Bishop: Life and the Memory of It* by Brett C. Millier (University of California Press, 1993). Lines from the first draft of "One Art" are quoted by permission of the Special Collections of the Vassar College Libraries and Elizabeth Bishop's literary executor, Alice H. Methfessell.

N. Scott Momaday: "Similie" from *Angle of Geese and Other Poems* by N. Scott Momaday. Reprinted by permission of David R. Godine, Publisher, Inc. Copyright © 1974 by N. Scott Momaday.

Marianne Moore: "Silence." Copyright 1935 by Marianne Moore; copyright renewed © 1963 by Marianne Moore and T. S. Eliot. "The Mind is an Enchanting Thing." Copyright 1944 by Marianne Moore; copyright renewed © 1972 by Marianne Moore. Both poems reprinted with the permission of Simon & Schuster from *Collected Poems of Marianne Moore*.

Frederick Morgan: "The Master" from *Poems: New and Selected*. Copyright 1987 by Frederick Morgan. Used with the permission of the author and the University of Illinois Press.

Arakida Moritake: "The Falling Flower." Translated by Babette Deutsch. Reprinted from *Poetry Handbook: A Dictionary of Terms*. The Universal Library, Grosset & Dunlap. © 1957 and 1962 by Babette Deutsch. Second edition, revised and enlarged. Reprinted by permission of HarperCollins Publishers, Inc.

Howard Moss: "Shall I Compare Thee to a Summer's Day?" from *A Swim off the Rocks*. Copyright © 1976 by Howard Moss. Reprinted by permission of Richard Evans.

Howard Nemerov: "The Snow Globe" from *The Collected Poems of Howard Nemerov*. Copyright © 1977 by Howard Nemerov. "The War in the Air" from *Trying Conclusions* by Howard Nemerov. Reprinted by permission of Margaret Nemerov.

Pablo Neruda: "Muchos Somos" from *Extravagaria* by Pablo Neruda. Translated by Alastair Reid. Translation copyright © 1974 by Alastair Reid. Originally published as *Estravagario* copyright © 1958 by Editorial Losada, S.A., Buenos Aires. Reprinted by permission of Farrar, Straus & Giroux, Inc.

Lorine Niedecker: "Popcorn-can cover" from *From This Condensery: The Complete Writings of Lorine Niedecker*. Edited by Robert J. Bertolf. Copyright © Cid Corman, Literary Executor of the Lorine Niedecker Estate. Reprinted by permission.

Naomi Shihab Nye: "Famous" from *Hugging the Jukebox*. Reprinted by permission of Theodore W. Macri, as agent for Naomi Shihab Nye.

Sharon Olds: "Rites of Passage" from *The Dead and the Living* by Sharon Olds. Copyright © 1983 by Sharon Olds. Reprinted by permission of Alfred A. Knopf, Inc. "The One Girl at the Boys Party" from *The Dead and the Living* by Sharon Olds. Copyright © 1975, 1978, 1979, 1980, 1981, 1982, 1983 by Sharon Olds. Reprinted by permission of Alfred A. Knopf, Inc.

Wilfred Owen: "Dulce et Decorum Est," "Anthem for Doomed Youth," and "On War Poems" from *Collected Poems* by Wilfred Owen. Copyright 1946, 1963 by Chatto & Windus Ltd. Reprinted by permission of New Directions Publishing Corporation.

José Emilio Pacheco: "High Treason." Written in Spanish by José Emilio Pacheco and translated by Alastair Reid. From *Weathering* (E. P. Dutton). © 1977, 1978 by Alastair Reid. Reprinted by permission.

Dorothy Parker: "Resumé" coypyright 1926, 1928, renewed 1954 © 1956 by Dorothy Parker, from *The Portable Dorothy Parker* by Dorothy Parker, Introduction by Brendan Gill. Used by permission of Viking Penguin, a division of Penguin Books USA, Inc.

Linda Pastan. "Ethics" from *Waiting for My Life* by Linda Pastan. Copyright © 1981 by Linda Pastan. Reprinted by permission of W. W. Norton & Company, Inc. "Jump Cabling" from *Light Year '85*. Copyright © 1984 by Linda Pastan. Reprinted by permission of the author.

Octavio Paz: "With Our Eyes Shut" from *The Collected Poems of Octavio Paz 1957–1987*. Copyright © 1986 by Octavio Paz and Eliot Weinberger. Reprinted by permission of New Directions Publishing Corporation. Translation reprinted by permission of John Felstiner.

Robert Phillips: "Running on Empty" from *Personal Accounts: New and Selected Poems 1966–1986* (Princeton: Ontario Review Press, 1986). Copyright © 1981, 1986 by Robert Phillips. Reprinted by permission.

Daryl Pinckney: "Langston Hughes." Excerpted from "Suitcase in Harlem" by Daryl Pickney, *The New York Review of Books*, February 16, 1989. Reprinted by permission from *The New York Review of Books*. Copyright © 1989 Nyrev, Inc.

Sylvia Plath: "Metaphors" (Copyright © 1960 by Ted Hughes), "Lady Lazarus" (Copyright © 1963 by Ted Hughes), and "Daddy" (Copyright © 1963 by Ted Hughes) from *The Collected Poems of Sylvia Plath*, edited by Ted Hughes. Reprinted by permission of HarperCollins Publishers and Faber and Faber Ltd.

Ezra Pound: "The River-Merchant's Wife: a Letter" and "The Garret" from *Personae* by Ezra Pound. Copyright © 1926 by Ezra Pound. Reprinted by permission of New Directions Publishing Corporation.

Craig Raine: "A Martian Sends a Postcard Home" from *A Martian Sends a Postcard Home* by Craig Raine. Reprinted by permission of Oxford University Press.

Dudley Randall: "A Different Image from Cities Burning" by Dudley Randall (Broadside Press). Copyright ©

1966 by Dudley Randall. Reprinted by permission of Broadside Press. "Ballad of Birmingham" from *Cities Burning* reprinted by permission of the author.

John Crowe Ransom: "Bells for John Whiteside's Daughter" from *Selected Poems* by John Crowe Ransom. Copyright © 1924 by Alfred A. Knopf, Inc. Copyright renewed 1952 by John Crowe Ransom. Reprinted by permission of Alfred A. Knopf, Inc.

Henry Reed: "Naming of Parts" from *A Map of Verona* by Henry Reed. © 1946 The Executor of the Estate of Henry Reed. Reprinted by permission of John Tydeman.

Alastair Reid: "High Treason," "Speaking a Foreign Language," and excerpt from "Neruda and Borges." Reprinted by permission; © 1996 Alastair Reid. Originally in *The New Yorker*. All rights reserved.

Carter Revard: "Birch Canoe" from *An Eagle Nation*. Sun Tracks, Vol. 24. Copyright © 1993 by University of Arizona Press . Reprinted by permission of University of Arizona Press.

Adrienne Rich: "Aunt Jennifer's Tigers," "Peeling Onions," "Power," and "Women" from *The Fact of a Doorframe: Poems Selected and New, 1950–1984* by Adrienne Rich. Copyright © 1984 by Adrienne Rich. Copyright © 1975, 1978 by W. W. Norton & Company, Inc. Copyright © 1981 by Adrienne Rich. Excerpt from "When We Dead Awaken: Writing as Re-Vision" from *On Lies, Secrets, and Silence: Selected Prose 1966–1978* by Adrienne Rich. Copyright © 1979 by W. W. Norton & Company, Inc. Reprinted by permission of the author and W. W. Norton & Company, Inc.

John Ridland: "The Lazy Man's Haiku." Reprinted by permission of the author.

Theodore Roethke: "Elegy for Jane." Copyright 1950 by Theodore Roethke. "I Knew a Woman." Copyright 1954 by Theodore Roethke. "Root Cellar." Copyright 1943 by Modern Poetry Association, Inc. "My Papa's Waltz." Copyright 1942 by Hearst Magazines, Inc., from *The Collected Poems of Theodore Roethke* by Theodore Roethke. Used by permission of Doubleday, a division of Bantam Doubleday Dell Publishing Group, Inc.

Wendy Rose: "For the White Poets Who Would Be Indian" from *Bone Dance: New and Selected Poems 1965–1993*. Sun Tracks, Vol. 27. © 1994 by University of Arizona Press.

Run, D.M.C: "Peter Piper," words and music by J. Simmons and D. McDaniels, as performed by Run-D.M.C from the album "Raising Hell." © 1986 Protoons, Inc. All Rights Reserved. International Copyright Secured. Used by Permission.

Kay Ryan: "Turtle" from *Flamingo Watching*. Reprinted by permission of Copper Beech Press.

Mary Jo Salter: "Welcome to Hiroshima" from *Henry Purcell in Japan* by Mary Jo Salter. Copyright © 1984 by Mary Jo Salter. Reprinted by permission of Alfred A. Knopf, Inc.

Carl Sandburg: "Fog" from *Chicago Poems* by Carl Sandburg. Copyright 1916 by Holt, Rinehart and Winston, Inc. and renewed 1944 by Carl Sandburg. Reprinted by permission of Harcourt Brace & Company.

Carole Satyamurti: "I Shall Paint My Nails Red" © Carole Satyamurti 1990. Reprinted from *Changing the Subject* by Carole Satyamurti (1990) by permission of Oxford University Press.

Gertrude Schnackenberg: "Signs" from The Lamplite Answer. Copyright © 1982, 1985 by Gjertrud Schnackenberg. Reprinted by permission of Farrar, Straus & Giroux, Inc.

Robert Scholes: "How Do We Make a Poem?" Excerpt from *Semiotics and Interpretation* by Robert Scholes. Copyright © 1982 by Yale University. Reprinted by permission of Yale University Press.

Bertie Sellers: "In the Counselor's Waiting Room" from *Morning of the Red-Tailed Hawk* by Bertie Sellers. (University Center, MI: GreenRiver Press, 1981). Reprinted by permission.

Anne Sexton: "Cinderella" from *Transformations*. Copyright © 1971 by Anne Sexton. "Her Kind" from *To Bedlam and Part Way Back*. Copyright © 1960 by Anne Sexton, © renewed 1988 by Linda G. Sexton. Letter from *Anne Sexton: A Self-Portrait in Letters*. Edited by Linda Gray Sexton and Lois Ames. Copyright © 1977 by Linda Gray Sexton and Loring Conant, Jr., executors of the will of Anne Sexton. Reprinted by permission of Houghton Mifflin Co. All rights reserved.

Elaine Showalter: Excerpt from "Toward a Feminist Criticism." Copyright © 1979 by Elaine Showalter. From Elaine Showalter, ed., *Feminist Criticism: Essays on Women, Literature, and Theory* (Pantheon, 1985). Reprinted by permission of the author.

Stephen Shu-Ning Liu: Excerpt from "My Father's Martial Art." Copyright © 1981 by the *Antioch Review, Inc.* First appeared in the *Antioch Review*, Vol. 39, No. 3 (Summer, 1981). Reprinted by permission of the Editors.

Charles Simic: "Butcher Shop" from *Dismantling the Silence* by Charles Simic. Copyright © 1971 by Charles Simic. Reprinted by permission of the publisher, George Braziller.

Paul Simon: Lyrics from "Richard Cory" by Paul Simon. Copyright © 1966 by Paul Simon. Reprinted by permission of Paul Simon Music.

David R. Slavitt: "Titanic." Reprinted by permission of Louisiana State University Press from *Big Nose: Poems* by David R. Slavitt. Copyright © 1983 by David R. Slavitt. Reprinted by permission of Louisiana State University Press.

Stevie Smith: "This Englishwoman" and "Not Waving but Drowning" from *The Collected Poems of Stevie Smith*. Copyright © 1972 by Stevie Smith. Reprinted by permission of New Directions Publishing Corporation.

William Jay Smith: "American Primitive" from *Collected Poems 1939–1989* by William Jay Smith. Published in 1990 by Charles Scribner's Sons. Copyright © 1990 by William Jay Smith. Reprinted by permission.

W. D. Snodgrass: "Disposal." © 1970 by W. D. Snodgrass. Reprinted from *Selected Poems 1957–1987* by W. D. Snodgrass, courtesy of Soho Press, Inc.

Gary Snyder: "After weeks of watching the roof leak" from "Hitch Haiku" from *The Back Country*. Copyright © 1968 by Gary Snyder. Reprinted by permission of New Directions Publishing Corporation. "Mid-August at Sourdough Mountain Lookout" from *Riprap* by Gary Snyder. Copyright © 1959 by Gary Snyder. Reprinted by permission of the author.

Richard Snyder: "A Mongoloid Child Handling Shells on the Beach" from *Keeping in Touch* by Richard Snyder (Ashland Poetry Press, 1991). Reprinted by permission of the publisher.

Cathy Song. "Stamp Collecting." From *Frameless Windows, Squares of Light: Poems by Cathy Song.* Copyright © 1988 by Cathy Song. Reprinted by permission of W. W. Norton & Company, Inc.

William Stafford: "Ask Me," "At the Klamath Berry Festival," and "Traveling Through the Dark." Copyright © 1977 William Stafford, from *Stories That Could Be True* (Harper & Row). Reprinted by permission of The Estate of William Stafford. "At the Un-National Monument Along the Canadian Border." Copyright © 1977 by Willliam Stafford. From *Stories That Could Be True.* Reprinted by permission of the author. "A Paraphrase of 'Ask Me' " from *Fifty Contemporary Poets: The Creative Process,* edited by Alberta T. Turner. David McKay Company.

Jon Stallworthy: "Singhi Woman" from *The Aztec Sonata: New and Selected Poems* by Jon Stallworthy. Copyright © 1986 by Jon Stallworthy. Reprinted by permission of W. W. Norton & Company, Inc. and Chatto & Windus.

George Starbuck: "Margaret Are You Drug" from "Translations from the English" from *White Paper* by George Starbuck. Copyright © 1965 by George Starbuck. By permission of Little, Brown and Company.

Timothy Steele: "Epitaph" from *Uncertanties and Rest* by Timothy Steele. Copyright © 1979. "Summer" from *Sapphics Against Anger and Other Poems* by Timothy Steele. Random House, 1986. Copyright © 1986 by Timothy Steele. Reprinted by permission of the author.

James Stephens: "The Wind" and "A Glass of Beer" from *Collected Poems* by James Stephens. Reprinted by permission of The Society of Authors as the literary representative of the Estate of James Stephens.

Wallace Stevens: "Disillusionment of Ten O'Clock," "Anecdote of the Jar," "Peter Quince at the Clavier" "The Emperor of Ice Cream," and "Thirteen Ways of Looking at a Blackbird" from *Collected Poems of Wallace Stevens* by Wallace Stevens. Copyright © 1923 and renewed 1951 by Wallace Stevens. Reprinted by permission of Alfred A. Knopf, Inc.

Anne Stevenson: "Sous-Entendu" and "The Victory" from *The Collected Poems of Anne Stevenson 1955–1995.* Reprinted by permission of Oxford University Press.

Michael Stillman: "Lying in the field" from *In an Eye of Minnows* by Michael Stillman. Copyright © 1976 by Michael Stillman. "In Memoriam John Coltrane" from *Occident,* Fall, 1971. Copyright © 1976 by Michael Stillman. Reprinted by permission of the author.

Ruth Stone: "Second Hand Coat" from *The Iowa Review,* Vol. 12: 2/3, Spring/Summer 1981. Reprinted by permission of the author.

Dabney Stuart: "Crib Death" from *Don't Look Back,*

Poems by Dabney Stuart. Copyright © 1987 by Dabney Stuart. Reprinted by permission of Louisiana State University Press.

Terese Svoboda: "On My First Son" from *All Aberration.* © 1985 by Terese Svoboda. Reprinted by permission of Georges Borchardt, Inc.

May Swenson: "Four-Word Lines" from *The Love Poems of May Swenson.* Copyright © 1991 by the Literary Estate of May Swenson. Reprinted by permission of Houghton Mifflin Co. All rights reserved.

Henry Taylor: "Riding a One-Eyed Horse" from *An Afternoon of Pocket Billiards* by Henry Taylor (Salt Lake City: University of Utah Press Poetry Series, 1975). Copyright © 1975 by Henry Taylor. Reprinted by permission of the publisher.

Sara Teasdale: "The Flight" from *The Collected Poems of Sara Teasdale* (New York: Macmillan, 1937).

Cornelius J. Ter Maat: "Etienne de Silhouette." Reprinted by permission of the author.

Dylan Thomas: "Do Not Go Gentle into That Good Night" and "Fern Hill" from *The Poems of Dylan Thomas.* Copyright 1939, 1946 by New Directions Publishing Corporation, 1952 by Dylan Thomas. Reprinted by permission of New Directions Publishing Corporation and David Higham Associates Ltd.

Frederick Turner: "On the Death of an Infant." Reprinted by permission of the author.

John Updike: "Ex-Basketball Player" from *The Carpentered Hen and Other Tame Creatures* by John Updike. Copyright © 1957, 1982 by John Updike. "Recital" from *Telephone Poles and Other Poems* by John Updike. Reprinted by permission of Alfred A. Knopf, Inc.

Amy Uyematsu: "Red Rooster, Yellow Sky" from *30 Miles from J-Town* by Amy Uyematsu. Copyright © 1992 by Amy Uyematsu. Reprinted by permission of Story Line Press.

Mona Van Duyn: "Earth Tremors Felt In Missouri" from *If It Be Not I* by Mona Van Duyn. Copyright © 1964 by Mona Van Duyn. Reprinted by permission of Alfred A. Knopf, Inc.

Derek Walcott: "The Virgins" from *Sea Grapes* by Derek Walcott. Copyright © 1976 by Derek Walcott. Reprinted by permission of Farrar, Straus & Giroux, Inc.

Robert Wallace: "The Girl Writing Her English Paper" from *The Common Summer: New and Selected Poems* by Robert Wallace. Copyright © 1989 by Robert Wallace. Reprinted by permission of Carnegie Mellon University Press.

Emma Lee Warrior: "How I Came to Have a Man's Name" from *Harper's Anthology of 20th Century Native American Poetry.* Edited by Duane Niatum. Copyright © 1988 by Duane Niatum. Reprinted by permission of HarperCollins Publishers.

Ruth Whitman: "Castoff Skin" from *The Passion of Lizzie Borden* by Ruth Whitman. Reprinted by permission of the author.

Richard Wilbur: "In the Elegy Season" from *Ceremony and Other Poems.* Copyright 1950 and renewed 1978 by Richard Wilbur. "Love Calls Us to the Things of This World" from *Things of This World.* Copyright © 1956 and renewed 1984 by Richard Wilbur. "The

dressed to William Craver, Writers and Artists Agency, 19 West 44th Street, Suite 1000, New York, NY 10036.

Garrison Keillor: *The Prodigal Son* from *Plays In One Act*, edited by Daniel Halpern. Reprinted by permission of Garrison Keillor. Copyright © 1991 by Garrison Keillor.

Terrence McNally: *Andre's Mother*. Copyright © 1994 by Terrence McNally. All rights reserved. CAUTION: Professionals and amateurs are hereby warned that *Andre's Mother* is subject to a royalty. It is fully protected under the copyright laws of the United States of America and of all countries covered by the International Copyright Union (including the Dominion of Canada and the rest of the British Commonwealth), the Berne Convention, the Pan-American Copyright Convention and the Universal Copyright Convention as well as all countries with which the United States has reciprocal copyright relations. All rights, including professional/amateur state rights, motion picture, recitation, lecturing, public reading, radio broadcasting, television, video or sound recording, all other forms of mechanical or electronic reproduction, such as CD-ROM, CD-I, information storage and retrieval systems and photocopying, and the rights of translation into foreign languages, are strictly reserved. Particular emphasis is laid upon the matter of readings, permission for which must be secured from the author's agent in writing. Inquiries concerning rights should be addressed to: William Morris Agency, Inc., 1325 Avenue of the Americas, New York, NY 10019. Attn: Gilbert Parker. Reprinted by permission of the William Morris Agency, Inc., "Terrence McNally on Drama: How to Write a Play," an interview with Joy Zinoman excerpted from *The Playwright's Art: Conversations with Contemporary American Dramatists*, edited by Jackson R. Bryer, Rutgers University Press, 1995.

Arthur Miller: *Death of a Salesman* from *Death of a Salesman* by Arthur Miller. Copyright 1949, renewed © 1977 by Arthur Miller. Reprinted by permission of Viking Penguin, a division of Penguin Books USA, Inc. "Tragedy and the Common Man" copyright 1949, renewed © 1977 by Arthur Miller, from *The Theater Essays Of Arthur Miller* by Arthur Miller, edited by Robert A. Martin. Reprinted by permission of Viking Penguin, a division of Penguin Books USA, Inc.

Milcha Sanchez-Scott: *The Cuban Swimmer*. Copyright © 1994 by Milcha Sanchez-Scott. All rights reserved. CAUTION: Professionals and amateurs are hereby warned that *The Cuban Swimmer* is subject to a royalty. It is fully protected under the copyright laws of the United States of America and of all countries covered by the International Copyright Union (including the Dominion of Canada and the rest of the British Commonwealth), the Berne Convention, the Pan-American Copyright Convention and the Universal Copyright Convention as well as all countries with which the United States has reciprocal copyright relations. All rights, including professional/amateur state rights, motion picture, recitation, lecturing, public reading,

radio broadcasting, television, video or sound recording, all other forms of mechanical or electronic reproduction, such as CD-ROM, CD-I, information storage and retrieval systems and photocopying, and the rights of translation into foreign languages, are strictly reserved. Particular emphasis is laid upon the matter of readings, permission for which must be secured from the author's agent in writing. Inquiries concerning rights should be addressed to: William Morris Agency, Inc., 1325 Avenue of the Americas, New York, NY 10019. Attn: George Lane. Reprinted by permission of the William Morris Agency, Inc. Excerpt from Milcha Sanchez-Scott's introductory essay in *On New Ground: Contemporary Hispanic-American Plays*. Copyright © 1987 by Milcha Sanchez-Scott. Reprinted by permission of Theatre Communications Group.

William Shakespeare: Notes to *Hamlet* and *Othello* by David Bevington. From *The Complete Works of Shakespeare*, fourth edition, edited by David Bevington. Copyright © 1992. Reprinted by permission of Addison Wesley Educational Publishers, Inc.

Sophocles: *The Antigonê of Sophocles* from *Sophocles the Oedipus Cycle: An English Version* by Dudley Fitts and Robert Fitzgerald. Copyright 1939 by Harcourt Brace & Company and renewed 1967 by Dudley Fitts and Robert Fitzgerald. *The Oedipus Rex of Sophocles* from *Sophocles the Oedipus Cycle: An English Version* by Dudley Fitts and Robert Fitzgerald. Copyright 1949 by Harcourt Brace & Company and renewed 1977 by Cornelia Fitts and Robert Fitzgerald. Both plays are reprinted by permission of the publisher. CAUTION: All rights, including professional, amateur, motion picture, recitation, lecturing, performance, public reading, radio broadcasting, and television are strictly reserved. Inquiries on all rights should be addressed to Harcourt Brace & Company, Permissions Department, Orlando, Florida 32887. Robert Fitzgerald on "Translating Sophocles" from *The Oedipus Cycle: An English Version*. Copyright © 1939, 1941, 1949 by Harcourt Brace & Company. Reprinted by permission of Harcourt Brace & Company.

Tennessee Williams: *The Glass Menagerie* and "How to Stage The Glass Menagerie" from *The Glass Menagerie* by Tennessee Williams. Copyright 1945 by Tennessee Williams and Edwina D. Williams and renewed 1973 by Tennessee Williams. Reprinted by permission of Random House, Inc.

August Wilson: *Joe Turner's Come and Gone*. Copyright © 1988 by August Wilson. Reprinted by arrangement with New American Library, a division of Penguin Books USA, Inc. "Black Experience in America" excerpted from an interview with August Wilson. From *Bill Moyers: A World Of Ideas* by Bill Moyers. Copyright © 1989 by Public Affairs Television, Inc. Reprinted by permission of Doubleday, a division of Bantam Doubleday Dell Publishing Group.

Joel Wingard: Excerpt entitled "Reading and Responding: A Shakespearean Tragedy" from *Literature: Reading and Responding to Fiction, Poetry, Drama, and the Essay* by Joel Wingard. Reprinted by permission of the author.

Photo Acknowledgments

FICTION

6, Brown Brothers; 17, Corbis-Bettmann; 26, Bern Keating/Black Star; 33, Corbis-Bettmann; 38, Scott, Foresman and Company; 53, Courtesy Alfred A. Knopf, Inc.; 63, Jill Krementz; 71, AP/Wide World Photos, Inc.; 89, Jerry Bauer; 95, Missouri Historical Society; 100, Corbis-Bettmann; 111, Pablo Campos; 134, Courtesy Putman; 160, Archive Photos; 167, UPI/Corbis-Bettmann; 172, UPI/Corbis-Bettmann; 177, Newark Public Library; 196, Peabody Essex Museum, Salem; 214, Nancy Crampton; 219, Scott, Foresman and Company; 228, Erich Hartmann/Magnum Photos; 241, Marian Wood; 262, Mikki Ansin; 272, The Dial Press. Photo by Mottke Weissman; 330, AP/Wide World Photos, Inc.; 379, AP/Wide World Photos, Inc.; 385, AP/Wide World Photos, Inc.; 389, Corbis-Bettmann; 397, Philip Gould/Corbis; 406, Willa Cather Pioneer Memorial Collection/Nebraska State Historical Society; 421, Corbis-Bettmann; 432, Corbis-Bettmann; 446, Robin Guzman; 448, Nancy Crampton; 459, Nancy Crampton; 463, AP/Wide World Photos, Inc.; 469, UPI/Corbis-Bettmann; 481, UPI/Corbis-Bettmann; 492, UPI/Corbis-Bettmann; 496, Scott, Foresman and Company; 506, Marion Ettlinger; 517, Berenice Abbott/Commerce Graphics Ltd., Inc.; 522, Sigrid Estrada; 524, Corbis-Bettmann; 536, Jaqueline Frewin; 547, UPI/Corbis-Bettmann; 555, David Lees/Archive Photos; 563, Jerry Bauer; 574, Jerry Bauer, courtesy Alfred A. Knopf, Inc.; 587, Jill Krementz; 600, Jerry Bauer, courtesy Penguin Putnam, Inc.; 613, Elliot Erwitt/Magnum Photos; 619, AP/Wide World Photos, Inc.; 626, Nancy Crampton; 629, Nancy Crampton; 632, AP/Wide World Photos, Inc.; 638, AP/Wide World Photos, Inc.; 643, John D. Schiff, courtesy New Directions

POETRY

664, Stanford University News Service; 692, The Trustees of the Imperial War Museum , London; 724, Brown Brothers; 738, AP/Wide World Photos, Inc.; 756, Boris De Rachewiltz, courtesy New Directions; 784, Brown Brothers; 804, Reuters/Corbis-Bettmann; 828, Houghton Library, Harvard University, Cambridge, Massachusetts; 851, AP/Wide World Photos, Inc.; 876, UPI/Corbis-Bettmann; 885, Kunsthistorisches Museum, Vienna; 899, Gabriel Harrison/Library of Congress; 916, Culver Pictures, Inc.; 937, Rollie McKenna, courtesy Houghton Mifflin Company; 964, Dorothy Alexander; 977, Scott, Foresman and Company; 1006, Scott, Foresman and Company; 1018, Trustees of Amherst College/Amherst College Library; 1025, Scott, Foresman and Company; 1027, Berg Collection of English and American Literature. The New York Public Library. Astor, Tilden and Lenox Foundation; 1033, Laurance Acland, courtesy Doubleday & Co., Inc.; 1034, UPI/Corbis-Bettmann; 1036, Musées Royaux des Beaux-Arts de Belgique; 1039, Thomas Victor, courtesy Farrar, Straus & Giroux, Inc.; 1041, Berg Collection of English and American Literature. The New York Public Library. Astor, Tilden and Lenox Foundation; 1044, National Portrait Gallery, London, England/SuperStock; 1053, National Portrait Gallery, London, and the Marquess of Lothian; 1056, Fred Viebahn, courtesy Vintage Books; 1059, AP/Wide World Photos, Inc.; 1072, National Portrait Gallery, London; 1075, Scott, Foresman and Company; 1076, AP/Wide World Photos, Inc.; 1078, Dorothy Alexander; 1080, Corbis-Bettmann; 1081, Dorothy Alexander; 1083, Scott, Foresman and Company; 1086, Ted Russell; 1093, National Portrait Gallery, London; 1095, Fay Godwin/Network Photographers; 1106, Scott, Foresman and Company; 1109, Gail Roub; 1112, George Murphy, courtesy W.W. Norton & Co., Inc.; 1114, Gordon LaMeyer, courtesy HarperCollins Publishers; 1119, Miriam Berkley; 1120, Willie Williams, courtesy Broadside Press; 1124, Corbis-Bettmann; 1126, Imogen Cunningham, courtesy Doubleday & Co., Inc.; 1127, Jerry Bauer; 1128, National Portrait Gallery, London; 1136, John Eddy, courtesy University of Pittsburgh Press; 1138, Corbis-Bettmann; 1143, National Portrait Gallery, London; 1148, Amy Uyematus, courtesy Broadside Press; 1149, UPI/Corbis-Bettmann; 1151, Corbis-Bettmann; 1153, Scott, Foresman and Company; 1155, John D. Schiff, courtesy New Directions; 1157, National Portrait Gallery, London; 1158, AP/Wide World Photos, Inc.; 1161, Pirie MacDonald/The Royal Photographic Society

DRAMA

1215, Corbis-Bettmann; 1227, Courtesy Writers & Artists Agency; 1237, AP/Wide World Photos, Inc.; 1243, AP/Wide World Photos, Inc.; 1252, Scott, Foresman and Company; 1254, Corbis-Bettman; 1255, John Vickers; 1297, Culver Pictures, Inc./Superstock; 1302, G. Swann/Sygma; 1303, Martha Swope (T); 1303, National Portrait Gallery, London (B); 1402, Library of Congress/Corbis; 1413, Corbis-Bettmann; 1414, Harvard Theatre Collection; 1470, Popperfoto/Archive Photos; 1479, Scott, Foresman and Company; 1520, John G. Ross; 1522, Martha Swope (T); 1522, Photofest (B); 1634, Archive Photos; 1707, Reuters/Corbis-Bettmann; 1711, New York Public Library, The Billy Rose Theater Collection; 1759, Film Archives/Springer/Corbis-Bettmann; 1777, Ted Thai/Sygma; 1781, AP/Wide World Photos, Inc.; 1783, Richard Devin; 1796, Courtesy Milcha Sanchez-Scott; 1846, AP/Wide World Photos, Inc.

Index of Major Themes

In case you prefer to study by theme or want to research possible subjects for an essay, below is a comprehensive listing of stories, poems, and plays by thirteen major themes.

ART, LANGUAGE, AND IMAGINATION

STORIES

POEMS

PLAYS

CHILDHOOD AND ADOLESCENCE

STORIES

POEMS

COMEDY AND SATIRE

STORIES

POEMS

PLAYS

DEATH

STORIES

POEMS

PLAYS

FAITH, DOUBT, AND RELIGIOUS VISION

STORIES

POEMS

PLAY

FAMILIES /PARENTS AND CHILDREN

STORIES

INDIVIDUAL VS. SOCIETY

STORIES

POEMS

PLAYS

LONELINESS
AND ALIENATION

STORIES

LOVE AND DESIRE

STORIES

RACE, CLASS, AND CULTURE

STORIES

POEMS

PLAYS

WAR, MURDER, AND VIOLENCE

STORIES

Index of First Lines of Poetry

I caught a tremendous fish, 744
I caught this morning morning's minion, 1084
I do not love my country. Its abstract lustre, 690
If but some vengeful god would call to me, 1073
I feel, 1141
I felt a Funeral, in my Brain, 1014
I found a ball of grass among the hay, 709
I found a dimpled spider, fat and white, 1894
I go, 750
If you wander far enough, 681
I had come to the house, in a cave of trees, 924
I hardly ever tire of love or rhyme—, 871
I have been one acquainted with the night, 865
I have done it again, 946
I have eaten, 700
I have gone out, a possessed witch, 679
I heard a Fly buzz – when I died –, 909
I knew a woman, lovely in her bones, 779
"I lift my lamp beside the golden door", 975
I like to see it lap the Miles –, 671
I like to touch your tattoos in complete, 866
I'm a riddle in nine syllables, 770
I met the Bishop on the road, 1161
I met a traveler from an antique land, 994
"I'm Mark's alone!" you swore. Given cause to doubt you, 870
I'm Nobody! Who are you?, 1015
Imperial Adam, naked in the dew, 931
I'm tired of Love: I'm still more tired of Rhyme, 871
In a solitude of the sea, 1070
In Breughel's great picture, The Kermess, 884
I need a bare sufficiency—red wine, 972
In ethics class so many years ago, 1112
In her room at the prow of the house, 1152
in Just-, 896
Inside a cave in a narrow canyon near Tassajara, 783
In the desert, 886
In the old stone pool, 750
In the Shreve High football stadium, 1159
In things a moderation keep, 869
In this strange labyrinth how shall I turn?, 1159
In Xanadu did Kubla Khan, 1050
I placed a jar in Tennessee, 915

I pray you not, Leuconoe, to pore, 970
I read you in a stranger's tongue, 959
I remember the neckcurls, limp and damp as tendrils, 1126
is an enchanted thing, 1106
I saw a jolly hunter, 686
I saw in Louisiana a live-oak growing, 1151
I shoot the Hippopotamus, 820
I started Early – Took my Dog –, 1016
"Is there anybody there?" said the Traveller, 734
I Stop Writing the Poem, 686
is what you first see, stepping off the train, 1127
It dropped so low – in my Regard –, 772
I tell you, hopeless grief is passionless, 1046
I thought you were my victory, 746
It is a cold and snowy night. The main street is deserted, 753
It is important that a son should know, 868
It is not the moon, I tell you, 754
It little profits that an idle king, 1143
I, too, sing America, 1021
It's a good thing Dad deserted Mom, 715
It sometimes happens, 930
It's wonderful how I jog, 1097
It was in and about the Martinmas time, 795
It was many and many a year ago, 1005
I've known rivers, 1019
I wakened on my hot, hard bed, 811
I wandered lonely as a cloud, 676
I wander through each chartered street, 729
I went back in the alley, 672
I will arise and go now, and go to Innisfree, 653
I will consider the outnumbering dead, 733
I work all day, and get half-drunk at night, 962

James Watt, 872
Jenny kissed me when we met, 873
Just as my fingers on these keys, 1138
Just off the highway to Rochester, Minnesota, 1158
just once, 954

Kisses are for the living, 988

Latecomer, first to go, 988

On my boat on Lake Cayuga, 817
On the one-ton temple bell, 750
O Rose, thou art sick!, 1041
out in the night, 751
O wind, rend open the heat, 753

Paper come out—done strewed de news, 722
Pearl Avenue runs past the high-school lot, 1147
Popcorn-can cover, 915

Quinquireme of Nineveh from distant Ophir, 728
Quite unexpectedly as Vasserot, 1100

Razors pain you, 839
Readers and listeners praise my books, 869
Red men embraced my body's whiteness, 673
Red river, red river, 827
Rose-cheeked Laura, come, 845

Said, Pull her up a bit will you, Mac, I want to unload there, 712
Season of mists and mellow fruitfulness, 1093
"See, here's the workbox, little wife, 687
September rain falls on the house, 874
Shall I compare thee to a summer's day?, 765
Shall the water not remember *Ember*, 823
She even thinks that up in heaven, 669
She is as in a field a silken tent, 780
She lay in her girlish sleep at ninety-six, 771
She sat down below a thorn, 789
She turns them over in her slow hands, 732
She wanted a little room for thinking, 1056
Shlup, shlup, the dog, 879
Should our day's portion be one mancel loaf, 972
Silver bark of beech, and sallow, 847
Since there's no help, come let us kiss and part, 864
Sir Christopher Wren, 872
Slated for demolition, 778
Slow, slow, fresh fount, keep time with my salt tears, 837
Snaggle-Tooth, Maytag, Taylor Falls—, 719
Snow falling and night falling fast, oh, fast,
Softly, in the dusk, a woman is singing to me, 656

Some for the Glories of this world; and some, 973
Some keep the Sabbath going to Church –, 1017
Some say the world will end in fire, 735
Something there is that doesn't love a wall, 1065
Sometimes walking late at night, 1131
Sometimes you hear, fifth-hand, 1095
Some time when the river is ice ask me, 665
somewhere i have never travelled,gladly beyond, 1052
Somewhere someone is traveling furiously toward you, 1032
so much depends, 680
Sorrow moves in wide waves, 1109
So smooth, so sweet, so silv'ry is thy voice, 814
Stone-cutters fighting time with marble, you foredefeated, 1088
Stop all the clocks, cut off the telephone, 801
Success is counted sweetest, 1014
Sundays too my father got up early, 1074

Take, O, take those lips away, 792
Tears, idle tears, I know not what they mean, 736
Tell all the Truth but tell it slant –, 1018
Tell me not, fans, I am unkind, 976
Tell me not, Sweet, I am unkind, 691
That civilization may not sink, 1162
That is no country for old men. The young, 991
That's my last Duchess painted on the wall, 661
That time of year thou mayst in me behold, 1129
The age, 1120
The Angel that presided o'er my birth, 818
The apparition of these faces in the crowd, 741
The art of losing isn't hard to master, 1039
The buzz-saw snarled and rattled in the yard, 660
The curfew tolls the knell of parting day, 999
Thee for my recitative, 670
The eyes open to a cry of pulleys, 736
The falling flower, 749
The fog comes, 999
The golf links lie so near the mill, 685
The grandmother who never spoke, 1148

Index of Authors and Titles

Each page number immediately following a writer's name indicates a quotation from or reference to that writer. A number in **bold** refers you to the page on which you will find the author's biography.